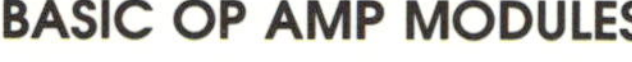

BASIC OP AMP MODULES

 Circuit	Block Diagram	Gains
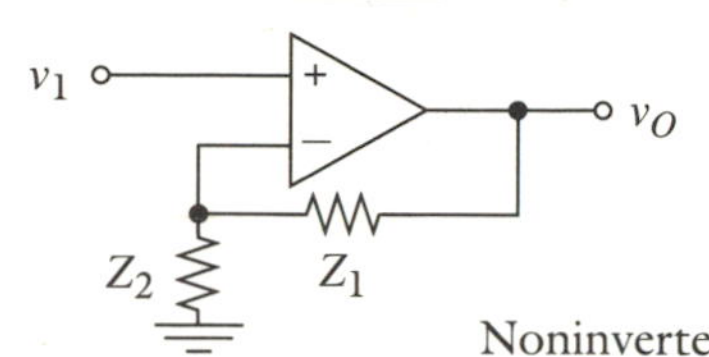	v_1 → K → v_O	$K = \frac{Z_1 + Z_2}{Z_2}$
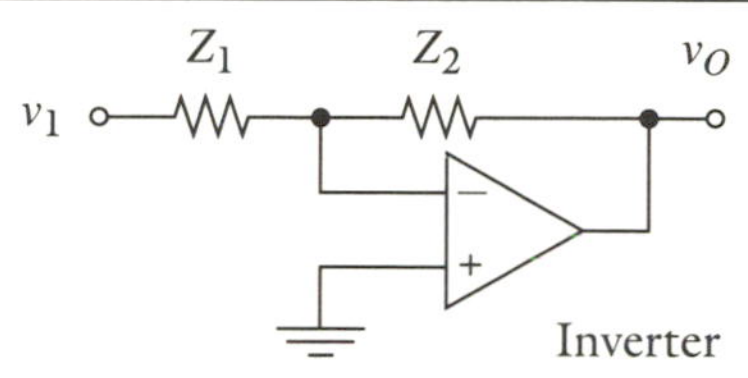	v_1 → K → v_O	$K = -\frac{Z_2}{Z_1}$
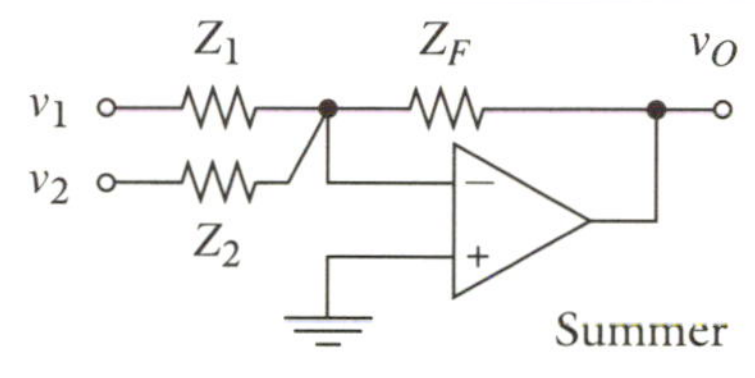	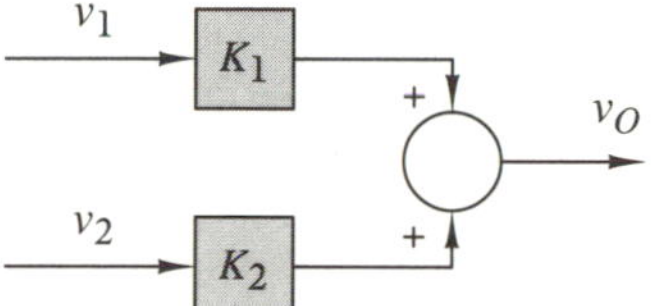	$K_1 = -\frac{Z_F}{Z_1}$ $K_2 = -\frac{Z_F}{Z_2}$
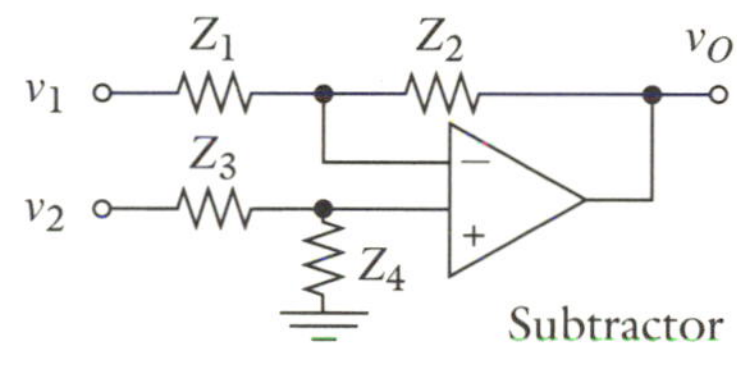	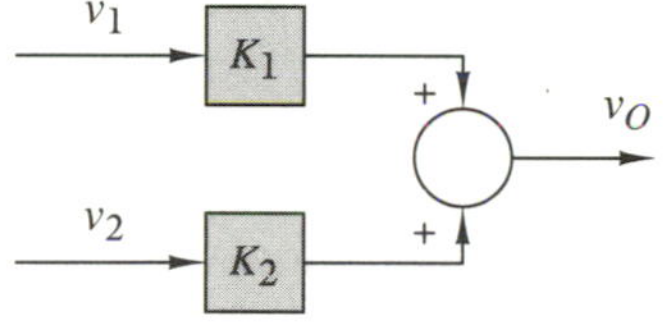	$K_1 = -\frac{Z_2}{Z_1}$ $K_2 = \left(\frac{Z_1 + Z_2}{Z_1}\right)\left(\frac{Z_4}{Z_3 + Z_4}\right)$
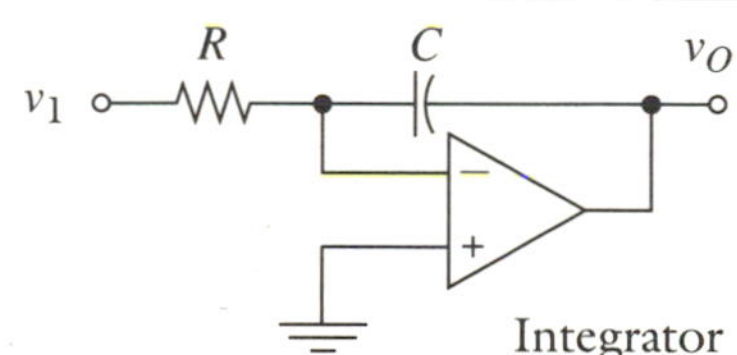	v_1 → K → $\int$ → v_O	$K = -\frac{1}{RC}$
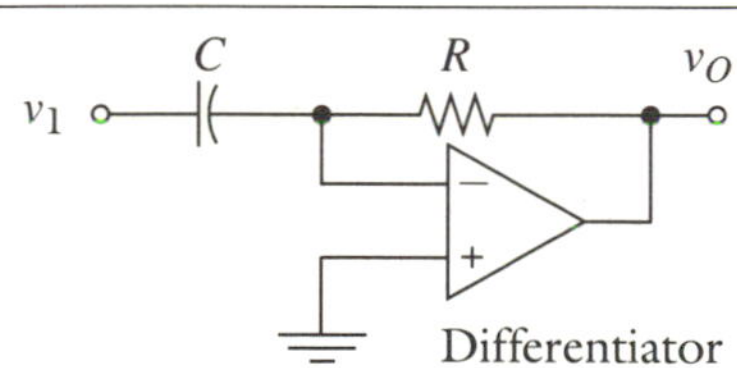	v_1 → K → $\frac{d}{dt}$ → v_O	$K = -RC$

of Congress Cataloging-in-Publication Data

omas, Roland E.
The analysis and design of linear circuits / Roland E. Thomas, Albert J. Rosa.—2nd ed.
p. cm.
Includes bibliographical references and index.
ISBN 0-13-535279-7
1. Electric circuits, Linear-Design and construction.
2. Electric circuit analysis. I. Rosa, Albert J.
II.Title.
TK454.T466 1998
621.319'2–dc21 97-6794
CIP

Acquisitions editor: Eric Svendsen
Editor-in-chief: Marcia Horton
Director of production and manufacturing: David W. Riccardi
Production manager: Bayani Mendoza de Leon
Production editor: Ann Marie Longobardo
Manufacturing buyer: Julia Meehan
Creative director: Paula Maylahn
Art director: Amy Rosen
Art manager: Gus Vibal
Cover and interior design: Kevin Kall
Copy editor: Patricia M. Daly
Editorial assistant: Andre Au

Printed in The United States of America
10 9 8 7 6 5 4 3 2

ISBN 0-13-535279-7

Prentice-Hall International (UK) Limited, *London*
Prentice-Hall of Australia Pty. Limited, *Sydney*
Prentice-Hall Canada Inc., *Toronto*
Prentice-Hall Hispanoamericana, S.A., *Mexico*
Prentice-Hall of India. Private Limited, *New Delhi*
Prentice-Hall of Japan, Inc., *Tokyo*
Simon & Shuster Asia Pte. Ltd., *Singapore*
Editora Prentice-Hall do Brasil, Ltda., *Rio de Janerio*

THE ANALYSIS AND DESIGN OF LINEAR CIRCUITS

SECOND EDITION

ROLAND E. THOMAS
Professor Emeritus
UNITED STATES AIR FORCE ACADEMY

ALBERT J. ROSA
Professor and Chairman of Engineering
UNIVERSITY OF DENVER

PRENTICE HALL, Upper Saddle River, New Jersey 07458

To our wives
Juanita and Kathleen

PREFACE

The Analysis and Design of Linear Circuits, second edition, builds on the three premises that guided the development of the first edition. First, we believe the introductory circuit courses should emphasize the analysis techniques used in subsequent upper division courses in electronics, signal processing, control, and communication systems. As a result this text introduces students to OP AMPs and systems points of view through the use of block diagrams and transform methods of describing signals and circuits. Second, we believe that design problems provide early student motivation and offer a valid alternative method of verifying comprehension of basic circuit concepts. While this book thoroughly threats the basic principles of circuit analysis, it goes beyond analysis to show the applications of these principles to real-world design and evaluation problems. Third, we believe that problem solving skills are best developed when the learning objectives are explicitly stated. Consequently, this book is built around nine overarching Course Objectives supported by a structured set of 74 En Route Objectives. Our experience is that the structured objectives together with the signal processing and design elements included in this book make the subject of circuit analysis more interesting to students.

What's New in the Second Edition

The revisions in the second edition have been guided by feedback from the many users of the first edition. The primary goal of the second edition is to provide more flexibility in topical coverage and course organization.

Content and Organization Changes

The second edition contains the following changes in topical coverage:

- The node-voltage and mesh-current methods of circuit analysis are introduced in Chapter 3. This earlier introduction allows these techniques to be applied to circuit theorems in Chapter 3 and active circuits in Chapter 4. It also eliminates the need for the stand-alone first edition Chapter 5 devoted to formal circuit analysis.
- The treatment of OP AMP circuit design in Chapter 4 has been broadened to include differential amplifiers, instrumentation systems, and worst-case component tolerances.

- The treatment of phasors and ac circuits has been moved forward to Chapter 8. This change allows schools to treat phasors in the first semester without first covering Laplace transforms. Schools that prefer the first edition's "Laplace first" approach can still do so by simply delaying Chapter 8 until after Chapter 11 (Network Functions).
- The relationship between network functions and sinusoidal steady-state responses has been moved forward into Chapter 11. This change allows greater flexibility in the selection of application chapters in Part 3 of the book.
- Chapter 12 (Frequency Response) has been expanded to include resonant *RLC* circuit concepts previously treated in the chapter on sinusoidal steady-state response. This change allows the concepts of resonant circuits to be integrated with the frequency response techniques based on network functions and Bode plots.
- In the second edition the analog filter design chapter has been moved forward so it immediately follows the discussion of frequency response in Chapter 12.
- A discussion of wattmeters and the two-wattmeter method of measuring three-phase power has been added to Chapter 14. The treatment of single- and three-phase power in this chapter can be treated immediately after the new Chapter 8 for schools that cover ac power in the first semester.
- The first edition Chapter 16 on Fourier methods has been divided into two chapters. The new Chapter 15 covers the Fourier series and its applications in circuit analysis. This chapter can also be treated immediately after the new Chapter 8 for those schools that emphasize ac circuits.

INTEGRATION OF COMPUTER-AIDED CIRCUIT ANALYSIS

In the second edition we illustrate computer-aided circuit analysis using three types of programs: a spreadsheet (Quattro Pro®), a math solver (Mathcad®), and a circuit simulator (PSpice®). Some 35 Examples illustrating the application of these tools to circuit problems are distributed throughout the book. Computer tools are routinely used by practicing engineers and in most cases our students already know how to use some of these programs. It is up to us to help them learn how to use these tools effectively. Thus, our purpose in having computer examples in the book is not to teach students how to use specific software packages, but to help them develop an analysis style that includes the intelligent use of computer tools. These tools are an intrinsic part of the engineering environment that can significantly enhance student understanding of circuit phenomena.

COMPUTER EXAMPLES TABLE OF CONTENTS 

KEY FEATURES

Some of the key features retained in the second edition are:

CIRCUIT DESIGN

Early involvement in design provides motivation because students can apply their new knowledge to practical situations. Although we include design for pedagogical reasons, it also allows introductory circuit courses to have some design content meeting the ABET/EAC Engineering Accreditation Criteria. The book includes 35 worked-out design examples, 10 design exercises, and about 150 design homework problems all of which are identified with a (D) for design. Students are first introduced to circuit design in Chapter 3. Important design coverage also appears in Chapters 4, 6, 7, 8, 11, 12, and 13. Many of the design examples involve evaluating alternate designs, while others emphasize a modular approach to circuit realization.

THE OP AMP

The OP AMP is the predominant linear active element whose treatment at this early stage promotes the development of the student's circuit design capability. After being introduced in Chapter 4, the OP AMP is used to realize various signal processing functions. The formal method of writing node equations for OP AMP circuits is presented in Chapter 4 for dc circuits and in Chapter 10 for dynamic circuits. OP AMPs occur frequently throughout the text, especially in Chapter 13 on analog filter design.

CIRCUIT PARAMETERS

In some examples and homework problems circuit parameters are assigned numerical values and in others they are left in symbolic form. Leaving parameters in symbolic form reminds students that in a design situation the circuit parameters are the unknowns. We use realistic values whenever numerical values are used or are unavoidable, as in second-order circuits. The ubiquitous scientific calculator eliminates the need for the archaic practice of scaling circuit parameters into numerically convenient, but patently impractical ranges. Using realistic values is also consistent with our emphasis on OP AMPs and circuit design.

LEARNING OBJECTIVES

A major pedagogical feature is the incorporation of explicitly stated objectives. This framework of objectives allows students to identify the ultimate goals and focus on the intermediate steps required to achieve those goals. The ultimate goals are the *Course Objectives* given at the beginning of each of the three parts of the book. Course Objectives represent the type of learning a student should be able to demonstrate at major checkpoints in a course. Each chapter has four to six *En Route Objectives* that cover the intermediate stepping stones needed to reach the level of achievement defined by the course objectives. En route Objectives are given at the end of each chapter and are immediately followed by homework problems that test the students' ability to meet these enabling objectives.

EXAMPLES AND EXERCISES

The second edition includes over 300 worked-out examples that apply basic chapter concepts to specific problems. Forty-five of these examples are Application Notes and Design Examples that illustrate practical application and real world constraints. There are over 240 in-text exercises that allow students to practice the analysis or design techniques discussed in the preceding example. The examples and exercises are designed to help students develop the problem solving abilities needed to meet the En Route and Course objectives.

HOMEWORK PROBLEMS

The book includes over 950 homework problems, most of them new to the second edition. Many of these problems are directly related to En Route Objectives and are designed to validate students' understanding. To help students integrate their knowledge we included 78 *Chapter-Integrating Problems* and 30 *Course-Integrating Problems*. These integrating problems test mastery of the Course Objectives and require proficiency of several En Route Objectives. Integrating Problems may require analysis, design, or evaluation and are labeled with (A), (D), or (E) icons to indicate the technique required. About thirty percent of the homework problems have answers in the back of the book.

The solutions manual for the second edition has been prepared using Quattro Pro, Mathcad, and PSpice. In this sense, all of the end-of-chapter problems can be solved using the computer tools illustrated in the book. However, most of the problems can be solved using traditional methods and do not actually require a computer tool. Those problems for which a computer tool offers a significant advantage are marked with a computer icon.

COURSE DESIGN OPTIONS

The primary goal of the second edition is to provide greater flexibility in course design. The book contains enough material for a full-year sequence in circuit analysis. Assuming three lectures per week, a two-semester sequence can cover Chapters 1–8 in the first semester leaving the Chapters 9–16 for the second semester. Chapter 8 (Sinusoidal Steady-State Response) can be delayed to the second semester and replaced by Chapter 9 (Laplace Transforms) for schools preferring the Laplace before phasors approach in the first edition. For a three-quarter sequence the logical break points are Chapters 1–6, Chapters 7–11, and Chapters 12–16. Again, schools preferring the Laplace first approach can slide Chapter 12 (Frequency Response) into the second quarter and delay Chapter 8 to the third quarter.

A two-quarter sequence can cover Chapters 1–6 is the first quarter. The instructor has several options for the second quarter. For example, covering Chapters 7, 8, 14, 15, and 16 produces a strong ac circuit emphasis, while treating Chapters 7, 9, 10, 11, and 12 produces a transform/systems emphasis. Other areas of emphasis are possible.

A one-semester course obviously requires that some material in the first eight chapters be deferred to other courses in order to make room for application topics. With careful selection of subsequent topics and homework problems, the following sections in the first eight chapters can be deferred: Section 3-6 (Interface Circuit Design), Section 4-3 (The Transistor), Section 4-6 (OP AMP Circuit Design), Section 4-7 (The Comparator), Section 5-7 (Signal Spectra), Section 6-3 (Dynamic OP AMP Circuits), Section 6-5 (Mutual Inductance), Section 6-6 (The Ideal Transformer), and Section 8-6 (The Linear Transformer). With these omissions, a cohesive one-semester course can designed by covering Chapters 1–8 and then adding one or more areas of emphasis such as:

- Electronics and Design—Sections 3-6, 4-3, 4-6, and 4-7.
- Mutual Inductance—Sections 6-5, 6-6, and 8-6.
- Frequency Response—Chapter 12 (omitting Section 12-7)
- ac Power-Chapter 14.
- Fourier Series—Chapter 15 (omitting Section 15-6).

INSTRUCTIONAL AIDS

The following supplementary materials are available for use with this book.

SOLUTIONS MANUAL

Complete set of detailed solutions to all of the end-of-chapter problems is available free to all adopting faculty. Solutions were prepared and documented using Quattro Pro, Mathcad, and PSpice, and were given two independent accuracy checks.

HTTP://WWW.PRENHALL.COM/THOMAS

The Second Edition of this text will be supported by a web site keeping the community informed about the book and its supplements. Please access this site to download *electronic files of the book's figures* for use in class, and to ask the authors any questions you may have about the book. In the future, look to this site to provide updates on the textual material and homework problems.

ACKNOWLEDGMENTS

The authors acknowledge their indebtedness to the many colleagues who have given valuable assistance in one or both editions of this book: Doran J. Baker, Utah State University; William E. Bennett, United States Naval Academy; Maqsood A. Chaudhry, California State University at Fullerton;

Don E. Cottrell, University of Denver; Michael L. Daley, University of Memphis; James G. Gottling, Ohio State University; K.S.P. Kumar, University of Minnesota; Michael Lightner, University of Colorado at Boulder; Jerry I. Lubell, Jaycor; Lloyd Massengill, Vanderbilt University; Frank L. Merat, Case Western Reserve University; Richard L. Moat, Motorola; William Rison, New Mexico Institute of Mining and Technology; Martin S. Roden, California State University at Los Angeles; Pat Sannuti, the State University of New Jersey; Jacob Shekel, Northeastern University; Kadagattur Srinidhi, Northeastern University; Len Trombetta, University of Houston; David Voltmer, Rose-Hulman Institute of Technology; and Bruce F. Wollenberg, University of Minnesota. We are also indebted to John C. Getty of the University of Denver for his assistance in developing an associated laboratory manual. The editorial assistance of Sondra Chavez, Alan Apt, Ann Marie Longobardo, and Eric Svendsen is also acknowledged. The copy editing provided by Patricia M. Daly made our task immeasurably easier. Finally, we again thank our wives for their patience and understanding.

DESIGN CONTENT

DESIGN EXAMPLES

DESIGN EXERCISE

CONTENTS

PART 1

PART 1 RESISTANCE CIRCUITS

COURSE OBJECTIVES

A Analysis Given a resistance circuit with dc input signals, select an analysis technique and find the circuit's response in terms of output signals or input–output relationships.

D Design Given a dc signal or power processing function stated in terms of output signals or input–output relationships, design one or more circuits that implement the specified function within stated constraints.

E Evaluation Given several resistance circuits that reportedly perform the same dc signal or power processing function, verify the claim and rank order the circuits using stated evaluation criteria.

INTRODUCTION

The electromotive action manifests itself in the form of two effects which I believe must be distinguished from the beginning by a precise definition. I will call the first of these "electric tension," the second "electric current."

André-Marie Ampère, 1820,
French Mathematician/Physicist

This book deals with the analysis and design of linear electric circuits. A circuit is an interconnection of electric devices that processes energy or information. Understanding circuits is important because energy and information are the underlying technological commodities in electrical engineering. The study of circuits provides a foundation for areas of electrical engineering such as electronics, power systems, communication systems, and control systems.

This chapter describes the structure of this book, introduces basic notation, and defines the primary physical variables in electric circuits—voltage and current. André Ampère (1775–1836) was the first to recognize the importance of distinguishing between the electrical effects now called voltage and current. He also invented the galvanometer, the forerunner of today's voltmeter and ammeter. A natural genius who had mastered all the then-known mathematics by age 12, he is best known for defining the mathematical relationship between electric current and magnetism. This relationship, now known as Ampère's law, is one of the basic concepts of modern electromagnetics.

The first section of this chapter describes the pedagogical framework and terminology that must be understood to use this book effectively. It describes how the learning objectives are structured to help the student develop the problem-solving abilities needed to analyze and design circuits. The second section provides some of the standard scientific notation and conventions used throughout the book. The last section introduces electric voltage, current, and power—the physical variables used throughout the book to describe the signal-processing and energy-transfer capabilities of linear circuits.

1-1 About This Book

The basic purpose of this book is to introduce the analysis and design of linear circuits. Circuits are important in electrical engineering because they process electrical signals that carry energy and information. For the present we can define a **circuit** as an interconnection of electrical devices, and a **signal** as a time-varying electrical entity. For example, the information stored on a compact disk is recovered in the CD-ROM player as electronic signals that are processed by circuits to generate audio and video outputs. In an electrical power system some form of stored energy is converted to electrical form and transferred to loads, where the energy is converted into the form required by the customer. The CD-ROM player and the electrical power system both involve circuits that process and transfer electrical signals carrying energy and information.

In this text we are primarily interested in **linear circuits**. An important feature of a linear circuit is that the amplitude of the output signal is proportional to the input signal amplitude. The proportionality property of linear circuits greatly simplifies the process of circuit analysis and design. Most circuits are only linear within a restricted range of signal levels. When driven outside this range they become nonlinear, and proportionality no longer applies. Although we will treat a few examples of nonlinear circuits, our attention is focused on circuits operating within their linear range.

Our study also deals with interface circuits. For the purposes of this book, we define an **interface** as a pair of accessible terminals at which signals may be observed or specified. The interface idea is particularly important with integrated circuit (IC) technology. Integrated circuits involve many thousands of interconnections, but only a small number are accessible to the user. Designing systems using integrated circuits involves interconnecting complex circuits that have only a few accessible terminals. This often involves relatively simple circuits whose purpose is to change signal levels or formats. Such interface circuits are intentionally introduced to ensure that the appropriate signal conditions exist at the connections between complex integrated circuits.

COURSE OBJECTIVES

This book has a set of learning objectives and related homework that can be used to verify your progress. The overarching course objectives are defined at three levels: analysis, design, and evaluation. The **analysis** level involves determining the output signals of a given circuit with known input signals. Analysis has the important feature that a unique solution exists in linear circuits. Circuit analysis will occupy the bulk of our attention, since it provides the foundation for understanding the interaction of signals and circuits. The **design** level involves devising circuits that perform a prescribed signal-processing function. In contrast to analysis, a design problem may have no solution or several solutions. The latter possibility leads to the **evaluation** level: namely, rank-order circuits that perform the same function using factors such as cost, power consumption, and part counts. In real life the engineer's role is a blend of analysis, design, and evaluation, and the boundaries between these levels are often blurred. By explicitly stating our analysis, design, and evaluation objectives, we intend to help to prepare you for that role.

This book is divided into three parts: (1) resistance circuits (Chapters 1 through 4), (2) dynamic circuits (Chapters 5 through 11), and (3) applications (Chapters 12 through 16). The course objectives are listed at the beginning of the three parts of the book. The course-integrating problems given at the end of each part are designed to test your mastery of the course objectives.

EN ROUTE OBJECTIVES

The course objectives are built on a foundation of intermediate milestones called en route objectives (EROs). The EROs are listed at the end of each chapter together with homework problems designed to test your understanding of basic concepts and techniques. Although they are listed at the end of each chapter, the EROs are an integral part of the chapter and are keyed to one or more sections of the text. Collectively, the en route objectives specify the basic knowledge and understanding needed to achieve the course objectives. At the very end of each chapter there are a number of chapter-integrating problems. These problems combine several en route objectives and offer an opportunity to deal with more complex problems before attempting the broad course-integrating problems described previously. The primary purpose of the course- and chapter-integrating problems is indicated by the symbols **A** for analysis, **D** for design, and **E** for evaluation.

This book contains many worked examples to help you master the en route objectives. These examples describe the steps needed to obtain the final answer. They usually treat analysis problems, although design examples and application notes are also included. There are in-text exercises that include only the problem statement and the final answer. These exercises provide immediate feedback on your ability to apply the ideas discussed in a particular section. You should work out the solution in detail, and then check your results with the answers given in the exercise.

1–2 SYMBOLS AND UNITS

Throughout this text we will use the international system (SI) of units. The SI system includes six fundamental units: meter (m), kilogram (kg), second (s), ampere (A), kelvin (K), and candela (cd). All the other units of measure can be derived from these six.

Like all disciplines, electrical engineering has its own terminology and symbology. The symbols used to represent some of the more important physical quantities and their units are listed in Table 1–1. It is not our purpose to define these quantities here, nor to offer this list as an item for memorization. Rather, the purpose of this table is merely to list in one place all the electrical quantities used in this book.

Numerical values in engineering range over many orders of magnitude. Consequently, the system of standard decimal prefixes in Table 1–2 is used. These prefixes on a unit abbreviation symbol indicate the power of 10 that is applied to the numerical value of the quantity.

Exercise 1–1

Given the pattern in the statement 1 kΩ = 1 kilohm = 1×10^3 ohms, fill in the blanks in the following statements using the standard decimal prefixes.

(a) ______ = ______ = 5×10^{-3} watts
(b) 10.0 dB = ______ = ______
(c) 3.6 ps = ______ = ______
(d) ______ = 0.03 microfarads = ______
(e) ______ = ______ gigahertz = 6.6×10^9 Hertz

Answers:
(a) 5.0 mW = 5 milliwatts
(b) 10.0 decibels = 1.0 bel
(c) 3.6 picoseconds = 3.6×10^{-12} seconds
(d) 30 nF or 0.03 μF = 30.0×10^{-9} Farads
(e) 6.6 GHz = 6.6 gigahertz

1–3 CIRCUIT VARIABLES

The underlying physical variables in the study of electronic systems are **charge** and **energy**. The idea of electrical charge explains the very strong electrical forces that occur in nature. To explain both attraction and repulsion, we say that there are two kinds of charge—positive and negative.

TABLE 1–1 SOME IMPORTANT QUANTITIES, THEIR SYMBOLS, AND UNIT ABBREVIATIONS

QUANTITY	SYMBOL	UNIT	UNIT ABBREVIATION
Time	t	second	s
Frequency	f	hertz	Hz
Radian frequency	ω	radian/second	rad/s
Phase angle	θ,ϕ	degree or radian	° or rad
Energy	w	joule	J
Power	p	watt	W
Charge	q	coulomb	C
Current	i	ampere	A
Electric field	$\mathcal{E}$	volt/meter	V/m
Voltage	v	volt	V
Impedance	Z	ohm	Ω
Admittance	Y	siemens	S
Resistance	R	ohm	Ω
Conductance	G	siemens	S
Reactance	X	ohm	Ω
Susceptance	B	siemens	S
Inductance, self	L	henry	H
Inductance, mutual	M	henry	H
Capacitance	C	farad	F
Magnetic flux	ϕ	weber	wb
Flux linkages	λ	weber-turns	wb-t
Power ratio	$\log_{10}(p_2/p_1)$	bel	B

Like charges repel, while unlike charges attract one another. The symbol q is used to represent charge. If the amount of charge is varying with time, we emphasize the fact by writing $q(t)$. In the international system (SI), charge is measured in **coulombs** (abbreviated C). The smallest quantity of charge in nature is an electron's charge ($q_E = 1.6 \times 10^{-19}$C). Thus, there are $1/q_E = 6.25 \times 10^{18}$ electrons in 1 coulomb of charge.

Electrical charge is a rather cumbersome variable to measure in practice. Moreover, in most situations the charges are moving, so we find it more convenient to measure the amount of charge passing a given point per unit time. If $q(t)$ is the cumulative charge passing through a point, we define a signal variable i called **current** as follows:

$$i = \frac{dq}{dt} \tag{1-1}$$

Current is a measure of the flow of electrical charge. It is the time rate of change of charge passing a given point in a circuit. The physical dimen-

TABLE 1–2 STANDARD DECIMAL PREFIXES

MULTIPLIER	PREFIX	ABBREVIATION
10^{18}	exa	E
10^{15}	peta	P
10^{12}	tera	T
10^{9}	giga	G
10^{6}	mega	M
10^{3}	kilo	k
10^{-1}	deci	d
10^{-2}	centi	c
10^{-3}	milli	m
10^{-6}	micro	μ
10^{-9}	nano	n
10^{-12}	pico	p
10^{-15}	femto	f
10^{-18}	atto	a

sions of current are coulombs per second. In the SI system, the unit of current is the **ampere** (abbreviated A). That is,

$$1 \text{ coulomb/second} = 1 \text{ ampere}$$

Since there are two types of electrical charge, there is a bookkeeping problem associated with the direction assigned to the current. In engineering it is customary to define the direction of current as the direction of the net flow of positive charge.

A second signal variable called **voltage** is related to the change in energy that would be experienced by a charge as it passes through a circuit. The symbol w is commonly used to represent energy. In the SI system of units, energy carries the units of **joules** (abbreviated J). If a small charge dq was to experience a change in energy dw in passing from point A to point B in a circuit, then the voltage v between A and B is defined as the change in energy per unit charge. We can express this definition in differential form as

$$v = \frac{dw}{dq} \tag{1–2}$$

Voltage does not depend on the path followed by the charge dq in moving from point A to point B. Furthermore, there can be a voltage between two points even if there is no charge motion, since voltage is a measure of how much energy dw would be involved if a charge dq was moved. The dimensions of voltage are joules per coulomb. The unit of voltage in the SI system is the **volt** (abbreviated V). That is,

$$1 \text{ joule/coulomb} = 1 \text{ volt}$$

The general definition of physical variable called **power** is the time rate of change of energy:

$$p = \frac{dw}{dt} \tag{1-3}$$

The dimensions of power are joules per second, which in the SI system is called a **watt** (abbreviated W). In electrical circuits it is useful to relate power to the signal variables current and voltage. Using the chain rule, Eq. (1–3) can be written as

$$p = \left(\frac{dw}{dq}\right)\left(\frac{dq}{dt}\right) \tag{1-4}$$

Now using Eqs. (1–1) and (1–2), we obtain

$$p = vi \tag{1-5}$$

The electrical power associated with a situation is determined by the product of voltage and current. The total energy transferred during the period from t_1 to t_2 is found by solving for dw in Eq. (1–3) and then integrating

$$w_T = \int_{w_1}^{w_2} dw = \int_{t_1}^{t_2} p\, dt \tag{1-6}$$

EXAMPLE 1–1

The electron beam in the cathode-ray tube shown in Figure 1–1 carries 10^{14} electrons per second and is accelerated by a voltage of 50 kV. Find the power in the electron beam.

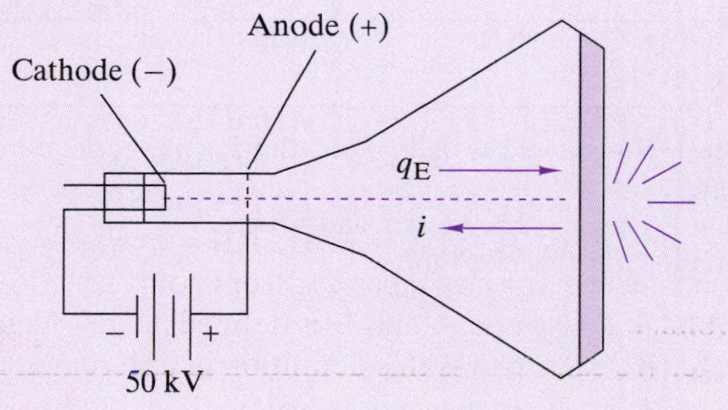

FIGURE 1–1

SOLUTION:

Since current is the rate of charge flow, we can find the net current by multiplying the charge of the electron q_E by the rate of electron flow dn_E/dt.

$$i = q_E\frac{dn_E}{dt} = (1.6 \times 10^{-19})(10^{14}) = 1.6 \times 10^{-5}\text{ A}$$

Therefore, the beam power is

$$p = vi = (50 \times 10^3)(1.6 \times 10^{-5}) = 0.8\text{ W}$$ ■

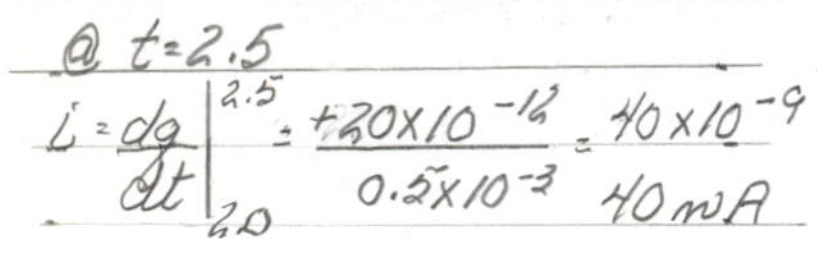

EXAMPLE 1–2

The current through a circuit element is 50 mA. Find the total charge and the number of electrons transferred during a period of 100 ns.

SOLUTION:

The relationship between current and charge is given in Eq. (1–1) as

$$i = \frac{dq}{dt}$$

Since the current i is given, we calculate the charge transferred by solving this equation for dq and then integrating

$$q_T = \int_{q_1}^{q_2} dq = \int_0^{10^{-7}} i\,dt$$

$$= \int_0^{10^{-7}} 50 \times 10^{-3}\,dt = 50 \times 10^{-10}\text{C} = 5\text{ nC}$$

There are $1/q_E = 6.25 \times 10^{18}$ electrons/coulomb, so the number of electrons transferred is

$$n_E = (5 \times 10^{-9}\text{ C})(6.25 \times 10^{18}\text{ electrons/C}) = 31.2 \times 10^9\text{ electrons}$$ ■

Exercise 1–2

A device dissipates 100 W of power. How much energy is delivered to it in 10 seconds?

Answer: 1 kJ

Exercise 1–3

The graph in Figure 1–2(a) shows the charge $q(t)$ flowing past a point in a wire as a function of time.

(a) Find the current $i(t)$ at $t = 1$, 2.5, 3.5, 4.5, and 5.5 ms.
(b) Sketch the variation of $i(t)$ versus time.

Answers:

(a) –10 nA, +40 nA, 0 nA, –20 nA, 0 nA.
(b) The variations in $i(t)$ are shown in Figure 1–2(b).

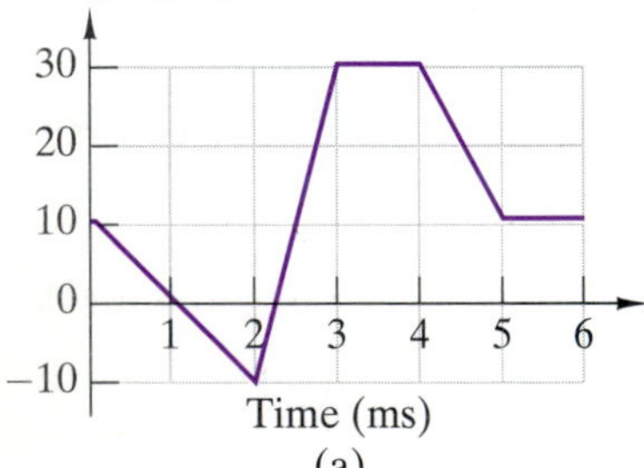

(a)

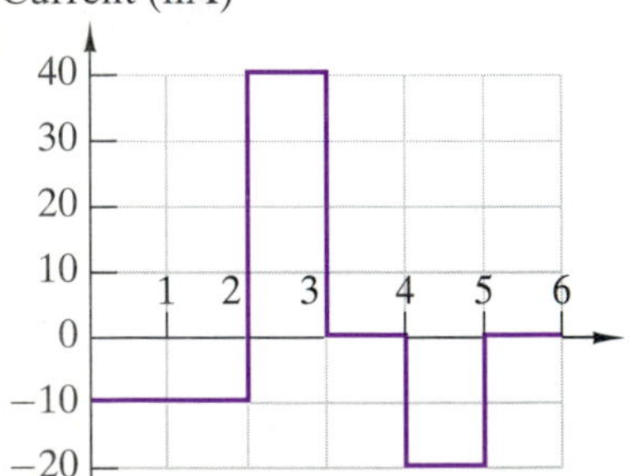

(b)

FIGURE 1–2

THE PASSIVE SIGN CONVENTION

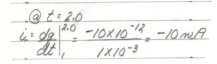

We have defined three circuit variables (current, voltage, and power) using two basic variables (charge and energy). Charge and energy, like mass, length, and time, are basic concepts of physics that provide the scientific foundation for electrical engineering. However, engineering problems rarely involve charge and energy directly, but are usually stated in terms of voltage, current, and power. The reason for this is simple: The circuit variables are much easier to measure and therefore are the most useful working variables in engineering practice.

At this point, it is important to stress the physical differences between current and voltage variables. Current is a measure of the time rate of charge passing a point in a circuit. We think of current as a *through variable,* since it describes the flow of electrical charge through a point in a circuit. On the other hand, voltage is not measured at a single point, but rather between two points or across an electrical device. Consequently, we think of voltage as an *across variable* that inherently involves two points.

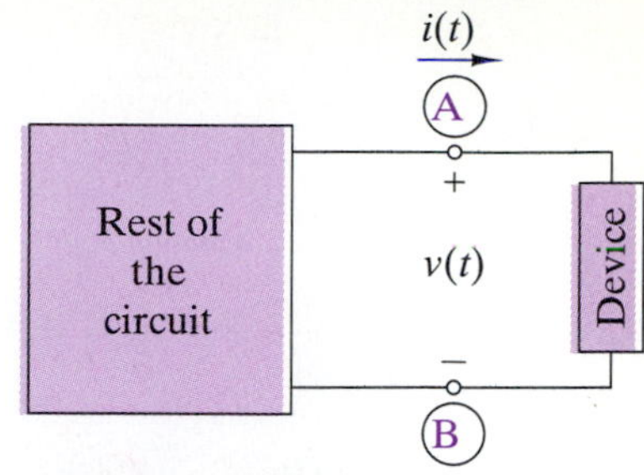

FIGURE 1–3 *Voltage and current reference marks for a two-terminal device.*

The arrow and the plus and minus symbols in Figure 1–3 are *reference marks* that define the positive directions for the current and voltage associated with an electrical device. These reference marks do not represent an assertion about what is happening physically in the circuit. The response of an electrical circuit is determined by physical laws, and not by the reference marks assigned to the circuit variables.

The reference marks are benchmarks assigned at the beginning of the analysis. When the actual direction and reference direction agree, the answers found by circuit analysis will have positive algebraic signs. When they disagree, the algebraic signs of the answers will be negative. For example, if circuit analysis reveals that the current variable in Figure 1–3 is positive [i.e., $i(t) > 0$], then the sign of this answer, together with the assigned reference direction, indicates that the current passes through point A in Figure 1–3 from left to right. Conversely, when analysis reveals that the current variable is negative, then this result, combined with the assigned reference direction, tells us that the current passes through point A from right to left. In summary, the algebraic sign of the answer together with arbitrarily assigned reference marks tell us the actual directions of a voltage or current variable.

In Figure 1–3, the current reference arrow enters the device at the terminal marked with the plus voltage reference mark. This orientation is called the **passive sign convention**. Under this convention, the power $p(t)$ is positive when the device absorbs power and is negative when it delivers power to the rest of the circuit. Since $p(t) = v(t) \times i(t)$, a device absorbs power when the voltage and current variables have the same algebraic sign and delivers power when they have opposite signs. Certain devices, such as heaters (a toaster, for example), can only absorb power. The voltage and current variables associated with these devices must always have the same algebraic sign. On the other hand, a battery absorbs power [$p(t) > 0$] when it is being charged and delivers power [$p(t) < 0$] when it is discharging. Thus, the voltage and current variables for a battery can have the same or the opposite algebraic signs.

The passive sign convention is used throughout this book. It is also the convention used by circuit simulation computer programs, such as SPICE and MICRO-CAP.[1] To interpret correctly the results of circuit analysis, it

1 We discuss computer-aided circuit analysis in subsequent chapters. MICRO-CAP is a trademark of Spectrum Software, Inc.

is important to remember that the reference marks (arrows and plus/minus signs) are reference directions, not indications of the circuit response. The actual direction of a response is determined by comparing its reference direction with the algebraic signs of the result predicted by circuit analysis based on physical laws.

GROUND

$v_A(t)$ + A $v_B(t)$ + B $v_C(t)$ + C – G

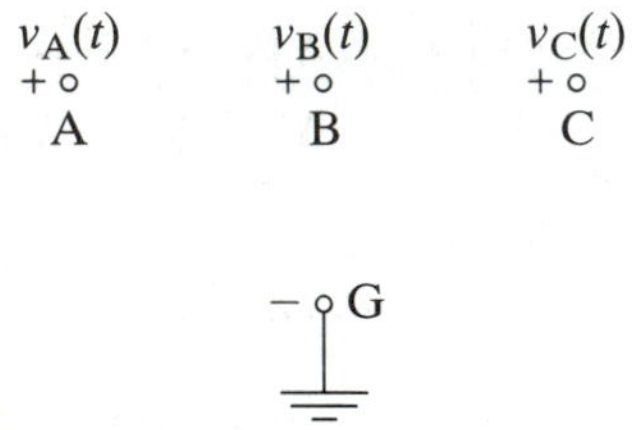

FIGURE 1–4 *Ground symbol indicates a common voltage reference point.*

Since voltage is defined between two points, it is often useful to define a common voltage reference point called **ground**. The voltages at all other points in a circuit are then defined with respect to this common reference point. We indicate the voltage reference point using the ground symbol shown in Figure 1–4. Under this convention we sometimes refer to the variables $v_A(t)$, $v_B(t)$, and $v_C(t)$ as the voltages at points A, B, and C, respectively. This terminology appears to contradict the fact that voltage is an across variable that involves two points. However, the terminology means that the variables $v_A(t)$, $v_B(t)$, and $v_C(t)$ are the voltages defined between points A, B, and C, and the common voltage reference point at point G.

Using a common reference point for across variables is not an idea unique to electrical circuits. For example, the elevation of a mountain is the number of feet or meters between the top of the mountain and a common reference point at sea level. If a geographic point lies below sea level, then its elevation is assigned a negative algebraic sign. So it is with voltages. If circuit analysis reveals that the voltage variable at point A is negative [i.e., $v_A(t) < 0$], then this fact together with the reference marks in Figure 1–4 indicate that the potential at point A is less than the ground potential.

EXAMPLE 1–3

Figure 1–5 shows a circuit formed by interconnecting five devices, each of which has two terminals. A voltage and current variable has been assigned to each device using the passive sign convention. The working variables for each device are observed to be as follows:

	DEVICE 1	DEVICE 2	DEVICE 3	DEVICE 4	DEVICE 5
v	+100 V	?	+25 V	+75 V	–75 V
i	?	+5 mA	+5 mA	?	+5 mA
p	–1 W	+0.5 W	?	0.75 W	?

(a) Find the missing variable for each device and state whether the device is absorbing or delivering power.
(b) Check your work by showing that the sum of the device powers is zero.

FIGURE 1-5

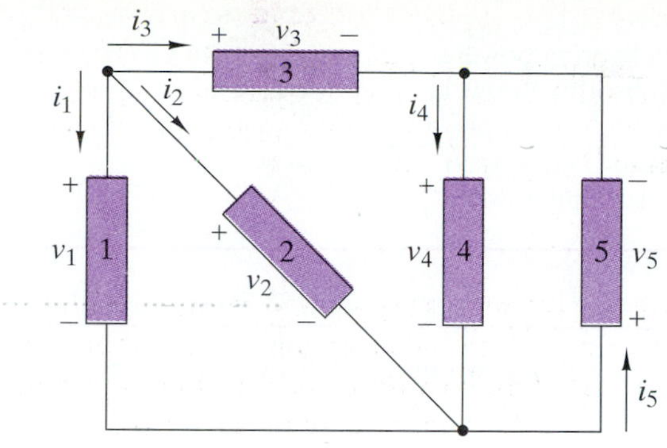

SOLUTION:

(a) We use $p = vi$ to solve for the missing variable since two of the three circuit variables are given for each device.

Device 1: $i_1 = p_1/v_1 = -1/100 = -10$ mA [$p(t) < 0$, delivering power]

Device 2: $v_2 = p_2/i_2 = 0.5/0.005 = 100$ V [$p(t) > 0$, absorbing power]

Device 3: $p_3 = v_3 i_3 = 25 \times 0.005 = 0.125$ W [$p(t) > 0$, absorbing power]

Device 4: $i_4 = p_4/v_4 = 0.75/75 = 10$ mA [$p(t) > 0$, absorbing power]

Device 5: $p_5 = v_5 i_5 = -75 \times 0.005 = -0.375$ W [$p(t) < 0$, delivering power]

(b) Summing the device powers yields

$$p_1 + p_2 + p_3 + p_4 + p_5 = -1 + 0.5 + 0.125 + 0.75 - 0.375$$
$$= +1.375 - 1.375 = 0$$

This example shows that the sum of the power absorbed by devices is equal in magnitude to the sum of the power supplied by devices. A power balance always exists in the types of circuits treated in this book and can be used as an overall check of circuit analysis calculations. ■

Exercise 1–4

The working variables of a set of two-terminal electrical devices are observed to be as follows:

	DEVICE 1	DEVICE 2	DEVICE 3	DEVICE 4	DEVICE 5
v	+10 V	?	−15 V	+5 V	?
i	−3 A	−3 A	+10 mA	?	−12 mA
p	?	+40 W	?	+10 mW	−120 mW

Using the passive sign convention, find the magnitude and sign of the unknown variable and state whether the device is absorbing or delivering power.

Answers:

Device 1: $p = -30$ W (delivering power)
Device 2: $v = -13.3$ V (absorbing power)
Device 3: $p = -150$ mW (delivering power)
Device 4: $i = +2$ mA (absorbing power)
Device 5: $v = +10$ V (absorbing power)

Exercise 1–5

Figure 1–6 shows a circuit with six two-terminal devices and their assigned voltage and current variables. The working variables for each element are observed to be as follows:

	Device 1	Device 2	Device 3	Device 4	Device 5	Device 6
v	+7.5 V	+5 V	?	+7.5 V	?	+12.5 V
i	−3 A	?	+0.5 A	+1.5 A	+2.5 A	+1 A
p	?	+10 W	+1.25 W	?	−12.5 W	?

(a) Using the passive sign convention, find the missing variable for each device and state whether the device is absorbing or delivering power.
(b) Use the power balance to check your work.

FIGURE 1–6

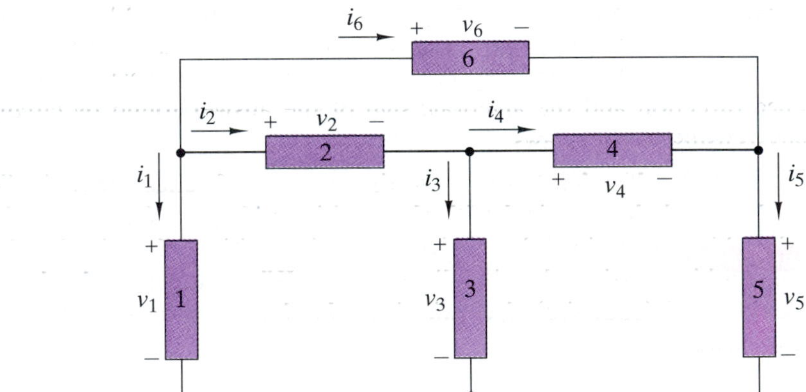

Answers:

(a) Device 1: p_1 = −22.5 W (delivering power)
Device 2: i_2 = +2 A (absorbing power)
Device 3: v_3 = +2.5 V (absorbing power)
Device 4: p_4 = +11.25 W (absorbing power)
Device 5: v_5 = −5 V (delivering power)
Device 6: p_6 = +12.5 W (absorbing power)

(b) 35 − 35 = 0

SUMMARY

- Circuits are important in electrical engineering because they process signals that carry energy and information. A **circuit** is an interconnection of electrical devices. A **signal** is an electrical current or voltage that carries energy or information. An **interface** is a pair of accessible terminals at which signals may be observed or specified.
- This book defines overall course objectives at the analysis, design, and evaluation levels. In **circuit analysis** the circuit and input signals are given and the object is to find the output signals. The object of **circuit design** is to devise one or more circuits that produce prescribed output signals for given inputs signals. The **evaluation** problem involves appraising alternative circuit designs using criteria such as cost, power consumption, and parts count.
- Charge (q) and energy (w) are the basic physical variables involved in electrical phenomena. Current (i), voltage (v), and power (p) are the derived variables used in circuit analysis and design. In the SI system, charge is measured in coulombs (C), energy in joules (J), current in amperes (A), voltage in volts (V), and power in watts (W).
- **Current** is defined as dq/dt and is a measure of the flow of electrical charge. **Voltage** is defined as dw/dq and is a measure of the energy required to move a small charge from one point to another. **Power** is defined as dw/dt and is a measure of the rate at which energy is being transferred. Power is related to current and voltage as $p = vi$.
- The **reference marks** (arrows and plus/minus signs) assigned to a device are reference directions, not indications of the way a circuit responds. The actual direction of the response is determined by comparing the reference direction and the algebraic sign of the answer found by circuit analysis using physical laws.
- Under the **passive sign convention**, the current reference arrow is directed toward the terminal with the positive voltage reference mark. Under this convention, the device power is positive when it absorbs power and is negative when it delivers power. When current and voltage have the same (opposite) algebraic signs, the device is absorbing (delivering) power.

EN ROUTE OBJECTIVES AND ASSOCIATED PROBLEMS

ERO 1–1 ELECTRICAL SYMBOLS AND UNITS (SECT. 1–2)

Given an electrical quantity described in terms of words, scientific notation, or decimal prefix notation, convert the quantity to an alternate description.

1–1 Write the following statements in symbolic form:

(a) twelve milliamperes

(b) four hundred fifty five kilohertz

(c) two hundred picoseconds
(d) two thousand one hundred volts

1–2 Write out the meaning of the following symbols in words:
(a) 66 kHz
(b) 10 krad/s
(c) 2.02 MW
(d) 2.02 J
(e) 1.1 MΩ

1–3 Express the following quantities using appropriate engineering prefixes (i.e., state the numeric to the nearest standard prefix).
(a) 2,200,000 volts
(b) 2300×10^{-9} farads
(c) 6200 ohms
(d) 7.52×10^{5} joules
(e) 0.000235 henrys

1–4 Commercial electrical power companies measure energy consumption in kilowatt-hours, denoted kWh. One kilowatt-hour is the amount of energy transferred by 1 kW of power in a time period of 1 hour. During a one-month time period, a power company billing statement reports a user's total energy usage to be 2128 kWh. Determine the number of joules used during the billing period.

1–5 Fill in the blanks in the following statements.
(a) To convert capacitance from microfarads to picofarads, multiply by ______.
(b) To convert resistance from kilohms to megohms, multiply by ______.
(c) To convert current from amperes to milliamperes, multiply by ______.
(d) To convert power from watts to megawatts, multiply by ______.

1–6 The decibel (dB) is one tenth of a bel. The number of dB in a power ratio is defined to be $10 \log_{10}(p_2/p_1)$. Signal power levels are often specified in dBm, which is the number of decibels referenced to a power level of $p_1 = 1$ milliwatt.
(a) Express the following power levels in dBm: 60 W, 10 μW, and 8 kW.
(b) Express the following power levels in W: 60 dBm, –35 dBm, and 200 dBm.

ERO 1–2 CIRCUIT VARIABLES (SECT. 1–3)

Given any two of the three signal variables (i, v, p) or the two basic variables (q, w), find the magnitude and direction (sign) of the unspecified variables.

1–7 An ampere-hour (Ah) meter measures the integral, with respect to time, of the current in a conductor. During a 12-hour period a certain meter records 3000 Ah.
(a) Find the number of coulombs that flowed through the meter during the recording period.
(b) Find the average current during the recording period.

1–8 Figure P1–8 shows a plot of the net positive charge flowing in a wire versus time. Sketch the corresponding current during the same time period.

1–9 The net positive charge flowing through a device varies as $q(t) = 3t^2$ C. Find the current through the device at $t = 0$ s, $t = 1$ s, and $t = 3$ s.

1–10 The current through a device is given by $i(t) = 0.05t$ A. How many coulombs enter the device between time $t = 0$ s and $t = 5$ s?

1–11 Figure P1–11 shows a plot of the net positive charge flowing in a wire versus time. Sketch the corresponding current during the same time period.

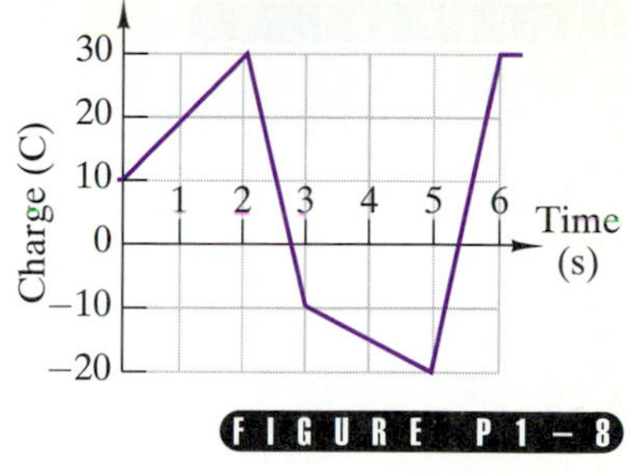

FIGURE P1–8

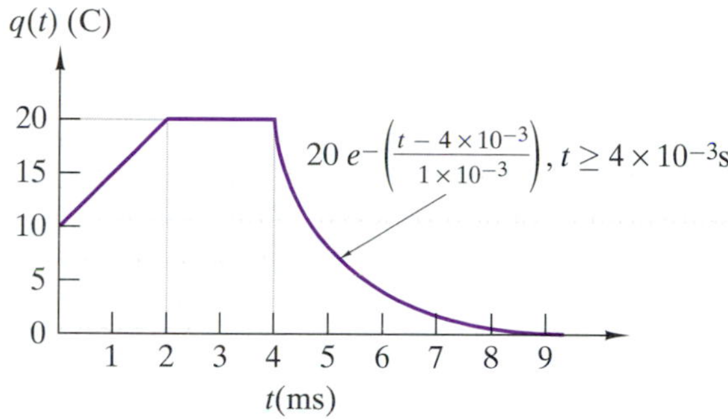

FIGURE P1–11

1–12 An incandescent lamp absorbs 75 W when connected to a 120-V source.

(a) Find the current through the lamp.

(b) Find the cost of operating the lamp for 8 hours when electricity costs 7.2 cents/kW-hr.

1–13 The 12-V automobile battery in Figure P1–13 has an output capacity of 200 ampere-hours (Ah) when connected to a headlamp that absorbs 50 watts of power. Assume the battery voltage is constant.

(a) Find the current supplied by the battery.

(b) How long can the battery power the headlight?

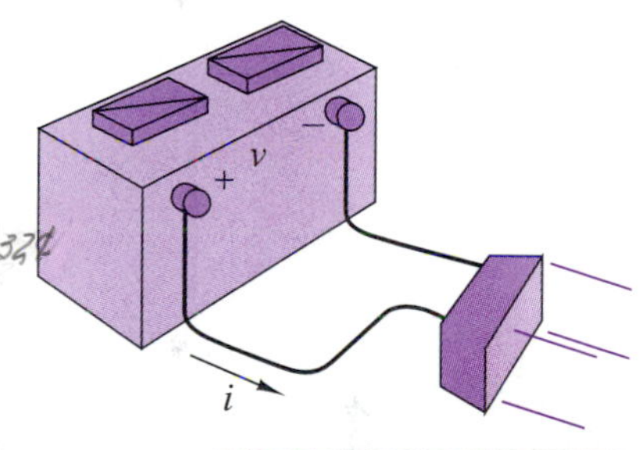

FIGURE P1–13

1–14 A certain semiconductor material carries a current density 4×10^4 A per square meter (m^2) and has 5×10^{22} free electrons/m^3. Find the average velocity of the electrons flowing in the material. *Hint:* the charge on an electron is 1.6×10^{-19} C.

1–15 A total of 50 ampere-hours are supplied to a 12-V battery during recharging. Determine the number of joules supplied to the battery. Assume battery voltage is constant.

1–16 The voltage between two points is 100 V. How much energy is required to move a charge of 3 μJ from one point to the other?

1–17 A two-terminal device has the current versus voltage characteristics shown in Figure P1–17. Assuming the passive sign convention,

(a) Determine the device power when it operates at point A and state whether the device is absorbing or delivering power.

(b) Repeat part (a) when the device operates at points B and C.

(c) Identify the operating point on the curve (it could be a point other than A, B, or C) at which the device delivers the most power.

FIGURE P1–17

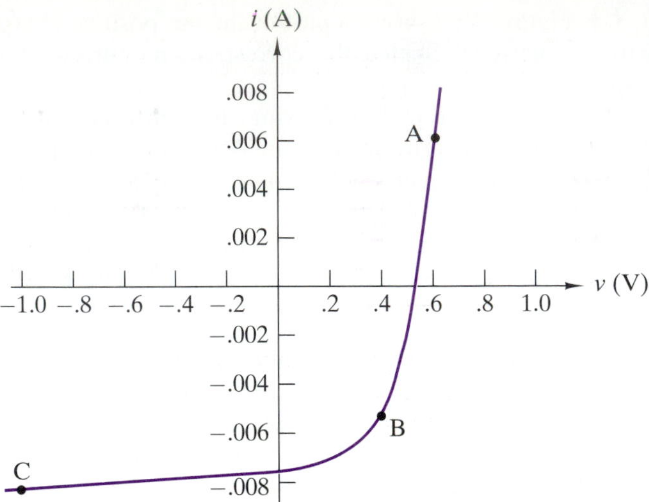

1–18 Under the passive sign convention, the current through and voltage across a two-terminal device are $i = 20$ mA and $v = 5$ V.

(a) Find the device power and state whether the device is absorbing or delivering power.

(b) Repeat (a) when $i = -20$ mA.

1–19 The voltage across a two-terminal device is always 15 V. The maximum power the device can dissipate is 0.5 W. Determine the maximum current magnitude allowed by the device power rating.

1–20 A laser produces 10-kW bursts of power that last 20 ns. If the burst rate is 50 bursts per second, what is the average power in the laser's output?

1–21 Two electrical devices are connected at an interface, as shown in Figure P1–21. Using the reference marks shown in the figure, find the power transferred and state whether the power is transferred from A to B or B to A when

(a) $v = +12$ V and $i = -2.2$ A

(b) $v = -33$ V and $i = -1.2$ mA

(c) $v = +15$ V and $i = +40$ mA

(d) $v = -37.5$ V and $i = -43$ mA

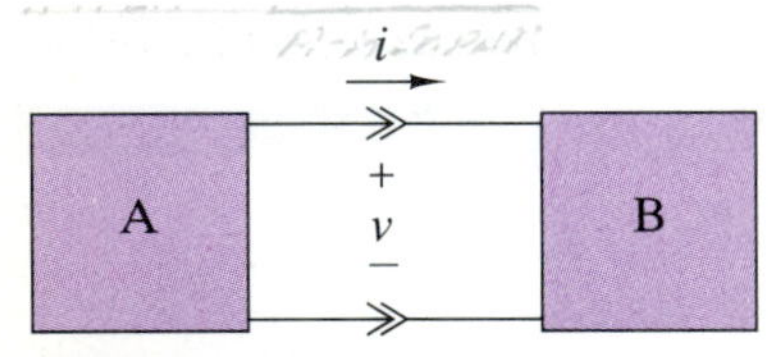

FIGURE P1–21

1–22 Figure P1–22 shows an electric circuit with a voltage and current variable assigned to each of the six devices. The device signal variables are observed to be as follows:

	DEVICE 1	DEVICE 2	DEVICE 3	DEVICE 4	DEVICE 5	DEVICE 6
v	+15 V	+10 V	?	+15 V	?	?
i	−3 A	?	+0.5 A	+2.5 A	+3.5 A	−1 A
p	?	+30W	+2.5 W	?	−35 W	+10 W

FIGURE P1–22

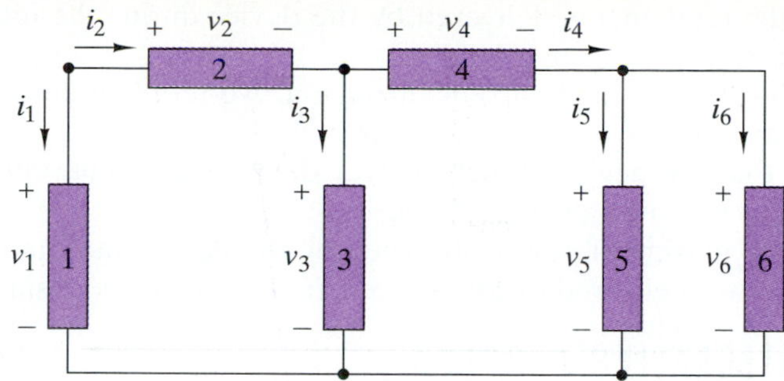

Find the unknown signal variable associated with each device and state whether the device is absorbing or delivering power. Use the power balance to check your work.

1–23 Figure P1–23 shows an electric circuit with a voltage and current variable assigned to each of the eight devices. The device signal variables are observed to be as follows:

	Device 1	Device 2	Device 3	Device 4	Device 5	Device 6	Device 7	Device 8
v	+12 V	?	?	−12 V	+12 V	+8 V	?	+1 V
i	+2 A	−4 A	−8 A	−2 A	2 A	?	2 A	?
p	?	+32 W	−160 W	?	?	48 W	+6 W	+2 W

Find the unknown signal variable associated with each device and state whether the device is absorbing or delivering power. Use the power balance to check your work.

FIGURE P1–23

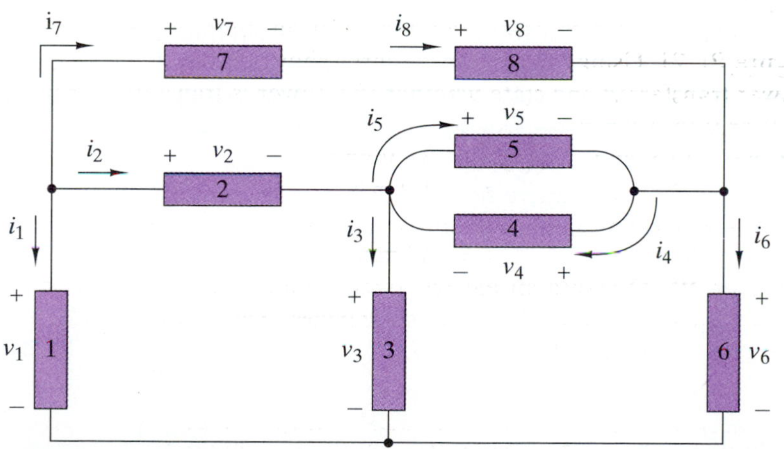

1–24 The voltage across and current through a two-terminal device are $v(t) = 5e^{-100t}$ V and $i(t) = -5e^{-100t}$ mA.

(a) Find the power delivered by the device at $t = 0$, $t = 5$ ms, and $t = 25$ ms.

(b) Find the total energy delivered by the device during the interval $0 < t < \infty$.

✓ **1–25** The voltage across and current through a two-terminal device are $v(t) = 120 \cos 1000t$ V and $i(t) = 4 \sin 1000t$ A.

(a) Show that the device absorbs power during some time intervals and delivers power during others.

(b) Find the maximum power absorbed by the device and the maximum power delivered by the device. *Hint*: $\cos x \sin x = \frac{1}{2} \sin 2x$.

CHAPTER-INTEGRATING PROBLEMS

✓ **1–26 POWER RATIO IN dB**

In complete darkness the voltage across and current through a two-terminal light detector are +5.6 V and +8 nA. In full sunlight the voltage and current are +0.9 V and +4 mA. Express the light/dark power ratio of the device in decibels (dB). (See Problem 1–6 for the definition of a decibel.)

$P_{LIGHT} = (0.9V)(4ma) = 3.6\ mW$
$P_{DARK} = (5.6V)(8nA) = 44.8\ nW$
$P_{dB} = 10 \log_{10}(P_{LIGHT}/P_{DARK}) = 10 \log_{10}\left(\frac{3.6 \times 10^{-3}}{44.8 \times 10^{-9}}\right) = 49.05\ dB$

✓ **1–27 INCREMENTAL SENSITIVITY**

Incremental sensitivity is an indication of the smallest change that can be detected by a measuring device or system. It is defined as the change in output indication caused by a specified change in the input stimulus. A temperature measuring system produces outputs of 1 mA and 2.5 V when the input temperature is 10°C. At 200°C the outputs are 5 mA and 7.5 V. Determine the sensitivity of the system in mW per °C.

$P_1 = (2.5V)(1ma) = 2.5\ mW$ @ $T_1 = 10°C$
$P_2 = (7.5V)(5ma) = 37.5\ mW$ @ $T_2 = 200°C$
$SENSITIVITY = \frac{(P_2-P_1)}{(T_2-T_1)} = \frac{37.5-2.5}{200°-10°} = \frac{35\ mW}{190°C} = 0.184\ mW/°C$

✓ **1–28 STORAGE BATTERY EFFICIENCY**

The ampere-hour efficiency of a storage battery is the ratio of its ampere-hour output to the ampere-hour input required to recharge the battery. A certain 24-V battery has a rated output of 500 ampere-hours. When the battery is completely drained, a battery charger must deliver 65 A for 8 hours to recharge the battery. Assume the battery voltage is constant.

(a) Determine the ampere-hour efficiency of the battery.

(b) Determine the number of joules required to recharge the battery.

(a) $A\text{-}h\ EFF = \frac{A\text{-}h\ OUTPUT}{A\text{-}h\ INPUT} = \frac{500}{(65)(8)} = 96.2\%$
(b) $ENERGY = (65)(8)(24) = 12{,}480\ J\text{-}HRS/SEC = (12{,}480\ J\text{-}HRS/SEC)(3600\ SEC/HR) = 44.928\ MJ$

CHAPTER 2

BASIC CIRCUIT ANALYSIS

The equation S = A/L *shows that the current of a voltaic circuit is subject to a change, by each variation originating either in the magnitude of a tension or in the reduced length of a part, which latter is itself again determined, both by the actual length of the part as well as its conductivity and its section.*

Georg Simon Ohm, 1827,
German Mathematician/Physicist

This chapter begins our study of the ideal models used to describe the physical devices in electrical circuits. Foremost among these is the renowned Ohm's law, defining the model of a linear resistor. Georg Simon Ohm (1789–1854) originally discovered the law that now bears his name in 1827. His results drew heavy criticism and were not generally accepted for many years. Fortunately, the importance of his contribution was eventually recognized during his lifetime. He was honored by the Royal Society of England in 1841 and appointed a Professor of Physics at the University of Munich in 1849.

The first section of this chapter deals with the element constraints derived from the ideal models of resistors, voltage sources, and current sources. The models for other linear devices, such as amplifiers, inductors, capacitors, and transformers, are introduced in later chapters. When devices are interconnected to form a circuit, they are subject to connection constraints based on fundamental conservation principles known as Kirchhoff's laws. The remainder of the chapter uses the combined element and connection constraints to develop a basic set of circuit analysis tools that include equivalent circuits, voltage and current division, and circuit reduction. The basic circuit analysis tools developed in this chapter are used frequently in the rest of the book and by practicing engineers. These analysis tools promote basic understanding because they involve working directly with the circuit model.

2–1 ELEMENT CONSTRAINTS

A **circuit** is a collection of interconnected electrical devices. An electrical **device** is a component that is treated as a separate entity. The rectangular box in Figure 2–1 is used to represent any one of the two-terminal devices used to form circuits. A two-terminal device is described by its ***i–v* characteristic**; that is, by the relationship between the voltage across and current through the device. In most cases the relationship is complicated and nonlinear, so we use a linear model that approximates the dominant features of a device.

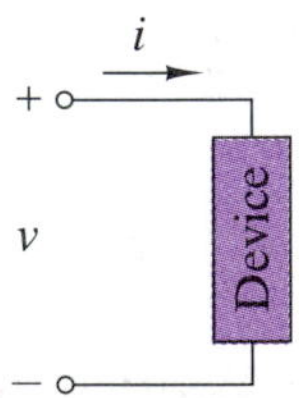

FIGURE 2–1 *Voltage and current reference marks for a two-terminal device.*

To distinguish between a device (the real thing) and its model (an approximate stand-in), we call the model a circuit **element**. Thus, a device is an article of hardware described in manufacturers' catalogs and parts specifications. An element is a model described in textbooks on circuit analysis. This book is no exception, and a catalog of circuit elements will be introduced as we go on. A discussion of real devices and their models is contained in Appendix A.

THE LINEAR RESISTOR

The first element in our catalog is a linear model of the device described in Figure 2–2. The actual *i–v* characteristic of this device is the blue curve shown in Figure 2–2(b). To model this curve accurately across the full operating range shown in the figure would require at least a cubic equation. However, the graph in Figure 2–4 shows that a straight line is a good approximation to the i–v characteristic if we operate the device within its linear range. The power rating of the device limits the range over which the i–v characteristics can be represented by a straight line through the origin.

For the passive sign convention used in Figure 2–2(a), the equations describing the *linear resistor* element are

$$v = Ri \quad \text{or} \quad i = Gv \tag{2-1}$$

where R and G are positive constants that are reciprocally related.

$$G = \frac{1}{R} \tag{2-2}$$

The relationships in Eq. (2–1) are collectively known as **Ohm's law**. The parameter R is called **resistance** and has the unit **ohms**, Ω. The parameter G is called **conductance**, with the unit **siemens**, S. In earlier times the unit of conductance was cleverly called the mho, with a unit abbreviation symbol ℧ (ohm spelled backward and the ohm symbol upside down). Note that Ohm's law presumes that the passive sign convention is used to assign the reference marks to voltage and current.

The Ohm's law model is represented graphically by the black straight line in Figure 2–2(b). The i–v characteristic for the Ohm's law model defines a circuit element that is said to be linear and bilateral. **Linear** means that the defining characteristic is a straight line through the origin. Elements whose characteristics do not pass through the origin or are not a straight line are said to be **nonlinear**. **Bilateral** means that the i–v characteristic curve has odd symmetry about the origin.[1] With a bilateral resistor, reversing the polarity of the applied voltage reverses the direction but not the magnitude of the current, and vice versa. The net result is that we can connect a bilateral resistor into a circuit without regard to which terminal is which. This is important because devices such as diodes and batteries are not bilateral, and we must carefully identify each terminal.

Figure 2–2(c) shows sketches of discrete resistor devices. Detailed device characteristics and fabrication techniques are discussed in Appendix A.

The power associated with the resistor can be found from $p = vi$. Using Eq. (2–1) to eliminate v from this relationship yields

$$p = i^2R \tag{2-3}$$

or using the same equations to eliminate i yields

$$p = v^2G = \frac{v^2}{R} \tag{2-4}$$

Since the parameter R is positive, these equations tell us that the power is always nonnegative. Under the passive sign convention, this means that the resistor **always absorbs power**.

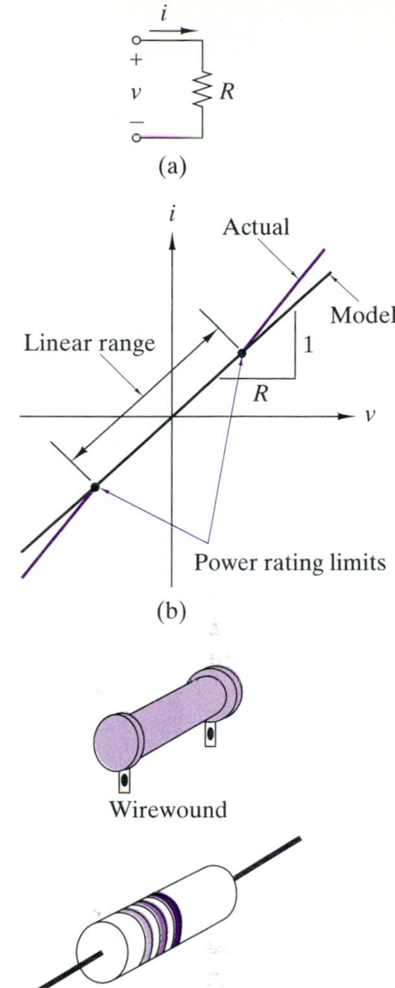

FIGURE 2–2 *The resistor: (a) Circuit symbol. (b) i–v characteristics. (c) Some actual devices.*

1 A curve $i = f(v)$ has odd symmetry if $f(-v) = -f(v)$.

EXAMPLE 2–1

A resistor operates as a linear element as long as the voltage and current are within the limits defined by its power rating. Suppose we have a 47-kΩ resistor with a power rating of 0.25 W. Determine the maximum current and voltage that can be applied to the resistor and remain within its linear operating range.

SOLUTION:

Using Eq. (2–3) to relate power and current, we obtain

$$I_{\text{MAX}} = \sqrt{\frac{P_{\text{MAX}}}{R}} = \sqrt{\frac{0.25}{47 \times 10^3}} = 2.31 \text{ mA}$$

Similarly, using Eq. (2–4) to relate power and voltage, we obtain

$$V_{\text{MAX}} = \sqrt{RP_{\text{MAX}}} = \sqrt{47 \times 10^3 \times 0.25} = 108 \text{ V}$$ ■

FIGURE 2–3 *Circuit symbols: (a) Open-circuit symbol. (b) Short-circuit symbol.*

OPEN AND SHORT CIRCUITS

The next two circuit elements can be thought of as limiting cases of the linear resistor. Consider a resistor R with a voltage v applied across it. Let's calculate the current i through the resistor for different values of resistance. If $v = 10$ V and $R = 1$ Ω, using Ohm's law we readily find that $i = 10$ A. If we increase the resistance to 100 Ω, we find i has decreased to 0.1 A or 100 mA. If we continue to increase R to 1 MΩ, i becomes a very small 10 μA. Continuing this process, we arrive at a condition where R is very nearly infinite and i just about zero. When the current $i = 0$, we call the special value of resistance (i.e., $R = \infty$ Ω), an **open circuit**. Similarly, if we reduce R until it approaches zero, we find that the voltage is very nearly zero. When $v = 0$, we call the special value of resistance (i.e., $R = 0$ Ω), a **short circuit**. The circuit symbols for these two elements are shown in Figure 2–3. In circuit analysis the elements in a circuit model are assumed to be interconnected by zero-resistance wire (that is, by short circuits).

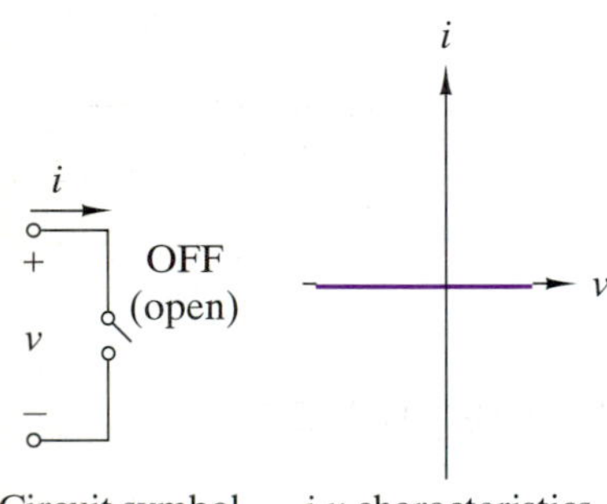

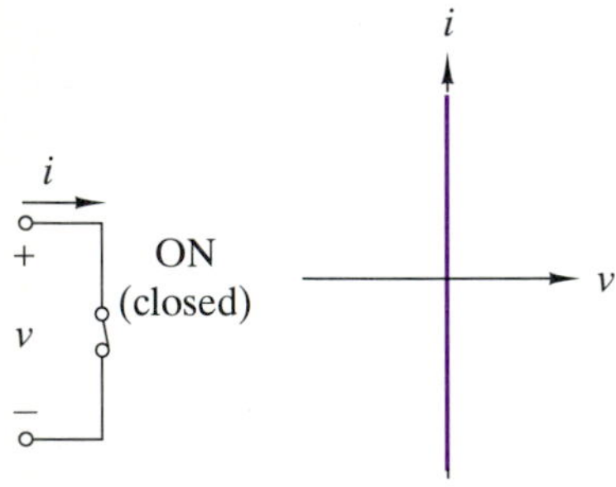

FIGURE 2–4 *The circuit symbol and i–v characteristics of an ideal switch: (a) Switch OFF. (b) Switch ON.*

THE IDEAL SWITCH

A switch is a familiar device with many applications in electrical engineering. The **ideal switch** can be modeled as a combination of an open- and a short-circuit element. Figure 2–4 shows the circuit symbol and the i–v characteristic of an ideal switch. When the switch is closed,

$$v = 0 \quad \text{and} \quad i = \text{any value} \tag{2–5a}$$

and when it is open,

$$i = 0 \quad \text{and} \quad v = \text{any value} \tag{2–5b}$$

When the switch is closed, the voltage across the element is zero and the element will pass any current that may result. When open, the current is zero and the element will withstand any voltage across its terminals. The power is always zero for the ideal switch, since the product $vi = 0$ when the switch is either open ($i = 0$) or closed ($v = 0$). Actual switch devices have limitations, such as the maximum current they can safely carry when closed and the maximum voltage they can withstand when open. The switch is operated (opened or closed) by some external influence, such as a mechanical motion, temperature, pressure, or an electrical signal.

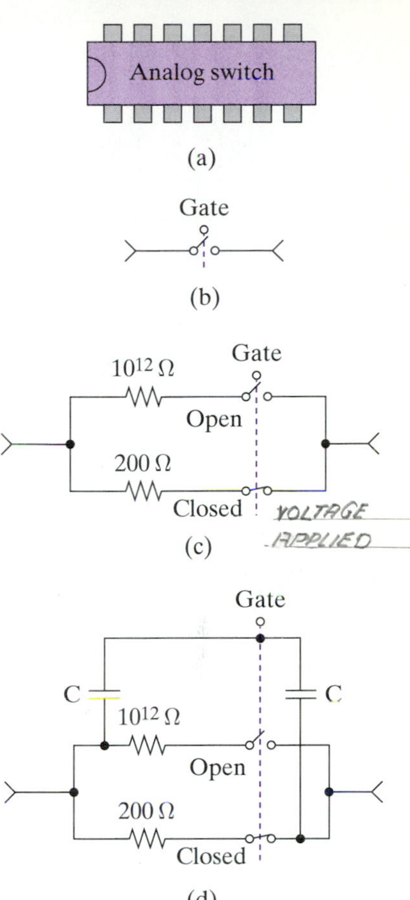

FIGURE 2-5 *The analog switch: (a) Actual device. (b) Basic curcuit model. (c) Intermediate circuit model. (d) Advanced model.*

APPLICATION NOTE: EXAMPLE 2-2

The **analog switch** is an important device found in analog-to-digital interfaces. Figure 2–5(a) shows an actual integrated circuit device in a dual-inline package (DIP). Figures 2–5(b), 2–5(c), and 2–5(d) show various circuit models of the device. In all models the switch is actuated by applying a voltage to the terminal labeled "gate."

In the basic model in Figure 2–5(b) the ideal switch closes when voltage is applied to the gate terminal and opens when no voltage is applied. The intermediate model in Figure 2–5(c) includes two ideal switch elements. When voltage is applied to the gate the upper switch opens and the lower switch closes. In the closed state a resistance of 200 Ω is connected between the terminals of the analog switch. Any current carried by the closed switch must pass through this resistance, causing an i^2R power loss. When voltage is removed from the gate the upper switch closes and the lower switch opens. In the open state a very high resistance (10^{12} Ω) is connected between the terminals of the analog switch. In the open state the voltage across the analog switch causes a very small current that is usually negligible. The advanced model in Figure 2–5(d) includes two capacitance elements labeled "C." These dynamic circuit elements are needed to account for transient effects and are discussed in a later chapter.

This example illustrates how a few basic circuit elements can be combined to model other electrical devices. It also suggests that no single model can serve in all applications. It is up to the engineer to select a model that adequately represents the actual device in each application.

IDEAL SOURCES

The signal and power sources required to operate electronic circuits are modeled using two elements: **voltage sources** and **current sources**. These sources can produce either constant or time-varying signals. The circuit symbols and the i–v characteristic of an ideal voltage source are shown in Figure 2–6, while the circuit symbol and i–v characteristic of an ideal current source are shown in Figure 2–7. The symbol in Figure 2–6(a) represents either a time-varying or constant voltage source. The battery symbol in Figure 2–6(b) is used exclusively for a constant voltage source. There is no separate symbol for a constant current source.

The i–v characteristic of an **ideal voltage source** in Figure 2–6(c) is described by the following element equations:

$$v = v_S \quad \text{and} \quad i = \text{any value} \tag{2-6}$$

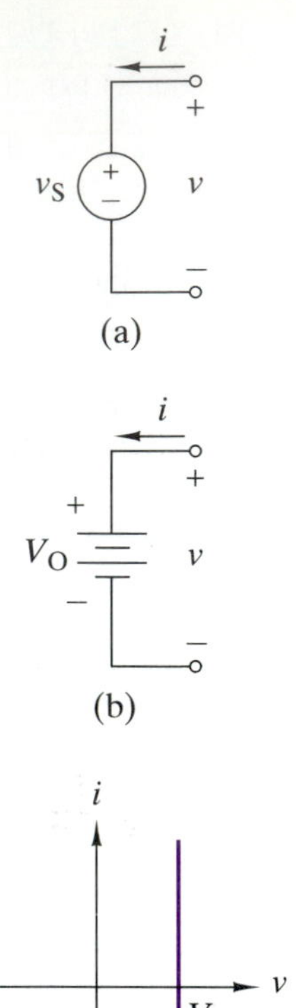

FIGURE 2–6 *Circuit symbols and* i–v *characteristics of an ideal independent voltage source: (a) Time varying. (b) Constant (battery). (c) Constant source* i–v *characteristics.*

FIGURE 2–7 *Circuit symbols and* i–v *characteristic of an ideal independent current source: (a) Time-varying or constant source. (b) Constant source* i–v *characteristics.*

The element equations mean that the ideal voltage source produces v_S volts across its terminals and will supply whatever current may be required by the circuit to which it is connected.

The *i–v* characteristic of an **ideal current source** in Figure 2–7(b) is described by the following element equations:

$$i = i_S \quad \text{and} \quad v = \text{any value} \tag{2-7}$$

The ideal current source produces i_S amperes in the direction of its arrow symbol and will furnish whatever voltage is required by the circuit to which it is connected. The voltage or current produced by these ideal sources is called a **forcing function** or a **driving function** because it represents an input that causes a circuit response.

EXAMPLE 2–3

Given an ideal voltage source with the time-varying voltage shown in Figure 2–8(a), sketch its *i–v* characteristic at the times $t = 0$, 1, and 2 ms.

FIGURE 2–8

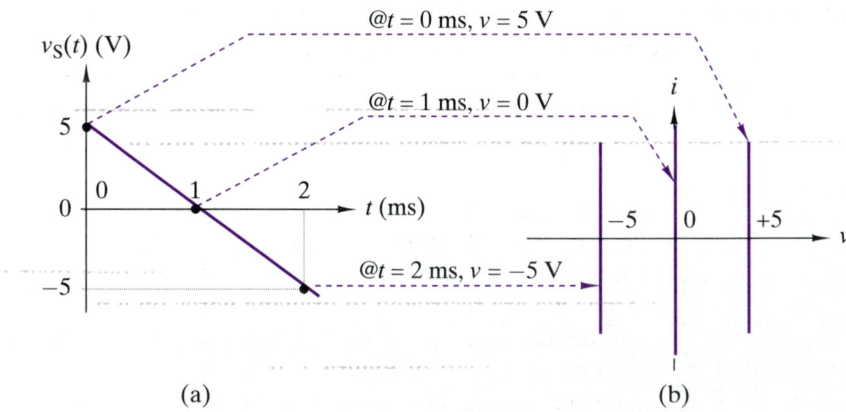

SOLUTION:
At any instant of time, the time-varying source voltage has only one value. We can treat the voltage and current at each instant of time as constants representing a snapshot of the source i–v characteristic. For example, at $t = 0$, the equations defining the i–v characteristic are $v_S = 5$ V and i = any value. Figure 2–8(b) shows the i–v relationship at the other instants of time. Curiously, the voltage source i–v characteristic at $t = 1$ ms ($v_S = 0$ and i = any value) is the same as that of a short circuit [see Eq. (2–5a) or Figure 2–3(b)]. ■

PRACTICAL SOURCES

The practical models for voltage and sources in Figure 2–9 may be more appropriate in some situations than the ideal models used up to this point. These circuits are called practical models because they more accurately represent the characteristics of real-world sources than do the ideal models. It is important to remember that models are interconnections of elements, not devices. For example, the resistance in a model does not always represent an actual resistor. As a case in point, the resistances R_S in the practical source models in Figure 2–9 do not represent physical resistors but are circuit elements used to account for resistive effects within the devices being modeled.

The linear resistor, open circuit, short circuit, ideal switch, ideal voltage source, and ideal current source are the initial entries in our catalog of circuit elements. In Chapter 4 we will develop models for active devices like the transistor and OP AMP. Models for dynamic elements like capacitors and inductors are introduced in Chapter 6.

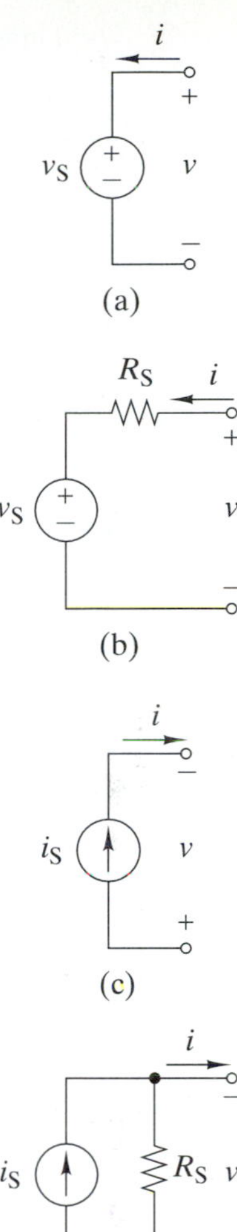

FIGURE 2–9 *Circuit symbols for ideal and practical independent sources: (a) Ideal voltage source. (b) Practical voltage source. (c) Ideal current source. (d) Practical current source.*

2–2 CONNECTION CONSTRAINTS

In the previous section, we considered individual devices and models. In this section, we turn our attention to the constraints introduced by interconnections of devices to form circuits. The laws governing circuit behavior are based on the meticulous work of the German scientist Gustav Kirchhoff (1824–1887). **Kirchhoff's laws** are derived from conservation laws as applied to circuits. They tell us that element voltages and currents are forced to behave in certain ways when the devices are interconnected to form a circuit. These conditions are called **connection constraints** because they are based only on the circuit connections and not on the specific devices in the circuit.

In this book, we will indicate that crossing wires are connected (electrically tied together) using the dot symbol, as in Figure 2–10(a). Sometimes crossing wires are not connected (electrically insulated) but pass over or under each other. Since we are restricted to drawing wires on a planar surface, we will indicate unconnected crossovers by *not* placing a dot at their intersection, as indicated in the left of Figure 2–10(b). Other books sometimes show unconnected crossovers using the semicircular "hopover" shown on the right of Figure 2–10(b). In engineering systems two or more

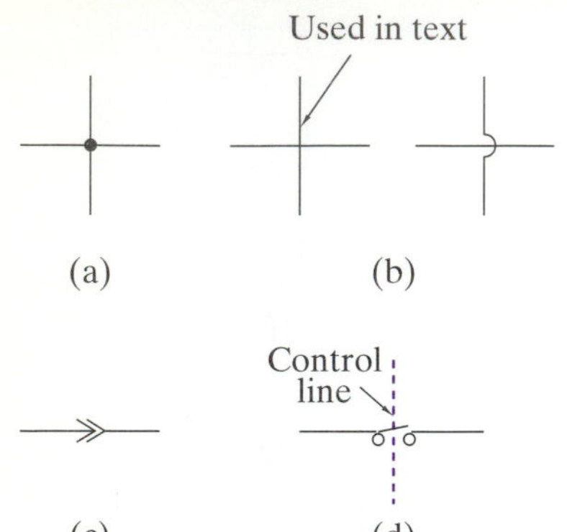

FIGURE 2–10 *Symbols used in circuit diagrams: (a) Electrical connection. (b) Crossover with no connection. (c) Jack connection. (d) Control line.*

separate circuits are often tied together to form a larger circuit (for example, the interconnection of two integrated circuit packages). Interconnecting different circuits forms an interface between the circuits. The special jack or interface symbol in Figure 2–10(c) is used in this book because interface connections represent important points at which the interaction between two circuits can be observed or specified. On certain occasions a control line is required to show a mechanical or other nonelectrical dependency. Figure 2–10(d) shows how this dependency is indicated in this book.

The treatment of Kirchhoff's laws uses the following definitions:

- A **circuit** is an interconnection of electrical devices.
- A **node** is an electrical juncture of two or more devices.
- A **loop** is a closed path formed by tracing through an ordered sequence of nodes without passing through any node more than once.

While it is customary to designate the juncture of two or more elements as a node, it is important to realize that a node is not confined to a point but includes all the zero-resistance wire from the point to each element. In the circuit of Figure 2–11, there are only three different nodes: A, B, and C. The points 2, 3, and 4, for example, are part of node B, while the points 5, 6, 7, and 8 are all part of node C.

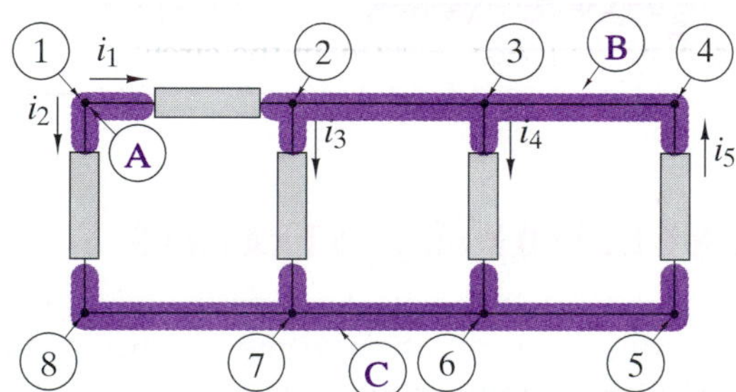

FIGURE 2–11 *Circuit for demonstrating Kirchhoff's current law.*

KIRCHHOFF'S CURRENT LAW

Kirchhoff's first law is based on the principle of conservation of charge. **Kirchhoff's current law (KCL)** states that

> ***the algebraic sum of the currents entering a node is zero at every instant.***

In forming the algebraic sum of currents, we must take into account the current reference direction associated with each device. If the current reference direction is into the node, then we assign a positive sign to the corresponding current in the algebraic sum. If the reference direction is away from the node, we assign a negative sign. Applying this convention to the nodes in Figure 2–11, we obtain the following set of KCL connection equations:

$$\begin{aligned}\text{Node A: } & -i_1 - i_2 = 0 \\ \text{Node B: } & i_1 - i_3 - i_4 + i_5 = 0 \\ \text{Node C: } & i_2 + i_3 + i_4 - i_5 = 0\end{aligned} \qquad (2-8)$$

The KCL equation at node A does not mean that the currents i_1 and i_2 are both negative. The minus signs in this equation simply mean that the reference direction for each current is directed away from node A. Likewise, the equation at node B could be written as

$$i_3 + i_4 = i_1 + i_5 \qquad (2-9)$$

This form illustrates an alternate statement of KCL:

The sum of the currents entering a node equals the sum of the currents leaving the node.

There are two algebraic signs associated with each current in the application of KCL. First is the sign given to a current in writing a KCL connection equation. This sign is determined by the orientation of the current reference direction relative to a node. The second sign is determined by the actual direction of the current relative to the reference direction. The actual direction is found by solving the set of KCL equations, as illustrated in the following example.

EXAMPLE 2–4

Given $i_1 = +4$ A, $i_3 = +1$ A, $i_4 = +2$ A in the circuit shown in Figure 2–11, find i_2 and i_5.

SOLUTION:

Using the node A constraint in Eq. (2–8) yields

$$-i_1 - i_2 = -(+4) - i_2 = 0$$

The sign outside the parentheses comes from the node A KCL connection constraint in Eq. (2–8). The sign inside the parentheses comes from the actual direction of the current. Solving this equation for the unknown current, we find that $i_2 = -4$ A. In this case, the minus sign indicates that the actual direction of the current i_2 is directed upward in Figure 2–11, which is opposite to the reference direction assigned. Using this current in the second KCL equation in Eq. (2–8), we can write

$$i_1 - i_3 - i_4 + i_5 = (+4) - (+1) - (+2) + i_5$$

which yields the result $i_5 = -1$ A.

Again, the signs inside the parentheses are associated with the actual direction of the current, and the signs outside come from the node B KCL connection constraint in Eq. (2–8). The minus sign in the final answer means that the current i_5 is directed in the opposite direction from its assigned reference direction. We can check our work by substituting the values found into the node C constraint in Eq. (2–8). These substitutions yield

$$+ i_2 + i_3 + i_4 - i_5 = (-4) + (+1) + (+2) - (-1) = 0$$

as required by KCL. Given three currents, we determined all the remaining currents in the circuit using only KCL without knowing the element constraints. ■

In Example 2–4, the unknown currents were found using only the KCL constraints at nodes A and B. The node C equation was shown to be valid, but it did not add any new information. If we look back at Eq. (2–8), we see that the node C equation is the negative of the sum of the node A and B equations. In other words, the KCL connection constraint at node C is not independent of the two previous equations. This example illustrates the following general principle:

In a circuit containing a total of* N *nodes there are only* N – 1 *independent KCL connection equations.

Current equations written at $N - 1$ nodes contain all the independent connection constraints that can be derived from KCL. To write these equations, we select one node as the reference or ground node and then write KCL equations at the remaining $N - 1$ nonreference nodes.

Exercise 2–1

Refer to Figure 2–12.

(a) Write KCL equations at nodes A, B, C, and D.
(b) Given $i_1 = -1$ mA, $i_3 = 0.5$ mA, $i_6 = 0.2$ mA, find i_2, i_4, and i_5.

FIGURE 2–12

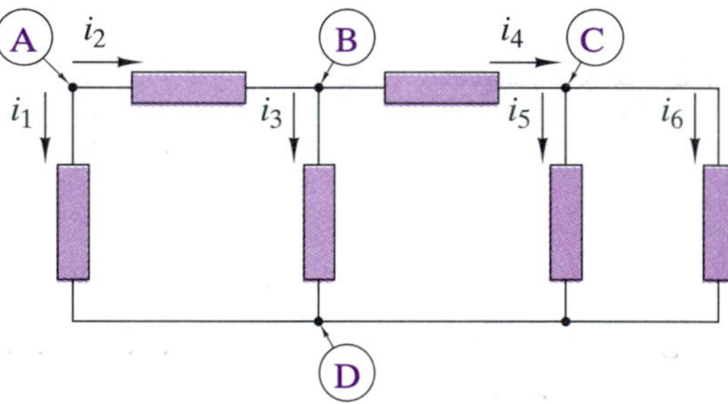

Answers:

(a) Node A: $-i_1 - i_2 = 0$; node B: $i_2 - i_3 - i_4 = 0$; node C: $i_4 - i_5 - i_6 = 0$; node D: $i_1 + i_3 + i_5 + i_6 = 0$
(b) $i_2 = 1$ mA, $i_4 = 0.5$ mA, $i_5 = 0.3$ mA

KIRCHHOFF'S VOLTAGE LAW

The second of Kirchhoff''s circuit laws is based on the principle of conservation of energy. **Kirchhoff's voltage law** (abbreviated **KVL**) states that

the algebraic sum of all the voltages around a loop is zero at every instant.

For example, three loops are shown in the circuit of Figure 2–13. In writing the algebraic sum of voltages, we must account for the assigned reference marks. As a loop is traversed, a positive sign is assigned to a voltage when we go from a "+" to "–" reference mark. When we go from "–" to "+", we use a minus sign. Traversing the three loops in Figure 2–13 in the indicated clockwise direction, yields the following set of KVL connection equations:

$$\begin{aligned}
\text{Loop 1: } & -v_1 + v_2 + v_3 = 0 \\
\text{Loop 2: } & -v_3 + v_4 + v_5 = 0 \\
\text{Loop 3: } & -v_1 + v_2 + v_4 + v_5 = 0
\end{aligned} \quad (2\text{–}10)$$

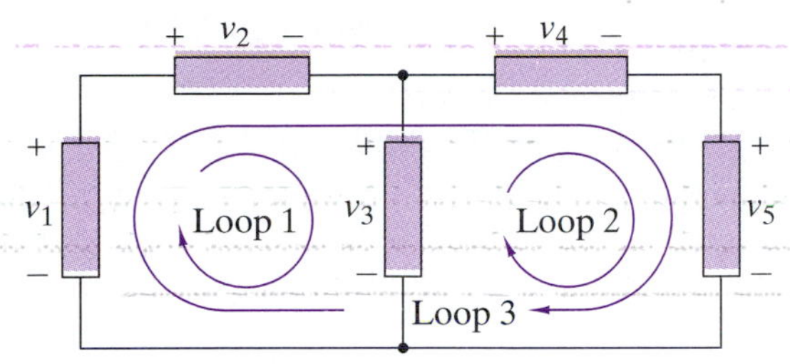

FIGURE 2–13 *Circuit for demonstrating Kirchhoff's voltage law.*

There are two signs associated with each voltage. The first is the sign given the voltage when writing the KVL connection equation. The second is the sign determined by the actual polarity of a voltage relative to its assigned reference polarity. The actual polarities are found by solving the set of KVL equations, as illustrated in the following example.

EXAMPLE 2–5

Given $v_1 = 5$ V, $v_2 = -3$ V, and $v_4 = 10$ V in the circuit shown in Figure 2–13, find v_3 and v_5.

SOLUTION:

Inserting the given numerical values into Eq. (2–10) yields the following KVL equation for loop 1:

$$-v_1 + v_2 + v_3 = -(+5) + (-3) + (v_3) = 0$$

The sign outside the parentheses comes from the loop 1 KVL constraint in Eq. (2–10). The sign inside comes from the actual polarity of the voltage. This equation yields $v_3 = +8$ V. Using this value in the loop 2, KVL constraint in Eq. (2–10) produces

$$-v_3 + v_4 + v_5 = -(+8) + (+10) + v_5 = 0$$

The result is $v_5 = -2$ V. The minus sign here means that the actual polarity of v_5 is the opposite of the assigned reference polarity indicated in Figure 2–13. The results can be checked by substituting all the aforementioned values into the loop 3 KVL constraint in Eq. (2–10). These substitutions yield

$$-(+5)+(-3)+(+10)+(-2)=0$$

as required by KVL. ■

In Example 2–5, the unknown voltages were found using only the KVL constraints for loops 1 and 2. The loop 3 equation was shown to be valid, but it did not add any new information. If we look back at Eq. (2–10), we see that the loop 3 equation is equal to the sum of the loop 1 and 2 equations. In other words, the KVL connection constraint around loop 3 is not independent of the previous two equations. This example illustrates the following general principle:

> ***In a circuit containing a total of* E *two-terminal elements and* N *nodes, there are only* E – N +1 *independent KVL connection equations.***

Writing voltage summations around a total of $E - N + 1$ *different* loops produces all the independent connection constraints that can be derived from KVL. A *sufficient condition* for loops to be different is that each contains at least one element that is not contained in any other loop. In simple circuits with no crossovers the open space between elements produces $E - N + 1$ independent loops. However, finding all the loops in a more complicated circuit can be a nontrivial problem.

Exercise 2–2

Find the voltages v_x and v_y in Figure 2–14. E-N+1 = 5-4+1 = 2

FIGURE 2–14

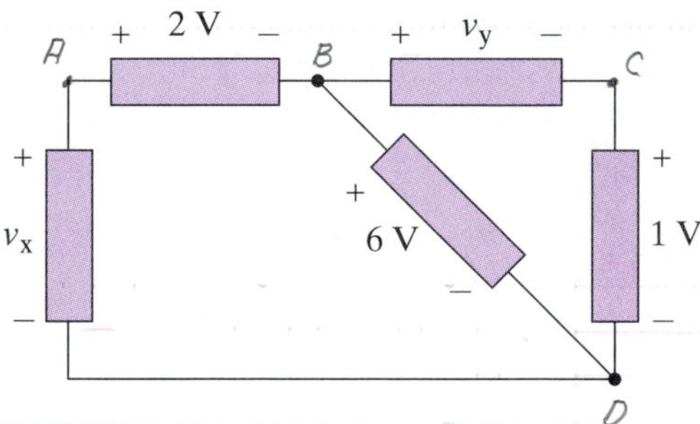

Answers: $v_x = +8$ V, $v_y = +5$ V

Exercise 2–3

Find the voltages v_x, v_y, and v_z in Figure 2–15.

Answers: $v_x = +25$ V; $v_y = +5$ V; $v_z = +10$ V. *Note:* KVL yields the voltage v_z even though it appears across an open circuit.

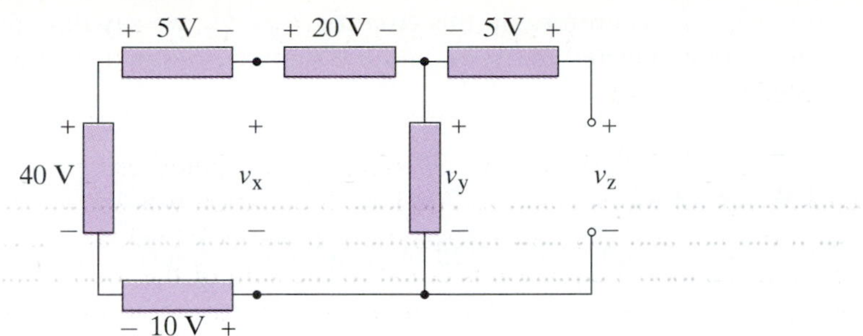

FIGURE 2–15

PARALLEL AND SERIES CONNECTIONS

Two types of connections occur so frequently in circuit analysis that they deserve special attention. Elements are said to be connected in **parallel** when they form a loop containing no other elements. For example, loop A in Figure 2–16 contains only elements 1 and 2. As a result, the KVL connection constraint around loop A is

$$-v_1 + v_2 = 0 \tag{2-11}$$

which yields $v_1 = v_2$. In other words, in a parallel connection KVL requires equal voltages across the elements. The parallel connection is not restricted to two elements. For example, loop B in Figure 2–16 contains only elements 2 and 3; hence, by KVL $v_2 = v_3$. As a result, in this circuit we have $v_1 = v_2 = v_3$, and we say that elements 1, 2, and 3 are connected in parallel. In general, then, any number of elements connected between two common nodes are in parallel, and as a result, the same voltage appears across each of them. Existence of a parallel connection does not depend on the graphical position of the elements. For example, the position of elements 1 and 3 could be switched, and the three elements are still connected in parallel.

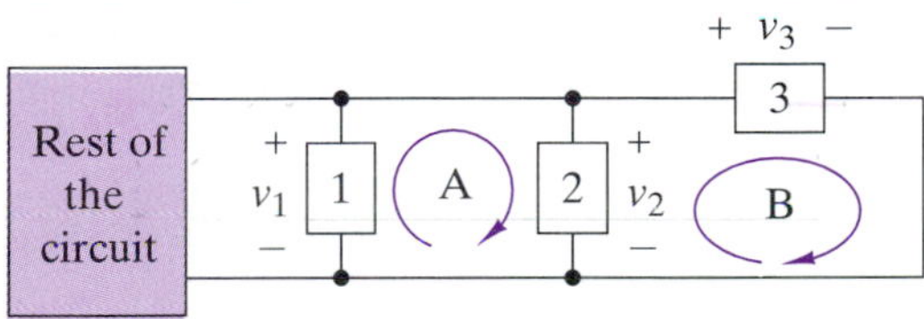

FIGURE 2–16 *A parallel connection.*

Two elements are said to be connected in **series** when they have one common node to which no other element is connected. In Figure 2–17 elements 1 and 2 are connected in series, since only these two elements are connected at node A. Applying KCL at node A yields

$$i_1 - i_2 = 0 \quad \text{or} \quad i_1 = i_2 \tag{2-12}$$

In a series connection, KCL requires equal current through each element. Any number of elements can be connected in series. For example, element 3 in Figure 2–17 is connected in series with element 2 at node B, and KCL

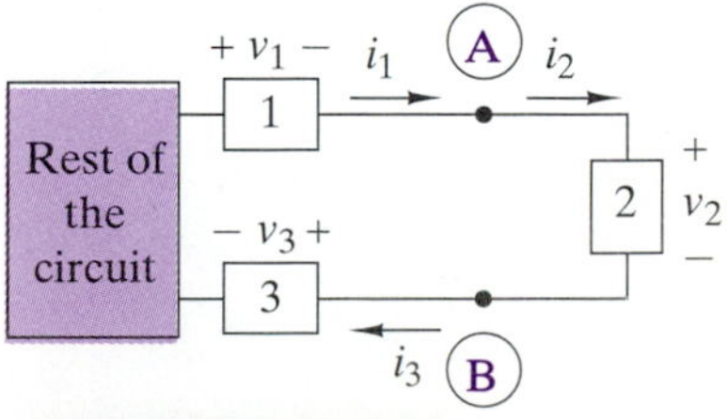

FIGURE 2–17 *A series connection.*

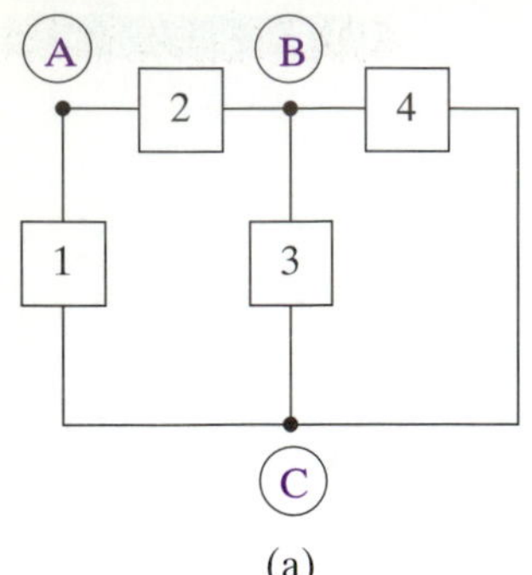

(a)

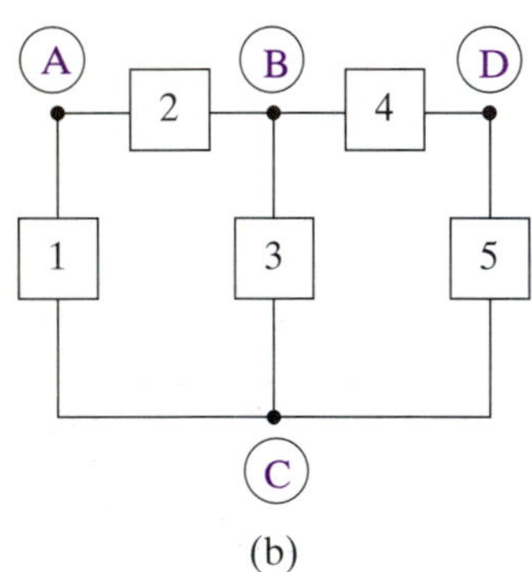

(b)

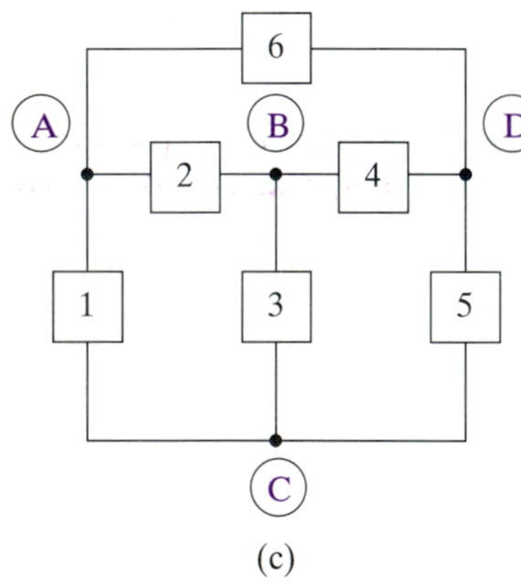

(c)

FIGURE 2–18

requires $i_2 = i_3$. Therefore, in this circuit $i_1 = i_2 = i_3$, we say that elements 1, 2, and 3 are connected in series, and the same current exists in each of the elements.

EXAMPLE 2–6

Identify the elements connected in parallel and in series in each of the circuits in Figure 2–18.

SOLUTION:

In Figure 2–18(a) elements 1 and 2 are connected in series at node A and elements 3 and 4 are connected in parallel between nodes B and C. In Figure 2–18(b) elements 1 and 2 are connected in series at node A, as are elements 4 and 5 at node D. There are no single elements connected in parallel in this circuit. In Figure 2–18(c) there are no elements connected in either series or parallel. It is important to realize that in some circuits there are elements that are not connected in either series or in parallel. ■

Exercise 2–4

Identify the elements connected in series or parallel when a short circuit is connected between nodes A and B in each of the circuits of Figure 2–18.

Answers:

Circuit in Figure 2–18(a): Elements 1, 3, and 4 are all in parallel.
Circuit in Figure 2–18(b): Elements 1 and 3 are in parallel; elements 4 and 5 are in series.
Circuit in Figure 2–18(c): Elements 1 and 3 are in parallel; elements 4 and 6 are in parallel.

Exercise 2–5

Identify the elements in Figure 2–19 that are connected in (a) parallel, (b) series, or (c) neither.

Answers:

(a) The following elements are in parallel: 1, 8, and 11; 3, 4, and 5.
(b) The following elements are in series: 9 and 10; 6 and 7.
(c) Only element 2 is not in series or parallel with any other element.

DISCUSSION: *The ground symbol indicates the reference node. When ground symbols are shown at several nodes, the nodes are connected by a short circuit and form a single node.*

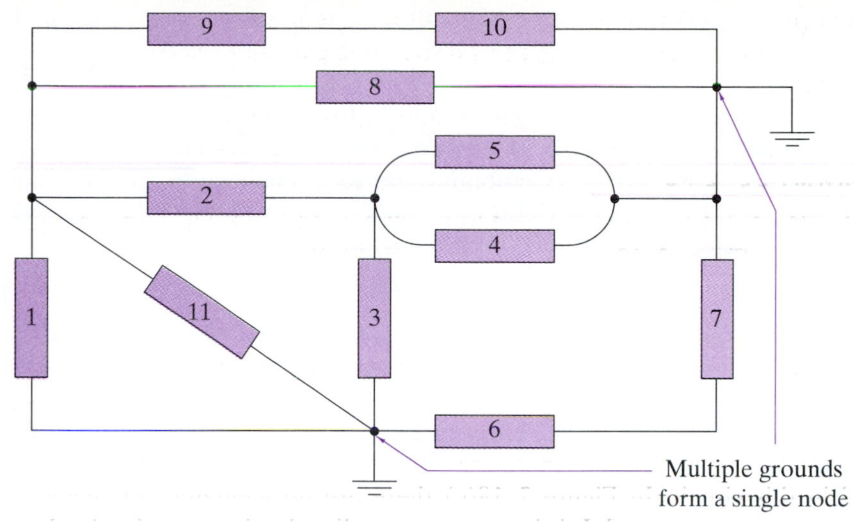

FIGURE 2–19

2–3 COMBINED CONSTRAINTS

The usual goal of circuit analysis is to determine the currents or voltages at various places in a circuit. This analysis is based on constraints of two distinctly different types. The element constraints are based on the models of the specific devices connected in the circuit. The connection constraints are based on Kirchhoff's laws and the circuit connections. The element equations are independent of the circuit connections. Likewise, the connection equations are independent of the devices in the circuit. Taken together, however, the combination of the element and connection constraints supply the equations needed to describe a circuit.

Our study of the combined constraints begins by considering the simple but important example in Figure 2–20. This circuit is driven by a current source i_S and the resulting responses are current/voltage pairs (i_X, v_X) and (i_O, v_O). The reference marks for the response pairs have been assigned using the passive sign convention.

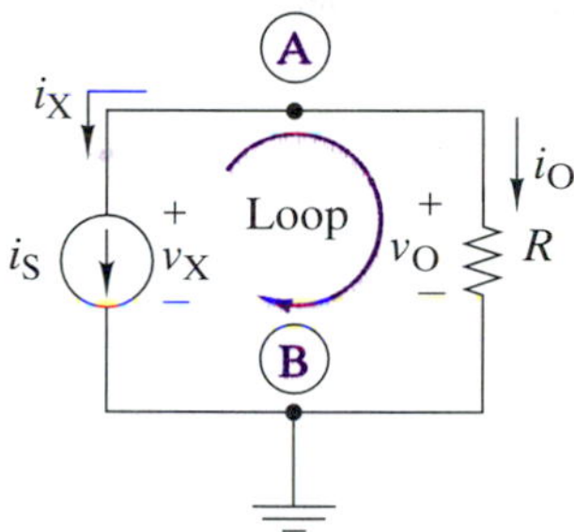

FIGURE 2–20 ***Circuit used to demonstrate combined constraints.***

To solve for all four responses, we must write four equations. The first two are the element equations

$$i_X = i_S$$
$$v_O = Ri_O \qquad (2\text{–}13)$$

The first element equation states that the response current i_X and the input driving force i_S are equal in magnitude and direction. The second element equation is Ohm's law relating v_O and i_O under the passive sign convention.

The connection equations are obtained by applying Kirchhoff's laws. The circuit in Figure 2–20 has two elements ($E = 2$) and two nodes ($N = 2$), so we need $E - N + 1 = 1$ KVL equation and $N - 1 = 1$ KCL equation. Selecting node B as the reference node, we apply KCL at node A and apply KVL around the loop to write

$$\text{KCL: } -i_X - i_O = 0$$

$$\text{KVL: } -v_X + v_O = 0 \qquad (2\text{–}14)$$

We now have two element constraints in Eq. (2–13) and two connection constraints in Eq. (2–14), so we can solve for all four responses in terms of the input driving force i_S. Combining the KCL connection equation and the first element equation yields $i_O = -i_X = -i_S$. Substituting this result into the second element equations (Ohm's law) produces

$$v_O = -Ri_S \qquad (2\text{–}15)$$

The minus sign in this equation does not mean that v_O is always negative. Nor does it mean the resistance is negative. It means that when the input driving force i_S is positive, then the response v_O is negative, and vice versa. This sign reversal is a result of the way we assigned reference marks at the beginning of our analysis. The reference marks defined the circuit input and outputs in such a way that i_S and v_O always have opposite algebraic signs. Put differently, Eq. (2–15) is an input–output relationship, not an element *i–v* relationship.

EXAMPLE 2–7

(a) Find the responses i_X, v_X, i_O, and v_O in the circuit in Figure 2–20 when $i_S = +2$ mA and $R = 2$ kΩ.
(b) Repeat for $i_S = -2$ mA.

SOLUTION:

(a) From Eq. (2–13) we have $i_X = i_S = +2$ mA and $v_O = 2000\, i_O$. From Eq. (2–14) we have $i_O = -i_X = -2$ mA and $v_X = v_O$. Combining these results, we obtain

$$v_X = v_O = 2000 i_O = 2000(-0.002) = -4 \text{ V}$$

(b) In this case $i_X = i_S = -2$ mA, $i_O = -i_X = -(-0.002) = +2$ mA, and

$$v_X = v_O = 2000 i_O = 2000(+0.002) = +4 \text{ V}$$

This example confirms that the algebraic signs of the outputs v_X, v_O, and i_O are always the opposite sign from that of the input driving force i_S. ■

Analyzing the circuit in Figure 2–21 illustrates the formulation of combined constraints. We first assign reference marks for all the voltages and currents using the passive sign convention. Then, using these definitions we can write the element constraints as

$$v_A = V_O$$

$$v_1 = R_1 i_1 \qquad (2\text{–}16)$$

$$v_2 = R_2 i_2$$

These equations describe the three devices and do not depend on how the devices are connected in the circuit.

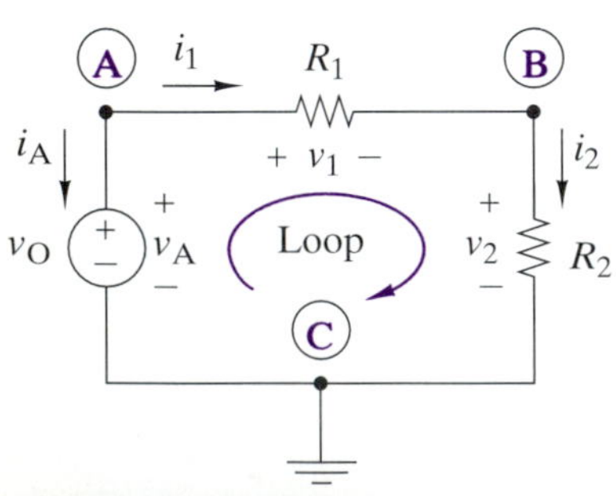

FIGURE 2–21 *Circuit used to demonstrate combined constraints.*

The connection equations are obtained from Kirchhoff's laws. To apply these laws, we must first label the different loops and nodes. The circuit contains $E = 3$ elements and $N = 3$ nodes, so there are $E - N + 1 = 1$ independent KVL constraints and $N - 1 = 2$ independent KCL constraints. There is only one loop, but there are three nodes in this circuit. We will select one node as the reference point and write KCL equations at the other two nodes. Any node can be chosen as the reference, so we select node C as the reference node and indicate this choice by drawing the ground symbol there. The connection constraints are

$$\begin{aligned} &\text{KCL: Node A} \quad -i_A - i_1 = 0 \\ &\text{KCL: Node B} \quad i_1 - i_2 = 0 \\ &\text{KVL: Loop} \quad -v_A + v_1 + v_2 = 0 \end{aligned} \tag{2-17}$$

These equations are independent of the specific devices in the circuit. They depend only on Kirchhoff's laws and the circuit connections.

This circuit has six unknowns: three element currents and three element voltages. Taken together, the element and connection equations give us six independent equations. For a network with (N) nodes and (E) two-terminal elements, we can write ($N - 1$) independent KCL connection equations, ($E - N + 1$) independent KVL connection equations, and (E) element equations. The total number of equations generated is

Element equations	E
KCL equations	$N - 1$
KVL equations	$E - N + 1$
Total	$2E$

The grand total is then ($2E$) combined connection and element equations, which is exactly the number of equations needed to solve for the voltage across and current through every element—a total of ($2E$) unknowns.

EXAMPLE 2–8

Find all of the element currents and voltages in Figure 2–21 for $V_O = 10$ V, $R_1 = 2000\ \Omega$, and $R_2 = 3000\ \Omega$.

SOLUTION:

Substituting the element constraints from Eq. (2–16) into the KVL connection constraint in Eq. (2–17) produces

$$-V_O + R_1 i_1 + R_2 i_2 = 0$$

This equation can be used to solve for i_1 since the second KCL connection equation requires that $i_2 = i_1$.

$$i_1 = \frac{V_O}{R_1 + R_2} = \frac{10}{2000 + 3000} = 2 \text{ mA}$$

In effect, we have found all of the element currents since the elements are connected in series. Hence, collectively the KCL connection equations require that

$$-i_A = i_1 = i_2$$

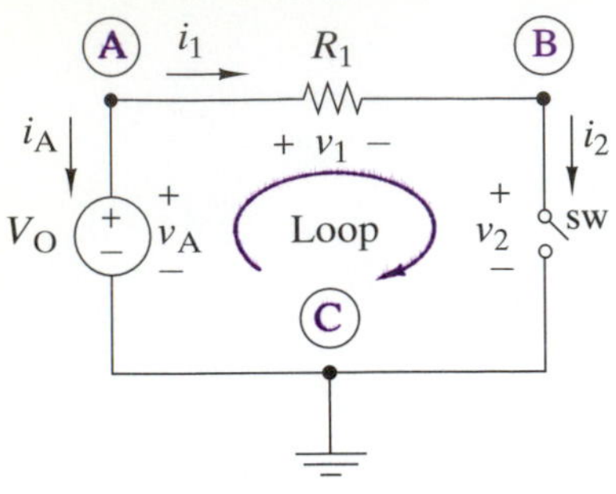

FIGURE 2–22

Substituting all of the known values into the element equations gives

$$v_A = 10\text{ V} \quad v_1 = R_1 i_1 = 4\text{ V} \quad v_2 = R_2 i_2 = 6\text{ V}$$

Every element voltage and current has been found. Note the analysis strategy used. We first found all the element currents and then used these values to find the element voltages. ■

EXAMPLE 2–9

Consider the source-resistor-switch circuit of Figure 2–22 with V_O = 10 V and R_1 = 2000 Ω. Find all the element voltages and currents with the switch open and again with the switch closed.

SOLUTION:

The connection equations for the circuit are

$$\text{KCL: Node A} \quad -i_A - i_1 = 0$$

$$\text{KCL: Node B} \quad i_1 - i_2 = 0$$

$$\text{KVL: Loop} \quad -v_A + v_1 + v_2 = 0$$

These connection equations are the same as those in Eq. (2–17) for the circuit in Figure 2–21. The two circuits have the same connections but different devices. When the switch is open, the current through the switch is zero, so $i_2 = 0$. The KCL connection equation at node B requires $i_1 = i_2$, and therefore $i_1 = 0$. The element equation for R_1 yields $v_1 = R_1 i_1 = 0$, and the KVL connection equation yields $v_1 + v_2 = v_2 = v_A = 10$ V. Thus, when the switch is open, the current is zero and all the source voltage appears across the switch. When the switch is closed, its element equations require $v_2 = 0$. The KVL connection equation gives $v_1 + v_2 = v_1 = v_A = 10$ V. When the switch is closed, all the source voltage appears across R_1 rather than across the switch. So the current through the circuit is

$$i_1 = \frac{v_1}{R_1} = \frac{10}{2000} = 5\text{ mA}$$ ■

Exercise 2–6

For the circuit of Figure 2–23,

FIGURE 2–23

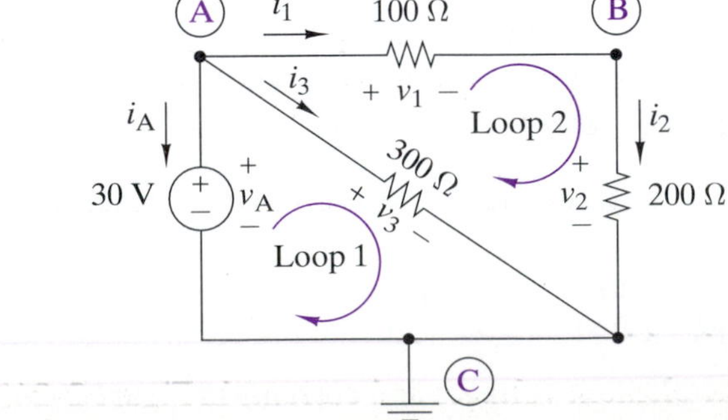

(a) Write a complete set of element equations.
(b) Write a complete set of connection equations.
(c) Solve the equations in (a) and (b) for all element currents and voltages.

Answers:

(a) $v_A = 30$ V; $v_3 = 300\, i_3$; $v_1 = 100\, i_1$; $v_2 = 200\, i_2$
(b) $-i_A - i_1 - i_3 = 0$; $+ i_1 - i_2 = 0$; $-30 + v_3 = 0$; $v_1 + v_2 - v_3 = 0$
(c) $v_A = 30$ V; $v_1 = 10$ V; $v_2 = 20$ V; $v_3 = 30$ V; $i_A = -200$ mA; $i_1 = i_2 = 100$ mA; $i_3 = 100$ mA

ASSIGNING REFERENCE MARKS

In all of our previous examples and exercises, the reference marks for the element currents (arrows) and voltages (+ and –) were given. When reference marks are not shown on a circuit diagram, they must be assigned by the person solving the problem. Beginners sometimes wonder how to assign reference marks when the actual voltage polarities and current directions are unknown. It is important to remember that the reference marks do not indicate what is actually happening in the circuit. They are benchmarks assigned at the beginning of the analysis. If it turns out that the actual direction and reference direction agree, then the algebraic sign of the response will be positive. If they disagree, the algebraic sign will be negative. In other words, the sign of the answer together with assigned reference marks tell us the actual voltage polarity or current direction.

In this book the reference marks always follow the passive sign convention. This means that for any given two-terminal element we can arbitrarily assign either the + voltage reference mark or the current reference arrow, but not both. For example, we can arbitrarily assign the voltage reference marks to the terminals of a two-terminal device. Once the voltage reference is assigned, however, the passive sign convention requires that the current reference arrow be directed into the element at the terminal with the + mark. On the other hand, we could start by arbitrarily selecting the terminal at which the current reference arrow is directed into the device. Once the current reference is assigned, however, the passive sign convention requires that the + voltage reference be assigned to the selected terminal.

Following the passive sign convention avoids confusion about the direction of power flow in a device. In addition, the element constraints, such as Ohm's law, assume that the passive sign convention is used to assign the voltage and current reference marks to a device. Finally, computer circuit analysis programs such as SPICE and MICRO-CAP use this convention.

The next example illustrates the assignment of reference marks.

EXAMPLE 2–10

Find all of the element voltages and currents in Figure 2–24(a).

FIGURE 2–24

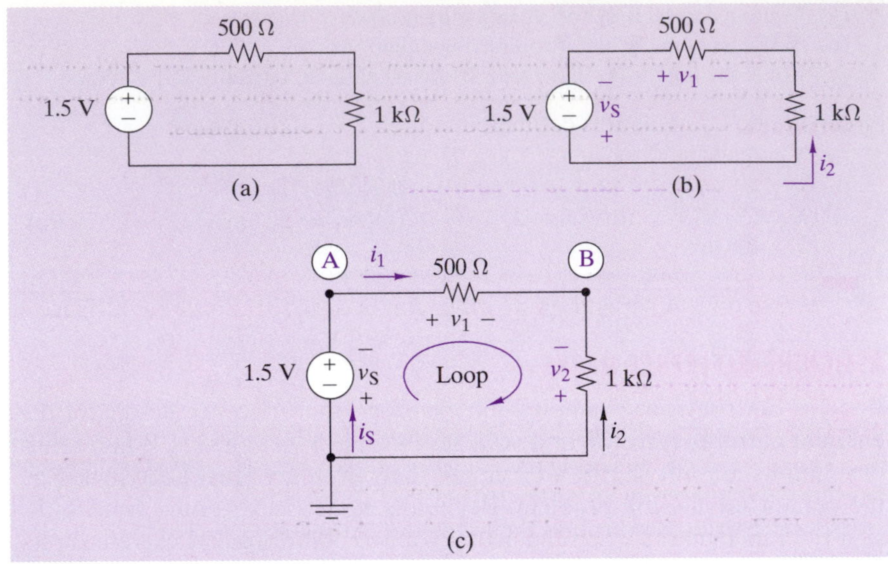

SOLUTION:

Since no reference marks are shown in Figure 2–24(a), we assign references to two voltages and one current, as shown in Figure 2–22(b). Other choices are possible, of course, but once these marks are selected, the passive sign convention dictates the reference marks for the remaining voltage and currents, as shown in Figure 2–22(c). Using all of these reference marks, we write the element equations as

$$v_1 = 500 i_1$$

$$v_2 = 1000 i_2$$

$$v_S = -1.5 \text{ V}$$

Using the indicated reference node, we write two KCL and one KVL equations:

$$\text{KCL: Node A} \quad +i_S - i_1 = 0$$

$$\text{KCL: Node B} \quad +i_1 + i_2 = 0$$

$$\text{KVL: Loop} \quad +v_S + v_1 - v_2 = 0$$

Solving the combined element and connection equations yields

$$v_S = -1.5 \text{ V}, \quad i_S = +1.0 \text{ mA}$$

$$v_1 = +0.5 \text{ V}, \quad i_1 = +1.0 \text{ mA}$$

$$v_2 = -1.0 \text{ V}, \quad i_2 = -1.0 \text{ mA}$$

These results show that the reference marks for v_1, i_S, and i_1 agree with the actual voltage polarities and current directions, while the minus signs on the other responses indicate disagreement. It is important to realize that this disagreement does not mean that assigned reference marks are wrong. ■

2–4 EQUIVALENT CIRCUITS

The analysis of a circuit can often be made easier by replacing part of the circuit with one that is equivalent but simpler. The underlying basis for two circuits to be equivalent is contained in their i–v relationships.

> ***Two circuits are said to be equivalent if they have identical* i–v *characteristics at a specified pair of terminals.***

In other words, when two circuits are equivalent the voltage and current at an interface do not depend on which circuit is connected to the interface.

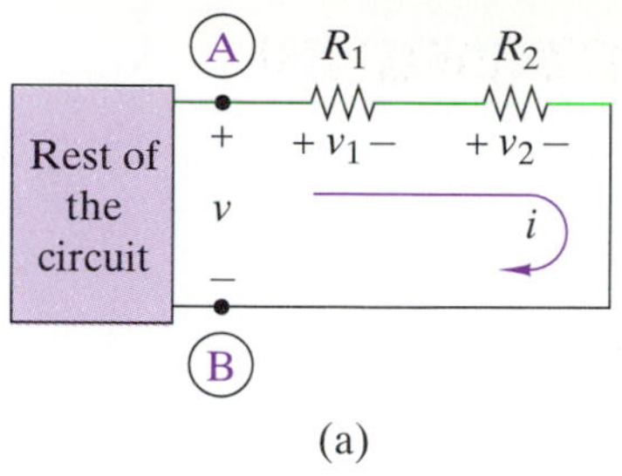

(a)

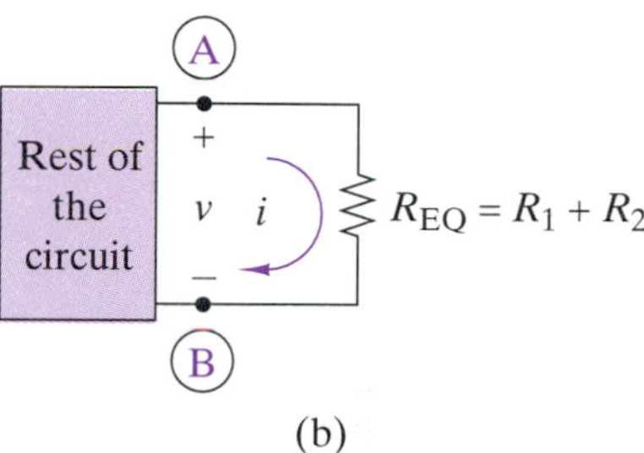

(b)

FIGURE 2–25 *A series resistance circuit: (a) Original circuit. (b) Equivalent circuit.*

EQUIVALENT RESISTANCE

The two resistors in Figure 2–25(a) are connected in series between a pair of terminals A and B. The objective is to simplify the circuit without altering the electrical behavior of the rest of the circuit.

The KVL equation around the loop from A to B is

$$v = v_1 + v_2 \tag{2–18}$$

Since the two resistors are connected in series, the same current i exists in both. Applying Ohm's law, we get $v_1 = R_1 i$ and $v_2 = R_2 i$. Substituting these relationships into Eq. (2–18) and then simplifying yields

$$v = R_1 i + R_2 i = i(R_1 + R_2)$$

We can write this equation in terms of an equivalent resistance R_{EQ} as

$$v = iR_{EQ} \quad \text{where} \quad R_{EQ} = R_1 + R_2 \tag{2–19}$$

This result means the circuits in Figs. 2–25(a) and 2–25(b) have the same i–v characteristic at terminals A and B. As a result, the response of the rest of the circuit is unchanged when the series connection of R_1 and R_2 is replaced by a resistance R_{EQ}.

The parallel connection of two conductances in Figure 2–26(a) is the dual[2] of the series circuit in Figure 2–25(a). Again the objective is to replace the parallel connection by a simpler equivalent circuit without altering the response of the rest of the circuit.

A KCL equation at node A produces

$$i = i_1 + i_2 \tag{2–20}$$

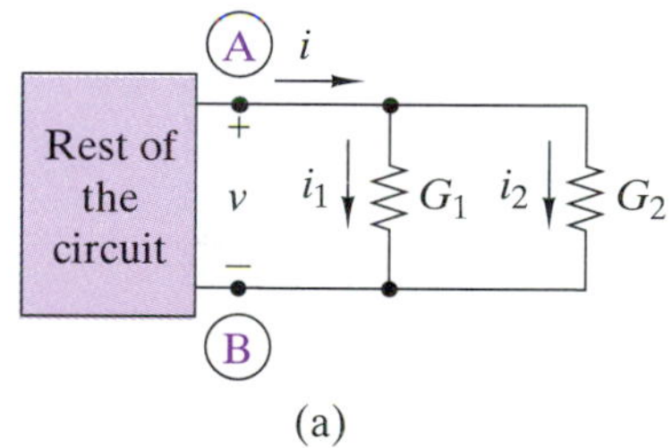

(a)

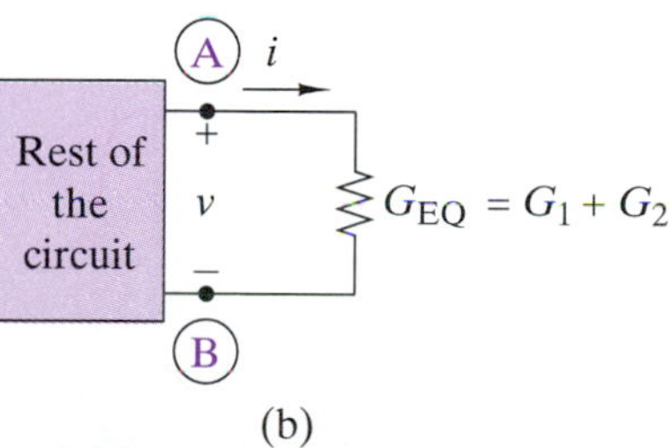

(b)

FIGURE 2–26 *A parallel resistance circuit: (a) Original circuit. (b) Equivalent circuit.*

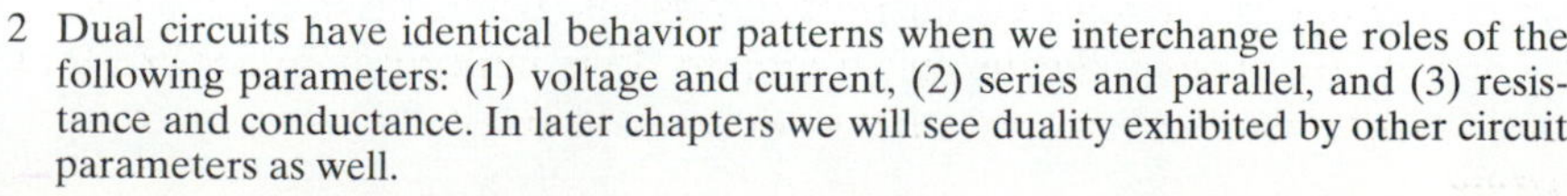
2 Dual circuits have identical behavior patterns when we interchange the roles of the following parameters: (1) voltage and current, (2) series and parallel, and (3) resistance and conductance. In later chapters we will see duality exhibited by other circuit parameters as well.

Since the conductances are connected in parallel, the voltage v appears across both. Applying Ohm's law, we obtain $i_1 = G_1 v$, and $i_2 = G_2 v$. Substituting these relationships into Eq. (2–20) and then simplifying yields

$$i = vG_1 + vG_2 = v(G_1 + G_2)$$

This result can be written in terms of an equivalent conductance G_{EQ} as follows:

$$i = vG_{EQ}, \quad \text{where} \quad G_{EQ} = G_1 + G_2 \tag{2–21}$$

This result means the circuits in Figures 2–26(a) and 2–26(b) have the same i–v characteristic at terminals A and B. As a result, the response of the rest of the circuit is unchanged when the parallel connection of G_1 and G_2 is replaced by a conductance G_{EQ}.

Since conductance is not normally used to describe a resistor, it is sometimes useful to rewrite Eq. (2–21) as an equivalent resistance $R_{EQ} = 1/G_{EQ}$. That is,

$$R_1 \| R_2 = R_{EQ} = \frac{1}{G_{EQ}} = \frac{1}{G_1 + G_2} = \frac{1}{\dfrac{1}{R_1} + \dfrac{1}{R_2}} = \frac{R_1 R_2}{R_1 + R_2} \tag{2–22}$$

where the symbol "||" is shorthand for "in parallel." The expression on the far right in Eq. (2–22) is called the product over the sum rule for two resistors in parallel. This rule is useful in derivations in which the resistances are left in symbolic form (see Example 2–11), but it is not an efficient algorithm for calculating numerical values of equivalent resistance.

Caution: The product over sum rule only applies to two resistors connected in parallel. When more than two resistors are in parallel, we must use the following general result to obtain the equivalent resistance:

$$R_{EQ} = \frac{1}{G_{EQ}} = \frac{1}{\dfrac{1}{R_1} + \dfrac{1}{R_2} + \dfrac{1}{R_3} + \cdots} \tag{2–23}$$

EXAMPLE 2–11

Given the circuit in Figure 2–27(a),

(a) Find the equivalent resistance R_{EQ1} connected between terminals A and B.

(b) Find the equivalent resistance R_{EQ2} connected between terminals C and D.

FIGURE 2–27

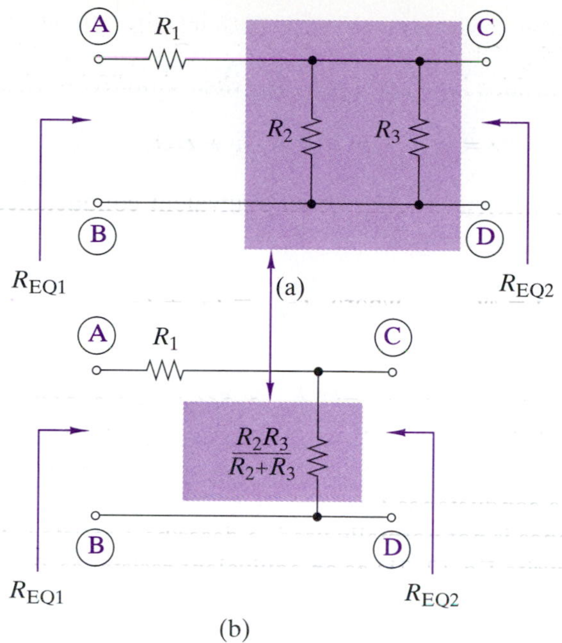

SOLUTION:

First we note that resistors R_2 and R_3 are connected in parallel. Applying the product over sum rule [Eq. (2–22)], we obtain

$$R_2||R_3 = \frac{R_2R_3}{R_2 + R_3}$$

As an interim step, we redraw the circuit, as shown in Figure 2–27(b).

(a) To find the equivalent resistance between terminals A and B, we note that R_1 and the equivalent resistance $R_2||R_3$ are connected in series. The total equivalent resistance R_{EQ1} between terminals A and B is

$$R_{EQ1} = R_1 + (R_2||R_3)$$

$$R_{EQ1} = R_1 + \frac{R_2R_3}{R_2 + R_3}$$

$$R_{EQ1} = \frac{R_1R_2 + R_1R_3 + R_2R_3}{R_2 + R_3}$$

(b) Looking between terminals C and D yields a different result. In this case R_1 is not involved, since there is an open circuit (an infinite resistance) between terminals A and B. Therefore, only $R_2 \parallel R_3$ affect the resistance between terminals C and D. As a result, R_{EQ2} is simply

$$R_{EQ2} = R_2||R_3 = \frac{R_2R_3}{R_2 + R_3}$$

This example shows that equivalent resistance depends on the pair of terminals involved. ■

Exercise 2–7

Find the equivalent resistance between terminals A–C, B–D, A–D, and B–C in the circuit in Figure 2–27.

Answers: $R_{A\text{-}C} = R_1$, $R_{B\text{-}D} = 0\ \Omega$ (a short circuit), $R_{A\text{-}D} = R_1 + R_2 \parallel R_3$, and $R_{B\text{-}C} = R_2 \parallel R_3$.

Exercise 2–8

Find the equivalent resistance between terminals A–B, A–C, A–D, B–C, B–D, and C–D in the circuit of Figure 2–28.

Answers: $R_{A\text{-}B} = 100\ \Omega$, $R_{A\text{-}C} = 70\ \Omega$, $R_{A\text{-}D} = 65\ \Omega$, $R_{B\text{-}C} = 90\ \Omega$, $R_{B\text{-}D} = 85\ \Omega$, and $R_{C\text{-}D} = 55\ \Omega$.

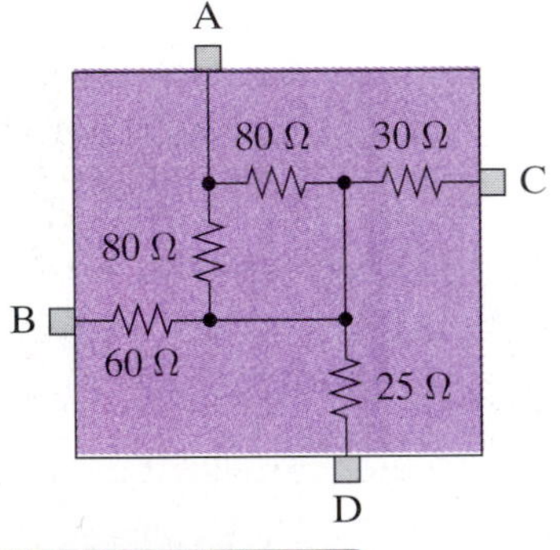

FIGURE 2–28

EQUIVALENT SOURCES

The practical source models introduced previously are shown in Figure 2–29. These models consist of an ideal voltage source in series with a resistance and an ideal current source in parallel with a resistance. We now determine the conditions under which the practical voltage source and the practical current sources are equivalent.

Figure 2–29 shows the two practical sources connected between terminals labeled A and B. A parallel analysis of these circuits yields the conditions for equivalency at terminals A and B. First, Kirchhoff's laws are applied as

Circuit A	Circuit B
KVL	KCL
$v_S = v_R + v$	$i_S = i_R + i$

Next, Ohm's law is used to obtain

Circuit A	Circuit B
$v_R = R_1 i$	$i_R = \dfrac{v}{R_2}$

Combining these results, we find that the i–v relationships of each of the circuits at terminals A and B are

Circuit A	Circuit B
$i = -\dfrac{v}{R_1} + \dfrac{v_S}{R_1}$	$i = -\dfrac{v}{R_2} + i_S$

These i–v characteristics take the form of the straight lines shown in Figure 2–30. The two lines are identical when the intercepts are equal. This requires that $v_S/R_1 = i_S$ and $v_S = i_S R_2$, which, in turn, requires that

$$R_1 = R_2 = R \quad \text{and} \quad v_S = i_S R \tag{2–24}$$

When conditions in Eq. (2–24) are met, the response of the rest of the circuit is unaffected when we replace a practical voltage source by an equiva-

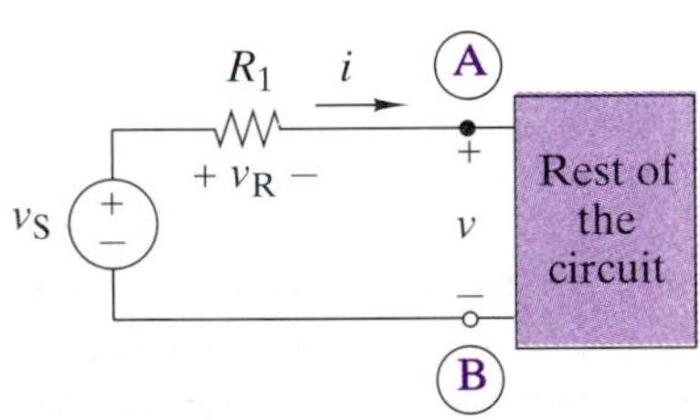

Circuit A

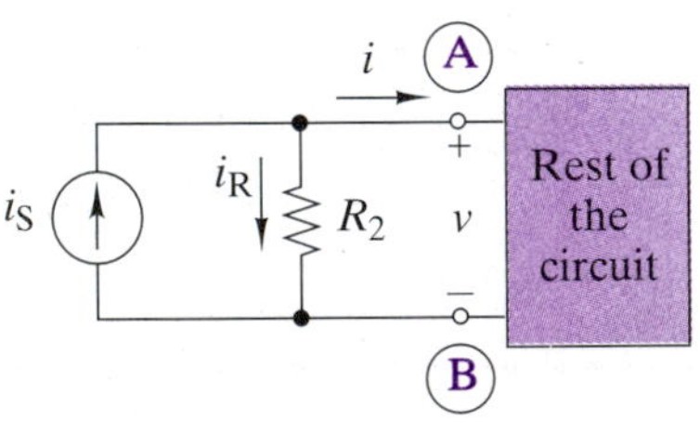

Circuit B

FIGURE 2–29 *Practical source models that are equivalent when Eq. (2–24) is statisfied.*

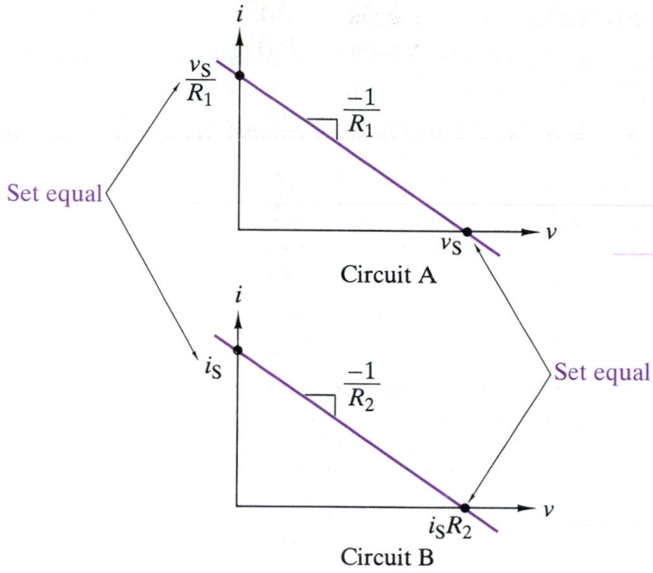

FIGURE 2–30 *The i–v characteristics of practical sources in Figure 2–29.*

lent practical current source, or vice versa. Exchanging one practical source model for an equivalent model is called *source transformation.*

Source transformation means that either model will deliver the same voltage and current to the rest of the circuit. It does not mean the two models are identical in every way. For example, when the practical voltage source drives an open circuit, there is no i^2R power loss since the current in the series resistance is zero. However, the current in the parallel resistance of a practical current source is not zero when the load is an open circuit. Thus, equivalent sources do not have the same internal power loss even though they deliver the same current and voltage to the rest of the circuit.

EXAMPLE 2–12

Convert the practical voltage source in Figure 2–31(a) into an equivalent current source.

SOLUTION:

Using Eq. (2–24), we have

$$R_1 = R_2 = R = 10\ \Omega$$

$$i_S = v_S/R = 5\text{ A}$$

The equivalent practical current source is shown in Figure 2–31(b). ■

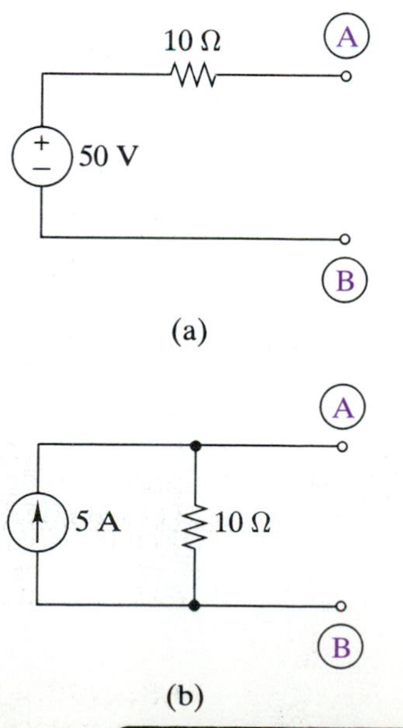

FIGURE 2–31

Exercise 2–9

A practical current source consists of a 2-mA ideal current source in parallel with a 0.002-S conductance. Find the equivalent practical voltage source.

Answer: The equivalent is a 1-V ideal voltage source in series with a 500-Ω resistance.

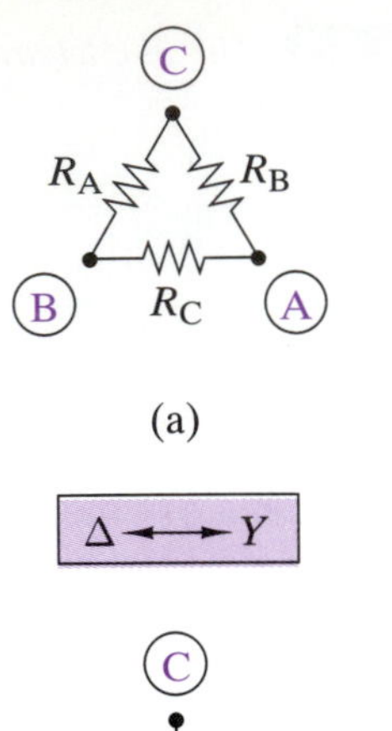

FIGURE 2–32 *The Y-to-Δ transformation: (a) Δ-configuration. (b) Y-configuration.*

Y ⇌ Δ TRANSFORMATIONS

In some circuits the methods of series and parallel equivalence do not apply because there are no resistors connected in series or parallel. Such nonseries/parallel circuits contain three-terminal subcircuits connected in the Δ-configuration or the Y-configuration shown in Figure 2–32. Replacing a Δ-connected subcircuit by an equivalent Y-configuration, or vice versa, changes connections so the modified circuit has series or parallel resistors. As a result, series and parallel equivalence can again be used to simplify the circuit model.

Interchanging these equivalent subcircuits is called a Δ–Y transformation or a Y–Δ transformation, depending on the starting and ending configurations. Our immediate task is to find the conditions under which Δ and Y subcircuits are equivalent. By definition, circuits are equivalent if they have the same *i–v* characteristics between specified terminals. Three-terminal Y- and Δ-resistive subcircuits will have the identical *i–v* characteristics if the same equivalent resistance is seen between terminal pairs A–B, B–C, and C–A. Equating the equivalent resistance seen between these terminals yields the following requirements:

$$\begin{aligned} R_{A-B} &= \frac{R_C(R_A + R_B)}{R_A + R_B + R_C} = R_1 + R_2 \\ R_{B-C} &= \frac{R_A(R_B + R_C)}{R_A + R_B + R_C} = R_2 + R_3 \\ R_{C-A} &= \frac{R_B(R_C + R_A)}{R_A + R_B + R_C} = R_3 + R_1 \end{aligned} \qquad (2\text{–}25)$$

Solving Eq. (2–25) for R_1, R_2, and R_3 yields the equations for a Δ to Y transformation:

$$\begin{aligned} R_1 &= \frac{R_B R_C}{R_A + R_B + R_C} \\ R_2 &= \frac{R_C R_A}{R_A + R_B + R_C} \\ R_3 &= \frac{R_A R_B}{R_A + R_B + R_C} \end{aligned} \qquad (2\text{–}26)$$

Solving Eq. (2–25) for R_A, R_B, and R_C yields the equations for a Y to Δ transformation:

$$\begin{aligned} R_A &= \frac{R_1 R_2 + R_2 R_3 + R_1 R_3}{R_1} \\ R_B &= \frac{R_1 R_2 + R_2 R_3 + R_1 R_3}{R_2} \\ R_C &= \frac{R_1 R_2 + R_2 R_3 + R_1 R_3}{R_3} \end{aligned} \qquad (2\text{–}27)$$

It is important to realize that the Y–Δ transformation depends on the electrical connections in a circuit and not the geometric layout of the circuit diagram. In some circuit diagrams the Y-connected subcircuit may appear as a T-connection or the Δ-connection as a Π-connection. Regardless of how a circuit diagram is drawn, a Y-configuration involves three resistors connected at a single node, while a Δ-configuration involves a single loop containing three resistors.

EXAMPLE 2–13

Find the equivalent resistance seen by the voltage source in Figure 2–33(a).

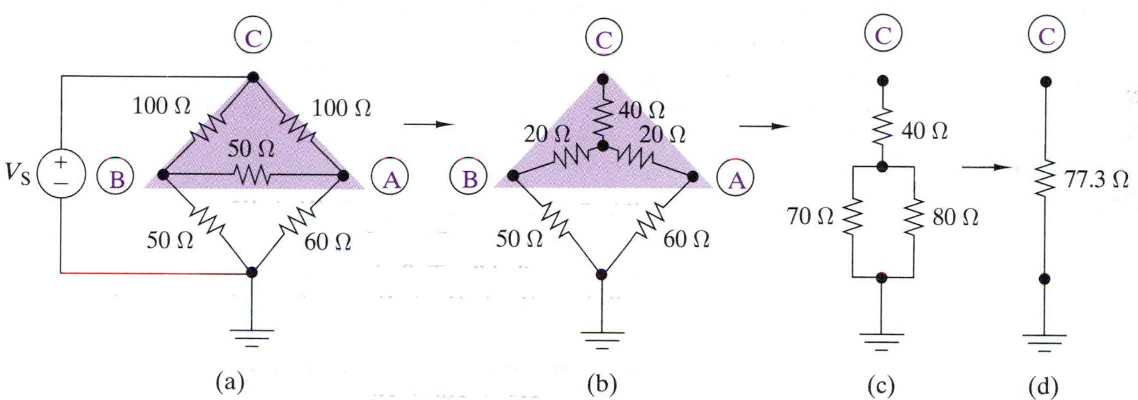

FIGURE 2–33

SOLUTION:
The circuit shown is called a **Wheatstone bridge**. There are no series or parallel connected resistors, so a Δ-to-Y or a Y-to-Δ transformation is needed to find the required resistance. Using Eq. (2–26), we convert the Δ-connected subcircuit in the upper part of the bridge into the equivalent Y subcircuit shown in Figure 2–33(b). The modified circuit has series and parallel connected resistors so it can be reduced to a single equivalent resistance, as shown in Figures 2–33(c) and 2–33(d).

The aforementioned method is not the only way to simplify the circuit model. We could have performed a Y-to-Δ transformation on the three leftmost resistors of the Wheatstone bridge to obtain an equivalent circuit with resistors connected in parallel. It is left to the reader to show that the alternative approach produces the same equivalent resistance shown in Figure 2–33(d). ■

In principle, Y–Δ and Δ–Y transformations allow us to reduce a resistive circuit of arbitrary complexity to an equivalent series/parallel circuit. In a complicated circuit, however, the computational burden involved in repeatedly applying Eqs. (2–26) and (2–27) usually outweighs whatever advantage the resulting series/parallel equivalent may offer. In other words, these transformations are usually only applied in special situations, such as balanced conditions. The Y and Δ subcircuits in Figure 2–32 are said to be *balanced* when $R_1 = R_2 = R_3 = R_Y$ and $R_A = R_B = R_C = R_\Delta$. Under balanced conditions, Eqs. (2–26) and (2–27) simplify to $R_Y = R_\Delta/3$ and $R_\Delta = 3R_Y$, results which are often used to analyze power systems.

SUMMARY OF EQUIVALENT CIRCUITS

Figure 2–34 is a summary of two-terminal equivalent circuits involving resistors and sources connected in series or parallel. The series and parallel equivalences in the first row and the source transformations in the second row are used regularly in subsequent discussions. The last two rows in Figure 2–34 present additional source transformations that reduce series or parallel connections to a single ideal current or voltage source. Proof of

FIGURE 2–34 *Summary of two-terminal equivalent circuits.*

Series	Parallel
R_1, R_2 — R_1+R_2 (a)	R_1, R_2 — $\frac{R_1R_2}{R_1+R_2}$ (b)
R, v_S — $\frac{v_S}{R}$, R (c)	i_S, R — R, i_SR (d)
R, i_S — i_S (e)	v_S, R — v_S (f)
v_{S2}, v_{S1} — $v_{S1}+v_{S2}$ (g)	i_{S1}, i_{S2} — $i_{S1}+i_{S2}$ (h)

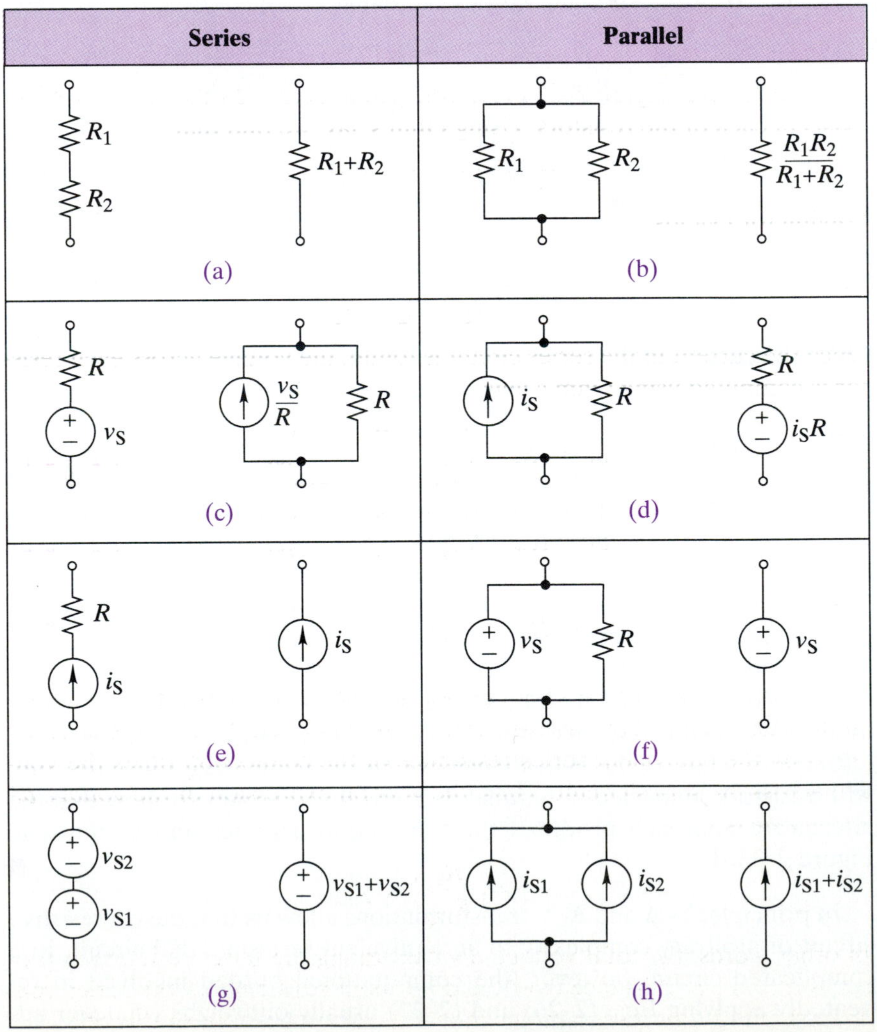

these equivalences involves showing that the final single-source circuits have the same open-circuit voltage or short-circuit current as the original connections. The details of such a derivation are left as an exercise for the reader.

2–5 VOLTAGE AND CURRENT DIVISION

We complete our treatment of series and parallel circuits with a discussion of voltage and current division. These two analysis tools find wide application in circuit analysis and design.

VOLTAGE DIVISION

Voltage division provides a simple way to find the voltage across each element in a series circuit. Figure 2–35 shows a circuit that lends itself to solution by voltage division. Applying

KVL around the loop in Figure 2–35 yields

$$v_S = v_1 + v_2 + v_3 \quad (2-28)$$

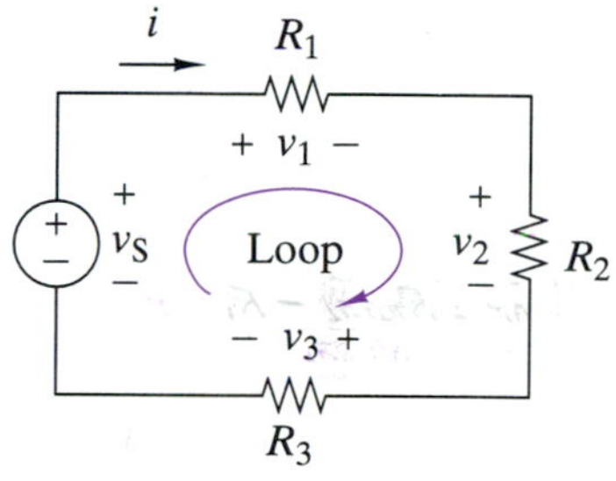

FIGURE 2–35 *A voltage-divider circuit.*

The elements in Figure 2–35 are connected in series, so the same current i exists in each of the resistors. Using Ohm's, law we find that

$$v_S = R_1 i + R_2 i + R_3 i \quad (2-29)$$

Solving for i yields

$$i = \frac{v_S}{R_1 + R_2 + R_3} \quad (2-30)$$

Once the current in the series circuit is found, the voltage across each resistor is computed using Ohm's law:

$$v_1 = R_1 i = \left(\frac{R_1}{R_1 + R_2 + R_3}\right) v_S \quad (2-31)$$

$$v_2 = R_2 i = \left(\frac{R_2}{R_1 + R_2 + R_3}\right) v_S \quad (2-32)$$

$$v_3 = R_3 i = \left(\frac{R_3}{R_1 + R_2 + R_3}\right) v_S \quad (2-33)$$

Looking over these results, we see an interesting pattern. In a series connection, the voltage across each resistor is equal to its resistance divided by the equivalent series resistance of the connection times the voltage across the series circuit. Thus, the general expression of the *voltage division rule* is

$$v_k = \left(\frac{R_k}{R_{EQ}}\right) v_{TOTAL} \quad (2-34)$$

In other words, the total voltage divides among the series resistors in proportion to their resistance over the equivalent resistance of the series connection. The following examples show several applications of this rule.

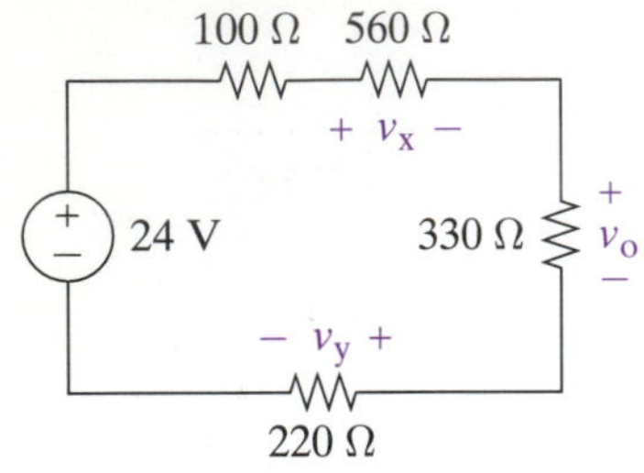

FIGURE 2–36

EXAMPLE 2–14

Find the voltage across the 330-Ω resistor in the circuit of Figure 2–36.

SOLUTION:
Applying the voltage division rule, we find that

$$v_o = \left(\frac{330}{100 + 560 + 330 + 220}\right)24 = 6.55 \text{ V}$$ ■

Exercise 2–10

Find the voltages v_x and v_y in Figure 2–36.

Answers: $v_x = 11.1$ V, $v_y = 4.36$ V

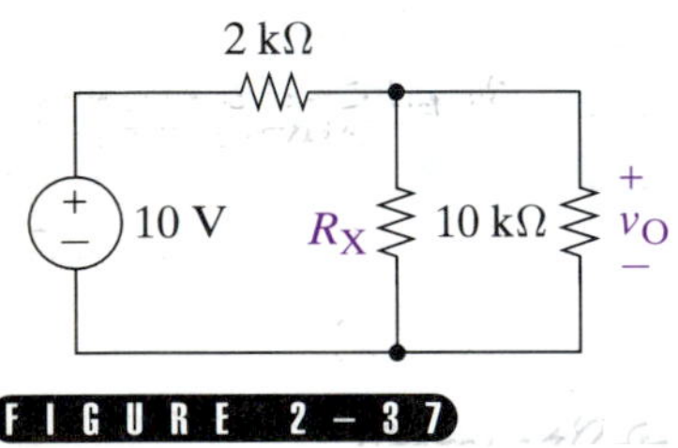

FIGURE 2–37

EXAMPLE 2–15

Select a value for the resistor R_X in Figure 2–37 so $v_O = 8$ V.

SOLUTION:
The unknown resistor is in parallel with the 10-kΩ resistor. Since voltages across parallel elements are equal, the voltage $v_O = 8$ V appears across both. We first define an equivalent resistance $R_{EQ} = R_X \parallel 10$ kΩ as

$$R_{EQ} = \frac{R_X \times 10000}{R_X + 10000}$$

We write the voltage division rule in terms of R_{EQ} as

$$v_O = 8 = \left(\frac{R_{EQ}}{R_{EQ} + 2000}\right)10$$

which yields $R_{EQ} = 8$ kΩ. Finally, we substitute this value into the equation defining R_{EQ} and solve for R_X to obtain $R_X = 40$ kΩ. ■

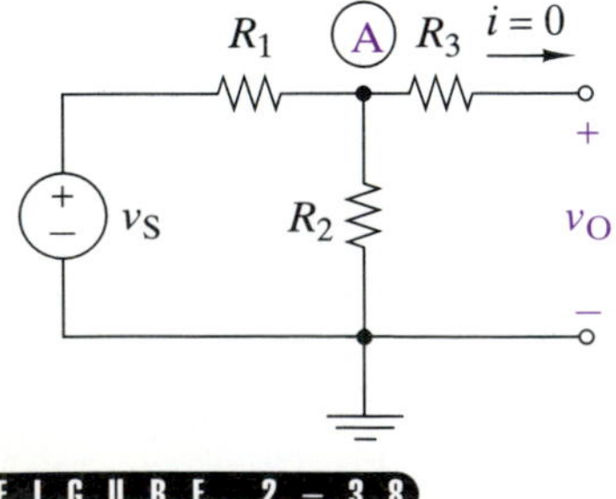

FIGURE 2–38

EXAMPLE 2–16

Use the voltage division rule to find the output voltage v_O of the circuit in Figure 2–38.

SOLUTION:
At first glance it appears that the voltage division rule does not apply, since the resistors are not connected in series. However, the current through R_3 is zero since the output of the circuit is an open circuit. Therefore, Ohm's law shows that $v_3 = R_3 i_3 = 0$. Applying KCL at node A shows that the same current exists in R_1 and R_2, since the current through R_3 is zero. Applying

KVL around the output loop shows that the voltage across R_2 must be equal to v_O since the voltage across R_3 is zero. In essence, it is as if R_1 and R_2 were connected in series. Therefore, voltage division can be used and yields the output voltage as

$$v_O = \left(\frac{R_2}{R_1 + R_2}\right) v_S$$

The reader should carefully review the logic leading to this result because voltage division applications of this type occur frequently. ■

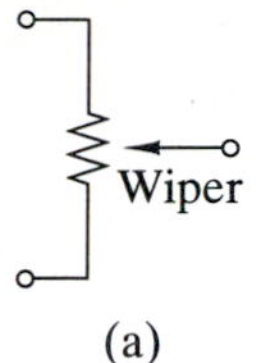

(a)

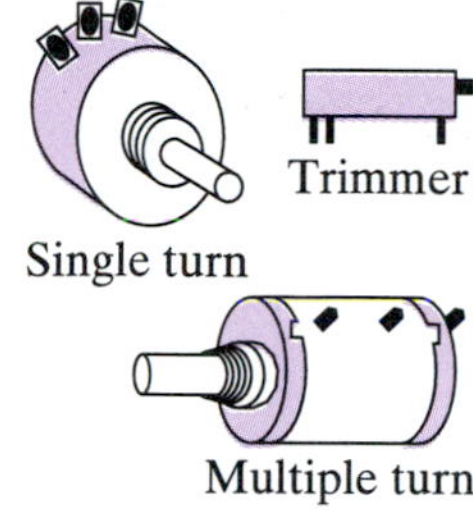

(b)

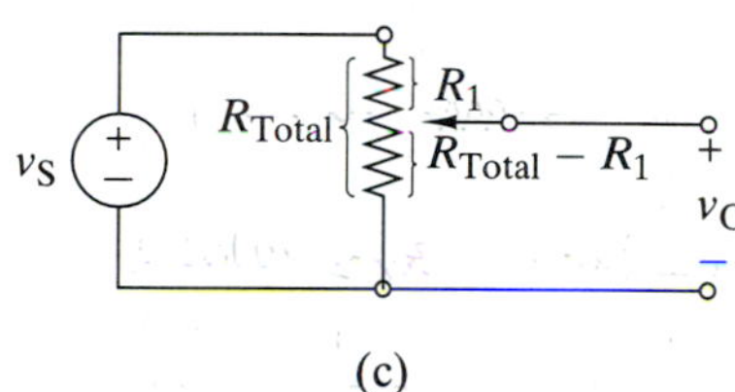

(c)

FIGURE 2–39 *The potentiometer: (a) Circuit symbol. (b) Actual device. (c) An application.*

APPLICATION NOTE: EXAMPLE 2–17

The operation of a potentiometer is based on the voltage division rule. The device is a three-terminal element that uses voltage (potential) division to meter out a fraction of the applied voltage. Simply stated, a **potentiometer** is an adjustable voltage divider. Figure 2–39 shows the circuit symbol of a potentiometer, sketches of three different types of actual potentiometers, and a typical application.

The voltage v_O in Figure 2–39(c) can be adjusted by turning the shaft on the potentiometer to move the wiper arm contact. Using the voltage division rule, the voltage v_O is found as

$$v_O = \left(\frac{R_{TOTAL} - R_1}{R_{TOTAL}}\right) v_S \tag{2-35}$$

Adjusting the movable wiper arm all the way to the top makes R_1 zero, and voltage division yields

$$v_O = \left(\frac{R_{TOTAL} - 0}{R_{TOTAL}}\right) v_S = v_S \tag{2-36}$$

In other words, 100% of the applied voltage is delivered to the rest of the circuit. Moving the wiper all the way to the bottom makes R_1 equal to R_{TOTAL}, and voltage division yields

$$v_O = \left(\frac{R_{TOTAL} - R_{TOTAL}}{R_{TOTAL}}\right) v_S = 0 \tag{2-37}$$

This opposite extreme delivers zero voltage. By adjusting the wiper arm position, we can obtain an output voltage anywhere between zero and the applied voltage v_S. When the wiper is positioned halfway between the top and bottom, we naturally expect to obtain half of the applied voltage. Setting $R_1 = \frac{1}{2}R_{TOTAL}$ yields

$$v_O = \left(\frac{R_{TOTAL} - \frac{1}{2}R_{TOTAL}}{R_{TOTAL}}\right) v_S = \frac{v_S}{2} \tag{2-38}$$

as expected. The many applications of the potentiometer include volume controls, voltage balancing, and fine-tuning adjustment.

Exercise 2–11

A device with an equivalent input resistance of 50 Ω requires 9 V to operate. A 12-V source with a 10-Ω internal resistance is available to power the device. Design the interface circuit in Figure 2–40(a) so that the 9-V device can be safely powered by the 12-V source.

FIGURE 2–40

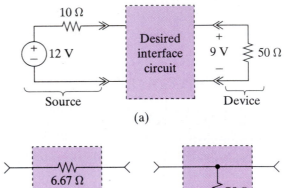

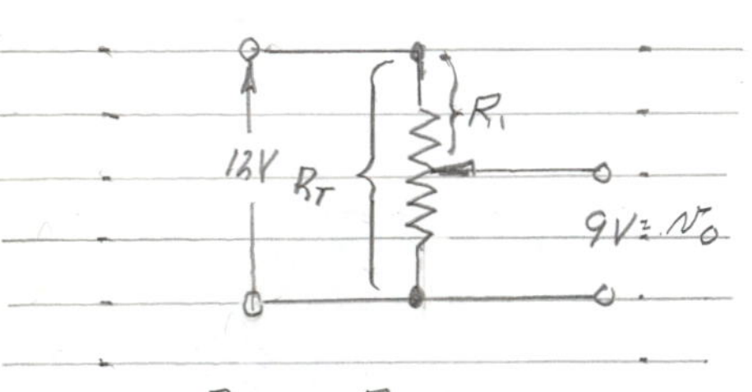

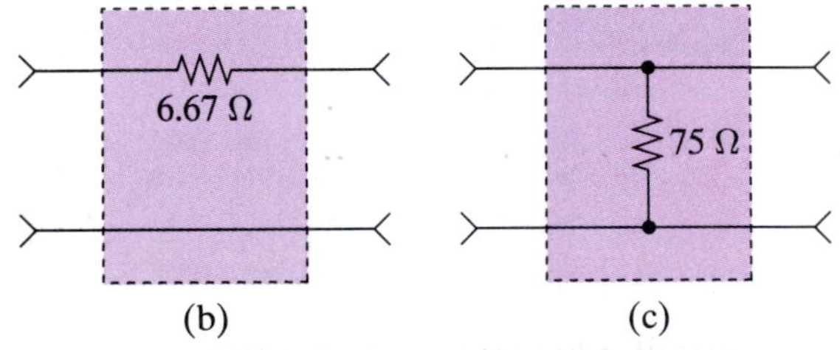

Answer: Two possible solutions are shown in Figures 2–40(b) and 2–40(c). Can you think of a reason for choosing one solution over the other?

CURRENT DIVISION

Current division provides a simple way to find the current through each element in a parallel circuit. Figure 2–41 shows a parallel circuit that lends itself to solution by current division. Applying KCL at node A yields

$$i_S = i_1 + i_2 + i_3$$

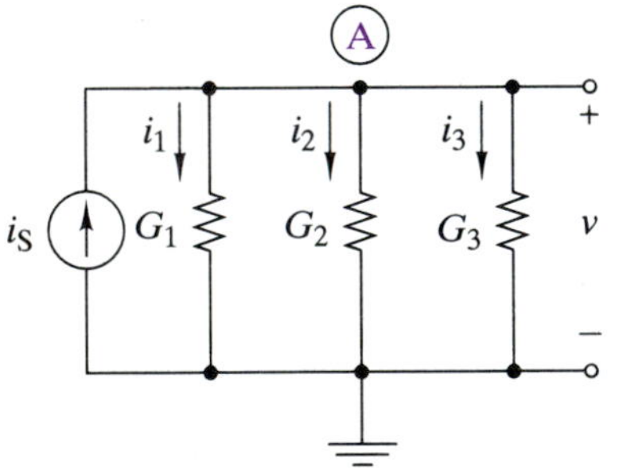

FIGURE 2–41 *A current divider circuit.*

The voltage v appears across all three conductances since they are connected in parallel. Using Ohm's law, we can write

$$i_S = vG_1 + vG_2 + vG_3$$

Solving for v yields

$$v = \frac{i_S}{G_1 + G_2 + G_3}$$

Given the voltage v, the current through any element is found using Ohm's law as

$$i_1 = vG_1 = \left(\frac{G_1}{G_1 + G_2 + G_3}\right) i_S \qquad (2\text{–}39)$$

$$i_2 = vG_2 = \left(\frac{G_2}{G_1 + G_2 + G_3}\right) i_S \qquad (2\text{–}40)$$

$$i_3 = vG_3 = \left(\frac{G_3}{G_1 + G_2 + G_3}\right) i_S \qquad (2\text{–}41)$$

These results show that the source current divides among the parallel resistors in proportion to their conductances divided by the equivalent conductances in the parallel connection. Thus, the general expression for the *current division rule* is

$$i_k = \left(\frac{G_k}{G_{EQ}}\right) i_{TOTAL} \qquad (2\text{–}42)$$

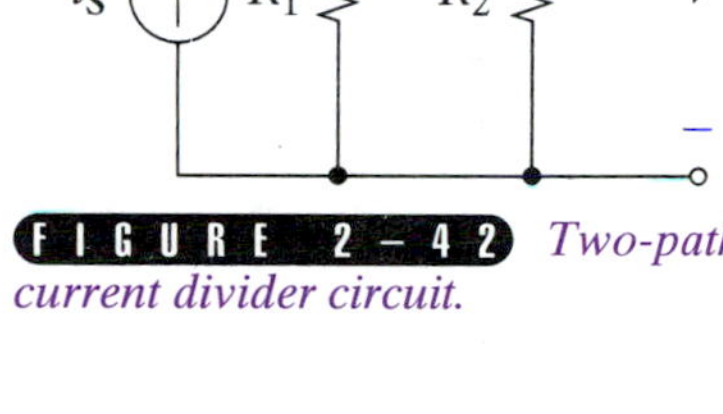

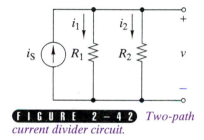

FIGURE 2–42 *Two-path current divider circuit.*

Sometimes it is useful to express the current division rule in terms of resistance rather than conductance. For the two-resistor case in Figure 2–42, the current i_1 is found using current division as

$$i_1 = \left(\frac{G_1}{G_1 + G_2}\right) i_S = \frac{\frac{1}{R_1}}{\frac{1}{R_1} + \frac{1}{R_2}} i_S = \left(\frac{R_2}{R_1 + R_2}\right) i_S \qquad (2\text{–}43)$$

Similarly, the current i_2 in Figure 2–42 is found to be

$$i_2 = \left(\frac{G_2}{G_1 + G_2}\right) i_S = \frac{\frac{1}{R_2}}{\frac{1}{R_1} + \frac{1}{R_2}} i_S = \left(\frac{R_1}{R_1 + R_2}\right) i_S \qquad (2\text{–}44)$$

These two results lead to the following *two-path current division rule:* When a circuit can be reduced to two equivalent resistances in parallel, the current through one resistance is equal to the other resistance divided by the sum of the two resistances times the total current entering the parallel combination.

Caution: Equations (2–43) and (2–44) only apply when the circuit is reduced to two parallel paths in which one path contains the desired current and the other path is the equivalent resistance of all other paths.

EXAMPLE 2–18

Find the current i_x Figure 2–43(a).

FIGURE 2–43

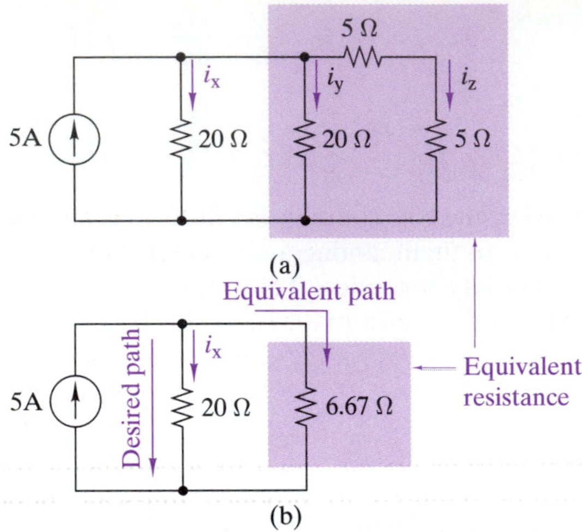

SOLUTION:

To find i_x, we reduce the circuit to two paths, a path containing i_x and a path equivalent to all other paths, as shown in Figure 2–43(b). Now we can use the two-path current divider rule as

$$i_x = \frac{6.67}{20 + 6.67} \times 5 = 1.25 \text{ A}$$

Exercise 2–12

(a) Find i_y and i_z in the circuit of Figure 2–43(a).
(b) Show that the sum of i_x, i_y, and i_z equals the source current.

Answers:
(a) $i_y = 1.25$ A, $i_z = 2.5$ A
(b) $i_x + i_y + i_z = 5$ A

Exercise 2–13

The circuit in Figure 2–44 shows a delicate device that is modeled by a 90-Ω equivalent resistance. The device requires a current of 1 mA to operate properly. A 1.5-mA fuse is inserted in series with the device to protect it from overheating. The resistance of the fuse is 10 Ω. Without the shunt resistance R_X, the source would deliver 5 mA to the device, causing the fuse to blow. Inserting a shunt resistor R_X diverts a portion of the available source current around the fuse and device. Select a value of R_X so only 1 mA is delivered to the device.

FIGURE 2–44

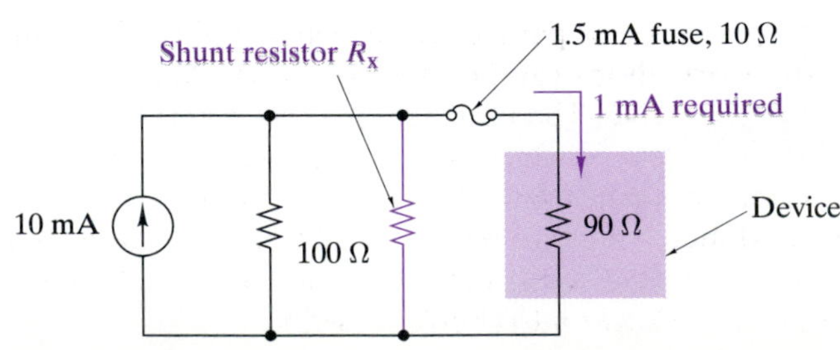

Answer: $R_X = 12.5\ \Omega$.

APPLICATION NOTE: EXAMPLE 2–19

The **D'Arsonval meter** shown in Figure 2–45(a) is a device used to measure electrical currents or voltages. In simple terms, a coil of wire is mounted between the poles of a permanent magnet so it is free to rotate. The magnet produces a magnetic field that interacts with the coil current to produce a torque, which causes the coil to turn. The deflection of the pointer attached to the coil is linearly proportional to the current.

D'Arsonval movements are rated by a parameter I_{FS}, which is the electrical current required to produce full-scale deflection of the pointer. Ratings range from a few microamperes to several milliamperes depending on the structure of the device. To measure larger currents, a very precise shunt resistance R_S is connected in parallel with the meter movement, as shown in Figure 2–45(b). The current i_x divides between the shunt resistance and the meter. The shunt resistance diverts a precisely known fraction of i_x around the coil to keep the meter current i_M within the meter's full-scale deflection rating. Different current ranges can be measured with the same D'Arsonval movement by using different values of R_S.

For example, suppose currents up to 10 A are to be measured using a D'Arsonval movement with a full-scale rating of $I_{FS} = 10$ mA and a coil resistance of $R_M = 20\ \Omega$. Using the circuit model in Figure 2–45(b), the problem is to find the value of R_S that will shunt current around the meter so that $i_M = I_{FS} = 10$ mA when $i_x = 10$ A. From the model it is evident the problem can be solved using the two-path current division rule:

$$i_M = \frac{R_S i_x}{R_M + R_S}$$

$$10^{-2} = \frac{R_S(10)}{20 + R_S}$$

Solving the last equation yields $R_S = 20.02\ \text{m}\Omega$.

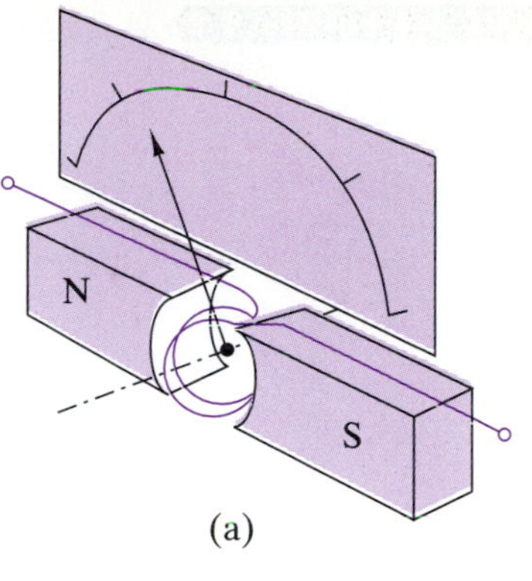

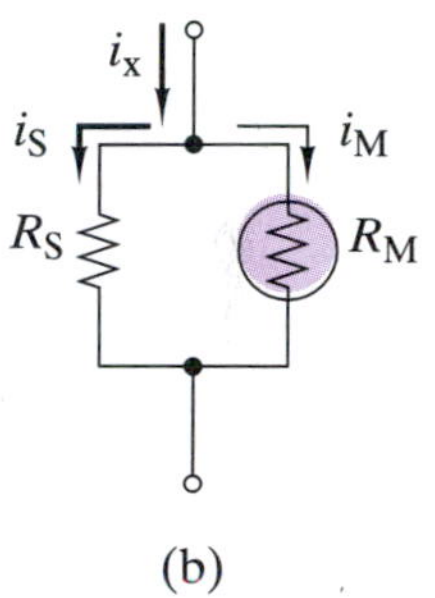

FIGURE 2–45 *The d'Arsonval meter: (a) Meter movement. (b) Equivalent circuit.*

2–6 CIRCUIT REDUCTION

The concepts of series/parallel equivalence, voltage/current division, and source transformations can be used to analyze **ladder circuits** of the type shown in Figure 2–46. The basic analysis strategy is to reduce the circuit to a simpler equivalent in which the output is easily found by voltage or current division or Ohm's law. There is no fixed pattern to the reduction process, and much depends on the insight of the analyst. In any case, with circuit reduction we work directly with the circuit model, and so the process gives us insight into circuit behavior.

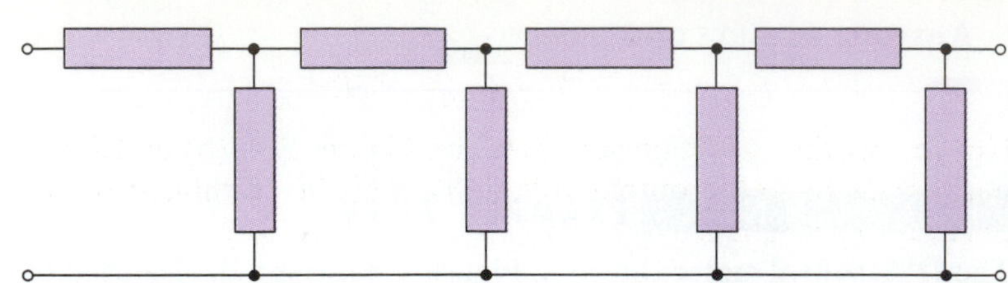

FIGURE 2–46 A ladder circuit.

With circuit reduction the desired unknowns are found by simplifying the circuit and, in the process, eliminating certain nodes and elements. However, we must be careful not to eliminate a node or element that includes the desired unknown voltage or current. The next three examples illustrate circuit reduction. The final example shows that rearranging the circuit can simplify the analysis.

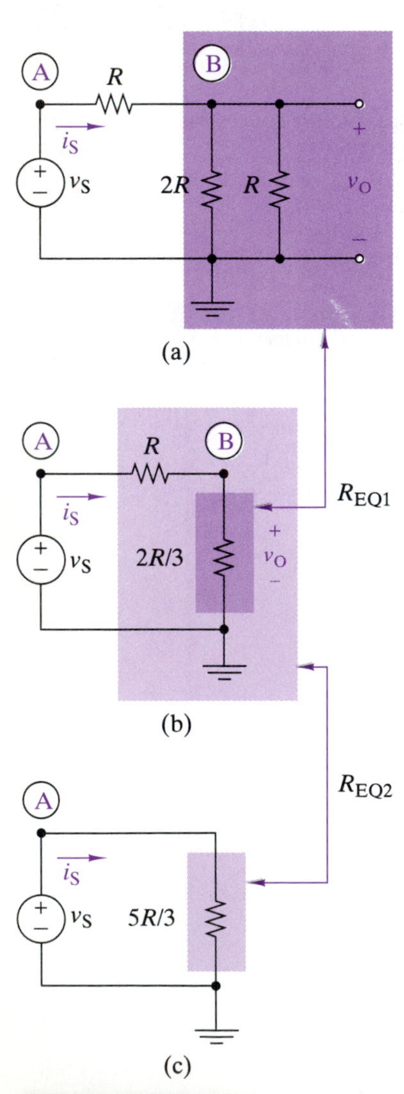

FIGURE 2–47

EXAMPLE 2–20

Use series and parallel equivalence to find the output voltage v_O and the input current i_S in the ladder circuit shown in Figure 2–47(a).

SOLUTION:

One approach is to combine parallel resistors and use voltage division to find v_O, and then combine all resistances into a single equivalent to find the input current i_S. Figure 2–47(b) shows the step required to determine the equivalent resistance between the terminals B and ground. The equivalent resistance of the parallel $2R$ and R resistors is

$$R_{EQ1} = \frac{R \times 2R}{R + 2R} = \frac{2}{3}R$$

The reduced circuit in Figure 2–47(b) is a voltage divider. Notice that the two nodes needed to find the voltage v_O have been retained. The unknown voltage is found in terms of the source voltage as

$$v_O = \frac{\frac{2}{3}R}{\frac{2}{3}R + R} v_S = \frac{2}{5}v_S$$

The input current is found by combining the equivalent resistance found previously with the remaining resistor R to obtain

$$R_{EQ2} = R + R_{EQ1}$$
$$= R + \frac{2}{3}R = \frac{5}{3}R$$

Application of series/parallel equivalence has reduced the ladder circuit to the single equivalent resistance shown in Figure 2–47(c). Using Ohm's law, the input current is

$$i_S = \frac{v_S}{R_{EQ2}} = \frac{3}{5}\frac{v_S}{R}$$

Notice that the reduction step between Figures 2–47(b) and 2–47(c) eliminates node B, so the output voltage v_O must be calculated before this reduction step is taken. ■

EXAMPLE 2–21

Use source transformations to find the output voltage v_O and the input current i_S in the ladder circuit shown in Figure 2–48(a).

FIGURE 2–48

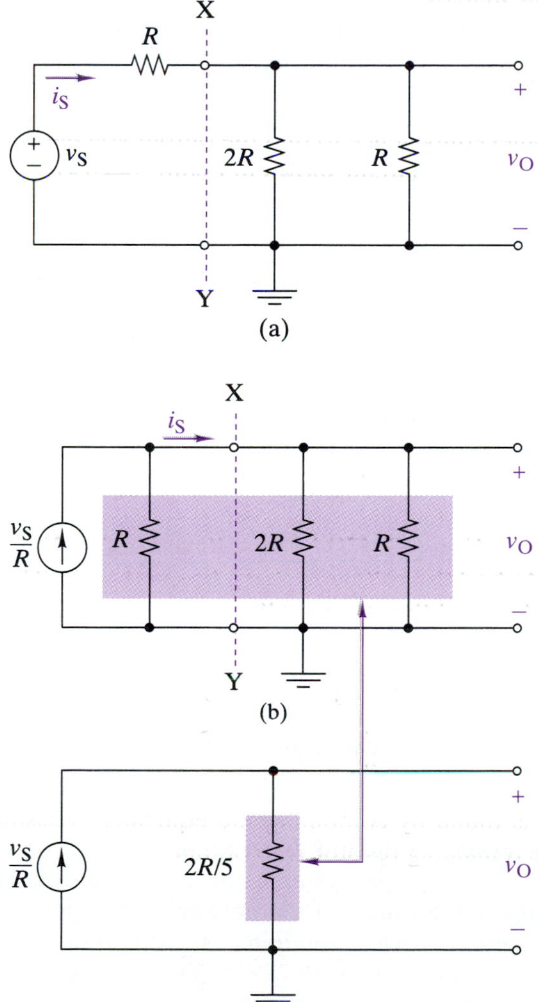

SOLUTION:

Figure 2–48 shows another way to reduce the circuit analyzed in Example 2–20. Breaking the circuit at points X and Y in Figure 2–48(a) produces a voltage source v_S in series with a resistor R. Using source transformation, this combination can be replaced by an equivalent current source in parallel with the same resistor, as shown in Figure 2–48(b).

Caution: The current source v_S/R is *not* the input current i_S, as is indicated in Figure 2–48(b). Applying the two-path current division rule to the circuit in Figure 2–48(b) yields the input current i_S as

$$i_S = \frac{R}{\frac{2}{3}R + R} \times \frac{v_S}{R} = \frac{v_S}{\frac{5}{3}R} = \frac{3}{5}\frac{v_S}{R}$$

The three parallel resistances in Figure 2–48(b) can be combined into a single equivalent conductance without eliminating the node pair used to define the output voltage v_O. Using parallel equivalence, we obtain

$$\begin{aligned} G_{EQ} &= G_1 + G_2 + G_3 \\ &= \frac{1}{R} + \frac{1}{2R} + \frac{1}{R} = \frac{5}{2R} \end{aligned}$$

which yields the equivalent circuit in Figure 2–48(c). The current source v_S/R determines the current through the equivalent resistance in Figure 2–48(c). The output voltage is found using Ohm's law.

$$v_O = \left(\frac{v_S}{R}\right) \times \left(\frac{2R}{5}\right) = \frac{2}{5}v_S$$

Of course, these results are the same result obtained in Example 2–20, except that here they were obtained using a different sequence of circuit reduction steps. ■

EXAMPLE 2–22

Find v_x in the circuit shown in Figure 2–49(a).

SOLUTION:

In the two previous examples the unknown responses were defined at the circuit input and output. In this example the unknown voltage appears across a 10-Ω resistor in the center of the network. The approach is to reduce the circuit at both ends while retaining the 10-Ω resistor defining v_x. Applying a source transformation to the left of terminals X–Y and a series reduction to the two 10-Ω resistors on the far right yields the reduced circuit shown in Figure 2–49(b). The two pairs of 20-Ω resistors connected in parallel can be combined to produce the circuit in Figure 2–49(c). At this point there are several ways to proceed. For example, a source transforma-

FIGURE 2–49

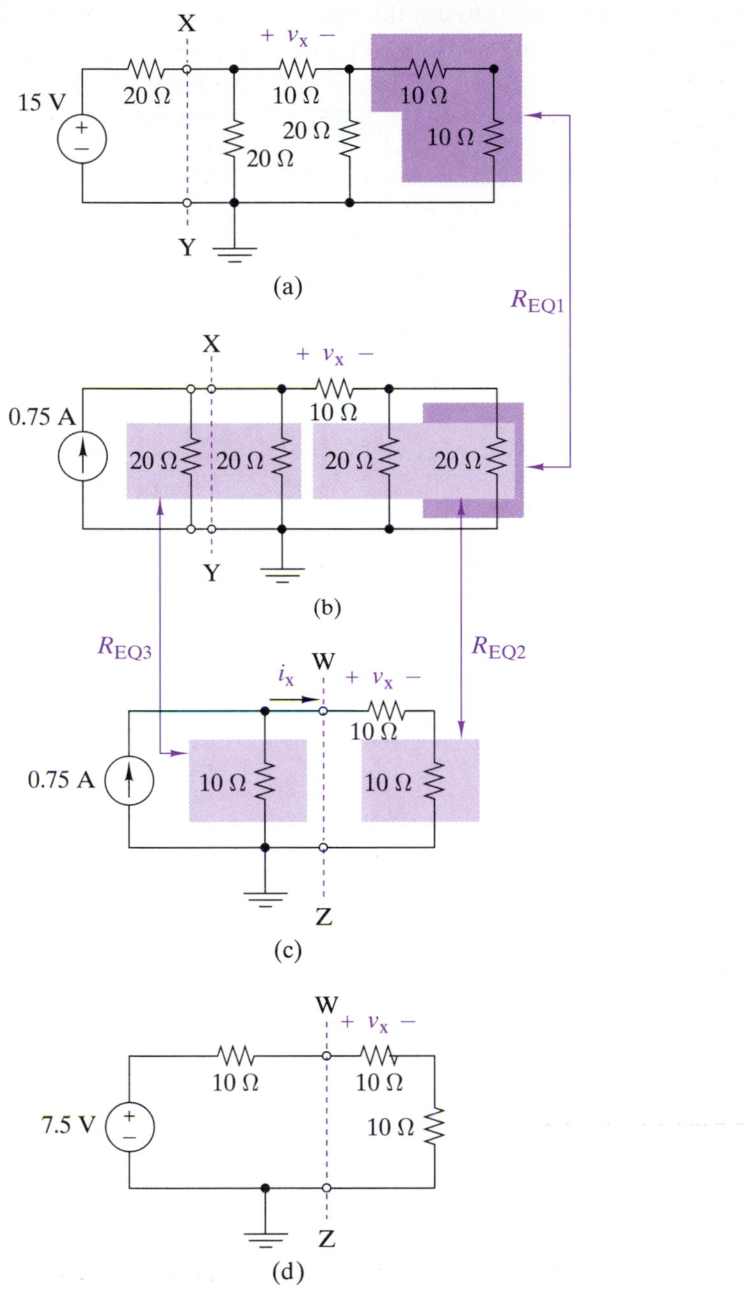

tion at the points W–Z in Figure 2–49(c) produces the circuit in Figure 2–49(d). Using voltage division in Figure 2–49(d) yields v_x.

$$v_x = \frac{10}{10 + 10 + 10} \times 7.5 = 2.5 \text{ V}$$

Yet another approach is to use the two-path current division rule in Figure 2–49(c) to find the current i_x.

$$i_x = \frac{10}{10 + 10 + 10} \times \frac{3}{4} = \frac{1}{4}\ \text{A}$$

Then, applying Ohm's law to obtain v_x,

$$v_x = 10 \times i_x = 2.5\ \text{V}$$

■

Exercise 2–14

Find v_x and i_x using circuit reduction on the circuit in Figure 2–50.

FIGURE 2–50

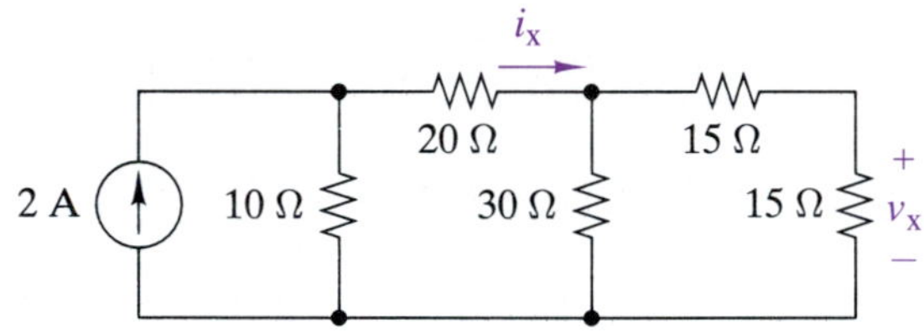

Answers: $v_x = 3.33$ V, $i_x = 0.444$ A

Exercise 2–15

Find v_x and v_y using circuit reduction on the circuit in Figure 2–51.

FIGURE 2–51

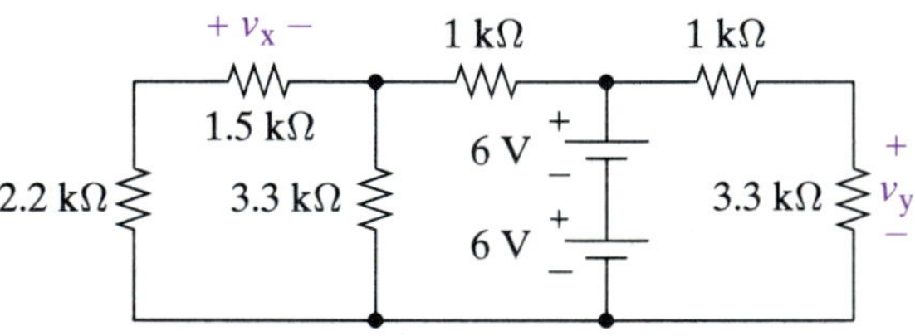

Answers: $v_x = Ω3.09$ V, $v_y = 9.21$ V

EXAMPLE 2–23

Using circuit reduction, find v_O in Figure 2–52(a).

SOLUTION:
One way to solve this problem is to notice that the source branch and the leftmost two-resistor branch are connected in parallel between node A and ground. Switching the order of these branches and replacing the two resistors by their series equivalent yields the circuit of Figure 2–52(b). A source transformation yields the circuit in Figure 2–52(c). This circuit contains a current source $v_S/2R$ in parallel with two $2R$ resistances whose equivalent resistance is

$$R_{EQ} = 2R \| 2R = \frac{2R \times 2R}{2R + 2R} = R$$

Applying a source transformation to the current source $v_S/2R$ in parallel with R_{EQ} results in the circuit of Figure 2–52(d), where

$$V_{EQ} = \left(\frac{v_S}{2R}\right) \times R_{EQ} = \left(\frac{v_S}{2R}\right) R = \frac{v_S}{2}$$

Finally, applying voltage division in Figure 2–52(d) yields

$$v_O = \left(\frac{2R}{R + R + 2R}\right)\frac{v_S}{2} = \frac{v_S}{4}$$

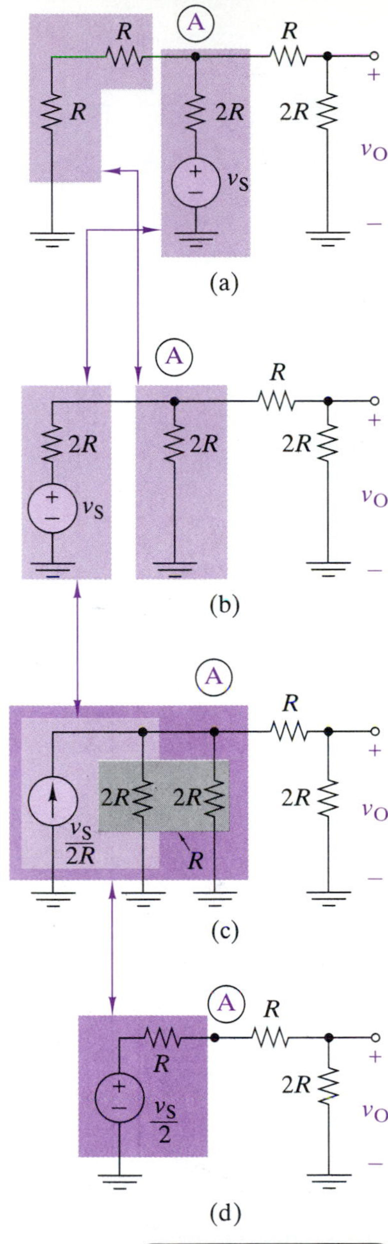

FIGURE 2–52

Exercise 2–16

Find the voltage across the current source in Figure 2–53.

Answer: $v_S = -0.225$ V

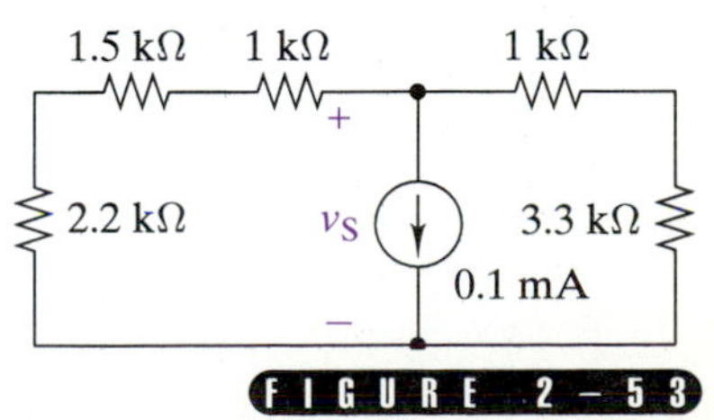

FIGURE 2–53

2–7 COMPUTER-AIDED CIRCUIT ANALYSIS

In this book we illustrate computer-aided circuit analysis using three types of programs: a spreadsheet, a math solver, and a circuit simulator. Practicing engineers routinely apply these computer tools to analysis and design problems, so you must learn when to apply them as well. The purpose of having computer examples in this book is to help you develop an analysis style that includes the intelligent use of computer tools. As you develop your style, you must always keep in mind that computer tools are not problem solvers. *You* are the problem solver. Computer tools can be very useful once the problem is defined, but they do not substitute for an understanding of the fundamentals needed to formulate the problem.

The spreadsheet examples in this book use Quattro Pro for WINDOWS version 6.0. The math solver examples use Mathcad for WINDOWS version 5.0, and the circuit simulation examples use programs in the MicroSim Design Center family version 6.0.[3] The following discussion gives a brief

3 Quattro Pro is a registered trademark of Novell, Inc. Mathcad is copyrighted by MathSoft, Inc. MicroSim Design Center is a registered trademark of MicroSim Corporation. WINDOWS is a registered trademark of Microsoft Corporation.

overview of circuit simulation, since you may be less familiar with this tool. However, this book does not treat the details of how to operate any of these software tools. We assume that you learned how to operate computer tools in previous courses or have enough familiarity with the WINDOWS operating environment to learn how to do so using on-line tutorials or the references given in Appendix E.

CIRCUIT SIMULATION

Most circuit simulation programs are based on a circuit analysis package called SPICE. The term *SPICE* is an acronym for *S*imulation *P*rogram with *I*ntegrated *C*ircuit *E*mphasis. The original SPICE program was developed in the 1970s at the University of California at Berkeley. Since that time, various companies have added proprietary features to the basic SPICE program to produce an array of SPICE-based commercial products for personal computer and workstation platforms.

Figure 2–54 is a block diagram summarizing the major features of a SPICE-based circuit simulation program. The inputs are a circuit diagram and the type of analysis to be carried out. In contemporary programs, the circuit diagram is drawn on the monitor screen using a graphical schematic editor. When the circuit diagram is complete, the input processor performs *schematic capture,* a process that documents the circuit with what is called a netlist. To initiate circuit simulation, the input processor sends the simulation processor the netlist and analysis commands by means of a circuit file. The simulation processor uses the circuit file together with data from the device library to formulate a set of equations that describe the circuit. The simulation processor then solves the equations, writes a dc analysis summary to a standard SPICE output file, and writes the other analysis results to a response data file. For simple dc analysis, the desired response data are easily accessible by simply examining the SPICE output file. For other types of analysis, the output processor can be used to generate graphical plots of the data in the response data file.

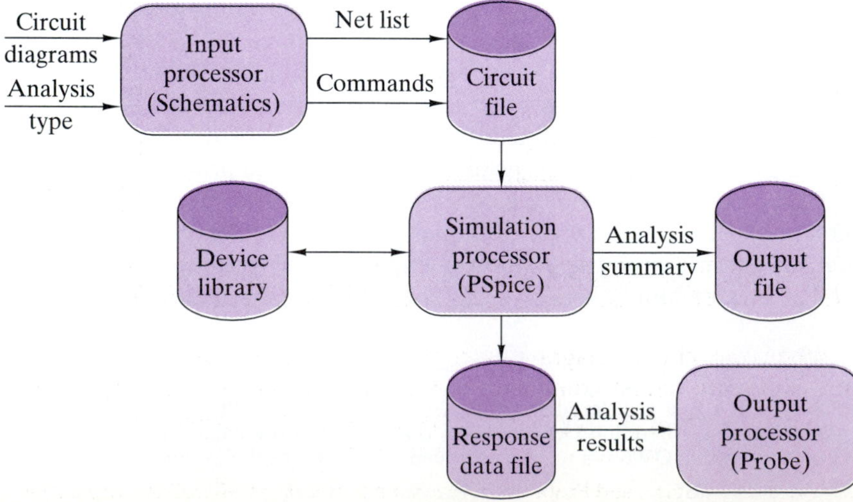

FIGURE 2–54 *Computer flow diagram for circuit simulation programs.*

In MicroSim Design Center, the input processor is called *Schematics*, the simulation processor is a version of SPICE called *PSpice*, and the output processor is called *Probe*.[4] Working together, these three programs create a graphical environment in which the circuit diagram and analysis objectives are entered using *Schematics*, the circuit is analyzed using *PSpice*, and the resulting circuit responses viewed using *Probe*.

The following example provides a simple illustration of circuit simulation using MicroSim Design Center.

EXAMPLE 2–24

Use MicroSim Design Center to find the voltage v_x across the 50-Ω resistor in the circuit of Figure 2–55.

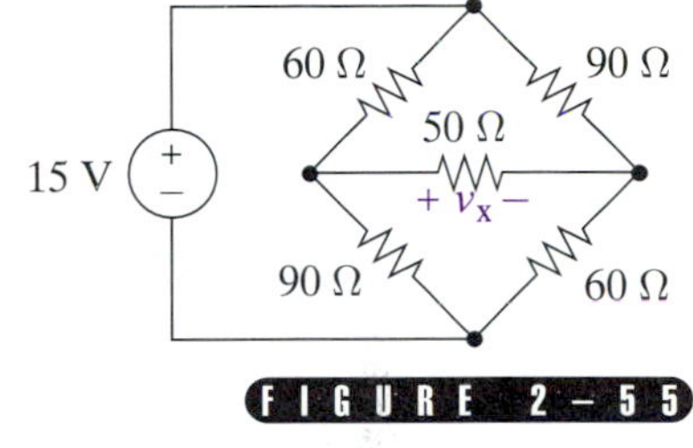

FIGURE 2–55

SOLUTION:

The purpose of this example is to illustrate the steps involved in using MicroSim Design Center to analyze a circuit. Figure 2–56 shows the circuit diagram as it might appear in MicroSim Schematics. The circuit diagram is entered by selecting elements using the **draw/get new part** commands, and then by placing the selected parts on the screen. Once all the parts are in place, the interconnecting wires are entered using the **draw/wire** commands. The circuit diagram in Figure 2–56 differs from the diagram in Figure 2–55 in two ways. First, Figure 2–56 includes both the element values and the reference designators (V_1, R_1, R_2, R_3, R_4, R_5). Second, the nodes are labeled A, B, C, and 0, and the reference node is indicated by the ground symbol. In the MicroSim PSpice syntax the node names can be numbers or letters, except for the ground node, which is automatically labeled with a zero (0).

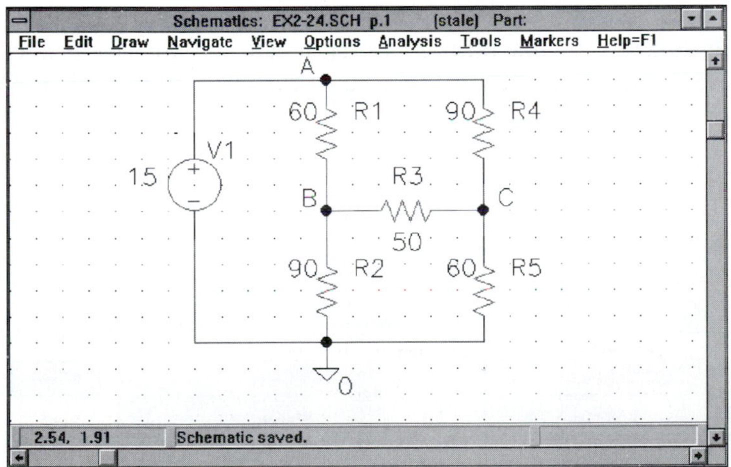

FIGURE 2–56

When the circuit diagram is completed, it is documented using the **analysis/create netlist** command. If there are mistakes, the program will issue error messages. Beginning users are likely to receive an error mes-

4 Schematics, PSpice, and Probe are registered trademarks of MicroSim Corporation.

sage reporting that one or more nodes are "floating." This message generally indicates a violation of one of the following SPICE rules: (1) There must be at least two elements connected to every node, or (2) the circuit must include a reference (ground) node.

Using the **analysis/examine netlist** command produces the netlist display shown in Figure 2–57. A netlist is a sequence of statements that define the circuit elements and connections. The first entry in each statement is the element name. The next two entries are the nodes to which the element is connected. The remaining entries define the element value. For example, the third statement in netlist says that the circuit contains a resistor named R_3, connected between node B and node C, and whose value is 50 Ω. All SPICE-based programs assign the positive reference mark for the element voltage to the first node in the element statement. For example, the plus reference mark for resistor R_2 is at node B and the minus mark is at the ground node. SPICE-based programs use the passive sign convention, so the reference direction for element current is from the first node toward the second node. For example, the reference direction for the current in resistor R_4 is from node A toward node C.

FIGURE 2–57

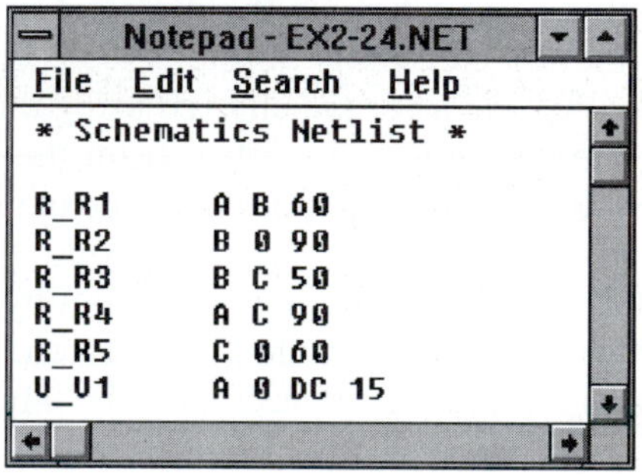

```
Notepad - EX2-24.NET
File  Edit  Search  Help
* Schematics Netlist *

R_R1        A B 60
R_R2        B 0 90
R_R3        B C 50
R_R4        A C 90
R_R5        C 0 60
V_V1        A 0 DC 15
```

The **analysis/setup** command produces the menu in Figure 2–58, which shows the various types of analysis that PSpice performs. In later chapters, we will use the AC Sweep, DC Sweep, Transfer Function, and Transient analysis options on this menu. The Bias Point Detail option produces a dc analysis of the circuit and writes the results to the output file. This analysis type is the default option, so PSpice always performs a dc analysis even when another analysis type is selected.

FIGURE 2–58

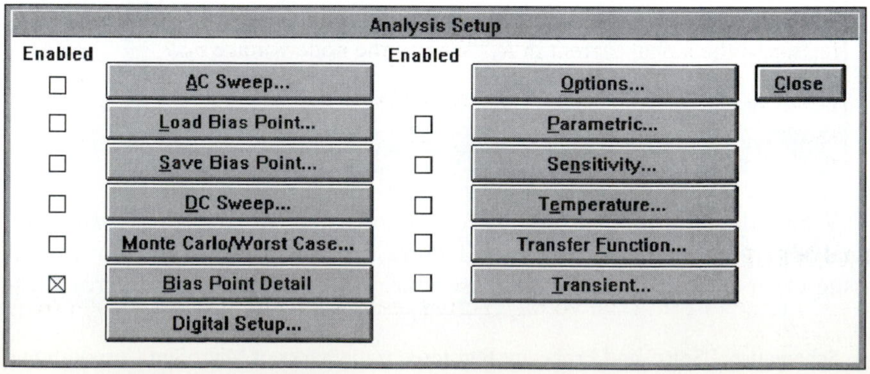

Enabled		Enabled		
☐	AC Sweep...		Options...	Close
☐	Load Bias Point...	☐	Parametric...	
☐	Save Bias Point...	☐	Sensitivity...	
☐	DC Sweep...	☐	Temperature...	
☐	Monte Carlo/Worst Case...	☐	Transfer Function...	
☒	Bias Point Detail	☐	Transient...	
	Digital Setup...			

The **analysis/simulate** command causes PSpice to analyze the circuit defined by the netlist and to write the calculated dc responses in the output file. When the analysis is completed, the **analysis/examine output** command causes the output file to appear on the screen. Paging down through the file, we find the data shown in Figure 2–59. The output file lists the voltage between the lettered nodes and ground; that is, $v_{A0} = 15$ V, $v_{B0} = 8.1148$ V, and $v_{C0} = 6.8852$ V. The problem statement asks for the voltage v_x across resistor R_3 in Figure 2–56 . To find this voltage, we apply KVL to the loop formed by R_2, R_3, and R_5.

$$-v_{A0} + v_x + v_{C0} = 0$$

Hence,

$$v_x = 8.1148 - 6.8852 = 1.2296 \text{ V}$$

Figure 2–59 also shows that the total power dissipated in the circuit is 3.07 W and that the current through the voltage source V_1 is $-2.049E-01$, or –0.2049 A. The minus sign means that the actual direction of the current through the voltage source is directed in at the minus terminal and out at the plus terminal, as you would expect. ■

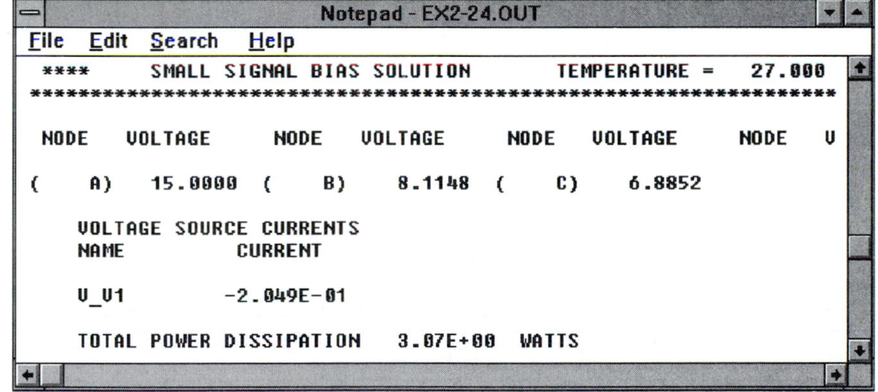
```
Notepad - EX2-24.OUT
File  Edit  Search  Help
 ****      SMALL SIGNAL BIAS SOLUTION          TEMPERATURE =    27.000
******************************************************************************

 NODE    VOLTAGE      NODE    VOLTAGE      NODE    VOLTAGE      NODE    V

(    A)    15.0000  (     B)     8.1148  (     C)     6.8852

     VOLTAGE SOURCE CURRENTS
     NAME            CURRENT

     V_V1           -2.049E-01

     TOTAL POWER DISSIPATION    3.07E+00  WATTS
```

FIGURE 2–59

Exercise 2–17

A PSpice netlist contains the following element statement:

```
R_R3 0 B 10K
```

The output file reports that the current through R_3 is –3.3 mA. What is the direction of the actual current in R_3? What is the node voltage v_{B0}?

Answers: The actual current is directed in at node B; $v_{B0} = 33$ V.

EXAMPLE 2–25

Use Mathcad to find the voltage across the 50-Ω resistor in the circuit of Figure 2–60.

FIGURE 2–60

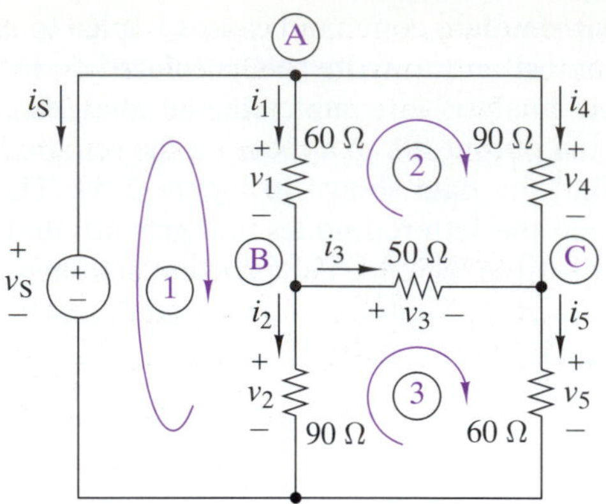

SOLUTION:

This problem was solved in the preceding example using MicroSim Design Center. The given circuit is not a ladder network, so we cannot use circuit reduction techniques. The only general analysis tool we have at this point is to write the full set of six connection equations plus six element equations for this circuit.

CONNECTION EQUATIONS:

Node A $+ i_S + i_1 + i_2 = 0$	Loop 1 $- v_S + v_1 + v_2 = 0$
Node B $- i_1 + i_2 + i_3 = 0$	Loop 2 $- v_1 - v_3 + v_4 = 0$
Node C $- i_3 - i_4 + i_5 = 0$	Loop 3 $- v_2 + v_3 + v_5 = 0$

ELEMENT EQUATIONS:

$$v_S = 15 \qquad v_1 = 60i_1 \qquad v_2 = 90i_2$$

$$v_3 = 50i_3 \qquad v_4 = 90i_4 \qquad v_5 = 60i_5$$

This set of 12 equations must be solved simultaneously to obtain the unknown element currents and voltages. Solving these 12 simultaneous equations by hand analysis is simply not practical. In the next chapter we develop analysis techniques that greatly reduce the number of circuit equations that must be dealt with simultaneously. However, in this example we use Mathcad to solve these 12 equations.

Figure 2–61 shows a Mathcad "solve block" for the 12 simultaneous equations just given. The block begins with initial guesses for all the unknowns. The reserve word **Given** tells Mathcad that what follows is a system of equations to be solved. In Figure 2–61 the statements following the **Given** are the foregoing six connection equations and six element equations. The reserve word **Find** ends the solve block. Mathcad iteratively solves the system of equations listed between the **Given** and the **Find** using the initial guesses listed before the **Given** as a starting point. In the present case, the **Find** statement loads the answers into a column vector containing all the element currents and voltages. Two specific entries in the column vector are shown to be $v_3 = 1.23$ V and $i_S = -0.205$ A. Summing the product of the voltages and currents for each resistor shows that the total power dissipated is 3.074 W. Note that these Mathcad answers agree with the PSpice results in Example 2–24 within round-off errors. ■

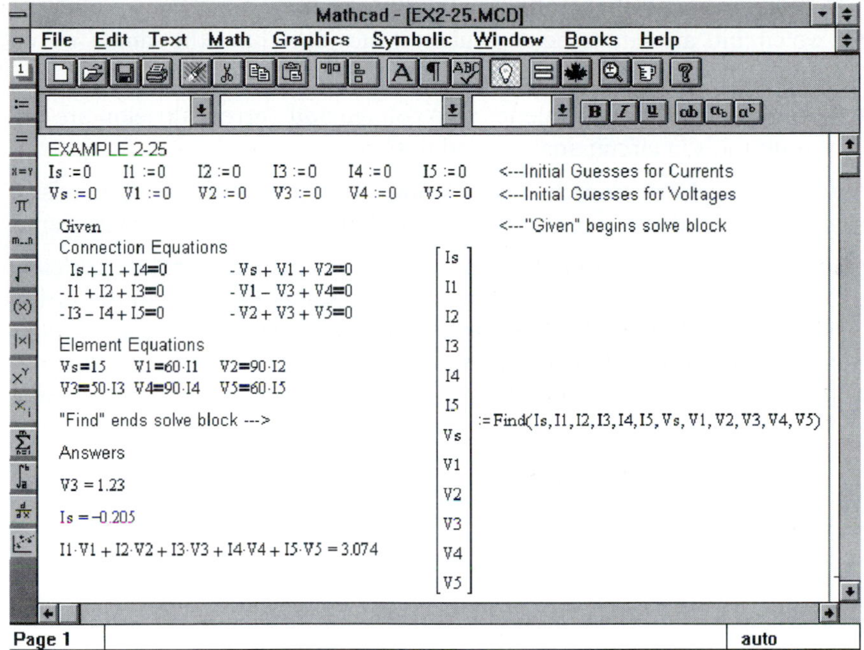

FIGURE 2–61

SUMMARY

- An **electrical device** is a real physical entity, while a **circuit element** is a mathematical or graphical model that approximates major features of the device.
- Two-terminal circuit elements are represented by a circuit symbol and are characterized by a single constraint imposed on the associated current and voltage variables.
- An **electrical circuit** is an interconnection of electrical devices. The interconnections form nodes and loops.
- A **node** is an electrical juncture of the terminals of two or more devices. A **loop** is a closed path formed by tracing through a sequence of devices without passing through any node more than once.
- Device interconnections in a circuit lead to two connection constraints: **Kirchhoff's current law (KCL)** states that the algebraic sum of currents at a node is zero at every instant; and **Kirchhoff's voltage law (KVL)** states that the algebraic sum of voltages around any loop is zero at every instant.

- A pair of two-terminal elements are connected in **parallel** if they form a loop containing no other elements. The same voltage appears across any two elements connected in parallel.
- A pair of two-terminal elements are connected in **series** if they are connected at a node to which no other elements are connected. The same current exists in any two elements connected in series.
- Two circuits are said to be **equivalent** if they each have the same i–v constraints at a specified pair of terminals.
- Series and parallel equivalence and voltage and current division are important tools in circuit analysis and design.
- **Source transformation** changes a voltage source in series with a resistor into an equivalent current source in parallel with a resistor, or vice versa.
- **Circuit reduction** is a method of solving for selected signal variables in ladder circuits. The method involves sequential application of the series/parallel equivalence rules, source transformations, and the voltage/current division rules. The reduction sequence used depends on the variables to be determined and the structure of the circuit and is not unique.

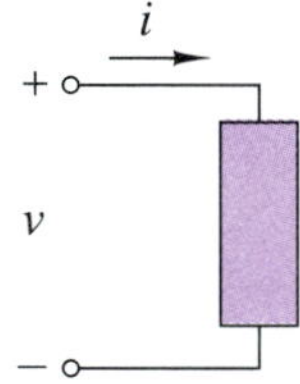

FIGURE P2–1

EN ROUTE OBJECTIVES AND ASSOCIATED PROBLEMS

ERO 2–1 ELEMENT CONTRAINTS (SECT. 2–1)

Given a two-terminal element with one or more electrical variables specified, use the element i–v constraint to find the magnitude and direction of the unknown variables.

2–1 Figure P2–1 shows a general two-terminal element with voltage and current reference marks assigned. Find the unknown electrical variables when the element is

(a) A linear 10-kΩ resistor with $v = 12$ V.
(b) An ideal 10-mA current source with the arrow directed upward and $p = 20$ mW.
(c) An ideal 15-V voltage source with the plus terminal at the top and $i = -8$ mA.
(d) An ideal switch with $i = -20$ A.

2–2 Figure P2–1 shows a general two-terminal element. Determine as much as you can about the element value and signal variables when the element is

(a) A linear resistor with $v = 15$ V and $p = 50$ mW.
(b) An ideal current source with $p = -150$ mW and $v = 10$ V.
(c) An ideal voltage source with $i = -4$ mA and $v = 8$ V.
(d) An ideal switch with $v = 0$ V.

2–3 Find the current through, the voltage across, and the power dissipated in each of the elements in Figure P2–3.

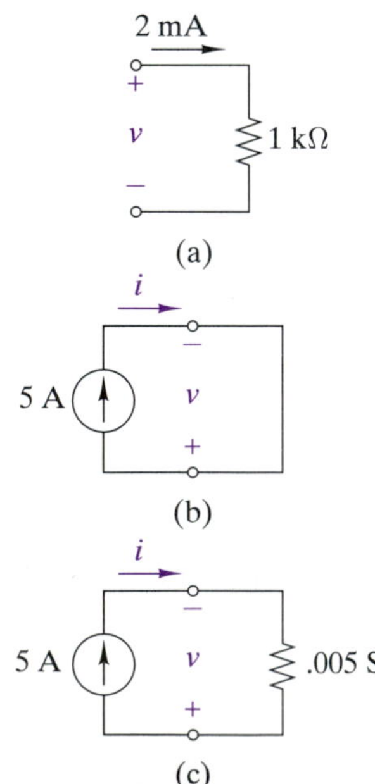

FIGURE P2–3

2–4 The design guidelines for a circuit call for using only ⅛-W resistors. The maximum voltage level in the circuit is known to be 30 V. Determine the smallest allowable value of resistance.

2–5 Fifty thousand devices have arrived at your plant's shipping and receiving department. The two-terminal devices are enclosed in identical containers, except that some are red and some are black. The shipping invoice indicates there are 20,000 identical resistors and 30,000 identical batteries in the shipment. The manufacturing department desperately needs these devices to meet its product delivery schedule, but needs to know which is which. As the junior engineer, you are asked to identify the device types. To start, you connect a red device into a test circuit and measure the device voltage and current. You then reverse the connections and again measure both the voltage and the current. You perform the same measurements with a black device. Like all dutiful junior engineers, you are careful to follow company Policy B-1742C (Revised), which states that voltage and current reference marks must always be assigned to two-terminal devices using the passive sign convention. Like every well-trained engineer, you keep meticulous records, as shown:

DEVICE NUMBER	CONNECTION	VOLTAGE (V)	CURRENT (MA)
2387A(RED)	Original	–1.5	4.0
2387A(RED)	Reversed	–1.5	–1.0
B38(BLACK)	Original	2.0	0.5
B38(BLACK)	Reversed	–2.0	–0.5

Determine the color code used by the shipper, the resistance value, and the battery voltage.

2–6 The i–v characteristic of a nonlinear resistor is $v = 100i + 0.2i^2$.

(a) Calculate v and p for $i = \pm 0.5, \pm 1, \pm 2, \pm 5$, and ± 10 A.

(b) If the operating range of the device is limited to $|i| < 0.5$ A, what is the maximum error in v when the device is approximated by a 100-Ω linear resistance?

2–7 Figure P2–7 shows the circuit symbol for an electronic switch controlled by the voltage between gate G and ground. The manufacturer's data sheet for this device contains the following information:

PARAMETER	SYMBOL	MIN	TYPICAL	MAX	UNITS
Gate voltage for analog switch ON	V_{GH}	2	4.5	5.5	V
Gate voltage for analog switch OFF	V_{GL}			0.8	V
Analog switch ON resistance	R_{ON}		75	200	Ω
Analog switch OFF resistance	R_{OFF}		100		GΩ

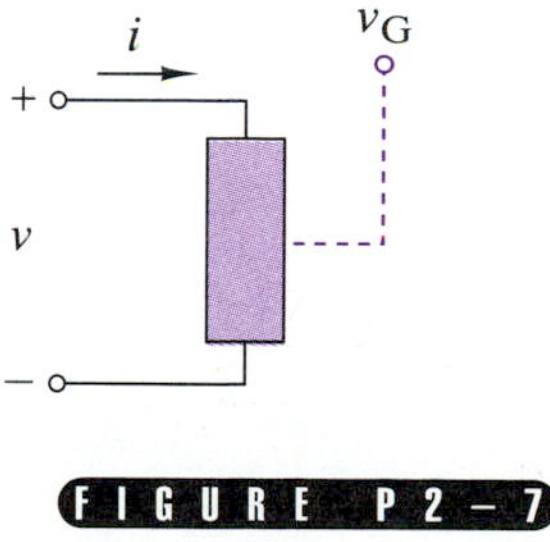

FIGURE P2–7

Devise a circuit model of a typical device using linear resistors and an ideal switch.

2–8 A certain type of film resistor is available with resistance values between 10 Ω and 100 MΩ. The maximum ratings for all resistors of this type are 500 V and 1 W. Show that the voltage rating is the controlling limit when $R > 250$ kΩ, and that the power rating is the controlling limit when $R < 250$ kΩ.

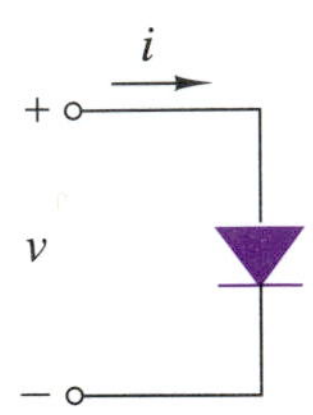

FIGURE P2–9

2–9 Figure P2–9 shows the circuit symbol for a two-terminal device called a diode. For a *p–n* junction diode, theoretical analysis yields the following *i–v* relationship:

$$i = 10^{-15}(e^{40v} - 1)$$

(a) Use this equation to find i and p for $v = 0$, ±0.1, ±0.2, ±0.4, and ±0.8 V. Use these data to plot the i–v characteristic of the element.
(b) Is the diode linear or nonlinear, bilateral or nonbilateral, and active or passive?
(c) Use the diode model to predict i and p for $v = 5$ V. Do you think the model applies to voltages in this range? Explain.
(d) Repeat (c) for $v = -5$ V.

2–10 A fuse contains a metal link that melts to create an open circuit when the current through the device exceeds I_{BLOW}. When the current is less than I_{BLOW}, the fuse acts like a fixed resistor R_{FUSE}. For a certain fuse, $I_{BLOW} = 20$ mA and $R_{FUSE} = 10\,\Omega$. Sketch the current through the fuse versus time when the voltage across the fuse increases linearly with time (i.e., $v = t$).

ERO 2–2 CONNECTION CONSTRAINTS (SECT. 2–2)

Given a circuit composed of two-terminal elements,
(a) Identify nodes and loops in the circuit.
(b) Identify elements connected in series and in parallel.
(c) Use Kirchhoff's laws (KCL and KVL) to find selected signal variables.

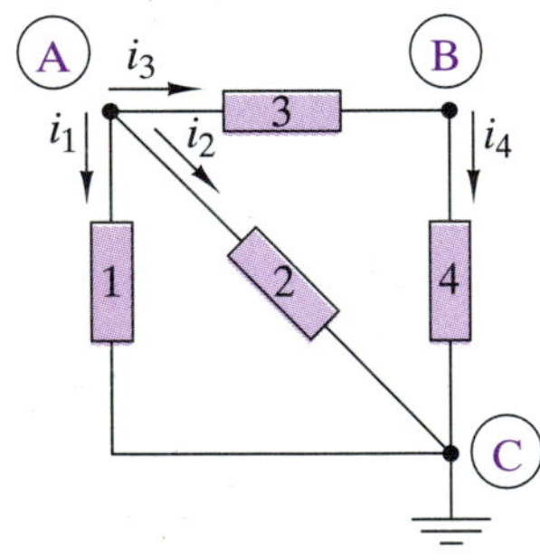

FIGURE P2–11

2–11 For the circuit in Figure P2–11,
(a) Identify the nodes and at least two loops.
(b) Identify any elements connected in series or in parallel.
(c) Write KCL and KVL connection equations for the circuit.
(d) If $i_1 = 6$ mA and $i_2 = -4$ mA, find the other element currents.

2–12 Repeat Prob. 2–11 when a short circuit is connected between nodes A and B.

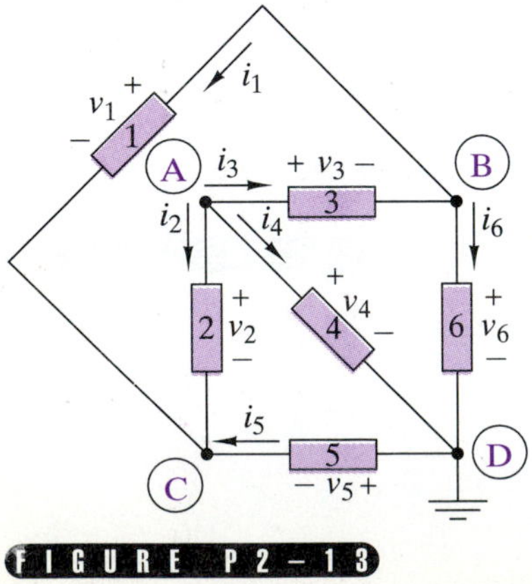

FIGURE P2–13

2–13 For the circuit in Figure P2–13,
(a) Identify the nodes and at least three loops in the circuit.
(b) Identify any elements connected in series or in parallel.
(c) Write KCL and KVL connection equations for the circuit.
(d) If $v_3 = -8$ V, $v_4 = -8$ V, and $v_5 = 9$ V, find the other element voltages.

2–14 Repeat Prob. 2–13 when a short circuit is connected between node B and ground.

2–15 The circuit in Figure P2–15 is organized around the three signal lines A, B, and C.
(a) Identify the nodes and at least three loops in the circuit.
(b) Write KCL connection equations for the circuit.
(c) If $i_3 = 15$ mA, $i_4 = -12$ mA, and $i_5 = 5$ mA, find the other element currents.

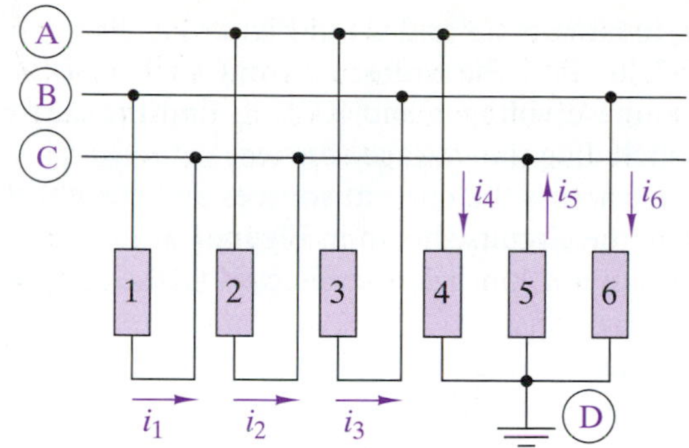

FIGURE P2–15

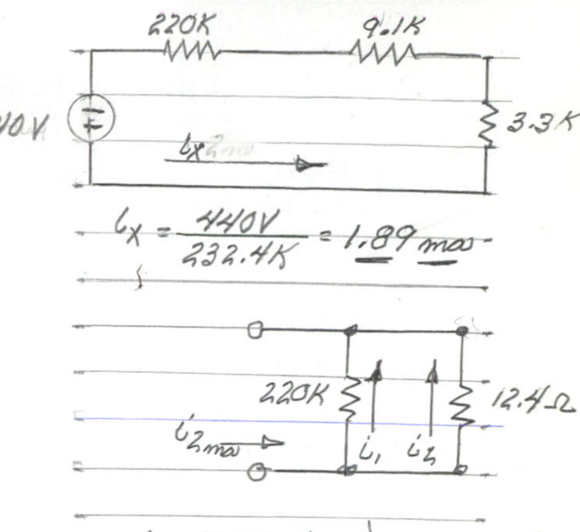

2–16 Repeat Prob. 2–15 when an additional element E_7 is connected between line B and ground. The current through the new element is 8 mA directed from line B to ground.

2–17 The circuit in Figure P2–17 is called a multitap voltage divider. Use KVL to find the output voltage when the switch is in positions A, B, C, D, and E. *Hint:* The output voltage is defined relative to ground.

FIGURE P2–17

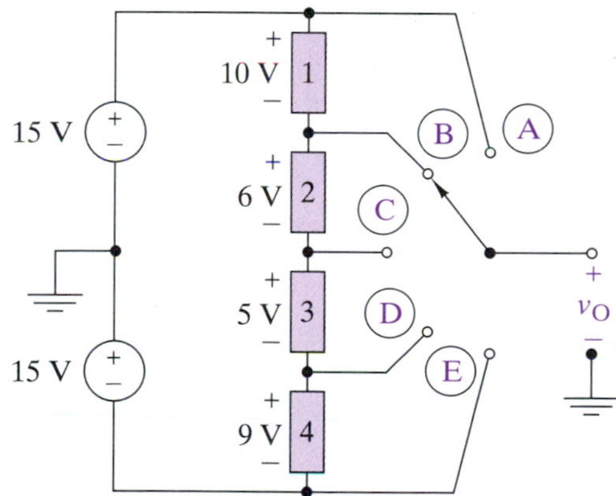

2–18 The connection equations for a certain circuit are

$$i_1 + i_2 - i_3 = 0 \qquad v_1 - v_2 = 0$$

$$i_3 + i_4 + i_5 = 0 \qquad v_2 + v_3 - v_4 = 0$$

$$v_4 - v_5 = 0$$

Using the passive sign convention, draw the circuit diagram and indicate the reference marks for the element voltages and currents.

2–19 Show that the circuits in Figures P2–13 and P2–15 have identical KCL and KVL connection constraints.

ERO 2–3 COMBINED CONSTRAINTS (SECT. 2–3)

Given a circuit consisting of independent sources and linear resistors, use the element constraints and connection constraints to find selected signal variables.

2–20 Find v_x and i_x in circuits C1 and C2 of Figure P2–20.

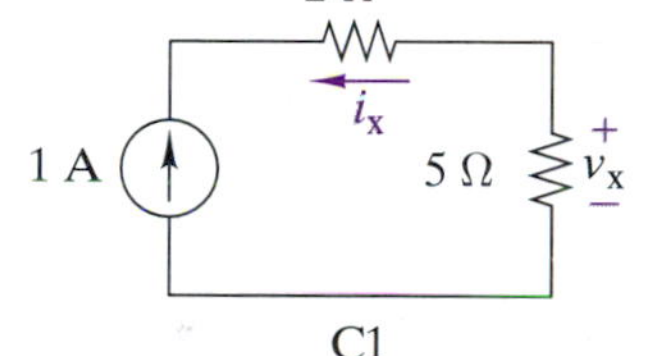

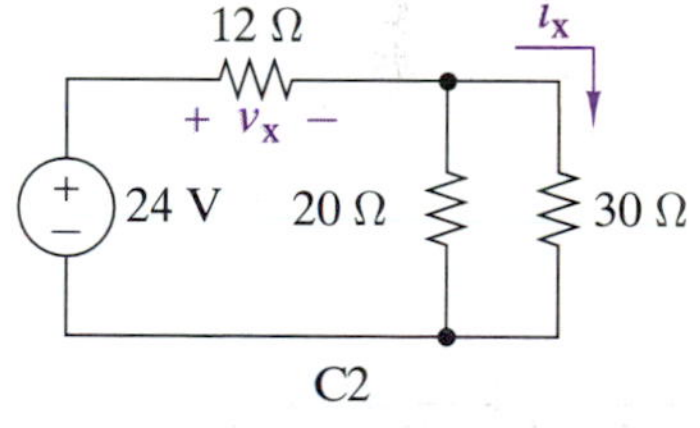

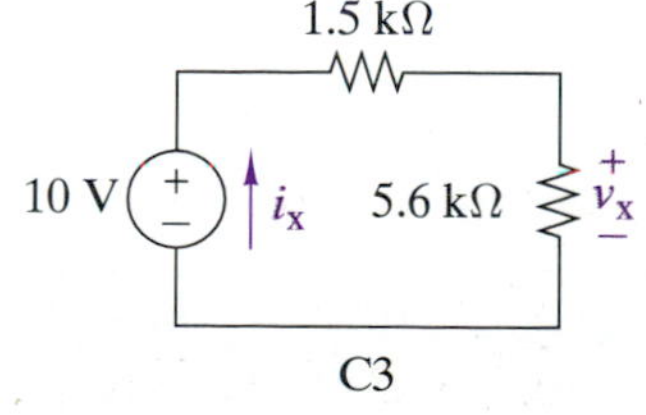

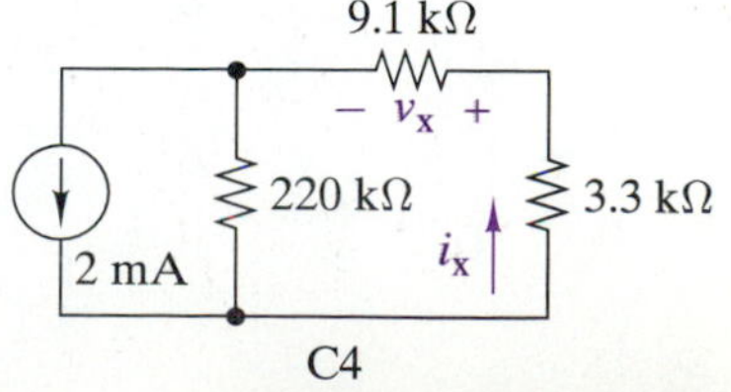

FIGURE P2–20

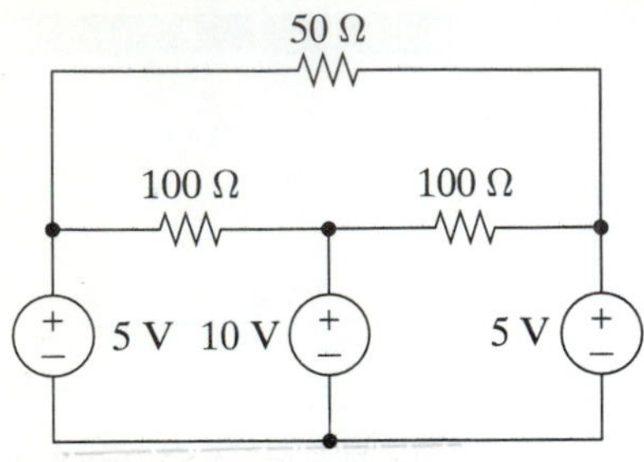

FIGURE P2–22

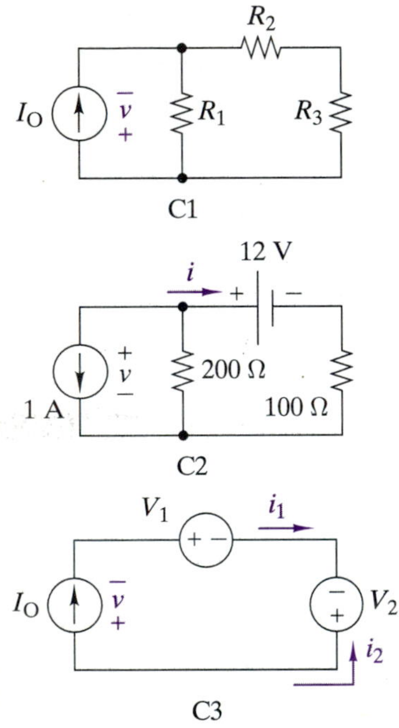

FIGURE P2–23

2–21 Find v_x and i_x in circuits C3 and C4 of Figure P2–20.

2–22 First use KVL to find the voltage across each resistor in Figure P2–22. Then use these voltages and KCL to find the current through every element, including the voltage sources.

2–23 Find the voltage across the current sources and current through the voltage sources in the circuits shown in Figure P2–23.

2–24 Figure P2–24 shows a subcircuit connected to the rest of the circuit at four points.

(a) Use element and connection constraints to find v_x and i_x.

(b) Show that the sum of the currents into the rest of the circuit is zero.

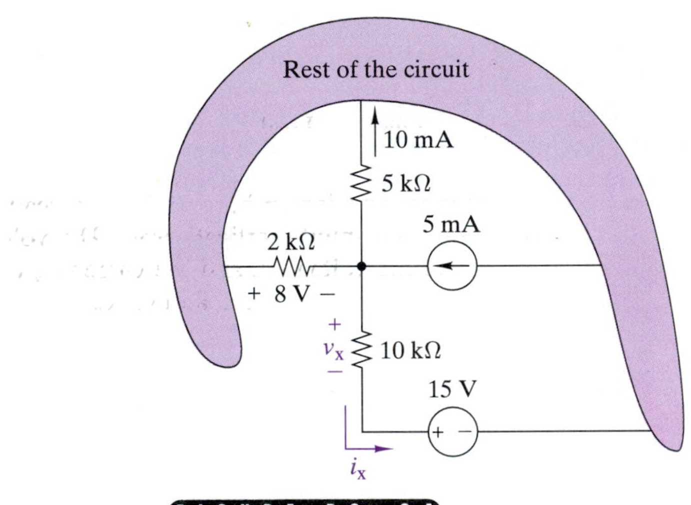

FIGURE P2–24

2–25 The circuit in Figure P2–25 is a model of the feedback path in an electronic amplifier circuit. The current i_x is known to be –0.5 mA.

(a) Find the value of R.

(b) Show that the sum of currents into the rest of the circuit is zero.

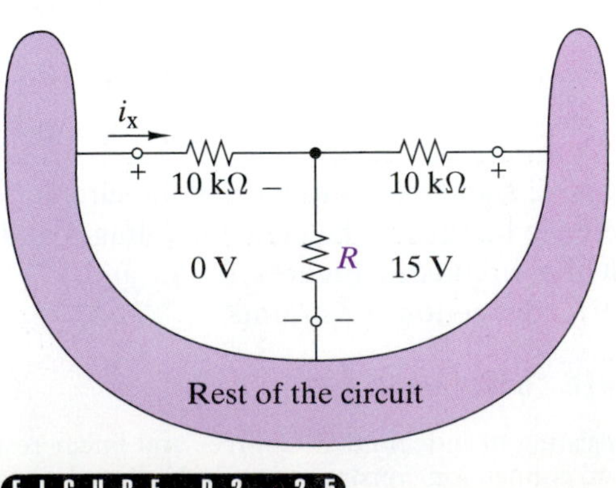

FIGURE P2–25

2–26 The circuit in Figure P2–26 is a model of a dc transmission line connecting a source and load. The current i_x at the line input is known to be 0.2 A.

(a) Find the line input voltage v_x and output voltage v_y.

(b) Find the power delivered at the line input and the power delivered to the load.

(c) Calculate the line efficiency defined as $\eta = (p_{OUT}/p_{IN}) \times 100$.

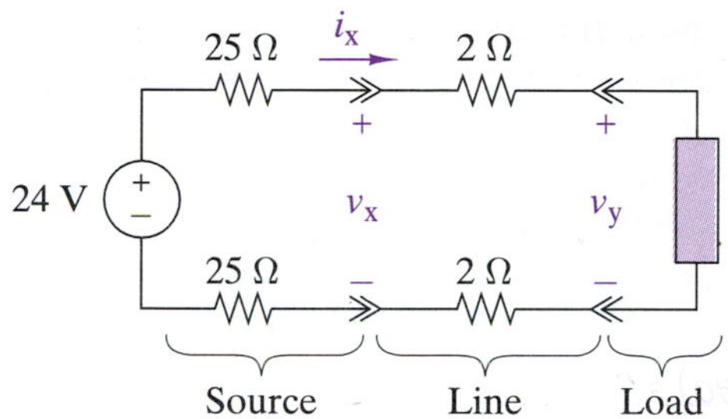

FIGURE P2–26

2–27 The circuit in Figure P2–27 is called a ladder because it is a cascade of alternating series (horizontal) and shunt (vertical) arms. The voltage v_O is known to be 5 V. Find the voltage v_x and the current i_x by successive application of element constraints, KCL, and KVL.

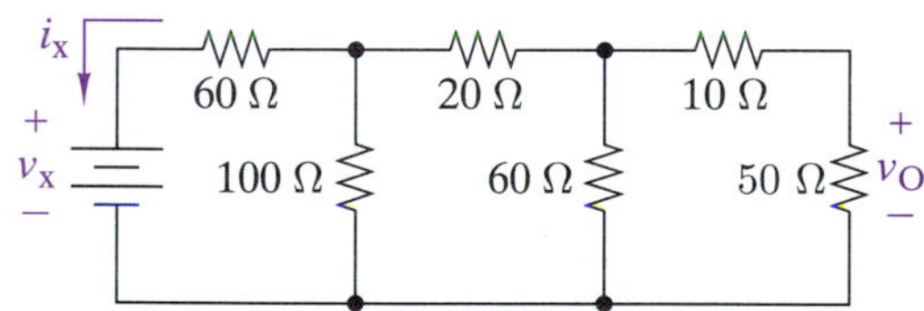

FIGURE P2–27

2–28 The circuit in Figure P2–28 is organized around the power supply lines A, B, and C. Find the input currents i_A, i_B, and i_C and the power supplied by each source.

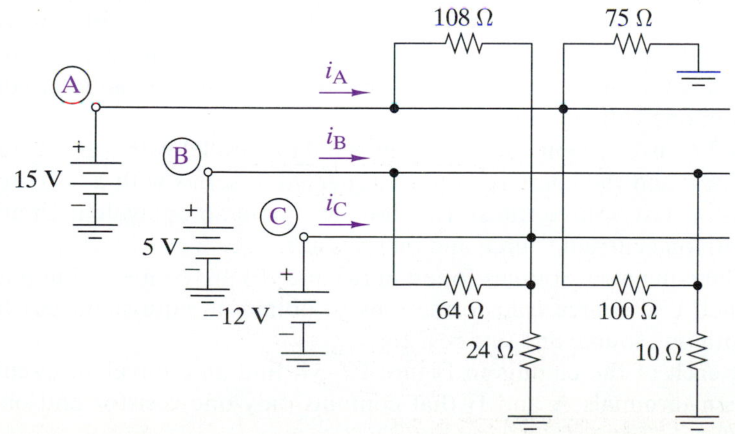

FIGURE P2–28

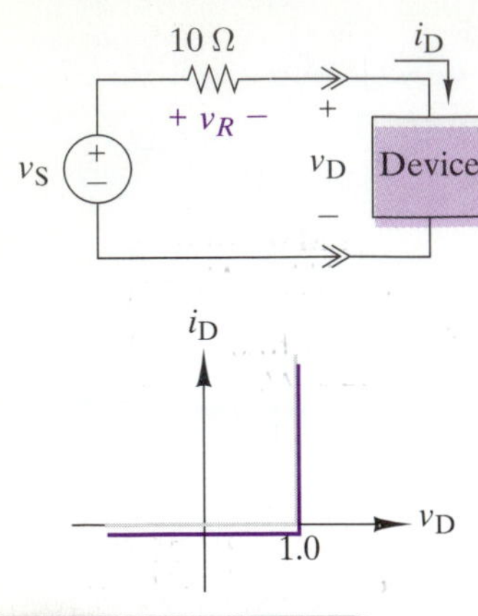

FIGURE P2–29

2–29 The box in Figure P2–29 represents a device whose idealized i–v characteristic is shown in the figure.
 (a) Find the device power for $v_S = -2$, 0.5, and 2 V.
 (b) Is the device linear or nonlinear, bilateral or nonbilateral, and active or passive?

ERO 2–4 EQUIVALENT CIRCUITS AND SOURCE TRANSFORMATIONS (SECT. 2–4)

(a) Given a circuit consisting of linear resistors, find the equivalent resistance between a specified pair of terminals.
(b) Given a circuit consisting of a source-resistor combination, find an equivalent source-resistor circuit.

2–30 Find the equivalent resistance between terminals A–B, B–C, A–C, C–D, B–D, and A–D in the circuit of Figure P2–30.

2–31 Find the equivalent resistance between terminals A–B, A–C, A–D, B–C, B–D, and C–D in the circuit of Figure P2–31.

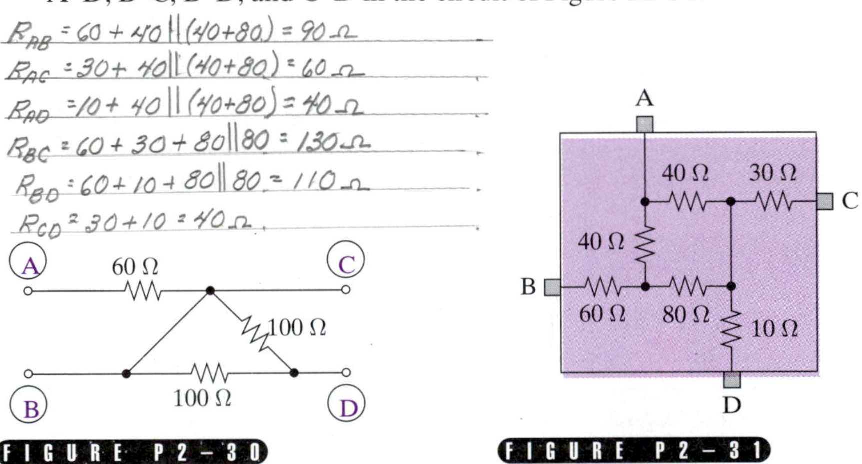

FIGURE P2–30

FIGURE P2–31

2–32 Find the equivalent resistance at terminals A–B in each circuit of Figure P2–32.

2–33 **(a)** A 10-V voltage source is connected in series with a 50-Ω resistor, and the combination is connected in parallel with a 200-Ω resistor. Use source transformations to obtain an equivalent circuit with one voltage source and one resistor.
 (b) A 200-mA current source is connected in parallel with a 100-Ω resistor, and the combination is connected in series with a 33-Ω resistor. Use source transformations to obtain an equivalent circuit with one current source and one resistor.
 (c) The equivalent sources found in (a) and (b) are connected in parallel. Use source transformations to obtain an equivalent circuit with one source and one resistor.

2–34 For each of the circuits in Figure P2–34, find an equivalent circuit between terminals A and B that contains only one resistor and one source.

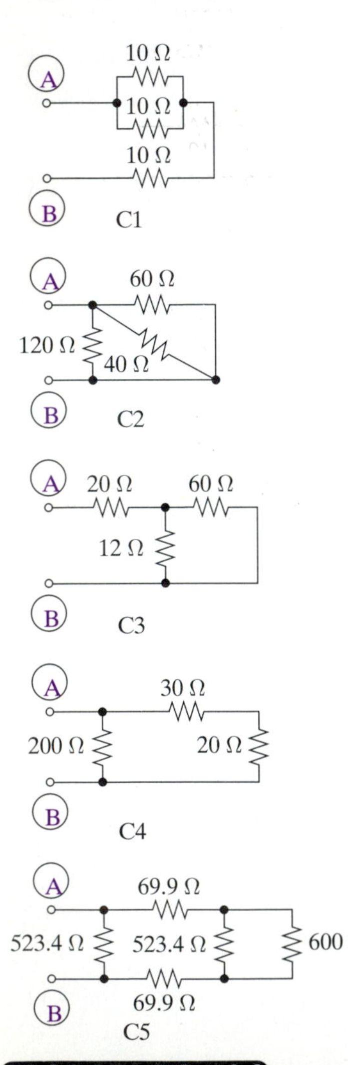

FIGURE P2–32

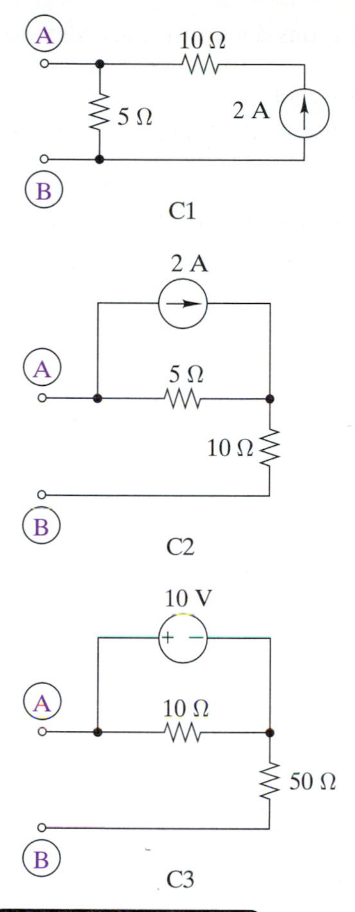

FIGURE P2–34

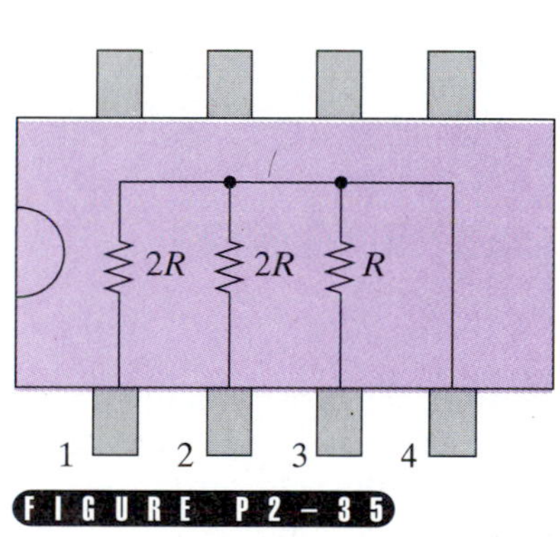

FIGURE P2–35

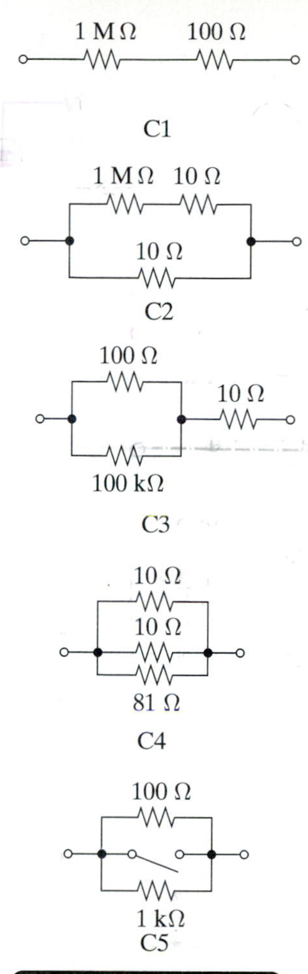

FIGURE P2–36

2–35 The circuit of Figure P2–35 is an R-$2R$ resistance array package. All of the following equivalent resistances can be obtained by making proper connections of the array *except for one:* $R/2$, $2R/3$, R, $8R/3$, $5R/3$, $2R$, $3R$, and $4R$. Show how to interconnect the terminals of the array to produce the equivalent resistances, and identify the one that cannot be obtained using this array.

2–36 Resistance values may differ by several orders of magnitude, so engineers often use approximations to estimate circuit parameters. Estimate the equivalent resistance of the circuits in Figure P2–36 considering that the resistors have ±5% tolerance.

2–37 **D** Show how to interconnect standard 3.9-kΩ resistors to obtain equivalent resistances that are within ±5% of 1 kΩ, 5 kΩ, and 10 kΩ. The total number of 3.9-kΩ resistors required to obtain all three equivalent resistances must not exceed 14.

2–38 Use a Δ-to-Y or a Y-to-Δ transformation to find the equivalent resistance seen by the source in Figure P2–38.

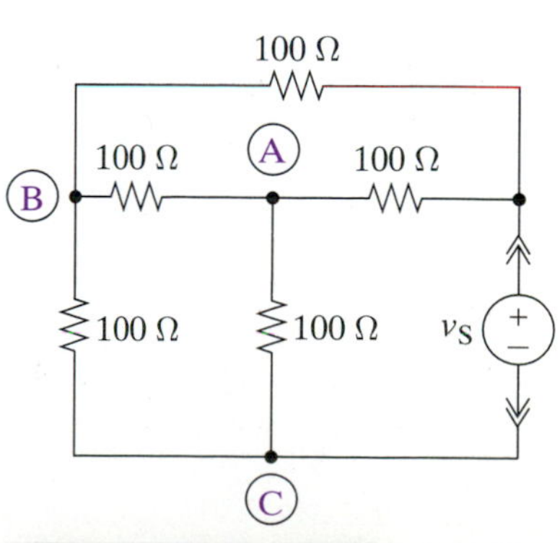

FIGURE P2–38

2–39 The circuit of Figure P2–39 is the pin diagram of a resistance array. Find the equivalent resistance between the following pins:

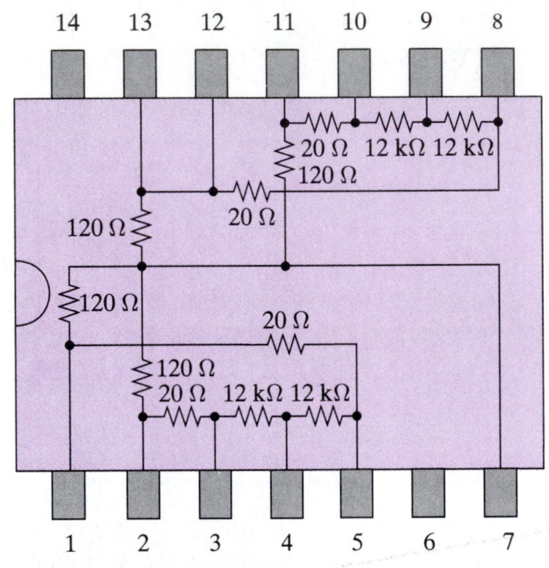

FIGURE P2–39

PINS
10–11
11–12
2–3
1–2
1–13
1–6
5–7
4–5
4–12
1–7
8–13
12–13

2–40 Each resistor in Figure P2–40 has the same resistance R. The equivalent resistance measured between terminals A and B is 90 Ω. Determine the value of R.

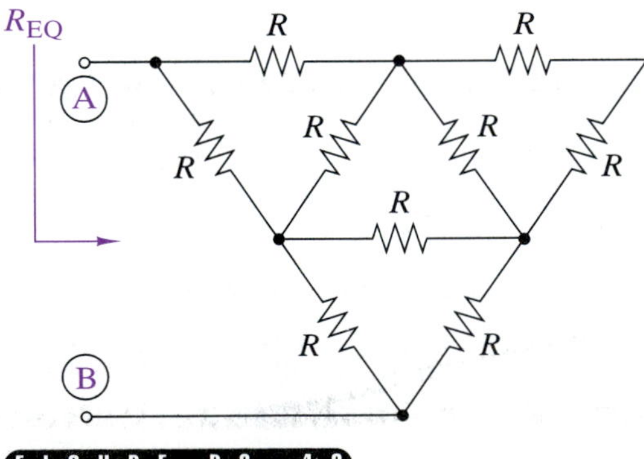

FIGURE P2–40

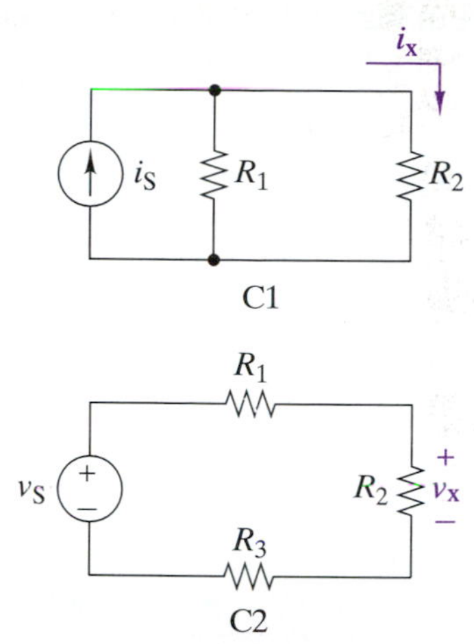

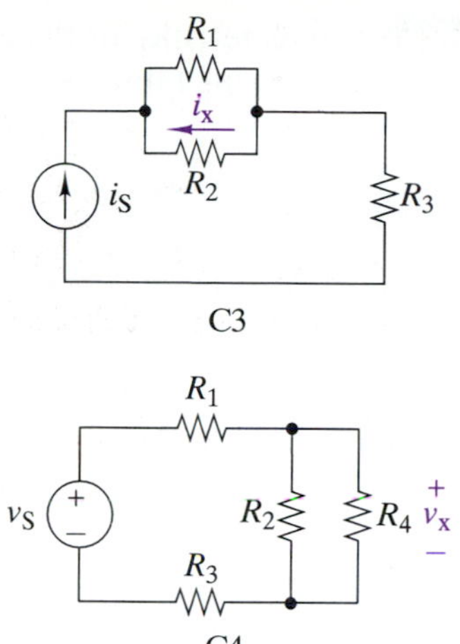

FIGURE P2–41

ERO 2–5 VOLTAGE AND CURRENT DIVISION (SECT. 2–5)

(a) Given a circuit with elements connected in series or parallel, use voltage or current division to find specified voltages or currents.
(b) Design a voltage or current divider that delivers specified output signals within stated constraints.

2–41 Use voltage or current division to obtain an expression for the indicated unknown signal in each of the circuits of Figure P2–41.

2–42 Find v_x in each of the circuits of Figure P2–42.

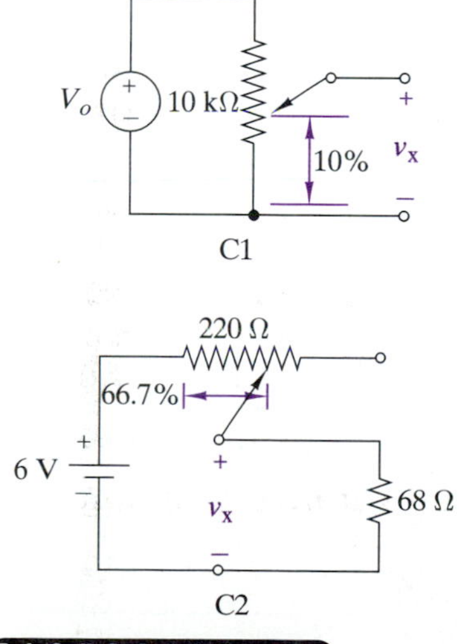

FIGURE P2–42

2–43 Use voltage or current division to find the indicated unknown signal in circuits C1 and C2 of Figure P2–43.

2–44 Use voltage or current division to find the indicated unknown signal in circuits C3 and C4 of Figure P2–43.

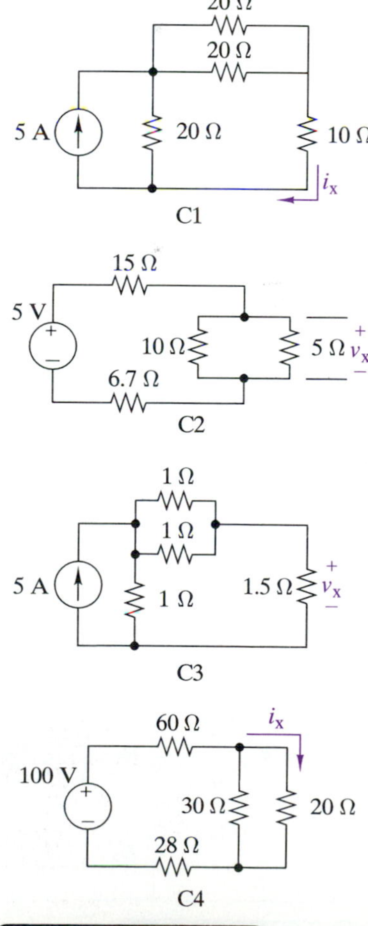

FIGURE P2–43

2–45 Characteristics of the electronic switch in Figure P2–45 are given in the following table:

FIGURE P2–45

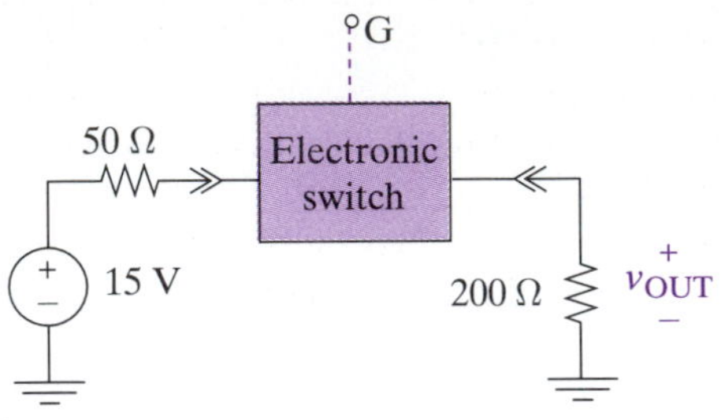

PARAMETER	SYMBOL	MIN	TYPICAL	MAX	UNITS
Gate voltage for analog switch ON	V_{GH}	2	4.5	5.5	V
Gate voltage for analog switch OFF	V_{GL}			0.8	V
Analog switch ON resistance	R_{ON}		75	200	Ω
Analog switch OFF resistance	R_{OFF}		100		MΩ

Use these data to model the switch and find v_O in Figure P2–45 with the switch ON and OFF.

2–46 Figure P2–46 shows a resistance divider connected in a general circuit.

(a) What is the relationship between v_1 and v_2 when $i_1 = 0$?
(b) What is the relationship between v_1 and v_2 when $i_2 = 0$?
(a) What is the relationship between i_1 and i_2 when $v_1 = 0$?
(b) What is the relationship between i_1 and i_2 when $v_2 = 0$?

FIGURE P2–46

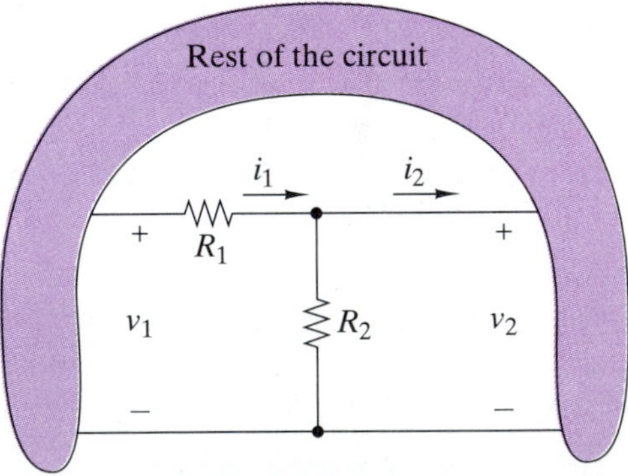

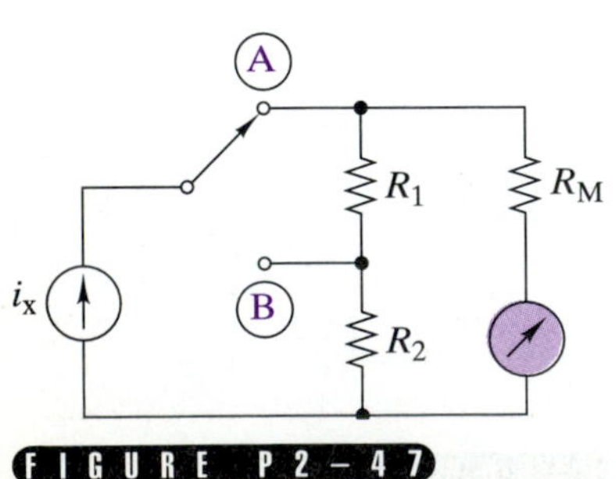

FIGURE P2–47

2–47 **D** Figure P2–47 shows an ammeter circuit consisting of a D'Arsonval meter, a two-position selector switch, and two shunt resistors. A current of 0.5 mA produces full-scale deflection of the D'Arsonval meter, whose internal resistance is $R_M = 50\ \Omega$. Select the shunt resistance R_1 and R_2 so that $i_x = 10$ mA produces full-scale deflection when the switch is in position A and $i_x = 50$ mA produces full-scale deflection when the switch is in position B.

2–48 **D** Figure P2–48 shows the R-$2R$ package described in Prob. 2–35 configured as a voltage divider and connected across a 12-V source. The divider output is 6 V for the connections shown in the figure. Show how to interconnect the source and the R-$2R$ package to obtain outputs of 3 V, 4 V, 8 V, and 9 V.

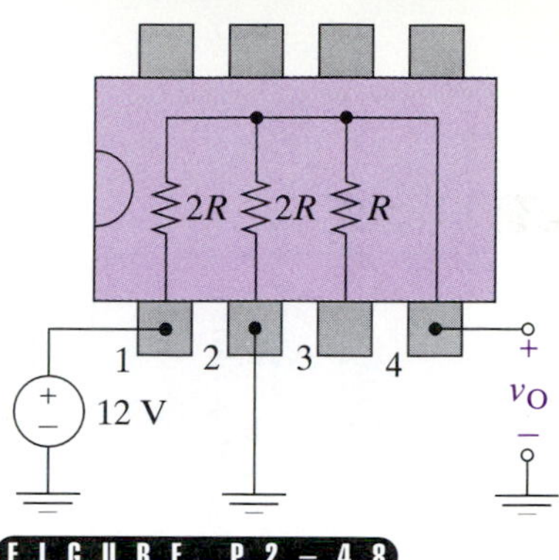

FIGURE P2–48

2–49 **D** This problem involves designing the interface circuit in Figure P2–49 to meet specified load conditions.

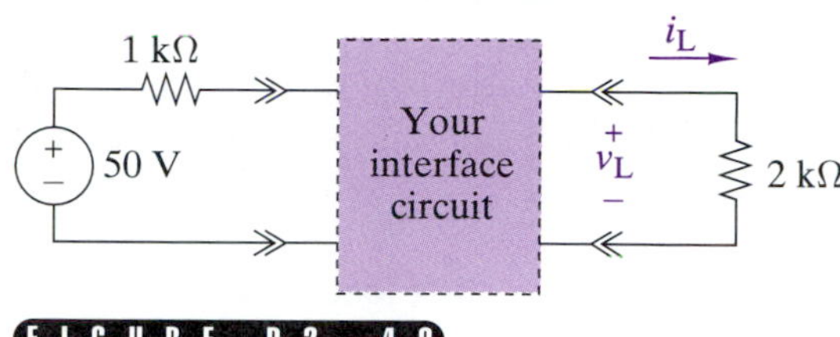

FIGURE P2–49

(a) Design the interface circuit so the current through the 2-kΩ load is 1 mA.

(b) Design the interface circuit so the voltage across the 2-kΩ load is 10 V.

(c) Design the interface circuit so the voltage across the 2-kΩ load is 10 ± 0.5 V using only 1-kΩ ± 5% resistors.

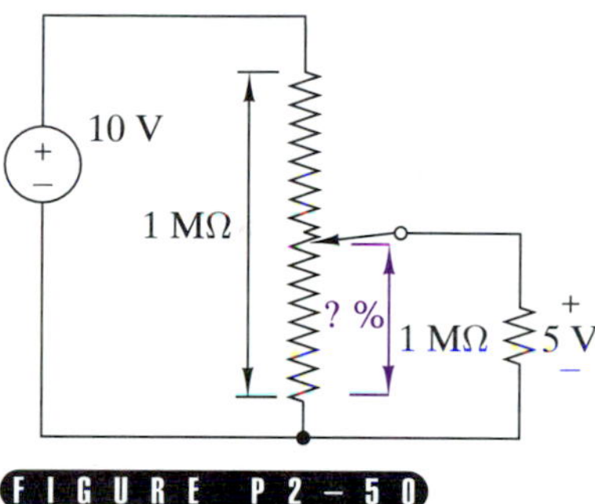

FIGURE P2–50

2–50 The 1-MΩ potentiometer in Figure P2–50 is adjusted until the voltage across the 1-MΩ load is 5 V. What is the position of the wiper arm in percent?

ERO 2–6 CIRCUIT REDUCTION (SECT. 2–6)

Given a circuit consisting of linear resistors and an independent source, find selected signal variables using successive application of series/parallel equivalence, source transformations, and voltage/current division.

2–51 Use circuit reduction to determine the indicated signal variables in the circuit shown in Figure P2–51.

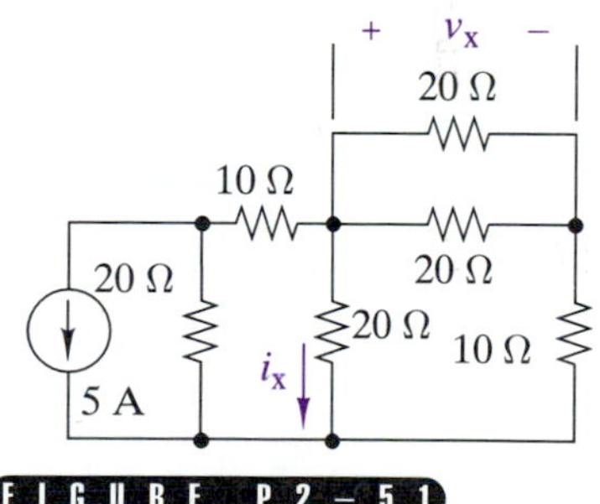

FIGURE P2–51

2–52 Use circuit reduction to find the indicated signal variables in the circuit shown in Figure P2–52.

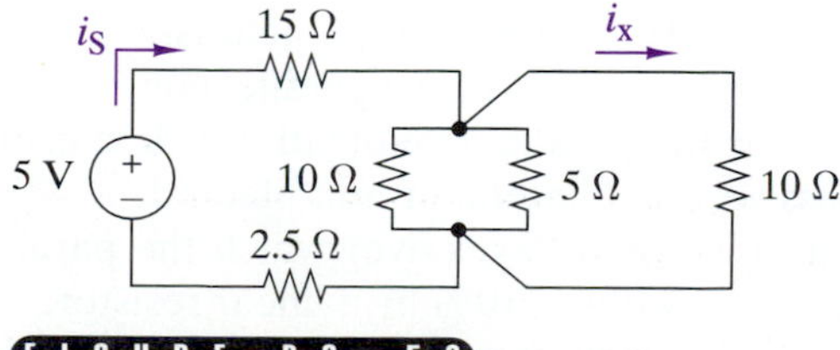

FIGURE P2–52

2–53 Use circuit reduction to find the indicated signal variables in the circuit shown in Figure P2–53.

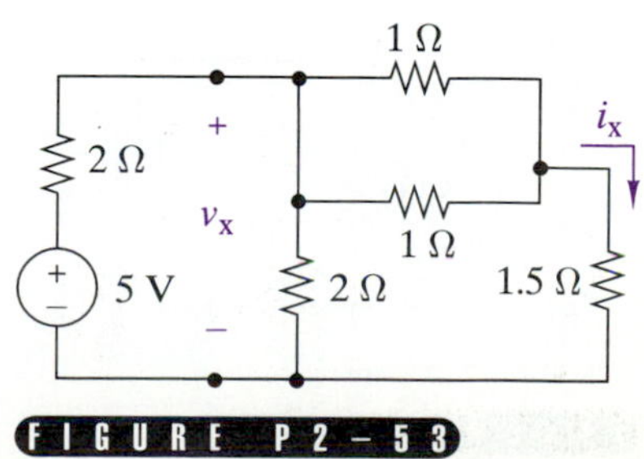

FIGURE P2–53

2–54 Use circuit reduction to find the indicated signal variables in the circuit shown in Figure P2–54.

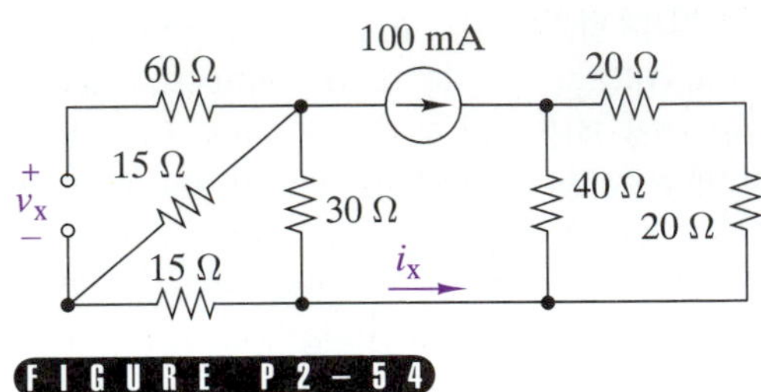

FIGURE P2–54

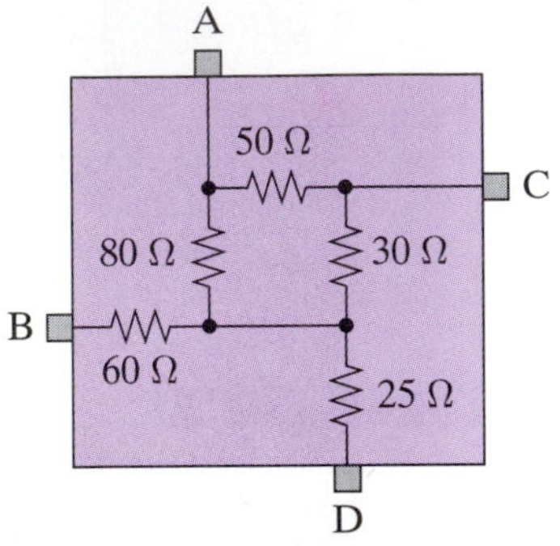

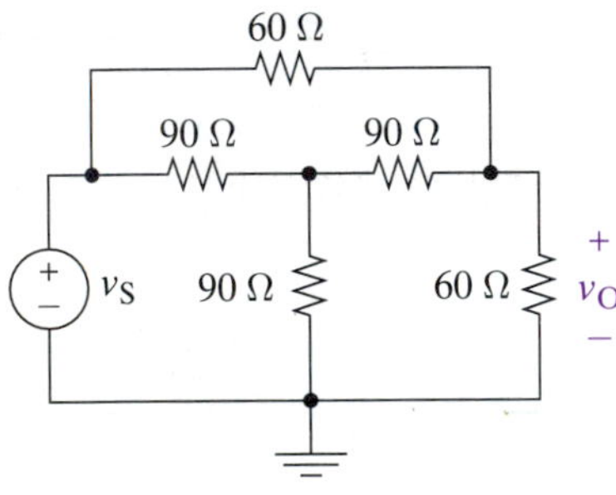

FIGURE P2–55

2–55 The resistance array circuit in Figure P2–55 has external terminals at pads A, B, C, and D. Connect the "+" terminal of a 10-V voltage to terminal A and the "–" to terminal B. Find the voltages v_{DB}, v_{AC}, and v_{CD}.

2–56 Repeat Prob. 2–55 when a 50-Ω load resistor is connected between terminals C and D.

2–57 A 5-V source is connected to terminal C of the resistance array in Figure P2–55 with the plus terminal at terminal C and the minus terminal connected to ground. Terminal B of the array is also connected to ground. Find v_{AD}.

2–58 A 50-Ω load is connected between terminals A and B of the resistance array in Figure P2–55. A second 50-Ω load is connected between terminals C and D, and a 10-V source is connected between terminals B and D with the + terminal at terminal D. Find v_{AB}, v_{CD}, and the power delivered by the source.

2–59 The circuit in Figure P2–59 is called a bridged T. Use a Y-to-Δ transformation and circuit reduction to show that $v_O = v_S/2$.

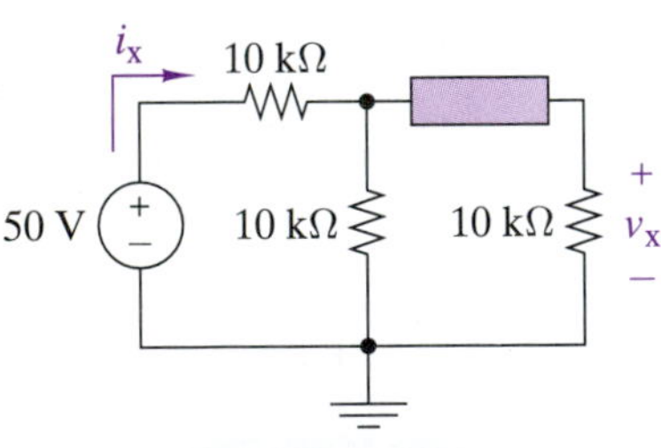

FIGURE P2–59

2–60 The box in the circuit in Figure P2–60 is a resistor whose value can be anywhere between 1 kΩ and 100 kΩ. Use circuit reduction to place upper and lower bounds on v_x and i_x.

FIGURE P2–60

CHAPTER-INTEGRATING PROBLEMS

2–61 A DEVICE MODELING

The circuit in Figure P2–61 consists of a 50-Ω linear resistor in parallel with a nonlinear varistor whose i–v characteristic is $i_V = 1.6 \times 10^{-5} v^3$.

(a) Plot the i–v characteristic of the parallel combination.

(b) State whether the parallel combination is linear or nonlinear, active or passive, and bilateral or nonbilateral.

(c) Identify a range of voltages over which the parallel combination can be modeled within ±10% by a linear resistor.

(d) Identify a range of voltages over which the parallel combination can be safely operated if both devices are rated at 50 W. Which device limits this range?

(e) The parallel combination is connected in series with a 50-Ω resis-

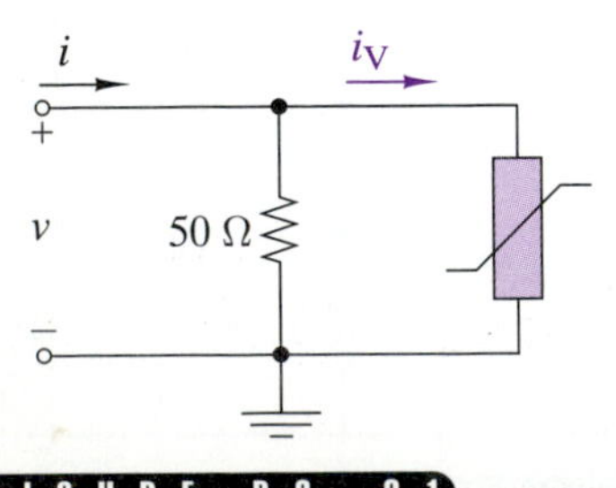

FIGURE P2–61

tor and a 5-V voltage source. In this circuit, how would you model the parallel combination and why?

2–62 A WHEATSTONE BRIDGE

The Wheatstone bridge circuit in Figure P2–62(a) occurs extensively in electrical instrumentation. The resistance R_X is the equivalent resistance of a transducer (a device that converts energy from one form to another). The value of R_X varies in relation to an external physical phenomenon such as temperature, pressure, or light. The resistance R_M is the equivalent resistance of a measuring instrument, often a D'Arsonval meter. Prior to any measurements, one of the other resistors (usually R_3) is adjusted until the current i_M is zero. The resistance of the transducer changes when exposed to the physical phenomenon it is designed to measure. This change causes the bridge to become unbalanced, and the meter indicates the resulting current through R_M. The deflection of the meter is calibrated to indicate the value of the physical phenomenon measured by the transducer.

(a) A Derive the relationship between R_1, R_2, R_3, and R_X when $i_M = 0$ A.

(b) A Suppose the transducer resistance R_X varies with temperature, as shown in Figure P2–62(b). With $R_1 = R_2 = 2.2$ kΩ, find the value of R_3 that produces $i_M = 0$ at a temperature of 57.5°C.

(c) A A current $i_M = -1.5$ mA is observed when $R_1 = R_2 = 2.2$ kΩ and R_3 is set to the value found in part (b). Is the temperature higher or lower than 57.5°C?

(d) A For $R_1 = R_2 = 2.2$ kΩ and $R_3 = 2.4$ kΩ, find the temperature at which $i_M = 0$.

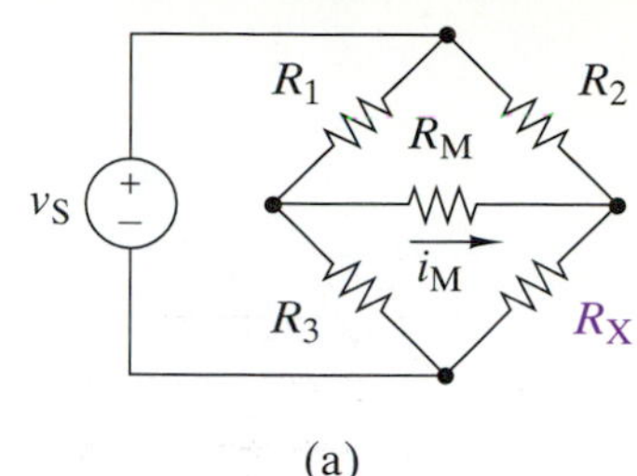

(a)

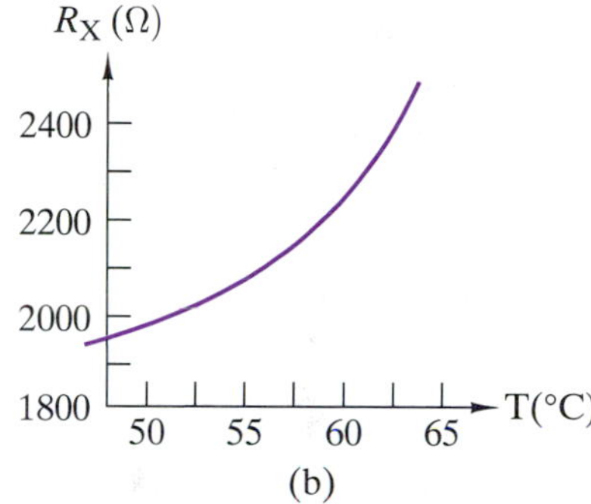

(b)

FIGURE P2–62

2–63 A D E FILM RESISTORS

Film resistors are fabricated by depositing a thin film of conducting materials in a vacuum chamber. A film resistor consisting of a simple rectangle of length ℓ and width w has a resistance of $R = (\omega/d)(\ell/w)$, where d is the film thickness and ρ is the resistivity of the material in ohms-cm. Sheet resistance defined as ρ/d is a basic material property of the film. For a given sheet resistance, different values of resistance are obtained by adjusting the film length ℓ and width w. The ratio ℓ/w is called the number of squares since $\ell w/w^2 = \ell/w$ represents the number of w by w squares that fit in a rectangle of length ℓ and width w. Note that "squares" is a dimensionless quantity. Although sheet resistance ρ/d has units of ohms, it is convenient to use ohms per square (Ω/□) since sheet resistance times the "number of squares" equals the resistance of a film resistor. Once the sheet resistance is established, the designer then lays out a pattern of "squares" to achieve the resistance desired. For example, suppose a certain thickness of a material produces 500 Ω/□. The layout pattern in Figure P2–63(a) has a length of 2 units and a width of 1 unit. This pattern produces two squares in series, so the resistance between metal pads A and B is 500 + 500 = 1000 Ω. The layout pattern in Figure P2–63(b) is 1 unit length by 2

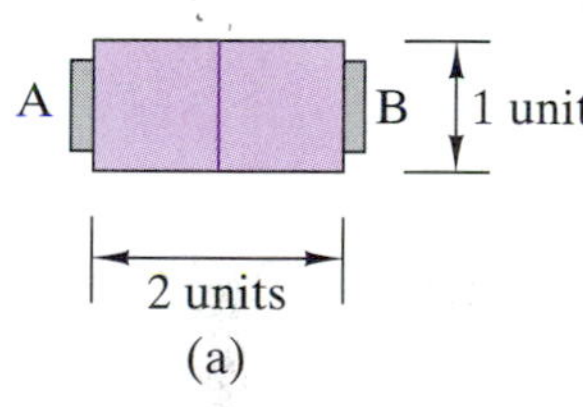

(a)

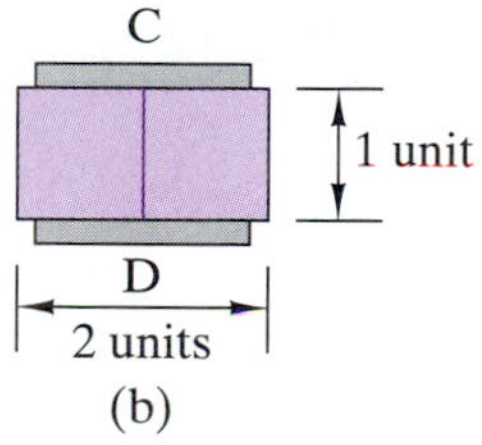

(b)

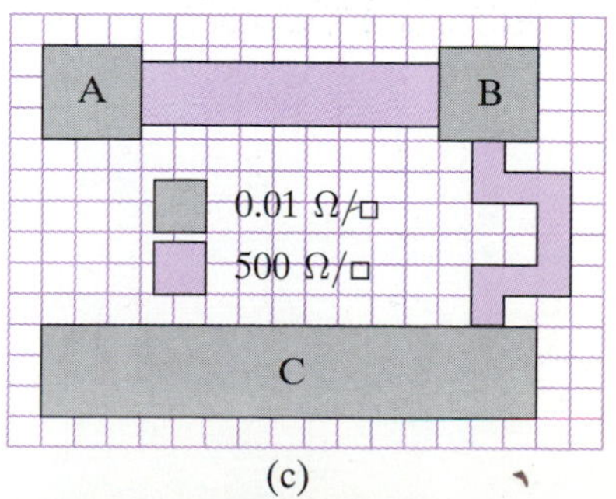

(c)

FIGURE P2–63

units width and produces two squares in parallel, so the resistance between pads C and D is 500||500 = 250 Ω.

(a) A Consider the thin-film circuit in Figure P2–63(c) with the ohms per square shown. Find the voltage measured between pads B and C when 10 V is applied between A and C. Assume that the film thickness is uniform.

(b) D Using Nichrome (a nickel-chromium alloy with $\rho = 150 \times 10^{-6}$ Ω-cm) and any film thickness between 0.05 and 5 μm, design film layout patterns to obtain resistances of 50 Ω, 250 Ω, and 12.5 Ω.

(c) D Suppose the voltage between points B and C is too small. How can the circuit be modified to increase the voltage without redesigning the film layout masks and redepositing the film?

(d) E A thin-film resistance array is to be fabricated as part of a system. The resistors must all use the same sheet resistance so that the array can be fabricated in a single evaporation. The circuit design department of your company reports that either of two arrays will meet their performance requirements. The total resistance in the first array is 100 kΩ. The total resistance in the second array is 70 kΩ. The controllable production costs are strongly influenced by the area occupied by the film array. As production manager, which of the two candidate arrays do you recommend?

2–64 D E VOLTAGE DIVIDER DESIGN

The purpose of the voltage divider in Figure P2–64(a) is to reduce the 15-V power supply output to the 5-V level required by the 8-kΩ loads. Any combination, from no load (all switches open) up to full load (all four switches closed), can be connected across the voltage reduction circuit output.

FIGURE P2–64

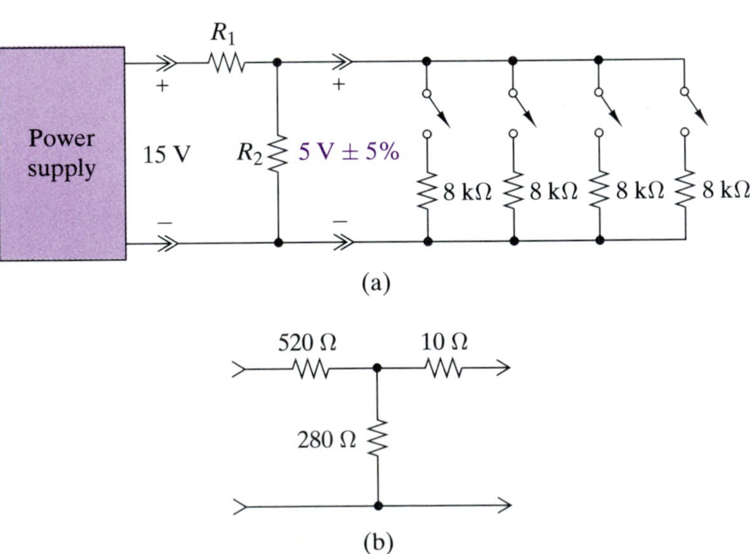

(a) D Using only 1/2-W resistors, select R_1 and R_2 so that the load voltage is always within ±5% of 5 V for any combination of loads.

(b) E It is claimed that all requirements in part (a) are met when the voltage divider is replaced by the T-circuit in Figure P2–64(b). Verify this claim.

(c) E Compare your voltage divider design in part (a) with the T-circuit in part (b) in terms of the total power consumed in the voltage reduction circuit during no-load operation.

2–65 A D E ANALOG VOLTMETER DESIGN

A voltmeter can be obtained by connecting suitably chosen resistors in series with a D'Arsonval meter. Figure P2–65(a) shows a voltmeter circuit consisting of a D'Arsonval meter, a two-position selector switch, and two series resistors. A current of 0.5 mA produces full-scale deflection of the D'Arsonval meter, whose internal resistance is $R_M = 50\ \Omega$.

(a) D Select the series resistance R_1 and R_2, so a voltage $v_x = 50$ V produces full-scale deflection when the switch is in position A and $v_x = 10$ V produces full-scale deflection when the switch is in position B.

(b) A By voltage division, the voltage across the 20-kΩ resistor in Figure P2–65(b) is 20 V when the voltmeter is disconnected. What voltage reading is obtained when the voltmeter designed in (a) is connected across the 20-kΩ resistor? What is the percentage error in the voltmeter reading?

(c) E A D'Arsonval meter with an internal resistance of 200 Ω and a full-scale deflection current of 100 μA is available. If the voltmeter in (a) were redesigned using this D'Arsonval meter, would the error found in part (b) be smaller or larger? Explain.

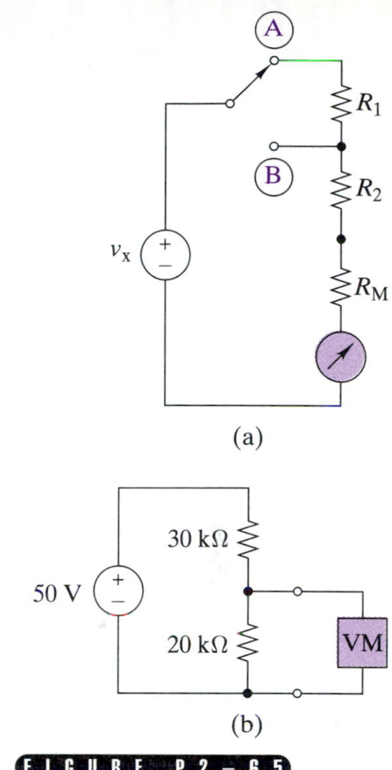

FIGURE P2–65

CHAPTER 3

CIRCUIT ANALYSIS TECHNIQUES

Assuming any system of linear conductors connected in such a manner that to the extremities of each one of them there is connected at least one other, a system having electromotive forces $E_1, E_2 \ldots E_3$, *no matter how distributed, we consider two points* A *and* A′ *belonging to the system and having potentials* V *and* V′. *If the points* A *and* A′ *are connected by a wire* ABA′, *which has a resistance* r, *with no electromotive forces, the potentials of points* A *and* A′ *assume different values from* V *and* V′, *but the current* i *flowing through this wire is given by* $i = (V - V')/(r + R)$ *in which* R *represents the resistance of the original wire, this resistance being measured between the points* A *and* A′, *which are considered to be electrodes.*

Leon Charles Thévenin, 1883,
French Telegraph Engineer

Thévenin's theorem is one of the important circuit analysis concepts developed in this chapter. Leon Charles Thévenin (1857–1926), a distinguished French telegraph engineer and teacher, was led to his theorem in 1883 following an extensive study of Kirchhoff's laws. Norton's theorem, which is the dual of Thévenin's theorem, was not proposed until 1926 by Edward L. Norton, an American electrical engineer working on long-distance telephony. Curiously, it turns out that the basic concept had been discovered in 1853 by Herman von Helmholtz. The earlier discovery by Helmholtz is not recognized in engineering terminology possibly because Thévenin and Norton both worked in areas of technology that offered immediate applications for their results, whereas Helmholtz was studying electricity in animal tissue at the time.

The analysis methods developed in the previous chapter offer insight into circuit analysis and design because we work directly with the circuit model to find responses. With practice and experience we learn which tools to use and in what order to avoid going down blind alleys. This ad hoc approach is practical as long as the circuits are fairly simple. As circuit complexity increases, however, a more systematic approach is needed.

Two basic methods of systematic circuit analysis—node-voltage analysis and mesh-current analysis—are developed in the first two sections of this chapter. With these methods the device and connection constraints are used to formulate a set of linear algebraic equations that characterize the circuit. Solving these equations simultaneously then yields the desired circuit responses. General methods of circuit analysis are necessarily more abstract because we manipulate sets of equations, rather than the circuit itself. In doing so we lose some contact with the more intuitive approach developed in the previous chapter. However, systematic methods make it possible for us to treat a wider range of applications and provide a framework for exploiting other properties of linear circuits.

Two key properties of linear circuits are developed in the third section. The superposition and proportionality properties lead to new circuit analysis techniques and are often used to derive other properties of linear circuits. For example, the superposition property is used in the fourth section to derive Thévenin's theorem. This theorem provides a viewpoint for dealing with circuit interfaces, and that leads directly to the maximum signal transfer properties developed in the fifth section. In the final section, circuit design is introduced by showing how the maximum signal transfer principles guide the design of interface circuit.

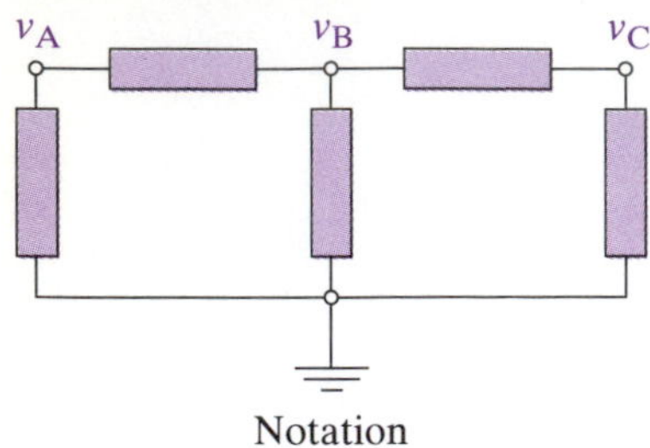

Notation

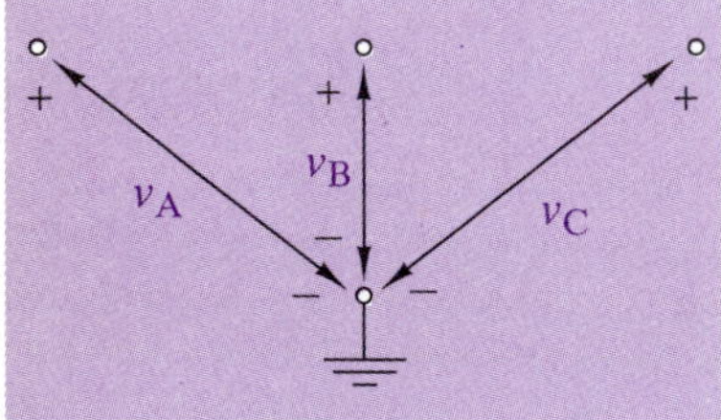

Interpretation

FIGURE 3–1 *Node voltage definition and notation.*

3–1 NODE-VOLTAGE ANALYSIS

Before describing node-voltage analysis, we first review the foundation for every method of circuit analysis. As noted in Sec. 2–3, circuit behavior is based on constraints of two types: (1) connection constraints (Kirchhoff's laws) and (2) device constraints (element *i–v* relationships). As a practical matter, however, using element voltages and currents to express the circuit constraints produces a large number of equations that must be solved simultaneously to find the circuit responses. In Example 2–25, we found that a circuit with only six devices requires us to treat 12 equations with 12 unknowns. Although this is not an impossible task using software tools like Mathcad, it is highly desirable to reduce the number of equations that must be solved simultaneously.

You should not abandon the concept of element and connection constraints. This method is vital because it provides the foundation for all methods of circuit analysis. In subsequent chapters, we use element and connection constraints many times to develop important ideas in circuit analysis.

Using node voltages instead of element voltages as circuit variables can reduce the number of equations that must be treated simultaneously. To define a set of node voltages we first select a reference node. The **node voltages** are then defined as the voltages between the remaining nodes and the selected reference node. Figure 3–1 shows the notation used to define node-voltage variables. In this figure the reference node indicated by the ground symbol and the node voltages are identified by a voltage symbol next to all the other nodes. This notation means that the positive reference mark for the node voltage is located at the node in question while the negative mark is at the reference node. Obviously, any circuit with N nodes involves $N-1$ node voltages.

A fundamental property of node voltages needs to be covered at the outset. Suppose we are given a two-terminal element whose element voltage is labeled v_1. Suppose further that the terminal with the plus reference mark is connected to a node, say node A. The two cases shown in Figure 3–2 are the only two possible ways the other element terminal can be connected. In case A, the other terminal is connected to the reference node, in which case KVL requires $v_1 = v_A$. In case B, the other terminal is connected to a nonreference node, say node B, in which case KVL requires $v_1 = v_A - v_B$. This example illustrates the following fundamental property of node voltages:

If the* K*th two-terminal element is connected between nodes X and Y, then the element voltage can be expressed in terms of the two node voltages as

$$v_K = v_X - v_Y \tag{3-1}$$

***where* X *is the node connected to the positive reference for element voltage* v_K.**

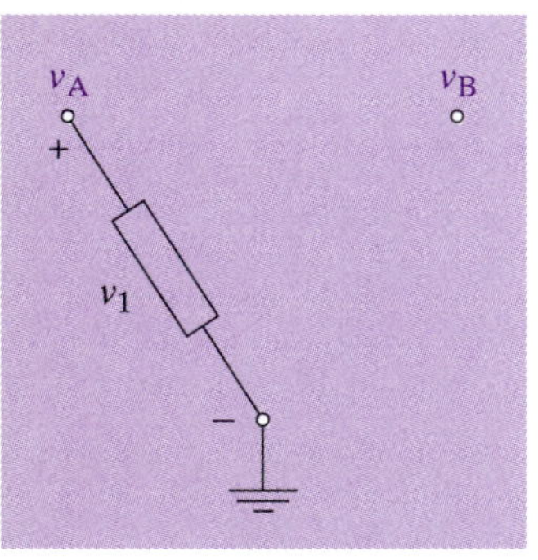

Case A

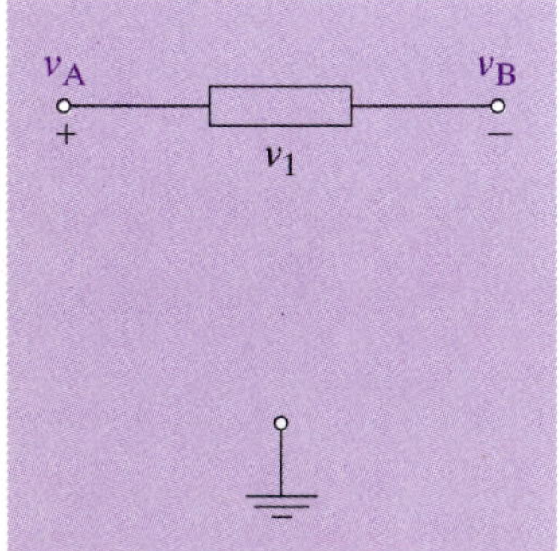

Case B

FIGURE 3–2 *Two possible connections of a two-terminal element.*

Equation (3–1) is a KVL constraint at the element level. If node Y is the reference node, then by definition $v_Y = 0$ and Eq. (3–1) reduces to $v_K = v_X$.

On the other hand, if node X is the reference node, then $v_X = 0$ and therefore $v_K = -v_Y$. The minus sign occurs here because the positive reference for the element is connected to the reference node. In any case, the important fact is that the voltage across any two-terminal element can be expressed as the difference of two node voltages, one of which may be zero.

Exercise 3–1

The reference node and node voltages in the bridge circuit of Figure 3–3 are $v_A = 5$ V, $v_B = 10$ V, and $v_C = -3$ V. Find the element voltages.

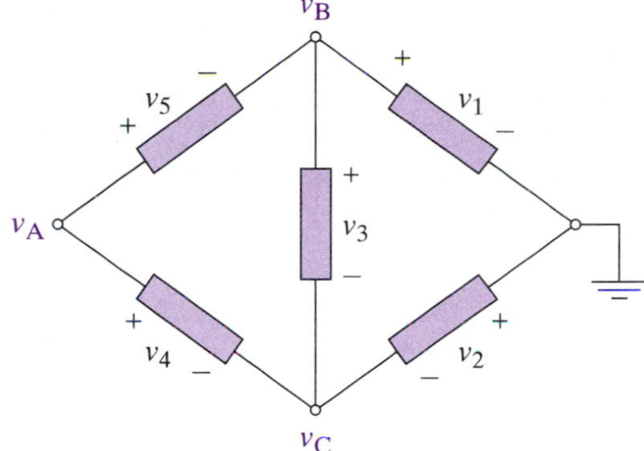

FIGURE 3–3

Answers:

$v_1 = 10$ V, $v_2 = 3$ V, $v_3 = 13$ V, $v_4 = 8$ V, and $v_5 = -5$ V.

FORMULATING NODE-VOLTAGE EQUATIONS

To formulate a circuit description using node voltages, we use element and connection constraints, except that the KVL connection equations are not explicitly written. Instead we use the fundamental property of node analysis to express the element voltages in terms of the node voltages.

The circuit in Figure 3–4 will demonstrate the formulation of node-voltage equations. In Figure 3–4 we have identified a reference node (indicated by the ground symbol), four element currents (i_0, i_1, i_2, and i_3), and two node voltages (v_A and v_B).

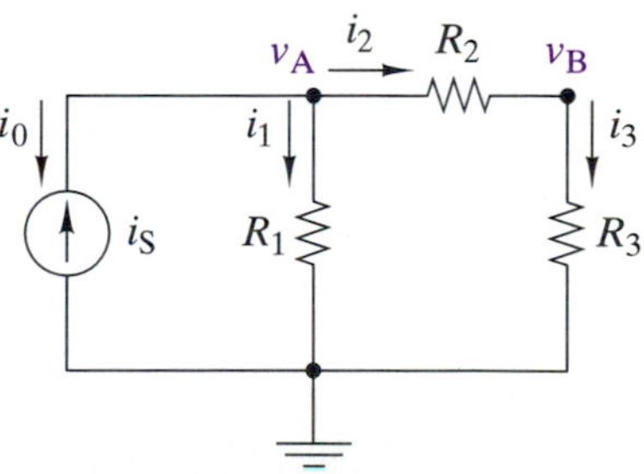

FIGURE 3–4 *Circuit for demonstrating node-voltage analysis.*

The KCL constraints at the two nonreference nodes are

$$\text{Node A: } -i_0 - i_1 - i_2 = 0$$

$$\text{Node B: } i_2 - i_3 = 0 \tag{3-2}$$

Using the fundamental property of node analysis, we use the element equations to relate the element currents to the node voltages.

$$\text{Resistor } R_1\text{: } i_1 = G_1 v_A$$
$$\text{Resistor } R_2\text{: } i_2 = G_2(v_A - v_B)$$

$$\text{Resistor } R_3\text{: } i_3 = G_3 v_B$$

$$\text{Current source: } i_0 = -i_S \qquad (3-3)$$

We have written six equations in six unknowns—four element currents and two node voltages. The right side of the element equations in Eq. (3–3) involves unknown node voltages and the input signal i_S. Substituting the element constraints in Eq. (3–3) into the KCL connection constraints in Eq. (3–2) yields

$$\text{Node A: } i_S - G_1 v_A - G_2(v_A - v_B) = 0$$

$$\text{Node B: } \qquad G_2(v_A - v_B) - G_3 v_B = 0$$

which can be arranged in the following standard form:

$$\text{Node A: } \quad (G_1 + G_2)v_A - G_2 v_B = i_S$$

$$\text{Node B: } \quad -G_2 v_A + (G_2 + G_3)v_B = 0 \qquad (3-4)$$

In this standard form all of the unknown node voltages are grouped on one side and the independent sources on the other.

By systematically eliminating the element currents, we have reduced the circuit description to two linear equations in the two unknown node voltages. The coefficients in the equations on the left side ($G_1 + G_2$, G_2, $G_2 + G_3$) depend only on circuit parameters, while the right side contains the known input driving force i_S.

As noted previously, every method of circuit analysis must satisfy KVL, KCL, and the element i–v relationships. In developing the node-voltage equations in Eq. (3–4), it may appear that we have not used KVL. However, KVL is satisfied because the equations $v_1 = v_A$, $v_2 = v_A - v_B$, and $v_3 = v_B$ were used to write the right side of the element equations in Eq. (3–3). The KVL constraints do not appear explicitly in the formulation of node equations, but are implicitly included when the fundamental property of node analysis is used to write the element voltages in terms of the node voltages.

In summary, four steps are needed to develop node-voltage equations.

STEP 1 Select a reference node. Identify a node voltage at each of the remaining $N - 1$ nodes and a current with every element in the circuit.

STEP 2 Write KCL connection constraints in terms of the element currents at the $N - 1$ nonreference nodes.

STEP 3 Use the element i–v relationships and the fundamental property of node analysis to express the element currents in terms of the node voltages.

STEP 4 Substitute the element constraints from step 3 into the KCL connection constraints from step 2 and arrange the resulting $N - 1$ equations in a standard form.

Writing node-voltage equations leads to $N - 1$ equations that must be solved simultaneously. If we write the element and connection constraints in terms of element voltages and currents, we must solve $2E$ simultaneous equations. The reduction from $2E$ to $N - 1$ is particularly impressive in circuits with a large number of elements (large E) connected in parallel (small N).

EXAMPLE 3–1

Formulate node-voltage equations for the bridge circuit in Figure 3–5.

SOLUTION:

Step 1: The reference node, node voltages, and element currents are shown in Figure 3–5.

Step 2: The KCL constraints at the three nonreference nodes are:

$$\text{Node A: } i_0 - i_1 - i_2 = 0$$

$$\text{Node B: } i_1 - i_3 + i_5 = 0$$

$$\text{Node C: } i_2 - i_4 - i_5 = 0$$

Step 3: We write the element equations in terms of the node voltages and input signal sources.

$$i_0 = i_{S1} \qquad i_3 = G_3 v_B$$

$$i_1 = G_1(v_A - v_B) \quad i_4 = G_4 v_C$$

$$i_2 = G_2(v_A - v_C) \quad i_5 = i_{S2}$$

Step 4: Substituting the element equations into the KCL constraints and arranging the result in standard form yields three equations in the three unknown node voltages.

$$\text{Node A: } (G_1 + G_2)v_A - G_1 v_B - G_2 v_C = i_{S1}$$

$$\text{Node B: } -G_1 v_A + (G_1 + G_3)v_B = i_{S2}$$

$$\text{Node C: } -G_2 v_A + (G_2 + G_4)v_C = -i_{S2}$$

■

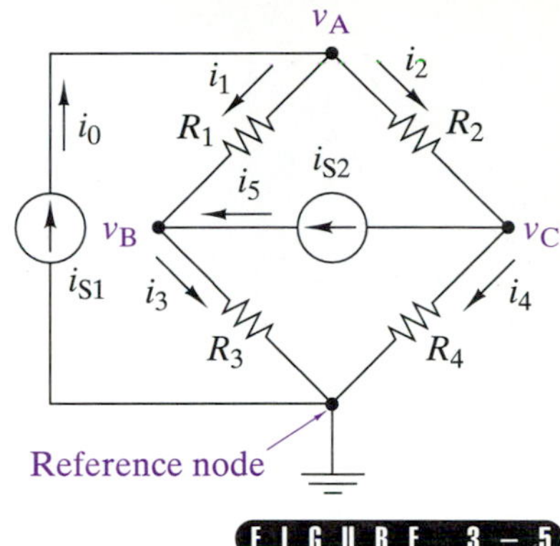

FIGURE 3–5

WRITING NODE-VOLTAGE EQUATIONS BY INSPECTION

The node-voltage equations derived in Example 3–1 have a symmetrical pattern. The coefficient of v_B in the node A equation and the coefficient of v_A in the node B equation are both the negative of the conductance connected between the nodes ($-G_1$). Likewise, the coefficients of v_A in the node C equation and v_C in the node A equation are both $-G_2$. Finally, coefficients of v_A in the node A equation, v_B in the node B equation, and v_C in the node C equation are the sum of the conductances connected to the node in question.

The symmetrical pattern always occurs in circuits containing only resistors and independent current sources. To understand why, consider any general two-terminal conductance G with one terminal connected to, say, node A. According to the fundamental property of node analysis, there are only two possibilities. Either the other terminal of G is connected to the reference node, in which case the current *leaving* node A via conductance G is

$$i = G(v_A - 0) = Gv_A$$

or else it is connected to another nonreference node, say, node B, in which case the current *leaving* node A via G is

$$i = G(v_A - v_B)$$

The pattern for node equations follows from these observations. The sum of the currents leaving any node A via conductances involves the following terms:

1. v_A times the sum of conductances connected to node A
2. Minus v_B times the sum of conductances connected between nodes A and B and similar terms for all other nodes connected to node A by conductances.

Because of KCL, the sum of currents leaving node A via conductances plus the sum of currents directed away from node A by independent current sources must equal zero.

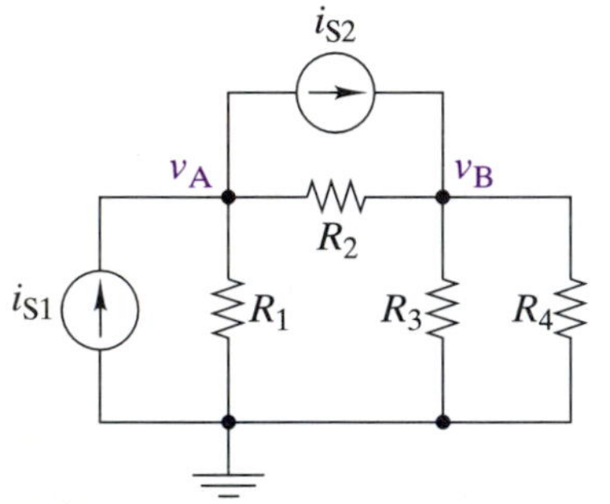

The aforementioned process allows us to write node-voltage equations by inspection without going through the intermediate steps involving the KCL constraints and the element equations. For example, the circuit in Figure 3–6 contains two independent current sources and four resistors. Starting with node A, the sum of conductances connected to node A is $G_1 + G_2$. The conductances between nodes A and B is G_2. The reference direction for the source current i_{S1} is into node A, while the reference direction for i_{S2} is directed away from node A. Pulling all of the observations together, we write the sum of currents directed out of node A as

FIGURE 3–6 *Circuit for demonstrating writing node-voltage equations by inspection.*

$$\text{Node A: } (G_1 + G_2)v_A - G_2 v_B - i_{S1} + i_{S2} = 0 \qquad (3-5)$$

Similarly, the sum of conductances connected to node B is $G_2 + G_3 + G_4$, the conductance connected between nodes B and A is again G_2, and the source current i_{S2} is directed away from node B. These observations yield the following node-voltage equation:

$$\text{Node B: } (G_2 + G_3 + G_4)v_B - G_2 v_A - i_{S2} = 0 \qquad (3-6)$$

Rearranging Eqs. (3–5) and (3–6) in standard form yields

$$\begin{aligned} &\text{Node A:} \quad (G_1 + G_2)v_A - G_2 v_B = i_{S1} - i_{S2} \\ &\text{Node B:} \quad -G_2 v_A + (G_2 + G_3 + G_4)v_B = i_{S2} \end{aligned} \qquad (3-7)$$

We have two symmetrical equations in the two unknown node voltages. The equations are symmetrical because the conductance G_2 connected between nodes A and B appears as the cross-coupling term in each equation.

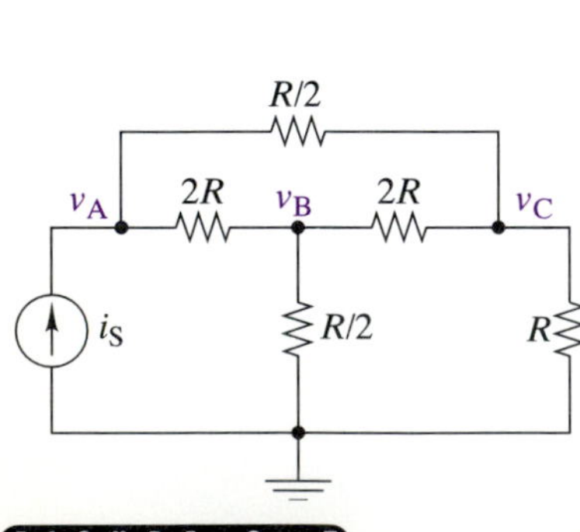

FIGURE 3–7

EXAMPLE 3–2

Formulate node-voltage equations for the circuit in Figure 3–7.

SOLUTION:

The total conductance connected to node A is $1/2R + 2/R = 2.5G$, to node B is $1/2R + 1/2R + 2/R = 3G$, and to node C is $1/R + 2/R + 1/2R = 3.5G$. The conductance connected between nodes A and B is $1/2R = 0.5G$, between nodes A and C is $2/R = 2G$, and between nodes B and C is $1/2R = 0.5G$. The independent current source is directed into node A. By inspection, the node-voltage equations are

$$\text{Node A:} \quad 2.5Gv_A - 0.5Gv_B - 2Gv_C = i_S$$
$$\text{Node B:} \quad -0.5Gv_A + 3Gv_B - 0.5Gv_C = 0$$
$$\text{Node C:} \quad -2Gv_A - 0.5Gv_B + 3.5Gv_C = 0$$

Written in matrix form,

$$\begin{bmatrix} 2.5G & -0.5G & -2G \\ -0.5G & 3G & -0.5G \\ -2G & -0.5G & 3.5G \end{bmatrix} \begin{bmatrix} v_A \\ v_B \\ v_C \end{bmatrix} = \begin{bmatrix} i_S \\ 0 \\ 0 \end{bmatrix}$$

This matrix equation is of the form $\mathbf{Ax} = \mathbf{b}$, where $\mathbf{A}$ is a 3×3 square matrix describing the circuit, $\mathbf{x}$ is a 3×1 column matrix of unknown node voltages, and $\mathbf{b}$ is a 3×1 column matrix of known inputs. Note that the $\mathbf{A}$ matrix is symmetrical about its main diagonal.[1] ■

Exercise 3–2

Formulate node-voltage equations for the circuit in Figure 3–8.

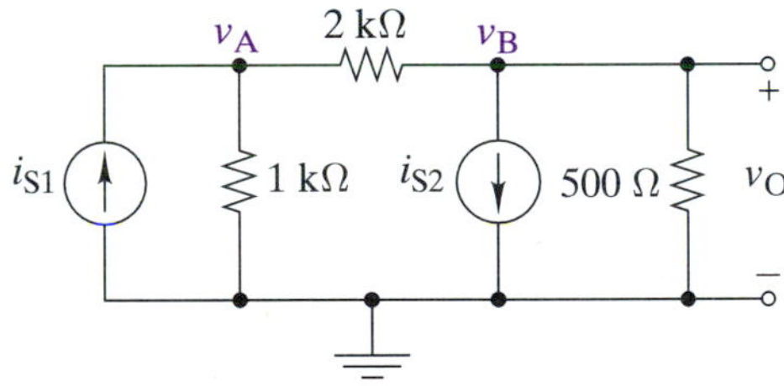

FIGURE 3–8

Answers:

$$(1.5 \times 10^{-3})v_A - (0.5 \times 10^{-3})v_B = i_{S1}$$
$$-(0.5 \times 10^{-3})v_A + (2.5 \times 10^{-3})v_B = -i_{S2}$$

SOLVING LINEAR ALGEBRAIC EQUATIONS

So far, we have only dealt with the problem of formulating node-voltage equations. To complete a circuit analysis problem, we must solve these linear equations for selected responses. Cramer's rule and Gaussian elimination are standard mathematical tools commonly used for hand solution of circuit equations. These tools are assumed to be part of the reader's math-

1 See Appendix B for a discussion of matrix algebra, including the definition of a symmetrical matrix.

ematical background. Those needing a review of these matters are referred to Appendix B.

Cramer's rule and Gaussian elimination are suitable for hand calculations involving three or four simultaneous equations. Cramer's rule is generally easier when the circuit parameters are left in symbolic form, while the Gaussian method is more efficient when numerical values of circuit parameters are given. The efficiency advantage of the Gaussian method is not very important for two or three equations, but increases dramatically for four or more equations.

At about four or five simultaneous equations, numerical solutions are best obtained using computer-aided analysis. Many scientific hand-held calculators have a built-in capability to solve up to five linear equations. Virtually all PC-based mathematical software can solve systems of linear equations or, what is equivalent, perform matrix manipulations. Appendix B describes how Mathcad and Quartro Pro are used to solve linear equations.

In this book we generally use Cramer's rule because our examples often leave the circuit parameters in symbolic form and usually involve no more than three equations. This does not mean Cramer's rule is the optimum method, but only that it can easily handle the class of problems treated in this book. The argument for Gaussian elimination is only compelling for four or more equations. The ready availability of computer-aided tools for this class of problem makes the hand solution of linear equations by Gaussian elimination an obsolete skill.

Earlier in this section we formulated node-voltage equations for the circuit in Figure 3–4 [See Eq. (3–4).]

$$\begin{aligned}\text{Node A:}\quad & (G_1 + G_2)v_A - G_2v_B = i_S \\ \text{Node B:}\quad & -G_2v_A + (G_2 + G_3)v_B = 0\end{aligned}$$

We use Cramer's rule to solve these equations because it easily handles the case in which the circuit parameters are left in symbolic form:

$$v_A = \frac{\Delta_A}{\Delta} = \frac{\begin{vmatrix} i_S & -G_2 \\ 0 & G_2 + G_3 \end{vmatrix}}{\begin{vmatrix} G_1 + G_2 & -G_2 \\ -G_2 & G_2 + G_3 \end{vmatrix}} = \left(\frac{G_2 + G_3}{G_1G_2 + G_1G_3 + G_2G_3}\right)i_S \tag{3-8}$$

$$v_B = \frac{\Delta_B}{\Delta} = \frac{\begin{vmatrix} G_1 + G_2 & i_S \\ -G_2 & 0 \end{vmatrix}}{\Delta} = \left(\frac{G_2}{G_1G_2 + G_1G_3 + G_2G_3}\right)i_S \tag{3-9}$$

These results express the two node voltages in terms of the circuit parameters and the input signal. Given the two node voltages v_A and v_B, we can now determine every element voltage and every current using Ohm's law and the fundamental property of node voltages.

$$\begin{aligned} v_1 &= v_A & v_2 &= v_A - v_B & v_3 &= v_B \\ i_1 &= G_1v_A & i_2 &= G_2(v_A - v_B) & i_3 &= G_3v_B \end{aligned}$$

In solving the node equations, we left everything in symbolic form to emphasize that responses depend on the values of the circuit parameters (G_1, G_2, G_3) and the input signal (i_S). Even when numerical values are given, it is sometimes useful to leave some parameters in symbolic form to obtain input–output relationships or to reveal the effect of specific parameters on circuit response.

EXAMPLE 3–3

Given the circuit in Figure 3–9, find the input resistance R_{IN} seen by the current source and the output voltage v_O.

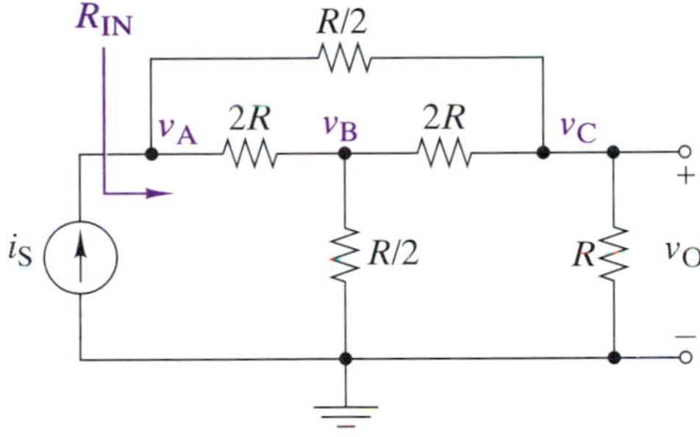

FIGURE 3–9

SOLUTION:

In Example 3–2 we formulated node-voltage equations for this circuit as follows:

$$\text{Node A:}\quad 2.5Gv_A - 0.5Gv_B - 2Gv_C = i_S$$

$$\text{Node B:}\quad -0.5Gv_A + 3Gv_B - 0.5Gv_C = 0$$

$$\text{Node C:}\quad -2Gv_A - 0.5Gv_B + 3.5Gv_C = 0$$

The input resistance is the ratio v_A/i_S, so we first solve for v_A:

$$v_A = \frac{\Delta_A}{\Delta} = \frac{\begin{vmatrix} i_S & -0.5G & -2G \\ 0 & 3G & -0.5G \\ 0 & -0.5G & 3.5G \end{vmatrix}}{\begin{vmatrix} 2.5G & -0.5G & -2G \\ -0.5G & 3G & -0.5G \\ -2G & -0.5G & 3.5G \end{vmatrix}}$$

$$= \frac{i_S \times G^2 \begin{vmatrix} 3 & -0.5 \\ -0.5 & 3.5 \end{vmatrix}}{2.5G^3 \begin{vmatrix} 3 & -0.5 \\ -0.5 & 3.5 \end{vmatrix} + 0.5G^3 \begin{vmatrix} -0.5 & -2 \\ -0.5 & 3.5 \end{vmatrix} - 2G^3 \begin{vmatrix} -0.5 & -2 \\ 3 & -0.5 \end{vmatrix}}$$

$$= \frac{10.25 i_S}{11.75G}$$

Hence the input resistance is

$$R_{IN} = \frac{v_A}{i_S} = \frac{10.25}{11.75G} = 0.872R$$

To find the output voltage, we solve for v_C:

$$v_C = \frac{\Delta_C}{\Delta} = \frac{\begin{vmatrix} 2.5G & -0.5G & i_S \\ -0.5G & 3G & 0 \\ -2G & -0.5G & 0 \end{vmatrix}}{\Delta} = \frac{i_S \times G^2 \begin{vmatrix} -0.5G & 3 \\ -2 & -0.5 \end{vmatrix}}{\Delta}$$

$$= \frac{6.25G^2 i_S}{11.75G^3} = 0.532 i_S R$$

■

Exercise 3–3

Solve for the node-voltage equations in Exercise 3–2 for v_O in Figure 3–8.

Answer:

$$v_O = 1000(i_{S1} - 3i_{S2})/7$$

Exercise 3–4

Use node-voltage equations to solve for v_1, v_2, and i_3 in Figure 3–10.

Answers:

$$v_1 = 12 \text{ V}, v_2 = 32 \text{ V}, \text{and } i_3 = -10 \text{ mA}$$

FIGURE 3–10

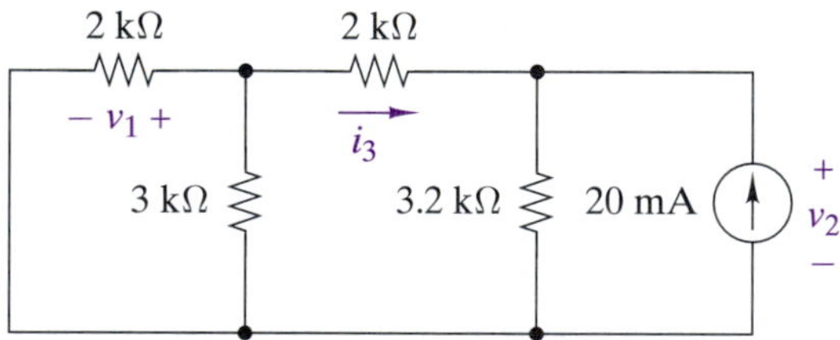

NODE ANALYSIS WITH VOLTAGE SOURCES

Up to this point we have analyzed circuits containing only resistors and independent current sources. Applying KCL in such circuits is simplified because the sum of currents at a node only involves the output of current sources or resistor currents expressed in terms of the node voltages. Adding voltage sources to circuits modifies node analysis procedures because the current through a voltage source is not directly related to the voltage across it. While initially it may appear that voltage sources complicate the situation, they actually simplify node analysis by reducing the number of equations required.

Figure 3–11 shows three ways to deal with voltage sources in node analysis. Method 1 uses a source transformation to replace the voltage source and series resistance with an equivalent current source and parallel resistance. We can then formulate node equations at the remaining nonreference nodes in the usual way. The source transformation eliminates node C, so there are only $N - 2$ nonreference nodes left in the circuit. Obviously, method 1 only applies when there is a resistance in series with the voltage source.

Method 2 in Figure 3–11 can be used whether or not there is a resistance in series with the voltage source. When node B is selected as the reference node, then by definition $v_B = 0$ and the fundamental property of node voltages says that $v_A = v_S$. We do not need a node-voltage equation at node A because its voltage is known to be equal to the source voltage. We write the node equations at the remaining $N - 2$ nonreference nodes in the usual way. In the final step, we move all terms involving v_A to the right side, since it is a known input and not an unknown response. Method 2 reduces the number of node equations by 1 since no equation is needed at node A.

The third method in Figure 3–11 is needed when neither node A nor node B can be selected as the reference and the source is not connected in series with a resistance. In this case we combine nodes A and B into a **supernode**, indicated by the boundary in Figure 3–11. We use the fact that

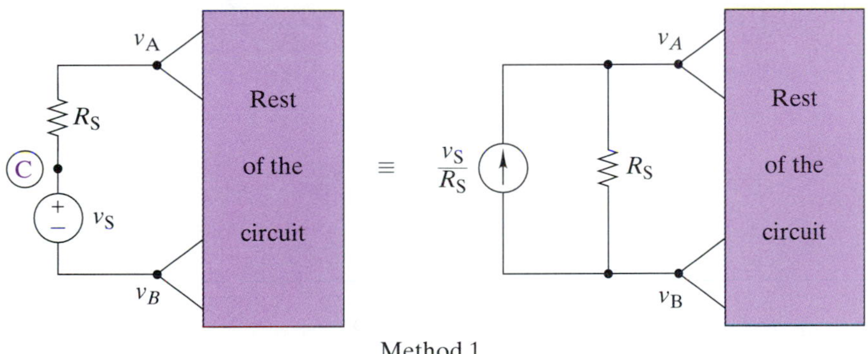

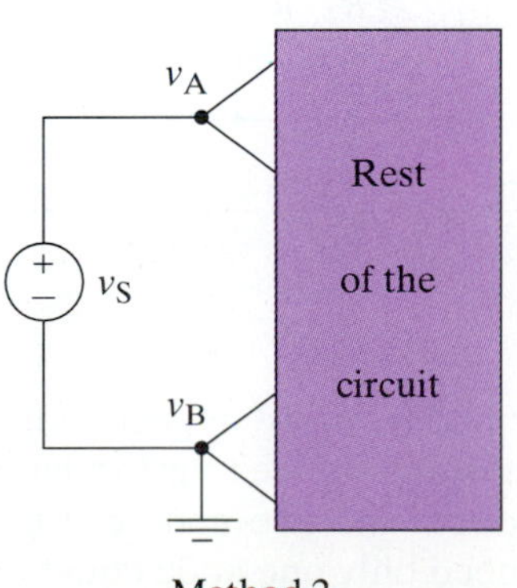

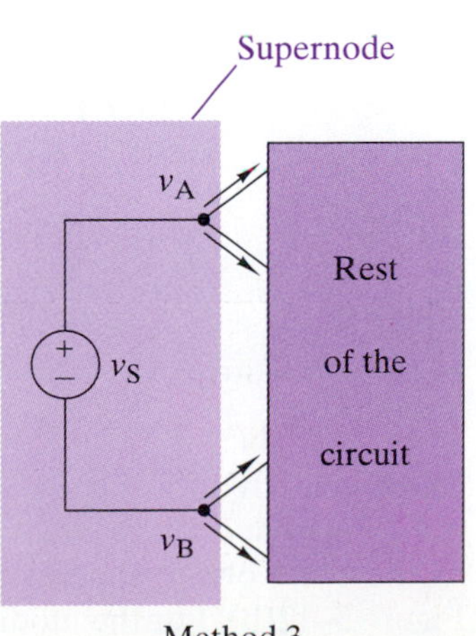

FIGURE 3–11 *Three methods of treating voltage sources in node analysis.*

KCL applies to the currents penetrating this boundary to write a node equation at the supernode. We then write node equations at the remaining $N-3$ nonreference nodes in the usual way. We now have $N-3$ node equations plus one supernode equation, leaving us one equation short of the $N-1$ required. Using the fundamental property of node voltages, we can write

$$v_A - v_B = v_S \tag{3-10}$$

The voltage source inside the supernode constrains the difference between the node voltages at nodes A and B. The voltage source constraint provides the additional relationship needed to write $N-1$ independent equations in $N-1$ node voltages.

For reference purposes we will call these modified node equations, since we either modify the circuit (method 1), use voltage source constraints to define node voltage at some nodes (method 2), or combine nodes to produce a supernode (method 3). The three methods are not mutually exclusive. We frequently use a combination of methods, as illustrated in the following examples.

EXAMPLE 3–4

Use node-voltage analysis to find v_O in the circuit in Figure 3–12(a).

FIGURE 3–12

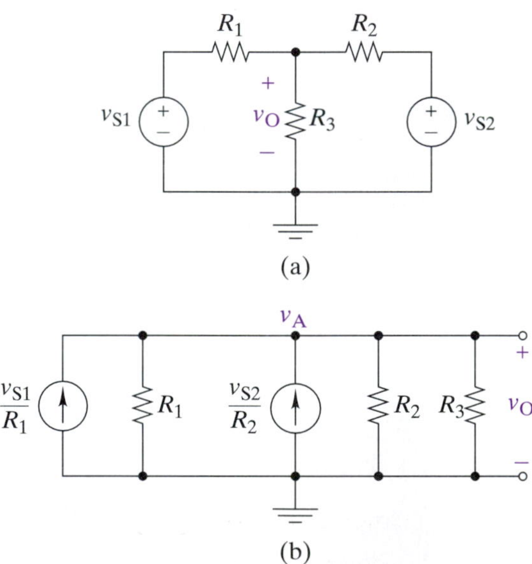

SOLUTION:

The given circuit in Figure 3–12(a) has four nodes, so we appear to need $N-1=3$ node-voltage equations. However, applying source transformations to the two voltage sources (method 1) produces the two-node circuit in Figure 3–12(b). For the modified circuit, we need only one node equation.

$$(G_1 + G_2 + G_3)v_A = G_1 v_{S1} + G_2 V_{S2}$$

To find the output voltage, we solve for v_A:

$$v_O = v_A = \frac{G_1 v_{S1} + G_2 v_{S2}}{G_1 + G_2 + G_3}$$

Because of the two voltage sources, we need only one node equation in what appears to be a three-node circuit. The two voltage sources have a common node, so the number of unknown node voltages is reduced from three to one. The general principle illustrated is that the number of independent KCL constraints in a circuit containing N nodes and N_V voltage sources is $N - 1 - N_V$.

EXAMPLE 3–5

Find the input resistance of the circuit in Figure 3–13.

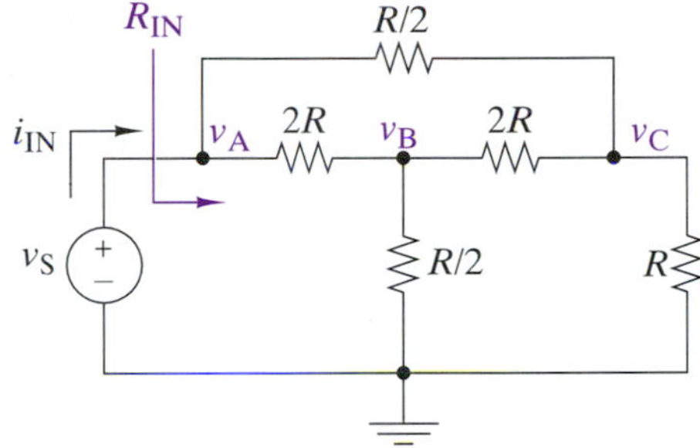

FIGURE 3–13

SOLUTION:

Method 1 of handling voltage sources will not work here because the source in Figure 3–13 is not connected in series with a resistor. Method 2 will work in this case because the voltage source is connected to the reference node. As a result, we only need node equations at nodes B and C since the node A voltage is $v_A = v_S$. By inspection, the two required node equations are

$$\text{Node B:} \quad -0.5Gv_A + 3Gv_B - 0.5Gv_C = 0$$

$$\text{Node C:} \quad -2Gv_A - 0.5Gv_B + 3.5Gv_C = 0$$

Since $v_A = v_S$, these equations can be written in standard form as follows:

$$\text{Node B:} \quad 3Gv_B - 0.5Gv_C = 0.5Gv_S$$

$$\text{Node C:} \quad -0.5Gv_B + 3.5Gv_C = 2Gv_S$$

Solving for the two unknown node voltages yields

$$v_B = \frac{\Delta_B}{\Delta} = \frac{\begin{vmatrix} 0.5Gv_S & -0.5G \\ 2Gv_S & 3.5G \end{vmatrix}}{\begin{vmatrix} 3G & -0.5G \\ -0.5G & 3.5G \end{vmatrix}} = \frac{2.75G^2 v_S}{10.25G^2} = \frac{2.75v_S}{10.25}$$

$$v_C = \frac{\Delta_C}{\Delta} = \frac{\begin{vmatrix} 3G & 0.5Gv_S \\ -0.5G & 2Gv_S \end{vmatrix}}{\Delta} = \frac{6.25G^2 v_S}{10.25G^2} = \frac{6.25v_S}{10.25}$$

Given the two node voltages, we can now solve for the input current.

$$i_{IN} = \frac{v_S - v_B}{2R} + \frac{v_S - v_C}{R/2} = \frac{3.75v_S}{10.25R} + \frac{8v_S}{10.25R} = \frac{11.75v_S}{10.25R}$$

Hence, the input resistance is

$$R_{IN} = \frac{v_S}{i_{IN}} = \frac{10.25R}{11.75} = 0.872R$$

This is the same answer as in Example 3–3, where the same circuit was driven by a current source rather than a voltage source. Input resistance is an intrinsic property of a circuit that does not depend on how the circuit is driven. ■

EXAMPLE 3–6

For the circuit in Figure 3–14,

(a) Formulate node-voltage equations.
(b) Solve for the output voltage v_O using $R_1 = R_4 = 2$ kΩ and $R_2 = R_3 = 4$ kΩ.

FIGURE 3–14

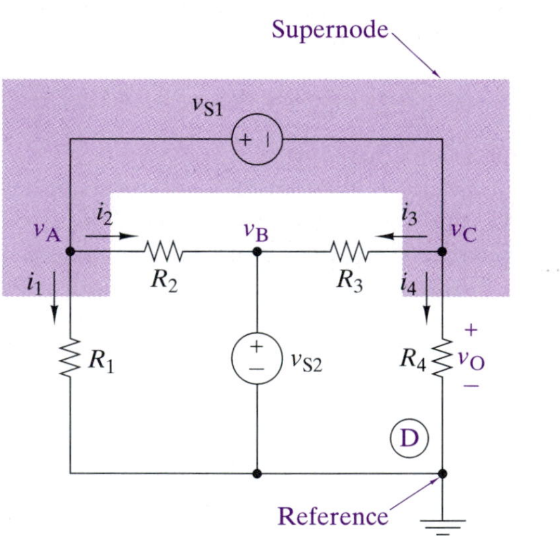

SOLUTION:

(a) The voltage sources in Figure 3–14 do not have a common node, and we cannot select a reference node that includes both sources. Selecting node D as the reference forces the condition $v_B = v_{S2}$ (method 2) but leaves the other source v_{S1} ungrounded. We surround the ungrounded source, and all wires leading to it, by the supernode boundary shown in Figure 3–14 (method 3). KCL applies to the four element currents that penetrate the supernode boundary, and we can write

$$i_1 + i_2 + i_3 + i_4 = 0$$

These currents can easily be expressed in terms of the node voltages.

$$G_1 v_A + G_2(v_A - v_B) + G_3(v_C - v_B) + G_4 v_C = 0$$

Since $v_B = v_{S2}$, the standard form of this equation is

$$(G_1 + G_2)v_A + (G_3 + G_4)v_C = (G_2 + G_3)v_{S2}$$

We have one equation in the two unknown node voltages v_A and v_C. Applying the fundamental property of node voltages inside the supernode, we can write

$$v_A - v_C = v_{S1}$$

That is, the ungrounded voltage source constrains the difference between the two unknown node voltages inside the supernode. It thereby supplies the relationship needed to obtain two equations in two unknowns.

(b) Inserting the given numerical values yields

$$(7.5 \times 10^{-4})v_A + (7.5 \times 10^{-4})v_C = (5 \times 10^{-4})v_{S2}$$

$$v_A - v_C = v_{S1}$$

To find the output v_O, we need to solve these equations for v_C. The second equation yields $v_A = v_C + v_{S1}$, which, when substituted into the first equation, yields the required output:

$$v_O = v_C = \frac{v_{S2}}{3} - \frac{v_{S1}}{2}$$ ■

Exercise 3–5

Find v_O in Figure 3–15 when the element E is

(a) A 10-kΩ resistance,
(b) A 4-mA independent current source with reference arrow pointing left.

Answers:

(a) 2.53 V
(b) –17.3 V

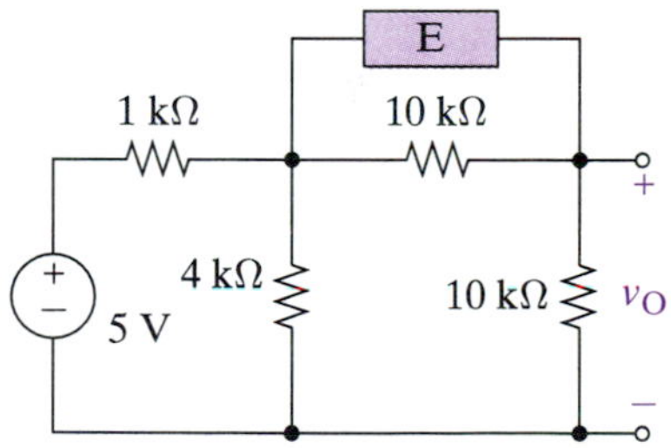

FIGURE 3–15

Exercise 3–6

Find v_O in Figure 3–15 when the element E is

(a) An open circuit
(b) A 10-V independent voltage source with the plus reference on the right.

Answers:

(a) 1.92 V
(b) 12.96 V

SUMMARY OF NODE-VOLTAGE ANALYSIS

We have seen that node-voltage equations are very useful in the analysis of a variety of circuits. These equations can always be formulated using KCL, the element constraints, and the fundamental property of node voltages. When in doubt, always fall back on these principles to formulate node equations in new situations. With practice and experience, however, we eventually develop an analysis approach that allows us to recognize shortcuts in the formulation process. The following guidelines summarize our approach and may help you develop your own analysis style:

1. Simplify the circuit by combining elements in series and parallel wherever possible.
2. If not specified, select a reference node so that as many voltage sources as possible are directly connected to the reference.
3. Node equations are required at supernodes and all other nonreference nodes except those that are directly connected to the reference by voltage sources.
4. Use KCL to write node equations at the nodes identified in step 3. Express element currents in terms of node voltages or the currents produced by independent current sources.
5. Write expressions relating the node voltages to the voltages produced by independent voltage sources.
6. Substitute the expressions from step 5 into the node equations from step 4 and arrange the resulting equations in standard form.
7. Solve the equations from step 6 for the node voltages of interest. Cramer's rule is often useful when circuit parameters are left in symbolic form. Computer tools are useful when there are four or more equations and numerical values are given.

3–2 MESH-CURRENT ANALYSIS

Mesh currents are analysis variables that are useful in circuits containing many elements connected in series. To review terminology, a loop is a closed path formed by passing through an ordered sequence of nodes without passing through any node more than once. A mesh is a special type of loop that does not enclose any elements. For example, loops A and B in Figure 3–16 are meshes, while the loop X is not a mesh because it encloses an element.

Mesh-current analysis is resistricted to planar circuits. A **planar circuit** can be drawn on a flat surface without crossovers in the "window pane" fashion shown in Figure 3–16. To define a set of variables, we associate a **mesh current** (i_A, i_B, i_C, etc.) with each window pane and assign a reference direction. The reference directions for all mesh currents are customarily taken in a clockwise sense. There is no momentous reason for this, except perhaps tradition.

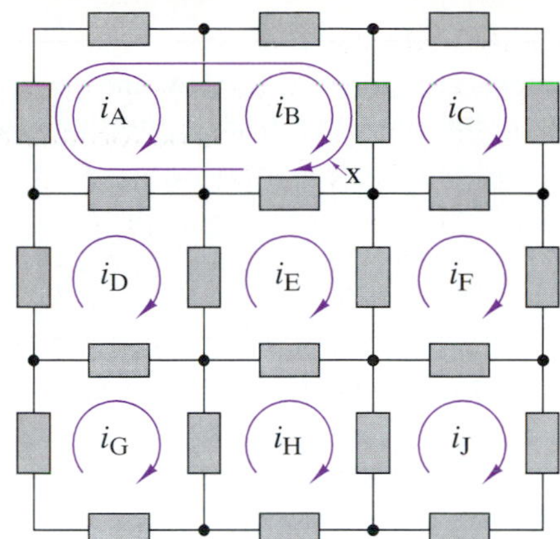

FIGURE 3–16 *Meshes in a planar circuit.*

We think of these mesh currents as circulating through the elements in their respective meshes, as suggested by the reference directions shown in Figure 3–16. We should emphasize that this viewpoint is not based on the physics of circuit behavior. There are not red and blue electrons running around that somehow get assigned to mesh currents i_A or i_B. Mesh currents are variables used in circuit analysis. They are only somewhat abstractly related to the physical operation of a circuit and may be impossible to measure directly. For example, there is no way to cut the circuit in Figure 3–16 to insert an ammeter that only measures i_E.

Mesh currents have a unique feature that is the dual of the fundamental property of node voltages. If we examine Figure 3–16, we see the elements around the perimeter are contained in only one mesh, while those in the interior are in two meshes. In a planar circuit any given element is contained in at most two meshes. When an element is in two meshes, the two mesh currents circulate through the element in opposite directions. In such cases KCL declares that the net current through the element is the difference of the two mesh currents.

These observations lead us to the fundamental property of mesh currents:

> ***If the Kth two-terminal element is contained in meshes X and Y, then the element current can be expressed in terms of the two mesh currents as***
>
> $$i_K = i_X - i_Y \tag{3-11}$$
>
> ***where X is the mesh whose reference direction agrees with the reference direction of i_K.***

Equation (3–11) is a KCL constraint at the element level. If the element is contained in only one mesh, then $i_K = i_X$ or $i_K = -i_Y$, depending on whether the reference direction for the element current agrees or disagrees with the reference direction of the mesh current. The key idea is that the current through every two-terminal element in a planar circuit can be expressed in terms of no more than two mesh currents.

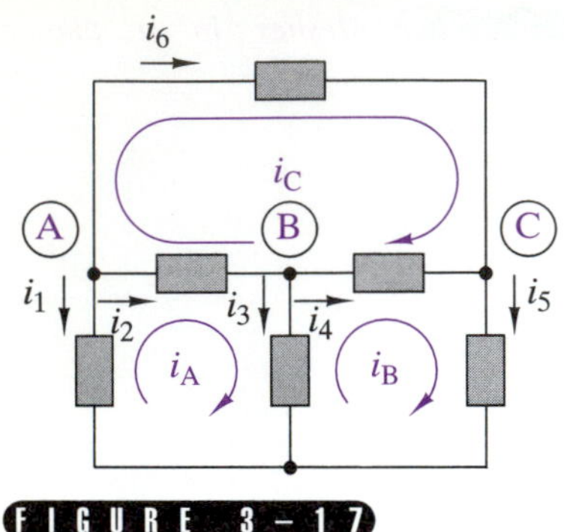

FIGURE 3–17

Exercise 3–7

In Figure 3–17 the mesh currents are $i_A = 10$ A, $i_B = 5$ A, and $i_C = -3$ A. Find the element currents i_1 through i_6 and show that KCL is satisfied at nodes A, B, and C.

Answers:

$i_1 = -10$ A, $i_2 = 13$ A, $i_3 = 5$ A, $i_4 = 8$ A, $i_5 = 5$ A, and $i_6 = -3$ A.

To use mesh currents to formulate circuit equations, we use elements and connection constraints, except that the KCL constraints are not explicitly written. Instead, we use the fundamental property of mesh currents to express the element voltages in terms of the mesh currents. By doing so we avoid using the element currents and work only with the element voltages and mesh currents.

For example, the planar circuit in Figure 3–18 can be analyzed using the mesh-current method. In the figure we have defined two mesh currents and five element voltages. We write KVL constraints around each mesh using the element voltages.

FIGURE 3–18 *Circuit for demonstrating mesh-current analysis.*

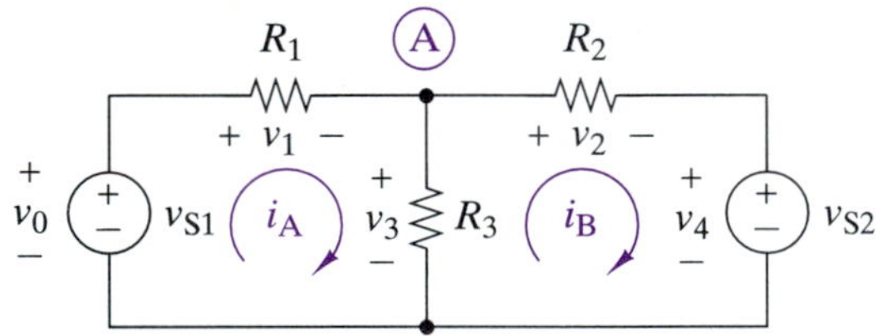

$$\text{Mesh A: } -v_0 + v_1 + v_3 = 0$$

$$\text{Mesh B: } -v_3 + v_2 + v_4 = 0 \quad (3\text{–}12)$$

Using the fundamental property of mesh currents, we write the element voltages in terms of the mesh currents and input voltages:

$$v_1 = R_1 i_A \qquad v_0 = v_{S1}$$

$$v_2 = R_2 i_B \qquad v_4 = v_{S2} \quad (3\text{–}13)$$

$$v_3 = R_3(i_A - i_B)$$

We substitute these element equations into the KVL connection equations and arrange the result in standard form.

$$(R_1 + R_3)i_A - R_3 i_B = v_{S1}$$

$$-R_3 i_A + (R_2 + R_3)i_B = -v_{S2} \quad (3\text{–}14)$$

We have completed the formulation process with two equations in two unknown mesh currents.

As we have previously noted, every method of circuit analysis must satisfy KCL, KVL, and the element i–v relationships. When formulating mesh equations, it may appear that we have not used KCL. However, writing the element constraints in the form in Eq. (3–13) requires the KCL equations $i_1 = i_A$, $i_2 = i_B$, and $i_3 = i_A - i_B$. Mesh-current analysis implicitly satisfies KCL when the element constraints are expressed in terms of the mesh currents. In effect, the fundamental property of mesh currents ensures that the KCL constraints are satisfied.

We use Cramer's rule to solve for the mesh currents in Eq. (3–14):

$$i_A = \frac{\Delta_A}{\Delta} = \frac{\begin{vmatrix} v_{S1} & -R_3 \\ -v_{S2} & R_2 + R_3 \end{vmatrix}}{\begin{vmatrix} R_1 + R_3 & -R_3 \\ -R_3 & R_2 + R_3 \end{vmatrix}} = \frac{(R_2 + R_3)v_{S1} - R_3 v_{S2}}{R_1R_2 + R_1R_3 + R_2R_3} \tag{3-15}$$

and

$$i_B = \frac{\Delta_B}{\Delta} = \frac{\begin{vmatrix} R_1 + R_3 & v_{S1} \\ -R_3 & -v_{S2} \end{vmatrix}}{\begin{vmatrix} R_1 + R_3 & -R_3 \\ -R_3 & R_2 + R_3 \end{vmatrix}} = \frac{R_3 v_{S1} - (R_1 + R_3)v_{S2}}{R_1R_2 + R_1R_3 + R_2R_3} \tag{3-16}$$

Equations (3–15) and (3–16) can now be substituted into the element constraints in Eq. (3–13) to solve for every voltage in the circuit. For instance, the voltage across R_3 is

$$v_A = v_3 = R_3(i_A - i_B) = \frac{R_2R_3v_{S1} + R_1R_3v_{S2}}{R_1R_2 + R_1R_3 + R_2R_3} \tag{3-17}$$

You are invited to show that the result in Eq. (3–17) agrees with the node analysis result obtained in Example 3–4 for the same circuit.

The mesh-current analysis approach just illustrated can be summarized in four steps:

STEP 1: Identify a mesh current with every mesh and a voltage across every circuit element.

STEP 2: Write KVL connection constraints in terms of the element voltages around every mesh.

STEP 3: Use KCL and the *i–v* relationships of the elements to express the element voltages in terms of the mesh currents.

STEP 4: Substitute the element constraints from step 3 into the connection constraints from step 2 and arrange the resulting equations in standard form.

The number of mesh-current equations derived in this way equals the number of KVL connection constraints in step 2. When discussing combined constraints in Chapter 2, we noted that there are $E - N + 1$ independent KVL constraints in any circuit. Using the window panes in a planar circuit generates $E - N + 1$ independent mesh currents. Mesh analysis works best when the circuit has many elements (E large) connected in series (N also large).

WRITING MESH-CURRENT EQUATIONS BY INSPECTION

The mesh equations in Eq. (3–14) have a symmetrical pattern that is similar to the coefficient symmetry observed in node equations. The coefficients of i_B in the first equation and i_A in the second equation are the negative of the resistance common to meshes A and B. The coefficients of i_A in the first equation and i_B in the second equation are the sum of the resistances in meshes A and B, respectively.

This pattern will always occur in planar circuits containing resistors and independent voltage sources when the mesh currents are defined in the window panes of a planar circuit, as shown in Figure 3–16. To see why, consider a general resistance R that is contained in, say, mesh A. There are only two possibilities. Either R is not contained in any other mesh, in which case the voltage across it is

$$v = R(i_A - 0) = Ri_A$$

or else it is also contained in only one adjacent mesh, say mesh B, in which case the voltage across it is

$$v = R(i_A - i_B)$$

These observations lead to the following conclusions. The voltages across resistance in mesh A involves the following terms:

1. i_A times the sum of the resistances in mesh A
2. $-i_B$ times the sum of resistances common to mesh A and mesh B, and similar terms for any other mesh adjacent to mesh A.

The sum of the voltages across resistors plus the sum of the independent voltage sources around mesh A must equal zero.

The aforementioned process makes it possible for us to write mesh-current equations by inspection without going through the intermediate steps involving the KVL connection constraints and the element constraints.

EXAMPLE 3–7

For the circuit of Figure 3–19,

(a) Formulate mesh-current equations.
(b) Find the output v_O using $R_1 = R_4 = 2\ \text{k}\Omega$ and $R_2 = R_3 = 4\ \text{k}\Omega$.

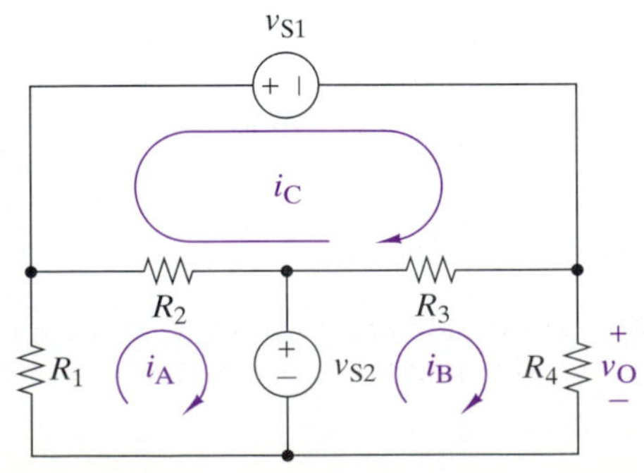

SOLUTION:

(a) To write mesh-current equations by inspection, we note that the total resistances in meshes A, B, and C are $R_1 + R_2$, $R_3 + R_4$, and $R_2 + R_3$, respectively. The resistance common to meshes A and C is R_2. The resistance common to meshes B and C is R_3. There is no resistance common to meshes A and B. Using these observations, we write the mesh equations as

$$\text{Mesh A: } (R_1 + R_2)i_A - 0\, i_B - R_2 i_C + v_{S2} = 0$$

$$\text{Mesh B: } (R_3 + R_4)i_B - 0\, i_A - R_3 i_C - v_{S2} = 0$$

$$\text{Mesh C: } (R_2 + R_3)i_C - R_2 i_A - R_3 i_B + v_{S1} = 0$$

The algebraic signs assigned to voltage source terms follow the passive convention for the mesh current in question. Arranged in standard form, these equations become

$$\begin{aligned} (R_1 + R_2)i_A - R_2 i_C &= -v_{S2} \\ +(R_3 + R_4)i_B - R_3 i_C &= +v_{S2} \\ -R_2 i_A - R_3 i_B + (R_2 + R_3)i_C &= -v_{S1} \end{aligned}$$

Coefficient symmetry greatly simplifies the formulation of these equations compared with the more fundamental, but time-consuming, process of writing element and connection constraints. (b) Inserting the numerical values into these equations yields

$$\begin{aligned} (6 \times 10^3)i_A - (4 \times 10^3)i_C &= -v_{S2} \\ (6 \times 10^3)i_B - (4 \times 10^3)i_C &= v_{S2} \\ -(4 \times 10^3)i_A - (4 \times 10^3)i_B + (8 \times 10^3)i_C &= -v_{S1} \end{aligned}$$

The output voltage v_O is the voltage across R_4. In terms of mesh currents, this voltage is $i_B R_4$. Using Cramer's rule to solve for i_B,

$$i_B = \frac{\Delta_B}{\Delta} = \frac{\begin{vmatrix} 6 \times 10^3 & -v_{S2} & -4 \times 10^3 \\ 0 & v_{S2} & -4 \times 10^3 \\ -4 \times 10^3 & -v_{S1} & 8 \times 10^3 \end{vmatrix}}{\begin{vmatrix} 6 \times 10^3 & 0 & -4 \times 10^3 \\ 0 & 6 \times 10^3 & -4 \times 10^3 \\ -4 \times 10^3 & -4 \times 10^3 & 8 \times 10^3 \end{vmatrix}}$$

$$= \frac{(16 \times 10^6)v_{S2} - (24 \times 10^6)v_{S1}}{96 \times 10^9} = 10^{-3}\left(\frac{v_{S2}}{6} - \frac{v_{S1}}{4}\right)$$

Using Ohm's law, the output voltage is

$$v_O = R_4 i_B = \frac{v_{S2}}{3} - \frac{v_{S1}}{2}$$

The same result was obtained in Example 3–6 using node equations. Either approach produces the same answer, but which method do you think is easier? ■

MESH EQUATIONS WITH CURRENT SOURCES

In developing mesh analysis, we assumed that circuits contain only voltage sources and resistors. This assumption simplifies the formulation process because the sum of voltages around a mesh is determined by voltage sources and the mesh currents through resistors. A current source complicates the picture because the voltage across it is not directly related to its current. We need to adapt mesh analysis to accommodate current sources just as we revised node analysis to deal with voltage sources.

There are three ways to handle current sources in mesh analysis:

1. If the current source is connected in parallel with a resistor, then it can be converted to an equivalent voltage source by source transformation. Each source conversion eliminates a mesh and reduces the number of equations required by 1. This method is the dual of method 1 for node analysis.
2. If a current source is contained in only one mesh, then that mesh current is determined by the source current and is no longer an unknown. We write mesh equations around the remaining meshes in the usual way and move the known mesh current to the source side of the equations in the final step. The number of equations obtained is one less than the number of meshes. This method is the dual of method 2 for node analysis.
3. Neither of the first two methods will work when a current source is contained in two meshes or is not connected in parallel with a resistance. In this case we create a **supermesh** by excluding the current source and any elements connected in series with it, as shown in Figure 3–20. We write one mesh equation around the

FIGURE 3–20 *Example of a supermesh.*

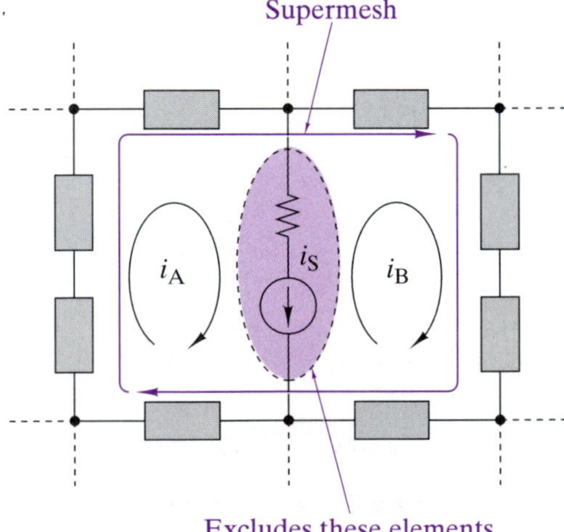

supermesh using the currents i_A and i_B. We then write mesh equations of the remaining meshes in the usual way. This leaves us one equation short because parts of meshes A and B are included in the supermesh. However, the fundamental property of mesh currents relates the currents i_S, i_A, and i_B as

$$i_A - i_B = i_S$$

This equation supplies the one additional relationship needed to get the requisite number of equations in the unknown mesh currents.

The aforementioned three methods are not mutually exclusive. We can use more than one method in a circuit, as the following examples illustrate.

EXAMPLE 3–8

Use mesh-current equations to find i_O in the circuit in Figure 3–21(a).

FIGURE 3–21

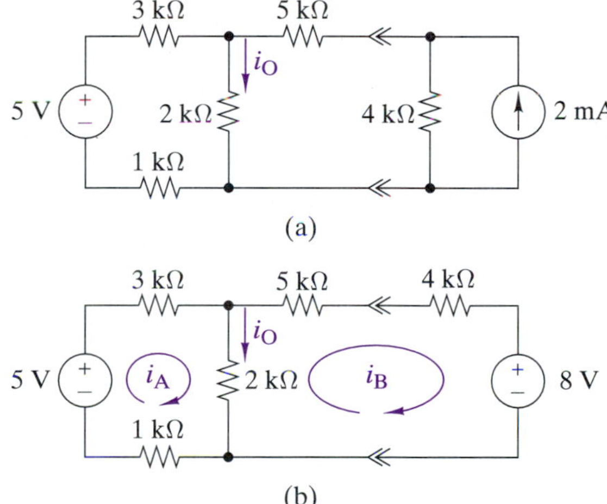

SOLUTION:

The current source in this circuit can be handled by a source transformation (method 1). The 2-mA source in parallel with the 4-kΩ resistor in Figure 3–21(a) can be replaced by an equivalent 8-V voltage source in series with the same resistor, as shown in Figure 3–21(b). In this circuit the total resistance in mesh A is 6 kΩ, the total resistance in mesh B is 11 kΩ, and the resistance contained in both meshes is 2 kΩ. By inspection, the mesh equations for this circuit are

$$(6000)i_A - (2000)i_B = 5$$

$$-(2000)i_A + (11000)i_B = -8$$

Solving for the two mesh currents yields $i_A = 0.6290$ mA and $i_B = -0.6129$ mA. By KCL the desired current is $i_O = i_A - i_B = 1.2419$ mA. The given circuit in Figure 3–21(a) has three meshes and one current source. The source transformation leading to Figure 3–21(b) produces a circuit with only two meshes. The general principle illustrated is that the number of independent mesh equations in a circuit containing E elements, N nodes, and N_I currents sources is $E - N + 1 - N_I$. ■

EXAMPLE 3–9

Use mesh-current equations to find the v_O in Figure 3–22.

FIGURE 3–22

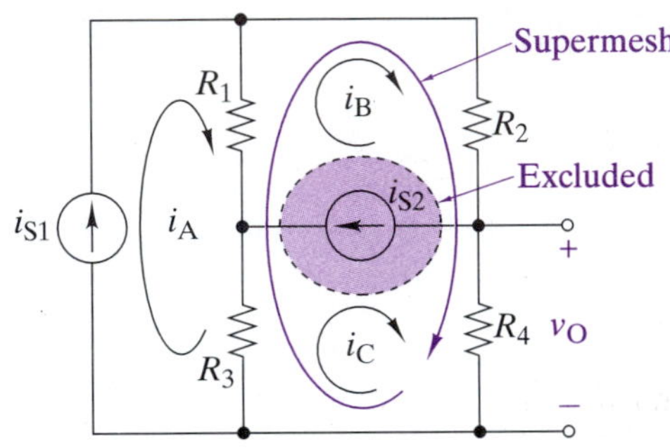

SOLUTION:

Source transformation (method 1) is not possible here since neither current source is connected in parallel with a resistor. The current source i_{S2} is in both mesh B and mesh C, so we exclude this element and create the supermesh (method 3) shown in the figure. The sum of voltages around the supermesh is

$$R_1(i_B - i_A) + R_2(i_B) + R_4(i_C) + R_3(i_C - i_A) = 0$$

The supermesh voltage constraint yields one equation in the three unknown mesh currents. Applying KCL to each of the current sources yields

$$i_A = i_{S1}$$

$$i_B - i_C = i_{S2}$$

Because of KCL the two current sources force constraints that supply two more equations. Using these two KCL constraints to eliminate i_A and i_B from the supermesh KVL constraint yields

$$(R_1 + R_2 + R_3 + R_4)i_C = (R_1 + R_3)i_{S1} - (R_1 + R_2)i_{S2}$$

Hence, the required output voltage is

$$v_O = R_4 i_C = R_4 \times \left[\frac{(R_1 + R_3)i_{S1} - (R_1 + R_2)i_{S2}}{R_1 + R_2 + R_3 + R_4}\right]$$ ■

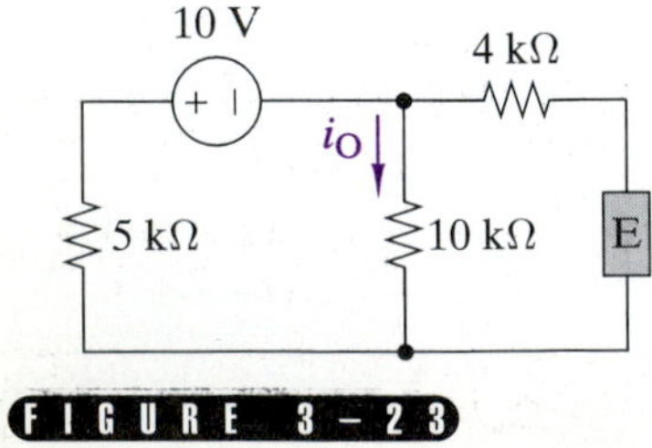

FIGURE 3–23

Exercise 3–8

Use mesh analysis to find the current i_O in Figure 3–23 when the element E is

(a) A 5-V voltage source with the positive reference at the top
(b) A 10-kΩ resistor.

Answers:

(a) –0.136 mA
(b) –0.538 mA

Exercise 3–9

Use mesh analysis to find the current i_O in Figure 3–23 when the element E is

(a) A 1-mA current source with the reference arrow directed down
(b) Two 20-kΩ resistors in parallel.

Answers:

(a) –1 mA
(b) –0.538 mA

Exercise 3–10

Use mesh-current equations to find v_O in Figure 3–24.

Answer:

$$v_O = (v_1 + v_2)/4$$

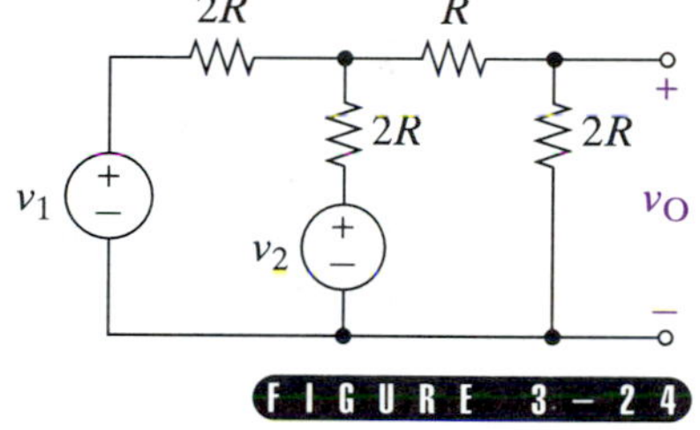

FIGURE 3–24

SUMMARY OF MESH-CURRENT ANALYSIS

Mesh-current equations can always be formulated from KVL, the element constraints, and the fundamental property of mesh currents. When in doubt, always fall back on these principles to formulate mesh equations in new situations. The following guidelines summarize an approach to formulating mesh equations for resistance circuits:

1. Simplify the circuit by combining elements in series or parallel wherever possible.
2. Mesh equations are required for supermeshes and all other meshes except those where current sources are contained in only one mesh.
3. Use KVL to write mesh equations for the meshes identified in step 2. Express element voltages in terms of mesh currents or the voltage produced by independent voltage sources.
4. Write expressions relating the mesh currents to the currents produced by independent current sources.
5. Substitute the expressions from step 4 into the mesh equations from step 3 and place the result in standard form.
6. Solve the equations from step 5 for the mesh currents of interest. Cramer's rule is often useful when circuit parameters are left in symbolic form. Computer tools are useful when there are four or more equations and numerical values are given.

3–3 LINEARITY PROPERTIES

This book treats the analysis and design of **linear circuits**. A circuit is said to be linear if it can be adequately modeled using only linear elements and independent sources. The hallmark feature of a linear circuit is that outputs are linear functions of the inputs. Circuit **inputs** are the signals produced by independent sources, and **outputs** are any other designated signals. Mathematically, a function is said to be linear if it possesses two properties—homogeneity and additivity. In linear circuits, **homogeneity** means that the output is proportional to the input. **Additivity** means that the output due to two or more inputs can be found by adding the outputs obtained when each input is applied separately. Mathematically, these properties are written as follows:

$$f(Kx) = Kf(x) \quad \text{(homogeneity)} \tag{3–18}$$

and

$$f(x_1 + x_2) = f(x_1) + f(x_2) \quad \text{(additivity)} \tag{3–19}$$

where K is a scalar constant. In circuit analysis the homogeneity property is called **proportionality**, while the additivity property is called **superposition**.

THE PROPORTIONALITY PROPERTY

The **proportionality property** applies to linear circuits with one input. For linear resistive circuits, proportionality states that every input–output relationship can be written as

$$y = Kx \tag{3–20}$$

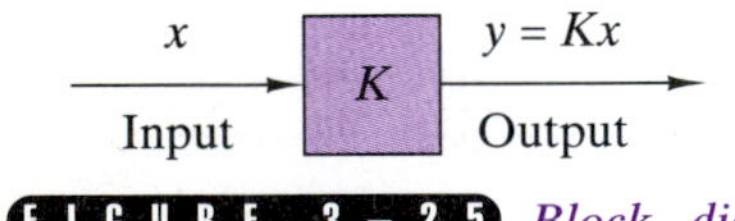

FIGURE 3–25 *Block diagram representation of the proportionality property.*

where x is the input current or voltage, y is an output current or voltage, and K is a constant. The block diagram in Figure 3–25 describes this linear input–output relationship. In a block diagram the lines headed by arrows indicate the direction of signal flow. The arrow directed into the block indicates the input, while the output is indicated by the arrow directed out of the block. The variable names written next to these lines identify the input and output signals. The scalar constant K written inside the block indicates that the input signal x is multiplied by K to produce the output signal as $y = Kx$.

Caution: Proportionality only applies when the input and output are current or voltage. It does not apply to output power since power is equal to the product of current and voltage. In other words, output power is not linearly related to the input current or voltage.

We have already seen several examples of proportionality. For instance, using voltage division in Figure 3–26(a) produces

$$v_O = \left(\frac{R_2}{R_1 + R_2}\right)v_S$$

which means

$$x = v_S \qquad y = v_O$$

$$K = \frac{R_2}{R_1 + R_2}$$

Similarly, applying current division in Figure 3–26(b) yields

$$i_O = \left(\frac{G_2}{G_1 + G_2}\right) i_S$$

so that

$$x = i_S \qquad y = i_O$$

$$K = \frac{G_2}{G_1 + G_2}$$

In these two examples the proportionality constant K is dimensionless because the input and output have the same units. In other situations K could have the units of ohms or siemens when the input and output have different units.

The next example illustrates that the proportionality constant K can be positive, negative, or even zero.

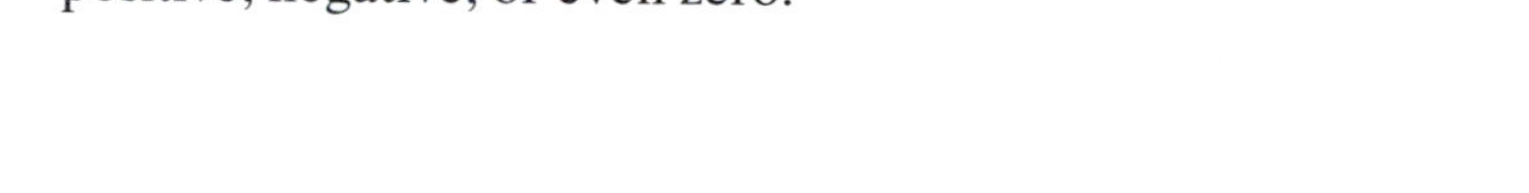

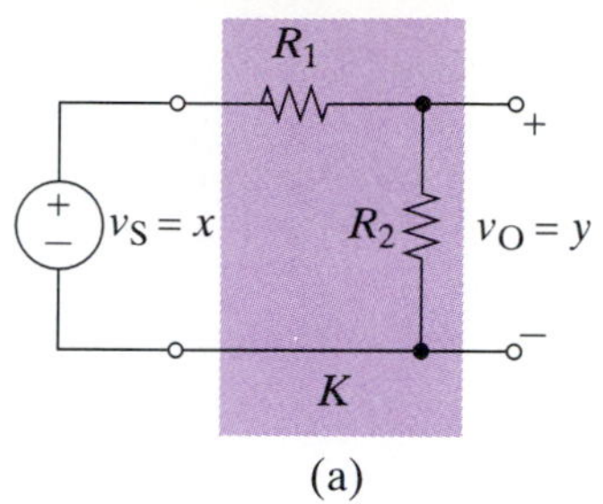

(a)

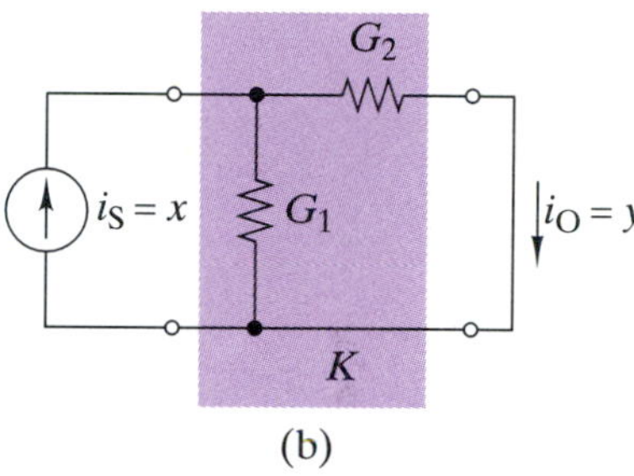

(b)

FIGURE 3–26 *Examples of circuit exhibiting of proportionality: (a) Voltage divider. (b) Current divider.*

EXAMPLE 3–10

Given the bridge circuit of Figure 3–27,

(a) Find the proportionality constant K in the input–output relationship $v_O = Kv_S$

(b) Find the sign of K when $R_2R_3 > R_1R_4$, $R_2R_3 = R_1R_4$, and $R_2R_3 < R_1R_4$.

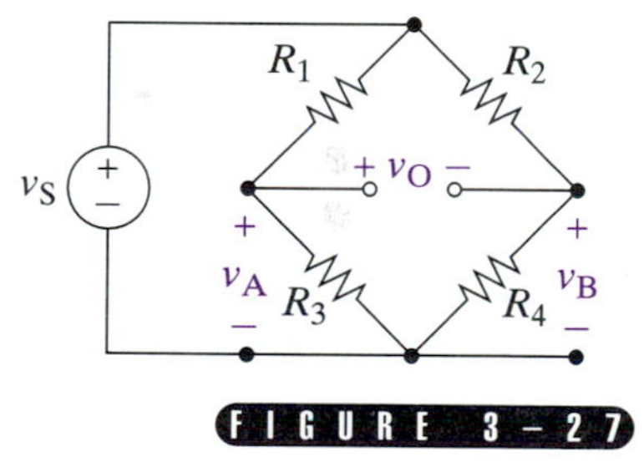

FIGURE 3–27

SOLUTION:

(a) We observe that the circuit consists of two voltage dividers. Applying the voltage division rule to each side of the bridge circuit yields

$$v_A = \frac{R_3}{R_1 + R_3} v_S \quad \text{and} \quad v_B = \frac{R_4}{R_2 + R_4} v_S$$

The fundamental property of node voltages allows us to write

$$v_O = v_A - v_B$$

Substituting the equations for v_A and v_B into this KVL equation yields

$$\begin{aligned} v_O &= \left(\frac{R_3}{R_1 + R_3} - \frac{R_4}{R_2 + R_4}\right) v_S \\ &= \left(\frac{R_2R_3 - R_1R_4}{(R_1 + R_3)(R_2 + R_4)}\right) v_S \\ &= \qquad (K) \qquad v_S \end{aligned}$$

(b) The proportionality constant K can be positive, negative, or zero. Specifically,

$$\text{If } R_2R_3 > R_1R_4 \text{ then } K > 0$$
$$\text{If } R_2R_3 = R_1R_4 \text{ then } K = 0$$
$$\text{If } R_2R_3 < R_1R_4 \text{ then } K < 0$$

When the products of the resistances in opposite legs of the bridge are equal, then $K = 0$ and the bridge is said to be balanced. ■

UNIT OUTPUT METHOD

The **unit output method** is an analysis technique based on the proportionality property of linear circuits. The method involves finding the input–output proportionality constant K by assuming an output of one unit and determining the input required to produce that unit output. This technique is most useful when applied to ladder circuits, and it involves the following steps:

1. A unit output is assumed; that is, $v_O = 1$ V or $i_O = 1$ A.
2. The input required to produce the unit output is then found by successive application of KCL, KVL, and Ohm's law.
3. Because the circuit is linear, the proportionality constant relating input and output is

$$K = \frac{\text{Output}}{\text{Input}} = \frac{1}{\text{Input for unit output}}$$

Given the proportionality constant K, we can find the output for any input using Eq. (3–20).

In a way, the unit output method solves the circuit response problem backwards—that is, from output to input—as illustrated by the next example.

EXAMPLE 3–11

Use the unit output method to find v_O in the circuit shown in Figure 3–28(a).

SOLUTION:

We start by assuming $v_O = 1$, as shown in Figure 3–28(b). Then, using Ohm's law, we find i_O.

$$i_O = \frac{v_O}{20} = 0.05 \text{ A}$$

Next, using KCL at node B, we find i_1.

$$i_1 = i_O = 0.05 \text{ A}$$

Again, using Ohm's law, we find v_1.

$$v_1 = 10i_1 = 0.5 \text{ V}$$

FIGURE 3–28

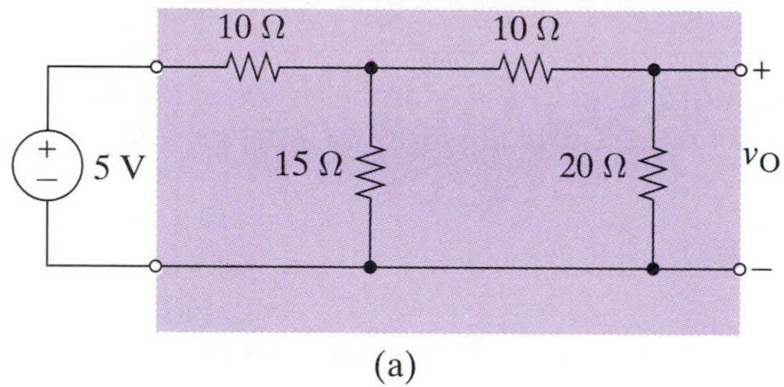

(a)

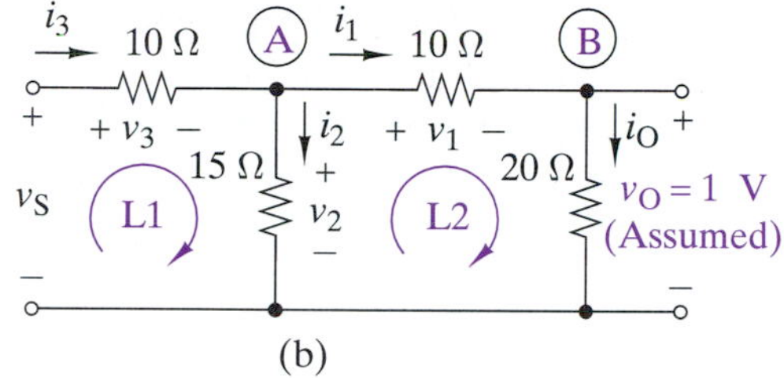

(b)

Then, writing a KVL equation around loop L2, we find v_2 as

$$v_2 = v_1 + v_O = 0.5 + 1.0 = 1.5 \text{ V}$$

Using Ohm's law once more produces

$$i_2 = \frac{v_2}{15} = \frac{1.5}{15} = 0.1 \text{ A}$$

Next, writing a KCL equation at node A yields

$$i_3 = i_1 + i_2 = 0.05 + 0.1 = 0.15 \text{ A}$$

Using Ohm's law one last time,

$$v_3 = 10i_3 = 1.5 \text{ V}$$

We can now find the source voltage v_S by applying KVL around loop L1:

$$v_S\big|_{\text{for } v_O = 1\text{V}} = v_3 + v_2 = 1.5 + 1.5 = 3 \text{ V}$$

A 3-V source voltage is required to produce a 1-V output. From this result, we calculate the proportionality constant K to be

$$K = \frac{v_O}{v_S} = \frac{1}{3}$$

Once K is known, the output for the specified 5-V input is $v_O = (1/3)5 = 1.667$ V. ■

Exercise 3–11

Find v_O in the circuit of Figure 3–28(a) when v_S is –5 V, 10 mV, and 3 kV.

Answers:

$v_O = -1.667$ V, 3.333 mV, and 1 kV

Exercise 3–12

Use the unit output method to find $K = i_O/i_{IN}$ for the circuit in Figure 3–29. Then use the proportionality constant K to find i_O for the input current shown in the figure.

FIGURE 3–29

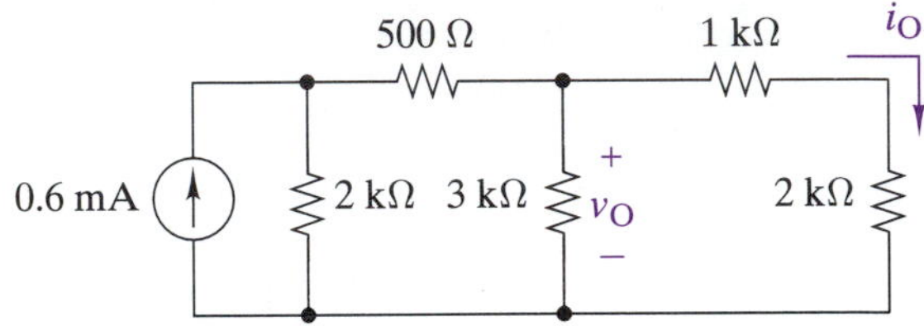

Answers:

$K = ¼$; $i_O = 0.15$ mA

Exercise 3–13

Use the unit output method to find $K = v_O/i_{IN}$ for the circuit in Figure 3–29. Then use K to find v_O for the input current shown in the figure.

Answers:

$K = 750\ \Omega$; $v_O = 450$ mV

Note: In this exercise K has the dimensions of ohms because the input is a current and the output a voltage.

ADDITIVITY PROPERTY

The **additivity property** states that any output current or voltage of a linear resistive circuit with multiple inputs can be expressed as a linear combination of the several inputs:

$$y = K_1x_1 + K_2x_2 + K_3x_3 + \ldots \tag{3–21}$$

where x_1, x_2, x_3, . . . are current or voltage inputs, and K_1, K_2, K_3 . . . are constants that depend on the circuit parameters. Figure 3–30 shows how we represent this relationship in block diagram form. Again the arrows indicate the direction of signal flow and the K's within the blocks are scalar multipliers. The circle in Figure 3–30 is a new block diagram element called a summing point that implements the operation $y = \Sigma K_ix_i$. Although the block diagram in Figure 3–30 is nothing more than a pictorial representation of Eq. (3–21), the diagram often helps us gain a clearer picture of how signals interact in different parts of a circuit.

To illustrate this property, we analyze the two-input circuit in Figure 3–31 using node-voltage analysis. Applying KCL at node A, we obtain

$$\frac{v_A - v_S}{R_1} + i_S + \frac{v_A}{R_2} = 0$$

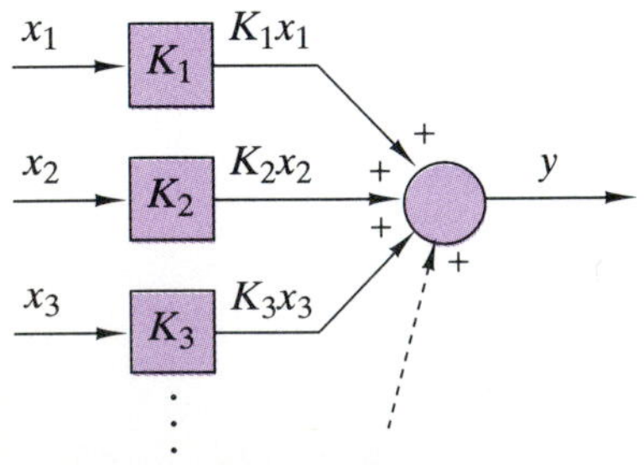

FIGURE 3–30 *Block diagram representation of the additivity property.*

Moving the inputs to the right side of this equation yields

$$\left[\frac{1}{R_1} + \frac{1}{R_2}\right]v_A = \frac{v_S}{R_1} + i_S$$

Since $v_O = v_A$, we obtain the input-output relationship in the form

$$v_O = \left[\frac{R_2}{R + R_2}\right]v_S + \left[\frac{R_1 R_2}{R_1 + R_2}\right]i_S$$

$$y = [K_1]x_1 + [K_2]x_2 \qquad (3-22)$$

This result shows that the output is a linear combination of the two inputs. Note that K_1 is dimensionless since its input and output are voltages, and that K_2 has the units of ohms since its input is a current and its output is a voltage.

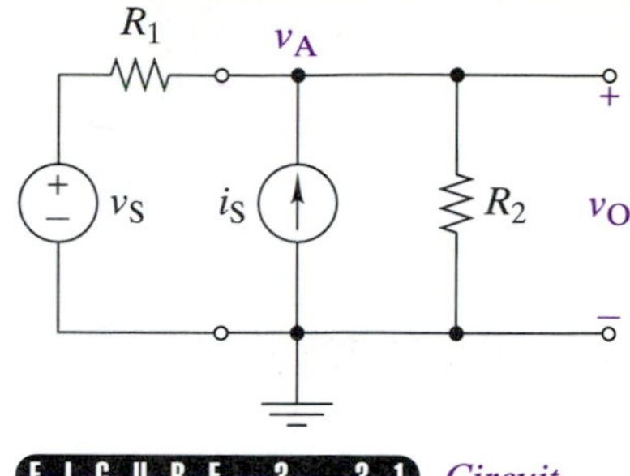

FIGURE 3–31 Circuit used to demonstrate superposition.

SUPERPOSITION PRINCIPLE

Since the output in Eq. (3–21) is a linear combination, the contribution of each input source is independent of all other inputs. This means that the output can be found by finding the contribution from each source acting alone and then adding the individual response to obtain the total response. This suggests that the output of a multiple-input linear circuit can be found by the following steps:

STEP 1: "Turn off" all independent sources except one and find the output of the circuit due to that source acting alone.

STEP 2: Repeat the process in step 1 until each independent source has been turned on and the output due to that source found.

STEP 3: The total output with all independent sources turned on is the algebraic sum of the outputs caused by each source acting alone.

These steps describe a circuit analysis technique called the **superposition principle**. Before applying this method, we must discuss what happens when a voltage or current source is "turned off."

The *i–v* characteristics of voltage and current sources are shown in Figure 3–32. A voltage source is "turned off" by setting its voltage to zero ($v_S = 0$). This step translates the voltage source *i–v* characteristic to the *i*–axis, as shown in Figure 3–32(a). In Chapter 2 we found that a vertical line on the *i*–axis is the *i–v* characteristic of a short circuit. Similarly, "turning off" a current source ($i_S = 0$) in Figure 3–32(b) translates its *i–v* characteristic to the *v*-axis, which is the *i–v* characteristic of an open circuit. Therefore, when a voltage source is "turned off" we replace it by a short circuit, and when a current source is "turned off" we replace it by an open circuit.

The superposition principle is now applied to the circuit in Figure 3–31 to duplicate the response in Eq. (3–22), which was found by node analysis. Figure 3–33 shows the steps involved in applying superposition to the circuit in Figure 3–31. Figure 3–33(a) shows that the circuit has two input sources. We will first "turn off" i_S and replace it with an open circuit, as shown in Figure 3–33(b). The output of the circuit in Figure 3–33(b) is

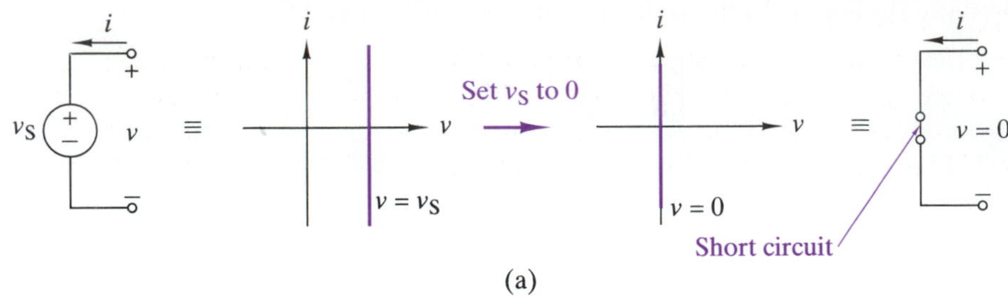

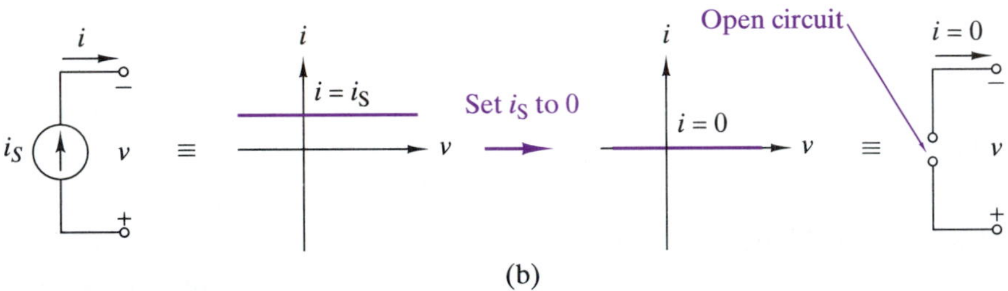

FIGURE 3–32 *Turning off an independent source: (a) Voltage source. (b) Current source.*

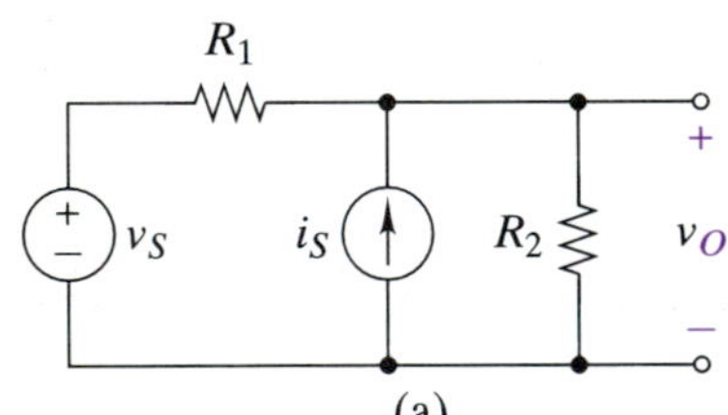

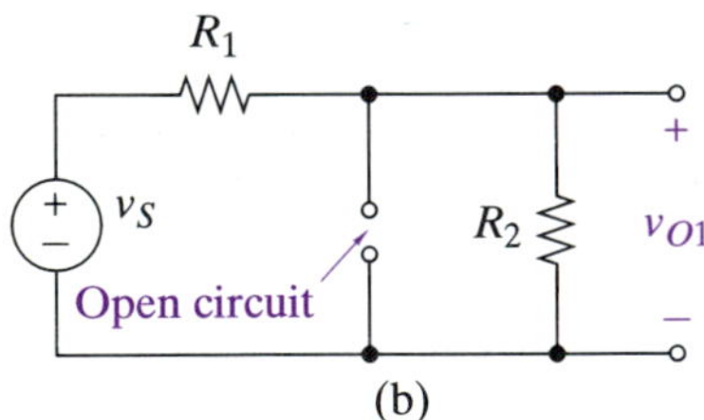

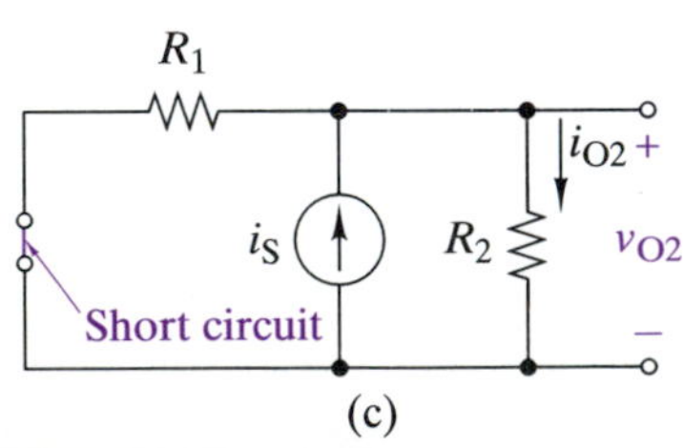

FIGURE 3–33 *Circuit analysis using superposition: (a) Current source off. (b) Voltage source off.*

called v_{O1} and represents that part of the total output caused by the voltage source. Using voltage division in Figure 3–33(b) yields v_{O1} as

$$v_{O1} = \frac{R_2}{R_1 + R_2} v_S$$

Next we "turn off" the voltage source and "turn on" the current source, as shown in Figure 3–33(c). Using Ohm's law, we get $v_{O2} = i_{O2}R_2$. We use current division to express i_{O2} in terms of i_S to obtain v_{O2}:

$$v_{O2} = i_{O2}R_2 = \left[\frac{R_1}{R_1 + R_2} i_S\right] R_2 = \frac{R_1 R_2}{R_1 + R_2} i_S$$

Applying the superposition principle, we find the response with both sources "turned on" by adding the two responses v_{O1} and v_{O2}.

$$\begin{aligned} v_O &= v_{O1} + v_{O2} \\ &= \left[\frac{R_2}{R_1 + R_2}\right] v_S + \left[\frac{R_1 R_2}{R_1 + R_2}\right] i_S \end{aligned}$$

This superposition result is the same as the circuit reduction result given in Eq. (3–22).

EXAMPLE 3–12

Figure 3–34(a) shows a resistance circuit used to implement a signal-summing function. Use superposition to show that the output v_O is a weighted sum of the inputs v_{S1}, v_{S2}, and v_{S3}.

SOLUTION:

To determine v_O using superposition, we first turn off sources 1 and 2 ($v_{S1} = 0$ and $v_{S2} = 0$) to obtain the circuit in Figure 3–34(b). This circuit is a voltage divider in which the output leg consists of two equal resistors in parallel. The equivalent resistance of the output leg is $R/2$, so the voltage division rule yields

$$v_{O3} = \frac{R/2}{R + R/2}v_{S3} = \frac{v_{S3}}{3}$$

Because of the symmetry of the circuit, it can be seen that the same technique applies to all three inputs; therefore

$$v_{O2} = \frac{v_{S2}}{3} \text{ and } v_{O1} = \frac{v_{S1}}{3}$$

Applying the superposition principle, the output with all sources "turned on" is

$$\begin{aligned} v_O &= v_{O1} + v_{O2} + v_{O3} \\ &= \frac{1}{3}[v_{S1} + v_{S2} + v_{S3}] \end{aligned}$$

That is, the output is proportional to the sum of the three input signals with $K_1 = K_2 = K_3 = 1/3$. ■

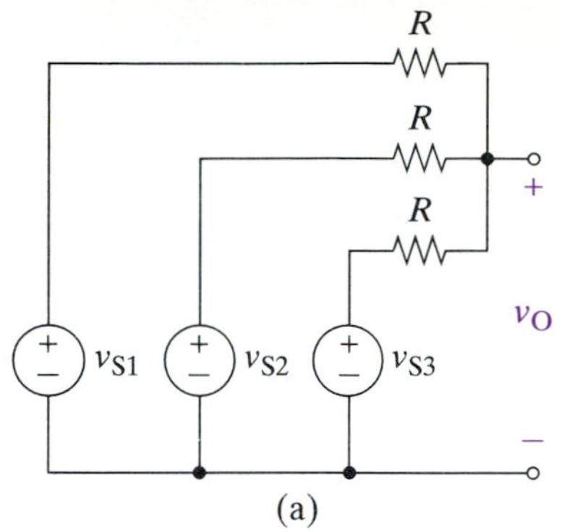

(a)

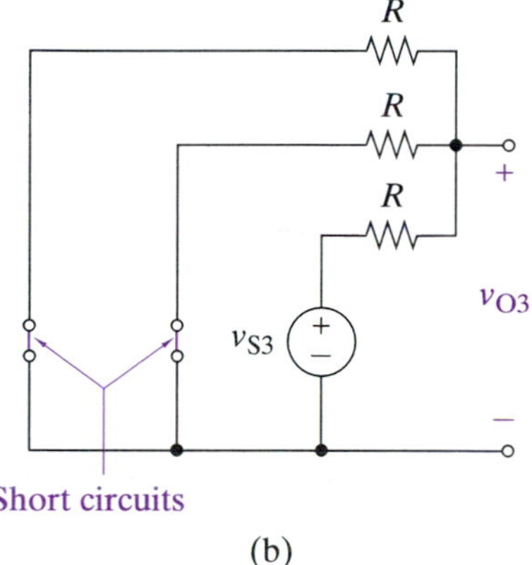

(b)

FIGURE 3–34

Exercise 3–14

The circuit of Figure 3–35 contains two of the R-$2R$ modules discussed in Problem 2–35. Use superposition to find v_O.

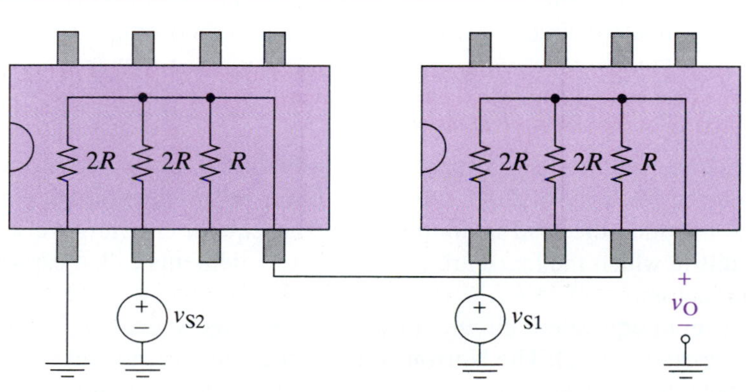

FIGURE 3–35

Answer:

$$v_O = \tfrac{1}{2}v_{S1} + \tfrac{1}{4}v_{S2}$$

Exercise 3–15

Repeat Exercise 3–14 with the voltage source v_{S2} replaced by a current source i_{S2} with the current reference arrow directed toward ground.

Answer:

$$v_O = 3v_{S1}/5 - 4i_{S2}R/5$$

The preceding examples and exercises illustrate the applications of the superposition principle. You should not conclude that superposition is used primarily to solve for the response of circuits with multiple independent sources. In fact, superposition is not a particularly attractive method of analysis since a circuit with N sources requires N different circuit analyses to obtain the final result. Unless the circuit is relatively simple, superposition does not reduce the analysis effort compared with, say, node-voltage analysis. Superposition is still an important property of linear circuits because it is often used as a conceptual tool to develop other circuit analysis techniques. For example, superposition is used in the next section to prove Thévenin's theorem.

3–4 THÉVENIN AND NORTON EQUIVALENT CIRCUITS

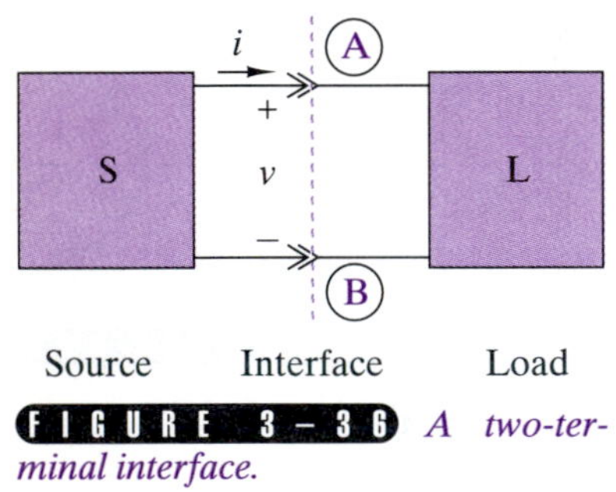

FIGURE 3–36 *A two-terminal interface.*

An *interface* is a connection between circuits. Circuit interfaces occur frequently in electrical and electronic systems, so special analysis methods are used to handle them. For the two-terminal interface shown in Figure 3–36, we normally think of one circuit as the source S and the other as the load L. We think of signals as being produced by the source circuit and delivered to the load circuit. The source-load interaction at an interface is one of the central problems of circuit analysis and design.

The Thévenin and Norton equivalent circuits shown in Figure 3–37 are valuable tools for dealing with circuit interfaces. The conditions under which these equivalent circuits exist can be stated as a theorem:

> ***If the source circuit in a two-terminal interface is linear, then the interface signals v and i do not change when the source circuit is replaced by its Thévenin or Norton equivalent circuit.***

The equivalence requires the source circuit to be linear, but places no restriction on the linearity of the load circuit. Later in this section we consider cases in which the load is nonlinear. In subsequent chapters we will study circuits in which the loads are energy storage elements called capacitors and inductors.

The Thévenin equivalent circuit consists of a voltage source (v_T) in series with a resistance (R_T). The Norton equivalent circuit is a current source (i_N) in parallel with a resistance (R_N). Note that the Thévenin and Norton equivalent circuits are practical sources in the sense discussed in Chapter 2.

The two circuits have the same i–v characteristics, since replacing one by the other leaves the interface signals unchanged. To derive the equivalency conditions, we apply KVL and Ohm's law to the Thévenin equivalent in Figure 3–37(a) to obtain its i–v relationship at the terminals A and B:

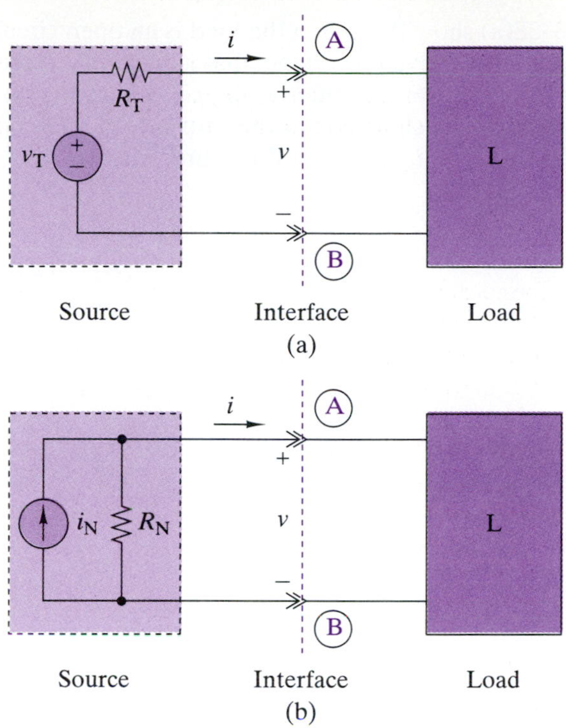

FIGURE 3–37 *Equivalent circuits for the source: (a) Thévenin equivalent. (b) Norton equivalent.*

$$v = v_T - iR_T \tag{3–23}$$

Next, applying KCL and Ohm's law to the Norton equivalent in Figure 3–37(b) yields its *i*–*v* relationship at terminals A–B:

$$i = i_N - \frac{v}{R_N} \tag{3–24}$$

Solving Eq. (3–24) for v yields

$$v = i_N R_N - iR_N \tag{3–25}$$

The Thévenin and Norton circuits have identical *i*–*v* relationships. Comparing Eqs. (3–23) and (3–25), we conclude that

$$R_N = R_T$$
$$i_N R_N = v_T \tag{3–26}$$

In essence, the Thévenin and Norton equivalent circuits are related by the source transformation studied in Chapter 2. We do not need to find both equivalent circuits. Once one of them is found, the other can be determined by a source transformation. The Thévenin and Norton circuits involve four parameters (v_T, R_T, i_N, R_N) and Eq. (3–26) provides two relations between the four parameters. Therefore, only two parameters are needed to specify either equivalent circuit.

In circuit analysis problems it is convenient to use the short-circuit current and open-circuit voltage to specify Thévenin and Norton circuits. The circuits in Figure 3–38(a) show that when the load is an open circuit the interface voltage equals the Thévenin voltage; that is, $v_{OC} = v_T$, since there is no voltage across R_T when $i = 0$. Similarly, the circuits in Figure 3–38(b) show that when the load is a short circuit the interface current equals the Norton current; that is, $i_{SC} = i_N$, since all the source current i_N is diverted through the short-circuit load.

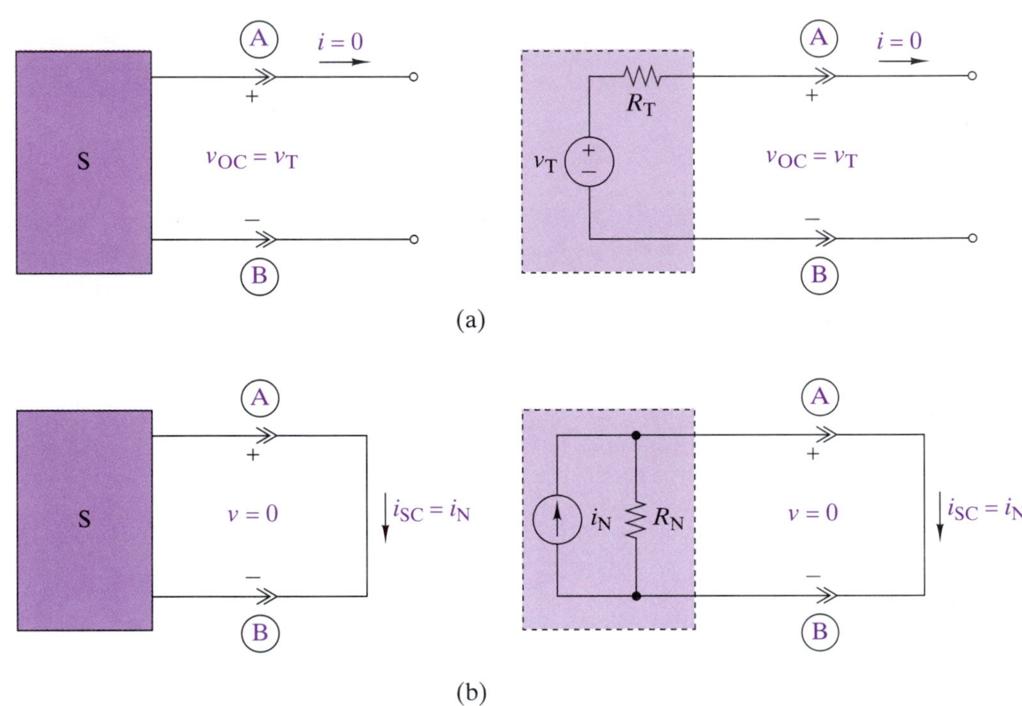

FIGURE 3–38 *Loads used to find Thévenin and Norton equivalent circuits: (a) Open circuit yields the Thévenin voltage. (b) Short circuit yields the Norton current.*

In summary, the parameters of the Thévenin and Norton equivalent circuits at a given interface can be found by determining the open-circuit voltage and the short-circuit current.

$$\begin{aligned} v_T &= v_{OC} \\ i_N &= i_{SC} \\ R_N = R_T &= v_{OC}/i_{SC} \end{aligned} \tag{3-27}$$

APPLICATIONS OF THÉVENIN AND NORTON EQUIVALENT CIRCUITS

Replacing a complex circuit by its Thévenin or Norton equivalent can greatly simplify the analysis and design of interface circuits. For example, suppose we need to select a load resistance in Figure 3–39(a) so the source circuit to the left of the interface A–B delivers 4 volts to the load. This task is easily handled once we have the Thévenin or Norton equivalent for the source circuit.

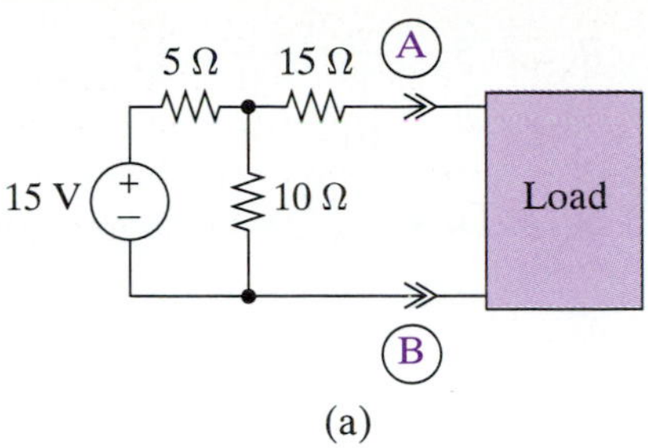

(a)

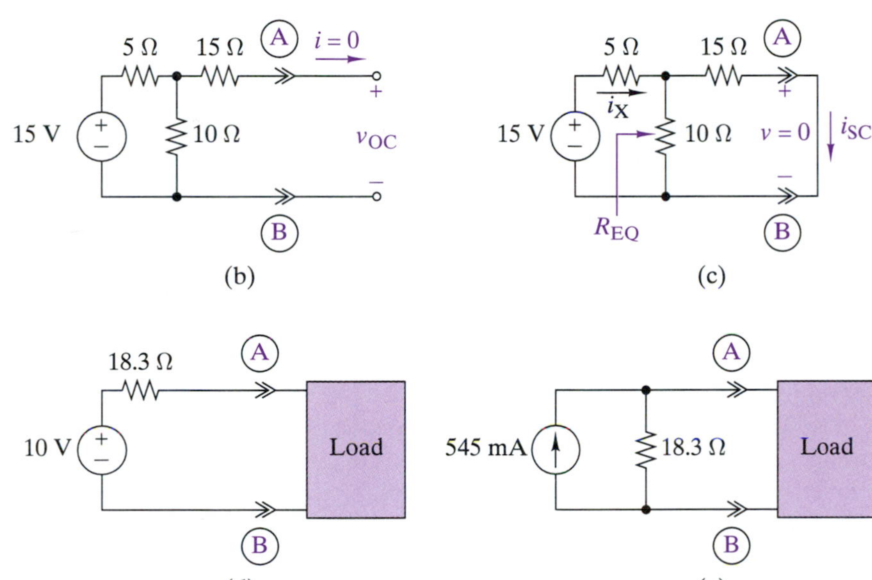

FIGURE 3–39 *Example of finding the Thévenin and Norton equivalent circuits: (a) The given circuit. (b) Open circuit yields the Thévenin voltage. (c) Short circuit yields the Norton current. (d) Thévenin equivalent circuit. (e) Norton equivalent circuit.*

To obtain the Thévenin and Norton equivalents, we need v_{OC} and i_{SC}. The open-circuit voltage v_{OC} is found by disconnecting the load at the terminals A and B, as shown in Figure 3–39(b). The voltage across the 15-Ω resistor is zero because the open circuit causes the current through the resistor to be zero. The open-circuit voltage at the interface is the same as the voltage across the 10-Ω resistor. Using voltage division, this voltage is

$$v_T = v_{OC} = \frac{10}{10+5} \times 15 = 10 \text{ V}$$

Next we find the short-circuit current i_{SC} using the circuit in Figure 3–39(c). The total current i_X delivered by the 15-V voltage source is

$$i_X = 15/R_{EQ}$$

where R_{EQ} is the equivalent resistance seen by the voltage source with a short circuit at the interface.

$$R_{EQ} = 5 + \frac{1}{\frac{1}{10} + \frac{1}{15}} = 11\ \Omega$$

We find $i_X = 15/11 = 1.36$ A. Given i_X, we now use current division to obtain the short-circuit current:

$$i_N = i_{SC} = \frac{10}{10 + 15} \times i_X = 0.545\ \text{A}$$

Finally, we compute the Thévenin and Norton resistances:

$$R_T = R_N = \frac{v_{OC}}{i_{SC}} = 18.3\ \Omega$$

The resulting Thévenin and Norton equivalent circuits are shown in Figures 3–39(d) and 3–39(e).

It now is an easy matter to select a load R_L so 4 V is supplied to the load. Using the Thévenin equivalent circuit, the problem reduces to a voltage divider:

$$\frac{R_L}{R_L + R_T} \times v_T = \frac{R_L}{R_L + 18.3} \times 10 = 4\ \text{V}$$

Solving for R_L yields $R_L = 12.2\ \Omega$.

The Thévenin or Norton equivalent can always be found from the open-circuit voltage and short-circuit current at the interface. The following examples illustrate other methods of determining these equivalent circuits.

EXAMPLE 3–13

(a) Find the Thévenin equivalent circuit of the source circuit to the left of the interface in Figure 3–40(a).

(b) Use the Thévenin equivalent to find the power delivered to two different loads. The first load is a 10-kΩ resistor and the second is a 5-V voltage source whose positive terminal is connected to the upper interface terminal.

SOLUTION:

(a) To find the Thévenin equivalent, we use the sequence of circuit reductions shown in Figure 3–40. In Figure 3–40(a) the 15-V voltage source in series with the 3-kΩ to the left of terminals A and B is replaced by a 3-kΩ resistor in parallel with an equivalent current source with i_S = 15/3000 = 5 mA. In Figure 3–40(b), looking to the left at terminals C and D, we see two resistors in parallel whose equivalent resistance is (3 kΩ)||(6 kΩ) = 2 kΩ. We also see two current sources in parallel whose equivalent is i_S = 5 mA − 2 mA = 3 mA. This equivalent current source is shown in Figure 3–40(c) to the left of terminals C and D. Figure 3–40(d) shows this current source converted to an equivalent volt-

FIGURE 3–40

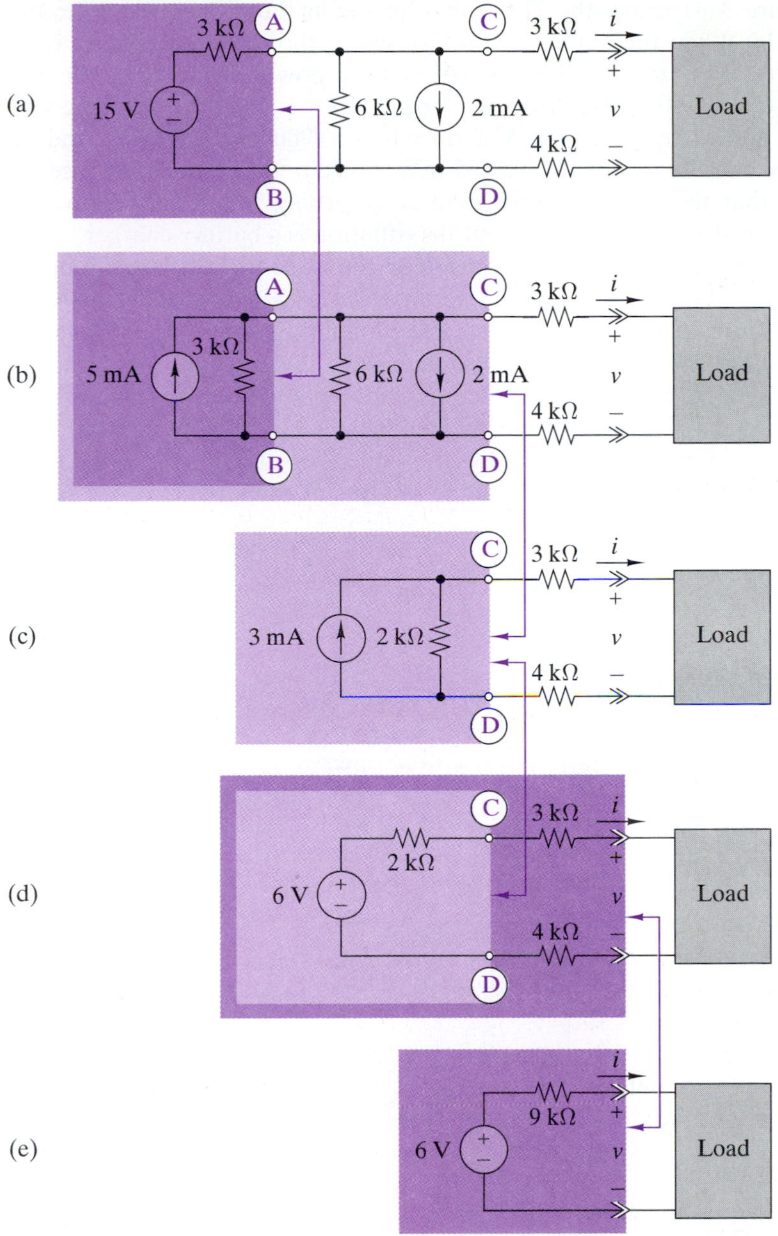

age source v_S = (3 ma) × (2 kΩ) = 6 V in series with 2 kΩ. In Figure 3–40(d) the three resistors are connected in series and can be replaced by an equivalent resistance R_{EQ} = 2 kΩ + 3 kΩ + 4 kΩ = 9 kΩ. This step produces the Thévenin equivalent shown in Figure 3–40(e).

Note: The steps leading from Figure 3–40(a) to 3–40(e) involve circuit reduction techniques studied in Chapter 2, so we know that this approach only works on ladder circuits like the one in Figure 3–40(a).

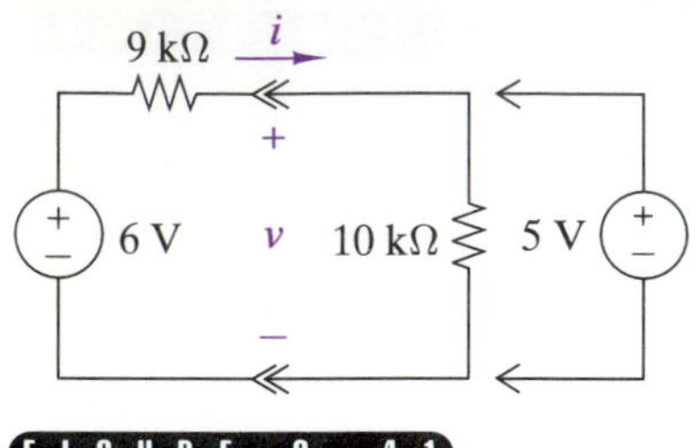

FIGURE 3–41

(b) Figure 3–41 shows the Thévenin equivalent found in (a) and the two loads. When the load is a 10-kΩ resistor, the interface current is $i = (6)/(9000 + 10{,}000) = 0.3158$ mA, and the power delivered to the load is $i^2R_L = 0.9973$ mW. When the load is a 5-V source, the interface voltage and current are $v = 5$ V and $i = (6 - 5)/9000 = 0.1111$ mA, and the power to the load is $vi = 0.5555$ mW. Since $p > 0$ in the latter case, we see that the voltage source load is absorbing rather than delivering power. A practical example of this situation is a battery charger.

Caution: The Thévenin equivalent allows us to calculate the power delivered to a load, but it does not tell us what power is dissipated in the source circuit. For instance, if the load in Figure 3–40(e) is an open circuit, then no power is dissipated in the Thévenin equivalent since $i = 0$. This does not mean that the power dissipated in the source circuit is zero, as we can easily see by looking back at Figure 3–40(a). The Thévenin equivalent circuit has the same i–v characteristic at the interface, but it does not duplicate the internal characteristics of the source circuit. ■

EXAMPLE 3–14

(a) Find the Norton equivalent of the source circuit to the left of the interface in Figure 3–42.

(b) Find the interface current i when the power delivered to the load is 5 W.

FIGURE 3–42

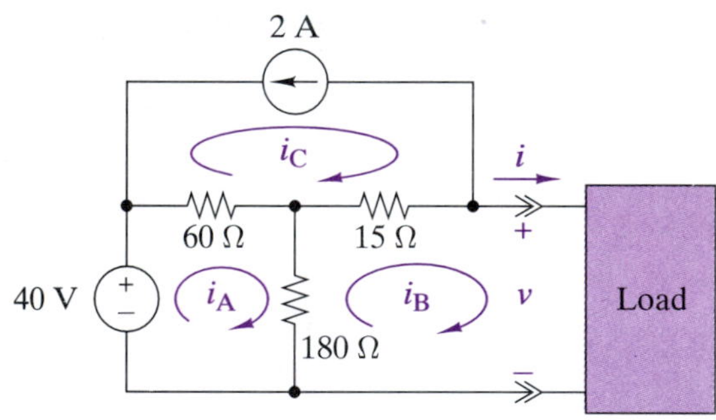

SOLUTION:

(a) The circuit reduction method will not work here since the source circuit is not a ladder. In this example we write mesh-current equations and solve directly for the source circuit i–v relationship. We only need to write equations for meshes A and B since the 2-A current source determines the mesh C current. The voltages sums around these meshes are

$$\text{Mesh A:}\quad -40 + 60(i_A - i_C) + 180(i_A - i_B) = 0$$

$$\text{Mesh B:}\quad -180(i_A - i_B) + 15(i_B - i_C) + v = 0$$

But since $i_B = i$ and the current source forces the condition $i_C = -2$, these equations have the form

$$240i_A - 180i = -80$$
$$-180i_A + 195i = -30 - v$$

Solving for i in terms of v yields

$$i = \frac{\begin{vmatrix} 240 & -80 \\ -180 & -30 - v \end{vmatrix}}{\begin{vmatrix} 240 & -180 \\ -180 & 195 \end{vmatrix}} = \frac{-21600 - 240v}{14400}$$
$$= -1.5 - \frac{v}{60}$$

At the interface the i–v relationship of the source circuit is $i = -1.5 - v/60$. Equation (3–24) gives the i–v relationship of the Norton circuit as $i = i_N - v/R_N$. By direct comparison, we conclude that $i_N = -1.5$ A and $R_N = 60\ \Omega$. This equivalent circuit is shown in Figure 3–43.

(b) When 5 W is delivered to the load, we have $vi = 5$ or $v = 5/i$. Substituting $v = 5/i$ into the source i–v relationship $i = -1.5 - v/60$ yields a quadratic equation

$$12i^2 + 18i + 1 = 0$$

whose roots are $i = -0.05778$ A and -1.442 A. Thus, there are two values of interface current that deliver 5 W to the load. ■

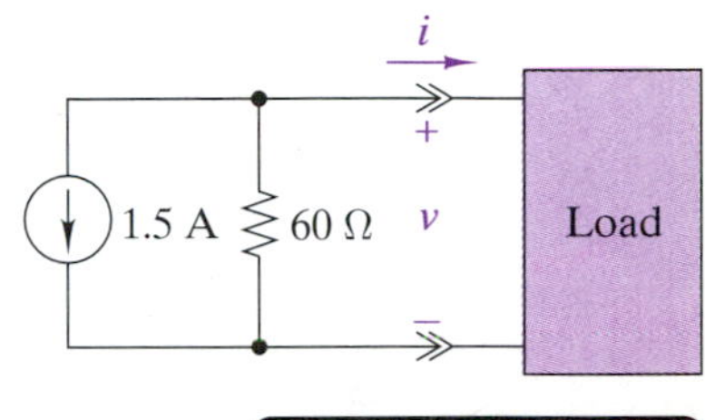

FIGURE 3–43

DERIVATION OF THÉVENIN'S THEOREM

The derivation of Thévenin's theorem is based on the superposition principle. We begin with the circuit in Figure 3–44(a), where the source circuit S is linear. Our approach is to use superposition to show that the source circuit and the Thévenin circuit have the same i–v relationship at the interface. To find the source circuit i–v relationship, we first disconnect the load and apply a current source i_{TEST}, as shown in Figure 3–44(b). Using superposition to find v_{TEST}, we first turn i_{TEST} off and leave all the sources inside S on, as shown in Figure 3–44(c). Turning a current source off leaves an open circuit, so

$$v_{TEST1} = v_{OC}$$

Next we turn i_{TEST} back on and turn off all of the sources inside S. Since the source circuit S is linear, it reduces to the equivalent resistance shown in Figure 3–44(d) when all internal sources are turned off. Using Ohm's law, we write

$$v_{TEST2} = (R_{EQ})(-i_{TEST})$$

The minus sign in this equation results from the reference directions originally assigned to i_{TEST} and v_{TEST} in Figure 3–44(b). Using the superposition principle, we find the i–v relationship of the source circuit at the interface to be

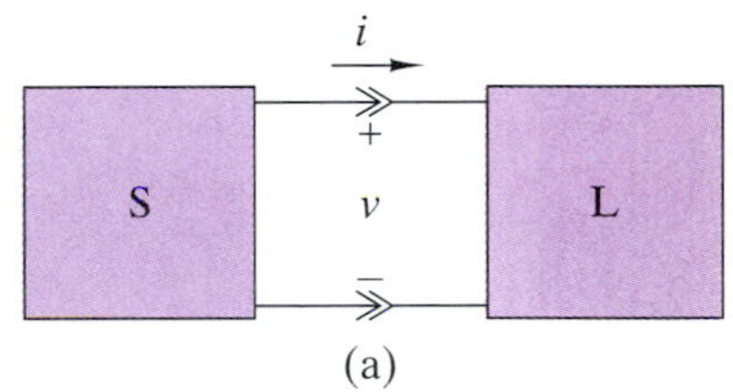

(a)

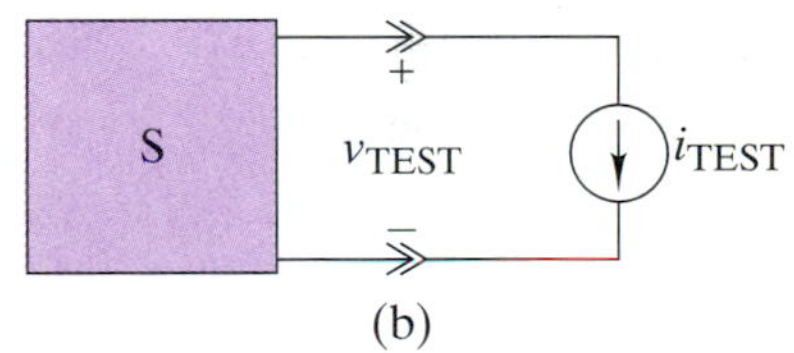

(b)

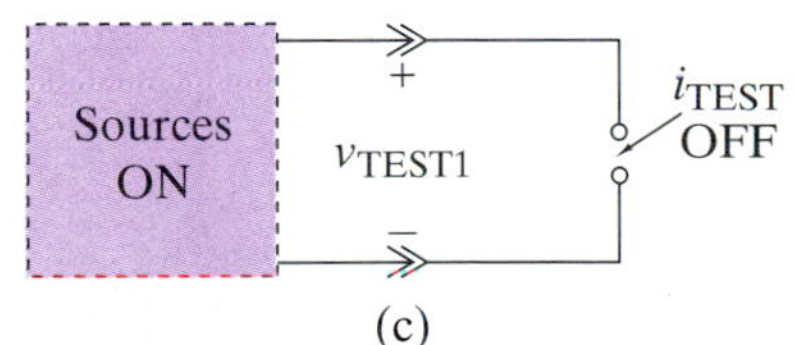

(c)

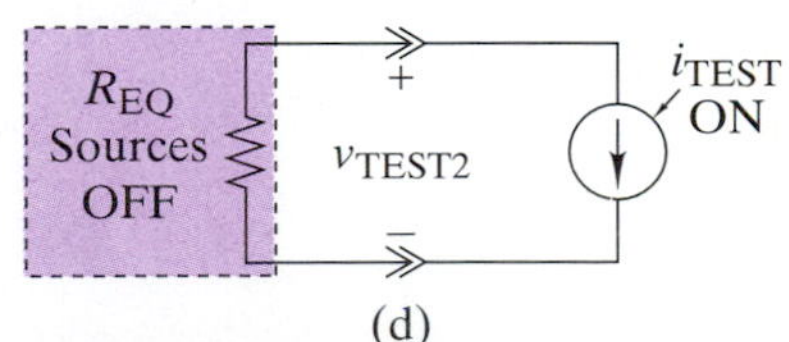

(d)

FIGURE 3–44 *Using superposition to prove Thévenin's theorem.*

$$v_{TEST} = v_{TEST1} + v_{TEST2}$$
$$= v_{OC} - R_{EQ}i_{TEST}$$

This equation has the same form as the i–v relationship of the Thévenin equivalent circuit in Eq. (3–23) when $v_{TEST} = v$, $i_{TEST} = i$, $v_{OC} = v_T$, and $R_T = R_{EQ}$.

The derivation points out another method of finding the Thévenin resistance. As indicated in Figure 3–44(d), when all the sources are turned off the i–v relationship of the source circuit reduces to $v = -iR_{EQ}$. Similarly, the i–v relationship of a Thévenin equivalent circuit reduces to $v = -iR_T$ when $v_T = 0$. We conclude that

$$R_T = R_{EQ} \tag{3–28}$$

We can find the value of R_T by determining the resistance seen looking back into the source circuit with all sources turned off. For this reason the Thévenin resistance R_T is sometimes called the **lookback resistance**.

The next example shows how lookback resistance contributes to finding a Thévenin equivalent circuit.

EXAMPLE 3–15

(a) Find the Thévenin equivalent of the source circuit to the left of the interface in Figure 3–45.

(b) Use the Thévenin equivalent to find the voltage delivered to the load.

FIGURE 3–45

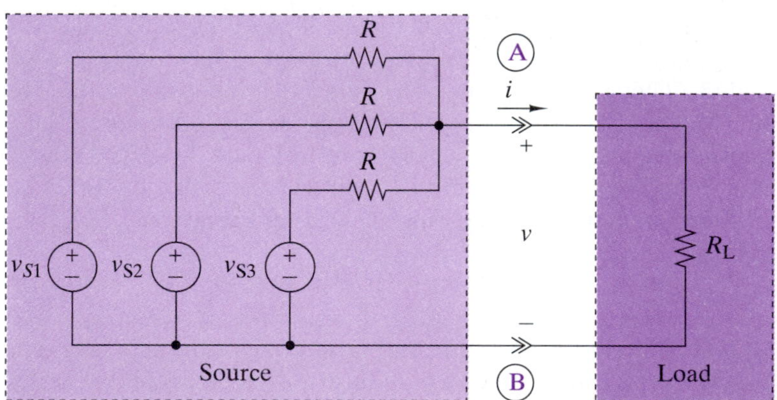

SOLUTION:

(a) The source circuit in Figure 3–45 is treated in Example 3–12 by using superposition to calculate the open-circuit voltage between terminals A and B. Using the results from Example 3–12, we have

$$v_T = v_{OC} = \frac{1}{3}(v_{S1} + v_{S2} + v_{S3})$$

Turning all sources off in the Figure 3–45 leads to the resistance circuit in Figure 3–46. Looking back into the source circuit in Figure 3–46, we see three equal resistances connected in parallel whose equivalent resistance is $R/3$. Hence, the Thévenin resistance is

$$R_T = R_{EQ} = \frac{R}{3}$$

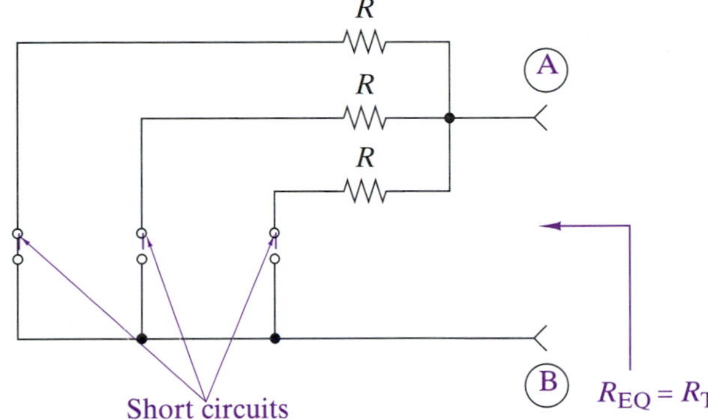

FIGURE 3–46

(b) Given the Thévenin circuit parameters v_T and R_T, we apply voltage division in Figure 3–45 to find the interface voltage.

$$v = \frac{R_L}{R_L + R_T} v_T = \left(\frac{R_L}{R_L + R/3}\right)\left(\frac{v_{S1} + v_{S2} + v_{S3}}{3}\right)$$

$$= \left(\frac{R_L}{3R_L + R}\right)(v_{S1} + v_{S2} + v_{S3})$$

The interface voltage is proportional to the sum of the three source voltages. The proportionality constant $K = R_L/(3R_L + R)$ depends on both the source and the load since these two circuits are connected at the interface. ■

Exercise 3–16

(a) Find the Thévenin and Norton equivalent circuits seen by the load in Figure 3–47.
(b) Find the voltage, current, and power delivered to a 50-Ω load resistor.

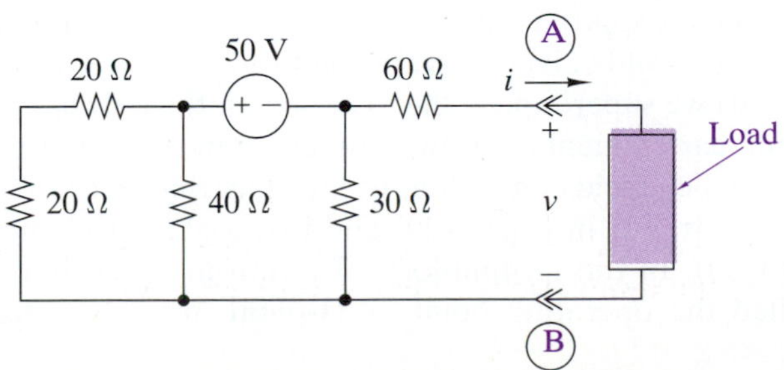

FIGURE 3–47

Answers:

(a) $v_T = -30$ V, $i_N = -417$ mA, $R_N = R_T = 72\ \Omega$
(b) $v = -12.3$ V, $i = -246$ mA, $p = 3.03$ W

Exercise 3–17

Find the current and power delivered to an unknown load in Figure 3–47 when $v = +6$ V.

Answers:

$i = -½\text{A}, p = -3\text{ W}$

APPLICATION TO NONLINEAR LOADS

Thévenin and Norton equivalent circuits can be used to find the response of a two-terminal nonlinear element (NLE). The method of analysis is a straightforward application of device and interface *i–v* characteristics. An interface is defined at the terminals of the nonlinear element, and the linear part of the circuit is reduced to the Thévenin equivalent in Figure 3–48(a). The *i–v* relationship of the Thévenin equivalent can be written with interface current as the dependent variable:

$$i = \left(-\frac{1}{R_T}\right)v + \left(\frac{v_T}{R_T}\right) \qquad (3-29)$$

This is the equation of a straight line in the *i–v* plane shown in Figure 3–48(b). The line intersects the *i*-axis ($v = 0$) at $i = v_T/R_T = i_{SC}$ and intersects the *v*–axis ($i = 0$) at $v = v_T = v_{OC}$. This line could logically be called the source line since it is determined by the Thévenin parameters of the source circuit. Logic notwithstanding, electrical engineers call this the **load line** for reasons that have blurred with the passage of time.

The nonlinear element has the *i–v* characteristic shown in Figure 3–48(c). Mathematically, this nonlinear characteristic has the form

$$i = f(v) \qquad (3-30)$$

To find the circuit response, we must solve Eqs. (3–29) and (3–30) simultaneously. Computer software tools like Mathcad can easily solve this problem when a numerical expression for the function $f(v)$ is known explicitly. However, in practice an approximate graphical solution is often adequate, particularly when $f(v)$ is only given in graphical form.

In Figure 3–48(d) we superimpose the load line on the *i–v* characteristic curve of the nonlinear element. The two curves intersect at the point $i = i_{NLE}$ and $v = v_{NLE}$, which yields the values of interface variables that satisfy both the source constraints in Eq. (3–29) and the nonlinear element constraints in Eq. (3–30). In the terminology of electronics, the point of intersection is called the operating point or **Q-point**, where Q stands for quiescent.

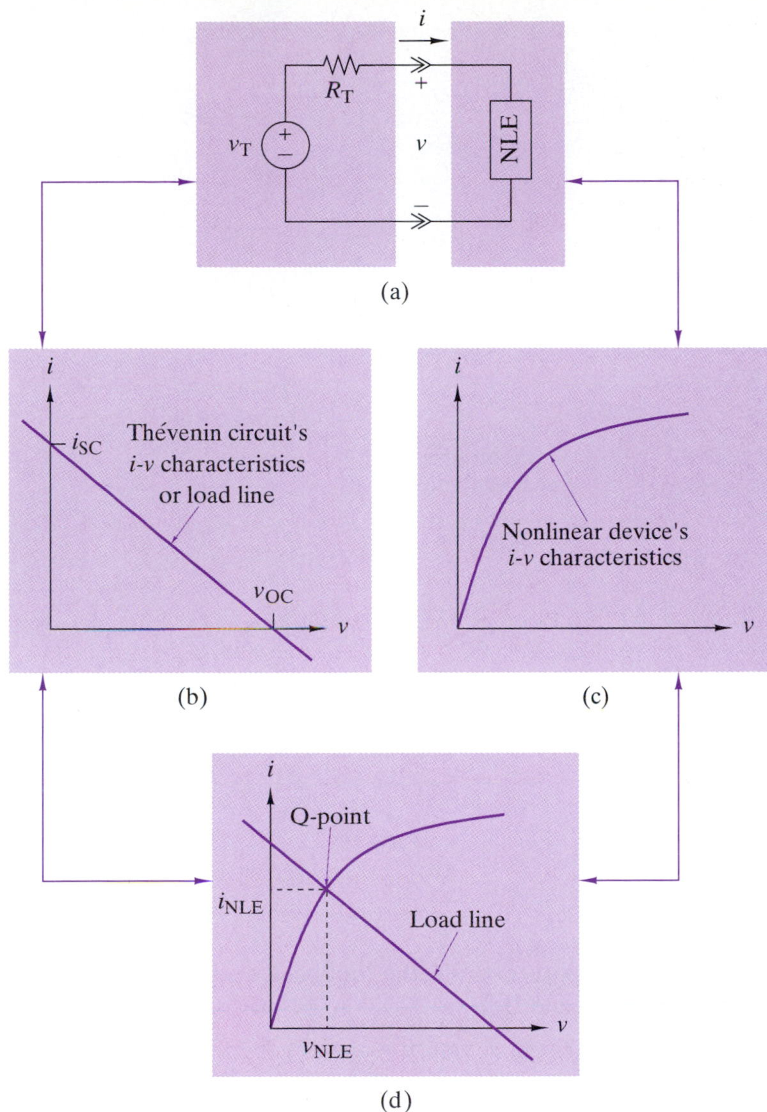

FIGURE 3–48 *Graphical analysis of a nonlinear circuit: (a) Given circuit. (b) Load line. (c) Nonlinear device i–v characteristics. (d) Q-point.*

EXAMPLE 3–16

Find the voltage, current, and power delivered to the diode in Figure 3–49(a).

SOLUTION:

We first find the Thévenin equivalent of the circuit to left of the terminals A and B. By voltage division, the open-circuit voltage is

$$v_T = v_{OC} = \frac{100}{100 + 100} \times 5 = 2.5 \text{ V}$$

FIGURE 3–49

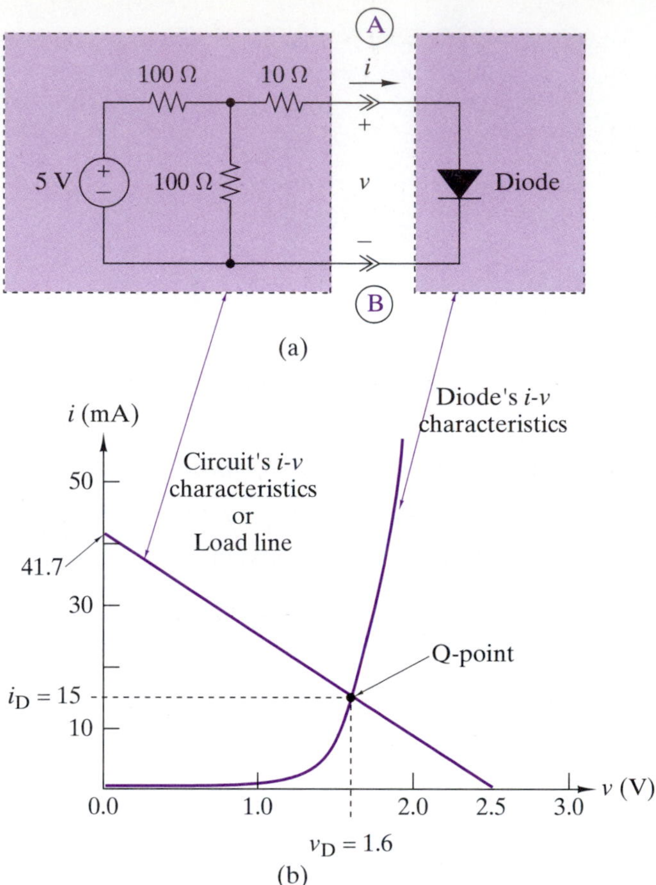

When the voltage source is turned off, the lookback equivalent resistance seen between terminals A and B is

$$R_T = 10 + 100 \| 100 = 60\ \Omega$$

The source circuit load line is given by

$$i = -\frac{1}{60}v + \frac{1}{60} \times 2.5$$

This line intersects the i-axis ($v = 0$) at $i = i_{SC} = 2.5/60 = 41.7$ mA and intersects the v–axis ($i = 0$) at $v = v_{OC} = 2.5$ V. Figure 3–49(b) superimposes the source circuit load line on the diode's i–v curve. The intersection (Q-point) is at $i = i_D = 15$ mA and $v = v_D = 1.6$ V. This is the point (i_D,v_D) at which both the source and diode device constraints are satisfied. Finally, the power delivered to the diode is

$$p_D = i_D v_D = (15 \times 10^{-3})(1.6) = 24 \text{ mW}$$

Because of the nonlinear element, the proportionality and superposition properties do not apply to this circuit. For instance, if the source voltage in

Figure 3–49 is decreased from 5 V to 2.5 V, the diode current and voltage do not decrease by one-half. Try it. ■

Exercise 3–18

Find the voltage, current, and power delivered to the diode in Figure 3–49(a) when the 10-Ω resistor is replaced by a short circuit.

Answer:

$v_D = 1.7$ V, $i_D = 18$ mA, and $p_D = 30.6$ mW

In summary, any two of the following parameters determine the Thévenin or Norton equivalent circuit at a specified interface:

- The open-circuit voltage at the interface
- The short-circuit current at the interface
- The source circuit lookback resistance.

Alternatively, for ladder circuits the Thévenin or Norton equivalent circuit can be found by a sequence of circuit reductions (see Example 3–13). For general circuits they can always be found by directly solving for the *i–v* relationship of the source circuit using node-voltage or mesh-current equations that include the interface current and voltage as unknowns (see Example 3–14).

3–5 MAXIMUM SIGNAL TRANSFER

An interface is a connection between two circuits at which the signal levels may be observed or specified. In this regard an important consideration is the maximum signal levels that can be transferred across a given interface. This section defines the maximum voltage, current, and power available at an interface between a *fixed source* and an *adjustable load.*

For simplicity we will treat the case in which both the source and load are linear resistance circuits. The source can be represented by a Thévenin equivalent and the load by an equivalent resistance R_L, as shown in Figure 3–50. For a fixed source, the parameters v_T and R_T are given and the interface signal levels are functions of the load resistance R_L.

By voltage division, the interface voltage is

$$v = \frac{R_L}{R_L + R_T} v_T \tag{3-31}$$

For a fixed source and a variable load, the voltage will be a maximum if R_L is made very large compared with R_T. Ideally, R_L should be made infinite (an open circuit), in which case

$$v_{MAX} = v_T = v_{OC} \tag{3-32}$$

Therefore, the maximum voltage available at the interface is the source open-circuit voltage v_{OC}.

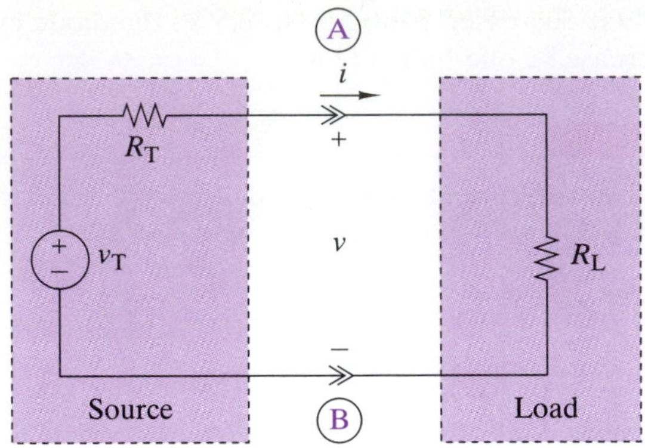

FIGURE 3–50 *Two-terminal interface for deriving the maximum signal transfer conditions.*

The current delivered at the interface is

$$i = \frac{v_T}{R_L + R_T} \tag{3–33}$$

For a fixed source and a variable load, the current will be a maximum if R_L is made very small compared with R_T. Ideally, R_L should be zero (a short circuit), in which case

$$i_{MAX} = \frac{v_T}{R_T} = i_N = i_{SC} \tag{3–34}$$

Therefore, the maximum current available at the interface is the source short-circuit current i_{SC}.

The power delivered at the interface is equal to the product $v \times i$. Using Eqs. (3–31) and (3–33), the power is

$$\begin{aligned} p &= v \times i \\ &= \frac{R_L v_T^2}{(R_L + R_T)^2} \end{aligned} \tag{3–35}$$

For a given source, the parameters v_T and R_T are fixed and the delivered power is a function of a single variable R_L. The condition for maximum voltage ($R_L \to \infty$) and the condition for maximum current ($R_L = 0$) both produce zero power. The value of R_L that maximizes the power lies somewhere between these two extremes. To find this value, we differentiate Eq. (3–35) with respect to R_L and solve for the value of R_L for which $dp/dR_L = 0$.

$$\frac{dp}{dR_L} = \frac{[(R_L + R_T)^2 - 2R_L(R_L + R_T)]v_T^2}{(R_L + R_T)^4} = \frac{R_T - R_L}{(R_L + R_T)^3} v_T^2 = 0 \tag{3–36}$$

Clearly, the derivative is zero when $R_L = R_T$. Therefore, **maximum power transfer** occurs when the load resistance equals the Thévenin resistance of the source. When the condition $R_L = R_T$ exists, the source and load are said to be **matched**.

Substituting the condition $R_L = R_T$ back into Eq. (3–35) shows the maximum power to be

$$p_{MAX} = \frac{v_T^2}{4R_T} \quad (3\text{–}37)$$

Since $v_T = i_N R_T$, this result can also be written as

$$p_{MAX} = \frac{i_N^2 R_T}{4} \quad (3\text{–}38)$$

or

$$p_{MAX} = \frac{v_T i_N}{4} = \left[\frac{v_{OC}}{2}\right]\left[\frac{i_{SC}}{2}\right] \quad (3\text{–}39)$$

These equations are consequences of what is known as the **maximum power transfer theorem**:

A source with a fixed Thévenin resistance R_T delivers maximum power to an adjustable load R_L when $R_L = R_T$.

To summarize, at an interface with a fixed source,

1. The maximum available voltage is the open-circuit voltage.
2. The maximum available current is the short-circuit current.
3. The maximum available power is the product of one-half the open-circuit voltage times one-half the short-circuit current.

Figure 3–51 shows plots of the interface voltage, current, and power as functions of R_L/R_T. The plots of v/v_{OC}, i/i_{SC}, and p/p_{MAX} are normalized to the maximum available signal levels, so the ordinates in Figure 3–51 range from 0 to 1. The plot of the normalized power p/p_{MAX} in the neighborhood of the maximum is not a particularly strong function of R_L/R_T. Changing the ratio R_L/R_T by a factor of 2 in either direction from the maximum reduces p/p_{MAX} by less than 20%. The normalized voltage v/v_{OC} is within 20% of its maximum when $R_L/R_T = 4$. Similarly, the normalized current is within 20% of its maximum when $R_L/R_T = ¼$. In other words, for engineering purposes we can get close to the maximum signal levels with load resistances that only approximate the theoretical requirements.

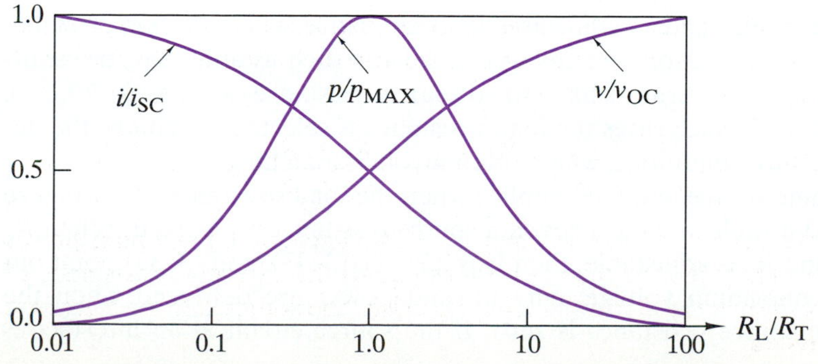

FIGURE 3–51 *Normalized plots of current, voltage, and power versus R_L/R_T.*

EXAMPLE 3–17

Determine the maximum signals available from the source circuit in Example 3–16.

SOLUTION:

In Example 3–16 we found $v_T = 2.5$ V and $R_T = 60\ \Omega$. The maximum available voltage and current are

$$v_{MAX} = v_{OC} = v_T = 2.5\text{ V } (R_L \to \infty)$$

$$i_{MAX} = i_{SC} = \frac{v_T}{R_T} = 41.7\text{ mA } (R_L = 0)$$

Using Eq. (3–39), the maximum available power is

$$p_{MAX} = \left[\frac{v_{OC}}{2}\right]\left[\frac{i_{SC}}{2}\right] = 26.0\text{ mW } (R_L = R_T = 60\ \Omega)$$

In Example 3–16 we found that a nonlinear element actually drew the following signal levels from the source:

$$v_D = 1.6\text{ V}$$

$$i_D = 15\text{ mA}$$

$$p_D = 24\text{ mW}$$

These levels are less than the maximum available values. However, the power delivered to the diode is nearly the same as the maximum available even though the nonlinear diode clearly does not "match" the source resistance. ■

Exercise 3–19

A resistive source circuit delivers 4 V when a 50-Ω resistor is connected across its output and 5 V when a 75-Ω resistor is connected. Find the maximum voltage, current, and power available from the source.

Answers:

10 V, 133 mA, and 333 mW

Remember that the maximum signal levels just derived are for a fixed source resistance and an adjustable load resistance. This situation often occurs in communication systems where devices such as antennas, transmitters, and signal generators have fixed source resistances such as 50, 75, 300, or 600 ohms. In such cases the load resistance is selected to achieve the desired interface conditions, which often involves matching.

Matching source and load applies when the load resistance R_L in Figure 3–50 is adjustable and the Thévenin source resistance R_T is fixed. When R_L is fixed and R_T is adjustable, then Eqs. (3–31), (3–33), and (3–35) point out that the maximum voltage, current, and power are delivered when the Thévenin source resistance is zero. If the source circuit at an interface is adjustable, then ideally the Thévenin source resistance should be zero. In the next chapter we will see that OP AMP circuits approach this ideal.

3–6 INTERFACE CIRCUIT DESIGN

The maximum signal levels discussed in the previous section place bounds on what is achievable at an interface. However, those bounds are based on a fixed source and an adjustable load. In practice, there are circumstances in which the source or the load, or both, can be adjusted to produce prescribed interface signal levels. Sometimes it is necessary to insert a circuit between the source and the load to achieve the desired results. Figure 3–52 shows the general situations and some examples of resistive interface circuits. By its nature, the inserted circuit has two terminal pairs, or interfaces, at which voltage and current can be observed or specified. These terminal pairs are also called *ports,* and the interface circuit is referred to as a **two-port network**. The port connected to the source is called the input, and the port connected to the load is called the output. The purpose of this two-port network is to make certain that the source and load interact in a prescribed way.

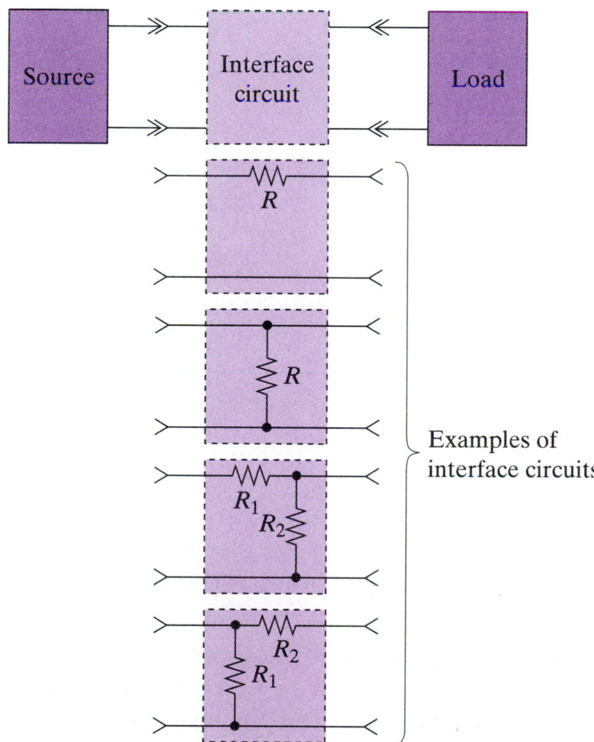

FIGURE 3–52 *A general interface circuit and some examples.*

BASIC CIRCUIT DESIGN CONCEPTS

Before we treat examples of different interface situations, you should recognize that we are now discussing a limited form of circuit design, as contrasted with circuit analysis. Although we use circuit analysis tools in design, there are important differences. A linear circuit analysis problem generally has a unique solution. A circuit design problem may have many solutions or even no solution. The maximum available signal levels found in the preceding section provide bounds that help us test for the existence of a solution. Generally there will be several ways to meet the interface constraints, and it then becomes necessary to evaluate the alternatives using other factors, such as cost, power consumption, or reliability.

At this point in our study, resistors are the only elements we can use to design interface circuits. In subsequent chapters we will introduce other devices, such as OP AMPs (Chapter 4) and capacitors and inductors (Chapter 6). In a design situation the engineer must choose the resistance values in a proposed circuit. This decision is influenced by a host of practical considerations, such as standard values and tolerances, power ratings, temperature sensitivity, cost, and fabrication methods. Some of these issues are discussed in Appendix A. We will occasionally introduce some of these considerations into our design examples. Gaining a full understanding of these practical matters is not one of our en route objectives. Rather, our goal is simply to illustrate how different constraints can influence the design process.

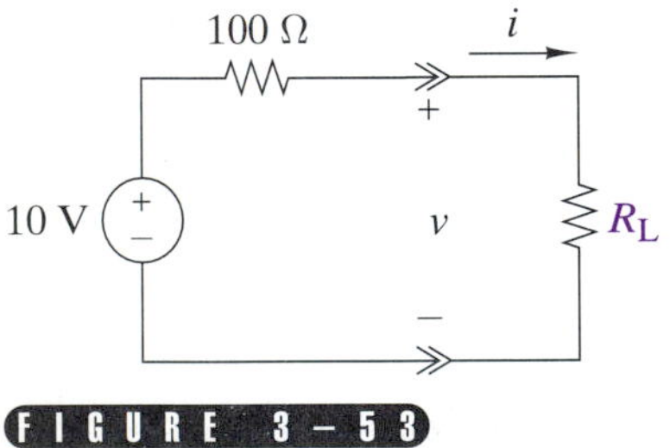

FIGURE 3–53

D DESIGN EXAMPLE 3–18

Selecting a Load Resistance

Select the load resistance in Figure 3–53 so that the interface signals are in the range defined by $v \geq 4$ V and $i \geq 30$ mA.

SOLUTION:

In this design problem, the source circuit is given and we are free to select the load. For a fixed source the maximum signal levels available at the interface are

$$v_{MAX} = v_T = 10 \text{ V}$$

$$i_{MAX} = \frac{v_T}{R_T} = 100 \text{ mA}$$

The bounds given as design requirements are below the maximum available signal levels, so we should be able to find a suitable resistor. Using voltage division, the interface voltage constraint requires

$$\frac{R_L}{100 + R_L} \times 10 \geqslant 4$$

or

$$10R_L \geqslant 4R_L + 400$$

This condition yields $R_L \geq 400/6 = 66.7\ \Omega$. The interface current constraint can be written as

$$\frac{10}{100 + R_L} \geqslant 0.03$$

or

$$10 \geqslant 3 + 0.03R_L$$

which requires $R_L \leq 7/0.03 = 233\ \Omega$. In theory, any value of R_L between 66.7 Ω and 233 Ω will work. However, to allow for parameter variations we select $R_L = 150\ \Omega$ because it lies at the arithmetic midpoint of the allowable range and is a standard value of resistance (see Table A–1, Appendix A). ■

D DESIGN EXAMPLE 3–19

Designing with Standard Values

Select the load resistor in Figure 3–53 so that the voltage delivered to the load is 3 V ±10%. Use only a the standard resistance value given in Appendix A for ±10% tolerance.

SOLUTION:

The ±10% voltage tolerance means that the interface voltage must fall between 2.7 V and 3.3 V. The required range can be achieved since the open-circuit voltage of the source circuit is 10 V. Using voltage division, we can write the constraints on the value of R_L:

$$2.7 \leqslant \frac{R_L}{100 + R_L} \times 10 \leqslant 3.3$$

The left inequality requires

$$270 + 2.7R_L \leqslant 10R_L$$

or $R_L \geq 270/7.3 = 37.0\ \Omega$. The right inequality requires

$$10R_L \leqslant 330 + 3.3R_L$$

or $R_L \leq 330/6.7 = 49.2\ \Omega$. Thus, R_L must lie in the range from 37.0 Ω to 49.2 Ω, which has a midpoint at 43.1 Ω.

Commercial resistors are not available in infinitely many values. To limit inventory costs, the electronic industry has agreed on a finite set of standard resistance values. For resistors with ±10% tolerance the standard values are

10 12 15 18 22 27 33 39 47 56 68 82 Ω

and multiples of 10 times these values. The standard values of 39 Ω and 47 Ω fall within the required 37.0 to 49.2 Ω range. However, these nominal values and the ±10% tolerance could carry the actual resistance value outside the range. Various series and parallel combinations of standard ±10% resistors produce values that fall in the desired range even with 10% tolerance. For example, two 22-Ω resistors connected in series produce a nominal equivalent resistance of 44 Ω with a ±10% range from 39.6 Ω to 48.4 Ω. Finally, it turns out that 43 Ω is a standard value for resistors with ±5% tolerance (see Appendix A, Table A–1). This option is attractive since 43 Ω falls almost exactly at the midpoint of the desired resistance range and the 5% tolerance easily meets the interface voltage range requirement.

In summary, either a standard 39-Ω resistor or a standard 47-Ω resistor produces nominal designs that meet the design requirements, but the 10% tolerance on the resistance could cause the voltage to fall outside the specified range. Series and parallel combinations of two 10% resistors meet all requirements but lead to a more complicated and costly design. A single 43-Ω 5% resistor meets all requirements, but its tighter tolerance could mean higher parts costs than two 10% resistors. The final design decision must take into account many factors, particularly the sensitivity of the system to changes in the specified interface voltage. ■

D DESIGN EXAMPLE 3–20

Designing with Resistance Arrays

The resistance array package shown in Figure 3–54 includes seven nearly identical resistors with nominal resistances of 1 kΩ. Use this resistance array to design a voltage divider that reduces the output of a 10-V dc power supply to 4.3 V.

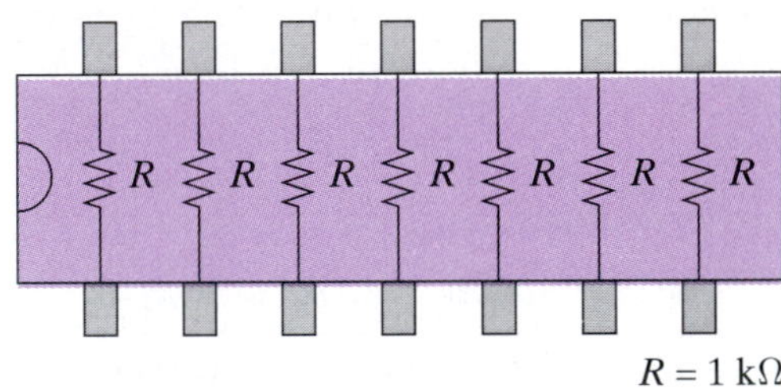

SOLUTION:

The required interface voltage is well within the capability of a 10-V source. Using voltage division, we can express the design requirement as

$$\frac{R_2}{R_1 + R_2} \times 10 = 4.3$$

where R_1 and R_2 are the series and shunt legs of the divider, respectively. This design constraint can be rearranged as

$$\frac{R_1}{R_2} = 1.33$$

In other words, the design requirement imposes a constraint on the ratio of R_1 and R_2.

Resistance array packages are particularly useful when the design constraints involve resistance ratios. The nominal resistance can change from one array to the next, but within a given array the resistances are all nearly equal, so their ratios are nearly unity. In effect, the resistance array in Figure 3–54 contains seven identical resistors, although we do not know the exact value of their resistance. Constructing the series leg using three resistors in parallel and the shunt leg using four resistors in parallel produces $R_1 = R/3$ and $R_2 = R/4$, where R is nominally 1 kΩ. But regardless of the actual value of R, the ratio $R_1/R_2 = 1.33$ as required.

The final design shown in Figure 3–55 may seem wasteful of resistors. However, in large-volume production an integrated circuit resistance array can cost less than a discrete resistor design. Resistance array packages are better suited to automated manufacturing than discrete resistors. The point is that estimating the cost of producing a circuit is not simply a matter of counting the number of resistors. ■

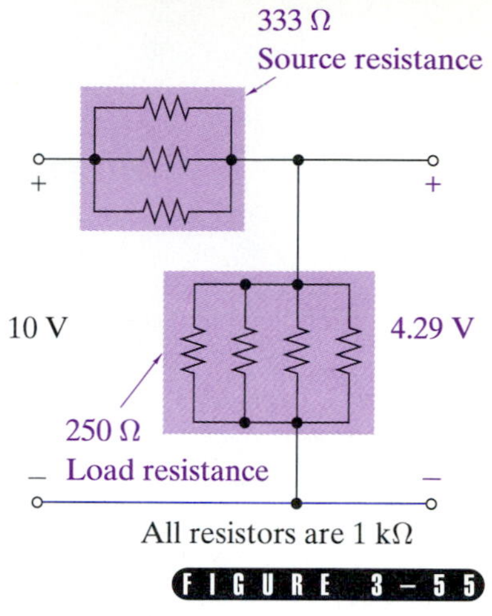

FIGURE 3–55

DESIGN EXAMPLE 3–21

Two-Port Circuit Design

Design the two-port interface circuit in Figure 3–56 so the 10-A source delivers 100 V to the 50-Ω load.

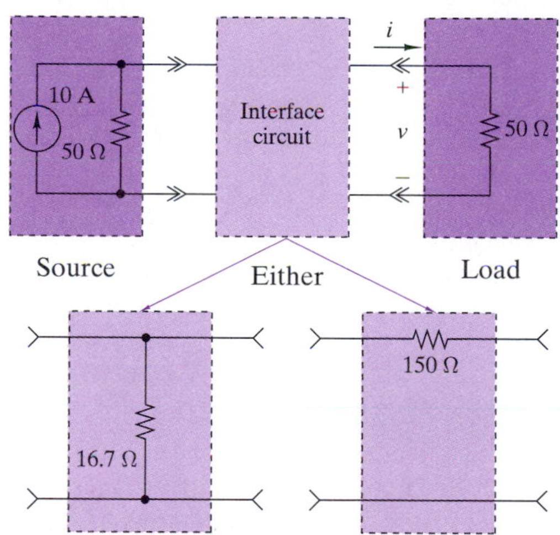

FIGURE 3–56

SOLUTION:

The problem requires that the current delivered to the load to be $i = 100/50 = 2$ A, which is well within the maximum value of current available from the source. In fact, if the 10-A source is connected directly to the load, the source current divides equally between two 50-Ω resistances, producing 5 A through the load. Therefore, an interface circuit is needed to reduce the load current to the specified 2-A level. Two possible design solutions are shown in Figure 3–56. Applying current division to the parallel resistor case yields the following constraint:

$$i = \frac{1/50}{1/50 + 1/50 + 1/R_{PAR}} \times 10$$

After inserting the $i = 2$ A design requirement, this equation becomes

$$2 = \frac{10}{2 + 50/R_{PAR}}$$

Solving for R_{PAR} yields

$$R_{PAR} = \frac{50}{3} = 16.7\ \Omega$$

Applying the two-path current division rule to the series resistor case yields the following constraint:

$$i = \frac{50}{50 + (50 + R_{SER})} \times 10 = 2\text{ A}$$

Solving for R_{SER} yields

$$R_{SER} = 150\ \Omega$$

We have two designs that meet the basic $i = 2$ A requirement. In practice, engineers evaluate alternative designs using additional criteria. One such consideration is the required power ratings of the resistors in each design. The voltage across the parallel resistor is $v = 100$ V, so the power loss is

$$p_{PAR} = \frac{100^2}{50/3} = 600\text{ W}$$

The current through the series resistor interface is $i = 2$ A, so the power loss is

$$p_{SER} = 2^2 \times 150 = 600\text{ W}$$

In either design the resistors must have a power rating of at least 600 W. Other factors besides power rating determine which design should be selected. ■

D DESIGN EXAMPLE 3–22

Nonlinear Device Circuit Design

An application calls for a nonlinear element (NLE) to be driven by the source circuit shown in Figure 3–57(a). The manufacturer's data sheet provides the element i–v characteristic shown as the heavy blue line in Figure 3–57(b). The maximum allowable power dissipation in the device is listed as 20 mW. The data sheet also states that at least 1 V must appear across the device for optimal performance. Design the two-port interface circuit in Figure 3–57(a) to produce an operating point for the NLE with $v > 1$ V and $p = vi < 20$ mW.

SOLUTION:

The operating point must lie within the unshaded region shown in Figure 3–57(b). The left boundary of the unshaded region is determined by the requirement that $v > 1$ V. Curves of constant power dissipation are shown in Figure 3–57(b). The curve corresponding to $p = 20$ mW forms the right boundary of the unshaded region.

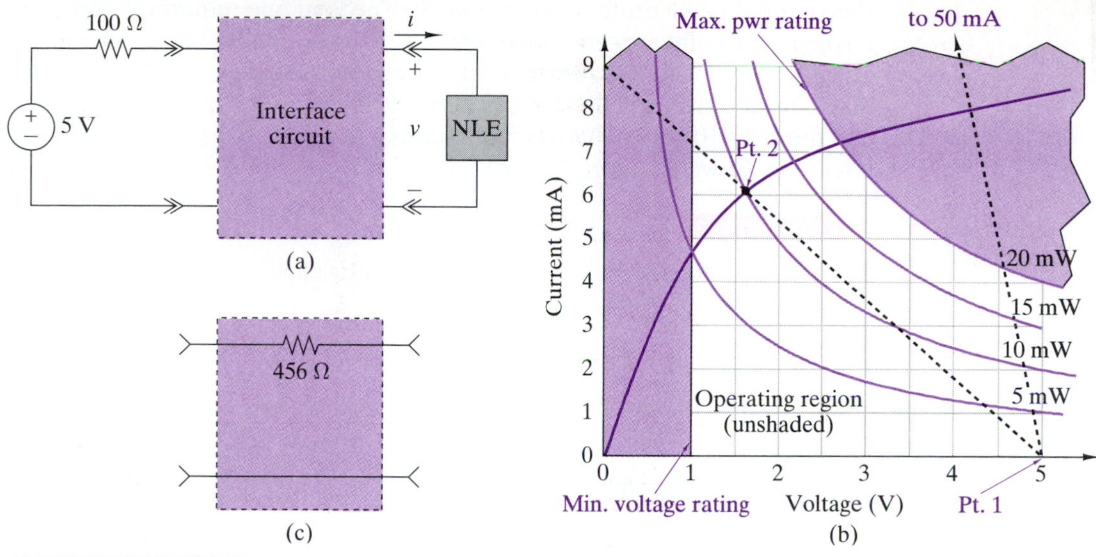

FIGURE 3–57

We first check to see if an interface circuit is actually required. This is accomplished by finding the operating point in Figure 3–57(b) when the 5-V source is connected directly to the NLE. With no interface circuit, the NLE sees a source with v_{OC} = 5 V and i_{SC} = 5/100 = 50 mA. The corresponding load line intercepts the abscissa in Figure 3–57(b) at $v = v_{OC}$ = 5 V and the ordinate axis at $i = i_{SC}$ = 50 mA. The 50-mA intercept is well off the graph in Figure 3–57(b). Nevertheless, we see that the intersection of this load line and the NLE i–v characteristic fall inside the shaded region. In other words, with no interface circuit the source delivers more than 20 mW to the NLE.

We can reduce the power dissipated in the NLE by inserting a series resistor in the interface circuit. The series resistor reduces the available short-circuit current but does not change the open-circuit voltage available at the terminals of the NLE. In effect, a series resistance causes the load line to pivot about point 1 (Pt. 1) in Figure 3–57(b). For example, 900-Ω of series resistance rotates the load line so it intercepts the ordinate at $i = i_{SC}$ = 5/1000 = 5 mA. The design problem reduces to selecting a series resistance that pivots the load line about point 1 until it goes through the desired operating point. The question is, where should we locate the device, at the operating or at the Q-point?

The manufacturer's data sheet states that the device cannot dissipate more than 20 mW. To prolong their useful life, it is common practice to "derate" devices (that is, to operate devices below their maximum power rating). Curves of constant power dissipation are shown on the NLE characteristic in Figure 3–57(b). The curve corresponding to 10 mW dissipation crosses the device's i–v characteristics at point 2 (Pt. 2) in the figure. This point offers a reasonable operating point, since the device voltage is greater than 1 V and the power dissipation is "derated" by a factor of 2. When the load line is pivoted until it intersects the NLE i–v characteristics at point 2, it then intersects the ordinate axis at 9 mA. The load line required to produce an operating point at point 2 in Figure 3–57(b) is defined by $v_{OC} = 5$ V and $i_{SC} = 9$ mA. The total series resistance required to produce $v_{OC} = 5$ V and $i_{SC} = 9$ mA at the terminal of the NLE is $R_{SER} = 5/0.009 = 556\ \Omega$. Since the source circuit provides 100 Ω, we add a 456-Ω series resistor in the interface two-port circuit, as shown in Figure 3–57(c). ■

Exercise 3–20

Find the value of series resistance so the NLE in Example 3–22 operates with 5 mW of power dissipation.

Answer:

733 Ω

D DESIGN EXAMPLE 3–23

Matching Two-Port Design

Design the two-port interface circuit in Figure 3–58 so the load "sees" a Thévenin resistance of 50 Ω between terminals C and D, while simultaneously the source "sees" a load resistance of 300 Ω between A and B.

SOLUTION:

We first try a single resistor in the interface circuit. A 60-Ω parallel resistor in the interface circuit would make the load see 50 Ω Thévenin resistance, but then the source would see a load resistance much less than 300 Ω. A 250-Ω series resistor in the interface circuit would make the source see a 300-Ω load, but then the load would see a Thévenin resistance much greater than 50 Ω.

We next try an interface circuit containing two resistors. Since the load must see a smaller resistance than the source, it should "look" into a parallel resistor. On the other hand, since the source must see a larger resistance than the load, it should look into a series resistor. A configuration that meets these conditions is the L-circuit shown in Figures 3–58(b) and 3–58(c).

The preceding discussion can be summarized mathematically. Using the L-circuit, the design requirement at terminals C and D is

$$\frac{(R_1 + 300)\,R_2}{R_1 + 300 + R_2} = 50\ \Omega$$

At terminals A and B, the requirement is

$$R_1 + \frac{50\,R_2}{R_2 + 50} = 300\ \Omega$$

The design requirements yield two equations in two unknowns; what could be simpler? It turns out that solving these nonlinear equations by hand analysis is a bit of a chore. These equations can easily be solved using a math solver, as we will shortly demonstrate. However, at this point in your development we encourage you to think about the problem in physical terms.

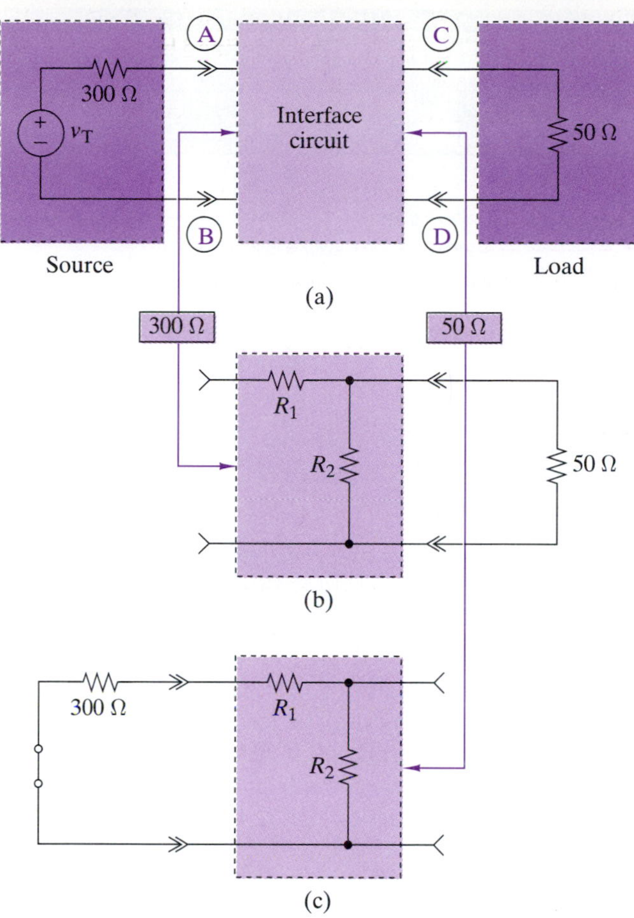

FIGURE 3–58

Given the L-circuits in Figure 3–58(b), one approach goes as follows. If we let $R_2 = 50$ ohms, then the requirement at terminals C and D will be met, at least approximately. Similarly, if $R_1 + R_2 = 300\ \Omega$, the requirements at terminals A and B will be approximately satisfied. In other words, try $R_1 = 250\ \Omega$ and $R_2 = 50\ \Omega$ as a first cut. These values yield equivalent resistances of $R_{CD} = 50 \| 550 = 45.8\ \Omega$ and $R_{AB} = 250 + 50 \| 50 = 275\ \Omega$. These equivalent resistances are not the exact values specified, but are within ± 10%. Since the tolerance on electrical components may be at least this high, a design using these values could be adequate.

Figure 3–59 shows how Mathcad solves the two design equations to find the exact values of R_1 and R_2. The approximate values derived previously are used as the first estimates required by a Mathcad solve block. Mathcad uses these estimates in an iterative process to solve the design equations listed between the Given and the Find statements. The final results at the bottom in Figure 3–59 show that the approximate values derived from physical reasoning are within 10% of the exact values derived using Mathcad.

In this example we used physical reasoning to find an approximation solution of a problem. Using physical reasoning to find practical solutions is what engineering is all about. ■

FIGURE 3–59

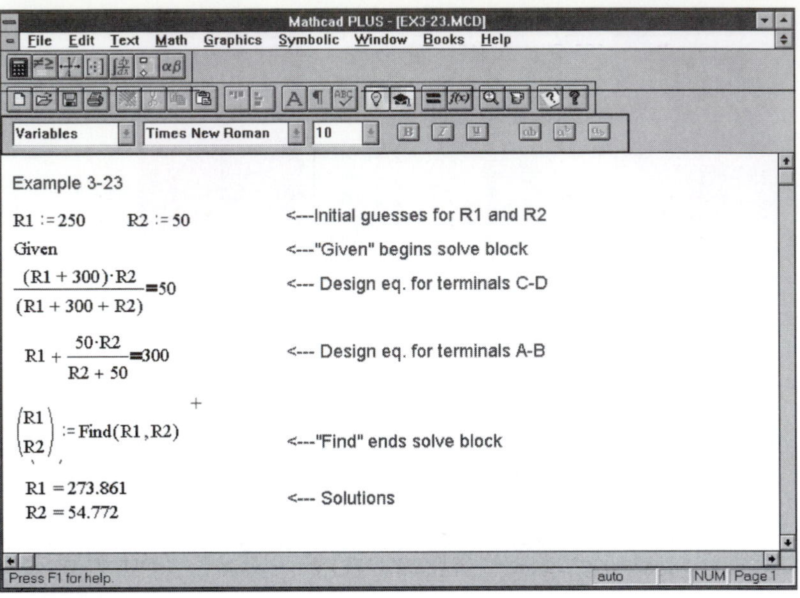

APPLICATION NOTE: EXAMPLE 3–24

An **attenuation pad** is a two-port resistance circuit that provides a non-adjustable reduction in signal level and provides resistance matching at the input and output ports. An example of an attenuation pad is shown in Figure 3–60. The manufacturer's data sheet states that the pad in Figure 3–60 has the following characteristics:

CHARACTERISTICS	PORT	CONDITION	VALUE	UNITS
Thévenin voltage	Output	600-Ω source connected at the input port	$v_S/4$	V
Thévenin resistance	Output	600-Ω source connected at the input port	600	Ω
Input resistance	Input	600-Ω load connected at the output port	600	Ω

Verify these characteristics.

SOLUTION:

MicroSim Design Center can be used to calculate the two-port circuit characteristics. Figure 3–61 shows the circuit diagram created using MicroSim Schematics. A 600-Ω source is connected at the input port (node A). The 600-Ω load is not connected since we want to find the Thévenin equivalent circuit seen looking back into the output port (node C). Under the **Analysis** menu we select **Analysis Set Up** and activate the **Transfer Function** option. Selecting the Transfer Function option produces the menu at the bottom left in Figure 3–61. Here we identify the output variable as V(C)—the voltage at node C. Note that V(C) is the open-circuit voltage at the output port. We also identify the input as the voltage source V1. With these selections PSpice will calculate three things: (1) the transfer function V(C)/V1, (2) the input resistance seen by V1, and (3) the output resistance at node C.

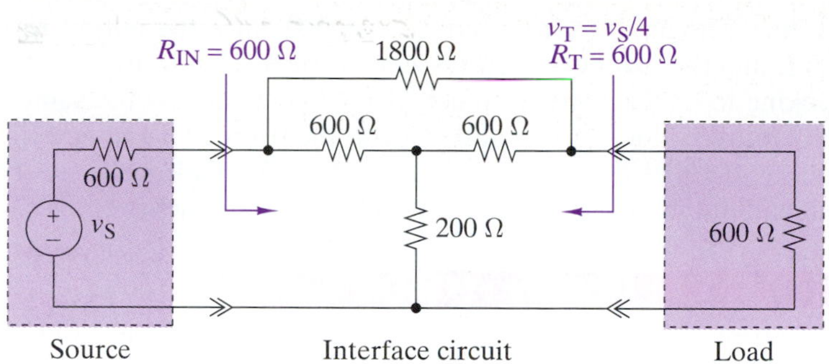

Returning to the **Analysis** menu, we select the **Simulate** command. MicroSim PSpice performs a dc analysis of the circuit and writes the results to an output file. Included in the output file are the small signal characteristics shown at the bottom right in Figure 3–61. PSpice reports that the transfer function V(C)/V1 is 2.500E–01, the input resistance is 1.280E+03, and the output resistance is 6.000E+02. That is, the open-circuit (Thévenin) voltage at the output port is exactly one-fourth of the source voltage and the output (Thévenin) resistance is 600 Ω, as advertised. The input resistance (1280 Ω) given in the output file is the resistance seen by the source V1 when the output port is an open circuit. The manufacturer specifies the input resistance looking in at node A when a 600-Ω load is connected at

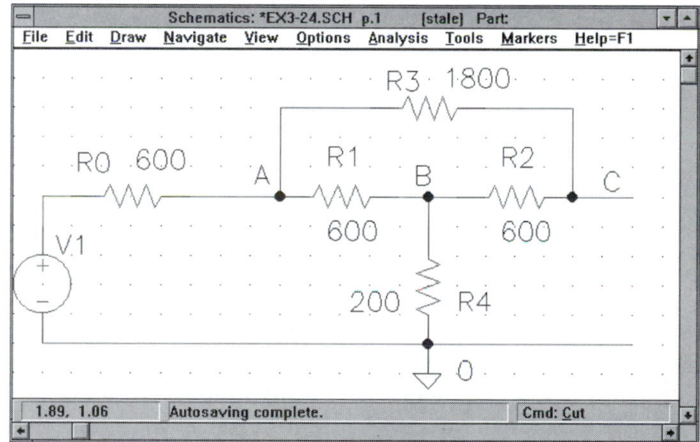

Transfer Function

Output Variable: V(C)

Input Source: V1

OK Cancel

Notepad - EX3-24.OUT

File Edit Search Help

```
****     SMALL-SIGNAL CHARACTERISTICS

         V(C)/V_V1 =   2.500E-01

         INPUT RESISTANCE AT V_V1 =   1.280E+03

         OUTPUT RESISTANCE AT V(C) =   6.000E+02
```

FIGURE 3-61

the output port. The input port resistance is 600 Ω since the output resistance is 600 Ω and the two-port circuit is symmetrical. That is, the input resistance looking in at node A with a 600-Ω load connected is the same as the output resistance looking in at node C with the source V1 turned off.

In summary, the pad reduces the signal voltage by one-fourth and has 600-Ω input and output resistances, as stated by the manufacturer. ■

D DESIGN EXERCISE: EXERCISE 3–21

Using only standard ±5% resistors, design the two-port interface circuit in Figure 3–62 to meet the following requirements:

(a) The power delivered to the 50-Ω load is 0.2 W ±5%.
(b) Repeat (a) for $p = 0.6$ W ±5%.

FIGURE 3–62

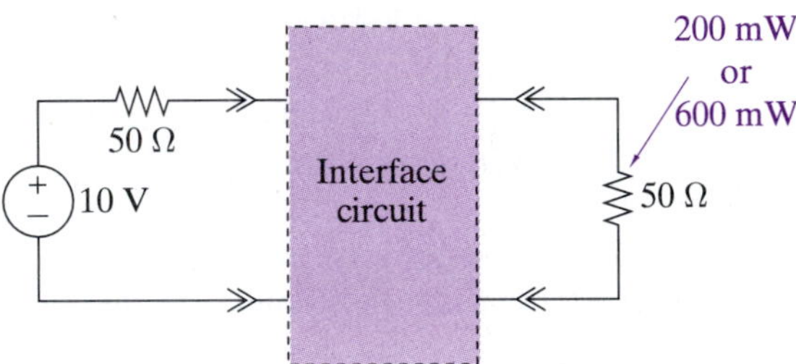

Answer: There are no unique answers to this problem. Some possibilities are discussed next.

DISCUSSION: *(a) A standard 56-Ω resistor in series (ideally 58.1 Ω) yields 200 mW ±5% into the 50-Ω load. (b) No resistive interface will work since the maximum power available from the source is only 0.5 W. Delivering more power than the signal source can provide requires an active device, such as an OP AMP or transistor (treated in the next chapter).*

SUMMARY

- Node-voltage analysis involves identifying a reference node and the node to datum voltages at the remaining $N - 1$ nodes. The KCL connection constraints at the $N - 1$ nonreference nodes combined with the element constraints written in terms of the node voltages produce $N - 1$ linear equations in the unknown node voltages.
- Mesh-current analysis involves identifying mesh currents that circulate around the perimeter of each mesh in a planar circuit. The KVL connection constraints around $E - N + 1$ meshes combined with the element constraints written in terms of the mesh currents produce $E - N + 1$ linear equations in the unknown mesh currents.
- Node and mesh analysis can be modified to handle both types of independent sources using a combination of three methods: (1) source transformations, (2) selecting circuit variables so independent sources specify the values of some of the unknowns, and (3) using supernodes or supermeshes.

- A circuit is linear if it contains only linear elements and independent sources. For single-input linear circuits, the proportionality property states that any output is proportional to the input. For multiple-input linear circuits, the superposition principle states that any output can be found by summing the output produced when each input acts alone.
- A Thévenin equivalent circuit consists of a voltage source in series with a resistance. A Norton equivalent circuit consists of a current source in parallel with a resistance. The Thévenin and Norton equivalent circuits are related by a source transformation.
- The parameters of the Thévenin and Norton equivalent circuits can be determined using any two of the following: (1) the open-circuit voltage at the interface, (2) the short-circuit current at the interface, and (3) the equivalent resistance of the source circuit with all sources turned off.
- The parameters of the Thévenin and Norton equivalent circuits can also be determined using circuit reduction methods or by directly solving for the source i–v relationship using node-voltage or mesh-current analysis.
- For a fixed source and an adjustable load, the maximum interface signal levels are $v_{MAX} = v_{OC}$ $(R_L = \infty)$, $i_{MAX} = i_{SC}$ $(R_L = 0)$, and $p_{MAX} = v_{OC}i_{SC}/4$ $(R_L = R_T)$. When $R_L = R_T$, the source and load are said to be matched.
- Interface signal transfer conditions are specified in terms of the voltage, current, or power delivered to the load. The design constraints depend on the signal conditions specified and the circuit parameters that are adjustable. Some design requirements may require a two-port interface circuit. An interface design problem may have one, many, or no solutions.

EN ROUTE OBJECTIVES AND ASSOCIATED PROBLEMS

ERO 3–1 GENERAL CIRCUIT ANALYSIS (SECTS. 3–1 TO 3–2)

Given a circuit consisting of linear resistors and independent sources,

(a) (Formulation) Write node-voltage or mesh-current equations for the circuit.
(b) (Solution) Solve the equations from (a) for selected signal variables or input–output relationships.

3–1 Given the circuit in Figure P3–1,

(a) How many node-voltage equations are needed to describe the circuit?

(b) Formulate (but do not solve) a set of node-voltage equations for this circuit.

(c) Given $v_x = 5$ V and $i_x = 0.5$ A, use the node-voltage equations to find all of the element currents and voltages in the circuit.

3–2 Given the circuit in Figure P3–1,

(a) How many mesh-current equations are needed to describe the circuit?

(b) Formulate (but do not solve) a set of mesh-current equations for this circuit.

(c) Given $v_x = 5$ V and $i_x = 0.5$ A, use the mesh-current equations to find all of the element currents and voltages in the circuit.

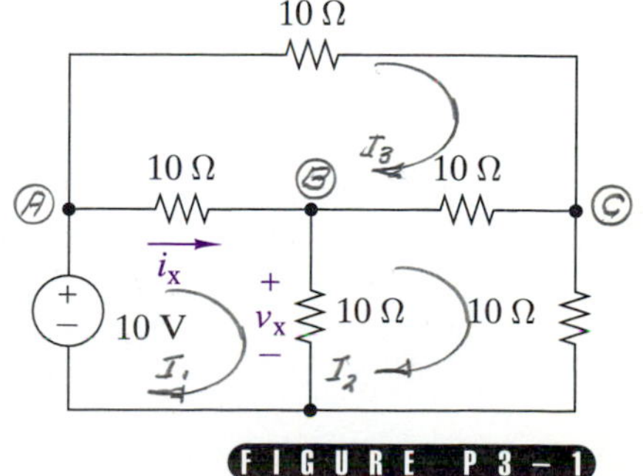

FIGURE P3–1

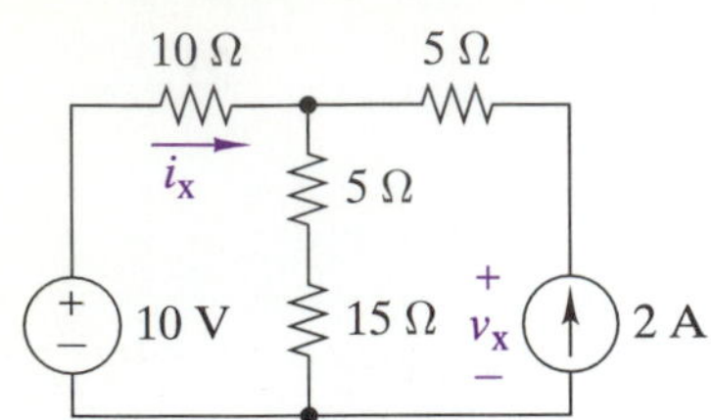

FIGURE P3–3

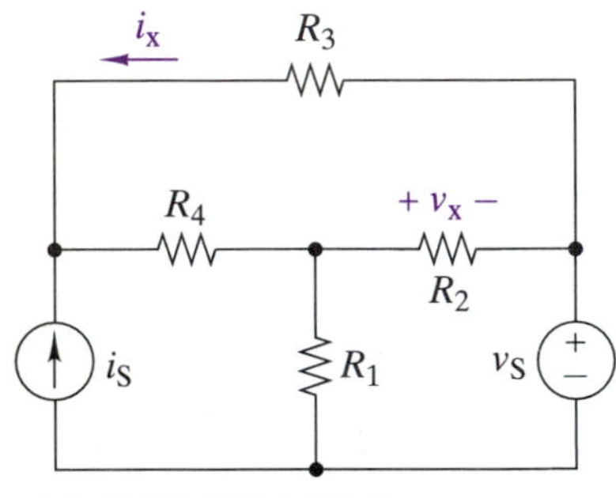

FIGURE P3–5

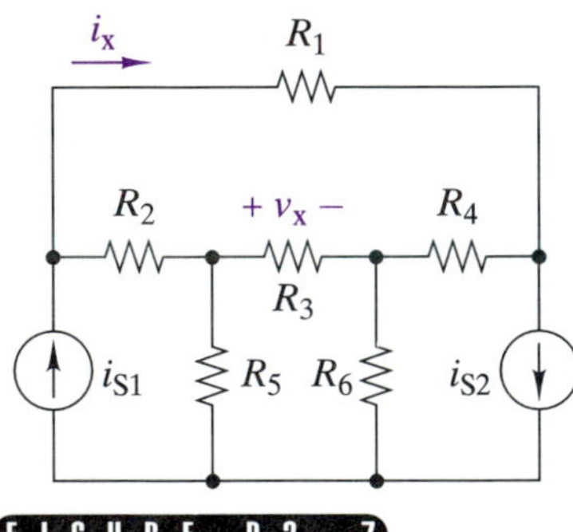

FIGURE P3–7

✓ **3–3** Given the circuit in Figure P3–3, EXAMPLE 3.4 (METHOD I) SOURCE XF

(a) How many node-voltage equations are needed to describe the circuit?

(b) Formulate (but do not solve) a set of node-voltage equations for this circuit.

(c) Given $v_x = 30$ V and $i_x = -1$ A, use the node-voltage equations to find all of the element currents and voltages in the circuit.

✓ **3–4** Given the circuit in Figure P3–3,

(a) How many mesh-current equations are needed to describe the circuit?

(b) Formulate (but do not solve) a set of mesh-current equations for this circuit.

(c) Given $v_x = 30$ V and $i_x = -1$ A, use the mesh-current equations to find all of the element currents and voltages in the circuit.

✓ **3–5** **(a)** Formulate node-voltage equations for the circuit in Figure P3–5.

(b) Solve for v_x and i_x when $v_S = 5$ V, $i_S = 1$ mA, $R_1 = R_2 = 10$ kΩ, and $R_3 = R_4 = 5$ kΩ.

✓ **3–6** **(a)** Formulate mesh-current equations for the circuit in Figure P3–5.

(b) Solve for v_x and i_x when $v_S = 25$ V, $i_S = 10$ A, $R_1 = R_2 = 10$ Ω, and $R_3 = R_4 = 15$Ω.

3–7 **(a)** Formulate node-voltage equations for the circuit in Figure P3–7.

(b) Solve for v_x and i_x for $R_1 = R_2 = R_3 = R_4 = 1$ kΩ, $R_5 = R_6 = 2$ kΩ, and $i_{S1} = i_{S2} = 100$ mA.

(c) Find the total power delivered to the circuit by the two current sources.

3–8 **(a)** Formulate node-voltage equations for the circuit in Figure P3–8.

(b) Solve for v_x and i_x using $R_1 = 10$ kΩ, $R_2 = 20$ kΩ, $R_3 = 30$ kΩ, $R_4 = 40$ kΩ, $R_x = 3$ kΩ, and $v_S = 10$ V.

(c) Find the power absorbed by resistor R_2.

3–9 **(a)** Formulate node-voltage equations for the circuit in Figure P3–9.

(b) Solve for v_x and i_x using $R_1 = 10$ kΩ, $R_2 = 10$ kΩ, $R_3 = 40$ kΩ, $R_4 = 20$ kΩ, and $v_1 = v_2 = v_3 = 15$ V.

(c) Find the power delivered to resistor R_1.

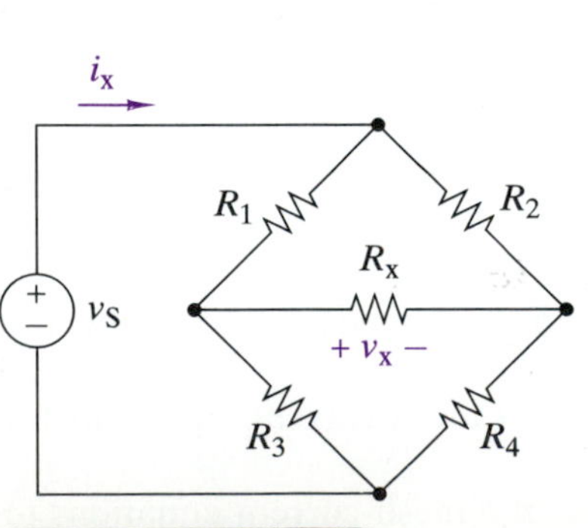

FIGURE P3–8

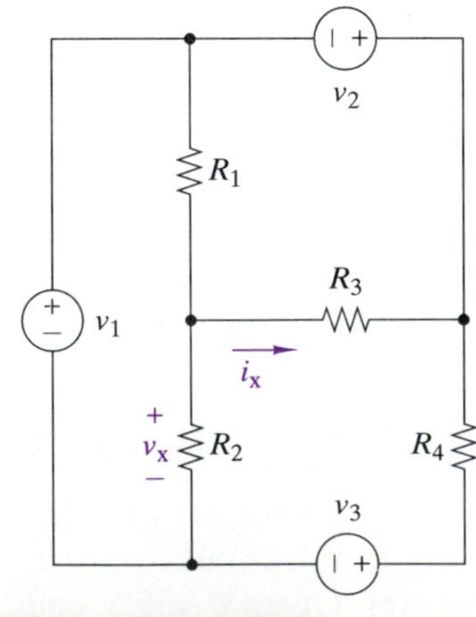

FIGURE P3–9

3–10 **(a)** Formulate node-voltage equations for the circuit in Figure P3–10.

(b) Solve for v_x and i_x using $R_1 = 10\ \Omega$, $R_2 = 20\ \Omega$, $R_3 = 10\ \Omega$, $R_4 = 20\ \Omega$, $R_5 = 5\ \Omega$, $R_x = 30\ \Omega$, $i_S = 2$ A, and $v_S = 10$ V.

(c) Find the power delivered by the voltage source.

FIGURE P3–10

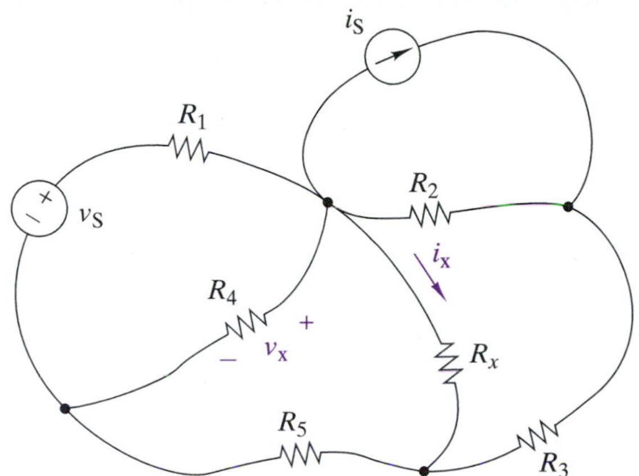

3–11 **(a)** Formulate mesh-current equations for the circuit in Figure P3–10.

(b) Solve for v_x and i_x using $R_1 = 10\ \Omega$, $R_2 = 20\ \Omega$, $R_3 = 10\ \Omega$, $R_4 = 20\ \Omega$, $R_5 = 5\ \Omega$, $R_x = 30\ \Omega$, $i_S = 2$ A and $v_S = 10$ V.

(c) Find the power delivered by the voltage source.

3–12 **(a)** Formulate mesh-current equations for the circuit in Figure P3–12.

(b) Solve for v_x and i_x using $R_1 = 300\ \Omega$, $R_2 = 500\ \Omega$, $R_3 = 60\ \Omega$, $R_4 = 240\ \Omega$, $R_5 = 180\ \Omega$, $i_S = 5$ mA, and $v_S = 12$ V.

(c) Find the total power dissipated in the circuit.

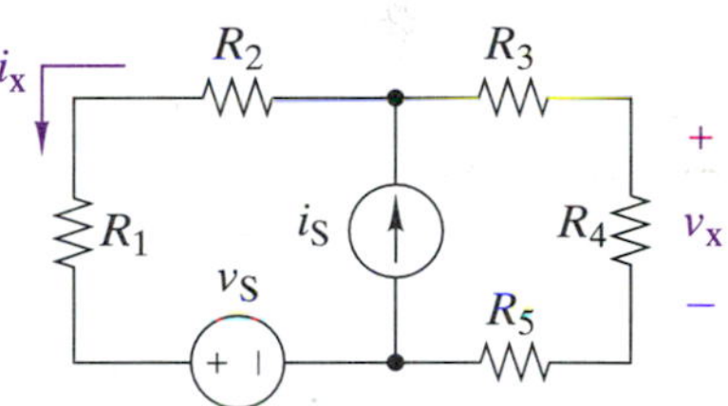

FIGURE P3–12

3–13 **(a)** Formulate mesh-current equations for the circuit in Figure P3–13.

(b) Solve for v_x and i_x using $R_1 = R_2 = 10\ \text{k}\Omega$, $R_3 = 2\ \text{k}\Omega$, $R_4 = 1\ \text{k}\Omega$, $i_S = 2.5$ mA, $v_{S1} = 12$ V, and $v_{S2} = 0.5$ V.

(c) Find the power supplied by v_{S1}.

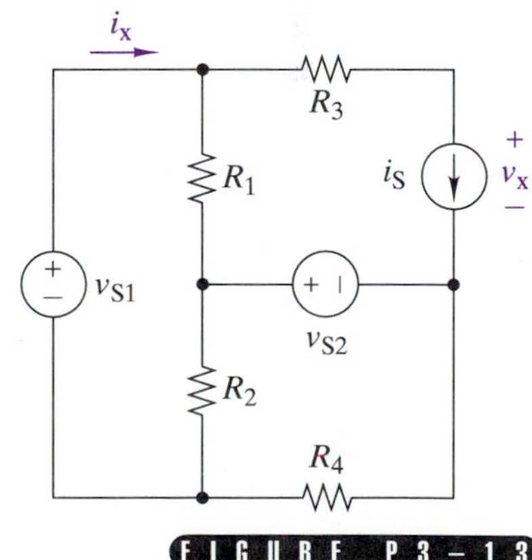

FIGURE P3–13

3–14 A circuit diagram can sometimes be rearranged to eliminate the need for a supermesh equation. For example, as drawn the circuit in Figure P3–14 requires a supermesh. However, the requirement can be eliminated by relocating the resistor R_6.

(a) Show that the supermesh can be eliminated by connecting resistor R_6 between nodes A and D via a different path than the one used in the figure.

FIGURE P3–14

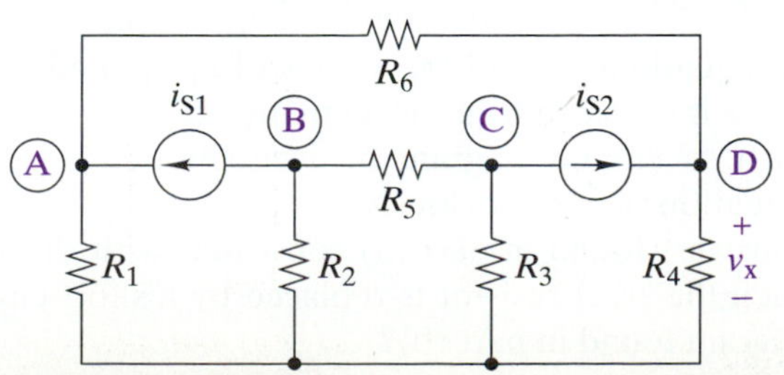

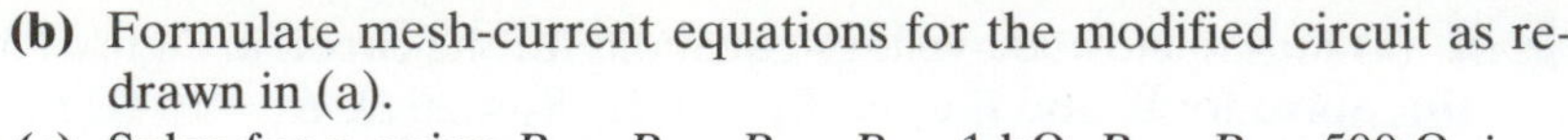

(b) Formulate mesh-current equations for the modified circuit as redrawn in (a).

(c) Solve for v_x using $R_1 = R_2 = R_3 = R_4 = 1\ \text{k}\Omega$, $R_5 = R_6 = 500\ \Omega$, $i_{S1} = 20$ mA, and $i_{S2} = 40$ mA.

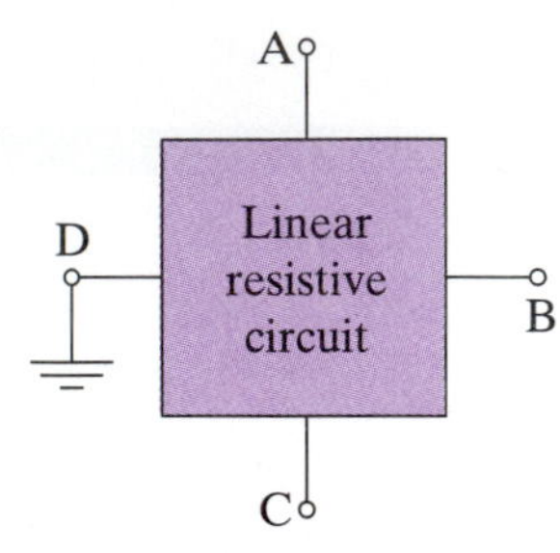

FIGURE P3–15

3–15 Figure P3–15 shows a linear resistive circuit with four nodes. When node D is selected as the reference, the node-voltage equations for the circuit are

$$\begin{aligned}
&\text{Node A:} && 3v_A - v_B = 2\\
&\text{Node B:} && -v_A + 5v_B - 2v_C = 0\\
&\text{Node C:} && -2v_B + 3v_C = 0
\end{aligned}$$

(a) Modify these equations to describe the circuit when node B is shorted to ground. Use these modified equations to find the values of v_A and v_C.

(b) Construct a schematic diagram of a circuit that has the node-voltage equations given previously.

(c) Are the answers found in part (a) consistent with the results obtained when node B is shorted to ground in the circuit diagram found in part (b)?

3–16 Figure P3–15 shows a linear resistive circuit with four nodes. When node D is selected as the reference, the node-voltage equations for the circuit are

$$\begin{aligned}
&\text{Node A:} && 2.5v_A - 0.5v_B - v_C = 0\\
&\text{Node B:} && -0.5v_A + 1.5v_B = -0.5\\
&\text{Node C:} && -v_A + 1.5v_C = 0.5
\end{aligned}$$

(a) Modify these equations to describe the circuit when the plus terminal of a 1-V source is connected to node B and the minus terminal is connected to ground. Use these modified equations to find the values of v_A and v_C.

(b) Construct a schematic diagram of a circuit that has the node-voltage equations given previously.

(c) Are the answers found in part (a) consistent with the results obtained when a 1-V source is connected between node B and ground in the circuit found in part (b)?

3–17 Figure P3–17 shows part of a linear resistive circuit with three meshes. The mesh-current equations for the circuit are

$$\begin{aligned}
&\text{Mesh A:} && 30i_A - 10i_B = 15\\
&\text{Mesh B:} && -10i_A + 50i_B - 20i_C = 0\\
&\text{Mesh C:} && -20i_B + 30i_C = 0
\end{aligned}$$

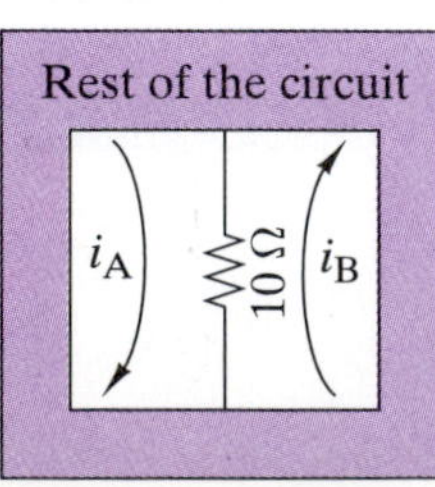

FIGURE P3–17

(a) Use these equations to find the values of i_A, i_B, and i_C when the 10-Ω resistor is replaced by a short circuit.

(b) Construct a schematic diagram of a circuit that has the mesh-current equations given previously.

(c) Are the answers found in part (a) consistent with the results obtained when the 10-Ω resistor is replaced by a short circuit in the circuit diagram found in part (b)?

3–18 When the switch is open the node-voltage equations for the circuit in Figure P3–18 are

$$(G_1 + G_3 + G_5)v_A - G_5 v_C = G_3 v_S$$

$$(G_2 + G_4 + G_5)v_C - G_5 v_A = G_4 v_S$$

How would you modify these equations to describe the circuit when the switch is closed?

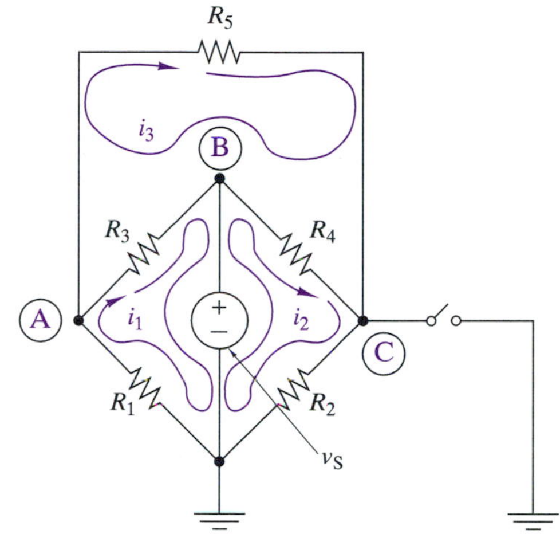

FIGURE P3–18

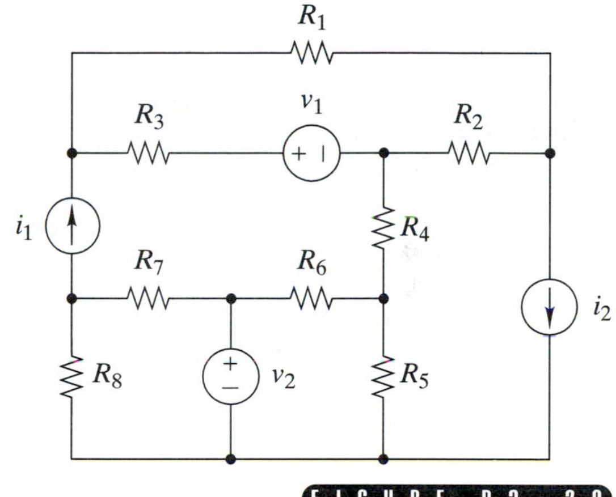

FIGURE P3–20

3–19 The mesh-current equations for the circuit in Figure P3–18 with the switch open are

$$(R_1 + R_3)i_1 - R_3 i_3 = -v_S$$

$$(R_2 + R_4)i_2 - R_4 i_3 = v_S$$

$$(R_3 + R_4 + R_5)i_3 - R_3 i_1 - R_4 i_2 = 0$$

How would you modify these equations to describe the circuit when the switch is closed?

3–20 How many node-voltage equations and mesh-current equations are needed to describe the circuit in Figure P3–20?

ERO 3–2 LINEARITY PROPERTIES (SECT. 3–3)

(a) Given a circuit containing linear resistors and one independent source, use the proportionality principle to find selected signal variables.
(b) Given a circuit containing linear resistors and two or more independent sources, use the superposition principle to find selected signal variables.

3–21 Find the proportionality constant $K = v_O/i_S$ for the circuit in Figure P3–21.

3–22 Find the proportionality constant $K = v_O/v_S$ for the circuit in Figure P3–22.

3–23 Find the proportionality constant $K = v_O/i_S$ for the circuit in Figure P3–23.

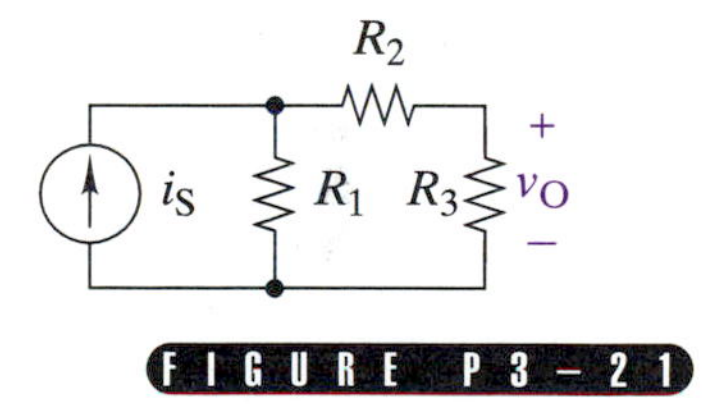

FIGURE P3–21

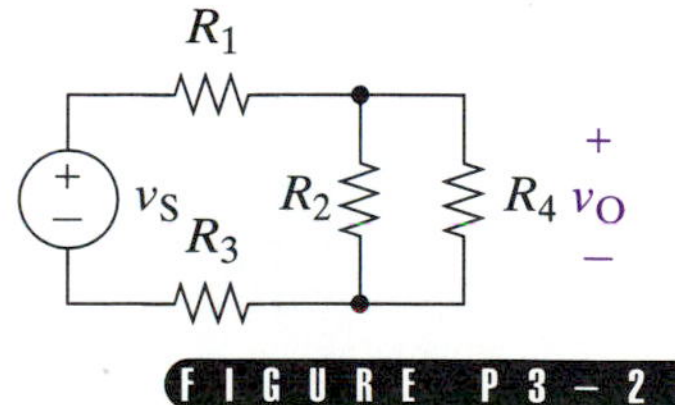

FIGURE P3–22

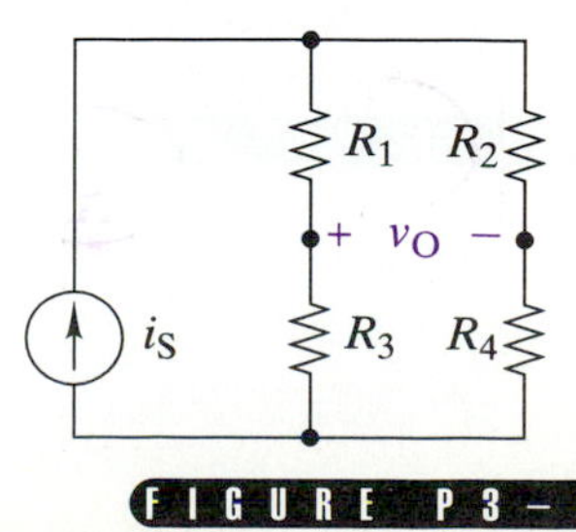

FIGURE P3–23

3–24 Use the unit output method to find v_O in the circuit in Figure P3–24.

FIGURE P3–24

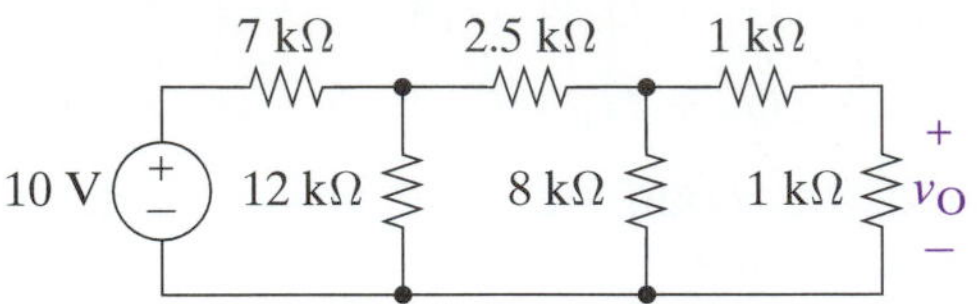

3–25 Use the unit output method to find i_O in the circuit in Figure P3–25.

FIGURE P3–25

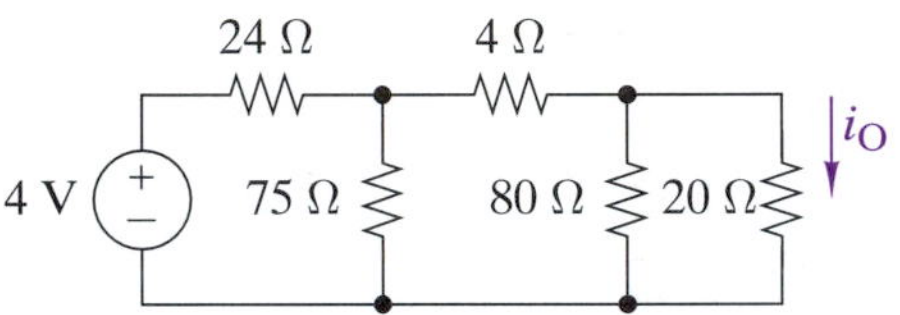

3–26 Use the unit output method to select R in the circuit in Figure P3–26 so that the proportionality constant $K = v_O/v_S = 1/30$. Find the largest possible value of K for any value of R.

FIGURE P3–26

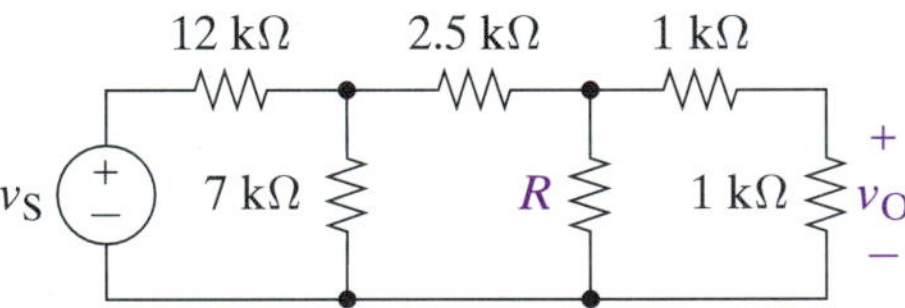

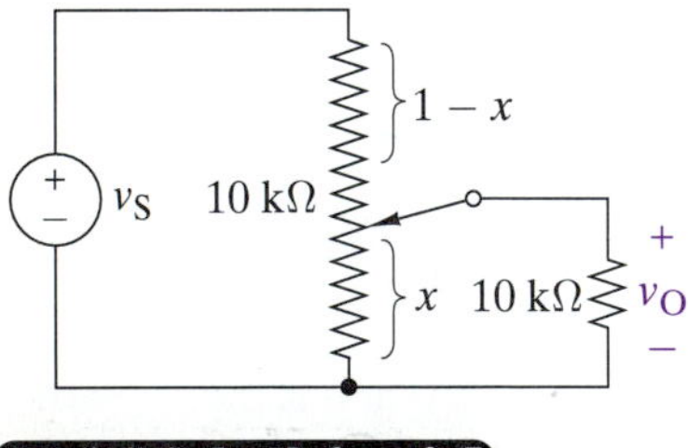

FIGURE P3–27

3–27 For the potentiometer circuit in Figure P3–27,

(a) Derive an expression for $K = v_O/v_S$ in terms of the movable contact position x.

(b) Is the plot of K versus x linear or nonlinear?

(c) If your answer in (b) is nonlinear, does this mean the circuit is nonlinear? Explain.

3–28 Use the superposition principle in the circuit of Figure P3–28 to find v_O.

FIGURE P3–28

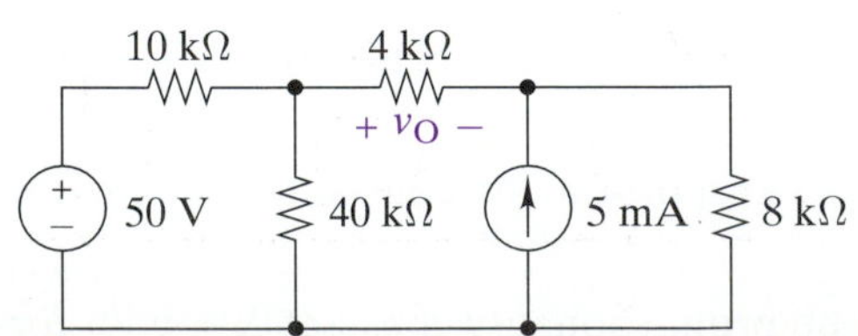

3–29 Use the superposition principle in the circuit of Figure P3–29 to find i_O.

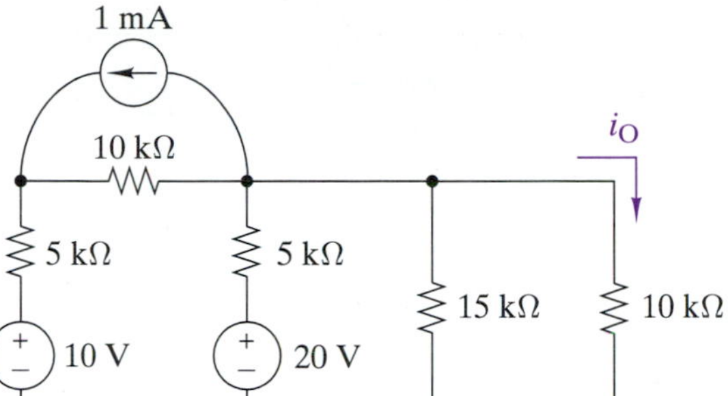

FIGURE P3–29

3–30 Use the superposition principle in the circuit of Figure P3–30 to find the output v_O in terms of v_1, v_2, and R.

3–31 Use the superposition principle in the circuit of Figure P3–31 to find the output v_O in terms of i_1, i_2, and R.

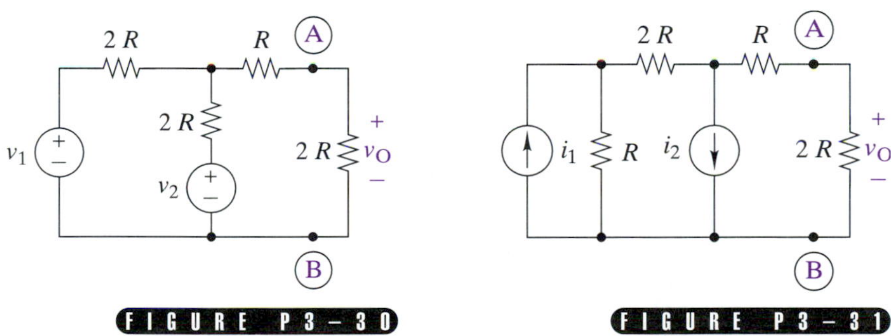

FIGURE P3–30

FIGURE P3–31

3–32 Superposition is not necessarily the best way to analyze circuits with several inputs.

(a) Use superposition in Figure P3–32 to find v_O in terms of the three inputs and R.

(b) Repeat part (a) using successive source transformations.

(c) Which method do you think is easier and why?

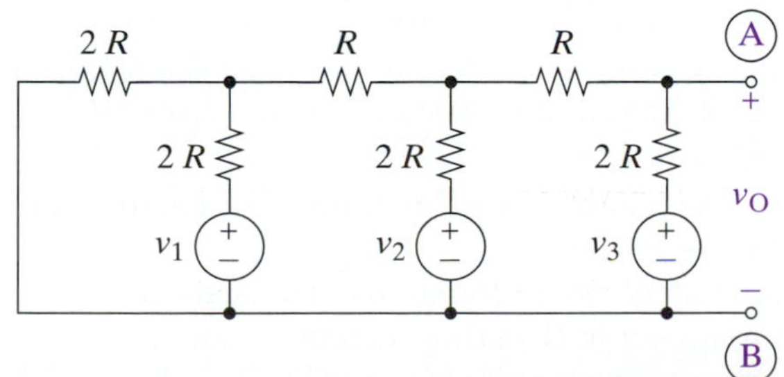

FIGURE P3–32

3–33 The linear load resistor in Figure P3–33 absorbs 400 mW. Find the value of the load resistance.

FIGURE P3–33

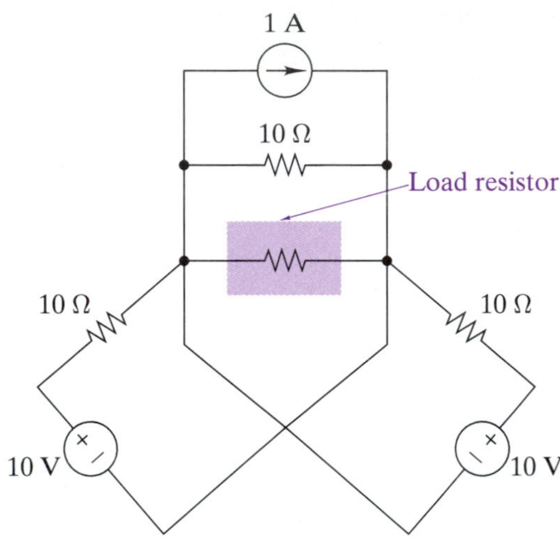

3–34 The following table of test data lists the output of a linear resistive circuit for different values of its three inputs. Find the input–output relationship for the circuit.

v_{S1}(V)	v_{S2}(V)	v_{S3}(V)	v_O(V)
0	4	–6	0
2	0	–3	1.5
2	4	0	2

3–35 **D** This problem involves designing a resistive circuit with two inputs v_{S1} and v_{S2} and a single output voltage v_O. Design the circuit so that $v_O = K(v_{S1} + 4v_{S2})$ is delivered across a 50-Ω load. The value of K is not specified but should be greater than 1/20.

ERO 3–3 THÉVENIN AND NORTON EQUIVALENT CIRCUITS (SECT. 3–4)

Given a circuit containing linear resistors and independent sources,

(a) Find the Thévenin or Norton equivalent at a specified pair of terminals.
(b) Use the Thévenin or Norton equivalent to find the signals delivered to linear or nonlinear loads.

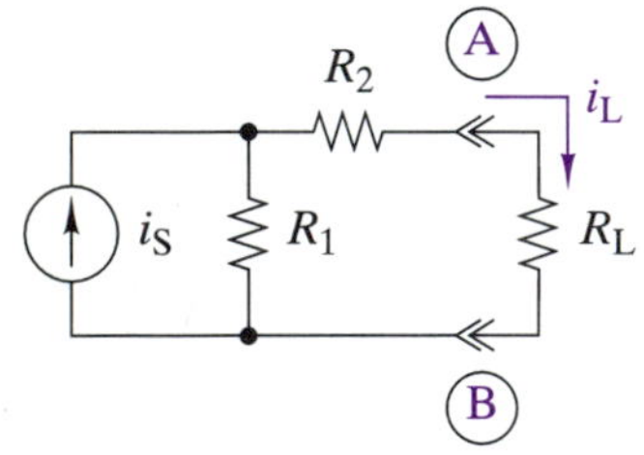

FIGURE P3–36

3–36 **(a)** Find the Thévenin or Norton equivalent circuit seen by R_L in the circuit in Figure P3–36.
(b) Use the equivalent circuit found in (a) to find i_L.
(c) Check your answer in (b) using current division.

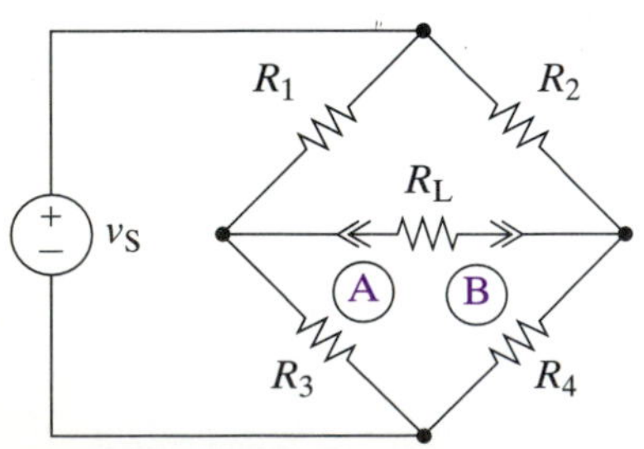

FIGURE P3–37

3–37 Find the Norton equivalent circuit seen by R_L in Figure P3–37.

3–38 **(a)** Find the Thévenin or Norton equivalent seen by R_L in the circuit in Figure P3–38.

(b) Use the equivalent circuit to find the load power for $R_L = 10\text{ k}\Omega$.

(c) Repeat (b) for $R_L = 20\text{ k}\Omega$, 40 kΩ, and 80 kΩ.

(d) Which value of R_L draws the most output power?

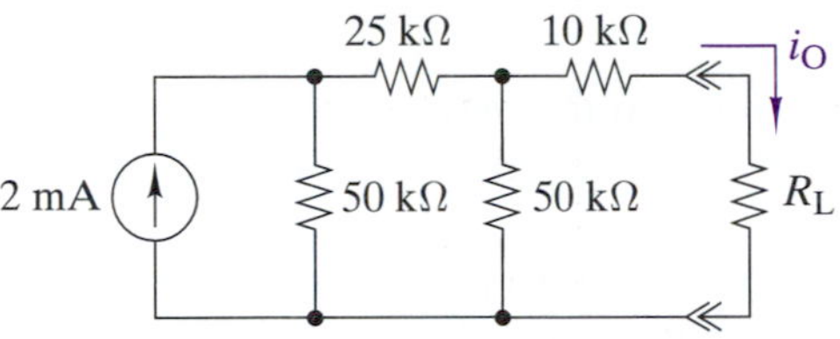

FIGURE P3–38

3–39 **(a)** Find the Thévenin or Norton equivalent seen by R_L in the circuit in Figure P3–39.

(b) Use the equivalent circuit to find i_O for $R_L = 5\text{ k}\Omega$.

(c) Repeat (b) for $R_L = 10\text{ k}\Omega$, 20 kΩ, and 40 kΩ.

(d) Which load draws the most output current?

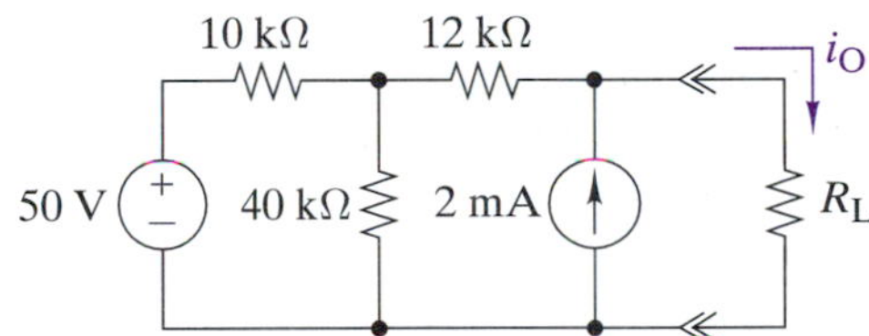

FIGURE P3–39

3–40 **(a)** Find the Thévenin or Norton equivalent at terminals A and B in the circuit in Figure P3–40.

(b) Use the equivalent circuit to find interface power when a 10-Ω load is connected between terminals A and B.

(c) Repeat (b) when a 5-V source is connected between terminals A and B with the plus terminal at terminal A.

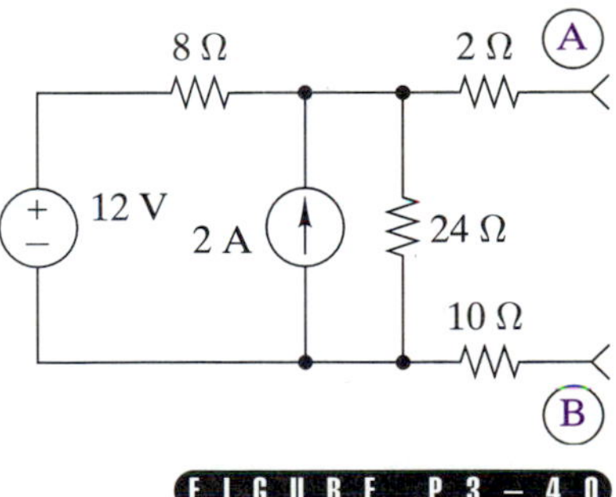

FIGURE P3–40

3–41 Find the Thévenin or Norton equivalent seen between terminals A and B of the R-$2R$ ladder circuit in Figure P3–32. (*Hint:* Use source transformations and circuit reduction.)

3–42 The open-circuit voltage of a two-terminal source is 8 V. When a 3-kΩ resistor is connected across the source, the output drops to 6 V.

(a) Find the Thévenin equivalent of the source.

(b) Use the equivalent circuit to find the power delivered to loads of 500 Ω, 1 kΩ, and 2 kΩ.

(c) Which load draws the most output power?

3–43 The open-circuit voltage of a two-terminal source is 5 V. When a diode is connected across the source, the output drops to 0.7 V. The diode i–v relationship is

$$i_D = 10^{-15}(e^{40v_D} - 1)$$

Find the Thévenin equivalent of the source.

3–44 Some measurements of the i–v characteristic of a two-terminal source are as follows:

v (V)	−10	−5	0	+5	+10	12	13	14
i(mA)	+5	+4	+3	+2	+1	0	−1	−2

(a) Plot the source i–v characteristic.
(b) Develop a Thévenin equivalent circuit valid on the range $|v| < 10$ V.
(c) Use the equivalent circuit to predict the source v_{OC} and i_{SC}.
(d) Compare your results in (c) with the measurements given and explain any differences.

3–45 For the circuit in Figure P3–45,
(a) Show that the load R_L sees a Thévenin resistance of R.
(b) Find v_O/v_S when $R_L = R$.

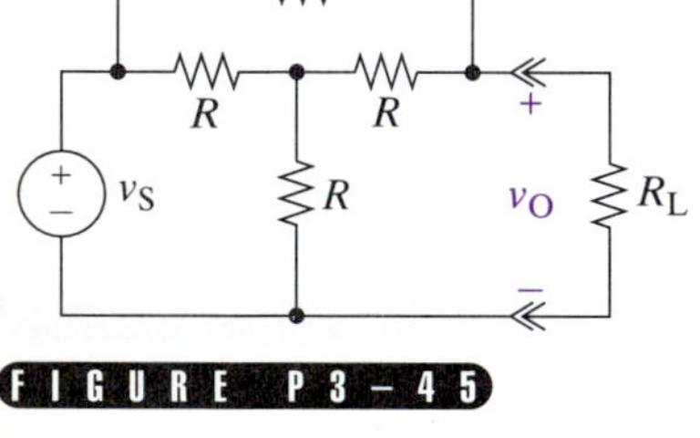

FIGURE P3–45

3–46 The two dc power supplies in Figure P3–46 operate in parallel to supply a load R_L.
(a) Find the smallest value of R_L for which $v_L \geq 5$ V.
(b) Find the power delivered to the load when $v_L = 5$ V.
(c) Find the power delivered by each source when $v_L = 5$ V.

3–47 **D** Select values for V_{CC} and R so the circuit in Figure P3–47 approximates (±5%) the i–v characteristic of the 10-mA current source for any load resistance from zero to 200 Ω.

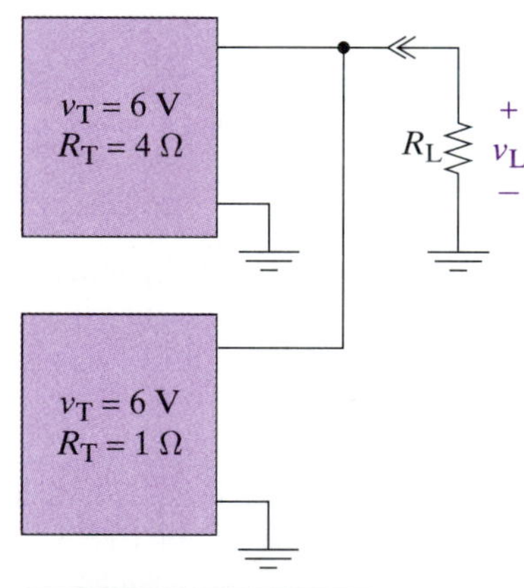

FIGURE P3–46

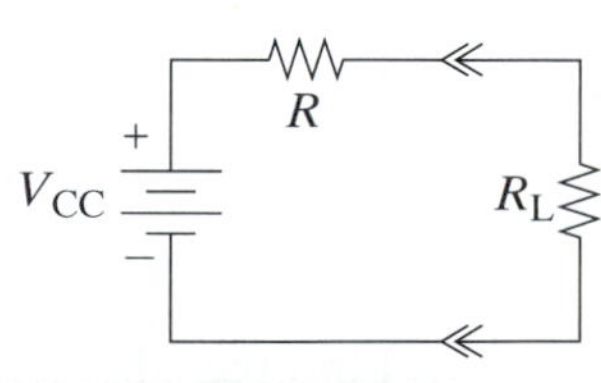

FIGURE P3–47

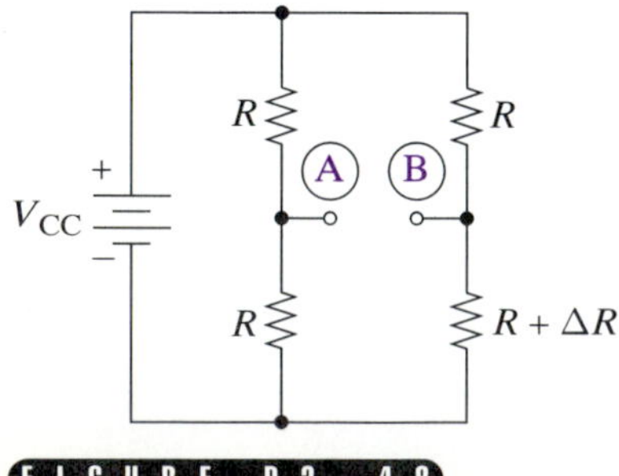

FIGURE P3–48

3–48 The Wheatstone bridge in Figure P3–48 would be balanced, except that the lower right leg is slightly out of balance by a small amount ΔR.
(a) Show that for $\Delta R << R$, the Thévenin equivalent seen between terminals A and B is $v_T = (\Delta R/R)(V_{CC}/4)$ and $R_T = R$.
(b) An ammeter with $R_M = 20$ Ω is connected between A and B. Calculate the meter reading for $V_{CC} = 15$ V, $R = 10$ kΩ, and $\Delta R/R = 1\%$.

3–49 The diode in the circuit of Figure P3–49(a) has the i–v characteristic shown in Figure P3–49(b). Find the power dissipated in the diode. Repeat if the source voltage is increased to 2.0 V.

3–50 A nonlinear resistor with the i–v characteristic shown in Figure P3–50 is connected to a circuit with the Thévenin equivalent shown in Figure P3–50. With the nonlinear resistor connected to the source, the interface voltage is $v = 30$ V. With the nonlinear resistor disconnected, the interface voltage is $v = 40$ V. Find v_S and R_S.

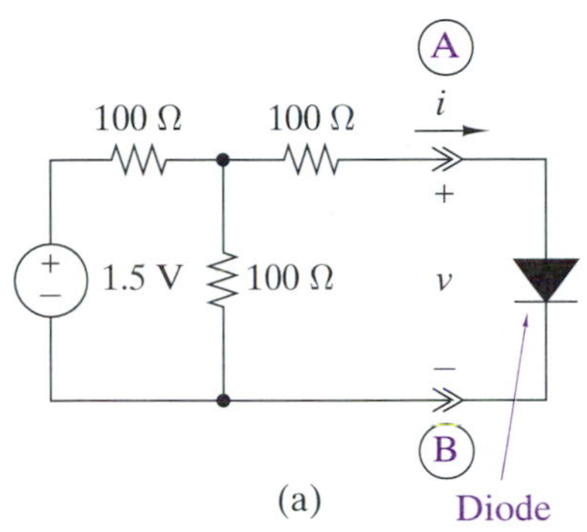

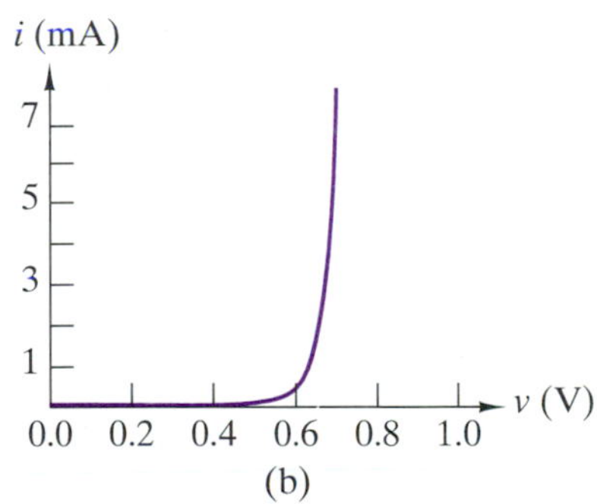

FIGURE P3–49

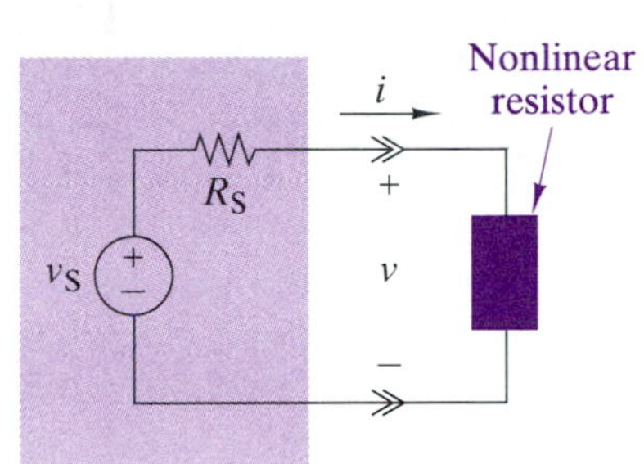

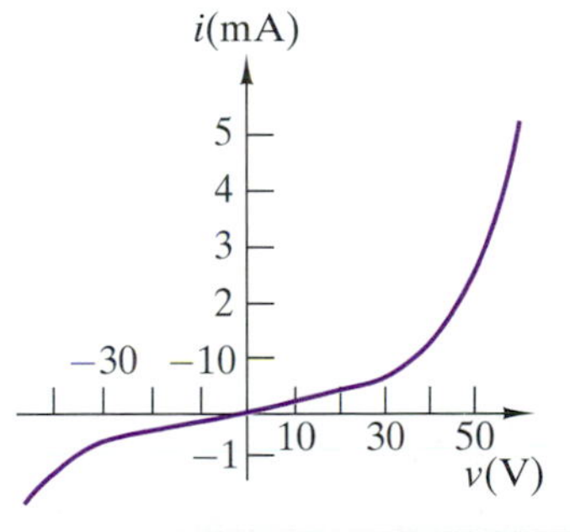

FIGURE P3–50

ERO 3–4 MAXIMUM SIGNAL TRANSFER (SECT. 3–5)

Given a circuit containing linear resistors and independent sources,

(a) Find the maximum voltage, current, and power available at a specified pair of terminals.

(b) Find the resistive loads required to obtain the maximum available signal levels.

3–51 **(a)** The load resistance in Figure P3–51 is adjusted until the maximum power is delivered. Find the power delivered and the value of R_L.

(b) The load resistance is adjusted until maximum voltage is delivered. Find the voltage delivered and the value of R_L.

(c) The load resistance is adjusted until maximum current is delivered. Find the current delivered and the value of R_L.

FIGURE P3–51

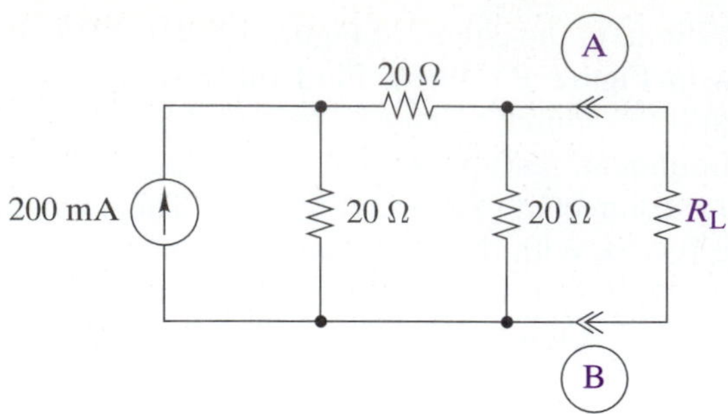

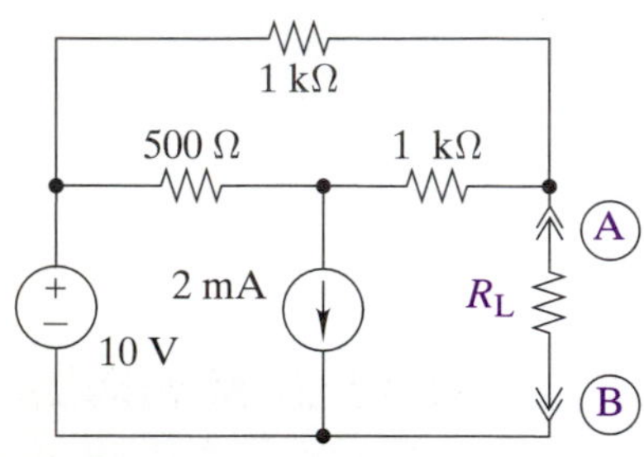

FIGURE P3–52

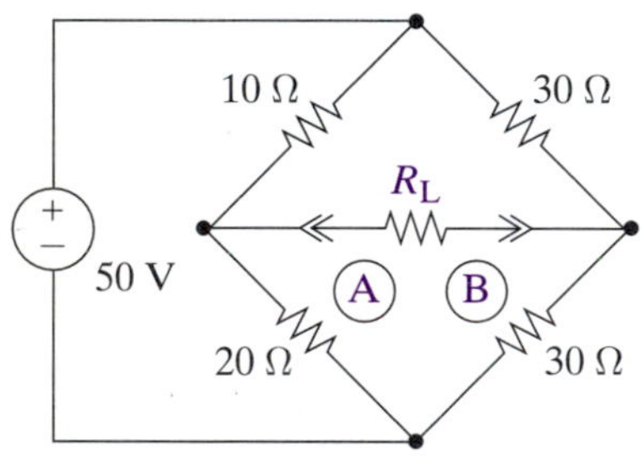

FIGURE P3–53

3–52 **(a)** The load resistance in Figure P3–52 is adjusted until maximum power is delivered. Find the power delivered and the value of R_L.

(b) The load resistance is adjusted until maximum voltage is delivered. Find the voltage delivered and the value of R_L.

(c) The load resistance is adjusted until maximum current is delivered. Find the current delivered and the value of R_L.

3–53 **(a)** The load resistance in Figure P3–53 is adjusted until maximum power is delivered. Find the power delivered and the value of R_L.

(b) The load resistance is adjusted until maximum voltage is delivered. Find the voltage delivered and the value of R_L.

(c) The load resistance is adjusted until maximum current is delivered. Find the current delivered and the value of R_L.

3–54 The resistance R in Figure P3–54 is adjusted until maximum power is delivered across the interface to the load consisting of R and the 6-kΩ resistor in parallel. Find the voltage and power delivered to the load and the value of R.

FIGURE P3–54

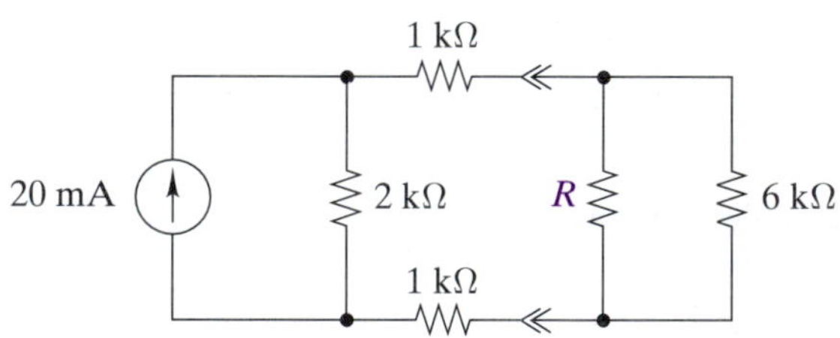

3–55 A current of 2 mA is delivered when a 10-kΩ resistor is connected across a two-terminal source. A total current of 3 mA is delivered when a second 10-kΩ resistor is connected in parallel with the first. Find the maximum power available from the source and specify the load resistance required to extract maximum power from the source.

3–56 For the potentiometer circuit in Figure P3–56, find wiper position x that delivers maximum power to the 2-kΩ load.

3–57 A stereo speaker can be modeled as an 8-Ω linear resistance. A 50-W stereo amplifier with an output resistance of 8 Ω is connected to the speaker via two wires each 75 meters long. The wire resistance is 0.01 Ω/meter.

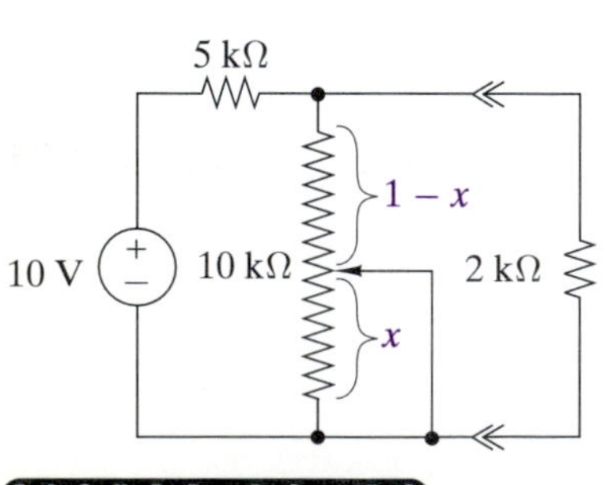

FIGURE P3–56

(a) Find the amplifier's Thévenin voltage when its volume control is set to deliver 50 W to an 8-Ω load.

(b) Find the maximum power available at the speaker when the amplifier volume control is set to the level in part (a).

(c) Find the power delivered to the speaker when the amplifier volume control is set to the level in part (a).

3–58 **(a)** The resistance R in Figure P3–58 is adjusted until the maximum power is delivered to the load. Find the voltage and power delivered to the load and the value of R.

(b) The resistance R is adjusted until the maximum voltage is delivered to the load. Find the voltage and power delivered to the load and the value of R.

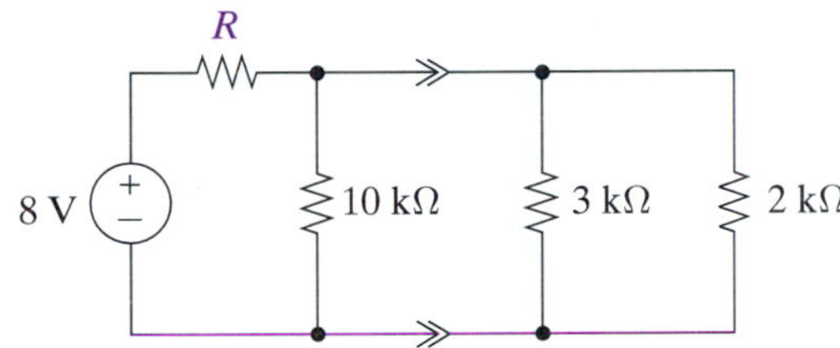

FIGURE P3–58

3–59 A 20-V source with negligible internal resistance is connected in series with a resistor R_S. Select the value of R_S so that outputs of the series combination are bounded by $i < 100$ mA and $p < 500$ mW for any load resistance.

3–60 The maximum power available from a practical source is 100 W. Find the maximum power available from N identical versions of the source when they are connected in parallel. Repeat for N identical versions connected in series.

ERO 3–5 INTERFACE CIRCUIT DESIGN (SECT. 3–6)

Given the signal transfer objectives at a source-load interface, adjust the circuit parameters or design one or more two-port interface circuits that achieve the specified objectives within stated constraints.

3–61 **D** Figure P3–61 shows a two-port interface circuit connecting source and load circuits. In this problem $v_S = 10$ V, $R_S = 50$ Ω, and the load is a 50-Ω resistor. To avoid damaging the source, its output current must be less than 100 mA. Design a resistive interface circuit so

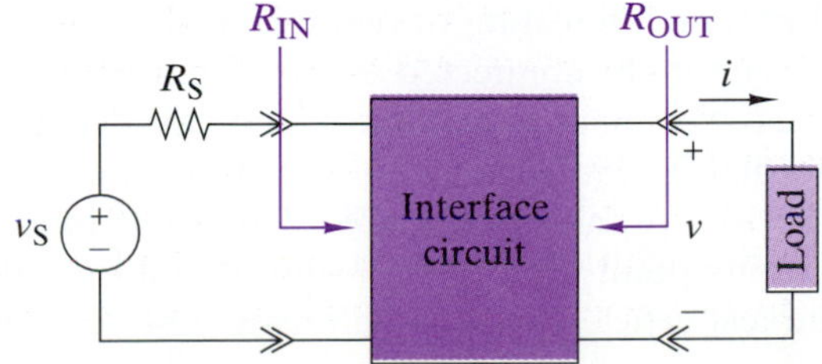

FIGURE P3–61

that the voltage delivered to the load is 4 V and the source current is less than 100 mA.

3–62 D Figure P3–61 shows a two-port interface circuit connecting source and load circuits. In this problem, $v_S = 10$ V, $R_S = 200\ \Omega$, and the load is a diode whose i–v characteristic is

$$i_D = 10^{-15}(e^{40v_D} - 1)$$

Design an interface circuit that dissipates less than 50 mW and produces an interface voltage of $v = 0.7$ V.

3–63 D Figure P3–61 shows a two-port interface circuit connecting source and load circuits. In this problem, $v_S = 15$ V, $R_S = 100\ \Omega$, and the load is a 1-kΩ resistor. Design a resistive interface circuit so that the voltage delivered to the load is 10 V ±10% using only the following standard resistors: 68 Ω, 100 Ω, 220 Ω, 330 Ω, 470 Ω, and 680 Ω. The resistors all have a tolerance of ± 5%, which you must account for in your design.

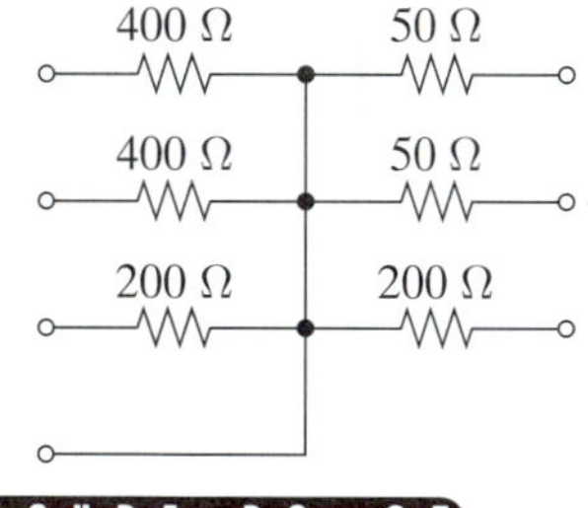

FIGURE P3–65

3–64 D In Figure P3–61 the load is a 600-Ω resistor and $R_S = 25\ \Omega$. Design an interface circuit so that the input resistance of the two-port is 25 Ω ± 5% and the output resistance seen by the load is 600 Ω ± 5%.

3–65 D Figure P3–61 shows a two-port interface circuit connecting source and load circuits. In this problem $v_S = 12$ V, $R_S = 300\ \Omega$, and the load is a 500-Ω resistor. Design an interface circuit using the resistor array in Figure P3–65 so that $v < 2$ V and $i > 5$ mA. *Hint:* Compare the design constraints with the i–v characteristics of the 500-Ω load.

3–66 D Use the resistor array in Figure P3–65 to design a two-port resistance circuit whose voltage gain $K = v_O/v_{IN}$ is at least 0.2 and whose input resistance is as close to 100 Ω as possible.

3–67 D It is sometimes important for a circuit to have at least some degraded performance when one or more of its components malfunctions. Suppose we have a large number of identical 10-kΩ resistors. Assume that the resistors become open circuits when they malfunction. Use the 10-kΩ resistors to design a voltage divider that meets the following requirements:

(a) A 15-V input produces a 5-V output when there are no resistor malfunctions.

(b) A 15-V input produces an output between 4 V and 7 V when one resistor malfunctions.

Hint: Connect resistors in parallel.

3–68 D Figure P3–61 shows a two-port interface circuit connecting a source and load. In this problem the source with $v_S = 5$ V and $R_S = 5\ \Omega$ is to be used in production testing of two-terminal semiconductor devices. The devices are to be connected as the load in Figure P3–61 and have i–v characteristics that are nonlinear and vary from one unit to the next. The normal operating range for acceptable devices is defined by $\{i > 5 \text{ mA or } v > 0.4 \text{ V}\}$ and $\{p < 5 \text{ mW}\}$. Design an interface circuit so that the operating point always lies within the normal range given regardless of the test article's i–v characteristic. Use resistors rated at 1/2 W or less.

3–69 The novel device in Figure P3–69 allows the operator to set up a variety of source and load conditions by selecting different switch positions. Find the switch positions required to obtain each of the following conditions:

(a) Maximum power to R_L when $R_L = 100\ \Omega$
(b) $v_O = 6$ volts when $R_L = 100\ \Omega$
(c) Maximum voltage when $R_L = 1\ k\Omega$
(d) Maximum current through R_L when $R_L = 50\ \Omega$
(e) 40 mA current through R_L when $R_L = 100\ \Omega$
(f) 60 mA current through R_L when $R_L = 100\ \Omega$
(g) $v_O = 4$ volts when $R_L = 50\ \Omega$

FIGURE P3–69

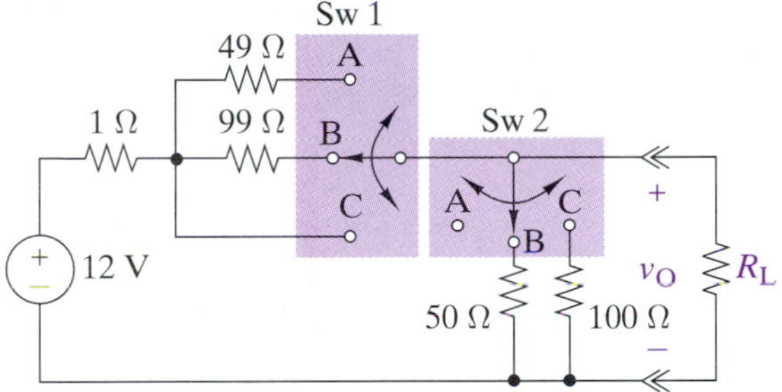

3–70 **D** To avoid damage, the source circuit in Figure P3–70 must always "see" an equivalent resistance of about 50 Ω. Design an interface circuit whose input resistance is about 50 Ω both when the electronic switch is on and when it is off. The interface circuit must transfer at least 1% of the source open-circuit voltage to the load when the switch is on. The switch characteristics are $R_{switch} = 100\ \Omega$ when $v_G = 5$ V (on) and $R_{switch} = 10^{10}\ \Omega$ when $V_G = 0$ V (off).

FIGURE P3–70

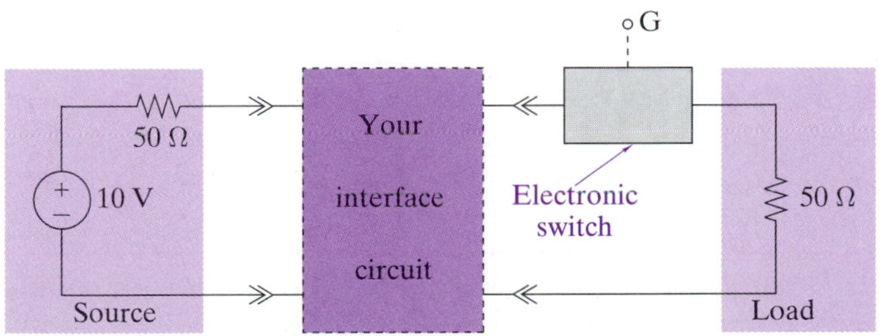

CHAPTER-INTEGRATING PROBLEMS

3–71 A NONLINEAR THREE-TERMINAL DEVICE

The i–v characteristics of a three-terminal nonlinear device are shown in Figures P3–71(a) and P3–71(b). Figure P3–71(c) shows the device connected in a circuit.

(a) Find the Thévenin equivalent seen by the device between terminals A and B. Construct the corresponding load line in Figure P3–71(a).

(b) Find the Thévenin equivalent seen by the device between terminals C and B. Construct the corresponding load line in Figure P3–71(b).

(c) Use the load lines in (a) to find i_A and v_{AB}.

(d) Use the load line in (b) and the results of (c) to find v_{CB} and i_C.

(e) Calculate the total power delivered to the three-terminal device.

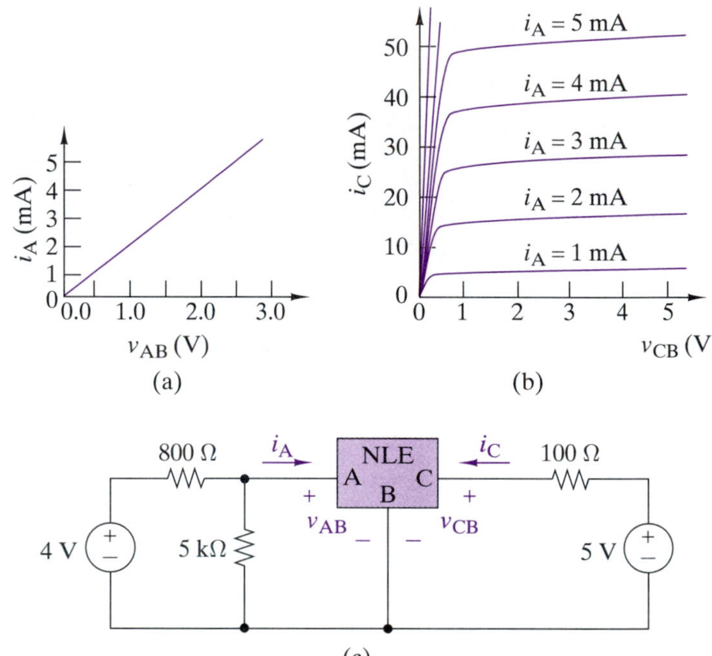

FIGURE P3–71

3–72 A THREE-TERMINAL DEVICE MODELING

The following data are measurements of the input–output relationship of the three-terminal resistive circuit shown in Figure P3–72.

v_S(V)	–12	–9	–6	–3	0	+3	+6	+9	+12
v_O(V)	–2	–2	–2	–1	0	+1	+2	+2.5	+3

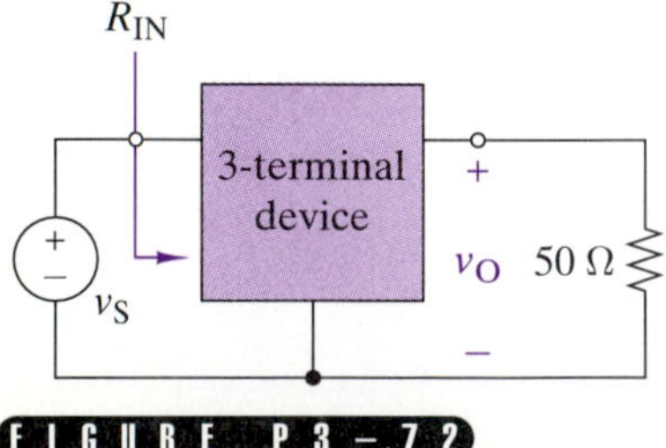

FIGURE P3–72

With the 50-Ω load connected the circuit input resistance is R_{IN} = 1 kΩ.

(a) Plot the input–output relationship and state whether the relationship is linear or nonlinear.

(b) Devise a linear model of the form $v_O = Kv_S$ that approximates the data for $|v_S| < 6$ V.

(c) Use your model from part (c) to predict the circuit output for $v_S = \pm 10$ V and explain why the predictions do not agree with the data given previously.

(d) For $v_S = 1$ V use your model from part (c) to find the circuit power gain = P_O/P_{IN}.

(e) In view of the result in (e), is the device active or is it passive?

3–73 A ADJUSTABLE THÉVENIN EQUIVALENT

Figure P3–73 shows an ideal voltage source in parallel with an adjustable potentiometer. This problem concerns the effect of adjusting the potentiometer on the interface Thévenin equivalent circuit and the signals available at the interface.

(a) Find the parameters v_T and R_T of the Thévenin equivalent circuit at the interface in terms of circuit parameters k, v_S, and R.

(b) Find the value of R_T for $k = 0$, $k = 0.5$, and $k = 1$. Explain your results physically in terms of the position of the movable arm of the potentiometer.

(c) What is the power available at the interface for $k = 0$, $k = 0.5$, and $k = 1$? Justify your answers physically in terms of the position of the movable arm of the potentiometer.

(d) A load resistor $R_L = R/4$ is connected across the interface. Where should the potentiometer be positioned (k = ?) to transfer the maximum power to this load?

(e) A load resistor $R_L = R/4$ is connected across the interface. Where should the potentiometer be positioned (k = ?) to deliver an interface voltage $v = v_S/4$ to this load?

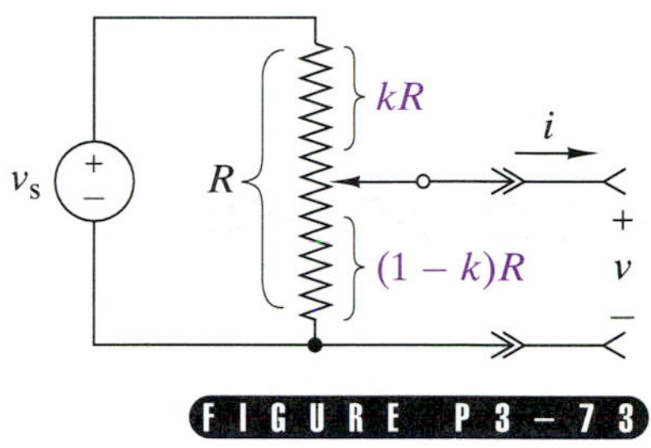

FIGURE P3–73

3–74 D POWER CHANGE-OVER DESIGN

The 1-kΩ resistor in Figure P3–74 is normally powered by the 110-V source. In case of 110-V power failure, a 12-V backup source is pro-

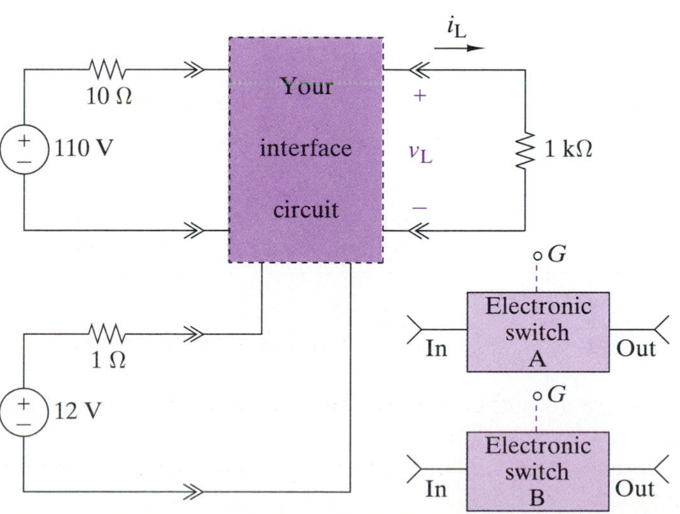

FIGURE P3–74

vided. Design an interface that delivers $v_L = 10$ V to the 1-kΩ resistor under normal and backup power conditions. Use the electronic switches shown in the figure. Switch A characteristics are $R_{switch} = 100$ Ω when $V_G < 10$ V and $R_{switch} = 10^{10}$ Ω when $V_G > 10$ V. Switch B characteristics are $R_{switch} = 100$ Ω when $V_G > 10$ V and $R_{switch} = 10^{10}$ Ω when $V_G < 10$ V. The switch gates draw negligible current, but you must show how to connect the gates to the main source.

3–75 E TTL TO ECL CONVERTER

It is claimed that the resistive circuit in Figure P3–75 converts transistor-transistor logic (TTL) input signals into output signals compatible with emitter coupled logic (ECL). The circuit characteristics are summarized in the following data sheet. The claim is that the circuit converts any input in the specified TTL logic low (high) range into an output in the specified ECL logic low (high) range for any output load current in the specified range.

CHARACTERISTIC	SYMBOL	MIN	TYPICAL	MAX	UNITS
TTL input logic "low"	V_{IL}	0	0.2	0.4	V
TTL input logic "high"	V_{IH}	3.0	3.4	3.8	V
ECL output logic "low"	V_{OL}	–1.7	–1.6	–1.5	V
ECL output logic "high"	V_{OH}	–0.9	–0.75	–0.6	V
Output load current	I_O	–100		+100	μA

Verify that ECL output voltages are in the stated ranges for any allowed combination of TTL inputs and load currents. *Hint:* Find the Thévenin equivalent circuit at the output interface in terms of v, i, and v_S.

FIGURE P3–75

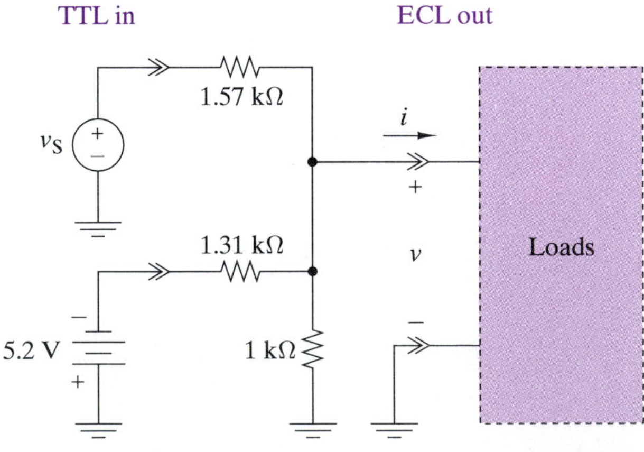

CHAPTER 4

ACTIVE CIRCUITS

Then came the morning of Tuesday, August 2, 1927, when the concept of the negative feedback amplifier came to me in a flash while I was crossing the Hudson River on the Lacakawana Ferry, on my way to work.

Harold S. Black, 1927,
American Electrical Engineer

The integrated circuit operational amplifier (OP AMP) is the workhorse of present-day linear electronic circuits. However, to operate as a linear amplifier the OP AMP must be provided with "negative feedback." The negative feedback amplifier is one of the key inventions of all time. During the 1920s, Harold S. Black (1898–1983) worked for several years without much success on the problem of improving the performance of vacuum tube amplifiers in telephone systems. The feedback amplifier solution came to him suddenly on his way to work. He documented his invention by writing the key concepts of negative feedback on his morning copy of the *New York Times*. His invention paved the way for the development of worldwide communication systems and spawned whole new areas of technology, such as feedback control systems and robotics.

An **active circuit** contains one or more devices that require an external power supply to operate correctly. These active devices control the flow of electrical power from the external supply and can operate in both linear and nonlinear modes. In their linear range active devices can be modeled using the four dependent source elements introduced in the first section. The second section shows how dependent sources change the properties of resistive circuits and how we modify our methods of analysis to cover these new linear elements. Dependent sources and resistors are used to model many active devices, including the transistor and OP AMP devices discussed in the third and fourth sections. The fourth section also develops an ideal OP AMP model that is useful in circuit analysis and design. In the fifth section the ideal OP AMP model is used to analyze circuit realizations of basic analog signal-processing functions, such as amplifiers, summers, subtractors, and inverters. These basic building blocks are then used to design OP AMP circuits that realize specified signal-processing functions. The comparator section treats a case in which the OP AMP intentionally operates as a nonlinear element. The final section summarizes and compares the various circuit analysis techniques.

4–1 LINEAR DEPENDENT SOURCES

This chapter treats the analysis and design of circuits containing active devices, such as transistors or operational amplifiers (OP AMPs). An **active device** is a component that requires an external power supply to operate correctly. An **active circuit** is one that contains one or more active devices. An important property of active circuits is that they are capable of providing signal amplification, one of the most important signal-processing functions in electrical engineering. Linear active circuits are governed by the proportionality property, so their input–output relationships are of the form $y = Kx$. The term **signal amplification** means the proportionality factor K is greater than 1 when the input x and output y have the same dimensions. Thus, active circuits can deliver more signal voltage, current, and power at their output than they receive from the input signal. The passive resistance circuits studied thus far cannot produce voltage, current, or power gains greater than unity.

Active devices operating in a linear mode are modeled using resistors and one or more of the dependent sources shown in Figure 4–1. A **dependent source** is voltage or current source whose output is controlled by a voltage or current in a different part of the circuit. As a result, there are four possible types of dependent sources: a current-controlled voltage source (CCVS), a voltage-controlled voltage source (VCVS), a current-controlled current source (CCCS), and a voltage-controlled current source (VCCS). The properties of these dependent sources are very different from those of the independent sources described in Chapter 2. The output voltage (current) of an independent voltage (current) source is a specified value that does not depend on the circuit to which it is connected. To distinguish between the two types of sources, the dependent sources are represented by the diamond symbol in Figure 4–1, in contrast to the circle symbol used for independent sources.

Caution: This book uses the diamond symbol to indicate a dependent source and the circle to show an independent source. However, some books and circuit analysis programs, like SPICE and MICRO-CAP, use the circle symbol for both dependent and independent sources.

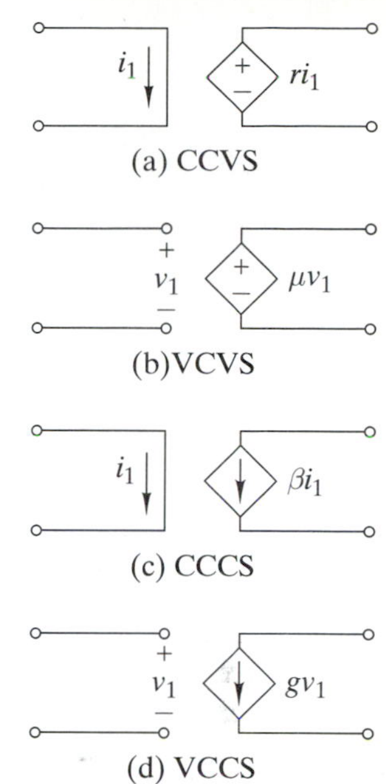

FIGURE 4–1 *Dependent source circuit symbols: (a) Current-controlled voltage source. (b) Voltage-controlled voltage source. (c) Current-controlled current source. (d) Voltage-controlled current source.*

A **linear dependent source** is one whose output is proportional to the controlling voltage or current. The defining relationship for dependent sources in Figure 4–1 are all of the form $y = Kx$, where x is the controlling variable, y is the source output variable, and K is the proportionality factor. Each type of dependent source is characterized by a proportionality factor, either μ, β, r, or g. These parameters are often called simply the **gain** of the controlled source. Strictly speaking, the parameters μ and β are dimensionless quantities called the **voltage gain** and **current gain**, respectively. The parameter r has the dimensions of ohms and is called the **transresistance**, a contraction of transfer resistance. The parameter g is then called **transconductance** and has the dimensions of siemens.

Although dependent sources are elements used in circuit analysis, they are conceptually different from the other circuit elements we have studied. The linear resistor and ideal switch are models of actual devices called resistors and switches. However, you will not find dependent sources listed in electronic part catalogs. For this reason, dependent sources are more abstract, since they are not models of identifiable physical devices. Dependent sources are used in combination with other resistive elements to create models of active devices.

In Chapter 3 we found that a voltage source acts as a short circuit when it is turned off. Likewise, a current source behaves as an open circuit when it is turned off. The same results apply to dependent sources, with one important difference. Dependent sources cannot be turned on and off individually because they depend on excitation supplied by independent sources.

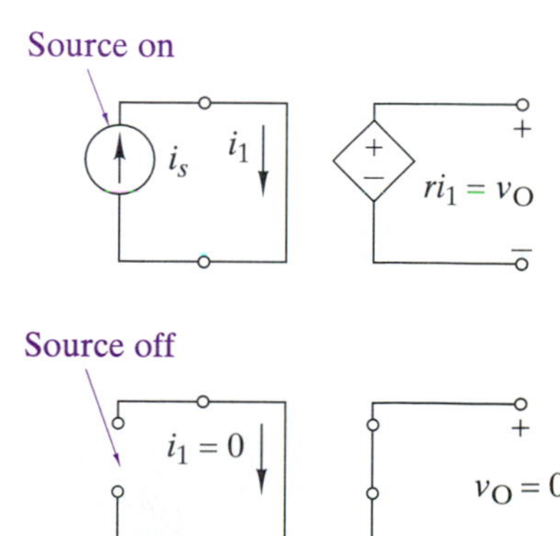

FIGURE 4–2 *Turning off the independent source affects the dependent source.*

Some consequences of this dependency are illustrated in Figure 4–2. When the independent current source is turned on, KCL requires that $i_1 = i_S$. Through controlled source action, the current controlled voltage source is on and its output is

$$v_O = ri_1 = ri_S$$

When the independent current source is off ($i_S = 0$), it acts as an open circuit and KCL requires that $i_1 = 0$. The dependent source is now off and its output is

$$v_O = ri_1 = 0$$

When the independent voltage source is off, the dependent source acts as a short circuit.

In other words, turning the independent source on and off turns the dependent source on and off as well. We must be careful when applying the superposition principle and Thévenin's theorem to active circuits, since the state of a dependent source depends on the excitation supplied by independent sources. To account for this possibility, we modify the superposition principle to state that the response due to all *independent* sources acting simultaneously is equal to the sum of the responses due to each *independent* source acting one at a time.

EXAMPLE 4–1

Figure 4–3 shows the symbols used in MicroSim Schematics to represent the four dependent sources. These elements are found on the **Analog** symbol library as part names starting with the letters:

E for a voltage-controlled voltage source

F for a current-controlled current source

G for a voltage-controlled current source

H for a current-controlled voltage source

FIGURE 4–3

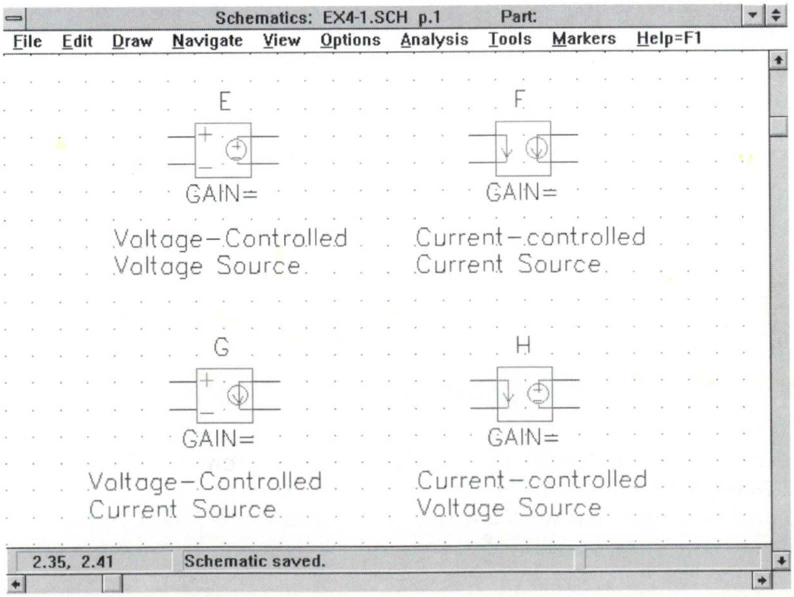

Schematics: EX4-1.SCH p.1 Part:

File Edit Draw Navigate View Options Analysis Tools Markers Help=F1

E

GAIN=

Voltage-Controlled
Voltage Source

F

GAIN=

Current-controlled
Current Source

G

GAIN=

Voltage-Controlled
Current Source

H

GAIN=

Current-controlled
Voltage Source

2.35, 2.41 Schematic saved.

The input ports are open circuits for the voltage-controlled elements and short circuits for the current-controlled elements. The output ports are voltage sources or current sources depending on the controlled variable. Note that the controlled sources are indicated by circles rather than diamonds. All four dependent sources are characterized by a single parameter called GAIN. The units of the GAIN depend on the units of the signals at the input and output ports. As we will see in subsequent examples, these PSpice elements are combined with other resistive elements to model active devices, such as transistors and OP AMPs.

4–2 ANALYSIS OF CIRCUITS WITH DEPENDENT SOURCES

With certain modifications the analysis tools developed for passive circuits apply to active circuits as well. Circuit reduction applies to active circuits, but in so doing we must not eliminate the control variable for a dependent source. As noted previously, when applying the superposition principle or Thévenin's theorem, we must remember that dependent sources cannot be turned on and off independently since their states depend on excitation supplied by one or more independent sources. Applying a source transformation to a dependent source is sometimes helpful, but again we must not lose the identify of a controlling signal for a dependent source. Methods like node and mesh analysis can be adapted to include dependent sources as well.

However, the main difference is that the properties of active circuits can be significantly different from those of the passive circuits treated in Chapters 2 and 3. Our analysis examples are chosen to highlight these differences.

In our first example the objective is to determine the current, voltage, and power delivered to the 500-Ω output load in Figure 4–4. The control current i_X is found using current division in the input circuit:

$$i_X = \left(\frac{50}{50 + 25}\right) i_S = \frac{2}{3} i_S \tag{4-1}$$

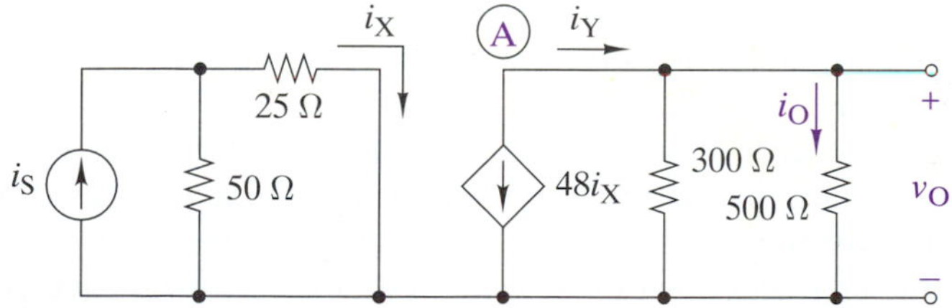

FIGURE 4–4 A circuit with a dependent source.

Similarly, the output current i_O is found using current division in the output circuit:

$$i_O = \left(\frac{300}{300 + 500}\right) i_Y = \frac{3}{8} i_Y \tag{4-2}$$

At node A, KCL requires that $i_Y = -48i_X$. Combining this result with Eqs. (4–1) and (4–2) yields the output current:

$$\begin{aligned} i_O &= \left(\frac{3}{8}\right)(-48)i_X = (-18)\left(\frac{2}{3}i_S\right) \\ &= -12\, i_S \end{aligned} \qquad (4-3)$$

The output voltage v_O is found using Ohm's law:

$$v_O = i_O\, 500 = -6000\, i_S \qquad (4-4)$$

The input–output relationships in Eqs. (4–3) and (4–4) are of the form $y = Kx$ with $K < 0$. The proportionality constants are negative because the reference direction for i_O in Figure 4–4 is the opposite of the orientation of the dependent source reference arrow. Active circuits often produce negative values of K, which means that the input and output signals have opposite algebraic signs. Circuits for which $K < 0$ are said to provide **signal inversion.** In the analysis and design of active circuits, it is important to keep track of signal inversions.

Using Eqs. (4–3) and (4–4), the power delivered to the 500-Ω load in Figure 4–4 is

$$p_O = v_O i_O = (-6000\, i_S)(-12\, i_S) = 72{,}000 i_S^2 \qquad (4-5)$$

The independent source at the input delivers its power to the parallel combination of 50 Ω and 25 Ω. Hence, the input power supplied by the independent source is

$$p_S = (50 \,||\, 25) i_S^2 = \left(\frac{50}{3}\right) i_S^2$$

Given the input power and output power, we find the power gain in the circuit:

$$\text{Power gain} = \frac{p_O}{p_S} = \frac{72{,}000 i_S^2}{(50/3) i_S^2} = 4320$$

A power gain greater than unity means that the circuit delivers more power at its output than it receives from the input source. At first glance this appears to be a violation of energy conservation, until we remember that dependent sources are models of active devices that require an external power supply to operate. Usually the external power supply is not shown in circuit diagrams. When using a dependent source to model an active circuit, we assume that the external supply and the active device itself can handle whatever power is required by the circuit. When designing the actual circuit, the engineer must make certain that the active device and its power supply operate within their power ratings.

Exercise 4–1

Find the output v_O in terms of the input v_S in the circuit in Figure 4–5.

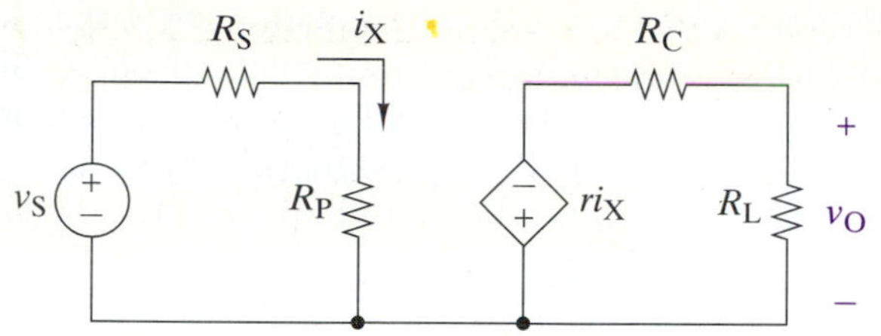

FIGURE 4–5

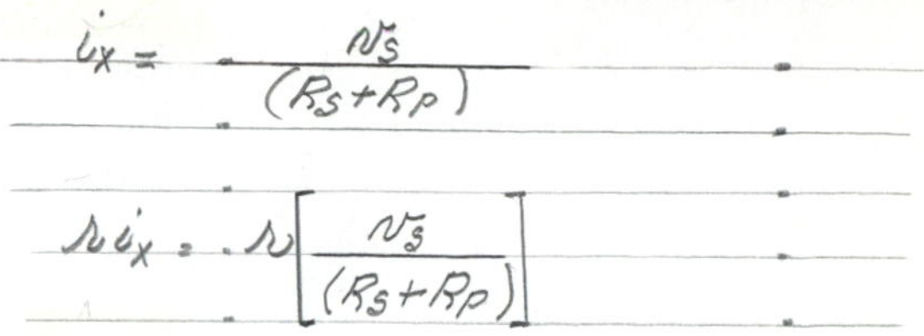

Answer:

$$v_O = \left[\frac{-R_L r}{(R_S + R_P)(R_C + R_L)}\right] v_S$$

NODE-VOLTAGE ANALYSIS WITH DEPENDENT SOURCES

Node analysis of active circuits is much the same as for passive circuits except that we must account for the additional constraints caused by the dependent sources. For example, the circuit in Figure 4–6 has five nodes. With node E as the reference, each independent voltage source has one terminal connected to ground. These connections force the conditions $v_A = v_{S1}$ and $v_B = v_{S2}$. Therefore, we only need to write node equations at nodes C and D because voltages at nodes A and B are already known.

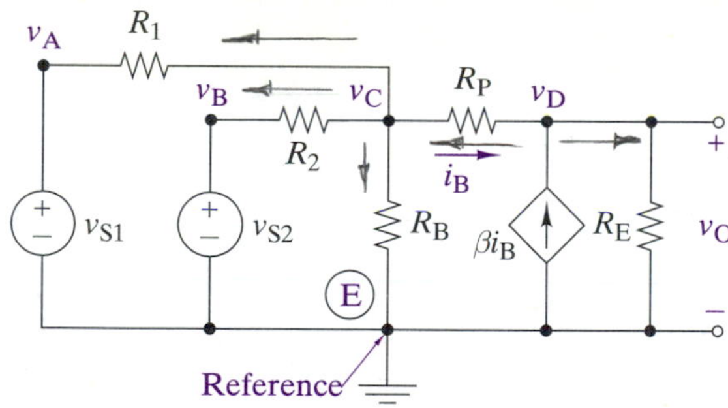

FIGURE 4–6 *Circuit used to demonstrate node-voltage analysis with dependent sources.*

Node analysis involves expressing element currents in terms of the node voltages and applying KCL at each unknown node. The sum of the currents leaving node C is

$$G_1(v_C - v_{S1}) + G_2(v_C - v_{S2}) + G_B v_C + G_P(v_C - v_D) = 0$$

Similarly, the sum of currents leaving node D is

$$G_P(v_D - v_C) + G_E v_D - \beta i_B = 0$$

These two node equations can be rearranged into the form

$$\text{Node C: } (G_1 + G_2 + G_B + G_P)v_C - G_P v_D = G_1 v_{S1} + G_2 v_{S2}$$

$$\text{Node D: } \quad -G_P v_C + (G_P + G_E)v_D = \beta i_B \tag{4–6}$$

We could write these two symmetrical node equations by inspection if the dependent current source βi_B had been an independent source. Since it is not independent, we must express its controlling variable i_B in terms of the unknown node voltages. Using the fundamental property of node voltages and Ohm's law, we express the current i_B in terms of the node voltages as

$$i_B = G_P(v_C - v_D)$$

Substituting this expression for i_B into Eq. (4–6) and putting the results in standard form yields

$$\text{Node C:}\quad (G_1 + G_2 + G_B + G_P)v_C - G_P v_D = G_1 v_{S1} + G_2 v_{S2}$$

$$\text{Node D:}\quad -(\beta + 1)G_P v_C + [(\beta + 1)G_P + G_E]v_D = 0 \tag{4-7}$$

The result in Eq. (4–7) involves two equations in the two unknown node voltages and includes the effect of the dependent source. Note that including the dependent source constraint destroys the coefficient symmetry in Eq. (4–6).

This example illustrates a general approach to writing node-voltage equations for circuits with dependent sources. We start out treating the dependent sources as if they are independent sources and write node equations for the resulting passive circuit using the inspection method developed in Chapter 3. This step produces a set of symmetrical node-voltage equations with the independent and dependent source terms on the right-hand side. Then we express the dependent source terms in terms of the unknown node voltages and move them to the left-hand side of the equations with the other terms involving the unknown node voltages. This step destroys the coefficient symmetry but leads to a set of node-voltage equations that describe the active circuit.

EXAMPLE 4–2

For the circuit in Figure 4–6, use the node-voltage equations in Eq. (4–7) to find the output voltage v_O when $R_1 = 1\ \text{k}\Omega$, $R_2 = 3\ \text{k}\Omega$, $R_B = 100\ \text{k}\Omega$, $R_P = 1.3\ \text{k}\Omega$, $R_E = 3.3\ \text{k}\Omega$, and $\beta = 50$.

SOLUTION:

Substituting the given numerical values into Eq. (4–7) yields

$$(2.11 \times 10^{-3})v_C - (7.69 \times 10^{-4})v_D = (10^{-3})v_{S1} + (3.33 \times 10^{-4})v_{S2}$$

$$-(3.92 \times 10^{-2})v_C + (3.95 \times 10^{-2})v_D = 0$$

We solve the second equation for $v_C = 1.008v_D$. When this equation is substituted into the first equation, we obtain

$$v_O = v_D = 0.736v_{S1} + 0.245v_{S2}$$

This circuit is as a signal summer that does not involve a signal inversion. The fact that the output is a linear combination of the two inputs reminds us that the circuit is linear. ■

EXAMPLE 4–3

The circuit in Figure 4–7(a) is a model of an inverting OP AMP circuit.

FIGURE 4–7

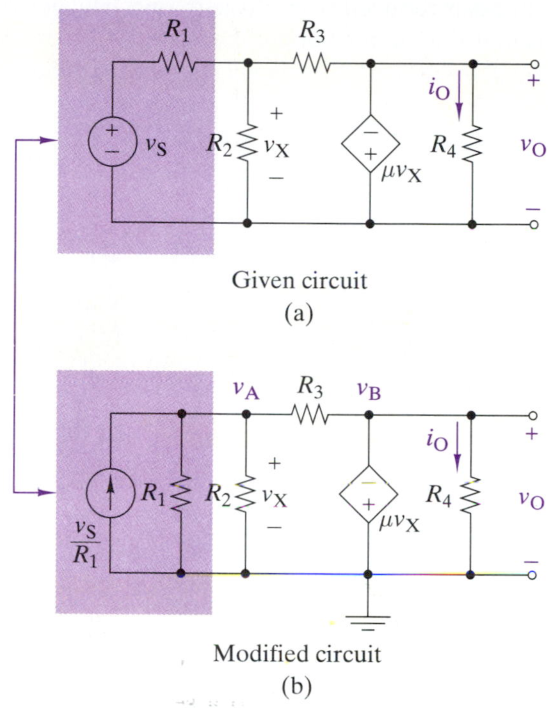

(a) Use node-voltage analysis to find the output v_O in terms of the input v_S.
(b) Evaluate the input–output relationship found in (a) as the gain μ becomes very large.

SOLUTION:

(a) Applying a source transformation to the independent source leads to the modified three-node circuit shown in Figure 4–7(b). With the indicated reference node the dependent voltage source constrains the voltage at node B. The control voltage is $v_X = v_A$, and the controlled source forces the node B voltage to be

$$v_B = -\mu v_X = -\mu v_A$$

Thus, node A is the only independent node in the circuit. We can write the node A equation by inspection as

$$(G_1 + G_2 + G_3)v_A - G_3 v_B = G_1 v_S$$

Substituting in the control source constraint yields the standard form for this equation:

$$[G_1 + G_2 + G_3(1 + \mu)]\, v_A = G_1 v_S$$

We end up with only one node equation even though at first glance the given circuit appears to need three node equations. The reason is that there are two voltage sources in the original circuit in Figure 4–7(a). Since the two sources share the reference node, the number of unknown node voltages is reduced from three to one. The general principle illustrated is that the number of independent KCL constraints in a circuit containing N nodes and N_V voltage sources (dependent or independent) is $N - 1 - N_V$.

The one-node equation can easily be solved for the output voltage $v_O = v_B$.

$$v_O = v_B = -\mu v_A = \left(\frac{-\mu G_1}{G_1 + G_2 + G_3(1+\mu)}\right) v_S$$

The minus sign in the numerator means that the circuit provides signal inversion. The output voltage does not depend on the value of the load resistor R_4, since the load is connected across an ideal (though dependent) voltage source.

(b) For large gains μ we have $(1+\mu)G_3 >> G_1 + G_2$ and the input–output relationship reduces to

$$v_O \approx \left[\frac{-\mu G_1}{(1+\mu)\, G_3}\right] v_S \approx -\left[\frac{R_3}{R_1}\right] v_S$$

That is, when the active device gain is large, the voltage gain of the active circuit depends on the ratio of two resistances. We will see this situation again with OP AMP circuits. ■

Exercise 4–2

(a) Formulate node-voltage equations for the circuit in Figure 4–8.

(b) Solve the node-voltage equations for v_O and i_O in terms of i_S.

FIGURE 4–8

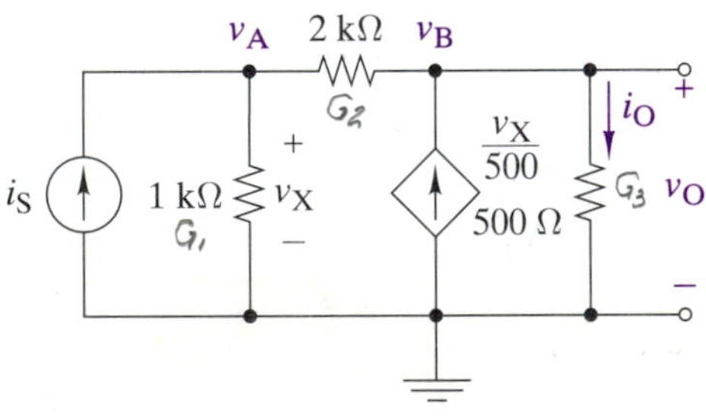

Answers:

(a)

$$(1.5 \times 10^{-3})\, v_A - (0.5 \times 10^{-3})\, v_B = i_S$$

$$-(2.5 \times 10^{-3})\, v_A + (2.5 \times 10^{-3})\, v_B = 0$$

(b) $v_O = 1000 i_S$; $i_O = 2 i_S$.

Exercise 4–3

Use node-voltage analysis to find v_O in Figure 4–9.

Answer:

$$v_O = \frac{G_X + \mu G_2}{G_X + G_L + (\mu + 1)G_2} v_S$$

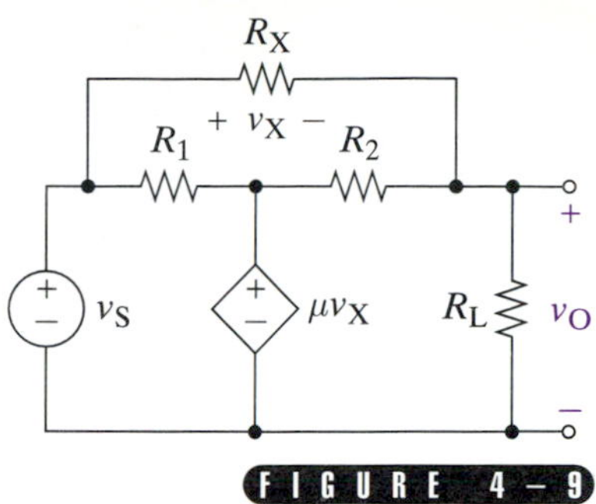

FIGURE 4–9

MESH-CURRENT ANALYSIS WITH DEPENDENT SOURCES

Mesh-current analysis of active circuits follows the same pattern noted for node-voltage analysis. We initially treat the dependent sources as independent sources and write the mesh equations of the resulting passive circuit using the inspection method from Chapter 3. We then account for the dependent sources by expressing their constraints in terms of unknown mesh currents. The following example illustrates the method.

EXAMPLE 4–4

(a) Formulate mesh-current equations for the circuit in Figure 4–10.
(b) Use the mesh equations to find v_O and R_{IN} when $R_1 = 50\ \Omega$, $R_2 = 1\ k\Omega$, $R_3 = 100\ \Omega$, $R_4 = 5\ k\Omega$, and $g = 100$ mS.

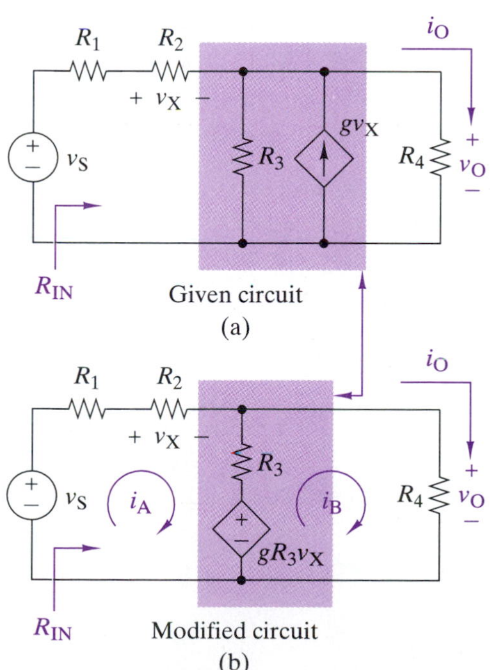

FIGURE 4–10

SOLUTION:

(a) Applying source transformation to the parallel combination of R_3 and gv_X in Figure 4–10(a) produces the dependent voltage source $R_3gv_X =$

μv_X in Figure 4–10(b). In the modified circuit we have identified two mesh currents. Initially treating the dependent source $(gR_3)v_X$ as an independent source leads to two symmetrical mesh equations.

$$\text{Mesh A: } (R_1 + R_2 + R_3)i_A - R_3 i_B = v_S - (gR_3)v_X$$

$$\text{Mesh B: } \quad -R_3 i_A + (R_3 + R_4)i_B = (gR_3)v_X$$

The control voltage v_X can be written in terms of mesh currents.

$$v_X = R_2 i_A$$

Substituting this equation for v_X into the mesh equations and putting the equations in standard form yields

$$(R_1 + R_2 + R_3 + gR_2R_3)i_A - R_3 i_B = v_S$$

$$-(R_3 + gR_2R_3)i_A + (R_3 + R_4)i_B = 0$$

The resulting mesh equations are not symmetrical because of the controlled source.

(b) Substituting the numerical values into the mesh equations gives

$$(1.115 \times 10^4)i_A - (10^2)i_B = v_S$$

$$-(1.01 \times 10^4)i_A + (5.1 \times 10^3)i_B = 0$$

Solving for the two mesh currents yields

$$i_A = \frac{\Delta_A}{\Delta} = \frac{\begin{vmatrix} v_S & -10^2 \\ 0 & 5.1 \times 10^3 \end{vmatrix}}{\begin{vmatrix} 1.115 \times 10^4 & -10^2 \\ -1.01 \times 10^4 & 5.1 \times 10^3 \end{vmatrix}} = \frac{5.1 \times 10^3 v_S}{5.5855 \times 10^7}$$

$$= 0.9131 \times 10^{-4} v_S$$

$$i_B = \frac{\Delta_B}{\Delta} = \frac{\begin{vmatrix} 1.115 \times 10^4 & v_S \\ -1.01 \times 10^4 & 0 \end{vmatrix}}{5.5885 \times 10^7} = 1.808 \times 10^{-4} v_S$$

The output voltage and input resistance are found using Ohm's law.

$$v_O = R_4 i_B = 0.904 v_S$$

$$R_{IN} = \frac{v_S}{i_A} = 10.95\ \text{k}\Omega$$ ■

EXAMPLE 4–5

The circuit in Figure 4–11 is a large signal model of a bipolar junction transistor operating in the active mode. Use mesh analysis to find the transistor base current i_B.

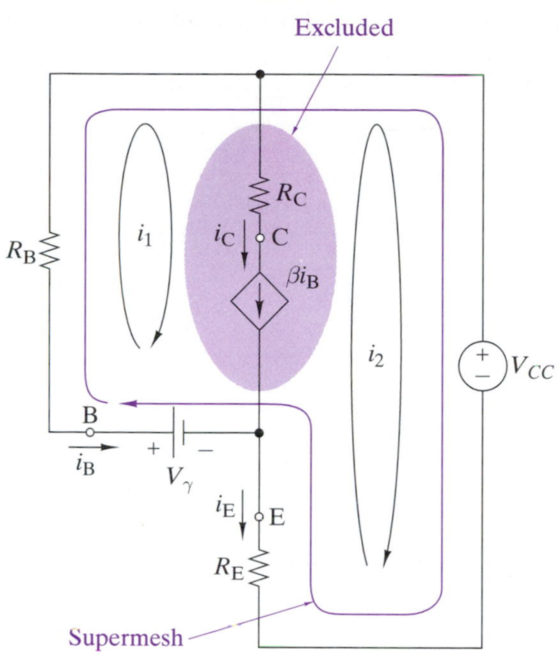

FIGURE 4–11 *Junction transistor circuit model*

SOLUTION:

The two mesh currents in Figure 4–11 are labeled i_1 and i_2 to avoid possible confusion with the transistor base current i_B. As drawn, the circuit requires a supermesh since the dependent current source βi_B is included in both meshes and is not connected in parallel with a resistance. A supermesh is created by combining meshes 1 and 2 after excluding the series subcircuit consisting of βi_B and R_C. Beginning at the bottom of the circuit, we write a KVL mesh equation around the supermesh using unknowns i_1 and i_2:

$$i_2 R_E - V_\gamma + i_1 R_B + V_{CC} = 0$$

This KVL equation provides one equation in the two unknown mesh currents. Since the two mesh currents have opposite directions through the dependent current source βi_B, the currents i_1, i_2, and βi_B are related by KCL as

$$i_1 - i_2 = \beta i_B$$

This constraint supplies the additional relationship needed to obtain two equations in the two unknown mesh-current variables. Since $i_B = -i_1$, the preceding KCL constraint means that $i_2 = (\beta + 1)i_1$. Substituting $i_2 = (\beta + 1)i_1$ into the supermesh KVL equation and solving for i_B yields

$$i_B = -i_1 = \frac{V_{CC} - V_\gamma}{R_B + (\beta + 1)R_E}$$ ■

Exercise 4–4

Use mesh analysis to find the current i_O in Figure 4–12 when the element E is a dependent current source $2i_X$ with the reference arrow directed down.

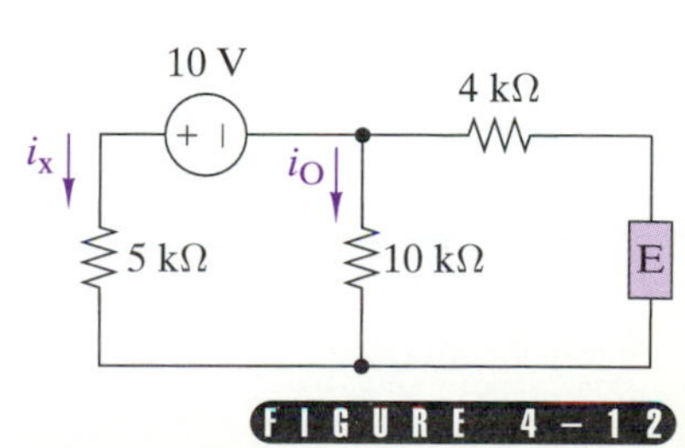

FIGURE 4–12

Answer:
–0.857 mA

Exercise 4–5

Use mesh analysis to find the current i_O in Figure 4–12 when the element E is a dependent voltage source $2000i_X$ with the plus reference at the top.

Answer:
–0.222 mA

EXAMPLE 4–6

The circuit in Figure 4–13 is a small signal model of a field effect transistor (FET) amplifier with two inputs v_{S1} and v_{S2}. Use MicroSim Design Center to solve for the input–output relationship of the circuit.

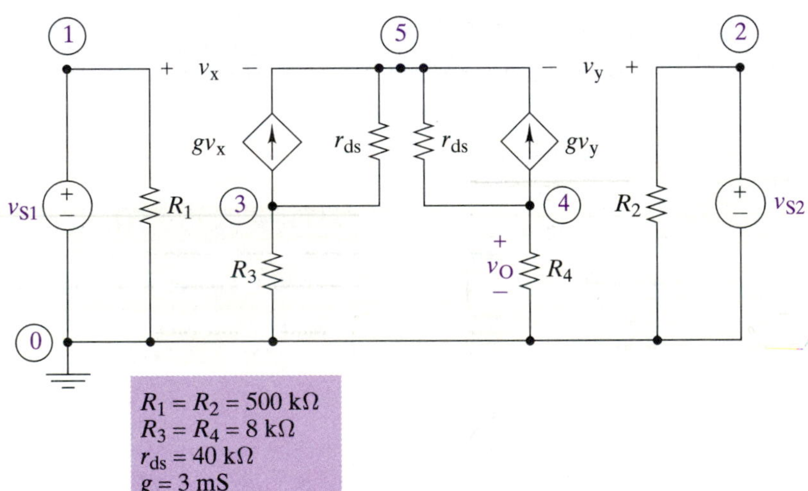

FIGURE 4–13 *Field effect transistor amplifier*

SOLUTION:

Since the circuit is linear, the input–output relationship is of the form

$$v_O = K_1 v_{S1} + K_2 v_{S2}$$

We can use the superposition principle to find the gain K_1 by setting $v_{S1} = 1$ and $v_{S2} = 0$ and solving for the node voltage V(4). The gain K_2 is then found by setting $v_{S1} = 0$ and $v_{S2} = 1$ and again solving for V(4). Figure 4–14 shows a MicroSim Schematics circuit diagram for the case $v_{S1} = 1$ and $v_{S2} = 0$. The figure also shows the resulting net list and a portion of the output file that includes the dc solution for the five node voltages. For this case the output file reports that V(4) = 10; therefore, gain $K_1 = V(4)/v_{S1} = 10$.

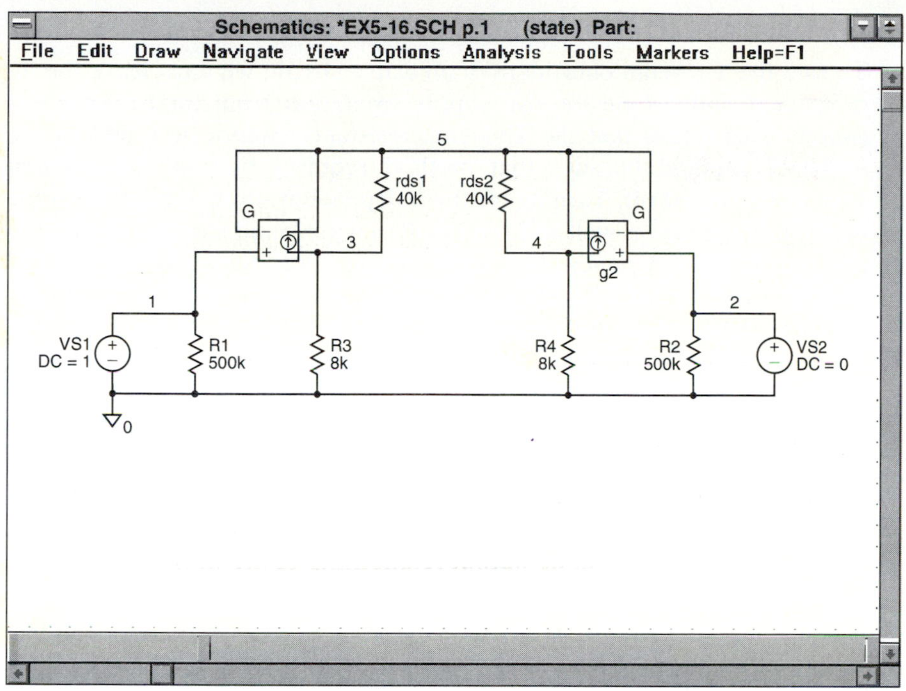

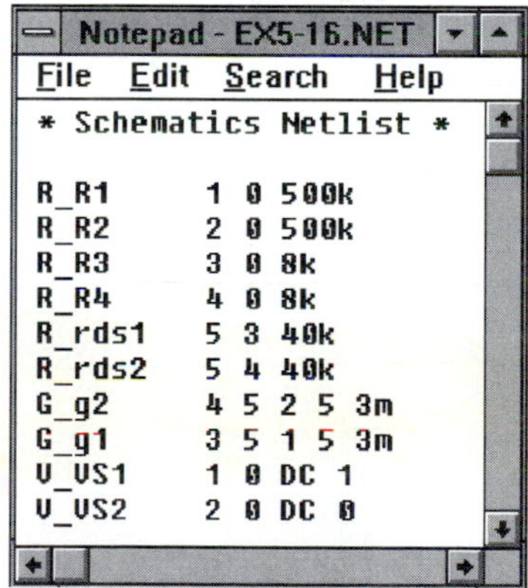
Notepad - EX5-16.NET

File Edit Search Help

```
* Schematics Netlist *

R_R1      1 0 500k
R_R2      2 0 500k
R_R3      3 0 8k
R_R4      4 0 8k
R_rds1    5 3 40k
R_rds2    5 4 40k
G_g2      4 5 2 5 3m
G_g1      3 5 1 5 3m
V_VS1     1 0 DC 1
V_VS2     2 0 DC 0
```

Notepad - EX5-16.OUT

File Edit Search Help

```
**SMALL SIGNAL BIAS SOLUTION
****************************
 NODE    VOLTAGE
(    1)     1.0000
(    2)     0.0000
(    3)   -10.0000
(    4)    10.0000
(    5)      .4959
```

FIGURE 4–14 *MicroSim Schematic diagram of the circuit in Figure 4–13.*

To find K_2, we change the source attributes to $v_{S1} = 0$ and $v_{S2} = 1$ and again simulate the circuit using MicroSim PSpice. For this case the output file reports V(4) = –10.000, and therefore $K_2 = V(4)/v_{S2} = -10$. The input–output relationship for the circuit is

$$v_O = 10(v_{S1} - v_{S2})$$

The circuit is a differential amplifier of a type often used as the input circuit of an OP AMP. ■

THÉVENIN EQUIVALENT CIRCUITS WITH DEPENDENT SOURCES

To find the Thévenin equivalent of an active circuit, we must leave the independent sources on or else supply excitation from an external test source. This means that the Thévenin resistance cannot be found by the lookback method because that method requires that all independent sources be turned off. Turning off the independent sources deactivates the dependent sources as well and can result in a profound change in the input and output characteristics of an active circuit. Thus, there are two ways of finding active circuit Thévenin equivalents. We can either find the open-circuit voltage and short-circuit current at the interface or directly solve for the interface i–v relationship.

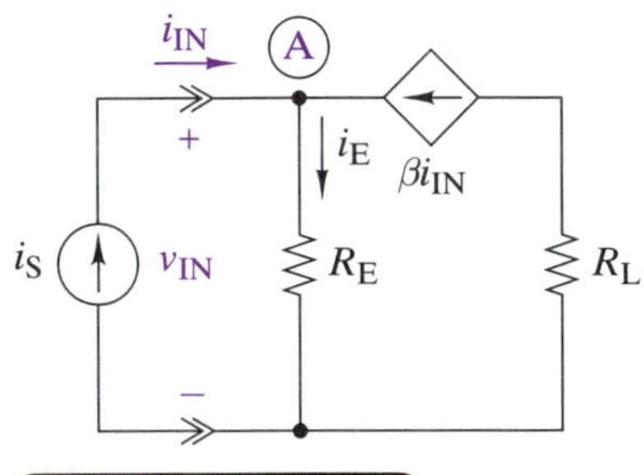

FIGURE 4–15

EXAMPLE 4–7

Find the input resistance of the circuit in Figure 4–15.

SOLUTION:

With the independent source turned off ($i_{IN} = i_S = 0$), the resistance seen at the input port is R_E since the dependent current source βi_{IN} is inactive and acts like an open circuit. Applying KCL at node A with the input source turned on yields

$$i_E = i_{IN} + \beta i_{IN} = (\beta + 1)i_{IN}$$

By Ohm's law, the input voltage is

$$v_{IN} = i_E R_E = (\beta + 1)i_{IN}R_E$$

Hence, the active input resistance is

$$R_{IN} = \frac{v_{IN}}{i_{IN}} = (\beta + 1)R_E$$

The circuit in Figure 4–15 is a model of a transistor circuit in which the gain parameter β typically lies between 50 and 100. The input resistance with external excitation is $(\beta + 1)R_E$, which is significantly different from the value of R_E without external excitation. ■

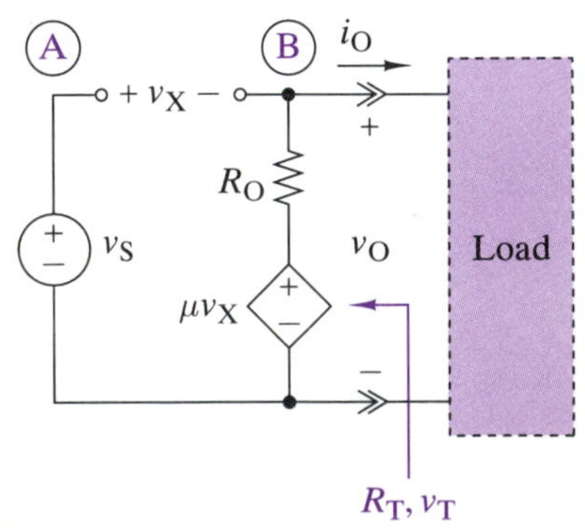

FIGURE 4–16

EXAMPLE 4–8

Find the Thévenin equivalent at the output interface of the circuit in Figure 4–16.

SOLUTION:

In this circuit the controlled voltage v_X appears across an open circuit between nodes A and B. By the fundamental property of node voltages, $v_X = v_S - v_O$. With the load disconnected and the input source turned off ($v_X = 0$), the dependent voltage source μv_X acts like a short circuit, and the Thévenin resistance looking back into the output port is R_O. With the load connected and the input source turned on, the sum of currents leaving node B is

$$\frac{v_O - \mu v_X}{R_O} + i_O = 0$$

Using the relationship $v_X = v_S - v_O$ to eliminate v_X and then solving for v_O produces the i–v characteristics at the output interface as

$$v_O = \frac{\mu v_S}{\mu + 1} - i_O\left[\frac{R_O}{\mu + 1}\right]$$

The i–v relationship of a Thévenin circuit is $v = v_T - iR_T$. By direct comparison, we find the Thévenin parameters of the active circuit to be

$$v_T = \frac{\mu v_S}{\mu + 1} \quad \text{and} \quad R_T = \frac{R_O}{\mu + 1}$$

The circuit in Figure 4–16 is a model of an OP AMP circuit called a voltage follower. The resistance R_O for a general-purpose OP AMP is around 100 Ω, while the gain μ is about 10^5. Thus, the active Thévenin resistance of the voltage follower is not 100 Ω, as the lookback method suggests, but is only a milliohm.

Exercise 4–6

Find the input resistance and output Thévenin equivalent circuit of the circuit Figure 4–17.

Answers:

$$R_{IN} = (1 + \mu)R_F$$

$$v_T = \frac{\mu}{\mu + 1}v_S$$

$$R_T = R_O$$

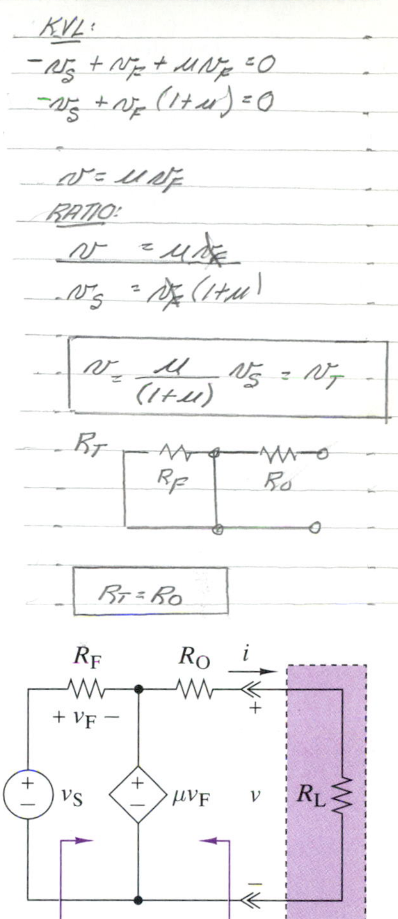

FIGURE 4–17

4–3 THE TRANSISTOR

The development of the **bipolar junction transistor (BJT)** in 1947 marked one of the major milestones in the history of technology. The term *bipolar* means that the i–v characteristics of the BJT depend on the action of both positive (holes) and negative (electrons) charge carriers. Initially, all transistors were fabricated and utilized as discrete components. Since the 1960s, integrated circuit technology has been the predominant method. With this technology the transistors and other devices are fabricated and interconnected on a tiny wafer of silicon called a chip. Detailed description of the physical properties of transistors is left to subsequent courses in semiconductor electronics.

The purpose of this section is to show how dependent sources are used to model an active device—the BJT. The BJT has several models for different applications, but we limit our study to the **large-signal model**. Although this model has a limited domain of application, it serves as a bridge

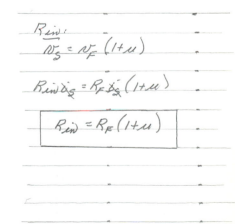

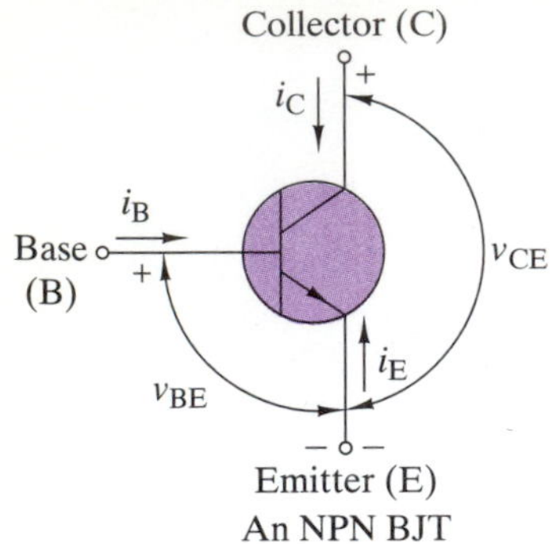

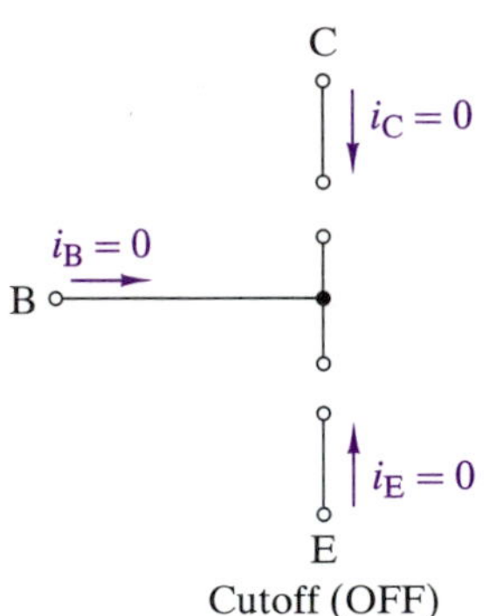

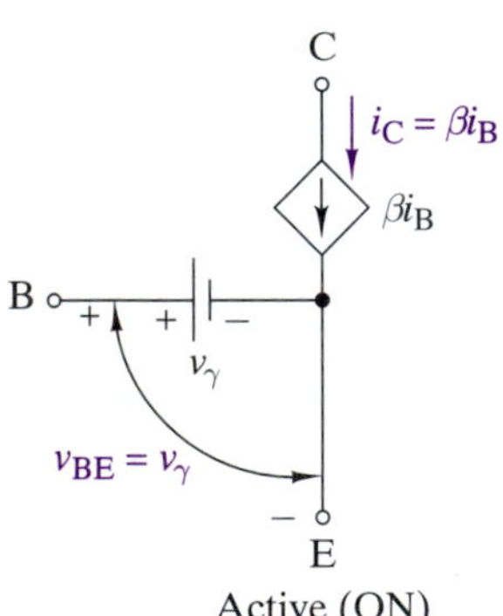

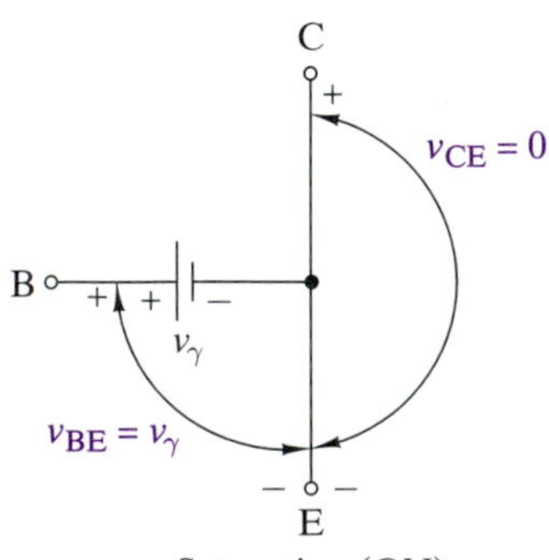

FIGURE 4–18 *Large signal model of the bipolar junction transistor.*

between the dependent sources in the previous sections and the OP AMP device in the next section.

The circuit symbol of the BJT is shown in Figure 4–18. The device has three terminals called the **emitter (E)**, the **base (B)**, and the **collector (C)**. The two voltages v_{BE} and v_{CE} shown in the figure are called the base-emitter voltage and the collector-emitter voltage, respectively. The three currents i_E, i_B, and i_C shown in Figure 4–18 are called the emitter, base, and collector currents. Writing a global KCL equation at the circle in the transistor circuit symbol yields

$$i_C + i_E + i_B = 0$$

This KCL constraint means that only two of the three transistor currents shown in Figure 4–18 can be independently specified.

LARGE-SIGNAL MODEL OF THE BJT

The model divides the nonlinear *i–v* characteristics of the BJT into three regions, or modes, called **cutoff**, **active**, and **saturation**. Figure 4–18 shows the equivalent circuit for each of these modes. In the cutoff mode the equivalent circuit consists of two open circuits; therefore, the currents i_B, i_E, and i_C are zero. In the saturation mode the open circuits are replaced by short circuits and an independent voltage source V_γ is added to produce the voltage constraints $v_{BE} = V_\gamma$ and $v_{CE} = 0$. In the active mode the equivalent circuit contains an independent voltage source V_γ and a current-controlled current source whose gain is β. Because of the orientation of these sources, we have $v_{BE} = V_\gamma$ and $i_C = \beta i_B$ when the transistor is in the active mode.

In summary, the large-signal model produces three sets of element equations:

$$\text{Cutoff mode:} \quad i_B = i_E = i_C = 0 \tag{4–8}$$

GAMMA

$$\text{Active mode:} \quad v_{BE} = V_\gamma \text{ and } i_C = \beta i_B \tag{4–9}$$

$$\text{Saturation mode:} \quad v_{BE} = V_\gamma \text{ and } v_{CE} = 0 \tag{4–10}$$

The large signal model has two parameters: (1) the **threshold voltage** $\mathbf{V_\gamma}$ which typically is around 0.7 V for a BJT; and (2) The **forward current gain** β, which ranges from about 50 to several hundred.

In linear circuits we usually analyze and design transistor circuits using the *i–v* characteristics of the active mode. When the operating mode is not given, we use a self-consistent approach to find the actual mode. Under this approach we assume that the transistor is in the active mode and use the element constraints in Eq. (4–9) together with normal circuit analysis methods to calculate the responses i_B and v_{CE}. We then use the following criteria to check whether the calculated responses are consistent with our assumption:

1. If $i_B > 0$ and $v_{CE} > 0$, the assumption is correct and the transistor is in the active mode.

2. If $i_B < 0$, the assumption is incorrect and the transistor is in cutoff with $i_B = 0$ and $i_C = 0$.
3. If $v_{CE} < 0$, the assumption is incorrect and the transistor is in saturation with $v_{CE} = 0$ and $v_{BE} = V_\gamma$.

The following examples illustrate circuit analysis using the large-signal model.

EXAMPLE 4–9

The parameters of the transistor circuit of Figure 4–19 are $V_\gamma = 0.7$ V, $\beta = 100$, $R_B = 100$ kΩ, $R_C = 1$ kΩ, and $V_{CC} = 5$ V. The dc source V_{CC} is necessary since the transistor is an active device that requires an external power supply to operate correctly.

(a) Find i_C and v_{CE} when $v_S = 3$ V.
(b) Find the range of the input voltage v_S over which the transistor operates in the active mode.
(c) Plot the output voltage v_{CE} versus the input voltage for v_S on the range from 0 to 10 V.

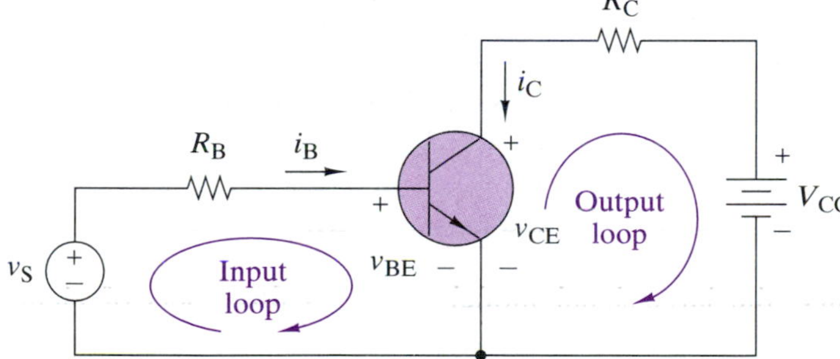

FIGURE 4–19 *Common emitter transistor circuit.*

SOLUTION:

(a) First we assume that the transistor is operating in the active mode. Under this assumption $v_{BE} = V_\gamma = 0.7$ V and the transistor base current is

$$i_B = \frac{v_S - V_\gamma}{R_B} = \frac{3 - 0.7}{10^5} = 23\ \mu\text{A} \qquad (4\text{–}11)$$

With the transistor in the active mode, the collector current $i_C = \beta i_B = 100 \times 23 \times 10^{-6} = 2.3$ mA. Writing a KVL equation around the output loop in Figure 4–19 yields

$$-v_{CE} - i_C R_C + V_{CC} = 0$$

from which we obtain v_{CE}:

$$v_{CE} = V_{CC} - i_C R_C = 5 - 2.3 = 2.7\ \text{V} \qquad (4\text{–}12)$$

This analysis yields $i_B = 23\ \mu\text{A} > 0$ and $v_{CE} = 2.7\ \text{V} > 0$. These results are consistent with our assumption and confirm that the transistor is operating in the active mode.

(b) The transistor operates in the active mode as long as $i_B > 0$ and $v_{CE} > 0$. Looking back at Eq. (4–11), we see that the base current is positive when $v_S > V_\gamma = 0.7$ V. Next, by looking at Eq. (4–12), we see that $v_{CE} > 0$ requires that $i_C < V_{CC}/R_C = 5$ mA. With the transistor in the active mode, $i_C < 5$ mA means that $i_B < i_C/\beta = 5 \times 10^{-3}/100 = 50\ \mu$A. Again invoking Eq. (4–11), we have

$$i_B = \frac{v_S - V_\gamma}{R_B} = \frac{v_S - 0.7}{10^5} < 50\ \mu\text{A}$$

This constraint requires that $v_S - 0.7 < 50 \times 10^{-6} \times 10^5$ or $v_S < 5.7$ V. The upshot is that the transistor is in the active mode when the input voltage is in the range $0.7 < v_S < 5.7$ V. This constraint also shows that $i_B < 0$ when $v_S < 0.7$ V. Negative base current is not consistent with the active mode. Hence, using the aforementioned criterion 2, we conclude that the transistor is in cutoff with $i_B = i_C = i_E = 0$ when $v_S < 0.7$ V.

(c) To complete this part of the problem, we must create a plot of v_{CE} versus v_S for $0 < v_S < 10$. When $0.7 < v_S < 5.7$, the transistor is in the active mode with $i_C = \beta i_B$. Using this result together with Eqs. (4–11) and (4–12), we find that

$$\begin{aligned} v_{CE} &= V_{CC} - \beta\, i_B R_C = V_{CC} - \beta \frac{R_C}{R_B}(v_S - V_\gamma) \\ &= 5.7 - v_S \end{aligned}$$

In the active mode the input-output relationship is $v_{CE} = 5.7 - v_S$, which is the equation of a straight line passing through $v_{CE} = 5$ when $v_S = 0.7$ and $v_{CE} = 0$ when $v_S = 5.7$ V. Note that when $v_S > 5.7$ this relationship predicts that $v_{CE} < 0$, which is not consistent with the active mode. Using criterion 3, we conclude that when $v_S > 5.7$ the transistor is in the saturation mode with $v_{CE} = 0$ V. When $0 < v_S < 0.7$, the transistor is in cutoff with $i_C = 0$, in which case Eq. (4–12) points out that $v_{CE} = V_{CC} = 5$ V. Figure 4–20 shows the resulting plot of the output in the cutoff, active, and saturation modes.

FIGURE 4–20

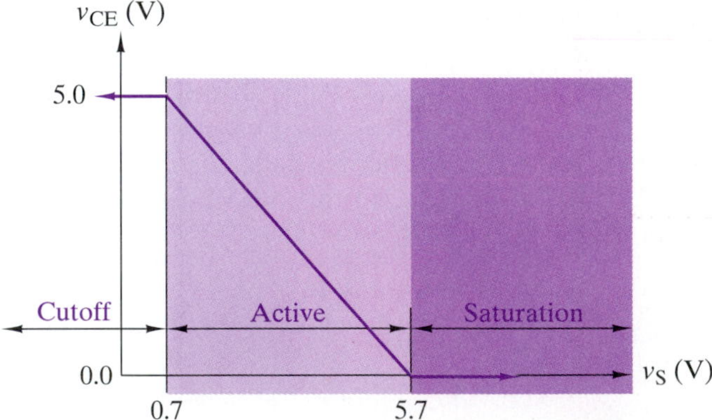

Comment: The plot in Figure 4–20 is called the transfer characteristic of the transistor circuit in Figure 4–19. In digital applications the input drives the transistor between the cutoff and saturation modes, passing quickly through the active mode. In analog applications the transistor remains in the active mode and operates as an amplifier. In the next section we see that the OP AMP also has a similar transfer characteristic. ■

EXAMPLE 4–10

In the transistor circuit in Figure 4–21, $V_{CC} = 10$ V, $R_C = 2.2$ kΩ, $V_\gamma = 0.7$ V, $\beta = 50$, and $v_S = 5$ V. Select the value of R_B so that $v_{CE} = 5$ V.

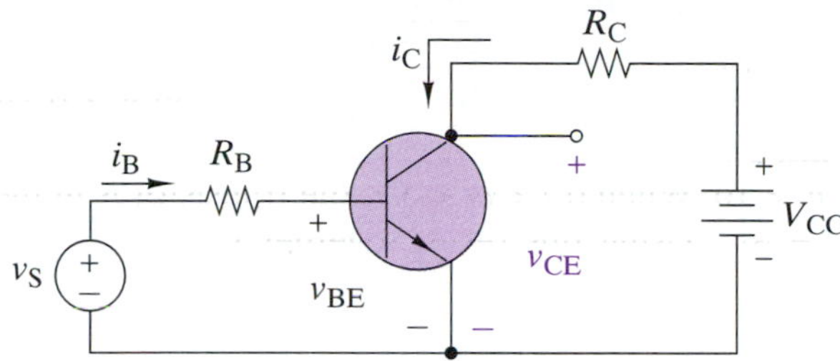

FIGURE 4–21

SOLUTION:

In the active mode collector voltage falls in the range $0 < v_{CE} < V_{CC}$. Since the specified value is in this range, the transistor must operate in the active mode. By KVL the voltage across R_C is $V_{CC} - v_{CE} = 10 - 5 = 5$ V, and hence the collector current is $i_C = 5/R_C = 2.27$ mA. In the active mode $i_C = \beta i_B$, and hence the base current is $i_B = i_C/50 = 45.5$ μA. In the active mode $v_{BE} = V_\gamma = 0.7$ V. By KVL, the voltage across R_B is $v_S - v_{BE} = 5 - 0.7 = 4.3$ V. So finally we have

$$R_B = \frac{v_S - v_{BE}}{i_B} = \frac{4.3}{45.5 \times 10^{-6}} = 94.5 \text{ k}\Omega$$

Note that for $R_B = 94.5$ kΩ the transistor is in the active mode since $i_B > 0$ and $v_{CE} > 0$. ■

Exercise 4–7

In the transistor circuit in Figure 4–21, $V_{CC} = 10$ V, $R_C = 2.2$ kΩ, $V_\gamma = 0.7$ V, $\beta = 50$, and $R_B = 100$ kΩ. Find the i_C and v_{CE} for $v_S = 3$ V.

Answer:
$i_C = 1.15$ mA; $v_{CE} = 7.47$ V.

Exercise 4–8

In the transistor circuit in Figure 4–21, $V_{CC} = 10$ V, $R_C = 2.2$ kΩ, $V_\gamma = 0.7$ V, $\beta = 50$, and $v_S = 5$ V. Select the value of R_B so that the transistor operates in the saturated mode.

Answer:
$R_B < 47.3$ kΩ

EXERCISE 4-7:
INPUT CURRENT:
$i_B = \frac{v_S - V_\gamma}{R_B} = \frac{3-0.7}{100K} = 2.3 \times 10^{-5}$
$= 23$ uamp
$i_C = \beta i_B = 50(23\times10^{-6})$
$= 1150\times10^{-6}$
$= 1.15$ ma
$v_{CE} = V_{CC} - i_C R_C$
$= 10 - (1.15\text{ma})(2.2K)$
$= 10 - 2.53 = 7.47$V

EXERCISE 4.8:
⇒ SATURATION MODE:
$v_{CE} = V_{CC} - i_C R_C$
⇒ $0 = V_{CC} - i_C R_C$
$i_C R_C = V_{CC} \Rightarrow i_C = \frac{V_{CC}}{R_C}$
$i_C = \frac{10V}{2.2K} = 4.545$ ma
$i_C = \beta i_B$
$i_B = \frac{i_C}{\beta} = \frac{4.545 \text{ ma}}{50}$
$= 90.9$ uamp
$i_B = \frac{v_S - V_\gamma}{R_B} = \frac{5-0.7}{R_B}$
$R_B = \frac{4.3}{i_B} = \frac{4.3V}{90.9 \text{uAmp}}$
$= 0.0473 \times 10^6$
$= 47.3K$

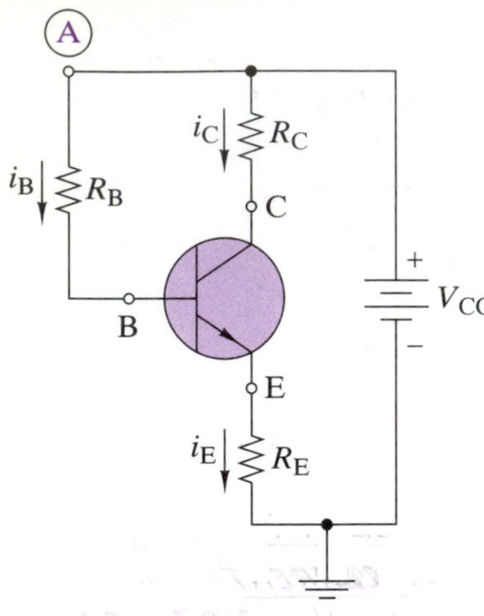

FIGURE 4–22

EXAMPLE 4–11

Derive an expression for the base current of the transistor in Figure 4–22. Assume that the transistor is in the active mode.

SOLUTION:

This problem is solved in Example 4–5 using formal mesh analysis. Here we use an informal method of analysis that is less structured but more representative of the ad hoc methods often used in electronic circuits analysis.

In the active mode $i_C = \beta i_B$. Applying KCL at node E yields $i_E = i_C + i_B = (\beta + 1)i_B$. Using Ohm's law, the voltage at node E is $v_E = i_E R_E = (\beta + 1)i_B R_E$. In the active mode $v_{BE} = V_\gamma$. Applying KVL, we express the voltage at node B as $v_B = v_{BE} + v_E = V_\gamma + (\beta + 1)i_B R_E$. For the indicated reference node, the voltage at node A is $v_A = V_{CC}$. Since $i_B = (v_A - v_B)/R_B$, we can now express the base current in the form

$$i_B = \frac{V_{CC} - [V_\gamma + (\beta + 1)i_B R_E]}{R_B}$$

Solving this expression for the base current yields

$$i_B = \frac{V_{CC} - V_\gamma}{R_B + (\beta + 1)R_E}$$

This equation is the same as the result obtained in Example 4–5 using mesh analysis. Which method do you think is easier? ■

4–4 THE OPERATIONAL AMPLIFIER

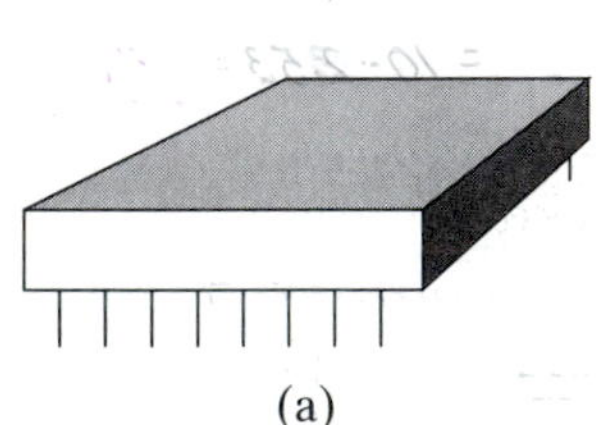

(a)

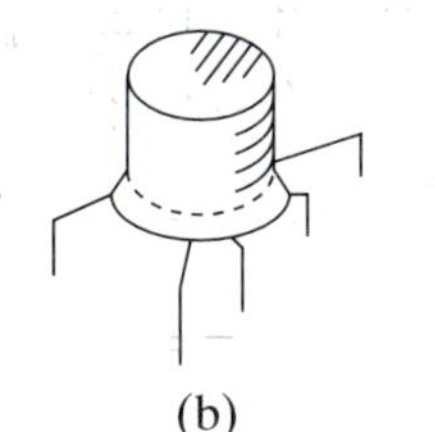

(b)

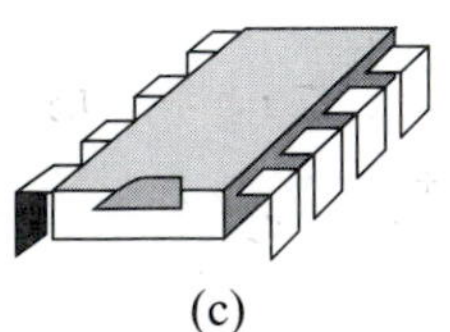

(c)

FIGURE 4–23 *Examples of integrated circuit OP AMP packages: (a) Encapsulated hybrid. (b) TO-5 can. (c) Dual in-line package.*

The integrated circuit operational amplifier is the premier linear active device in present-day analog circuit applications. The term *operational amplifier* was apparently first used in a 1947 paper by John R. Ragazzini and his colleagues, who reported on work carried out for the National Defense Research Council during World War II. The paper described high-gain dc amplifier circuits that perform mathematical operations (addition, subtraction, multiplication, division, integration, etc.), hence the name *operational amplifier.* For more than a decade the most important applications were general- and special-purpose analog computers using vacuum tube amplifiers. In the early 1960s general-purpose, discrete-transistor operational amplifiers became readily available, and by the mid-1960s the first commercial integrated circuit OP AMPs entered the market. The transition from vacuum tubes to integrated circuits decreased the size, power consumption, and cost of OP AMPs by nearly three orders of magnitude. By the early 1970s the integrated circuit version became the dominant active device in analog circuits.

The device itself is a complex array of transistors, resistors, diodes, and capacitors all fabricated and interconnected on a silicon chip less than 0.5 mm^2 in area and about 1 mm thick. Figure 4–23 shows examples of ways OP AMPs are packaged for use in circuits. In spite of its complexity, the device can be modeled by rather simple *i–v* characteristics. We do not need to concern ourselves with what is going on inside the package; rather, we can treat the OP AMP as a circuit element with a particular set of constraints between the voltages and currents at its external terminals.

OP AMP NOTATION

Certain matters of notation and nomenclature must be discussed before developing a circuit model for the OP AMP. The OP AMP is a five-terminal device, as shown in Figure 4–24(a). The "+" and "–" symbols identify the input terminals and are a shorthand notation for the noninverting and inverting input terminals, respectively. These "+" and "–" symbols identify the two input terminals and have nothing to do with the polarity of the voltages applied. The other terminals are the output and the positive and negative supply voltages, usually labeled $+V_{CC}$ and $-V_{CC}$. While some OP AMPs have more than five terminals, these five are always present and are the only ones we will use in this text. Figure 4–24(b) show how these terminals are arranged in a common eight-pin integrated circuit package.

The two power supply terminals in Figure 4–24 are not usually shown in circuit diagrams. Be assured that they are always there because the external power supplies are required for the OP AMP to operate as an active device. The power required for signal amplification comes through these terminals from an external power source. The $+V_{CC}$ and $-V_{CC}$ voltages applied to these terminals also determine the upper and lower limits on the OP AMP output voltage.

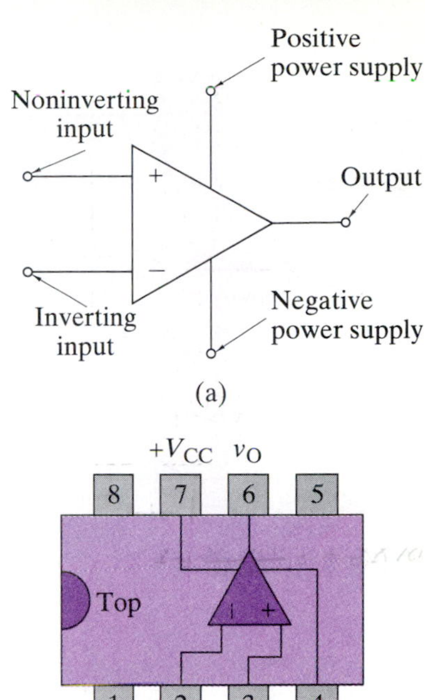

FIGURE 4–24 *The OP AMP: (a) Circuit symbol. (b) Pin-out diagram for an 8-pin package.*

Figure 4–25(a) shows a complete set of voltage and current variables for the OP AMP, while Figure 4–25(b) shows the abbreviated set of signal variables we will use. All voltages are defined with respect to a common reference node, usually ground. Voltage variables v_P, v_N, and v_O are defined by writing a voltage symbol beside the corresponding terminals. This notation means the "+" reference mark is at the terminal in question and the "–" reference mark is at the reference or ground terminal. In this book the reference directions for the currents are directed in at input terminals and out at the output. At times the abbreviated set of current variables may appear to violate KCL. For example, a global KCL equation for the complete set of variables in Figure 4–25(a) is

$$i_O = I_{C+} + I_{C-} + i_P + i_N \quad \text{(correct equation)} \qquad (4-13)$$

A similar equation using the shorthand set of current variables in Figure 4–25(b) reads

$$i_O = i_N + i_P \quad \text{(incorrect equation)} \qquad (4-14)$$

This equation is *not* correct, since it does not include all the currents. What is more important, it implies that the output current comes from the inputs. In fact, this is wrong. The input currents are very small, ideally zero. The output current comes from the supply voltages, as Eq. (4–13) points out, even though these terminals are not shown on the abbreviated circuit diagram.

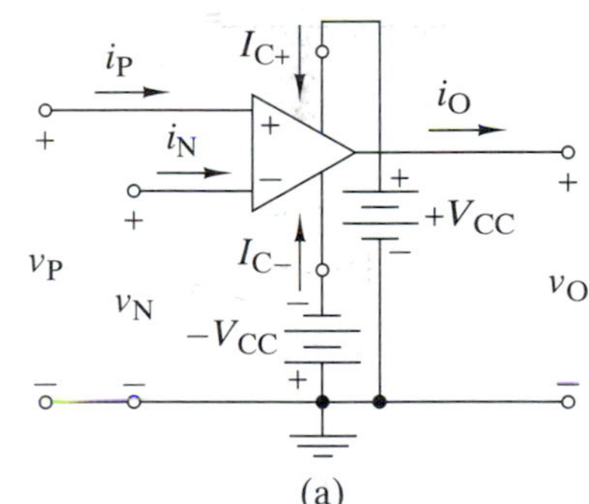

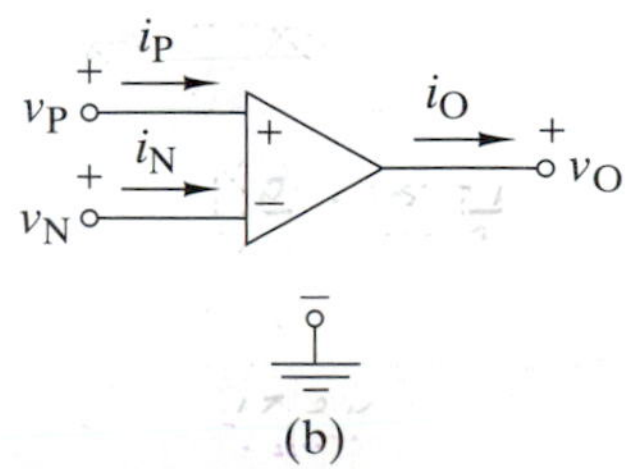

FIGURE 4–25 *OP AMP voltage and current definitions: (a) Complete set. (b) Shorthand set.*

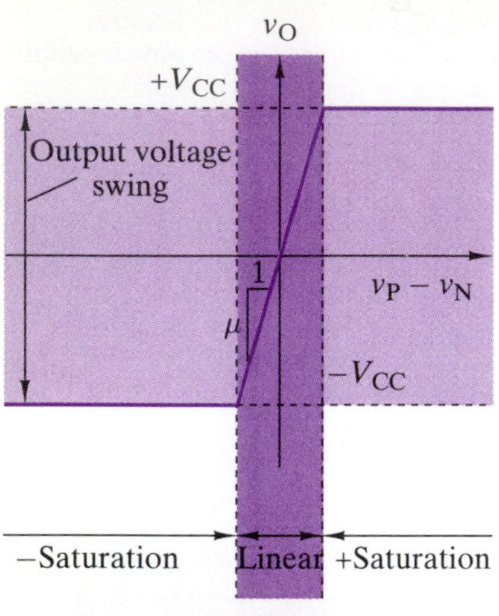

FIGURE 4–26 *OP AMP transfer characteristics.*

TRANSFER CHARACTERISTICS

The dominant feature of the OP AMP is the transfer characteristic shown in Figure 4–26. This characteristic provides the relationships between the **noninverting input** v_P, the **inverting input** v_N, and the **output voltage** v_O. The transfer characteristic is divided into three regions or modes called **+saturation**, **–saturation**, and **linear**. In the linear region the OP AMP is a **differential amplifier** because the output is proportional to the difference between the two inputs. The slope of the line in the linear range is called the voltage gain. In this linear region the input–output relation is

$$v_O = \mu(v_P - v_N) \tag{4-15}$$

The voltage gain of an OP AMP is very large, usually greater than 10^5. As long as the net input $(v_P - v_N)$ is very small, the output will be proportional to the input. However, when $\mu|v_P - v_N| > V_{CC}$, the OP AMP is saturated and the output voltage is limited by the supply voltages (less some small internal losses).

In the previous section, we found that the transistor has three operating modes. The input–output characteristic in Figure 4–26 points out that the OP AMP also has three operating modes:

1. +Saturation mode when $\mu(v_P - v_N) > V_{CC}$ and $v_O = +V_{CC}$.
2. –Saturation mode when $\mu(v_P - v_N) < -V_{CC}$ and $v_O = -V_{CC}$.
3. Linear mode when $\mu|v_P - v_N| < V_{CC}$ and $v_O = \mu(v_P - v_N)$.

Usually we analyze and design OP AMP circuits using the model for the linear mode. When the operating mode is not given, we use a self-consistent approach similar to the one used for the transistor. That is, we assume that the OP AMP is in the linear mode and then calculate the output voltage v_O. If it turns out that $-V_{CC} < v_O < +V_{CC}$, then the assumption is correct and the OP AMP is indeed in the linear mode. If $v_O < -V_{CC}$, then the assumption is wrong and the OP AMP is in the –saturation mode with $v_O = -V_{CC}$. If $v_O > +V_{CC}$, then the assumption is wrong and the OP AMP is in the +saturation mode with $v_O = +V_{CC}$.

IDEAL OP AMP MODEL

A dependent-source model of an OP AMP operating in its linear range is shown in Figure 4–27. This model includes an input resistance (R_I), an output resistance (R_O), and a voltage-controlled voltage source whose gain is μ. Numerical values of these OP AMP parameters typically fall in the following ranges:

$$10^6 < R_I < 10^{12}\ \Omega$$

$$10 < R_O < 100\ \Omega$$

$$10^5 < \mu < 10^8$$

Clearly, high input resistance, low output resistances, and high voltage gain are the key attributes of an OP AMP.

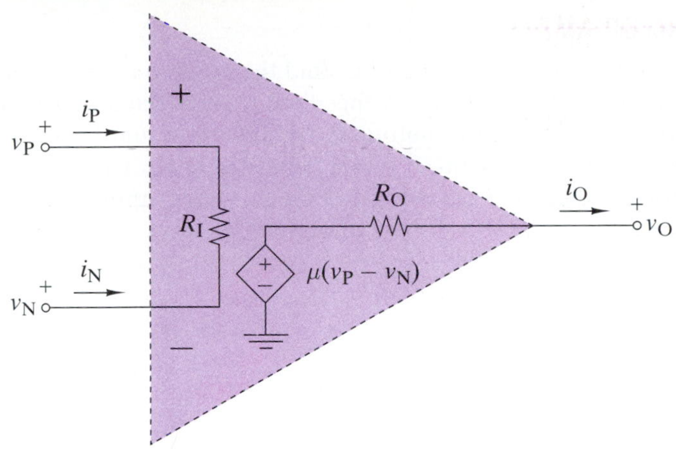

FIGURE 4–27 *Dependent-source model of an OP AMP operating in the linear mode.*

The dependent-source model can be used to develop the i–v relationships of the ideal model. For the OP AMP to operate in its linear mode, the output voltage is bounded by

$$-V_{CC} \leqslant v_O \leqslant +V_{CC}$$

Using Eq. (4–15), we can write this bound as

$$-\frac{V_{CC}}{\mu} \leqslant (v_P - v_N) \leqslant +\frac{V_{CC}}{\mu}$$

The supply voltage V_{CC} is typically about 15 V, while μ is a very large number, usually 10^5 or greater. Consequently, linear operation requires that $v_P \approx v_N$. In the ideal OP AMP model, the voltage gain is assumed to be infinite ($\mu \to \infty$), in which case linear operation requires $v_P = v_N$. The input resistance R_I of the ideal OP AMP is assumed to be infinite, so the currents entering both input terminals are both zero. In summary, the i–v relationships of the **ideal model** of the OP AMP are

$$v_P = v_N$$
$$i_P = i_N = 0 \qquad (4–16)$$

The implications of these element equations are illustrated on the OP AMP circuit symbol in Figure 4–28.

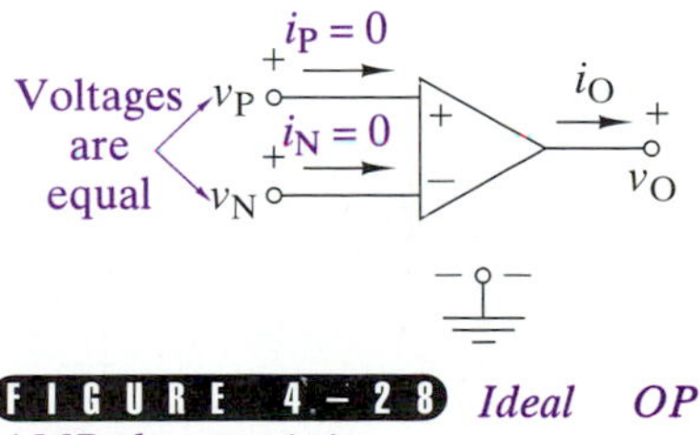

FIGURE 4–28 *Ideal OP AMP characteristics.*

At first glance the element constraints of the ideal OP AMP appear to be fairly useless. They look more like connection constraints and are totally silent about the output quantities (v_O and i_O), which are usually the signals of greatest interest. They seem to say that the OP AMP input terminals are simultaneously a short circuit ($v_P = v_N$) and an open circuit ($i_P = i_N = 0$). In practice, however, the ideal model of the OP AMP is very useful because in linear applications feedback is always present. That is, for the OP AMP to operate in a linear mode, it is necessary for there to be feedback paths from the output to one or both of the inputs. These feedback paths ensure that $v_P \approx v_N$ and make it possible for us to analyze OP AMP circuits using the ideal OP AMP element constraints in Eq. (4–16).

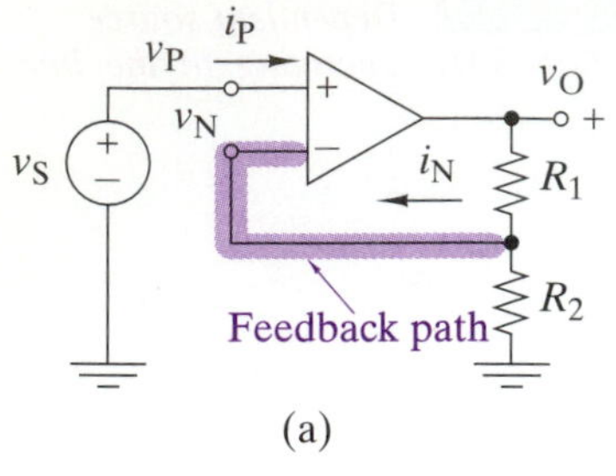

(a)

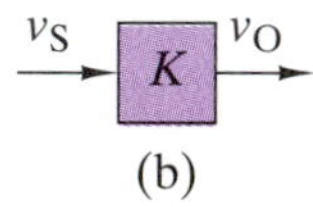

(b)

FIGURE 4–29 *The noninverting amplifier circuit.*

NONINVERTING OP AMP

To illustrate the effects of feedback, let us find the input–output characteristics of the circuit in Figure 4–29. In this circuit the voltage divider provided a feedback path from the output to the inverting input.[1] Since the ideal OP AMP draws no current at either input ($i_P = i_N = 0$), we can use voltage division to determine the voltage at the inverting input:

$$v_N = \frac{R_2}{R_1 + R_2} v_O \tag{4-17}$$

The input source connection at the noninverting input requires the condition

$$v_P = v_S \tag{4-18}$$

The ideal OP AMP element constraints demand that $v_P = v_N$, therefore, we can equate the right sides of Eqs. (4–17) and (4–18) to obtain the input–output relationship of the overall circuit.

$$v_O = \frac{R_1 + R_2}{R_2} v_S \tag{4-19}$$

The preceding analysis illustrates a general strategy for analyzing OP AMP circuits. We use normal circuit analysis methods to express the OP AMP input voltages v_P and v_N in terms of circuit parameters. We then use the ideal OP AMP constraint $v_P = v_N$ to solve for the overall circuit input–output relationship.

The circuit in Figure 4–29(a) is called a **noninverting amplifier**. The input–output relationship is of the form $v_O = Kv_S$, which reminds us that the circuit is linear. Figure 4–29(b) shows the functional building block for this circuit, where the proportionality constant K is

$$K = \frac{R_1 + R_2}{R_2} \tag{4-20}$$

In an OP AMP circuit the proportionality constant K is sometimes called the **closed-loop** gain, because it defines the input–output relationship when the feedback loop is connected (closed).

When discussing OP AMP circuits, it is necessary to distinguish between two types of gains. The first is the large voltage gain provided by the OP AMP device itself. The second is the voltage gain of the OP AMP circuit with a negative feedback path. Note that Eq. (4–20) indicates that the circuit gain is determined by the resistors in the feedback path and not by the value of the OP AMP gain. The gain in Eq. (4–20) is really the voltage division rule upside down. Variation of the value of K depends on the tolerance on the resistors in the feedback path, and not the variation in the value of the OP AMP's gain. In effect, feedback converts the OP AMP's very large but variable gain into a much smaller but well-defined gain.

1 The feedback must always be to the noninverting input, otherwise the circuit will be unstable for reasons that cannot be explained by what we have learned up to now.

D DESIGN EXAMPLE 4–12

Gain 10 Amplifier Design

Design an amplifier with a gain of $K = 10$.

SOLUTION:

Using a noninverting OP AMP circuit, the design problem is to select the values of the resistors in the feedback path. From Eq. (4–20) the design constraint is

$$10 = \frac{(R_1 + R_2)}{R_2}$$

We have one constraint with two unknowns. Arbitrarily selecting $R_2 = 10\ \text{k}\Omega$, we find $R_1 = 90\ \text{k}\Omega$. These resistors would normally have low tolerances (± 1% or less) to produce a precisely controlled closed-loop gain.

Comment: The problem of choosing resistance values in OP AMP circuit design problems deserves some discussion. Although values of resistance from a few ohms to several hundred megohms are commercially available, we generally limit ourselves to the range from about 1 kΩ to perhaps 1 MΩ. The lower limit of 1 kΩ is imposed in part because of power dissipation in the resistors. Typically, we use resistors with ¼-W power ratings or less. The maximum voltage in OP AMP circuits is often around 15 V. The smallest ¼-W resistance we can use is $R_{\text{MIN}} \geq (15)^2/0.25 = 900\ \Omega$, or about 1 kΩ. The upper bound of 1 MΩ comes about because surface leakage make it is difficult to maintain the tolerance in a high-value resistance. High-value resistors are also noisy, which leads to problems when they are connected in the feedback path. The 1-kΩ to 1-MΩ range should be used as a guideline and not an inviolate design rule. Actual design choices are influenced by system-specific factors and changes in technology. ■

Exercise 4–9

The noninverting amplifier circuit in Figure 4–29(a) is operating with $R_1 = 2R_2$ and $V_{CC} = \pm 12$ V. Over what range of input voltages v_S is the OP AMP in the linear mode?

Answer:

$-4\text{ V} < v_S < +4\text{ V}$

EFFECTS OF FINITE OP AMP GAIN

The ideal OP AMP model has an infinite gain. Actual OP AMP devices have very large, but finite voltage gains. We now address the effect of large but finite gain on the input–output relationships of OP AMP circuits.

The circuit in Figure 4–30 shows a finite gain OP AMP circuit model in which the input resistance R_I is infinite. The actual values of OP AMP input resistance range from 10^6 to 10^{12} Ω, so no important effect is left out by ignoring this resistance. Examining the circuit, we see that the noninverting input voltage is determined by the independent voltage source.

The inverting input can be found by voltage division, since the current i_N is zero. In other words, Eqs. (4–17) and (4–18) apply to this circuit as well.

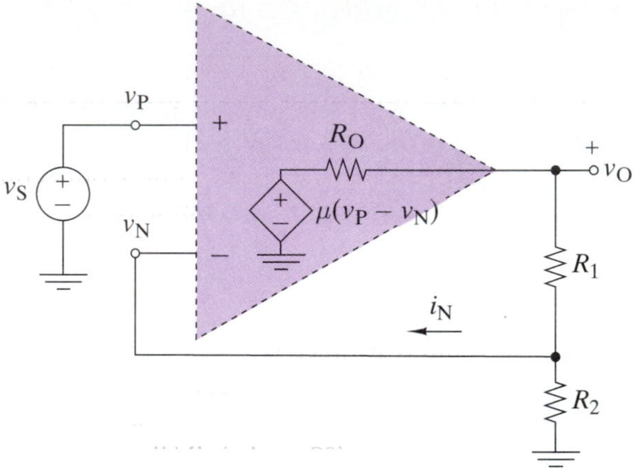

FIGURE 4–30 *The noninverting amplifier circuit with a dependent-source model.*

We next determine the output voltage in terms of the controlled source voltage using voltage division on the series connection of the three resistors R_O, R_1, and R_2:

$$v_O = \frac{R_1 + R_2}{R_O + R_1 + R_2}\mu(v_P - v_N)$$

Substituting v_P and v_N from Eqs. (4–17) and (4–18) yields

$$v_O = \left[\frac{R_1 + R_2}{R_O + R_1 + R_2}\right]\mu\left[v_S - \frac{R_2}{R_1 + R_2}v_O\right] \qquad (4\text{–}21)$$

The intermediate result in Eq. (4–21) shows that feedback is present since v_O appears on both sides of the equation. Solving for v_O yields

$$v_O = \frac{\mu(R_1 + R_2)}{R_O + R_1 + R_2(1 + \mu)}v_S \qquad (4\text{–}22)$$

In the limit, as $\mu \to \infty$, Eq. (4–22) reduces to

$$v_O = \frac{R_1 + R_2}{R_2}v_S = Kv_S$$

where K is the closed-loop gain we previously found using the ideal OP AMP model.

To see the effect of a finite μ, we ignore R_O in Eq. (4–22) since it is generally quite small compared with $R_1 + R_2$. With this approximation Eq. (4–22) can be written in the following form:

$$v_O = \frac{K}{1 + (K/\mu)}v_S \qquad (4\text{–}23)$$

When written in this form, we see that the closed-loop gain reduces to K as $\mu \to \infty$. Moreover, we see that the finite-gain model yields a good approximation to the ideal model results as long as $K << \mu$. In other words, the ideal model yields good results as long as the closed-loop gain is much less than the gain of the OP AMP device. One practical rule of thumb is to limit the closed-loop gain to less than 1% of the OP AMP gain (i.e., $K < \mu/100$).

The feedback path also affects the active output resistance. To see this, we construct a Thévenin equivalent circuit using the open-circuit voltage and the short-circuit current. Equation (4–23) is the open-circuit voltage, and we need only find the short-circuit current. Connecting a short-circuit at the output in Figure 4–30 forces $v_N = 0$ but leaves $v_P = v_S$. Therefore, the short-circuit current is

$$i_{SC} = \mu(v_S/R_O)$$

As a result, the Thévenin resistance is

$$R_T = \frac{v_{OC}}{i_{SC}} = \frac{K/\mu}{1 + K/\mu}R_O$$

When $K << \mu$, this expression reduces to

$$R_T = \frac{K}{\mu}R_O \approx 0\ \Omega$$

The OP AMP circuit with feedback has an output Thévenin resistance that is much smaller than the output Thévenin resistance of the OP AMP device itself. In fact, the Thévenin resistance is very small since R_O is typically less 100 Ω and μ is greater than 10^5.

At this point we can summarize our discussion. We introduced the OP AMP as an active five-terminal device including two supply terminals not normally shown on the circuit diagram. We then developed an ideal model of this device that is used to analyze and design circuits that have feedback. Feedback must be present for the device to operate in the linear mode. The most dramatic feature of the ideal model is the assumption of infinite gain. Using a finite-gain model, we found that the ideal model predicts the circuit input–output relationship quite closely as long as the circuit gain K is much smaller than the OP AMP gain μ. We also discovered that the Thévenin output resistance of an OP AMP with feedback is essentially zero.

In the rest of this book we use the ideal *i–v* constraints in Eq. (4–16) to analyze OP AMP circuits. The OP AMP circuits have essentially zero output resistance, which means that the output voltage does not change with different loads. Unless otherwise stated, from now on the term *OP AMP* refers to the ideal model.

4–5 OP AMP CIRCUIT ANALYSIS

This section introduces OP AMP circuit analysis using examples that are building blocks for analog signal-processing systems. We have already introduced one of these circuits—the noninverting amplifier discussed in the preceding section. The other basic circuits are the voltage follower, the inverting amplifier, the summer, and the subtractor. The key to using the building block approach is to recognize the feedback pattern and to isolate the basic circuit as a building block. The first example illustrates this process.

EXAMPLE 4–13

Find the input–output relationship of the circuit in Figure 4–31(a).

FIGURE 4–31

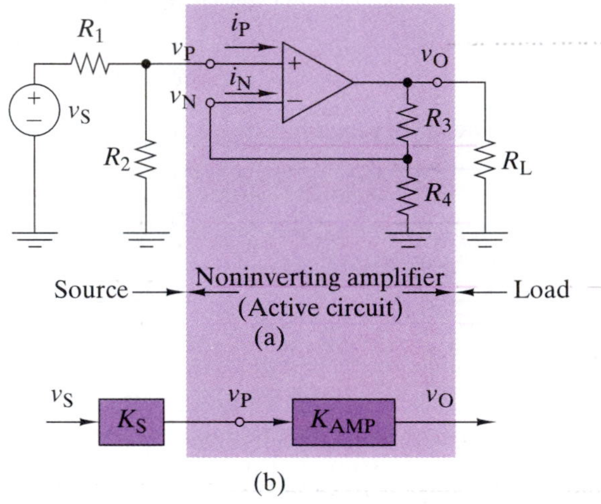

SOLUTION:

When the circuit is partitioned as shown in Figure 4–31(a), we recognize two building block gains: (1) K_S, the proportionality constant of the source circuit, and (2) K_{AMP}, the gain of the noninverting amplifier. The OP AMP circuit input current $i_P = 0$; hence, we can use voltage division to find K_S as

$$K_S = \frac{v_P}{v_S} = \frac{R_2}{R_1 + R_2}$$

Since the noninverting amplifier has zero output resistance, the load R_L has no effect on the output voltage v_O. Using Eq. (4–19), the gain of the noninverting amplifier circuit is

$$K_{AMP} = \frac{v_O}{v_P} = \frac{R_3 + R_4}{R_4}$$

The overall circuit gain is found as

$$\begin{aligned} K_{CIRCUIT} &= \frac{v_O}{v_S} = \left[\frac{v_P}{v_S}\right]\left[\frac{v_O}{v_P}\right] \\ &= K_S \times K_{AMP} \\ &= \left[\frac{R_2}{R_1 + R_2}\right]\left[\frac{R_3 + R_4}{R_4}\right] \end{aligned}$$

The gain $K_{CIRCUIT}$ is the product of K_S times K_{AMP} because the amplifier circuit does not load the source circuit since $i_P = 0$. ■

VOLTAGE FOLLOWER

The OP AMP in Figure 4–32(a) is connected as a **voltage follower** or **buffer**. In this case, the feedback path is a direct connection from the output to the inverting input. The feedback connection forces the condition $v_N = v_O$. The input current $i_P = 0$, so there is no voltage across the source resistance R_S. Applying KVL, we have the input condition $v_P = v_S$. The ideal OP AMP model requires $v_P = v_N$, so we conclude that $v_O = v_S$. By inspection, the closed-loop gain is $K = 1$. Since the output exactly equals the input, we say that the output follows the input (hence the name *voltage follower*).

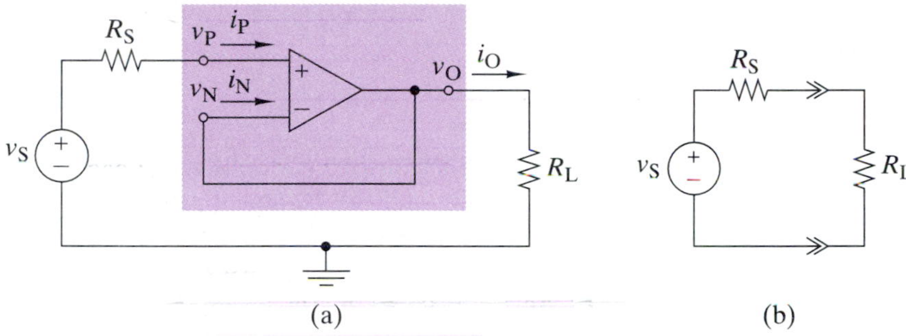

FIGURE 4–32 *The OP AMP voltage follower: (a) Connected at an interface. (b) Interface with the voltage follower.*

The voltage follower is used in interface circuits because it isolates the source from the load. Note that the input–output relationship $v_O = v_S$ does not depend on the source or load resistance. When the source is connected directly to the load, as in Figure 4–32(b), the voltage delivered to the load depends on R_S and R_L. The source and load interaction limits the signals that can be transferred across the interface, as discussed in Chapter 3. When the voltage follower is inserted between the source and load, the signal levels are limited by the capability of the OP AMP.

By Ohm's law, the current delivered to the load is $i_O = v_O/R_L$. But since $v_O = v_S$, the output current can be written in the form

$$i_O = v_S/R_L$$

Applying KCL at the reference node, we discover an apparent dilemma:

$$i_P = i_O$$

For the ideal model $i_P = 0$, but the preceding equations say that i_O cannot be zero unless v_S is zero. It appears that KCL is violated.

The dilemma is resolved by noting that the circuit diagram does not include the supply terminals. The output current comes from the power supply and not from the input. This dilemma arises only at the reference node (the ground terminal). In OP AMP circuits, as in all circuits, KCL must be satisfied. However, we must be alert to the fact that a KCL equation at the reference node could yield misleading results because the power supply terminals are not usually included in circuit diagrams.

EXERCISE 4-10
$v_S = 1.5V$ $R_S = 2K$ $R_L = 1K$

(a) FIG. 4-32(a) VOLTAGE FOLLOWER
$v_O = v_S = 1.5V$
$P_O = \frac{(v_O)^2}{R_L} = \frac{(1.5)^2}{1K} = \frac{2.250}{1K}$
$= 2.250 \times 10^{-3} = 2{,}250\ \mu W$

(b) FIG. 4-32(b) SOURCE CONNECTED DIRECTLY TO LOAD
$v_O = \frac{R_L}{R_L+R_S}(v_S) = \frac{1}{1+2}(1.5) = 0.5V$
$P = \frac{v_O^2}{R} = \frac{(0.5)^2}{1K} = 0.25 \times 10^{-3}$
$= 250\ \mu W$

(c) FIG 4-32(b)
MAX POWER TO LOAD
$R_L = R_S$
$v_O = \frac{R_L}{R_L+R_L} v_S = \frac{1}{2} v_S = 0.75V$
$P_O = \frac{(v_O)^2}{R_L} = \frac{(0.75)^2}{2K} = \frac{0.5625}{2K}$
$= 0.28125 \times 10^{-3}$
$= 281.25\ \mu W$

Exercise 4–10

The circuits in Figure 4–32 have $v_S = 1.5$ V, $R_S = 2$ kΩ, and $R_L = 1$ kΩ. Compute the maximum power available from the source. Compute the power absorbed by the load resistor in the direct connection in Figure 4–32(b) and in the voltage follower circuit in Figure 4–32(a). Discuss any differences.

Answers:
281 μW; 250 μW; 2250 μW.

DISCUSSION: *With the direct connection, the power delivered to the load is less than the maximum power available. With the voltage follower circuit, the power delivered to the load is greater than the maximum value specified by the maximum power transfer theorem. However, the maximum power transfer theorem does not apply to the voltage follower circuit since the load power comes from the OP AMP power supply rather than the signal source.*

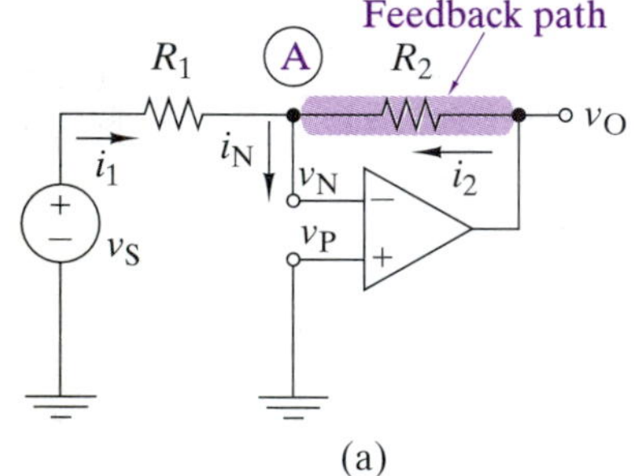

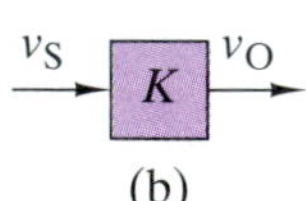

FIGURE 4–33 *The inverting amplifier circuit.*

THE INVERTING AMPLIFIER

The circuit in Figure 4–33 is called an **inverting amplifier**. The key feature of this circuit is that the input signal and the feedback are both applied at the inverting input. Since the noninverting input is grounded, we have $v_P = 0$, an observation we will use shortly. The sum of currents entering node A can be written as

$$\frac{v_S - v_N}{R_1} + \frac{v_O - v_N}{R_2} - i_N = 0 \qquad (4\text{–}24)$$

The element constraints for the OP AMP are $v_P = v_N$ and $i_P = i_N = 0$. Since $v_P = 0$, it follows that $v_N = 0$. Substituting the OP AMP constraints into Eq. (4–24) and solving for the input–output relationship yields

$$v_O = -\left(\frac{R_2}{R_1}\right) v_S \qquad (4\text{–}25)$$

This result is of the form $v_O = Kv_S$, where K is the closed-loop gain. However, in this case the voltage gain $K = -R_2/R_1$ is negative, indicating a signal inversion (hence the name *inverting amplifier*). We use the block diagram symbol in Figure 4–33(b) to indicate either the inverting or the noninverting OP AMP configuration.

The OP AMP constraints mean that the input current i_1 in Figure 4–33(a) is

$$i_1 = \frac{v_S - v_N}{R_1} = \frac{v_S}{R_1}$$

This, in turn, shows that the input resistance seen by the source v_S is

$$R_{IN} = \frac{v_S}{i_1} = R_1 \qquad (4\text{–}26)$$

In other words, the inverting amplifier has a finite input resistance determined by the external resistor R_1.

The next example shows that the finite input resistance must be taken into account when analyzing circuits with OP AMPs in the inverting amplifier configuration.

EXAMPLE 4–14

Find the input–output relationship of the circuit in Figure 4–34(a).

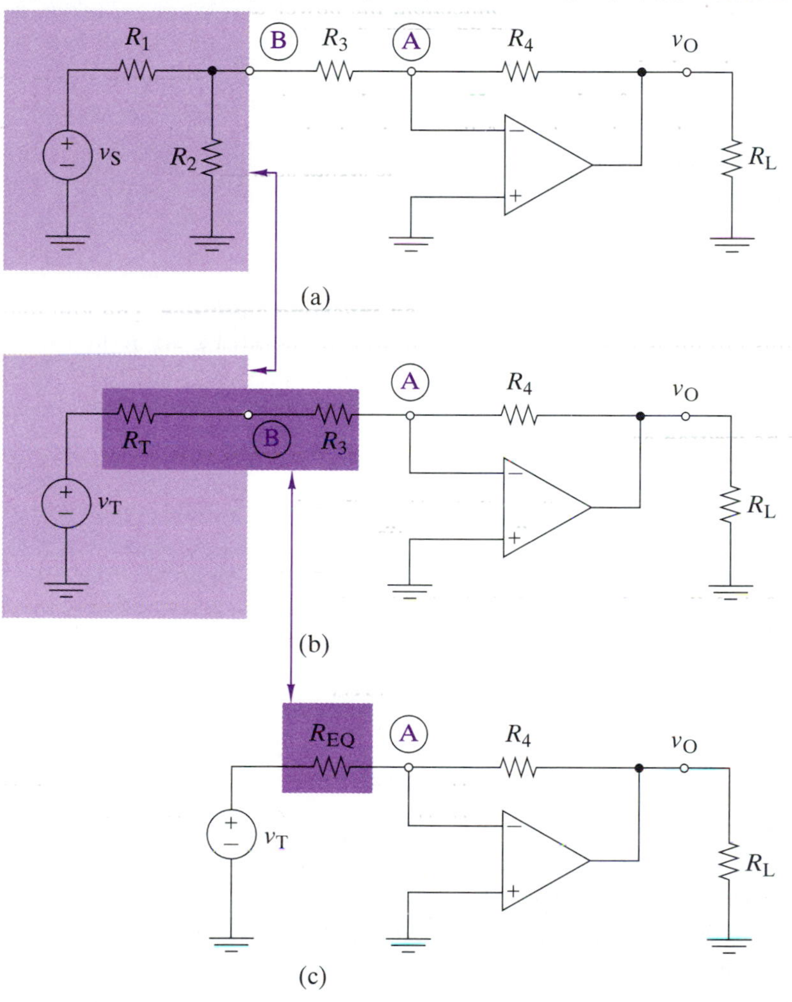

FIGURE 4–34

SOLUTION:

The circuit to the right of node B is an inverting amplifier. The load resistance R_L has no effect on the circuit transfer characteristics since the OP AMP has zero output resistance. However, the source circuit to the left of node B is influenced by the input resistance of the inverting amplifier circuit. The effect can be seen by constructing a Thévenin equivalent of the circuit to the left of node B, as shown in Figure 4–34(b). By inspection of Figure 4–34(a),

$$v_T = \frac{R_2}{R_1 + R_2} v_S$$

$$R_T = \frac{R_1 R_2}{R_1 + R_2}$$

In Figure 4–34(b) this Thévenin resistance is connected in series with the input resistor R_3, yielding the equivalence resistance $R_{EQ} = R_T + R_3$ shown in Figure 4–34(c). This reduced circuit is in the form of an inverting amplifier, so we can write the input–output relationship relating v_O and v_T as

$$K_1 = \frac{v_O}{v_T} = -\frac{R_4}{R_{EQ}} = -\frac{R_4(R_1 + R_2)}{R_1R_2 + R_1R_3 + R_2R_3}$$

The overall input–output relationship from the input source v_S to the OP AMP output v_O is obtained by writing

$$K_{CIRCUIT} = \frac{v_O}{v_S} = \left[\frac{v_O}{v_T}\right]\left[\frac{v_T}{v_S}\right]$$

$$= -\left[\frac{R_4(R_1 + R_2)}{R_1R_2 + R_1R_3 + R_2R_3}\right]\left[\frac{R_2}{R_1 + R_2}\right]$$

$$= -\left[\frac{R_2R_4}{R_1R_2 + R_1R_3 + R_2R_3}\right]$$

It is important to note that the overall gain is *not* the product of the source circuit voltage gain $R_2/(R_1 + R_2)$ and the inverting amplifier gain $-R_4/R_3$. In this circuit the two building blocks interact because the input resistance of the inverting amplifier circuit loads the source circuit. ■

Exercise 4–11

Sketch the transfer characteristic of the OP AMP circuit in Figure 4–35(a) for $-10\text{ V} < v_S < 10\text{ V}$.

Answer:
The solution is shown in Figure 4–35(b).

THE SUMMING AMPLIFIER

The **summing amplifier** or **adder** circuit is shown in Figure 4–36(a). This circuit has two inputs connected at node A, which is called the **summing point**. Since the noninverting input is grounded, we have the condition $v_P = 0$. This configuration is similar to the inverting amplifier, so we start by applying KCL to write the sum of currents entering the node A summing point.

$$\frac{v_1 - v_N}{R_1} + \frac{v_2 - v_N}{R_2} + \frac{v_O - v_N}{R_F} - i_N = 0 \qquad (4-27)$$

With the noninverting input grounded, the OP AMP element constraints are $v_N = v_P = 0$ and $i_N = 0$. Substituting these OP AMP constraints into Eq. (4–27), we can solve for the circuit input–output relationship.

FIGURE 4–35

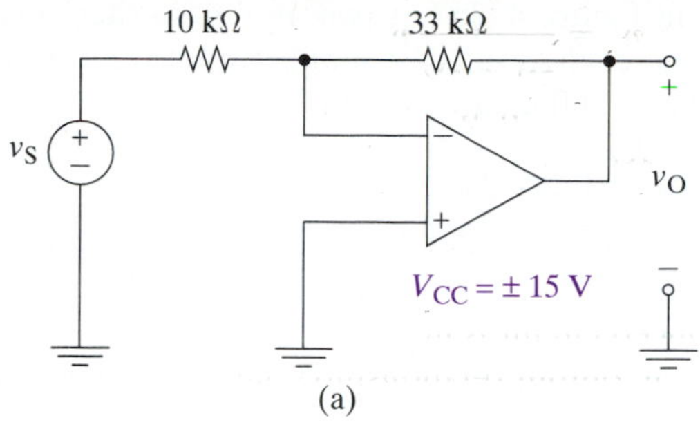

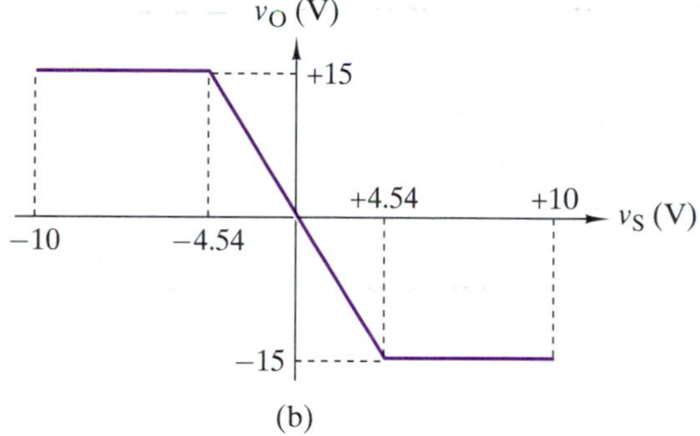

$$v_O = \left(-\frac{R_F}{R_1}\right) v_1 + \left(-\frac{R_F}{R_2}\right) v_2 \qquad (4\text{–}28)$$

$$= (K_1)\, v_1 + (K_2)\, v_2$$

The output is a weighted sum of the two inputs. The scale factors (or gains, as they are called) are determined by the ratio of the feedback resistor R_F to the input resistor for each input: that is, $K_1 = -R_F/R_1$ and $K_2 = -R_F/R_2$. In the special case $R_1 = R_2 = R$, Eq. (4–28) reduces to

$$v_O = -\frac{R_F}{R}(v_1 + v_2)$$

In this special case the output is proportional to the sum of the two inputs (hence the name *summing amplifier* or, more precisely, *inverting summer*). A block diagram representation of this circuit is shown in Figure 4–36(b).

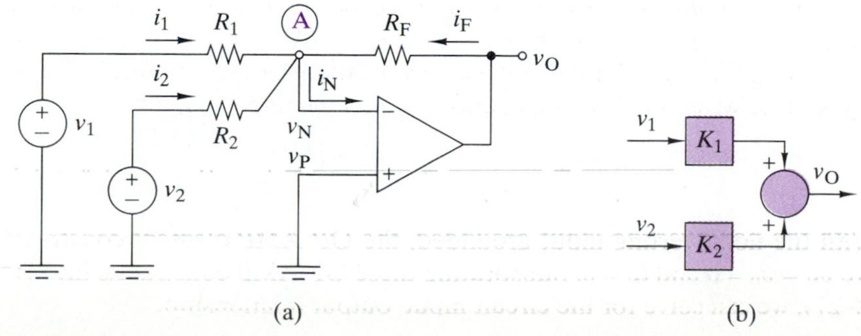

FIGURE 4–36 *The inverting summer.*

The summing amplifier in Figure 4–36 has two inputs, so there are two gains to contend with, one for each input. The input–output relationship in Eq. (4–28) is easily generalized to the case of n inputs as

$$v_O = \left(-\frac{R_F}{R_1}\right) v_1 + \left(-\frac{R_F}{R_2}\right) v_2 + \cdots + \left(-\frac{R_F}{R_n}\right) v_n$$
$$= K_1 v_1 + K_2 v_2 + \cdots + K_n v_n \tag{4–29}$$

where R_F is the feedback resistor and $R_1, R_2, \ldots R_n$ are the input resistors for the n input voltages $v_1, v_2, \ldots v_n$. You can easily verify this result by expanding the KCL sum in Eq. (4–27) to include n inputs, invoking the OP AMP constraints, and then solving for v_O.

DESIGN EXAMPLE 4–15

Inverting Summer Design

Design an inverting summer that implements the input–output relationship

$$v_O = -(5\,v_1 + 13\,v_2)$$

SOLUTION:

The design problem involves selecting the input and feedback resistors so that

$$\frac{R_F}{R_1} = 5 \quad \text{and} \quad \frac{R_F}{R_2} = 13$$

One solution is arbitrarily to select R_F = 65 kΩ, which yields R_1 = 13 kΩ and R_2 = 5 kΩ. The resulting circuit is shown in Figure 4–37(a). The design can be modified to use standard resistance values for resistors with ±5% tolerance (see Appendix A, Table A-1). Selecting the standard value R_F = 56 kΩ requires R_1 = 11.2 kΩ and R_2 = 4.31 kΩ. The nearest standard values are 11 kΩ and 4.3 kΩ. The resulting circuit shown in Figure 4–37(b) incorporates standard value resistors and produces gains of K_1 = 56/11 = 5.09 and K_2 = 56/4.3 = 13.02. These nominal gains are within 2% of the values in the specified input–output relationship. ■

FIGURE 4–37

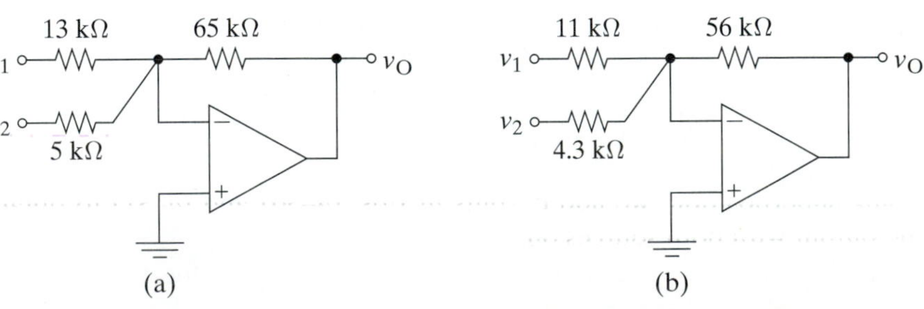

Exercise 4–12

(a) Find v_O in Figure 4–37(a) when $v_1 = 2$ V and $v_2 = -0.5$ V.
(b) If $v_1 = 400$ mV and $V_{CC} = \pm 15$ V, what is the maximum value of v_2 for linear mode operation?
(c) If $v_1 = 500$ mV and $V_{CC} = \pm 15$ V, what is the minimum value of v_2 for linear mode operation?

Answers:
(a) –3.5 V; (b) 1 V; (c) –1.346 V

THE DIFFERENTIAL AMPLIFIER

The circuit in Figure 4–38(a) is called a **differential amplifier** or **subtractor**. Like the summer, this circuit has two inputs, one applied at the inverting input and one at the noninverting input of the OP AMP. The input–output relationship can be obtained using the superposition principle.

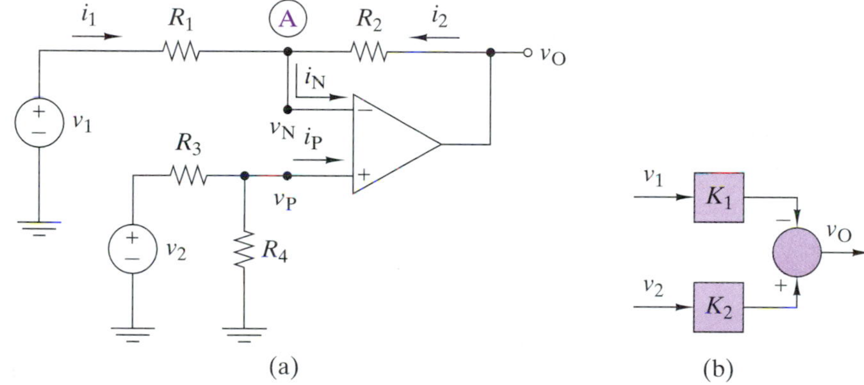

FIGURE 4–38 *The differential amplifier.*

First, we turn off source v_2, in which case there is no excitation at the noninverting input and $v_P = 0$. In effect, the noninverting input is grounded and the circuit acts like an inverting amplifier with the result that

$$v_{O1} = -\frac{R_2}{R_1}v_1 \tag{4–30}$$

Next, turning v_2 back on and turning v_1 off, we see that the circuit looks like a noninverting amplifier with a voltage divider connected at its input. This case was treated in Example 4–13, so we can write

$$v_{O2} = \left[\frac{R_4}{R_3 + R_4}\right]\left[\frac{R_1 + R_2}{R_1}\right]v_2 \tag{4–31}$$

Using superposition, we add outputs in Eqs. (4–30) and (4–31) to obtain the output with both sources on:

$$
\begin{aligned}
v_O &= v_{O1} + v_{O2} \\
&= -\left[\frac{R_2}{R_1}\right] v_1 + \left[\frac{R_4}{R_3 + R_4}\right]\left[\frac{R_1 + R_2}{R_1}\right] v_2 \qquad (4-32) \\
&= -[K_1]\, v_1 + [K_2] v_2
\end{aligned}
$$

where K_1 and K_2 are the inverting and noninverting gains. Figure 4–38(b) shows how the differential amplifier is represented in a block diagram.

For the special case of $R_3/R_1 = R_4/R_2$, Eq. (4–32) reduces to

$$v_O = \frac{R_2}{R_1}(v_2 - v_1) \qquad (4-33)$$

In this case the output is proportional to the difference between the two inputs (hence the name *differential amplifier* or *subtractor*).

Exercise 4–13

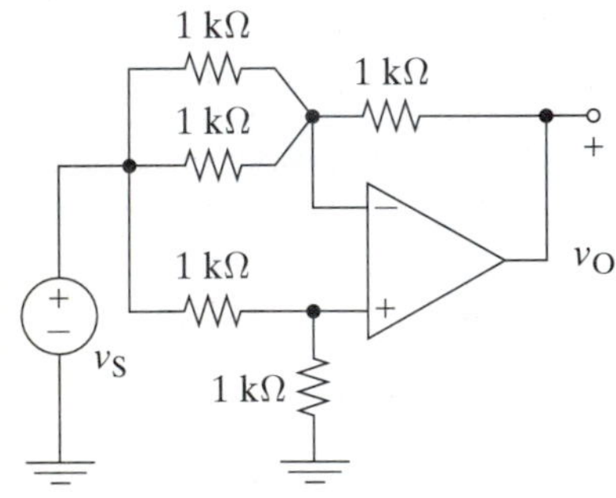

FIGURE 4–39

(a) Find v_O in Figure 4–39 when v_S = 10 V.
(b) When V_{CC} = ±15 V, find the maximum value of v_S for linear mode operation.
(c) When V_{CC} = ±15 V, find the minimum value of v_S for linear mode operation.

Answers:
(a) –5 V; (b) 30 V; (c) –30 V

BASIC OP AMP BUILDING BLOCKS

The block diagram representations of the basic OP AMP circuit configurations are shown in Figure 4–40. The noninverting and inverting amplifiers are represented as gain blocks. The summing amplifier and differential amplifier require both gain blocks and the summing point symbol. Considerable care must be used when translating from a block diagram to a circuit, or vice versa, since some gain blocks involve negative gains. For example, the gains of the inverting summer are negative. The required minus sign is sometimes moved to the summing point and the value of K within the gain block changed to a positive number. Since there is no standard convention for doing this, it is important to keep track of the signs associated with gain blocks and summing points.

EXAMPLE 4–16

Find the input–output relationship of the circuit in Figure 4–41(a).

SOLUTION:

This circuit is a cascade connection of three OP AMP circuits. The first circuit is an inverting amplifier with $K_1 = -0.33$, the second is a unity-gain inverting summer, and the final circuit is another inverting amplifier with $K_3 = -5/9$. Given these observations, we construct the block diagram shown in

Circuit	Block diagram	Gains
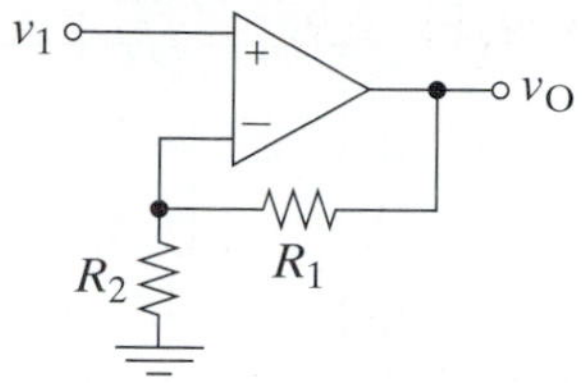		$K = \dfrac{R_1 + R_2}{R_2}$
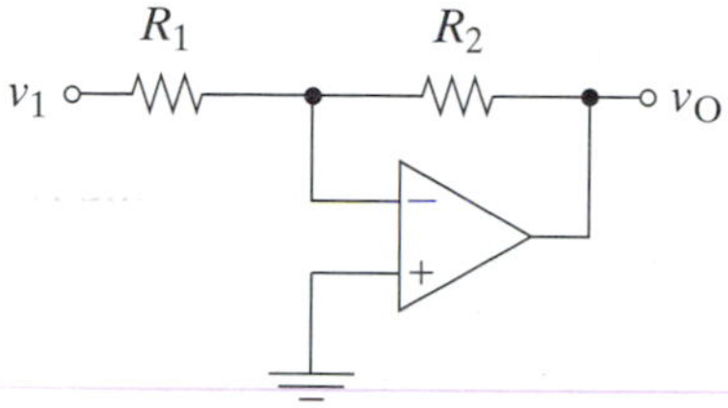		$K = -\dfrac{R_2}{R_1}$
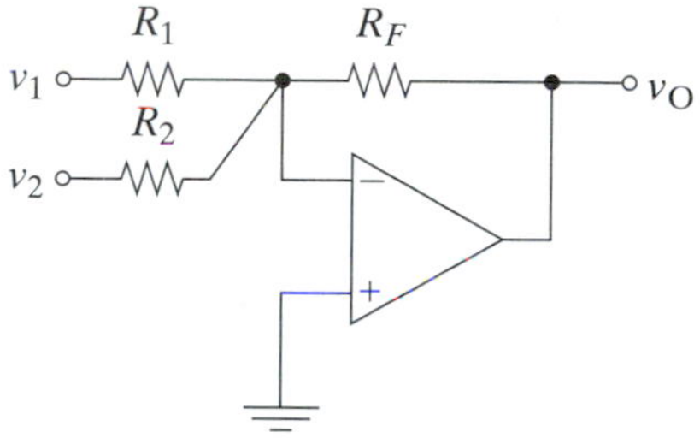	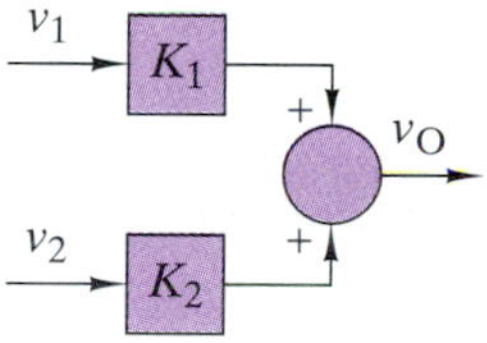	$K_1 = -\dfrac{R_F}{R_1}$ $K_2 = -\dfrac{R_F}{R_2}$
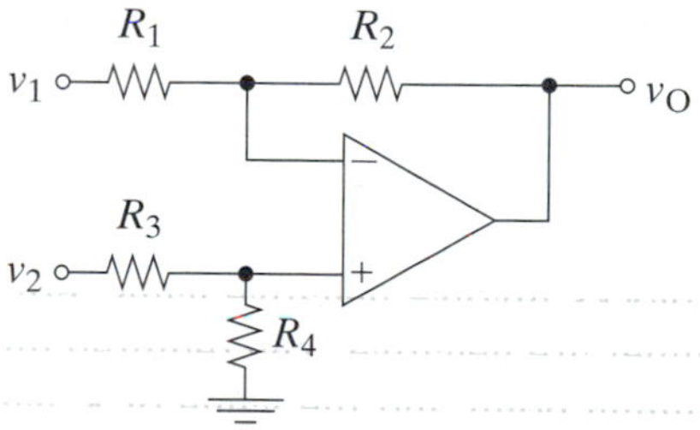	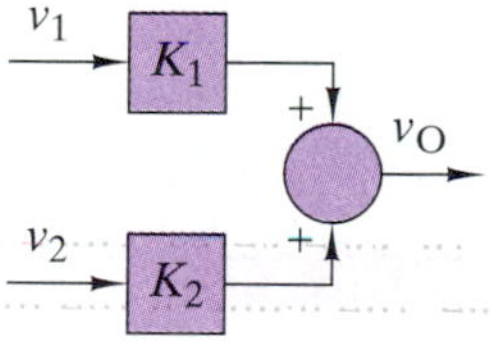	$K_1 = -\dfrac{R_2}{R_1}$ $K_2 = \left(\dfrac{R_1 + R_2}{R_1}\right)\left(\dfrac{R_4}{R_3 + R_4}\right)$

FIGURE 4–40 *Summary of basic OP AMP signal-processing circuits.*

Figure 4–41(b). To trace the signal from input to output, we note that the input to the first circuit is 9.7 V and its output is $K_1 \times 9.7 = (-0.33) \times (9.7) = -3.2$ V. This voltage is added to the variable input v_F in the second circuit to produce $(-1) \times (-3.2) + (-1) \times (v_F) = 3.2 - v_F$. This result is then multiplied by the gain of the final circuit ($K_3 = -5/9$) to obtain the overall circuit output.

$$v_C = -\frac{5}{9}(3.2 - v_F) = \frac{5}{9}(v_F - 3.2)$$

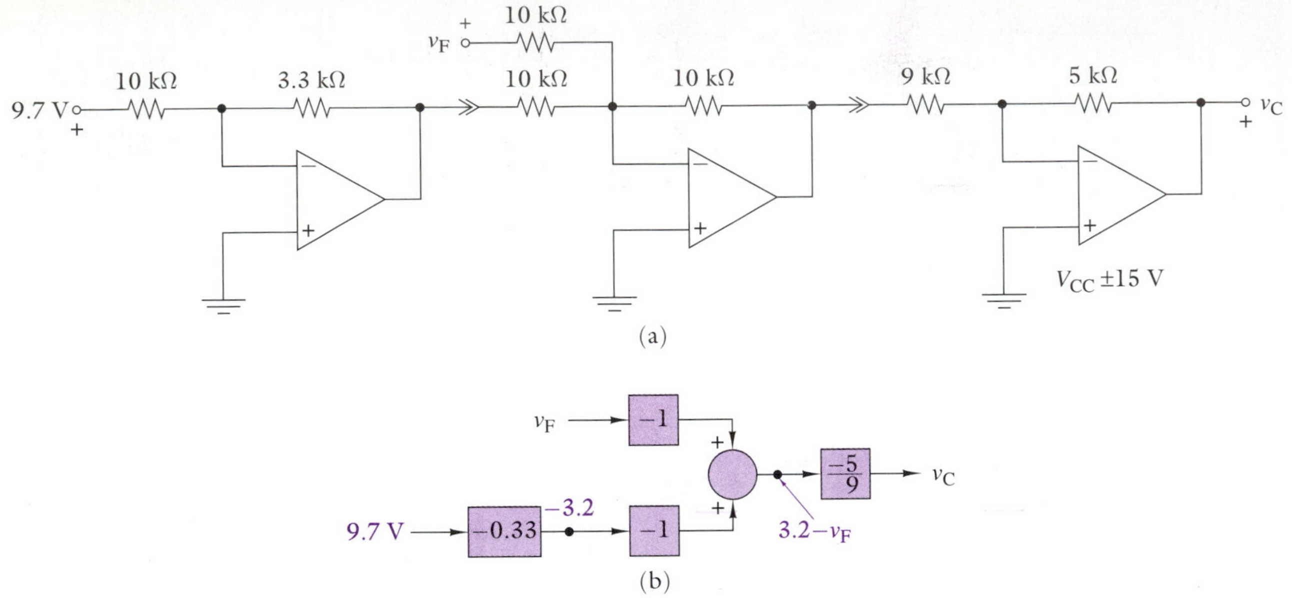

FIGURE 4–41

This circuit implements a conversion of temperature from degrees Fahrenheit to degrees Celsius. Specifically, when the input voltage is $v_F = \theta_F/10$, where θ_F is a temperature in degrees Fahrenheit, then the output voltage is $v_C = \theta_C/10$, where θ_C is the equivalent temperature in degrees Celsius.

Each circuit in Figure 4–41 is an inverting amplifier with input resistances of about 10 kΩ. Since $V_{CC} = 15$ V, this means that the maximum current drawn at the input of any stage is about $15 \div 10^4 = 1.5$ mA, which is well within the power capabilities of general-purpose OP AMP devices.

Show that all OP AMPs are in the linear mode when the input temperature is in the range from −128°F to +182°F. ■

Exercise 4–14

Construct a block diagram for the circuit in Figure 4–42(a).

Answer:

Figures 4–42(b) and 4–42(c) show acceptable solutions.

NODE-VOLTAGE ANALYSIS WITH OP AMPS

In many applications we encounter OP AMP circuits that are more complicated than the four basic configurations in Figure 4–40. In such cases we use a modified form of node-voltage analysis that is based on the OP AMP connections in Figure 4–43. The overall circuit contains N nodes, including the three associated with the OP AMP. Normally the objective is to find the OP AMP output voltage (v_O) relative to the reference node (ground). We assign node voltage variables to the $N-1$ nonreference nodes, includ-

FIGURE 4–42

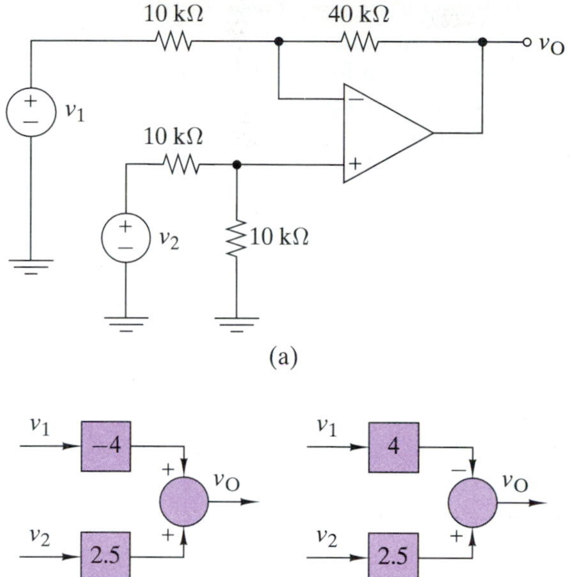

ing a variable at the OP AMP output. However, an ideal OP AMP acts like a dependent voltage source connected between the output terminal and ground. As a result, the OP AMP output voltage is determined by the other node voltages, so we do not need to write a node equation at the OP AMP output node.

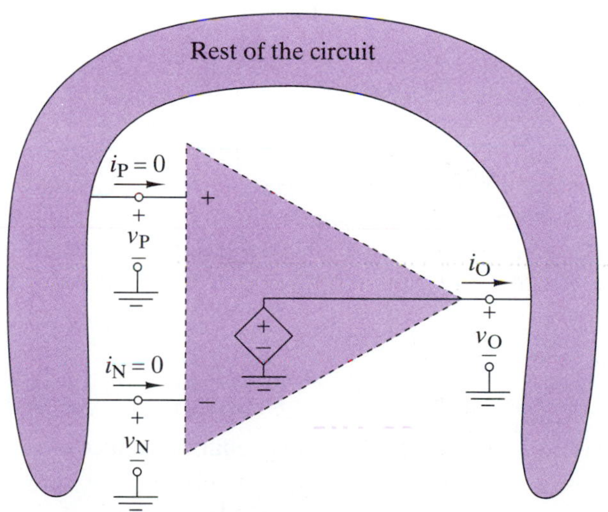

FIGURE 4–43 *General OP AMP circuit analysis.*

We formulate node equations at the other $N - 2$ nonreference nodes in the usual way. Since there are $N - 1$ node voltages, we seem to have more unknowns than equations. However, the OP AMP forces the condition $v_P = v_N$ in Figure 4–43. This eliminates one unknown node voltage since these two nodes are forced to have identical voltages. Finally, remember that the ideal OP AMP draws no current at its inputs ($i_P = i_N = 0$) in Figure 4–43, so these currents can be ignored when formulating node equations.

The following steps outline an approach to the formulation of node equations for OP AMP circuits:

STEP 1: Identify a node voltage at all nonreference nodes, including OP AMP outputs, but do *not* formulate node equations at the OP AMP output nodes.

STEP 2: Formulate node equations at the remaining nonreference nodes and then use the ideal OP AMP voltage constraint $v_P = v_N$ to reduce the number of unknowns.

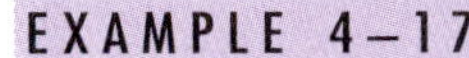

EXAMPLE 4–17

Find the input–output relationship of the circuit in Figure 4–44.

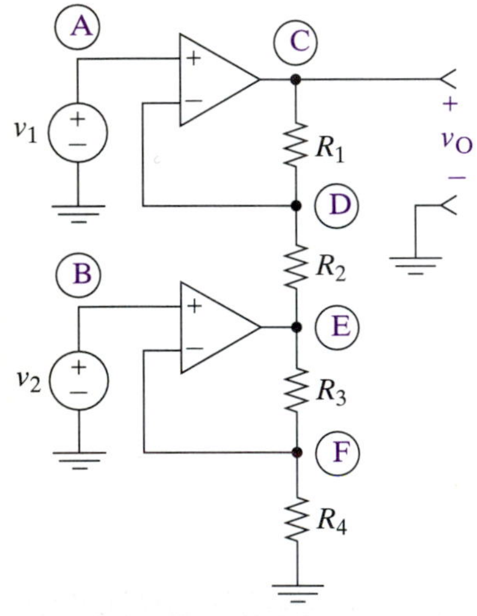

FIGURE 4–44

SOLUTION:

The circuit contains two OP AMPs and a total of six nonreference nodes. Nodes C and E are connected to OP AMP outputs, and nodes A and B are connected to the grounded independent voltage sources. As a result, we only require node equations at nodes D and F. By inspection,

$$\text{Node D: } (G_1 + G_2)v_D - G_1 v_C - G_2 v_E = 0$$

$$\text{Node F: } (G_3 + G_4)v_F - G_3 v_E = 0$$

This formulation yields two equations in four unknowns. However, the noninverting inputs are connected to independent voltage sources, so $v_A = v_1$ and $v_B = v_2$. The OP AMP voltage constraint ($v_P = v_N$) means $v_D = v_A = v_1$ and $v_F = v_B = v_2$. Substituting these constraints reduces the two node equations to

$$G_1 v_C + G_2 v_E = (G_1 + G_2)\, v_1$$

$$G_3\, v_E = (G_3 + G_4) v_2$$

Node analysis quickly reduces this rather formidable appearing OP AMP circuit to two equations in two unknowns.

The circuit output voltage is $v_O = v_C$, so we use the second equation to eliminate v_E from the first equation and then solve for the input–output relationship as

$$v_O = v_C = \left[\frac{G_1 + G_2}{G_1}\right] v_1 - \frac{G_2}{G_1}\left[\frac{G_3 + G_4}{G_3}\right] v_2$$

For the special case $R_1 = R_4$ and $R_2 = R_3$, this equation reduces to

$$v_O = \frac{R_1 + R_2}{R_2}\,[v_1 - v_2]$$

The configuration in Figure 4–44 is a two-OP-AMP subtractor. The advantage of this circuit over the one-OP-AMP configuration in Figure 4–40 is that both inputs are connected to noninverting inputs, so the two-OP-AMP subtractor does not load the input sources. ■

Exercise 4–15

Find the input–output relationship for the circuit in Figure 4–45.

Answer:

$$v_O = -\left[\frac{R_2R_3 + R_2R_4 + R_3R_4}{R_1R_3}\right] v_S$$

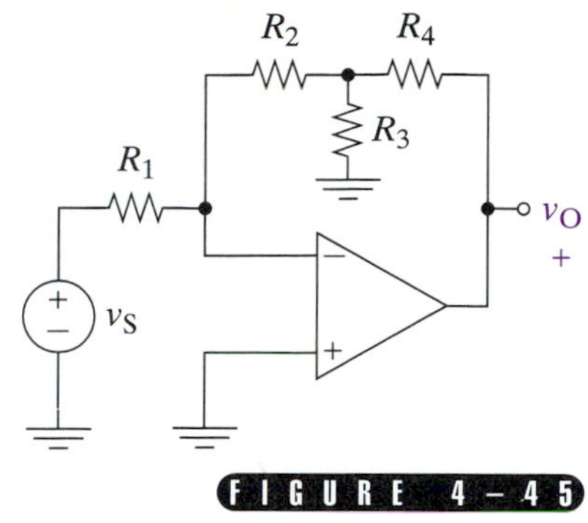

FIGURE 4–45

EXAMPLE 4–18

Most of the analysis and design problems in this book can be solved using the ideal model of the OP AMP. However, MicroSim Design Center does not support the ideal model. The Design Center device library file contains models for specific device types, such as the uA741 or the LM111. These device-specific models are reasonably accurate, but involve device properties that are more appropriately studied in courses on semiconductor electronics.

In different sections of this book we use PSpice to verify design results obtained using the ideal OP AMP model. To do this we use the dependent-source model shown in Figure 4–46 to simulate the ideal model. The numerical values shown in the figure are not those of the ideal model, but are much better than the parameters available in actual devices. To validate this model, we carry out the following steps:

(a) Use Schematics to create a circuit file implementing the controlled source model in Figure 4–46.

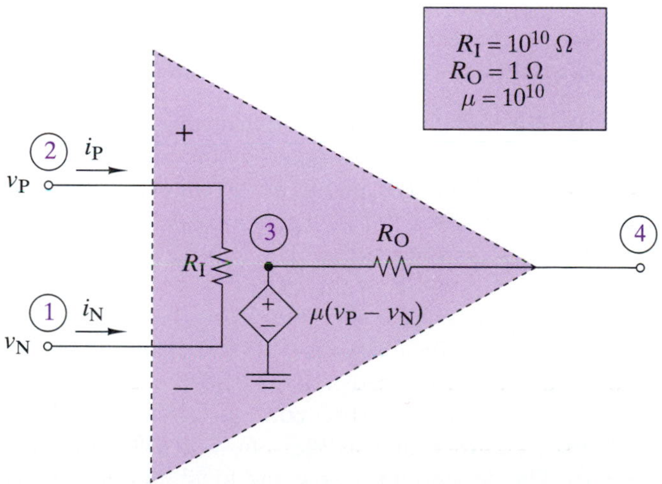

FIGURE 4–46

(b) Use the file developed in (a) and PSpice to calculate the voltage gain, input resistance, and output resistance of an inverting OP AMP circuit with $R_1 = 10$ kΩ and $R_2 = 50$ kΩ.

(c) Evaluate the dependent-source model by comparing the PSpice results found in (b) with those predicted by the ideal model.

SOLUTION:

(a) Figure 4–47 shows a circuit that implements the dependent-source model using the elements available in MicroSim Schematics. The only accessible terminals in this model are the input nodes labelled *p* and *n* plus the output node *O*. The circuit is stored in a file called OPAMP.SCH. To use this circuit in other files, we first open OPAMP.SCH, highlight the entire circuit, and use the standard **EDIT/COPY** command. Copies of the circuit can then be inserted into other files using the standard **EDIT/PASTE** command.

FIGURE 4–47

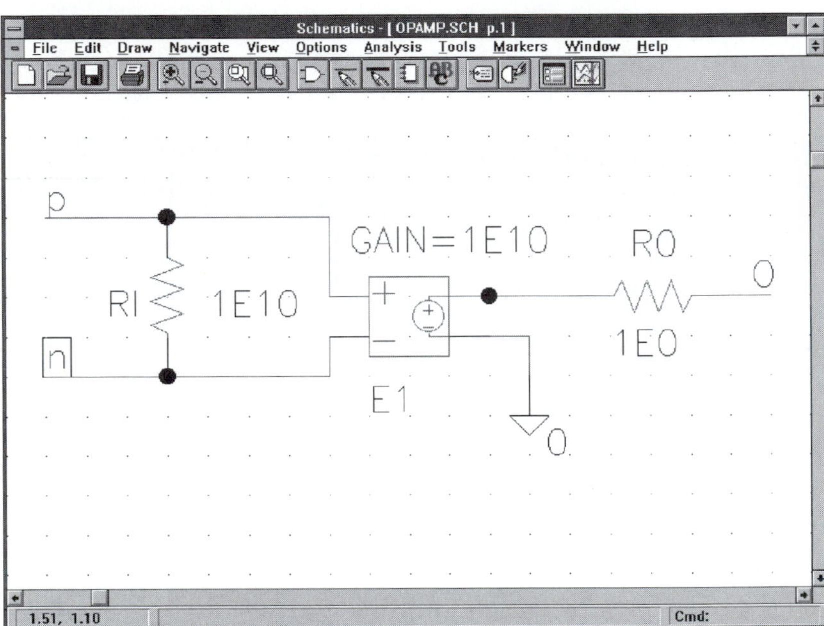

(b) Figure 4–48 shows the circuit diagram of an inverting amplifier configuration in which the OP AMP is represented by the model developed in (a). In the **ANALYSIS/SET UP** menu we activate the **TRANSFER FUNCTION** option and select the voltage source VS as the input and the node voltage V(O) as the output. The **ANALYSIS/SIMULATE** command performs a dc analysis of the circuit. A portion of the resulting output file is shown in Figure 4–48. Thus, using the finite-gain model, PSpice predicts that the voltage gain is –5.000, the input resistance is 1.000E4 = 10 kΩ, and the output resistance is 6.000E – 11 = 60 pΩ.

(c) For an ideal OP AMP in the inverting configuration, the voltage gain is $-R_2/R_1 = -5$, the input resistance is $R_{IN} = R_1 = 10$ kΩ, and the output resistance is zero. The dependent source and ideal model results agree for voltage gain and input resistance to within the four significant figures given in the output file. The output resistance for the dependent model is not exactly zero, but 60 pΩ is negligible compared with other circuit resistances. In summary, both our dependent-source model in Figure 4–47 and the ideal model predict equivalent results in a typical OP AMP circuit application. ■

FIGURE 4–48

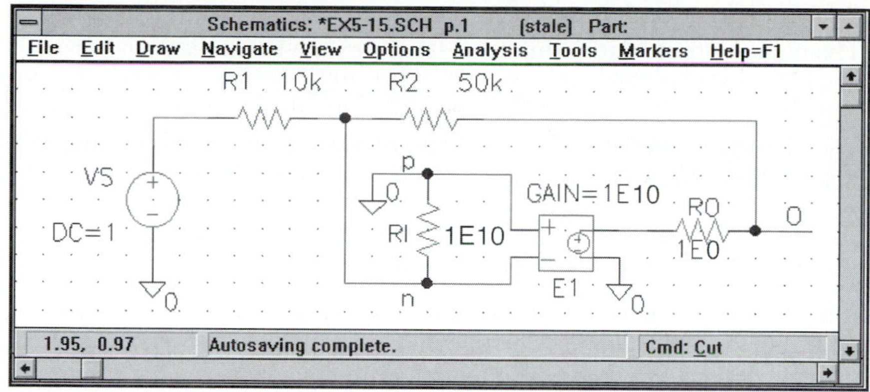

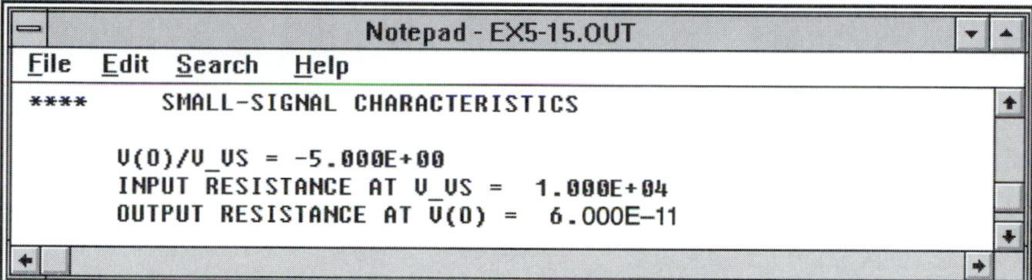

Notepad - EX5-15.OUT

```
****     SMALL-SIGNAL CHARACTERISTICS

      V(O)/V_VS = -5.000E+00
      INPUT RESISTANCE AT V_VS =   1.000E+04
      OUTPUT RESISTANCE AT V(O) =   6.000E-11
```

4–6 OP AMP CIRCUIT DESIGN

With OP AMP circuit analysis, we are asked to find the input–output relationship for a given circuit configuration. An OP AMP circuit analysis problem has a unique answer. In OP AMP circuit design, we are given an equation or block diagram representation of a signal-processing function and asked to devise a circuit configuration that implements the desired function. Circuit design can be accomplished by interconnecting the amplifier, summer, and subtractor building blocks shown in Figure 4–40. The design process is greatly simplified by the nearly one-to-one correspondence between the OP AMP circuits and the elements in a block diagram. However, a design problem may not have a unique answer since often there are several OP AMP circuits that meet the design objective. The following example illustrates the design process.

D DESIGN EXAMPLE 4–19

OP AMP Circuit Design

Design an OP AMP circuit that implements the block diagram in Figure 4–49.

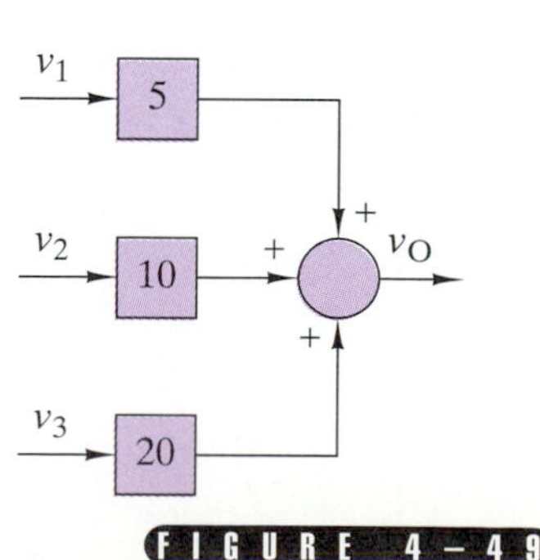

FIGURE 4–49

SOLUTION:

The input–output relationship represented by the block diagram is

$$v_O = 5v_1 + 10v_2 + 20v_3$$

The inverting summer can be used to produce the summation required in this relationship. A three-input adder implements the relationship

$$v_O = -\left[\frac{R_F}{R_1}v_1 + \frac{R_F}{R_2}v_2 + \frac{R_F}{R_3}v_3\right]$$

The required scale factors are obtained by first selecting $R_F = 100\ \text{k}\Omega$, and then choosing $R_1 = 20\ \text{k}\Omega$, $R_2 = 10\ \text{k}\Omega$, and $R_3 = 5\ \text{k}\Omega$. However, the circuit involves a signal inversion. To implement the block diagram, we must add an inverting amplifier ($K = -R_2/R_1$) with $R_1 = R_2 = 100\ \text{k}\Omega$. The final implementation is shown in Figure 4–50. ■

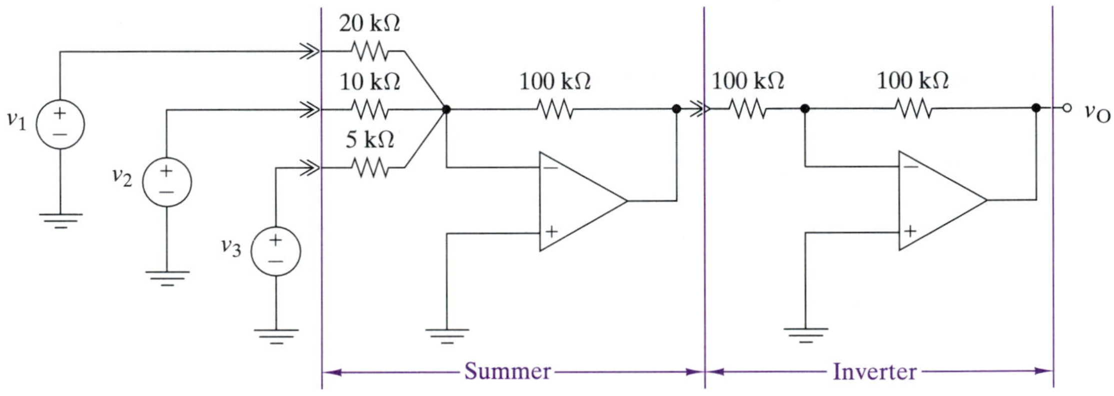

FIGURE 4–50

EVALUATION EXAMPLE 4–20

It is claimed that the OP AMP circuit in Figure 4–51 implements the same input–output function as the circuit in Figure 4–50. Verify this claim and compare the two circuits in terms of element count.

FIGURE 4–51

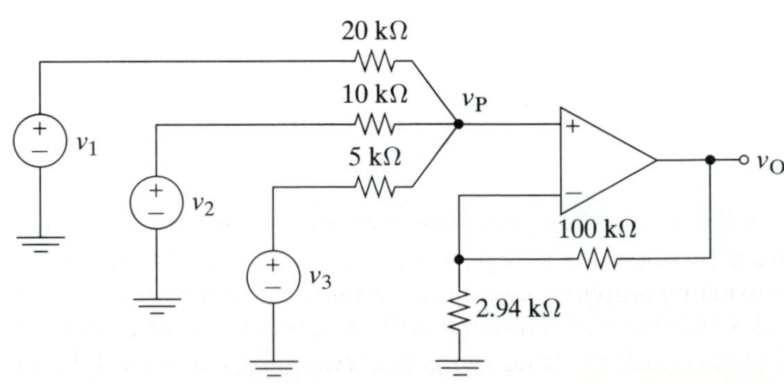

SOLUTION:

The circuit in Figure 4–51 is a modification of the OP AMP subtractor in Figure 4–40. In the modified circuit, several inputs are connected to the noninverting input and the negative input is grounded. The output voltage is related to the signal v_P by a noninverting amplifier gain; that is,

$$v_O = Kv_P = \frac{100 \times 10^3 + 2.94 \times 10^3}{2.94 \times 10^3} v_P$$
$$= 35v_P$$

Applying KCL, the sum of currents entering the noninverting input is

$$\frac{v_1 - v_P}{2 \times 10^4} + \frac{v_2 - v_P}{10^4} + \frac{v_3 - v_P}{0.5 \times 10^4} = 0$$

Multiplying this equation by 10^4 and solving for v_P yields

$$v_P = \frac{0.5}{3.5} v_1 + \frac{1}{3.5} v_2 + \frac{2}{3.5} v_3$$

Thus the overall input–output relationship is

$$v_O = 35v_P = 5v_1 + 10v_2 + 20v_3$$

and the claim is verified. The circuit in Figure 4–51 has the same input–output relationship as the circuit in Figure 4–50. The circuit in Figure 4–51 requires only one OP AMP since the inverting stage in Figure 4–50 is not required.

The circuit in Figure 4–51 is an example of a **noninverting summer**. The input–output relationship for a general noninverting summer in Figure 4–52 is (see Problem 4–35)

$$v_O = K\left[\left(\frac{R_{EQ}}{R_1}\right) v_1 + \left(\frac{R_{EQ}}{R_2}\right) v_2 + \cdots + \left(\frac{R_{EQ}}{R_n}\right) v_n\right] \quad (4-34)$$

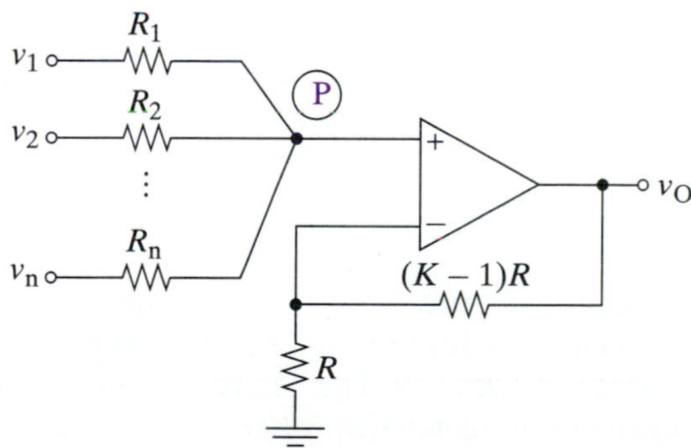

FIGURE 4–52

where R_{EQ} is the Thévenin resistance looking to the left at point P with all sources turned off (i.e., $R_{EQ} = R_1 \| R_2 \| R_3 \ldots \| R_n$) and K is the gain of the noninverting amplifier circuit to the right of point P. There are several similarities between this equation and the general inverting summer result in Eq. (4–29). In both cases the gain factor assigned to each input voltage is inversely proportional to the input resistance to which it is connected. The gain factor is directly proportional to the feedback resistor R_F in the inverting summer and is directly proportional to R_{EQ} in the noninverting summer. ■

DIGITAL-TO-ANALOG CONVERTERS

A **digital-to-analog converter** (DAC) is a signal processor whose input is an n-bit digital word and whose output is an analog signal proportional to the binary value of the digital input. For example, the parallel four-bit digital signal in Figure 4–53 represents the value of a signal. Each bit can only have two values: (1) a high or "1" (e.g., +5 V) and (2) a low or "0" (e.g., 0 V). The bits have binary weights, so v_1 is worth $(2)^3 = 8$ times as much v_4, v_2 is worth $(2)^2 = 4$ times as much as v_4, and v_3 is worth $(2)^1$ times as much v_4. We call v_4 the **least significant bit** (LSB) and call v_1 the **most significant bit** (MSB). To convert the digital representation of the signal to analog form, we must weight the bits so that the analog output v_O is

$$v_O = \pm K(8v_1 + 4v_2 + 2v_3 + v_4) \tag{4-35}$$

where K is an overall scale factor. This result is the input–output relationship of a 4-bit DAC.

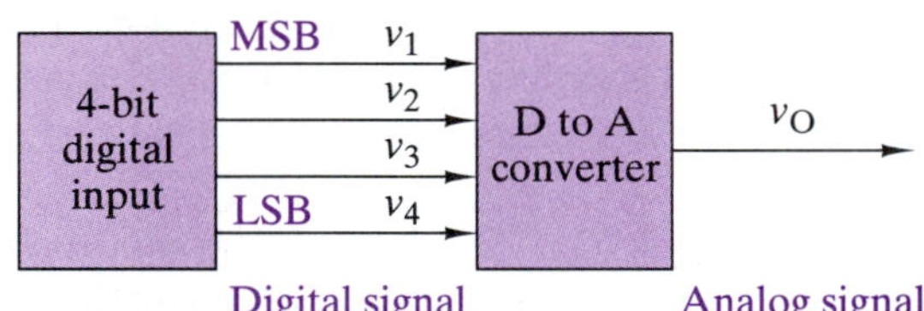

FIGURE 4–53 *A digital-to-analog converter (DAC).*

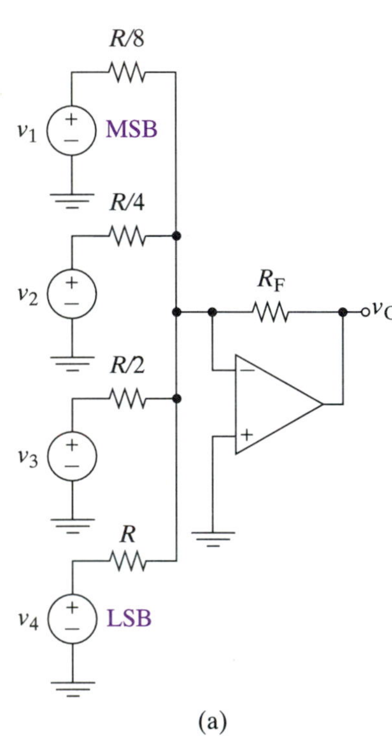

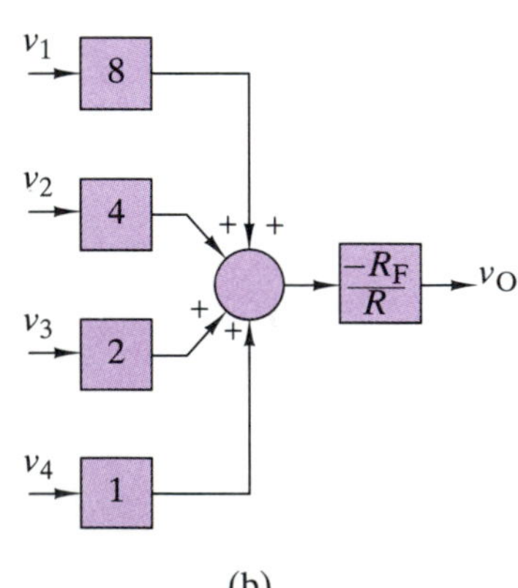

FIGURE 4–54 *A binary-weighted DAC: (a) Circuit diagram. (b) Block diagram.*

One way to implement Eq. (4–35) is to use an inverting summer with binary-weighted input resistors. Figure 4–54 shows the OP AMP circuit and a block diagram of the circuit input–output relationship. In either form, the output is seen to be a binary-weighted sum of the digital input scaled by $-R_F/R$. That is, the output voltage is

$$v_O = \frac{-R_F}{R}(8v_1 + 4v_2 + 2v_3 + v_4) \tag{4-36}$$

The R-2R ladder circuit in Figure 4–55(a) also produces a 4-bit DAC. The resistance seen looking back into the R-2R ladder at point A, with all sources turned off, is seen to be $R_T = R$. The Thévenin equivalent circuit of the R-2R circuit is shown in Figure 4–55(b), where

$$v_T = \frac{v_1}{2} + \frac{v_2}{4} + \frac{v_3}{8} + \frac{v_4}{16}$$

The output voltage is found using the inverting amplifier gain relationship:

$$v_O = \frac{-R_F}{R}v_T = \frac{-R_F}{R}\left(\frac{v_1}{2} + \frac{v_2}{4} + \frac{v_3}{8} + \frac{v_4}{16}\right) \tag{4-37}$$

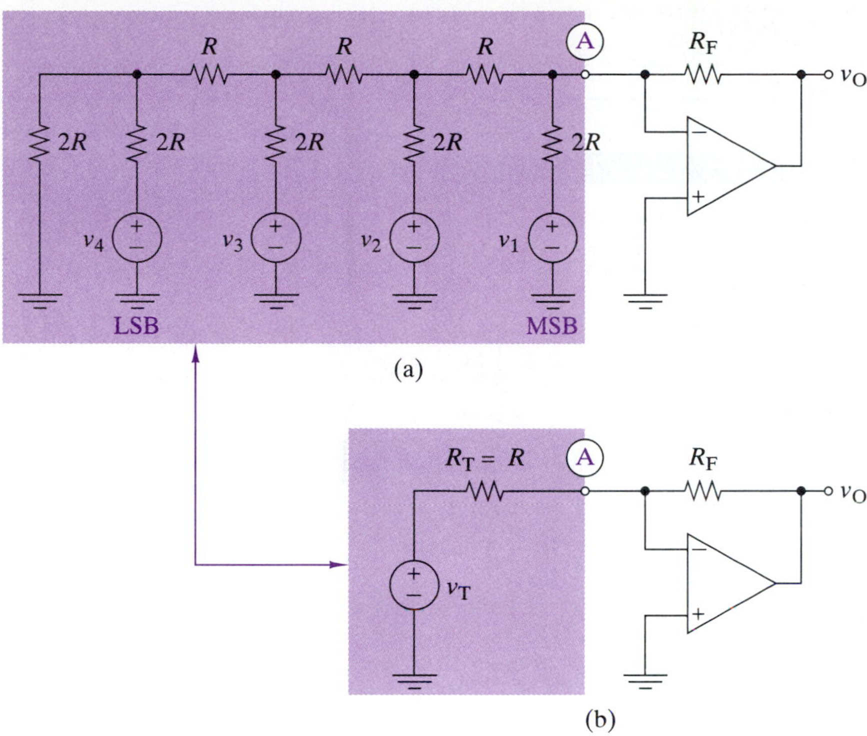

FIGURE 4–55 An R-2R ladder DAC: (a) Circuit diagram. (b) Thévenin equivalent.

Using $R_F = R$ yields

$$v_O = -\frac{1}{16}(8v_1 + 4v_2 + 2v_3 + v_4) \tag{4-38}$$

This equation shows that the ladder assigns the correct binary weights to the digital inputs—namely, 8, 4, 2, and 1.

In theory, the circuits in Figures 4–54 and 4–55 perform the same signal-processing function—namely, a 4-bit DAC. However, there are important practical differences between the two circuits. The inverting summer in Figure 4–54 requires precision resistors with four different values spanning an 8:1 range. An 8-bit converter would require eight precision resistors spanning a 256:1 range. Moreover, the digital voltage sources in Figure 4–54 see input resistances that span an 8:1 range; therefore, the source-load interface is not the same for each bit. On the other hand, the resistances in the *R*-2*R* ladder converter in Figure 4–55 only span a 2:1 range regardless of the number of digital bits. Another desirable feature of the *R*-2*R* ladder is that it presents the same input resistance to each binary input.

Exercise 4–16

Find the output voltage when the following inputs are applied to the *R*-2*R* ladder D/A converter in Figure 4–55(a) with $R_F = 16R/5$.

(a) $v_1 = 0$ V; $v_2 = 0$ V; $v_3 = 0$ V; $v_4 = 5$ V.
(b) $v_1 = 0$ V; $v_2 = 0$ V; $v_3 = 5$ V; $v_4 = 5$ V.
(c) $v_1 = 0$ V; $v_2 = 5$ V; $v_3 = 0$ V; $v_4 = 5$ V.
(d) $v_1 = 5$ V; $v_2 = 0$ V; $v_3 = 0$ V; $v_4 = 5$ V.

Answers:
(a) $v_O = -1$ V, (b) $v_O = -3$ V, (c) $v_O = -5$ V, (d) $v_O = -9$ V.

D DESIGN EXAMPLE 4–21

D/A Converter Design

Design a noninverting summer that implements a 3–bit D/A converter defined by

$$v_O = \frac{1}{5}[4v_1 + 2v_2 + v_3]$$

SOLUTION:

From Eq. (4–34) the input–output relationship for a three-input noninverting summer is

$$v_O = K\left[\left(\frac{R_{EQ}}{R_1}\right)v_1 + \left(\frac{R_{EQ}}{R_2}\right)v_2 + \left(\frac{R_{EQ}}{R_3}\right)v_3\right]$$

To implement the given relationship, we first select the input resistors so that the correct weight is assigned to each input. One way to accomplish this is to assign $R_1 = 10$ kΩ, $R_2 = 20$ kΩ, and $R_3 = 40$ kΩ. For this assignment $R_{EQ} = R_1 \| R_2 \| R_3 = 1/0.175$ kΩ, and the input-output relationship is

$$v_O = K\left[\frac{1}{1.75}v_1 + \frac{1}{3.5}v_2 + \frac{1}{7}v_3\right]$$

$$= \frac{K}{7}[4v_1 + 2v_2 + v_3]$$

To achieve the specified scale factor, we need $K = 7/5 = 1.4$. Figure 4–56 shows the circuit diagram for the noninverting summer design. ■

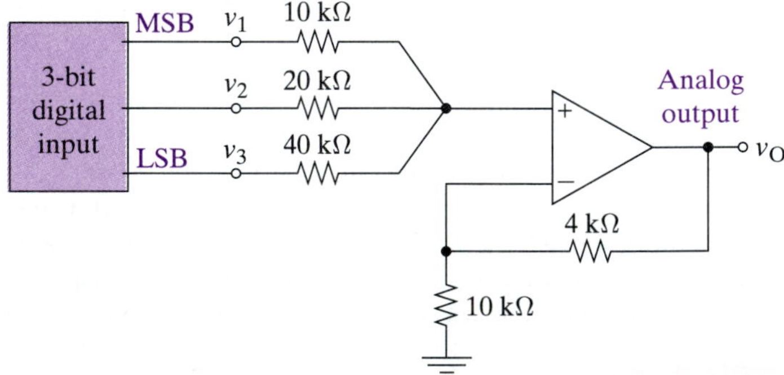

FIGURE 4–56

INSTRUMENTATION SYSTEMS

One of the most interesting and useful applications of OP AMP circuits is in the design of instrumentation systems that collect and process data about physical phenomena. In such a system an **input transducer** (a device that converts some physical quantity, such as temperature or pressure, into an electrical signal) generates an electrical signal that describes some physical process. In a simple system the transducer signal is processed by OP AMP circuits and displayed on an **output transducer**, such as a meter or a strip chart recorder. In other cases the output signal is fed to an analog-to-digital converter and sent to a digital computer for further processing and display. The output signal can also be used in a feedback control system to monitor and regulate the physical process itself.

The block diagram in Figure 4–57 shows an instrumentation system in its simplest form. The objective of the system is to deliver an output signal that is directly proportional to the value of the physical variable measured by the input transducer. The input transducer converts a physical variable x into an electrical voltage v_{TR}. For many transducers this voltage is of the form

$$v_{TR} = mx + b$$

where m is a calibration constant and b is a constant offset or bias. The transducer voltage is usually quite small and must be amplified by the gain K, as indicated in Figure 4–57. The amplified signal includes both a signal component $K(mx)$ and a bias component $K(b)$. The amplified bias $K(b)$ is then removed by subtracting a constant electrical signal. The resulting output voltage $K(mx)$ is directly proportional to the variable measured and goes to an output transducer for display.

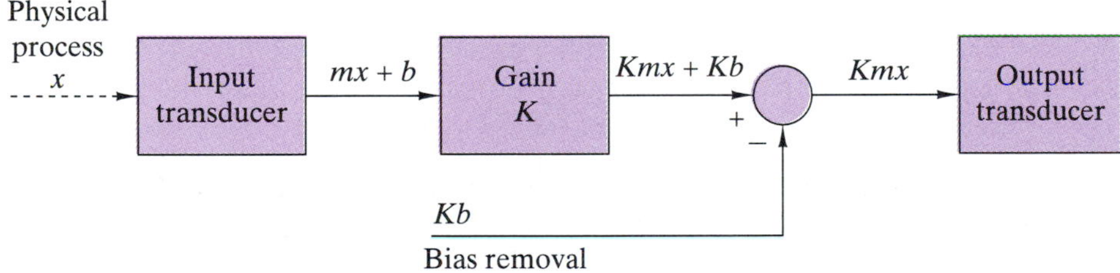

FIGURE 4–57 *Block diagram of a basic instrumentation system.*

To put these concepts into practice, let's look at an example. In a laboratory experiment the amount (5 to 20 lumens) of incident light is to be measured using a photocell as the input transducer. The system output is to be displayed on the 0- to 10-V scale of a voltmeter. The photocell characteristics are shown in Figure 4–58(a). The design requirements are that 5 lumens indicate 0 V, and 20 lumens indicate 10 V on the voltmeter. From the transducer characteristics we see that a light intensity range $\Delta\Phi = (20 - 5) = 15$ lumens will produce a range of $\Delta v = (0.6 - 0.2) = 0.4$ mV at the system input. This 0.4-mV change must be translated into a 10-V change at the system output. To accomplish this, the transducer voltage must be amplified by a gain of

$$K = \frac{\text{output range}}{\text{input range}} = \frac{(10 - 0)}{(0.6 - 0.2) \times 10^{-3}} = 2.5 \times 10^{4}$$

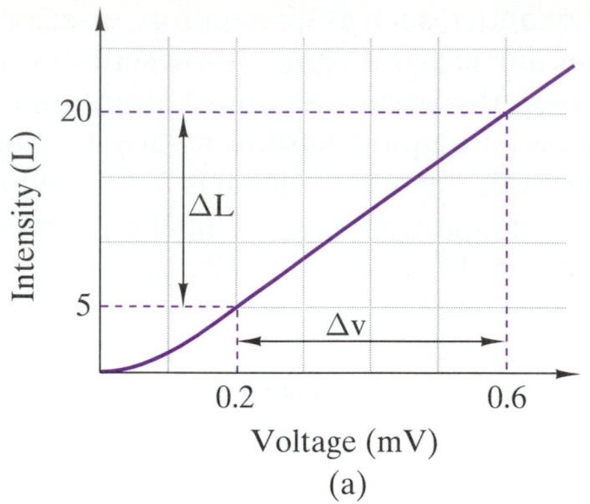

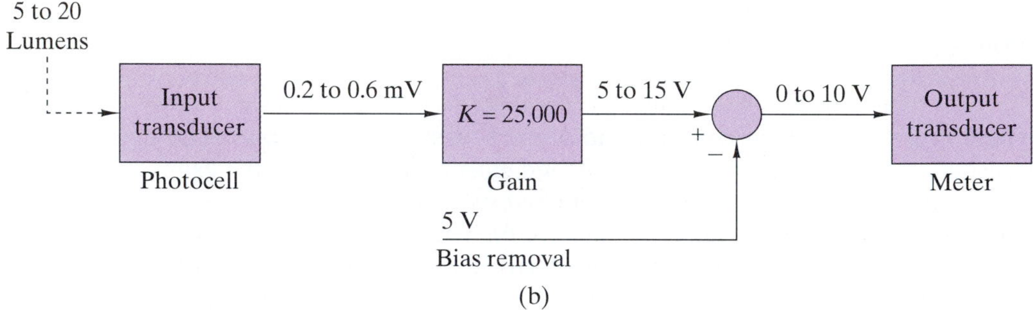

FIGURE 4–58 *Photocell transducer design example: (a) Transducer chracteristics. (b) Block diagram.*

When the transducer's output voltage range (0.2 to 0.6 mV) is multiplied by the gain K found previously, we obtain a voltage range of 5 to 15 V. This range is shifted to the required 0- to 10-V range by subtracting the 5-V bias from the amplified signal. Figure 4–58(b) shows a block diagram of the required signal-processing functions.

We use a cascade connection of OP AMP circuits to realize the signal-processing functions shown in the block diagram. Figure 4–59 shows one possible design using an inverting amplifier and an inverting adder. This design includes two inverting circuits in cascade so that the signal inversions cancel in the output signal. Part of the overall gain of $K = 2.5 \times 10^4$ is realized in the inverting amplifier ($K_1 = -200$) and the remainder is provided by the inverting summer ($K_2 = -125$). The overall gain is realized in two stages since a voltage gain of $K = 25{,}000$ is too large compared with the

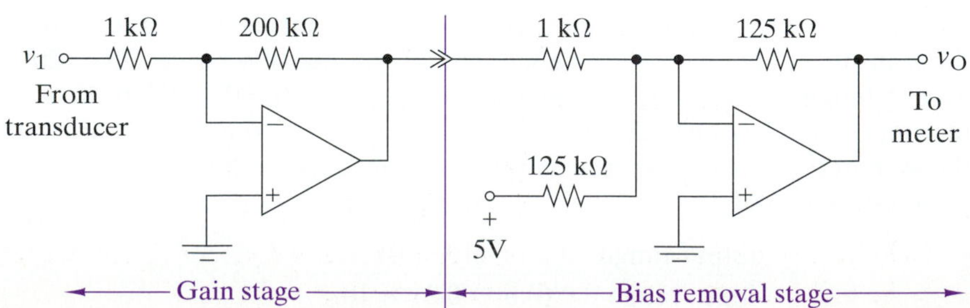

FIGURE 4–59 *Interface circuit design for the photocell transducer problem.*

open-loop gain of most OP AMPs. The high open-loop gain would also require a small input resistance and a large feedback resistance (for example, 100 Ω and 2.5 MΩ). This small input resistance could load the input transducer and change its calibration.

D DESIGN EXAMPLE 4–22

Strain Gauge Signal Conditioner

A strain gauge is a resistive device that measures the elongation (strain) of a solid material caused by applied forces (stress). A typical strain gauge consists of a thin film of conducting material deposited on an insulating substrate. When bonded to a member under stress, the resistance of the gauge changes by an amount

$$\Delta R = 2R_G \frac{\Delta L}{L}$$

where R_G is the resistance of the gauge with no applied stress and $\Delta L/L$ is the elongation of the material expressed as a fraction of the unstressed length L. The change in resistance ΔR is only a few tenths of a milliohm, far too small a value to be measured with a standard ohmmeter. To detect such a small change, the strain gauge is placed in a Wheatstone bridge circuit like the one shown in Figure 4–60. The bridge contains fixed resistors R_A and R_B, matched strain gages R_{G1} and R_{G2}, and a precisely controlled reference voltage V_{REF}. The values of R_A and R_B are chosen so that the bridge is balanced ($v_1 = v_2$) when no stress is applied. When stress is applied, the resistance of the stressed gauge changes to $R_{G2} + \Delta R$, and the bridge is unbalanced ($v_1 \neq v_2$). The differential signal ($v_2 - v_1$) indicates the strain resulting from the applied stress.

Design an OP AMP circuit to translate strains over the range $0 < \Delta L/L < 0.02\%$ into an output voltage on the range $0 < v_O < 4$ V, for $R_G = 120\ \Omega$ and $V_{REF} = 25$ V.

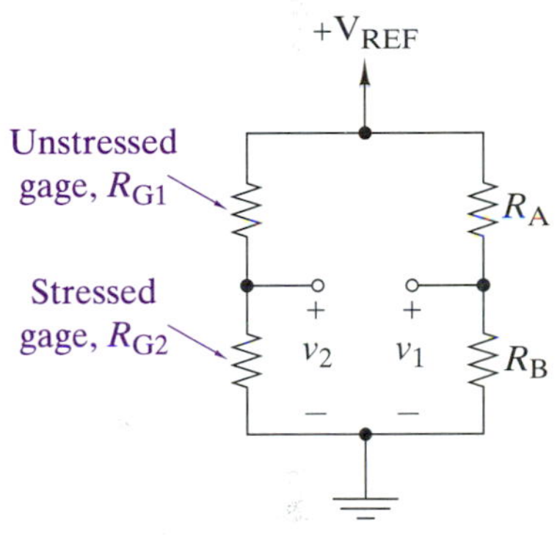

FIGURE 4–60 *Strain guages in a Wheatstone bridge.*

SOLUTION:

When an external stress is applied, the resistance R_{G2} changes to $R_{G2} + \Delta R$. Applying voltage division to each leg of the bridge yields

$$v_2 = \frac{R_{G2} + \Delta R}{R_{G1} + R_{G2}} V_{REF}$$

$$v_1 = \frac{R_B}{R_A + R_B} V_{REF}$$

The differential voltage ($v_2 - v_1$) can be written as

$$v_2 - v_1 = V_{REF}\left[\frac{R_{G2} + \Delta R}{R_{G1} + R_{G2}} - \frac{R_A}{R_A + R_B}\right]$$

To achieve bridge balance in the unstressed state, we select $R_{G1} = R_{G2} = R_A = R_B = R_G$, in which case the differential voltage reduces to

$$v_2 - v_1 = V_{REF}\left[\frac{\Delta R}{2R_G}\right] = V_{REF}\left[\frac{\Delta L}{L}\right]$$

Thus, the differential voltage is directly proportional to the strain $\Delta L/L$. However, for $V_{REF} = 25$ V and $\Delta L/L = 0.02\%$, the differential voltage is only $(V_{REF})(\Delta L/L) = 25 \times 0.0002 = 5$ mV. To obtain the required 4-V output, we need a voltage gain of $K = 4/0.005 = 800$.

The OP AMP subtractor in Figure 4–40 is ideally suited to the task of amplifying differential signals. Selecting $R_1 = R_3 = 10$ kΩ and $R_2 = R_4 = 8$ MΩ produces an input–output relationship for the subtractor circuit of

$$v_O = 800(v_2 - v_1)$$

Figure 4–61 shows the basic design.

FIGURE 4–61

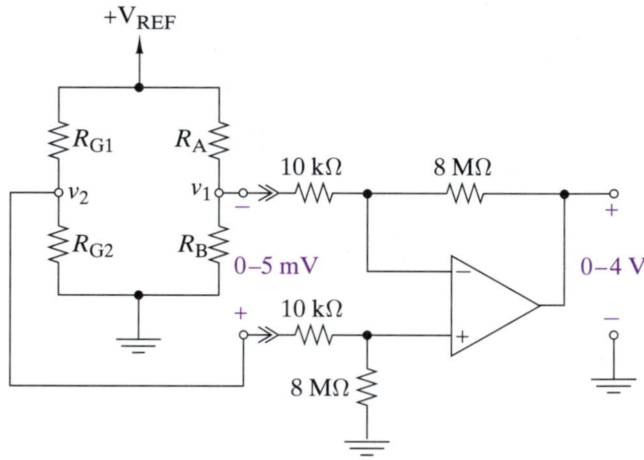

The input resistance of the subtractor circuit must be large to avoid loading the bridge circuit. The Thévenin resistance looking back into the bridge circuit is

$$\begin{aligned} R_T &= R_{G1}\|R_{G2} + R_A\|R_B \\ &= R_G\|R_G + R_G\|R_G \\ &= R_G = 120\ \Omega \end{aligned}$$

This value is small compared with the 10-kΩ input resistance of the subtractor's inverting input.

Comment: The transducer in this example is the resistor R_{G2}. In the unstressed state the voltage across this resistor is $v_2 = 12.5$ V. In the stressed state the voltage is $v_2 = 12.5$ V plus a 5-mV signal. In other words, the transducer's 5-mV signal component is accompanied by a much larger bias component. We cannot afford to amplify the 12.5-V bias component by $K = 800$ before subtracting it out. The bias is eliminated at the input by using a bridge circuit in which $v_1 = 12.5$ V, and then processing the differential signal $v_2 - v_1$. The situation illustrated in this example is quite common.

Consequently, the first stage in most instrumentation systems is a differential amplifier that removes the transducer bias. ■

D DESIGN EXERCISE: 4–17

Design an OP AMP circuit to translate the temperature range from –20°C to +120°C onto a 0- to 1-V output signal using the transducer characteristics shown in Figure 4–62(a). The transducer has a Thévenin resistance of 880 Ω.

Answer: One possible design is shown in Figure 4–62(b).

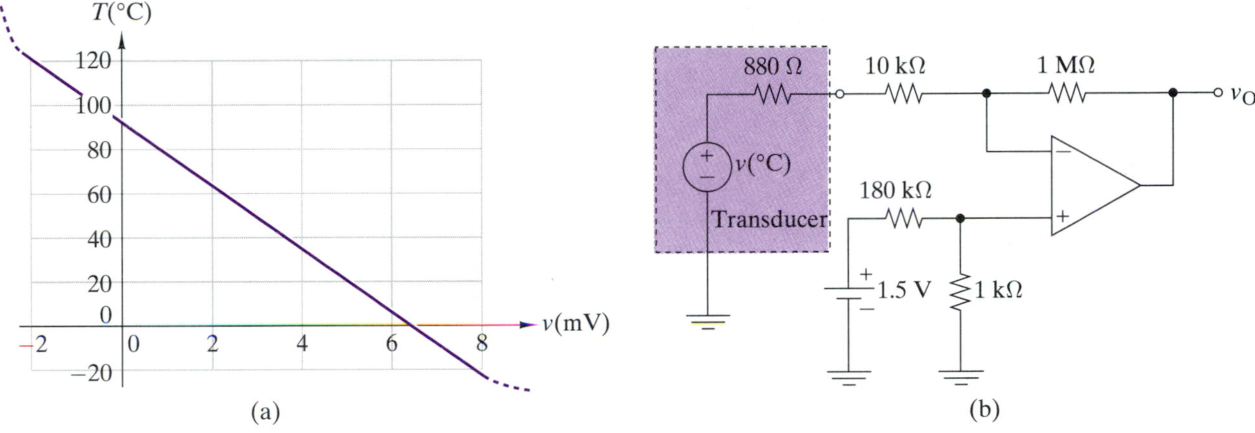

FIGURE 4–62

DISCUSSION: *It is important for the input resistor of the inverting amplifier to be at least 10 times as large as the Thévenin resistance of the transducer. Our design uses an input resistance of 10 kΩ compared with a transducer Thévenin resistance of 880 Ω.*

RESISTOR TOLERANCES

Parameter **tolerance** is the total amount by which the value of a parameter is allowed to vary. Specifying a tolerance of, say, 10% means that the parameter is allowed to vary by ±10% from its nominal value. In linear OP AMP circuits the gain tolerance is determined by the resistors in the feedback path. A logical question is what tolerance must be placed on these resistors to ensure that the gain remains within a specified tolerance.

We use **worst-case analysis** to introduce the component tolerance assignment problem. Under worst-case analysis, it is assumed that every component value lies at one of its extreme values: either $X_{MAX} = X(1 + \Delta X)$ or $X_{MIN} = X(1 - \Delta X)$, where X is the nominal value and ΔX is the parameter tolerance. Moreover, it is assumed that these extreme values combine in such a way as to produce the worst possible outcome, hence the term *worst case.*

To use a concrete example, consider the gain of the noninverting amplifier configuration in Figure 4–40.

$$K = \frac{R_1 + R_2}{R_2} = 1 + \frac{R_1}{R_2} \qquad (4-39)$$

Clearly the gain K will be a maximum when R_1 is at a maximum and R_2 is at a minimum. In worst-case analysis notation the maximum gain is written as

$$K(1 + \Delta K) = 1 + \frac{R_1(1 + \Delta R)}{R_2(1 - \Delta R)}$$

where ΔK is the gain tolerance resulting from a resistor tolerance ΔR. Looking back at Eq. (4–39), we see that $R_1/R_2 = K - 1$, so the preceding equation can be written as

$$K(1 + \Delta K) = 1 + (K - 1)\frac{1 + \Delta R}{1 - \Delta R}$$

Solving this equation for ΔK yields

$$\Delta K = \frac{K - 1}{K}\,\frac{2\,\Delta R}{1 - \Delta R} \quad \text{for } K_{\text{MAX}} \qquad (4-40)$$

This equation yields the worst-case gain tolerance when the component tolerances combine to produce the maximum gain.

By similar reasoning, in Eq. (4–39) the minimum gain occurs when R_1 is at a minimum and R_2 is at a maximum. In worst-case notation the minimum gain is

$$K(1 - \Delta K) = 1 + \frac{R_1(1 - \Delta R)}{R_2(1 + \Delta R)}$$

Again, recognizing that $R_1/R_2 = K - 1$ and solving for ΔK yields

$$\Delta K = \frac{K - 1}{K}\,\frac{2\Delta R}{1 + \Delta R} \quad \text{for } K_{\text{MIN}} \qquad (4-41)$$

This equation yields the worst-case gain tolerance when the component tolerances combine to produce the minimum gain.

Comparing Eqs. (4–40) and (4–41), we see that the "worst of the worst" occurs when the gain is at a maximum. Since $(K - 1)/K < 1$, we can place an upper bound on the worst-case gain tolerance of

$$\Delta K \leq \frac{2\Delta R}{1 - \Delta R} \quad \text{worst case} \qquad (4-42)$$

We used the noninverting amplifier to obtain this result. It turns out that the same bound applies to the inverting amplifier as well (see Problem 4–45).

For $\Delta R << 1$, Eq. (4–42) reduces to $\Delta K < 2\Delta R$, which suggests the following rule of thumb:

The worst-case gain tolerance for a single-stage OP AMP amplifier circuit is roughly twice the resistor tolerance.

If we use 1% resistors, then the worst-case gain tolerance will be about 2%. Conversely, if we want a worst case gain tolerance of 3%, the rule of thumb suggests a resistor tolerance of 1.5%. Unfortunately, commercially available standard resistors have tolerances of 0.5%, 1%, 2%, 5%, 10%, and 20%. Hence, for practical reasons we are forced to use 1% resistors to achieve 3% gain tolerance.

The following example illustrates the impact of multistage designs on worst-case analysis.

D DESIGN EXAMPLE 4–23

Circuit Design with Tolerance Specified

Design an OP AMP circuit with an overall gain of $K_{\text{TOTAL}} = +10^4 \pm 5\%$. The circuit must be designed to accommodate general-purpose OP AMPs with $\mu = 10^5$.

SOLUTION:

The overall gain cannot be achieved in a single-stage design since the circuit gain would not be small compared with the OP AMP's gain. One simple approach is a two-stage design using identical noninverting amplifiers, each realizing $K = 100$. The cascade connection of two such amplifiers yields an overall gain of $K^2 = K_{\text{TOTAL}} = 10^4$. A gain $K = 100$ can be obtained in the noninverting OP AMP configuration in Figure 4–40 using $R_1 = 99$ kΩ and $R_2 = 1$ kΩ.

What tolerance should be placed on these resistors to achieve an overall gain tolerance of 5%? Our rule of thumb suggests 2% resistor tolerance. However, Eq. (4–40) points out that 2% resistor tolerance yields a worst-case gain tolerance of

$$\Delta K = \frac{99}{100}\frac{2 \times 0.02}{1 - 0.02} = 0.040$$

For a resistor tolerance of 2%, the worst-case gain per stage is 100 (1 + 0.04). Hence, a cascade connection of two such amplifiers yields a worst-case overall gain of

$$100\,(1 + 0.04) \times 100\,(1 + 0.04) \approx 10^4\,(1 + 0.08)$$

In summary, 2% resistors produce a worst-case tolerance of 8% on the overall gain. Thus, to achieve a 5% gain tolerance in a two-stage design, we must use 1% resistors. ■

In the preceding analysis and example, it is a simple matter to determine the component values that lead to worst-case performance. In more complicated circuits it is generally not practical to determine analytically the combination of extreme values that produce the worst case. For this reason, circuit analysis programs like SPICE include a worst-case analysis option. Under this option user-specified components are sequentially assigned their extreme values and the worst-case combination identified. Finding the worst of the worst takes two passes, one to find the worst maximum and the other to find the worst minimum. Component tolerances derived from worst-case analysis are very conservative since they depend on an unlikely combination of extreme value events.

4–7 THE COMPARATOR

Up to this point we have treated circuits in which negative feedback keeps the OP AMP in the linear mode with $v_P \approx v_N$. When v_P and v_N differ by more than a few millivolts, the OP AMP is driven into one of its two saturation modes:

1. +Saturation with $v_O = +V_{CC}$ when $(v_P - v_N) > 0$
2. –Saturation with $v_O = -V_{CC}$ when $(v_P - v_N) < 0$.

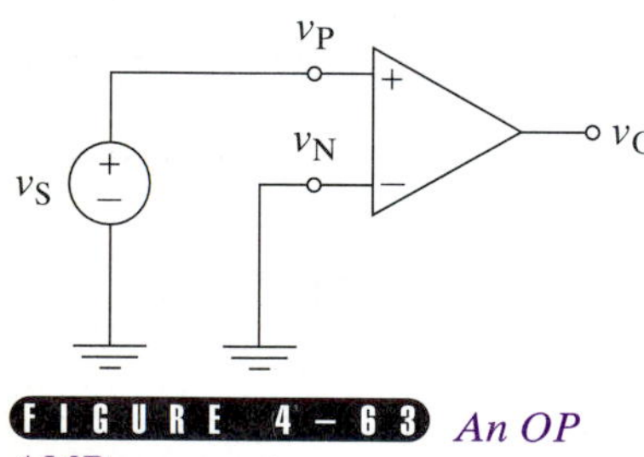

FIGURE 4–63 *An OP AMP comparator.*

With no feedback the OP AMP operates in one of these two saturation modes whenever the inputs are not equal. Under saturation conditions the output voltage indicates whether $v_P > v_N$ or $v_P < v_N$. A device that discriminates between two unequal voltages is called a **comparator**.

Figure 4–63 shows an example of an OP AMP operating as a comparator. First note that there is no feedback and $v_N = 0$, since the inverting input is grounded. The voltage source connected to the noninverting input means that when $v_P = v_S > 0$, the OP AMP is driven into +saturation with $v_O = +V_{CC}$. Conversely, when $v_P = v_S < 0$, the OP AMP is in –saturation with $v_O = -V_{CC}$. Figure 4–64 shows an example of a plot of $v_S(t)$ versus time plus the resulting comparator output. The circuit in Figure 4–63 is called a **zero crossing detector** because the comparator output changes its saturation state whenever the input v_S crosses through zero. Notice that the comparator output is not proportional to the input, which shows that the comparator is a nonlinear device.

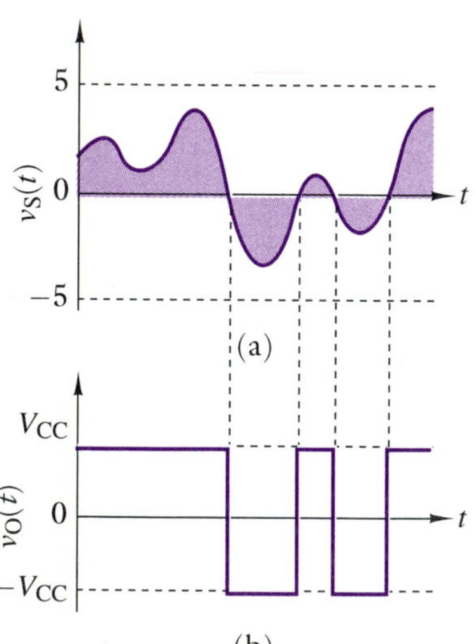

FIGURE 4–64 *Input and output signals of an OP AMP comparator.*

A modified version of the zero-crossing detector is shown in Figure 4–65. In this circuit a constant 2-V source is applied at the inverting input and the input signal v_S from Figure 4–64 is applied to the noninverting input. The input signal is now compared with 2 V rather than with zero. When $v_P = v_S > 2$ V, the OP AMP is in +saturation with $v_O = +V_{CC}$, and when $v_P = v_S < 2$ V, the OP AMP is in –saturation with $v_O = -V_{CC}$. A plot of the resulting output voltage is shown in Figure 4–65(c). The value of the fixed source determines the input signal level at which the comparator switches from one saturation state to the other. For example, connecting a 10-V fixed source to the inverting input causes the comparator output to remain at $-V_{CC}$, since v_S never exceeds 10 V.

Although ordinary OP AMPs can be used as comparators, there are integrated circuit devices specifically designed to operate in saturation. These comparator devices are designed to switch rapidly from one saturation state to the other and to have output saturation levels that are compatible with digital circuits.

Using digital circuit terminology, the input–output characteristics of an **ideal comparator** can be written as

$$\text{If } v_P > v_N, \text{ then } v_O = V_{OH}, \text{ else}$$
$$\text{If } v_P < v_N, \text{ then } v_O = V_{OL} \quad (4-43)$$

where V_{OH} and V_{OL} are the high and low saturation levels of the element. For example, a comparator with V_{OH} = +5 V and V_{OL} = 0 V is compatible with commonly used TTL (transistor–transistor logic) digital circuits. Note that the equal sign is omitted in the conditional part of the statement because we cannot be certain what the output will be if $v_P = v_N$.

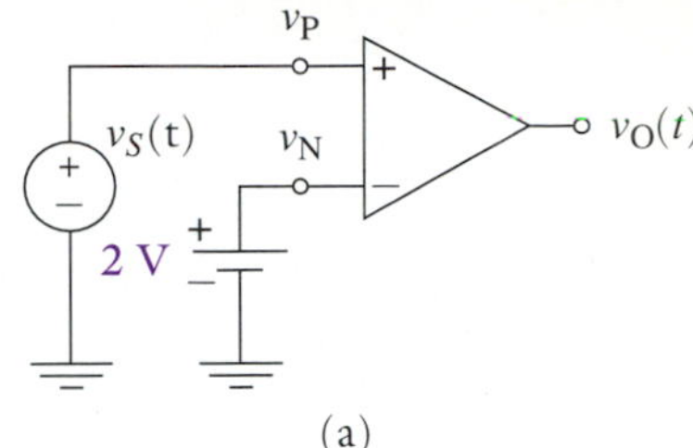

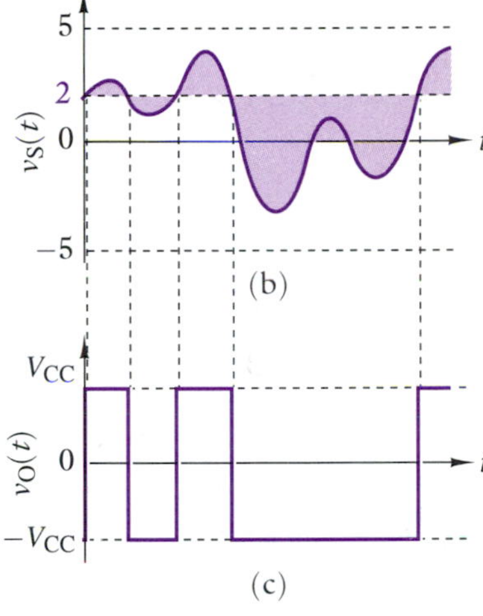

FIGURE 4–65 *Comparator with a 2-V offset: (a) Circuit diagram. (b) Input voltage. (c) Output voltage.*

EXAMPLE 4–24

Figure 4–66 shows an OP AMP whose output is connected to two 15-V lamps. Analyze the circuit and find the input signal condition required to turn each of the lamps on.

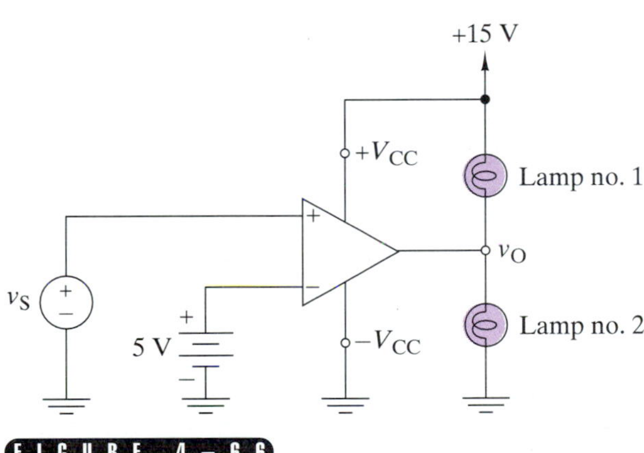

FIGURE 4–66

SOLUTION:

The circuit has no feedback so the OP AMP operates as a comparator. Figure 4–66 shows the power supply inputs to the OP AMP. The positive supply terminal is connected to a +15-V source and the negative supply terminal is grounded. Therefore, the two output saturation levels are V_{OH} = +15 V and V_{OL} = 0 V.

Because the 5-V source is connected to the inverting input, the comparator changes its state whenever the input voltage v_S passes through 5 V. When v_S < 5 V, the comparator is in negative saturation with $v_O = V_{OL}$ = 0 V. In this case, the voltages across lamps 1 and 2 are 15 V and 0 V, respectively. Conversely, when v_S > 5 V, the comparator is in positive saturation with $v_O = V_{OH}$ = +15 V, and hence the voltages across lamps 1 and 2 are 0 V and 15 V, respectively. These observations can be summarized as follows:

INPUT RANGE	COMPARATOR STATE	OUTPUT VOLTAGE	LAMP 1	LAMP 2
$v_S < 5$ V	–Saturation	$v_O = 0$ V	On	Off
$v_S > 5$ V	+Saturation	$v_O = 15$ V	Off	On

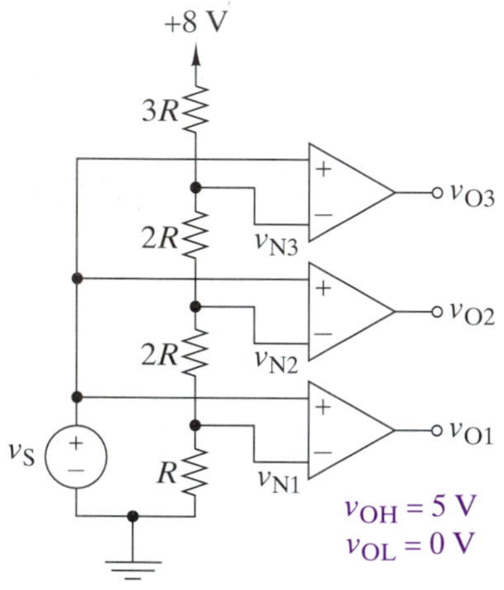

FIGURE 4–67

APPLICATION NOTE: EXAMPLE 4–25

The circuit in Figure 4–67 is an analog-to-digital converter (ADC) that changes the analog voltage v_S into a 3-bit digital output v_{O1}, v_{O2}, and v_{O3}. The inverting inputs to the comparators are connected to a voltage divider. Using voltage division, we see that $v_{N1} = 1$ V, $v_{N2} = 3$ V, and $v_{N3} = 5$ V. The analog input v_S is applied simultaneously to the noninverting inputs of all three comparators. When $v_S < 1$ V, all three comparators are in –saturation with $v_{O1} = v_{O2} = v_{O3} = V_{OL} = 0$. When the analog input is in the range $3 > v_S > 1$, comparator 1 switches to +saturation and the three outputs are $v_{O1} = V_{OH} = 5$ V and $v_{O2} = v_{O3} = V_{OL} = 0$ V. When $5 > v_S > 3$, comparators 1 and 2 are in +saturation so the three outputs are $v_{O1} = v_{O2} = V_{OH} = 5$ V and $v_{O3} = V_{OL} = 0$ V. Finally, when $v_S > 5$ V, all three comparators are in +saturation with $v_{O1} = v_{O2} = v_{O3} = V_{OH} = 5$ V. These observations can be summarized as follows:

INPUT RANGE	COMPARATOR 1 v_{O1}	COMPARATOR 2 v_{O2}	COMPARATOR 3 v_{O3}
$1 > v_S$	0	0	0
$3 > v_S > 1$	5	0	0
$5 > v_S > 3$	5	5	0
$v_S > 5$	5	5	5

Note that each analog voltage range is converted into a unique 3-bit digital word. This 3-bit code can be converted to a 2-bit binary code using standard combinatorial logic design methods. The circuit is called a flash converter because the comparators operate in parallel and the analog-to-digital conversion takes place almost instantaneously.

4–8 COMPARISON OF ANALYSIS METHODS

We have completed our study of resistance circuits, so it is important to reflect on what we have learned. We began by describing how the voltages and currents in a circuit are constrained by Kirchhoff's laws and device characteristics. Using the device and connection method as a foundation, we studied a variety of circuit analysis techniques, including circuit reduction, unit output, superposition, Thévenin's and Norton's theorems, node analysis, mesh analysis, and computer-aided analysis. Are all of these methods really necessary? Why don't we learn one method and apply it to every situation?

The short answer is that we cannot. All of these methods are useful because each offers a different perspective of circuit behavior. To illustrate the point, consider the circuit in Figure 4–68. If we need a general characterization, then writing two node equations is preferable to three mesh equations. On the other hand, mesh currents might be better if the purpose of the analysis is to determine the current through R_F. Similarly, if the purpose is to determine R_L for maximum power transfer, then either Thévenin's or Norton's equivalent is needed. Superposition would be used if the objective is to isolate the effects of v_{S1} and v_{S2} on the circuit responses. Still another approach is to use successive source conversions and circuit reductions to reduce the circuit to only three elements connected in parallel—a resistor, a dependent current source, and an independent current source (try it). An engineer must understand and know how to use different tools because some tools may work better than others on any given problem.

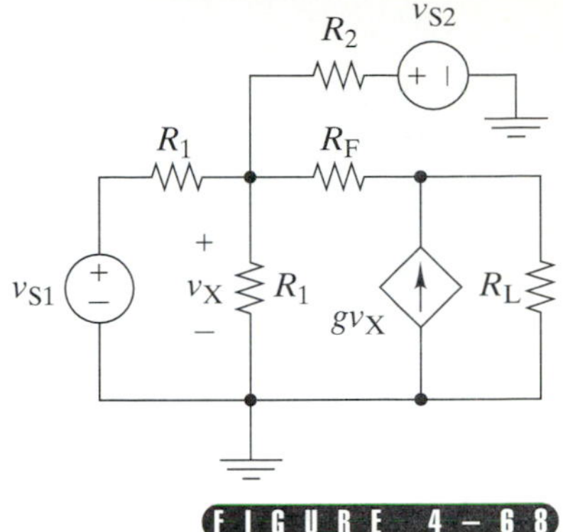

FIGURE 4–68

Conversely, each method has limitations that make it difficult or impossible to apply in every situation. Some of these limitations are fundamental and some arise from practical considerations. An example of a fundamental limitation is that the unit output method only works on ladder circuits. A practical limitation is that the algebraic burden of hand computations begins to get out of hand for circuits with four or more nodes or meshes, making computer-aided analysis a practical necessity.

Of what use are hand analysis methods that become impractical at such a modest level of complexity? Why not just use SPICE or MICRO-CAP and forget everything else? It is certainly true that large-scale circuits are best handled by computer-aided techniques. Programs like SPICE are probably the right tool for circuits of even modest complexity when numerical values of all parameters are known and a numerical value of the response is the desired end product. However, circuit analysis is not an end product, but a means to an end. What hand analysis does that SPICE cannot do is generate an analytical solution with the circuit parameters left in symbolic form. A symbolic solution often gives us greater insight into circuit operation because we can see how parameters affect the response.

In other words, hand analysis and computer-aided analysis are not simply alternative ways to solve the same old problems. Computer-aided analysis is appropriate when we already have a basic understanding of how a circuit works and need to examine the numerical details of its operation. The basic understanding needed to use programs like SPICE intelligently is gained through hand analysis of the relatively simple circuits that form the building blocks of large-scale circuits.

Some general guidelines for using these analysis tools are as follows:

1. Simplify the circuit by combining elements in series or parallel wherever possible.
2. Single-input ladder circuits are easily treated using circuit reduction or the unit output method.
3. Superposition is useful in multiple-input circuits to isolate the ef-

fect of individual inputs. It is not always the best way to find the combined effects of several inputs.

4. Thévenin's or Norton's theorems are useful in interface circuits to examine the effect of different loads or nonlinear loads. They are not particularly useful for a fixed linear load.
5. OP AMP circuits can be treated using functional block diagrams for the standard configurations. Node analysis can be used for more complex configurations.
6. Node analysis works best in circuits with many elements connected in parallel and all voltage sources connected to the reference node.
7. Mesh analysis works best in circuits with many elements connected in series and only one mesh current passing through each current source.
8. Computer-aided analysis is appropriate when you have a basic understanding of how a circuit works and need to check the numerical details of its operation, including worst-case analysis.

No single technique fits every task. In most circuit problems several different techniques will be needed. Only practice and experience will give you the insight needed to select the best set of tools in each new situation. Table 4–1 summarizes the major advantages and disadvantages of various methods of circuit analysis.

TABLE 4–1 A SUMMARY OF CIRCUIT ANALYSIS TECHNIQUES

TECHNIQUE	ADVANTAGE	DISADVANTAGE
Circuit reduction	Involves working directly with the circuit model	Nonseries/parallel circuits not easily handled
Unit output	Simple and direct application of KCL, KVL, and Ohm's law	Only works for ladder circuits
Superposition	Isolates the effect of different sources on circuit responses	Requires repeated analysis
Thévenin/Norton	Useful for interface situations with many different loads	May require two analyses to find v_{OC} and i_{SC}
Device and connection analysis	Equations are easy to formulate. Useful as a conceptual foundation	Generates many equations
Node analysis	Equations are easy to formulate and apply to electronic circuits	Transformers (Chapter 6) not easily handled
Mesh analysis	Equations are easy to formulate and apply to planar circuits	OP AMPs not easily handled
Computer-aided circuit analysis	Can easily handle simple or large-scale electronic circuits	Requires numerical values for all circuit parameters

SUMMARY

- The output of a dependent source is controlled by a signal in a different part of the circuit. Linear dependent sources are circuit elements used to model active devices and are represented in this text by a diamond-shaped source symbol. Each type of controlled source is characterized by a single-gain parameter μ, β, r, or g.
- The Thévenin resistance of a circuit containing dependent sources can be found using the open-circuit voltage and the short-circuit current, or by directly solving for the interface i–v characteristic. The active Thévenin resistance may be significantly different from the passive lookback resistance.
- The large-signal model divides the transistor operating characteristics into cutoff, active, and saturation modes. Each mode has a unique set of i–v characteristics. The operating mode can be found by assuming the transistor is in the active mode and checking the signs of i_B and v_{CE}. The operating mode is active if $i_B > 0$ and $v_{CE} > 0$, cutoff if $i_B < 0$, and saturation if $v_{CE} < 0$.
- The OP AMP is an active device with at least five terminals: the inverting input, the noninverting input, the output, and two power supply terminals. The power supply terminals are not usually shown in circuit diagrams. The integrated circuit OP AMP is a differential amplifier with a very high voltage gain.
- The OP AMP can operate in a linear mode when there is a feedback path from the output to the inverting input. To remain in the linear mode, the output voltage is limited to the range $-V_{CC} \leq v_O \leq +V_{CC}$, where $\pm V_{CC}$ are the supply voltages.
- The i–v characteristics of the ideal model of an OP AMP are $i_P = i_N = 0$ and $v_P = v_N$. The ideal OP AMP has an infinite voltage gain, an infinite input resistance, and zero output resistance. The ideal model is a good approximation to real devices as long as the circuit gain is much smaller than the OP AMP gain.
- Four basic signal-processing functions performed by OP AMP circuits are the inverting amplifier, noninverting amplifier, inverting summer, and differential amplifier. These arithmetic operations can also be represented in block diagram form.
- OP AMP circuits can be connected in cascade to obtain more complicated signal-processing functions. The analysis and design of the individual stages in the cascade can be treated separately, provided the input resistance of the following stage is kept sufficiently high.
- OP AMP circuits are easily treated using node analysis. A node voltage is identified at each OP AMP output, but a node equation is not written at these nodes. Node equations are then written at the remaining nodes, and the ideal OP AMP input voltage constraint ($v_N = v_P$) is used to reduce the number of unknowns.

- The comparator is a nonlinear signal-processing device obtained by operating an OP AMP device without feedback. The comparator has two analog inputs and a two-state digital output.
- Table 4–1 summarizes the major advantages and disadvantages of the circuit analysis techniques studied in the first four chapters of this book. Some general guidelines can be given, but only experience and practice develop the ability to select the best technique in a given situation.

EN ROUTE OBJECTIVES AND ASSOCIATED PROBLEMS

ERO 4–1 LINEAR ACTIVE CIRCUITS (SECTS. 4–1, 4–2)

Given a circuit containing linear resistors, dependent sources, and independent sources,

(a) Find selected output signal variables, input–output relationships, or equivalent circuits.
(b) Select circuit parameters so that a specified signal is delivered to a load.

4–1 For the circuit in Figure P4–1,

(a) Find the voltage gain v_O/v_S .
(b) Find the current gain i_O/i_X.
(c) For $v_S = 0.1$ V, find the power supplied by the input source v_S and the power delivered to the 1-kΩ load resistor.

FIGURE P4–1

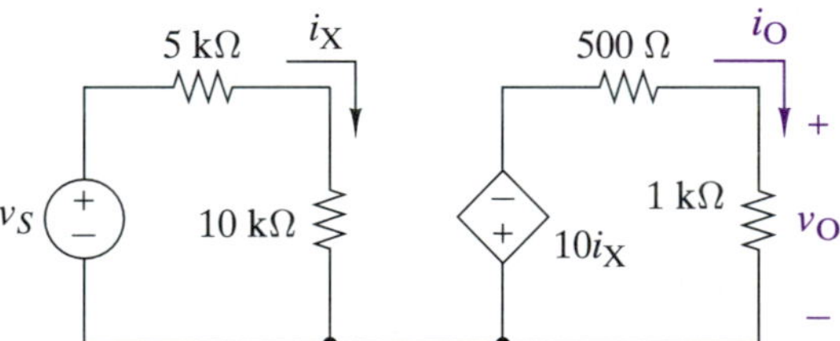

4–2 For the circuit in Figure P4–2,

(a) Find the voltage gain v_O/v_1 .
(b) Find the current gain i_O/i_S.
(c) For $i_S = 2$ mA, find the power supplied by the input source i_S and the power delivered to the 2-kΩ load resistor.

FIGURE P4–2

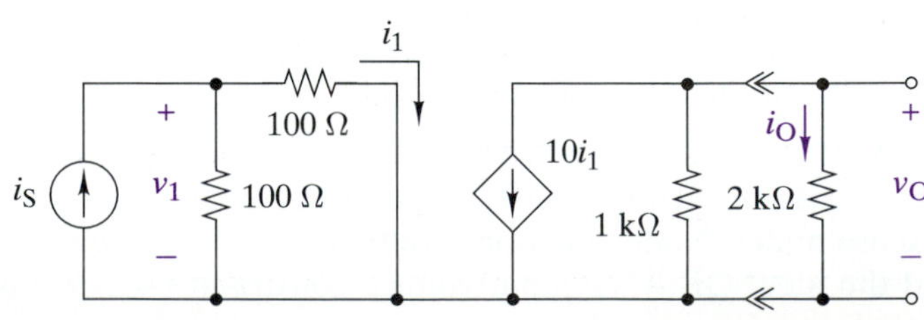

4–3 The circuit in Figure P4–3 is a dependent-source model of a two-stage amplifier. For $v_S = 1$ mV, find the output voltage v_3 and the current gain i_3/i_1.

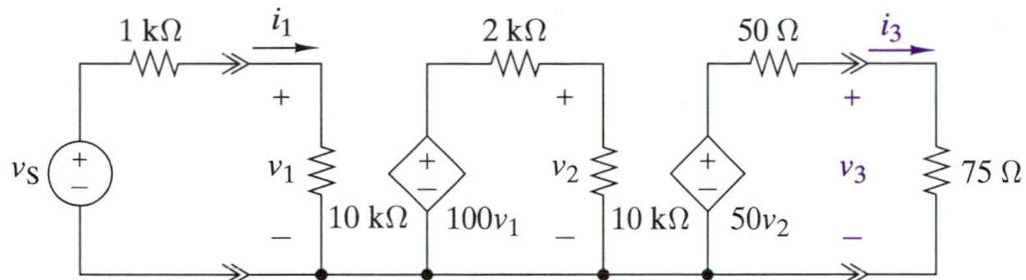

FIGURE P4–3

4–4 The circuit in Figure P4–4 is an ideal voltage amplifier with negative feedback via the resistor R_F.

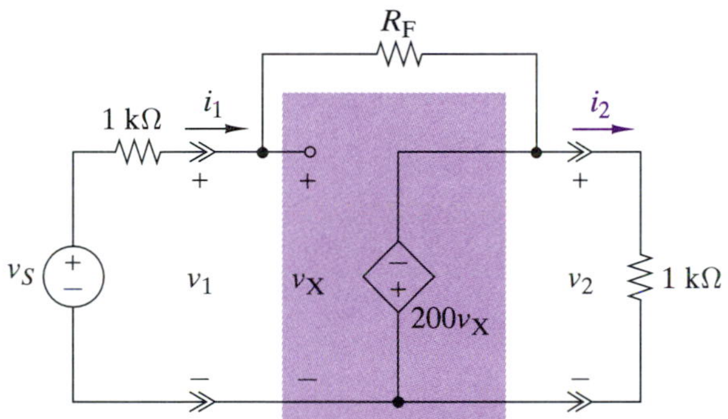

FIGURE P4–4

(a) For $v_S = 10$ mV and $R_F = 50$ kΩ, find the output voltage v_2 and the current gain i_2/i_1.

(b) Find the input resistance $R_{IN} = v_1/i_1$.

4–5 The circuit in Figure P4–5 is an ideal current amplifier with negative feedback via the resistor R_E.

(a) For $i_S = 25$ μA and $R_E = 250$ Ω, find the output current i_2 and the voltage gain v_2/v_1.

(b) Find the input resistance $R_{IN} = v_1/i_1$.

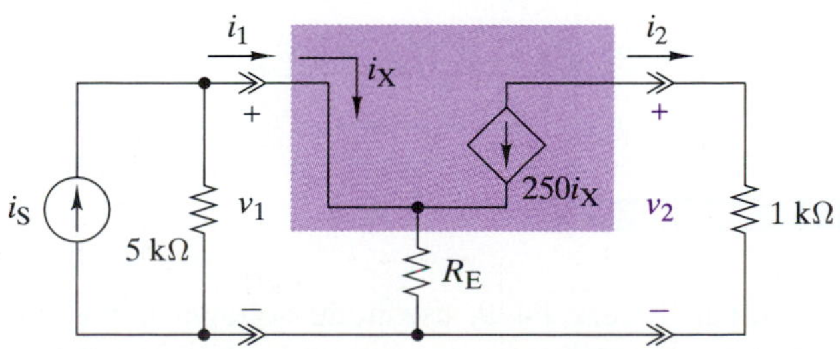

FIGURE P4–5

4–6 Find the Norton equivalent seen by the load resistor R_L in the circuit in Figure P4–6.

FIGURE P4–6

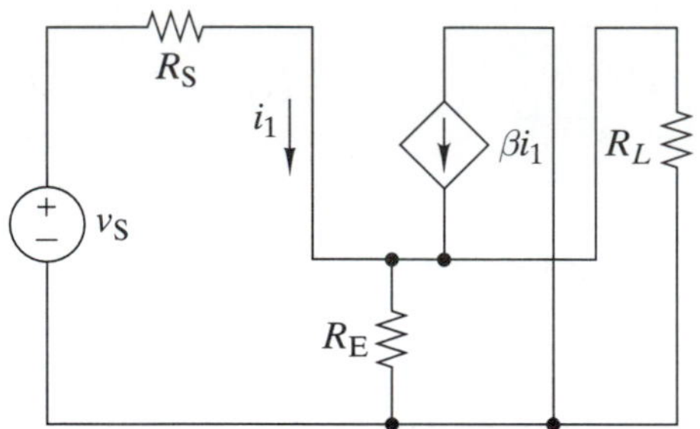

4–7 The circuit in Figure P4–7 is a model of a two-stage amplifier using identical transistors. Formulate node-voltage or mesh-current equations for this circuit. Use these equations to solve for the input–output relationship $v_O = Kv_S$ using $R_S = 50\ \Omega$, $r_\pi = 1\ \text{k}\Omega$, $\beta = 100$, and $R_L = 1\ \text{k}\Omega$.

FIGURE P4–7

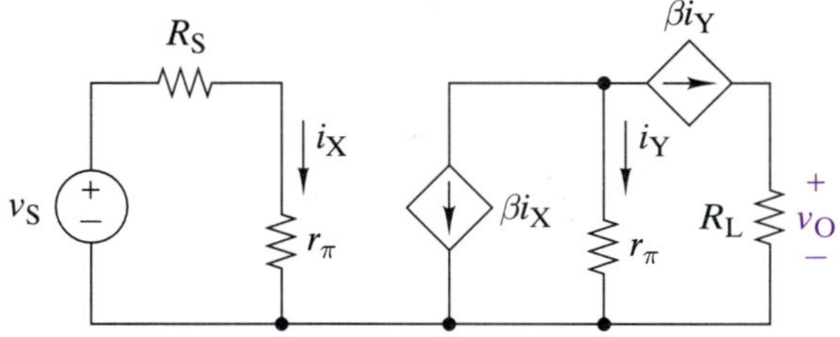

4–8 The circuit in Figure P4–8 is a model of a feedback amplifier using two identical transistors. Formulate either node-voltage or mesh-current equations for this circuit. Use these equations to solve for the input–output relationship $v_O = Kv_S$ using $r_\pi = 1\ \text{k}\Omega$, $R_E = 100\ \Omega$, $R_C = 10\ \text{k}\Omega$, $R_L = 5\ \text{k}\Omega$, $R_F = 5\ \text{k}\Omega$, and $\beta = 50$.

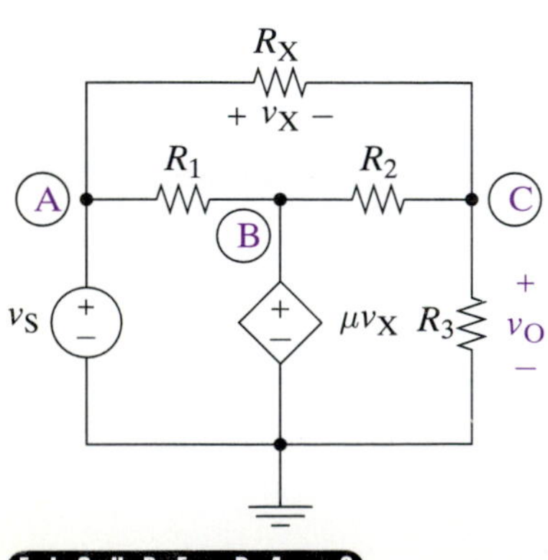

FIGURE P4–9

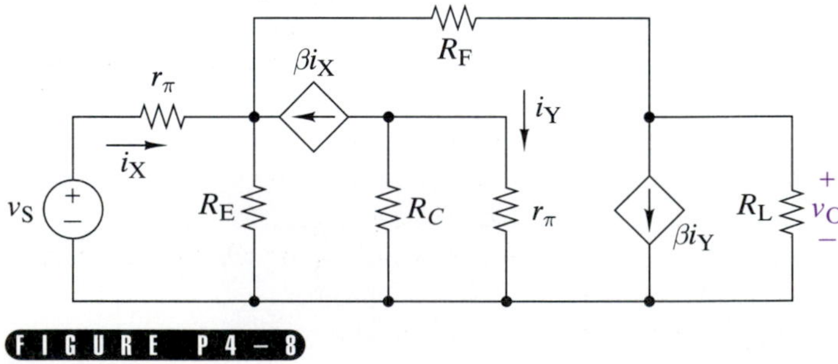

FIGURE P4–8

4–9 For the circuit in Figure P4–9, use node-voltage or mesh-current analysis to solve for the voltage gain v_O/v_S in terms of circuit parameters R_1, R_2, R_3, R_X, and μ.

4–10 **D** Select the value of R_F in Figure P4–4 so that the voltage gain $K = v_2/v_S = -10$.

4–11 **D** Select the value of R_E in Figure P4–5 so that the current gain $K = i_2/i_S = -10$.

4–12 The input resistance of the circuit in Figure P4–12(a) is found to be 200 Ω.

(a) Explain why the rest of the circuit must contain at least one active device.

(b) Suppose the rest of the circuit in Figure P4–12(a) has the form shown in Figure P4–12(b). Select the values of R and β so that $R_{IN} = 200\ \Omega$.

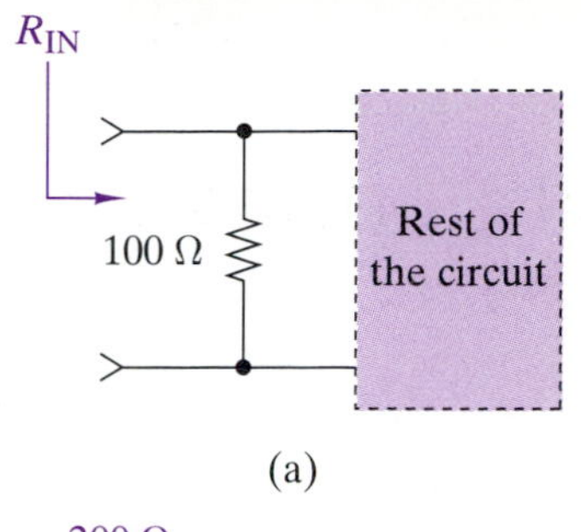

(a)

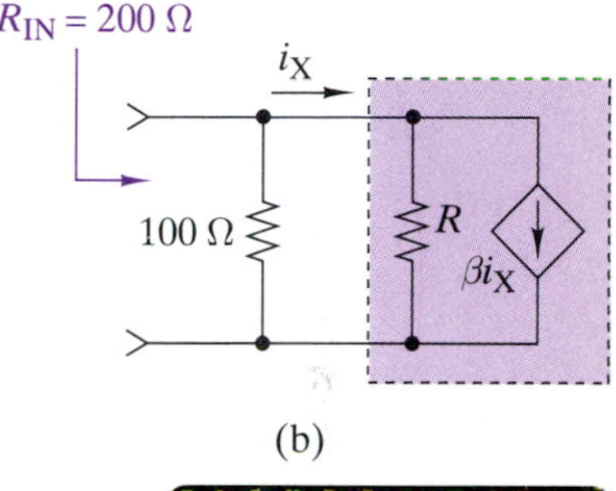

(b)

FIGURE P4–12

ERO 4–2 TRANSISTOR CIRCUITS (SECT. 4–3)

Given a circuit containing linear resistive elements and one transistor, use the large-signal model to

(a) Find the transistor operating mode and selected circuit responses or transfer characteristics.

(b) Select circuit parameters to obtain a specified transistor operating mode.

4–13 The parameters of the circuit in Figure P4–13 are $R_B = 50\ \text{k}\Omega$, $R_C = 2\ \text{k}\Omega$, $\beta = 100$, $V_\gamma = 0.6$ V, and $V_{CC} = 10$ V:

(a) Find i_B, i_C, and v_{CE} for $v_S = 2$ V.

(b) Repeat part (a) with β = 200.

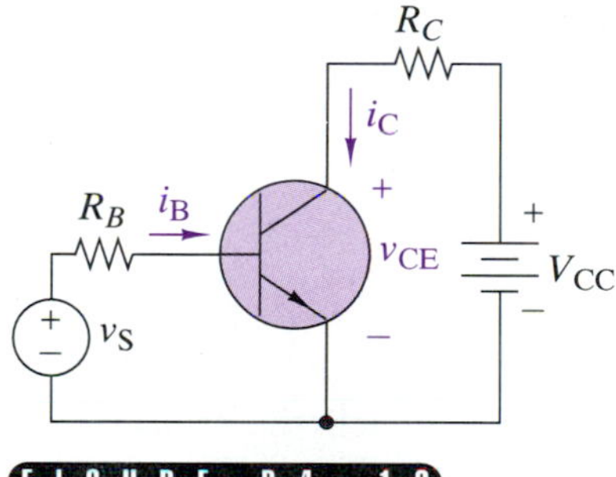

FIGURE P4–13

4–14 The parameters of the circuit in Figure P4–13 are $R_B = 100\ \text{k}\Omega$, $R_C = 5\ \text{k}\Omega$, $\beta = 50$, $V_\gamma = 0.6$ V, and $V_{CC} = 20$ V:

(a) Find the range of values of v_S for which the transistor operates in the active mode.

(b) Repeat part (a) with β = 100.

4–15 The parameters of the circuit in Figure P4–13 are $R_B = 250\ \text{k}\Omega$, $R_C = 4.7\ \text{k}\Omega$, $\beta = 150$, $V_\gamma = 0.7$ V, and $V_{CC} = 15$ V:

(a) Find the range of values of v_S for which the transistor operates in the active mode.

(b) Repeat part (a) with β = 250.

4–16 **D** The parameters of the circuit in Figure P4–13 are $R_C = 4.7\ \text{k}\Omega$, $\beta = 100$, $V_\gamma = 0.7$ V, and $V_{CC} = 15$ V:

(a) With $v_S = 2.5$ V, select a value of R_B so that the transistor is in the active mode and $v_{CE} = V_{CC}/2$.

(b) Repeat part (a) with β = 200.

4–17 **D** The parameters of the circuit in Figure P4–13 are $R_C = 3.3\ k\Omega$, $\beta = 150$, $V_\gamma = 0.6$ V, and $V_{CC} = 12$ V:

(a) Select a value of R_B so that the transistor is in the active mode when $1\ V \leq v_S \leq 5$ V and is in the saturation mode for $v_S \geq 6$ V.

(b) For the value of R_B found in (a), plot the transfer characteristic v_{CE} versus v_S as the input voltage sweeps across the range $0 \leq v_S \leq 10$ V.

4–18 **D** Transistor circuit design must allow for variation in circuit parameters, especially the forward current gain β. For the circuit in Figure P4–13 the nominal values and tolerances on the circuit parameters are $R_C = 6\ k\Omega \pm 10\%$, $V_\gamma = 0.6$ to 0.7 V, $\beta = 100 \pm 50\%$, and $V_{CC} = 10\ V \pm 1\%$. Select a value of R_B so that the transistor is always in the active mode when $v_S = 5$ V and is always in the saturation mode when $v_S = 20$ V for any set of circuit parameters within the tolerance ranges.

4–19 The element values for the circuit in Figure P4–13 are $R_B = 800\ k\Omega$, $R_C = 10\ k\Omega$, and $V_{CC} = 10$ V. The following data are measured in the laboratory:

v_S (V)	1	2	5	10
v_{CE} (V)	9.7	8.7	5.7	0.7

Sketch the circuit transfer characteristic and estimate the values of the transistor parameters V_γ and β.

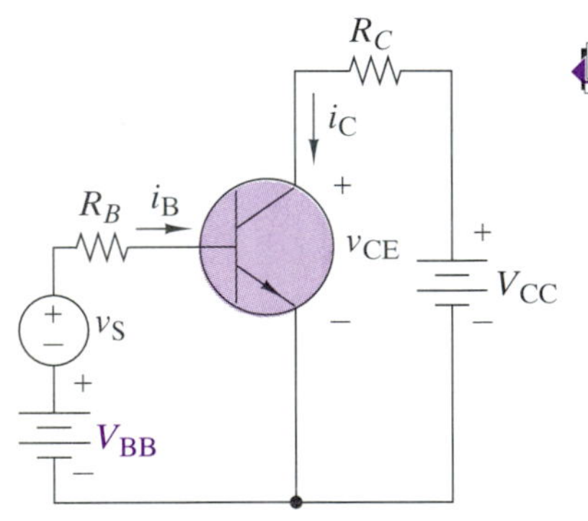

FIGURE P4–20

4–20 The input source in Figure P4–20 is a series connection of a dc source V_{BB} and a signal source v_S. The circuit parameters are $R_B = 500\ k\Omega$, $R_C = 7.5\ k\Omega$, $\beta = 200$, $V_\gamma = 0.7$ V, and $V_{CC} = 15$ V.

(a) With $v_S = 0$, select the value of V_{BB} so that the dc operating point of the transistor is in the active mode with $v_{CE} = V_{CC}/2$.

(b) Using the value of V_{BB} found in (a), find the range of values of the signal voltage v_S for which the transistor remains in the active mode.

(c) Plot the transfer characteristic v_{CE} versus v_S as the signal voltage sweeps across the range from −5 V to +5 V.

4–21 The output of the transistor circuit of Figure P4–21 is defined across the resistor R_E connected in series with the emitter. For $R_B = 100\ k\Omega$, $R_E = 1\ k\Omega$, $V_{CC} = 10$ V, $\beta = 100$, and $V_\gamma = 0.7$ V, plot the transfer characteristic v_O versus v_S as the input sweeps across the range $0 \leq v_S \leq 25$ V.

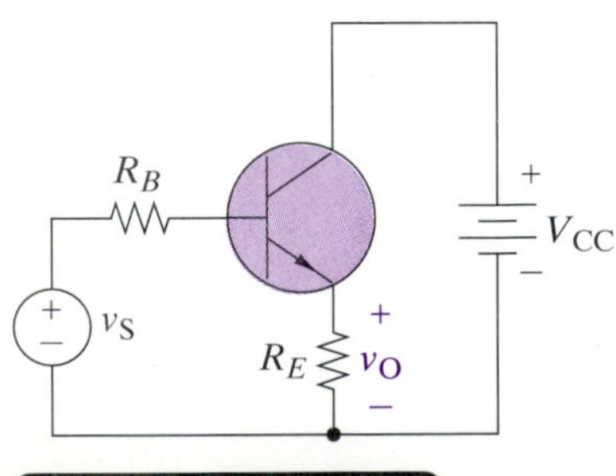

FIGURE P4–21

4–22 The incandescent lamp in Figure P4–22 must be on when the Thévenin voltage of the digital circuit is 5 V. The 5-V Thévenin source cannot supply the power needed to drive the lamp directly. In the saturation mode the transistor acts like a closed switch ($v_{CE} = 0$) and the lamp power is supplied by the 10-V dc source. Assume $V_\gamma = 0.7$ V.

(a) Explain why the 5-V Thévenin source cannot power the lamp directly.

(b) Explain why the 5-V Thévenin will turn the lamp on if $R_B \leq 575\ \Omega$.

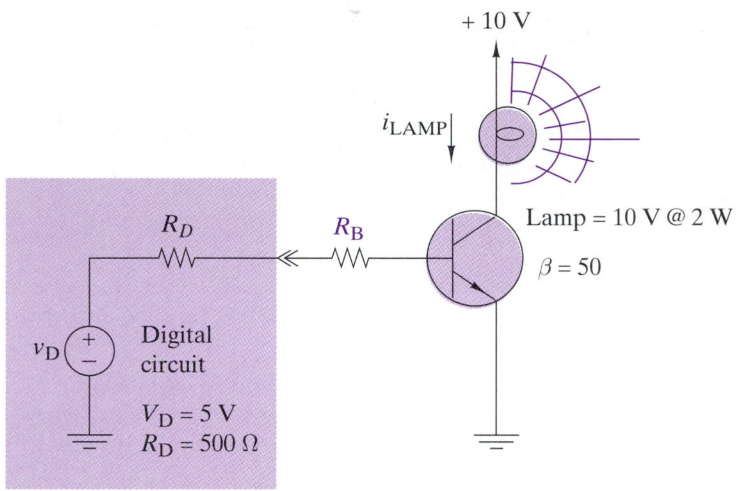

FIGURE P4–22

ERO 4–3 OP AMP CIRCUIT ANALYSIS (SECTS. 4–4, 4–5)

Given a circuit consisting of linear resistors, OP AMPs, and independent sources, find selected output signals or input–output relationships in equation or block diagram form.

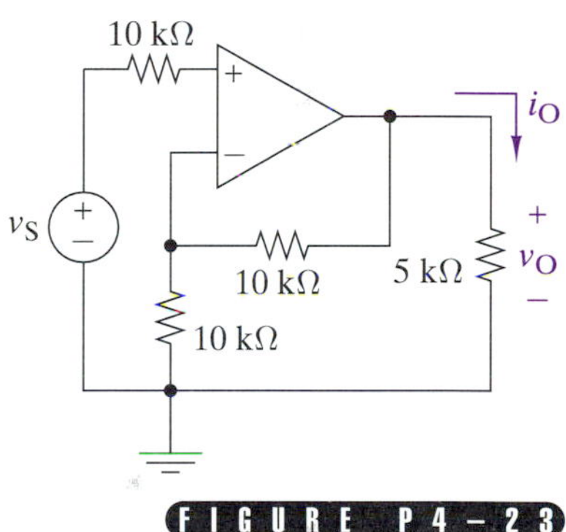

FIGURE P4–23

4–23 For the circuit in Figure P4–23,

(a) Find the relationship between the output v_O and input v_S.

(b) For $v_S = 1.5$ V, find the power delivered to the 5-kΩ load resistor and the power supplied by the input voltage source.

(c) For $V_{CC} = \pm 12$ V, sketch the circuit transfer characteristic v_O versus v_S for an input voltage on the range $-10\text{ V} < v_S < 10\text{ V}$.

4–24 For the circuit in Figure P4–24,

(a) Derive a relationship between the output v_O and the inputs v_{S1} and v_{S2}.

(b) Draw a block diagram of the input–output relationship found in (a).

(c) For $V_{CC} = \pm 15$ V and $v_{S1} = 10$ V, find the allowable range of v_{S2} for linear operation.

(d) If v_{S1} is known to fall in the range from 0 to 10 V, select a value for v_{S2} that ensures that v_O remains in the range from −10 V to +10 V.

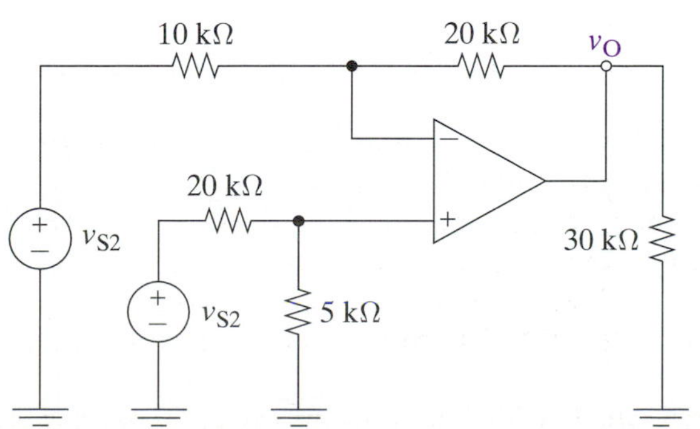

FIGURE P4–24

4–25 The input–output relationship for a three-input inverting summer is

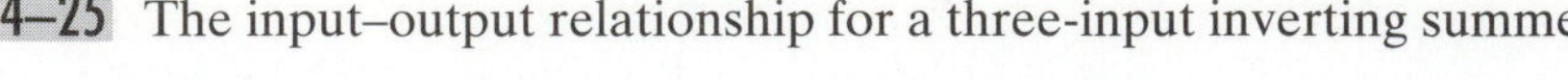

$$v_O = -[v_1 + 3v_2 + 6v_3]$$

The resistance of the feedback resistor is 54 kΩ and the supply voltages are $V_{CC} = \pm 15$ V.

(a) Find the values of the input resistors R_1, R_2, and R_3.

(b) For $v_2 = 0.5$ V and $v_3 = -1$ V, find the allowable range of v_1 for linear operation.

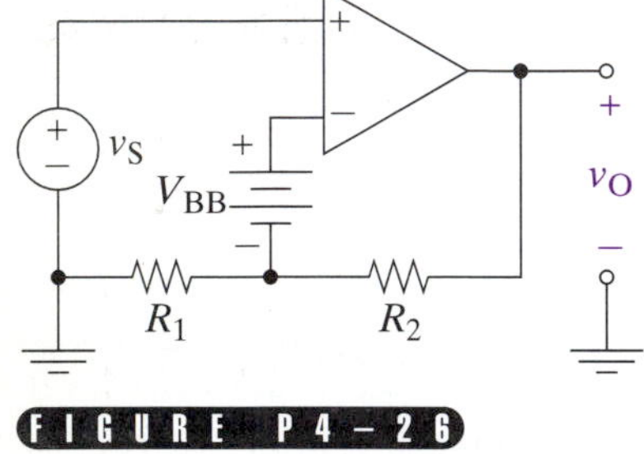

FIGURE P4–26

4–26 For the circuit in Figure P4–26,

(a) Find the input–output relationship between v_O and v_S in terms of R_1, R_2, and V_{BB}.

(b) Draw a block diagram of the relationship found in part (a).

(c) For $V_{CC} = \pm 15$ V, $V_{BB} = 5$ V, and $R_1 = R_2$, sketch the circuit transfer relationship v_O versus v_S for v_S over the range from –15 V to +15 V.

4–27 For the circuit in Figure P4–27,

(a) Find the maximum voltage, current, and power available from the 5-V source.

(b) Find the voltage, current, and power delivered to the 5-kΩ load resistor.

(c) Explain why the voltage, current, and power found in part (b) exceed the maximum available values found in part (a).

(d) Express the ratio of the power found in part (b) to the power found in part (a) in decibels.

FIGURE P4–27

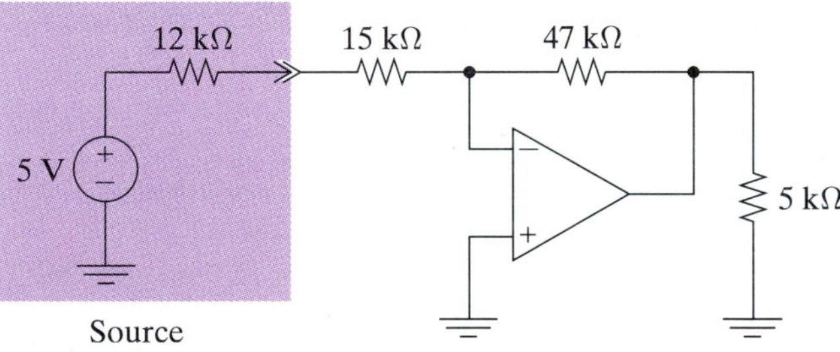

4–28 **E** It is claimed that the OP AMP circuit in Figure P4–28 operates as a voltage follower with $v_O = v_S$ when the switch S is open and operates as an inverter with $v_O = -v_S$ when the switch S is closed. Prove or disprove this claim.

FIGURE P4–28

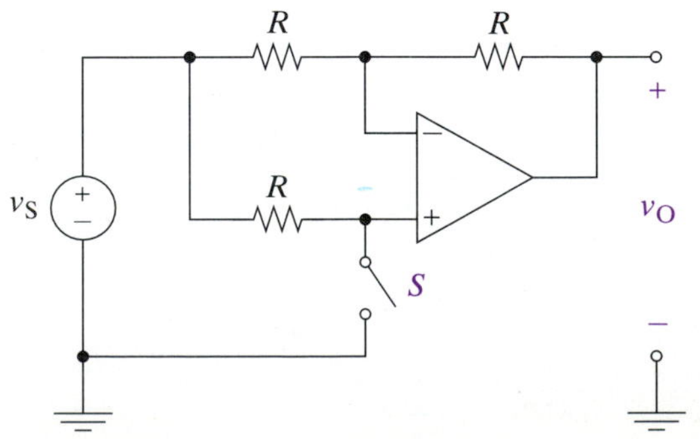

4–29 The circuit in Figure P4–29 has $V_{CC} = \pm 15$ V.

(a) Show that when the OP AMP is in the linear mode, the circuit to the left of the interface operates as an ideal current source with $i_L = v_S/R$ regardless of the value of load resistance.

(b) For $v_S = 5$ V, find the maximum load voltage that the current source can deliver without saturating the OP AMP.

(c) For $v_S = 5$ V and $R = 10$ kΩ, find the maximum load resistance R_L that the current source can drive without saturating the OP AMP.

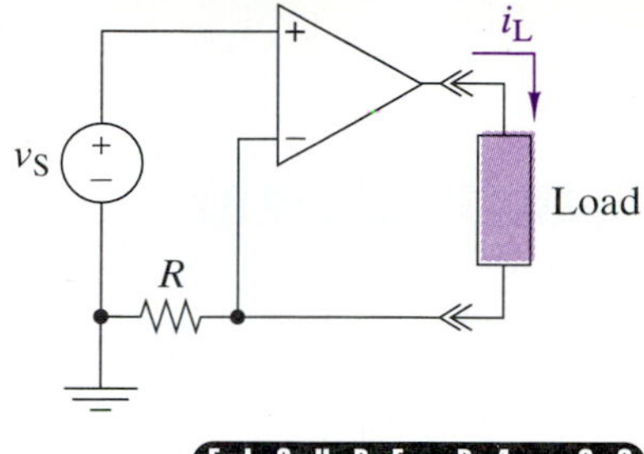

FIGURE P4–29

4–30 The power supply voltages for the circuit in Figure P4–30 are $V_{CC} = \pm 15$ V. Show that the voltage across the load R_L can range from –30 V to +30 V without saturating either OP AMP.

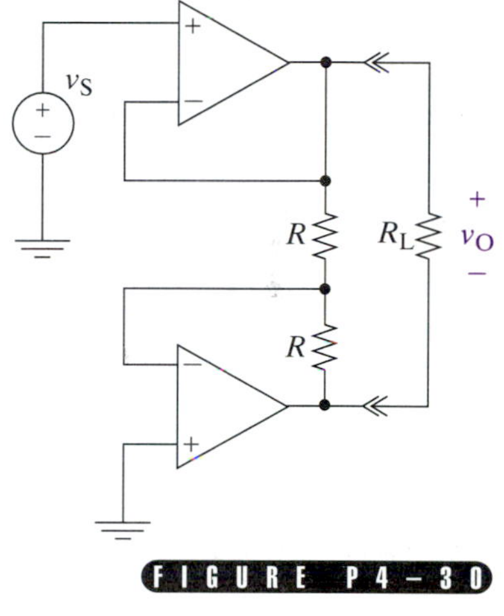

FIGURE P4–30

4–31 For the circuit in Figure P4–31, show that the input resistance $R_{IN} = -R$ when $R_1 = R_2$.

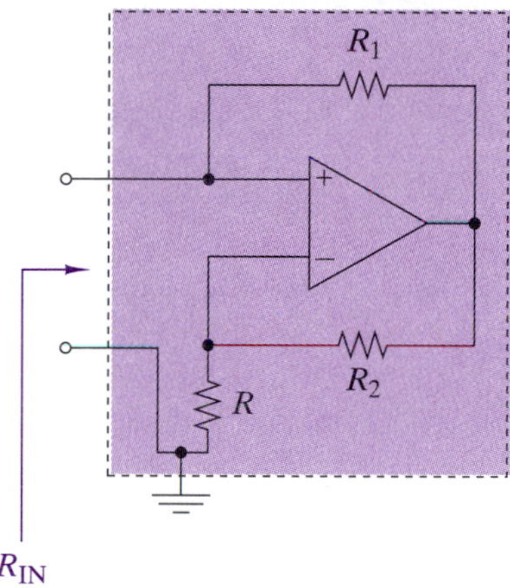

FIGURE P4–31

4–32 Identify the signal processing function preformed by each stage of the circuit in Figure P4–32. Draw a block diagram representing each stage. Use the diagrams to find the input-output relationship of the circuit.

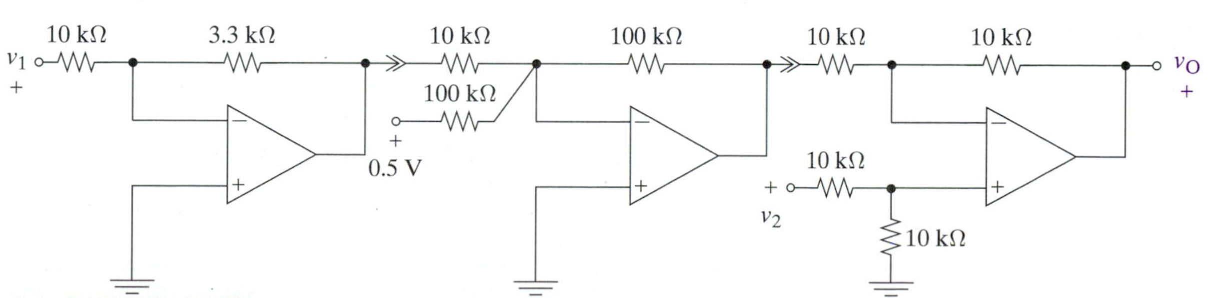

FIGURE P4–32

4–33 Use node-voltage analysis to solve for the voltage gain v_O/v_S of the circuit in Figure P4–33.

FIGURE P4–33

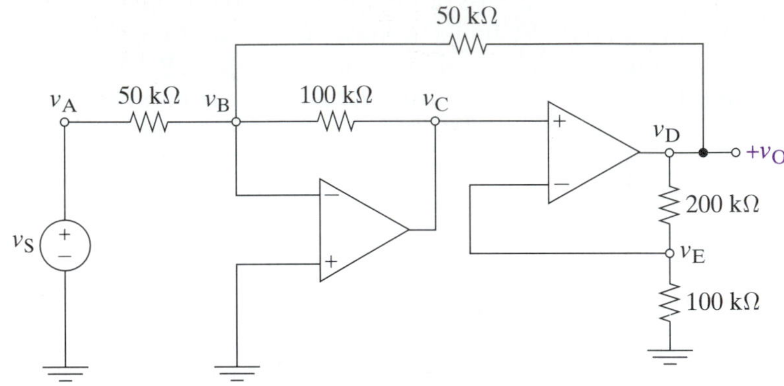

4–34 The circuit in Figure P4–34 is a simplified diagram of a standard instrumentation amplifier that is commercially available in a single integrated circuit package. The objective is to show that the circuit is a differential amplifier whose input–output relationship is of the form $v_O = K(v_{S2} - v_{S1})$ and to find the gain K in terms of the circuit resistances.

(a) Write node-voltage equations at nodes B, C, E, and F.

(b) Solve the equations at nodes E and F to show that the circuit to the right of nodes A and D is a subtractor with $v_O = v_D - v_A$.

(c) Solve the equations at nodes B and C for v_A and v_D in terms of v_{S1} and v_{S2}.

(d) Substitute the results from (c) into the result found in (b) to derive the overall input–output relationship of the entire circuit.

FIGURE P4–34

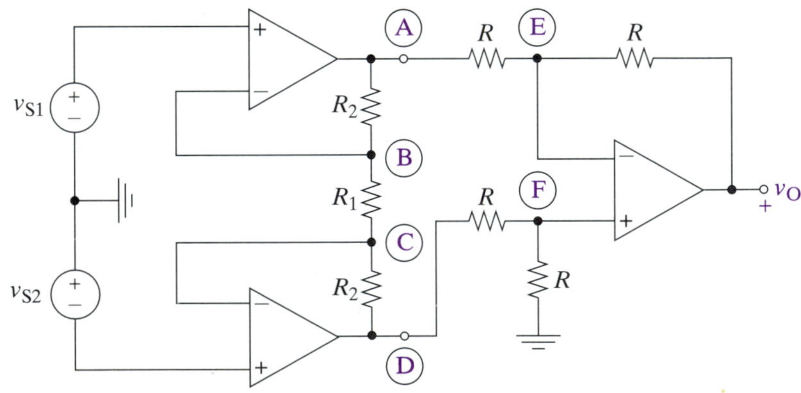

4–35 The circuit diagram of an n-input noninverting summer is shown in Figure 4–52 of Sect. 4–6. Use node-voltage analysis to derive the input–output relationship in Eq. (4–34).

ERO 4–4 OP AMP CIRCUIT DESIGN (SECT. 4–6)

Given an input–output relationship, use resistors and OP AMPs to design one or more circuits that implement the relationship within stated constraints.

4–36 **D** Show how to interconnect a single OP AMP and the *R*-2*R* resistor array shown in Figure P4–36 to obtain closed-loop voltage gains of ± 3, ± 2, ± 1, and ± 0.5.

4–37 **D** Design circuits using resistors and OP AMPs to implement each of the following input–output relationships:

(a) $v_O = 3v_1 - 3v_2$

(b) $v_O = 2v_1 - v_2$

(c) $v_O = 2v_1 + 4v_2$

4–38 **D** Design an instrumentation system to process the output of a temperature transducer whose characteristics are shown in Figure P4–38. The output voltage must be –1 V when the temperature is –300°C and +1 V at –100°C. The closed-loop gains for all stages must be less than 1000.

4–39 **D** A five-bit parallel binary-coded digital signal (v_1, v_2, v_3, v_4, v_5) is to be converted into an analog signal. The digital signal represents a logic "1" as 0 V and a logic "0" as +5 V. When all five bits are one (11111) the analog output voltage must be v_O = 23.25 V. When all five bits are zero (00000) the analog output must be v_O = 0 V. The digital signals are written with the most significant bit first. Use OP AMPs with V_{CC} = ±25 V and resistors with ± 1 % tolerance.

(a) Determine the input–output relationship required to implement the D to A conversion.

(b) Design an OP AMP circuit that implements the required relationship.

(c) Check your design by applying the digital inputs corresponding to 00000, 01111, and 11111 and comparing the analog output with the result predicted by your input–output relationship.

(d) Calculate the difference between analog outputs corresponding to 01111 and 10000, and comment on the adequacy of ±1% tolerance on the resistors.

4–40 **D** Design OP AMP circuits that implement each of the block diagrams in Figure P4–40 using only the standard resistance values for ± 5% tolerance (see Appendix A, Table A–1).

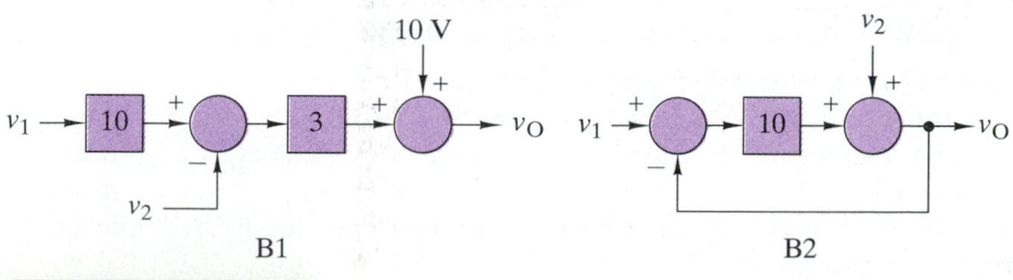

FIGURE P4–40

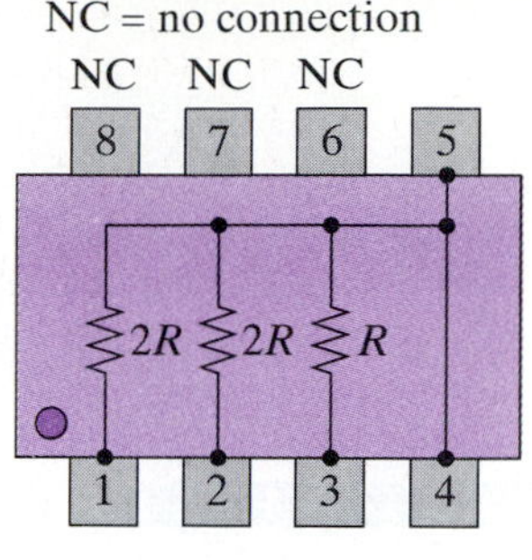

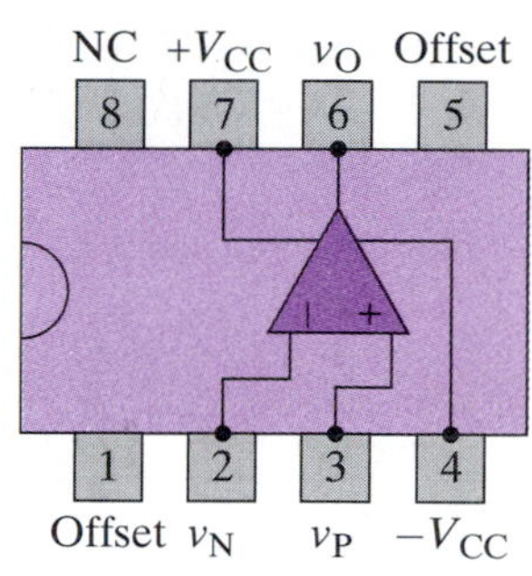

FIGURE P4–36

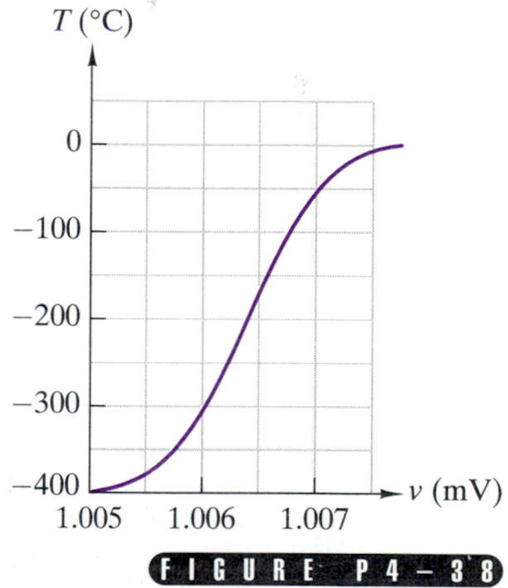

FIGURE P4–38

4–41 **D** Design an OP AMP circuit with a voltage gain $K = -50$ and an input resistance of at least 500 Ω using only 1-kΩ, 10-kΩ, 100-kΩ resistors.

4–42 **D** The circuit in Figure P4–42 is designed to implement a certain input–output relationship. Find the relationship and develop an alternative design using only a single OP AMP device.

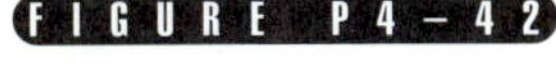
FIGURE P4–42

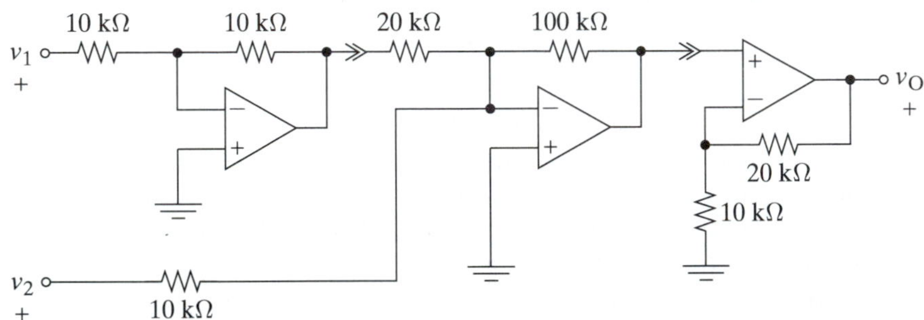

4–43 **D** A requirement exists for an amplifier with a voltage gain of −20,000 and an input resistance of at least 250 kΩ. Design an OP AMP circuit that meets the requirements using a general-purpose OP AMP with a voltage gain of $\mu = 10^5$, input resistance of $R_I = 10^8$ Ω, and output resistance $R_O = 25$ Ω.

4–44 **D** An OP AMP circuit is to be designed to implement the relationship $v_O = 100v_S$. The output voltage must be within ±7.5% of the value predicted by this relationship. Find the allowable standard resistor tolerance and design a circuit.

4–45 Show that the worst-case gain change ΔK for an inverting amplifier is

$$\Delta K = \frac{2\Delta R}{1 - \Delta R}$$

where ΔR is the worst-case change in the resistors.

ERO 4–5 THE COMPARATOR (SECT. 4–7)

(a) Given a circuit with one or more comparators, find the circuit input–output relationship.
(b) Given an input–output relationship, use resistors, voltage sources, and comparators to design circuits that realize the desired relationship.

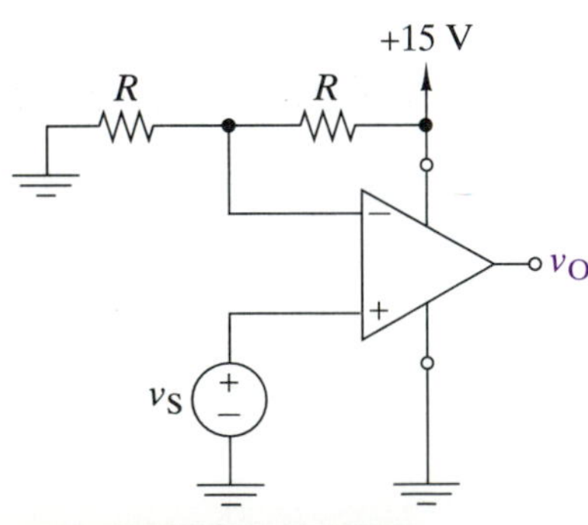

FIGURE P4–46

4–46 For the circuit in Figure P4–46,

(a) Estimate the values of V_{OH} and V_{OL}.

(b) Determine the input voltage ranges for which $v_O = V_{OH}$ and $v_O = V_{OL}$.

(c) Sketch the circuit transfer characteristics for v_S over the range −15 V to +15 V.

4–47 Repeat Problem 4–46 for the circuit of Figure P4–47.

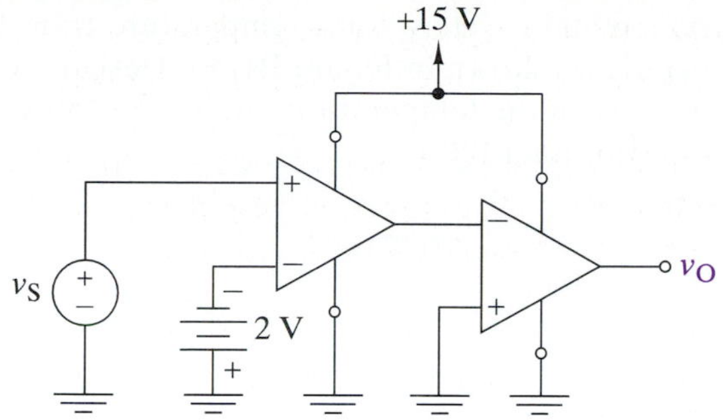

FIGURE P4–47

4–48 The OP AMP circuit in Figure P4–48 is called a window detector. In this circuit the OP AMP saturation levels are $V_{OL} = -V_{CC}$ and $V_{OH} = +V_{CC}$.

(a) Use node analysis to show that $v_O = (v_A + v_B)/2$.

(b) Show that $v_O = V_{OH}$ when the input is in the range $-V_{BB} < v_S < V_{AA}$ and is zero outside this range.

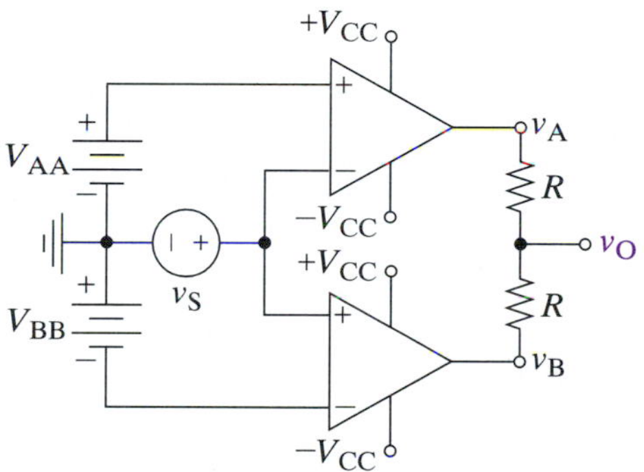

FIGURE P4–48

4–49 **D** The circuit in Figure P4–49 is an automatic tester that lights a 15-V green lamp when a resistor inserted at the interface is in the range 4.7 kΩ ±5% and a 15-V red lamp otherwise. Select the values of the resistors in the Wheatstone bridge and design an interface circuit to light the appropriate lamp.

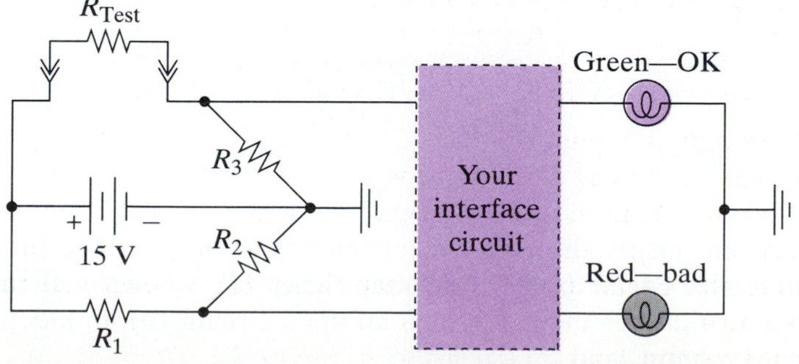

FIGURE P4–49

4–50 **D** An instrumentation system for a temperature transducer produces the characteristics shown in Figure P4–50. Design a circuit that lights a green lamp when the temperature is less than 150°C and a red lamp when it is greater than 120°C.

FIGURE P4–50

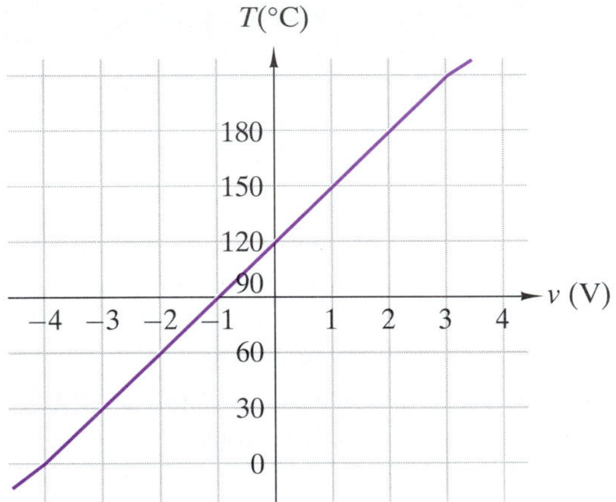

ERO 4–6 COMPARISON OF ANALYSIS METHODS (SECT. 4–8)

Given a linear circuit, identify and compare alternative analysis techniques for finding specified circuit parameters or the values of specified circuit variables.

4–51 Identify and justify the analysis techniques you would use on the circuit in Figure P4–51 to solve for the value of the following parameters.

(a) The voltage across R_4
(b) The current through R_2
(c) The value of R_3 that will extract maximum power from the circuit
(d) The contribution of v_2 to the current through R_2
(e) The value of v_1 that makes the voltage across R_2 zero

FIGURE P4–51

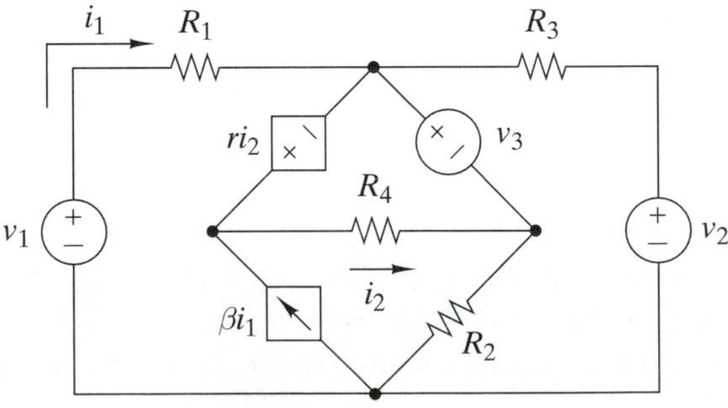

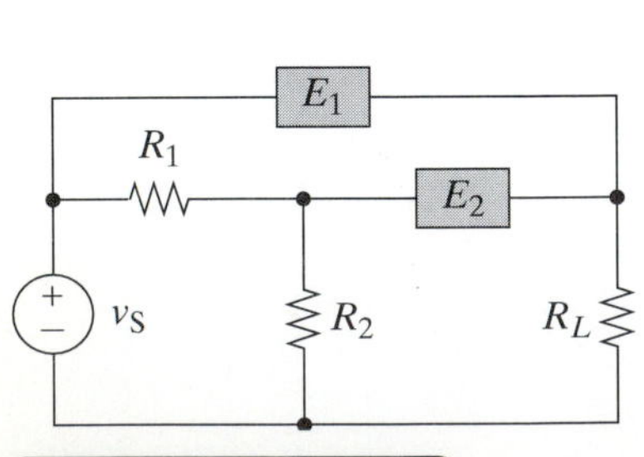

FIGURE P4–52

4–52 Identify and justify the analysis techniques you would use on the circuit in Figure P4–52 to find the voltage across R_L when the element E_2 is a resistor and element E_1 is (a) an open circuit, (b) an independent current source, and (c) a resistor.

4–53 Identify and justify the analysis techniques you would use on the circuit in Figure P4–52 to find the current through R_2 when the element E_1 is an independent voltage source and element E_2 is (a) an open circuit, (b) an independent current source, and (c) a resistor.

4–54 Identify and justify the analysis techniques you would use on the circuit in Figure P4–52 to find the voltage across R_1 when the element E_1 is an independent voltage source and element E_2 is (a) an independent voltage source, (b) an independent current source, and (c) a short circuit.

4–55 In Figure P4–52, $R_1 = R_2 = 10\ \Omega$, $v_S = 10$ V, and element E_2 is a 1/4-A fuse. Identify and justify the analysis technique you would use to find the value of R_L that will blow the fuse when element E_1 is (a) an open circuit, (b) a 10-Ω resistor, and (c) a short circuit.

4–56 Identify and justify the analysis approach you would use on the circuit in Figure P4–52 to find the Thévenin voltage and resistance seen by resistance R_2 when element E_1 is an open circuit and E_2 is (a) an independent voltage source, (b) an independent current source, and (c) a resistor.

4–57 Identify and justify the analysis approach you would use to find to find the Thévenin equivalent circuit seen by R_L Figure P4–8.

4–58 Identify and justify the analysis approach you would use to find the value of R_F in Figure P4–8 that produces a voltage gain $v_O/v_S = 50$.

4–59 **(a)** Identify and justify the analysis method you would use to find the voltage gain of the circuit in Figure P4–59.
(b) Repeat (a) when resistor R_4 is replaced by an open circuit.

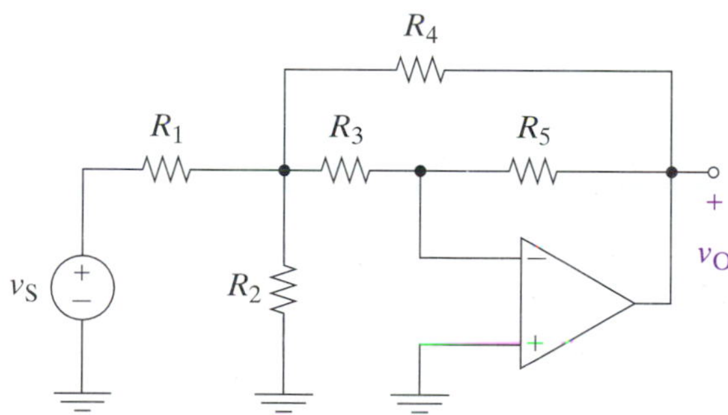

FIGURE P4–59

4–60 Identify and justify the analysis method you would use to find the input–output relationship of the circuit in Figure P4–42
(a) Using the ideal OP AMP model.
(b) Using the dependent-source model of a general-purpose OP AMP.

CHAPTER-INTEGRATING PROBLEMS

4–61 A D E BRIDGED-T INVERTING AMPLIFIER

Using the basic inverting OP AMP configuration to obtain a large voltage gain requires a small input resistor, a large feedback resistor,

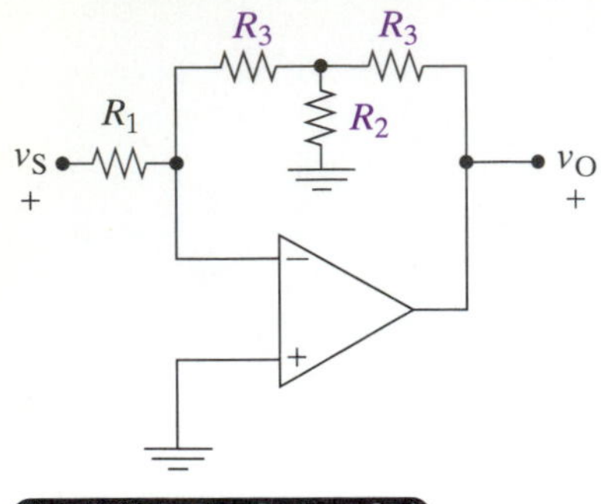

FIGURE P4–61

or both. Small input resistors load the input source, and large ($R > 1$ MΩ) feedback resistors have more noise and exhibit greater life-cycle variations. The circuit in Figure P4–61 circumvents these problems by using a bridged-T circuit in the feedback path. Note that R_3 occurs twice in this diagram.

(a) A Show that the gain of the circuit in Figure P4–61 can be written as $K = -R_{FDBK}/R_1$, where R_{FDBK} is the effective feedback resistance:

$$R_{FDBK} = R_3\left(2 + \frac{R_3}{R_2}\right)$$

(b) D Design a basic inverting amplifier to achieve $K = -500$ and $R_{IN} \geq 10$ kΩ.

(c) D Design a bridged-T inverting amplifier to achieve $K = -500$ and $R_{IN} \geq 10$ kΩ.

(d) E Compare the two designs in terms of element count, element spread (ratio of largest over smallest resistance), and total resistance (sum of all resistances).

4–62 A HYBRID CIRCUIT ANALYSIS

The two-port interface circuit in Figure P4–62 is a small-signal model of a bipolar junction transistor using what are called hybrid parameters. The analysis of this circuit illustrates that it can be useful to use a mixture (or hybrid) of mesh-current and node-voltage equations.

(a) Using the symbolic notation in the figure, write a mesh-current equation for the input circuit and a node-voltage equation for the output circuit.

(b) Using $R_S = 5$ kΩ, $R_1 = 2$ kΩ, $R_2 = 50$ kΩ, $R_L = 100$ kΩ, $\mu = 10^{-3}$, and $\beta = 100$, solve the equations from part (a) for the input current i_1 and the output voltage v_2 in terms of the input v_S.

(c) Using the results from part (b), solve for the input resistance and the voltage gain of the circuit.

(d) Calculate the power gain defined as the ratio of the power delivered to R_L divided by the power supplied by v_S.

FIGURE P4–62

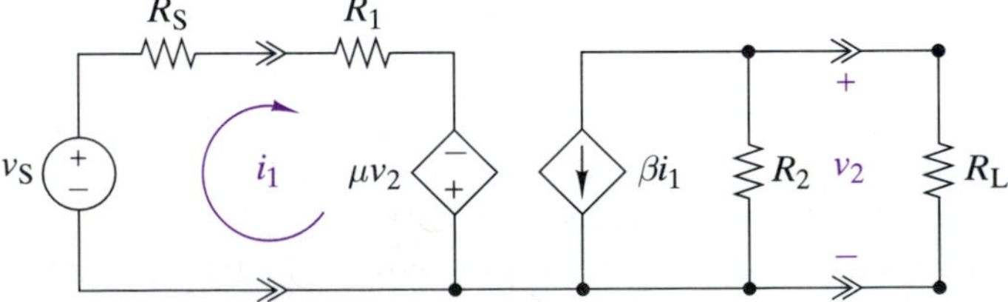

4–63 A D WHEATSTONE BRIDGE AMPLIFIER

The circuit in Figure P4–63 shows a Wheatstone bridge consisting of three equal resistors and a fourth resistor that is a transducer whose resistance is $R + \Delta R$, where $\Delta R << R$. The bridge is excited by a constant reference voltage source V_{REF} and is connected to the inputs of an OP AMP. For $\Delta R << R$ the OP AMP output voltage can be expressed in the form

$$\frac{v_O}{V_{Ref}} = K\frac{\Delta R}{R}$$

(a) A Verify that the preceding expression is correct and express K in terms of circuit parameters.

(b) D For $R = 100\ \Omega$ and $\Delta R/R$ in the range $\pm0.04\%$, select values of $V_{REF} < 25$ V and $R_F < 250$ kΩ so that the output voltage v_O is in the range ±3 V.

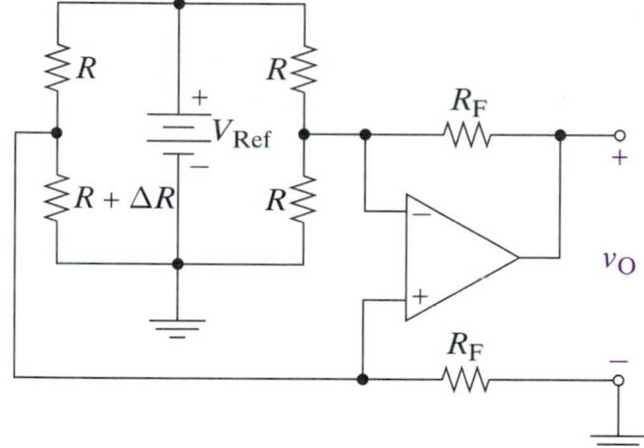

FIGURE P4–63

4–64 A OP AMP POWER BOOST

Inserting an OP AMP voltage follower at an interface isolates the source and load, but may result in a load current that exceeds the OP AMP rating. In such cases we can use the voltage follower with the transistor power boost shown in Figure P4–64. In this circuit the OP AMP output current is reduced since the transistor supplies the load current. Note that the transistor base-emitter port is included inside the OP AMP feedback path. For this analysis use the large-signal model of the transistor with a forward current gain β and turnout voltage V_γ. Use the ideal OP AMP model with output saturations levels of $\pm V_{CC}$.

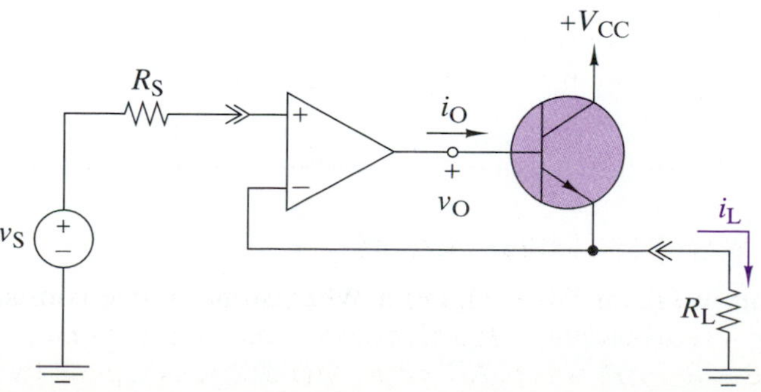

FIGURE P4–64

When the transistor is in the active mode and the OP AMP is in the linear mode:

(a) Show that the load current is given by $i_L = v_S/R_L$.

(b) Show that the OP AMP output current is $i_L/(\beta + 1)$

(c) Show that the OP AMP output voltage is $v_S + V_\gamma$.

(d) Show that the transistor is in the active mode, and that the OP AMP is in the linear mode when the input is in the range $0 < v_S < V_{CC} - V_\gamma$.

4–65 A PATHOLOGICAL CIRCUITS

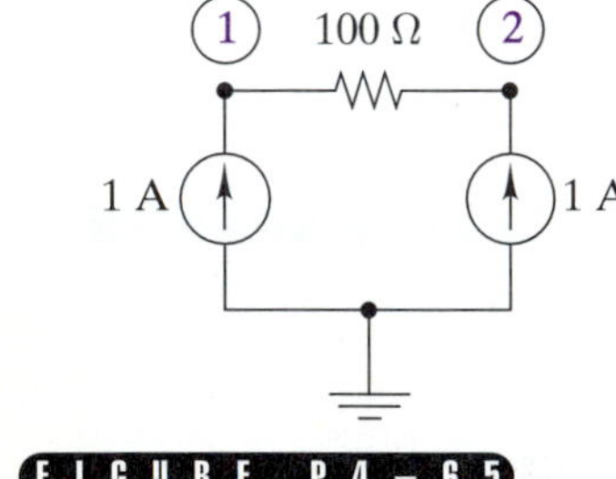

FIGURE P4–65

In theory, there are circuit element interconnections that produce irreconcilable conflicts between the device and connection constraints. An example is shown in Figure P4–65. Try using node analysis to solve for the voltage at node 1. Try using SPICE and see what error message is generated. Insolvable circuits, such as this one, are easy to draw on paper but are impossible to assemble in the laboratory. In the laboratory the response of such a circuit is controlled by parasitic components not included in the models of our ideal circuit elements. These parasitic components resolve the irreconcilable conflict, often in a blinding flash. For example, connect a 1000-MΩ resistor (almost an open circuit) between node 1 and ground, and then solve for the node 1 voltage.

RESISTANCE CIRCUITS

COURSE-INTEGRATING PROBLEMS
COURSE OBJECTIVES

A Analysis Given a resistance circuit with dc input signals, select an analysis technique and find the circuit's response in terms of output signals or input-output relationships.

D Design Given a dc signal or power processing function stated in terms of either output signals or input–output relationships, design one or more circuits that implement the specified function within stated constraints.

E Evaluation Given several resistance circuits that reportedly perform the same dc signal or power processing function, verify the claim and rank order the circuits using stated evaluation criteria.

I–1 A D E SUBTRACTOR CIRCUITS

The input–output relationship for the circuit C1 in Figure PI–1 is of the form $v_O = K_2v_2 + K_1v_1$. When $R_3 = R_6 = 10\ \Omega$ and $R_4 = R_5 = 90\ \Omega$,

FIGURE PI–1

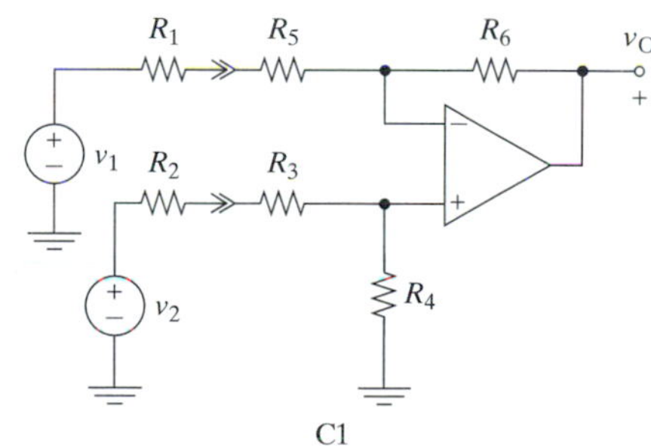

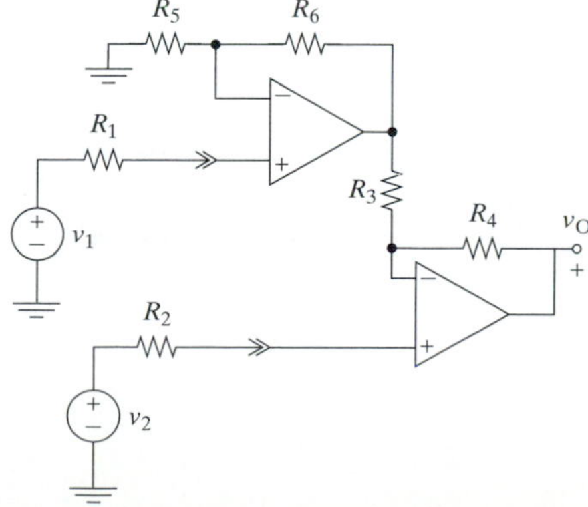

(a) A Determine the constants K_1 and K_2 in terms of circuit parameters.

(b) D For $R_1 = 1$ kΩ and $R_2 = 2$ kΩ, select the values of the remaining circuit resistances to achieve $v_O = 10(v_2 - v_1)$.

(c) E Show that the circuit C2 in Figure PI–1 meets the design requirement listed in (b). Compare these two designs on the basis of the number of devices required and the load each presents to the input signal sources.

I–2 A D E PHOTORESISTOR INSTRUMENTATION

Circuit C1 in Figure PI–2 contains a photoresistor whose resistance varies inversely with the intensity of the incident light. In complete darkness its resistance is 10 kΩ. In bright sunlight its resistance is 1 kΩ.

(a) A At any given light level the circuit is linear, so its input–output relationship is of the form $v_O = Kv_1$. Determine the constant K in terms of circuit resistances.

(b) D For $v_1 = +15$ V, select the values of R and R_F so that $v_O = -10$ V in bright sunlight and +10 V in complete darkness.

(c) E Show that circuit C2 in Figure PI–2 meets the design requirement given in (b) when $R = 4.71$ kΩ and $R_F = 2.96$ kΩ. Compare these two designs on the basis of the number of devices required and the total power dissipated in each design.

FIGURE PI–2

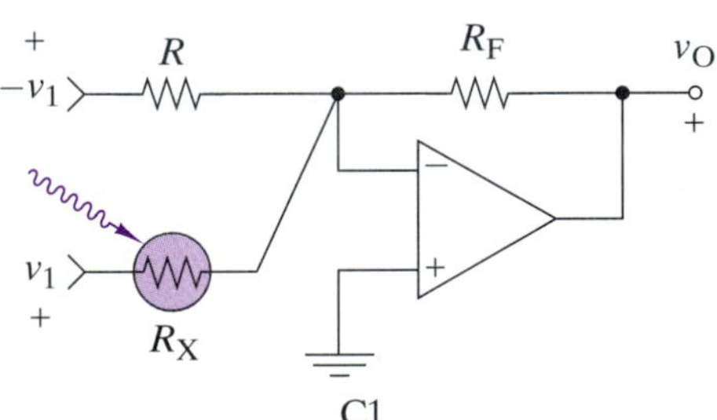

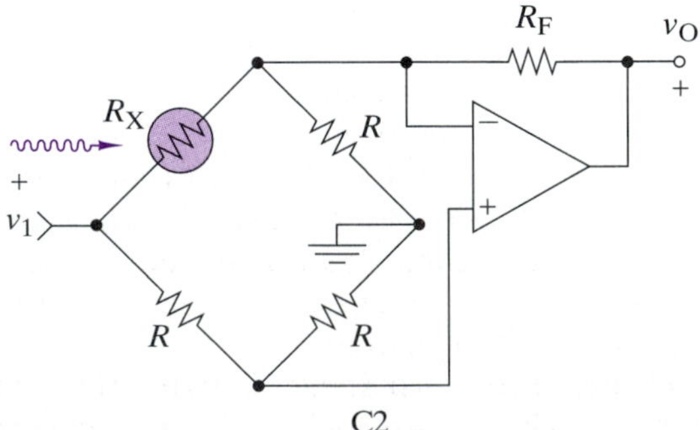

I–3 A D MAXIMUM SIGNAL TRANSFER

The source circuit in Figure PI–3 is to be connected to the load R_L.

(a) A Select the value of R_L so that maximum power is delivered to the load.

(b) A Select the value of R_L so that maximum voltage is delivered to the load.

(c) A Select the value of R_L so that the load current is 10 mA.

(d) D For $R_L = 1\ k\Omega$, design an interface circuit so the load current is 5 mA.

(e) D Repeat (d) for a load current of 10 mA.

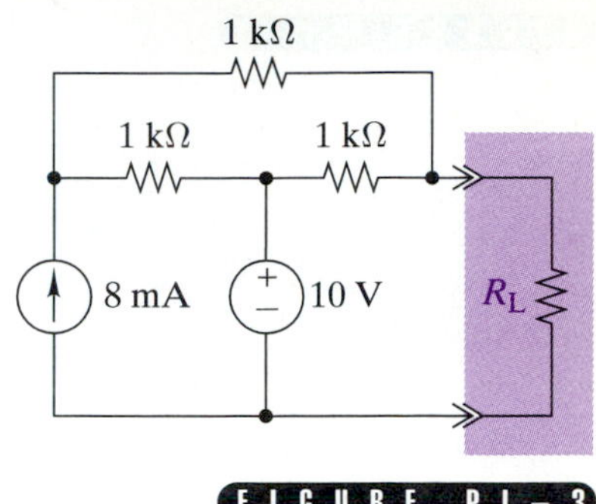

FIGURE PI–3

I–4 A D INTERFACE CIRCUIT DESIGN

The source circuit in Figure PI–4 contains an adjustable potentiometer. The load resistance is fixed. An interface circuit is required so that the power delivered to the load varies between 0 and 20 mW as the potentiometer is adjusted over its full range.

(a) A Show that the interface circuit must contain an amplifier with a voltage gain of at least 4.

(b) D Design an interface circuit to meet the objective given.

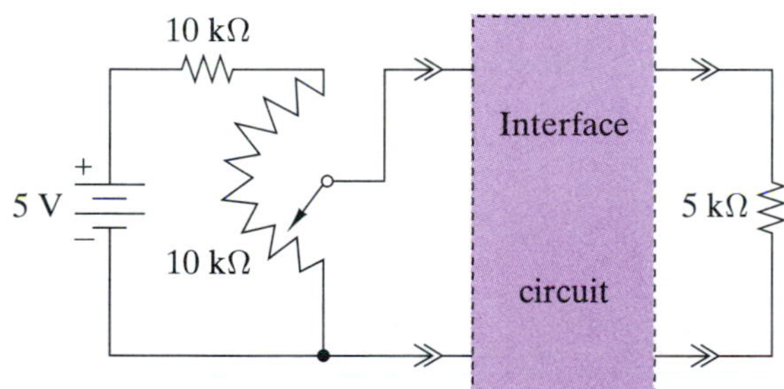

FIGURE PI–4

I–5 D E INTERFACE CIRCUIT DESIGN AND EVALUATION

A system in Figure PI–5 contains a sensor that requires an excitation voltage of 10 ± 0.1 V. The input resistance of the sensor varies from 1 kΩ to 1 MΩ. The system contains a power supply that provides ± 15 and +5 V. Figure PI–5 shows two integrated circuit packages on the approved parts list for the system. These parts must be used in the design.

(a) D Design at least two interface circuits using only the two IC packages in the figure. You may use any number of packages, but try to minimize the total package count. There are at least a half dozen two-package designs.

(b) E Compare your two designs in terms of the power dissipated in the *R*-2*R* package. Two-package designs range from 5 to 100 mW.

FIGURE PI–5

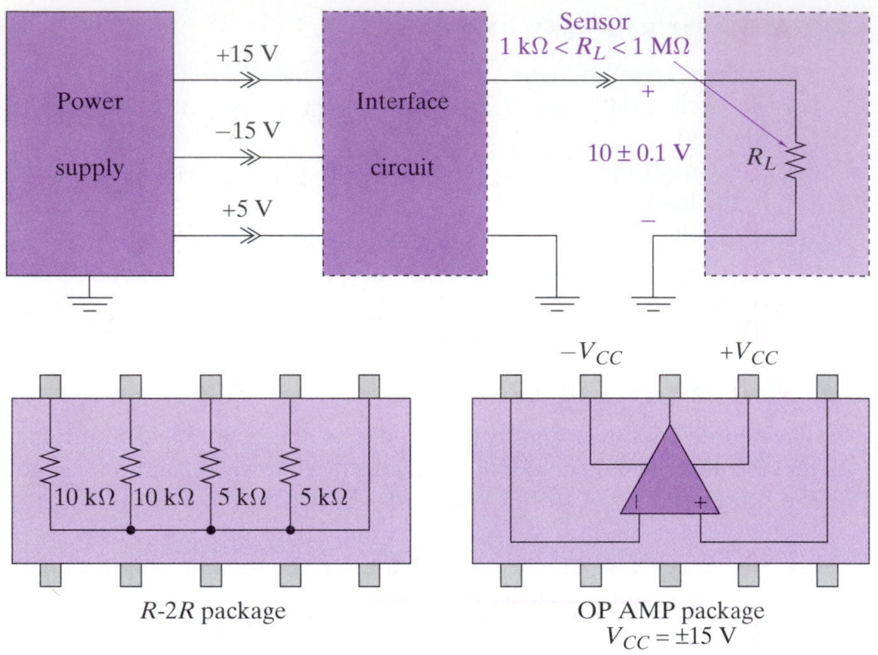

I–6 A LOGIC ANALYZER ANALYSIS

Figure PI–6 shows a simplified version of an electronic test system called a logic analyzer. When the probe is connected to a test point, the analyzer detects whether the voltage (relative to ground) is

FIGURE PI–6

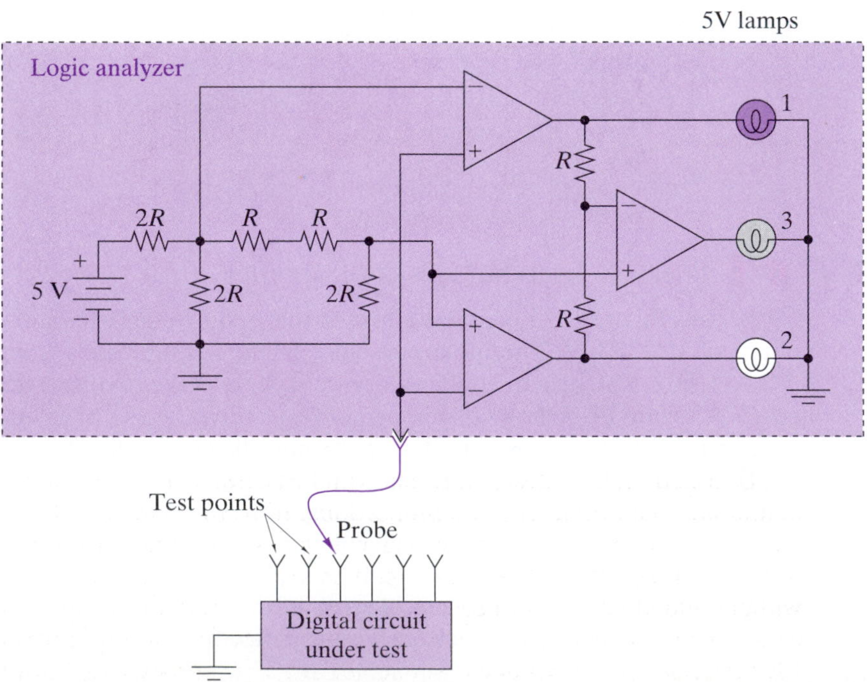

greater than 2 V (logic "1"), less than 1 V (logic "0"), or between 1 V and 2 V (an ambiguous case indicating a circuit fault). All three comparators have $V_{OH} = 5$ V and $V_{OL} = 0$ V.

(a) Show that if the test point voltage is greater than 2 V, then lamp 1 is on and lamps 2 and 3 are off.

(b) Show that if the test point voltage is less than 1 V, then lamp 2 is on and lamps 1 and 3 are off.

(c) Show that if the test point voltage is between 1 V and 2 V, then lamp 3 is on and lamps 1 and 2 are off.

(d) Identify three points within the logic analyzer that could be used to perform a self-test of the analyzer.

I–7 A E DESIGN EVALUATION

As chief engineer of a small electronics company, you find yourself with a dilemma. Your two engineering interns have worked independently and have produced different solutions for the design problem you gave them. Their proposed solutions are shown in Figure PI–7.

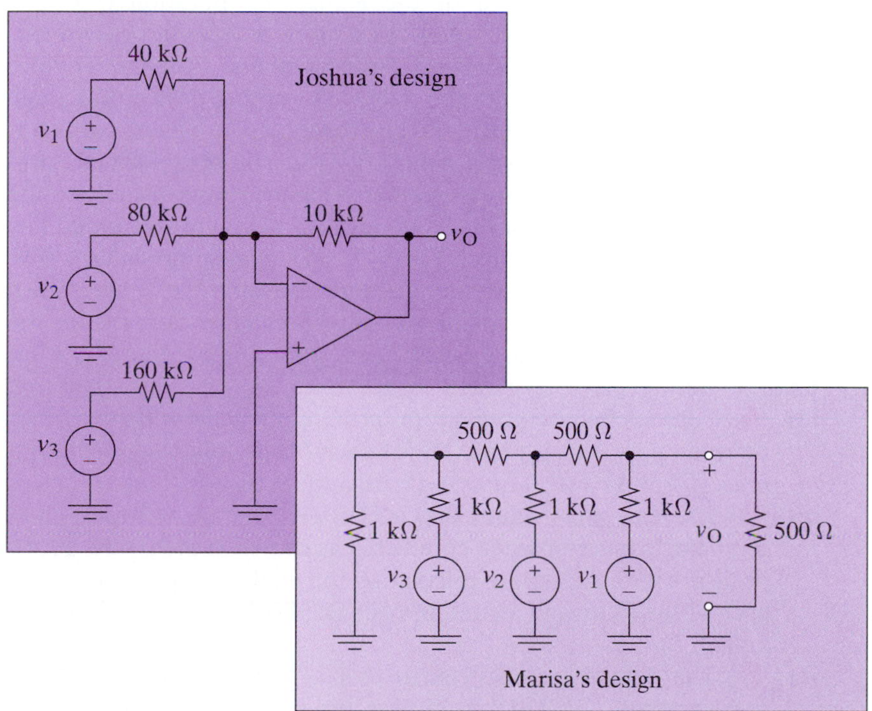

FIGURE PI–7

You asked them to design a circuit with three inputs v_1, v_2, v_3, and an output v_O. The output is to be proportional to $v_1/16 + v_2/8 + v_3/4$. The output can be either positive or negative, but must be able to drive a 500-Ω load. A ±15-V dc power supply is available within the system without added cost. You need to manufacture 2 million of these circuits, so part costs are a concern, but performance is the top priority. Electrical characteristics and cost data for available parts are as follows.

PART TYPE	PART CHARACTERISTICS	RELATIVE COST
Standard resistors	1.0, 1.5, 2.2, 3.3, 4.7, 6.8 Ω and multiples of 10 thereof	$4000 per 100,000
Custom resistors	Values to three significant figures from 100 Ω to 200 kΩ	$4500 per 100,000
OP AMPs	Minimum open-loop gain 100,000 Output voltage range ±15 V Maximum output current 10 mA	$11,500 per 100,000

(a) A Verify whether both circuits comply with the performance requirements. If not, explain how one or both can be modified to comply.

(b) E Which of the two circuits would you select for production and why?

I–8 A E VERIFYING A NEW PRODUCT CLAIM

The New Products Division of the RonAl Corporation (founded by two well-known authors) has announced a new integrated circuit package called the Two-Bit Programmable Voltage Divider (TBPVD). Figure PI–8 shows the data sheet on the device plus some typical applications. The TBPVD has three analog signal pins (A1, A2, A3) and two digital signal pins (D1, D2). The digital signals control a ganged set of analog switches. It is claimed that this allows the voltage divider between pins A1, A2, and A3 to be "programmed" by applying digital signals to pins D1 and D2. When a digital signal is 0 V, the switches it controls are in the positions shown in the figure. When a digital signal is 5 V, the switches it controls change state; that is, the open switches in the diagram are closed and the closed switches are open.

(a) A Construct a circuit diagram of the equivalent voltage divider between pins A1, A2, and A3 for each of the following digital inputs: (D2, D1) = (0, 0), (0, 5), (5, 0), and (5, 5).

(b) E The data sheet claims that a TBPVD becomes a 2-bit digital-to-analog converter when connected as shown in the figure. Prove or disprove this claim by calculating the analog output voltage for each of the following digital inputs: (D2, D1) = (0, 0), (0, 5), (5, 0), and (5, 5).

(c) E The data sheet also claims that a TBPVD together with a user-supplied OP AMP become a programmable gain amplifier when connected as shown in the figure. Find the amplifier gain for each of the following digital inputs: (D2, D1) = (0, 0), (0, 5), (5, 0), and (5, 5).

I–9 A E RONAL STRIKES AGAIN

The RonAl Corporation has issued Application Note No. 1 on its new and exciting TBPVD device, whose data sheet is shown in Figure PI–8. The note claims that connecting two such devices, as shown in

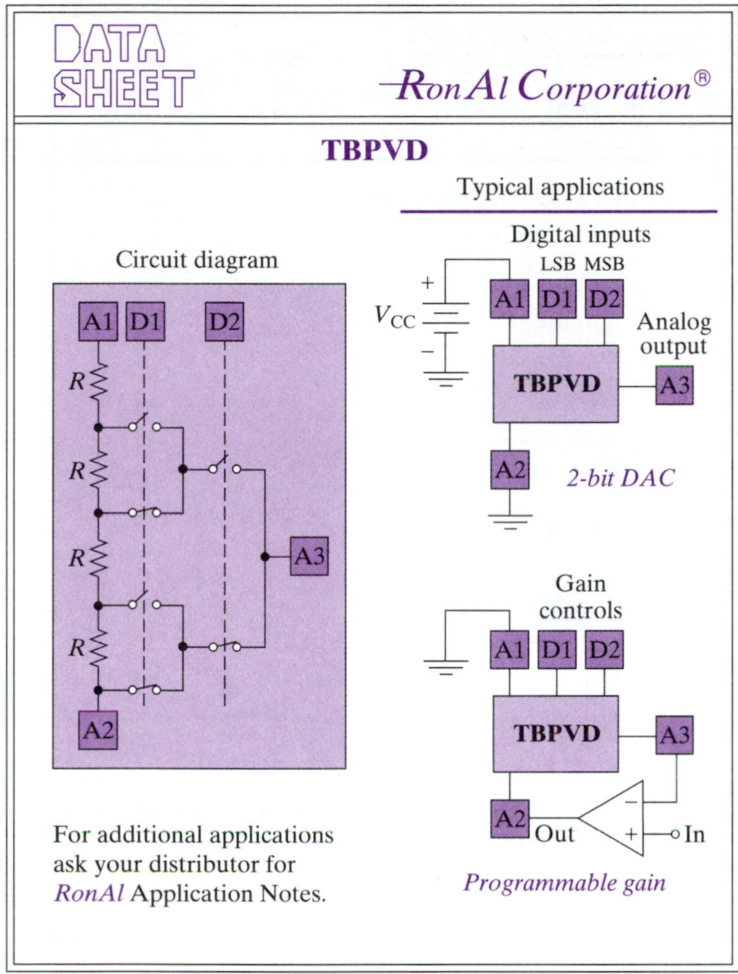

Figure PI–9 produces an amplifier whose gain is controlled by the 3-bit digital signal (B2, B1, B0) applied to the control inputs of the TVPDs. The individual bits in the digital signal are either 0 V or 5 V. Note that the most significant bit (MSB) on TBPVD No. 2 is permanently tied to +5 V.

(a) **E** The table in Application Note No. 1 claims that applying the digital signals shown produces analog gains of K = 0, ±0.5, and ±1. Evaluate the claim.

(b) **A** The 3-bit digital signal (B2, B1, B0) has $2^3 = 8$ possible combinations ranging from (0, 0, 0) to (5, 5, 5). The table in Figure PI–9 shows only five of the eight possible combinations. What three combinations are missing in the table, and what analog gains do they produce?

FIGURE PI–9

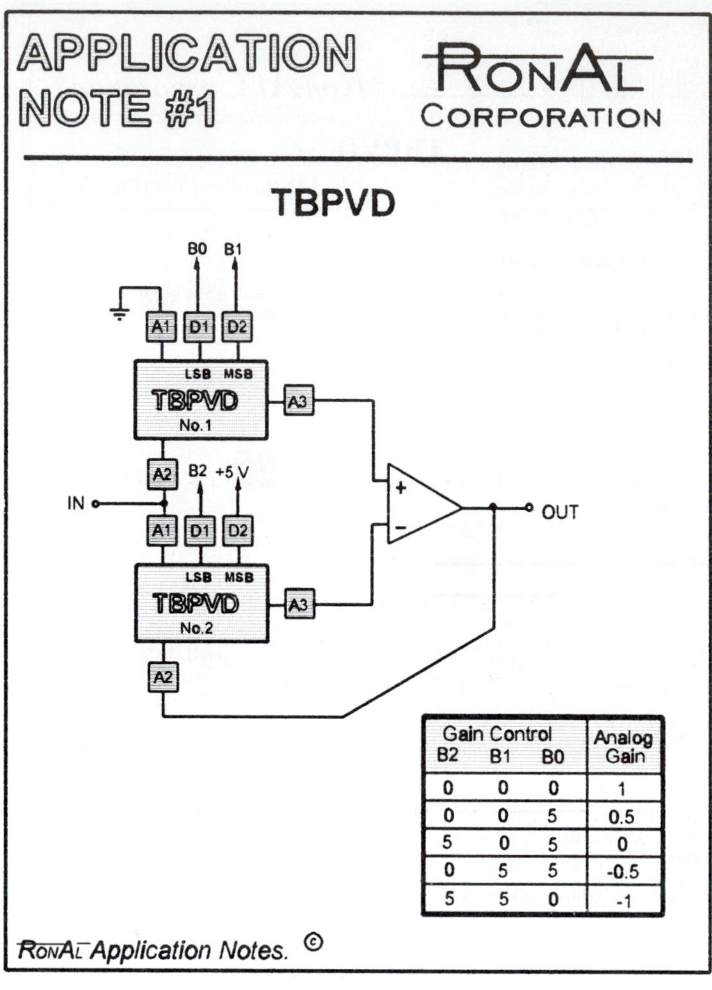

Gain Control B2	B1	B0	Analog Gain
0	0	0	1
0	0	5	0.5
5	0	5	0
0	5	5	-0.5
5	5	0	-1

I–10 D COMPUTER-AIDED CIRCUIT DESIGN

Use computer-aided circuit analysis to find the value of R_F in Figure PI–10 that causes the input resistance seen by i_S to be 50 Ω. Find the current gain i_O/i_S for this value of R_F. Use $\beta = 50$, $r_\pi = 1.1$ kΩ, $R_C = 10$ kΩ, and $R_E = R_L = 100$ Ω.

FIGURE PI–10

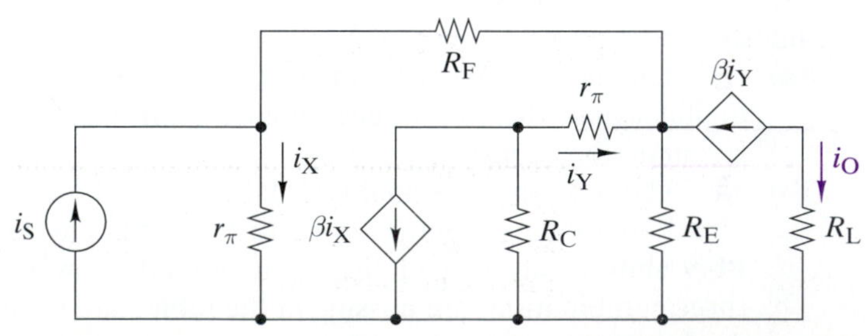

PART 2

DYNAMIC CIRCUITS

COURSE OBJECTIVES

A Analysis Given a dynamic circuit with time-varying input signals, select an appropriate analysis technique and find the circuit's response in terms of output signal waveforms, phasors, or transforms.

D Design Given a specified dynamic signal- or power-processing function stated in terms of output signal waveforms, phasors, or transforms, design one or more circuits that implement the specified function within stated constraints.

E Evaluation Given several dynamic circuits that reportedly perform the same dynamic signal- or power-processing function, verify the claim and rank order the circuits using stated evaluation criteria.

CHAPTER 5

SIGNAL WAVEFORMS

Under the sea, under the sea
mark how the telegraph motions to me.
Under the sea, under the sea
signals are coming along.

James Clerk Maxwell, 1873,
Scottish Physicist and
Occasional Humorous Poet

James Clerk Maxwell (1831–1879) is considered the unifying founder of the mathematical theory of electromagnetics. This genial Scotsman often communicated his thoughts to friends and colleagues via whimsical poetry. In the preceding short excerpt, Maxwell reminds us that the purpose of a communication system (the submarine cable telegraph in this case) is to transmit signals and that those signals must be changing, or *in motion,* as he put it.

This chapter marks the beginning of a new phase of our study of circuits. Up to this point we have dealt with resistive circuits, in which voltages and currents are constant (for example, +15 V or –3 mA). From this point forward we will be dealing with dynamic circuits, in which voltages and currents vary as functions of time. To analyze dynamic circuits, we need models for the time-varying signals and models for devices that describe the effects of time-varying signals in circuits. Signal models are introduced in this chapter. The dynamic circuit elements called capacitance and inductance are introduced in the next chapter. Chapters 7, 8, 9, and 10 then show how we combine signal models and device models to analyze dynamic circuits.

This chapter introduces the basic signal models used in the remainder of the book. We devote a chapter to this so you can master these models prior to launching into the complexities of dynamic circuits. We first introduce three key waveforms: the step, exponential, and sinusoid functions. By combining these three models we can build composite waveforms for all signals encountered in this book. Descriptors used to classify and describe waveforms are introduced because they highlight important signal attributes. The concept of a signal spectrum is briefly introduced to begin developing an understanding of how signals and signal processing can be studied using either time or a new parameter called frequency as the independent variables.

5–1 INTRODUCTION

We normally think of a signal as an electrical current $i(t)$ or voltage $v(t)$. The time variation of the signal is called a waveform. More formally,

> ***A* waveform *is an equation or graph that defines the signal as a function of time.***

Up to this point our study has been limited to the type of waveform shown in Figure 5–1. Waveforms that are constant for all time are called **dc signals**. The abbreviation *dc* stands for direct current, but it applies to either voltage or current. Mathematical expressions for a dc voltage $v(t)$ or current $i(t)$ take the form

$$\left.\begin{aligned} v(t) &= V_0 \\ i(t) &= I_0 \end{aligned}\right\} \quad \text{for } -\infty < t < \infty \qquad (5-1)$$

This equation is only a model. No physical signal can remain constant forever. It is a useful model, however, because it approximates the signals produced by physical devices such as batteries.

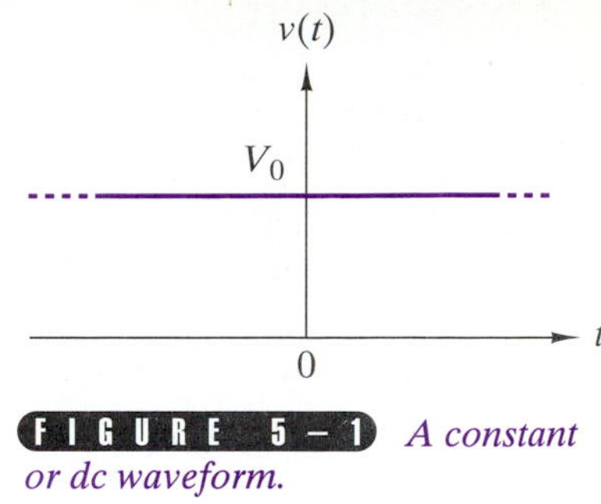

FIGURE 5–1 *A constant or dc waveform.*

There are two matters of notation and convention that must be discussed before continuing. First, quantities that are constant (non-time-varying) are usually represented by uppercase letters (V_A, I, T_O) or lowercase letters in the early part of the alphabet (a, b_7, f_0). Time-varying electrical quantities are represented by the lowercase letters i, v, p, q, and w. The time variation is expressly indicated when we write these quantities as $v_1(t)$, $i_A(t)$, or $w_C(t)$. Time variation is implicit when they are written as v_1, i_A, or w_C.

Second, in a circuit diagram signal variables are normally accompanied by the reference marks (+, –) for voltage and (→) for current. It is important to remember that these reference marks *do not* indicate the polarity of a voltage or the direction of current. The marks provide a baseline for determining the sign of the numerical value of the actual waveform. When the actual voltage polarity or current direction coincides with the reference directions, the signal has a positive value. When the opposite occurs, the value is negative. Figure 5–2 shows examples of voltage waveforms, including some that assume both positive and negative values. The bipolar waveforms indicate that the actual voltage polarity is changing as a function of time.

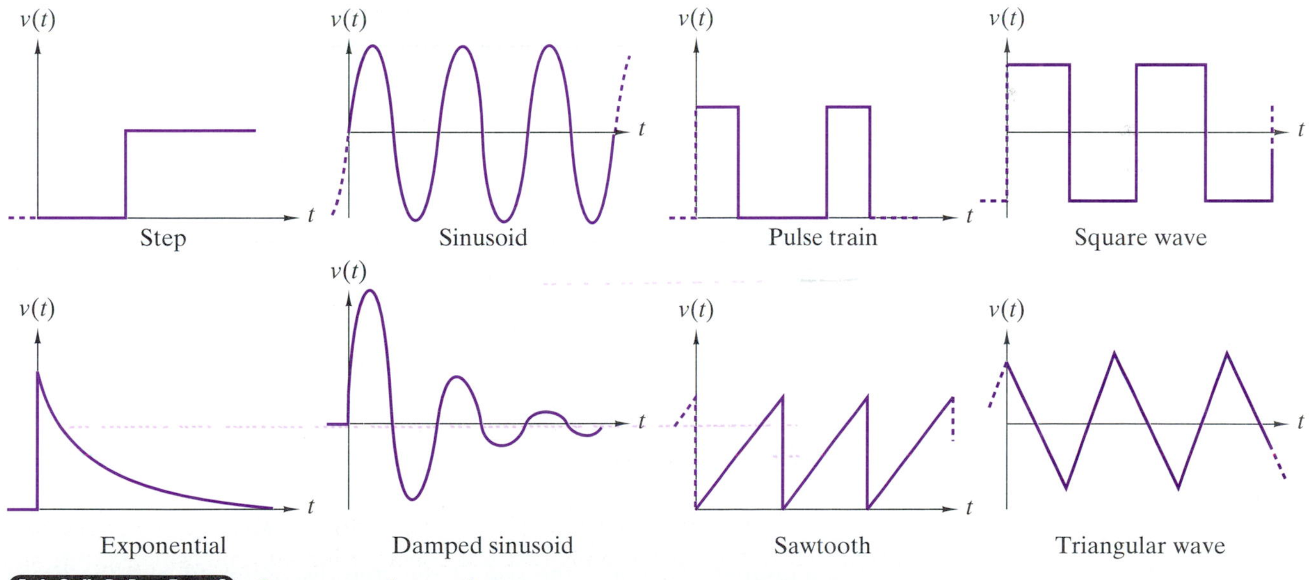

FIGURE 5–2 *Some example waveforms.*

The waveforms in Figure 5–2 are examples of signals used in electrical engineering. Since there are many such signals, it may seem that the study of signals involves the uninviting task of compiling a lengthy catalog of waveforms. However, it turns out that a long list is not needed. In fact, we can derive most of the waveforms of interest using just three basic signal models: the step, exponential, and sinusoidal functions. The small number of basic signals illustrates why models are so useful to engineers. In reality, waveforms are very complex, but their time variation can be approximated adequately using only a few basic building blocks.

Finally, in this chapter we will generally use voltage $v(t)$ to represent a signal waveform. Remember, however, that a signal can be either a voltage $v(t)$ or current $i(t)$.

5–2 THE STEP WAVEFORM

The first basic signal in our catalog is the step waveform. The general step function is based on the **unit step function** defined as

$$u(t) = \begin{cases} 0 & \text{for } t < 0 \\ 1 & \text{for } t > 0 \end{cases} \tag{5–2}$$

The step function waveform is equal to zero when its argument t is negative, and is equal to unity when its argument is positive. Mathematically, the function $u(t)$ has a jump discontinuity at $t = 0$.

Strictly speaking, it is impossible to generate a true step function since signal variables like current and voltage cannot jump from one value to another in zero time. Practically speaking, we can generate very good approximations to the step function. What is required is that the transition time be short compared with other response times in the circuit. Actually, the generation of approximate step functions is an everyday occurrence since people frequently turn things like TVs, stereos, and lights on and off.

On the surface, it may appear that the step function is not a very exciting waveform or, at best, only a source of temporary excitement. However, the step waveform is a versatile signal used to construct a wide range of useful waveforms. Multiplying $u(t)$ by a constant V_A produces the waveform

$$V_A u(t) = \begin{cases} 0 & \text{for } t < 0 \\ V_A & \text{for } t \geq 0 \end{cases} \tag{5–3}$$

Replacing t by $(t - T_S)$ produces a waveform $V_A u(t - T_S)$, which takes on the values

$$V_A u(t - T_S) = \begin{cases} 0 & \text{for } t < T_S \\ V_A & \text{for } t \geq T_S \end{cases} \tag{5–4}$$

The **amplitude** V_A scales the size of the step discontinuity, and the **time-shift** parameter T_S advances or delays the time at which the step occurs.

Amplitude and time-shift parameters are required to define the general step function. The amplitude V_A carries the units of volts. The amplitude of step function in electric current is I_A and carries the units of amperes. The constant T_S carries the units of time, usually seconds. The parameters V_A (or I_A) and T_S can be positive, negative, or zero, as shown in Figure

5–3. By combining several step functions, we can represent a number of important waveforms. One possibility is illustrated in the following example:

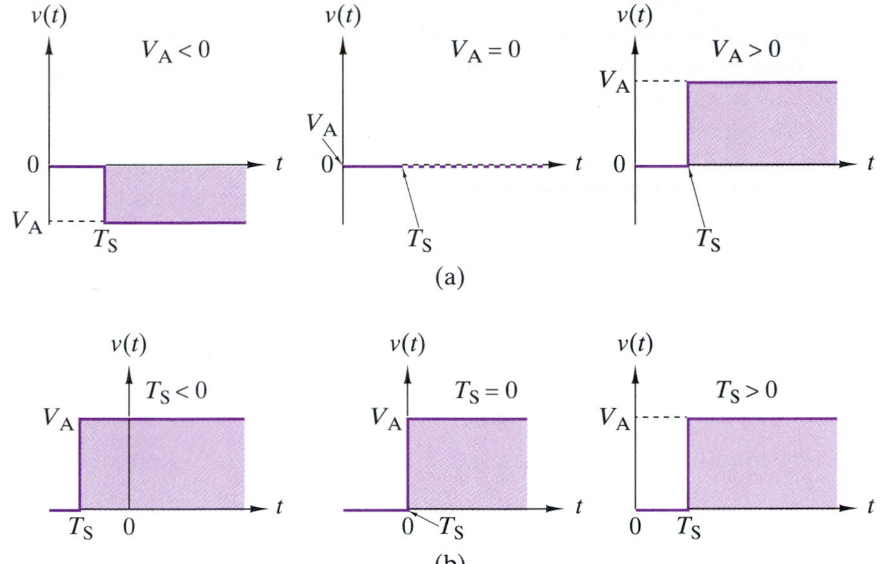

FIGURE 5–3 *Effect of changing the amplitude and time shift on step function waveforms.*

EXAMPLE 5–1

Express the waveform in Figure 5–4(a) in terms of step functions.

SOLUTION:

The amplitude of the pulse jumps to a value of 3 V at $t = 1$ s; therefore, 3 $u(t-1)$ is part of the equation for the waveform. The pulse returns to zero at $t = 3$ s, so an equal and opposite step must occur at $t = 3$ s. Putting these observations together, we express the rectangular pulse as

$$v(t) = 3u\,(t-1) - 3u\,(t-3)$$

Figure 5–5(b) shows how the two step functions combine to produce the given rectangular pulse. ■

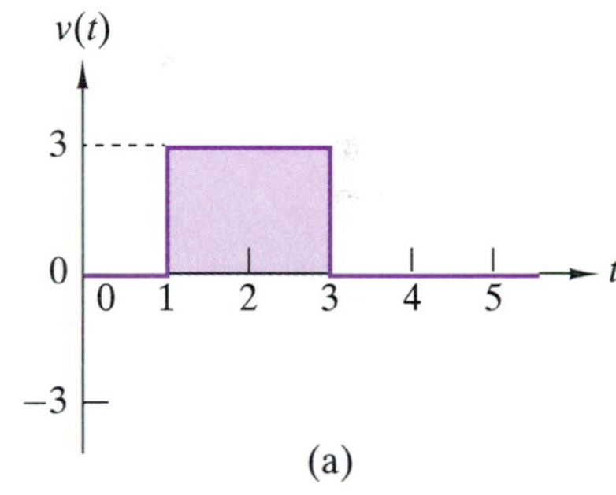

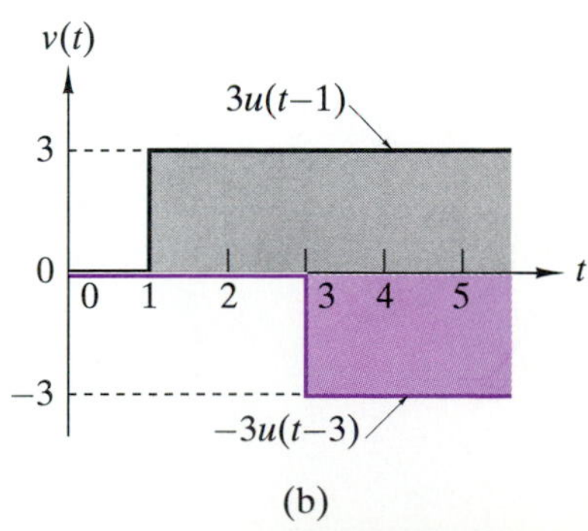

FIGURE 5–4

THE IMPULSE FUNCTION

The generalization of Example 5–1 is the waveform

$$v(t) = V_A[u(t-T_1) - u(t-T_2)]$$

This waveform is a rectangular pulse of amplitude V_A that turns on at $t = T_1$ and off at $t = T_2$. The pulse train and square wave signals in Figure 5–2 can be generated by a series of these pulses. Pulses that turn on at some time T_1 and off at some later time T_2 are sometimes called **gating functions** because they are used in conjunction with electronic switches to enable or inhibit the passage of another signal.

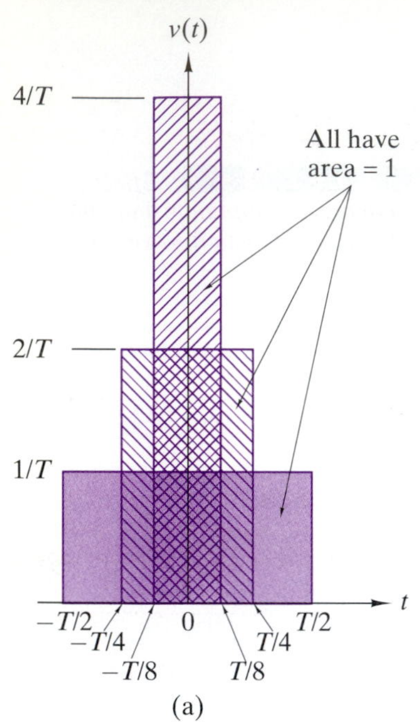

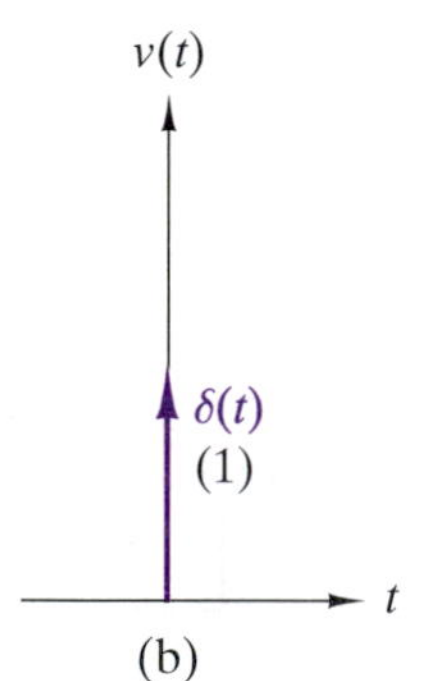

FIGURE 5–5 *Rectangular phase waveforms and the impulse.*

A unit-area pulse centered on $t = 0$ is written in terms of step functions as

$$v(t) = \frac{1}{T}\left[u\left(t + \frac{T}{2}\right) - u\left(t - \frac{T}{2}\right)\right] \tag{5-5}$$

The pulse in Eq. (5–5) is zero everywhere except in the range $-T/2 \leq t \leq T/2$, where its value is $1/T$. The area under the pulse is 1 because its scale factor is inversely proportional to its duration. As shown in Figure 5–5(a), the pulse becomes narrower and higher as T decreases but maintains its unit area. In the limit as $T \to 0$ the scale factor approaches infinity but the area remains 1. The function obtained in the limit is called a **unit impulse**, symbolized as $\delta(t)$. The graphical representation of $\delta(t)$ is shown in Figure 5–5(b). The impulse is an idealized model of a large-amplitude, short-duration pulse.

A formal definition of the unit impulse is

$$\delta(t) = 0 \text{ for } t \neq 0 \quad \text{and} \quad \int_{-\infty}^{t} \delta(x)dx = u(t) \tag{5-6}$$

The first condition says the impulse is zero everywhere except at $t = 0$. The second condition suggests that the unit impulse is the derivative of a unit step function:

$$\delta(t) = \frac{du(t)}{dt} \tag{5-7}$$

The conclusion in Eq. (5–7) cannot be justified using elementary mathematics since the function $u(t)$ has a discontinuity at $t = 0$ and its derivative at that point does not exist in the usual sense. However, the concept can be justified using limiting conditions on continuous functions, as discussed in texts on signals and systems.[1] Accordingly, we defer the question of mathematical rigor to later courses and think of the unit impulse as the derivative of a unit step function. Note that this means that the unit impulse $\delta(t)$ has units of reciprocal time, or s^{-1}.

An impulse of strength K is denoted $v(t) = K\delta(t)$. Consequently, the scale factor K has the units of V-s and is the area under the impulse $K\delta(t)$. In the graphical representation of the impulse the value of K is written in parentheses beside the arrow, as shown in Figure 5–5(b).

EXAMPLE 5–2

Calculate and sketch the derivative of the pulse in Figure 5–6(a).

SOLUTION:

In Example 5–1 the pulse waveform was written as

$$v(t) = 3u(t - 1) - 3u(t - 3) \text{ V}$$

1 For example, see Alan V. Oppenheim and Allan S. Willsky, *Signals and Systems Analysis*, (Englewood Cliffs, N.J.: Prentice Hall, 1983), pp. 22–23.

Using the derivative property of the step function, we write

$$\frac{dv(t)}{dt} = 3\delta(t-1) - 3\delta(t-3)$$

The derivative waveform consists of a positive-going impulse at $t = 1$ s and a negative-going impulse at $t = 3$ s. Figure 5–6(b) shows how the impulse train is represented graphically. The waveform $v(t)$ has the units of volts (V), so its derivative $dv(t)/dt$ has the units of V/s. ■

FIGURE 5–6

THE RAMP FUNCTION

The **unit ramp** is defined as the integral of a step function:

$$r(t) = \int_{-\infty}^{t} u(x)dx = tu(t) \tag{5-8}$$

The unit ramp waveform $r(t)$ in Figure 5–7(a) is zero for $t < 0$ and is equal to t for $t > 0$. Notice that the slope of $r(t)$ is 1 and has the units of time, or s. A ramp of strength K is denoted $v(t) = Kr(t)$, where the scale factor K has the units of V/s and is the slope of the ramp. The general ramp waveform shown in Figure 5–7(b) written as $v(t) = Kr(t - T_S)$ is zero for $t < T_S$ and equal to $K(t - T_S)$ for $t > 0$. By adding a sequence of ramps, we can create the triangular and sawtooth waveforms shown in Figure 5–2.

SINGULARITY FUNCTIONS

The unit impulse, unit step, and unit ramp form a triad of related signals that are referred to as **singularity functions**. They are related by integration as

$$u(t) = \int_{-\infty}^{t} \delta(x)dx$$
$$r(t) = \int_{-\infty}^{t} u(x)dx \tag{5-9}$$

or by differentiation as

$$\delta(t) = \frac{du(t)}{dt}$$
$$u(t) = \frac{dr(t)}{dt} \tag{5-10}$$

These signals are used to generate other waveforms and as test inputs to linear systems to characterize their responses. When applying the singularity functions in circuit analysis, it is important to remember that $u(t)$ is a dimensionless function. But Eqs. (5–9) and (5–10) point out that $\delta(t)$ carries the units of s^{-1} and $r(t)$ carries units of seconds.

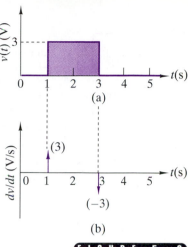

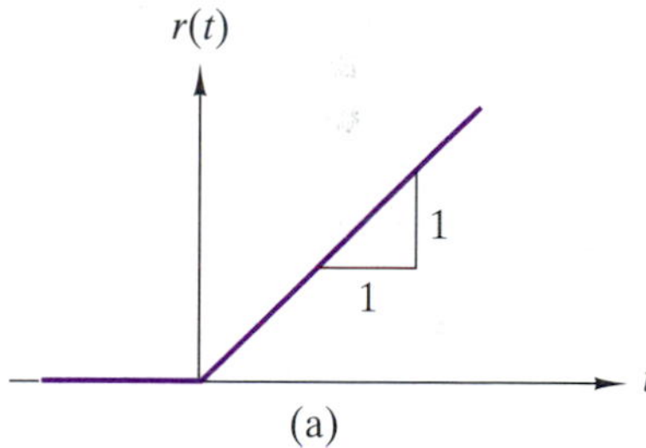

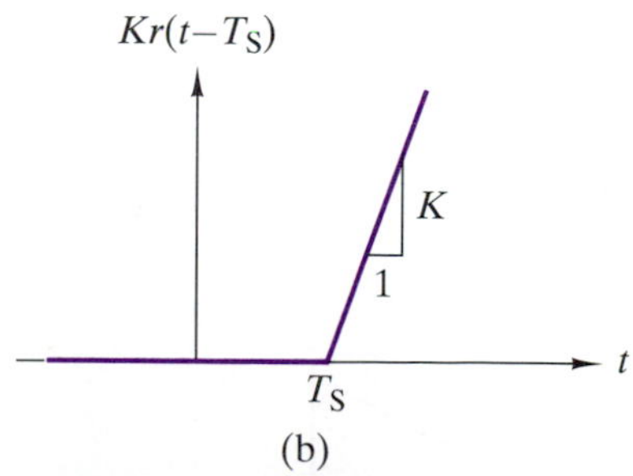

FIGURE 5–7 *(a) Unit ramp waveform. (b) General ramp waveform.*

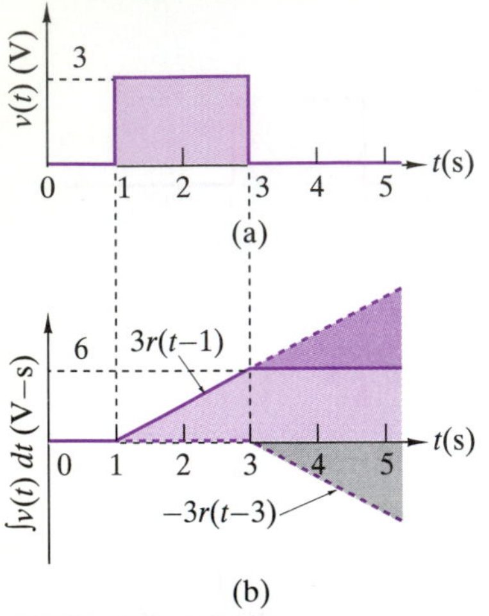

FIGURE 5–8

EXAMPLE 5–3

Derive an expression for the waveform for the integral of the pulse in Figure 5–8(a).

SOLUTION:

In Example 5–1 the pulse waveform was written as

$$v(t) = 3u(t-1) - 3u(t-3) \text{ V}$$

Using the integration property of the step function, we write

$$\int_{-\infty}^{t} v(x)dx = 3r(t-1) - 3r(t-3)$$

The integral is zero for $t < 1$ s. For $1 < t < 3$ the waveform is $3(t-1)$. For $t > 3$ it is $3(t-1) - 3(t-3) = 6$. These two ramps produce the pulse integral shown in Figure 5–8(b). The waveform $v(t)$ has the units of volts (V), so the units of its integral are V-s. ■

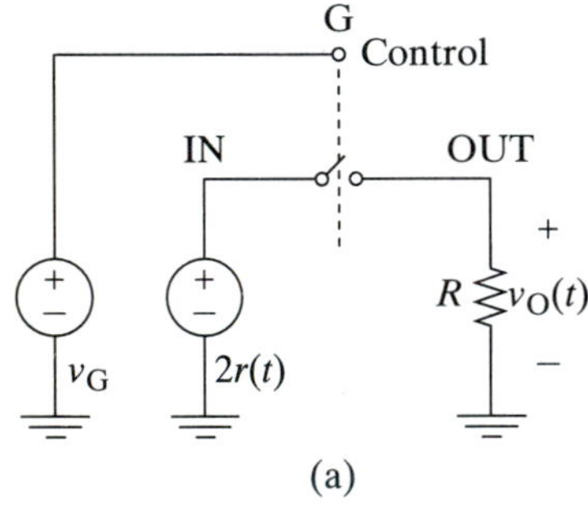

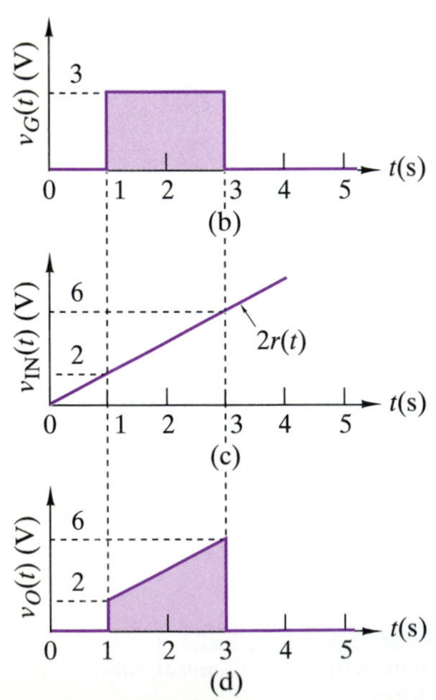

FIGURE 5–9

EXAMPLE 5–4

Figure 5–9(a) shows an ideal electronic switch whose input is a ramp $2r(t)$, where the scale factor $K = 2$ carries the units of V/s. Find the switch output $v_O(t)$ when the gate function in Example 5–1 is applied to the control terminal (G) of the switch.

SOLUTION:

In Example 5–1 the gate function was written as

$$v_G(t) = 3u(t-1) - 3u(t-3) \text{ V}$$

The gate function turns the switch turn on at $t = 1$ s and off at $t = 3$ s. The output voltage of the switch is

$$v_O(t) = \begin{cases} 0 & t < 1 \\ 2t & 1 < t < 3 \\ 0 & 3 < t \end{cases}$$

Only the portion of the input waveform within the gate interval appears at the output. Figures 5–9(b), 5–9(c), and 5–9(d) show how the gate function $v_G(t)$ controls the passage of the input signal through the electronic switch. ■

Exercise 5–1

Express the following signals in terms of singularity functions:

$$\text{(a) } v_1(t) = \begin{cases} 0 & t < 2 \\ 4 & 2 < t < 4 \\ -4 & 4 < t \end{cases} \qquad \text{(b) } v_2(t) = \begin{cases} 0 & t < 2 \\ 4 & 2 < t < 4 \\ -2t + 12 & 4 < t \end{cases}$$

$$\text{(c) } v_3(t) = \int_{-\infty}^{t} v_1(x)dx \qquad \text{(d) } v_4(t) = \frac{dv_2(t)}{dt}$$

Answers:

(a) $v_1(t) = 4\,u(t-2) - 8\,u(t-4)$ (b) $v_2(t) = 4\,u(t-2) - 2\,r(t-4) + 8u(t-4)$
(c) $v_3(t) = 4\,r(t-2) - 8\,r(t-4)$ (d) $v_4(t) = 4\,\delta(t-2) - 2\,u(t-4)$

Exercise 5–2

(a) Write an expression for a rectangular pulse with an amplitude of 15 V that begins at $t = -5$ s and ends at $t = 10$ s.
(b) Write an expression for the derivative of the pulse defined in (a).
(c) Write an expression for the integral of the pulse in (a).

Answers:

(a) $15[u(t+5) - u(t-10)]$
(b) $15[\delta(t+5) - \delta(t-10)]$
(c) $15(t+5)u(t+5) - 15(t-10)u(t-10) = 15[r(t+5) - r(t-10)]$

5–3 THE EXPONENTIAL WAVEFORM

The **exponential waveform** is a step function whose amplitude factor gradually decays to zero. The equation for this waveform is

$$v(t) = [V_A e^{-t/T_C}]\,u(t) \tag{5-11}$$

A graph of $v(t)$ versus t/T_C is shown in Figure 5–10. The exponential starts out like a step function. It is zero for $t < 0$ and jumps to a maximum amplitude of V_A at $t = 0$. Thereafter it monotonically decays toward zero as time marches on. The two parameters that define the waveform are the **amplitude** V_A (in volts) and the **time constant** T_C (in seconds). The amplitude of a current exponential would be written I_A and carry the units of amperes. Figure 5–11 shows how the exponential waveform changes for different values of the amplitude and time constant.

The time constant is of special interest, since it determines the rate at which the waveform decays to zero. An exponential decays to about 37% of its initial amplitude $v(0) = V_A$ in one time constant, because at $t = T_C$, $v(T_C) = V_A e^{-1}$, or approximately $0.368 \times V_A$. At $t = 5T_C$, the value of the waveform is $V_A e^{-5}$, or approximately $0.00674\ V_A$. An exponential signal decays to less than 1% of its initial amplitude in a time span of five time constants. In theory, an exponential endures forever, but practically speak-

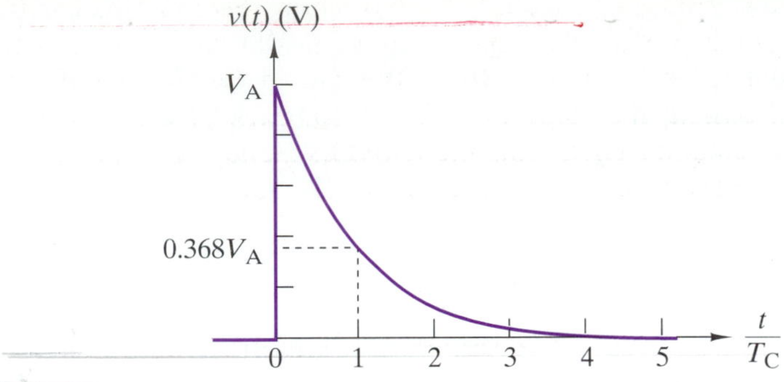

FIGURE 5-10 *The exponential waveform.*

ing after about $5T_C$ the waveform amplitude becomes negligibly small. We define the **duration** of a waveform to be the interval of time outside of which the waveform is everywhere less than a stated value. Using this concept, we say the duration of an exponential waveform is $5T_C$.

EXAMPLE 5-5

Plot the waveform $v(t) = [-17e^{-100t}]u(t)$ V.

SOLUTION:

From the form of $v(t)$, we recognize that $V_A = -17$ V and $T_C = 1/100$ s or 10 ms. The minimum value of $v(t)$ is $v(0) = -17$ V, and the maximum value is approximately 0 V as t approaches $5T_C = 50$ ms. These observations define appropriate scales for plotting the waveform. Spreadsheet programs are especially useful for the repetitive calculations and graphical functions in-

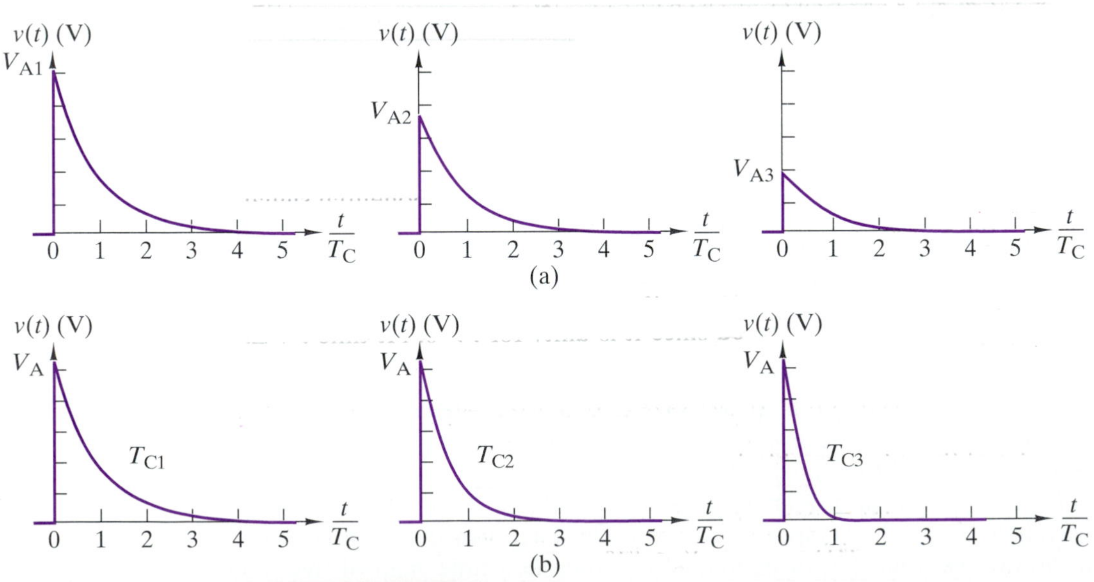

FIGURE 5-11 *Effect of changing the amplitude and time constant on step function waveforms.*

volved in waveform plotting. Figure 5–12 shows how this example can be handled using Quattro Pro. We begin by filling in the "A" column with time values ranging from $t = 0$ to $t = 50$ ms. The data in the "B" column are obtained by calculating the value of $-17e^{-1001t}$ for each of the values of t (ms) in the "A" column. Then using the **Graphics** menu, we create a plot showing that the waveform starts out at $v(t) = -17$ V at $t = 0$ and then increases toward $v(t) = 0$ as $t \to 50$ ms. ■

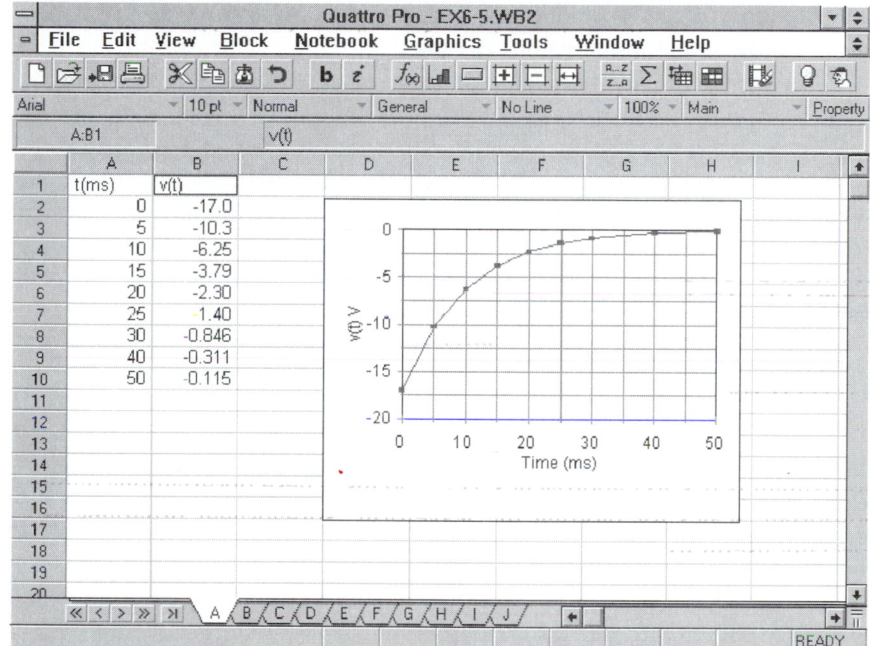

	A	B
1	t(ms)	v(t)
2	0	-17.0
3	5	-10.3
4	10	-6.25
5	15	-3.79
6	20	-2.30
7	25	-1.40
8	30	-0.846
9	40	-0.311
10	50	-0.115

FIGURE 5–12

PROPERTIES OF EXPONENTIAL WAVEFORMS

The **decrement property** describes the decay rate of an exponential signal. For $t > 0$ the exponential waveform is given by

$$v(t) = V_A e^{-t/T_C} \tag{5-12}$$

The step function can be omitted since it is unity for $t > 0$. At time $t + \Delta t$ the amplitude is

$$v(t + \Delta t) = V_A e^{(t+\Delta t)/T_C} = V_A e^{-t/T_C} e^{-\Delta t/T_C} \tag{5-13}$$

The ratio of these two amplitudes is

$$\frac{v(t + \Delta t)}{v(t)} = \frac{V_A e^{-t/T_C} e^{-\Delta t/T_C}}{V_A e^{-t/T_C}} = e^{-\Delta t/T_C} \tag{5-14}$$

The decrement ratio is independent of amplitude and time. In any fixed time period Δt, the fractional decrease depends only on the time constant.

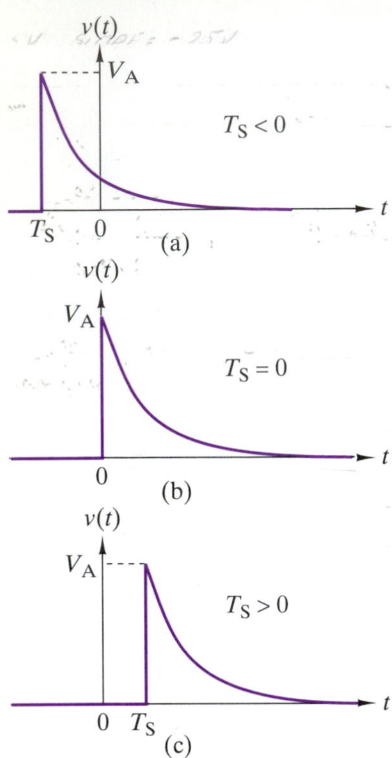

FIGURE 5–13 *Effect of time shifting on the exponential waveform.*

The decrement property states that the same percentage decay occurs in equal time intervals.

The slope of the exponential waveform (for $t > 0$) is found by differentiating Eq. (5–12) with respect to time:

$$\frac{dv(t)}{dt} = -\frac{V_A}{T_C}e^{-t/T_C} = -\frac{v(t)}{T_C} \quad (5-15)$$

The **slope property** states that the time rate of change of the exponential waveform is inversely proportional to the time constant. Small time constants lead to large slopes or rapid decays, while large time constants produce shallow slopes and long decay times.

Equation (5–15) can be rearranged as

$$\frac{dv(t)}{dt} + \frac{v(t)}{T_C} = 0 \quad (5-16)$$

When $v(t)$ is an exponential of the form in Eq. (5–12), then $dv/dt + v/T_C = 0$. That is, the exponential waveform is a solution of the first-order linear differential equation in Eq. (5–16). We will make use of this fact in Chapter 7.

The time-shifted exponential waveform is obtained by replacing t in Eq. (5–11) by $t - T_S$. The general exponential waveform is written as

$$v(t) = [V_A e^{-(t-T_S)/T_C}]\,u(t - T_S) \quad (5-17)$$

where T_S is the time-shift parameter for the waveform. Figure 5–13 shows exponential waveforms with the same amplitude and time constant but different values of T_S. Time shifting translates the waveform to the left or right depending on whether T_S is negative or positive. *Caution:* The factor $t - T_S$ must appear in both the argument of the step function and the exponential, as shown in Eq. (5–17).

EXAMPLE 5–6

An oscilloscope is a laboratory instrument that displays the instantaneous value of waveform versus time. Figure 5–14 shows an oscilloscope display of a portion of an exponential waveform. In the figure the vertical (amplitude) axis is calibrated at 2 V per division, and the horizontal (time) axis is calibrated at 1 ms per division. Find the time constant of the exponential.

SOLUTION:

For $t > 0$ the general expression for an exponential in Eq. (5–17) becomes

$$v(t) = V_A e^{-(t-T_S)/T_C}$$

We have only a portion of the waveform, so we do not know the location of the $t = 0$ time origin; hence, we cannot find the amplitude V_A or the time shift T_S from the display. But, according to the decrement property, we

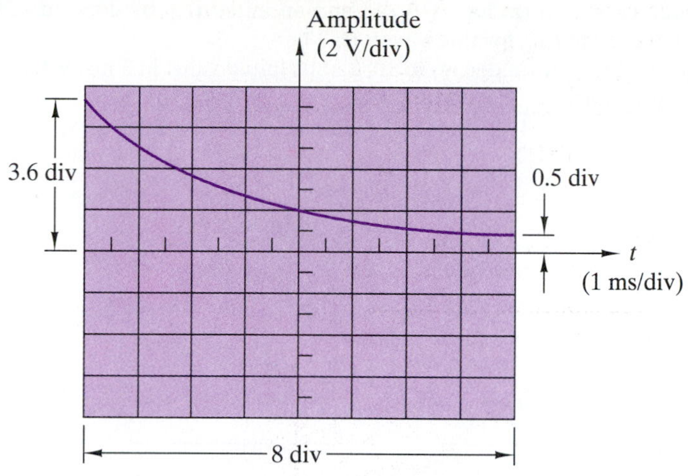

FIGURE 5–14

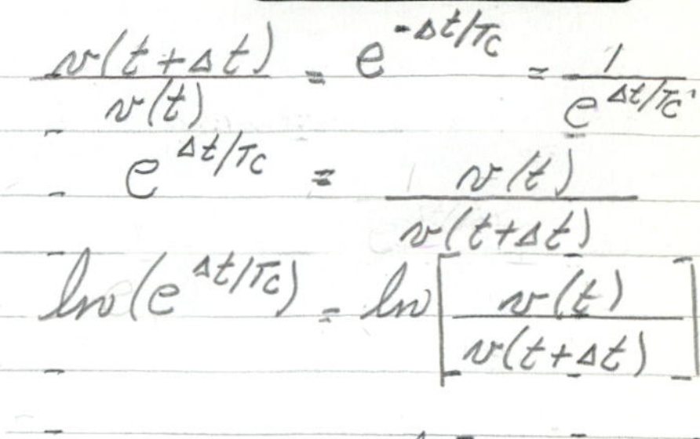

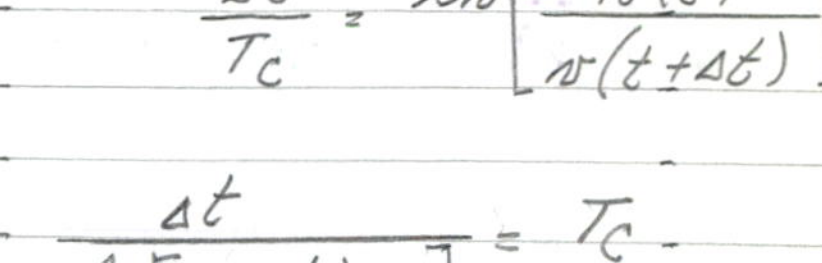

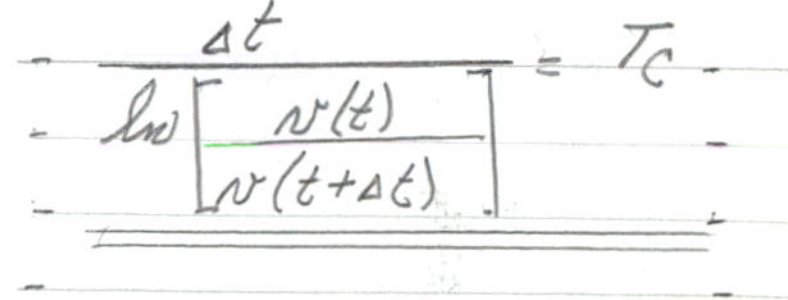

should be able to determine the time constant since the decrement ratio is independent of amplitude and time. Specifically, Eq. (5–14) points out that

$$\frac{v(t+\Delta t)}{v(t)} = e^{-\Delta t/T_C}$$

Solving for the time constant T_C yields

$$T_C = \frac{\Delta t}{\ln\left[\dfrac{v(t)}{v(t+\Delta t)}\right]}$$

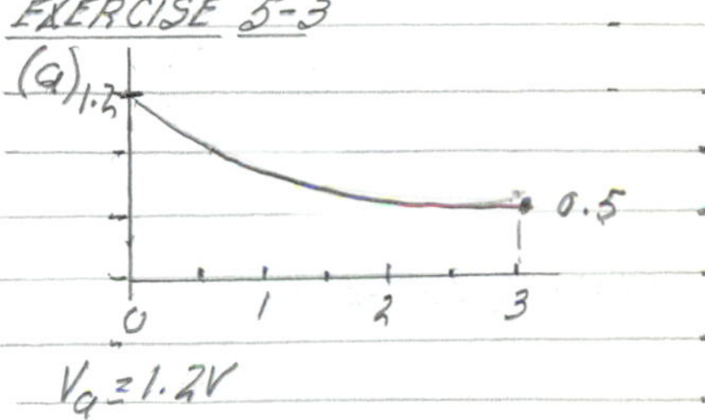

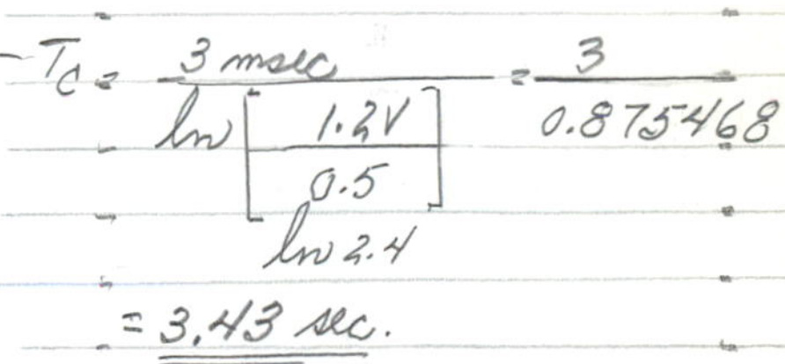

Taking the starting point at the left edge of the oscilloscope display yields

$$v(t) = (3.6 \text{ div})(2 \text{ V/div}) = 7.2 \text{ V}$$

Next, defining Δt to be the full width of the display produces

$$\Delta t = (8 \text{ div})(1 \text{ ms/div}) = 8 \text{ ms}$$

and

$$v(t+\Delta t) = (0.5 \text{ div})(2 \text{ V/div}) = 1 \text{ V}$$

As a result, the time constant of the waveform is found to be

$$T_C = \frac{\Delta t}{\ln\left[\dfrac{v(t)}{v(t+\Delta t)}\right]} = \frac{8 \times 10^{-3}}{\ln(7.2/1)} = 4.05 \text{ ms}$$ ■

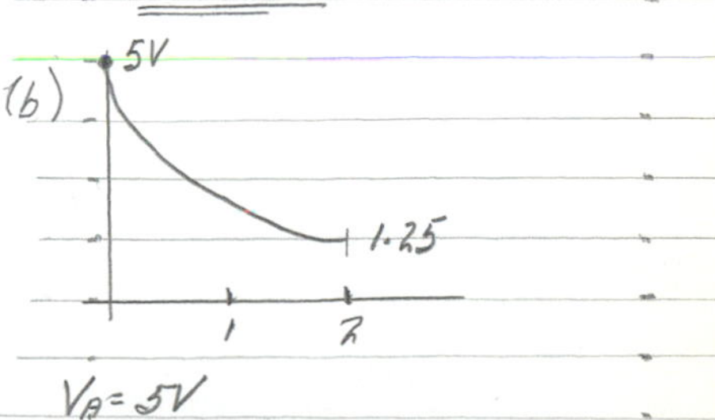

Exercise 5–3

(a) An exponential waveform has $v(0) = 1.2$ V and $v(3) = 0.5$ V. What are V_A and T_C for this waveform?

(b) An exponential waveform has $v(0) = 5$ V and $v(2) = 1.25$ V. What are values of $v(t)$ at $t = 1$ and $t = 4$?

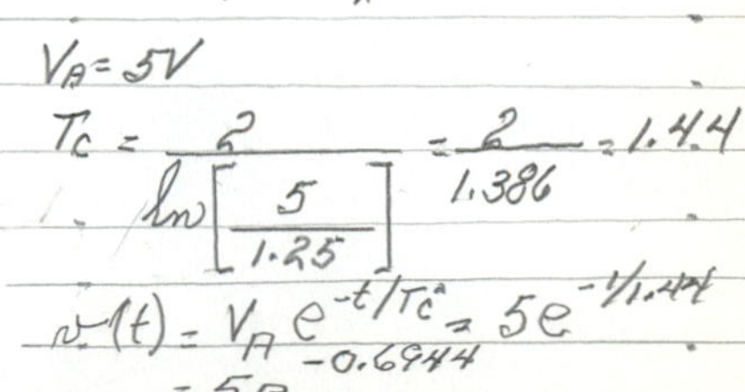

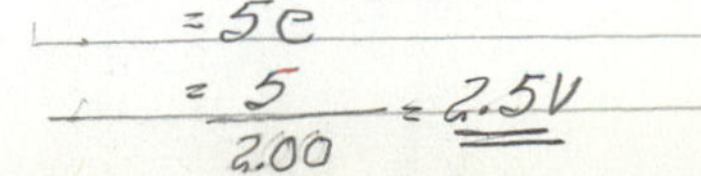

(c) An exponential waveform has $v(0) = 5$ and an initial ($t = 0$) slope of -25 V/s. What are V_A and T_C for this waveform?
(d) An exponential waveform decays to 10% of its initial value in 3 ms. What is T_C for this waveform?
(e) A waveform has $v(2) = 4$ V, $v(6) = 1$ V, and $v(10) = 0.5$ V. Is it an exponential waveform?

Answers:

(a) $V_A = 1.2$ V, $T_C = 3.43$ s
(b) $v(1) = 2.5$ V, $v(4) = 0.3125$ V
(c) $V_A = 5$ V, $T_C = 200$ ms
(d) $T_C = 1.303$ ms
(e) No, it violates the decrement property

Exercise 5–4

Find the amplitude and time constant of the following exponential signals:

(a) $v_1(t) = [-15e^{-1000t}]u(t)$ V
(b) $v_2(t) = [+12e^{-t/10}]u(t)$ mV
(c) $i_3(t) = [15e^{-500t}]u(-t)$ mA
(d) $i_4(t) = [4e^{-200(t-100)}]u(t-100)]$ A

Answers:

(a) $V_A = -15$ V, $T_C = 1$ ms (b) $V_A = 12$ mV, $T_C = 10$ s

(c) $I_A = 15$ mA, $T_C = 2$ ms (d) $I_A = 4$ A, $T_C = 5$ ms

5–4 THE SINUSOIDAL WAVEFORM

The cosine and sine functions are important in all branches of science and engineering. The corresponding time-varying waveform in Figure 5–15 plays an especially prominent role in electrical engineering.

In contrast with the step and exponential waveforms studied earlier, the sinusoid, like the dc waveform in Figure 5–1, extends indefinitely in time in both the positive and negative directions. The sinusoid has neither a beginning nor an end. Of course, real signals have finite durations. They were turned on at some finite time in the past and will be turned off at some time in the future. While it may seem unrealistic to have a signal model that lasts forever, it turns out that the eternal sinewave is a very good approximation in many practical applications.

The sinusoid in Figure 5–15 is an endless repetition of identical oscillations between positive and negative peaks. The **amplitude** V_A (in volts) defines the maximum and minimum values of the oscillations. The **period** T_0 (usually seconds) is the time required to complete one cycle of the oscillation. The sinusoid can be expressed mathematically using either the sine or the cosine function. The choice between the two depends on where we

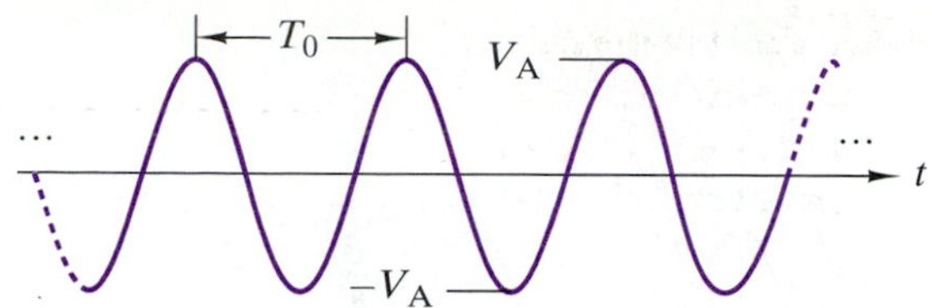

FIGURE 5–15 *The eternal sinusoid.*

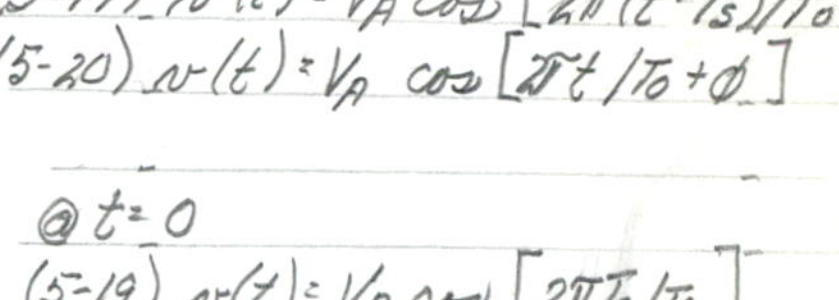

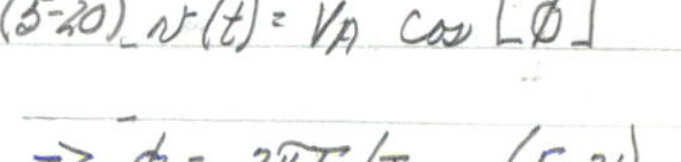

choose to define $t = 0$. If we choose $t = 0$ at a point where the sinusoid is zero, then it can be written as

$$v(t) = V_A \sin(2\pi t/T_0) \tag{5–18a}$$

On the other hand, if we choose $t = 0$ at a point where the sinusoid is at a positive peak, we can write an equation for it in terms of a cosine function:

$$v(t) = V_A \cos(2\pi t/T_0) \tag{5–18b}$$

Although either choice will work, it is common practice to choose $t = 0$ at a positive peak; hence Eq. (5–18b) applies. Thus, we will continue to call the waveform a sinusoid even though we use a cosine function to describe it.

As in the case of the step and exponential functions, the general sinusoid is obtained by replacing t by $(t - T_S)$. Inserting this change in Eq. (5–18) yields a general expression for the sinusoid as

$$v(t) = V_A \cos[2\pi(t - T_S)/T_0] \tag{5–19}$$

where the constant T_S is the time-shift parameter. Figure 5–16 shows that the sinusoid shifts to the right when $T_S > 0$ and to the left when $T_S < 0$. In effect, time shifting causes the positive peak nearest the origin to occur at $t = T_S$.

The time-shifting parameter can also be represented by an angle:

$$v(t) = V_A \cos[2\pi t/T_0 + \phi] \tag{5–20}$$

The parameter ϕ is called the **phase angle**. The term *phase angle* is based on the circular interpretation of the cosine function. We think of the period as being divided into 2π radians. In this sense the phase angle is the angle between $t = 0$ and the nearest positive peak. Comparing Eqs. (5–19) and (5–20), we find the relation between T_S and ϕ to be

$$\phi = -2\pi \frac{T_S}{T_0} \tag{5–21}$$

Changing the phase angle moves the waveform to the left or right, revealing different phases of the oscillating waveform (hence the name *phase angle*).

The phase angle should be expressed in radians, but is often reported in degrees. Care must be used when numerically evaluating the argument of the cosine $(2\pi t/T_0 + \phi)$ to ensure that both terms have the same units. The term $2\pi t/T_0$ has the units of radians, so it is necessary to convert ϕ to radians when it is given in degrees.

FIGURE 5–16 *Effect of time shifting on the sinusoidal waveform.*

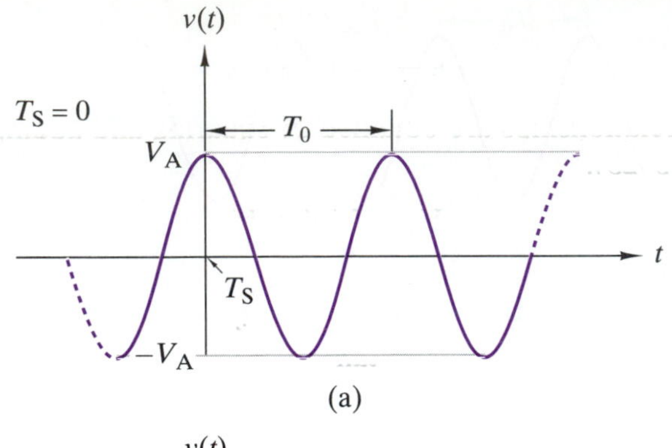

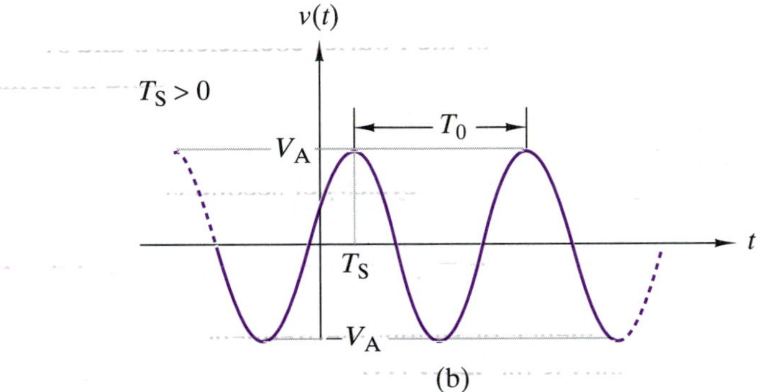

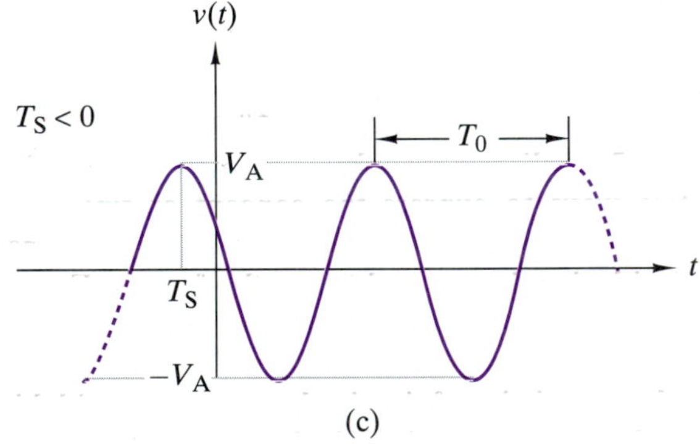

An alternative form of the general sinusoid is obtained by expanding Eq. (5–20) using the identity $\cos(x + y) = \cos(x)\cos(y) - \sin(x)\sin(y)$,

$$v(t) = [V_A \cos\phi]\cos(2\pi t/T_0) + [-V_A \sin\phi]\sin(2\pi t/T_0)$$

The quantities inside the brackets in this equation are constants; therefore, we can write the general sinusoid in the form

$$v(t) = a\cos(2\pi t/T_0) + b\sin(2\pi t/T_0) \qquad (5\text{–}22)$$

The two amplitudelike parameters a and b have the same units as the waveform (volts in this case) and are called Fourier coefficients. By definition, the Fourier coefficients are related to the amplitude and phase parameters by the equations

$$a = V_A \cos\phi$$

$$b = -V_A \sin\phi \qquad (5\text{–}23)$$

The inverse relationships are obtained by squaring and adding the expressions in Eq. (5–23):

$$V_A = \sqrt{a^2 + b^2} \qquad (5\text{–}24)$$

and by dividing the second expression in Eq. (5–23) by the first:

$$\phi = \tan^{-1}\frac{-b}{a} \qquad (5\text{–}25)$$

Caution: The inverse tangent function has a ±180° ambiguity that can be resolved by considering the signs of the Fourier coefficients a and b.

It is customary to describe the time variation of the sinusoid in terms of a frequency parameter. **Cyclic frequency** f_0 is defined as the number of periods per unit time. By definition, the period T_0 is the number of seconds per cycle; consequently, the number of cycles per second is

$$f_0 = \frac{1}{T_0} \qquad (5\text{–}26)$$

where f_0 is the cyclic frequency or simply the frequency. The unit of frequency (cycles per second) is the **hertz** (Hz). The **angular frequency** ω_0 in radians per second is related to the cyclic frequency by the relationship

$$\omega_0 = 2\pi f_0 = \frac{2\pi}{T_0} \qquad (5\text{–}27)$$

because there are 2π radians per cycle.

There are two ways to express the concept of sinusoidal frequency: cyclic frequency (f_0, hertz) and angular frequency (ω_0, radians per second). When working with signals, we tend to use the former. For example, radio stations transmit carrier signals at frequencies specified as 690 kHz (AM band) or 101 MHz (FM band). Radian frequency is more convenient when describing the characteristics of circuits driven by sinusoidal inputs.

In summary, there are several equivalent ways to describe the general sinusoid:

$$v(t) = V_A \cos\left[\frac{2\pi(t - T_S)}{T_0}\right] = V_A \cos\left(\frac{2\pi t}{T_0} + \phi\right) = a \cos\left(\frac{2\pi t}{T_0}\right) + b \sin\left(\frac{2\pi t}{T_0}\right)$$

$$= V_A \cos[2\pi f_0(t - T_S)] = V_A \cos(2\pi f_0 t + \phi) = a\cos(2\pi f_0 t) + b \sin(2\pi f_0 t)$$

$$= V_A \cos[\omega_0(t - T_S)] = V_A \cos(\omega_0 t + \phi) = a \cos(\omega_0 t) + b \sin(\omega_0 t)$$

To use any one of these expressions, we need three types of parameters:

1. *Amplitude:* either V_A or the Fourier coefficients a and b
2. *Time shift:* either T_S or the phase angle ϕ
3. *Time/frequency:* either T_0, f_0, or ω_0.

In different parts of this book we use different forms to represent a sinusoid. Therefore, it is important for you to understand thoroughly the relationships among the various parameters in Eqs. (5–21) through (5–27).

EXAMPLE 5–7

Figure 5–17 shows an oscilloscope display of a sinusoid. The vertical axis (amplitude) is calibrated at 5 V per division, and the horizontal axis (time) is calibrated at 0.1 ms per division. Derive an expression for the sinusoid displayed in Figure 5–17.

FIGURE 5–17

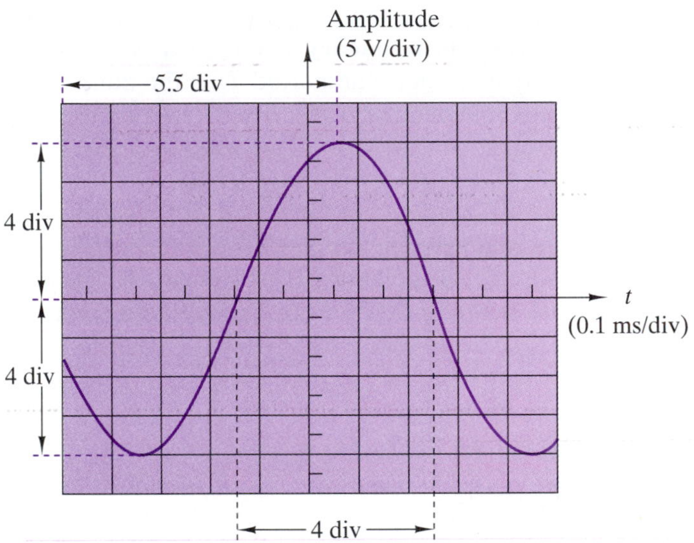

SOLUTION:

The maximum amplitude of the waveform is seen to be four vertical divisions; therefore,

$$V_A = (4 \text{ div})(5 \text{ V/div}) = 20 \text{ V}$$

There are four horizontal divisions between successive zero crossings, which means there are a total of eight divisions in one cycle. The period of the waveform is

$$T_0 = (8 \text{ div})(0.1 \text{ ms/div}) = 0.8 \text{ ms}$$

The two frequency parameters are $f_0 = 1/T_0 = 1.25$ kHz and $\omega_0 = 2\pi f_0 = 7854$ rad/s. The parameters V_A, T_0, f_0, and ω_0 do not depend on the location of the $t = 0$ axis.

To determine the time shift T_S, we need to define a time origin. The $t = 0$ axis is arbitrarily taken at the left edge of the display in Figure 5–17. The positive peak shown in the display is 5.5 divisions to the right of $t = 0$, which is more than half a cycle (four divisions). The positive peak closest to $t = 0$ is not shown in Figure 5–17 because it must lie beyond the left edge of the display. However, the positive peak shown in the display is located at $t = T_S + T_0$ since it is one cycle after $t = T_S$. We can write

$$T_S + T_0 = (5.5 \text{ div})(0.1 \text{ ms/div}) = 0.55 \text{ ms}$$

which yields $T_S = 0.55 - T_0 = -0.25$ ms. As expected, T_S is negative because the nearest positive peak is to the left of $t = 0$.

Given T_S, we can calculate the remaining parameters of the sinusoid as follows:

$$\phi = -\frac{2\pi T_S}{T_0} = 1.96 \text{ rad or } 112.5°$$

$$a = V_A \cos\phi = -7.65 \text{ V}$$

$$b = -V_A \sin\phi = -18.5 \text{ V}$$

Finally, the three alternative expressions for the displayed sinusoid are

$$\begin{aligned} v(t) &= 20 \cos[(7854\,(t + 0.25 \times 10^{-3})] \\ &= 20 \cos(7854\,t + 112.5°) \\ &= -7.65 \cos 7854t - 18.5 \sin 7854t \end{aligned}$$

■

Exercise 5–5

Derive an expression for the sinusoid displayed in Figure 5–17 when $t = 0$ is placed in the middle of the display.

Answer: $v(t) = 20 \cos(7854t - 22.5°)$

PROPERTIES OF SINUSOIDS

In general, a waveform is said to be **periodic** if

$$v(t + T_0) = v(t)$$

for all values of t. The constant T_0 is called the period of the waveform if it is the smallest nonzero interval for which $v(t + T_0) = v(t)$. Since this equality must be valid for all values of t, it follows that periodic signals must have eternal waveforms that extend indefinitely in time in both directions. Signals that are not periodic are called **aperiodic**.

The sinusoid is a periodic signal since

$$\begin{aligned} v(t + T_0) &= V_A \cos[2\pi\,(t + T_0)/T_0 + \phi] \\ &= V_A \cos[2\pi\,(t)/T_0 + \phi + 2\,\pi] \end{aligned}$$

But $\cos(x + 2\pi) = \cos(x)$. Consequently,

$$v(t + T_0) = V_A \cos(2\pi t/T_0 + \phi) = v(t)$$

for all t.

The **additive property** of sinusoids states that summing two or more sinusoids with the same frequency yields a sinusoid with different amplitude and phase parameters but the same frequency. To illustrate, consider two sinusoids

$$v_1(t) = a_1 \cos(2\pi f_0 t) + b_1 \sin(2\pi f_0 t)$$

$$v_2(t) = a_2 \cos(2\pi f_0 t) + b_2 \sin(2\pi f_0 t)$$

The waveform $v_3(t) = v_1(t) + v_2(t)$ can be written as

$$v_3(t) = (a_1 + a_2) \cos(2\pi f_0 t) + (b_1 + b_2) \sin(2\pi f_0 t)$$

because cosine and sine are linearly independent functions. We obtain the Fourier coefficients of the sum of two sinusoids by adding their Fourier coefficients, provided the two have the same frequency. *Caution:* The summation must take place with the sinusoids in Fourier coefficient form. Sums of sinusoids *cannot* be found by adding amplitudes and phase angles.

The **derivative** and **integral** properties state that when we differentiate or integrate a sinusoid, the result is another sinusoid with the same frequency:

$$\frac{d(V_A \cos \omega t)}{dt} = -\omega V_A \sin \omega t = \omega V_A \cos(\omega t + \pi/2)$$

$$\int V_A \cos(\omega t)\, dt = \frac{V_A}{\omega} \sin \omega t = \frac{V_A}{\omega} \cos(\omega t - \pi/2)$$

These operations change the amplitude and phase angle but do not change the frequency. The fact that differentiation and integration preserve the underlying waveform is a key property of the sinusoid. No other periodic waveform has this shape-preserving property.

EXAMPLE 5–8

(a) Find the periods cyclic and radian frequencies of the sinusoids
$v_1(t) = 17 \cos(2000t - 30°)$
$v_2(t) = 12 \cos(2000t + 30°)$.
(b) Find the waveform of $v_3(t) = v_1(t) + v_2(t)$.

SOLUTION:

(a) The two sinusoids have the same frequency $\omega_0 = 2000$ rad/s since a term $2000t$ appears in the arguments of $v_1(t)$ and $v_2(t)$. Therefore, $f_0 = \omega_0/2\pi = 318.3$ Hz and $T_0 = 1/f_0 = 3.14$ ms.

(b) We use the additive property, since the two sinusoids have the same frequency. Beyond this checkpoint, the frequency plays no further role in the calculation. The two sinusoids must be converted to the Fourier coefficient form using Eq. (5–23).

$$a_1 = 17\cos(-30°) = +14.7\text{ V}$$
$$b_1 = -17\sin(-30°) = +8.50\text{ V}$$
$$a_2 = 12\cos(30°) = +10.4\text{ V}$$
$$b_2 = -12\sin(30°) = -6.00\text{V}$$

The Fourier coefficients of the signal $v_3 = v_1 + v_2$ are found as

$$a_3 = a_1 + a_2 = 25.1\text{ V}$$
$$b_3 = b_1 + b_2 = 2.50\text{ V}$$

The amplitude and phase angle of $v_3(t)$ are found using Eqs. (5–24) and (5–25):

$$V_A = \sqrt{a_3^2 + b_3^2} = 25.2\text{ V}$$
$$\phi = \tan^{-1}(2.5/25.1) = 5.69°$$

Two equivalent representations of $v_3(t)$ are

$$v_3(t) = 25.1\cos(2000t) + 2.5\sin(2000t)\text{ V}$$

and

$$v_3(t) = 25.2\cos(2000t + 5.69°)\text{ V}$$ ■

EXAMPLE 5–9

The balanced three-phase voltages used in electrical power systems can be written as

$$v_A(t) = V_m\cos(2\pi f_0 t)$$
$$v_B(t) = V_m\cos(2\pi f_0 t + 120°)$$
$$v_C(t) = V_m\cos(2\pi f_0 t + 240°)$$

Show that the sum of these voltages is zero.

SOLUTION:

The three voltages are given in amplitude/phase angle form. They can be converted to the Fourier coefficient form using Eq. (5–23):

$$v_A(t) = +V_m\cos(2\pi f_0 t)$$
$$v_B(t) = -\frac{V_m}{2}\cos(2\pi f_0 t) + \frac{\sqrt{3}V_m}{2}\sin(2\pi f_0 t)$$
$$v_C(t) = -\frac{V_m}{2}\cos(2\pi f_0 t) - \frac{\sqrt{3}V_m}{2}\sin(2\pi f_0 t)$$

The sum of the cosine and sine terms is zero; consequently, $v_A(t) + v_B(t) + v_C(t) = 0$. The zero sum occurs because the three sinusoids have equal amplitudes and are disposed at 120° intervals. If the amplitudes are not equal or the phase angles do not differ by 120°, then the voltages are said to be unbalanced. ■

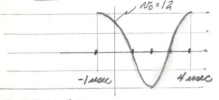

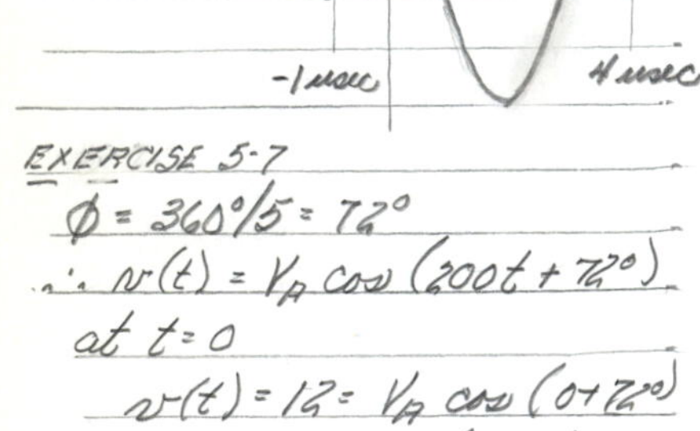

Exercise 5–6

Write an equation for the waveform obtained by integrating and differentiating the following signals:

$$\text{(a) } v_1(t) = 30\cos(10t - 60°)$$

$$\text{(b) } v_2(t) = 3\cos(4000\pi t) - 4\sin(4000\pi t)$$

Answers:

$$\text{(a) } \frac{dv_1}{dt} = 300\cos(10t + 30°)$$

$$\int v_1(t)\,dt = 3\cos(10t - 150°)$$

$$\text{(b) } \frac{dv_2}{dt} = 2\pi \times 10^4 \cos(4000\pi t + 143.1°)$$

$$\int v_2\,dt = \frac{1}{800\pi}\cos(4000\pi t - 36.87°)$$

Exercise 5–7

A sinusoid has a period of 5 μs. At $t = 0$ the amplitude is 12 V. The waveform reaches its first positive peak after $t = 0$ at $t = 4$ μs. Find its amplitude, frequency, and phase angle.

Answers: $V_A = 38.8$ V, $f_0 = 200$ kHz, $\phi = +72°$

5–5 COMPOSITE WAVEFORMS

In the previous sections we introduced the step, exponential, and sinusoidal waveforms. These waveforms are basic signals because they can be combined to synthesize all other signals used in this book. Signals generated by combining the three basic waveforms are called **composite signals**. This section provides examples of composite waveforms.

EXAMPLE 5–10

Characterize the composite waveform generated by subtracting an exponential from a step function with the same amplitude.

SOLUTION:
The equation for this composite waveform is

$$v(t) = V_A u(t) - [V_A e^{-t/T_C}]u(t)$$
$$= V_A[1 - e^{-t/T_C}]u(t)$$

For $t < 0$ the waveform is zero because of the step function. At $t = 0$ the waveform is still zero since the step and exponential cancel:

$$v(0) = V_A[1 - e^0](1) = 0$$

For $t >> T_C$ the waveform approaches a constant value V_A because the exponential term decays to zero. For practical purposes $v(t)$ is within less than 1% of its final value V_A when $t = 5T_C$. At $t = T_C$, $v(T_C) = V_A(1 - e^{-1}) = 0.632V_A$. The waveform rises to about 63% of its final value in one time constant. All of the observations are summarized in the plot shown in Figure 5–18. This waveform is called an **exponential rise**. It is also sometimes referred to as a "charging exponential," since it represents the behavior of signals that occur during the buildup of voltage in resistor-capacitor circuits studied in Chapter 7. ■

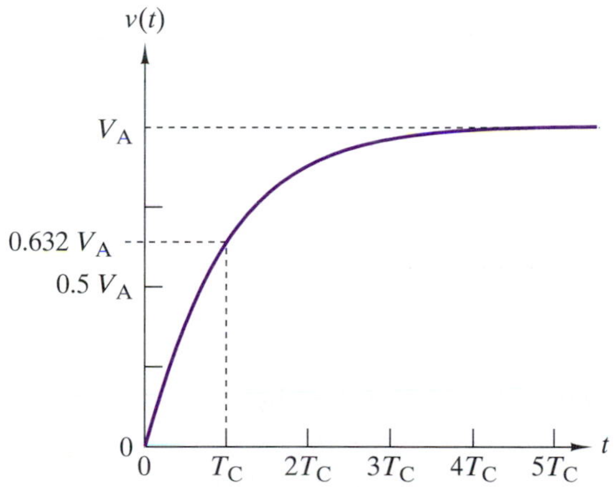

FIGURE 5–18 *The exponential rise waveform.*

EXAMPLE 5–11

Characterize the composite waveform obtained by multiplying the ramp $r(t)/T_C$ times an exponential.

SOLUTION:
The equation for this composite waveform is

$$v(t) = \frac{r(t)}{T_C}[V_A e^{-t/T_C}]u(t)$$
$$= V_A[(t/T_C)\, e^{-t/T_C}]u(t)$$

For $t < 0$ the waveform is zero because of the step function. At $t = 0$ the waveform is zero because $r(0) = 0$. For $t > 0$ there is a competition between two effects—the ramp increases linearly with time while the exponential decays to zero. Since the composite waveform is the product of these terms, it is important to determine which effect dominates. In the limit, as $t \to \infty$, the product of the ramp and exponential takes on the indeterminate form of infinity times zero. A single application of *l'Hôpital's* rule, then, shows that the exponential dominates, forcing the $v(t)$ to zero as t becomes large. That is, the exponential decay overpowers the linearly increasing ramp, as shown by the graph in Figure 5–19. The waveform obtained by multiplying a ramp by a decaying exponential is called a **damped ramp**. ■

FIGURE 5–19 *The damped ramp waveform.*

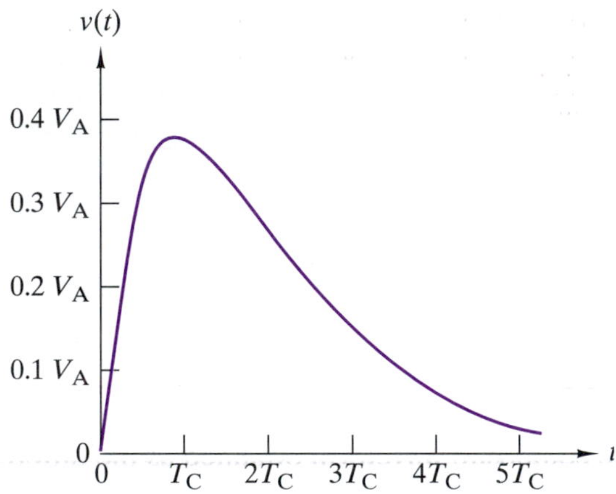

EXAMPLE 5–12

Characterize the composite waveform obtained by multiplying $\sin \omega_0 t$ by an exponential.

SOLUTION:

In this case the composite waveform is expressed as

$$\begin{aligned} v(t) &= \sin \omega_0 t [V_A e^{-t/T_C}]\, u(t) \\ &= V_A [e^{-t/T_C} \sin \omega_0 t]\, u(t) \end{aligned}$$

Figure 5–20 shows a graph of this waveform for $T_0 = 2T_C$. For $t < 0$ the step function forces the waveform to be zero. At $t = 0$, and periodically thereafter, the waveform passes through zero because $\sin(n\pi) = 0$. The waveform is not periodic, however, because the decaying exponential gradually reduces the amplitude of the oscillation. For all practical purposes the oscillations become negligibly small for $t > 5T_C$. The waveform obtained by multiplying a sinusoid by a decaying exponential is called a **damped sine**. ■

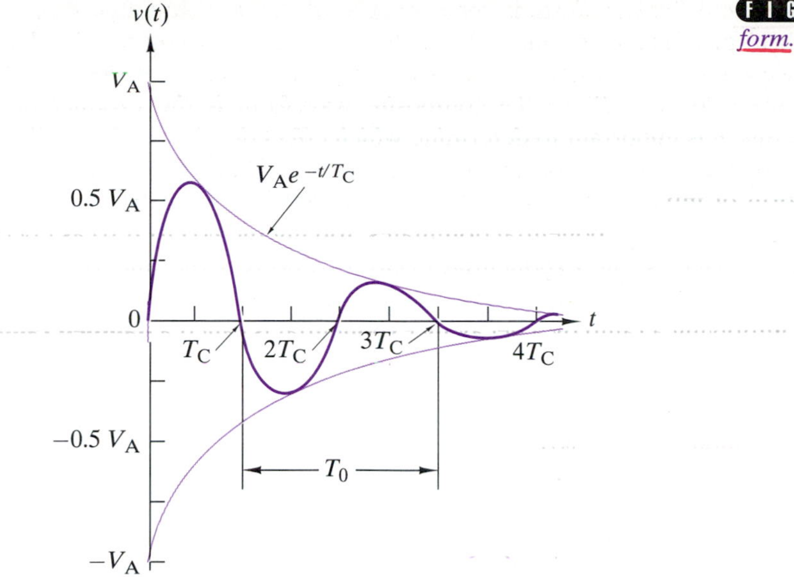

FIGURE 5–20 The damped sine waveform.

EXAMPLE 5–13

Characterize the composite waveform obtained as the difference of two exponentials with the same amplitude.

SOLUTION:

The equation for this composite waveform is

$$v(t) = [V_A e^{-t/T_1}]u(t) - [V_A e^{-t/T_2}]\,u(t)$$
$$= V_A\,(e^{-t/T_1} - e^{-t/T_2})\,u(t)$$

For $T_1 > T_2$ the resulting waveform is illustrated in Figure 5–21 (plotted for $T_1 = 2T_2$). For $t < 0$ the waveform is zero. At $t = 0$ the waveform is still zero, since

$$v(0) = V_A\,(e^{-0} - e^{-0})$$
$$= V_A\,(1 - 1) = 0$$

For $t >> T_1$ the waveform returns to zero because both exponentials decay to zero. For $5T_1 > t > 5T_2$ the second exponential is negligible and the waveform essentially reduces to the first exponential. Conversely, for $t << T_1$ the first exponential is essentially constant, so the second exponential determines the early time variation of the waveform. The waveform is called a **double exponential**, since both exponential components make important contributions to the waveform. ■

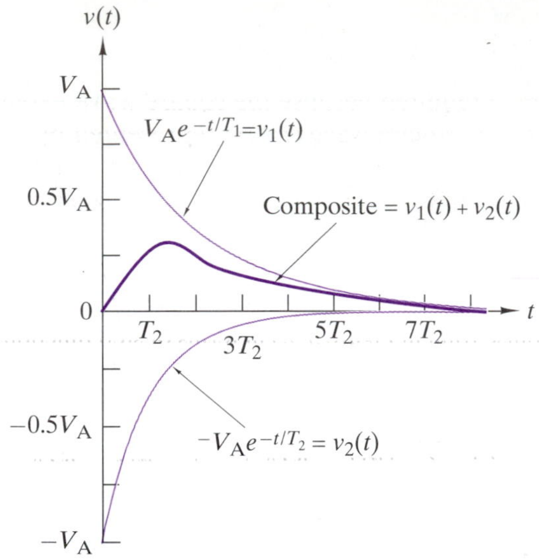

FIGURE 5–21 The double exponential waveform.

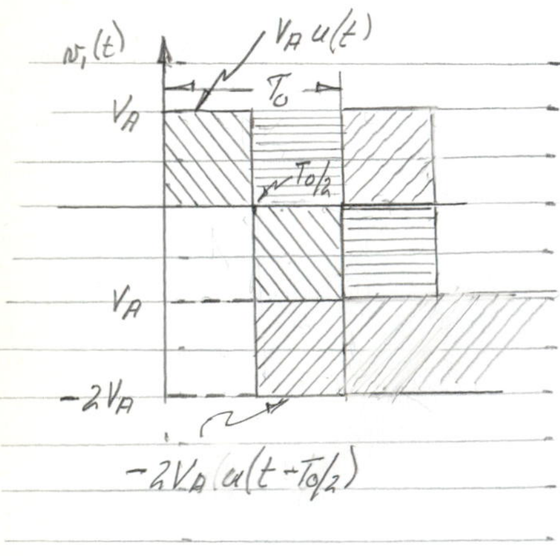

EXAMPLE 5–14

Develop an equation for the square wave in Figure 5–22 using step functions.

SOLUTION:

An equation for the square wave can be developed by summing the expressions for each cycle since it is periodic. The first cycle after $t = 0$ can be written as the sum of three step functions:

$$v_1(t) = V_A u(t) - 2V_A u(t - T_0/2) + V_A u(t - T_0)$$

Similarly, the second cycle after $t = 0$ is

$$v_2(t) = V_A u(t - T_0) - 2V_A u(t - 3T_0/2) + V_A u(t - 2T_0)$$

From these results we see that the kth cycle is

$$v_k(t) = V_A u(t - [k - 1]T_0) - 2V_A u(t - [k - {}^1/_2]T_0) + V_A u(t - kT_0)$$

We can produce the square wave $v(t)$ cycle by cycle, by summing $v_k(t)$ from $k = -\infty$ to $k = \infty$:

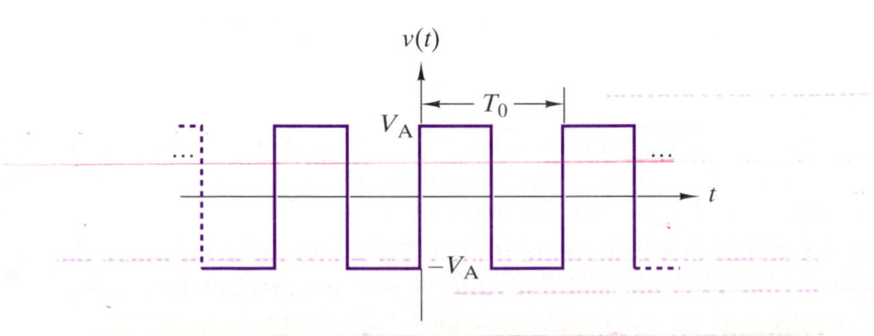

FIGURE 5–22 The square wave.

$$v(t) = \sum_{k=-\infty}^{k=\infty} v_k(t)$$

An infinite sum is required because the square wave extends to infinity in both directions. The square wave can be represented by an infinite sum of step functions. In Chapter 15 we will see that the square wave and other periodic signals can be constructed using an infinite sum of sinusoids called a Fourier series. ■

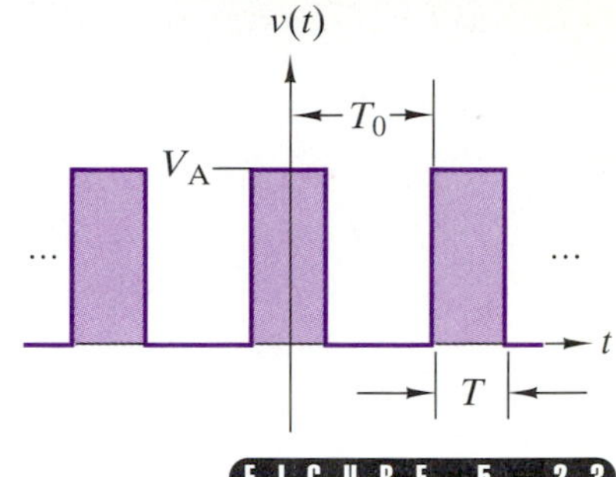

FIGURE 5–23

Exercise 5–8

Express the pulse train in Figure 5–23 in terms of step functions.

Answer:

$$v(t) = V_A \sum_{k=-\infty}^{k=\infty} \left[u\left(t - kT_0 + \frac{T}{2}\right) - u\left(t - kT_0 - \frac{T}{2}\right)\right]$$

Exercise 5–9

Find the maximum amplitude and the approximate duration of the following composite waveforms:

(a) $v_1(t) = [25 \sin 1000t][u(t) - u(t - 10)]$ V
(b) $v_2(t) = [50 \cos 1000t][e^{-200t}]u(t)$ V
(c) $i_3(t) = [3000te^{-1000t}]u(t)$ mA
(d) $i_4(t) = [10e^{5000t}]u(-t) + [10e^{-5000t}]u(t)$ A

Answers:

(a) 25 V, 10 s
(b) 50 V, 25 ms
(c) 1.10 mA, 5 ms
(d) 10 A, 2 ms

5–6 WAVEFORM PARTIAL DESCRIPTORS

An equation or graph defines a waveform for all time. The value of a waveform $v(t)$ or $i(t)$ at time t is called the **instantaneous value** of the waveform. We often use parameters called **partial descriptors** that characterize important features of a waveform but do not give a complete description. These partial descriptors fall into two categories: (1) those that describe temporal features and (2) those that describe amplitude features.

TEMPORAL DESCRIPTORS

Temporal descriptors identify waveform attributes relative to the time axis. For example, waveforms that repeat themselves at fixed time intervals are said to be **periodic**. Stated formally,

A signal $v(t)$ is periodic if $v(t + T_0) = v(t)$ for all t, where the period T_0 is the smallest value that meets this condition. Signals that are not periodic are called aperiodic.

The fact that a waveform is periodic provides important information about the signal, but does not specify all of its characteristics. Thus, the fact that a signal is periodic is itself a partial description, as is the value of the period. The eternal sinewave is the premier example of a periodic signal. The square wave and triangular wave in Figure 5–2 are also periodic. Examples of aperiodic waveforms are the step function, exponential, and damped sine.

Waveforms that are identically zero prior to some specified time are said to be **causal**. Stated formally,

> ***A signal v(t) is causal if there exists a value of T such that v(t) ≡ 0 for all t < T; otherwise it is noncausal.***

It is usually assumed that a causal signal is zero for $t < 0$, since we can always use time shifting to make the starting point of a waveform at $t = 0$. Examples of causal waveforms are the step function, exponential, and damped sine. The eternal sinewave is, of course, noncausal.

Causal waveforms play a central role in circuit analysis. When the input driving force $x(t)$ is causal, the circuit response $y(t)$ must also be causal. That is, a physically realizable circuit cannot anticipate and respond to an input before it is applied. Causality is an important temporal feature, but only a partial description of the waveform.

AMPLITUDE DESCRIPTORS

Amplitude descriptors are positive scalars that describe signal strength. Generally, a waveform varies between two extreme values denoted as V_{MAX} and V_{MIN}. The **peak-to-peak value** (V_{pp}) describes the total excursion of $v(t)$ and is defined as

$$V_{pp} = V_{MAX} - V_{MIN} \tag{5-28}$$

Under this definition V_{pp} is always positive even if V_{MAX} and V_{MIN} are both negative. The **peak value** (V_p) is the maximum of the absolute value of the waveform. That is,

$$V_p = \text{Max}\{|V_{MAX}|, |V_{MIN}|\} \tag{5-29}$$

The peak value is a positive number that indicates the maximum absolute excursion of the waveform from zero. Figure 5–24 shows examples of these two amplitude descriptors.

The peak and peak-to-peak values describe waveform variation using the extreme values. The average value smooths things out to reveal the underlying waveform baseline. Average value is the area under the waveform over some period of time T, divided by that time period. Mathematically, we define **average value** (V_{avg}) over the time interval T as

$$V_{avg} = \frac{1}{T}\int_{t}^{t+T} v(x)dx \tag{5-30}$$

For periodic signals the period T_0 is used as the averaging interval T.

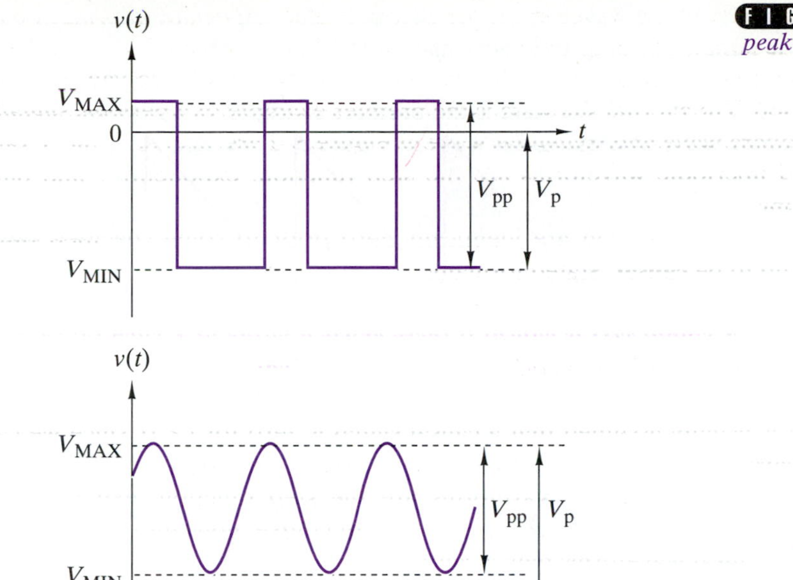

FIGURE 5–24 Peak value (V_p) and peak-to-peak value (V_{pp}).

For some periodic waveforms the integral in Eq. (5–30) can be evaluated graphically. The net area under the waveform is the area above the time axis minus the area below the time axis. For example, the sinusoid in Figure 5–25 has zero average value, since the area above the axis is exactly equal to the area below. The sawtooth in Figure 5–25 clearly has a positive average value. By geometry, the net area under one cycle of the sawtooth waveform is $V_A T_0/2$, so its average value is $(1/T_0)(V_A T_0/2) = V_A/2$.

The average value indicates whether the waveform contains a constant, non-time-varying component. The average value is also called the **dc component** of the waveform because dc signals are constant for all t.

EXAMPLE 5–15

Find the peak, peak-to-peak, and average values of the periodic input and output waveforms in Figure 5–26.

SOLUTION:

The input waveform is a sinusoid whose amplitude descriptors are

$$V_{pp} = 2V_A \quad V_p = V_A \quad V_{avg} = 0$$

The output waveform is obtained by clipping off the negative half-cycle of the input sinusoid. The amplitude descriptors of the output waveform are

$$V_{pp} = V_p = V_A$$

FIGURE 5–25 *Average value (V_{avg}) of periodic waveforms.*

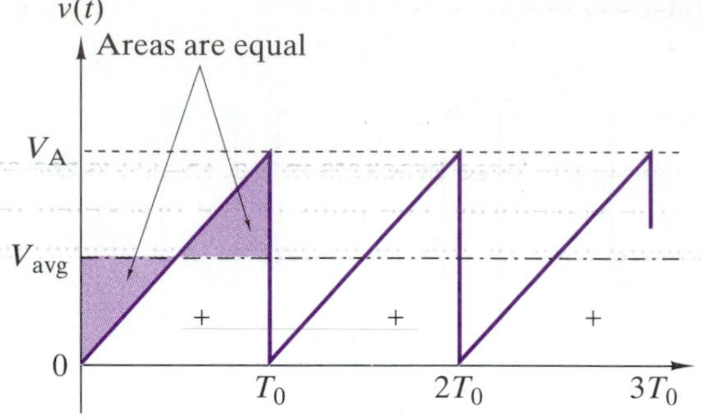

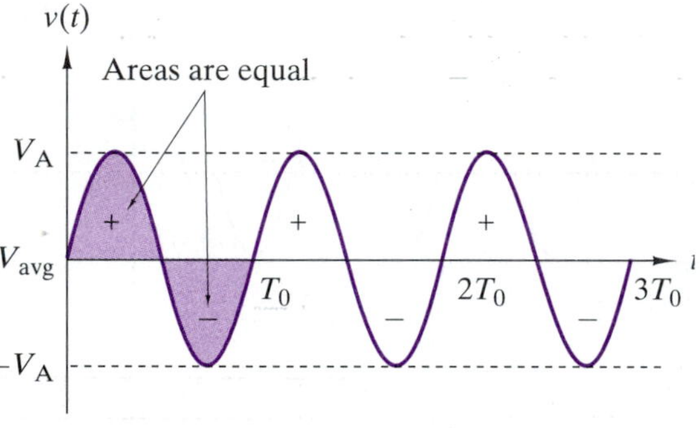

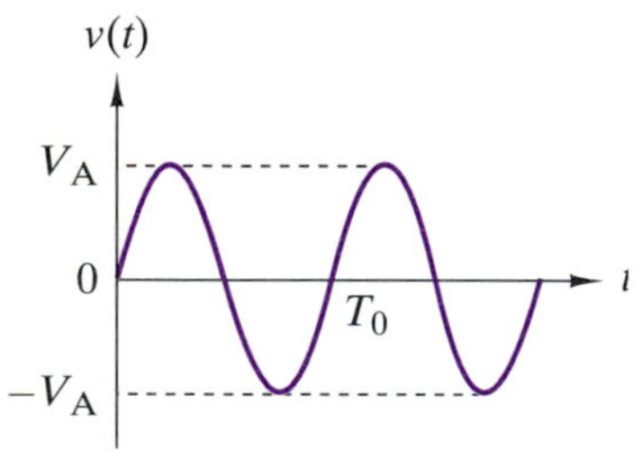

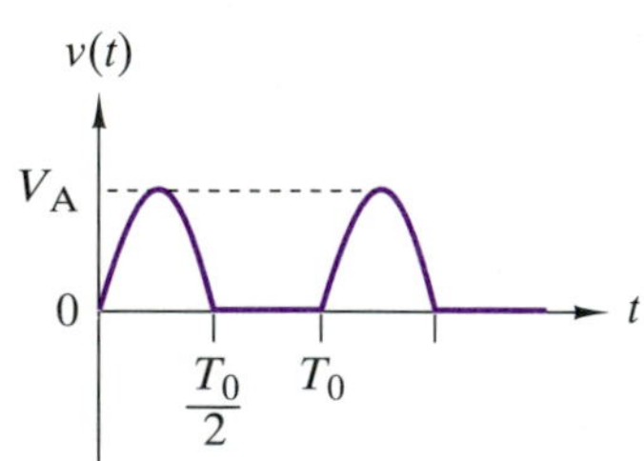

FIGURE 5–26

The output has a nonzero average value, since there is a net positive area under the waveform. The upper limit in Eq. (5–30) can be taken as $T_0/2$, since the waveform is zero from $T_0/2$ to T_0.

$$V_{\text{avg}} = \frac{1}{T_0}\int_0^{T_0/2} V_{\text{A}} \sin(2\pi t/T_0)dt = -\frac{V_{\text{A}}}{2\pi}\cos(2\pi\, t/T_0)\Big|_0^{T_0/2}$$
$$= \frac{V_{\text{A}}}{\pi}$$

The signal processor produces an output with a dc value from an input with no dc component. Rectifying circuits described in electronics courses produce waveforms like the output in Figure 5–26. ■

ROOT-MEAN-SQUARE VALUE

The **root-mean-square value** (V_{rms}) is a measure of the average power carried by the signal. The instantaneous power delivered to a resistor R by a voltage $v(t)$ is

$$p(t) = \frac{1}{R}[v(t)]^2 \qquad (5-31)$$

The average power delivered to the resistor in time span T is defined as

$$P_{\text{avg}} = \frac{1}{T}\int_t^{t+T} p(t)dt \qquad (5-32)$$

Combining Eqs. (5–31) and (5–32) yields

$$P_{\text{avg}} = \frac{1}{R}\left[\frac{1}{T}\int_{t}^{t+T} [v(t)]^2\, dt\right] \tag{5–33}$$

The quantity inside the large brackets in Eq. (5–33) is the average value of the square of the waveform. The units of the bracketed term are volts squared. The square root of this term defines the amplitude partial descriptor V_{rms}:

$$V_{\text{rms}} = \sqrt{\frac{1}{T}\int_{t}^{t+T} [v(t)]^2\, dt} \tag{5–34}$$

The amplitude descriptor V_{rms} is called the root-mean-square (rms) value because it is obtained by taking the square root of the average (mean) of the square of the waveform. For periodic signals the averaging interval is one cycle since such a waveform repeats itself every T_0 seconds.

We can express the average power delivered to a resistor in terms of V_{rms} as

$$P_{\text{avg}} = \frac{1}{R}V_{\text{rms}}^2 \tag{5–35}$$

The equation for average power in terms of V_{rms} has the same form as the power delivered by a dc signal. For this reason the rms value was originally called the **effective value**, although this term is no longer common. If the waveform amplitude is doubled, its rms value is doubled, and the average power is quadrupled. Commercial electrical power systems use transmission voltages in the range of several hundred kilovolts (rms).

EXAMPLE 5–16

Find the rms value of the sinusoid and sawtooth in Figure 5–25.

SOLUTION:

Applying Eq. (5–34) the sinusoid yields an rms value of

$$V_{\text{rms}} = \sqrt{\frac{V_A^2}{T_0}\int_0^{T_0} \sin^2(2\pi t/T_0)dt}$$

$$= \sqrt{\frac{V_A^2}{T_0}\left[\frac{t}{2} - \frac{\sin(4\pi t/T_0)}{8\pi/T_0}\right]_0^{T_0}} = \frac{V_A}{\sqrt{2}}$$

For the sawtooth the rms value is found as follows:

$$V_{\text{rms}} = \sqrt{\frac{1}{T_0}\int_0^{T_0} (V_A t/T_0)^2\, dt} = \sqrt{\frac{V_A^2}{T_0^3}\left[\frac{t^3}{3}\right]_0^{T_0}} = \frac{V_A}{\sqrt{3}}$$ ■

APPLICATION NOTE: EXAMPLE 5–17

In the United States residential ac power is supplied at 60 Hz and voltages of 115 and 230 V. These voltages are the rms values of the sinusoidal waveforms supplied by the power company. An oscilloscope displaying the waveform at a 115 V (rms) outlet indicates that the peak value of the sinusoid is larger than 115 V. Example 5–16 showed that the rms value of a sinusoid equals its peak divided by $\sqrt{2}$. If the rms value is 115 V, then the peak value is $115\sqrt{2}$ or about 163 V. Most ac voltmeters are calibrated to indicate the rms value of a sinusoid. If we measure a sinusoid with a peak value of 200 V using an ac voltmeter, the meter will indicate $200/\sqrt{2}$, or about 141 V (rms). In general, ac voltmeters are designed to measure pure sinusoids and will not correctly measure the rms value of nonsinusoidal waveforms such as a square wave.

The concept of rms value applies to sinusoidal currents as well. You are invited to return to Eq. (5–31) and write the instantaneous power delivered to the resistor in terms of the current through it. Continuing the derivation in terms of current shows that

$$I_{\text{rms}} = \sqrt{\frac{1}{T}\int_{t}^{t+T} [i(x)]^2\, dx}$$

and

$$P_{\text{avg}} = RI^2_{\text{rms}}$$

This power relationship has the same form as the dc case studied in Chapter 2. Most ac ammeters are calibrated to display the rms value of the current. Similarly, the ampere ratings of devices such as fuses, motors, and circuit breakers refer to rms current.

Since rms values relate to the average power, it should come as no surprise to discover that ac power ratings of devices refer to average power. A 75-W lightbulb will draw an average power of 75 W at its rated (rms) voltage. The instantaneous power delivered to the bulb has a constant average value and an oscillatory component. As a result, its light output fluctuates slightly, although the variation is not noticeable to most people. We will return to the concept of average power again in Chapter 8 when we study maximum power transfer conditions. The consequences of the oscillatory component of the instantaneous power will also be studied in Chapter 14.

EXAMPLE 5–18

A pulse train consists of a periodic sequence of exponential waveforms. The first cycle of the pulse train can be written as

$$v(t) = [u(t) - u(t - T_0)]\, V_A e^{-t/T_C}$$

Use Mathcad to calculate the V_{rms} of the pulse train for $V_A = 10$ V, $T_C =$ 2 ms, and $T_0 = 5T_C$.

SOLUTION:

Figure 5–27 shows a Mathcad worksheet. The first line assigns numerical values to the waveform parameters. The second line is the general form of the first cycle of the exponential pulse train. The third line is a general expression for the rms value of any waveform $v(t)$. Note that Mathcad evaluates the definite integral in this expression using the waveform and parameters in the previous two lines. The last line reports a final result of V_{rms} = 3.162 V. You can easily reconstruct this Matchcad worksheet and experiment using different numerical values in the first line or even try a different waveform in the second line. ■

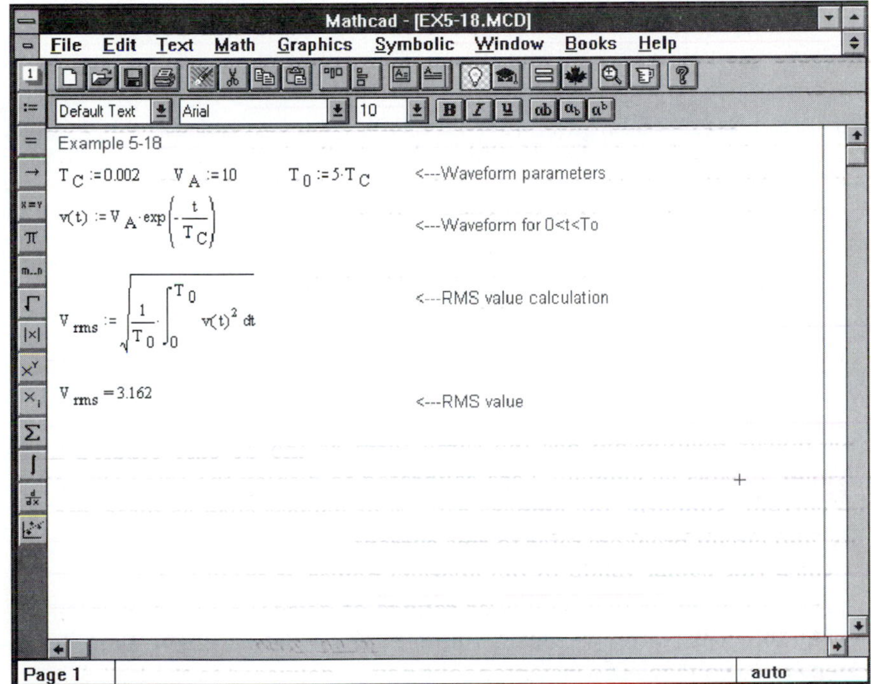

FIGURE 5–27

Exercise 5–10

Find the peak, peak-to-peak, average, and rms values of the periodic waveform in Figure 5–28.

Answers:

$$V_p = 2V_A, \quad V_{pp} = 3V_A, \quad V_{avg} = \frac{V_A}{4}, \quad V_{rms} = \frac{\sqrt{5}}{2}V_A$$

Exercise 5–11

Classify each of the following signals as periodic or aperiodic and causal or noncausal. Then calculate the average and rms values of the periodic waveforms, and the peak and peak-to-peak values of the other waveforms.

(a) $v_1(t) = 99 \cos 3000t - 132 \sin 3000t$ V

FIGURE 5–28

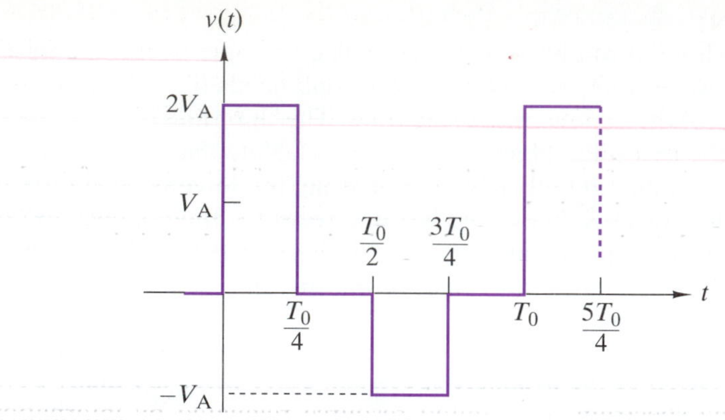

(b) $v_2(t) = 34\,[\sin 800\pi t][u(t) - u(t - 0.03)]$ V
(c) $i_3(t) = 120[u(t + 5) - u(t - 5)]$ mA
(d) $t_4(t) = 50$ A

Answers:

(a) Periodic, noncausal, $V_{avg} = 0$ and $V_{rms} = 117$ V
(b) Aperiodic, causal, $V_p = 34$ V and $V_{pp} = 68$ V
(c) Aperiodic, causal, $V_p = V_{pp} = 120$ mA
(d) Aperiodic, noncausal, $V_p = 50$ A and $V_{pp} = 0$

Exercise 5–12

Construct waveforms that have the following characteristics:

(a) Aperiodic and causal with $V_p = 8$ V and $V_{pp} = 15$ V
(b) Periodic and noncausal with $V_{avg} = 10$ V and $V_{pp} = 50$ V
(c) Periodic and noncausal with $V_{avg} = V_p/2$ ½bh = ½BH
(d) Aperiodic and causal with $V_p = V_{pp} = 10$ V

Answers: There are many possible correct answers since the given parameters are only partial descriptions of the required waveforms. Some examples that meet the requirements are as follows:

(a) $v(t) = 8\,u(t) - 15\,u(t - 1) + 7\,u(t - 2)$
(b) $v(t) = 10 + 25 \sin 1000t$
(c) A sawtooth wave
(d) $v(t) = 10[e^{-100t}]u(t)$

5–7 SIGNAL SPECTRA

Up to this point we have described signals as waveforms, where a waveform is an equation or graph that characterizes a signal as a function of time. The waveform is the appropriate starting place for studying signals because we live in a world in which time is the independent variable. But signals have a dual nature. They can also be described by a **spectrum**, which characterizes the signal as a function of frequency. Accordingly, a signal can be studied either in the time domain as a waveform or in the frequency domain as a spectrum.

The dual nature of signals and circuits is one of the most profound and useful concepts in electrical engineering. While we cannot fully develop the frequency domain concept at this point in our study, it is important to introduce the concept of a signal spectrum.

All signals occupy a portion of the electromagnetic spectrum. The signals emitted by radio, television, radar, and telephone systems are assigned a portion of the available spectrum. Since there are many potential users, the spectrum is a limited resource regulated by international agreements and governmental agencies. As a result, electrical engineers are required to optimize system performance within specified spectral limits.

To quantify spectral limitations, we use the concept of **signal bandwidth**, defined as frequency interval outside of which the magnitude of a signal spectrum is smaller than some specified value. For engineering purposes, **bandwidth** (B) can be written as

$$B = f_U - f_L \tag{5-36}$$

where f_U and f_L are the upper and lower limits on the bandwidth interval. Bandwidth is a partial signal descriptor that places an upper bound on the amplitude of the spectrum that falls outside the interval from f_L to f_U. *Caution:* This definition allows the magnitude of a spectrum to be smaller than the specified upper bound at some frequencies inside the bandwidth interval, but it must be less than the bound everywhere outside the bandwidth interval.

The sinusoid is an important signal because it is the building block for describing the spectra of all signals of interest. Consider the general sinusoid described by

$$v(t) = V_A \cos(2\pi f_0 t + \phi)$$

This signal has an amplitude of V_A volts, a frequency of f_0 hertz, and a phase angle of ϕ radians or degrees. It contains a single discrete frequency f_0; hence $f_U = f_L = f_0$ and $B = 0$. To visualize graphically the spectrum of the sinusoid, we plot the values shown in Figure 5–29(b). The plot of V_A versus frequency is called an **amplitude spectrum** and a plot of ϕ versus frequency is called **phase spectrum**. Both plots are called **line spectra** because component amplitudes and phase angles exist only at discrete frequencies. Note that the sinusoid is completely described by its waveform in Figure 5–29(a) or by its spectrum in Figure 5–29(b).

A discrete spectrum plot consists of vertical lines that are topped by dots. The length of the lines varies to indicate the amplitude or phase of each of the signal's spectral components. These lines have different meanings from the vertical lines topped by arrows, which are used to indicate an impulse function.

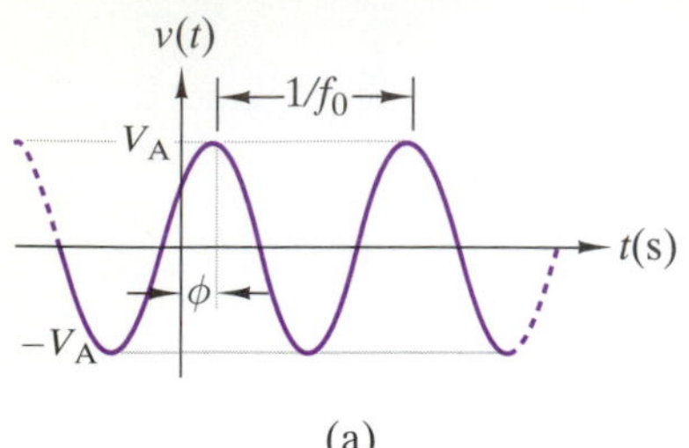

(a)

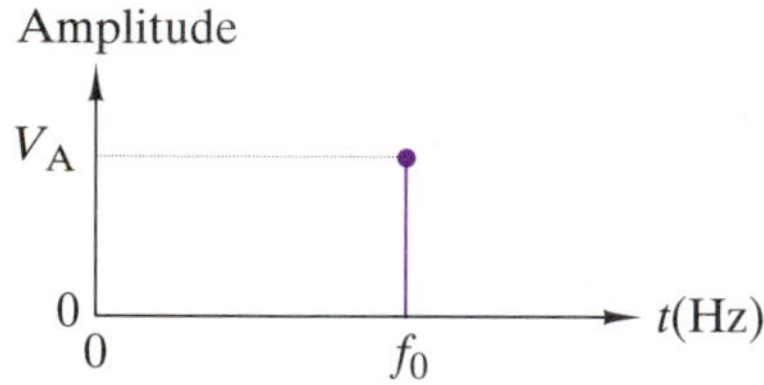

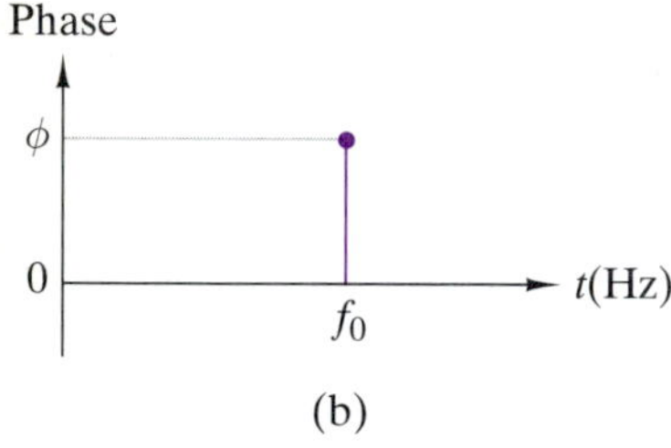

(b)

FIGURE 5–29 *(a) Sinusoidal waveform. (b) Sinusoidal spectrum.*

In many applications signals are composites of two or more sinusoids of different frequencies. For example, the touch-tone telephone dial shown in Figure 5–30 represents each digit as a mixture of two sinusoidal at different frequencies. When the "3" button is pressed the instrument transmits a mixture of sinusoids at 697 Hz and 1477 Hz. When the "5" button is pressed, the dial signal is a mixture of 770 Hz and 1336 Hz. The exact time-domain waveform of the transmitted signal is not important here. The important point is that the touch-tone dial produces signals whose frequency spectrum lies in the range from 697 Hz to 1477 Hz. Thus, we can describe the bandwidth of the dial signal as

$$B = f_U - f_L = 1477 - 697 = 780 \text{ Hz}$$

since the amplitudes of spectral components outside of this interval are essentially zero. Although the value of the bandwidth is clear in this case, it is usually not so easily calculated.

One of the sinusoid's most important properties is that periodic signals arising in engineering applications can be decomposed into a sum of sinusoids with different amplitudes, phase angles, and frequencies. The decomposition includes a dc component (the signal's average value) and sinusoids at a **fundamental frequency** f_0 and at **harmonic frequencies** nf_0 that are integer multiples of the fundamental. The frequency f_0 is called the fundamental because it determines the period of the signal $T_0 = 1/f_0$ and vice versa. The harmonic frequencies begin with the second harmonic $(2f_0)$, followed by the third harmonic $(3f_0)$, or, in general, the nth harmonic (nf_0). For example, the periodic signal

$$v(t) = 10 + 30\cos(2\pi f_0 t) + 15\sin(2\pi 2 f_0 t) - 7.5\cos(2\pi 4 f_0 t) \quad (5\text{–}37)$$

is the sum of a dc component plus three sinusoidal ac components. A plot of the waveform in Figure 5–31 reveals the periodic nature of the signal.

We associated zero frequency with the dc component in Eq. (5–37) because when $f = 0$ the sinusoidal signal $v(t) = V_A\cos(0) = V_A$. The frequency of the first ac component is the fundamental frequency, since it is the lowest nonzero frequency. The third and fourth terms in Eq. (5–37) are the

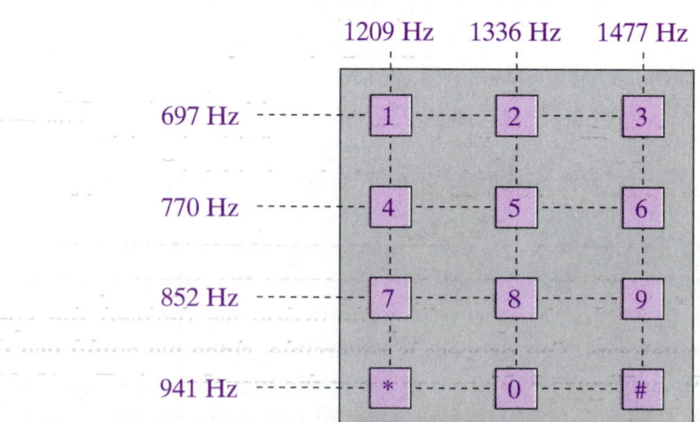

FIGURE 5–30 *Touch-tone dialing frequencies.*

second harmonic and fourth harmonic since their frequencies are $2f_0$ and $4f_0$, respectively.

The periodic signal in Eq. (5–37) contains four frequencies; 0, f_0, $2f_0$, and $4f_0$. To obtain the correct phase spectrum, we must write each term in Eq. (5–37) in the form $V_A \cos(2\pi ft + \phi)$. Using the identities $\sin x = \cos(x - 90°)$ and $-\cos x = \cos(x + 180°)$, we rewrite Eq. (5–37) in the following way:

$$v(t) = 10 + 30\cos(2\pi f_0 t) + 15\cos(2\pi 2f_0 t - 90°) + 7.5\cos(2\pi 4f_0 t + 180°) \tag{5–38}$$

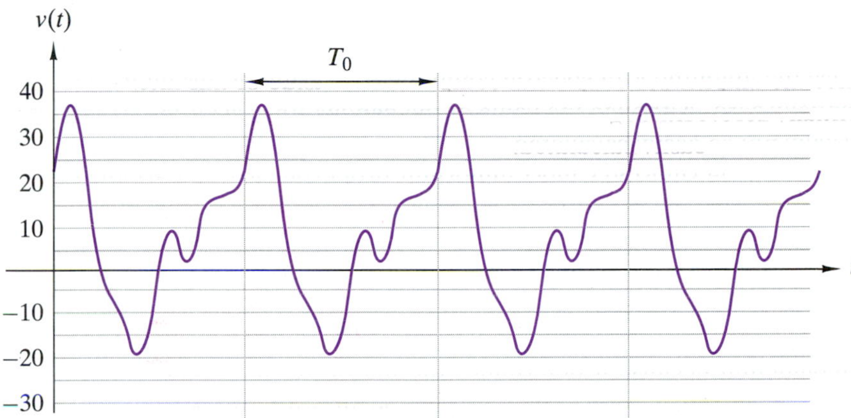

FIGURE 5–31 Periodic waveform in Eq. (5–37).

Each term is now in a standard form, so we can list the amplitude and phase angle of each component using the following format:

Frequency	0	f_0	$2f_0$	$4f_0$
Amplitude V	10	30	15	7.5
Phase angle	NA	0°	−90°	180°

(5–39)

where NA indicates that a phase angle is not applicable or does not exist.

The listing in Eq. (5–39) gives the amplitudes and phase angles of the sinusoidal components as functions of frequency. In so doing, the list defines the spectrum of the signal in Eq. (5–38). Figure 5–32 uses the data in Eq. (5–39) to display the spectrum of the signal graphically. In this case the signal contains four separate frequencies: a zero frequency or dc component, a fundamental frequency component at f_0, a second harmonic at $2f_0$, and a fourth harmonic at $4f_0$. The amplitude spectrum of this signal is zero outside the range from $f_L = 0$ to $f_U = 4f_0$; hence its bandwidth is $B = 4f_0$.

The preceding example illustrates the dual nature of periodic signals. Equation (5–38) and Figure 5–31 describe the signal waveform in the time domain, while Eq. (5–39) and Figure 5–32 describe the signal spectrum in the frequency domain. In the preceding discussion we derived the spectrum from the waveform. The process is reversible, since we could use the data in Eq. (5–39) or Figure 5–32 to construct the waveform in Eq. (5–38). The waveform and the spectrum are seen to be two sides of the same coin.

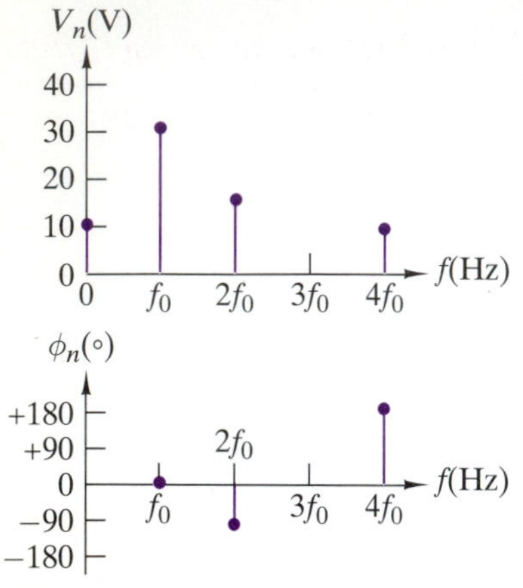

FIGURE 5–32 *Amplitude and phase plots of the spectrum in Eq. (5–39).*

They are two equivalent ways of representing and studying periodic signals.

The decomposition of signals into sums of harmonic sinusoids can be extended to any of the periodic waveforms shown in Figure 5–2. For example, the first four terms in the decomposition of the square wave are

$$v(t) = V_1 \cos(2\pi f_0 t - 90°) + \frac{V_1}{3}\cos(2\pi 3f_0 t - 90°)$$
$$+ \frac{V_1}{5}\cos(2\pi 5f_0 t - 90°) + \frac{V_1}{7}\cos(2\pi 7f_0 t - 90°) + \cdots \quad (5\text{–}40)$$

In this case the harmonics all have the same phase angle, and their amplitudes decrease with frequency as $1/n$. There is no dc component, and there are no terms at the even harmonics $2f_0$, $4f_0$, $6f_0$, ... Therefore, the spectrum of the square wave contains only odd harmonics beginning with the fundamental:

Frequency	0	f_0	$2f_0$	$3f_0$	$4f_0$	$5f_0$	. . .	nf_0	. . .
Amplitude	0	V_1	0	$V_1/3$	0	$V_1/5$	. . .	V_1/n	. . .
Phase angle	NA	−90°	NA	−90°	NA	−90°	. . .	−90°	. . .

(5–41)

Figure 5–33 shows the amplitude and phase spectrum of the square wave.

A summation of harmonic sinusoids is called a **Fourier series**. We will study Fourier analysis in Chapter 15, where we develop methods of determining the amplitude and phase angle of each of the harmonic components. At this point we are concerned not with the mathematical details of these methods, but simply the fact that such a Fourier series decomposition is possible.

The square wave can be thought of as being generated by a set of signal sources, with one source for each harmonic, as indicated by the block diagram in Figure 5–34. Once we know how to find circuit responses for a single-frequency sinusoidal input (Chapter 8), we can then use superposition to treat periodic input signals, like the square wave, containing many sinusoids. That is, we find the response to each harmonic frequency separately and then sum the individual responses to obtain the total response.

Mathematically, the decomposition in Eq. (5–41) is an infinite sum, so theoretically the square wave contains infinitely many discrete frequencies. However, the amplitudes decrease as $1/n$, so at some point the high-frequency components become negligibly small. This fact allows us to define an upper frequency f_U and a lower frequency f_L that define the bandwidth of the square wave.

In general, the lower limit for a periodic waveform is $f_L = f_0$ unless the signal has a dc component, in which case $f_L = 0$. The upper limit f_U is the frequency above which all harmonic amplitudes are less than some specified value. The specified value is usually some fraction of the amplitude of

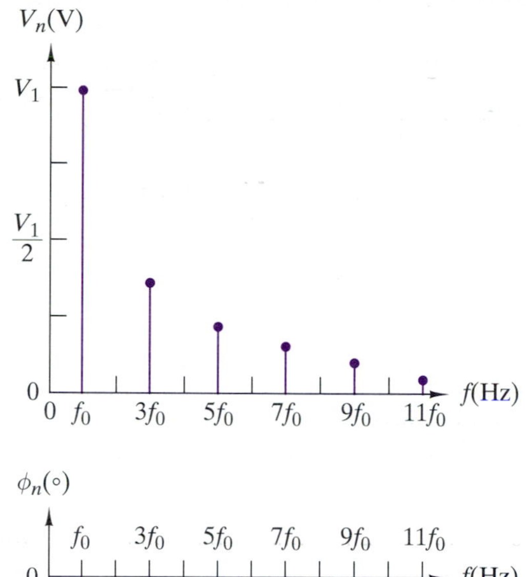

FIGURE 5–33 *Amplitude and phase plots for the square wave spectrum.*

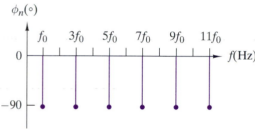

the largest ac component, which is usually the fundamental component. Using this rule, we say that f_U is the harmonic above which all higher harmonics amplitudes are less than, say, 2% of the fundamental.

The same idea is used to define the time duration of an exponential waveform. In principle, the exponential waveform endures forever. However, after about $5T_C$ the amplitude becomes negligible, and we define a finite duration. Similarly, in principle a Fourier series decomposition contains infinitely many frequencies, but in practice the spectrum has a finite bandwidth because the higher order harmonics become negligibly small.

The fact that periodic waveforms have finite bandwidths gives us important insight into signal transmission requirements. To transmit a periodic signal through a system, its bandwidth must fall within the system bandwidth. Since the system bandwidth is generally a limited and expensive resource, it is desirable to reduce the signal bandwidth as much as possible. As a case in point, for full fidelity human speech has a bandwidth of around 18 kHz, yet the telephone system works well using a reduced voice bandwidth of only about 3 kHz.

EXAMPLE 5–19

(a) Find the spectrum of the following waveform $v(t)$.
(b) Determine its bandwidth using a 5% criterion.

$$v(t) = 10 + 20\cos(2\pi 500t - 45°) + 5\sin(2\pi 1500t - 90°) + 0.25\cos(2\pi 5000t)\text{ V}$$

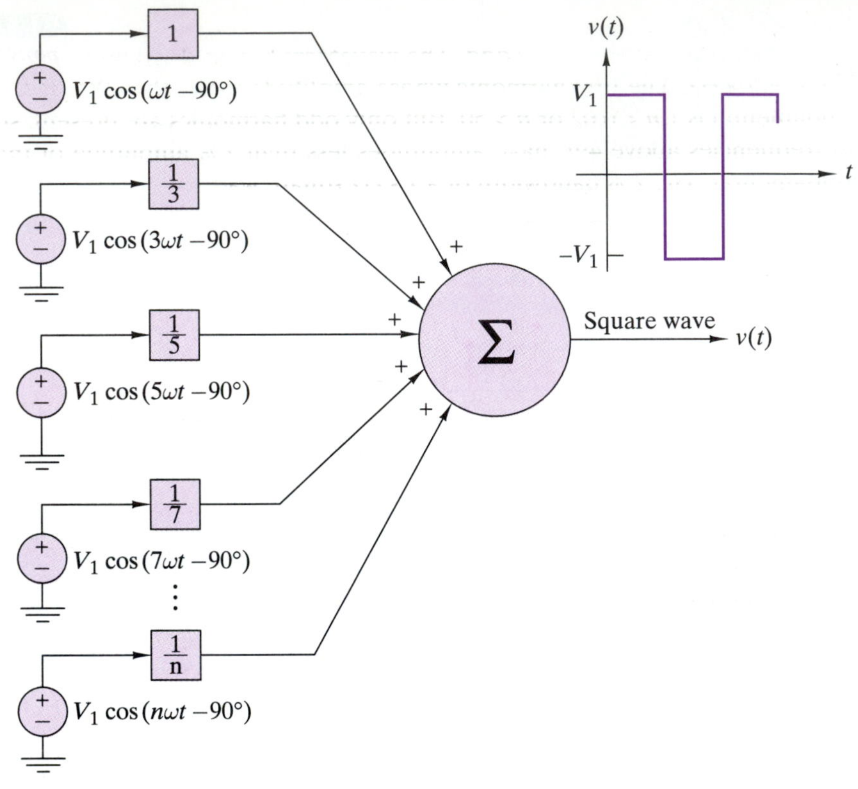

FIGURE 5–34 *Conceptual block diagram for generating a square wave.*

SOLUTION:

(a) The signal has a dc component, a fundamental frequency of 500 Hz, a third harmonic at 1500 Hz, and a tenth harmonic at 5 kHz. The third harmonic term is not written as a cosine. Using the identities

$$\sin(x - 90°) = -\cos x = \cos(x + 180°)$$

we rewrite $v(t)$ as

$$v(t) = 10 + 20\cos(2\pi 500t - 45°) + 5\cos(2\pi 1500t + 180°) + 0.25\cos(2\pi 5000t)$$

The spectrum corresponding to the waveform $v(t)$ is

Frequency (kHz)	0	0.5	1.5	5
Amplitude (V)	10	20	5	0.25
Phase angle	NA	–45°	180°	0°

(b) The spectrum has a dc component, so $f_L = 0$. The amplitude of the 5-kHz component is less than 5% of the amplitude of the fundamental $(0.05 \times 20 = 1\text{ V})$. Hence $f_U = 1.5$ kHz and $B = f_U - f_L = 1.5$ kHz. ■

EXAMPLE 5–20

Determine the bandwidth of a 1-kHz square wave using a 2% criterion.

SOLUTION:

From Eq. (5–40), $V_n = V_1/n$, n odd. The waveform has no dc component, so $f_L = f_0 = 1$ kHz. The first harmonic whose amplitude is less than 2% of the fundamental is $1/n < 0.02$ or $n > 50$. But only odd harmonics are present, so all frequencies above $49f_0$ have amplitudes less than 2% amplitude of the fundamental. The 2% bandwidth of a 1 kHz square wave is

$$B = 49f_0 - f_0 = 48f_0 = 48 \text{ kHz}$$

Exercise 5–13

Find the bandwidth of the following signals using a 10% criterion:

(a) $v(t) = 25 \sin 2\pi 20t + 10 \cos(2\pi 40t - 60°) + 5 \sin 2\pi 60t + 2 \cos 2\pi 100t$
(b) $v(t) = -5 + 10 \cos 1000t + 3 \cos 3000t + 2 \sin 9000t$
(c) $v(t) = 40 + 20 \cos 200t + 20 \sin 200t + 5 \cos 600t + 2.5 \sin(1200t + 60°)$

Answers:
(a) 40 Hz
(b) 1.432 kHz
(c) 95.5 Hz

SUMMARY

- A waveform is an equation or graph that describes a voltage or current as a function of time. Most signals of interest in electrical engineering can be derived using three basic waveforms: the step, exponential, and sinusoid.
- The step function is defined by its amplitude and time-shift parameters. The impulse, step, and ramp are called singularity functions and are often used as test inputs for circuit analysis purposes.
- The exponential waveform is defined by its amplitude, time constant, and time-shift parameter. For practical purposes, the duration of the exponential waveform is five time constants.
- A sinusoid can be defined in terms of three types of parameters: *amplitude* (either V_A or the Fourier coefficients a and b), *time shift* (either T_S or the phase angle ϕ), and *time/frequency* (either T_0 or f_0 or ω_0).
- Many composite waveforms can be derived using the three basic waveforms. Some examples are the impulse, ramp, damped ramp, damped sinusoid, exponential rise, and double exponential.
- Partial descriptors are used to classify or describe important signal attributes. Two important temporal attributes are periodicity and causality. Periodic waveforms repeat themselves every T_0 seconds. Causal signals are zero for $t < 0$. Some important amplitude descriptors are peak value V_p, peak-to-peak value V_{pp}, average value V_{avg}, and root-mean-square value V_{rms}.

EXERCISE (5-13)
(a) $v(t) = 25\sin(2\pi 20t) + 10\cos(2\pi 40t - 60°) + 5\sin(2\pi 60t) + 2\cos(2\pi 100t)$
sin → cos
$= 25\cos(2\pi 20t - 90°) + 10\cos(2\pi 40t - 60°) + 5\cos(2\pi 60t - 90°) + 2\cos(2\pi 100t)$
$2\pi 20t = 2\pi f_0 t \Rightarrow f_0 = 20$ HZ
$2\pi 40t = 2f_0$ $2\pi 60t = 3f_0$
$2\pi 100t = 5f_0$
10% Rule
$\frac{1}{n} < 0.10 \Rightarrow \frac{1}{0.10} = n = 10$
$V_n = \frac{V}{n} = \frac{25}{10} = 2.5$
⇒ FIRST COMPONENT < 10%
$= 5\cos(2\pi 60t - 90°) = 3f_0$
$BW = 3f_0 - f_0 = 2f_0 = 2(20) = 40HZ$
$f_L - f_u = f_0 - f_u = 40KHZ$
(b) $-5 + 10\cos(1000t) + 3\cos(3000t) + 2\sin(9000t)$
sin → cos
$v(t) = -5 + 10\cos(1000t) + 3\cos(3000t) + 2\cos(9000t - 90°)$
$1000t = 2\pi f_0 t \Rightarrow f_0 = \frac{1000}{2\pi} = 159.155$
$9000t = 9(159.155) = 1432.9$ HZ
COMPONENT < 10%
$V_n = \frac{V_1}{n} = \frac{10}{10} = 1$
(c) $200 = 2\pi f_0 \Rightarrow f_0 = 31.83$ HZ
$V_n = \frac{V_1}{10} = \frac{20}{10} = 2$
$3(31.83) = 95.5$ HZ
$6(31.83) = 190.98$ HZ

- A spectrum is an equation or graph that defines the amplitudes and phase angles of sinusoidal components contained in a signal. The signal bandwidth (B) is a partial descriptor that defines the range of frequencies outside of which the component amplitudes are less than a specified value. Periodic signals can be resolved into a dc component and a sum of ac components at harmonic frequencies.

EN ROUTE OBJECTIVES AND ASSOCIATED PROBLEMS

ERO 5–1 BASIC WAVEFORMS (SECTS. 5–2, 5–3, 5–4)

Given an equation, graph, or word description of a step, exponential, or sinusoid waveform,

(a) Construct an alternative description of the waveform.
(b) Find new waveforms by summing, integrating, or differentiating the given waveform.

5–1 Graph the following step function waveforms:
(a) $v_1(t) = 5u(t)$
(b) $v_2(t) = -5u(t-1)$
(c) $v_3(t) = 5u(t+1)$
(d) $v_4(t) = -10u(t-1)$

5–2 Graph the waveforms obtained by adding the waveforms in Problem 5–1.
(a) $v_A(t) = v_1(t) + v_2(t)$
(b) $v_B(t) = v_1(t) + v_3(t)$
(c) $v_C(t) = v_1(t) + v_4(t)$
(d) $v_D(t) = v_2(t) + v_3(t)$

5–3 Graph the waveforms obtained by integrating and differentiating each of the waveforms in Problem 5–1.

5–4 A waveform $v(t)$ is zero for t in the range $5 \text{ ms} \geq t \geq 3 \text{ ms}$ and +5 V elsewhere. Write an equation for the waveform using step functions.

5–5 Figure P5–5 shows an approximation to a unit step function that increases linearly from zero to one during the interval $0 \leq t \leq \Delta t$ and is unity for $t > \Delta t$. Plot the derivative of the waveform and show that it has an area of unity. What waveform does the derivative approach as Δt approaches zero?

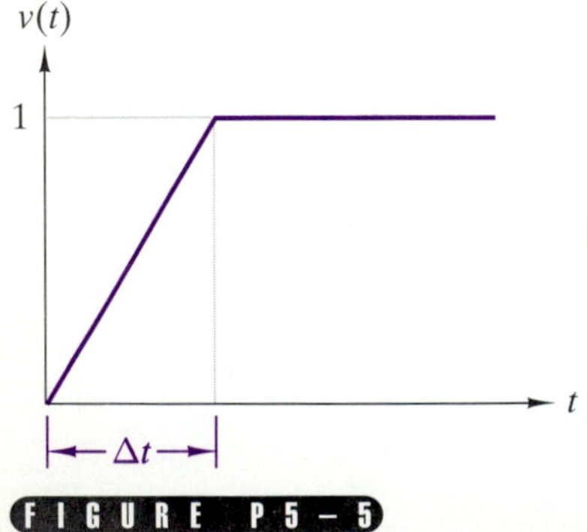

FIGURE P5–5

5–6 Determine the amplitude and time constant of each of the following exponential waveforms. Graph each of the waveforms.
(a) $v_1(t) = [10\, e^{-2t}]u(t)$ **(b)** $v_2(t) = [10\, e^{-t/2}]u(t)$
(c) $v_3(t) = [-10\, e^{-20t}]u(t)$ **(d)** $v_4(t) = [-10\, e^{-t/20}]u(t)$

5–7 Graph the exponential waveform obtained by differentiating and integrating the exponential waveforms in Problem 5–6.

5–8 An exponential waveform starts at $t = 0$ and decays to 5 V at $t = 4$ ms and 3 V at $t = 6$ ms. Find the amplitude and time constant of the waveform.

5–9 An exponential waveform with $T_C = 5$ ms has a value of 5 V at $t = 2.5$ ms. What is its value when $t = 3.5$ ms?

5–10 Show that the exponential waveform $v(t) = V_A e^{-\alpha t}u(t)$ is a solution of the following first-order differential equation:

$$\frac{dv(t)}{dt} + \alpha v(t) = 0$$

5–11 Determine the period, frequency, amplitude, time shift, and phase angle of the following sinusoids. Graph the waveform.

(a) $v_1(t) = 10\cos(2000\pi t) + 10\sin(2000\pi t)$
(b) $v_2(t) = -30\cos(2000\pi t) - 20\sin(2000\pi t)$
(c) $v_3(t) = 10\cos(2\pi t/10) - 10\sin(2\pi t/10)$
(d) $v_4(t) = -20\cos(800\pi t) + 30\sin(800\pi t)$

5–12 Determine the frequency, period, amplitude, time shift, and phase angle of the sum of the first two sinusoids in Problem 5–11.

5–13 Write an equation for a sinusoid with an amplitude of 150 V, a period of 200 ms, and its first positive peak at $t = 50$ ms. Graph the waveform.

5–14 A sinusoid has a frequency of 5 MHz, a value of 10 V at $t = 0$, and reaches its first positive peak at $t = 25$ ns. Determine its amplitude, phase angle, and Fourier coefficients.

5–15 Determine the frequency, period, and Fourier coefficients of the following sinusoids:

(a) $v_1(t) = 20\cos(4000\pi t - 180°)$
(b) $v_2(t) = 20\cos(4000\pi t - 90°)$
(c) $v_3(t) = 30\cos(2\pi t/400 - 45°)$
(d) $v_4(t) = 60\sin(2000\pi t + 45°)$

5–16 Determine the frequency, period, phase angle, and amplitude of the sum of the first two sinusoids in Problem 5–15.

5–17 Show that the sinusoid $v(t) = a\cos\omega t + b\sin\omega t$ is a solution of the following second-order differential equation:

$$\frac{d^2v(t)}{dt^2} + \omega^2 v(t) = 0$$

ERO 5–2 COMPOSITE WAVEFORMS (SECT. 5–5)

Given an equation, graph, or word description of a composite waveform,

(a) Construct an alternative description of the waveform.
(b) Find new waveforms by summing, integrating, differentiating, or clipping the given waveform.

5–18 Graph the following waveforms:

(a) $v_1(t) = 20\,[1 - e^{-1000t}]u(t)$
(b) $v_2(t) = [10 - 20e^{-1000t}]u(t)$
(c) $v_3(t) = 20\,[1 - 2\sin(100\pi t)]u(t)$
(d) $v_4(t) = 20\,[1 - e^{-20t}\sin(100\pi t)]u(t)$

5–19 Graph the following ramp waveforms. Then graph and write an equation for the derivative of each waveform.

(a) $v_1(t) = tu(t) - (t-2)u(t-2)$
(b) $v_2(t) = tu(t) - 2(t-1)u(t-1) + (t-2)u(t-2)$

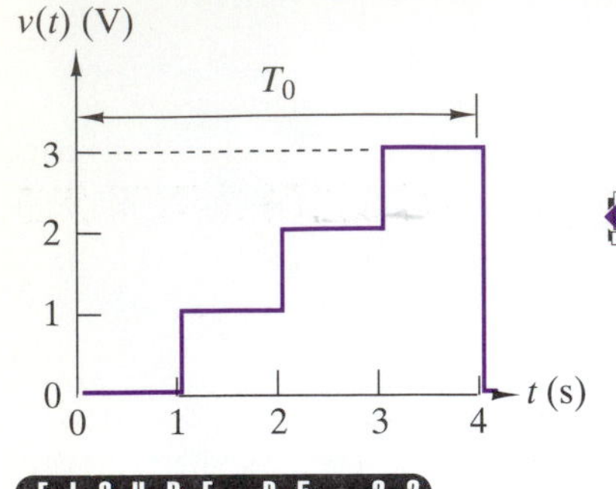

FIGURE P5–22

5–20 A waveform is known to be of the form $v(t) = V_A - V_B\, e^{-\alpha t}$. At $t = 0$ the value of the waveform is 5 V, at $t = 5$ μs its value is 7.5 V, and it approaches 10 V for large values of t. Find the values of the parameters V_A, V_B, and α, and then graph the waveform.

5–21 A waveform is known to be of the form $v(t) = V_A e^{-\alpha t} \sin \beta t$. The waveform periodically passes through zero every 2.5 ms. At $t = 1$ ms its value is 3.5 V and at $t = 2$ ms it is 0.8 V. Find the values of the parameters V_A, α, and β, and then graph the waveform.

5–22 Write an equation for the first cycle of the waveform in Figure P5–22, and then graph the waveform obtained by differentiating the signal.

5–23 Write an equation for the first cycle of the waveform in Figure P5–23, and then graph the waveform obtained by integrating the signal.

FIGURE P5–23

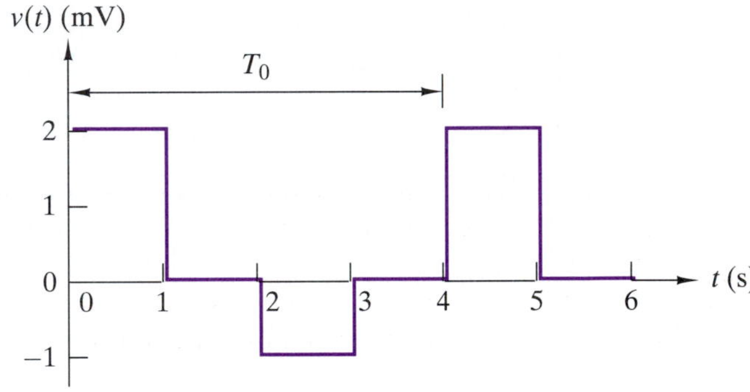

5–24 A waveform is known to be of the form $v(t) = V_A - V_B \sin \beta t$. At $t = 0$ the value of the waveform is 10 V, and it periodically reaches a minimum value of –2 V every 25 μs. Find the value of the parameters V_A, V_B, and β, and then graph the waveform.

5–25 Write an equation for a waveform that has the same V_{pp}, V_{avg}, and T_0 as the signal in Figure P5–25. Graph the waveform obtained by differentiating your signal.

FIGURE P5–25

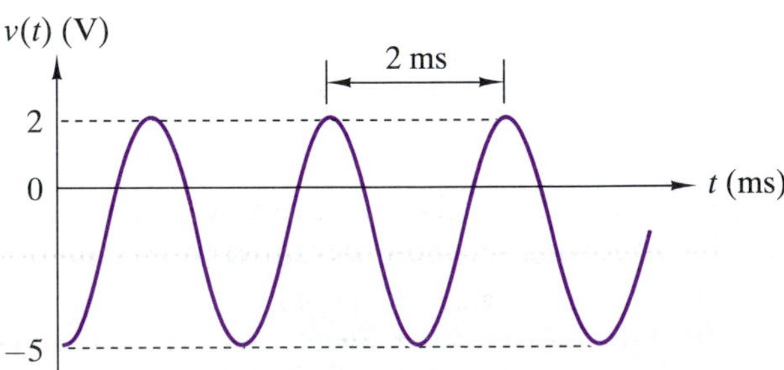

5–26 A waveform is known to be a damped ramp of the form $v(t) = V_A(t/T_C)e^{-\alpha t}$. The value of the waveform is 5 V at $t = 1$ ms and again at $t = 3$ ms. Find the value of the parameters V_A and T_C, and then graph the waveform.

5–27 Write an equation for the first cycle of the waveform in Figure P5–27 and then graph the waveform obtained by differentiating the signal.

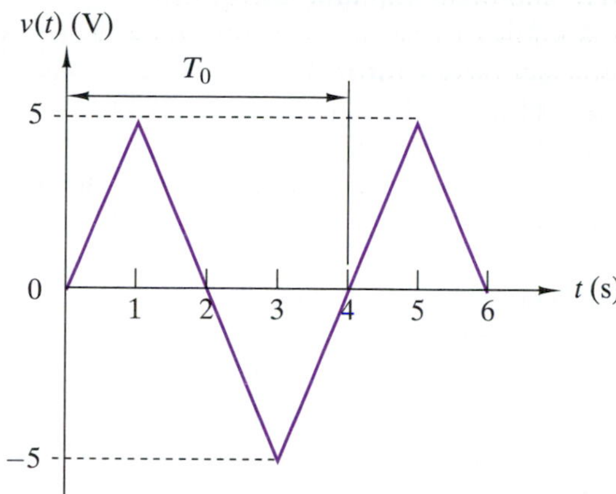

FIGURE P5–27

5–28 The waveform defined as $\text{sgn}(t) = u(t) - u(-t)$ is called a signum function. Construct graphs of the waveforms $v_1(t) = V_A[\text{sgn}(t) - \text{sgn}(t - T_0)]$ and $v_2(t) = V_A\,[\sin(2\pi t/T_0)]\text{sgn}(t - T_0)$.

5–29 Figure P5–29 shows a plot of the waveform $v(t) = V_A[e^{-\alpha t} \sin \beta t]u(t)$. Find the value of the parameters V_A, α, and β.

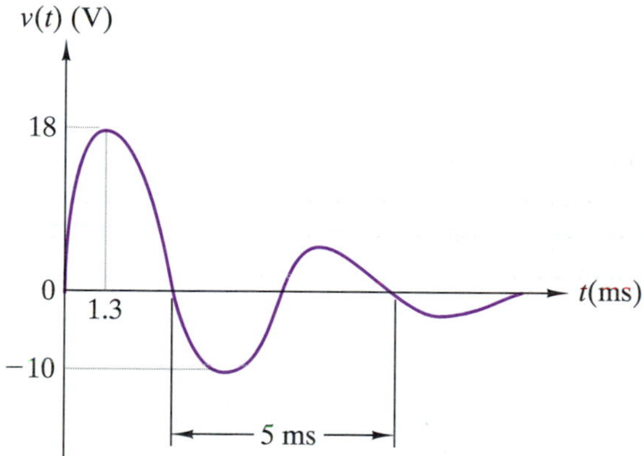

FIGURE P5–29

5–30 Show that the damped sinusoid $v(t) = V_A e^{-\alpha t} \sin \beta t$ is a solution of the following second-order differential equation:

$$\frac{d^2v(t)}{dt^2} + 2\alpha \frac{dv(t)}{dt} + (\alpha^2 + \beta^2)v(t) = 0$$

ERO 5–3 WAVEFORM PARTIAL DESCRIPTORS (SECT. 5–6)

Given a complete description of a basic or composite waveform,

(a) Classify the waveform as periodic or aperiodic and causal or noncausal.
(b) Find the applicable partial waveform descriptors.

5–31 Classify the waveforms as periodic or aperiodic and causal or noncausal. Determine V_p and V_{pp} for all of the waveforms. Determine V_{rms} and V_{avg} for those waveforms that are periodic. Determine the duration of those waveforms that are causal.

(a) $v_1(t) = [10 - 5e^{-100t}]u(t)$

(b) $v_2(t) = 100[e^{-20t}\sin(2000\pi t)]u(t)$

(c) $v_3(t) = 15\cos(2000\pi t) - 5\sin(2000\pi t)$

(d) $v_4(t) = 10\cos(1000\pi t)[u(t) - u(t-1)]$

5–32 Classify the waveforms as periodic or aperiodic and causal or noncausal. Determine V_p, V_{pp}, V_{rms}, and V_{avg} for each of the following waveforms:

(a) $v_1(t) = 10\cos(2000\pi t) + 10\sin(2000\pi t)$

(b) $v_2(t) = -30\cos(2000\pi t) - 20\sin(2000\pi t)$

(c) $v_3(t) = 10\cos(2\pi t/10) - 10\sin(2\pi t/10)$

(d) $v_4(t) = -20\cos(800\pi t) + 30\sin(800\pi t)$

5–33 Classify the waveforms as periodic or aperiodic and causal or noncausal. Determine V_p and V_{pp} for all of the waveforms. Determine V_{rms} and V_{avg} for those waveforms that are periodic.

(a) $v_1(t) = 20\,[1 - e^{-1000t}]u(t)$

(b) $v_2(t) = [10 - 20e^{-1000t}]u(t)$

(c) $v_3(t) = 20\,[1 - 2\sin(100\pi t)]u(t)$

(d) $v_4(t) = 20\,[1 - 2\sin(100\pi t)]$

5–34 Determine V_p, V_{pp}, V_{rms}, and V_{avg} for the waveform in Figure P5–22.

5–35 Determine V_p, V_{pp}, V_{rms}, and V_{avg} for the waveform in Figure P5–23.

5–36 A signal of the form $v(t) = V_A + V_B\sin(\beta t)$ has $V_p = 15$ V and $V_{avg} =$ 5 V. Find the values of V_A and V_B.

5–37 The waveform $v(t) = V_0 + 10\sin 200\pi t$ is applied at the input of an OP AMP voltage follower with $V_{CC} = \pm 15$ V. What range of values of the dc component V_0 ensures that the OP AMP does not become saturate?

5–38 A loudspeaker has an average power rating of 100 W and a resistance of 8 Ω. What is the maximum rms voltage that can be applied to the speaker? If the applied waveform is a sinusoid, what is the maximum peak-to-peak voltage?

5–39 A sinusoidal signal passes through a squaring circuit whose output is

$$v_O(t) = V_A\sin^2(2\pi t/T_0)$$

Sketch the output waveform and find the values of V_p, V_{pp}, and V_{avg}.

5–40 The crest factor of a periodic waveform is defined as the ratio of its peak value to its rms value. What is the crest factor of a sinusoid? What is the crest factor of a square wave?

ERO 5–4 SIGNAL SPECTRA (SECT. 5–7)

(a) Given a waveform expressed as a sum of sinusoids, construct a plot of its spectrum and find its bandwidth using a specified criterion.

(b) Given an equation or graph of the spectrum of a periodic signal, find its bandwidth and write an expression for its waveform as a sum of harmonic sinusoids.

5–41 Construct the amplitude and phase plots of the spectrum of each of the following waveforms, and determine their bandwidths using a 5% criterion. Repeat using $v(t) = v_1(t) + v_2(t)$.

(a) $v_1(t) = 4 + 5\sin 2\pi 2500t - 2\cos 2\pi 5000t + 0.2\sin 2\pi 10^4 t$ V

(b) $v_2(t) = 3\cos(2\pi 1250t - 60°) - 2\sin 2\pi 2500t + \cos 2\pi 5000t$ V

5–42 Construct the amplitude and phase plots of the spectrum of each of the following waveforms, and determine their bandwidths using a 5% criterion. Repeat using $v(t) = v_1(t) + v_2(t)$.

(a) $v_1(t) = -20 + 40\cos 2\pi 1000t + 10\cos 2\pi 2000t + 2.5\cos 2\pi 4000t$ V

(b) $v_2(t) = 20 + 40\sin(2\pi 1000t - 90°) + 30\cos 2\pi 3000t - 1.6\cos 2\pi 5000t$ V

5–43 Figure P5–43 shows the amplitude and phase plots of the spectrum of a periodic signal. Write an equation for the signal waveform and sketch its time variation. Determine the signal bandwidth using a 10% criterion.

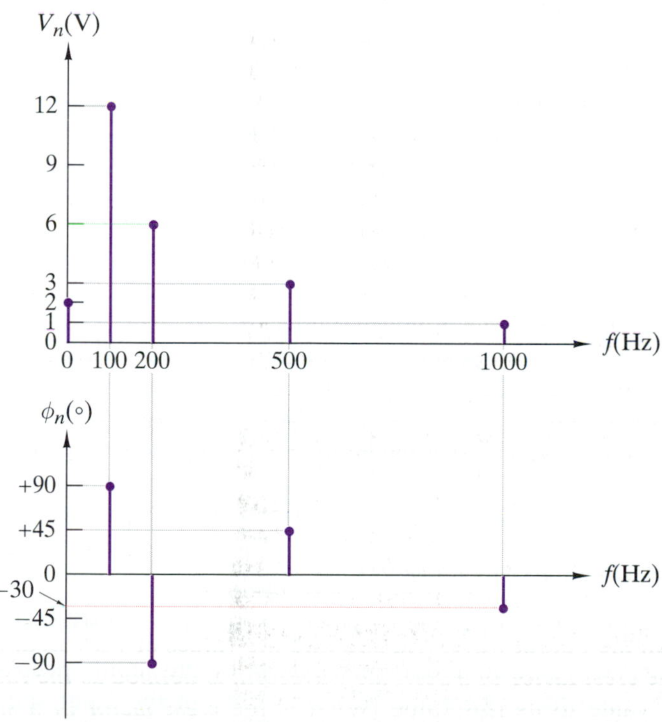

FIGURE P5–43

5–44 The amplitude and phase angles of the nth (n = 1, 2, 3, . . .) harmonic of a period waveform with an average value of $V_A/2$ are

$$V_n = \frac{V_A}{n\pi} \qquad \phi_n = 90°$$

Using $T_0 = 0.2$ ms and $V_A = 5$ V, determine the signal bandwidth using a 10% criterion. Write an equation for the waveform using only those frequency components that lie within this bandwidth.

5–45 The amplitude and phase angles of the nth ($n = 1, 2, 3, \ldots$) harmonic of a period waveform with zero average value are

$$V_n = \frac{8V_A}{(n\pi)^2} \qquad \phi_n = 0^\circ, \quad n \text{ odd}$$
$$V_n = 0, \qquad n \text{ even}$$

Using $T_0 = 0.2$ ms and $V_A = 5$ V, determine the signal bandwidth using a 10% criterion. Write an equation for the waveform using only those frequency components that lie within this bandwidth.

5–46 A differentiator is a linear signal processor whose output is proportional to the time derivative of its input. For example, the input–output relationship for a certain differentiator is

$$v_O = \frac{1}{1000}\frac{dv_{IN}(t)}{dt}$$

Using the input voltage

$$v_{IN}(t) = 10 \cos 200t + 2 \cos 600t + \cos 1000t + 0.3 \cos 3000t + 0.02 \cos 10^4 t$$

construct the amplitude and phase plots for the input spectrum and output spectrum. Determine the bandwidths of the input and output signals using a 5% criterion, and discuss the spectral changes caused by the differentiator.

5–47 An ideal lowpass filter acts like an amplifier with a gain $K = 1$ for sinusoidal inputs with $\omega \leq \omega_C$, and a gain $K = 0$ for input with $\omega > \omega_C$. For a filter with $\omega_C = 4$ krad/s and an input

$$v_{IN}(t) = 10 + 10\cos(2\pi 500t) + 3\cos(2\pi 1000t) + 2\cos(2\pi 4000t)$$

construct the amplitude plots of the input spectrum and output spectrum. Determine the bandwidths of the input and output signals using a 5% criterion, and discuss the spectral changes caused by the lowpass filter.

5–48 An ideal time delay is a signal processor whose output at any time t is equal to the earlier input at time $t - T_D$; that is, $v_O(t) = v_{IN}(t - T_D)$. For a time delay of $T_D = 1$ ms and an input

$$v_{IN}(t) = 10 + 10\cos(2\pi 500t) + 3\cos(2\pi 1000t) + 2\cos(2\pi 4000t)$$

construct the amplitude and phase plots of the input spectrum and output spectrum. Determine the bandwidths of the input and output signals using a 5% criterion, and discuss the spectral changes caused by the time delay.

5–49 Use a spreadsheet or math solver to plot of the sum of the first 10 harmonics of the periodic signal defined in Problem 5–44. Use a time interval $0 \leq t \leq 2T_0$. Can you recognize this waveform as one of the waveforms shown in Figure 5–2?

5–50 Repeat Problem 5–49 using the signal defined in Problem 5–45.

CHAPTER-INTEGRATING PROBLEMS

5–51 A RESISTOR POWER WAVEFORM

This problem deals with the waveform of the power delivered to a resistor by a sinusoidal current. Derive an expression for the waveform of the instantaneous power $p(t)$ delivered to a resistor R by a sinusoidal current $i(t) = I_A \sin(2\pi t/T_0)$. Show that $p(t)$ is periodic with a period of $T_0/2$. Find peak, peak-to-peak, and average values of $p(t)$.

5–52 A ANALOG-TO-DIGITAL CONVERSION

Figure P5–52 shows a circuit diagram of an analog-to-digital converter of the type discussed in Example 4–24. Each of the open-loop OP AMPs operates as a comparator whose output is $V_{OH} = 5$ V when $v_P > v_N$ and $V_{OL} = 0$ V when $v_P < v_N$. The input signal $v_S(t)$ is applied to all of the noninverting inputs simultaneously. The voltages applied to the inverting inputs come from the four-resistor voltage divider shown. For an input voltage of $v_S(t) = 20e^{-100t}$ V, express the output voltages $v_A(t)$, $v_B(t)$, $v_C(t)$, and $v_D(t)$ in terms of step functions.

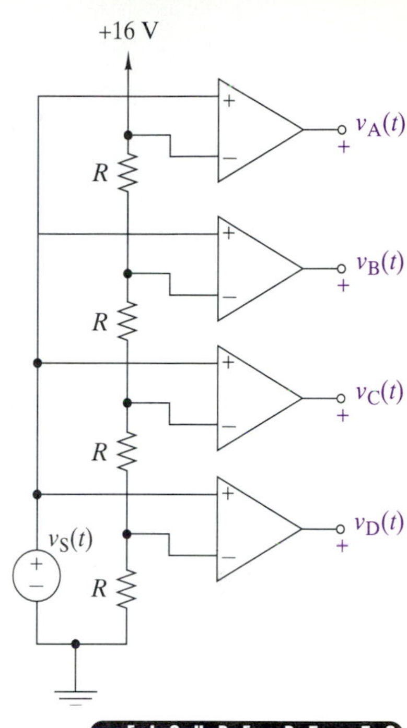

FIGURE P5–52

5–53 A DIGITAL-TO-ANALOG CONVERSION

Figure P5–53 shows a 3-bit digital-to-analog converter of the type discussed in Sect. 4–6. The circuit consists of an R-$2R$ ladder connected at the input to the inverting input to the OP AMP. The ladder circuit is driven by three digital input signals $v_1(t)$, $v_2(t)$, and $v_3(t)$. These input signals can be expressed in terms of step functions as follows:

$$v_1(t) = 5u(t) - 5u(t-1) \text{ V}$$

$$v_2(t) = 5u(t) - 5u(t-2) + 5u(t-4) - 5u(t-5) \text{ V}$$

$$v_3(t) = 5u(t-1) - 5u(t-4) + 5u(t-5) \text{ V}$$

(a) Show that the input–output relationship for the OP AMP circuit is

$$v_O(t) = -\frac{R_F}{8R}[4v_1 + 2v_2 + v_3]$$

(b) Plot the input waveforms on separate plots, and stack the plots on top of the other with $v_1(t)$ at the bottom and $v_3(t)$ at the top. Stacked plots of digital signals are termed a timing diagram.

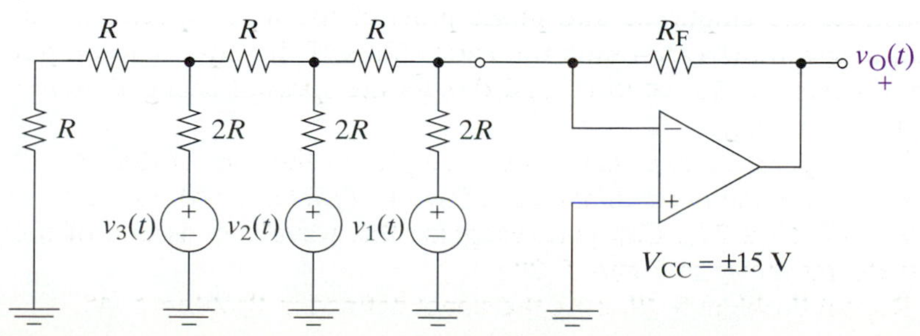

FIGURE P5–53

(c) For $R_F = R$, use the input timing diagram in (a) and the input–output relationship in (b) to obtain a plot of the output voltage in the range $0 < t < 6$ s.

5–54 D SIGNAL PROCESSOR DESIGN

An ac signal source produces a sinusoidal output with an amplitude of 1 mV (rms). The only dc source available produces ±15 V dc. Design an OP AMP circuit that uses these inputs and produces an output with an average value of –5 V and a 20-V peak-to-peak swing.

5–55 A PARTIAL SIGNAL DESCRIPTORS

A signal is defined as $v(t) = V_0 + v_A(t)$, where V_0 is a constant and $v_A(t)$ is periodic with zero average value.

(a) Show that $v(t)$ is periodic.

(b) Show that the peak-to-peak value of $v(t)$ is $V_{pp} = V_{App}$.

(c) Show that the average value of $v(t)$ is $V_{avg} = V_0$.

(d) Show that the rms value of $v(t)$ is $V_{rms} = \sqrt{V_0^2 + V_{Arms}^2}$.

CHAPTER 6

CAPACITANCE AND INDUCTANCE

From the foregoing facts, it appears that a current of electricity is produced, for an instant, in a helix of copper wire surrounding a piece of soft iron whenever magnetism is induced in the iron; also that an instantaneous current in one or the other direction accompanies every change in the magnetic intensity of the iron.

Joseph Henry, 1831,
American Physicist

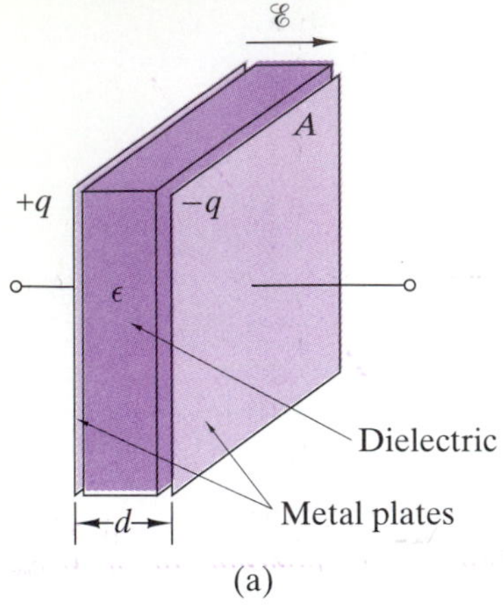

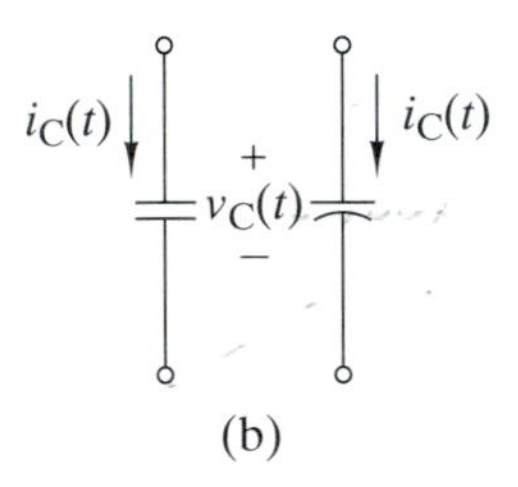

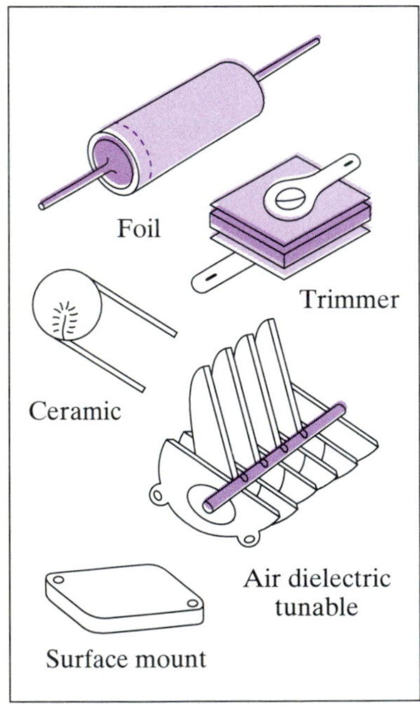

FIGURE 6–1 *The capacitor: (a) Parallel plate device. (b) Circuit symbol. (c) Example devices.*

Joseph Henry (1797–1878) and the British physicist Michael Faraday (1791–1867) independently discovered magnetic induction almost simultaneously. The foregoing quotation is Henry's summary of the experiments leading to his discovery of magnetic induction. Although Henry and Faraday used similar apparatus and observed almost the same results, Henry was the first to recognize the importance of the discovery. The unit of circuit inductance (henry) honors Henry, while the mathematical generalization of magnetic induction is called Faraday's law. Michael Faraday had wide-ranging interests and performed many fundamental experiments in chemistry and electricity. His electrical experiments often used capacitors, or Leyden jars as they were called in those days. Faraday was a meticulous experimenter, and his careful characterization of these devices may be the reason that the unit of capacitance (the farad) honors Faraday.

The dynamic circuit responses involve memory effects that cannot be explained by the circuit elements we included in resistance circuits. The two new circuit elements required to explain memory effects are the capacitor and the inductor. The purpose of this chapter is to introduce the *i–v* characteristics of these dynamic elements and to explore circuit applications that illustrate dynamic behavior.

The first two sections of this chapter develop the device constraints for the linear capacitor and inductor. The third section is a circuit application in which resistors, capacitors, and operational amplifiers (OP AMPs) perform waveform integration and differentiation. The fourth section shows that capacitors or inductors connected in series or parallel can be replaced by a single equivalent capacitance or inductance.

The fifth section covers mutual inductance effects in which a time-varying current in one inductor induces a voltage in another inductor. Mutual inductance is the basis for a widely used electrical device called a transformer, whose ideal model is developed in the last section.

6–1 THE CAPACITOR

A capacitor is a dynamic element involving the time variation of an electric field produced by a voltage. Figure 6–1(a) shows the parallel plate capacitor, which is the simplest physical form of a capacitive device. Figure 6–1 also shows two alternative circuit symbols and sketches of actual devices. Some of the physical features of commercially available devices are given in Appendix A.

Electrostatics shows that a uniform electric field $\mathscr{E}(t)$ exists between the metal plates in Figure 6–1(a) when a voltage exists across the capacitor.[1] The electric field produces charge separation with equal and opposite charges appearing on the capacitor plates. When the separation d is small compared with the dimension of the plates, the electric field between the plates is

1 An electric field is a vector quantity. In Figure 6-1(a) the field is confined to the space between the two plates and is perpendicular to the plates.

$$\mathscr{E}(t) = \frac{q(t)}{\varepsilon A} \quad (6\text{–}1)$$

where ε is the permittivity of the dielectric, A is the area of the plates, and $q(t)$ is the magnitude of the electric charge on each plate. The relationship between the electric field and the voltage across the capacitor $v_C(t)$ is given by

$$\mathscr{E}(t) = \frac{v_C(t)}{d} \quad (6\text{–}2)$$

Substituting Eq. (6–2) into Eq. (6–1) and solving for the charge $q(t)$ yields

$$q(t) = \left[\frac{\varepsilon A}{d}\right] v_C(t) \quad (6\text{–}3)$$

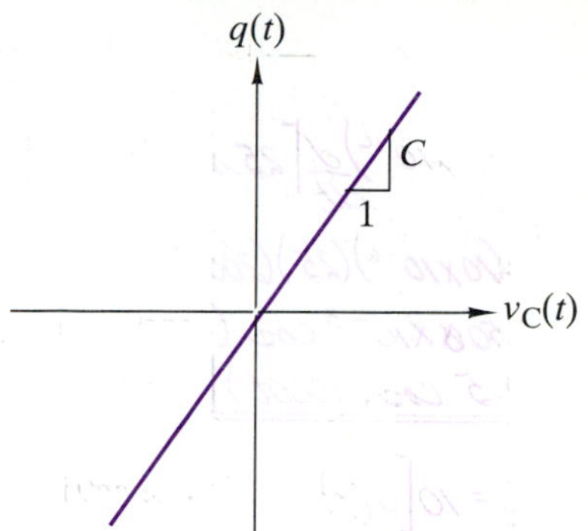

FIGURE 6–2 *Graph of the defining relationship of a linear capacitor.*

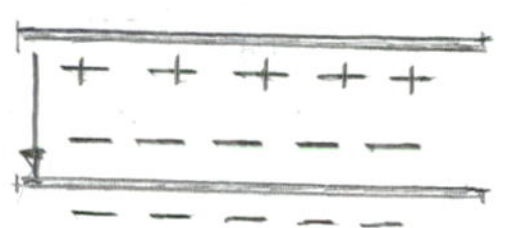

The proportionality constant inside the brackets in this equation is the **capacitance** C of the capacitor. That is, by definition,

$$C = \frac{\varepsilon A}{d} \quad (6\text{–}4)$$

The unit of capacitance is the **farad** (F), a term that honors the British physicist Michael Faraday. Values of capacitance range from a few pF (10^{-12} F) in semiconductor devices to tens of mF (10^{-3} F) in industrial capacitor banks. Using Eq. (6–4), the defining relationship for the capacitor becomes

$$q(t) = Cv_C(t) \quad (6\text{–}5)$$

Figure 6–2 graphically displays the element constraint in Eq. (6–5). The graph points out that the capacitor is a linear element since the defining relationship between voltage and charge is a straight line through the origin.

I–V RELATIONSHIP

To express the element constraint in terms of voltage and current, we differentiate Eq. (6–5) with respect to time t:

$$\frac{dq(t)}{dt} = \frac{d[Cv_C(t)]}{dt}$$

Since C is constant and $i_C(t)$ is the time derivative of $q(t)$, we obtain a capacitor i–v relationship in the form

$$i_C(t) = C\frac{dv_C(t)}{dt} \quad (6\text{–}6)$$

The relationship assumes that the reference marks for the current and voltage follow the passive sign convention shown in Figure 6–3.

+ $v_C(t)$ –
$i_C(t)$ C

FIGURE 6–3 *Capacitor current and voltage.*

The time derivative in Eq. (6–6) means the current is zero when the voltage across the capacitor is constant, and vice versa. In other words, the capacitor acts like an open circuit ($i_C = 0$) when dc excitations are applied. The capacitor is a dynamic element because the current is zero unless the voltage is changing. However, a discontinuous change in voltage would require an infinite current, which is physically impossible. Therefore, the capacitor voltage must be a continuous function of time.

Equation (6–6) relates the capacitor current to the rate of change of the capacitor voltage. To express the voltage in terms of the current, we multiply both sides of Eq. (6–6) by dt, solve for the differential dv_C, and integrate:

$$\int dv_C = \frac{1}{C}\int i_C(t)dt$$

Selecting the integration limits requires some discussion. We assume that at some time t_0 the voltage across the capacitor $v_C(t_0)$ is known and we want to determine the voltage at some later time $t > t_0$. Therefore, the integration limits are

$$\int_{v_C(t_0)}^{v_C(t)} dv_C = \int_{t_0}^{t} i_C(x)dx$$

where x is a dummy integration variable. Integrating the left side of this equation yields

$$v_C(t) = v_C(t_0) + \frac{1}{C}\int_{t_0}^{t} i_C(x)dx \tag{6–7}$$

In practice, the time t_0 is established by a physical event such as closing a switch or the start of a particular clock pulse. Nothing is lost in the integration in Eq. (6–7) if we arbitrarily define t_0 to be zero. Using $t_0 = 0$ in Eq. (6–7) yields

$$v_C(t) = v_C(0) + \frac{1}{C}\int_{0}^{t} i_C(x)dx \tag{6–8}$$

Equation (6–8) is the integral form of the capacitor i–v constraint. Both the integral form and the derivative form in Eq. (6–6) assume that the reference marks for current and voltage follow the passive sign convention in Figure 6–3.

POWER AND ENERGY

With the passive sign convention the capacitor power is

$$p_C(t) = i_C(t)v_C(t) \tag{6–9}$$

Using Eq. (6–6) to eliminate $i_C(t)$ from Eq. (6–9) yields the capacitor power in the form

$$p_C(t) = Cv_C(t)\frac{dv_C(t)}{dt} = \frac{d}{dt}[{}^1\!/_2 Cv_C^2(t)] \tag{6–10}$$

This equation shows that the power can be either positive or negative because the capacitor voltage and its time rate of change can have opposite signs. With the passive sign convention, a positive sign means the element absorbs power, while a negative sign means the element delivers power. The ability to deliver power implies that the capacitor can store energy.

To determine the stored energy, we note that the expression for power in Eq. (6–10) is a perfect derivative. Since power is the time rate of change of energy, the quantity inside the brackets must be the energy stored in the capacitor. Mathematically, we can infer from Eq. (6–10) that the energy at time t is

$$w_C(t) = {}^1/_2 C v_C^2(t) + \text{constant}$$

The constant in this equation is the value of stored energy at some instant t when $v_C(t) = 0$. At such an instant the electric field is zero; hence the stored energy is also zero. As a result, the constant is zero and we write the capacitor energy as

$$w_C(t) = \frac{1}{2} C v_C^2(t) \tag{6–11}$$

The stored energy is never negative, since it is proportional to the square of the voltage. The capacitor absorbs power from the circuit when storing energy and returns previously stored energy when delivering power to the circuit.

The relationship in Eq. (6–11) also implies that voltage is a continuous function of time, since an abrupt change in the voltage implies a discontinuous change in energy. Since power is the time derivative of energy, a discontinuous change in energy implies infinite power, which is physically impossible. The capacitor voltage is called a **state variable** because it determines the energy state of the element.

To summarize, the capacitor is a dynamic circuit element with the following properties:

1. The current through the capacitor is zero unless the voltage is changing. The capacitor acts like an open circuit to dc excitations.
2. The voltage across the capacitor is a continuous function of time. A discontinuous change in capacitor voltage would require infinite current and power, which is physically impossible.
3. The capacitor absorbs power from the circuit when storing energy and returns previously stored energy when delivering power. The net energy transfer is nonnegative, indicating that the capacitor is a passive element.

The following examples illustrate these properties.

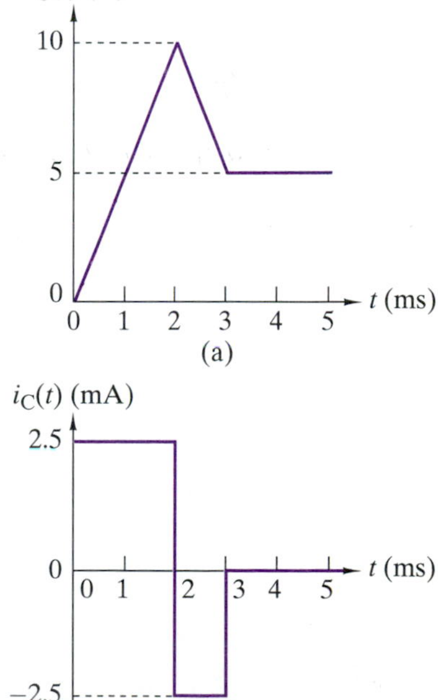

FIGURE 6–4

EXAMPLE 6–1

The voltage in Figure 6–4(a) appears across a ½-μF capacitor. Find the current through the capacitor.

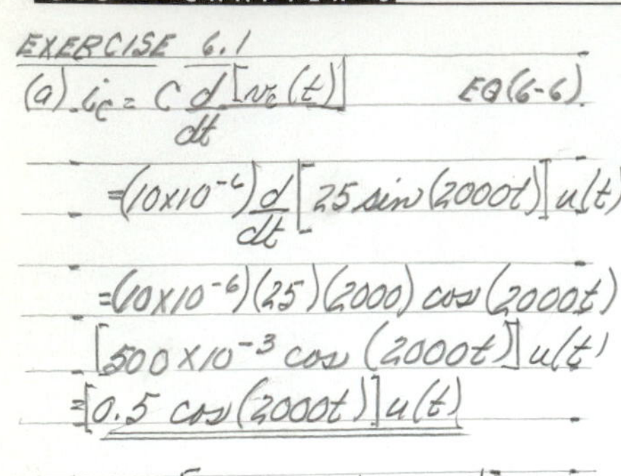

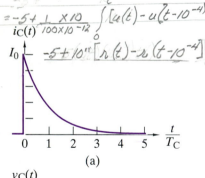

SOLUTION:

The capacitor current is proportional to the time rate of change of the voltage. For $0 < t < 2$ ms the slope of the voltage waveform has a constant value

$$\frac{dv_C}{dt} = \frac{10}{2 \times 10^{-3}} = 5000 \text{ V/s}$$

The capacitor current during this interval is

$$i_C(t) = C\frac{dv_C}{dt} = (0.5 \times 10^{-6}) \times (5 \times 10^3) = 2.5 \text{ mA}$$

For $2 < t < 3$ ms the rate of change of the voltage is –5000 V/s. Since the rate of change of voltage is negative, the current changes direction and takes on the value $i_C(t) = -2.5$ mA. For $t > 3$ ms, the voltage is constant, so its slope is zero; hence the current is zero. The resulting current waveform is shown in Figure 6–4(b). Note that the voltage across the capacitor (the state variable) is continuous, but the capacitor current can be, and in this case is, discontinuous. ■

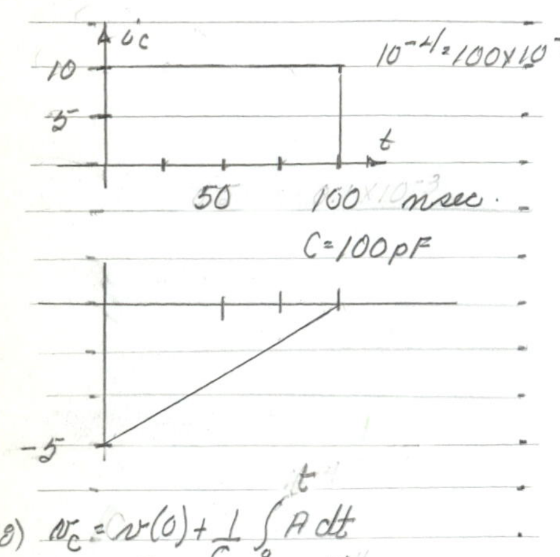

EXAMPLE 6–2

The $i_C(t)$ in Figure 6–5(a) is given by

$$i_C(t) = I_0(e^{-t/T_C})u(t)$$

Find the voltage across the capacitor if $v_C(0) = 0$ V.

SOLUTION:

Using the capacitor i–v relationship in integral form,

$$v_C(t) = v_C(0) + \frac{1}{C}\int_0^t i_C(x)dx$$

$$= 0 + \frac{1}{C}\int_0^t I_0 e^{-x/T_C}\,dx = \frac{I_0T_C}{C}(-e^{-x/T_C})\Big|_0^t$$

$$= \frac{I_0T_C}{C}(1 - e^{-t/T_C})$$

The graphs in Figure 6–5(b) show that the voltage is continuous while the current is discontinuous. ■

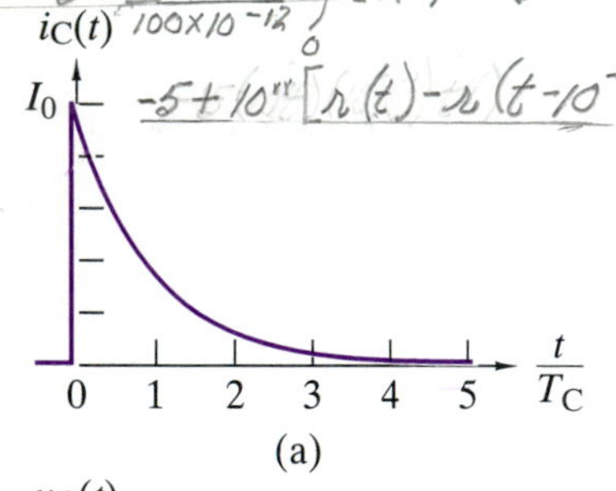

(a)

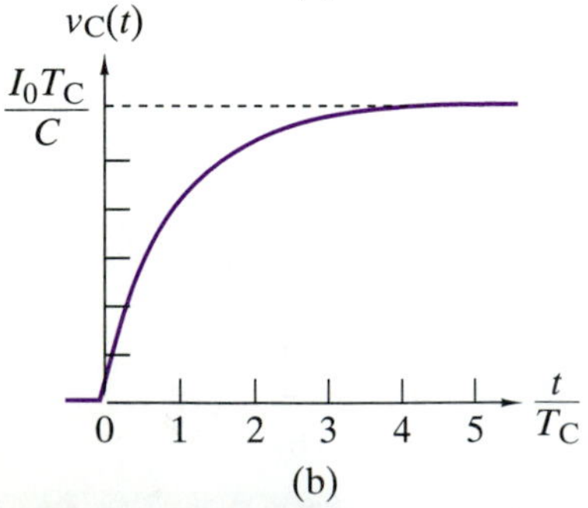

(b)

FIGURE 6–5

Exercise 6–1

(a) The voltage across a 10-μF capacitor is $25[\sin 2000t]u(t)$. Derive an expression for the current through the capacitor.

(b) At $t = 0$ the voltage across a 100-pF capacitor is –5 V. The current through the capacitor is $10[u(t) - u(t - 10^{-4})]$ μA. What is the voltage across the capacitor for $t > 0$?

Answers:

(a) $i_C(t) = 0.5\ [\cos 2000t]u(t)$ A.
(b) $v_C(t) = -5 + 10^5 t$ V for $0 < t < 0.1$ ms and $v_C(t) = 5$ V for $t > 0.1$ ms

Exercise 6–2

For $t \geq 0$ the voltage across a 200-pF capacitor is $5e^{-4000t}$ V.

(a) What is the charge on the capacitor at $t = 0$ and $t = +\infty$?
(b) Derive an expression for the current through the capacitor for $t \geq 0$.
(c) For $t > 0$ is the device absorbing or delivering power?

Answers:

(a) 1 nC and 0 C
(b) $i_C(t) = -4e^{-4000t}$ μA
(c) Delivering

EXAMPLE 6–3

Figure 6–6(a) shows the voltage across 0.5-μF capacitor. Find the capacitor's energy and power.

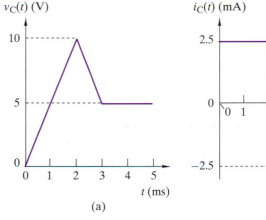

FIGURE 6–6

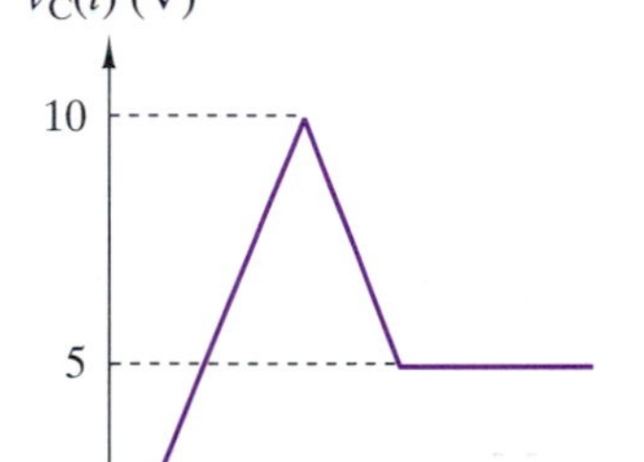
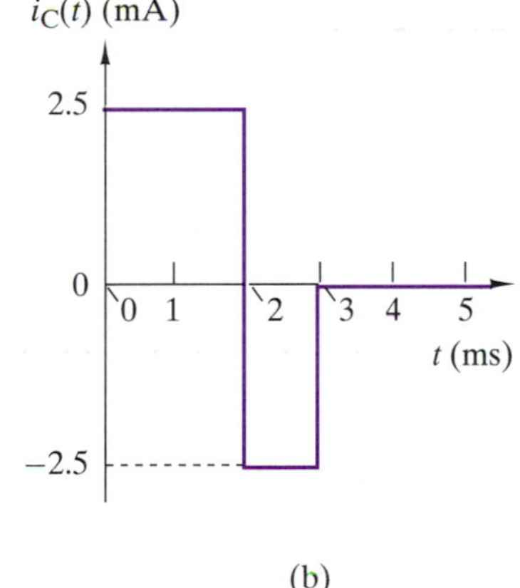

(a) (b)

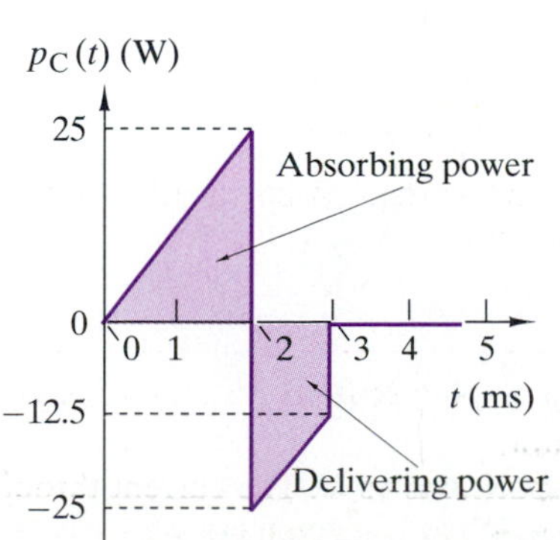
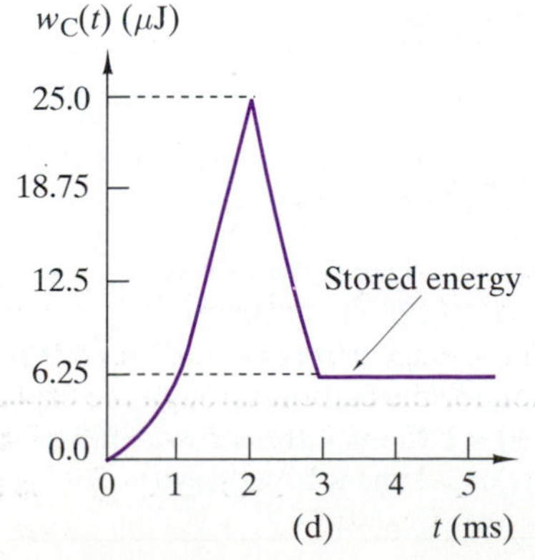

(c) (d)

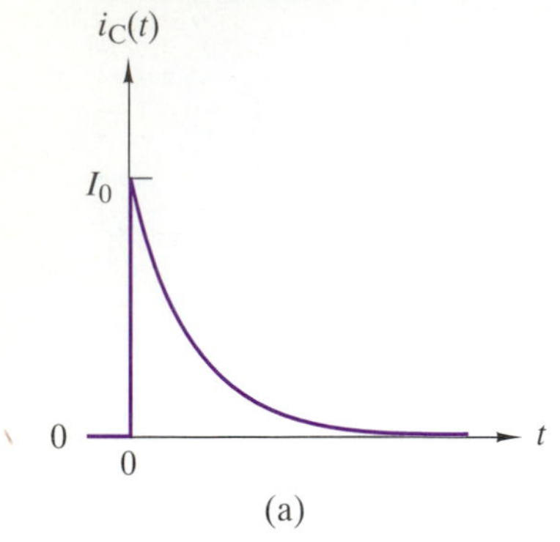

(a)

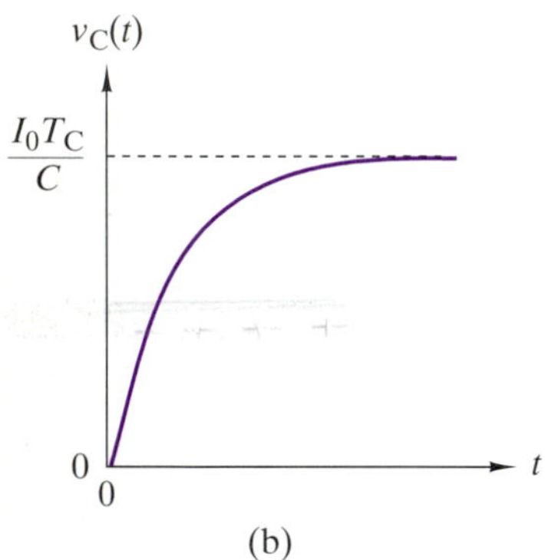

(b)

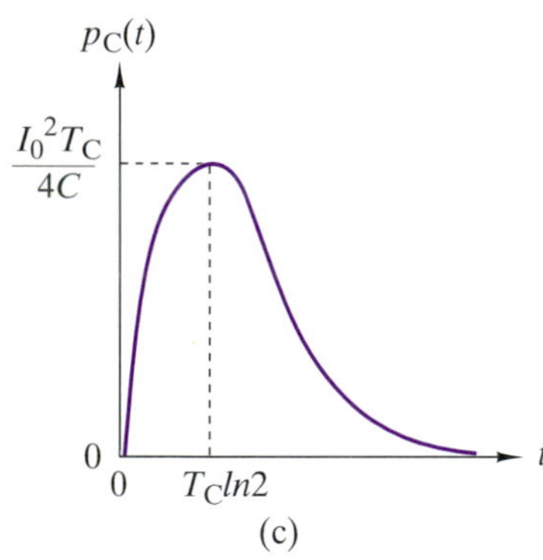

(c)

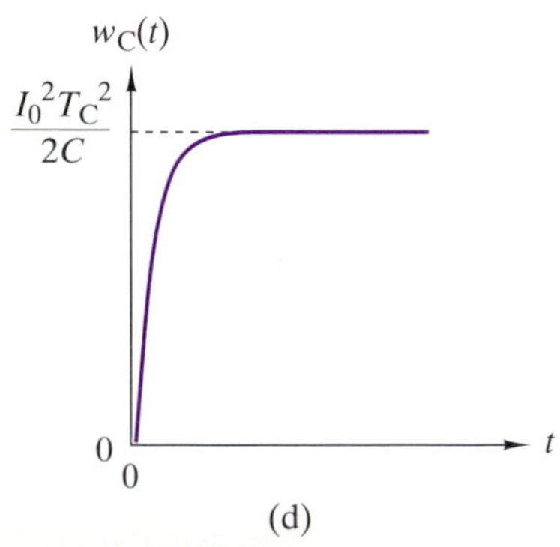

(d)

FIGURE 6–7

SOLUTION:

The current through the capacitor was found in Example 6–1. The power waveform is the point-by-point product of the voltage and current waveforms. The energy is found by either integrating the power waveform or by calculating $\frac{1}{2}C[v_C(t)]^2$ point by point. The current, power, and energy are shown in Figures 6–6(b), 6–6(c), and 6–6(d). Note that the capacitor energy increases when it is absorbing power $[p_C(t) > 0]$ and decreases when delivering power $[p_C(t) < 0]$. ■

EXAMPLE 6–4

The current through a capacitor is given by

$$i_C(t) = I_0[e^{-t/T_C}]u(t)$$

Find the capacitor's energy and power.

SOLUTION:

The current and voltage were found in Example 6–2 and are shown in Figures 6–7(a) and 6–7(b). The power waveform is found as the product of current and voltage:

$$\begin{aligned} p_C(t) &= i_C(t)v_C(t) \\ &= [I_0e^{-t/T_C}]\left[\frac{I_0T_C}{C}(1 - e^{-t/T_C})\right] \\ &= \frac{I_0^2T_C}{C}(e^{-t/T_C} - e^{-2t/T_C}) \end{aligned}$$

The waveform of the power is shown in Figure 6–7(c). The energy is

$$w_C(t) = \frac{1}{2}Cv_C^2(t) = \frac{(I_0T_C)^2}{2C}(1 - e^{-t/T_C})^2$$

The time history of the energy is shown in Figure 6–7(d). In this example both power and energy are always positive. ■

Exercise 6–3

Find the power and energy for the capacitors in Exercise 6–1.

Answers:

(a) $p_C(t) = 6.25[\sin 4000t]u(t)$ W
$w_C(t) = 3.125 \sin^2 2000t$ mJ

(b) $p_C(t) = -0.05 + 10^3 t$ mW for $0 < t < 0.1$ ms
$p_C(t) = 0$ for $t > 0.1$ ms
$w_C(t) = 1.25 - 5 \times 10^4 t + 5 \times 10^8 t^2$ nJ for $0 < t < 0.1$ ms
$w_C(t) = 1.25$ nJ for $t > 0.1$ ms

Exercise 6–4

Find the power and energy for the capacitor in Exercise 6–2.

Answers:

$$p_C(t) = -20e^{-8000t}\ \mu\text{W}$$

$$w_C(t) = 2.5e^{-8000t}\ \text{nJ}$$

APPLICATION NOTE: EXAMPLE 6–5

A track-hold circuit is usually found at the input to an analog-to-digital (A/D) converter. The purpose of the circuit is to follow continuously a time-varying input voltage and then to hold a constant value during the time needed to perform the A/D conversion. This example shows that a capacitor can perform the track-hold function.

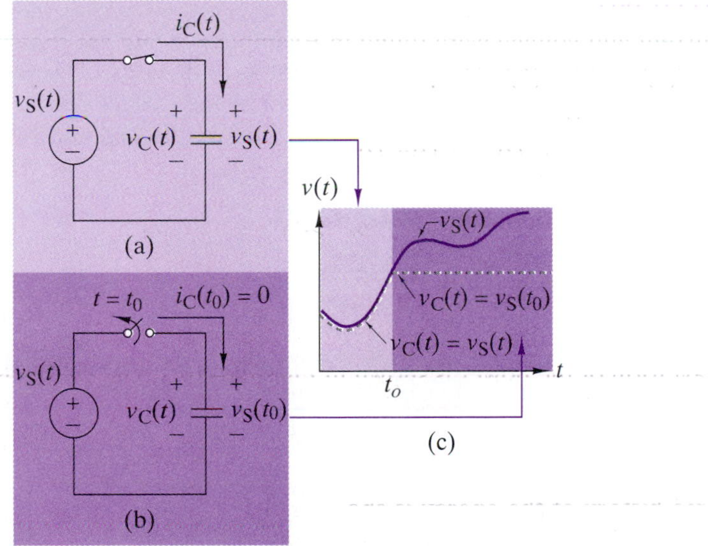

FIGURE 6–8

Figure 6–8(a) shows the simplest form of a capacitor track-hold circuit. When the switch is closed, the circuit is in the track mode and the voltage across the capacitor follows or tracks the input source voltage. At some time, $t = t_0$ the switch opens and the circuit changes to the hold mode shown in Figure 6–8(b). For $t > t_0$, the source voltage continues to change, producing the waveform $v_S(t)$ shown in blue in Figure 6–8(c). However, Figure 6–8(c) shows in black that the capacitor voltage $v_C(t)$ is constant for $t > t_0$. Opening the switch at $t = t_0$ forces the capacitor current to zero, and zero current means the voltage is constant. The capacitor holds or remembers the voltage existing across it at the instant the switch was opened—namely, $v_S(t_0)$.

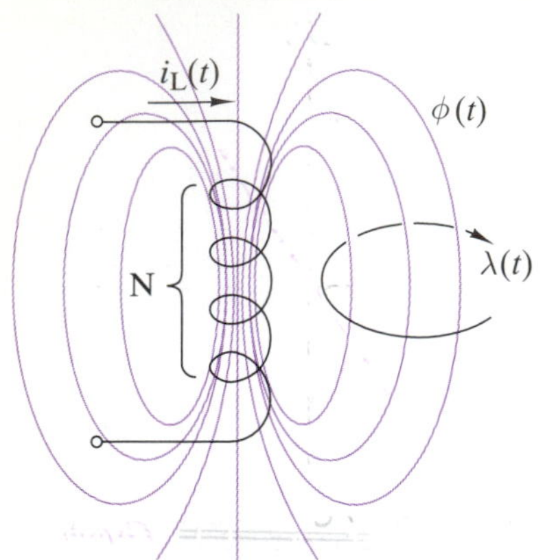

FIGURE 6–9 *Magnetic flux surrounding a current carrying coil.*

Theoretically, the capacitor holds $v_S(t_0)$ forever. In reality, some leakage occurs through the dielectric, so the capacitor gradually loses stored energy and the voltage decreases. The stored value in a track-hold circuit must be occasionally refreshed for long-term storage. The capacitor can hold or remember past events because it can store energy.

6–2 THE INDUCTOR

The inductor is a dynamic circuit element involving the time variation of the magnetic field produced by a current. Magnetostatics shows that a magnetic flux ϕ surrounds a wire carrying an electric current. When the wire is wound into a coil, the lines of flux concentrate along the axis of the coil, as shown in Figure 6–9. In a linear magnetic medium, the flux is proportional to both the current and the number of turns in the coil. Therefore, the total flux is

$$\phi(t) = k_1 N i_L(t) \qquad (6\text{–}12)$$

where k_1 is a constant of proportionality.

The magnetic flux intercepts or links the turns of the coil. The flux linkage in a coil is represented by the symbol λ, with units of webers (Wb), named after the German scientist Wilhelm Weber (1804–1891). The flux linkage is proportional to the number of turns in the coil and to the total magnetic flux, so $\lambda(t)$ is

$$\lambda(t) = N\phi(t) \qquad (6\text{–}13)$$

Substituting Eq. (6–12) into Eq.(6–13) gives

$$\lambda(t) = [k_1 N^2] i_L(t) \qquad (6\text{–}14)$$

The proportionality constant inside the brackets in this equation is the **inductance** L of the coil. That is, by definition

$$L = k_1 N^2 \qquad (6\text{–}15)$$

The unit of inductance is the henry (H) (plural henrys), a name that honors American scientist Joseph Henry. Figure 6–10 shows the circuit symbol for an inductor and some examples of actual devices. Some physical features of commercially available inductors are given in Appendix A.

Using Eq. (6–15), the defining relationship for the inductor becomes

$$\lambda(t) = L i_L(t) \qquad (6\text{–}16)$$

Figure 6–11 graphically displays the inductor's element constraint in Eq. (6–16). The graph points out that the inductor is a linear element since the defining relationship is a straight line through the origin.

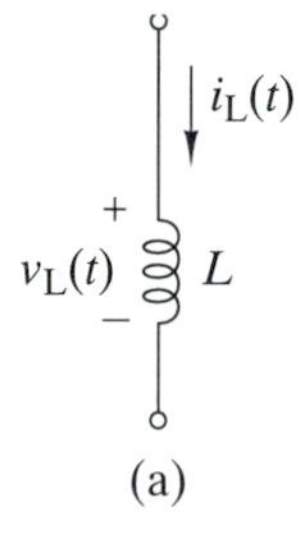

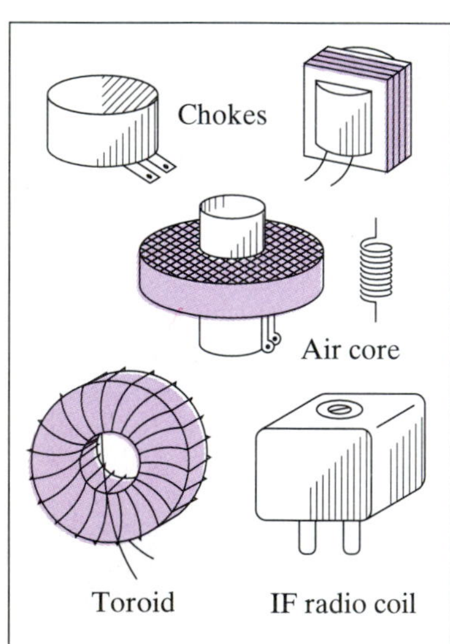

FIGURE 6–10 *The inductor: (a) Circuit symbol. (b) Example devices.*

I–V RELATIONSHIP

Equation (6–16) is the inductor element constraint in terms of current and flux linkage. To obtain the element characteristic in terms of voltage and current, we differentiate Eq. (6–16) with respect to time:

$$\frac{d[\lambda(t)]}{dt} = \frac{d[Li_L(t)]}{dt} \qquad (6\text{–}17)$$

The inductance L is a constant. According to Faraday's law, the voltage across the inductor is equal to the time rate of change of flux linkage. Therefore, we obtain an inductor i–v relationship in the form

$$v_L(t) = L\frac{di_L(t)}{dt} \qquad (6\text{–}18)$$

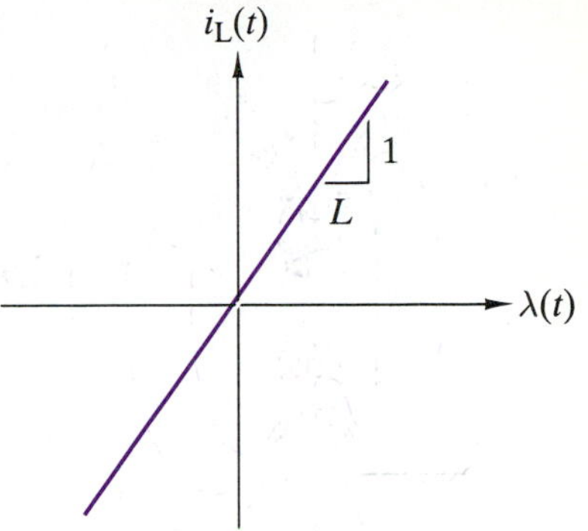

FIGURE 6–11 *Graph of the defining relationship of a linear inductor.*

The time derivative in Eq. (6–18) means that the voltage across the inductor is zero unless the current is time varying. Under dc excitation the current is constant and $v_L = 0$, so the inductor acts like a short circuit. The inductor is a dynamic element because only a changing current produces a nonzero voltage. However, a discontinuous change in current would produce an infinite voltage, which is physically impossible. Therefore, the current $i_L(t)$ must be a continuous function of time t.

Equation (6–18) relates the inductor voltage to the rate of change of the inductor current. To express the inductor current in terms of the voltage, we multiply both sides of Eq. (6–18) by dt, solve for the differential di_L, and integrate:

$$\int di_L = \frac{1}{L}\int v_L(t)dt \qquad (6\text{–}19)$$

To set the limits of integration, we assume that the inductor current $i_L(t_0)$ is known at some time t_0. Under this assumption the integration limits are

$$\int_{i_L(t_0)}^{i_L(t)} di_L = \frac{1}{L}\int_{t_0}^{t} v_L(x)dx \qquad (6\text{–}20)$$

where x is a dummy integration variable. The left side of Eq. (6–20) integrates to produce

$$i_L(t) = i_L(t_0) + \frac{1}{L}\int_{t_0}^{t} v_L(x)dx \qquad (6\text{–}21)$$

The reference time t_0 is established by some physical event, such as closing or opening a switch. Without losing any generality, we can assume $t_0 = 0$ and write Eq. (6–21) in the form

$$i_L(t) = i_L(0) + \frac{1}{L}\int_{0}^{t} v_L(x)dx \qquad (6\text{–}22)$$

Equation (6–22) is the integral form of the inductor i–v characteristic. Both the integral form and the derivative form in Eq. (6–18) assume that the reference marks for the inductor voltage and current follow the passive sign convention shown in Figure 6–10.

POWER AND ENERGY

With the passive sign convention the inductor power is

$$p_L(t) = i_L(t)v_L(t) \qquad (6\text{–}23)$$

Using Eq. (6–18) to eliminate $v_L(t)$ from this equation puts the inductor power in the form

$$p_L(t) = [i_L(t)]\left[L\frac{di_L(t)}{dt}\right] = \frac{d}{dt}[{}^1/_2 L i_L^2(t)] \qquad (6-24)$$

This expression shows that power can be positive or negative because the inductor current and its time derivative can have opposite signs. With the passive sign convention a positive sign means the element absorbs power, while a negative sign means the element delivers power. The ability to deliver power indicates that the inductor can store energy.

To find the stored energy, we note that the power relation in Eq. (6–24) is a perfect derivative. Since power is the time rate of change of energy, the quantity inside the brackets must represent the energy stored in the magnetic field of the inductor. From Eq. (6–24), we infer that the energy at time t is

$$w_L(t) = \frac{1}{2}L i_L^2(t) + \text{constant}$$

As is the case with capacitor energy, the constant in this expression is zero since it is the energy stored at an instant t at which $i_L(t) = 0$. As a result, the energy stored in the inductor is

$$w_L(t) = \frac{1}{2}L i_L^2(t) \qquad (6-25)$$

The energy stored in an inductor is never negative because it is proportional to the square of the current. The inductor stores energy when absorbing power and returns previously stored energy when delivering power, so that the net energy transfer is never negative.

Equation (6–25) implies that inductor current is a continuous function of time because an abrupt change in current causes a discontinuity in the energy. Since power is the time derivative of energy, an energy discontinuity implies infinite power, which is physically impossible. Current is called the **state variable** of the inductor because it determines the energy state of the element.

In summary, the inductor is a dynamic circuit element with the following properties:

1. The voltage across the inductor is zero unless the current through the inductor is changing. The inductor acts like a short circuit for dc excitations.
2. The current through the inductor is a continuous function of time. A discontinuous change in inductor current would require infinite voltage and power, which is physically impossible.
3. The inductor absorbs power from the circuit when storing energy and delivers power to the circuit when returning previously stored energy. The net energy is nonnegative, indicating that the inductor is a passive element.

EXAMPLE 6–6

The current through a 2-mH inductor is $i_L = 2 \sin 1000t$ A. Find waveforms of the resulting voltage, power, and energy.

SOLUTION:

The voltage is found from the derivative form of the i–v relationship:

$$v_L(t) = L\frac{di_L(t)}{dt} = 0.002\,[2 \times 1000 \cos 1000t]$$

$$= 4 \cos 1000t \text{ V}$$

The inductor power is

$$p_L(t) = i_L(t)v_L(t) = (2 \sin 1000t)\,(4 \cos 1000t)$$
$$= 4 \sin 2000t \text{ W}$$

The energy is given by

$$w_L(t) = {}^1/_2 Li_L^2(t) = 4 \sin^2 1000t \text{ mJ}$$

These waveforms are shown in Figure 6–12. Note that the power is alternately positive and negative, whereas the energy is nonnegative. ■

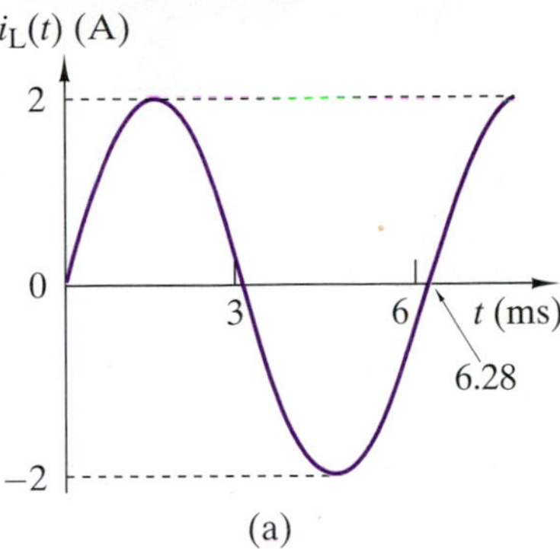

(a)

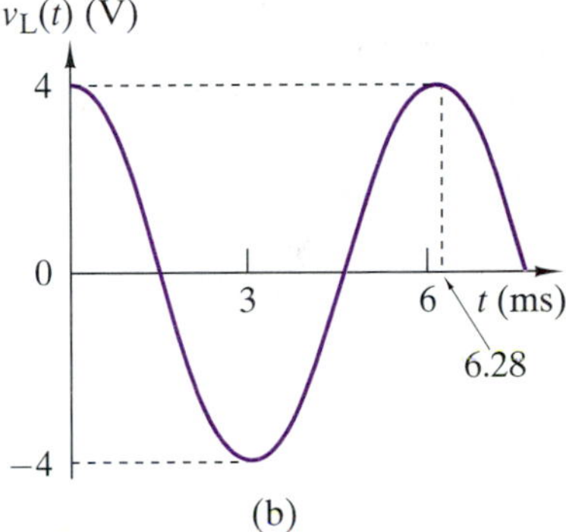

(b)

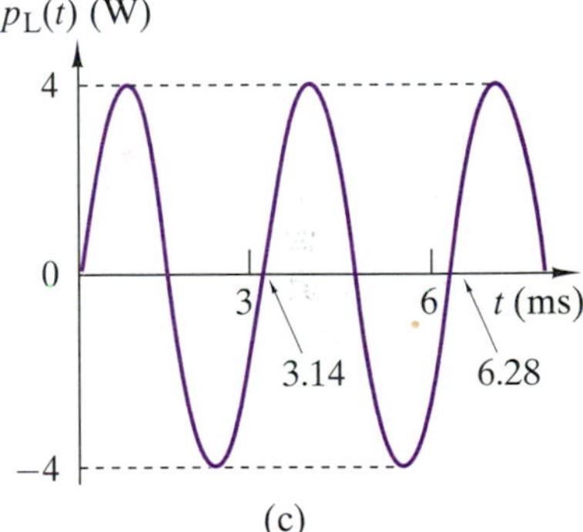

(c)

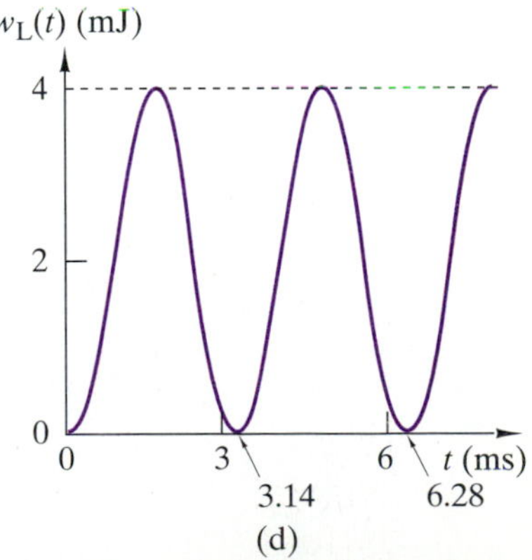

(d)

FIGURE 6–12

EXAMPLE 6–7

Figure 6–13 shows the current through and voltage across an unknown energy storage element.

(a) What is the element and what is its numerical value?
(b) If the energy stored in the element at $t = 0$ is zero, how much energy is stored in the element at $t = 1$ s?

SOLUTION:

(a) By inspection, the voltage across the device is proportional to the derivative of the current, so the element is a linear inductor. During the interval $0 < t < 1$ s, the slope of the current waveform is 10 A/s. During the same interval the voltage is a constant 100 mV. Therefore, the inductance is

$$L = \frac{v}{di/dt} = \frac{0.1 \text{ V}}{10 \text{ A/s}} = 10 \text{ mH}$$

(b) The energy stored at $t = 1$ s is

$$w_L(1) = \frac{1}{2}Li_L^2(1) = 0.5(0.01)(10)^2 = 0.5 \text{ J}$$ ■

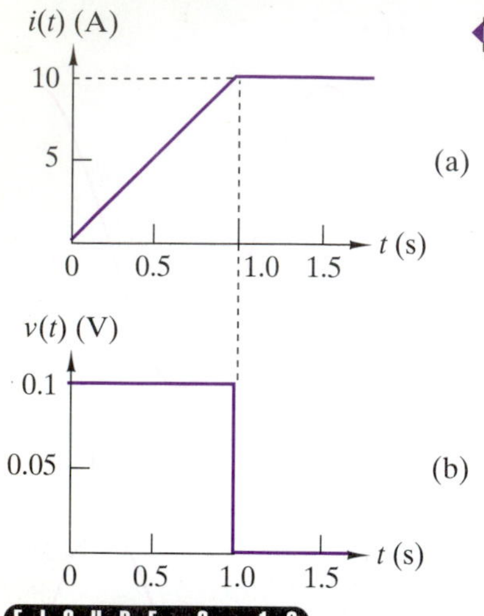

FIGURE 6–13

EXAMPLE 6–8

The current through a 2.5-mH inductor is a damped sine $i(t) = 10e^{-500t} \sin 2000t$. Plot the waveforms of the element current, voltage, power, and energy.

SOLUTION:

Figure 6–14 shows a Mathcad file that produces the required graphs. The first two lines in the file define the inductance and the current. The inductor voltage is found by differentiation, the power as the product of voltage and current, and the energy by integrating the power. In the plots shown in Figure 6–14, note that the current, voltage, and power alternate signs, whereas the total energy is always positive.

In Mathcad the time scale statement shown in the figure uses the following format:

$$t = T_{\text{Start}},\ T_{\text{Start}} + \Delta t \ldots T_{\text{Stop}}$$

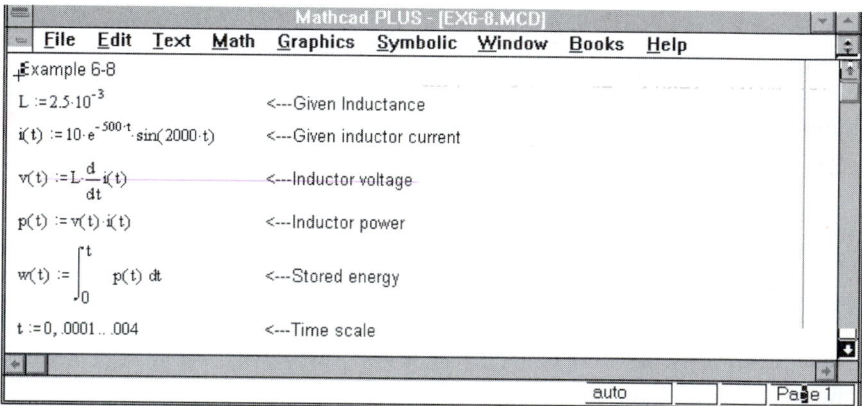

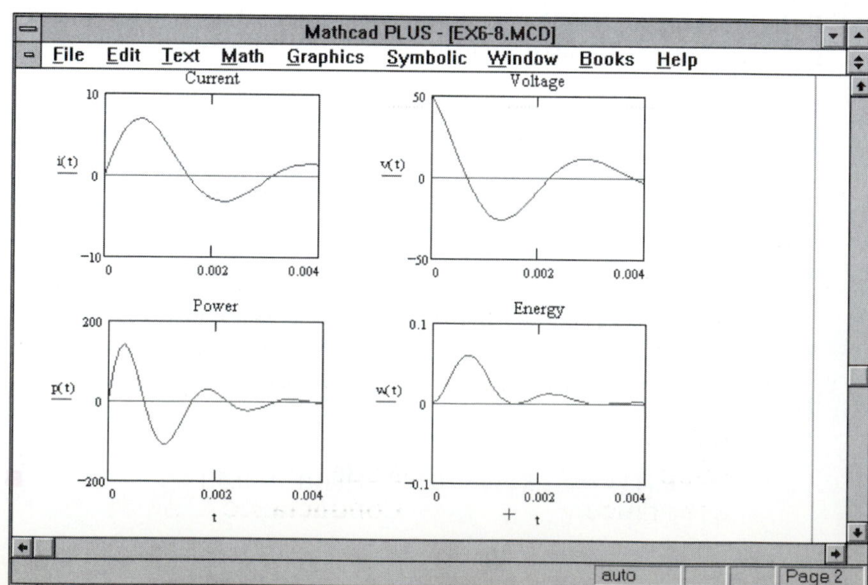

FIGURE 6–14

Numerical values for T_{Start}, Δt, and T_{Stop} are chosen by considering the damped sine waveform. The period of the sinusoid is

$$T_0 = \frac{2 \times \pi}{2000} = 0.00314 \text{ s}$$

The plots start at $T_{\text{Start}} = 0$. To include at least one cycle requires an end time of $T_{\text{End}} > T_0 = 0.00314$ s; hence we select $T_{\text{Stop}} = 0.004$ s. To include at least 20 points per cycle requires a time increment ($t < T_O/20 = 0.000158$; hence we select $\Delta t = 0.0001$ s. ■

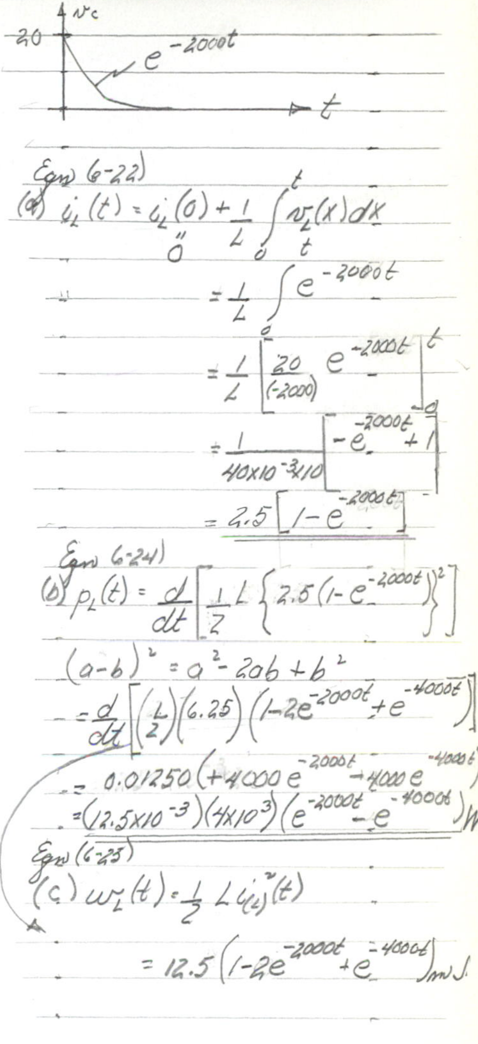

Exercise 6–5

For $t > 0$, the voltage across a 4-mH inductor is $v_L(t) = 20e^{-2000t}$ V. The initial current is $i_L(0) = 0$.

(a) What is the current through the inductor for $t > 0$?
(b) What is the power and (c) what is the energy for $t > 0$?

Answers:

(a) $i_L(t) = 2.5(1 - e^{-2000t})$ A
(b) $p_L(t) = 50(e^{-2000t} - e^{-4000t})$ W
(c) $w_L(t) = 12.5(1 - 2e^{-2000t} + e^{-4000t})$ mJ

Exercise 6–6

For $t < 0$, the current through a 100-mH inductor is zero. For $t \geq 0$, the current is $i_L(t) = 20e^{-2000t} - 20e^{-4000t}$ mA.

(a) Derive an expression for the voltage across the inductor for $t > 0$.
(b) Find the time $t > 0$ at which the inductor voltage passes through zero.
(c) Derive an expression for the inductor power for $t > 0$.
(d) Find the time interval over which the inductor absorbs power and the interval over which it delivers power.

Answers:

(a) $v_L(t) = -4e^{-2000t} + 8e^{-4000t}$ V
(b) $t = 0.347$ ms
(c) $p_L(t) = -80e^{-4000t} + 240e^{-6000t} - 160e^{-8000t}$ mW
(d) Absorbing for $0 < t < 0.347$ ms, delivering for $t > 0.347$ ms

MORE ABOUT DUALITY

The capacitor and inductor characteristics are quite similar. Interchanging C and L, and i and v converts the capacitor equations into the inductor equations, and vice versa. This interchangeability illustrates the principle of duality. Some the dual concepts seen so far are as follows:

KVL	KCL
Loop	Node
Resistance	Conductance

Voltage source	Current source
Thévenin	Norton
Short circuit	Open circuit
Series	Parallel
Capacitance	Inductance
Flux linkage	Charge

The term in one column is the dual of the term in the other column. The **principle of duality** states that

If every electrical term in a correct statement about circuit behavior is replaced by its dual, then the result is another correct statement.

This principle may help beginners gain confidence in their understanding of circuit analysis. When the concept in one column is understood, the dual concept in the other column becomes easier to remember and apply.

6–3 DYNAMIC OP AMP CIRCUITS

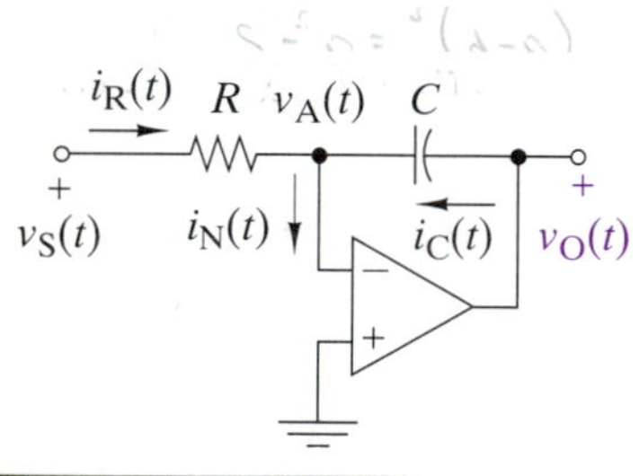

FIGURE 6–15 *The inverting OP AMP integrator.*

The dynamic characteristics of capacitors and inductors produce signal processing functions that cannot be obtained using resistors. The OP AMP circuit in Figure 6–15 is similar to the inverting amplifier circuit except for the capacitor in the feedback path. To determine the signal-processing function of the circuit, we need to find its input–output relationship.

We begin by writing a KCL equation at node A.

$$i_R(t) + i_C(t) = i_N(t)$$

The resistor and capacitor device equations are written using their i–v relationships and the fundamental property of node voltages:

$$i_C(t) = C\frac{d[v_O(t) - v_A(t)]}{dt}$$

$$i_R(t) = \frac{1}{R}[v_S(t) - v_A(t)]$$

The ideal OP AMP device equations are $i_N(t) = 0$ and $v_A(t) = 0$. Substituting all of the element constraints into the KCL connection constraint produces

$$\frac{v_S(t)}{R} + C\frac{dv_O(t)}{dt} = 0$$

To solve for the output $v_O(t)$, we multiply this equation by dt, solve for the differential dv_O, and integrate:

$$\int dv_0 = -\frac{1}{RC}\int v_S(t)dt$$

Assuming the output voltage is known at time $t_0 = 0$, the integration limits are

$$\int_{v_O(0)}^{v_O(t)} dv_O = -\frac{1}{RC}\int_0^t v_S(x)dx$$

which yields

$$v_O(t) = v_O(0) - \frac{1}{RC}\int_0^t v_S(x)dx$$

The initial condition $v_O(0)$ is actually the voltage on the capacitor at $t = 0$, since by KVL, we have $v_C(t) = v_O(t) - v_A(t)$. But $v_A = 0$ for the OP AMP, so in general $v_O(t) = v_C(t)$. When the voltage on the capacitor is zero at $t = 0$, the circuit input–output relationship reduces to

$$v_O(t) = -\frac{1}{RC}\int_0^t v_S(x)dx \qquad (6\text{–}26)$$

The output voltage is proportional to the integral of the input voltage when the initial capacitor voltage is zero. The circuit in Figure 6–15 is an **inverting integrator** since the proportionality constant is negative. The constant $1/RC$ has the units of reciprocal seconds (s^{-1}) so that both sides of Eq. (6–26) have the units of volts.

Interchanging the resistor and capacitor in Figure 6–15 produces the OP AMP differentiator in Figure 6–16. To find the input–output relationship of this circuit, we start by writing the element and connection equations. The KCL connection constraint at node A is

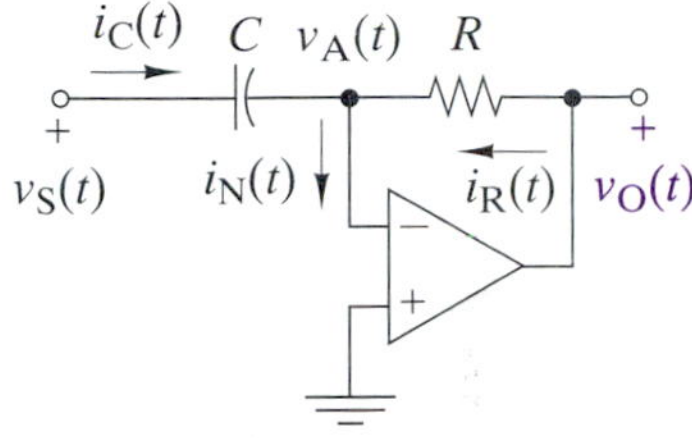

FIGURE 6–16 *The inverting OP AMP differentiator.*

$$i_R(t) + i_C(t) = i_N(t)$$

The device equations for the input capacitor and feedback resistor are

$$i_C(t) = C\frac{d[v_S(t) - v_A(t)]}{dt}$$

$$i_R(t) = \frac{1}{R}[v_O(t) - v_A(t)]$$

The device equations for the OP AMP are $i_N(t) = 0$ and $v_A(t) = 0$. Substituting all of these element constraints into the KCL connection constraint produces

$$\frac{v_O(t)}{R} + C\frac{dv_S(t)}{dt} = 0$$

Solving this equation for $v_O(t)$ produces the circuit input–output relationship:

$$v_O(t) = -RC\frac{dv_S(t)}{dt} \qquad (6\text{–}27)$$

The output voltage is proportional to the derivative of the input voltage. The circuit in Figure 6–16 is an **inverting differentiator** since the proportionality constant ($-RC$) is negative. The units of the constant RC are seconds so that both sides of Eq. (6–27) have the units of volts.

There are OP AMP inductor circuits that produce the inverting integrator and differentiator functions (see Problem 6–21); however, they are of little practical interest because of the physical size and resistive losses in real inductor devices.

Figure 6–17 shows OP AMP circuits and block diagrams for the inverting integrator and differentiator, together with signal-processing functions studied in Chapter 4. The term *operational amplifier* results from the vari-

Circuit	Block diagram	Gains
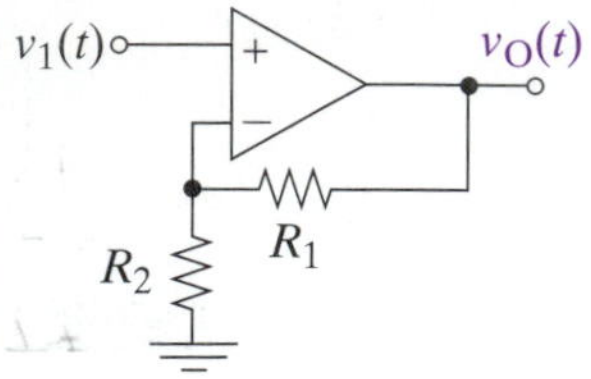 $v_1(t)$, +, −, $v_O(t)$, R_1, R_2	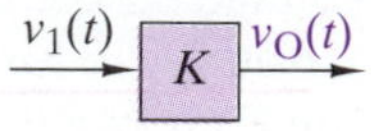 $v_1(t)$, K, $v_O(t)$	$K = \dfrac{R_1 + R_2}{R_2}$
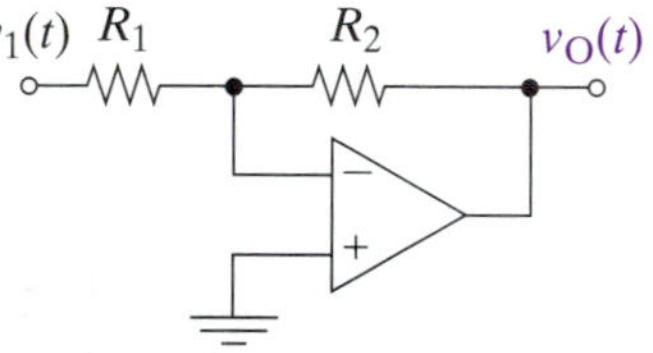 $v_1(t)$, R_1, R_2, $v_O(t)$, −, +	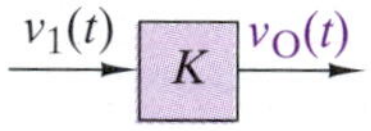 $v_1(t)$, K, $v_O(t)$	$K = -\dfrac{R_2}{R_1}$
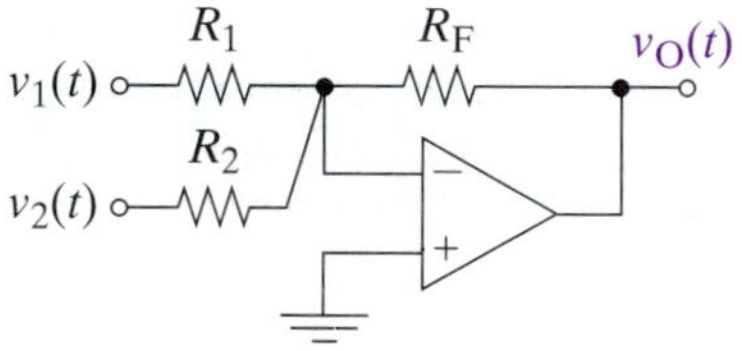 R_1, R_F, $v_O(t)$, $v_1(t)$, R_2, $v_2(t)$, −, +	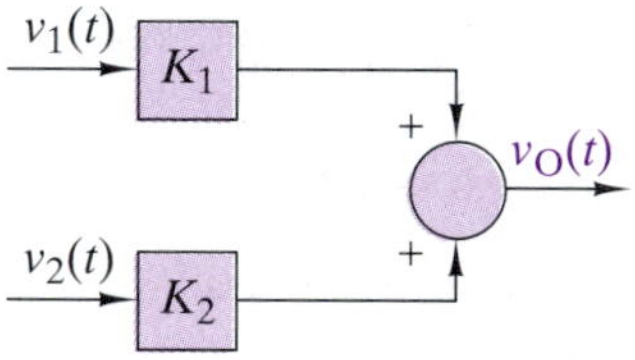 $v_1(t)$, K_1, +, $v_O(t)$, $v_2(t)$, K_2, +	$K_1 = -\dfrac{R_F}{R_1}$ $K_2 = -\dfrac{R_F}{R_2}$
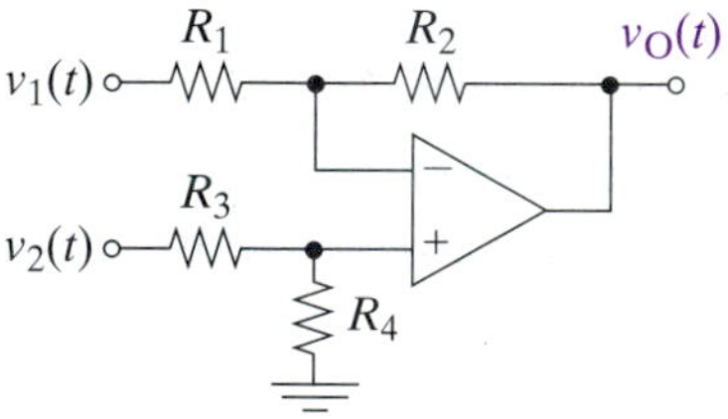 R_1, R_2, $v_O(t)$, $v_1(t)$, R_3, $v_2(t)$, −, +, R_4	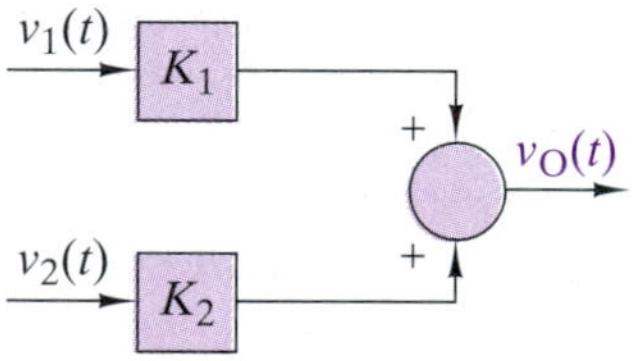 $v_1(t)$, K_1, +, $v_O(t)$, $v_2(t)$, K_2, +	$K_1 = -\dfrac{R_2}{R_1}$ $K_2 = \left(\dfrac{R_1 + R_2}{R_1}\right)\left(\dfrac{R_4}{R_3 + R_4}\right)$
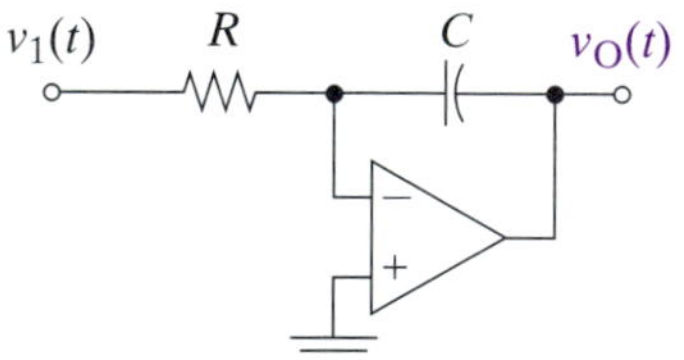 $v_1(t)$, R, C, $v_O(t)$, −, +	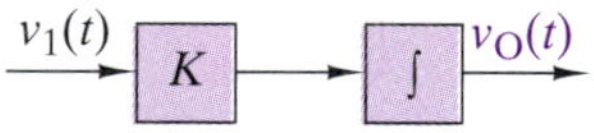 $v_1(t)$, K, $\int$, $v_O(t)$	$K = -\dfrac{1}{RC}$
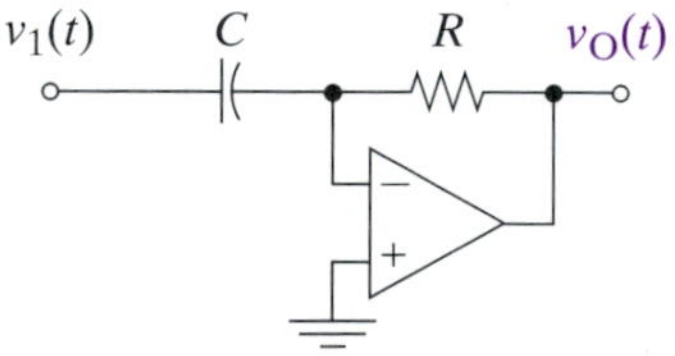 $v_1(t)$, C, R, $v_O(t)$, −, +	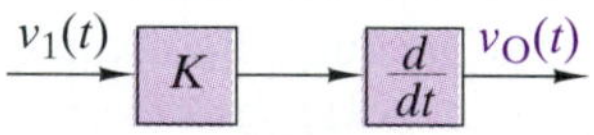 $v_1(t)$, K, $\dfrac{d}{dt}$, $v_O(t)$	$K = -RC$

FIGURE 6–17 *Summary of basic OP AMP signal-processing circuits.*

ous mathematical operations implemented by these circuits. The following examples illustrate using the collection of circuits in Figure 6–17 in the analysis and design of signal-processing functions.

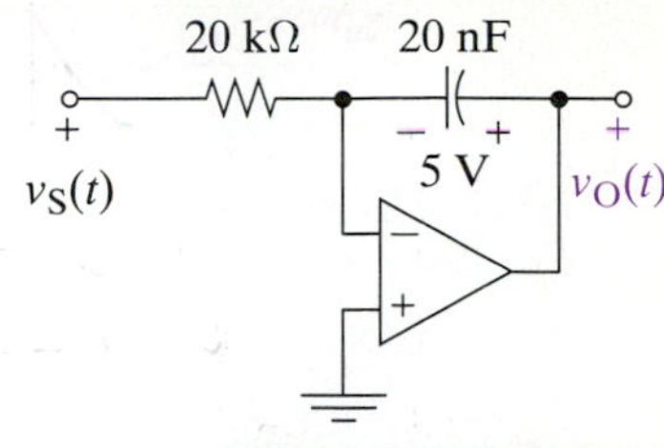

FIGURE 6–18

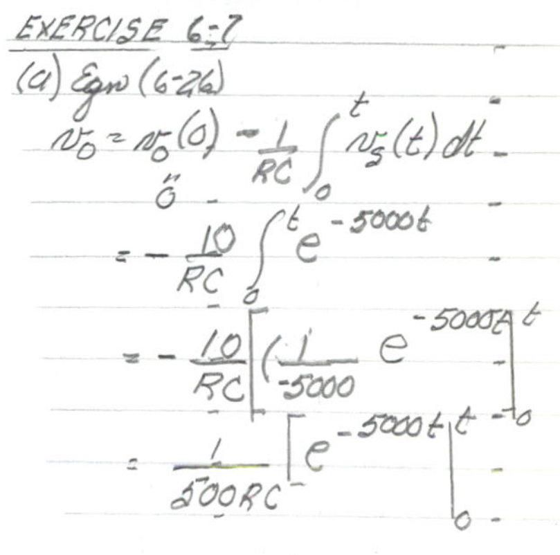

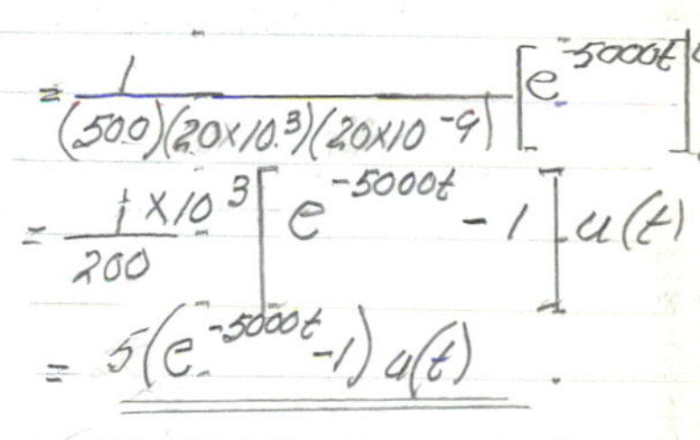

EXAMPLE 6–9

The input to the circuit in Figure 6–18 is $v_S(t) = 10u(t)$. Derive an expression for the output voltage. The OP AMP saturates when $v_O(t) = \pm 15$ V.

SOLUTION:

The circuit is the inverting integrator with an initial voltage of 5 V across the capacitor. For the reference marks shown in Figure 6–18, this means that $v_O(0) = +5$V. Assuming the OP AMP is operating in the linear mode, the output voltage is

$$\begin{aligned} v_O(t) &= v_O(0) - \frac{1}{RC}\int_0^t v_S \, dt \\ &= 5 - 2500\int_0^t 10 \, dt \\ &= 5 - 25{,}000t \quad t > 0 \end{aligned}$$

The output contains a negative going ramp because the circuit is an inverting integrator. The ramp output response is valid only as long as the OP AMP remains in its linear range. Negative saturation will occur when $5 - 25{,}000t = -15$, or at $t = 0.8$ ms. For $t > 0.8$ ms, the OP AMP is in the negative saturation mode with $v_O = -15$ V.

This example illustrates that dynamic circuits with bounded inputs may have unbounded responses. The circuit input here is a 10-V step function that has a bounded amplitude. The circuit output is a ramp whose output would be unbounded expect that the OP AMP saturates. ■

Exercise 6–7

The input to the circuit in Figure 6–18 is $v_S(t) = 10\,[e^{-5000t}]u(t)$ V.

(a) For $v_C(0) = 0$, derive an expression for the output voltage, assuming the OP AMP is in its linear range.
(b) Does the OP AMP saturate with the given input?

Answers:
(a) $v_O(t) = 5(e^{-5000t} - 1)u(t)$
(b) Does not saturate

EXAMPLE 6–10

The input to the circuit in Figure 6–19(a) is a trapezoidal waveform shown in (b). Find the output waveform. The OP AMP saturates when $v_O(t) = \pm 15$ V.

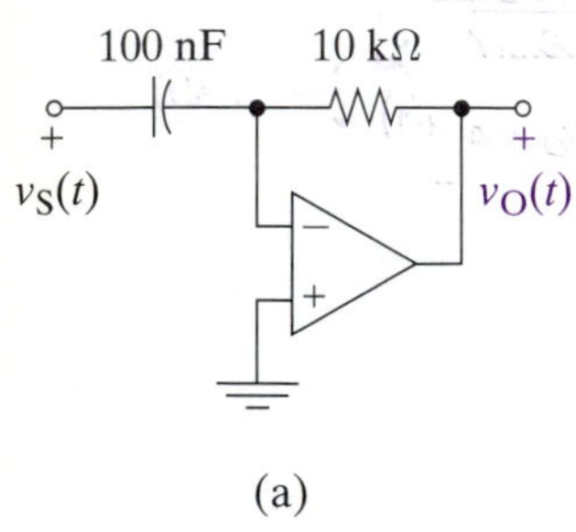

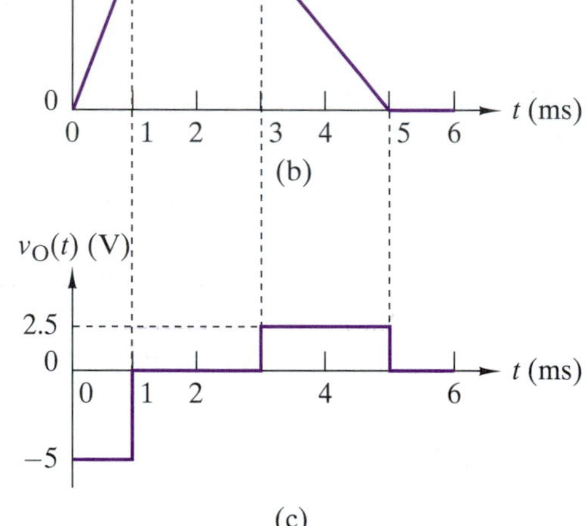

FIGURE 6–19

SOLUTION:

The circuit is the inverting differentiator with the following input–output relationship:

$$v_O(t) = -RC\frac{dv_S(t)}{dt} = -\frac{1}{1000}\frac{dv_S(t)}{dt}$$

The output voltage is constant over each of the following three time intervals:

1. For $0 < t < 1$ ms, the input slope is 5000 V/s and the output is $v_O = -5$ V.
2. For $1 < t < 3$ ms, the input slope is zero, so the output is zero as well.
3. For $3 < t < 5$ ms, the input slope is –2500 V/s and the output is +2.5 V.

The resulting output waveform is shown in Figure 6–19(c).

The output voltage remains within ±15-V limits, so the OP AMP operates in the linear mode. ■

Exercise 6–8

The input to the circuit in Figure 6–19 is $v_S(t) = V_A \cos 2000t$. The OP AMP saturates when $v_O = \pm 15$ V.

(a) Derive an expression for the output, assuming that the OP AMP is in the linear mode.

(b) What is the maximum value of V_A for linear operation?

Answers:

(a) $v_O(t) = 2V_A \sin 2000t$

(b) $|V_A| \leq 7.5$ V

EXAMPLE 6–11

Determine the input–output relationship of the circuit in Figure 6–20(a).

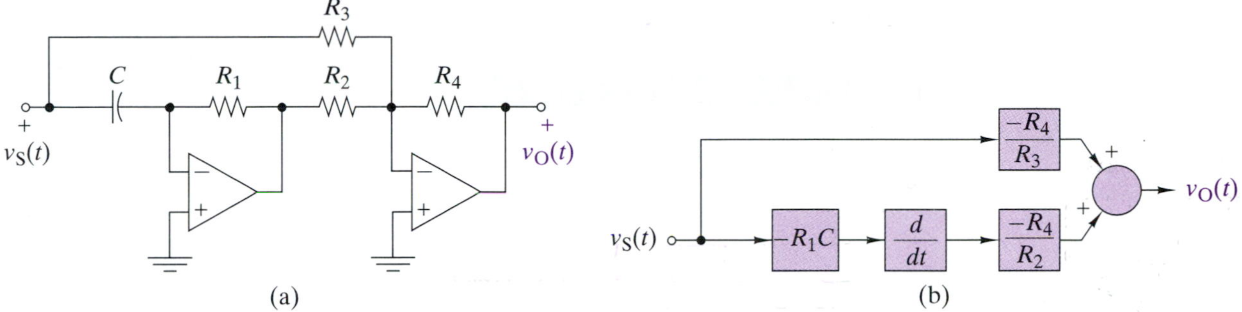

FIGURE 6–20

SOLUTION:

The circuit contains an inverting differentiator and an inverting summer. To find the input–output relationship, it is helpful to develop a block diagram for the circuit. Figure 6–20(b) shows a block diagram using the functional blocks in Figure 6–17. The product of the gains along the lower path yields its contribution to the output as

$$(-R_1C)\left[\frac{d}{dt}\left(-\frac{R_4}{R_2}\right)v_S(t)\right]$$

The upper path contributes $(-R_4/R_3)v_S(t)$ to the output. The total output is the sum of the contributions from each path:

$$v_O(t) = \left(\frac{R_1CR_4}{R_2}\right)\frac{dv_S(t)}{dt} - \left(\frac{R_4}{R_3}\right)v_S(t)$$

This equation assumes that both OP AMPs remain within their linear range. ■

Exercise 6–9

Find the input–output relationship of the circuit in Figure 6–21.

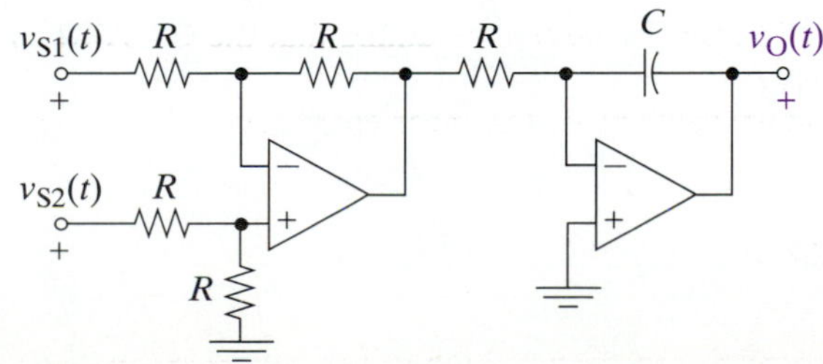

FIGURE 6–21

Answer:

$$v_O(t) = v_O(0) + \frac{1}{RC}\int_0^t (v_{S1} - v_{S2})dt$$

D DESIGN EXAMPLE 6–12

Implementing an Input–Output Relationship

Use the functional blocks in Figure 6–17 to design an OP AMP circuit to implement the following input–output relationship:

$$v_O(t) = 10v_S(t) + \int_0^t v_S\,dt$$

SOLUTION:

There is no unique solution to this design problem. We begin by drawing the block diagram in Figure 6–22(a), which shows that we need a gain block, an integrator, and a summer. However, the integrator and summer in Figure 6–17 are inverting circuits. Figure 6–22(b) shows how to overcome this problem by including an even number of signal inversions in each path. The inverting building blocks are realizable using OP AMP circuits in Figure 6–17, and the overall transfer characteristic is noninverting as required. One (of many) possible circuit realization of these processors is shown in Figure 6–22(c). The element parameter constraint on this circuit is $RC = 1$. Selecting the OP AMPs and the values of R and C depends on many additional factors, such as accuracy, internal resistance of the input source, and output load. ■

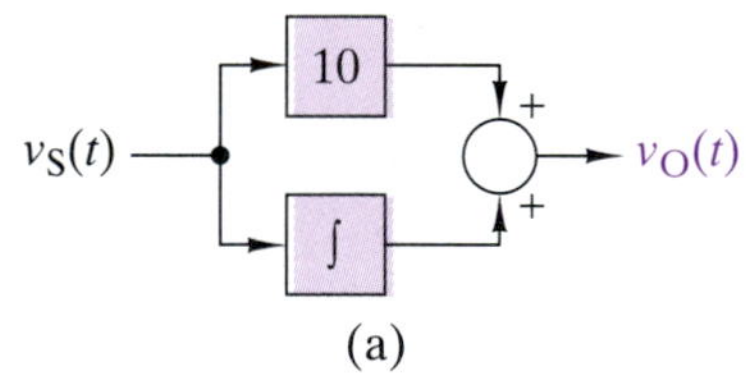

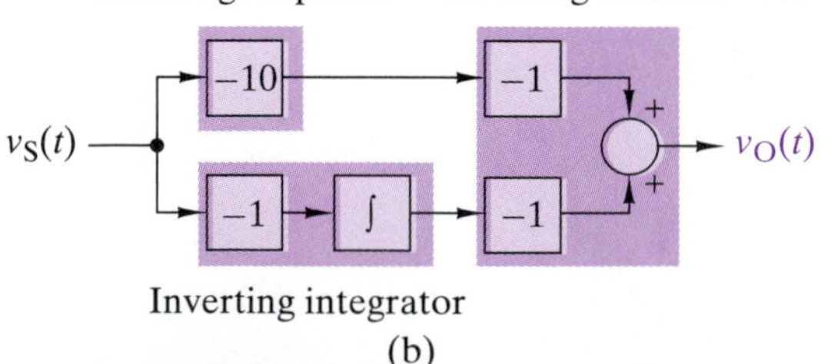

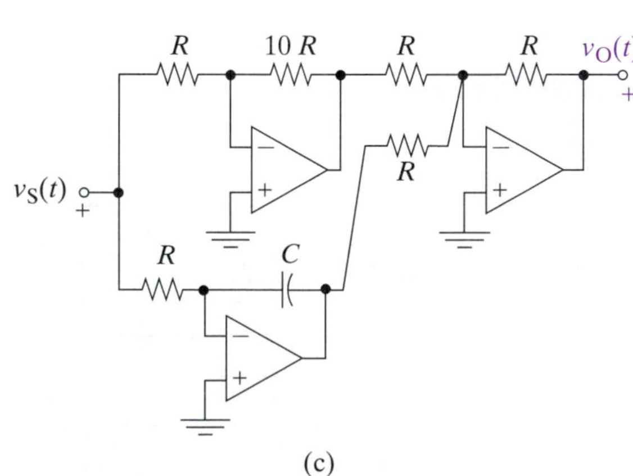

FIGURE 6–22

EXAMPLE 6–13

Draw a block diagram that implements the following input–output relationship:

$$100\frac{d^2v_O}{dt^2} + 20\frac{dv_O}{dt} + v_O = v_S$$

SOLUTION:

The relationship is a linear second-order differential equation of the type we will study in the next chapter. We can create a block diagram for linear differential equations using summers, integrators, and gain blocks. We begin by solving for the highest order derivative in the equation:

$$\frac{d^2v_O}{dt^2} = \frac{1}{100}v_S - \frac{1}{5}\frac{dv_O}{dt} - \frac{1}{100}v_O$$

The sum on the right side of this equation is shown in block diagram form in Figure 6–23(a). The summing operation generates the second derivative of the output, which is then integrated twice to generate the first derivative and the output itself, as shown in Figure 6–23(b). The two integrations generate the input signals in the original summing operation. Figure 6–23(c) shows how these signals are fed back to the summer via gain blocks, which provide the necessary scale factors and inversions. The net result is that the summer, integrators, and feedback gains produce the required input–output relationship.

FIGURE 6–23

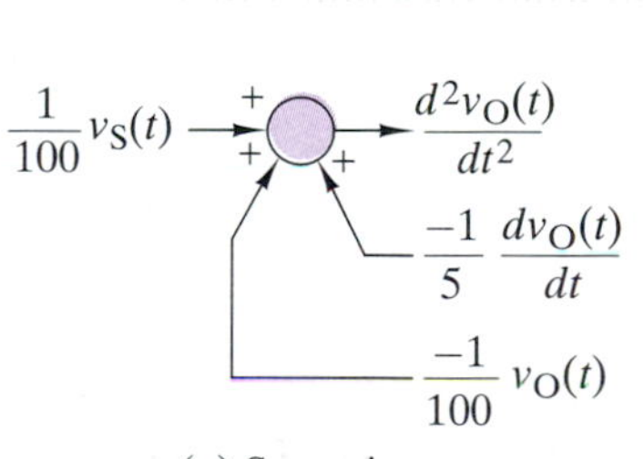

(a) Summing

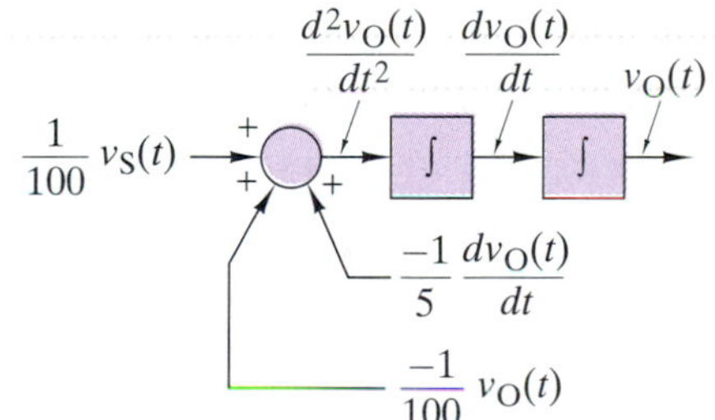

(b) Summing plus integration

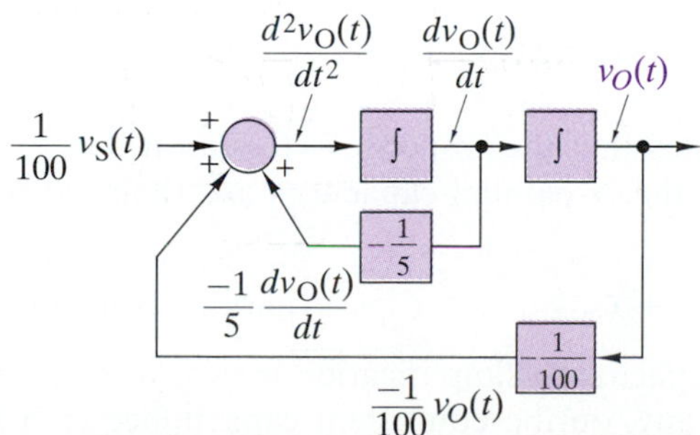

(c) Summing plus integration plus feedback

The OP-AMP building blocks in this example are commonly packaged in a general-purpose instrument called an **analog computer**. Prior to the 1960s, analog computers were the primary tool for simulating the differential equations arising in physical situations such as aircraft flight control. ■

6–4 EQUIVALENT CAPACITANCE AND INDUCTANCE

In Chapter 2 we found that resistors connected in series or parallel can be replaced by equivalent resistances. The same principle applies to connections of capacitors and inductors—for example, to the parallel connection of capacitors in Figure 6–24(a). Applying KCL at node A in Figure 6–24(a) yields

$$i(t) = i_1(t) + i_2(t) + \ldots + i_N(t)$$

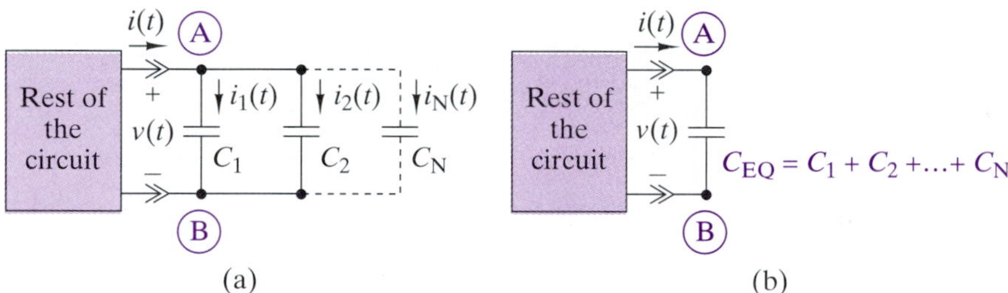

FIGURE 6–24 *Capacitors connected in parallel. (a) Given circuit. (b) Equivalent circuit.*

Since the elements are connected in parallel, KVL requires

$$v_1(t) = v_2(t) = \ldots = v_N(t) = v(t)$$

Because the capacitors all have the same voltage, their i–v relationships are all of the form $i_k(t) = C_k dv(t)/dt$. Substituting the i–v relationships into the KCL equation yields

$$i(t) = C_1\frac{dv(t)}{dt} + C_2\frac{dv(t)}{dt} + \ldots + C_N\frac{dv(t)}{dt}$$

Factoring the derivative out of each term produces

$$i(t) = (C_1 + C_2 + \ldots + C_N)\frac{dv(t)}{dt}$$

This equation states that the responses $v(t)$ and $i(t)$ in Figure 6–24(a) do not change when the N parallel capacitors are replaced by an equivalent capacitance:

$$C_{EQ} = C_1 + C_2 + \ldots + C_N \quad \text{(parallel connection)} \qquad (6-28)$$

The equivalent capacitance simplification is shown in Figure 6–24(b). The initial voltage, if any, on the equivalent capacitance is $v(0)$, the common voltage across all of the original N capacitors at $t = 0$.

Next consider the series connection of N capacitors in Figure 6–25(a). Applying KVL around loop 1 in Figure 6–25(a) yields the equation

$$v(t) = v_1(t) + v_2(t) + \ldots + v_N(t)$$

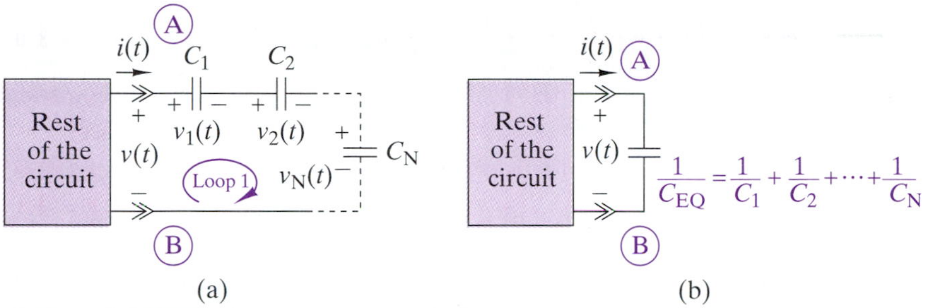

FIGURE 6–25 *Capacitors connected in series. (a) Given circuit. (b) Equivalent circuit.*

Since the elements are connected in series, KCL requires

$$i_1(t) = i_2(t) = \ldots = i_N(t) = i(t)$$

Since the same current exists in all capacitors, their i–v relationships are all of the form

$$v_k(t) = v_k(0) + \frac{1}{C_k}\int_0^t i(x)dx$$

Substituting these i–v relationships into the loop 1 KVL equation yields

$$v(t) = v_1(0) + \frac{1}{C_1}\int_0^t i(x)dx + v_2(0) + \frac{1}{C_2}\int_0^t i(x)dx$$

$$+ \cdots + v_N(0) + \frac{1}{C_N}\int_0^t i(x)dx$$

We can factor the integral out of each term to obtain

$$v(t) = [v_1(0) + v_2(0) + \ldots + v_N(0)] + \left(\frac{1}{C_1} + \frac{1}{C_2} + \ldots + \frac{1}{C_N}\right)\int_0^t i(x)dx$$

This equation indicates that the responses $v(t)$ and $i(t)$ in Figure 6–25(a) do not change when the N series capacitors are replaced by an equivalent capacitance:

$$\frac{1}{C_{EQ}} = \frac{1}{C_1} + \frac{1}{C_2} + \ldots + \frac{1}{C_N} \quad \text{(series connection)} \quad (6-29)$$

The equivalent capacitance is shown in Figure 6–25(b). The initial voltage on the equivalent capacitance is the sum of the initial voltages on each of the original N capacitors.

The equivalent capacitance of a parallel connection is the sum of the individual capacitances. The reciprocal of the equivalent capacitance of a series connection is the sum of the reciprocals of the individual capacitances. Since the capacitor and inductor are dual elements, the corresponding results for inductors are found by interchanging the series and parallel equivalence rules for the capacitor. That is, in a series connection the equivalent inductance is the sum of the individual inductances:

$$L_{EQ} = L_1 + L_2 + \ldots + L_N \qquad \text{(series connection)} \tag{6-30}$$

For the parallel connection, the reciprocals add to produce the reciprocal of the equivalent inductance:

$$\frac{1}{L_{EQ}} = \frac{1}{L_1} + \frac{1}{L_2} + \ldots + \frac{1}{L_N} \qquad \text{(parallel connection)} \tag{6-31}$$

Derivation of Eqs. (6–30) and (6–31) uses the approach given previously for the capacitor except that the roles of voltage and current are interchanged. Completion of the derivation is left as a problem for the reader. (See Problems 6–37 and 6–38.)

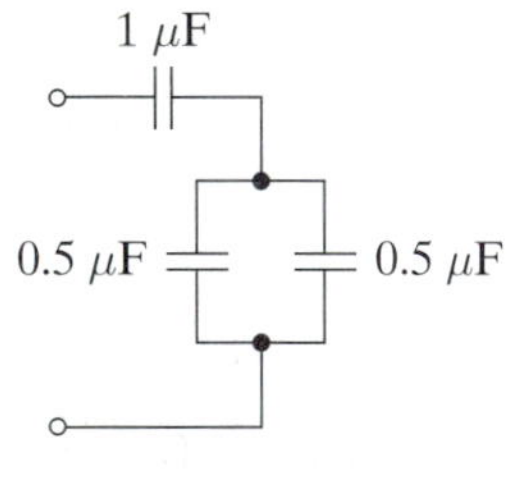

(a)

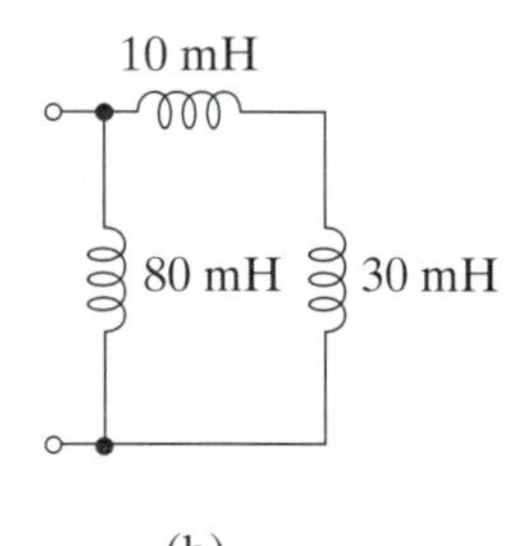

(b)

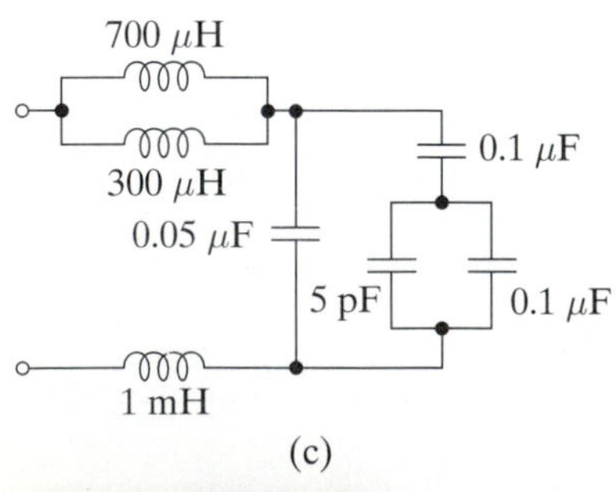

(c)

FIGURE 6–26

EXAMPLE 6–14

Find the equivalent capacitance and inductance of the circuits in Figure 6–26.

SOLUTION:

(a) For the circuit in Figure 6–26(a), the two 0.5-μF capacitors in parallel combine to yield an equivalent 0.5 + 0.5 = 1-μF capacitance. This 1-μF equivalent capacitance is in series with a 1-μF capacitor, yielding an overall equivalent of $C_{EQ} = 1/(1/1 + 1/1) = 0.5$ μF.

(b) For the circuit of Figure 6–26(b), the 10-mH and the 30-mH inductors are in series and add to produce an equivalent inductance of 40 mH. This 40-mH equivalent inductance is in parallel with the 80-mH inductor. The equivalent inductance of the parallel combination is $L_{EQ} = 1/(1/40 + 1/80) = 26.67$ mH.

(c) The circuit of Figure 6–26(c) contains both inductors and capacitors. In later chapters, we will learn how to combine all of these into a single equivalent element. For now, we combine the inductors and the capacitors separately. The 5-pF capacitor in parallel with the 0.1-μF capacitor yields an equivalent capacitance of 0.100005 μF. For all practical purposes, the 5-pF capacitor can be ignored, leaving two 0.1-μF capacitors in series with equivalent capacitance of 0.05 μF. Combining this equivalent capacitance in parallel with the remaining 0.05-μF capacitor yields an overall equivalent capacitance of 0.1 μF. The parallel 700-μH and 300-μH inductors yield an equivalent inductance of 1/(1/700 + 1/300) = 210 μH. This equivalent inductance is effectively in series with the 1-mH inductor at the bottom, yielding 1000 + 210 = 1210 μH as the overall equivalent inductance.

Figure 6–27 shows the simplified equivalent circuits for each of the circuits of Figure 6–26. ■

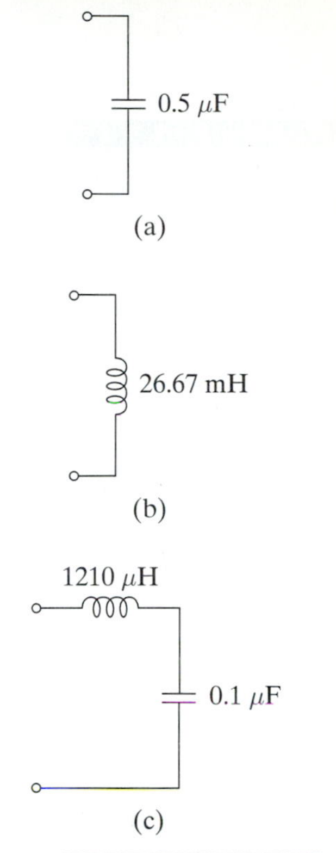

FIGURE 6–27

Exercise 6–10

The current through a series connection of two 1-μF capacitors is a rectangular pulse with an amplitude of 2 mA and a duration of 10 ms. At $t = 0$ the voltage across the first capacitor is +10 V and across the second is zero.

(a) What is the voltage across the series combination at $t = 10$ ms?
(b) What is the maximum instantaneous power delivered to the series combination?
(c) What is the energy stored on the first capacitor at $t = 0$ and $t = 10$ ms?

Answers:

(a) 50 V
(b) 100 mW at $t = 10$ ms
(c) 50 μJ and 450 μJ

DC EQUIVALENT CIRCUITS

Sometimes we need to find the dc response of circuits containing capacitors and inductors. In the first two sections of this chapter, we found that under dc conditions a capacitor acts like an open circuit and an inductor acts like a short circuit. In other words, under dc conditions, an equivalent circuit for a capacitor is an open circuit and an equivalent circuit of an inductor is a short circuit.

To determine dc responses, we replace capacitors by open circuits and inductors by short circuits and analyze the resulting resistance circuit using any of the methods in Chapters 2 through 4. The circuit analysis involves only resistance circuits and yields capacitor voltages and inductor currents along with any other variables of interest. Computer programs like SPICE and MICRO-CAP use this type of dc analysis to find the initial operating point of a circuit to be analyzed. The dc capacitor voltages and inductor currents become initial conditions for a transient response that begins at $t = 0$ when something in the circuit changes, such as the position of a switch.

EXAMPLE 6–15

Determine the voltage across the capacitors and current through the inductors in Figure 6–28(a).

SOLUTION:

The circuit is driven by a 5-V dc source. Figure 6–28(b) shows the equivalent circuit under dc conditions. The current in the resulting series circuit is 5/(50 + 50) = 50 mA. This dc current exists in both inductors, so $i_{L1} = i_{L2} =$ 50 mA. By voltage division the voltage across the 50-Ω output resistor is $v = 5 \times 50/(50 + 50) = 2.5$ V; therefore, $v_{C1}(0) = 2.5$ V. The voltage across C_2 is zero because of the short circuits produced by the two inductors. ■

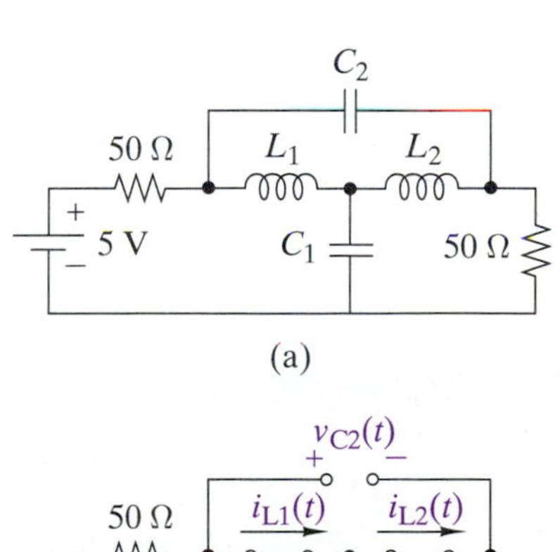

FIGURE 6–28

Exercise 6–11

Find the OP AMP output voltage in Figure 6–29.

FIGURE 6–29

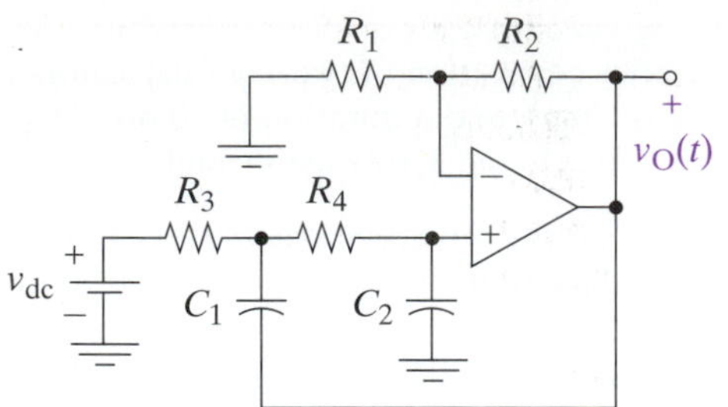

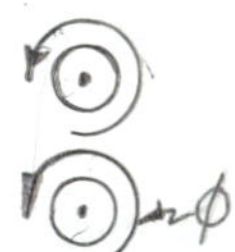

Answer:

$$v_O = \frac{R_2 + R_1}{R_1} V_{dc}$$

6–5 MUTUAL INDUCTANCE

The i–v characteristic of the inductor results from the magnetic field produced by current in a coil of wire. The magnetic flux spreads out around the coil, forming closed loops that cut or link with the turns in the coil. If the current is changing, then Faraday's law states that voltage across the coil is equal to the time rate of change of the total flux linkage.

Now suppose that a second coil is brought close to the first coil so that the flux from the first coil links with the turns of the second coil. If the current in the first coil is changing, then this flux linkage will generate a voltage in the second coil. The coupling between a changing current in one coil and a voltage across a second coil results in **mutual inductance**.

I–V CHARACTERISTICS

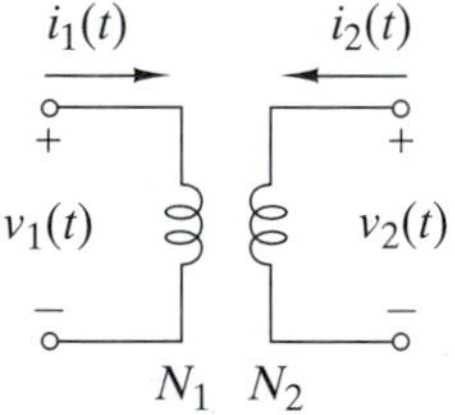

FIGURE 6–30 *Coupled coils.*

We assume that there is coupling between the two coils in Figure 6–30, and our objective is to develop the i–v characteristics of these coils. Such a derivation unavoidably involves describing the effects observed in one coil due to causes occurring in the other. We will use a double subscript notation because it clearly identifies the various cause-and-effect relationships. The first subscript indicates the coil in which the effect takes place, and the second identifies the coil in which the cause occurs. For example, $v_{11}(t)$ is the voltage across coil 1 due to causes occurring in coil 1 itself, while $v_{12}(t)$ is the voltage across coil 1 due to causes occurring in coil 2.

We begin by assuming that the coils in Figure 6–30 are far apart, so there is no mutual inductance between them. A current $i_1(t)$ passes through the N_1 turns of the first coil in Figure 6–30 and $i_2(t)$ through N_2 turns in the second. Each coil produces a flux

Coil 1	Coil 2	
$\phi_1(t) = k_1N_1i_1(t)$	$\phi_2(t) = k_2N_2i_2(t)$	(6–32)

where k_1 and k_2 are proportionality constants. The flux linkage in each coil is proportional to the number of turns:

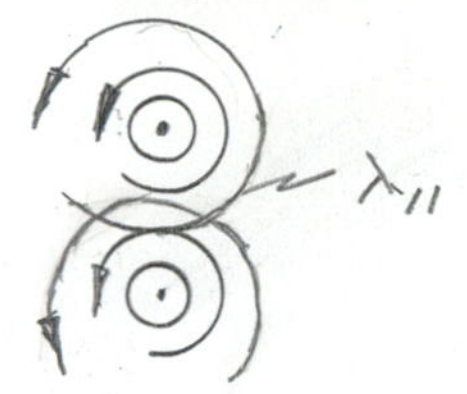

$$\text{Coil 1} \qquad \lambda_{11}(t) = N_1\phi_1(t) \qquad\qquad \text{Coil 2} \qquad \lambda_{22}(t) = N_2\phi_2(t) \tag{6-33}$$

By Faraday's law, the voltage across a coil is equal to the time rate of change of the flux linkage. Using Eqs. (6–32) and (6–33) and the derivative relationship between voltage and flux linkage gives

$$\begin{aligned} \text{Coil 1:}\ v_{11}(t) &= \frac{d\lambda_{11}(t)}{dt} = N_1\frac{d\phi_1(t)}{dt} = [k_1N_1^2]\frac{di_1(t)}{dt} \\ \text{Coil 2:}\ v_{22}(t) &= \frac{d\lambda_{22}(t)}{dt} = N_2\frac{d\phi_2(t)}{dt} = [k_2N_2^2]\frac{di_2(t)}{dt} \end{aligned} \tag{6-34}$$

Equations (6–34) provide the i–v relationships for the coils when there is no mutual coupling. These results are the same as previously found in Sect. 6–2.

Now suppose the coils are brought close together so that part of the flux produced by each coil intercepts the other. That is, part, but not all, of the fluxes $\phi_1(t)$ and $\phi_2(t)$ in Eq. (6–32) intercept the opposite coil. We describe the cross coupling using the double subscript notation:

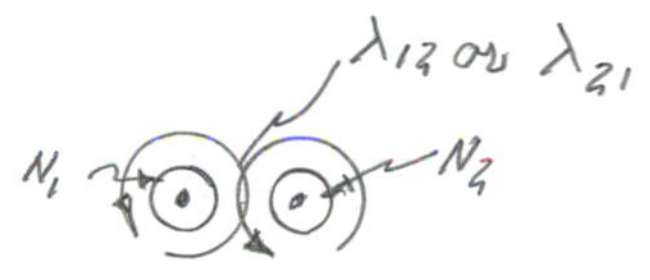

$$\text{Coil 1} \qquad \phi_{12}(t) = k_{12}N_2i_2(t) \qquad\qquad \text{Coil 2} \qquad \phi_{21}(t) = k_{21}N_1i_1(t) \tag{6-35}$$

The quantity $\phi_{12}(t)$ is the flux intercepting coil 1 due to the current in coil 2, and $\phi_{21}(t)$ is the flux intercepting coil 2 due to the current in coil 1. The total flux linkage in each coil is proportional to the number of turns:

$$\text{Coil 1} \qquad \lambda_{12}(t) = N_1\phi_{12}(t) \qquad\qquad \text{Coil 2} \qquad \lambda_{21}(t) = N_2\phi_{21}(t) \tag{6-36}$$

By Faraday's law, the voltage across a coil is equal to the time rate of change of the flux linkage. Using Eqs. (6–35) and (6–36) and the derivative relationship between flux linkages and voltages gives

$$\begin{aligned} \text{Coil 1:}\ v_{12}(t) &= \frac{d\lambda_{12}(t)}{dt} = N_1\frac{d\phi_{12}(t)}{dt} = [k_{12}N_1N_2]\frac{di_2(t)}{dt} \\ \text{Coil 2:}\ v_{21}(t) &= \frac{d\lambda_{21}(t)}{dt} = N_2\frac{d\phi_{21}(t)}{dt} = [k_{21}N_1N_2]\frac{di_1(t)}{dt} \end{aligned} \tag{6-37}$$

The expressions in Eq. (6–37) are the i–v relationships describing the cross coupling between coils when there is mutual coupling.

When the magnetic medium supporting the fluxes is linear, the superposition principle applies, and the total voltage across the coils is the sum of the results in Eqs. (6–34) and (6–37):

$$\text{Coil 1: } v_1(t) = v_{11}(t) + v_{12}(t)$$
$$= [k_1N_1^2]\frac{di_1(t)}{dt} + [k_{12}N_1N_2]\frac{di_2(t)}{dt} \quad (6\text{–}38)$$
$$\text{Coil 2: } v_2(t) = v_{21}(t) + v_{22}(t)$$
$$= [k_{21}N_1N_2]\frac{di_1(t)}{dt} + [k_2N_2^2]\frac{di_2(t)}{dt}$$

We can identify four inductance parameters in these equations:

$$L_1 = k_1N_1^2 \qquad L_2 = k_2N_2^2 \quad (6\text{–}39)$$

and

$$M_{12} = k_{12}N_1N_2 \qquad M_{21} = k_{21}N_2N_1 \quad (6\text{–}40)$$

The two inductance parameters in Eq. (6–39) are the **self-inductance** of the coils. The two parameters in Eq. (6–40) are the **mutual inductances** between the two coils. In a linear magnetic medium, $k_{12} = k_{21} = k_M$, so it is not necessary to use double subscripts to identify the mutual inductances. For a linear medium, there is a single mutual inductance parameter M defined as

$$M = M_{12} = M_{21} = k_M N_1 N_2 \quad (6\text{–}41)$$

Using the definitions in Eqs. (6–39) and (6–41), the i–v characteristics of two coupled coils are

$$\text{Coil 1: } v_1(t) = L_1\frac{di_1(t)}{dt} + M\frac{di_2(t)}{dt}$$
$$\text{Coil 2: } v_2(t) = M\frac{di_1(t)}{dt} + L_2\frac{di_2(t)}{dt} \quad (6\text{–}42)$$

Coupled coils involve three inductance parameters, the two self-inductances L_1 and L_2 and the mutual inductance M.

The preceding development assumes that the cross coupling is additive. Additive coupling means that a positive rate of change of current in coil 2 induces a positive voltage in coil 1, and vice versa. The additive assumption produces the positive sign on the mutual inductance terms in Eq. (6–42). Unhappily, it is possible for a positive rate of change of current in coil 2 to induce a negative voltage in coil 1, and vice versa. To account for additive and subtractive coupling, the general form of the coupled coil i–v characteristics includes a ± sign on the mutual inductance terms:

$$\text{Coil 1: } v_1(t) = L_1\frac{di_1(t)}{dt} \pm M\frac{di_2(t)}{dt}$$
$$\text{Coil 2: } v_2(t) = \pm M\frac{di_1(t)}{dt} + L_2\frac{di_2(t)}{dt} \quad (6\text{–}43)$$

When applying these element equations, it is necessary to know when to use a plus sign and when to use a minus sign.

THE DOT CONVENTION

We define the parameter M as a positive quantity. The question is, what sign should be put in front of this positive parameter in the i–v relationships in Eq. (6–43)? The correct sign depends on two things: (1) the spatial orientation of the two coils, and (2) the reference marks given to the coil currents and voltages.

Figure 6–31 shows the additive and subtractive spatial orientation of two coupled coils. In either case, the direction of the flux produced by a current is found using the right-hand rule treated in physics courses. In the additive case, currents i_1 and i_2 both produce clockwise fluxes ϕ_1 and ϕ_2. In the subtractive case, the currents produce opposing fluxes since ϕ_1 is clockwise and ϕ_2 is counterclockwise. The sign for the mutual inductance term is positive for the additive orientation and negative for the subtractive case.

In general, it is awkward to show the spatial features of the coils in circuit diagrams. The dots shown near one terminal of each coil in Figure 6–31 are special reference marks indicating the relative orientation of the coils. The reference directions for the coil currents and voltages are arbitrary. They can be changed as long as we follow the passive sign convention. However, the dots indicate physical attributes of the coils. They are not arbitrary. They cannot be changed.

The correct sign for the mutual inductance term hinges on how the reference marks for currents and voltages are assigned relative to the coil dots. For a given coil orientation, Figure 6–32 shows all four possible current and voltage reference assignments under the passive sign convention. In cases A and B the fluxes are additive, so the mutual inductance term is positive. In cases C and D the fluxes are subtractive and the mutual inductance term is negative. From these results we derive the following rule:

> ***Mutual inductance is additive when both current reference directions point toward or both point away from dotted terminals; otherwise, it is subtractive.***

Since we always use the passive sign convention, the rule can be stated in terms of voltages as follows:

> ***Mutual inductance is additive when the voltage reference marks are both positive or both negative at the dotted terminals; otherwise, it is subtractive.***

Since the current reference directions or voltage polarity marks can be changed, a corollary of this rule is that we can always assign reference directions so that the positive sign applies to the mutual inductance. This corollary is important because a positive sign is built into the mutual inductance models in computer-aided circuit analysis programs like SPICE and MICRO-CAP.

You may feel that all of this discussion about signs and dots is much ado about nothing. Not so. First, selecting the wrong sign can have nontrivial consequences because the polarity of the output signal is reversed. If the signal is a command to your car's autopilot, then you really need to know

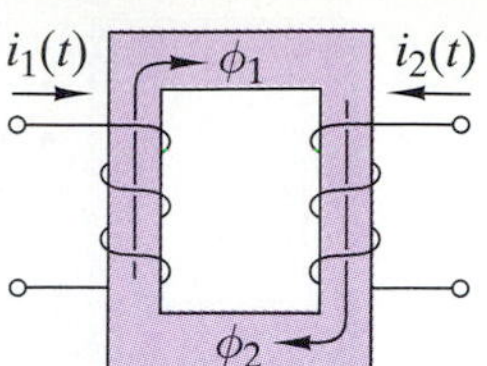

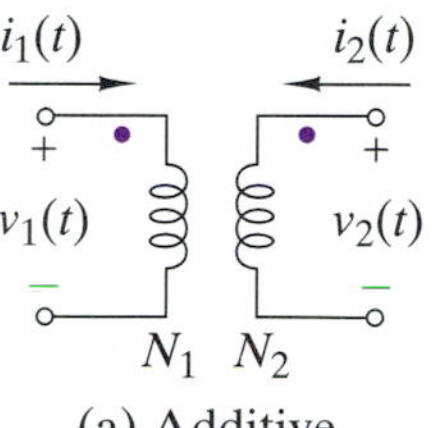

(a) Additive

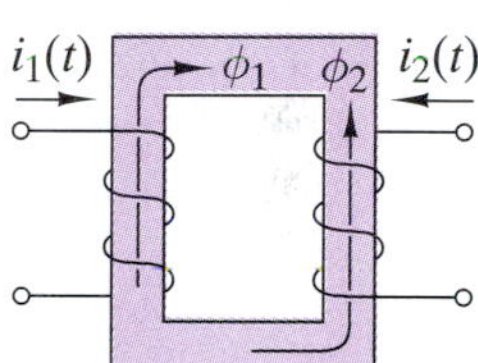

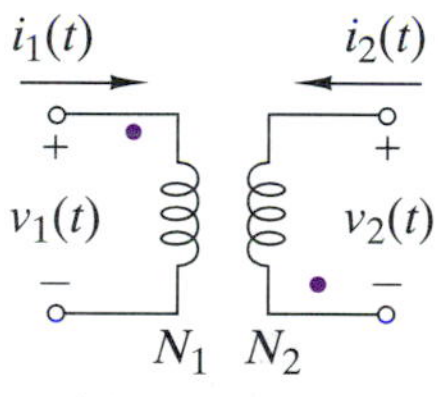

(b) Subtractive

FIGURE 6–31 *Coil orientations and corresponding reference dots. (a) Additive. (b) Subtractive.*

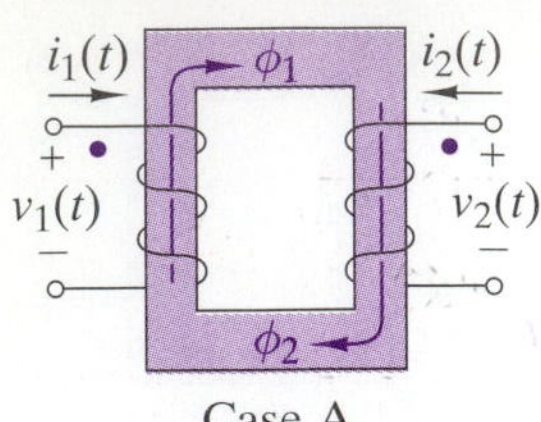

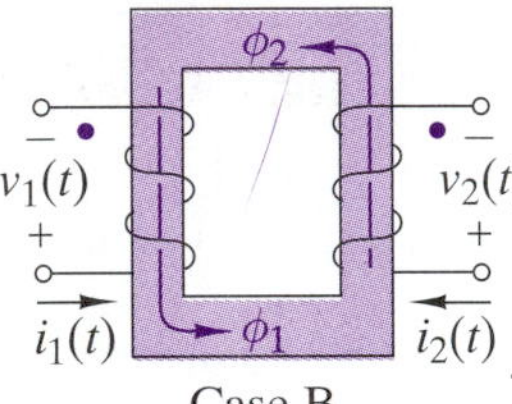

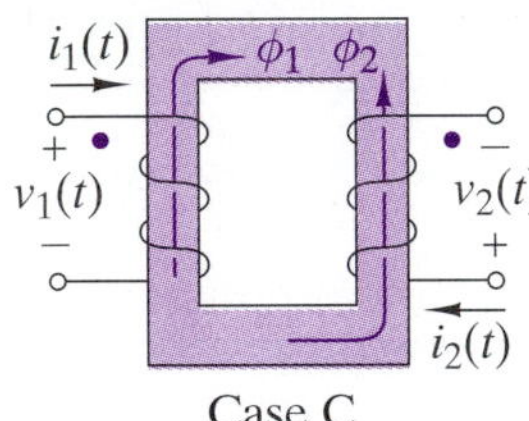

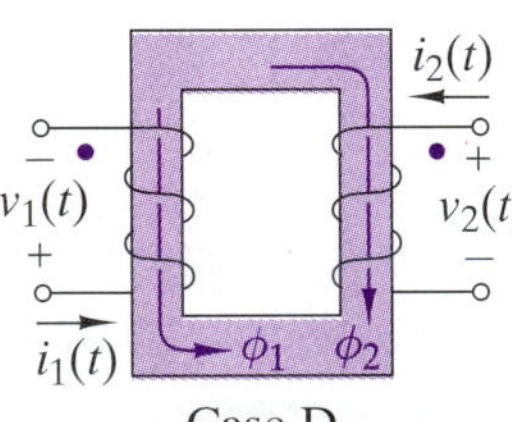

FIGURE 6–32 *All possible current and voltage reference mark assignments under the passive sign convention.*

whether stepping on the brake pedal will slow the car down or speed it up. Another problem is that the two coils may appear in different parts of a circuit diagram and may be assigned voltage and current reference marks for other reasons. In such circumstances it is important to understand the underlying principle to select the correct sign for the mutual inductance term.

The following examples and exercises illustrate selecting the correct sign and applying the *i–v* characteristics in Eq. (6–43).

EXAMPLE 6–16

In Figure 6–33 the source voltage is $v_S(t) = 10 \cos 100t$. Find the output voltage $v_2(t)$.

SOLUTION:

The sign of the mutual inductance term is positive because both current reference directions are toward the coil dots. Since the load on coil 2 is an open circuit, $i_2(t) = 0$ and the *i–v* equations of the coupled coils reduce to

$$\text{Coil 1: } 10 \cos 100t = 0.01\frac{di_1(t)}{dt} + 0$$

$$\text{Coil 2: } v_2(t) = 0.002\frac{di_1(t)}{dt} + 0$$

Solving the coil 1 equation for di_1/dt yields

$$\frac{di_1(t)}{dt} = 1000 \cos 100t$$

Substituting this equation for $i_1(t)$ into the coil 2 equation yields

$$v_2(t) = 2 \cos 100t \text{ (correct)}$$

Incorrectly choosing a minus sign for the mutual inductance term produces a coil 2 voltage of

$$v_2(t) = -2 \cos 100t \text{ (incorrect)}$$

Note that the incorrect and correct solutions differ by a signal inversion. ■

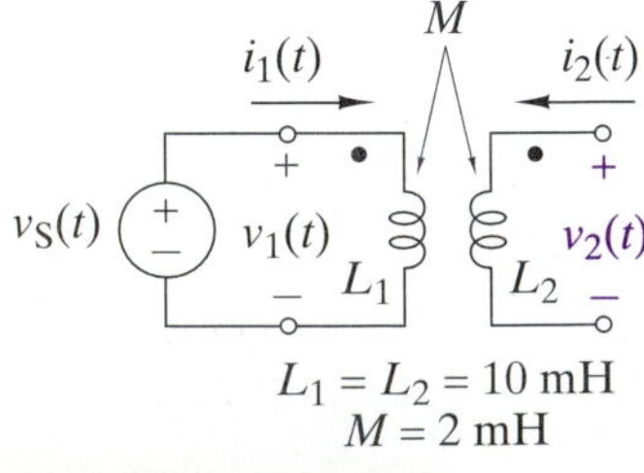

FIGURE 6–33

EXAMPLE 6–17

Solve for $v_X(t)$ in terms of $i_1(t)$ for the coupled coils in Figure 6–34.

SOLUTION:

In this case the signs of the mutual inductance terms are negative because the reference direction for $i_1(t)$ points toward the coil 1 dot and the reference direction for $i_2(t)$ points away from the coil 2 dot. The coupled coil *i–v* equations are

$$\text{Coil 1: } v_1(t) = L_1\frac{di_1(t)}{dt} - M\frac{di_2(t)}{dt}$$

$$\text{Coil 2: } v_2(t) = -M\frac{di_1(t)}{dt} + L_2\frac{di_2(t)}{dt}$$

A KCL constraint at node A requires that $i_1(t) = -i_2(t)$. Therefore, the coil i–v equations can be written in the form

$$\text{Coil 1: } v_1(t) = L_1\frac{di_1(t)}{dt} - M\frac{d[-i_1(t)]}{dt}$$

$$\text{Coil 2: } v_2(t) = -M\frac{di_1(t)}{dt} + L_2\frac{d[-i_1(t)]}{dt}$$

A KVL constraint around the loop requires that $v_X(t) = v_1(t) - v_2(t)$. Subtracting the second equation from the first yields

$$v_X(t) = L_1\frac{di_1(t)}{dt} + M\frac{di_1(t)}{dt} + M\frac{di_1(t)}{dt} + L_2\frac{di_1(t)}{dt}$$

$$= (L_1 + L_2 + 2M)\frac{di_1(t)}{dt}$$

The two mutual inductance terms add, producing an equivalent inductance of $L_1 + L_2 + 2M$. With a plus sign in the coil i–v relations the mutual inductance produces an equivalent inductance of $L_1 + L_2 - 2M$. Thus, it is important to have the right sign in the i–v relationship. ■

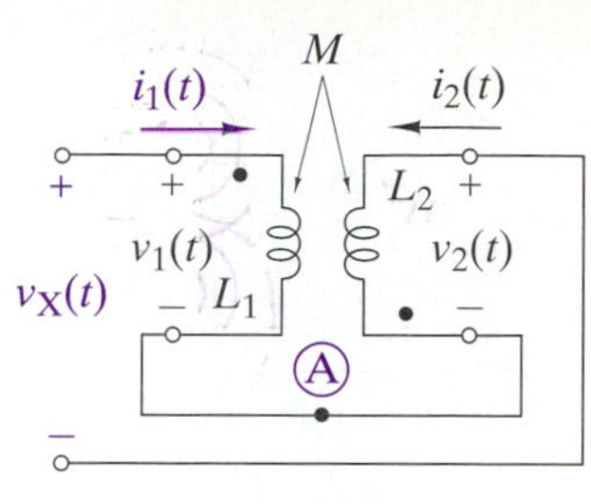

FIGURE 6–34

Exercise 6–12

Select the appropriate sign for the mutual inductance terms for each pair of coupled coils shown in Figure 6–35.

Answer:

All are negative.

Exercise 6–13

Assign a reference direction to i_X in Figure 6–36 so that the mutual inductance terms have a positive sign for each pair of coupled coils.

Answers:

C1: Either
C2: Counterclockwise
C3: To the right

Exercise 6–14

Find $v_1(t)$ and $v_2(t)$ for the circuit in Figure 6–37.

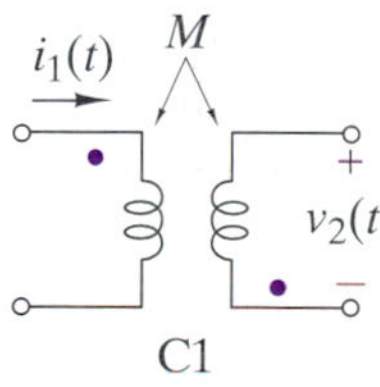

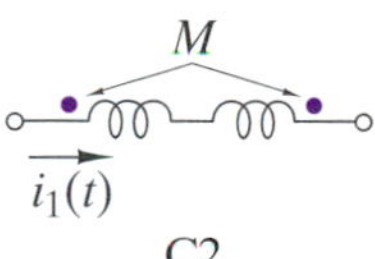

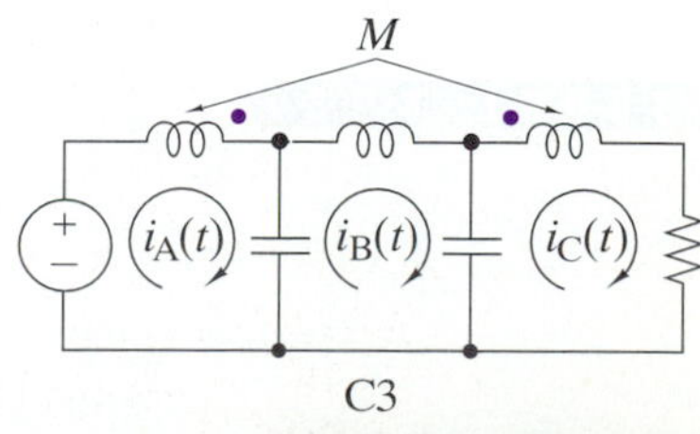

FIGURE 6–35

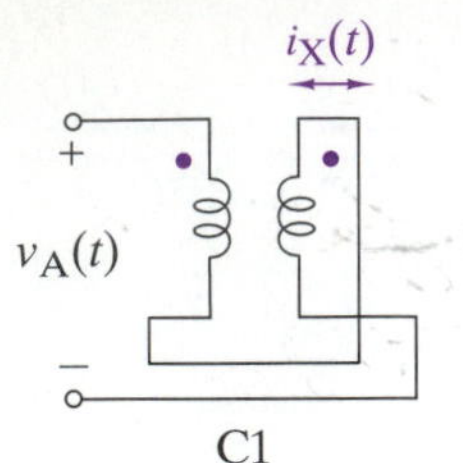

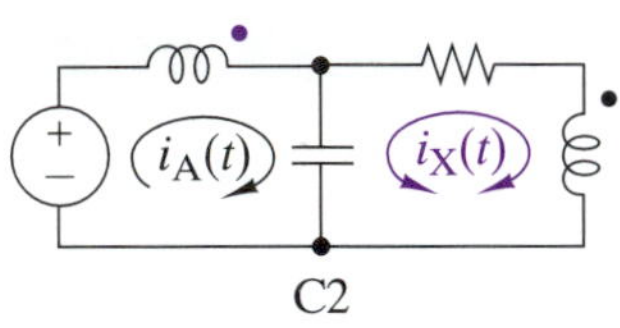

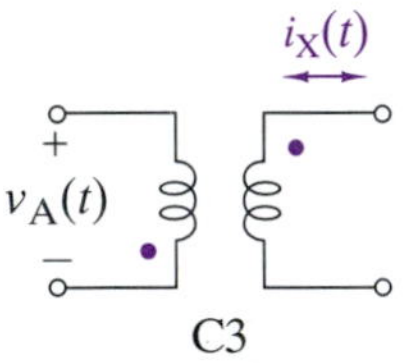

FIGURE 6–36

Answers:

$$v_1(t) = -10 \sin 10^4 t - 3 \cos 5 \times 10^3 t$$

$$v_2(t) = -15 \sin 10^4 t - 5 \cos 5 \times 10^3 t$$

ENERGY ANALYSIS

Calculating the total energy stored in a pair of coupled coils reveals a fundamental limitation on allowable values of the self- and mutual inductances. We first calculate the total power absorbed. Multiplying the coil 1 equation in Eq. (6–43) by $i_1(t)$ and the coil 2 equation by $i_2(t)$ produces

$$p_1(t) = v_1(t)i_1(t) = L_1 i_1(t)\frac{di_1(t)}{dt} \pm M i_1(t)\frac{di_2(t)}{dt}$$

$$p_2(t) = v_2(t)i_2(t) = \pm M i_2(t)\frac{di_1(t)}{dt} + L_2 i_2(t)\frac{di_2(t)}{dt} \qquad (6-44)$$

The quantities $p_1(t)$ and $p_2(t)$ are the powers absorbed with coils 1 and 2. The total power is the sum of the individual coil powers:

$$p(t) = p_1(t) + p_2(t)$$
$$= L_1\left[i_1(t)\frac{di_1(t)}{dt}\right] \pm M\left[i_1(t)\frac{di_2(t)}{dt} + i_2(t)\frac{di_1(t)}{dt}\right] + L_2\left[i_2(t)\frac{di_2(t)}{dt}\right] \qquad (6-45)$$

Each of the bracketed terms in Eq. (6–45) is a perfect derivative. Specifically,

$$i_1(t)\frac{di_1(t)}{dt} = \frac{1}{2}\frac{di_1^2(t)}{dt}$$

$$i_2(t)\frac{di_2(t)}{dt} = \frac{1}{2}\frac{di_2^2(t)}{dt} \qquad (6-46)$$

$$i_1(t)\frac{di_2(t)}{dt} + i_2(t)\frac{di_1(t)}{dt} = \frac{di_1(t)i_2(t)}{dt}$$

Therefore, the total power in Eq. (6–45) is

$$p(t) = \frac{d}{dt}\left[\frac{1}{2}L_1 i_1^2(t) \pm M i_1(t) i_2(t) + \frac{1}{2}L_2 i_2^2(t)\right] \qquad (6-47)$$

FIGURE 6–37

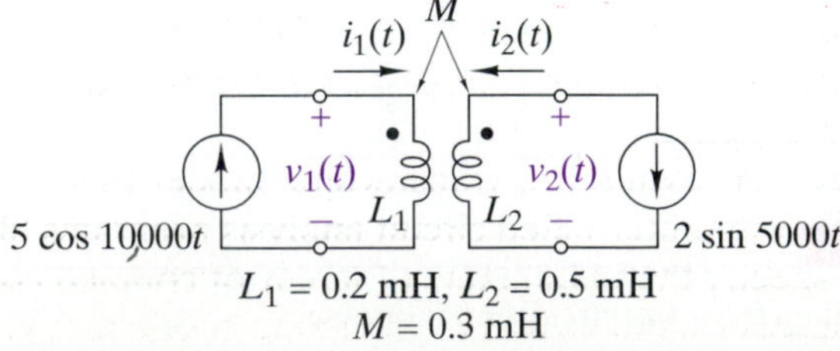

Since power is the time rate of change of energy, the quantity inside the brackets in Eq. (6–47) is the total energy stored in the two coils:

$$w(t) = \frac{1}{2}L_1 i_1^2(t) \pm M i_1(t) i_2(t) + \frac{1}{2}L_2 i_2^2(t) \qquad (6-48)$$

In Eq. (6–48) the self-inductance terms are always positive. However, the mutual inductance term can be either positive or negative. At first glance it appears that the total energy could be negative. But the total energy must be positive; otherwise the coils could deliver net energy to the outside world.

The condition $w(t) \geq 0$ places a constraint on the values of the self- and mutual inductances. First, if $i_2(t) = 0$, then $w(t) \geq 0$ in Eq. (6–48) requires $L_1 > 0$. Next, if $i_1(t) = 0$, then $w(t) \geq 0$ in Eq. (6–48) requires $L_2 > 0$. Finally, if $i_1(t) \neq 0$ and $i_2(t) \neq 0$, then we divide Eq. (6–48) by $[i_2(t)]^2$ and define a variable $x = i_1/i_2$. With these changes, the energy constraint $w(t) > 0$ becomes

$$\frac{w(t)}{i_2^2(t)} = f(x) = \frac{1}{2}L_1 x^2 \pm Mx + \frac{1}{2}L_2 \geqslant 0 \qquad (6-49)$$

The minimum value of $f(x)$ occurs when

$$\frac{df(x)}{dx} = L_1 x \pm M = 0, \quad \text{hence,} \quad x_{\text{MIN}} = \pm\frac{M}{L_1} \qquad (6-50)$$

The value x_{MIN} yields the minimum of $f(x)$ because the second derivative of $f(x)$ is positive. Substituting x_{MIN} back into Eq. (6–49) yields the condition

$$f(x_{\text{MIN}}) = \frac{1}{2}L_1\frac{M^2}{L_1^2} - \frac{M^2}{L_1} + \frac{1}{2}L_2 = \frac{1}{2}\left[-\frac{M^2}{L_1} + L_2\right] \geqslant 0 \qquad (6-51)$$

The constraint in Eq. (6–51) means, the stored energy in a pair of coils is positive if

$$L_1 L_2 \geqslant M^2 \qquad (6-52)$$

Energy considerations dictate that in any pair of coupled coils, the product of the self-inductances must exceed the square of the mutual inductance.

The constraint in Eq. (6–52) is usually written in terms of a new parameter called the **coupling coefficient** k:

$$k = \frac{M}{\sqrt{L_1 L_2}} \leqslant 1 \qquad (6-53)$$

The parameter k ranges from 0 to 1. If $M = 0$, then $k = 0$ and the coupling between the coils is zero. The condition $k = 1$ requires **perfect coupling**, in which all of the flux in coil 1 links coil 2, and vice versa. Perfect coupling is physically impossible, although careful design can produce coupling coefficients of 0.99 and higher.

The next section discusses a transformer model that assumes perfect coupling ($k = 1$). Computer-aided circuit analysis programs like SPICE and MICRO-CAP specify the parameters of a pair of coupled coils in terms of the self-inductances L_1 and L_2 and the coupling coefficient k.

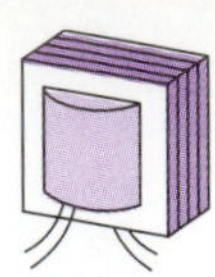

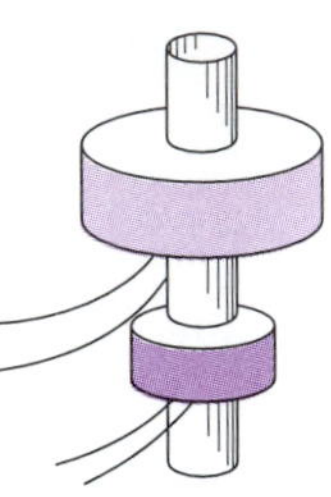

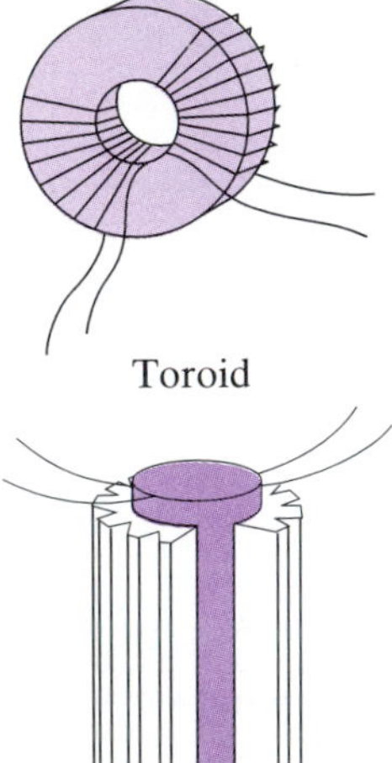

FIGURE 6–38 *Examples of transformer devices.*

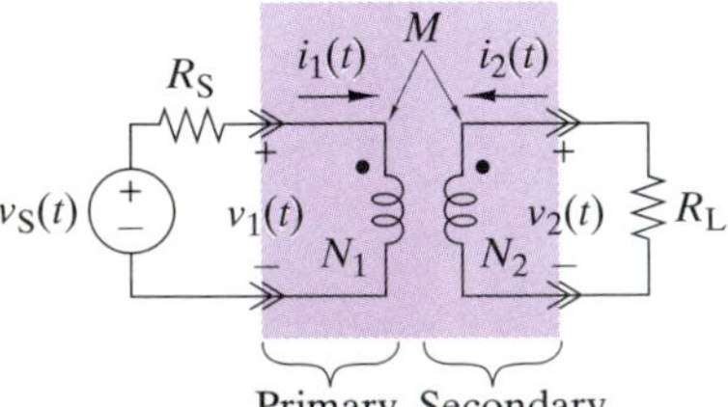

FIGURE 6–39 *A transformer connected as an interface circuit.*

Exercise 6–15

What is the coupling coefficient of the coils in Exercise 6–14?

Answer:

$k = 0.949$

6–6 THE IDEAL TRANSFORMER

A **transformer** is an electrical device that utilizes mutual inductance coupling between two coils. Transformers find application in virtually every type of electrical system, but especially in power supplies and commercial power grids. Some example devices from these applications are shown in Figure 6–38.

In Figure 6–39 the transformer is shown as an interface device between a source and a load. The coil connected to the source is called the **primary winding** and the coil connected to the load the **secondary winding**. In most applications the transformer is a coupling device that transfers signals (especially power) from the source to the load. The basic purpose of the device is to change voltage and current levels so that the conditions at the source and load are compatible.

Transformer design involves two primary goals: (1) to maximize the magnetic coupling between the two windings, and (2) to minimize the power loss in the windings. The first goal produces nearly perfect coupling ($k \approx 1$) so that almost all of the flux in one winding links the other. The second goal produces nearly zero power loss so that almost all of the power delivered to the primary winding transfers to the load. The **ideal transformer** is a circuit element in which coupled coils are assumed to have perfect coupling and zero power loss. We now wish to derive the i–v characteristics of a transformer with perfect coupling and no power loss.

PERFECT COUPLING

Perfect coupling means that all of the flux in the first coil links the second coil, and vice versa. Equation (6–32) defines the total flux in each coil as

$$\begin{array}{cc} \text{Coil 1} & \text{Coil 2} \\ \phi_1(t) = k_1 N_1 i_1(t) & \phi_2(t) = k_2 N_2 i_2(t) \end{array} \tag{6-54}$$

where k_1 and k_2 are proportionality constants. Equation (6–35) defines the cross coupling using the double subscript notation:

$$\begin{array}{cc} \text{Coil 1} & \text{Coil 2} \\ \phi_{12}(t) = k_{12} N_2 i_2(t) & \phi_{21}(t) = k_{21} N_1 i_1(t) \end{array} \tag{6-55}$$

In this equation $\phi_{12}(t)$ is the flux intercepting coil 1 due to the current in coil 2, and $\phi_{21}(t)$ is the flux intercepting coil 2 due to the current in coil 1. Perfect coupling means that

$$\phi_{21}(t) = \phi_1(t) \quad \text{and} \quad \phi_{12}(t) = \phi_2(t) \tag{6-56}$$

Comparing Eqs. (6–54) and (6–55) shows that perfect coupling requires $k_1 = k_{21}$ and $k_2 = k_{12}$. But in a linear magnetic medium $k_{12} = k_{21} = k_M$, so perfect coupling implies

$$k_1 = k_2 = k_{12} = k_{21} = k_M \tag{6–57}$$

Substituting the perfect coupling conditions in Eq. (6–57) into the coupled-coil *i–v* characteristics in Eq. (6–38) gives

$$v_1(t) = [k_M N_1^2]\frac{di_1(t)}{dt} \pm [k_M N_1 N_2]\frac{di_2(t)}{dt}$$

$$v_2(t) = \pm [k_M N_1 N_2]\frac{di_1(t)}{dt} + [k_M N_2^2]\frac{di_2(t)}{dt} \tag{6–58}$$

Factoring N_1 out of the first equation and $\pm N_2$ out of the second produces

$$v_1(t) = N_1\left([k_M N_1]\frac{di_1(t)}{dt} \pm [k_M N_2]\frac{di_2(t)}{dt}\right)$$

$$v_2(t) = \pm N_2\left([k_M N_1]\frac{di_1(t)}{dt} \pm [k_M N_2]\frac{di_2(t)}{dt}\right) \tag{6–59}$$

Dividing the second equation by the first shows that perfect coupling implies

$$\frac{v_2(t)}{v_1(t)} = \pm\frac{N_2}{N_1} = \pm n \tag{6–60}$$

where the parameter n is called the **turns ratio**.

With perfect coupling the secondary voltage is proportional to the primary voltage, so they have the same waveshape. For example, when the primary voltage is $v_1(t) = V_A \sin \omega t$, the secondary voltage is $v_2(t) = \pm nV_A \sin \omega t$. When the turns ratio $n > 1$, the secondary voltage amplitude is larger than the primary and the device is called a **step-up transformer**. Conversely, when $n < 1$, the secondary voltage is smaller than the primary and the device is called a **step-down transformer**. The ability to increase or decrease ac voltage levels is a basic feature of transformers. Commercial power systems use transmission voltages of several hundred kilovolts. For residential applications, the transmission voltage is reduced to safer levels (typically 220/110 V_{rms}) using step-down transformers.

The ± sign in Eq. (6–60) reminds us that mutual inductance can be additive or subtractive. Selecting the correct sign is important because of signal inversion. The sign depends on the reference marks given the primary and secondary currents relative to the dots indicating the relative coil orientations. The rule for the ideal transformer is a corollary of the rule for selecting the sign of the mutual inductance term in coupled-coil element equations:

The sign in Eq. (6–60) is positive when both current reference directions point toward or both point away from a dotted terminal; otherwise, it is negative.

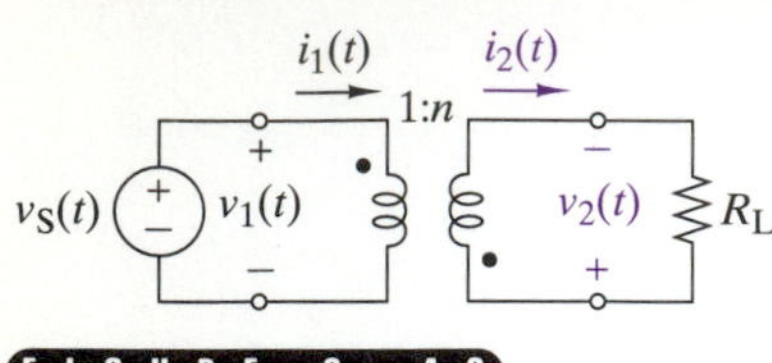

FIGURE 6–40

Exercise 6–16

The transformer in Figure 6–40 has perfect coupling and a turns ratio of $n = 0.1$. The input voltage is $v_S(t) = 120 \sin 377t$ V.

(a) What is the secondary voltage?
(b) What is the secondary current for a 50-Ω load?
(c) Is this a step-up or step-down transformer?

Answers:

(a) $+12 \sin 377t$ V
(b) $-0.24 \sin 377t$ A
(c) Step down

ZERO POWER LOSS

The ideal transformer model also assumes that there is no power loss in the transformer. With the passive sign convention, the powers in the primary winding and secondary windings are $v_1(t)i_1(t)$ and $v_2(t)i_2(t)$, respectively. Zero power loss requires

$$v_1(t)i_1(t) + v_2(t)i_2(t) = 0 \quad (6\text{–}61)$$

which can be rearranged into the form

$$\frac{i_2(t)}{i_1(t)} = -\frac{v_1(t)}{v_2(t)} \quad (6\text{–}62)$$

But under the perfect coupling assumption, $v_2(t)/v_1(t) = \pm n$. With zero power loss and perfect coupling, the primary and secondary currents are related as

$$\frac{i_2(t)}{i_1(t)} = \mp\frac{1}{n} \quad (6\text{–}63)$$

The correct sign in this equation depends on the orientation of the curent reference directions relative to the dots describing the transformer structure.

With both perfect coupling and zero power loss, the secondary current is inversely proportional to the turns ratio. A step-up transformer ($n > 1$) increases the voltage and decreases the current, which improves transmission line efficiency because the i^2R losses in the conductors are smaller.

Exercise 6–17

The transformer in Figure 6–40 has perfect coupling, zero power loss, and a turns ratio of $n = 10$. The input is $v_S = 120 \sin 377t$ V.

(a) What is the secondary voltage?
(b) What is the secondary current for a 50-Ω load?
(c) What is the primary current?
(d) What is the power absorbed by the load?
(e) Is this a step-up or step-down transformer?

Answers:

(a) $+1200 \sin 377t$ V
(b) $-24 \sin 377t$ A
(c) $240 \sin 377t$ A
(d) $28.8 \sin^2 377t$ kW
(e) Step up

I–V CHARACTERISTICS

Equations (6–60) and (6–63) define the i–v characteristics of the ideal transformer circuit element.

$$v_2(t) = \pm n v_1(t)$$
$$i_2(t) = \mp \frac{1}{n} i_1(t) \qquad (6-64)$$

where $n = N_2/N_1$ is the turns ratio. The correct sign in these equations depends on the assigned reference directions and transformer dots, as previously discussed.

Using the ideal transformer model requires some caution. The relationships in Eq. (6–64) state that the secondary signals are proportional to the primary signals. These element equations appear to apply to dc signals. This is, of course, wrong. The element equations are an idealization of mutual inductance, and mutual inductance requires time-varying signals to provide the coupling between two coils.

The lesson to remember is that it is up to the user to know and conform to the limitations of a circuit model. The model will not do this for you. If you apply a dc signal to the primary of an ideal transformer element, the model will happily report a proportional dc signal in the secondary. The point is that models do not tell you when they give nonsense for answers. The derivation of a circuit model is not simply an academic exercise: The derivation must be understood in order to know the limitations of a model.

EQUIVALENT INPUT RESISTANCE

Because a transformer changes the voltage and current levels, it effectively changes the load resistance seen by a source in the primary circuit. To derive the equivalent input resistance, we write the device equations for the ideal transformer shown in Figure 6–41:

$$\text{Resistor: } v_2(t) = R_L i_L(t)$$

$$\text{Transformer: } v_2(t) = n v_1(t) \text{ and } i_2(t) = -\frac{1}{n} i_1(t)$$

Dividing the first transformer equation by the second and inserting the load resistance constraint yields

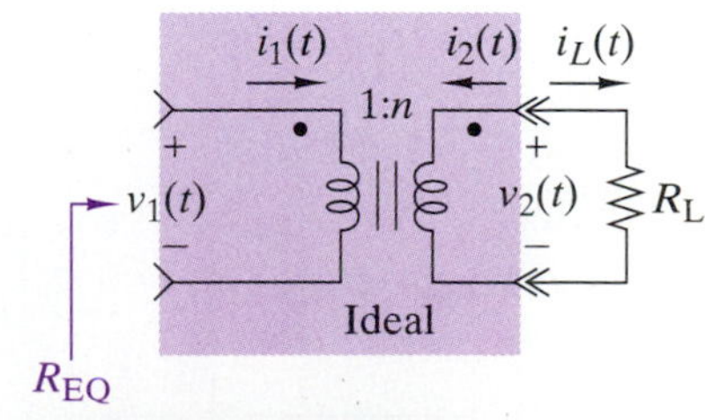

FIGURE 6–41 *Transformer input resistance.*

$$\frac{v_2(t)}{i_2(t)} = \frac{i_L(t)R_L}{i_2(t)} = -n^2\frac{v_1(t)}{i_1(t)}$$

Applying KCL at the output interface tells us that $i_L(t) = -i_2(t)$. Therefore, the equivalent resistance seen on the primary side is

$$R_{EQ} = \frac{v_1(t)}{i_1(t)} = \frac{1}{n^2}R_L \qquad (6-65)$$

The equivalent load resistance seen on the primary side depends on the turns ratio and the load resistance. Adjusting the turns ratio can make R_{EQ} equal to the source resistance. Transformer coupling can produce the resistance match condition for maximum power transfer when the source and load resistances are not equal.

The derivation leading to Eq. (6–65) used the ideal transformer with the dot markings and reference directions in Figure 6–41. However, the final result does not depend on the location of the dot marks relative to voltage and current reference directions. In other words, Eq. (6–65) yields the input resistance for any ideal transformer with a turns ratio of n and a load R_L.

EXAMPLE 6–18

A stereo amplifier has an output resistance of 600 Ω. The input resistance of the speaker (the load) is 8 Ω. Select the turns ratio of a transformer to obtain maximum power transfer.

SOLUTION:

The maximum power transfer theorem in Chapter 3 states that the source and load resistance must be matched (equal) to achieve maximum power. Directly connecting the amplifier (600 Ω) to the speaker (8 Ω) produces a mismatch. If a transformer is inserted as shown in Figure 6–42, then the equivalent load resistance seen by the amplifier is

$$R_{EQ} = \frac{1}{n^2}R_L = \frac{1}{n^2}8$$

To produce a resistance match, we need $R_{EQ} = 600 = 8/n^2$ or a turns ratio of $n = 1/8.66$. ■

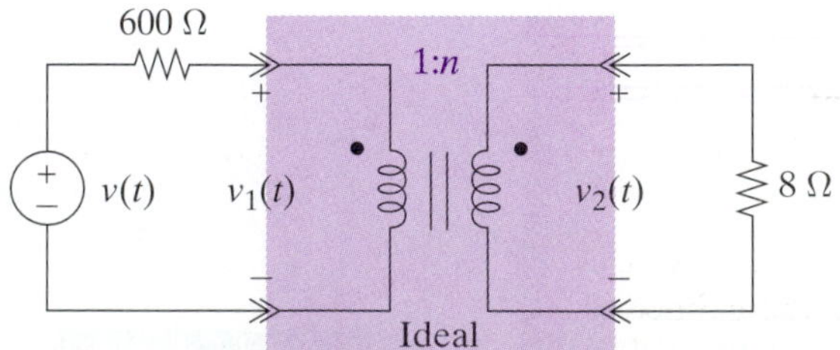

FIGURE 6–42

SUMMARY

- The linear capacitor and inductor are dynamic circuit elements that can store energy. The instantaneous element power is positive when they are storing energy and negative when they are delivering previously stored energy. The net energy transfer is never negative because inductors and capacitors are passive elements.
- The current through a capacitor is zero unless the voltage is changing. A capacitor acts like an open circuit to dc excitations.
- The voltage across an inductor is zero unless the current is changing. An inductor acts like an short circuit to dc excitations.
- Capacitor voltage and inductor current are called state variables because they define the energy state of a circuit. Circuit state variables are continuous functions of time as long as the circuit driving forces are finite.
- OP AMP capacitor circuits perform signal integration or differentiation. These operations, together with the summer and gain functions, provide the building blocks for designing dynamic input–output characteristics.
- Capacitors or inductors in series or parallel can be replaced with an equivalent element found by adding the individual capacitances or inductances or their reciprocals. The dc response of a dynamic circuit can be found by replacing all capacitors with open circuits and all inductors with short circuits.
- Mutual inductance describes magnetic coupling between two coils. The dot convention describes the physical orientation of the two magnetically coupled coils. Mutual inductance coupling is additive when both current reference arrows point toward or away from dotted terminals; otherwise, it is subtractive.
- The ideal transformer is a model that assumes perfect coupling and no power loss. An ideal transformer is characterized by its turns ratio.

EN ROUTE OBJECTIVES AND ASSOCIATED PROBLEMS

ERO 6–1 CAPACITOR AND INDUCTOR RESPONSES (SECTS. 6–1, 6–2)

Given the current through (voltage across) a capacitor or an inductor,

(a) Determine the voltage across (current through) the element.
(b) Determine the power absorbed and energy stored by the element.

6–1 The voltage across a 2-μF capacitor is $v_C(t) = 3\,e^{-4000t}u(t)$ V. Derive expressions for, and sketch, $i_C(t)$, $p_C(t)$, and $w_C(t)$. Is the capacitor absorbing power, delivering power, or both?

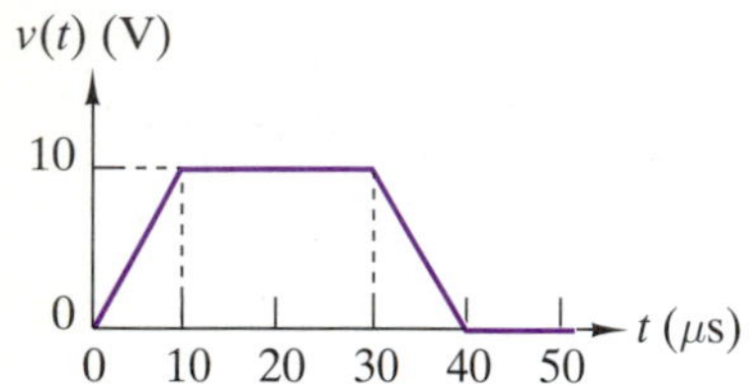

FIGURE P6–6

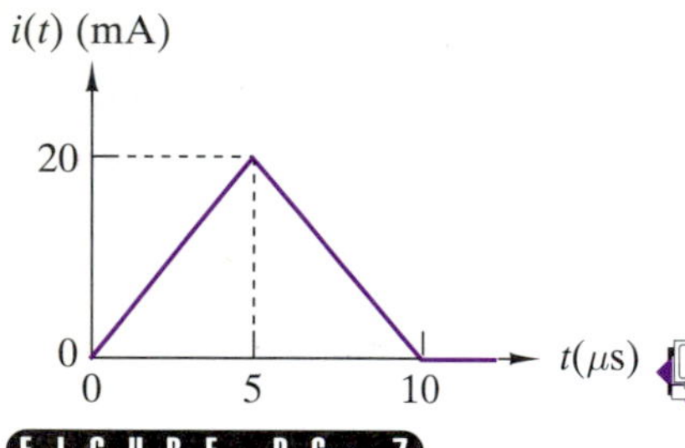

FIGURE P6–7

6–2 The voltage across a 100-nF capacitor is $v_C(t) = 30\cos(5000t)u(t)$ V. Derive expressions for, and sketch, $i_C(t)$, $p_C(t)$, and $w_C(t)$. Is the capacitor absorbing power, delivering power, or both?

6–3 The current through a 125-nF capacitor is $i_C(t) = 50e^{-5000t}u(t)$ mA. Derive expressions for, and sketch, $v_C(t)$, $p_C(t)$, and $w_C(t)$. Assume $v_C(0) = 0$. Is the capacitor absorbing power, delivering power, or both?

6–4 The current through a 25-μF capacitor is $i_C(t) = 50[u(t) - u(t - 5 \times 10^{-3})]$ mA. Derive expressions for, and sketch, $v_C(t)$, $p_C(t)$, and $w_C(t)$. Is the capacitor absorbing power, delivering power, or both?

6–5 At $t = 0$, the initial voltage across a 200-nF capacitor is 30 V. For $t > 0$, the current through the capacitor is $i_C(t) = 0.4\cos 10^5 t$ A. Derive expressions for and sketch $v_C(t)$, $p_C(t)$, and $w_C(t)$. Is the capacitor absorbing power, delivering power, or both?

6–6 The voltage across a 500-nF capacitor is shown in Figure P6–6. Derive expressions for, and sketch, $i_C(t)$, $p_C(t)$, and $w_C(t)$. Is the capacitor absorbing power, delivering power, or both?

6–7 The current through a 1-μF capacitor is shown in Figure P6–7. Given that $v_C(0) = 0$, find the value of $v_C(t)$ at $t = 5$, 10, and 20 μs.

6–8 The current through a 2-mH inductor is $i_L(t) = [1 - e^{-1000t}]u(t)$ A. Derive expressions for, and sketch, $v_L(t)$, $p_L(t)$, and $w_L(t)$. Is the capacitor absorbing power, delivering power, or both?

6–9 For $t > 0$, the current through a 500-mH inductor is $i_L(t) = 10\,e^{-1000t}\sin 2000t$ mA. Derive expressions for, and sketch, $v_L(t)$, $p_L(t)$, and $w_L(t)$. Is the inductor absorbing power, delivering power, or both?

6–10 A voltage pulse $v_L(t) = 5[u(t - 10^{-3}) - u(t - 2 \times 10^{-3})]$ V appears across a 50-mH inductor. Derive expressions for, and sketch, $i_L(t)$, $p_L(t)$, and $w_L(t)$. Assume $i_L(0) = 0$. Is the inductor absorbing power, delivering power, or both?

6–11 For $t > 0$, the voltage across a 50-mH inductor is $v_L(t) = e^{-1000t}u(t)$ V. Derive expressions for, and sketch, $i_L(t)$, $p_L(t)$, and $w_L(t)$. Assume $i_L(0) = 0$. Is the inductor absorbing power, delivering power, or both?

6–12 The current through a 20-mH inductor is shown in Figure P6–7. Derive expressions for, and sketch, $v_L(t)$, $p_L(t)$, and $w_L(t)$.

6–13 The voltage across a 100-μH inductor is shown in Figure P6–6. Given that $i_L(0) = 0$, find the value of $i_L(t)$ at $t = 5$, 10, and 20 μs. What is the value of $i_L(t)$ at $t > 40$ μs? Is the inductor absorbing power, delivering power, or both?

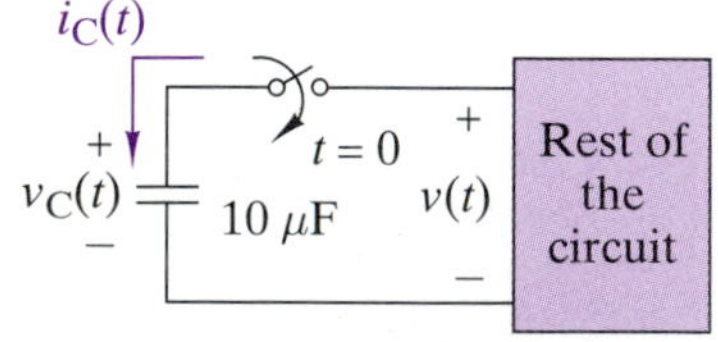

FIGURE P6–14

6–14 The capacitor in Figure P6–14 carries an initial voltage $v_C(0) = 25$ V. At $t = 0$, the switch is closed, and thereafter the voltage across the capacitor is $v_C(t) = 25\,e^{-5000t}$ V. For $t > 0$, derive expressions for $i_C(t)$ and $p_C(t)$. Is the capacitor absorbing power from or delivering power to the rest of the circuit?

6–15 The capacitor in Figure P6–14 carries an initial voltage $v_C(0) = 0$ V. At $t = 0$, the switch is closed, and thereafter the voltage across the capacitor is $v_C(t) = 10(1 - e^{-1000t})$ V. For $t > 0$, derive expressions for $i_C(t)$ and $p_C(t)$. Is the capacitor absorbing power from or delivering power to the rest of the circuit?

6–16 The inductor in Figure P6–16 carries an initial current of $i_L(0) = 20$ mA. At $t = 0$ the switch opens, and thereafter the current into the rest of the circuit is $i(t) = -20\, e^{-500t}$ mA. For $t > 0$, derive expressions for $v_L(t)$and $p_L(t)$. Is the inductor absorbing power from or delivering power to the rest of the circuit?

6–17 The inductor in Figure P6–16 carries an initial current of $i_L(0) = 20$ mA. At $t = 0$ the switch opens, and thereafter the current into the rest of the circuit is $i(t) = 20 - 40\, e^{-500t}$ mA. For $t > 0$, derive expressions for $v_L(t)$ and $p_L(t)$. Is the inductor absorbing power from or delivering power to the rest of the circuit?

6–18 Using the passive sign convention, we find that the voltage across and current through a linear energy storage element are $v(t) = 100 \cos 5000t$ V and $i(t) = \sin 5000t$ A. Is the element an inductor or a capacitor? What is the value of its inductance or capacitance?

6–19 Using the passive sign convention, we find that the voltage across and current through a linear energy storage element are $v(t) = 15[e^{-100t}]u(t)$ V and $i(t) = 0.1(1 - e^{-100t})u(t)$ A. Is the element an inductor or a capacitor? What is the value of its inductance or capacitance?

6–20 Using the passive sign convention, we find that the voltage across and current through a linear energy storage element are $v(t) = 100\,(1 - e^{-1000t})u(t)$ V and $i(t) = 0.1[e^{-1000t}]u(t)$ A. Is the element an inductor or a capacitor? What is the value of its inductance or capacitance?

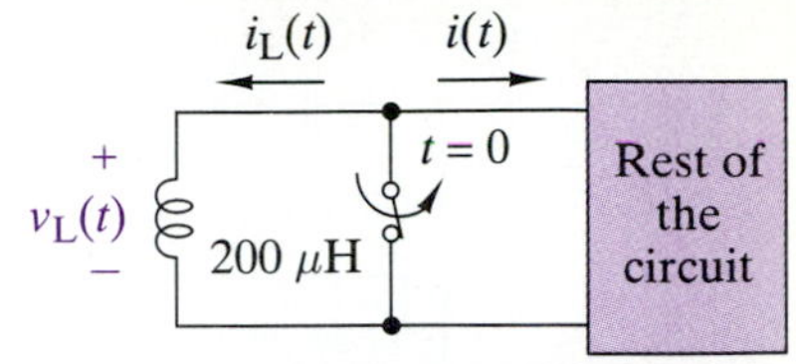

FIGURE P6–16

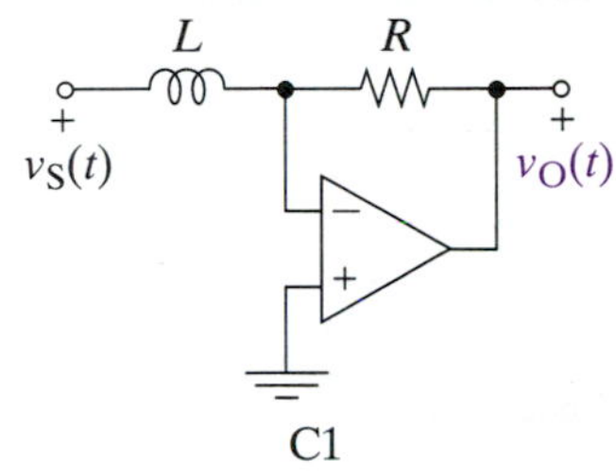

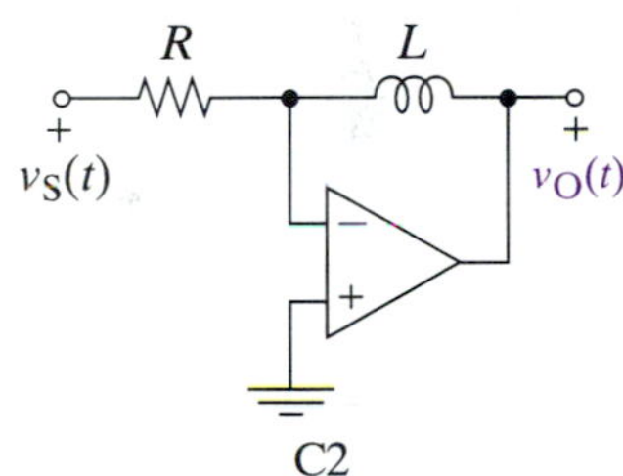

FIGURE P6–21

ERO 6–2 DYNAMIC OP AMP CIRCUITS (SECT. 6–3)

(a) Given a circuit consisting of resistors, capacitors, inductors, and OP AMPs, determine its input–output relationship and use the relationship to find the output for specified inputs.
(b) Design an OP AMP circuit to implement a given input–output relationship or a block diagram.

6–21 Show that the OP AMP inductor circuits in Figure P6–21 provide integration and differentiation of the input $v_S(t)$.

6–22 Show that the OP AMP capacitor circuit in Figure P6–22 is a noninverting integrator whose input–output relationship is

$$v_O(t) = \frac{2}{RC}\int_0^t v_S(x)dx$$

Hint: By voltage division, the voltage at the inverting input is $v_N(t) = v_O(t)/2$.

6–23 Show that the OP AMP circuit in Figure P6–23 has the input–output relationship

$$v_O(t) = \frac{v_S(t)}{2} - \frac{RC}{2}\frac{dv_S(t)}{dt}$$

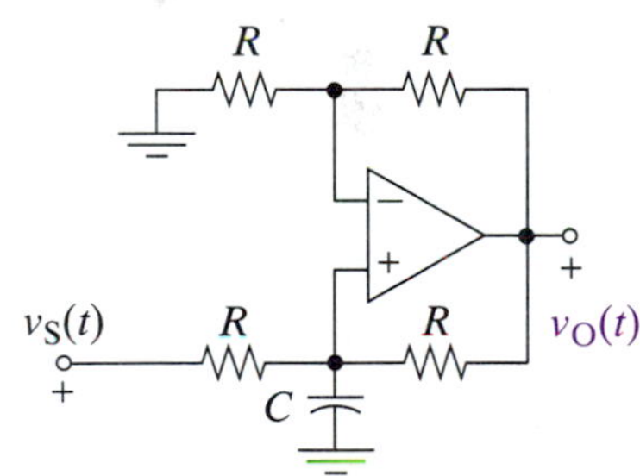

FIGURE P6–22

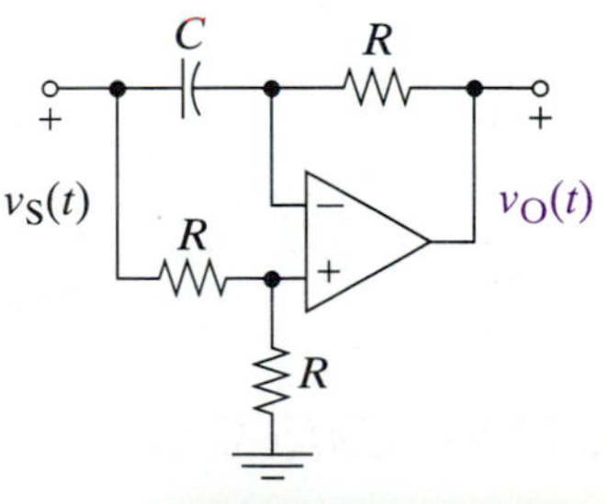

FIGURE P6–23

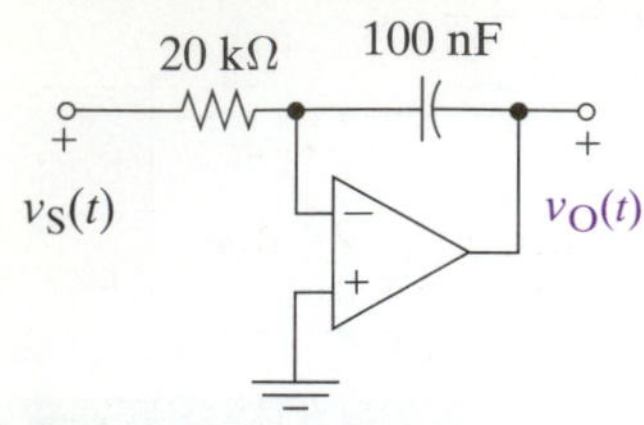

FIGURE P6–24

Hint: By voltage division, the voltage at the noninverting input is $v_P(t) = v_S(t)/2$.

6–24 In Figure P6–24, the voltage across the capacitor at $t = 0$ is such that $v_O(0) = +10$ V. The input signal is $v_S(t) = 5u(t)$ V. Derive an equation for the output voltage when the OP AMP is in its linear range. If the OP AMP saturates when $v_O(t) = \pm 15$ V, find the time $t > 0$ when the OP AMP saturates.

6–25 In Figure P6–24, the voltage across the capacitor at $t = 0$ is 0 V. The input signal is $v_S(t) = 5[u(t) - u(t - 0.005)]$. The OP AMP saturates when $v_O(t) = \pm 15$ V. Does the input signal saturate the OP AMP?

6–26 At $t = 0$, the voltage across the capacitor in Figure P6–24 is zero. The OP AMP saturates when $v_O(t) = \pm 15$ V. For $v_S(t) = V_A[\cos 2000t]u(t)$ V, derive an expression for the output voltage when the OP AMP is in its linear range. What is the maximum value of V_A for linear operation?

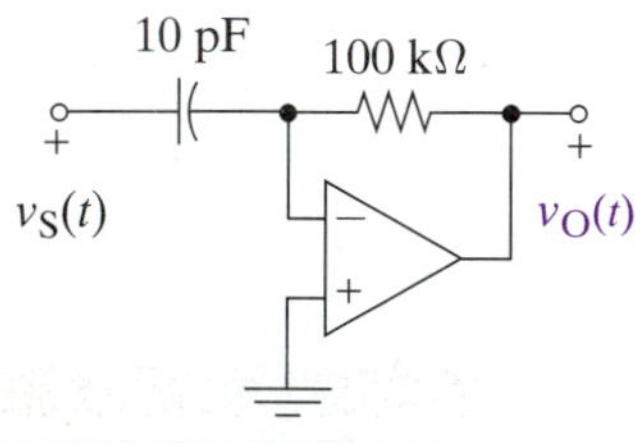

FIGURE P6–27

6–27 The input to the circuit in Figure P6–27 is $v_S(t) = V_A[\sin 10^6 t]u(t)$ V. Derive an expression for the output voltage when the OP AMP is in its linear range. The OP AMP saturates when $v_O(t) = \pm 15$ V. What is the maximum value of V_A for linear operation?

6–28 The input to the circuit in Figure P6–27 is $v_S(t) = 5[\sin 10^6 t]u(t)$ V. Derive an expression for the output voltage when the OP AMP is in its linear range. The OP AMP saturates when $v_O(t) = \pm 15$ V. What is the maximum value of the feedback resistor for linear operation?

6–29 Write an expression for the input–output relationship of each of the block diagrams in Figure P6–29.

FIGURE P6–29

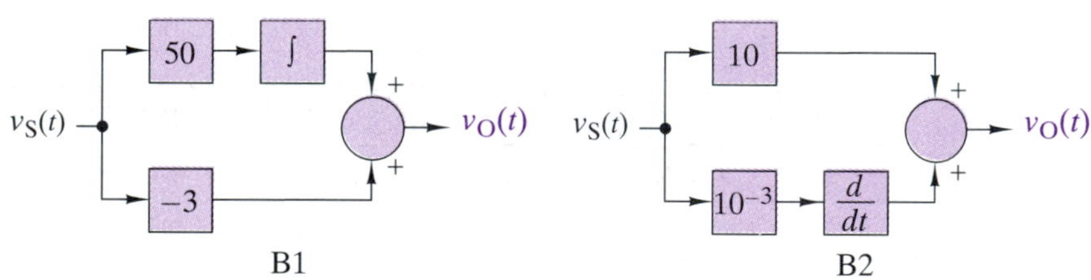

6–30 Construct block diagrams for the following input–output relationships:

$$\text{(a)}\ v_O(t) = -20v_S(t) + \frac{1}{250}\frac{dv_S(t)}{dt}$$

$$\text{(b)}\ v_O(t) = \frac{1}{300}v_S(t) - 200\int_0^t v_S(x)dx$$

6–31 Construct block diagrams for the following differential equations:

$$\text{(a)}\ \frac{dv_O(t)}{dt} + 200v_O(t) = v_S(t) + \frac{1}{200}\frac{dv_S(t)}{dt}$$

$$\text{(b)}\ \frac{d^2v_O(t)}{dt^2} + 40\frac{dv_O(t)}{dt} + 400v_O(t) = 800v_S(t)$$

6–32 **D** Design OP AMP RC circuits to implement the block diagrams in Figure P6–29.

6–33 **D** Design OP AMP RC circuits to implement the input–output relationships in Problem 6–30.

6–34 **D** Design OP AMP RC circuits to implement the differential equation in Problem 6–31(a).

6–35 **D** Design OP AMP RC circuits to implement the differential equation in Problem 6–31(b).

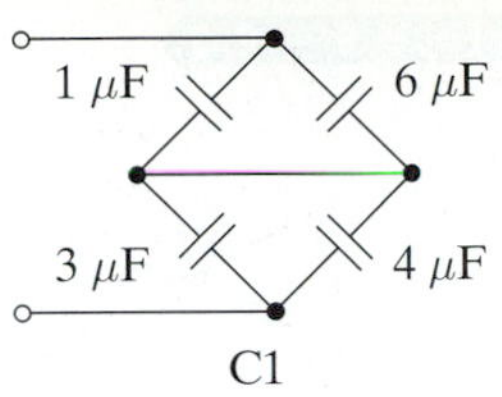

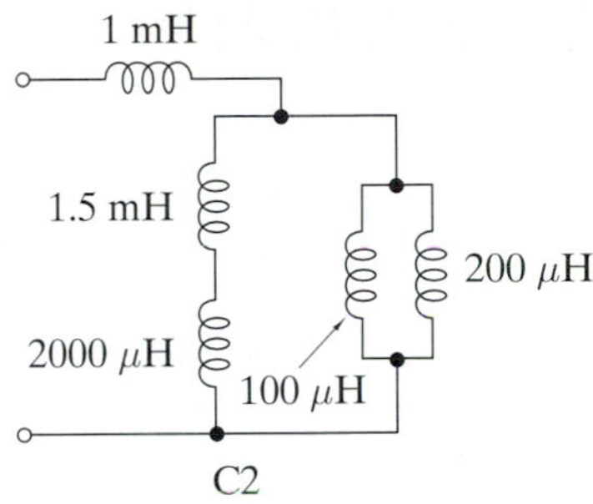

FIGURE P6–36

ERO 6–3 EQUIVALENT INDUCTANCE AND CAPACITANCE (SECT. 6–4)

(a) Derive equivalence properties of inductors and capacitors or use equivalence properties to simplify LC circuits.
(b) Solve for currents and voltages in RLC circuits with dc input signals.

6–36 Find a single equivalent element for each of the circuits in Figure P6–36.

6–37 Derive the expression in Eq. (6–30) for the equivalent inductance of a series connection of inductors.

6–38 Derive the expression in Eq. (6–31) for the equivalent inductance of a parallel connection of inductors.

6–39 Two 6.8-μF capacitors are connected in series and the combination is connected in parallel with a series connection of a 3.3-μF capacitor and a 4.7-μF capacitor. Find the equivalent capacitance of the connection.

6–40 Find the equivalent capacitance between terminals A and B in Figure P6–40.

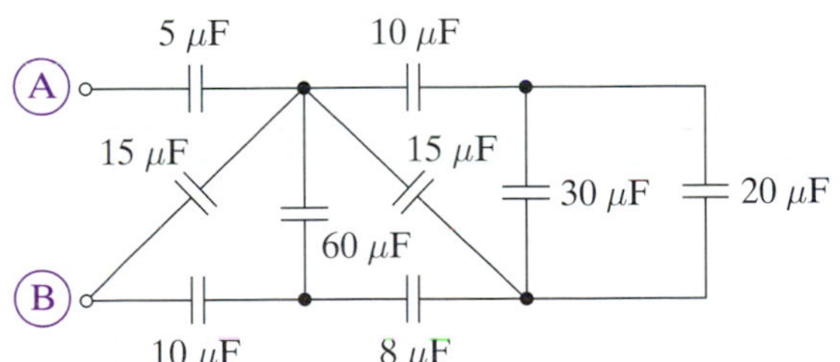

FIGURE P6–40

6–41 The standard values of capacitors with 20% tolerance are multiples of 10^{-N} times the factors 1.0, 1.5, 2.2, 3.3, 4.7, and 6.8. Using only standard values, show how to interconnect capacitors to obtain capacitances of 2, 4, 7, and 8 nF. You must use a total of no more than 10 standard value capacitors to obtain all 4 capacitances.

6–42 **D** A capacitor bank is required that can be charged to 5 kV and store at least 250 J of energy. Design a series/parallel combination that meets the voltage and energy requirements using 20-μF capacitors each rated at 1.5 kV max.

6–43 Reduce the circuit in Figure P6–43 to as few equivalent elements as possible.

FIGURE P6–43

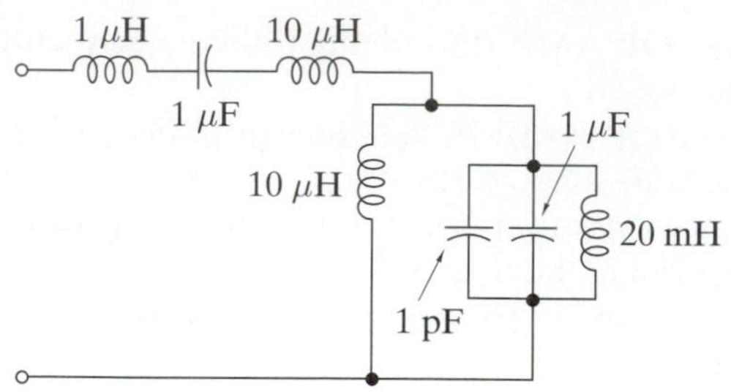

6–44 The circuits in Figure P6–44 are driven by dc sources. Find the voltage across capacitors and the current through inductors.

6–45 The OP AMP circuits in Figure P6–45 are driven by dc sources. Find the output voltage $v_O(t)$.

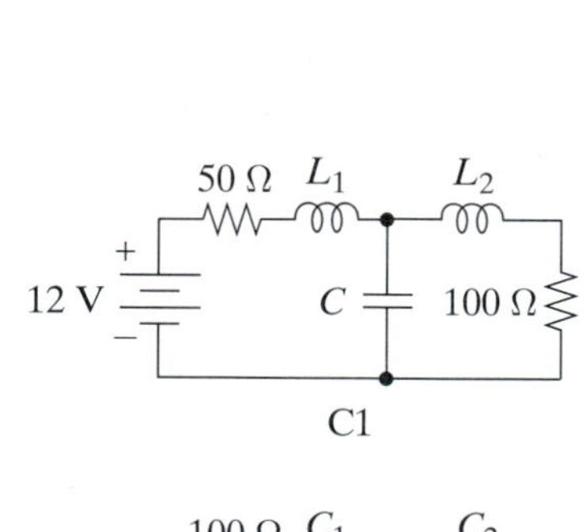

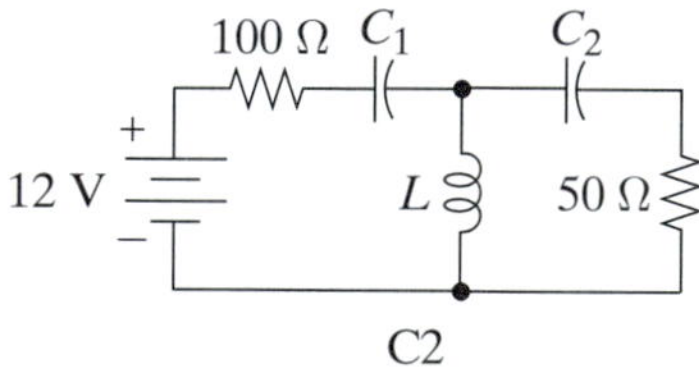

FIGURE P6–44

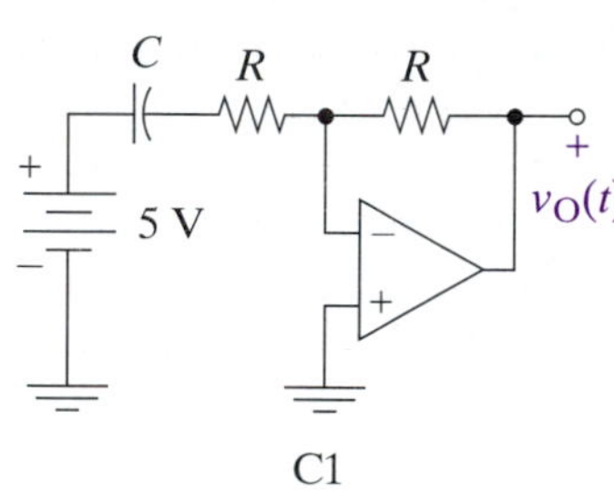

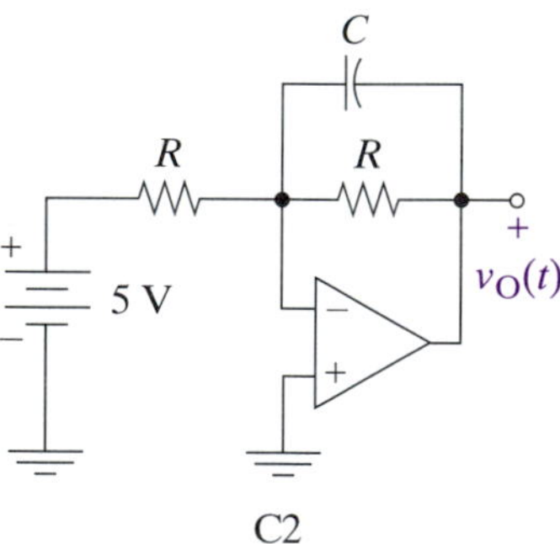

FIGURE P6–45

ERO 6–4 MUTUAL INDUCTANCE (SECT. 6–5)

(a) Given the current through or voltage across two coupled inductors, find the unspecified currents or voltages.
(b) Find the equivalent inductance of series and parallel connections of coupled coils.

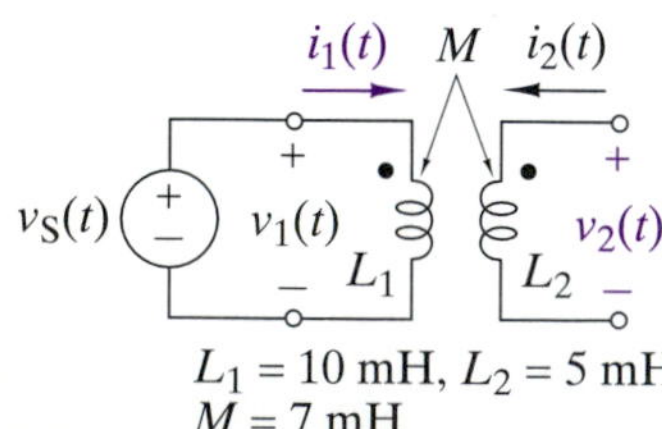

FIGURE P6–46

6–46 The input to the coupled coils in Figure P6–46 is a voltage source $v_S(t) = 10[\sin 2000t]u(t)$ V. The output is connected to an open circuit.

(a) Write the i–v relationships for the coupled inductors using the reference marks in the figure.

(b) Use the results in (a) and the specified input–output connections to solve for $v_2(t)$.

6–47 The input to the coupled coils in Figure P6–46 is a voltage source $v_S(t) = 25[\sin 1000t]u(t)$ V. The output is connected to a short circuit.

(a) Write the *i*–*v* relationships for the coupled inductors using the reference marks in the figure.

(b) Use the results in (a) and the input–output connections to solve for $i_1(t)$ and $i_2(t)$.

6–48 The input of the coupled coils in Figure P6–46 is a voltage source $v_S(t) = 10[1 - e^{-1000t}]u(t)$ V. The output is connected to an open circuit.

(a) Write the *i*–*v* relationships for the coupled inductors using the reference marks given.

(b) Use the results in (a) and the input–output connections to solve for $i_1(t)$ and $v_2(t)$.

6–49 The input to the coupled coils in Figure P6–49 is a current source $i_S(t) = 0.5[\sin 1000t]u(t)$ A. The output is connected to an open circuit.

(a) Write the *i*–*v* relationships for the coupled inductors using the reference marks given.

(b) Use the results in (a) and the input–output connections to solve for $v_1(t)$ and $v_2(t)$.

6–50 Figure P6–50 shows the physical layout of two pairs of coupled coils. Assign dot marks to the coils that are consistent with the physical layout.

6–51 When the switch in Figure P6–51 is closed, the secondary current is observed to be

$$i_2(t) = 10(e^{-2000t} - e^{-1000t})\text{ A}$$

Assign dot marks to the coils that are consistent with this observation. *Hint:* It is important to know whether $i_2(t)$ is positive or negative.

6–52 Derive an expression for $v_X(t)$ in terms of $i_1(t)$ for the circuit of Figure P6–52.

6–53 Find the equivalent inductance of the circuit of Figure P6–53.

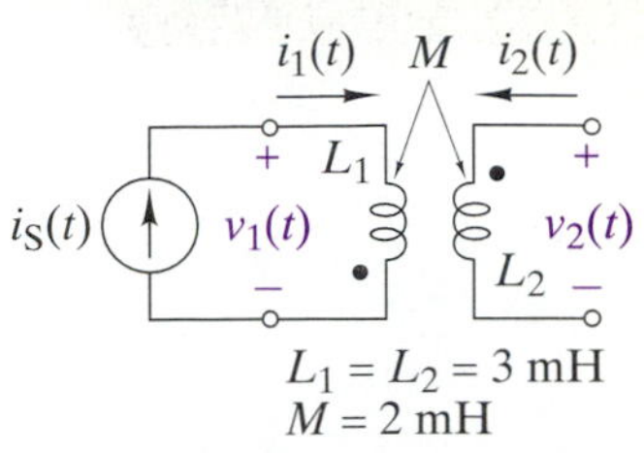

FIGURE P6–49

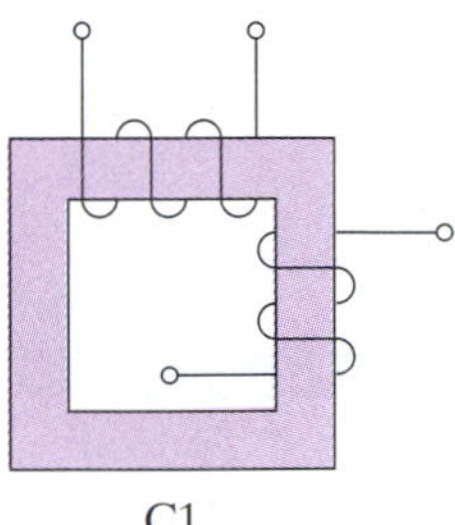

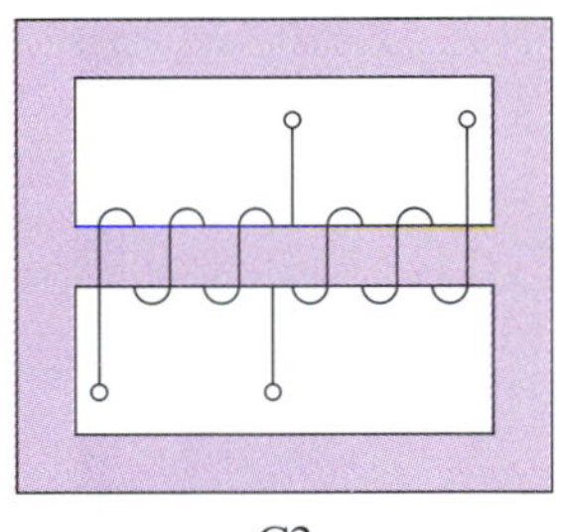

FIGURE P6–50

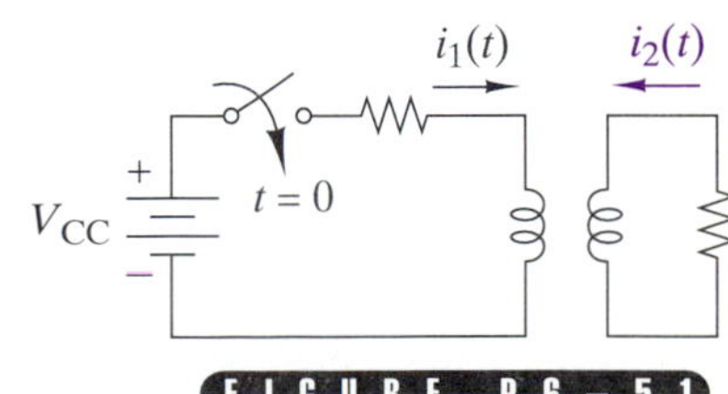

FIGURE P6–51

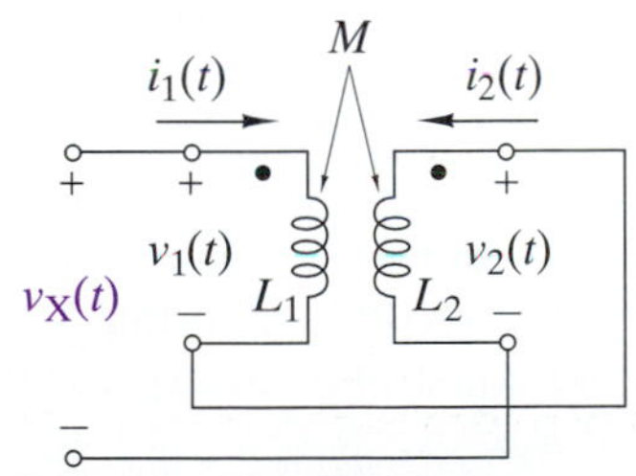

FIGURE P6–52

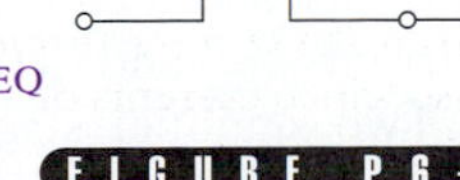

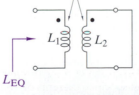

FIGURE P6–53

ERO 6–5 THE IDEAL TRANSFORMER (SECT. 6–6)

Given a circuit containing ideal transformers,

(a) Find the output current, voltage, and power.
(b) Select the turns ratio to meet prescribed conditions.

6–54 The primary voltage in an ideal transformer is a 120-V, 60-Hz sinusoid. The secondary voltage is a 24-V, 60-Hz sinusoid. The secondary terminals are connected to an 8-Ω resistive load.

(a) What is the transformer turns ratio?

(b) Write expressions for the primary current and voltage.

6–55 The number of turns in an ideal transformer are $N_1 = 50$ and $N_2 = 600$. The secondary current is observed to be $i_2(t) = 3 \sin 377t$ A. Write an expression for the primary current. Assume that the magnetic coupling is additive.

6–56 Figure P6–56 shows a voltage source supplying power to a 1-Ω load via a transmission line with transformers at each end. The purpose of this problem is to investigate the effect of the transformers on the voltage delivered to the load.

FIGURE P6–56

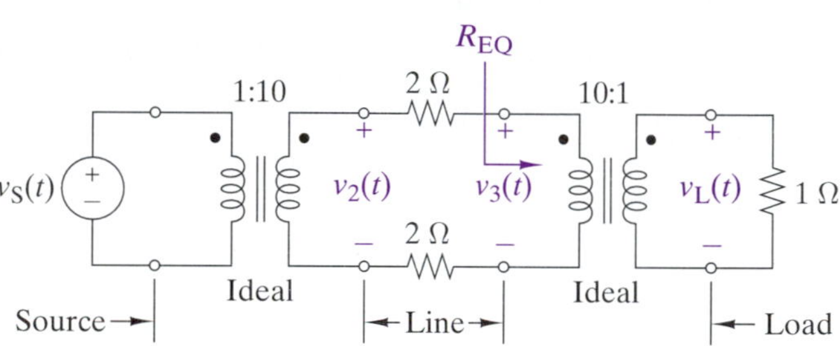

(a) Use ideal transformer relationships to express the voltage v_2 in terms of v_S and to find the equivalent resistance R_{EQ} seen in the primary of the second transformer.

(b) Use the results in (a) and voltage division to express the voltage v_3 in terms of v_S.

(c) Use the result in (b) and ideal transformer relationships to express the load voltage v_L in terms of the source v_S.

(d) Remove the two transformers and connect the source and to the load via the 2-Ω transmission line. Now use voltage division to express the load voltage v_L in terms of the source v_S.

(e) Compare the result in (d) and the result in (c) and comment on the effect of the transformers.

6–57 Figure P6–57 shows an ideal transformer connected as an autotransformer. Assign a consistent set of primary and secondary voltages and currents, and then use the ideal transformer constraints to express the currents $i_L(t)$ and $i_S(t)$ in terms of $v_S(t)$ and R_L.

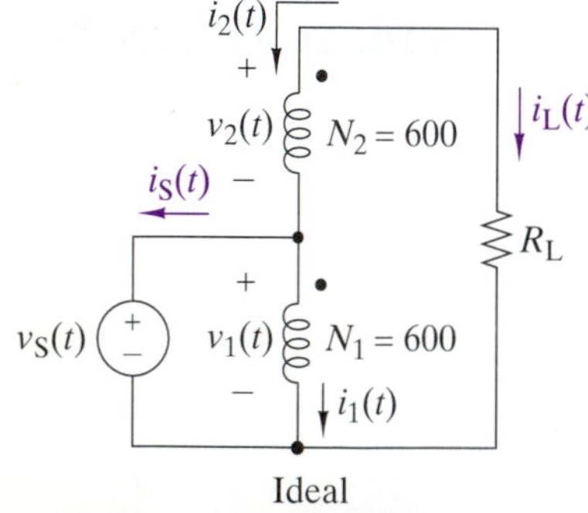

FIGURE P6–57

6–58 Two amplifier stages are to be coupled using a transformer. The output resistance of the first stage is 500 Ω and the input to the second is 4200 Ω. Select the transformer turns ratio so that maximum power is transferred.

6–59 Select the turns ratio of an ideal transformer in the interface circuit shown in Figure P6–59, so that the maximum available power is delivered to the 1-kΩ output resistor.

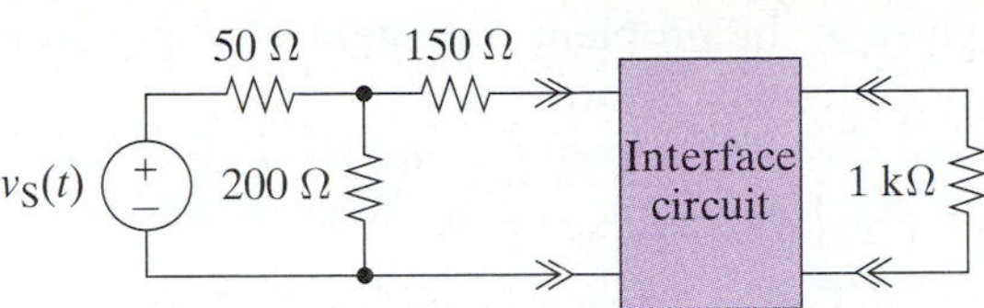

FIGURE P6–59

6–60 Show that the controlled source model in Figure P6–60(a) has the same *i–v* characteristics as an ideal transformer in Figure P6–60(b) when $\mu = \alpha = 1/n$.

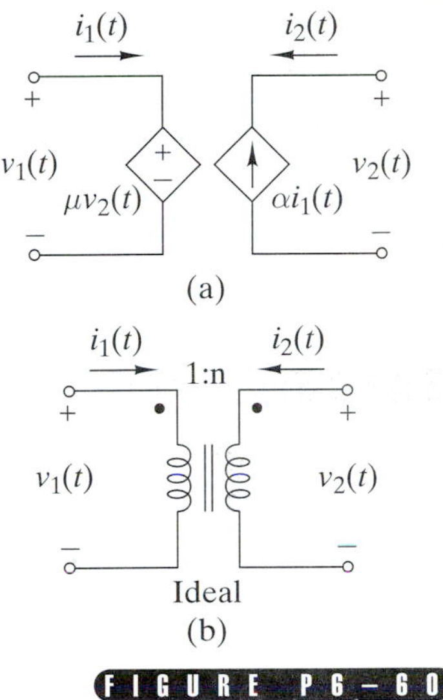

FIGURE P6–60

CHAPTER-INTEGRATING PROBLEMS

6–61 A CAPACITIVE DISCHARGE PULSER

A capacitor bank for a large pulse generator consists of 11 capacitor strings connected in parallel. Each string consists of 16 1.5-mF capacitors connected in series. The purpose of this problem is to calculate important characteristics of the pulser.

(a) What is the total equivalent capacitance of the bank?

(b) If each capacitor in a series string is charged to 300 V, what is the total energy stored in the bank?

(c) In the discharge mode, the voltage across the capacitor bank is $v(t) = 4.8[e^{-500t}]u(t)$ kV. What is the peak power delivered by the capacitor bank?

(d) For practical purposes the capacitor bank is completely discharged after about five time constants. What is the average power delivered during that interval?

6–62 A LC CIRCUIT RESPONSE

In the circuit shown in Figure P6–62, the initial capacitor voltage is $v_C(0) = 30$ V. At $t = 0$, the switch is closed, and thereafter the current into the rest of the circuit is

$$i(t) = 2(e^{-2000t} - e^{-8000t}) \text{ A}$$

The purpose of this problem is to find the voltage $v(t)$ and the equivalent resistance looking into the rest of the circuit.

FIGURE P6–62

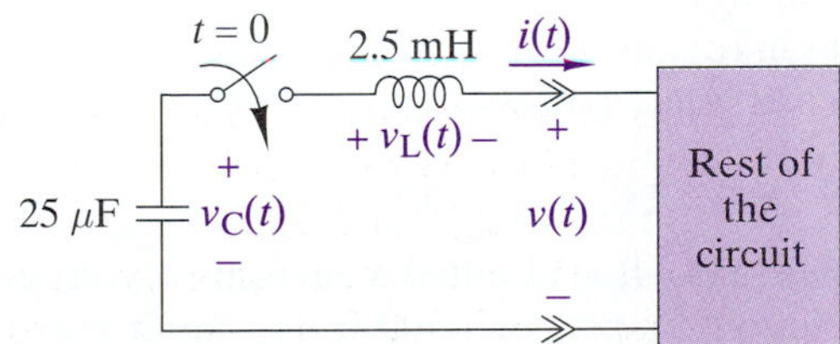

(a) Use the inductor's *i–v* characteristic to find $v_L(t)$ for $t \geq 0$. Find the value of $v_L(t)$ at $t = 0$.

(b) Use the capacitor's *i–v* characteristic to find $v_C(t)$ for $t \geq 0$. Find the value of $v_C(t)$ at $t = 0$. Does this value agree with the initial condition given in the problem statement? If not, you need to review your work to find the error.

(c) Use KVL and the results from (a) and (b) to find the voltage $v(t)$ delivered to the rest of the circuit. What is the value of $v(t)$ at $t = 0$?

(d) The $v(t)$ found in (c) should be proportional to the $i(t)$ given in the problem statement. If so, what is the equivalent resistance looking into the rest of the circuit?

6–63 A CAPACITOR MULTIPLIER

The i–v relationship at the input to RC OP AMP circuit in Figure P6–63 is

$$i(t) = C_{EQ}\frac{dv(t)}{dt}$$

where C_{EQ} can be larger than capacitance C. The purpose of this problem is to find an expression for C_{EQ} in terms of circuit parameters. Assume ideal OP AMPs operating in their linear range.

FIGURE P6–63

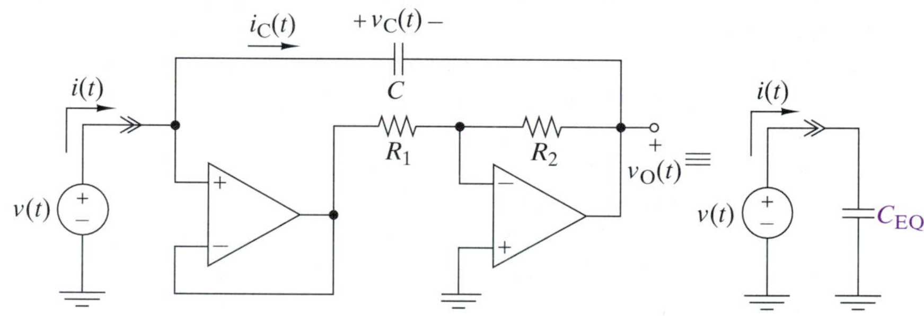

(a) Use basic OP AMP building blocks to express the output $v_O(t)$ in terms of the input $v(t)$.

(b) Use the result in (a) and the KVL to express the capacitor voltage $v_C(t)$ in terms of $v(t)$.

(c) Use the result in (b) and the capacitor's i–v relationship to express $i_C(t)$ in terms of $v(t)$.

(d) Use the result in (c) and KCL to express $i(t)$ in terms of $v(t)$.

(e) Use the result in (d) to express C_{EQ} in terms of circuit parameters.

6–64 A D CHARGE AMPLIFIER

The circuit in Figure P6–64(a) is called a current-to-voltage converter, since the output voltage is proportional to the input current. The circuit in Figure P6–64(b) is called a charge amplifier, since the voltage output is proportional to the charge delivered by the input current source. The purpose of this problem is to find the input–output relationships for these circuits and to design a charge amplifier for a simple application.

(a) **A** Show that the output $v_O(t)$ in Figure P6–64(a) is proportional to the input current $i_S(t)$.

(b) **A** Show that the output $v_O(t)$ in Figure P6–64(b) is proportional to charge $q_S(t)$ delivered by the input current $i_S(t)$.

(c) **D** An electric field sensor produces a charge $q_S(t) = K\mathscr{E}(t)$, where $\mathscr{E}(t) = \mathscr{E}_0 \sin \omega t$ in the incident electric field and $K = 10^{-15}$ is a calibration constant. Select the value of C for a charge amplifier, so the OP AMP produces at least 1 V output when $\mathscr{E}_0 = 5 \times 10^3$ V/m and does not saturate for $\mathscr{E}_0 = 5 \times 10^4$ V/m.

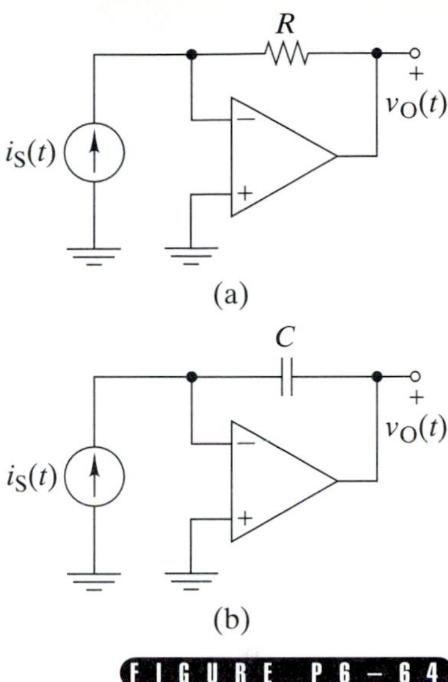

FIGURE P6–64

6–65 A D E RC OP AMP CIRCUIT DESIGN

An upgrade to one of your company's robotics products requires a proportional plus integral compensator that implements the input–output relationship

$$v_O(t) = v_S(t) + 200 \int_0^t v_S(x)dx$$

The input voltage $v_S(t)$ comes from an OP AMP, and the output voltage $v_O(t)$ drives a 10-kΩ resistive load. As the junior engineer in the company, you have been given the responsibility of developing a preliminary design.

(a) **D** Design a circuit that implements the relationship using the standard OP AMP building blocks in Figure 6–17. Minimize the parts count in your design.

(b) **A** The RonAl Corporation (founded by two well-known authors) has given you an unsolicited proposal claiming that their standard DIFF AMP-10 product can realize the required relationship. Their proposal is shown in Figure P6–65. Verify their claim.

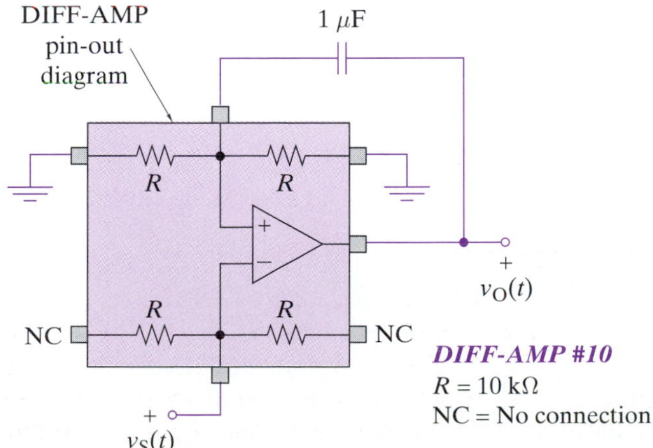

FIGURE P6–65

(c) E Compare your design in part (a) with the RonAl proposal in part (b) in terms of the total parts costs. Parts costs in your company are as follows: resistors, \$400 per 10,000; capacitors, \$1500 per 10,000; and OP AMPs, \$2500 per 10,000. RonAl's proposal offers to provide the company's standard DIFF AMP product for \$5000 per 10,000. Note that for the RonAl product you must supply the capacitor shown in Figure P6–65.

FIRST- AND SECOND-ORDER CIRCUITS

When a mathematician engaged in investigating physical actions and results has arrived at his own conclusions, may they not be expressed in common language as fully, clearly and definitely as in mathematical formula? If so, would it not be a great boon to such as we to express them so—translating them out of their hieroglyphics that we also might work upon them by experiment.

Michael Faraday, 1857,
British Physicist

Michael Faraday (1791–1867) was appointed a Fellow in the Royal Society at age 32 and was a lecturer at the Royal Institution in London for more than 50 years. During this time he published over 150 papers on chemistry and electricity. The most important of these papers was the series *Experimental Researches in Electricity,* which included a description of his discovery of magnetic induction. A gifted experimentalist, Faraday had no formal education in mathematics and apparently felt that mathematics obscured the physical truths he discovered through experimentation. The foregoing quotation is taken from a letter written by Faraday to James Clerk Maxwell in 1857. Faraday's comments are perhaps ironic because Maxwell is best known today for his formulation of the mathematical theory of electromagnetics, which he published in 1873.

Since Faraday's time, tremendous strides have been made in correlating mathematical theory and experiment. Electrical circuit analysis is one of the areas in which there is a close relationship between mathematical theory and laboratory measurements. The nearly one-to-one correspondence between the predictions of circuit analysis and hardware results enormously simplifies the design and development of electrical and electronic systems.

The *i–v* characteristics of capacitors and inductors were treated in Chapter 6. This chapter combines these device characteristics with the connection constraints to derive the differential equations governing the response of dynamic circuits. Mathematical methods for analytically solving these differential equations are also treated. The first four sections treat the formulation and solution of the first-order differential equations governing circuits with one capacitor or inductor. The next three sections treat circuits with two dynamic elements that lead to second-order differential equations.

7–1 *RC* AND *RL* CIRCUITS

The flow diagram in Figure 7–1 shows the two major steps in the analysis of a dynamic circuit. In the first step we use device and connection equations to formulate a differential equation describing the circuit. In the second step we solve the differential equation to find the circuit response. In this chapter we examine basic methods of formulating circuit differential equations and the time-honored, classical methods of solving for responses. Solving for the responses of simple dynamic circuits gives us insight into the physical behavior of the basic modules of the complex networks in subsequent chapters. This insight will help us correlate circuit behavior with the results obtained by other methods of dynamic circuit analysis. The treatment of other methods includes phasor circuit analysis (Chapter 8) and the Laplace transform methods (beginning in Chapter 9).

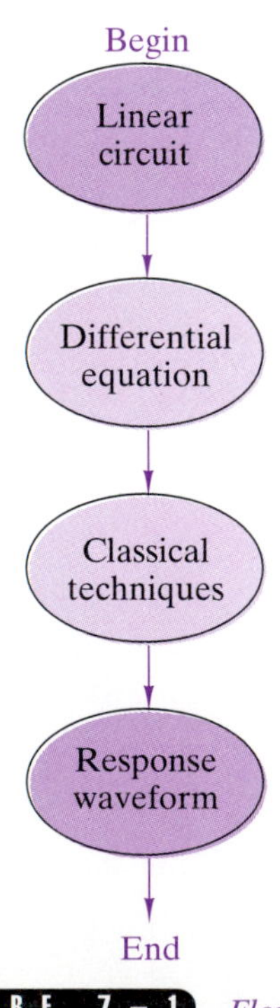

FIGURE 7–1 *Flow diagram for dynamic circuit analysis*

FORMULATING *RC* AND *RL* CIRCUIT EQUATIONS

RC and *RL* circuits contain linear resistors and a single capacitor or a single inductor. Figure 7–2 shows how we can divide *RC* and *RL* circuits into two parts: (1) the dynamic element and (2) the rest of the circuit, containing only linear resistors and sources. To formulate the equation governing either of these circuits, we replace the resistors and sources by their Thévenin and Norton equivalents shown in Figure 7–2.

Dealing first with the RC circuit in Figure 7–2(a), we note that the Thévenin equivalent source is governed by the constraint

$$R_T i(t) + v(t) = v_T(t) \qquad (7-1)$$

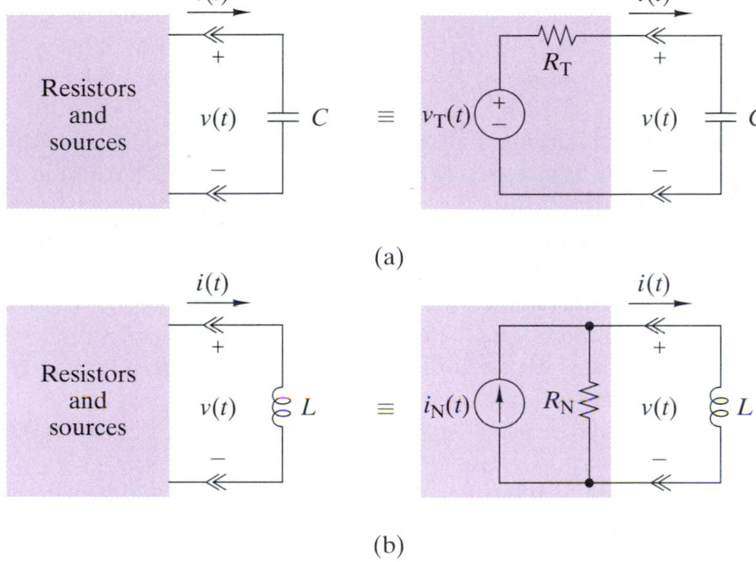

FIGURE 7–2 First-order circuits: (a) RC circuit. (b) RL circuit.

The capacitor i–v constraint is

$$i(t) = C\frac{dv(t)}{dt} \qquad (7-2)$$

Substituting the i–v constraint into the source constraint yields

$$R_T C\frac{dv(t)}{dt} + v(t) = v_T(t) \qquad (7-3)$$

Combining the source and element constraints produces the equation governing the RC series circuit. The unknown in Eq. (7–3) is the capacitor voltage $v(t)$, the **state variable** that determines the amount of energy stored in the RC circuit.

Mathematically, Eq. (7–3) is a first-order linear differential equation with constant coefficients. The equation is first order because the first derivative of the dependent variable is the highest order derivative in the equation. The product $R_T C$ is a constant coefficient because it depends on fixed circuit parameters. The signal $v_T(t)$ is the Thévenin equivalent of the independent sources driving the circuit. The voltage $v_T(t)$ is the input, and the capacitor voltage $v(t)$ is the circuit response.

The Norton equivalent source in the *RL* circuit in Figure 7–2(b) is governed by the constraint

$$G_N v(t) + i(t) = i_N(t) \tag{7-4}$$

The element constraint for the inductor can be written

$$v(t) = L\frac{di(t)}{dt} \tag{7-5}$$

Combining the element and source constraints produces the differential equation for the *RL* circuit:

$$G_N L\frac{di(t)}{dt} + i(t) = i_N(t) \tag{7-6}$$

The response of the *RL* circuit is also governed by a first-order linear differential equation with constant coefficients. The dependent variable in Eq. (7–6) is the inductor current. The circuit parameters enter as the constant product $G_N L$, and the driving forces are represented by a Norton equivalent current $i_N(t)$. The unknown in Eq. (7–6) is the inductor current, the state variable that determines the amount of energy stored in the *RL* circuit.

We observe that Eqs. (7–3) and (7–6) have the same form. In fact, interchanging the quantities

$$R_T \leftrightarrow G_N \qquad C \leftrightarrow L \qquad v \leftrightarrow i \qquad v_T \leftrightarrow i_N$$

converts one equation into the other. This interchange is another example of the principle of duality. Because of duality we do not need to study the *RC* and *RL* circuits as independent problems. Everything we learn by solving the *RC* circuit can be applied to the *RL* circuit as well.

We refer to the *RC* and *RL* circuits as **first-order circuits** because they are described by a first-order differential equation. The first-order differential equations in Eqs. (7–3) and (7–6) describe general *RC* and *RL* circuits shown in Figure 7–2. Any circuit containing a single capacitor or inductor and linear resistors and sources is a first-order circuit.

ZERO-INPUT RESPONSE OF FIRST-ORDER CIRCUITS

The response of a first-order circuit is found by solving the circuit differential equation. For the *RC* circuit the response $v(t)$ must satisfy the differential equation in Eq. (7–3) and the initial condition $v(0)$. By examining Eq. (7–3) we see that the response depends on three factors:

1. The inputs driving the circuit $v_T(t)$
2. The values of the circuit parameters R_T and C
3. The value of $v(t)$ at $t = 0$ (i.e., the initial condition).

The first two factors apply to any linear circuit, including resistance circuits. The third factor relates to the initial energy stored in the circuit. The initial energy can cause the circuit to have a nonzero response even when the input $v_T(t) = 0$ for $t \geq 0$. The existence of a response with no input is something new in our study of linear circuits.

To explore this discovery we find the **zero-input response**. Setting all independent sources in Figure 7–2 to zero makes $v_T = 0$ in Eq. (7–3):

$$R_T C \frac{dv}{dt} + v = 0 \qquad (7-7)$$

Mathematically, Eq. (7–7) is a **homogeneous equation** because the right side is zero. The classical approach to solving a linear homogeneous differential equation is to try a solution in the form of an exponential

$$v(t) = Ke^{st} \qquad (7-8)$$

where K and s are constants to be determined.

The form of the homogenous equation suggests an exponential solution for the following reasons. Equation (7–7) requires that $v(t)$ plus $R_T C$ times its derivative must add to zero for all time $t \geq 0$. This can only occur if $v(t)$ and its derivative have the same form. In Chapter 5 we saw that an exponential signal and its derivative are both of the form e^{-t/T_C}. Therefore, the exponential is a logical starting place.

If Eq. (7–8) is indeed a solution, then it must satisfy the differential equation in Eq. (7–7). Substituting the trial solution into Eq. (7–7) yields

$$R_T CKse^{st} + Ke^{st} = 0$$

or

$$Ke^{st}(R_T Cs + 1) = 0$$

The exponential function e^{st} cannot be zero for all t. The condition $K = 0$ is a trivial solution because it implies that $v(t)$ is zero for all time t. The only nontrivial way to satisfy the equation involves the condition

$$R_T Cs + 1 = 0 \qquad (7-9)$$

Equation (7–9) is the circuit **characteristic equation** because its root determines the attributes of $v(t)$. The characteristic equation has a single root at $s = -1/R_T C$ so the zero-input response of the RC circuit has the form

$$v(t) = Ke^{-t/R_T C} \qquad t \geqslant 0$$

The constant K can be evaluated using the value of $v(t)$ at $t = 0$. Using the notation $v(0) = V_0$ yields

$$v(0) = Ke^0 = K = V_0$$

The final form of the zero-input response is

$$v(t) = V_0 e^{-t/R_T C} \qquad t \geqslant 0 \qquad (7-10)$$

The zero-input response of the RC circuit is the familiar exponential waveform shown in Figure 7–3. At $t = 0$ the exponential response starts out at $v(0) = V_0$ and then decays to zero at $t \to \infty$. The time constant $T_C = R_T C$ depends only on fixed circuit parameters. From our study of the exponential signals in Chapter 5, we know that the $v(t)$ decays to about 37% of its initial amplitude in one time constant and to essentially zero after about five time constants. The zero-input response of the *RC* circuit is determined by two quantities: (1) the circuit time constant and (2) the value of the capacitor voltage at $t = 0$.

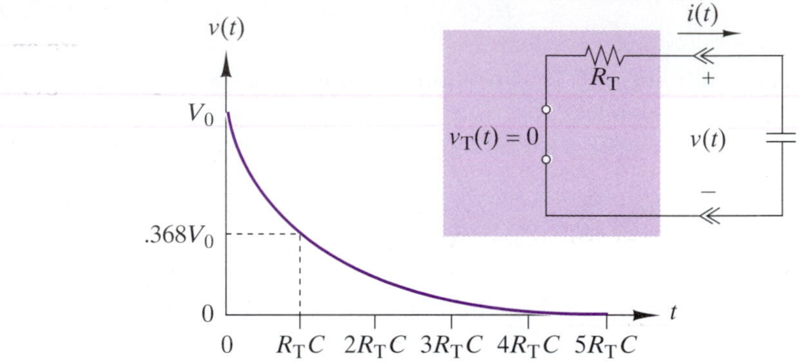

FIGURE 7–3 *First-order RC circuit zero-input response.*

The zero-input response of the *RL* circuit in Figure 7–2(b) is found by setting the Norton current $i_N(t) = 0$ in Eq. (7–6).

$$G_N L \frac{di}{dt} + i = 0 \qquad (7\text{–}11)$$

The unknown in this homogeneous differential equation is the inductor current $i(t)$. Equation (7–11) has the same form as the homogeneous equation for the *RC* circuit, which suggests a trial solution of the form

$$i(t) = Ke^{st}$$

where K and s are constant to be determined. Substituting the trial solution into Eq. (7–11) yields the *RL* circuit characteristic equation.

$$G_N Ls + 1 = 0 \qquad (7\text{–}12)$$

The root of this equation is $s = -1/G_N L$. Denoting the initial value of the inductor current by I_0, we evaluate the constant K:

$$i(0) = I_0 = Ke^0 = K$$

The final form of the zero-input response of the *RL* circuit is

$$i(t) = I_0 e^{-t/G_N L} \qquad t \geq 0 \qquad (7\text{–}13)$$

For the *RL* circuit the zero-input response of the state variable $i(t)$ is an exponential function with a time constant of $T_C = G_N L = L/R_T$. This response connects the initial state $i(0) = I_0$ with the final state $i(\infty) = 0$.

The zero-input responses in Eqs. (7–10) and (7–13) show the duality between first-order *RC* and *RL* circuits. These results point out that the zero-input response in a first-order circuit depends on two quantities: (1) the circuit time constant and (2) the value of the state variable at $t = 0$. Capacitor voltage and inductor current are called state variables because they determine the amount of energy stored in the circuit at any time t. The following examples show that the zero-input response of the state variable provides enough information to determine the zero-input response of every other voltage and current in the circuit.

EXAMPLE 7–1

The switch in Figure 7–4 is closed at $t = 0$, connecting a capacitor with an initial voltage of 30 V to the resistances shown. Find the responses $v_C(t)$, $i(t)$, $i_1(t)$, and $i_2(t)$ for $t \geq 0$.

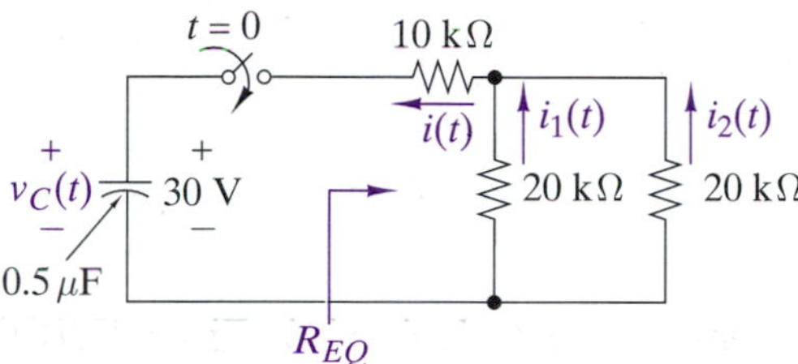

FIGURE 7–4

SOLUTION:

This problem involves the zero-input response of an *RC* circuit since there is no independent source in the circuit. To find the required responses, we first determine the circuit time constant with the switch closed ($t \geq 0$). The equivalent resistance seen by the capacitor is

$$R_{EQ} = 10 + (20 \| 20) = 20\ \text{k}\Omega$$

For $t \geq 0$ the circuit time constant is

$$T_C = R_T C = 20 \times 10^3 \times 0.5 \times 10^{-6} = 10\ \text{ms}$$

The initial capacitor voltage is given by $V_0 = 30$ V. Using Eq. (7–10), the zero-input response of the capacitor voltage is

$$v_C(t) = 30e^{-100t}\ \text{V} \quad t \geqslant 0$$

The capacitor voltage provides the information needed to solve for all other zero-input responses. The current $i(t)$ through the capacitor is

$$\begin{aligned} i(t) &= C\frac{dv_C}{dt} = (0.5 \times 10^{-6})(30)(-100)\,e^{-100t} \\ &= -1.5 \times 10^{-3}\,e^{-100t}\ \text{A} \qquad t \geqslant 0 \end{aligned}$$

The minus sign means the actual current direction is opposite of the reference direction shown in Figure 7–4. The minus sign makes physical sense because the initial voltage on the capacitor is positive, which forces current into the resistances to the right of the switch. The other current responses are found by current division.

$$i_1(t) = i_2(t) = \frac{20}{20 + 20}i(t) = -0.75 \times 10^{-3}e^{-100t}\ \text{A} \qquad t > 0$$

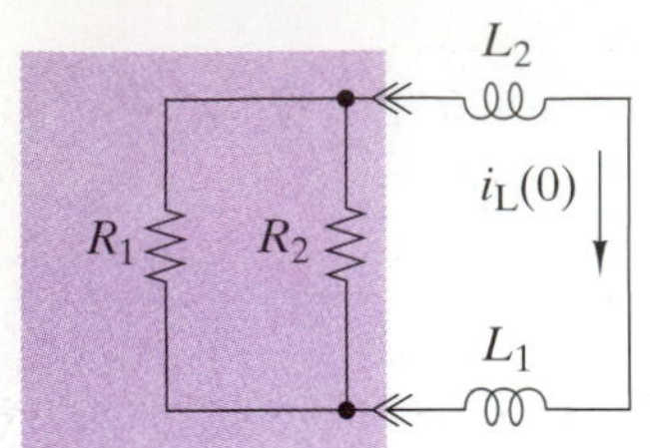

Given circuit

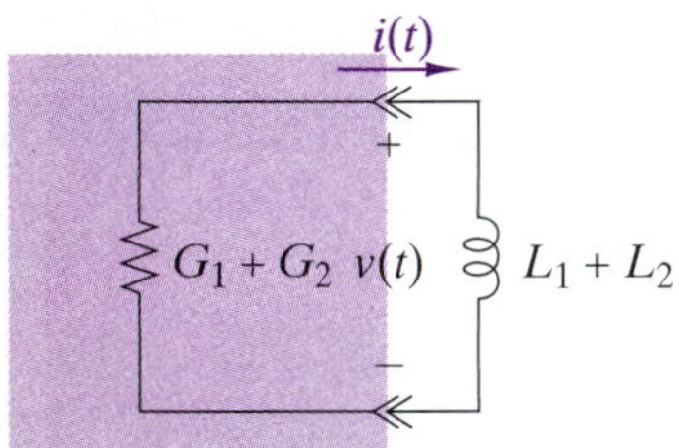

Equivalent circuit

FIGURE 7–5

Notice the analysis pattern. We first determine the zero-input response of the capacitor voltage. The state variable response together with resistance circuit analysis techniques were then used to find other voltages and currents. The circuit time constant and the value of the state variable at $t = 0$ provide enough information to determine the zero-input response of every voltage or current in the circuit. ■

EXAMPLE 7–2

Find the response of the state variable of the *RL* circuit in Figure 7–5 using $L_1 = 10$ mH, $L_2 = 30$ mH, $R_1 = 2$ kΩ, $R_2 = 6$ kΩ, and $i_L(0) = 100$ mA.

SOLUTION:

The inductors are connected in series and can be replaced by an equivalent inductor

$$L_{EQ} = L_1 + L_2 = 10 + 30 = 40 \text{ mH}$$

Likewise, the resistors are connected in parallel and the conductance seen by L_{EQ} is

$$G_{EQ} = G_1 + G_2 = 10^{-3}/2 + 10^{-3}/6 = 2 \times 10^{-3}/3 \text{ S}$$

Figure 7–5 shows the resulting equivalent circuit. The interface signals $v(t)$ and $i(t)$ are the voltage across and current through $L_{EQ} = L_1 + L_2$. The time constant of the equivalent *RL* circuit is

$$T_C = G_{EQ}L_{EQ} = 8 \times 10^{-5}/3 \text{ s} = 1/37500 \text{ s}$$

The initial current through L_{EQ} is $i_L(0) = 0.1$ A. Using Eq. (7–13) with $I_0 = 0.1$ yields the zero-state response of the inductor current.

$$i(t) = 0.1e^{-37500t} \text{ A} \qquad t \geq 0$$

Given the state variable response, we can find every other response in the original circuit. For example, by KCL and current division the currents through R_1 and R_2 are

$$i_{R_1}(t) = \frac{R_2}{R_1 + R_2} i(t) = 0.075\, e^{-37500t} \text{ A} \qquad t \geq 0$$

$$i_{R_2}(t) = \frac{R_1}{R_1 + R_2} i(t) = 0.025\, e^{-37500t} \text{ A} \qquad t \geq 0$$

■

Example 7–2 illustrates an important point. The *RL* circuit in Figure 7–5 is a first-order circuit even though it contains two inductors. The two inductors are connected in series and can be replaced by a single equivalent inductor. In general, capacitors or inductors in series and parallel can be replaced by a single equivalent element. Thus, any circuit containing the *equivalent* of a single inductor or a single capacitor is a first-order circuit.

Sometimes it may be difficult to determine the Thévenin or Norton equivalent seen by the dynamic element in a first-order circuit. In such cases we use other circuit analysis techniques to derive the differential equation in terms of a more convenient signal variable. For example, the OP AMP *RC* circuit in Figure 7–6 is a first-order circuit because it contains a single capacitor.

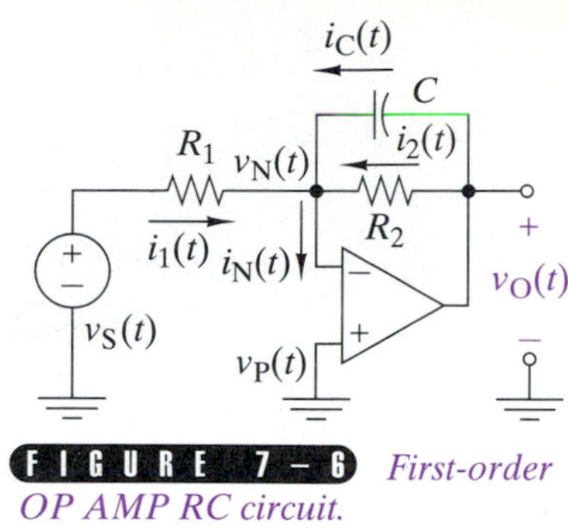

FIGURE 7–6 *First-order OP AMP RC circuit.*

From previous experience we know that the key to analyzing an inverting OP AMP circuit is to write a KCL equation at the inverting input. The sum of currents entering the inverting input is

$$\underbrace{G_1(v_S - v_N)}_{i_1(t)} + \underbrace{G_2(v_O - v_N)}_{i_2(t)} + \underbrace{C\frac{d(v_O - v_N)}{dt}}_{i_C(t)} - i_N(t) = 0$$

The element equations for the OP AMP are $i_N(t) = 0$ and $v_N(t) = v_P(t)$. However, the noninverting input is grounded; hence $v_N(t) = v_P(t) = 0$. Substituting the OP AMP element constraints into the KCL constraint yields

$$G_1 v_S + G_2 v_O + C\frac{dv_O}{dt} = 0$$

which can be rearranged in standard form as

$$R_2 C\frac{dv_O}{dt} + v_O = -\frac{R_2}{R_1}v_S(t) \qquad (7-14)$$

The unknown Eq. (7–14) is the OP AMP output voltage rather than the capacitor voltage. The form of the differential equation indicates that the circuit time constant is $T_C = R_2 C$.

EXAMPLE 7–3

Use MicroSim Design Center to calculate the response $v_C(t)$ in the circuit in Figure 7–4 for $t \geq 0$.

SOLUTION:

This problem was solved analytically in Example 7–1. The problem is repeated here to introduce computer simulation of dynamic circuits. The simulation option used is called **transient analysis**, which predicts the variation of currents and voltages as a function of time. Figure 7–7 shows the circuit diagram as drawn in MicroSim Schematics. This diagram does not include the switch in Figure 7–4 since for $t \geq 0$ the switch is closed. The net list in Figure 7–7 shows that the 0.5 μF connected between nodes 1 and 0 (ground) carries an initial condition of IC = 30 V. The Part Attribute dialog box in Figure 7–7 shows how the capacitor's initial condition attribute is given a numerical value. In circuit simulation programs the user must specify both the element value attributes and the initial condition attributes for dynamic elements.

Once the circuit diagram is complete, we must set up a transient analysis run. Selecting **Analysis/Setup/Transient** from the schematics menu bar brings up the dialog box in Figure 7–8. The key entry in this box is the

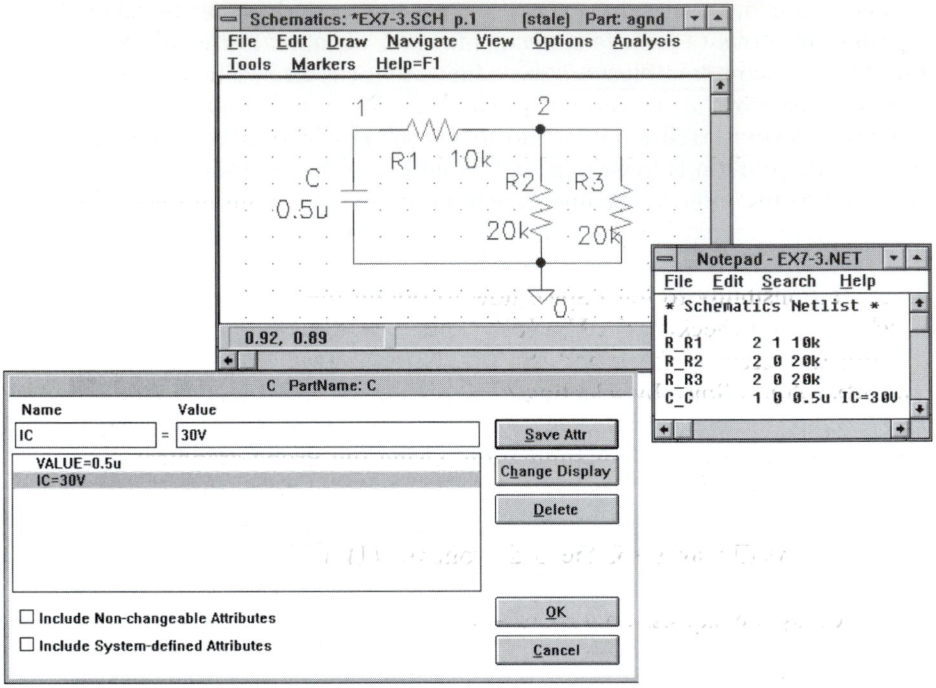

FIGURE 7–7 *MicroSim Design Center schematic and net list.*

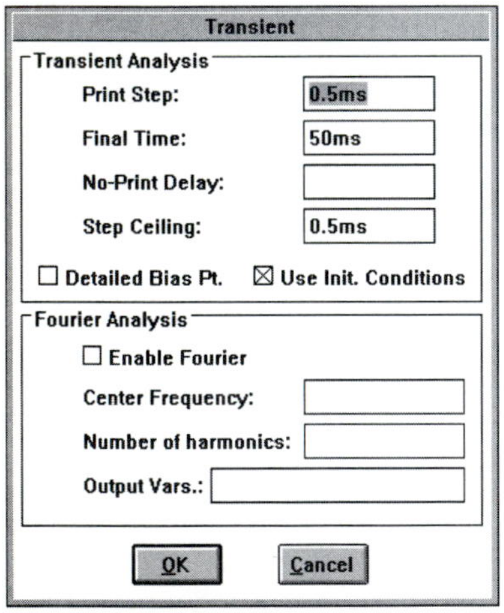

FIGURE 7–8 *Analysis setup.*

Final Time, which specifies the time duration of simulation since a PSpice transient analysis starts at $t = 0$ (always) and runs to $t =$ **Final Time**. In the present case we know that the circuit time constant is 10 ms (see Example 7–1), so we can safely specify **Final Time** $= 5T_C = 50$ ms.[1]

The **Print Step** parameter in Figure 7–8 is not important to us since we observe the calculated response using MicroSim Probe. The **Step Ceiling** parameter is important since it controls the minimum number of points included in the Probe plots. A useful rule of thumb is to let **Step Ceiling** = **Final Time**/100. This rule generates at least 101 points (counting $t = 0$) in the Probe plot, which is often adequate. In the present case this means that **Step Ceiling** = 0.050/100 = 0.5 ms. We must also assign a numerical value to **Print Step** even though this parameter does not affect the calculated responses observed in Probe. The reason is that originally SPICE outputs were produced by a printer, so SPICE-based programs will not run unless $0 <$ **Print Step** $<$ **Final Time**.

1 Specifying a value for **Final Time** presents a dilemma. We must have some knowledge about the response to specify an appropriate simulation time interval. If we have no knowledge, we may specify an interval that is too short or too long to observe the response. If we have complete knowledge, then there is no reason to run the simulaiton. Effectively using circuit simulation tools requires that we operate in a gray area between no knowledge and complete knowledge.

The transient analysis dialog box in Figure 7–8 includes a box labeled **Use Init. Conditions**. When this box is checked, PSpice uses the initial conditions specified when the circuit is created in Schematics. When this box is not checked, PSpice automatically calculates the initial conditions for all dynamic elements using the dc analysis method discussed in Chapter 6. The initial conditions calculated by PSpice can be different from those specified by the user in Schematics. For example, the circuit in Figure 7–7 has no dc sources, so PSpice dc analysis would report that the initial capacitor voltage is zero, whereas we specified IC = 30 V in Schematics. It is the user's responsibility to tell PSpice how to obtain the initial conditions by checking or not checking the **Use Init. Conditions** box.

With the circuit defined and the transient analysis run set up, we can start MicroSim PSpice by selecting **Analysis/Simulate** from the Schematics menu bar. MicroSim Probe is automatically started once PSpice successfully completes the transient simulation. Using the Probe graphical interface produces the plots shown in Figure 7–9. The legend at the bottom of the figure indicates that there are two traces in the plot. The trace indicated by the □ markers is the node voltage $v(1)$, which is the PSpice solution for the capacitor voltage. The trace indicated by the ◇ markers is generated by the expression 30*exp(–100*time), which is the Probe implementation of the analytical solution found in Example 7–1. On this scale of observation the two traces appear to be congruent, indicating close agreement between the PSpice numerical solution and the analytical solution.

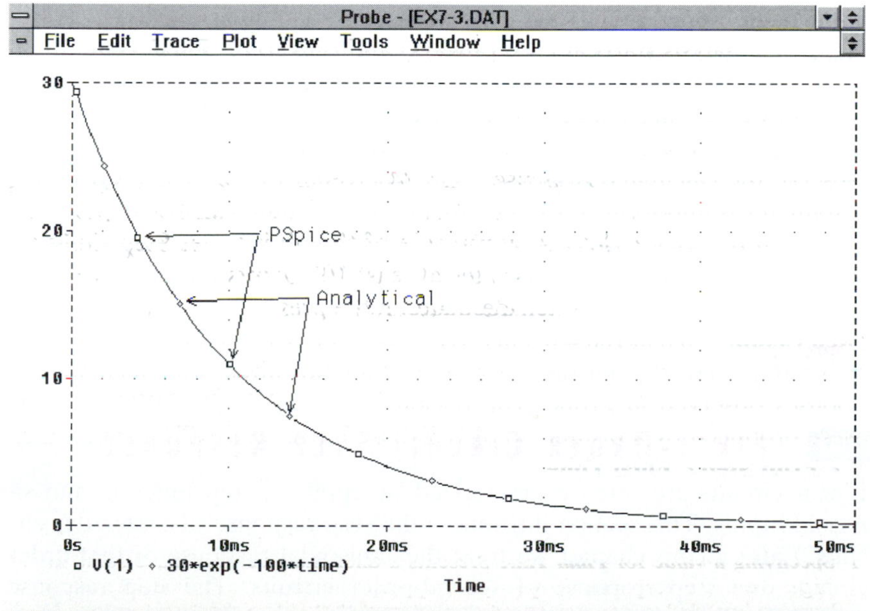

FIGURE 7–9 *MicroSim Probe response plots.*

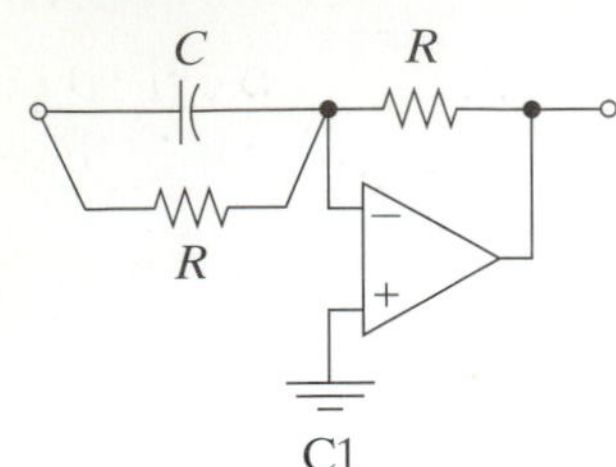

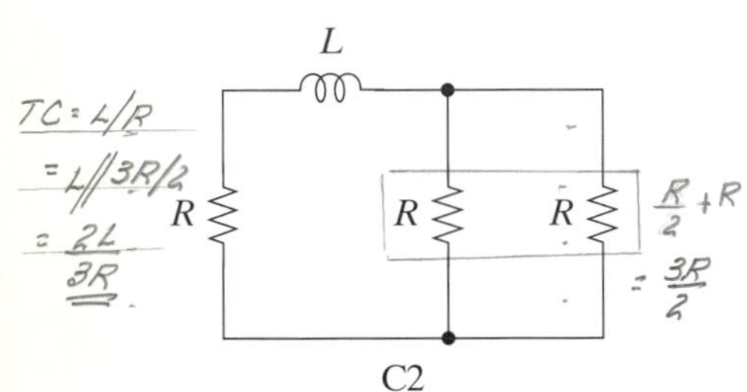

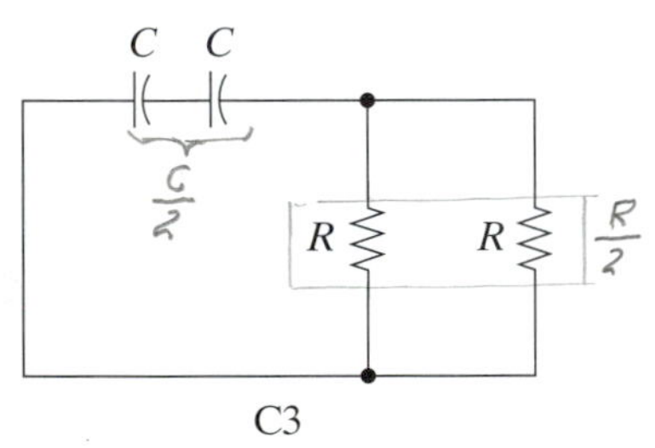

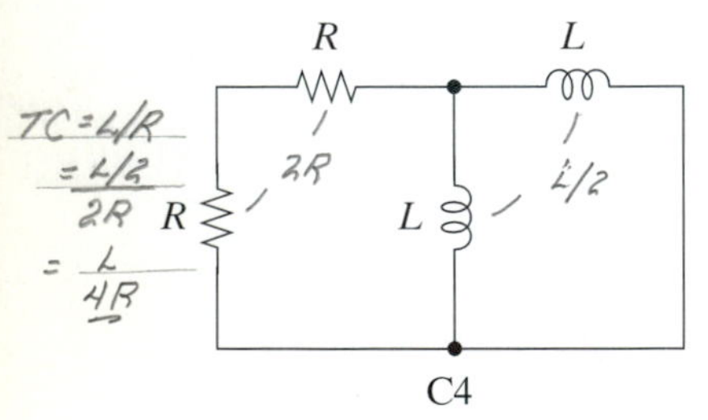

FIGURE 7–10

Exercise 7–1

What are the time constants of the circuits shown in Figure 7–10?

Answers:

C1: RC C2: $2L/3R$ C3: $RC/4$ C4: $L/4R$

Exercise 7–2

The switch in Figure 7–11 closes at $t = 0$. For $t \geq 0$ the current through the resistor is $i_R(t) = e^{-100t}$ mA.

(a) What is the capacitor voltage at $t = 0$?
(b) Write an equation for $v(t)$ for $t \geq 0$.
(c) Write an equation for the power absorbed by the resistor for $t \geq 0$.
(d) How much energy does the resistor dissipate for $t \geq 0$?
(e) How much energy is stored in the capacitor at $t = 0$?

Answers:

(a) 10 V
(b) $v(t) = 10e^{-100t}$ V
(c) $p_R(t) = 10e^{-200t}$ mW
(d) 50 μJ
(e) 50 μJ

Exercise 7–3

For $t > 0$ the current through the 40–mH inductor in a first-order circuit is $20e^{-500t}$ mA.

(a) What is the circuit time constant?
(b) How much energy is stored in the inductor at $t = 0$, $t = T_C$, and $t = 5T_C$?
(c) Write an equation for the voltage across the inductor.
(d) What is the equivalent resistance seen by the inductor?

Answers:

(a) 2 ms
(b) 8, 1.08, 0.000363 μJ
(c) $-400e^{-500t}$ mV
(d) 20 Ω

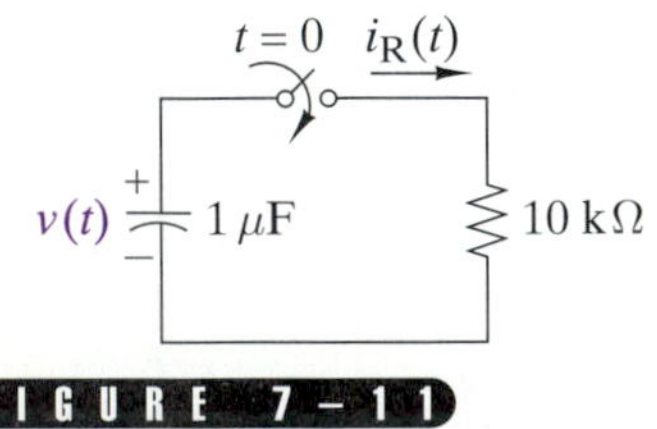

FIGURE 7–11

7–2 FIRST-ORDER CIRCUIT STEP RESPONSE

Linear circuits are often characterized by applying step function and sinusoid inputs. This section introduces the step response of first-order circuits. Later in this chapter we treat the sinusoidal response of first-order circuits and step response of second-order circuits. The step response analysis introduces the concepts of forced, natural, and zero-state responses that appear extensively in later chapters.

Our development of first-order step response treats the *RC* circuit in detail and then summarizes the corresponding results for its dual, the *RL* circuit. When the input to the *RC* circuit in Figure 7–2 is a step function, we can write the Thévenin source as $v_T(t) = V_A u(t)$. The circuit differential equation in Eq. (7–3) becomes

$$R_T C \frac{dv}{dt} + v = V_A u(t) \tag{7-15}$$

The step response is a function $v(t)$ that satisfies this differential equation for $t \geq 0$ and meets the initial condition $v(0)$. Since $u(t) = 1$ for $t \geq 0$ we can write Eq. (7–15) as

$$R_T C \frac{dv(t)}{dt} + v(t) = V_A \quad \text{for } t \geqslant 0 \tag{7-16}$$

Mathematics provides a number of approaches to solving this equation, including separation of variables and integrating factors. However, because the circuit is linear we chose a method that uses superposition to divide solution $v(t)$ into two components:

$$v(t) = v_N(t) + v_F(t) \tag{7-17}$$

The first component $v_N(t)$ is the **natural response** and is the general solution of Eq. (7–16) when the input is set to zero. The natural response has its origin in the physical characteristic of the circuit and does not depend on the form of the input. The component $v_F(t)$ is the **forced response** and is a particular solution of Eq. (7–16) when the input is the step function. We call this the forced response because it represents what the circuit is compelled to do by the form of the input.

Finding the natural response requires the general solution of Eq. (7–16) with the input set to zero:

$$R_T C \frac{dv_N(t)}{dt} + v_N(t) = 0 \qquad t \geqslant 0$$

But this is the homogeneous equation that produces the zero-input response in Eq. (7–8). Therefore, we know that the natural response takes the form

$$v_N(t) = Ke^{-t/R_T C} \qquad t \geqslant 0 \tag{7-18}$$

This is a general solution of the homogeneous equation because it contains an arbitrary constant K. At this point we cannot evaluate K from the initial condition, as we did for the zero-input response. The initial condition applies to the total response (natural plus forced), and we have yet to find the forced response.

Turning now to the forced response, we seek a particular solution of the equation

$$R_T C \frac{dv_F(t)}{dt} + v_F(t) = V_A \qquad t \geqslant 0 \tag{7-19}$$

The equation requires that a linear combination of $v_F(t)$ and its derivative equal a constant V_A for $t \geq 0$. Setting $v_F(t) = V_A$ meets this condition since $dv_F/dt = dV_A/dt = 0$. Substituting $v_F = V_A$ into Eq. (7–19) reduces it to the identity $V_A = V_A$.

Now combining the forced and natural responses, we obtain

$$\begin{aligned} v(t) &= v_N(t) + v_F(t) \\ &= Ke^{-t/R_T C} + V_A \qquad t \geqslant 0 \end{aligned}$$

This equation is the general solution for the step response because it satisfies Eq. (7–16) and contains an arbitrary constant K. This constant can now be evaluated using the initial condition:

$$v(0) = V_0 = Ke^0 + V_A = K + V_A$$

The initial condition requires that $K = (V_0 - V_A)$. Substituting this conclusion into the general solution yields the step response of the RC circuit.

$$v(t) = (V_0 - V_A)e^{-t/R_T C} + V_A \qquad t \geqslant 0 \qquad (7-20)$$

A typical plot of $v(t)$ is shown in Figure 7–12.

FIGURE 7–12 *Step response of first-order RC circuit.*

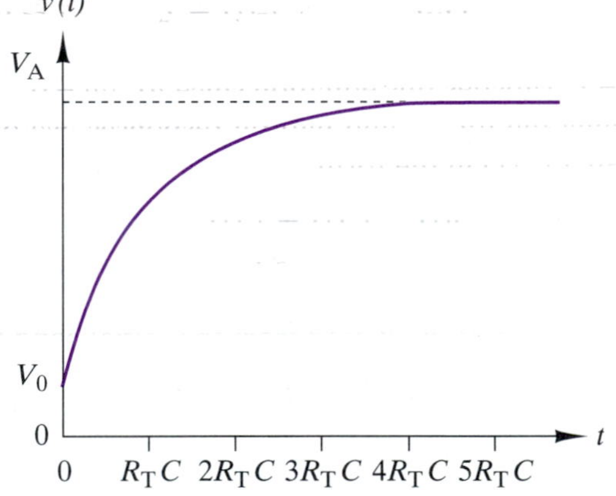

The RC circuit step response in Eq. (7–20) starts out at the initial condition V_0 and is driven to a final condition V_A, which is determined by the amplitude of the step function input. That is, the initial and final values of the response are

$$\lim_{t \to 0+} v(t) = (V_0 - V_A)e^{-0} + V_A = V_0$$
$$\lim_{t \to \infty} v(t) = (V_0 - V_A)e^{-\infty} + V_A = V_A$$

The path between the two end points is an exponential waveform whose time constant is the circuit time constant. We know from our study of exponential signals that the step response will reach its final value after about five time constants. In other words, after about five time constants the natural response decays to zero and we are left with a constant forced response caused by the step function input.

The RL circuit in Figure 7–2 is the dual of the RC circuit, so the development of its step responses follows the same pattern discussed previously. Briefly sketching the main steps, the Norton equivalent input is a step function $I_A u(t)$, and for $t \geq 0$ the RL circuit differential equation Eq. (7–6) becomes

$$G_N L \frac{di(t)}{dt} + i(t) = I_A \qquad t \geqslant 0 \qquad (7\text{–}21)$$

The solution of this equation is found by superimposing the natural and forced components. The natural response is the solution of the homogeneous equation [right side of Eq. (7–21) set to zero] and takes the same form as the zero-input response found in the previous section.

$$i_N(t) = Ke^{-t/G_N L} \qquad t \geqslant 0$$

where K is a constant to be evaluated from the initial condition once the complete response is known. The forced response is a particular solution of the equation

$$G_N L \frac{di_F(t)}{dt} + i_F(t) = I_A \qquad t \geqslant 0$$

Setting $i_F = I_A$ satisfies this equation since $dI_A/dt = 0$.

Combining the forced and natural responses, we obtain the general solution of Eq. (7–21) in the form

$$\begin{aligned} i(t) &= i_N(t) + i_F(t) \\ &= Ke^{-t/G_N L} + I_A \qquad t \geqslant 0 \end{aligned}$$

The constant K is now evaluated from the initial condition:

$$i(0) = I_0 = Ke^{-0} + I_A = K + I_A$$

The initial condition requires that $K = I_0 - I_A$, so the step response of the RL circuit is

$$i(t) = (I_0 - I_A)e^{-t/G_N L} + I_A \qquad t \geqslant 0 \qquad (7\text{–}22)$$

The RL circuit step response has the same form as the RC circuit step response in Eq. (7–20). At $t = 0$ the starting value of the response is $i(0) = I_0$, as required by the initial condition. The final value is the forced response $i(\infty) = i_F = I_A$, since the natural response decays to zero as time increases.

A step function input to the RC or RL circuit drives the state variable from an initial value determined by what happened prior to $t = 0$ to a final value determined by amplitude of the step function applied at $t = 0$. The time needed to transition from the initial to the final value is about $5T_C$, where T_C is the circuit time constant. We conclude that the step response of a first-order circuits depends on three quantities:

1. The amplitude of the step input (V_A or I_A)
2. The circuit time constant ($R_T C$ or $G_N L$)
3. The value of the state variable at $t = 0$ (V_0 or I_0).

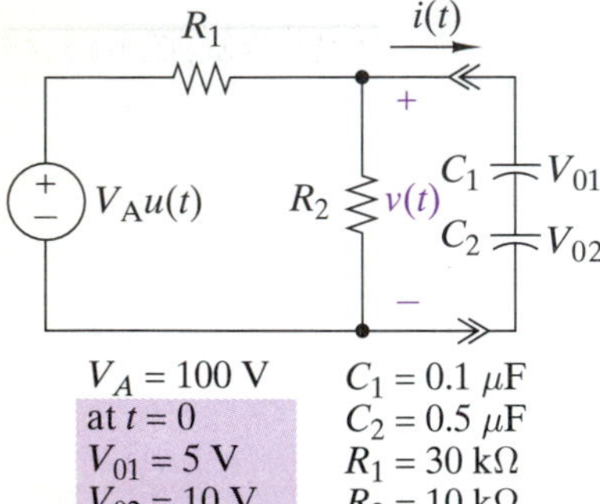

FIGURE 7–13

EXAMPLE 7–4

Find the response of the RC circuit in Figure 7–13.

SOLUTION:

The circuit is first order, since the two capacitors in series can be replaced by a single equivalent capacitor

$$C_{EQ} = \frac{1}{\dfrac{1}{C_1} + \dfrac{1}{C_2}} = 0.0833\ \mu\text{F}$$

The initial voltage on C_{EQ} is the sum of the initial voltages on the original capacitors.

$$V_0 = V_{01} + V_{02} = 5 + 10 = 15\ \text{V}$$

To find the Thévenin equivalent seen by C_{EQ}, we first find the open-circuit voltage. Disconnecting the capacitors in Figure 7–13 and using voltage division at the interface yields

$$v_T = v_{OC} = \frac{R_2}{R_1 + R_2} V_A u(t) = \frac{10}{40} 100u(t) = 25u(t)$$

Replacing the voltage source by a short circuit and looking to the left at the interface, we see R_1 in parallel with R_2. The Thévenin resistance of this combination is

$$R_T = \frac{1}{\dfrac{1}{R_1} + \dfrac{1}{R_2}} = 7.5\ \text{k}\Omega$$

The circuit time constant is

$$T_C = R_T C_{EQ} = (7.5 \times 10^3)(8.33 \times 10^{-8}) = \frac{1}{1600}\ \text{s}$$

For the Thévenin equivalent circuit, the initial capacitor voltage is $V_0 = 15$ V, the step input is $25u(t)$, and the time constant is 1/1600 s. Using the RC circuit step response in Eq. (7–20) yields

$$\begin{aligned} v(t) &= (15 - 25)\, e^{-1600t} + 25 \\ &= 25 - 10\, e^{-1600t}\ \text{V} \qquad t \geq 0 \end{aligned}$$

The initial ($t = 0$) value of $v(t)$ is $25 - 10 = 15$ V, as required. The equivalent capacitor voltage is driven to a final value of 25 V by the step input in the Thévenin equivalent circuit. For practical purposes, $v(t)$ reaches 25 V after about $5T_C = 3.125$ ms.

EXAMPLE 7–5

Find the step response of the RL circuit in Figure 7–14(a). The initial condition is $i(0) = I_0$.

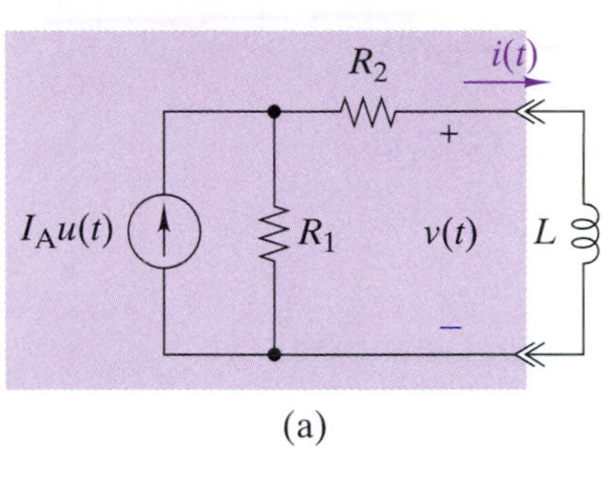

(a)

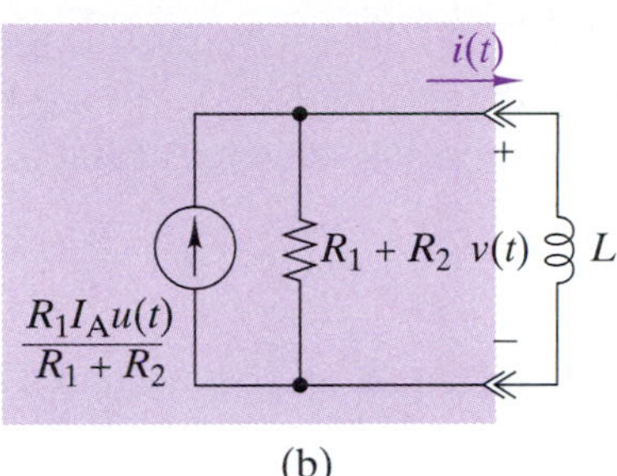

(b)

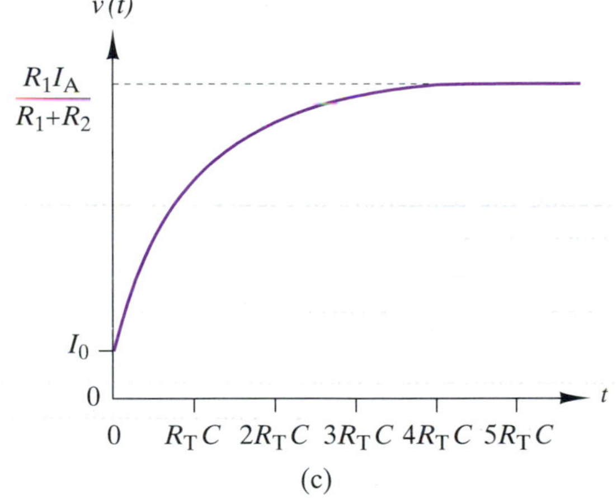

(c)

FIGURE 7–14

SOLUTION:

We first find the Norton equivalent to the left of the interface. By current division, the short-circuit current at the interface is

$$i_{SC}(t) = \frac{R_1}{R_1 + R_2} I_A u(t)$$

Looking to the left at the interface with the current source off (replaced by an open circuit), we see R_1 and R_2 in series producing a Thévenin resistance

$$R_T = \frac{1}{G_N} = R_1 + R_2$$

The time constant of the Norton equivalent circuit in Figure 7–14(b) is

$$T_C = G_N L = \frac{L}{(R_1 + R_2)}$$

The natural response of the Norton equivalent circuit is

$$i_N(t) = Ke^{-(R_1+R_2)t/L} \qquad t \geq 0$$

The short-circuit current $i_{SC}(t)$ is the step function input in the Norton circuit. Therefore, the forced response is

$$i_F(t) = i_{SC}(t) = \frac{R_1}{(R_1 + R_2)} I_A u(t)$$

Superimposing the natural and forced responses yields

$$i(t) = Ke^{-(R_1+R_2)t/L} + \frac{R_1 I_A}{R_1 + R_2} \qquad t \geq 0$$

The constant K can be evaluated from the initial condition:

$$i(0) = I_0 = K + \frac{R_1 I_A}{R_1 + R_2}$$

which requires that

$$K = I_0 - \frac{R_1 I_A}{R_1 + R_2}$$

So circuit step response is

$$i(t) = \left[I_0 - \frac{R_1 I_A}{R_1 + R_2}\right] e^{-(R_1+R_2)t/L} + \frac{R_1 I_A}{R_1 + R_2} \qquad t \geq 0$$

An example of this response is shown in Figure 7–14(c). ■

EXAMPLE 7–6

The state variable response of a first-order RC circuit for a step function input is

$$v_C(t) = 20e^{-200t} - 10 \text{ V} \qquad t \geq 0$$

(a) What is the circuit time constant?
(b) What is the initial voltage across the capacitor?
(c) What is the amplitude of the forced response?
(d) At what time is $v_C(t) = 0$?

SOLUTION:

(a) The natural response of a first-order circuit is of the form Ke^{-t/T_C}. Therefore, the time constant of the given responses is $T_C = 1/200 = 5$ ms.
(b) The initial ($t = 0$) voltage across the capacitor is

$$v_C(0) = 20e^{-0} - 10 = 20 - 10 = 10 \text{ V}$$

(c) The natural response decays to zero, so the forced response is the final value $v_C(t)$.

$$v_C(\infty) = 20e^{-\infty} - 10 = 0 - 10 = -10 \text{ V}$$

(d) The capacitor voltage must pass through zero at some intermediate time, since the initial value is positive and the final value negative. This time is found by setting the step response equal to zero:

$$20e^{-200t} + 10 = 0$$

which yields the condition $e^{200t} = 2$ or $t = \ln 2/200 = 3.47$ ms. ■

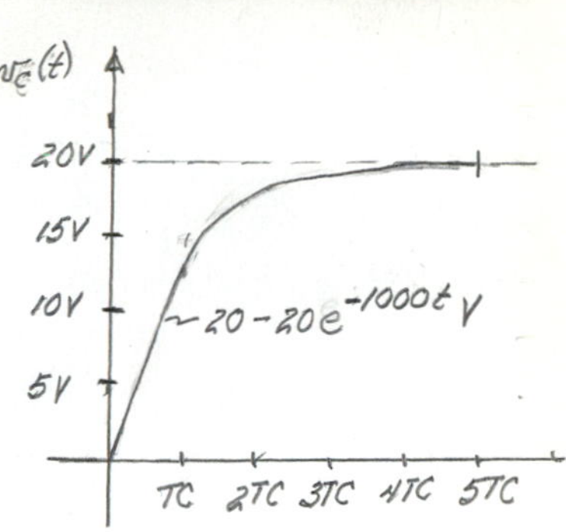

Exercise 7–4

Given the following first-order circuit step responses

(1) $v_C(t) = 20 - 20e^{-1000t}$ V $\quad t \geq 0$
(2) $i_L(t) = -3 + 3e^{-200t}$ A $\quad t \geq 0$
(3) $v_C(t) = -20 + 10e^{-t/10}$ V $\quad t \geq 0$
(4) $i_L(t) = 3e^{-10t}$ A $\quad t \geq 0$

(a) What is the amplitude of the step input?
(b) What is the circuit time constant?
(c) What is the initial value of the state variable?
(d) What is the circuit differential equation?

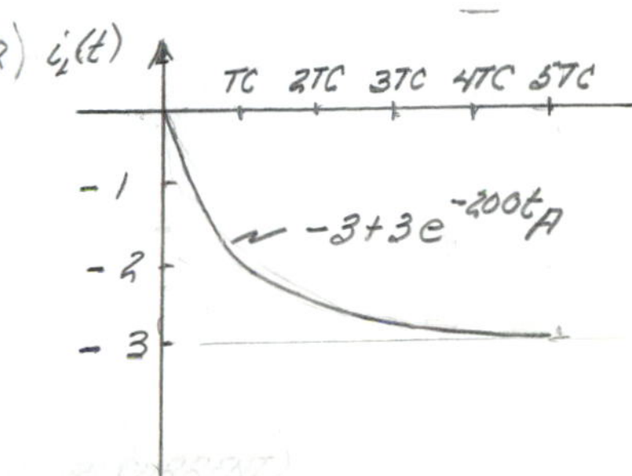

Answers:

(1) (a) 20 V
(b) 1 ms
(c) 0 V
(d) $10^{-3}\, dv_C/dt + v_C = 20u(t)$

(2) (a) −3 A
(b) 5 ms
(c) 0 A
(d) $di_L/dt + 200i_L = -600u(t)$

(3) (a) −20 V
(b) 10 s
(c) −10 V
(d) $10\, dv_C/dt + v_C = -20u(t)$

(4) (a) 0 A
(b) 100 ms
(c) 3 A
(d) $di_L/dt + 10i_L = 0$

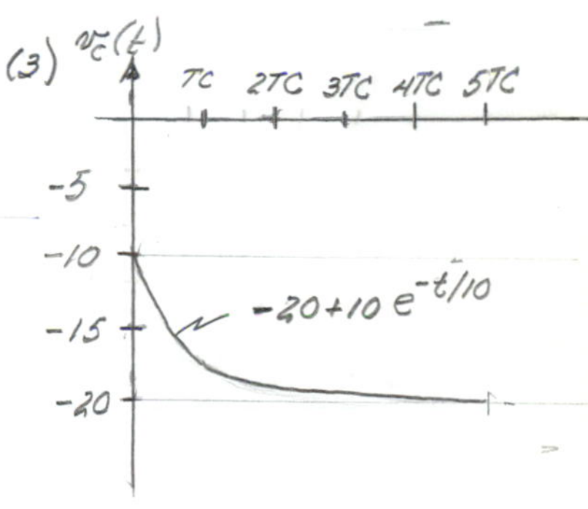

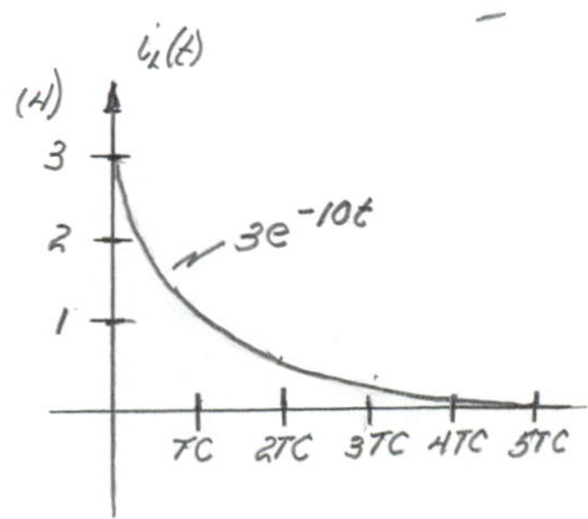

Exercise 7–5

Find the solution of the following first-order differential equations:

$$\text{(a)}\ 10^{-4}\frac{dv_C}{dt} + v_C = -5u(t) \qquad v_C(0) = 5\text{ V}$$

$$\text{(b)}\ 5 \times 10^{-2}\frac{di_L}{dt} + 2000\, i_L = 10u(t) \qquad i_L(0) = -5\text{ mA}$$

Answers:

(a) $v_C(t) = -5 + 10e^{-10000t}$ V $\quad t \geq 0$

(b) $i_L(t) = 5 - 10e^{-40000t}$ mA $\quad t \geq 0$

ZERO-STATE RESPONSE

Additional properties of dynamic circuit responses are revealed by rearranging the *RC* and *RL* circuit step responses in Eqs. (7–20) and (7–22) in the following way:

$$RC\text{ circuit: } v(t) = \underbrace{V_0 e^{-t/R_T C}}_{\text{Zero-input response}} + \underbrace{V_A(1 - e^{-t/R_T C})}_{\text{Zero-state response}} \qquad t \geq 0$$

$$RL\text{ circuit: } i(t) = \overbrace{I_0 e^{-t/G_N L}} + \overbrace{I_A(1 - e^{-t/G_N L})} \qquad t \geq 0$$

We recognize the first term on the right in each equation as the zero-input response discussed in Sect. 7–1. By definition, the **zero-input response** occurs when the step function input is zero ($V_A = 0$ or $I_A = 0$). The second term on the right in each equation is called the **zero-state response** because this part occurs when the initial state of the circuit is zero ($V_0 = 0$ or $I_0 = 0$).

The zero-state response is proportional to the amplitude of the input step function (V_A or I_A). However, the total response (zero input plus zero state) is not directly proportional to the input amplitude. When the initial state is not zero, the circuit appears to violate the proportionality property of linear circuits. However, bear in mind that the proportionality property applies to linear circuits with only one input.

The *RC* and *RL* circuits can store energy and have memory. In effect, they have two inputs: (1) the input that occurred before $t = 0$, and (2) the step function applied at $t = 0$. The first input produces the initial energy state of the circuit at $t = 0$, and the second causes the zero-state response for $t \geq 0$. In general, for $t \geq 0$, the total response of a dynamic circuit is the sum of two responses: (1) the zero-input response caused by the initial conditions produced by inputs applied before $t = 0$, and (2) the zero-state response caused by inputs applied after $t = 0$.

EXAMPLE 7-7

Find the zero-state response of the *RC* circuit of Figure 7–15(a) for an input

$$v_S(t) = V_A[u(t) - u(t - T)]$$

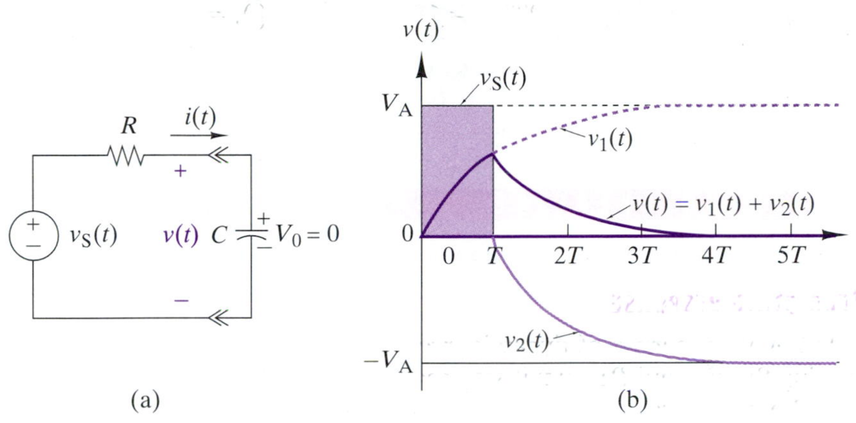

FIGURE 7-15

SOLUTION:

The input is the rectangular pulse shown by the shading in Figure 7–15(b). Since the initial condition is zero (zero state), the total response is the superposition of responses caused by two inputs:

1. A step function of amplitude V_A applied at $t = 0$
2. A step function of amplitude $-V_A$ applied at $t = T$

The first input causes a zero-state response of

$$v_1(t) = V_A(1 - e^{-t/RC})u(t)$$

The second input causes a zero-state response of

$$v_2(t) = -V_A(1 - e^{\frac{-(t-T)}{RC}})u(t - T)$$

The total response is the superposition of these two responses.

$$v(t) = v_1(t) + v_2(t)$$

Figure 7–15(b) shows how the two responses combine to produce the overall pulse response of the circuit. The first step function causes a response $v_1(t)$ that begins at zero and would eventually reach an amplitude of $+V_A$ for $t > 5RC$. However, at $t = T < 5T_C$ the second step function initiates an equal and opposite response $v_2(t)$. For $t > T + 5RC$ the second response reaches its final state and cancels the first response, so the total pulse response returns to zero. ■

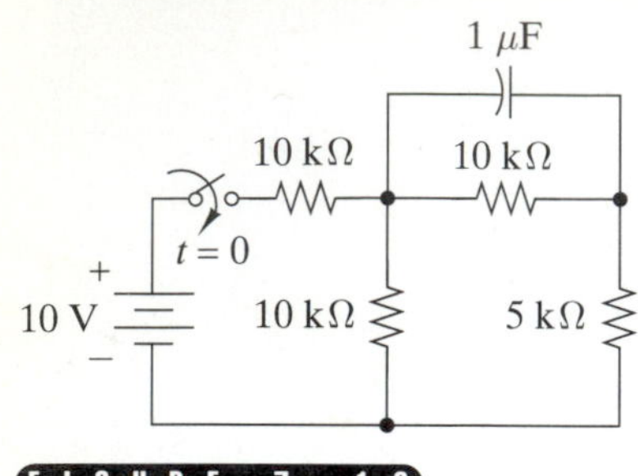

FIGURE 7–16

Exercise 7–6

The switch in Figure 7–16 closes at $t = 0$. SEE OPPOSITE PAGE

(a) Find the zero-state response of the capacitor voltage.
(b) Find the zero-state response of the current through the 10-V voltage source.

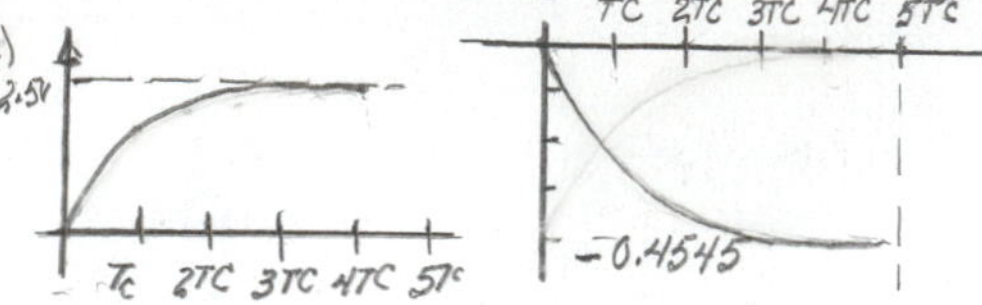

Answers:
(a) $2.5(1 - e^{-200t})$ V
(b) $-0.4545(1 - e^{-200t})$ mA

D DESIGN EXERCISE: 7–7

Given the following first-order circuit zero-state step responses:
(1) $v_C(t) = 10(1 - e^{-2000t})u(t)$ V
(2) $i_L(t) = 5(1 - e^{-5000t})u(t)$ mA
(a) Find the characteristic equation for each circuit.
(b) Find the circuit time constants.
(c) Design first-order circuits that realize each of these responses.

Answers:
(1) (a) $(s + 2000) = 0$ EQ (7-9)
(b) 0.5 ms
(c) There are no unique answers to the (c) part of this exercise because the time constants only specify the products RC and GL. Figure 7–17 shows some possible answers.
(2) (a) $(s + 5000) = 0$
(b) 0.2 ms
(c) See (c) above.

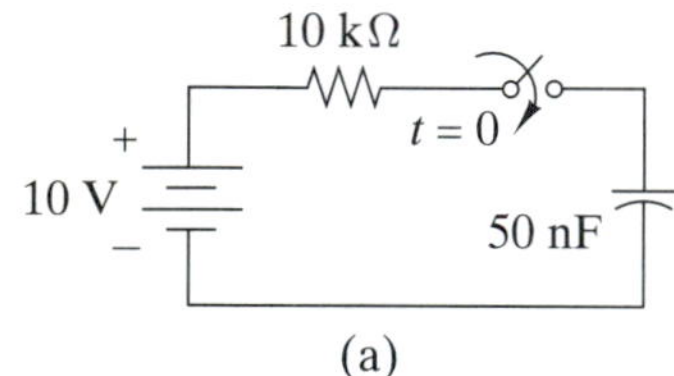

(a)

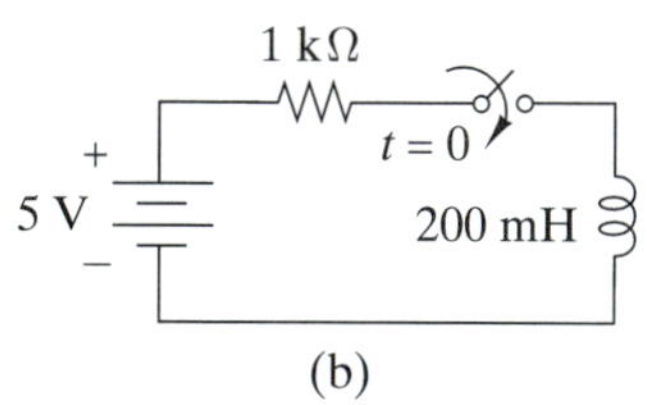

(b)

FIGURE 7–17

DISCUSSION: *The response in (1) is an* RC *circuit with* $V_A = 10$ *V and a time* $RC = 5 \times 10^{-4}$ *s. Selecting* $R = 10$ *kΩ yields* $C = 50$ *nF, producing the circuit in Figure 7–17(a). The response in (2) is an* RL *circuit with* $I_A = 5$ *mA and a time constant of* $GL = 2 \times 10^{-4}$ *s. Selecting* $R = 1$ *kΩ yields* $L = 200$ *mH. A source conversion changes the 5-mA current source in parallel with* R *into a* $(5 \times 10^{-3})(10^3) = 5$*-V voltage source in series with* R, *as shown in Figure 7–17(b).*

7–3 INITIAL AND FINAL CONDITIONS

Reviewing the first-order step responses of the last section shows that for $t \geq 0$ the state variable responses can be written in the form

$$\begin{aligned} RC \text{ circuit: } v_C(t) &= [v_C(0) - v_C(\infty)]e^{-t/T_C} + v_C(\infty) \qquad t \geqslant 0 \\ RL \text{ circuit: } i_L(t) &= [i_L(0) - i_L(\infty)]e^{-t/T_C} + i_L(\infty) \qquad t \geqslant 0 \end{aligned} \tag{7–23}$$

In both circuits the step response is of the general form

$$\text{The state variable response} = \left[\text{The initial value of the state variable} - \text{The final value of the state variable}\right] \times e^{-\frac{t}{T_C}} + \text{The final value of the state variable}$$

To determine the step response of a first-order circuit, we need three quantities: the initial value of the state variable, the final value of the state variable, and the time constant. Since we know how to get the time constant directly from the circuit, it would be useful to have a direct way to determine the initial and final values by inspecting the circuit itself.

The final value can be calculated directly from the circuit by observing that for $t > 5T_C$ the step responses approach a constant value or dc value. Under dc conditions a capacitor acts like an open circuit and an inductor acts like a short circuit. As a result, the final value of the state variable is found by applying dc analysis methods to the circuit configuration for $t > 0$, with capacitors replaced by open circuits and inductors replaced by short circuits.

We can also use dc analysis to determine the initial value in many practical situations. A common situation is a circuit containing dc sources and a switch that is in one position for a period of time much greater than the circuit time constant, and then is moved to a new position at $t = 0$. For example, if the switch is closed for a long period of time, then the dc sources drive the state variable to a final value. If the switch is now opened at $t = 0$, then the dc sources drive the state variable to a new final condition appropriate to the new circuit configuration for $t > 0$.

Note: The initial condition at $t = 0$ is the dc value of the state variable for the circuit configuration that existed before the switch changed positions at $t = 0$. The switching action cannot cause an instantaneous change in the initial condition because capacitor voltage and inductor current are continuous functions of time. In other words, opening a switch at $t = 0$ marks the boundary between two eras. The final condition of the state variable for the $t < 0$ era is the initial condition for the $t > 0$ era that follows.

The usual way to state a switched circuit problem is to say that a switch has been closed (open) for a long time and then is opened (closed) at $t = 0$. In this context, a long time means at least five time constants. Time constants rarely exceeds a few hundred milliseconds in electrical circuits, so a long time passes rather quickly.

The state variable response in switched dynamic circuits is found using the following steps:

STEP 1: Find the initial value by applying dc analysis to the circuit configuration for $t < 0$.

STEP 2: Find the final value by applying dc analysis to the circuit configuration for $t > 0$.

STEP 3: Find the time constant T_C of the circuit in the configuration for $t > 0$.

STEP 4: Write the step response directly using Eq. (7–23) without formulating and solving the circuit differential equation.

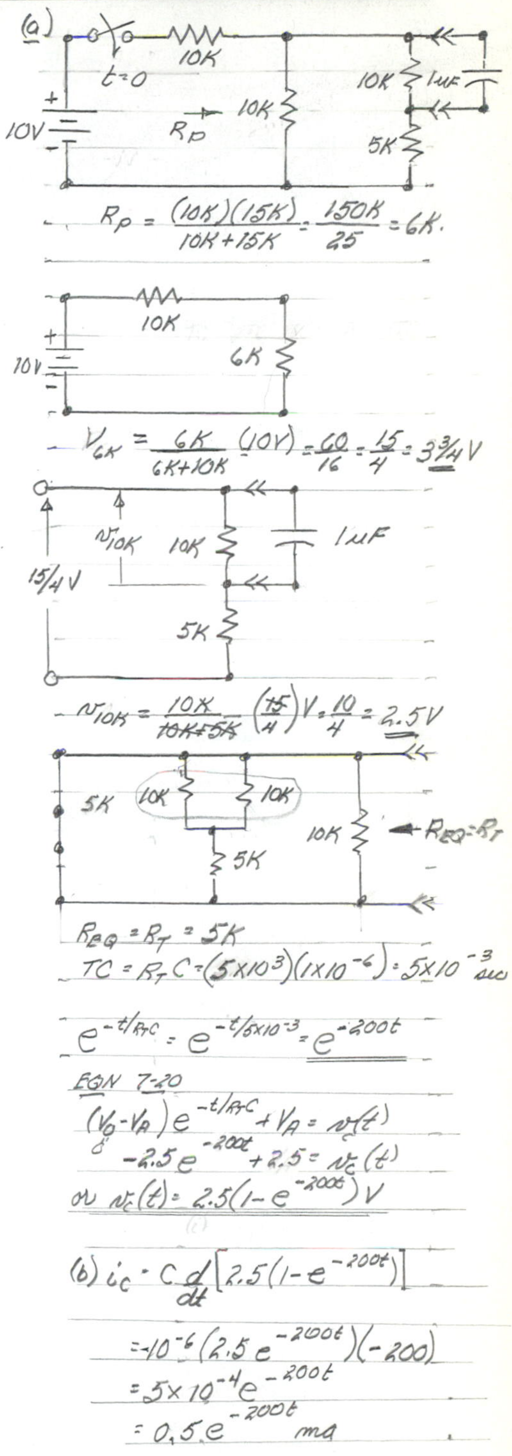

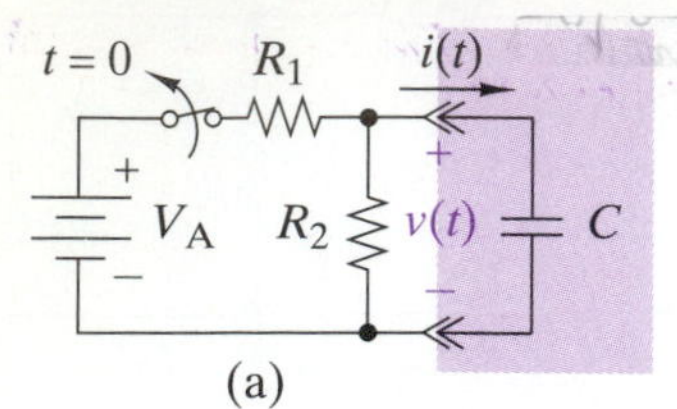

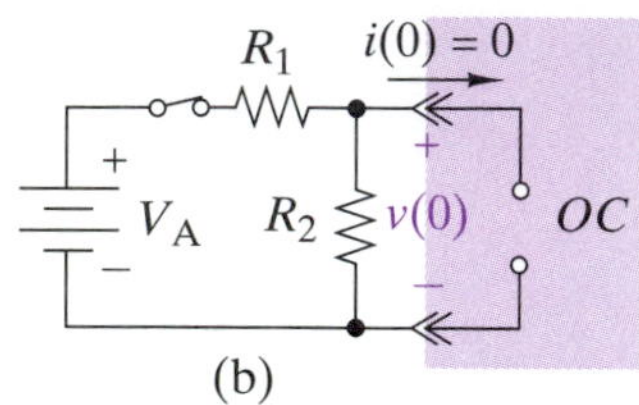

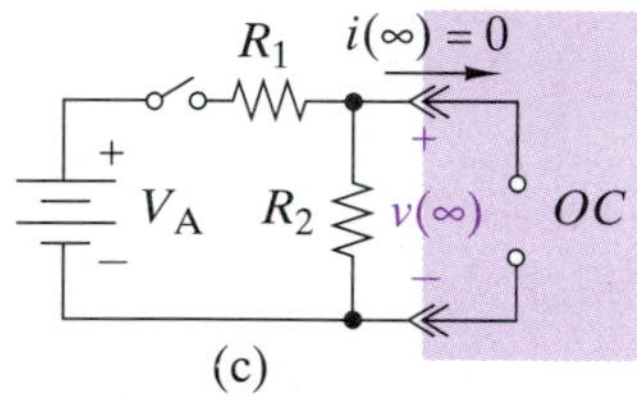

FIGURE 7–18 *Solving a switched dynamic circuit using the initial and final conditions.*

For example, the switch in Figure 7–18(a) has been closed for a long time and is opened at $t = 0$. We want to find the capacitor voltage $v(t)$ for $t \geq 0$.

STEP 1: The initial condition is found by dc analysis of the circuit configuration in Figure 7–18(b), where the switch is closed. Using voltage division, the initial capacitor voltage in found to be

$$v(0) = \frac{R_2 V_A}{R_1 + R_2}$$

STEP 2: The final condition is found by dc analysis of the circuit configuration in Figure 7–18(c), where the switch is open. When the switch is open the circuit has no dc excitation, so the final value of the capacitor voltage is zero.

STEP 3: The circuit in Figure 7–18(c) also gives us the time constant. Looking back at the interface, we see an equivalent resistance of R_2, since R_1 is connected in series with an open switch. For $t \geq 0$ the time constant is R_2C. Using Eq. (7–23), the capacitor voltage for $t \geq 0$ is

$$\begin{aligned} v(t) &= [v(0) - v(\infty)]e^{-t/T_C} + v_C(\infty) \\ &= \frac{R_2 V_A}{R_1 + R_2} e^{-t/R_2C} \qquad t \geqslant 0 \end{aligned}$$

The result is a zero-input response, since there is no excitation for $t \geq 0$. But now we see how the initial condition for the zero-input response could be produced physically by opening a switch that has been closed for a long time.

To continue the analysis, we find the capacitor current using its element constraint:

$$i(t) = C\frac{dv}{dt} = -\frac{V_A}{R_1 + R_2} e^{-t/R_2C} \qquad t \geqslant 0$$

This is the capacitor current for $t \geq 0$. For $t < 0$ the circuit in Figure 7–18(b) points out that the capacitor current is zero since the capacitor acts like an open circuit.

The capacitor voltage and current responses are plotted in Figure 7–19. The capacitor voltage is continuous at $t = 0$, but the capacitor current has a jump discontinuity at $t = 0$. In other words, state variables are continuous, but nonstate variables can have discontinuities at $t = 0$. Since the state variable is continuous, we first find the circuit state variable and then solve for other circuit variables using the element and connection constraints.

EXAMPLE 7–8

The switch in Figure 7–20(a) has been open for a long time and is closed at $t = 0$. Find the inductor current for $t > 0$.

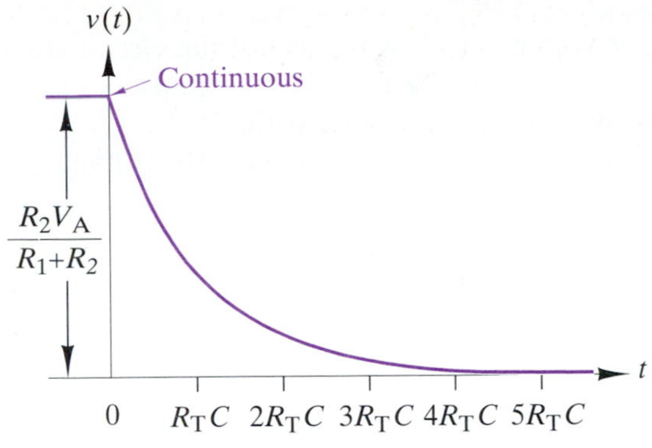

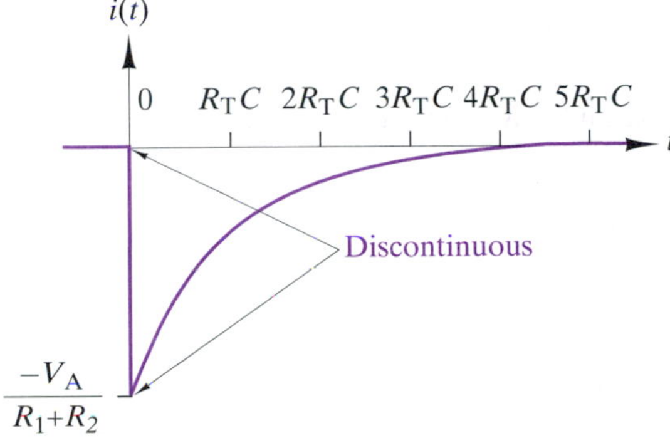

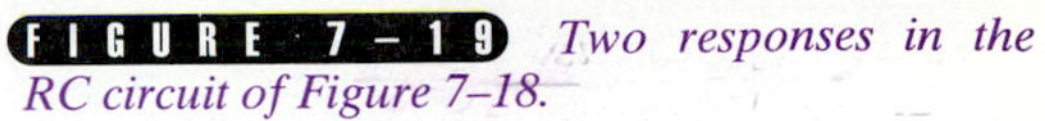
FIGURE 7–19 *Two responses in the RC circuit of Figure 7–18.*

SOLUTION:

We first find the initial condition using the circuit in Figure 7–20(b). By series equivalence the initial current is

$$i(0) = \frac{V_A}{R_1 + R_2}$$

The final condition and the time constant are determined from the circuit in Figure 7–17(c). Closing the switch shorts out R_2, and the final condition and time constant for $t > 0$ are

$$i(\infty) = \frac{V_A}{R_1} \quad \text{and} \quad T_C = G_N L = \frac{L}{R_1}$$

Using Eq. (7–23), the inductor current for $t \geq 0$ is

$$\begin{aligned} i(t) &= [i(0) - i(\infty)]e^{-t/T_C} + i(\infty) \\ &= \left[\frac{V_A}{R_1 + R_2} - \frac{V_A}{R_1}\right]e^{-R_1 t/L} + \frac{V_A}{R_1} \qquad t \geqslant 0 \end{aligned}$$

■

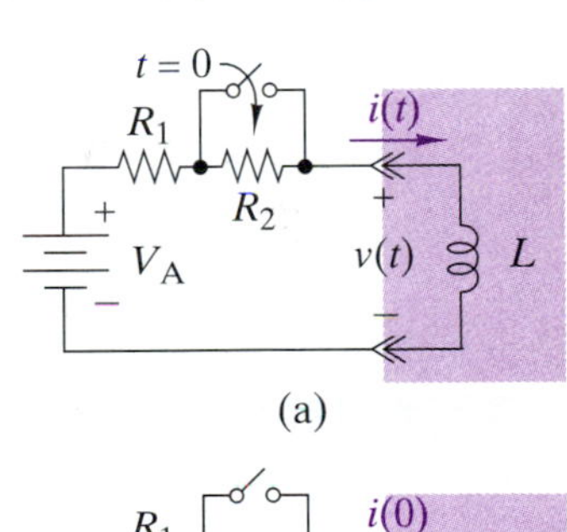

(a)

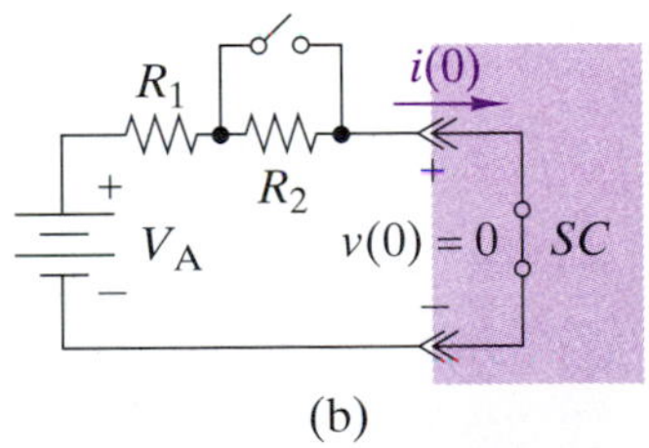

(b)

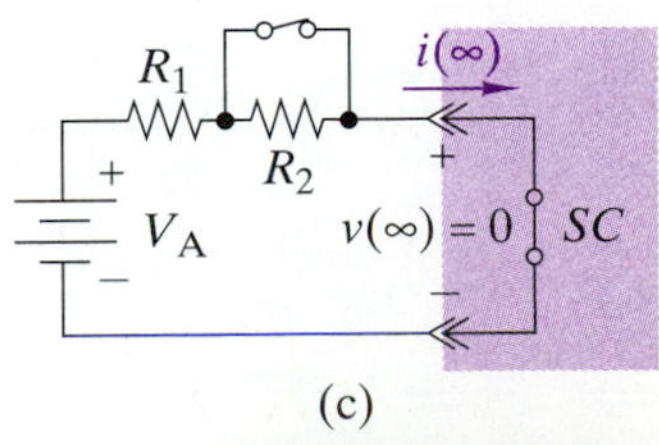

(c)

FIGURE 7–20

EXAMPLE 7–9

The switch in Figure 7–21(a) has been closed for a long time and is opened at $t = 0$. Find the voltage $v_O(t)$.

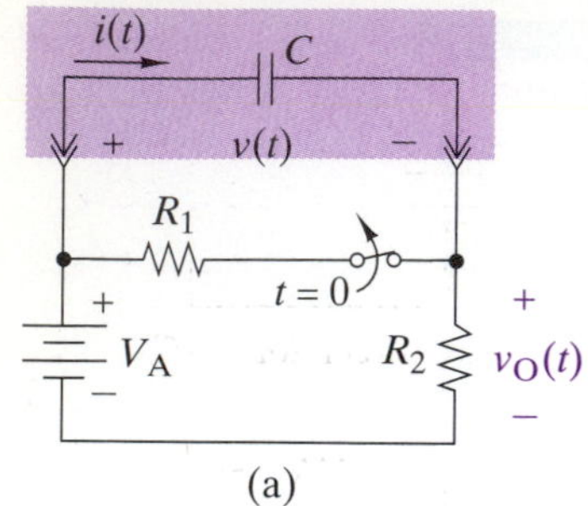

(a)

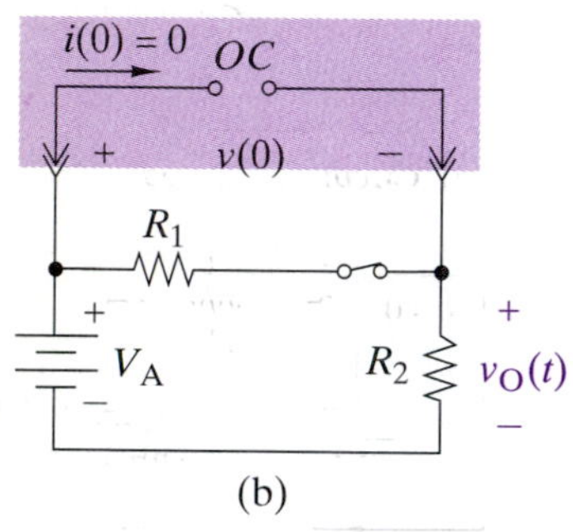

(b)

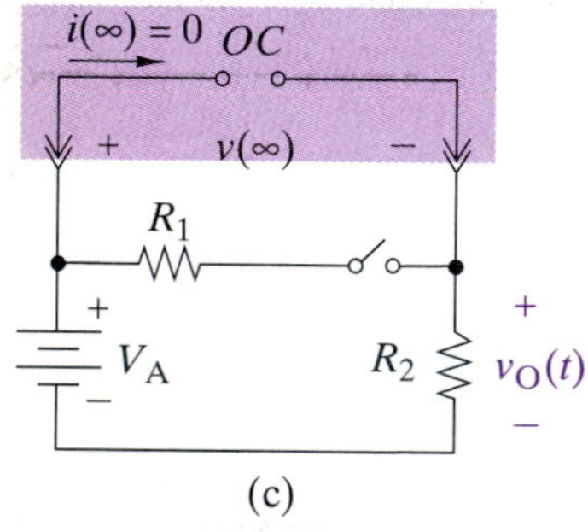

(c)

FIGURE 7–21

SOLUTION:

The problem asks for voltage $v_O(t)$, which is not the circuit state variable. Our approach is first to find the state variable response and then use this response to solve for the required nonstate variable.

For $t < 0$ the circuit in Figure 7–21(b) applies. By voltage division, the initial capacitor voltage is

$$v(0) = \frac{R_1 V_A}{R_1 + R_2}$$

The final value and time constant are found from the circuit in Figure 7–18(c).

$$v(\infty) = V_A \quad \text{and} \quad T_C = R_T C = R_2 C$$

Using Eq. (7–23), the capacitor voltage for $t \geq 0$ is

$$\begin{aligned} v(t) &= [v(0) - v(\infty)]e^{-t/T_C} + v(\infty) \\ &= \left[\frac{R_1 V_A}{R_1 + R_2} - V_A\right]e^{-t/R_2C} + V_A \\ &= V_A + \frac{R_2 V_A}{R_1 + R_2}e^{-t/R_2C} \qquad t \geqslant 0 \end{aligned}$$

Given the state variable, we can find the voltage $v_O(t)$ by writing a KVL equation around the perimeter of the circuit in Figure 7–21(a):

$$-V_A + v(t) + v_O(t) = 0$$

or

$$v_O(t) = V_A - v(t) = -\frac{R_2 V_A}{R_1 + R_2}e^{-t/R_2C} \qquad t \geqslant 0$$

The output voltage response looks like a zero-input response even though the circuit input is not zero for $t \geq 0$. However, $v_O(t)$ is not the state variable but the voltage across the resistor R_2. The voltage across R_2 is proportional to the capacitor current, which eventually decays to zero in the final circuit configuration in Figure 7–21(c) because the capacitor acts like an open circuit. ■

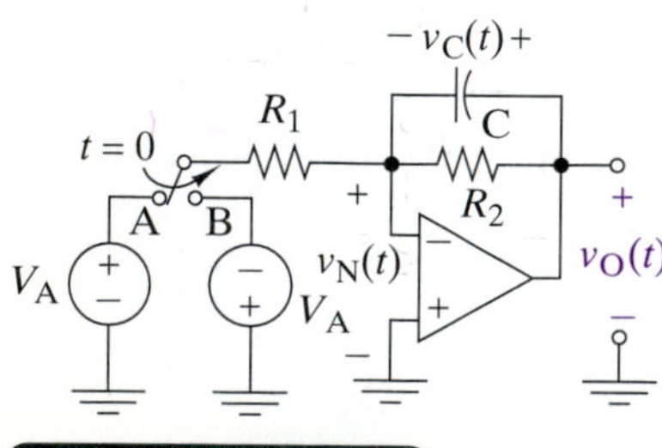

FIGURE 7–22

EXAMPLE 7–10

The switch in Figure 7–22 has been in position A for quite a while and is moved to position B at $t = 0$. Find the OP AMP output voltage $v_O(t)$.

SOLUTION:

Since $v_O(t)$ does not appear to be a state variable, we need to show that Eq. (7–23) applies to this problem. Applying the fundamental principle of node voltages to the capacitor voltage yields

$$v_C(t) = v_O(t) - v_N(t)$$

For the ideal OP AMP model, $v_N = v_p = 0$ since the noninverting input is grounded. In other words, the OP AMP output voltage equals the capacitor voltage, which is the state variable. Hence, we can use Eq. (7–23) to find $v_O(t)$. In Sect. 7–1 we showed that this OP AMP circuit is a first-order circuit with a time constant of R_2C. When the capacitor is replaced by an open circuit, the configuration is an inverting amplifier with a gain of $-R_2/R_1$. For $t < 0$ the switch is in position A and the initial output (and capacitor) voltage is

$$v_O(0) = -\frac{R_2}{R_1}V_A$$

For $t \geq 0$ the switch is in position B and the final output (and capacitor) voltage is

$$v_O(\infty) = -\frac{R_2}{R_1}(-V_A) = -v_O(0)$$

Applying Eq. (7–23), the step response is

$$v_O(t) = -2\frac{R_2}{R_1}V_A e^{-t/R_2C} + \frac{R_2}{R_1}V_A$$

$$= \frac{R_2}{R_1}V_A(1 - 2e^{-t/R_2C}) \qquad t \geq 0$$

■

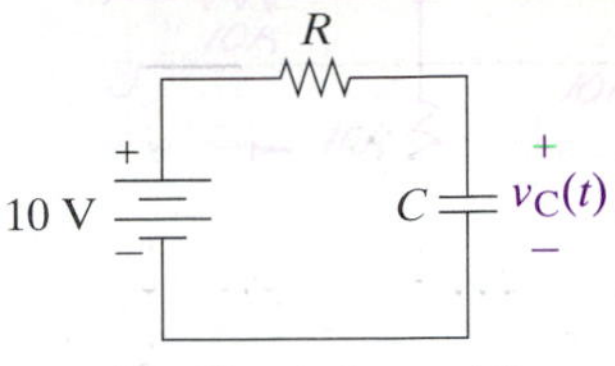

(a) Circuit for $v_C(0)$

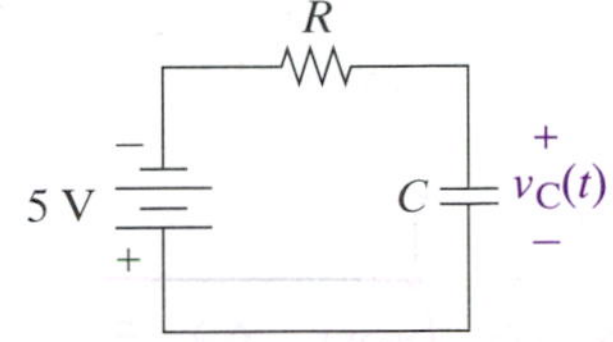

(b) Circuit for $v_C(\infty)$

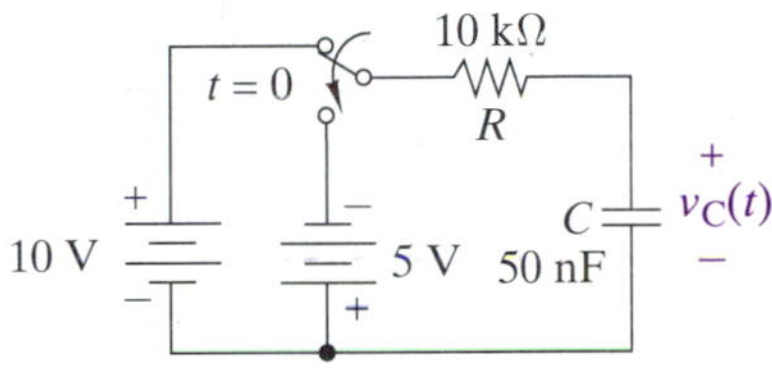

(c) Candidate design

FIGURE 7–23

D DESIGN EXAMPLE 7–11

First-Order RC Circuit Design

Design an RC circuit whose response is $v_C(t) = -5 + 15e^{-2000t}$ V for $t \geq 0$. The circuit can include one switch that is thrown at $t = 0$.

SOLUTION:

The required initial and final conditions for the specified response are

$$v_C(0) = 15e^{-0} - 5 = +10 \text{ V}$$

$$v_C(\infty) = 15e^{-\infty} - 5 = -5 \text{ V}$$

The time constant of the specified response is $T_C = 1/2000 = 0.5$ ms. The time constant of a simple RC circuit is $T_C = RC = 0.5$ ms. Choosing $R = 10$ kΩ yields $C = 50$ nF. Figure 7–23(a) shows a simple RC circuit that produces the required $v_C(0)$. Similarly, the RC circuit in Figure 7–23(b) produces the required $v_C(\infty)$. One switch is allowed, so we combine these two circuits, as indicated in Figure 7–23(c). Many other designs are possible. ■

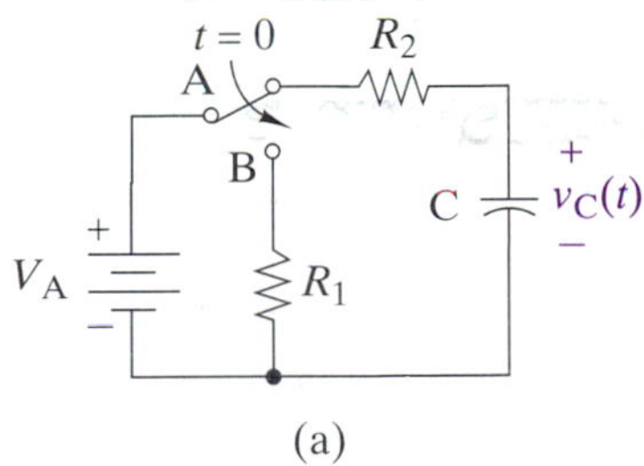

(a)

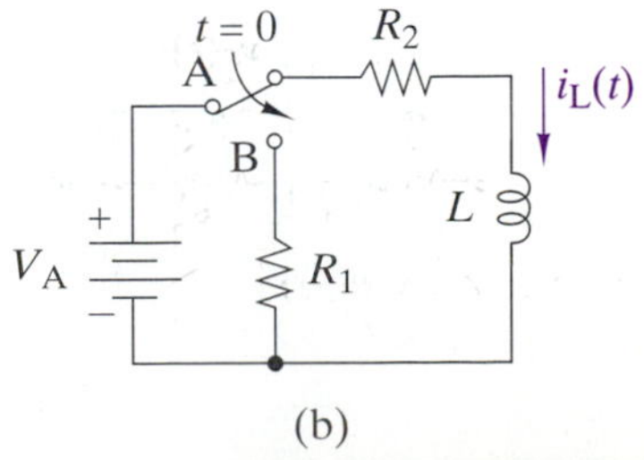

(b)

FIGURE 7–24

Exercise 7–8

In each circuit shown in Figure 7–24 the switch has been in position A for a long time and is moved to position B at $t = 0$. Find the circuit state variable for each circuit for $t \geq 0$.

Answers:

$$(a)\ v_C(t) = V_A e^{-t/(R_1+R_2)C}$$

$$(b)\ i_L(t) = \frac{V_A}{R_2} e^{-(R_1+R_2)t/L}$$

Exercise 7–9

In each circuit shown in Figure 7–24 the switch has been in position B for a long time and is moved to position A at $t = 0$. Find the circuit state variable for each circuit for $t \geq 0$.

Answers:

$$(a)\ v_C(t) = V_A(1 - e^{-t/R_2C})$$

$$(b)\ i_L(t) = \frac{V_A}{R_2}(1 - e^{-R_2t/L})$$

Exercise 7–10

In the circuit in Figure 7–25 the switch has been in position A for a long time and is moved to position B at $t = 0$. For $t \geq 0$ find

FIGURE 7–25

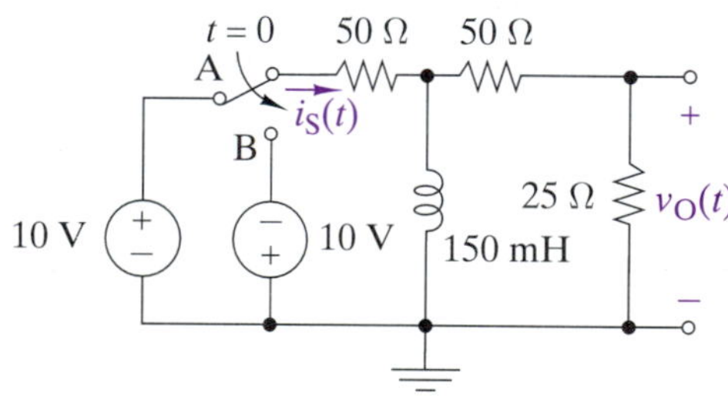

(a) The output voltage $v_O(t)$
(b) The current $i_S(t)$ through the switch.

Answers:
(a) $-4e^{-200t}$ V
(b) $-0.2 + 0.24e^{-200t}$ A

7–4 FIRST-ORDER CIRCUIT SINUSOIDAL RESPONSE

The response of linear circuits to sinusoidal inputs is one of the central themes of electrical engineering. In this introduction to the concept we treat the sinusoidal response of first-order circuits using differential equations. In later chapters we see that sinusoidal response can be found using other techniques, such as phasors and Laplace transforms. But for the moment, we concentrate on the classical method of finding the forced response from the circuit differential equation.

If the input to the *RC* circuit in Figure 7–2 is a casual sinusoid, then the circuit differential equation in Eq. (7–3) is written as

$$R_{\mathrm{T}}C\frac{dv(t)}{dt} + v(t) = V_{\mathrm{A}}[\cos \omega t]u(t) \tag{7–24}$$

The input on the right side of Eq. (7–24) is *not* an eternal sinewave but a casual sinusoid that starts at $t = 0$, through some action such as closing a switch. We seek a solution function $v(t)$ that satisfies Eq. (7–24) for $t \geq 0$ and that meets the prescribed initial condition $v(0) = V_0$.

As with the step response, we find the solution in two parts: natural response and forced response. The natural response is of the form

$$v_{\mathrm{N}}(t) = K e^{-t/R_{\mathrm{T}}C} \qquad t \geqslant 0$$

The natural response of a first-order circuit always has this form because it is a general solution of the homogeneous equation with input set to zero. The form of the natural response depends on the physical characteristics of the circuit and is independent of the input.

The forced response depends on both the circuit and the nature of the forcing function. The forced response is a particular solution of the equation

$$R_{\mathrm{T}}C\frac{dv_{\mathrm{F}}(t)}{dt} + v_{\mathrm{F}}(t) = V_{\mathrm{A}} \cos \omega t \qquad t \geqslant 0$$

This equation requires that $v_{\mathrm{F}}(t)$ plus $R_{\mathrm{T}}C$ times its first derivative add to produce a cosine function for $t \geq 0$. The only way this can happen is for $v_{\mathrm{F}}(t)$ and its derivative to be sinusoids of the same frequency. This requirement brings to mind the derivative property of the sinusoid. So we try a solution in the form of a general sinusoid. As noted in Chapter 5, a general sinusoid can be written in amplitude and phase angle form as

$$v_{\mathrm{F}}(t) = V_{\mathrm{F}} \cos(\omega t + \phi) \tag{7–25a}$$

or in terms of Fourier coefficients as

$$v_{\mathrm{F}}(t) = a \cos \omega t + b \sin \omega t \tag{7–25b}$$

While either form will work, it is somewhat easier to work with the Fourier coefficient format.

The approach we are using is called the method of undetermined coefficients, where the unknown coefficients are the Fourier coefficients a and b in Eq. (7–25b). To find these unknowns we insert the proposed forced response in Eq. (7–25b) into the differential equation to obtain

$$R_{\mathrm{T}}C\frac{d}{dt}(a \cos \omega t + b \sin \omega t) + (a \cos \omega t + b \sin \omega t) = V_{\mathrm{A}} \cos \omega t \qquad t \geqslant 0$$

Performing the differentiation gives

$$R_TC(-\omega a \sin \omega t + \omega b \cos \omega t) + (a \cos \omega t + b \sin \omega t) = V_A \cos \omega t$$

We next gather all sine and cosine terms on one side of the equation.

$$[R_TC\omega b + a - V_A]\cos \omega t + [-R_TC\omega a + b]\sin \omega t = 0$$

The left side of this equation is zero for all $t \geq 0$ only when the coefficients of the cosine and sine terms are identically zero. This requirement yields two linear equations in the unknown coefficients a and b:

$$a + (R_TC\omega)b = V_A$$

$$-(R_TC\omega)a + b = 0$$

The solutions of these linear equations are

$$a = \frac{V_A}{1 + (\omega R_TC)^2} \qquad b = \frac{\omega R_TCV_A}{1 + (\omega R_TC)^2}$$

These equations express the unknowns a and b in terms of known circuit parameters (R_TC) and known input signal parameters (ω and V_A).

We combine the forced and natural responses as

$$v(t) = Ke^{-t/R_TC} + \frac{V_A}{1 + (\omega R_TC)^2}(\cos \omega t + \omega R_TC \sin \omega t) \qquad t \geqslant 0 \tag{7-26}$$

The initial condition requires

$$v(0) = V_0 = K + \frac{V_A}{1 + (\omega R_TC)^2}$$

which means K is

$$K = V_0 - \frac{V_A}{1 + (\omega R_TC)^2}$$

We substitute this value of K into Eq. (7–26) to obtain the function $v(t)$ that satisfies the differential equation and the initial conditions.

$$v(t) = \underbrace{\left[V_0 - \frac{V_A}{1 + (\omega R_TC)^2}\right]e^{-t/R_TC}}_{\text{Natural response}} + \underbrace{\frac{V_A}{1 + (\omega R_TC)^2}(\cos \omega t + \omega R_TC \sin \omega t)}_{\text{Forced response}} \qquad t \geqslant 0$$

This expression is somewhat less formidable when we convert the forced response to an amplitude and phase angle format

$$v(t) = \underbrace{\left[V_0 - \frac{V_A}{1 + (\omega R_T C)^2}\right] e^{-t/R_T C}}_{\text{Natural Response}} + \underbrace{\frac{V_A}{\sqrt{1 + (\omega R_T C)^2}} \cos(\omega t + \theta)}_{\text{Forced Response}} \quad t \geq 0 \tag{7–27}$$

where

$$\theta = \tan^{-1}(-b/a) = \tan^{-1}(-\omega R_T C)$$

Equation (7–27) is the complete response of the *RC* circuit for an initial condition V_0 and a sinusoidal input $[V_A \cos \omega t]u(t)$. Several aspects of the response deserve comment:

1. After roughly five time constants the natural response decays to zero but the sinusoidal forced response persists.
2. The forced response is a sinusoid with the same frequency (ω) as the input but with a different amplitude and phase angle.
3. The forced response is proportional to V_A. This means that the amplitude of the forced component has the proportionality property because the circuit is linear.

In the terminology of electrical engineering, the forced component is called the **sinusoidal steady-state response**. The words *steady state* may be misleading since together they seem to imply a constant or "steady" value, whereas the forced response is a sustained oscillation. To electrical engineers *steady state* means the conditions reached after the natural response has died out. The sinusoidal steady-state response is also called the **ac steady-state response**. Often the words *steady state* are dropped and it is called simply the **ac response**. Hereafter, ac response, sinusoidal steady-state response, and the forced response for a sinusoidal input will be used interchangeably.

Finally, the forced response due to a step function input is called the **zero-frequency** or **dc steady-state response**. The zero-frequency terminology means that we think of a step function as a cosine $V_A[\cos \omega t]u(t)$ with $\omega = 0$. The reader can easily show that inserting $\omega = 0$ reduces Eq. (7–27) to the *RC* circuit step response in Eq. (7–20).

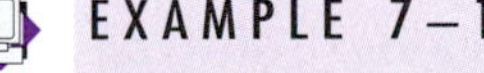

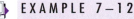

EXAMPLE 7–12

The switch in Figure 7–26 has been open for a long time and is closed at $t = 0$. Find the voltage $v(t)$ for $t \geq 0$ when $v_S(t) = [20 \sin 1000t]u(t)$ V.

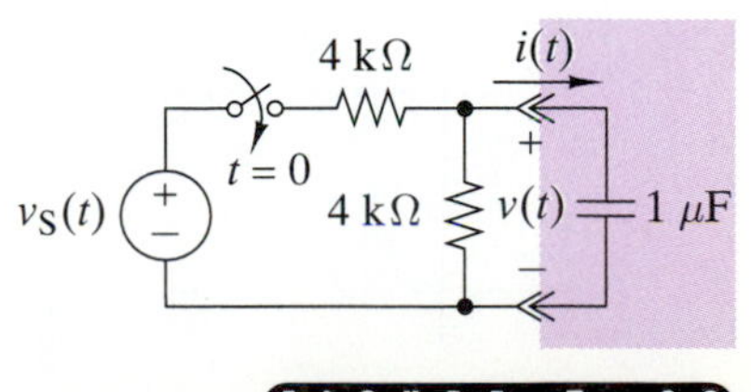

FIGURE 7–26

SOLUTION:

We first derive the circuit differential equation. By voltage division, the Thévenin voltage seen by the capacitor is

$$v_T(t) = \frac{4}{4 + 4} v_S(t) = 10 \sin 1000t \quad \text{V}$$

The Thévenin resistance (switch closed and source off) looking back into the interface is two 4-kΩ resistors in parallel, so $R_T = 2$ kΩ. The circuit time constant is

$$T_C = R_T C = (2 \times 10^3)(1 \times 10^{-6}) = 2 \times 10^{-3} = 1/500 \text{ s}$$

Given the Thévenin equivalent seen by the capacitor and the circuit time constant, the circuit differential is

$$2 \times 10^{-3}\frac{dv(t)}{dt} + v(t) = 10 \sin 1000t \qquad t \geq 0$$

Note that the right side of the circuit differential equation is the Thévenin voltage $v_T(t)$ and not the original source input $v_S(t)$. The natural response is of the form

$$v_N(t) = Ke^{-500t} \qquad t \geq 0$$

The forced response with undetermined Fourier coefficients is

$$v_F(t) = a \cos 1000t + b \sin 1000t$$

Substituting the forced response into the differential equation produces

$$2 \times 10^{-3}(-1000\, a \sin 1000t + 1000b \cos 1000t) +$$

$$a \cos 1000t + b \sin 1000t = 10 \sin 1000t$$

Collecting all sine and cosine terms on one side of this equation yields

$$(a + 2b) \cos 1000t + (-2a + b - 10)\sin 1000t = 0$$

The left side of this equation is zero for all $t \geq 0$ only when the coefficient of the sine and cosine terms vanish:

$$a + 2b = 0$$

$$-2a + b = 10$$

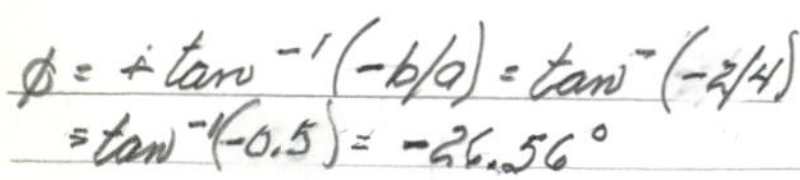

The solutions of these two linear equations are $a = -4$ and $b = 2$. We combine the forced and natural responses

$$v(t) = Ke^{-500t} - 4 \cos 1000t + 2 \sin 1000t \qquad t \geq 0$$

The constant K is found from the initial conditions

$$v(0) = V_0 = K - 4$$

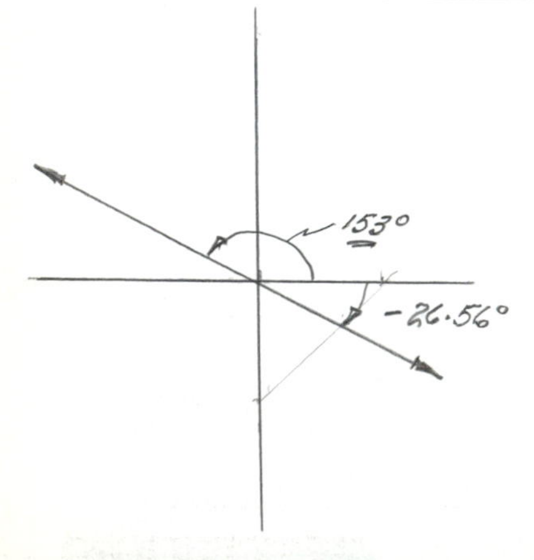

The initial condition is $V_0 = 0$ because with the switch open the capacitor had no input for a long time prior to $t = 0$. The initial condition $v(0) = 0$ requires $K = 4$, so we can now write the complete response in the form

$$v(t) = 4e^{-500t} - 4 \cos 1000t + 2 \sin 1000t \text{ V} \qquad t \geq 0$$

or, in an amplitude, phase angle format as

$$v(t) = 4e^{-500t} + 4.47 \cos(1000t + 153°) \text{ V} \qquad t \geq 0$$

Figure 7–27 shows a Quattro Pro worksheet that generates plots of the natural response, forced response, and total response. Column A is the

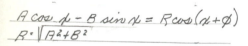

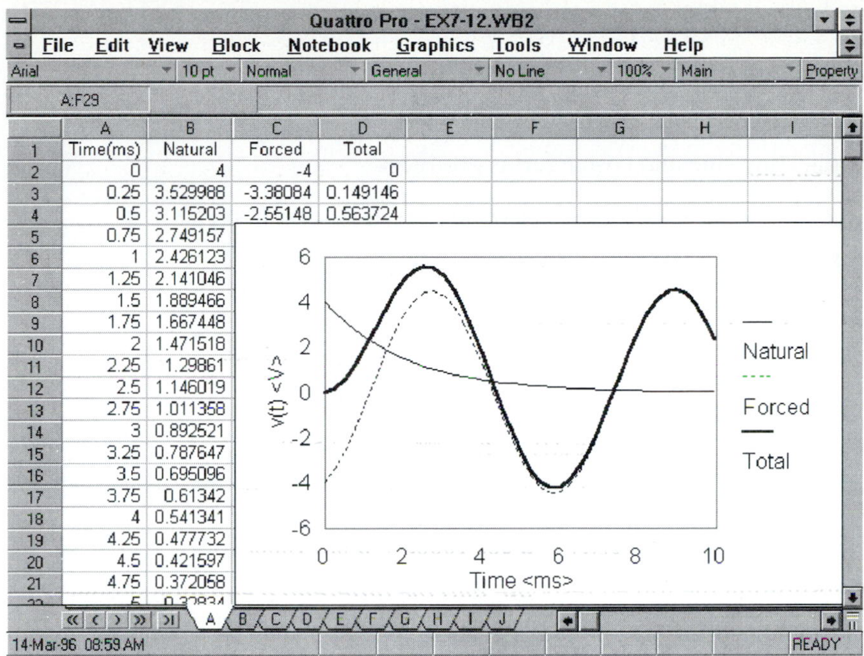

	A	B	C	D
1	Time(ms)	Natural	Forced	Total
2	0	4	-4	0
3	0.25	3.529988	-3.38084	0.149146
4	0.5	3.115203	-2.55148	0.563724
5	0.75	2.749157		
6	1	2.426123		
7	1.25	2.141046		
8	1.5	1.889466		
9	1.75	1.667448		
10	2	1.471518		
11	2.25	1.29861		
12	2.5	1.146019		
13	2.75	1.011358		
14	3	0.892521		
15	3.25	0.787647		
16	3.5	0.695096		
17	3.75	0.61342		
18	4	0.541341		
19	4.25	0.477732		
20	4.5	0.421597		
21	4.75	0.372058		

FIGURE 7–27

time at 0.25-ms intervals. Columns B and C calculate the natural response ($4e^{-500t}$) and the forced response ($-4 \cos 1000t + 2 \sin 1000t$) at each of the times given in column A. The total response in column D is the sum of the entries in columns B and C. The plots show that the total response merges into the sinusoidal forced response since the natural response decays to zero after about $5T_C = 10$ ms. That is, after about 10 ms or so the circuit settles down to an ac steady-state condition. ■

EXAMPLE 7–13

Find the sinusoidal steady-state response of the output voltage $v_O(t)$ in Figure 7–28 when the input current is $i_S(t) = [I_A \cos \omega t]u(t)$.

SOLUTION:

In keeping with our general analysis approach, we first find the steady-state response of the state variable $i(t)$ and use it to determine the required output voltage. The differential equation of the circuit in terms of the inductor current is

$$GL\frac{di}{dt} + i = I_A \cos \omega t \qquad t \geqslant 0$$

To find the steady-state response, we need to find the unknown Fourier coefficients a and b in the forced component:

$$i_F(t) = a \cos \omega t + b \sin \omega t \qquad t \geqslant 0$$

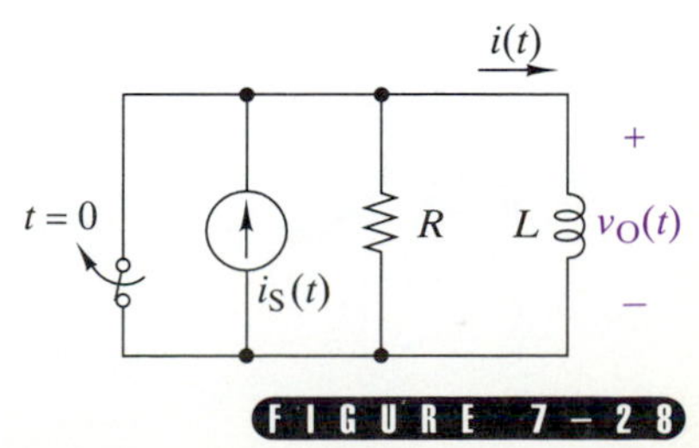

FIGURE 7–28

Substituting this expression into the differential equation yields

$$GL(-a\omega \sin \omega t + b\omega \cos \omega t) +$$
$$a \cos \omega t + b \sin \omega t = I_A \cos \omega t$$

Collecting sine and cosine terms produces

$$(a + GLb\omega - I_A)\cos \omega t + (-GLa\omega + b)\sin \omega t = 0$$

The left side of this equation is zero for all $t \geq 0$ only if

$$a + (GL\omega)b = I_A$$
$$-(GL\omega)a + b = 0$$

The solutions of these linear equations are

$$a = \frac{I_A}{1 + (GL\omega)^2} \qquad b = \frac{\omega GLI_A}{1 + (GL\omega)^2}$$

Therefore, the forced component of the inductor current is

$$i_F(t) = \frac{I_A}{1 + (\omega GL)^2}(\cos \omega t + \omega GL \sin \omega t) \qquad t \geqslant 0$$

The prescribed output is the voltage across the inductor. The steady-state output voltage is found using the inductor element equation:

$$v_0 = L\frac{di_F}{dt} = \left[\frac{I_A L}{1 + (\omega GL)^2}\right]\frac{d}{dt}[\cos \omega t + \omega GL \sin \omega t]$$
$$= \left[\frac{I_A L}{1 + (\omega GL)^2}\right][-\omega \sin \omega t + \omega^2 GL \cos \omega t]$$
$$= \frac{I_A \omega L}{\sqrt{1 + (\omega GL)^2}} \cos(\omega t + \theta) \qquad t \geqslant 0$$

where $\theta = \tan^{-1}(1/\omega GL)$. The output voltage is a sinusoid with the same frequency as the input signal, but with a different amplitude and phase angle. In fact, in the sinusoidal steady state every voltage and current in a linear circuit is sinusoidal with the same frequency. ■

Exercise 7–11

Find the forced component solution of the differential equation

$$10^{-3}\frac{dv}{dt} + v = 10 \cos \omega t$$

for the following frequencies:

(a) $\omega = 500$ rad/s
(b) $\omega = 1000$ rad/s
(c) $\omega = 2000$ rad/s

Answers:
(a) $v_F(t) = 8 \cos 500t + 4 \sin 500t \quad t \geq 0$
(b) $v_F(t) = 5 \cos 1000t + 5 \sin 1000t \quad t \geq 0$
(c) $v_F(t) = 2 \cos 2000t + 4 \sin 2000t \quad t \geq 0$

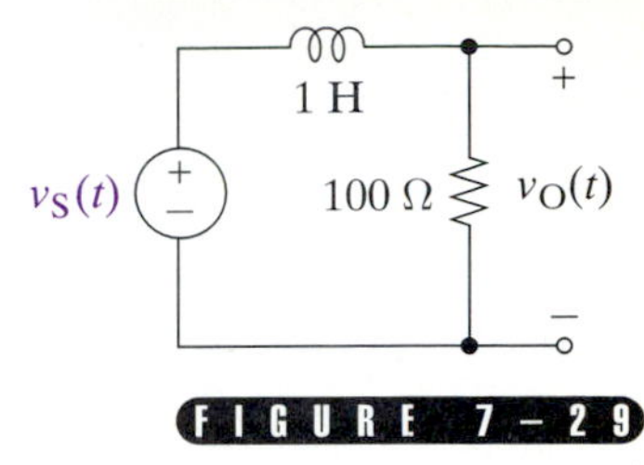

FIGURE 7–29

Exercise 7–12

The circuit in Figure 7–29 is operating in the sinusoidal steady state with

$$v_O(t) = 10 \cos(100t - 45°) \text{ V}$$

Find the source voltage $v_S(t)$.

Answer:
$10\sqrt{2} \cos 100t$ V

7–5 THE SERIES *RLC* CIRCUIT

Second-order circuits contain two energy storage elements that cannot be replaced by a single equivalent element. They are called **second-order circuits** because the circuit differential equation involves the second derivative of the dependent variable. Although there is an endless number of such circuits, in this chapter we will concentrate on two classical forms: (1) the series *RLC* circuit and (2) the parallel *RLC* circuit. These two circuits illustrate almost all of the basic concepts of second-order circuits and serve as vehicles for studying the solution of second-order differential equations. In subsequent chapters we use Laplace transform techniques to analyze any second-order circuit.

FORMULATING SERIES *RLC* CIRCUIT EQUATIONS

We begin with the circuit in Figure 7–30(a), where the inductor and capacitor are connected in series. The source-resistor circuit can be reduced to the Thévenin equivalent shown in Figure 7–25(b). The result is a circuit in which a voltage source, resistor, inductor, and capacitor are connected in series (hence the name **series *RLC* circuit**).

The first task is to develop the equations that describe the series *RLC* circuit. The Thévenin equivalent to the left of the interface in Figure 7–30(b) produces the KVL constraint

$$v + R_T i = v_T \tag{7-28}$$

Applying KVL around the loop on the right side of the interface yields

$$v = v_L + v_C \tag{7-29}$$

Finally, the *i–v* characteristics of the inductor and capacitor are

$$v_L = L\frac{di}{dt} \tag{7-30}$$

$$i = C\frac{dv_C}{dt} \tag{7-31}$$

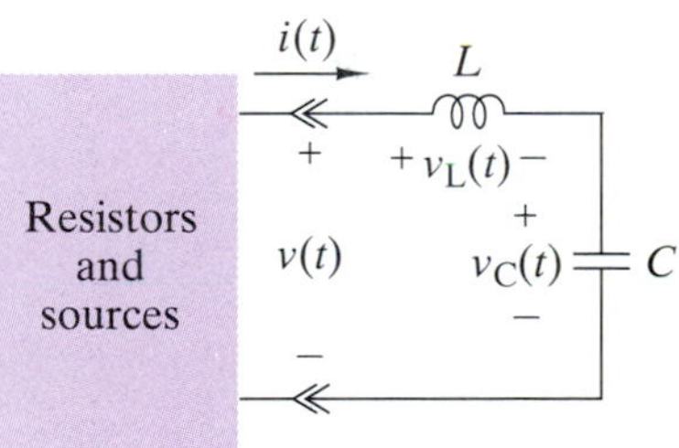

(a)

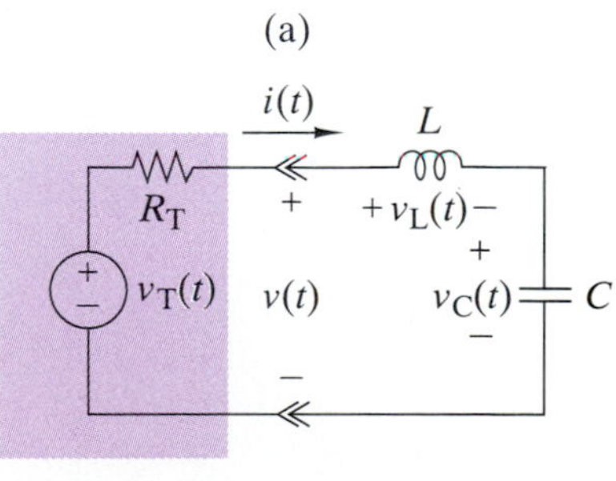

(b)

FIGURE 7–30 The series *RLC* circuit.

Equations (7–28) through (7–31) are four independent equations in four unknowns (i, v, v_L, v_C). Collectively, this set of equations provides a complete description of the dynamics of the series *RLC* circuit. To find the circuit response using classical methods, we must derive a circuit equation containing only one of these unknowns.

We use circuit state variables as solution variables because they are continuous functions of time. In the series *RLC* circuit in Figure 7–25(b), there are two state variables: (1) the capacitor voltage $v_C(t)$ and (2) the inductor current $i(t)$. We first show how to describe the circuit using the capacitor voltage as the solution variable:

To derive a single equation in $v_C(t)$, we substitute Eqs. (7–29) and (7–31) into Eq. (7–28).

$$v_L + v_C + R_T C\frac{dv_C}{dt} = v_T \tag{7-32}$$

These substitutions eliminate the unknowns except v_C and v_L. To eliminate the inductor voltage, we substitute Eq. (7–31) into Eq. (7–30) to obtain

$$v_L = LC\frac{d^2v_C}{dt^2}$$

Substituting this result into Eq. (7–32) produces

$$\begin{aligned} LC\frac{d^2v_C}{dt^2} &+ R_T C\frac{dv_C}{dt} + v_C = v_T \\ v_L \quad &+ \quad\; v_R \quad + v_C = v_T \end{aligned} \tag{7-33}$$

In effect, this is a KVL equation around the loop in Figure 7–30(b), where the inductor and resistor voltages have been expressed in terms of the capacitor voltage.

Equation (7–33) is a second-order linear differential equation with constant coefficients. It is a second-order equation because the highest order derivative is the second derivative of the dependent variable $v_C(t)$. The coefficients are constant because the circuit parameters L, C, and R_T do not change. The Thévenin voltage $v_T(t)$ is a known driving force. The initial conditions

$$v_C(0) = V_0 \text{ and } \frac{dv_C}{dt}(0) = \frac{1}{C}i(0) = \frac{I_0}{C} \tag{7-34}$$

are determined by the values of the capacitor voltage and inductor current at $t = 0$—namely, V_0 and I_0.

In summary, the second-order differential equation in Eq. (7–33) characterizes the response of the series *RLC* circuit in terms of the capacitor voltage $v_C(t)$. Once the solution $v_C(t)$ is found, we can solve for every other voltage or current, including the inductor current, using the element and connection constraints in Eqs. (7–28) to (7–31).

Alternatively, we can characterize the series *RLC* circuit using the inductor current. We first write the capacitor i–v characteristics in integral form:

$$v_C(t) = \frac{1}{C}\int_0^t i(x)dx + v_C(0) \quad (7\text{–}35)$$

Equations (7–35), (7–30), and (7–29) are inserted into the interface constraint of Eq. (7–28) to obtain a single equation in the inductor current $i(t)$:

$$\begin{aligned} L\frac{di}{dt} + \frac{1}{C}\int_0^t i(x)dx + v_C(0) + R_T i &= v_T \\ v_L + \qquad v_C \qquad + v_R &= v_T \end{aligned} \quad (7\text{–}36)$$

In effect, this a KVL equation around the loop in Figure 7–25(b), where the capacitor and resistor voltages have been expressed in terms of the inductor current.

Equation (7–36) is a second-order linear integro-differential equation with constant coefficients. It is second order because it involves the first derivative and the first integral of the dependent variable $i(t)$. The coefficients are constant because the circuit parameters L, C, and R_T do not change. The Thévenin equivalent voltage $v_T(t)$ is a known driving force, and the initial conditions are $v_C(0) = V_0$ and $i(0) = I_0$.

Equations (7–33) and (7–36) involve the same basic ingredients: (1) an unknown state variable, (2) three circuit parameters (R_T, L, C), (3) a known input $v_T(t)$, and (4) two initial conditions (V_0 and I_0). The only difference is that one expresses the sum of voltages around the loop in terms of the capacitor voltage, while the other uses the inductor current. Either equation characterizes the dynamics of the series *RLC* circuit because once a state variable is found, every other voltage or current can be found using the element and connection constraints.

ZERO-INPUT RESPONSE OF THE SERIES *RLC* CIRCUIT

The circuit dynamic response for $t \geq 0$ can be divided into two components: (1) the zero-input response caused by the initial conditions and (2) the zero-state response caused by driving forces applied after $t = 0$. Because the circuit is linear, we can solve for these responses separately and superimpose them to get the total response. We first deal with the zero-input response.

With $v_T = 0$ (zero-input) Eq. (7–33) becomes

$$LC\frac{d^2v_C}{dt^2} + R_T C\frac{dv_C}{dt} + v_C = 0 \quad (7\text{–}37)$$

This result is a second-order homogeneous differential equation in the capacitor voltage. Alternatively, we set $v_T = 0$ in Eq. (7–36) and differentiate once to obtain the following homogeneous differential equation in the inductor current:

$$LC\frac{d^2i}{dt^2} + R_T C\frac{di}{dt} + i = 0 \quad (7\text{–}38)$$

We observe that Eqs. (7–37) and (7–38) have exactly the same form except that the dependent variables are different. The zero-input response of the capacitor voltage and inductor current have the same general form. We do not need to study both to understand the dynamics of the series *RLC* circuit. In other words, in the series *RLC* circuit we can use either state variable to describe the zero-input response.

In the following discussion we will concentrate on the capacitor voltage response. Equation (7–37) requires the capacitor voltage, plus *RC* times its first derivative, plus *LC* times its second derivative to add to zero for all $t \geq 0$. The only way this can happen is for $v_C(t)$, its first derivative, and its second derivative to have the same waveform. No matter how many times we differentiate an exponential of the form e^{st}, we are left with a signal with the same waveform. This observation, plus our experience with first-order circuits, suggests that we try a solution of the form

$$v_C(t) = Ke^{st}$$

where the parameters K and s are to be evaluated. When the trial solution is inserted in Eq. (7–37), we obtain the condition

$$Ke^{st}(LCs^2 + R_TCs + 1) = 0$$

The function e^{st} cannot be zero for all $t \geq 0$. The condition $K = 0$ is not allowed because it is a trivial solution declaring that $v_C(t)$ is zero for all t. The only useful way to meet the condition is to require

$$LCs^2 + R_TCs + 1 = 0 \qquad (7\text{–}39)$$

Equation (7–39) is the **characteristic equation** of the series *RLC* circuit. The characteristic equation is a quadratic because the circuit contains two energy storage elements. Inserting Ke^{st} into the homogeneous equation of the inductor current in Eq. (7–38) produces the same characteristic equation. Thus, Eq. (7–39) relates the zero-input response to circuit parameters for both state variables (hence the name *characteristic equation*).

In general, a quadratic characteristic equation has two roots:

$$s_1,\ s_2 = \frac{-R_TC \pm \sqrt{(R_TC)^2 - 4LC}}{2LC} \qquad (7\text{–}40)$$

From the form of the expression under the radical in Eq. (7–40), we see that there are three distinct possibilities:

Case A: If $(R_TC)^2 - 4LC > 0$, there are two real, unequal roots ($s_1 = -\alpha_1 \neq s_2 = -\alpha_2$).

Case B: If $(R_TC)^2 - 4LC = 0$, there are two real, equal roots ($s_1 = s_2 = -\alpha$).

Case C: If $(R_TC)^2 - 4LC < 0$, there are two complex conjugate roots ($s_1 = -\alpha - j\beta$ and $s_2 = -\alpha + j\beta$).

Where the symbol j represents the imaginary number $\sqrt{-1}$.[2] Before dealing with the form of the zero-input response for each case, we consider an example.

2 Mathematicians use the letter i to represent $\sqrt{-1}$. Electrical engineers use j, since the letter i represents electric current.

EXAMPLE 7–14

A series *RLC* circuit has $C = 0.25\ \mu\text{F}$ and $L = 1$ H. Find the roots of the characteristic equation for $R_T = 8.5\ \text{k}\Omega$, $4\ \text{k}\Omega$, and $1\ \text{k}\Omega$.

SOLUTION:

For $R_T = 8.5\ \text{k}\Omega$, the characteristic equation is

$$0.25 \times 10^{-6}s^2 + 2.125 \times 10^{-3}s + 1 = 0$$

whose roots are

$$s_1, s_2 = -4250 \pm \sqrt{(3750)^2} = -500, \quad -8000$$

These roots illustrate case A. The quantity under the radical is positive, and there are two real, unequal roots at $s_1 = -500$ and $s_2 = -8000$.

For $R_T = 4\ \text{k}\Omega$, the characteristic equation is

$$0.25 \times 10^{-6}s^2 + 10^{-3}s + 1 = 0$$

whose roots are

$$s_1,\ s_2 = -2000 \pm \sqrt{4 \times 10^6 - 4 \times 10^6} = -2000$$

This is an example of case B. The quantity under the radical is zero, and there are two real, equal roots at $s_1 = s_2 = -2000$.

For $R_T = 1\ \text{k}\Omega$ the characteristic equation is

$$0.25 \times 10^{-6}s^2 + 0.25 \times 10^{-3}\ s + 1 = 0$$

whose roots are

$$s_1,\ s_2 = -\ 500 \pm 500\sqrt{-15}$$

The quantity under the radical is negative, illustrating case C.

$$s_1,\ s_2 = -500 \pm j500\sqrt{15}$$

In case C the two roots are complex conjugates. ■

Exercise 7–13

For a series *RLC* circuit:

(a) Find the roots of the characteristic equation when $R_T = 2\ \text{k}\Omega$, $L = 100$ mH, and $C = 0.4\ \mu\text{F}$.
(b) For $L = 100$ mH, select the values of R_T and C so the roots of the characteristic equation are $s_1, s_2 = -1000 \pm j2000$.
(c) Select the values of R_T, L, and C so $s_1 = s_2 = -10^4$.

Answers:
(a) –1340, –18,660
(b) $R_T = 200\ \Omega$, $C = 2\ \mu\text{F}$
(c) There is no unique answer to part (c) since the requirement

$$(10^{-4}s + 1)^2 = LCs^2 + R_TCs + 1$$
$$= 10^{-8}s^2 + 10^{-4}s + 1$$

gives two equations $R_T C = 10^{-4}$ and $LC = 10^{-8}$ in three unknowns. One solution is to select $C = 1\ \mu F$, which yields $L = 10$ mH and $R_T = 200\ \Omega$.

We have not introduced complex numbers simply to make things complex. Complex numbers arise quite naturally in practical physical situations involving nothing more than factoring a quadratic equation. The ability to deal with complex numbers is essential to our study. For those who need a review of such matters, there is a concise discussion in Appendix C.

FORM OF THE ZERO-INPUT RESPONSE

Since the characteristic equation has two roots, there are two solutions to the homogeneous differential equation:

$$v_{C1}(t) = K_1 e^{s_1 t}$$

$$v_{C2}(t) = K_2 e^{s_2 t}$$

That is,

$$LC\frac{d^2}{dt^2}(K_1 e^{s_1 t}) + R_T C\frac{d}{dt}(K_1 e^{s_1 t}) + K_1 e^{s_1 t} = 0$$

and

$$LC\frac{d^2}{dt^2}(K_2 e^{s_2 t}) + R_T C\frac{d}{dt}(K_2 e^{s_2 t}) + K_2 e^{s_2 t} = 0$$

The sum of these two solutions is also a solution since

$$LC\frac{d^2}{dt^2}(K_1 e^{s_1 t} + K_2 e^{s_2 t}) + R_T C\frac{d}{dt}(K_1 e^{s_1 t} + K_2 e^{s_2 t}) + K_1 e^{s_1 t} + K_2 e^{s_2 t} = 0$$

Therefore, the general solution for the zero-input response is of the form

$$v_C(t) = K_1 e^{s_1 t} + K_2 e^{s_2 t} \tag{7-41}$$

The constants K_1 and K_2 can be found using the initial conditions given in Eq. (7–34). At $t = 0$ the condition on the capacitor voltage yields

$$v_C(0) = V_0 = K_1 + K_2 \tag{7-42}$$

To use the initial condition on the inductor current, we differentiate Eq. (7–41).

$$\frac{dv_C}{dt} = K_1 s_1 e^{s_1 t} + K_2 s_2 e^{s_2 t}$$

Using Eq. (7–34) to relate the initial value of the derivative of the capacitor voltage to the initial inductor current $i(0)$ yields

$$\frac{dv_C(0)}{dt} = \frac{I_0}{C} = K_1 s_1 + K_2 s_2 \tag{7-43}$$

Equations (7–42) and (7–43) provide two equations in the two unknown constants K_1 and K_2:

$$K_1 + K_2 = V_0$$

$$s_1K_1 + s_2K_2 = I_0/C$$

The solutions of these equations are

$$K_1 = \frac{s_2V_0 - I_0/C}{s_2 - s_1} \text{ and } K_2 = \frac{-s_1V_0 + I_0/C}{s_2 - s_1}$$

Inserting these solutions back into Eq. (7–41) yields

$$v_C(t) = \frac{s_2V_0 - I_0/C}{s_2 - s_1}e^{s_1t} + \frac{-s_1V_0 + I_0/C}{s_2 - s_1}e^{s_2t} \qquad t \geq 0 \quad (7-44)$$

Equation (7–44) is the general zero-input response of the series *RLC* circuit. The response depends on two initial conditions V_0 and I_0, and the circuit parameters R_T, L, and C since s_1 and s_2 are the roots of the characteristic equation $LCs^2 + R_TCs + 1 = 0$. The response takes on different forms depending on whether the roots s_1 and s_2 fall under case A, B, or C.

For case A the two roots are real and distinct. Using the notation $s_1 = -\alpha_1$ and $s_2 = -\alpha_2$, the form zero-input response for $t \geq 0$ is

$$v_C(t) = \left[\frac{\alpha_2V_0 + I_0/C}{\alpha_2 - \alpha_1}\right]e^{-\alpha_1t} + \left[\frac{-\alpha_1V_0 - I_0/C}{\alpha_2 - \alpha_1}\right]e^{-\alpha_2t} \quad (7-45)$$

For case A the response is the sum of two exponential functions similar to the double exponential signal treated in Example 5–13. The function has two time constants $1/\alpha_1$ and $1/\alpha_2$. The time constants can be greatly different, or nearly equal, but they cannot be equal because we would have case B.

With case B the roots are real and equal. Using the notation $s_1 = s_2 = -\alpha$, the general form in Eq. (7–44) becomes

$$v_C(t) = \frac{(\alpha V_0 + I_0/C)e^{-\alpha t} + (-\alpha V_0 - I_0/C)e^{-\alpha t}}{\alpha - \alpha}$$

We immediately see a problem here because the denominator vanishes. However, a closer examination reveals that the numerator vanishes as well, so the solution reduces to the indeterminate form 0/0. To investigate the indeterminacy, we let $s_1 = -\alpha$ and $s_2 = -\alpha + x$, and we explore the situation as x approaches zero. Inserting s_1 and s_2 in this notation in Eq. (7–44) produces

$$v_C(t) = V_0e^{-\alpha t} + \left[\frac{-\alpha V_0 - I_0/C}{x}\right]e^{-\alpha t} + \left[\frac{\alpha V_0 + I_0/C}{x}\right]e^{-\alpha t}e^{xt}$$

which can be arranged in the form

$$v_C(t) = e^{-\alpha t}\left[V_0 - (\alpha V_0 + I_0/C)\frac{1 - e^{xt}}{x}\right]$$

We see that the indeterminacy comes from the term $(1 - e^{xt})/x$, which reduces to 0/0 as x approaches zero. Application of l'Hôpital's rule reveals

$$\lim_{x\to 0}\frac{1-e^{xt}}{x} = \lim_{x\to 0}\frac{-te^{xt}}{1} = -t$$

This result removes the indeterminacy, and as x approaches zero the zero-input response reduces to

$$v_C(t) = V_0 e^{-\alpha t} + (\alpha V_0 + I_0/C)\, te^{-\alpha t} \qquad t \geq 0 \qquad (7-46)$$

For case B the response includes an exponential and the damped ramp studied in Example 5–11. The damped ramp is required, rather than two exponentials, because in case B the two equal roots produce the same exponential function.

Case C produces complex conjugate roots of the form

$$s_1 = -\alpha - j\beta \text{ and } s_2 = -\alpha + j\beta$$

Inserting these roots into Eq. (7–44) yields

$$v_C(t) = \left[\frac{(-\alpha + j\beta)\, V_0 - I_0/C}{j2\beta}\right] e^{-\alpha t} e^{-j\beta t} + \left[\frac{(\alpha + j\beta)\, V_0 + I_0/C}{j2\beta}\right] e^{-\alpha t} e^{j\beta t}$$

which can be arranged in the form

$$v_C(t) = V_0 e^{-\alpha t}\left[\frac{e^{j\beta t} + e^{-j\beta t}}{2}\right] + \frac{\alpha V_0 + I_0/C}{\beta} e^{-\alpha t}\left[\frac{e^{j\beta t} - e^{-j\beta t}}{j2}\right] \qquad (7-47)$$

The expressions within the brackets have been arranged in a special way for the following reasons. Euler's relationships for an imaginary exponential are written as

$$e^{j\theta} = \cos\theta + j\sin\theta$$

and

$$e^{-j\theta} = \cos\theta - j\sin\theta$$

When we add and subtract these equations, we obtain

$$\cos\theta = \frac{e^{j\theta} + e^{-j\theta}}{2} \quad \text{and} \quad \sin\theta = \frac{e^{j\theta} - e^{-j\theta}}{2j}$$

Comparing these expressions for $\sin\theta$ and $\cos\theta$ with the complex terms in Eq. (7–47) reveals that we can write $v_C(t)$ in the form

$$v_C(t) = V_0\, e^{-\alpha t} \cos\beta t + \frac{\alpha V_0 + I_0/C}{\beta} e^{-\alpha t} \sin\beta t \qquad t \geq 0$$

For case C the response contains the damped sinusoid studied in Example 5–12. The real part of the roots (α) provides the exponent coefficient in the exponential function, while the imaginary parts (β) defines the frequency of the sinusoidal oscillation.

In summary, the roots of the characteristic equation affect the form of the zero-input response in the following ways. In case A the two roots are real and unequal ($s_1 = -\alpha_1 \neq s_2 = -\alpha_2$) and the zero-input response is the sum of two exponentials of the form

$$v_C(t) = K_1 e^{-\alpha_1 t} + K_2 e^{-\alpha_2 t} \quad (7-48a)$$

In case B the two roots are real and equal ($s_1 = s_2 = -\alpha$) and the zero-input response is the sum of an exponential and a damped ramp.

$$v_C(t) = K_1 e^{-\alpha t} + K_2 t e^{-\alpha t} \quad (7-48b)$$

In case C the two roots are complex conjugates ($s_1 = -\alpha - j\beta$, $s_2 = -\alpha + j\beta$) and the zero-input response is the sum of a damped cosine and a damped sine.

$$v_C(t) = K_1 e^{-\alpha t} \cos \beta t + K_2 e^{-\alpha t} \sin \beta t \quad (7-48c)$$

In determining the zero-input response we use the parameters s, α, and β. At various points in the development these parameters appear in expressions such as e^{st}, $e^{-\alpha t}$, and $e^{j\beta t}$. Since the exponent of e must be dimensionless, the parameters s, α, and β all have the dimensions of the reciprocal of time, or equivalently, frequency. Collectively, we say that s, α, and β define the **natural frequencies** of the circuit. When it is necessary to distinguish between these three parameters we say that s is the **complex frequency**, α is the **neper frequency**, and β is the **radian frequency**. The importance of this notation will become clear as we proceed through subsequent chapters of this book. To be consistent with expressions such as $s = -\alpha + j\beta$, we specify numerical values of s, α, and β in units of radians per second (rad/s).[3]

The constants K_1 and K_2 in Eqs. (7–48a). (7–48b), and (7–48c) are determined by the initial conditions on two state variables, as illustrated in the following example.

EXAMPLE 7–15

The circuit of Figure 7–31 has $C = 0.25$ μF and $L = 1$ H. The switch has been open for a long time and is closed at $t = 0$. Find the capacitor voltage for $t \geq 0$ for (a) $R = 8.5$ kΩ, (b) $R = 4$ kΩ, and (c) $R = 1$ kΩ. The initial conditions are $I_0 = 0$ and $V_0 = 15$ V.

SOLUTION:

The roots of the characteristic equation for these three values of resistance are found in Example 7–14. We are now in a position to use those results to find the corresponding zero-input responses.

(a) In Example 7–14 the value $R = 8.5$ kΩ yields case A with roots $s_1 = -500$ and $s_2 = -8000$. The corresponding zero-input solution takes the form in Eq. (7–48a).

$$v_C(t) = K_1 e^{-500t} + K_2 e^{-8000t}$$

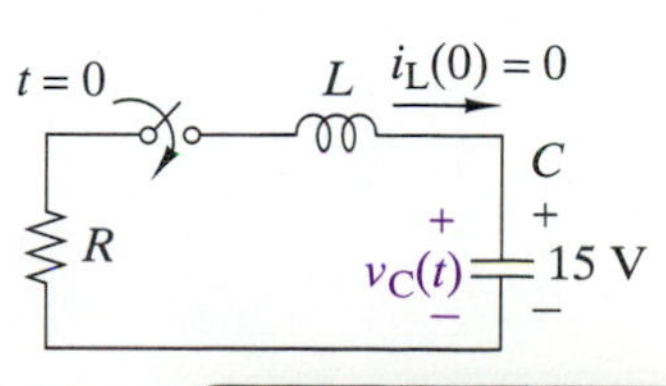

FIGURE 7–31

3 The term *neper frequency* honors the sixteenth-century mathematician John Napier, who invented the base e or natural logarithms. The term *complex frequency* was apparently first used about 1900 by the British engineer Oliver Heaviside.

The initial conditions yield two equations in the constants K_1 and K_2:

$$v_C(0) = V_0 = 15 = K_1 + K_2$$

$$\frac{dv_C(0)}{dt} = \frac{I_0}{C} = 0 = -500K_1 - 8000K_2$$

Solving these equations yields $K_1 = 16$ and $K_2 = -1$, so that the zero-input response is

$$v_C(t) = 16e^{-500t} - e^{-8000t} \text{ V} \qquad t \geq 0$$

(b) In Example 7–14 the value $R = 4$ kΩ yields case B with roots $s_1 = s_2 = -2000$. The corresponding zero-input response takes the form in Eq. (7–48b):

$$v_C(t) = K_1e^{-2000t} + K_2te^{-2000t}$$

The initial conditions yield two equations in the constants K_1 and K_2:

$$v_C(0) = V_0 = 15 = K_1$$

$$\frac{dv_C(0)}{dt} = \frac{I_0}{C} = 0 = -2000\,K_1 + K_2$$

Solving these equations yields $K_1 = 15$ and $K_2 = 2000 \times 15$, so the zero-input response is

$$v_C(t) = 15e^{-2000t} + 15(2000t)e^{-2000t} \text{ V} \qquad t \geq 0$$

(c) In Example 7–14 the value $R = 1$ kΩ yields case C with roots $s_1, s_2 = -500 \pm j500\sqrt{15}$. The corresponding zero-input response takes the form in Eq. (7–48c):

$$v_C(t) = K_1e^{-500t}\cos(500\sqrt{15})t + K_2e^{-500t}\sin(500\sqrt{15})t$$

The initial conditions yield two equations in the constants K_1 and K_2:

$$v_C(0) = V_0 = 15 = K_1$$

$$\frac{dv_C(0)}{dt} = \frac{I_0}{C} = 0 = -500K_1 + 500\sqrt{15}K_2$$

Solving these equations yields $K_1 = 15$ and $K_2 = \sqrt{15}$, so the zero-input response is

$$v_C(t) = 15e^{-500t}\cos(500\sqrt{15})t + \sqrt{15}\,e^{-500t}\sin(500\sqrt{15})t \text{ V} \qquad t \geq 0$$

Figure 7–32 shows plots of these responses. All three responses start out at 15 V (the initial condition) and all eventually decay to zero. The temporal decay of the responses is caused by energy loss in the circuit and is called **damping**. The case A response does not change sign and is called the **overdamped** response. The case C response undershoots and then oscillates about the final value. This response is said to be **underdamped** because there is not enough damping to prevent these oscillations. The case

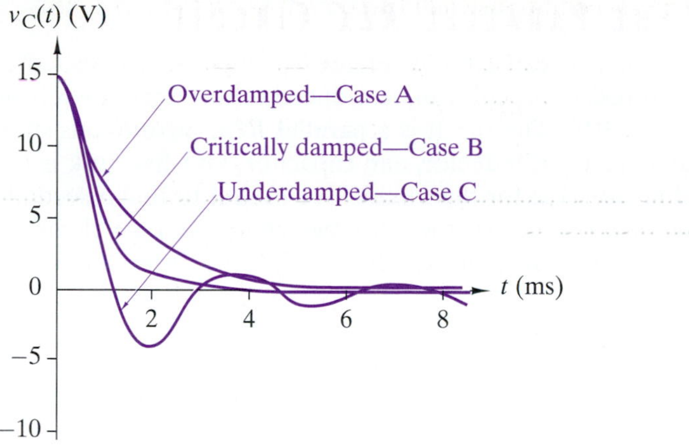

FIGURE 7–32

B response is said to be **critically damped** since it is a special case at the boundary between overdamping and underdamping.

Exercise 7–14

For a series RLC circuit, $R = 5\ \text{k}\Omega$, $C = 0.1\ \mu\text{F}$, $L = 100$ mH, $V_0 = 0$ V, and $I_0 =$ 25 mA.

(a) What is the capacitor voltage for $t \geq 0$?
(b) What is the inductor current for $t \geq 0$?
(c) What is the capacitor voltage if R is changed to 100 Ω?

Answers:
(a) $v_C(t) = 5.45(e^{-2087t} - e^{-47913t})$ V
(b) $i_L(t) = -1.14e^{-2087t} + 26.14e^{-47913t}$ mA
(c) $v_C(t) = 25.03e^{-500t} \sin 9987t$ V

Exercise 7–15

In a series RLC circuit, the zero-input responses are:

$$v_C(t) = 10e^{-1000t} \sin 1000t \text{ V}$$

$$i_L(t) = 10e^{-1000t}(\cos 1000t - \sin 1000t) \text{ mA}$$

(a) What is the circuit characteristic equation?
(b) What are the initial values of the state variables?
(c) What are the values of R, L, and C?

Answers:
(a) $s^2 + 2000s + 2 \times 10^6 = 0$
(b) $V_0 = 0$ V, $I_0 = 10$ mA
(c) $R = 1\ \text{k}\Omega$, $L = 0.5$ H, $C = 1\ \mu\text{F}$

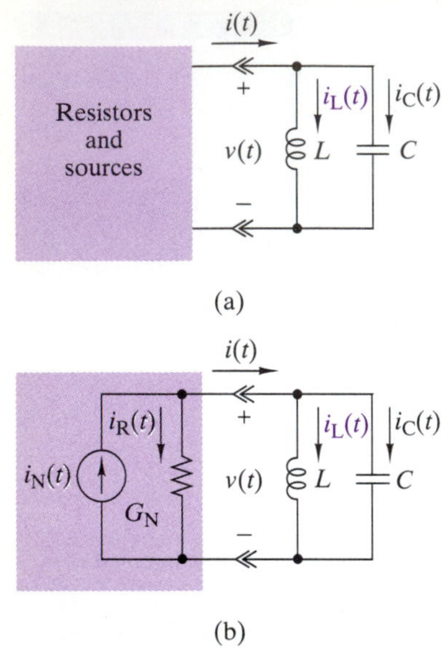

FIGURE 7–33
The parallel RLC *circuit.*

7–6 THE PARALLEL *RLC* CIRCUIT

The inductor and capacitor in Figure 7–33(a) are connected in parallel. The source-resistor circuit can be reduced to the Norton equivalent shown in Figure 7–33(b). The result is a **parallel *RLC* circuit** consisting of a current source, resistor, inductor, and capacitor. Our first task is to develop a differential equation for this circuit. We expect to find a second-order differential equation because there are two energy storage elements.

The Norton equivalent to the left of the interface introduces the constraint

$$i + G_N v = i_N \tag{7–49}$$

Writing a KCL equation at the interface yields

$$i = i_L + i_C \tag{7–50}$$

The i–v characteristics of the inductor and capacitor are

$$i_C = C\frac{dv}{dt} \tag{7–51}$$

$$v = L\frac{di_L}{dt} \tag{7–52}$$

Equations (7–49) through (7–52) provide four independent equations in four unknowns (i, v, i_L, i_C). Collectively these equations describe the dynamics of the parallel *RLC* circuit. To solve for the circuit response using classical methods, we must derive a circuit equation containing only one of these four variables.

We prefer using state variables because they are continuous. To obtain a single equation in the inductor current, we substitute Eqs. (7–50) and (7–52) into Eq. (7–49):

$$i_L + i_C + G_N L\frac{di_L}{dt} = i_N \tag{7–53}$$

The capacitor current can be eliminated from this result by substituting Eq. (7–52) into Eq. (7–51) to obtain

$$i_C = LC\frac{d^2 i_L}{dt^2} \tag{7–54}$$

Inserting this equation into Eq. (7–53) produces

$$\begin{aligned} LC\frac{d^2 i_L}{dt^2} &+ G_N L\frac{di_L}{dt} + i_L = i_N \\ i_C \quad &+ \qquad i_R \qquad + i_L = i_N \end{aligned} \tag{7–55}$$

This result is a KCL equation in which the resistor and capacitor currents are expressed in terms of the inductor current.

Equation (7–55) is a second-order linear differential equation of the same form as the series *RLC* circuit equation in Eq. (7–33). In fact, if we interchange the following quantities:

$$v_C \leftrightarrow i_L \qquad L \leftrightarrow C \qquad R_T \leftrightarrow G_N \qquad v_T \leftrightarrow i_N$$

we change one equation into the other. The two circuits are duals, which means that the results developed for the series case apply to the parallel circuit with the preceding duality interchanges.

However, it is still helpful to outline the major features of the analysis of the parallel *RLC* circuit. The initial conditions in the parallel circuit are the initial inductor current I_0 and capacitor voltage V_0. The initial inductor current provides the condition $i_L(0) = I_0$ for the differential equation in Eq. (7–55). By using Eq. (7–52), the initial capacitor voltage specifies the initial rate of change of the inductor current as

$$\frac{di_L(0)}{dt} = \frac{1}{L}v_C(0) = \frac{1}{L}V_0$$

These initial conditions are the dual of those obtained for the series *RLC* circuit in Eq. (7–34).

To solve for the zero-input response, we set $i_N = 0$ in Eq. (7–55) and obtain a homogeneous equation in the inductor current:

$$LC\frac{d^2i_L}{dt^2} + G_N L\frac{di_L}{dt} + i_L = 0$$

A trial solution of the form $i_L = Ke^{st}$ leads to the characteristic equation

$$LCs^2 + G_N Ls + 1 = 0 \qquad (7\text{–}56)$$

The characteristic equation is quadratic because there are two energy storage elements in the parallel *RLC* circuit. The characteristic equation has two roots:

$$s_1,\ s_2 = \frac{-G_N L \pm \sqrt{(G_N L)^2 - 4LC}}{2LC}$$

and, as in the series case, there are three distinct cases:

Case A: If $(G_N L)^2 - 4LC > 0$, there are two unequal real roots $s_1 = -\alpha_1$ and $s_2 = -\alpha_2$ and the zero-input response is the overdamped form

$$i_L(t) = K_1 e^{-\alpha_1 t} + K_2 e^{-\alpha_2 t} \qquad t \geq 0 \qquad (7\text{–}57)$$

Case B: If $(G_N L)^2 - 4LC = 0$, there are two real equal roots $s_1 = s_2 = -\alpha$ and the zero-input response is the critically damped form

$$i_L(t) = K_1 e^{-\alpha t} + K_2 te^{-\alpha t} \qquad t \geq 0 \qquad (7\text{–}58)$$

Case C: If $(G_N L)^2 - 4LC < 0$, there are two complex, conjugate roots $s_1, s_2 = -\alpha \pm j\beta$ and the zero-input response is the underdamped form

$$i_L(t) = K_1 e^{-\alpha t}\cos\beta t + K_2 e^{-\alpha t}\sin\beta t \qquad t \geq 0 \qquad (7\text{–}59)$$

The analysis results for the series *RLC* circuit apply to the parallel *RLC* case with the appropriate duality replacements. In particular, the form of overdamped, critically damped, and underdamped response applies to both circuits. The forms of the responses in Eqs. (7–57), (7–58), and (7–59) have been written with two arbitrary constants K_1 and K_2. The following example shows how to evaluate these constants using the initial conditions for the two state variables.

EXAMPLE 7–16

In a parallel *RLC* circuit $R_T = 1/G_N = 500\ \Omega$, $C = 1\ \mu F$, $L = 0.2$ H. The initial conditions are $I_0 = 50$ mA and $V_0 = 0$. Find the zero-input response of inductor current, resistor current, and capacitor voltage.

SOLUTION:

From Eq. (7–56) the circuit characteristic equation is

$$LCs^2 + G_N Ls + 1 = 2 \times 10^{-7}s^2 + 4 \times 10^{-4}s + 1 = 0$$

The roots of the characteristic equation are

$$s_1,\ s_2 = \frac{-4 \times 10^{-4} \pm \sqrt{16 \times 10^{-8} - 8 \times 10^{-7}}}{4 \times 10^{-7}} = -1000 \pm j2000$$

Since roots are complex conjugates, we have the underdamped case. The zero-input response of the inductor current takes the form of Eq. (7–59).

$$i_L(t) = K_1 e^{-1000t} \cos 2000t + K_2 e^{-1000t} \sin 2000t \qquad t \geqslant 0$$

The constants K_1 and K_2 are evaluated from the initial conditions. At $t = 0$ the inductor current reduces to

$$i_L(0) = I_0 = K_1 e^0 \cos 0 + K_2 e^0 \sin 0 = K_1$$

We conclude that $K_1 = I_0 = 50$ mA. To find K_2 we use the initial capacitor voltage. In a parallel *RLC* circuit the capacitor and inductor voltages are equal.

$$L\frac{di_L}{dt} = v_C(t)$$

In this example the initial capacitor voltage is zero, so the initial rate of change of inductor current is zero at $t = 0$. Differentiating the zero-input response produces

$$\begin{aligned}\frac{di_L}{dt} = &-2000K_1 e^{-1000t} \sin 2000t - 1000K_1 e^{-1000t} \cos 2000t \\ &- 1000K_2 e^{-1000t} \sin 2000t + 2000K_2 e^{-1000t} \cos 2000t\end{aligned}$$

Evaluating this expression at $t = 0$ yields

$$\begin{aligned}\frac{di_L}{dt}(0) &= -2000K_1 e^0 \sin 0 - 1000K_1 e^0 \cos 0 \\ &\quad - 1000K_2 e^0 \sin 0 + 2000K_2 e^0 \cos 0 \\ &= -1000K_1 + 2000K_2 = 0\end{aligned}$$

The derivative initial condition gives condition $K_2 = K_1/2 = 25$ mA. Given the values of K_1 and K_2, the zero-input response of the inductor current is

$$i_L(t) = 50e^{-1000t}\cos 2000t + 25e^{-1000t}\sin 2000t \text{ mA} \qquad t \geq 0$$

The zero-input response of the inductor current allows us to solve for every voltage and current in the parallel *RLC* circuit. For example, using the *i–v* characteristic of the inductor, we obtain the inductor voltage:

$$v_L(t) = L\frac{di_L}{dt} = -25e^{-1000t}\sin 2000t \text{ V} \qquad t \geq 0$$

Since the elements are connected in parallel, we obtain the capacitor voltage and resistor current as

$$v_C(t) = v_L(t) = L\frac{di_L}{dt} = -25e^{-1000t}\sin 2000t \text{ V} \qquad t \geq 0$$

$$i_R(t) = \frac{v_L(t)}{R} = -50e^{-1000t}\sin 2000t \text{ mA} \qquad t \geq 0$$

■

EXAMPLE 7–17

The switch in Figure 7–34 has been open for a long time and is closed at $t = 0$.

(a) Find the initial conditions at $t = 0$.
(b) Find the inductor current for $t \geq 0$.
(c) Find the capacitor voltage and current through the switch for $t \geq 0$.

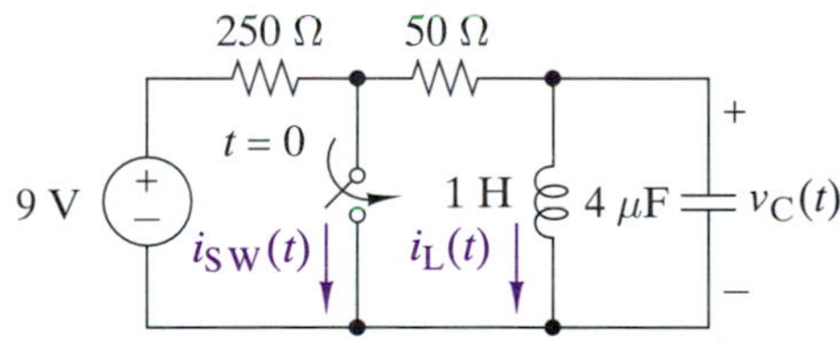

FIGURE 7–34

SOLUTION:

(a) For $t < 0$ the circuit is in the dc steady state, so the inductor acts like a short circuit and the capacitor like an open circuit. Since the inductor shorts out the capacitor, the initial conditions just prior to closing the switch at $t = 0$ are

$$v_C(0) = 0 \qquad i_L(0) = \frac{9}{250 + 50} = 30 \text{ mA}$$

(b) For $t \geq 0$ the circuit is a zero-input parallel *RLC* circuit with initial conditions found in (a). The circuit characteristic equation is

$$LCs^2 + GLs + 1 = 4 \times 10^{-6}s^2 + 2 \times 10^{-2}s + 1 = 0$$

The roots of this equation are

$$s_1 = -50.51 \quad \text{and} \quad s_2 = -4950$$

The circuit is overdamped (case A), since the roots are real and unequal. The general form of the inductor current zero-input response is

$$i_L(t) = K_1 e^{-50.51t} + K_2 e^{-4950t} \qquad t \geq 0$$

The constants K_1 and K_2 are found using the initial conditions. At $t = 0$ the zero-input response is

$$i_L(0) = K_1 e^0 + K_2 e^0 = K_1 + K_2 = 30 \times 10^{-3}$$

The initial capacitor voltage establishes an initial condition on the derivative of the inductor current since

$$L\frac{di_L}{dt}(0) = v_C(0) = 0$$

The derivative of the inductor response at $t = 0$ is

$$\begin{aligned}\frac{di_L}{dt}(0) &= (-50.51K_1 e^{-50.51t} - 4950K_2 e^{-4950t})\big|_{t=0}\\ &= -50.51K_1 - 4950K_2 = 0\end{aligned}$$

The initial conditions on inductor current and capacitor voltage produce two equations in the unknown constants K_1 and K_2:

$$\begin{aligned}K_1 + K_2 &= 30 \times 10^{-3}\\ -50.51K_1 - 4950K_2 &= 0\end{aligned}$$

Solving these equations yields $K_1 = 30.3$ mA and $K_2 = -0.309$ mA. The zero-input response of the inductor current is

$$i_L(t) = 30.3e^{-50.51t} - 0.309e^{-4950t} \text{ mA} \qquad t \geq 0$$

(c) Given the inductor current in (b), the capacitor voltage is

$$v_C(t) = L\frac{di_L}{dt} = -1.53e^{-50.51t} + 1.53e^{-4950t} \text{ V} \qquad t \geq 0$$

For $t \geq 0$ the current $i_{SW}(t)$ is the current through the 50-Ω resistor plus the current through the 250-Ω resistor.

$$\begin{aligned}i_{SW}(t) &= i_{250} + i_{50} = \frac{9}{250} + \frac{v_C(t)}{50}\\ &= 36 - 30.6e^{-50.51t} + 30.6e^{-4950t} \text{ mA} \qquad t \geq 0\end{aligned}$$

■

Exercise 7–16

The zero-input responses of a parallel *RLC* circuit are observed to be

$$\begin{aligned}i_L(t) &= 10te^{-2000t} \text{ A}\\ v_C(t) &= 10e^{-2000t} - 20000te^{-2000t} \text{ V} \qquad t \geq 0\end{aligned}$$

(a) What is the circuit characteristic equation?
(b) What are the initial values of the state variables?
(c) What are the values of R, L, and C?
(d) Write an expression for the current through the resistor.

Answers:

(a) $s^2 + 4000s + 4 \times 10^6 = 0$
(b) $i_L(0) = 0$, $v_C(0) = 10$ V
(c) $L = 1$ H, $C = 0.25$ μF, $R = 1$ kΩ
(d) $i_R(t) = 10e^{-2000t} - 20000te^{-2000t}$ mA $\quad t \geq 0$

7–7 SECOND-ORDER CIRCUIT STEP RESPONSE

The step response provides important insights into the response of dynamic circuits in general. So it is natural that we investigate the step response of second-order circuits. In Chapter 11 we will develop general techniques for determining the step response of any linear circuit. However, in this introduction we use classical methods of solving differential equations to find the step response of second-order circuits.

The general second-order linear differential equation with a step function input has the form

$$a_2 \frac{d^2y(t)}{dt^2} + a_1 \frac{dy(t)}{dt} + a_0 y(t) = Au(t) \tag{7-60}$$

where $y(t)$ is a voltage or current response, $Au(t)$ is the step function input, and a_2, a_1, and a_0 are constant coefficients. The step response is the general solution of this differential equation for $t \geq 0$. The step response can be found by partitioning $y(t)$ into forced and natural components:

$$y(t) = y_N(t) + y_F(t) \tag{7-61}$$

The natural response $y_N(t)$ is the general solution of the homogeneous equation (input set to zero), while the forced response $y_F(t)$ is a particular solution of the equation

$$a_2 \frac{d^2y_F}{dt^2} + a_1 \frac{dy_F}{dt} + a_0 y_F = A \qquad t \geqslant 0$$

Since A is a constant, it follows that dA/dt and d^2A/dt^2 are both zero, so it is readily apparent that $y_F = A/a_0$ is a particular solution of this differential equation. So much for the forced response.

Turning now to the natural response, we seek a general solution of the homogeneous equation. The natural response has the same form as the zero-state response studied in the previous section. In a second-order circuit the zero-state and natural responses take one of the three possible forms: overdamped, critically damped, or underdamped. To describe the three possible forms, we introduce two new parameters: ω_0 (omega zero) and ζ (zeta). These parameters are defined in terms of the coefficients of the general second-order equation in Eq. (7–60):

$$\omega_0^2 = \frac{a_0}{a_2} \quad \text{and} \quad 2\zeta\omega_0 = \frac{a_1}{a_2} \tag{7-62}$$

The parameter ω_0 is called the **undamped natural frequency** and ζ is called the **damping ratio**. Using these two parameters, the general homogeneous equation is written in the form

$$\frac{d^2y_N(t)}{dt^2} + 2\zeta\omega_0 \frac{dy_N(t)}{dt} + \omega_0^2 y_N(t) = 0 \tag{7-63}$$

The left side of Eq. (7–63) is called the **standard form** of the second-order linear differential equation. When a second-order equation is arranged in this format, we can determine its damping ratio and undamped natural frequency by equating its coefficients with those in the standard form. For example, in standard form the homogeneous equation for the series *RLC* circuit in Eq. (7–37) is

$$\frac{d^2v_C}{dt^2} + \frac{R_T}{L}\frac{dv_C}{dt} + \frac{1}{LC}v_C = 0$$

Equating like terms yields

$$\omega_0^2 = \frac{1}{LC} \quad \text{and} \quad 2\zeta\omega_0 = \frac{R_T}{L}$$

for the series *RLC* circuit. Note that the circuit elements determine the values of the parameters ω_0 and ζ.

To determine the form of the natural response using ω_0 and ζ, we insert a trial solution $y_N(t) = Ke^{st}$ into the standard form in Eq. (7–63). The trial function Ke^{st} is a solution provided that

$$Ke^{st}[s^2 + 2\zeta\omega_0 s + \omega_0^2] = 0$$

Since $K = 0$ is the trivial solution and $e^{st} \neq 0$ for all $t \geq 0$, the only useful way for the right side of this equation to be zero for all t is for the quadratic expression within the brackets to vanish. The quadratic expression is the characteristic equation for the general second-order differential equation:

$$s^2 + 2\zeta\omega_0 s + \omega_0^2 = 0$$

The roots of the characteristic equation are

$$s_1, s_2 = \omega_0(-\zeta \pm \sqrt{\zeta^2 - 1})$$

We begin to see the advantage of using the parameters ω_0 and ζ. The constant ω_0 is a scale factor that designates the size of the roots. The expression under the radical defines the form of the roots and depends only on the damping ratio ζ. As a result, we can express the three possible forms of the natural response in terms of the damping ratio.

Case A: For $\zeta > 1$ the discriminant is positive, there are two unequal, real roots

$$s_1, s_2 = -\alpha_1, -\alpha_2 = \omega_0(-\zeta \pm \sqrt{\zeta^2 - 1}) \tag{7-64a}$$

and the natural response has the overdamped form

$$y_N(t) = K_1 e^{-\alpha_1 t} + K_2 e^{-\alpha_2 t} \qquad t \geq 0 \tag{7-64b}$$

Case B: For $\zeta = 1$ the discriminant vanishes, there are two real, equal roots

$$s_1 = s_2 = -\alpha = -\zeta\omega_0 \tag{7-65a}$$

and the natural response has the critically damped form

$$y_N(t) = K_1 e^{-\alpha t} + K_2 t e^{-\alpha t} \qquad t \geq 0 \tag{7-65b}$$

Case C: For $\zeta < 1$ the discriminant is negative, leading to two complex, conjugate roots $s_1, s_2 = -\alpha \pm j\beta$, where

$$\alpha = \zeta\omega_0 \quad \text{and} \quad \beta = \omega_0\sqrt{1-\zeta^2} \tag{7-66a}$$

and the natural response has the underdamped form

$$y_N(t) = K_1 e^{-\alpha t}\cos\beta t + K_2 e^{-\alpha t}\sin\beta t \qquad t \geq 0 \tag{7-66b}$$

Equations (7–64a), (7–65a), and (7–66a) provide relationships between the natural frequency parameters α and β and the new parameters ζ and ω_0. The reasons for using two equivalent sets of parameters to describe the natural frequencies of a second-order circuit will become clear as we continue our study of dynamic circuits. Since the units of complex frequency s are radians per second, the standard form of the characteristic equation $s^2 + 2\zeta\omega_0 s + \omega_0^2$ shows that ω_0 is specified in radians per second and ζ is dimensionless.

Combining the forced and natural responses yields the step response of the general second-order differential equation in the form

$$y(t) = y_N(t) + A/a_0 \qquad t \geq 0 \tag{7-67}$$

The factor A/a_0 is the forced response. The natural response $y_N(t)$ takes one of the forms in Eqs. (7–64b), (7–65b), or (7–66b), depending on the value of the damping ratio. The constants K_1 and K_2 in natural response can be evaluated from the initial conditions.

In summary, the step response of a second-order circuit is determined by

1. The amplitude of the step function input $Au(t)$
2. The damping ratio ζ and natural frequency ω_0
3. The initial conditions $y(0)$ and $dy/dt\,(0)$.

In this regard the damping ratio and natural frequency play the same role for second-order circuits that the time constant plays for first-order circuits. That is, these circuit parameters determine the basic form of the natural response, just as the time constant defines the form of the natural response in a first-order circuit. It is not surprising that a second-order circuit takes two parameters, since it contains two energy storage elements.

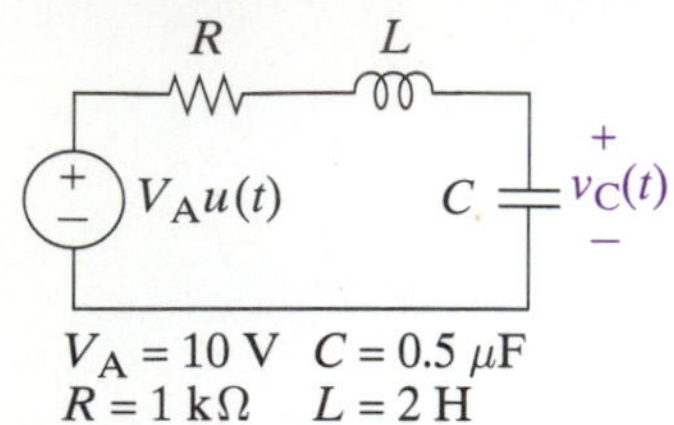

FIGURE 7–35

EXAMPLE 7–18

The series RLC circuit in Figure 7–35 is driven by a step function and is in the zero state at $t = 0$. Find the capacitor voltage for $t \geq 0$.

SOLUTION:

This is a series RLC circuit, so the differential equation for the capacitor voltage is

$$10^{-6}\frac{d^2v_C}{dt^2} + 0.5 \times 10^{-3}\frac{dv_C}{dt} + v_C = 10 \qquad t \geq 0$$

By inspection, the forced response is $v_{CF} = 10$ V. In standard format the homogeneous equation is

$$\frac{d^2v_{CN}}{dt^2} + 500\frac{dv_{CN}}{dt} + 10^6\, v_{CN} = 0 \qquad t \geq 0$$

Comparing this format the standard form in Eq. (7–63) yields

$$\omega_0^2 = 10^6 \quad \text{and} \quad 2\zeta\omega_0 = 500$$

so $\omega_0 = 1000$ and $\zeta = 0.25$. Since $\zeta < 1$, the natural response is underdamped (case C). Using Eqs. (7–66a) and (7–66b), we have

$$\alpha = \zeta\omega_0 = 250$$

$$\beta = \omega_0\sqrt{1 - \zeta^2} = 968$$

$$v_{CN}(t) = K_1e^{-250t}\cos 968t + K_2e^{-250t}\sin 968t$$

The general solution of the circuit differential equation is the sum of the forced and natural responses:

$$v_C(t) = 10 + K_1e^{-250t}\cos 968t + K_2e^{-250t}\sin 968t \qquad t \geq 0$$

The constants K_1 and K_2 are determined by the initial conditions. The circuit is in the zero state at $t = 0$, so the initial conditions are $v_C(0) = 0$ and $i_L(0) = 0$. Applying the initial condition constraints to the general solution yields two equations in the constants K_1 and K_2:

$$v_C(0) = 10 + K_1 = 0$$

$$\frac{dv_C}{dt}(0) = -250\,K_1 + 968\,K_2 = 0$$

These equations yield $K_1 = -10$ and $K_2 = -2.58$. The step response of the capacitor voltage step response is

$$v_C(t) = 10 - 10e^{-250t}\cos 968t - 2.58e^{-250t}\sin 968t \text{ V} \qquad t \geq 0$$

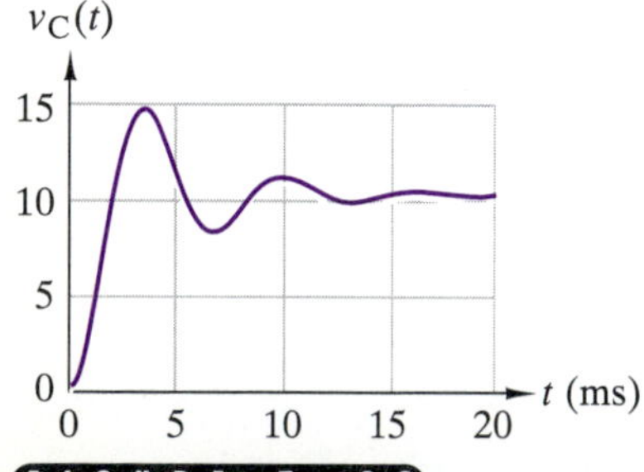

FIGURE 7–36

A plot of $v_C(t)$ versus time is shown in Figure 7–36. The response and its first derivative at $t = 0$ satisfy the initial conditions. The natural response decays to zero, so the forced response determines the final value of $v_C(\infty) = 10$ V. Beginning at $t = 0$ the response climbs rapidly but overshoots the mark several times before eventually settling down to the final value. The damped sinusoidal behavior results from the fact that $\zeta < 1$, producing an underdamped natural response. ■

EXAMPLE 7–19

The step response of the series *RLC* circuit in Figure 7–35 is found analytically in Example 7–18. In this example we explore the effect of varying the resistance on the step response. Use MicroSim Design Center to calculate the step response for $L = 2$ H, $C = 0.5$ μF, $V_A = 10$ V, and R varying from 500 Ω to 2000 Ω in 500-Ω steps.

SOLUTION:

The MicroSim Schematics circuit diagram in Figure 7–37 includes numerical values for the inductor, capacitor, and voltage source. The 10-V dc source simulates the step function input for $t \geq 0$. The circuit is in the zero state at $t = 0$ so the initial inductor current and capacitor voltage must be set to zero. A zero-state condition can be established by setting IC = 0 in the inductor and capacitor attributes dialog boxes, or by leaving these IC attributes blank. When the IC attribute is blank, PSpice assigns a default value that happens to be zero.

FIGURE 7–37

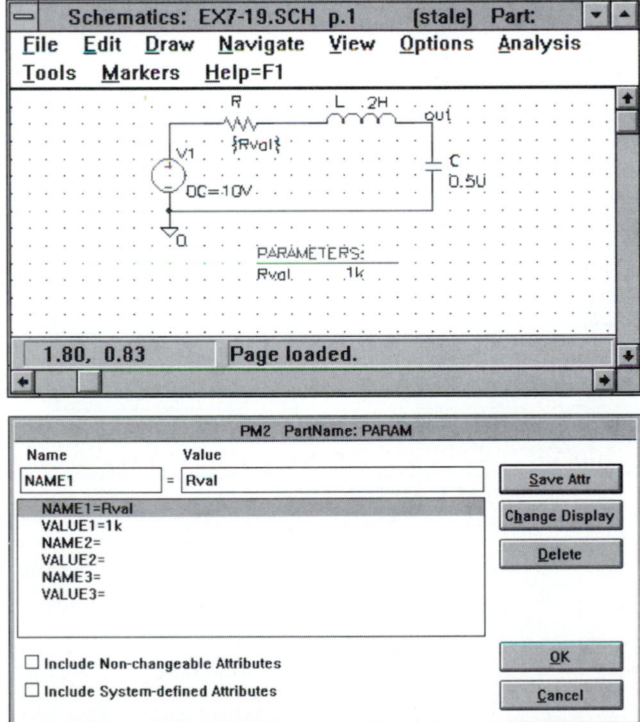

The value of the resistor R in Figure 7–37 is a text **{Rval}** rather than a numerical value. The condition R = **Rval** is obtained by double clicking the resistor symbol for R to bring up its attribute dialog box and then setting **value** = **{Rval}**. MicroSim PSpice treats text surrounded by the curly brackets {} as a parameter to be assigned numerical values. To assign a value to **{Rval}**, select **Draw/Get New Part/Browse** from the Schematics menu bar. Under the Special Library is a part called **PARAM** that is used to specify parameters. Placing the **PARAM** part at any convenient spot on the circuit diagram and double clicking on the part name brings up the **PARAM** attributes dialog box shown in Figure 7–37. Assigning the attribute **Name1=Rval** (no curly brackets) and **Value1** = 1k produces the final situation shown in the figure.

The aforementioned procedure sets up a single numerical value of R = **Rval** = 1 kΩ. We now set up a parametric analysis in which **Rval** is stepped from 500 Ω to 2000 Ω. Selecting **Analysis/Setup/Parametric** from the Schematics menu bar brings up the **Parametric Analysis** dialog box in Figure 7–38. In this box we identify a global parameter named **Rval** and set up a linear sweep that starts at **Rval** = 500 and runs to **Rval** = 2000 in increments of 500. Next we need to define the simulation interval for the transient analysis. Clicking on **Transient** brings up the **Transient Analysis** dialog box in Figure 7–38. Looking at Figure 7–36, we see that **Final Time** = 20 ms allows us to observe the step response of the circuit. Following our rule of thumb, we set **Step Ceiling = Final Time**/100 = 0.2 ms. Note that we must tell PSpice to use the zero-state initial conditions by checking the **Use Init. Condition** box. If we do not check this box, PSpice will automatically perform a dc analysis on the circuit in Figure 7–37 and conclude that $v_C(0)$ = 10 V, which is not what we want.

FIGURE 7–38

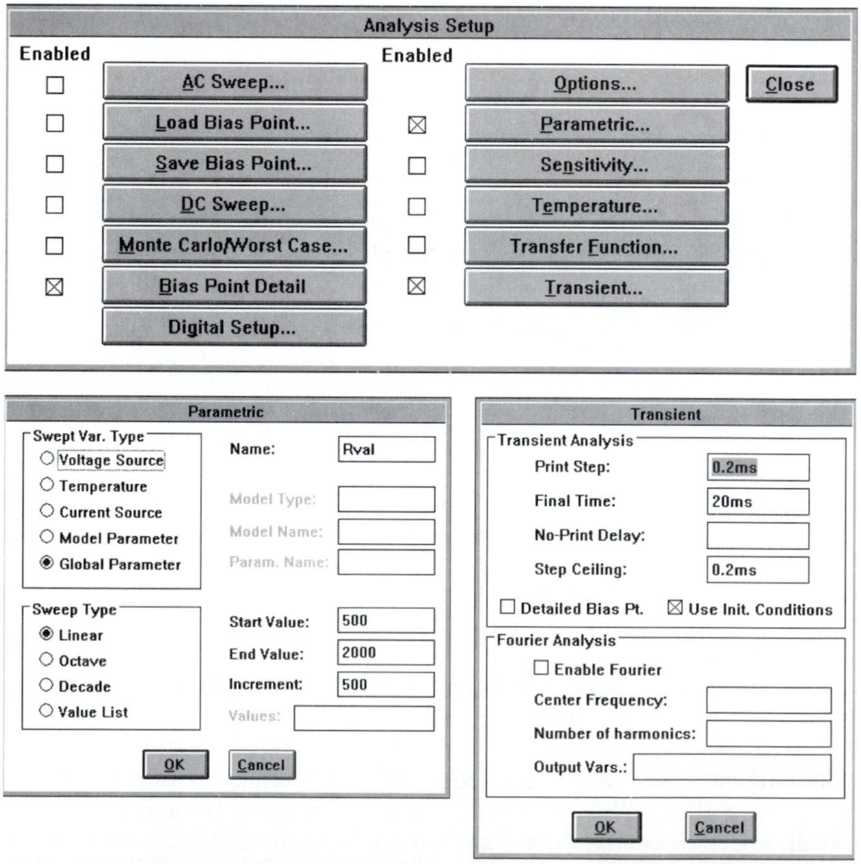

Analysis Setup
Enabled
AC Sweep...
Load Bias Point...
Save Bias Point...
DC Sweep...
Monte Carlo/Worst Case...
Bias Point Detail
Digital Setup...
Enabled
Options...
Parametric...
Sensitivity...
Temperature...
Transfer Function...
Transient...
Close

Parametric
Swept Var. Type
Voltage Source
Temperature
Current Source
Model Parameter
Global Parameter
Name: Rval
Model Type:
Model Name:
Param. Name:
Sweep Type
Linear
Octave
Decade
Value List
Start Value: 500
End Value: 2000
Increment: 500
Values:
OK
Cancel

Transient
Transient Analysis
Print Step: 0.2ms
Final Time: 20ms
No-Print Delay:
Step Ceiling: 0.2ms
Detailed Bias Pt.
Use Init. Conditions
Fourier Analysis
Enable Fourier
Center Frequency:
Number of harmonics:
Output Vars.:
OK
Cancel

The foregoing procedure sets up PSpice for transient analysis runs with R = **Rval** = 500, 1000, 1500, and 2000 Ω. Selecting **Analysis/Simulate** from the Schematics menu bar brings up the PSpice simulation window, and we see a transient analysis run four times, once for each value of **Rval**. When the four simulations are completed, MicroSim Probe is automatically invoked and we obtain the family of step responses shown in Figure 7–39. Note that increasing the resistance increases the damping in the step response and vice versa. ■

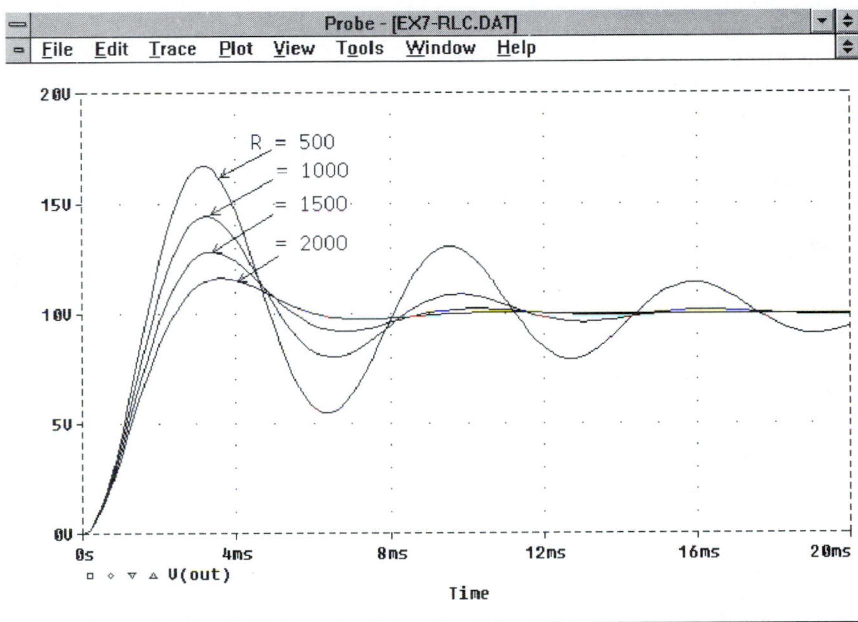

FIGURE 7–39

Exercise 7–17

Find the zero-state solution of the following differential equations:

$$\text{(a) } 10^{-4}\frac{d^2v}{dt^2} + 2 \times 10^{-2}\frac{dv}{dt} + v = 100u(t)$$

$$\text{(b) } \frac{d^2i}{dt^2} + 2500\frac{di}{dt} + 4 \times 10^6 i = 10^5 u(t)$$

Answers:

(a) $v(t) = 100 - 100e^{-100t} - 10^4 te^{-100t}$ V $\quad t \geq 0$

(b) $i(t) = \frac{1}{40} - \frac{1}{40}e^{-1250t}\cos 1561t - \frac{1}{50}e^{-1250t}\sin 1561t$ A $\quad t \geq 0$

Exercise 7–18

The step response of a series *RLC* circuit is observed to be

$$v_C(t) = 15 - 15e^{-1000t}\cos 1000t \text{ V} \qquad t \geq 0$$

$$i_L(t) = 45e^{-1000t}\cos 1000t + 45e^{-1000t}\sin 1000t \text{ mA} \qquad t \geq 0$$

(a) What is the circuit characteristic equation?
(b) What are the initial values of the state variables?
(c) What is the amplitude of the step input?
(d) What are the values of *R*, *L*, and *C*?
(e) What is the voltage across the resistor?

Answers:
(a) $s^2 + 2000s + 2 \times 10^6 = 0$
(b) $v_C(0) = 0$, $i_L(0) = 45$ mA
(c) $V_A = 15$ V
(d) $R = 333\ \Omega$, $L = 167$ mH, $C = 3\ \mu$F
(e) $v_R(t) = 15e^{-1000t}\cos 1000t + 15e^{-1000t}\sin 1000t$ V

SOME OTHER SECOND-ORDER CIRCUITS

Up to this point, the series and parallel *RLC* circuits are the only second-order circuits we have considered. Using the classical differential equation methods, we found that the form of the natural (zero-input) response can be overdamped, critically damped, or underdamped depending on the roots of the characteristic equation. We now show that these concepts apply to other second-order circuits besides the series and parallel *RLC*.

The OP AMP circuit in Figure 7–40 contains three equal resistors and two unequal capacitors. The circuit is second order because the two capacitors are not in series or parallel and cannot be replaced by a single equivalent capacitor. We use the basic concept of device and connection equations to formulate the circuit differential equation.

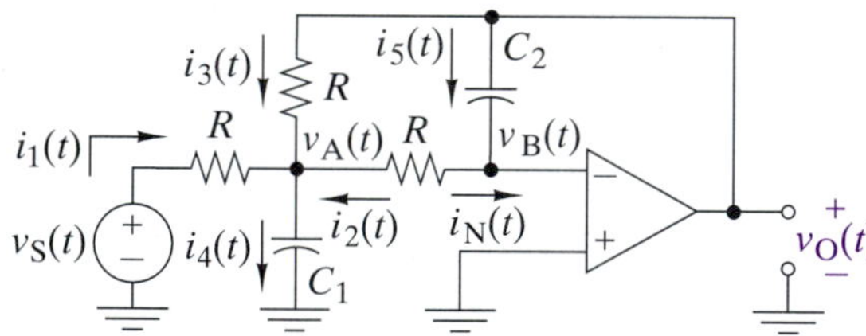

FIGURE 7–40 *A second-order OP AMP RC circuit.*

From our experience with OP AMP resistance circuits, we know that two node equations describe an OP AMP circuit of this type. We formulate these equations by writing KCL connection constraints at nodes A and B:

$$\text{Node A: } i_1 + i_2 + i_3 - i_4 = 0$$

$$\text{Node B: } -i_2 + i_5 - i_N = 0$$

The resistor and capacitor element constraints in terms of the node voltages are

$$i_1 = G(v_S - v_A) \quad i_4 = C_1 \frac{dv_A}{dt}$$

$$i_2 = G(v_B - v_A) \quad i_5 = C_2 \frac{d(v_O - v_B)}{dt}$$

$$i_3 = G(v_O - v_A)$$

The ideal OP AMP model requires $i_N = 0$ and $v_B = 0$ because the noninverting input is connected to ground. Substituting all of these element equations into the KCL connection equations at nodes A and B results in

$$-3Gv_A - C_1 \frac{dv_A}{dt} + Gv_O + Gv_S = 0$$

$$Gv_A + C_2 \frac{dv_O}{dt} = 0$$

Solving the second of these equations for v_A yields

$$v_A = -RC_2 \frac{dv_O}{dt}$$

Inserting this result into the first equation produces the circuit differential equation:

$$R^2C_1C_2 \frac{d^2v_O}{dt^2} + 3RC_2 \frac{dv_O}{dt} + v_O = -v_S$$

This expression is a second-order linear differential equation in which the OP AMP output voltage is the dependent variable.

In standard format the homogeneous equation for this circuit is

$$\frac{d^2v_O}{dt^2} + \frac{3}{RC_1} \frac{dv_O}{dt} + \frac{1}{R^2C_1C_2} v_O = 0$$

Comparing this expression with the standard form yields

$$\omega_0^2 = \frac{1}{R^2C_1C_2} \quad \text{and} \quad 2\zeta\omega_0 = \frac{3}{RC_1}$$

or

$$\omega_0 = \frac{1}{\sqrt{RC_1RC_2}} \quad \text{and} \quad \zeta = \frac{3}{2}\sqrt{\frac{C_2}{C_1}}$$

The natural frequency ω_0 of the circuit is determined by RC products and the damping ratio ζ is determined by C_2 and C_1. In particular, we see that the natural response has three forms.

Case A: If $9C_2 > 4C_1$ then $\zeta > 1$ and the natural response is overdamped.

Case B: If $9C_2 = 4C_1$ then $\zeta = 1$ and the natural response is critically damped.

Case C: If $9C_2 < 4C_1$ then $\zeta < 1$ and the natural response is underdamped.

The *RC* OP AMP circuit in Figure 7–40 produces the same response forms as the series and parallel *RLC* circuits without using an inductor. The next example shows that active *RC* circuits can produce responses that cannot be produced by passive *RLC* circuits.

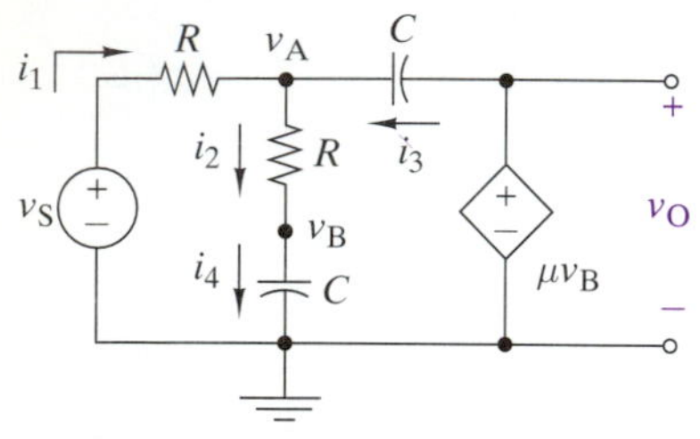

FIGURE 7–41

EXAMPLE 7–20

Find the damping ratio and natural frequency of the second-order circuit in Figure 7–41.

SOLUTION:

The circuit differential equation is obtained from the connection and element constraints. Writing KCL equations at nodes A and B, we obtain the following connection constraints:

$$\text{Node A: } i_1 - i_2 + i_3 = 0$$

$$\text{Node B: } \quad i_2 - i_4 = 0$$

The element constraints are

$$i_1 = G(v_S - v_A) \quad i_3 = C\frac{d(v_O - v_A)}{dt}$$

$$i_2 = G(v_A - v_B) \quad i_4 = C\frac{dv_B}{dt}$$

$$v_O = \mu v_B$$

Substituting the element equations into the connection equations yields

$$\text{Node A: } Gv_S - 2Gv_A + Gv_B + \mu C\frac{dv_B}{dt} - C\frac{dv_A}{dt} = 0$$

$$\text{Node B: } \quad Gv_A - Gv_B - C\frac{dv_B}{dt} = 0$$

We have two coupled first-order differential equations in node voltages v_A and v_B. To derive a single second-order equation, we need to eliminate one of these node voltages. Solving the node B equation for v_A produces

$$v_A = v_B + RC\frac{dv_B}{dt}$$

Substituting this result into the node A equation and using the fact that $v_O = \mu v_B$ yields the circuit differential equation.

$$\frac{d^2v_O}{dt^2} + \frac{3-\mu}{RC}\frac{dv_O}{dt} + \frac{1}{(RC)^2}v_O = \frac{\mu}{(RC)^2}v_S$$

Comparing this equation with the standard form of the second-order differential equation in Eq. (7–63) identities the damping ratio and undamped natural frequency of the circuit.

$$\omega_0 = \frac{1}{RC} \qquad \zeta = \frac{3-\mu}{2}$$

The natural frequency is determined by the RC product and the damping ratio by the dependent source gain μ. There are the usual three responses:

Case A: If $\mu < 1$ then $\zeta > 1$ and the circuit is overdamped.

Case B: If $\mu = 1$ then $\zeta = 1$ and the circuit is critically damped.

Case C: If $3 > \mu > 1$ then $0 < \zeta < 1$ and the circuit is underdamped.

In addition, this active circuit has two response forms that are not possible in passive RLC circuits. If $\mu = 3$ then $\zeta = 0$ and there is no damping. The natural response has the form

$$v_{ON}(t) = K_1 \cos \omega_0 t + K_2 \sin \omega_0 t \qquad t \geqslant 0$$

No damping corresponds to a sustained oscillation where the energy to overcome the losses in the resistors comes from the dependent source. Note that when $\zeta = 0$ the frequency of the undamped sinusoid is ω_0 (hence the name undamped natural frequency).

Even more dramatic is the case $\mu > 3$ and $\zeta < 0$. When $\zeta < 0$ there is negative damping, which means that the exponentials in the natural response

$$v_{ON}(t) = K_1 e^{-\zeta\omega_0 t} \cos \beta t + K_2 e^{-\zeta\omega_0 t} \sin \beta t \qquad t \geqslant 0$$

grow without bound. A circuit whose natural response increases without bound is said to be **unstable**. We will treat circuit stability again in Chapter 11. ■

EXAMPLE 7–21

(a) Select element values in the active circuit in Figure 7–41 so the circuit is unstable with $\zeta = -0.1$ and $\omega_0 = 1000$ rad/s.
(b) Use MicroSim Design Center to plot the zero-state output voltage for a unit step function input.

SOLUTION:

(a) In Example 7–20 we found that $\omega_0 = 1/RC$ and $\zeta = (3 - \mu)/2$. Selecting $R = 1$ kΩ, we can solve for the capacitance and gain as

$$C = \frac{1}{R\omega_0} = \frac{1}{1000 \times 1000} = 1 \mu\text{F}$$

$$\mu = 3 - 2\zeta = 3.2$$

(b) Figure 7–42 shows the resulting circuit diagram as constructed using MicroSim Schematics. The 1-V dc source simulates the step function input for $t \geq 0$. The zero-state condition is set up by leaving the IC attributes of the capacitors blank and checking the **Use Init. Conditions** box in the transient analysis dialog box. To observe the PSpice-generated response, we need to select an appropriate simulation interval. However, in this case the step response does not settle down on a final value since the circuit is unstable with $\zeta = -0.1$. The following analysis suggests a way to estimate an appropriate simulation interval when the response does not have a finite duration.

FIGURE 7–42

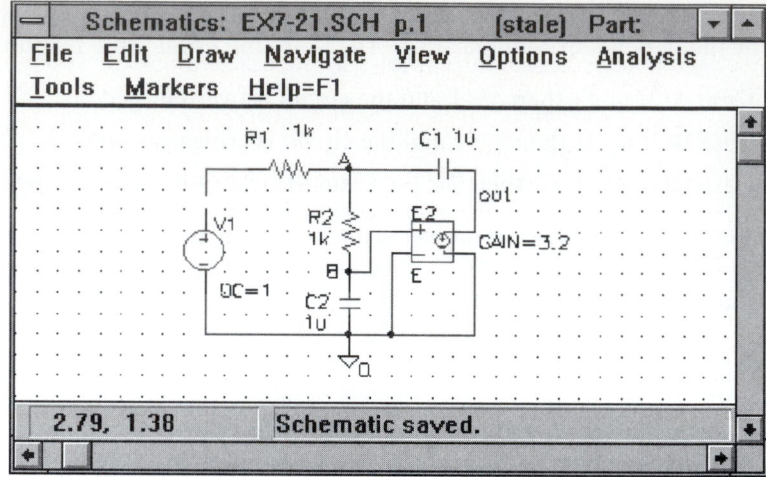

In this circuit the period of the undamped natural frequency is $2\pi/\omega_0$, or about $T_0 = 6.2$ ms. To observe about four cycles of the unstable response, we need a simulation time of $4T_0$ or about 25 ms. Therefore, in the **Transient Analysis** dialog box, where we set **Final Time** = 25 ms and **Step Ceiling** = **Final Time**/100 = 0.25 ms. Selecting **Analysis/Simulate** then produces a PSpice transient analysis, the results of which are shown in the Probe plot in Figure 7–43. Note that the step response is a negatively damped oscillation that, theoretically, increases in amplitude without bound. Practically speaking, the active element in the circuit will saturate at some finite level, leading to a sustained oscillation whose form cannot be predicted by the linear models we are using here. ■

FIGURE 7–43

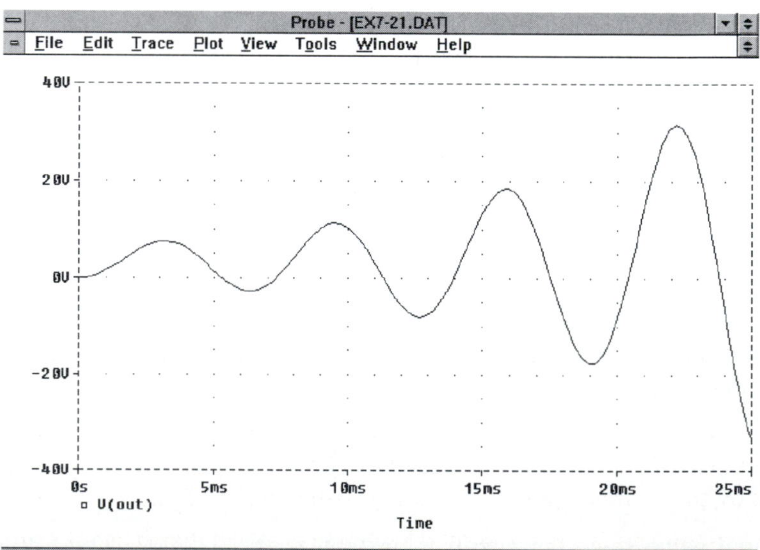

D **DESIGN EXERCISE: 7–19**

Given the following second-order circuit zero-state step responses

(1) $v_C(t) = (10 - 15e^{-1000t} + 5e^{-3000t})u(t)$ V

(2) $v_C(t) = (10 - 10e^{-1000t}\cos 3000t - 3.33e^{-1000t}\sin 3000t)u(t)$ V

(a) What are the characteristic equations?

(b) What are the damping ratios and undamped natural frequencies?

(c) Design series *RLC* circuits that realize these responses.

Answers:

For the response in (1):

(a) $s^2 + 4000s + 3 \times 10^6 = 0$

(b) $\omega_0 = 1732$ rad/s, $\zeta = 1.155$

(c) $C = 1/3\ \mu$F, $L = 1$ H, $R = 4$ kΩ

For the response in (2):

(a) $s^2 + 2000s + 10^7 = 0$

(b) $\omega_0 = 3000$, $\zeta = 0.333$

(c) $C = 100$ nF, $L = 1$ H, $R = 2$ kΩ.

DISCUSSION: *The answers in part (c) are not unique. The standard form of the characteristic equation for a second-order series* RLC *circuit is* $LCs^2 + RCs + 1$. *For the response in (1) the results from (a) require* $LC = 10^{-6}/3$ *and* $RC = 4 \times 10^{-3}/3$. *Selecting* $C = 1/3\ \mu F$ *yields* $L = 1\ H$ *and* $R = 4\ k\Omega$. *For the response in (2), part (a) requires* $LC = 10^{-7}$ *and* $RC = 2 \times 10^{-4}$. *Selecting* $C = 100\ nF$ *yields* $L = 1\ H$ *and* $R = 2\ k\Omega$.

SUMMARY

- Circuits containing linear resistors and the equivalent of one capacitor or one inductor are described by first-order differential equations in which the unknown is the circuit state variable.
- The zero-input response in a first-order circuit is an exponential whose time constant depends on circuit parameters. The amplitude of the exponential is equal to the initial value of the state variable.
- The natural response is the general solution of the homogeneous differential equation obtained by setting the input to zero. The forced response is a particular solution of the differential equation for the given input. For linear circuits the total response is the sum of the forced and natural responses.
- For linear circuits the total response is the sum of the zero-input and zero-state responses. The zero-input response is caused by the initial energy stored in capacitors or inductors. The zero-state response results from the input driving forces.
- The initial and final values of the step response of a first and second-order circuit can be found by replacing capacitors by open circuits and inductors by short circuits and then using resistance circuit analysis methods.
- For a sinusoidal input the forced response is called the sinusoidal steady-state response, or the ac response. The ac response is a sinusoid with the

same frequency as the input but with a different amplitude and phase angle. The ac response can be found from the circuit differential equation using the method of undetermined coefficients.

- Circuits containing linear resistors and the equivalent of two energy storage elements are described by second-order differential equations in which the dependent variable is one of the state variables. The initial conditions are the values of the two state variables at $t = 0$.
- The zero-input response of a second-order circuit takes different forms depending on the roots of the characteristic equation. Unequal real roots produce the overdamped response, equal real roots produce the critically damped response, and complex conjugate roots produce underdamped responses.
- The circuit damping ratio ζ and undamped natural frequency ω_0 determine the form of the zero-input and natural responses of any second-order circuit. The response is overdamped if $\zeta > 1$, critically damped if $\zeta = 1$, and underdamped if $\zeta < 1$. Active circuits can produce undamped ($\zeta = 0$) and unstable ($\zeta < 0$) responses.
- Computer-aided circuit analysis programs can generate numerical solutions for circuit transient responses. Some knowledge of analytical methods and an estimate of the general form of the expected response are necessary to use these analysis tools.

EN ROUTE OBJECTIVES AND ASSOCIATED PROBLEMS

ERO 7–1 FIRST-ORDER CIRCUITS (SECTS. 7–1, 7–2, 7–3, 7–4)

Given a first-order RC or RL circuit

(a) Find the circuit differential equation, the circuit characteristic equation, the circuit time constant, and the initial conditions (if not given).
(b) Find the zero-input response.
(c) Find the forced and natural responses for step function and sinusoidal inputs.

7–1 For each of the following differential equations, find the function that satisfies the equation and the initial condition.

$$\text{(a)}\ \frac{dv(t)}{dt} + 1500v(t) = 0,\ v(0) = -15\ \text{V}$$

$$\text{(b)}\ 10^{-4}\frac{di(t)}{dt} + 10^{-1}i(t) = 10^{-2}u(t),\ i(0) = -20\ \text{mA}$$

7–2 Find the function that satisfies the following differential equation and initial condition:

$$20\frac{dv(t)}{dt} + 500v(t) = 10(\cos 100t)u(t),\ v(0) = 0$$

7–3 Determine the time constant of each of the circuits in Figure P7–3.

7–4 Determine the time constant of each of the circuits in Figure P7–4.

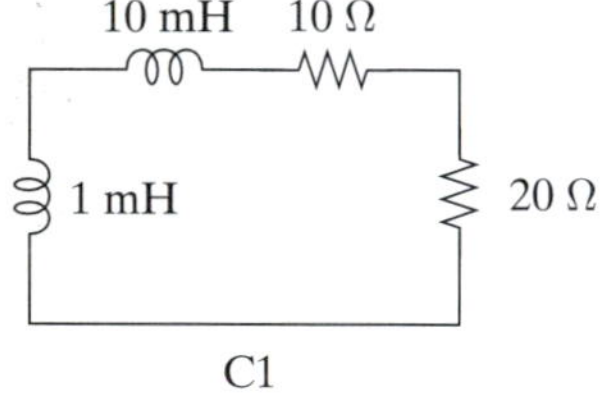

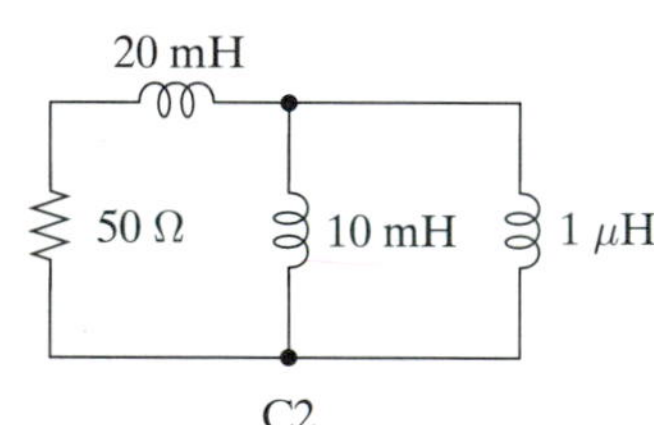

FIGURE P7–3

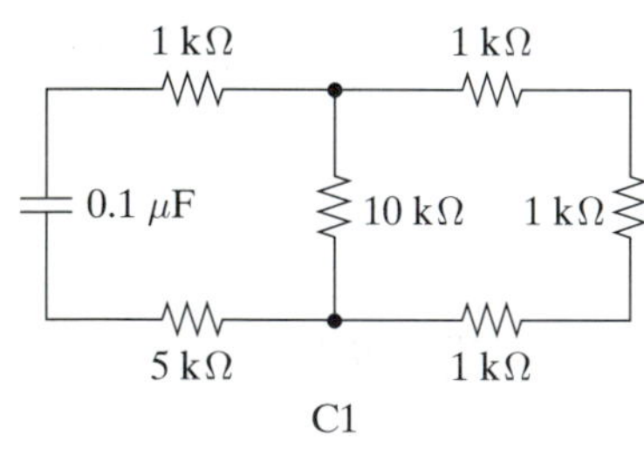

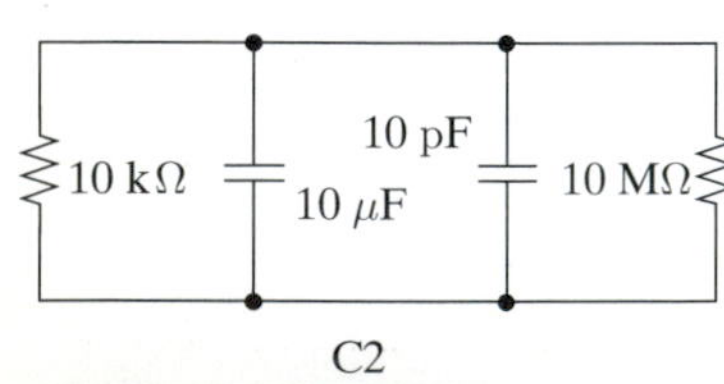

FIGURE P7–4

7–5 The switch in each circuit in Figure P7–5 has been open for a long time and is closed at $t = 0$. For each circuit

(a) Determine the value of the state variable at $t = 0$ and the value of the state variable as $t \to \infty$.

(b) Determine the circuit time constant.

(c) Write an expression for the state variable for $t \geq 0$ and sketch its waveform.

7–6 Repeat Problem 7–5 when the switch in each circuit has been closed for a long time and then is opened at $t = 0$.

7–7 The switch in each circuit in Figure P7–7 has been in position A for a long time and is moved to position B at $t = 0$. For each circuit write an expression for the state variable for $t \geq 0$ and sketch its waveform.

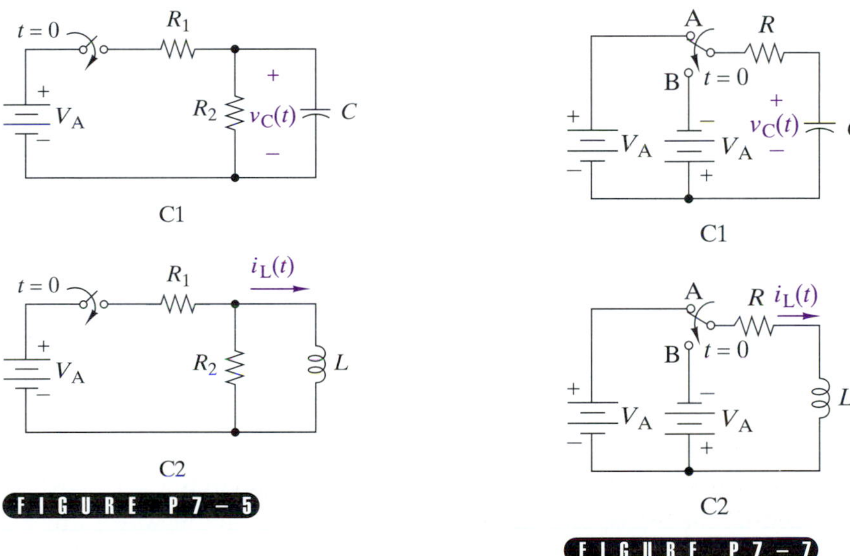

FIGURE P7–5

FIGURE P7–7

7–8 Repeat Problem 7–7 when the switch is each circuit has been in position B for a long time and is moved to position A at $t = 0$.

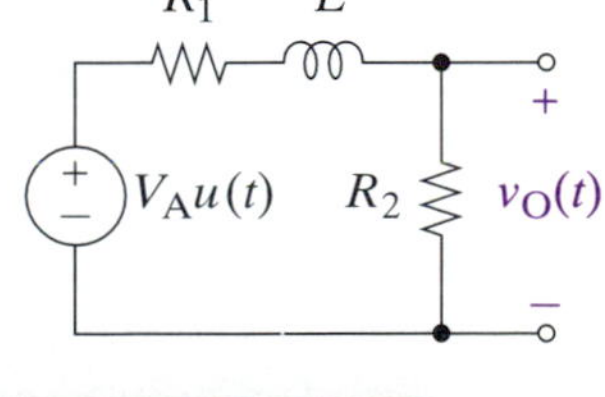

FIGURE P7–9

7–9 The circuit in Figure P7–9 is in the zero state when the step function $V_A u(t)$ is applied. Find the output voltage response $v_O(t)$ for $t \geq 0$. Identify the forced and natural components and sketch their waveforms.

7–10 The circuit in Figure P7–10 is in the zero state when the step function $V_A u(t)$ is applied. Find the output voltage response $v_O(t)$ for $t \geq 0$. Identify the forced and natural components and sketch their waveforms.

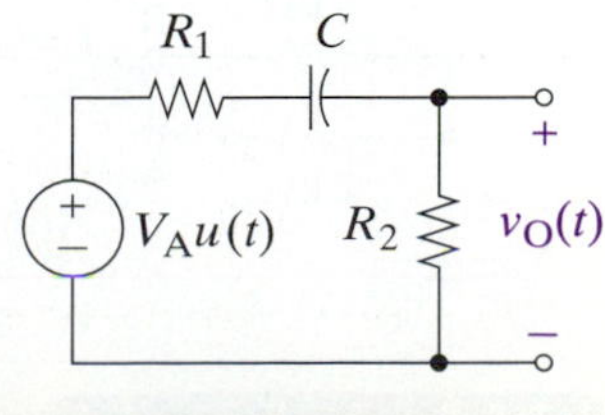

FIGURE P7–10

7–11 The switch in Figure P7–11 has been in position A for a long time and is moved to position B at $t = 0$. Write an expression for $v_C(t)$ for $t \geq 0$, identify the forced and natural components, and plot its waveform.

FIGURE P7–11

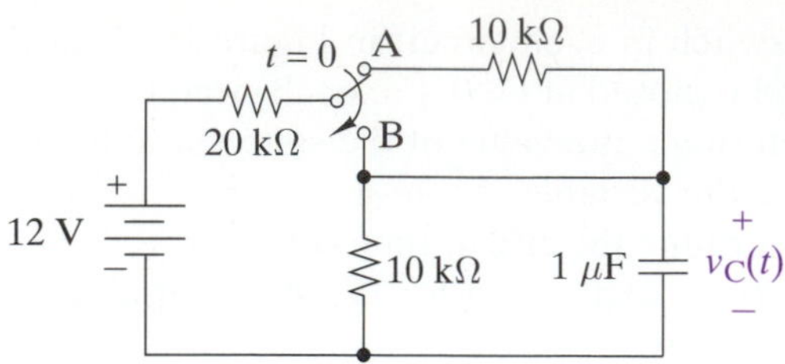

7–12 Repeat Problem 7–11 when the switch has been in position B for a long time and is moved to position A at $t = 0$.

7–13 The switch in Figure P7–13 has been open for a long time and is closed at $t = 0$. Solve for $v_C(t)$ for $t \geq 0$ when the input is $v_S(t) = 15$ V, identify the forced and natural components, and plot its waveform.

FIGURE P7–13

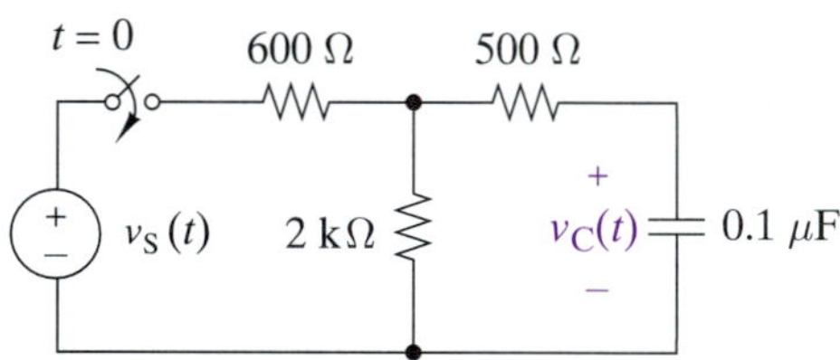

7–14 The switch in Figure P7–13 has been open for a long time and is closed at $t = 0$. The switch is subsequently reopened at $t = 100$ μs. Solve for $v_C(t)$ for $t \geq 0$ when the input is $v_S(t) = 15$ V and plots its waveform.

7–15 Repeat Problem 7–13 for an input $v_S(t) = 20 \cos 2500t$.

7–16 The switch in Figure P7–16 has been open for a long time and is closed at $t = 0$. Solve for $i_O(t)$ for $t \geq 0$ when the input is $v_S(t) = 12$ V, identify the forced and natural components, and plot its waveform.

FIGURE P7–16

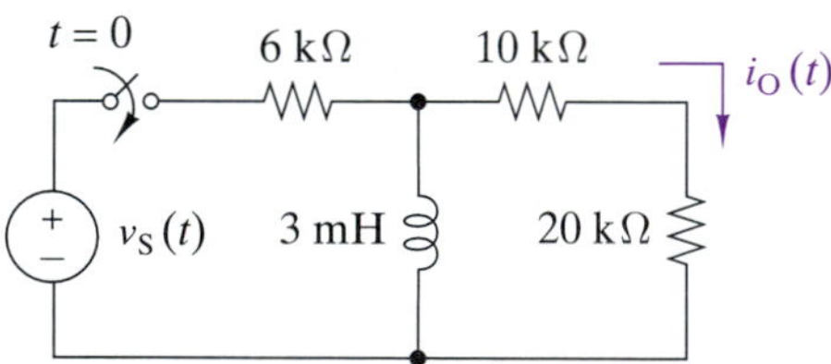

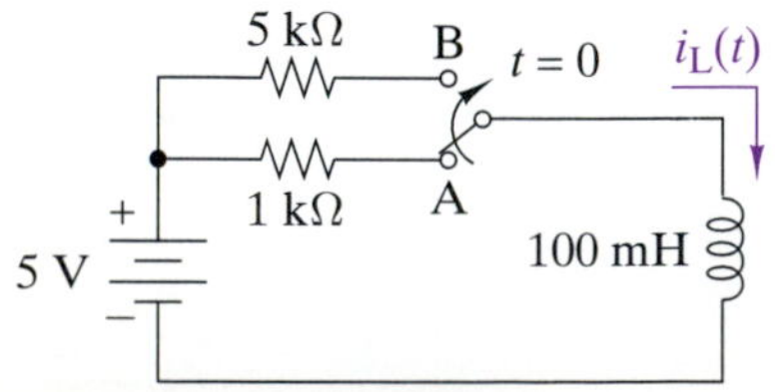

FIGURE P7–18

7–17 Repeat Problem 7–16 for an input $v_S(t) = 10(\cos 500{,}000t)$.

7–18 The switch in Figure P7–18 has been in position A for a long time and is moved to position B at $t = 0$. Find $i_L(t)$ for $t \geq 0$ and plot its waveform.

7–19 The switch in Figure P7–19 has been in position A for a long time and is moved to position B at $t = 0$. Find $v_C(t)$ for $t \geq 0$ and plot its waveform.

R/2

v_A 2R v_B 2R v_C

i_s

i_s R/2 R

Node A: $R_A = R/2 + 2R$

$$G_A = \frac{1}{R/2} + \frac{1}{2R} = \frac{2}{R} + \frac{1}{2R} = \frac{1}{R}\left(2 + \frac{1}{2}\right) = \frac{2.5}{R}$$

$$G = 1/R = \frac{2.5}{R} = \underline{2.5G.}$$

Node B: $R_B = 2R + 2R + R/2$

$$G_B = \frac{1}{2R} + \frac{1}{2R} + \frac{1}{R/2} = \frac{1}{2R} + \frac{1}{2R} + \frac{2}{R} = \underline{3.0G}$$

Node C: $R_C = 2R + R + R/2$

$$G_C = \frac{1}{2R} + \frac{1}{R} + \frac{1}{R/2} = \frac{1}{2R} + \frac{1}{R} + \frac{2}{R} = \underline{3.5G}$$

Node A-B: $R_{AB} = 2R \Rightarrow G_{AB} = \frac{1}{2R} = \underline{0.5G}$

Node B-C $R_{BC} = 2R \Rightarrow G_{BC} = \frac{1}{2R} = \underline{0.5G}$

Node A-C: $R_{AC} = R/2 \Rightarrow G_{AC} = \frac{1}{R/2} = \frac{2}{R} = \underline{2G}$

FIGURE P7–19

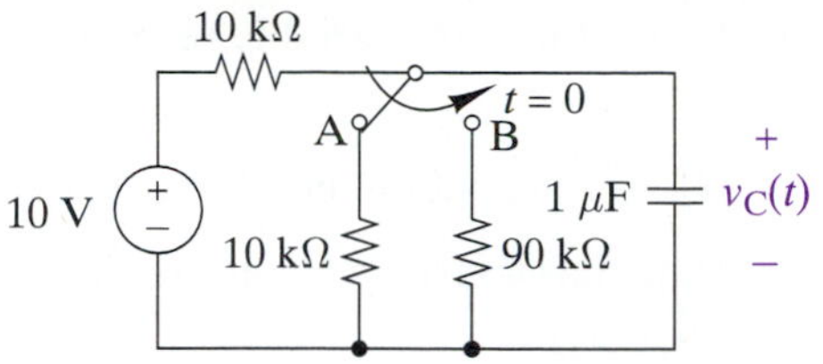

7–20 Switches 1 and 2 in Figure P7–20 have both been in position A for a long time. Switch 1 is moved to position B at $t = 0$ and switch 2 is moved to position B at $t = 20$ ms. Find the voltage across the 0.1-μF capacitor for $t > 0$ and plot its waveform.

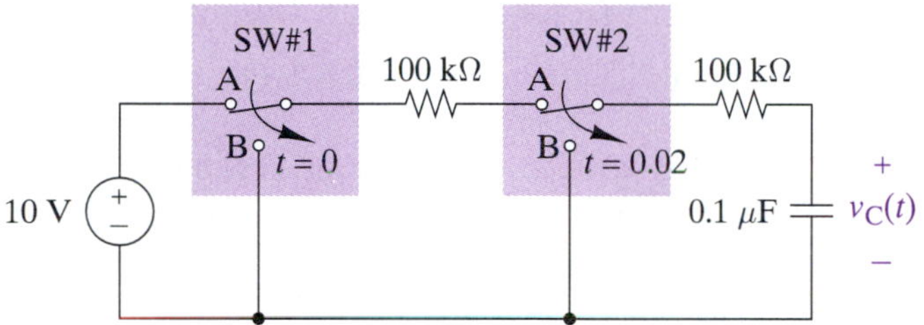

FIGURE P7–20

ERO 7–2 FIRST-ORDER RESPONSE (SECTS. 7–1, 7–2, 7–3)

Given the response of a first-order *RC* or *RL* circuit,

(a) Find the circuit characteristic equation, the circuit time constant, and the initial conditions.
(b) Design a first-order circuit that produces the given response.

7–21 The following function is the state variable response of a first-order *RC* circuit:

$$v_C(t) = 5 - 10e^{-1000t} \text{ V for } t \geqslant 0$$

(a) Determine the circuit characteristic equation, the circuit time constant, and the initial condition of the state variable.
(b) Determine the Thévenin equivalent input voltage.

7–22 The following function is the state variable response of a first-order *RL* circuit:

$$i_L(t) = 5 + 15e^{-6000t} \text{ mA for } t \geqslant 0$$

(a) Determine the circuit characteristic equation, the circuit time constant, and the initial condition of the state variable.
(b) Determine the Norton equivalent input current.

7–23 The following function is the state variable response of a first-order *RC* circuit:

$$v_C(t) = 10 \cos 1000t + 10 \sin 1000t - 5e^{-1000t} \text{ V for } t \geqslant 0$$

(a) Determine the circuit characteristic equation, the circuit time constant, and the initial condition.
(b) Determine the amplitude and phase angle of the Thévenin equivalent input voltage.

7–24 The following function is the state variable response of a first-order *RL* circuit:

$$i_L(t) = -6\cos 300t + 2\sin 300t + 6e^{-100t} \text{ mA for } t \geq 0$$

(a) Determine the circuit characteristic equation, the circuit time constant, and the initial condition.
(b) Determine the amplitude and phase angle of the Norton equivalent input current.

7–25 The following function is the zero-input response of a first-order *RC* circuit. The given response is *not* state variable, but the initial value of the state variable is given.

$$i_C(t) = -20e^{-1000t} \text{ mA for } t \geq 0 \text{ with } v_C(0) = 12 \text{ V}$$

(a) Determine the circuit characteristic equation and the circuit time constant.
(b) Determine the value of the circuit parameters *R* and *C*.

7–26 The following function is the zero-input response of a first-order *RL* circuit. The given response is *not* state variable, but the initial value of the state variable is given.

$$v_L(t) = 5e^{-5000t} \text{ V for } t \geq 0 \text{ with } i_L(0) = -10 \text{ mA}$$

(a) Determine the circuit characteristic equation and the circuit time constant.
(b) Determine the value of the circuit parameters *R* and *L*.

7–27 **D** Design a first-order *RC* circuit that produces the response given in Problem 7–21.

7–28 **D** Design a first-order *RL* circuit that produces the response given in Problem 7–22.

7–29 **D** Design a first-order *RC* circuit that produces the response given in Problem 7–25.

7–30 **D** Design a first-order *RL* circuit that produces the response given in Problem 7–26.

ERO 7–3 SECOND-ORDER CIRCUITS (SECTS. 7–5, 7–6, 7–7)

Given a second-order *RLC* or OP AMP *RC* circuit,

(a) Find the circuit differential equation, the circuit characteristic equation, circuit damping ratio and undamped natural frequency, and the initial conditions (if not given).
(b) Find the zero-input response.
(c) Find the forced and natural responses for a step function input.

7–31 For each of the following differential equations, find the function that satisfies the equation and meets the initial conditions.

$$\text{(a)} \frac{d^2v}{dt^2} + 6\frac{dv}{dt} + 8v = 0, \; v(0) = 0, \; \frac{dv}{dt}(0) = 15 \text{ V/s}$$

$$\text{(b)} \frac{d^2v}{dt^2} + 6\frac{dv}{dt} + 9v = 0, \; v(0) = 0, \; \frac{dv}{dt}(0) = 2 \text{ V/s}$$

7–32 Find the function that satisfies the following differential equation and the initial conditions:

$$\frac{d^2v}{dt^2} + 10\frac{dv}{dt} + 125v = 250u(t),\ v(0) = 5\text{ V},\ \frac{dv}{dt}(0) = 25\text{ V/s}$$

7–33 Determine the numerical value of the circuit damping ratio ζ and the undamped natural frequency ω_0 for each circuit in Figure P7–33. Specify whether the circuits are overdamped, underdamped, or critically damped.

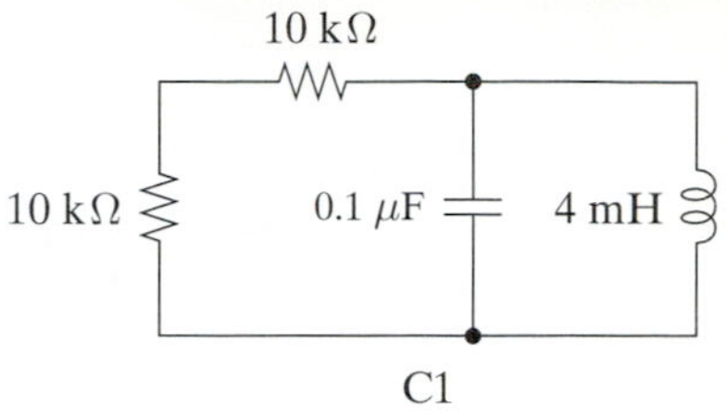

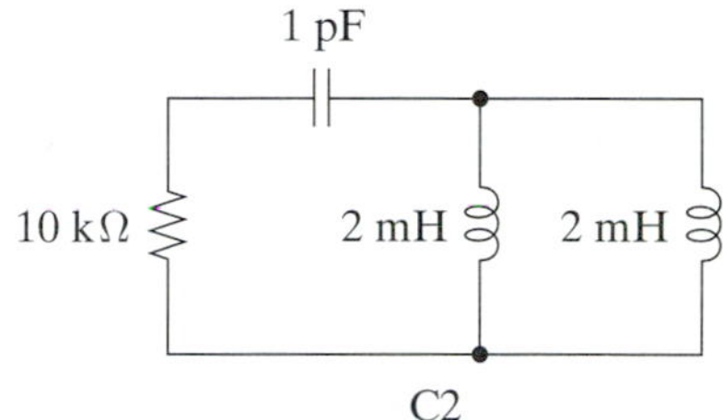

FIGURE P7–33

7–34 The switch in Figure P7–34 has been open for a long time and is closed at $t = 0$. The circuit parameters are $L = 0.1$ H, $C = 25$ nF, $R_1 = 5$ kΩ, $R_2 = 5$ kΩ, and $V_A = 10$ V.

(a) Find the initial values of v_C and i_L at $t = 0$ and the final values of v_C and i_L as $t \to \infty$.

(b) Find the differential equation for $v_C(t)$ and the circuit characteristic equation.

(c) Find $v_C(t)$ and $i_L(t)$ for $t \geq 0$, identify the forced and natural components of the responses, and plot $v_C(t)$ and $i_L(t)$. Is the circuit overdamped or underdamped?

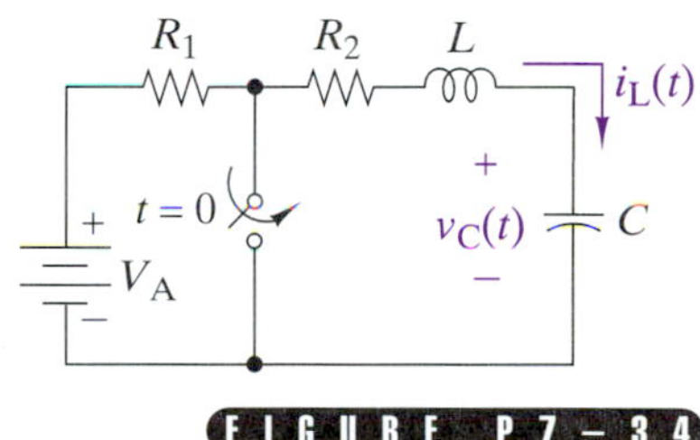

FIGURE P7–34

7–35 The switch in Figure P7–34 has been closed for a long time and is opened at $t = 0$. The circuit parameters are $L = 0.5$ H, $C = 250$ nF, $R_1 = 5$ kΩ, $R_2 = 5$ kΩ, and $V_A = 10$ V.

(a) Find the initial values of v_C and i_L at $t = 0$ and the final values of v_C and i_L as $t \to \infty$.

(b) Find the differential equation for $v_C(t)$ and the circuit characteristic equation.

(c) Find $v_C(t)$ and $i_L(t)$ for $t \geq 0$, identify the forced and natural components of the responses, and plot $v_C(t)$ and $i_L(t)$. Is the circuit overdamped or underdamped?

7–36 The switch in Figure P7–36 has been open for a long time and is closed at $t = 0$. The circuit parameters are $L = 0.5$ H, $C = 25$ pF, $R_1 = 5$ kΩ, $R_2 = 12$ kΩ, and $V_A = 10$ V.

(a) Find the initial values of v_C and i_L at $t = 0$ and the final values of v_C and i_L as $t \to \infty$.

(b) Find the differential equation for $v_C(t)$ and the circuit characteristic equation.

(c) Find $v_C(t)$ and $i_L(t)$ for $t \geq 0$, identify the forced and natural components of the responses, and $v_C(t)$ and $i_L(t)$. Is the circuit overdamped or underdamped?

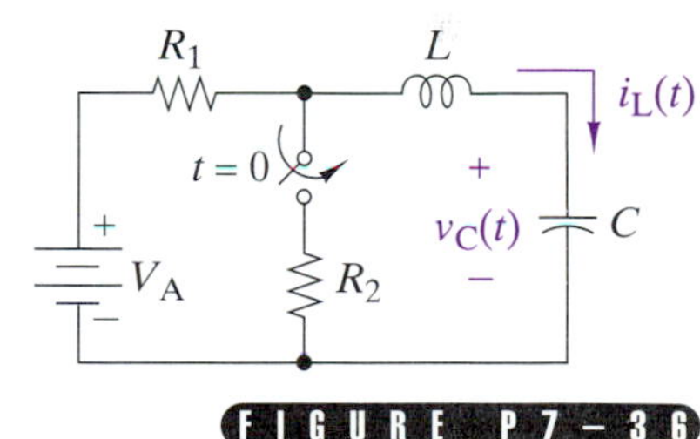

FIGURE P7–36

7–37 The switch in Figure P7–36 has been closed for a long time and is opened at $t = 0$. The circuit parameters are $L = 0.25$ H, $C = 8$ nF, $R_1 = 2$ kΩ, $R_2 = 3$ kΩ, and $V_A = 15$ V.

(a) Find the initial values of v_C and i_L at $t = 0$ and the final values of v_C and i_L as $t \to \infty$.

(b) Find the differential equation for $v_C(t)$ and the circuit characteristic equation.

(c) Find $v_C(t)$ and $i_L(t)$ for $t \geq 0$, identify the forced and natural components of the responses, and plot $v_C(t)$ and $i_L(t)$. Is the circuit overdamped or underdamped?

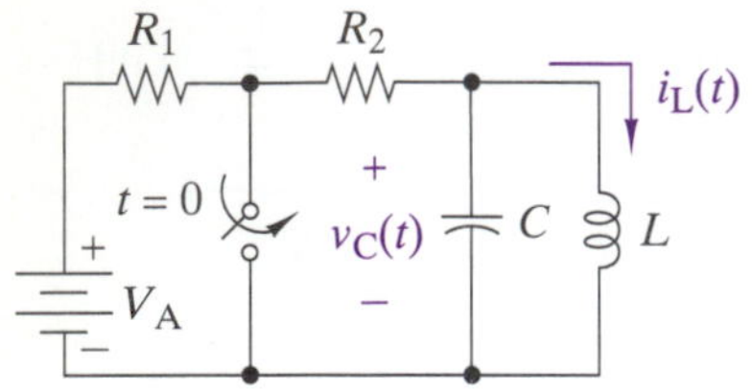

FIGURE P7–38

7–38 The switch in Figure P7–38 has been open for a long time and is closed at $t = 0$. The circuit parameters are $L = 0.1$ H, $C = 0.1$ μF, $R_1 = 3$ kΩ, $R_2 = 3$ kΩ, and $V_A = 10$ V.

(a) Find the initial values of v_C and i_L at $t = 0$ and the final values of v_C and i_L as $t \to \infty$.

(b) Find the differential equation for $i_L(t)$ and the circuit characteristic equation.

(c) Find $v_C(t)$ and $i_L(t)$ for $t \geq 0$, identify the forced and natural components of the responses, and plot $v_C(t)$ and $i_L(t)$. Is the circuit overdamped or underdamped?

7–39 The switch in Figure P7–38 has been closed for a long time and is opened at $t = 0$. The circuit parameters are $L = 0.5$ H, $C = 5$ nF, $R_1 = 2$ kΩ, $R_2 = 2$ kΩ, and $V_A = 10$ V.

(a) Find the initial values of v_C and i_L at $t = 0$ and the final values of v_C and i_L as $t \to \infty$.

(b) Find the differential equation for $i_L(t)$ and the circuit characteristic equation.

(c) Find $v_C(t)$ and $i_L(t)$ for $t \geq 0$, identify the forced and natural components of the responses, and plot $v_C(t)$ and $i_L(t)$. Is the circuit overdamped or underdamped?

7–40 The switch in Figure P7–38 has been open for a long time and is closed at $t = 0$. The circuit parameters are $R_1 = 20$ kΩ, $R_2 = 20$ kΩ, $L = 80$ mH, $C = 2.5$ nF, and $V_A = 12$ V. Find $v_C(t)$ and $i_L(t)$ for $t > 0$, identify the forced and natural components of the responses, and plot $v_C(t)$ and $i_L(t)$. Is the circuit overdamped or underdamped?

7–41 The switch in Figure P7–38 has been closed for a long time and is opened at $t = 0$. The circuit parameters are $R_1 = 20$ kΩ, $R_2 = 20$ kΩ, $L = 80$ mH, $C = 125$ pF, and $V_A = 12$ V. Find $v_C(t)$ and $i_L(t)$ for $t > 0$, identify the forced and natural components of the responses, and plot $v_C(t)$ and $i_L(t)$. Is the circuit overdamped or underdamped?

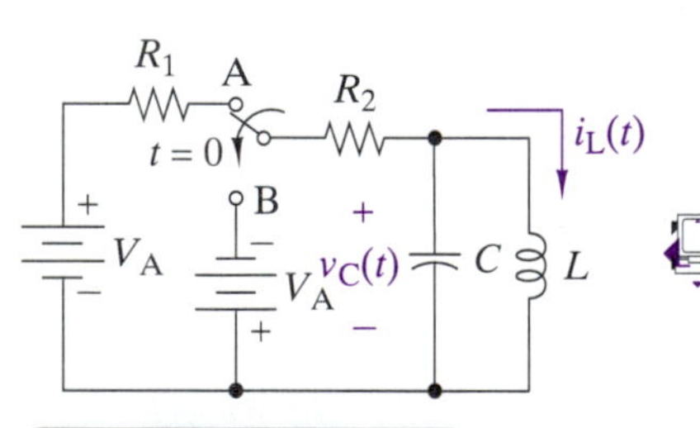

FIGURE P7–42

7–42 The switch in the circuit shown in Figure P7–42 has been in position A for a long time. At $t = 0$ it is moved to position B. The circuit parameters are $R_1 = 250$ Ω, $R_2 = 1$ kΩ, $L = 125$ mH, $C = 20$ nF, and $V_A = 15$ V. Find $v_C(t)$ and $i_L(t)$ for $t > 0$, identify the forced and natural components of the responses, and plot $v_C(t)$ and $i_L(t)$. Is the circuit overdamped or underdamped?

7–43 The switch in the circuit shown in Figure P7–42 has been in position B for a long time. At $t = 0$ it is moved to position A. The circuit parameters are $R_1 = 250$ Ω, $R_2 = 1$ kΩ, $L = 125$ mH, $C = 20$ nF, and $V_A = 15$ V. Find $v_C(t)$ and $i_L(t)$ for $t > 0$, identify the forced and natural components of the response, and plot $v_C(t)$ and $i_L(t)$. Is the circuit overdamped or underdamped?

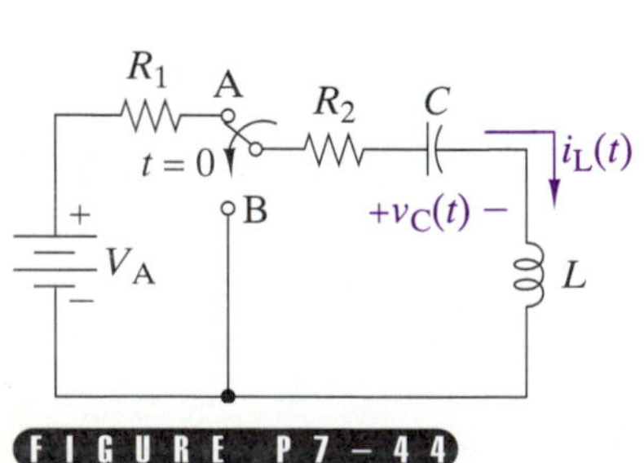

FIGURE P7–44

7–44 The switch in Figure P7–44 has been in position A for a long time and is moved to position B at $t = 0$. The circuit parameters are $R_1 = 500$ Ω, $R_2 = 2$ kΩ, $L = 50$ mH, $C = 50$ nF, and $V_A = 5$ V. Find $v_C(t)$

and $i_L(t)$ for $t > 0$, identify the forced and natural components of the responses, and plot $v_C(t)$ and $i_L(t)$. Is the circuit overdamped or underdamped?

7–45 The switch in Figure P7–44 has been in position B for a long time and is moved to position A at $t = 0$. The circuit parameters are $R_1 = 500\ \Omega$, $R_2 = 2\ \text{k}\Omega$, $L = 50$ mH, $C = 50$ nF, and $V_A = 5$ V. Find $v_C(t)$ and $i_L(t)$ for $t > 0$, identify the forced and natural components of the response, and plot $v_C(t)$ and $i_L(t)$. Is the circuit overdamped or underdamped?

7–46 The circuit in Figure P7–46 is in the zero state when the step function input is applied. Find the output $v_O(t)$ for $L = 50$ mH, $C = 50$ nF, $R = 4\ \text{k}\Omega$, and $V_A = 100$ V.

7–47 The circuit in Figure P7–47 is in the zero state when the step function input is applied. The circuit parameters are $L = 50$ mH, $C = 50$ nF, and $V_A = 100$ V. Plot the output $v_O(t)$ as R is stepped across the range from 2 kΩ to 6 kΩ in 2-kΩ steps. Comment on the effect of varying the resistance.

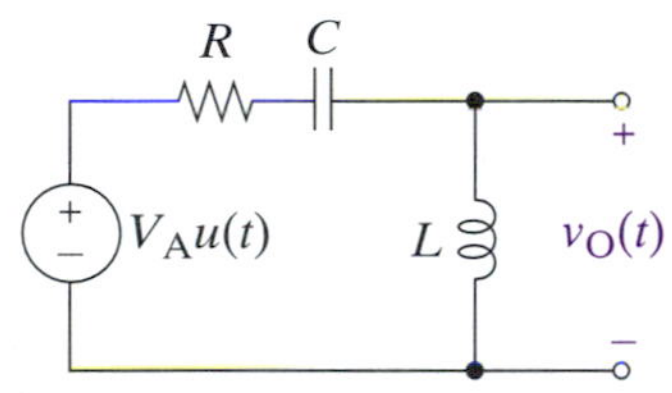

FIGURE P7–46

FIGURE P7–47

7–48 The circuit in Figure P7–48 is in the zero state when the step function input is applied. The circuit parameters are $R = 4\ \text{k}\Omega$, $L = 50$ mH, and $V_A = 100$ V. Plot the output $v_O(t)$ for $C = 5$ nF, 50 nF, and 500 nF. Comment on the effect of varying the capacitance.

7–49 Derive expressions for the damping ratio and natural frequency of the parallel *RLC* circuit in terms of circuit parameters. Comment on the effect of varying circuit parameters.

7–50 Show that the following differential equation describes the circuit in Figure P7–50.

$$(RC)^2\frac{d^2v_2(t)}{dt^2} + (2RC)\frac{dv_2(t)}{dt} + v_2(t) = v_S(t)$$

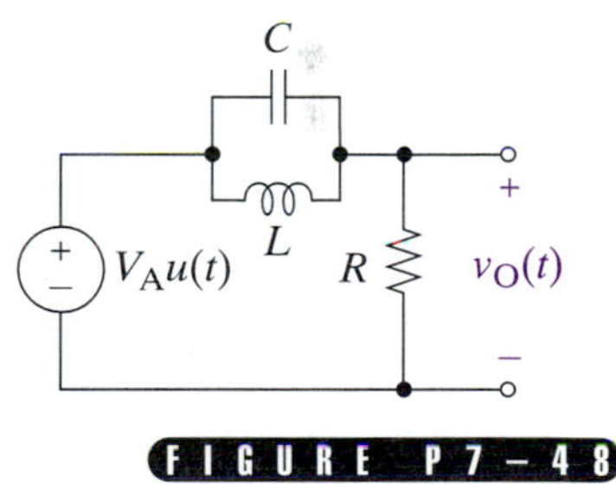

FIGURE P7–48

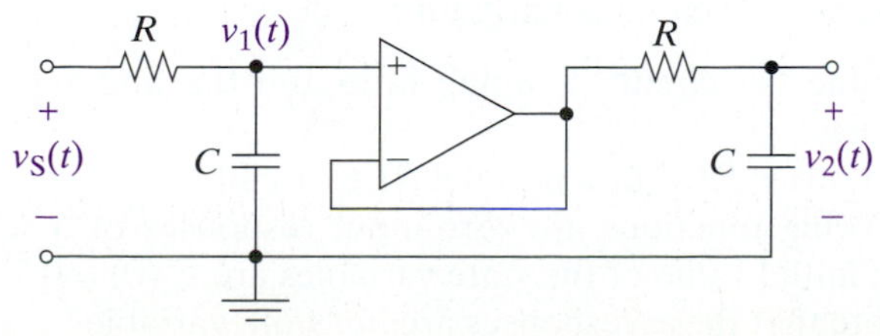

FIGURE P7–50

ERO 7–4 SECOND-ORDER RESPONSE (SECTS. 7–5, 7–6, 7–7)

Given the response of a second-order *RLC* circuit,

(a) Find the circuit differential equation, the circuit characteristic equation, circuit damping ratio and undamped natural frequency, and the initial conditions (if not given).
(b) Design a second-order circuit that produces the given response.

7–51 The following functions are the step responses of a series *RLC* circuit:

$$v_C(t) = 10 - 5e^{-3000t} - 5e^{-6000t}\text{ V for } t \geq 0$$

$$i_L(t) = 2e^{-3000t} + 4e^{-6000t}\text{ mA for } t \geq 0$$

(a) Determine the circuit damping ratio and undamped natural frequency.
(b) Find state variable initial and final conditions and the Thévenin equivalent input.
(c) Determine the value of *C*.

7–52 The following functions are the step responses of a series *RLC* circuit:

$$v_C(t) = 10 - 5e^{-100t}\sin 100t\text{ V for } t \geq 0$$

$$i_L(t) = 0.5e^{-100t}(\sin 100t - \cos 100t)\text{ mA for } t \geq 0$$

(a) Determine the circuit damping ratio and undamped natural frequency.
(b) Find state variable initial and final conditions and the Thévenin equivalent input.
(c) Determine the value of *C*.

7–53 The following functions are the step responses of a parallel *RLC* circuit:

$$v_C(t) = 2.5e^{-100t} - 2.5e^{-500t}\text{ V for } t \geq 0$$

$$i_L(t) = 20 - 25e^{-100t} + 5e^{-500t}\text{ mA for } t \geq 0$$

(a) Determine the circuit damping ratio and undamped natural frequency.
(b) Find state variable initial and final conditions and the Norton equivalent input.
(c) Determine the value of *L*.

7–54 The following functions are the zero-input responses of an *RLC* circuit:

$$v_C(t) = 2e^{-1000t}\cos 2000t - 4e^{-1000t}\sin 2000t\text{ V for } t \geq 0$$

$$i_L(t) = 5e^{-1000t}\cos 2000t\text{ mA for } t \geq 0$$

(a) Determine the circuit damping ratio and the undamped natural frequency.
(b) Is this a series *RLC* or a parallel *RLC* circuit?

7–55 The following functions are zero-input responses of a series *RLC* circuit. The initial value of the state variables are $v_C(0) = 0$ V and $i_L(0) = 2$ mA. Note that these responses are *not* state variables.

$$i_C(t) = 2e^{-2000t} - 4000te^{-2000t}\ \text{mA}$$
$$v_L(t) = -8e^{-2000t} + 8000te^{-2000t}\ \text{V}$$

(a) Determine the circuit characteristic equation, damping ratio, and undamped natural frequency.
(b) Use the inductor *i–v* characteristic to find the value of L.
(c) Use the value of L from (b) and the characteristic equation from (a) to find the values of R_T and C.

7–56 The response of a series *RLC* circuit with $\omega_0 = 2000$ rad/s and $\zeta = 1.25$ is

$$v_C(t) = 10e^{-500t} + 5e^{-1000t} - 10e^{-4000t}\ \ \text{V}$$

Find the Thévenin equivalent input.

7–57 The response of a series *RLC* circuit with $i_L(0) = -200$ mA is

$$v_C(t) = 10e^{-1000t}\cos(2000t)\ \ \text{V}$$

Find the values of L and C.

7–58 **D** Design a series *RLC* circuit whose zero-state output is

$$v_C(t) = V_A - 2V_Ae^{-200t} + V_Ae^{-400t}\ \text{for}\ t > 0$$

when the Thévenin equivalent input voltage is $v_T(t) = V_A u(t)$.

7–59 **D** Design a parallel *RLC* circuit whose zero-state output is

$$i_L(t) = I_A - I_Ae^{-100t} - I_A(100t)e^{-100t}\ \text{for}\ t > 0$$

when the Norton equivalent input current is $i_N(t) = I_A u(t)$.

7–60 **D** The circuit in Figure P7–60 is a simplified diagram of a pulser that simulates lightning transients. When the switch closes the short-circuit current delivered by the pulser must be of the form $i_{SC}(t) = I_A e^{-\alpha t}\cos \beta t$, with $\alpha = 2 \times 10^4$ rad/s, $\beta = 10^6$ rad/s, and $I_A = 2$ kA. Select the values of L, C, and the initial charge on the capacitor.

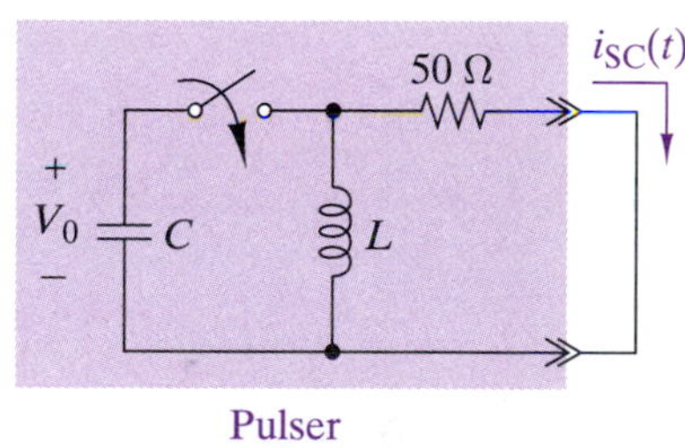

Pulser

FIGURE P7–60

CHAPTER-INTEGRATING PROBLEMS

7–61 **A** COUPLED COIL ANALYSIS

The circuit in Figure P7–61 shows a pair of coils with mutual inductance coupling.

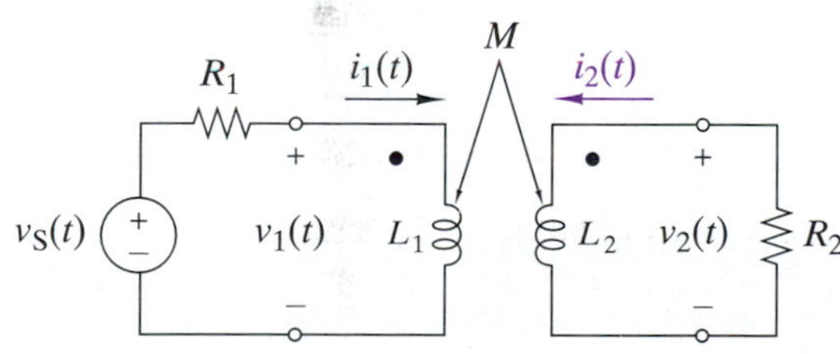

FIGURE P7–61

(a) Write the device and connection equations for the circuit.
(b) Reduce the equations in (a) to a single second-order differential equation in the current $i_2(t)$.

(c) Show that with perfect coupling ($L_1L_2 = M^2$)reduces the second-order equation in (b) to a first-order equation with a time constant of $L_1/R_1 + L_2/R_2$.

(d) With perfect coupling, find the sinusoidal steady-state component of $i_2(t)$ using $L_1 = L_2 = 100$ mH, $R_1 = R_2 = 100\ \Omega$, and $v_S(t) = 10 \sin 500t$ V.

7–62 A D CAPACITANCE TEST JIG

The circuit in Figure P7–62 is a production test jig used to determine whether a shipment of capacitors are all within ±10% of their nominal value of 220 nF. The signal generator at the input produces a 500-Hz square wave whose peak to peak value is 5 V and whose average value is 2.5 V. The oscilloscope at the output displays the response of the *RC* circuit so that a test technician can determine if the capacitor under test is within the ±10% tolerance.

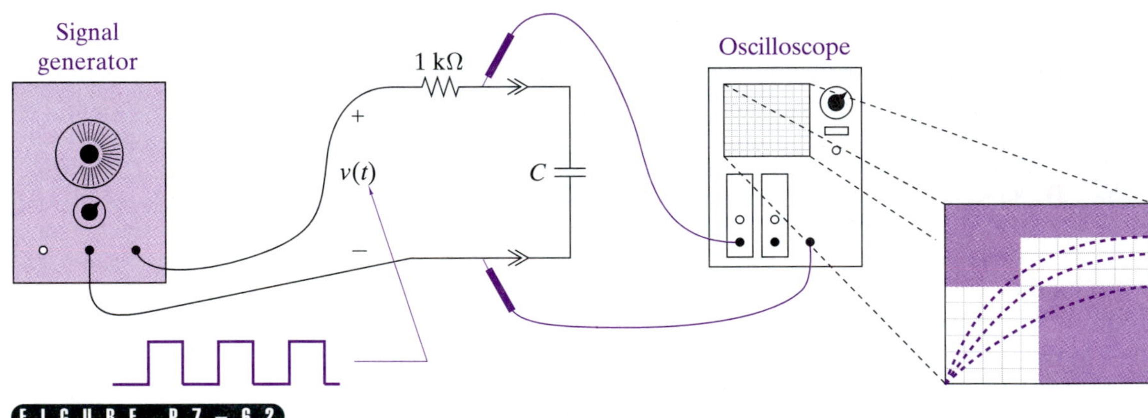

FIGURE P7–62

(a) A Calculate the period and dc offset of the input signal and sketch two cycles of its waveform.

(b) A Calculate the time constant of the *RC* circuit and sketch its zero-state response for a 5-V step function input.

(c) A Compare the period of the square wave input to the time constant of the *RC* circuit. Based on this comparison, sketch the *RC* circuit output for the square wave input.

(d) D Design the oscilloscope display template (solid area in the display) so the square wave response of the *RC* circuit lies is the clear area of the display when the capacitor is within the allowed tolerance and crosses the solid area when the capacitor is out of tolerance.

7–63 A EXPERIMENTAL SECOND-ORDER RESPONSE

Figure P7–63 shows an oscilloscope display of the voltage across the resistor in a series *RLC* circuit.

(a) Estimate the values of α and β of the damped sine signal.

(b) Use the values of α and β from (a) to write the characteristic equation of the circuit.

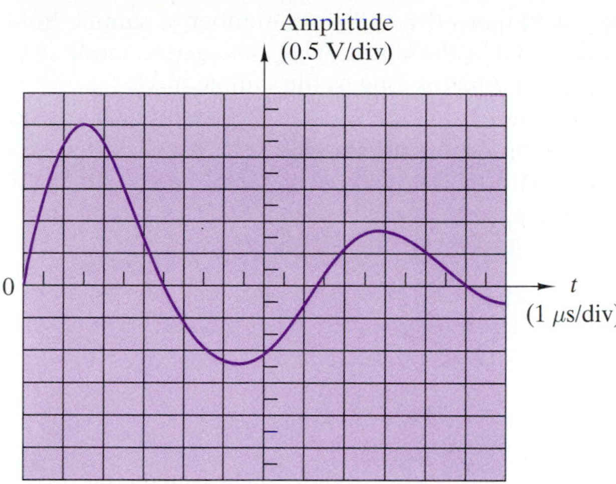

(c) The resistor is known to be 2.2 kΩ. Use the characteristic equation from (b) to determine the values of L and C.

(e) If the display shows the zero-input response of the circuit, what are the values of the initial conditions $v_C(0)$ and $i_L(0)$?

7–64 A SAMPLE HOLD CIRCUIT

Figure P7–64 shows a sample-hold circuit at the input of an analog-to-digital converter. In the sample mode the converter commands the analog switch to close (ON) and the capacitor charges up to the value of the input signal. In the hold mode the converter commands the analog switch to open (OFF), and the capacitor holds and feeds the input signal value to the converter via the OP AMP voltage follower. When conversion is completed the analog switch is turned ON again and the sample-hold cycle repeats.

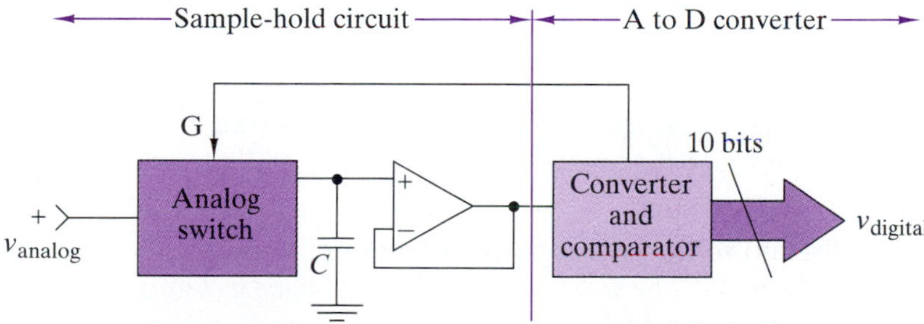

FIGURE P7–64

(a) The series resistances of the analog switch are $R_{ON} = 100\ \Omega$ and $R_{OFF} = 100\ \text{M}\Omega$. When $C = 10$ pF, what is the time constant in the sample mode and the time constant in the hold mode?

(b) The number of sample-hold cycles per second must be at least twice the highest frequency in the analog input signal. What is the minimum number of sample-hold cycles per second for an input $v_S(t) = 5 + 5 \sin 2\pi 1000t$?

(c) Sampling at 10 times the minimum number of sample-hold cycles per second, what is the duration of the sample mode if the hold mode lasts nine times as long as the sample mode?

(d) For the input in (b), will the capacitor voltage reach a steady-state condition during the sample mode?

(e) What fraction of the capacitor voltage will be lost during the hold mode?

7–65 A AUTO IGNITION SYSTEM

The circuit in Figure P7–65 models the ignition system of an vintage automobile. If the switch (the breaker points) has been closed for a long time and is suddenly opened at $t = 0$,

FIGURE P7–65

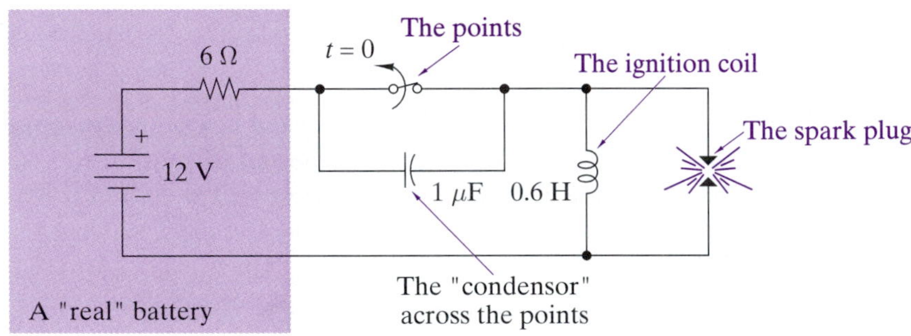

(a) Derive a second-order differential equation in $v_C(t)$ and determine the initial conditions.

(b) Show that the circuit damping ratio is very small.

(c) Assume zero damping ($R = 0$) ratio and show that the voltage across the capacitor is approximately

$$v_C(t) = 2\sqrt{\frac{L}{C}}\sin(\sqrt{LC})t$$

(d) Explain why the voltage across the inductor is approximately $-v_C(t)$.

(e) An arc occurs between the two electrodes (the spark plug) when the voltage between them exceeds 500 V. Will the spark plug fire?

SINUSOIDAL STEADY-STATE RESPONSE

The vector diagram of sine waves gives the best insight into the mutual relationships of alternating currents and emf's.

Charles P. Steinmetz, 1893,
American Engineer

In this chapter we introduce the vector representation of sinusoids as a tool for finding the response of a linear circuit. The vector model was first discussed in detail by Charles Steinmetz (1865–1923) at the International Electric Congress of 1893. Although there is some evidence of earlier use by Oliver Heaviside, Steinmetz is generally credited with popularizing the vector approach by demonstrating its many applications to alternating current devices and systems. By the turn of the century, the concept was well established in engineering practice and education. In the 1950s the Steinmetz vector representation of sinusoids came to be called *phasors* to avoid possible confusion with the space vectors used to describe electromagnetic fields.

The response of a linear circuit consists of a natural component and a forced component. In a stable circuit the natural response eventually vanishes, leaving a sustained response caused by the input driving force. When the input is a sinusoid, the forced response is a sinusoid, with the same frequency as the input but with a different amplitude and phase angle. In electrical engineering the forced sinusoidal component remaining after the natural component disappears is called the **sinusoidal steady-state response**. The sinusoidal steady-state response is also called the **ac response** since the driving force is an alternating current signal.

The phasor defined in the first section of this chapter is the key concept in sinusoidal steady-state analysis. The second section examines the form taken by the device and connection constraints when sinusoidal voltages and currents are represented by phasors. It turns out that the device and connection constraints have the same form as resistive circuits. As a result, we can analyze circuits in the sinusoidal steady state using the analysis tools developed in Chapters 2, 3, and 4. The basic circuit analysis techniques, such as series equivalence and voltage division, are treated in the third section. The phasor domain versions of circuit theorems, such as superposition and Thévenin's theorem, are treated in the fourth section. The fifth section treats general phasor analysis methods using node voltages and mesh currents. The last two sections treat linear transformers and power transfer, two important applications of phasor circuit analysis.

8–1 SINUSOIDS AND PHASORS

The phasor concept is the foundation for the analysis of linear circuits in the sinusoidal steady state. Simply put, a **phasor** is a complex number representing the amplitude and phase angle of a sinusoidal voltage or current. The connection between sinewaves and complex numbers is provided by Euler's relationship:

$$e^{j\theta} = \cos\theta + j\sin\theta \tag{8-1}$$

Equation (8–1) relates the sine and cosine functions to the complex exponential $e^{j\theta}$. To develop the phasor concept, it is necessary to adopt the point of view that the cosine and sine functions can be written in the form

$$\cos\theta = \text{Re}\{e^{j\theta}\} \tag{8-2}$$

and

$$\sin\theta = \mathrm{Im}\{e^{j\theta}\} \qquad (8-3)$$

where Re stands for the "real part of" and Im for the "imaginary part of." Development of the phasor concept can begin with either Eq. (8–2) or (8–3). The choice between the two involves deciding whether to describe the eternal sinewave using a sine or cosine function. In Chapter 5 we chose the cosine, so we will reference phasors to the cosine function.

When Eq. (8–2) is applied to the general sinusoid defined in Chapter 5, we obtain

$$\begin{aligned} v(t) &= V_A\cos(\omega t + \phi) \\ &= V_A\mathrm{Re}\{e^{j(\omega t+\phi)}\} = V_A\mathrm{Re}\{e^{j\omega t}e^{j\phi}\} \qquad (8-4) \\ &= \mathrm{Re}\{(V_A e^{j\phi})e^{j\omega t}\} \end{aligned}$$

In the last line of Eq. (8–4), moving the amplitude V_A inside the real part operation does not change the final result because it is a real constant.

By definition, the quantity $V_A e^{j\phi}$ in the last line of Eq. (8–4) is the **phasor representation** of the sinusoid $v(t)$. The phasor **V** is written as

$$\mathbf{V} = V_A e^{j\phi} = V_A\cos\phi + jV_A\sin\phi \qquad (8-5)$$

Note that **V** is a complex number determined by the amplitude and phase angle of the sinusoid. Figure 8–1 shows a graphical representation commonly called a phasor diagram.

The phasor is a complex number that can be written in either polar or rectangular form. An alternative way to write the polar form is to replace the exponential $e^{j\phi}$ by the shorthand notation $\angle\phi$. In subsequent discussions, we will often express phasors as $\mathbf{V} = V_A\angle\phi$, which is equivalent to the polar form in Eq. (8–5).

Two features of the phasor concept need emphasis:

1. Phasors are written in boldface type like **V** or $\mathbf{I}_1$ to distinguish them from signal waveforms such as $v(t)$ and i_1(t).
2. A phasor is determined by amplitude and phase angle and does not contain any information about the frequency of the sinusoid.

The first feature points out that signals can be described in different ways. Although the phasor **V** and waveform $v(t)$ are related concepts, they have different physical interpretations and our notation must clearly distinguish between them. The absence of frequency information in the phasors results from the fact that in the sinusoidal steady state, all currents and voltages are sinusoids with the same frequency. Carrying frequency information in the phasor would be redundant, since it is the same for all phasors in any given steady-state circuit problem.

In summary, given a sinusoidal signal $v(t) = V_A\cos(\omega t + \phi)$, the corresponding phasor representation is $\mathbf{V} = V_A e^{j\phi}$. Conversely, given the phasor $\mathbf{V} = V_A e^{j\phi}$, the corresponding sinusoid is found by multiplying the phasor by $e^{j\omega t}$ and reversing the steps in Eq. (8–4) as follows:

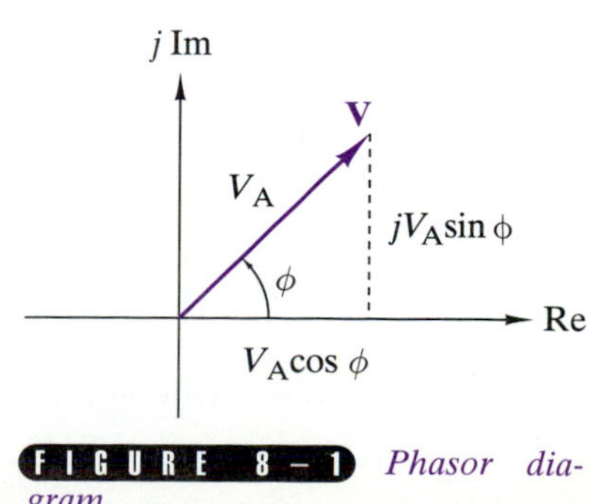

FIGURE 8–1 *Phasor diagram.*

$$\begin{aligned} v(t) &= \text{Re}\{\mathbf{V}e^{j\omega t}\} = \text{Re}\{(V_A e^{j\phi})e^{j\omega t}\} \\ &= V_A \text{Re}\{e^{j(\omega t+\phi)}\} = V_A \text{Re}\{\cos(\omega t + \phi) + j\sin(\omega t + \phi)\} \\ &= V_A \cos(\omega t + \phi) \end{aligned} \quad (8-6)$$

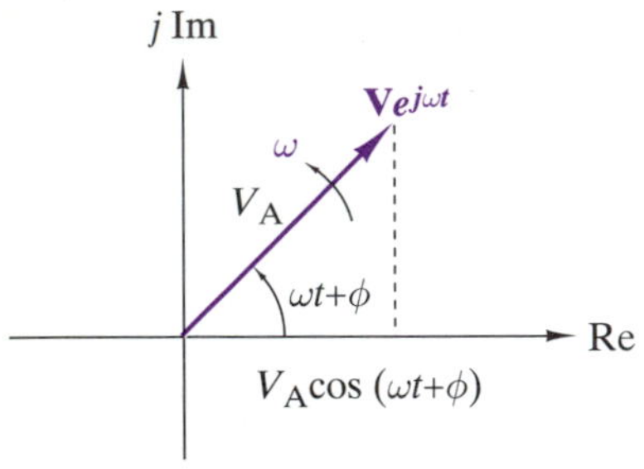

FIGURE 8–2 *Complex exponential* $\mathbf{V}e^{j\omega t}$.

The frequency ω in the complex exponential $\mathbf{V}e^{j\omega t}$ in Eq. (8–6) must be expressed or implied in a problem statement, since by definition it is not contained in the phasor. Figure 8–2 shows a geometric interpretation of the complex exponential $\mathbf{V}e^{j\omega t}$ as a vector in the complex plane of length V_A, which rotates counterclockwise with a constant angular velocity of ω. The real part operation projects the rotating vector onto the horizontal (real) axis and thereby generates $v(t) = V_A \cos(\omega t + \phi)$. The complex exponential is sometimes called a **rotating phasor**, and the phasor **V** is viewed as a snapshot of the situation at $t = 0$.

PROPERTIES OF PHASORS

Two important properties of phasors play key roles in circuit analysis. First, the **additive property** states that the phasor representing a sum of sinusoids of the same frequency is obtained by adding the phasor representations of the component sinusoids. To establish this property we write the expression

$$\begin{aligned} v(t) &= v_1(t) + v_2(t) + \ldots + v_N(t) \\ &= \text{Re}\{\mathbf{V}_1 e^{j\omega t}\} + \text{Re}\{\mathbf{V}_2 e^{j\omega t}\} + \ldots + \text{Re}\{\mathbf{V}_N e^{j\omega t}\} \end{aligned} \quad (8-7)$$

where $v_1(t)$, $v_2(t)$, . . . and $v_N(t)$ are sinusoids of the same frequency whose phasor representations are $\mathbf{V}_1$, $\mathbf{V}_2$, . . . and $\mathbf{V}_N$. The real part operation is additive, so the sum of real parts equals the real part of the sum. Consequently, Eq. (8–7) can be written in the form

$$\begin{aligned} v(t) &= \text{Re}\{\mathbf{V}_1 e^{j\omega t} + \mathbf{V}_2 e^{j\omega t} + \ldots + \mathbf{V}_N e^{j\omega t}\} \\ &= \text{Re}\{(\mathbf{V}_1 + \mathbf{V}_2 + \ldots + \mathbf{V}_N)e^{j\omega t}\} \end{aligned} \quad (8-8)$$

Comparing the last line in Eq. (8–8) with the definition of a phasor, we conclude that the phasor **V** representing $v(t)$ is

$$\mathbf{V} = \mathbf{V}_1 + \mathbf{V}_2 + \ldots + \mathbf{V}_N \quad (8-9)$$

The result in Eq. (8–9) applies only if the component sinusoids all have the same frequency so that $e^{j\omega t}$ can be factored out as shown in the last line in Eq. (8–8).

In Chapter 5 we found that the time derivative of a sinusoid is another sinusoid with the same frequency. Since they have the same frequency the signal and its derivative can be represented by phasors. The **derivative property** of phasors allows us easily to relate the phasor representing a sinusoid to the phasor representing its derivative.

Equation (8–6) relates a sinusoid function and its phasor representation as

$$v(t) = \text{Re}\{\mathbf{V}e^{j\omega t}\}$$

Differentiating this equation with respect time t yields

$$\begin{aligned}\frac{dv(t)}{dt} &= \frac{d}{dt}\text{Re}\{\mathbf{V}e^{j\omega t}\} = \text{Re}\left\{\mathbf{V}\frac{d}{dt}e^{j\omega t}\right\} \\ &= \text{Re}\{(j\omega\mathbf{V})e^{j\omega t}\}\end{aligned} \tag{8–10}$$

From the definition of a phasor, we see that the quantity ($j\omega\mathbf{V}$) on the right side of this equation is the phasor representation of the time derivative of the sinusoidal waveform. This phasor can be written in the form

$$\begin{aligned}j\omega\mathbf{V} &= (\omega e^{j90^\circ})(V_A e^{j\theta}) \\ &= \omega V_A e^{j(\theta + 90^\circ)}\end{aligned} \tag{8–11}$$

which points out that differentiating a sinusoid changes its amplitude by a multiplicative factor ω and shifts the phase angle by 90°.

In summary, the additive property states that adding phasors is equivalent to adding sinusoids of the same frequency. The derivative property states that multiplying a phasor by $j\omega$ is equivalent to differentiating the corresponding sinusoid. The following examples show applications of these two properties of phasors.

EXAMPLE 8–1

(a) Construct the phasors for the following signals:

$$v_1(t) = 10\cos(1000t - 45^\circ)$$

$$v_2(t) = 5\cos(1000t + 30^\circ)$$

(b) Use the additive property of phasors and the phasors found in (a) to find $v(t) = v_1(t) + v_2(t)$.

SOLUTION:

(a) The phasor representations of $v_1(t)$ and $v_2(t)$ are

$$\begin{aligned}\mathbf{V}_1 &= 10e^{-j45^\circ} = 10\cos(-45^\circ) + j10\sin(-45^\circ) \\ &= 7.07 - j7.07\end{aligned}$$

$$\begin{aligned}\mathbf{V}_2 &= 5\,e^{+j30^\circ} = 5\cos(30^\circ) + j5\sin(30^\circ) \\ &= 4.33 + j2.5\end{aligned}$$

(b) The two sinusoids have the same frequency so the additive property of phasors can be used to obtain their sum:

$$\mathbf{V} = \mathbf{V}_1 + \mathbf{V}_2 = 11.4 - j4.57 = 12.3e^{-j21.8^\circ}$$

The waveform corresponding to this phasor sum is

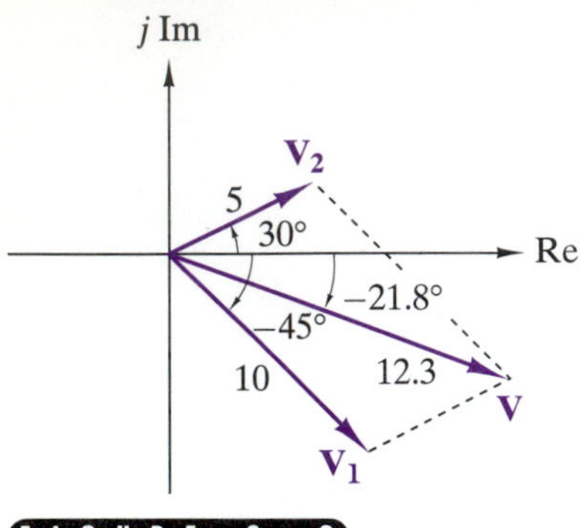

FIGURE 8–3

$$v(t) = \text{Re}\{(12.3e^{-j21.8°})e^{j1000t}\}$$
$$= 12.3\cos(1000t - 21.8°)$$

The phasor diagram in Figure 8–3 shows that summing sinusoids can be viewed geometrically in terms of phasors. ■

EXAMPLE 8–2

(a) Construct the phasors representing the following signals:

$$i_A(t) = 5\cos(377t + 50°)$$
$$i_B(t) = 5\cos(377t + 170°)$$
$$i_C(t) = 5\cos(377t - 70°)$$

(b) Use the additive property of phasors and the phasors found in (a) to find the sum of these waveforms.

SOLUTION:

(a) The phasor representation of the three sinusoidal currents are

$$\mathbf{I}_A = 5e^{j50°} = 5\cos(50°) + j5\sin(50°) = 3.21 + j3.83$$
$$\mathbf{I}_B = 5e^{j170°} = 5\cos(170°) + j5\sin(170°) = -4.92 + j0.87$$
$$\mathbf{I}_C = 5e^{-j70} = 5\cos(-70°) + j5\sin(-70°) = 1.71 - j4.70$$

(b) The currents have the same frequency, so the additive property of phasors applies. The phasor representing the sum of these currents is

$$\mathbf{I}_A + \mathbf{I}_B + \mathbf{I}_C = (3.21 - 4.92 + 1.71) + j(3.83 + 0.87 - 4.70)$$
$$= 0 + j0$$

It is not obvious by examining the waveforms that these three currents add to zero. However, the phasor diagram in Figure 8–4 makes this fact clear, since the sum of any two phasors is equal and opposite to the third. Phasors of this type occur in balanced three-phase power systems, which we study in Chapter 14. The balanced condition occurs when three equal-amplitude phasors are displaced in phase by exactly 120°. ■

FIGURE 8–4

EXAMPLE 8–3

Use the derivative property of phasors to find the time derivative of $v(t) = 15\cos(200t - 30°)$.

SOLUTION:

The phasor for the sinusoid is $\mathbf{V} = 15\angle-30°$. According to the derivative property, the phasor representing the dv/dt is found by multiplying $\mathbf{V}$ by $j\omega$.

$$(j200) \times (15\angle-30°) = (200e^{j90°}) \times (15e^{-j30°}) = 3000e^{j60°}$$

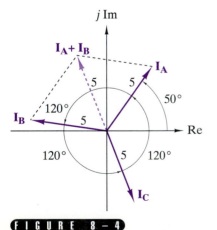

The sinusoid corresponding to the phasor $j\omega\mathbf{V}$ is

$$\frac{dv(t)}{dt} = \text{Re}\{(3000e^{j60^\circ})e^{j200t}\} = 3000\ \text{Re}\{e^{j(200t+60^\circ)}\}$$

$$= 3000 \cos(200t + 60^\circ)$$

Finding the derivative of a sinusoid is easily carried out in phasor form, since it only involves manipulating complex numbers. ■

EXAMPLE 8–4

Use phasors to find the forced response of a first-order *RC* circuit with an input $v_T = V_A \cos \omega t$.

SOLUTION:

In Chapter 7 we found that the forced response $v_F(t)$ must satisfy the differential equation

$$R_T C\frac{dv_F}{dt} + v_F = V_A \cos \omega t$$

In Chapter 7 the forced response is found by substituting a trial solution $v_F = a \cos \omega t + b \sin \omega t$ into this differential equation and then solving for the unknown Fourier coefficients a and b. The forced response can also be written in phasor form as $v_F = \text{Re}\{\mathbf{V}_F e^{j\omega t}\}$, where $\mathbf{V}_F$ is a phasor whose amplitude and phase angle are unknown. Substituting the phasor trial solution into the differential equation yields

$$(R_T C) \times \text{Re}\{j\omega\mathbf{V}_F e^{j\omega t}\} + \text{Re}\{\mathbf{V}_F e^{j\omega t}\} = \text{Re}\{V_A e^{j\omega t}\}$$

where we use the derivative property to get the phasor for dv_F/dt. The unknown in this equation is the phasor $\mathbf{V}_F$. To solve for $\mathbf{V}_F$, we move the real constant $R_T C$ inside the real part operation. Likewise, the real part operation is additive, so the sum of real parts equals the real part of the sum. Applying these observations reduces the left side of this equation to

$$\text{Re}\{(j\omega R_T C + 1)\mathbf{V}_F e^{j\omega t}\} = \text{Re}\{V_A e^{j\omega t}\}$$

The only way this equality can hold is for the quantities multiplying $e^{j\omega t}$ on each side of this equation to be equal. Hence,

$$(j\omega R_T C + 1)\mathbf{V}_F = V_A$$

Solving for the unknown phasor yields

$$\mathbf{V}_F = \frac{V_A}{j\omega R_T C + 1}$$

$$= \frac{V_A e^{j\theta}}{\sqrt{1 + (\omega R_T C)^2}}$$

where $\theta = -\tan^{-1}(\omega R_T C)$. Given the amplitude and phase of the phasor forced response, we can now obtain the forced response as

$$v_F(t) = \text{Re}\{\mathbf{V}_F e^{j\omega t}\} = \text{Re}\left\{\frac{V_A e^{j(\omega t+\theta)}}{\sqrt{1+(\omega R_T C)^2}}\right\}$$

$$= \frac{V_A}{\sqrt{1+(\omega R_T C)^2}}\cos(\omega t + \theta)$$

This solution agrees with the result given in Eq. (7–27) of Sect. 7–4. To see the advantages of using phasors, compare the classical methodology leading to Eq. (7–27) to the phasor approach used here. ■

Exercise 8–1

Convert the following sinusoids to phasors in polar and rectangular form:

(a) $v(t) = 20 \cos(150t - 60°)$ V
(b) $v(t) = 10 \cos(1000t + 180°)$ V
(c) $i(t) = -4 \cos 3t + 3 \cos(3t - 90°)$ A

Answers:

(a) $\mathbf{V} = 20\angle -60° = 10 - j17.3$ V
(b) $\mathbf{V} = 10\angle 180° = -10 + j0$ V
(c) $\mathbf{I} = 5\angle -143° = -4 - j3$ A

Exercise 8–2

Convert the following phasors to sinusoids:

(a) $\mathbf{V} = 169\angle -45°$ V at $f = 60$ Hz
(b) $\mathbf{V} = 10\angle 90° + 66 - j10$ V at $\omega = 10$ krad/s
(c) $\mathbf{I} = 15 + j5 + 10\angle 180°$ mA at $\omega = 1000$ rad/s

Answers:

(a) $v(t) = 169 \cos(377t - 45°)$ V
(b) $v(t) = 66 \cos 10^4 t$ V
(c) $i(t) = 7.07 \cos(1000t + 45°)$ mA

Exercise 8–3

Express the phasors for $V_A \cos \omega t$, $V_A \sin \omega t$, $-V_A \cos \omega t$, and $-V_A \sin \omega t$ in rectangular form. *Hint:* Use the identity $\sin \theta = \cos(\theta - 90°)$.

Answer:

$$V_A + j0,\ 0 - jV_A,\ -V_A + j0,\ 0 + jV_A.$$

Exercise 8–4

Express the phasors for the time derivatives of $V_A \cos \omega t$, $V_A \sin \omega t$, $-V_A \cos \omega t$, and $-V_A \sin \omega t$ in rectangular form. *Hint:* Use the results from Exercise 8–3.

Answers:

$$0 + j\omega V_A,\ \omega V_A + j0,\ 0 - j\omega V_A,\ -\omega V_A + j0.$$

8–2 PHASOR CIRCUIT ANALYSIS

Phasor circuit analysis is a method of finding sinusoidal steady-state responses directly from the circuit without using differential equations. How do we perform phasor circuit analysis? At several points in our study we have seen that circuit analysis is based on two kinds of constraints: (1) connection constraints (Kirchhoff's laws), (2) device constraints (element equations). To analyze phasor circuits, we must see how these constraints are expressed in phasor form.

CONNECTION CONSTRAINTS IN PHASOR FORM

The sinusoidal steady-state condition is reached after the circuit's natural response decays to zero. In the steady state all of the voltages and currents are sinusoids with the same frequency as the driving force. Under these conditions, the application of KVL around a loop could take the form

$$V_1 \cos(\omega t + \phi_1) + V_2 \cos(\omega t + \phi_2) \ldots + V_N \cos(\omega t + \phi_N) = 0$$

These sinusiods have the same frequency but have different amplitudes and phase angles. The additive property of phasors discussed in the preceding section shows that there is a one-to-one correspondence between waveform sums and phasor sums. Therefore, if the sum of the waveforms is zero, then the corresponding phasors must also sum to zero.

$$\mathbf{V}_1 + \mathbf{V}_2 \ldots + \mathbf{V}_N = 0$$

Clearly the same result applies to phasor currents and KCL. In other words, we can state Kirchhoff's laws in phasor form as follows:

KVL: The algebraic sum of phasor voltages around a loop is zero.

KCL: The algebraic sum of phasor currents at a node is zero.

DEVICE CONSTRAINTS IN PHASOR FORM

Turning now to the device constraints, we note that the i–v characteristics of the three passive elements are

$$\begin{aligned} \text{Resistor: } v_R(t) &= Ri_R(t) \\ \text{Inductor: } v_L(t) &= L\frac{di_L(t)}{dt} \\ \text{Capacitor: } i_C(t) &= C\frac{dv_C(t)}{dt} \end{aligned} \tag{8-12}$$

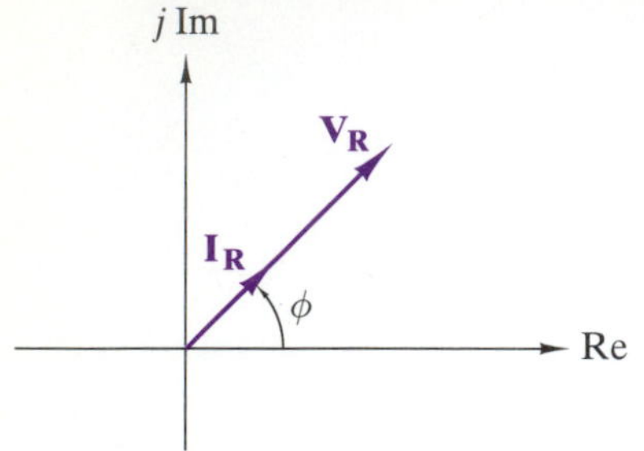

FIGURE 8–5 *Phasor i–v characteristics of the resistor.*

In the sinusoidal steady state, all of these currents and voltages are sinusoids. Given that the signals are sinusoid, how do these *i–v* relationships constrain the corresponding phasors?

In the sinusoidal steady state, the voltage and current of the resistor can be written in terms of phasors as $v_R(t) = \text{Re}\{\mathbf{V}_R e^{j\omega t}\}$ and $i_R(t) = \text{Re}\{\mathbf{I}_R e^{j\omega t}\}$. Consequently, the resistor *i–v* relationship in Eq. (8–12) can be expressed in terms of phasors as follows:

$$\text{Re}\{\mathbf{V}_R e^{j\omega t}\} = R \times \text{Re}\{\mathbf{I}_R e^{j\omega t}\}$$

Since R is a real constant, moving it inside the real part operation on the right side of this equation does not change things:

$$\text{Re}\{\mathbf{V}_R e^{j\omega t}\} = \text{Re}\{R\mathbf{I}_R e^{j\omega t}\}$$

This relationship holds only if the phasor voltage and current for a resistor are related as

$$\mathbf{V}_R = R\mathbf{I}_R \qquad (8–13)$$

To explore this relationship, we assume that the current through a resistor is $i_R(t) = I_A \cos(\omega t + \phi)$. Then the phasor current is $\mathbf{I}_R = I_A e^{j\phi}$, and according to Eq. (8–13), the phasor voltage across the resistor is

$$\mathbf{V}_R = RI_A e^{j\phi}$$

This result shows that the voltage has the same phase angle (ϕ) as the current. Phasors with the same phase angle are said to be **in phase**; otherwise they are said to be **out of phase**. Figure 8–5 shows the phasor diagram of the resistor current and voltage. Two scale factors are needed to construct a phasor diagram showing both voltage and current, since the two phasors do not have the same dimensions.

In the sinusoidal steady state, the voltage and phasor current for the inductor can be written in terms of phasors as $v_L(t) = \text{Re}\{\mathbf{V}_L e^{j\omega t}\}$ and $i_L(t) = \text{Re}\{\mathbf{I}_L e^{j\omega t}\}$. Using the derivative property of phasors, the inductor *i–v* relationship in Eq. (8–12) can be expressed as follows:

$$\begin{aligned}\text{Re}\{\mathbf{V}_L e^{j\omega t}\} &= L \times \text{Re}\{j\omega\mathbf{I}_L e^{j\omega t}\} \\ &= \text{Re}\{j\omega\mathbf{I}_L e^{j\omega t}\}\end{aligned}$$

Since L is a real constant, moving it inside the real part operation does not change things. Written this way, we see that the phasor voltage and current for an inductor are related as

$$\mathbf{V}_L = j\omega L\mathbf{I}_L \qquad (8–14)$$

When the current is $i_L(t) = I_A \cos(\omega t + \phi)$ the corresponding phasor is $\mathbf{I}_L = I_A e^{j\phi}$ and the *i–v* constraint in Eq. (8–14) yields

$$\begin{aligned}\mathbf{V}_L = j\omega L\mathbf{I}_L &= (\omega L e^{j90°})(I_A e^{j\phi}) \\ &= \omega L I_A e^{j(\phi + 90°)}\end{aligned}$$

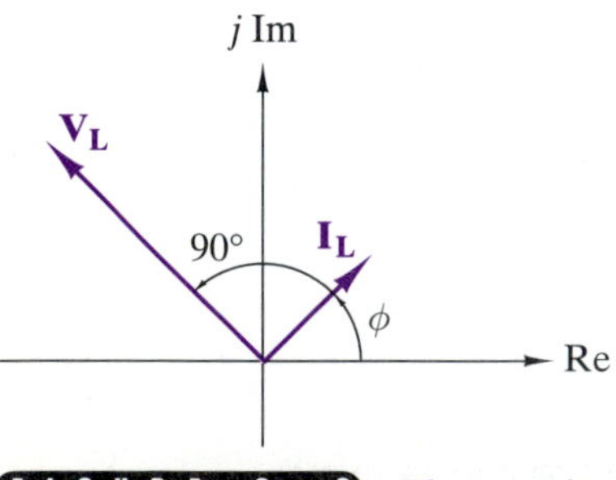

FIGURE 8–6 *Phasor i–v characteristics of the inductor.*

The resulting phasor diagram in Figure 8–6 shows that the inductor voltage and current are 90° out of phase. The voltage phasor is advanced by 90°

counterclockwise, which is in the direction of rotation of the complex exponential $e^{j\omega t}$. When the voltage phasor is advanced counterclockwise (that is, ahead of the rotating current phasor), we say that the voltage phasor *leads* the current phasor by 90° or, equivalently, the current *lags* the voltage by 90°.

Finally, the capacitor voltage and current in the sinusoidal steady state can be written in terms of phasors as $v_C(t) = \text{Re}\,\{\mathbf{V}_C e^{j\omega t}\}$ and $i_C(t) = \text{Re}\,\{\mathbf{I}_C e^{j\omega t}\}$. Using the derivative property of phasors, the i–v relationship of the capacitor in Eq. (8–12) becomes

$$\begin{aligned}\text{Re}\{\mathbf{I}_C e^{j\omega t}\} &= C \times \text{Re}\{j\omega \mathbf{V}_C e^{j\omega t}\} \\ &= \text{Re}\{j\omega C \mathbf{V}_C e^{j\omega t}\}\end{aligned}$$

Moving the real constant C inside the real part operation does not change the final result, so we conclude that the phasor voltage and current for a capacitor are related as

$$\mathbf{I}_C = j\omega C \mathbf{V}_C$$

Solving for $\mathbf{V}_C$ yields

$$\mathbf{V}_C = \frac{1}{j\omega C}\mathbf{I}_C \qquad (8\text{–}15)$$

When $i_C(t) = I_A \cos(\omega t + \phi)$, then according to Eq. (8–15), the phasor voltage across the capacitor is

$$\begin{aligned}\mathbf{V}_C &= \frac{1}{j\omega C}\mathbf{I}_C = \left(\frac{1}{\omega C}e^{-j90^\circ}\right)(I_A e^{j\phi}) \\ &= \frac{I_A}{\omega C}e^{j(\phi - 90^\circ)}\end{aligned}$$

The resulting phasor diagram in Figure 8–7 shows that voltage and current are 90° out of phase. In this case, the voltage phasor is retarded by 90° clockwise, which is in a direction opposite to rotation of the complex exponential $e^{j\omega t}$. When the voltage is retarded clockwise (that is, behind the rotating current phasor), we say that the voltage phasor *lags* the current phasor by 90° or, equivalently, the current *leads* the voltage by 90°.

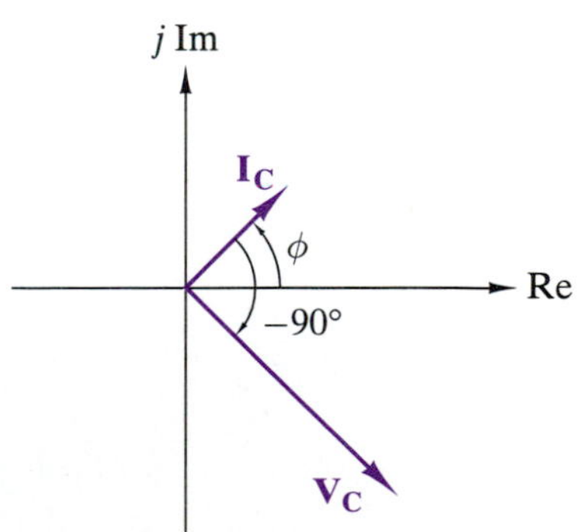

FIGURE 8–7 *Phasor i–v characteristics of the capacitor.*

THE IMPEDANCE CONCEPT

The **I–V** constraints Eqs. (8–13), (8–14), and (8–15) are all of the form

$$\mathbf{V} = Z\mathbf{I} \qquad (8\text{–}16)$$

where Z is called the impedance of the element. Equation (8–16) is analogous to Ohm's law in resistive circuits. **Impedance** is the proportionality constant relating phasor voltage and phasor current in linear, two-terminal elements. The impedances of the three passive elements are

$$\text{Resistor: } Z_R = R$$
$$\text{Inductor: } Z_L = j\omega L \qquad (8\text{–}17)$$
$$\text{Capacitor: } Z_C = \frac{1}{j\omega C} = -\frac{j}{\omega C}$$

Since impedance relates phasor voltage to phasor current, it is a complex quantity whose units are ohms. Although impedance can be a complex number, it is not a phasor. Phasors represent sinusoidal signals, while impedances characterize circuit elements in the sinusoidal steady state. Finally, it is important to remember that the generalized two-terminal device constraint in Eq. (8–16) assumes that the passive sign convention is used to assign the reference marks to the voltage and current.

EXAMPLE 8–5

The circuit in Figure 8–8 is operating in the sinusoidal steady state with $v_S(t) = 50 \cos(4000t - 20°)$ and $i_1(t) = 0.5 \cos(4000t)$. Find the impedance of the elements in the rectangular box.

FIGURE 8–8

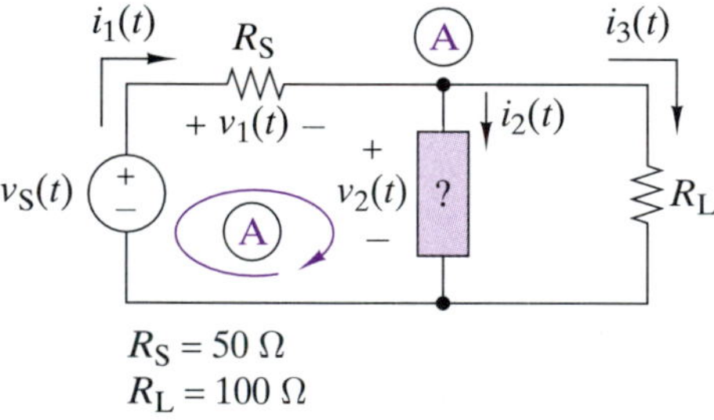

SOLUTION:

The purpose of this example is to show that we can apply basic circuit analysis tools to phasors. The phasors representing the given signals are $\mathbf{V}_S = 50\angle{-20°}$ V and $\mathbf{I}_1 = 0.5\angle 0°$ A. Using Ohm's law in phasor form, we find that $\mathbf{V}_1 = R_S \mathbf{I}_1 = 25\angle 0°$ V. Applying KVL around loop A yields $\mathbf{V}_S - \mathbf{V}_1 - \mathbf{V}_2 = 0$. Solving for the unknown voltage yields

$$\mathbf{V}_2 = \mathbf{V}_S - \mathbf{V}_1 = 50\angle{-20°} - 25\angle 0° = 27.8\angle{-37.9°} \text{ V}$$

This voltage appears across the load resistor R_L; hence $\mathbf{I}_3 = \mathbf{V}_2/R_L = 0.278\angle{-37.9°}$ A. Applying KCL at node A yields $\mathbf{I}_2 = \mathbf{I}_1 - \mathbf{I}_3 = 0.5\angle 0° - 0.278\angle{-37.9°} = 0.328\angle 31.4°$ A. Given the phasor voltage across and current through the unknown element, we find the impedance to be

$$Z = \frac{\mathbf{V}_2}{\mathbf{I}_2} = \frac{27.8\angle{-37.9°}}{0.328\angle 31.4} = 84.8\angle{-69.3°}$$
$$= 30.1 - j79.2 \ \Omega$$

Note that this complex number is not a phasor. It is the impedance of the unknown elements inside the rectangular box in Figure 8–8. ■

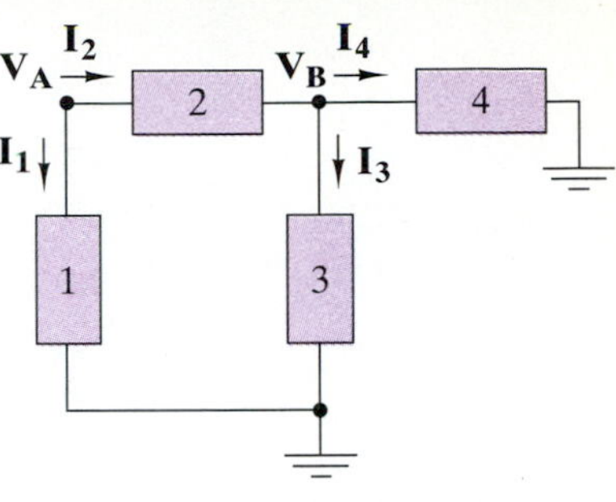

FIGURE 8–9

Exercise 8–5

The circuit in Figure 8–9 is operating in the sinusoidal steady state with $v_A(t) = 10 \cos \omega t$ V, $v_B(t) = 10 \sin \omega t$ V, $i_1 = \sqrt{2} \cos(\omega t + 135°)$ A, and $i_4 = \cos \omega t$ A. Use KCL and KVL to find the phasor voltage across and current through each element. Use the passive sign convention.

Answers:

$\mathbf{V}_1 = 10\angle 0°$ V, $\mathbf{V}_2 = 10 + j\,10$ V, $\mathbf{V}_3 = \mathbf{V}_4 = 10\angle{-90°}$ V, $\mathbf{I}_1 = -1 + j$ A, $\mathbf{I}_2 = 1 - j$ A,

$\mathbf{I}_3 = 1\angle{-90°}$ A, $\mathbf{I}_4 = 1 + j0$ A

Exercise 8–6

The current through a 12-mH inductor is $i_L(t) = 20 \cos(10^6 t)$ mA. Determine

(a) The impedance of the inductor
(b) The phasor voltage across the inductor
(c) The waveform of the voltage across the inductor.

Answers:
(a) $j12$ kΩ
(b) $240\angle 90°$ V
(c) $v_L = 240 \cos(10^6 t + 90°)$ V

Exercise 8–7

The current through a 20-pF capacitor is $i_C(t) = 0.3 \cos(10^6 t)$ mA.

(a) Find the impedance of the capacitor.
(b) Find the phasor voltage across the capacitor.
(c) Find the waveform of the voltage across the capacitor.

Answers:
(a) $-j50$ kΩ
(b) $15\angle{-90°}$ V
(c) $v_C = 15 \cos(10^6 t - 90°)$ V

8–3 BASIC CIRCUIT ANALYSIS WITH PHASORS

Functions of time like $v(t) = V_A \cos(\omega t + \phi_V)$ and $i(t) = I_A \cos(\omega t + \phi_I)$ are time-domain representations of sinusoidal signals. Producing the corresponding phasors can be thought of as a transformation that carries $v(t)$ and $i(t)$ into a complex-number domain where signals are represented as phasors **V** and **I**. We call this complex-number domain the **phasor domain**. When we analyze circuits in this phasor domain, we obtain sinusoidal steady-state responses in terms of phasors like **V** and **I**. Performing the inverse phasor transformation as $v(t) = \text{Re}\{\mathbf{V}e^{j\omega t}\}$ and $i(t) = \text{Re}\{\mathbf{I}e^{j\omega t}\}$ carries the responses back into the time domain. To perform ac circuit analysis in this way, we obviously need to develop methods of analyzing circuits in the phasor domain.

In the preceding section, we showed that KVL and KCL apply in the phasor domain and that the phasor element constraints all have the form $\mathbf{V} = Z\mathbf{I}$. These element and connection constraints have the same format as the underlying constraints for resistance circuit analysis as developed in Chapters 2, 3, and 4. Therefore, familiar algebraic circuit analysis tools, such as series and parallel equivalence, voltage and current division, proportionality and superposition, and Thévenin and Norton equivalent circuits, are applicable in the phasor domain. In other words, we do not need new analysis techniques to handle circuits in the phasor domain. The only difference is that circuit responses are phasors (complex numbers) rather than dc signals (real numbers).

We can think of phasor domain circuit analysis in terms of the flow diagram in Figure 8–10. The analysis begins in the time domain with a linear circuit operating in the sinusoidal steady state and involves three major steps:

STEP 1: The circuit is transformed into the phasor domain by representing the input and response sinusoids as phasors and the passive circuit elements by their impedances.

STEP 2: Standard algebraic circuit analysis techniques are applied to solve the phasor domain circuit for the desired unknown phasor responses.

STEP 3: The phasor responses are inverse transformed back into time-domain sinusoids to obtain the response waveforms.

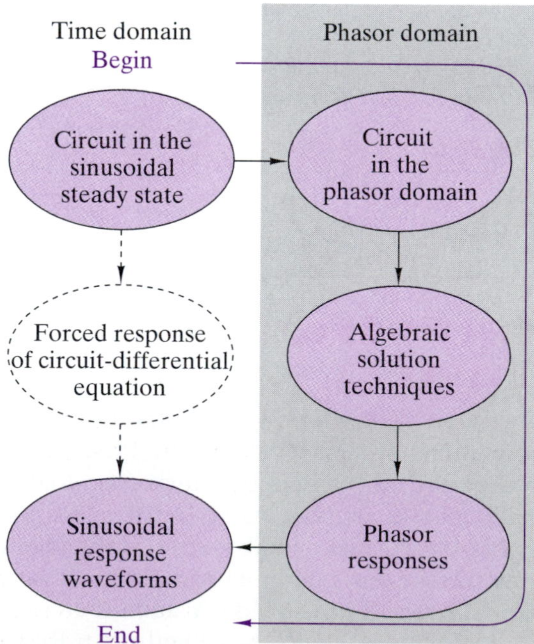

FIGURE 8–10 *Flow diagram for phasor circuit analysis.*

The third step assumes that the required end product is a time-domain waveform. However, a phasor is just another representation of a sinusoid. With some experience, we learn to think of the response as a phasor without converting it back into a time-domain waveform.

Figure 8–10 points out that there is another route to time-domain response using the classical differential equation method from Chapter 7. However, the phasor-domain method works directly with the circuit model and is far simpler. More important, phasor-domain analysis provides insights into ac circuit analysis that are essential to understanding much of the terminology and viewpoint of electrical engineering.

SERIES EQUIVALENCE AND VOLTAGE DIVISION

We begin the study of phasor-domain analysis with two basic analysis tools—series equivalence and voltage division. In Figure 8–11 the two-terminal elements are connected in series, so by KCL, the same phasor current **I** exists in impedances $Z_1, Z_2, \ldots Z_N$. Using KVL and the element constraints, the voltage across the series connection can be written as

$$\begin{aligned}\mathbf{V} &= \mathbf{V}_1 + \mathbf{V}_2 + \ldots + \mathbf{V}_N \\ &= Z_1\mathbf{I} + Z_2\mathbf{I} + \ldots + Z_N\mathbf{I} \\ &= (Z_1 + Z_2 + \ldots + Z_N)\mathbf{I}\end{aligned} \quad (8-18)$$

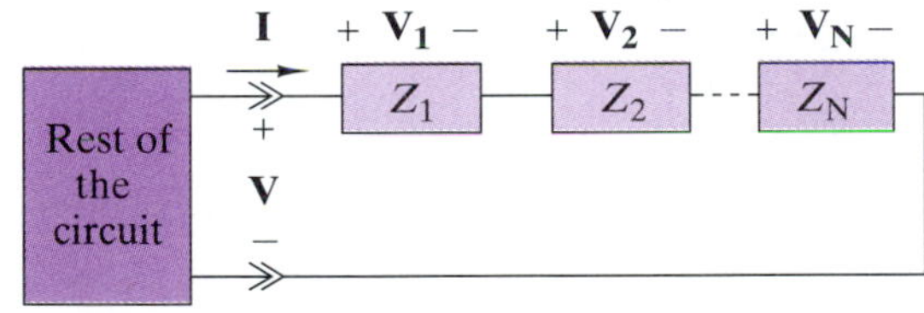

FIGURE 8–11 *A series connection of impedances.*

The last line in this equation points out that the phasor responses **V** and **I** do not change when the series connected elements are replaced by an equivalent impedance:

$$Z_{EQ} = Z_1 + Z_2 + \ldots + Z_N \quad (8-19)$$

In general, the equivalent impedance Z_{EQ} is a complex quantity of the form

$$Z_{EQ} = R + jX$$

where R is the real part and X is the imaginary part. The real part of Z is called **resistance** and the imaginary part (X, not jX) is called **reactance**. Both resistance and reactance are expressed in ohms (Ω), and both can be functions of frequency (ω). For passive circuits, resistance is always positive, while reactance X can be either positive or negative. A positive X is called an **inductive** reactance because the reactance of an inductor is ωL, which is always positive. A negative X is called a **capacitive** reactance because the reactance of a capacitor is $-1/\omega C$, which is always negative.

Combining Eqs. (8–18) and (8–19), we can write the phasor voltage across the kth element in the series connection as

$$\mathbf{V}_k = Z_k\mathbf{I}_k = \frac{Z_k}{Z_{EQ}}\mathbf{V} \tag{8–20}$$

Equation (8–20) is the phasor version of the voltage division principle. The phasor voltage across any element in a series connection is equal to the ratio of its impedance to the equivalent impedance of the connection times the total phasor voltage across the connection.

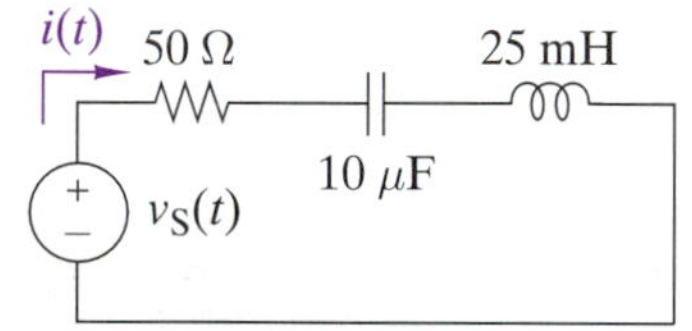

FIGURE 8–12

EXAMPLE 8–6

The circuit in Figure 8–12 is operating in the sinusoidal steady state with $v_S(t) = 35 \cos 1000t$ V.

(a) Transform the circuit into the phasor domain.
(b) Solve for the phasor current **I**.
(c) Solve for the phasor voltage across each element.
(d) Construct the waveforms corresponding to the phasors found in (b) and (c).

SOLUTION:

(a) The phasor representing the input source voltage is $\mathbf{V}_S = 35\angle 0°$. The impedances of the three passive elements are

$$Z_R = R = 50\ \Omega$$

$$Z_L = j\omega L = j1000 \times 25 \times 10^{-3} = j25\ \Omega$$

$$Z_C = \frac{1}{j\omega C} = \frac{1}{j1000 \times 10^{-5}} = -j100\ \Omega$$

Using these results, we obtain the phasor-domain circuit in Figure 8–13.

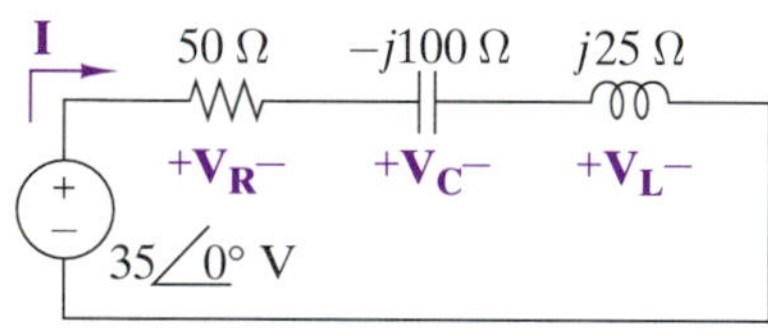

FIGURE 8–13

(b) The equivalent impedance of the series connection is

$$Z_{EQ} = 50 + j25 - j100 = 50 - j75 = 90.1\angle -56.3°\ \Omega$$

The current in the series circuit is

$$\mathbf{I} = \frac{\mathbf{V}_S}{Z_{EQ}} = \frac{35\angle 0°}{90.1\angle -56.3°} = 0.388\angle 56.3°\ \text{A}$$

(c) The current **I** exists in all three series elements, so the voltage across each passive element is

$$\mathbf{V}_R = Z_R\mathbf{I} = 50 \times 0.388\angle 56.3° = 19.4\angle 56.3°\ \text{V}$$

$$\mathbf{V}_L = Z_L\mathbf{I} = j25 \times 0.388\angle 56.3° = 9.70\angle 146.3°\ \text{V}$$

$$\mathbf{V}_C = Z_C\mathbf{I} = -j100 \times 0.388\angle 56.3° = 38.8\angle -33.7°\ \text{V}$$

(d) The sinusoidal steady-state waveforms corresponding to the phasors in (b) and (c) are

$$i(t) = \text{Re}\{0.388e^{j56.3°}e^{j1000t}\} = 0.388\cos(1000t + 56.3°) \text{ A}$$
$$v_R(t) = \text{Re}\{19.4e^{j56.3°}e^{j1000t}\} = 19.4\cos(1000t + 56.3°) \text{ V}$$
$$v_L(t) = \text{Re}\{9.70e^{j146.3°}e^{j1000t}\} = 9.70\cos(1000t + 146.3°) \text{ V}$$
$$v_C(t) = \text{Re}\{38.8e^{-j33.7°}e^{j1000t}\} = 38.8\cos(1000t - 33.7°) \text{ V}$$

■

D DESIGN EXAMPLE 8–7

AC Voltage Divider Design

Design the voltage divider in Figure 8–14 so that an input $v_S = 15\cos 2000t$ produces a steady-state output $v_O(t) = 2\sin 2000t$.

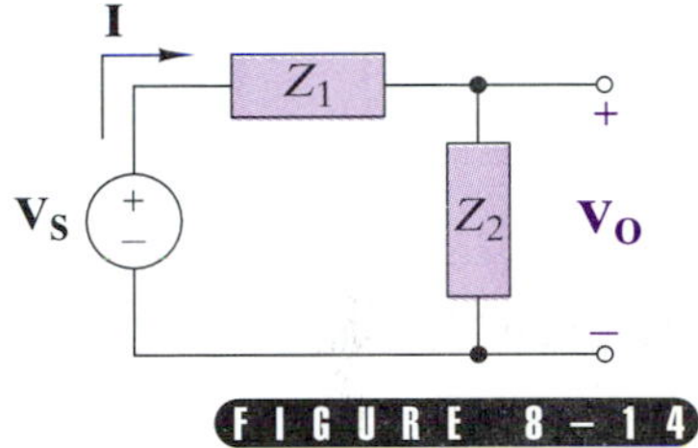

FIGURE 8–14

SOLUTION:
Using voltage division, we can relate the input and output phasor as follows:

$$\mathbf{V}_O = \frac{Z_2}{Z_1 + Z_2}\mathbf{V}_S$$

The phasor representation of the input voltage is $\mathbf{V}_S = 15\angle 0 = 15 + j0$. Using the identity $\cos(x - 90°) = \sin x$, we write the required output phasor as $\mathbf{V}_O = 2\angle -90° = 0 - j2$. The design problem is to select the impedances Z_1 and Z_2 so that

$$0 - j2 = \frac{Z_2}{Z_1 + Z_2}(15 + j0)$$

Solving this design constraint for Z_1 yields

$$Z_1 = \frac{15 + j2}{-j2}Z_2$$

Evidently, we can choose Z_2 and then solve for Z_1. In making this choice, we must keep some physical realizability conditions in mind. In general, an impedance has the form $Z = R + jX$. The reactance X can be either positive (an inductor) or negative (a capacitor), but the resistance R must be positive. With these constraints in mind, we select $Z_2 = -j1000$ (a capacitor) and solve for $Z_1 = 7500 + j1000$ (a resistor in series with an inductor). Figure 8–15 shows the resulting phasor circuit. To find the values of L and C, we note that the input is $v_S = 15\cos 2000t$ hence, the frequency is $\omega = 2000$. The inductive reactance $\omega L = 1000$ requires $L = 0.5$ H, while the capacitive reactance requires $-(\omega C)^{-1} = -1000$ or $C = 0.5$ μF. Other possible designs are obtained by selecting different values of Z_2. To be physically realizable, the selected value of Z_2 must produce $R \geq 0$ for Z_1 and Z_2. ■

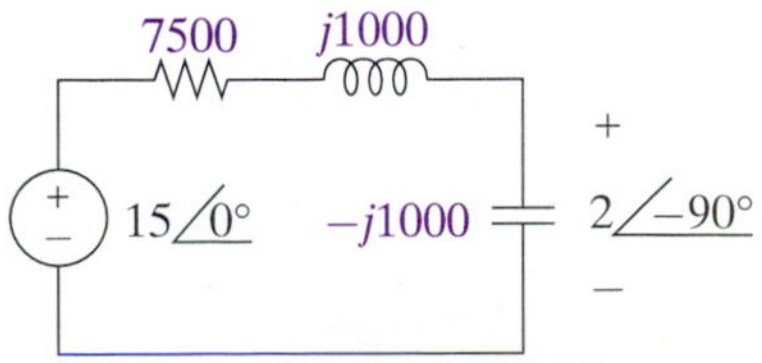

7500 $j1000$ + $15\angle 0°$ $-j1000$ $2\angle -90°$ –

FIGURE 8–15

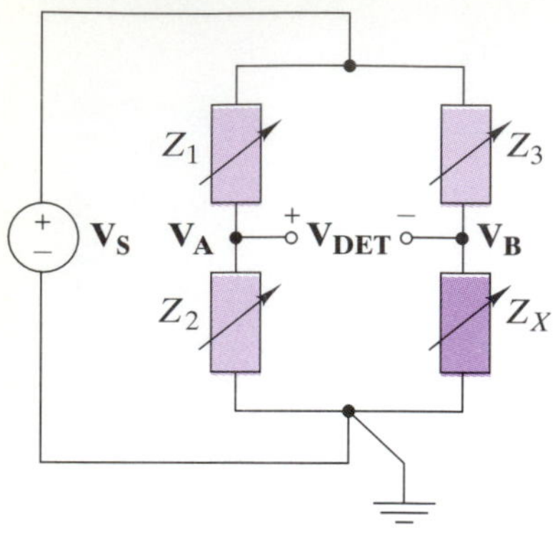

FIGURE 8–16
Impedance bridge.

APPLICATION NOTE:

EXAMPLE 8–8

The purpose of the impedance bridge in Figure 8–16 is to measure the unknown impedance Z_X by adjusting known impedances Z_1, Z_2, and Z_3 until the detector voltage $\mathbf{V}_{DET}$ is zero. The circuit consists of a sinusoidal source $\mathbf{V}_S$ driving two voltage dividers connected in parallel. Using the voltage division principle, we find that the detector voltage is

$$\mathbf{V}_{DET} = \mathbf{V}_A - \mathbf{V}_B = \frac{Z_2}{Z_1 + Z2}\mathbf{V}_S - \frac{Z_X}{Z_3 + Z_X}\mathbf{V}_S$$
$$= \left[\frac{Z_2Z_3 - Z_1Z_X}{(Z_1 + Z_2)(Z_3 + Z_X)}\right]\mathbf{V}_S$$

This equation shows that the detector voltage will be zero when $Z_2Z_3 = Z_1Z_X$. When the branch impedances are adjusted so that the detector voltage is zero, the unknown impedance can be written in terms of the known impedances as follows:

$$Z_X = R_X + jX_X = \frac{Z_2Z_3}{Z_1}$$

This equation is called the bridge balance condition. Since the equality involves complex quantities, at least two of the known impedances must be adjustable to balance both the resistance R_X and the reactance X_X of the unknown impedance. In practice, bridges are designed assuming that the sign of the unknown reactance is known. Bridges that measure only positive reactance are called inductance bridges, while those that measure only negative reactance are called capacitance bridges.

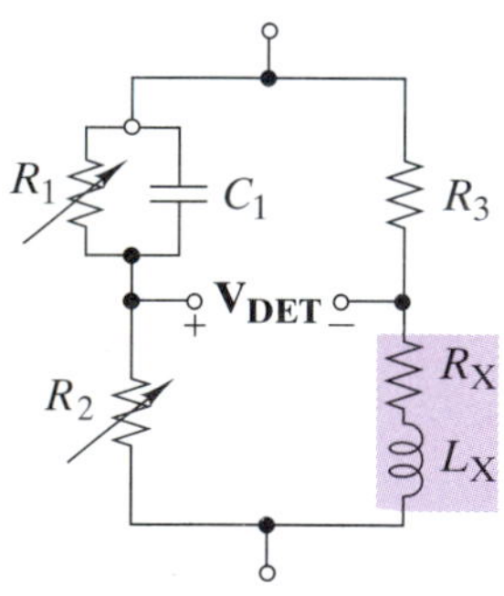

FIGURE 8–17
Maxwell bridge.

The Maxwell inductance bridge in Figure 8–17 is used to measure the resistance R_X and inductance L_X of an inductive device by alternately adjusting resistances R_1 and R_2 to balance the bridge circuit. The impedances of the legs of this bridge are

$$Z_1 = \frac{1}{j\omega C_1 + \dfrac{1}{R_1}}$$
$$Z_2 = R_2 \quad Z_3 = R_3$$

For the Maxwell bridge, the balance condition $Z_X = Z_2Z_3/Z_1$ yields

$$R_X + j\omega L_X = \frac{R_2R_3}{R_1} + j\omega C_1R_2R_3$$

Equating the real and imaginary parts on each side of this equation yields the parameters of the unknown impedance in terms of the known impedances:

$$R_X = \frac{R_2R_3}{R_1} \quad \text{and} \quad L_X = R_2R_3C_1$$

Note that adjusting R_1 only affects R_X. The Maxwell bridge measures inductance by balancing the positive reactance of an unknown inductive device with a calibrated fraction of negative reactance of the known capacitor C_1. If the reactance of the unknown device is actually capacitive (negative), then the Maxwell bridge cannot be balanced.

PARALLEL EQUIVALENCE AND CURRENT DIVISION

In Figure 8–18 the two-terminal elements are connected in parallel, so the same phasor voltage **V** appears across the impedances $Z_1, Z_2, \ldots Z_N$. Using the phasor element constraints, the current through each impedance is $\mathbf{I}_k = \mathbf{V}/Z_k$. Next, using KCL, the total current entering the parallel connection is

$$\begin{aligned}\mathbf{I} &= \mathbf{I}_1 + \mathbf{I}_2 + \ldots + \mathbf{I}_N \\ &= \frac{\mathbf{V}}{Z_1} + \frac{\mathbf{V}}{Z_2} + \ldots + \frac{\mathbf{V}}{Z_N} \\ &= \left(\frac{1}{Z_1} + \frac{1}{Z_2} + \ldots + \frac{1}{Z_N}\right)\mathbf{V}\end{aligned} \tag{8-21}$$

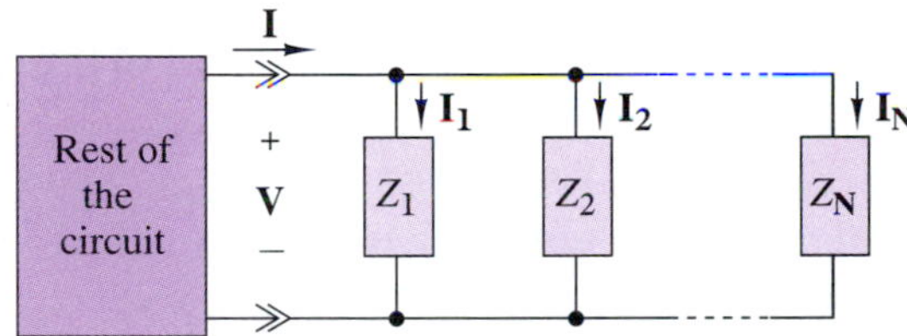

FIGURE 8–18 *Parallel connection of impedances.*

The same phasor responses **V** and **I** exist when the parallel connected elements are replaced by an equivalent impedance.

$$\frac{1}{Z_{EQ}} = \frac{\mathbf{I}}{\mathbf{V}} = \frac{1}{Z_1} + \frac{1}{Z_2} + \ldots + \frac{1}{Z_N} \tag{8-22}$$

These results can also be written in terms of admittance Y, which is defined as the reciprocal of impedance:

$$Y = \frac{1}{Z} = G + jB$$

The real part of Y is called **conductance** and the imaginary part B is called **susceptance** both of which are expressed in units of siemens (S).

Using admittances to rewrite Eq. (8–21) yields

$$\begin{aligned}\mathbf{I} &= \mathbf{I}_1 + \mathbf{I}_2 + \ldots + \mathbf{I}_N \\ &= Y_1\mathbf{V} + Y_2\mathbf{V} + \ldots + Y_N\mathbf{V} \\ &= (Y_1 + Y_2 + \ldots + Y_N)\mathbf{V}\end{aligned} \tag{8-23}$$

Hence, the equivalent admittance of the parallel connection is

$$Y_{EQ} = \frac{\mathbf{I}}{\mathbf{V}} = Y_1 + Y_2 + \ldots + Y_N \qquad (8-24)$$

Combining Eqs. (8–23) and (8–24), we find that the phasor current through the kth element in the parallel connection is

$$\mathbf{I}_k = Y_k\mathbf{V}_k = \frac{Y_k}{Y_{EQ}}\mathbf{I} \qquad (8-25)$$

Equation (8–25) is the phasor version of the current division principle. The phasor current through any element in a parallel connection is equal to the ratio of its admittance to the equivalent admittance of the connection times the total phasor current entering the connection.

EXAMPLE 8–9

The circuit in Figure 8–19 is operating in the sinusoidal steady state with $i_S(t) = 50 \cos 2000t$ mA.

(a) Transform the circuit into the phasor domain.
(b) Solve for the phasor voltage **V**.
(c) Solve for the phasor current through each element.
(d) Construct the waveforms corresponding to the phasors found in (b) and (c).

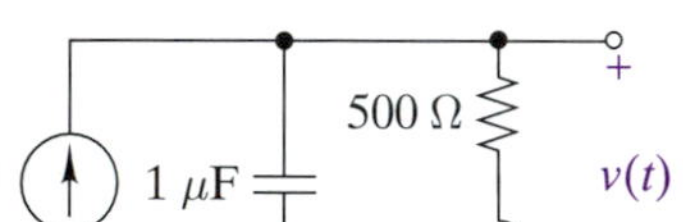

FIGURE 8–19

SOLUTION:

(a) The phasor representing the input source current is $\mathbf{I}_S = 0.05\angle 0°$ A. The impedances of the three passive elements are

$$Z_R = R = 500\ \Omega$$

$$Z_L = j\omega L = j2000 \times 0.5 = j1000\ \Omega$$

$$Z_C = \frac{1}{j\omega C} = \frac{1}{j2000 \times 10^{-6}} = -j500\ \Omega$$

Using these results, we obtain the phasor-domain circuit in Figure 8–20.

FIGURE 8–20

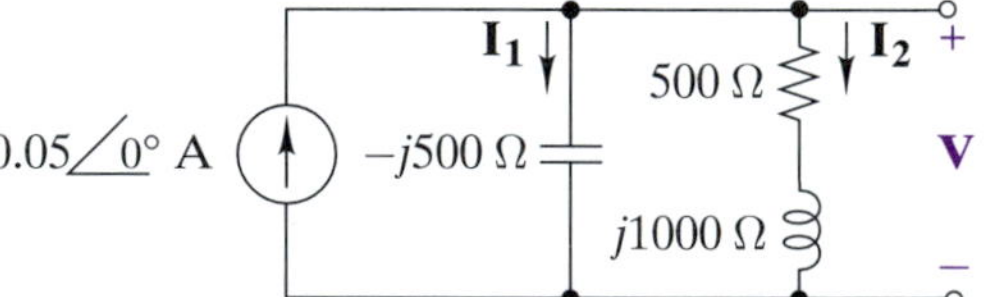

(b) The admittances of the two parallel branches are

$$Y_1 = \frac{1}{-j500} = j2 \times 10^{-3}\ \text{S}$$

$$Y_2 = \frac{1}{500 + j1000} = 4 \times 10^{-4} - j8 \times 10^{-4}\ \text{S}$$

The equivalent admittance of the parallel connection is

$$Y_{EQ} = Y_1 + Y_2 = 4 \times 10^{-4} + j12 \times 10^{-4}$$
$$= 12.6 \times 10^{-4}\angle 71.6° \text{ S}$$

and the voltage across the parallel circuit is

$$\mathbf{V} = \frac{\mathbf{I}_S}{Y_{EQ}} = \frac{0.05\angle 0°}{12.6 \times 10^{-4}\angle 71.6°}$$
$$= 39.7\angle -71.6° \text{ V}$$

(c) The current through each parallel branch is

$$\mathbf{I}_1 = Y_1\mathbf{V} = j2 \times 10^{-3} \times 39.7\angle -71.6° = 79.4\angle 18.4° \text{ mA}$$
$$\mathbf{I}_2 = Y_2\mathbf{V} = (4 \times 10^{-4} - j8 \times 10^{-4}) \times 39.7\angle -71.6°$$
$$= 35.5\angle -135° \text{ mA}$$

(d) The sinusoidal steady-state waveforms corresponding to the phasors in (b) and (c) are

$$v(t) = \text{Re}\{39.7e^{-j71.6°}e^{j2000t}\} = 39.7\cos(2000t - 71.6°) \text{ V}$$
$$i_1(t) = \text{Re}\{79.4e^{j18.4°}e^{j2000t}\} = 79.4\cos(2000t + 18.4°) \text{ mA}$$
$$i_2(t) = \text{Re}\{35.5e^{-j135°}e^{j2000t}\} = 35.5\cos(2000t - 135°) \text{ mA}$$ ■

EXAMPLE 8–10

Find the steady-state currents $i(t)$, $i_C(t)$, and $i_R(t)$ in the circuit of Figure 8–21 for $v_S = 100\cos 2000t$ V, $L = 250$ mH, $C = 0.5\ \mu$F, and $R = 3$ kΩ.

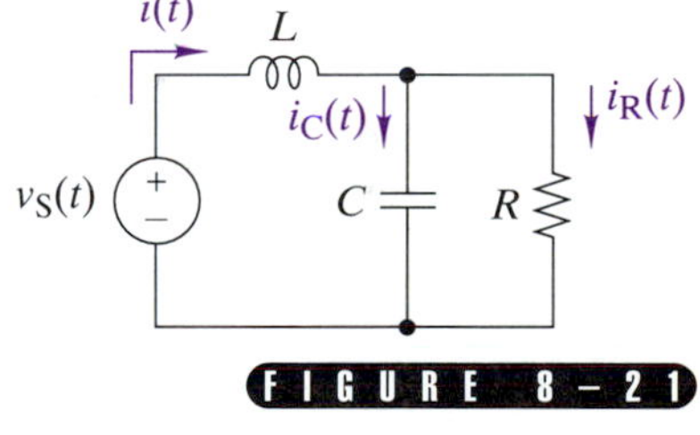

FIGURE 8–21

SOLUTION:

The phasor representation of the input voltage is $100\angle 0°$. The impedances of the passive elements are

$$Z_L = j500\ \Omega \quad Z_C = -j1000\ \Omega \quad Z_R = 3000\ \Omega$$

Figure 8–22(a) shows the phasor-domain circuit.

To solve for the required phasor responses, we reduce the circuit using a combination of series and parallel equivalence. Using parallel equivalence, we find that the capacitor and resistor can be replaced by an equivalent impedance

$$Z_{EQ1} = \frac{1}{Y_{EQ1}} = \frac{1}{\frac{1}{-j1000} + \frac{1}{3000}}$$
$$= 300 - j900\ \Omega$$

The resulting circuit reduction is shown in Figure 8–22(b). The equivalent impedance Z_{EQ1} is connected in series with the impedance $Z_L = j500$. This series combination can be replaced by an equivalent impedance

FIGURE 8–22

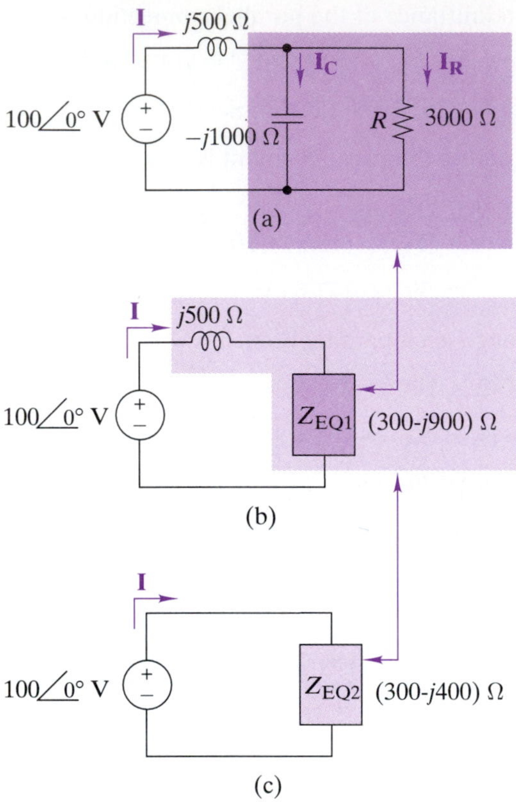

$$Z_{EQ2} = j500 + Z_{EQ1} = 300 - j400\ \Omega$$

This step reduces the circuit to the equivalent input impedance shown in Figure 8–22(c). The phasor input current in Figure 8–22(c) is

$$\mathbf{I} = \frac{100\angle 0^\circ}{Z_{EQ2}} = \frac{100\angle 0^\circ}{300 - j400} = 0.12 + j0.16 = 0.2\angle 53.1^\circ\ \text{A}$$

Given the phasor current **I**, we use current division to find $\mathbf{I}_C$:

$$\mathbf{I}_C = \frac{Y_C}{Y_C + Y_R}\mathbf{I} = \frac{\dfrac{1}{-j1000}}{\dfrac{1}{-j1000} + \dfrac{1}{3000}} 0.2\angle 53.1^\circ$$

$$= 0.06 + j0.18 = 0.19\angle 71.6^\circ\ \text{A}$$

By KCL, $\mathbf{I} = \mathbf{I}_C + \mathbf{I}_R$, so the remaining unknown current is

$$\mathbf{I}_R = \mathbf{I} - \mathbf{I}_C = 0.06 - j0.02 = 0.0632\angle -18.4^\circ\ \text{A}$$

The waveforms corresponding to the phasor currents are

$$i(t) = \text{Re}\{\mathbf{I}e^{j2000t}\} = 0.2\cos(2000t + 53.1°)\text{ A}$$
$$i_C(t) = \text{Re}\{\mathbf{I}_C e^{j2000t}\} = 0.19\cos(2000t + 71.6°)\text{ A}$$
$$i_R(t) = \text{Re}\{\mathbf{I}_R e^{j2000t}\} = 0.0632\cos(2000t - 18.4°)\text{ A}$$

APPLICATION NOTE:

EXAMPLE 8–11

In general, the equivalent impedance seen at any pair of terminals can be written in rectangular form as

$$Z_{EQ} = R_{EQ} + jX_{EQ}$$

For passive circuits, $R_{EQ} \geq 0$, but the reactance X_{EQ} can be either positive (inductive) or negative (capacitive). When inductance and capacitance are both present, their reactances may exactly cancel at certain frequencies. When $X_{EQ} = 0$, the impedance is purely resistive and the circuit is said to be in **resonance**. The frequency at which this occurs is called a **resonant frequency**, denoted by ω_0.

For example, suppose we want to find the resonant frequency of the circuit in Figure 8–23. We first find the equivalent impedance of the parallel resistor and capacitor:

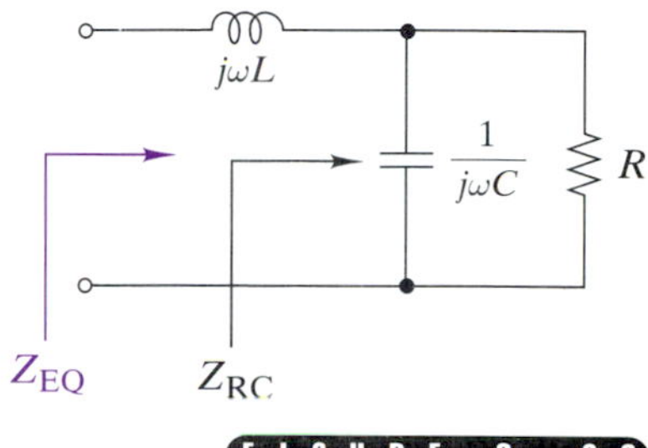

FIGURE 8–23

$$Z_{RC} = \frac{1}{Y_R + Y_C} = \frac{1}{\frac{1}{R} + j\omega C} = \frac{R}{1 + j\omega RC}$$

This expression can be put into rectangular form by multiplying and dividing by the conjugate of the denominator:

$$Z_{RC} = \frac{R}{1 + j\omega RC}\frac{1 - j\omega RC}{1 - j\omega RC} = \frac{R}{1 + (\omega RC)^2} - j\frac{\omega R^2 C}{1 + (\omega RC)^2}$$

The impedance Z_{RC} is connected in series with the inductor. Therefore, the overall equivalent impedance Z_{EQ} is

$$\begin{aligned} Z_{EQ} &= Z_L + Z_{RC} \\ &= \frac{R}{1 + (\omega RC)^2} + j\left[\omega L - \frac{\omega R^2 C}{1 + (\omega RC)^2}\right] \\ &= \qquad R_{EQ} \qquad\qquad + jX_{EQ} \end{aligned}$$

Note that the equivalent resistance R_{EQ} is positive for all ω. However, the equivalent reactance X_{EQ} can be positive or negative. The resonant frequency is found by setting the reactance to zero

$$X_{EQ}(\omega_0) = \omega_0 L - \frac{\omega_0 R^2 C}{1 + (\omega_0 RC)^2} = 0$$

and solving for the resonant frequency:

$$\omega_0 = \sqrt{\frac{1}{LC} - \frac{1}{(RC)^2}}$$

Note the reactance X_{EQ} is inductive (positive) when $\omega > \omega_0$ and capacitive (negative) with $\omega < \omega_0$.

Exercise 8–8

A 1-μF capacitor and 1-kΩ resistor are connected in parallel, and this parallel combination is connected in series with a 200-mH inductor.

(a) Find the equivalent impedance of the connection at $\omega = 1$ krad/s.
(b) Repeat (a) with $\omega = 4$ krad/s.

Answers:
(a) $500 - j300\ \Omega$
(b) $58.8 + j565\ \Omega$

Exercise 8–9

A voltage source $v_S = 15 \cos 2000t$ is applied across the circuit in Exercise 8–8.

(a) Find the steady-state current through the inductor.
(b) Find the steady-state voltage across the 1-kΩ resistor.

Answers:
(a) $75 \cos 2000t$ mA
(b) $33.5 \cos(2000t - 63.4°)$ V

Exercise 8–10

Two branches with impedances $500 - j125\ \Omega$ and $100 + j400\ \Omega$ are connected in parallel. The frequency is 10 krad/s.

(a) Find the equivalent impedance of the parallel combination.
(b) What element should be connected in series with the parallel combination to make the total reactance zero?

Answers:
(a) $322\angle 37.3°\ \Omega$
(b) A capacitor with $C = 513$ nF

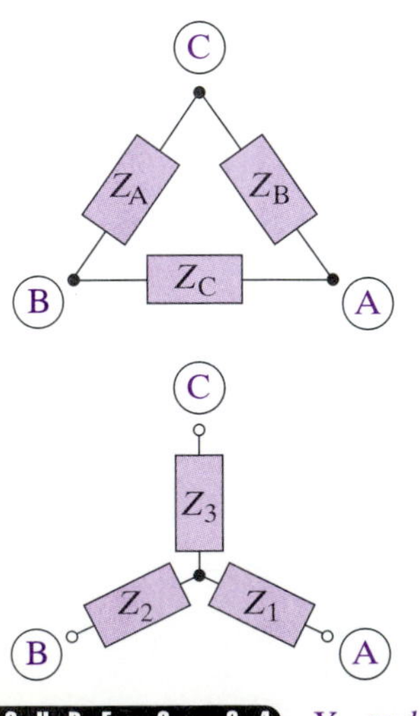

FIGURE 8–24 *Y- and Δ-connected subcircuits.*

Y⇌Δ TRANSFORMATIONS

In Chapter 2 we found that circuits that cannot be reduced by series or parallel equivalence can be handled by a Δ-to-Y or a Y-to-Δ transformation. The same basic concept can be applied to the Δ- and Y-connected impedances in Figure 8–24. Replacing a Δ-connected circuit by an equivalent Y, or vice versa, changes circuit connections so that series and parallel equivalence can again be used to reduce the circuit.

The equations for the Δ-to-Y transformation are

$$Z_1 = \frac{Z_B Z_C}{Z_A + Z_B + Z_C}$$

$$Z_2 = \frac{Z_C Z_A}{Z_A + Z_B + Z_C} \qquad (8-26)$$

$$Z_3 = \frac{Z_A Z_B}{Z_A + Z_B + Z_C}$$

The equations for a Y-to-Δ transformation are

$$Z_A = \frac{Z_1 Z_2 + Z_2 Z_3 + Z_1 Z_3}{Z_1}$$

$$Z_B = \frac{Z_1 Z_2 + Z_2 Z_3 + Z_1 Z_3}{Z_2} \qquad (8-27)$$

$$Z_C = \frac{Z_1 Z_2 + Z_2 Z_3 + Z_1 Z_3}{Z_3}$$

Equations (8–26) and (8–27) have the same form as Eqs. (2–26) and (2–27), except that here they involve impedances rather than resistances. Derivation of the impedance equations uses the same approach given for resistance circuits in Chapter 2. It is important to remember that the Y and Δ configurations are defined by electrical connections and not by the geometric shapes in the circuit diagram. That is, the circuit diagram does not have to show the circuits with geometric Y or Δ shapes for the transformation equations to apply.

Applying these transformation equations in phasor circuits involves manipulating complex numbers representing the impedances. While these manipulations are not conceptually difficult, they do involve a computational burden that generally outweighs any advantages gained by the resulting circuit simplification. In other words, there are easier ways to deal with phasor circuits that cannot be solved by series and parallel equivalence. An important exception occurs in electrical power systems that are made up of interconnections of Y- or Δ-connected circuits. Most often these circuits are balanced.

A Y- or Δ-connected circuit is said to be **balanced** when $Z_1 = Z_2 = Z_3 = Z_Y$ or $Z_A = Z_B = Z_C = Z_\Delta$. Under balanced conditions the transformation equations reduce to $Z_Y = Z_\Delta/3$ and $Z_\Delta = 3Z_Y$. We make use of the balanced circuit transformation equations in the study of three-phase power systems in Chapter 14.

EXAMPLE 8–12

Use a Δ-to-Y transformation to solve for the phasor current $\mathbf{I}_X$ in Figure 8–25.

FIGURE 8–25

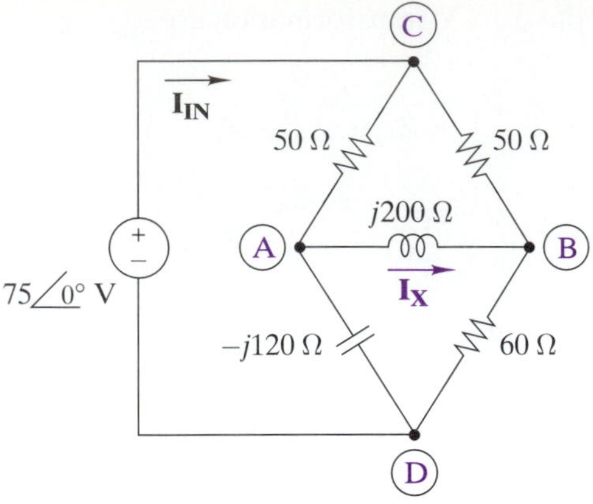

SOLUTION:

We cannot use basic reduction tools on the circuit in Figure 8–25 because no elements are connected in series or parallel. However, if we replace either the upper delta (A, B, C) or lower delta (A, B, D) by an equivalent Y subcircuit, then we can apply series and parallel reduction methods. We choose to transform the upper delta because it has two equal resistors, which simplifies the transformation equations. The sum of the impedances in the upper delta is $100 + j200\ \Omega$. This sum is the denominator in the expression in Eq. (8–26). Using the first expression in Eq. (8–26), we find the equivalent Y impedance connected at node A to be

$$Z_1 = \frac{(50)(j200)}{100 + j200} = 40 + j20\ \Omega$$

Using the second expression in Eq. (8–26), we obtain the equivalent Y impedance connected at node B:

$$Z_2 = \frac{(50)(j200)}{100 + j200} = 40 + j20\ \Omega$$

Using the third expression in Eq. (8–26), we obtain the equivalent Y impedance connected at node C:

$$Z_3 = \frac{(50)(50)}{100 + j200} = 5 - j10\ \Omega$$

Figure 8–26 shows the revised circuit with the equivalent Y inserted in place of the upper delta in Figure 8–25. Note that the transformation introduces a new node labeled N in Figure 8–26.

The revised circuit in Figure 8–26 can be reduced by series and parallel equivalence. The total impedance of the path NAD is $40 - j100\ \Omega$. The total impedance of the path NBD is $100 + j20\ \Omega$. These paths are connected in parallel, so the equivalent impedance between nodes N and D is

$$Z_{ND} = \frac{1}{\dfrac{1}{40 - j100} + \dfrac{1}{100 + j20}} = 60.6 - j31.1\ \Omega$$

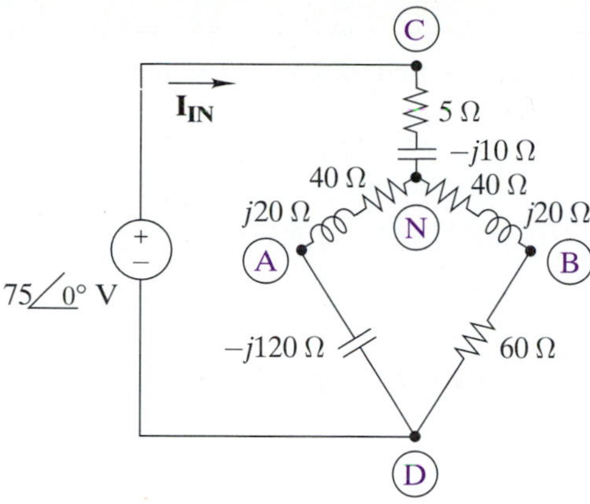

FIGURE 8–26

The impedance Z_{ND} is connected in series with the remaining leg of the equivalent Y, so the equivalent impedance seen by the voltage source is

$$Z_{EQ} = 5 - j10 + Z_{ND} = 65.6 - j41.1\ \Omega$$

The input current shown in Figure 8–26 is

$$\mathbf{I}_{IN} = \frac{75\angle 0^\circ}{Z_{EQ}} = 0.821 + j0.514\ \text{A}$$

Given the input current, we work backward through the equivalent circuit to find the required current $\mathbf{I}_X$. To calculate $\mathbf{I}_X$, we need the voltage $\mathbf{V}_{AB}$ between nodes A and B. To find $\mathbf{V}_{AB}$, we first calculate the voltage $\mathbf{V}_{CN}$ as

$$\begin{aligned}\mathbf{V}_{CN} &= \mathbf{I}_{IN}Z_{CN} = (0.821 + j0.514)(5 - j10)\\ &= 9.24 - j5.64\ \text{V}\end{aligned}$$

By KVL, $\mathbf{V}_{CN} + \mathbf{V}_{ND} = 75\angle 0^\circ$, therefore we can write

$$\mathbf{V}_{ND} = 75\angle 0^\circ - \mathbf{V}_{CN} = 65.8 + j5.64\ \text{V}$$

The voltage $\mathbf{V}_{ND}$ appears across two parallel voltage dividers. Using voltage division, the voltages $\mathbf{V}_{AD}$ and $\mathbf{V}_{BD}$ are

$$\mathbf{V}_{AD} = \frac{-j120}{40 - j100}\mathbf{V}_{ND} = 70.4 - j21.4\ \text{V}$$

$$\mathbf{V}_{BD} = \frac{60}{100 + j20}\mathbf{V}_{ND} = 38.6 - j4.34\ \text{V}$$

Using KVL, the voltage $\mathbf{V}_{AB}$ is

$$\begin{aligned}\mathbf{V}_{AB} &= \mathbf{V}_{AD} - \mathbf{V}_{BD}\\ &= 31.8 - j17.1 = 36.1\angle -28.3^\circ\ \text{V}\end{aligned}$$

Using the voltage $\mathbf{V}_{AB}$, the unknown current $\mathbf{I}_X$ is found to be

$$\mathbf{I}_X = \frac{\mathbf{V}_{AB}}{j200} = 0.18\angle -118^\circ\ \text{A}$$

■

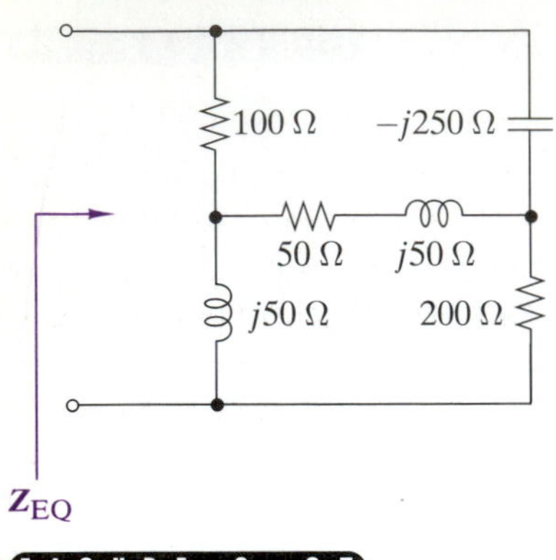

FIGURE 8–27

Exercise 8–11

Use a Y-Δ or Δ-Y transformation to find the equivalent impedance of the circuit in Figure 8–27.

Answer:

$$Z_{EQ} = 97.3 + j13.3\ \Omega$$

8–4 CIRCUIT THEOREMS WITH PHASORS

In this section we treat basic properties of phasor circuits that parallel the resistance circuit theorems developed in Chapter 3. Circuit linearity is the foundation for all of these properties. The proportionality and superposition properties are two fundamental consequences of linearity.

PROPORTIONALITY

The **proportionality** property states that phasor output responses are proportional to the input phasor. Mathematically, proportionality means that

$$\mathbf{Y} = K\mathbf{X} \tag{8-28}$$

where $\mathbf{X}$ is the input phasor, $\mathbf{Y}$ is the output phasor, and K is the proportionality constant. In phasor circuit analysis, the proportionality constant is generally a complex number.

The unit output method discussed in Chapter 3 is based on the proportionality property and is applicable to phasors. To apply the unit output method in the phasor domain, we assume that the output is a unit phasor $\mathbf{Y} = 1\angle 0°$. By successive application of KCL, KVL, and the element impedances, we solve for the input phasor required to produce the unit output. Because the circuit is linear, the proportionality constant relating input and output is

$$K = \frac{\text{Output}}{\text{Input}} = \frac{1\angle 0°}{\text{Input phasor for unit output}}$$

Once we have the constant K, we can find the output for any input or the input required to produce any specified output.

The next example illustrates the unit output method for phasor circuits.

EXAMPLE 8–13

Use the unit output method to find the input impedance, current $\mathbf{I}_1$, output voltage $\mathbf{V}_C$, and current $\mathbf{I}_3$ of the circuit in Figure 8–28 for $\mathbf{V}_S =$

SOLUTION:

The following steps implement the unit output method for the circuit in Figure 8–28:

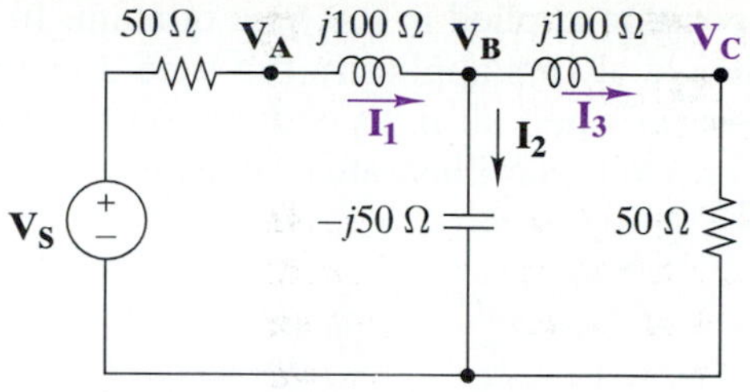

FIGURE 8-28

1. Assume a unit output voltage $\mathbf{V}_C = 1 + j0$ V.
2. By Ohm's law, $\mathbf{I}_3 = \mathbf{V}_C/50 = 0.02 + j0$ A.
3. By KVL, $\mathbf{V}_B = \mathbf{V}_C + (j100)\mathbf{I}_3 = 1 + j2$ V.
4. By Ohm's law, $\mathbf{I}_2 = \mathbf{V}_B/(-j50) = -0.04 + j0.02$ A.
5. By KCL, $\mathbf{I}_1 = \mathbf{I}_2 + \mathbf{I}_3 = -0.02 + j0.02$ A.
6. By KVL, $\mathbf{V}_S = (50 + j100)\mathbf{I}_1 + \mathbf{V}_B = -2 + j1$ V.

Given $\mathbf{V}_S$ and $\mathbf{I}_1$, the input impedance is

$$Z_{IN} = \frac{\mathbf{V}_S}{\mathbf{I}_1} = \frac{-2 + j1}{-0.02 + j0.02} = 75 + j25\ \Omega$$

The proportionality factor between the input $\mathbf{V}_S$ and output voltage $\mathbf{V}_C$ is

$$K = \frac{1}{\mathbf{V}_S} = \frac{1}{-2 + j} = -0.4 - j0.2$$

Given K and Z_{IN}, we can now calculate the required responses for an input $\mathbf{V}_S = 10\angle 0°$:

$$\mathbf{V}_C = K\mathbf{V}_S = -4 - j2 = 4.47\angle -153°\ \text{V}$$

$$\mathbf{I}_1 = \frac{\mathbf{V}_S}{Z_{IN}} = 0.12 - j0.04 = 0.126\angle -18.4°\ \text{A}$$

$$\mathbf{I}_3 = \frac{\mathbf{V}_C}{50} = -0.08 - j0.04 = 0.0894\angle -153°\ \text{A}$$

■

SUPERPOSITION

The superposition principle applies to phasor responses only if all of the independent sources driving the circuit have the *same frequency.* That is, when the input sources have the same frequency, we can find the phasor response due to each source acting alone and obtain the total response by adding the individual phasors. If the sources have different frequencies, then superposition can still be used but its application is different. With different frequency sources, each source must be treated in a separate steady-state analysis because the element impedances change with frequency. The phasor response for each source must be changed into wave-

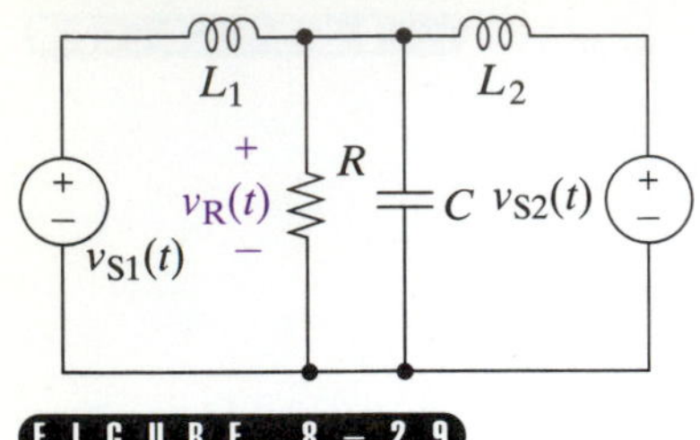

FIGURE 8–29

forms and then superposition applied in the time domain. In other words, the superposition principle always applies in the time domain. It also applies in the phasor domain when all independent sources have the same frequency. The following examples illustrate both cases.

EXAMPLE 8–14

Use superposition to find the steady-state voltage $v_R(t)$ in Figure 8–29 for $R = 20\ \Omega$, $L_1 = 2$ mH, $L_2 = 6$ mH, $C = 20\ \mu$F, $v_{S1} = 100 \cos 5000t$ V, and $v_{S2} = 120 \cos(5000t + 30°)$ V.

SOLUTION:

In this example, the two sources operate at the same frequency. Figure 8–30(a) shows the phasor domain circuit with source no. 2 turned off and replaced by a short circuit. The three elements in parallel in Figure 8–30(a) produce an equivalent impedance of

$$Z_{EQ} = \frac{1}{\dfrac{1}{20} + \dfrac{1}{-j10} + \dfrac{1}{j30}} = 7.20 - j9.60\ \Omega$$

FIGURE 8–30

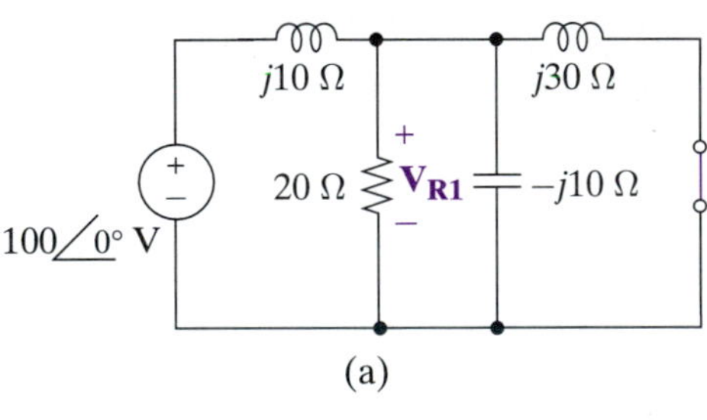

(a)

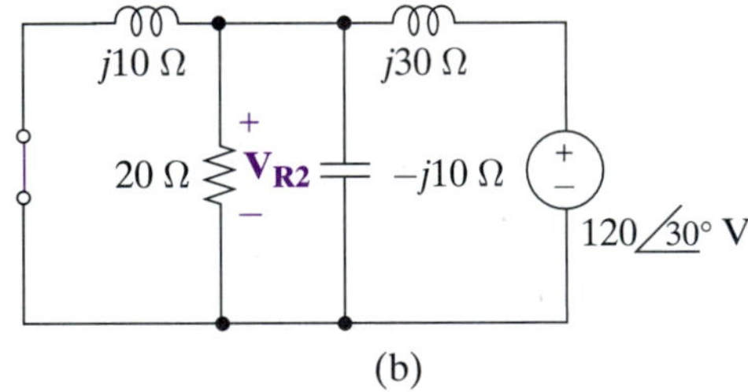

(b)

By voltage division, the phasor response $\mathbf{V}_{R1}$ is

$$\mathbf{V}_{R1} = \frac{Z_{EQ1}}{j10 + Z_{EQ1}} 100\angle 0°$$
$$= 92.3 - j138 = 166\angle -56.3°\ \text{V}$$

Figure 8–30(b) shows the phasor-domain circuit with source no. 1 turned off and source no. 2 on. The three elements in parallel in Figure 8–30(b) produce an equivalent impedance of

$$Z_{EQ2} = \frac{1}{\dfrac{1}{20} + \dfrac{1}{-j10} + \dfrac{1}{j10}} = 20 - j0\ \Omega$$

By voltage division, the response $\mathbf{V}_{R2}$ is

$$\mathbf{V}_{R2} = \frac{Z_{EQ2}}{j30 + Z_{EQ2}} 120\angle 30^\circ$$
$$= 59.7 - j29.5 = 66.6\angle -26.3^\circ \text{ V}$$

Since the sources have the same frequency, the total response can be found by adding the individual phasor responses $\mathbf{V}_{R1}$ and $\mathbf{V}_{R2}$:

$$\mathbf{V}_R = \mathbf{V}_{R1} + \mathbf{V}_{R2} = 152 - j167 = 226\angle -47.8^\circ \text{ V}$$

The time-domain function corresponding to the phasor sum is

$$v_R(t) = \text{Re}\{\mathbf{V}_R e^{j5000t}\} = 226\cos(5000t - 47.8^\circ) \text{ V}$$

The overall response can also be obtained by adding the time-domain functions corresponding to the individual phasor responses $\mathbf{V}_{R1}$ and $\mathbf{V}_{R2}$:

$$v_R(t) = \text{Re}\{\mathbf{V}_{R1} e^{j5000t}\} + \text{Re}\{\mathbf{V}_{R2} e^{j5000t}\}$$
$$= 166\cos(5000t - 56.3^\circ) + 66.6\cos(5000t - 26.3^\circ) \text{ V}$$

You are encouraged to show that the two expressions for $v_R(t)$ are equivalent using the additive property of sinusoids. ■

EXAMPLE 8–15

Use superposition to find the steady-state current $i(t)$ in Figure 8–31 for R = 10 kΩ, L = 200 mH, v_{S1} = 24 cos 20000t V, and v_{S2} = 8 cos(60000t + 30°) V.

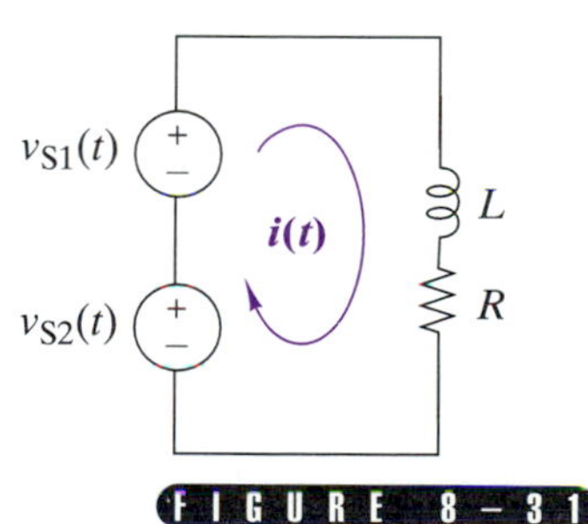

FIGURE 8–31

SOLUTION:

In this example the two sources operate at different frequencies. With source no. 2 off, the input phasor is $\mathbf{V}_{S1} = 24\angle 0^\circ$ V at a frequency of ω = 20 krad/s. At this frequency the equivalent impedance of the inductor and resistor is

$$Z_{EQ1} = R + j\omega L = 10 + j4\ k\Omega$$

The phasor current due to source no. 1 is

$$\mathbf{I}_1 = \frac{\mathbf{V}_{S1}}{Z_{EQ1}} = \frac{24\angle 0^\circ}{10000 + j4000} = 2.23\angle -21.8^\circ \text{ mA}$$

With source no. 1 off and source no. 2 on, the input phasor $\mathbf{V}_{S2} = 8\angle 30^\circ$ V at a frequency of ω = 60 krad/s. At this frequency the equivalent impedance of the inductor and resistor is

$$Z_{EQ2} = R + j\omega L = 10 + j12 \text{ k}\Omega$$

The phasor current due to source no. 2 is

$$\mathbf{I}_2 = \frac{\mathbf{V}_{S2}}{Z_{EQ2}} = \frac{8\angle 30°}{10{,}000 + j12{,}000} = 0.512\angle -20.2° \text{ mA}$$

The two input sources operate at different frequencies, so the phasors responses $\mathbf{I}_1$ and $\mathbf{I}_2$ cannot be added to obtain the overall response. In this case the overall response is obtained by adding the corresponding time-domain functions.

$$\begin{aligned} i(t) &= \text{Re}\{\mathbf{I}_1 e^{j20000t}\} + \text{Re}\{\mathbf{I}_2 e^{j60000t}\} \\ &= 2.23\cos(20000t - 21.8°) + 0.512\cos(60{,}000t - 20.2°) \text{ mA} \end{aligned}$$

■

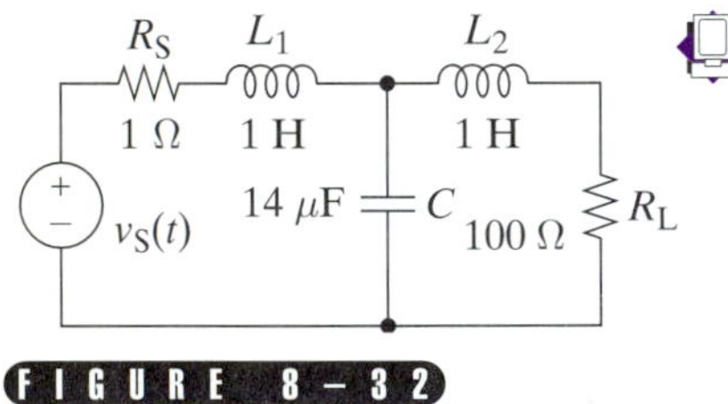

FIGURE 8–32

EXAMPLE 8–16

The voltage source in Figure 8–32 produces a 60-Hz sinusoid with a peak amplitude of 200 V plus a 180-Hz third harmonic with a peak amplitude of 10 V. The purpose of the *LC* circuit is to reduce the relative size of the third harmonic component delivered to the 100-Ω load resistor. Use MicroSim Design Center to calculate the amplitude of the 60-Hz and 180-Hz components in the output.

SOLUTION:

Figure 8–33 shows the circuit diagram as constructed in MicroSim Schematics. The value AC = 1 means that $\mathbf{V}_S$ is an AC voltage source with an amplitude of 1 V. The printer symbol attached to node 4 causes MicroSim PSpice to write the magnitude and phase of the node voltage V(4) in the output file. The problem involves ac analysis with input sinusoids at 60 Hz and 180 Hz. **Selecting Analysis/Setup/AC Sweep** from the Schematics menu bar brings up the AC sweep menu shown in Figure 8–33. We select a two-point linear sweep that starts at 60 Hz and ends at 180 Hz. Returning to the main menu and selecting **Analysis/Simulate** causes MicroSim PSpice to make two AC analysis runs, first at f = 60 Hz and then again at f = 180 Hz. The input phasor for each run is $\mathbf{V}_S = 1\angle 0°$. The relevant portion of the output file is shown at the bottom in Figure 8–33. The symbol VM(4) is the magnitude of the output voltage phasor in volts and VP(4) is the phase angle in degrees. These values are for the normalized input $\mathbf{V}_S = 1\angle 0°$. To get the actual output, we must scale the normalized results by the actual input amplitudes at each frequency.

FREQUENCY (HZ)	INPUT (V)	OUTPUT (V)
60	200	$200 \times 0.9994 = 199.9$
180	10	$10 \times 0.005534 = 0.05534$

The amplitude of the 60-Hz component is virtually unchanged, while the amplitude of the 180-Hz component is greatly reduced. This frequency selectivity occurs because the impedances of the inductor and capacitor change with frequency. ■

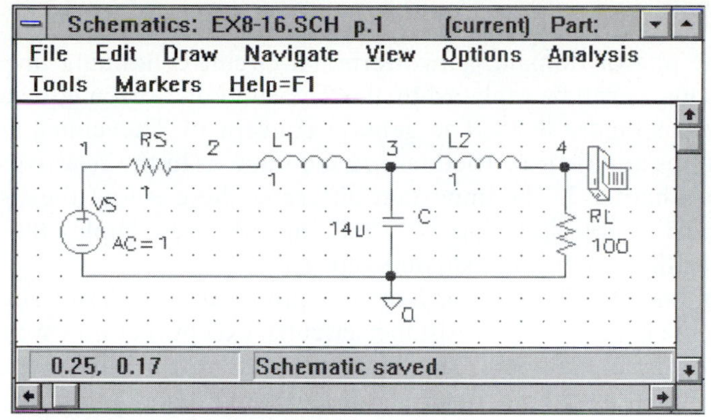

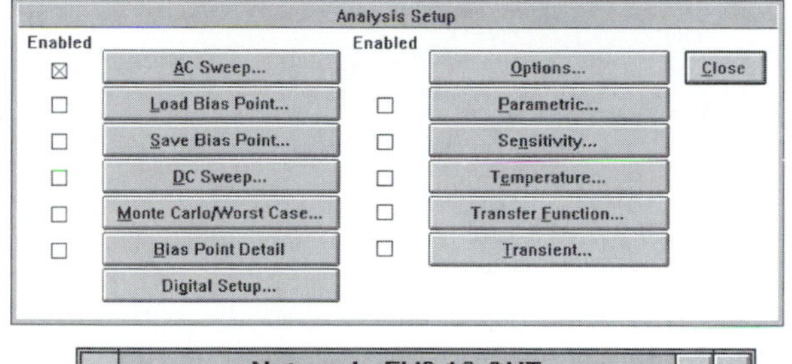

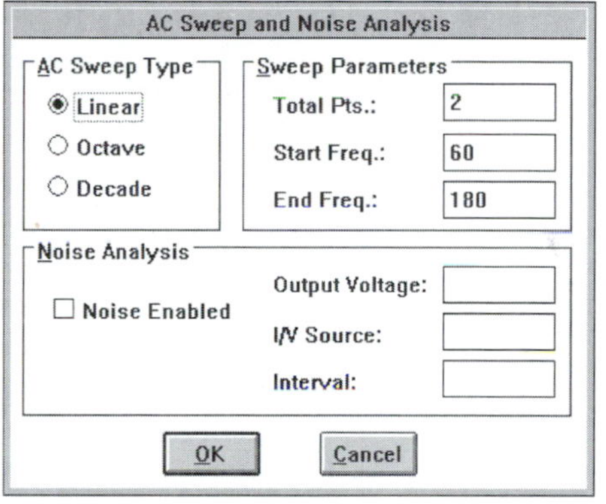

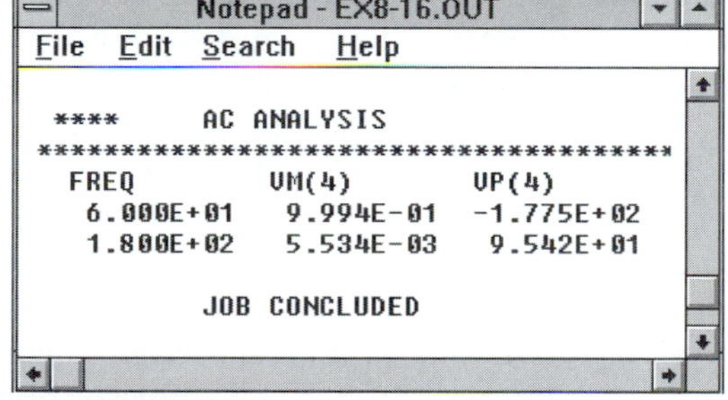

FIGURE 8–33

Exercise 8–12

The two sources in Figure 8–34 have the same frequency. Use superposition to find the phasor current $\mathbf{I}_X$.

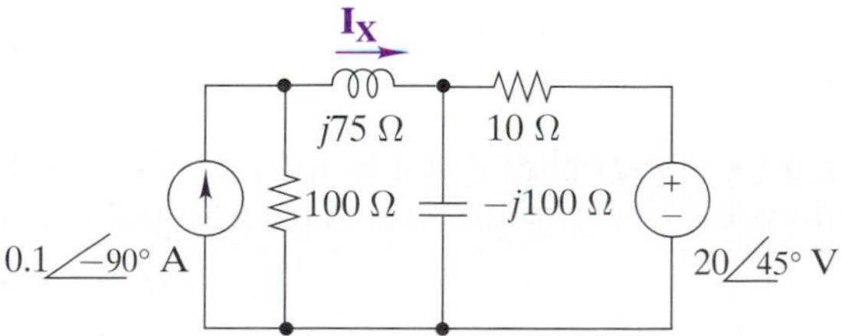

FIGURE 8–34

Answer:

$$\mathbf{I}_X = 0.206\angle{-158^\circ}\ \text{A}$$

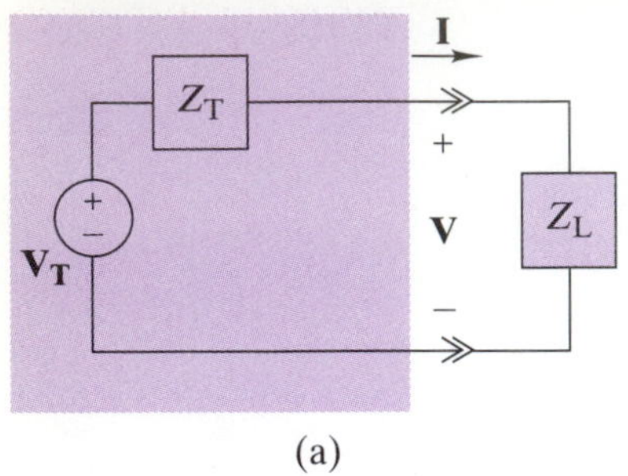

(a)

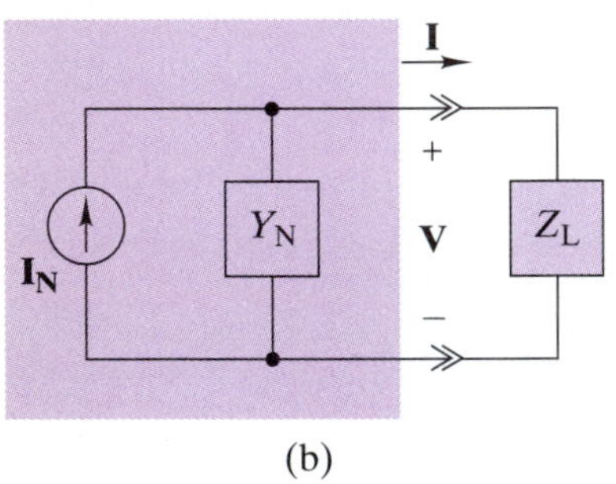

(b)

FIGURE 8–35 *Thévenin and Norton equivalent circuits in the phasor analysis.*

THÉVENIN AND NORTON EQUIVALENT CIRCUITS

In the phasor domain, a two-terminal circuit containing linear elements and sources can be replaced by the Thévenin or Norton equivalent circuits shown in Figure 8–35. The general concept of Thévenin's and Norton's theorems and their restrictions are the same as in the resistive circuit studied in Chapter 3. The important difference here is that the signals $\mathbf{V}_\text{T}$, $\mathbf{I}_\text{N}$, $\mathbf{V}$, and $\mathbf{I}$ are phasors, and $Z_\text{T} = 1/Y_\text{N}$ and Z_L are complex numbers representing the source and load impedances.

Finding the Thévenin or Norton equivalent of a phasor circuit involves the same process as for resistance circuits, except that now we must manipulate complex numbers. The Thévenin and Norton circuits are equivalent to each other, so their circuit parameters are related as follows:

$$\mathbf{V}_\text{OC} = \mathbf{V}_\text{T} = \mathbf{I}_\text{N} Z_\text{T}$$

$$\mathbf{I}_\text{SC} = \frac{\mathbf{V}_\text{T}}{Z_\text{T}} = \mathbf{I}_\text{N} \qquad (8-29)$$

$$Z_\text{T} = \frac{1}{Y_\text{N}} = \frac{\mathbf{V}_\text{OC}}{\mathbf{I}_\text{SC}}$$

Algebraically, the results in Eq. (8–29) are identical to the corresponding equations for resistance circuits. The important difference is that these equations involve phasors and impedances rather than waveforms and resistances. These equations point out that we can determine a Thévenin or Norton equivalent by finding any two of the following quantities: (1) the open-circuit voltage $\mathbf{V}_\text{OC}$, (2) the short-circuit current $\mathbf{I}_\text{SC}$, and (when there are no dependent sources) (3) the impedance Z_T looking back into the source circuit with all independent sources turned off.

The relationships in Eq. (8–29) define source transformations that allow us to convert a voltage source in series with an impedance into a current source in parallel with the same impedance, or vice versa. Phasor-domain source transformations simplify circuits and are useful in formulating general node-voltage or mesh-current equations, discussed in the next section.

The next two examples illustrate applications of source transformation and Thévenin equivalent circuits.

EXAMPLE 8–17

Both sources in Figure 8–36(a) operate at a frequency of $\omega = 5000$ rad/s. Find the steady-state voltage $v_\text{R}(t)$ using source transformations.

SOLUTION:

Example 8–14 solves this problem using superposition. In this example we use source transformations. We observe that the voltage sources in Figure 8–36(a) are connected in series with an impedance and can be converted into the following equivalent current sources:

FIGURE 8–36

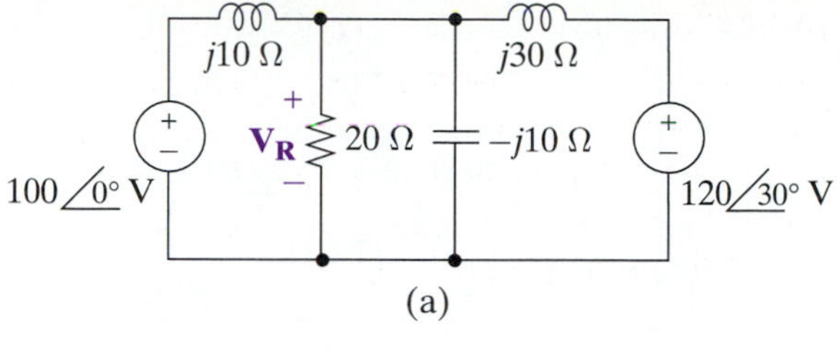

(a)

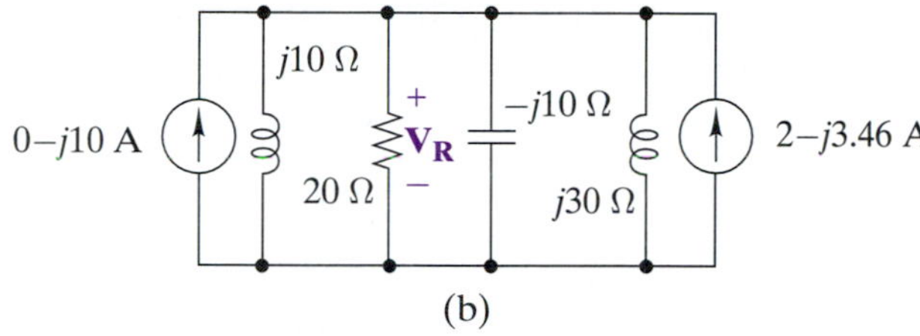

(b)

$$\mathbf{I}_{EQ1} = \frac{100\angle 0°}{j10} = 0 - j10 \text{ A}$$

$$\mathbf{I}_{EQ2} = \frac{120\angle 30°}{j30} = 2 - j3.46 \text{ A}$$

Figure 8–36(b) shows the circuit after these two source transformations. The two current sources are connected in parallel and can be replaced by a single equivalent current source:

$$\mathbf{I}_{EQ} = \mathbf{I}_{EQ1} + \mathbf{I}_{EQ2} = 2 - j13.46 = 13.6\angle -81.5° \text{ A}$$

The four passive elements are connected in parallel and can be replaced by an equivalent impedance:

$$Z_{EQ} = \frac{1}{\dfrac{1}{20} + \dfrac{1}{-j10} + \dfrac{1}{j10} + \dfrac{1}{j30}} = 16.6\angle 33.7° \ \Omega$$

The voltage across this equivalent impedance equals $\mathbf{V}_R$, since one of the parallel elements is the resistor R. Therefore, the unknown phasor voltage is

$$\mathbf{V}_R = \mathbf{I}_{EQ}Z_{EQ} = (13.6\angle -81.5°) \times (16.6\angle 33.7°) = 226\angle -47.8° \text{ V}$$

The value of $\mathbf{V}_R$ is the same as found in Example 8–14 using superposition. The corresponding time-domain function is

$$v_R(t) = \text{Re}\{\mathbf{V}_R e^{j5000t}\} = 226 \cos(5000t - 47.8°) \text{ V}$$ ■

EXAMPLE 8–18

Use Thévenin's theorem to find the current $\mathbf{I}_X$ in the bridge circuit shown in Figure 8–37.

FIGURE 8–37

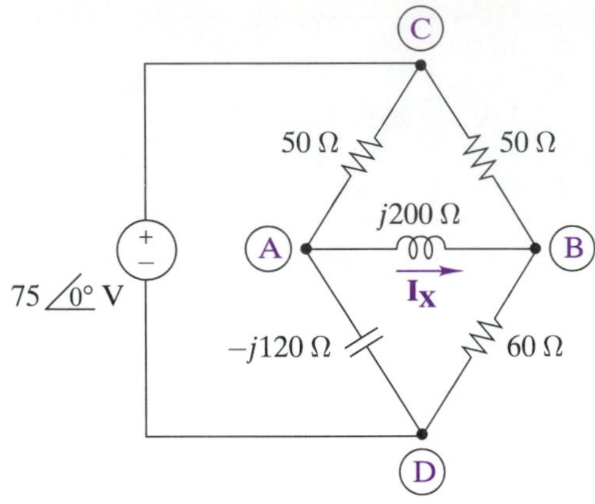

SOLUTION:

Example 8–12 solves this problem using a Δ-to-Y transformation. In this example, we determine $\mathbf{I}_X$ by finding the Thévenin equivalent circuit seen by the impedance $j200$. The Thévenin equivalent will be found by determining the open-circuit voltage and the lookback impedance.

Disconnecting the impedance $j200$ from the circuit in Figure 8–37 produces the circuit shown in Figure 8–38(a). The voltage between nodes A and B is the Thévenin voltage since removing the impedance $j200$ leaves an open circuit. The voltages at nodes A and B can each be found by voltage division. Since the open-circuit voltage is the difference between these node voltages, we have

$$\begin{aligned}\mathbf{V}_T &= \mathbf{V}_A - \mathbf{V}_B \\ &= \frac{-j120}{50 - j120} 75\angle 0^\circ - \frac{60}{60 + 50} 75\angle 0^\circ \\ &= 23.0 - j26.6 \text{ V}\end{aligned}$$

FIGURE 8–38

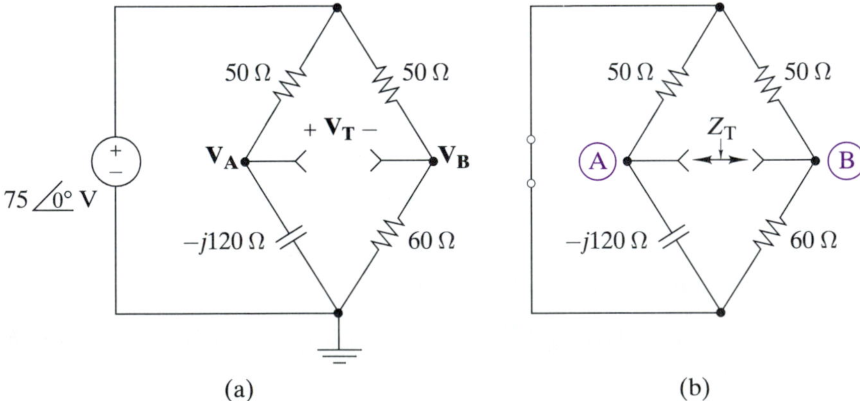

Turning off the voltage source in Figure 8–38(a) and replacing it by a short circuit produces the situation shown in Figure 8–38(b). The lookback impedance seen at the interface is a series connection of two pairs of elements connected in parallel. The equivalent impedance of the series/parallel combination is

$$Z_T = \frac{1}{\dfrac{1}{50} + \dfrac{1}{-j120}} + \frac{1}{\dfrac{1}{50} + \dfrac{1}{60}} = 69.9 - j17.8\ \Omega$$

Given the Thévenin equivalent circuit, we treat the impedance $j200$ as a load connected at the interface and calculate the resulting load current $\mathbf{I}_X$ as

$$\mathbf{I}_X = \frac{\mathbf{V}_T}{Z_T + j200} = \frac{23.0 - j26.6}{69.9 + j182} = 0.180\angle -118^\circ\ \text{A}$$

The value of $\mathbf{I}_X$ found here is the same as the answer obtained in Example 8–12 using a Δ-to-*Y* transformation. ■

EXAMPLE 8–19

In the steady state, the open-circuit voltage at an interface is observed to be

$$v_{OC}(t) = 12 \cos 2000t$$

When a 50-mH inductor is connected across the interface, the interface voltage is observed to be

$$v(t) = 17 \cos(2000t + 45^\circ)$$

Find the Thévenin equivalent circuit at the interface.

SOLUTION:

The phasors for $v_{OC}(t)$ and $v(t)$ are $\mathbf{V}_{OC} = 12\angle 0^\circ$ and $\mathbf{V} = 17\angle 45^\circ$. The phasor Thévenin voltage at the interface is $\mathbf{V}_T = \mathbf{V}_{OC} = 12\angle 0^\circ$. The impedance of the inductor is $Z_L = j\omega L = j2000 \times 0.050 = j100\ \Omega$. When the inductor load is connected across the interface, we use voltage division to express the interface voltage as

$$\mathbf{V} = \frac{Z_L}{Z_T + Z_L}\mathbf{V}_T$$

Inserting the known numerical values yields

$$17\angle 45^\circ = \frac{j100}{Z_T + j100} 12\angle 0^\circ$$

Solving for Z_T, we have

$$Z_T = j100 \times \frac{12\angle 0^\circ}{17\angle 45^\circ} - j100 = 49.9 - j50.1\ \Omega$$

The Thévenin equivalent circuit at the interface is defined by $\mathbf{V}_T = 12\angle 0^\circ$ and $Z_T = 49.9 - j50.1\ \Omega$. ■

Exercise 8–13

(a) Find the Thévenin equivalent circuit seen by the inductor in Figure 8–34.
(b) Use the Thévenin equivalent to calculate the current $\mathbf{I}_X$.

Answers:
(a) $\mathbf{V}_T = -15.4 - j22.6$ V, $Z_T = 109.9 - j0.990\ \Omega$
(b) $\mathbf{I}_X = 0.206\angle{-158^\circ}$ A

Exercise 8–14

By inspection, determine the Thévenin equivalent circuit seen by the capacitor in Figure 8–28 for $\mathbf{V}_S = 10\angle 0^\circ$ V.

Answer:
$\mathbf{V}_T = 5\angle 0^\circ$ V, $Z_T = 25 + j\,50\ \Omega$

Exercise 8–15

In the steady state the short-circuit current at an interface is observed to be

$$i_{SC}(t) = 0.75 \sin \omega t \text{ A}$$

When a 150-Ω resistor is connected across the interface, the interface current is observed to be

$$i(t) = 0.6 \cos(\omega t - 53.1^\circ) \text{ A}$$

Find the Norton equivalent phasor circuit at the interface.

Answer:

$$\mathbf{I}_N = 0 - j0.75 \text{ A},\ Z_N = 0 + j200\ \Omega$$

8–5 GENERAL CIRCUIT ANALYSIS WITH PHASORS

The previous sections discuss basic analysis methods based on equivalence, reduction, and circuit theorems. These methods are valuable because we work directly with element impedances and thereby gain insight into steady-state circuit behavior. We also need general methods, such as node and mesh analysis, to deal with more complicated circuits than the basic methods can easily handle. These general methods use node-voltage or mesh-current variables to reduce the number of equations that must be solved simultaneously.

Node-voltage equations involve selecting a reference node and assigning a node-to-datum voltage to each of the remaining nonreference nodes. Because of KVL, the voltage between any two nodes equals the difference of the two node voltages. This fundamental property of node voltages plus the element impedances allow us to write KCL constraints at each of the nonreference nodes.

For example, consider node A in Figure 8–39. The sum of currents leaving this node can be written as

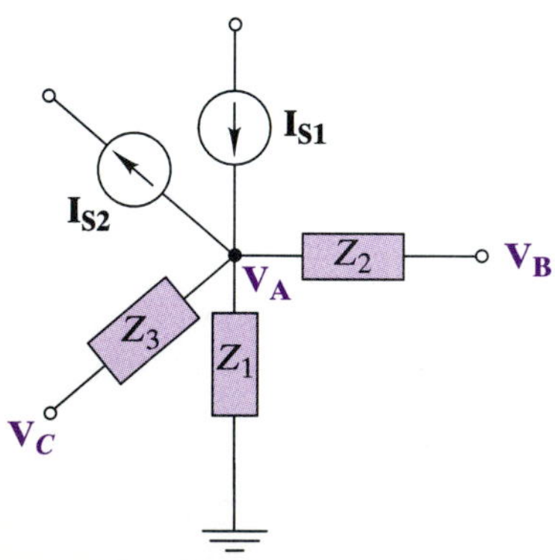

FIGURE 8–39 An example node.

$$\mathbf{I}_{S2} - \mathbf{I}_{S1} + \frac{\mathbf{V}_A}{Z_1} + \frac{\mathbf{V}_A - \mathbf{V}_B}{Z_2} + \frac{\mathbf{V}_A - \mathbf{V}_C}{Z_3} = 0$$

Rewriting this equation with unknowns grouped on the left and known inputs on the right yields

$$\left[\frac{1}{Z_1} + \frac{1}{Z_2} + \frac{1}{Z_3}\right]\mathbf{V}_A - \frac{1}{Z_2}\mathbf{V}_B - \frac{1}{Z_3}\mathbf{V}_C = \mathbf{I}_{S1} - \mathbf{I}_{S2}$$

Expressing this result in terms of admittances produces the following equation.

$$[Y_1 + Y_2 + Y_3]\mathbf{V}_A - [Y_2]\mathbf{V}_B - [Y_3]\mathbf{V}_C = \mathbf{I}_{S1} - \mathbf{I}_{S2}$$

This equation has a familiar pattern. The unknowns $\mathbf{V}_A$, $\mathbf{V}_B$, and $\mathbf{V}_C$ are the node-voltage phasors. The coefficient $[Y_1 + Y_2 + Y_3]$ of $\mathbf{V}_A$ is the sum of the admittances of all of the elements connected to node A. The coefficient $[Y_2]$ of $\mathbf{V}_B$ is admittance of the elements connected between nodes A and B, while $[Y_3]$ is the admittance of the elements connected between nodes A and C. Finally, $\mathbf{I}_{S1}$ and $\mathbf{I}_{S2}$ are the phasor current sources connected to node A, with $\mathbf{I}_{S1}$ directed into and $\mathbf{I}_{S2}$ directed away from the node. These observations suggest that we can write node-voltage equations for phasor circuits by inspection, just as we did with resistive circuits.

Circuits that can be drawn on a flat surface with no crossovers are called **planar** circuits. The mesh-current variables are the loop currents assigned to each mesh in a planar circuit. Because of KCL, the current through any two-terminal element is equal to the difference of the two adjacent meshes. This fundamental property of mesh currents together with the element impedances allow us to write KVL constraints around each of the meshes.

For example, the sum of voltages around mesh A in Figure 8–40 is

$$Z_1\mathbf{I}_A + Z_2[\mathbf{I}_A - \mathbf{I}_B] + Z_3[\mathbf{I}_A - \mathbf{I}_C] - \mathbf{V}_{S1} + \mathbf{V}_{S2} = 0$$

The mesh A equation is obtained by equating this sum to the sum of the source voltages produced in mesh A. Arranging this equation in standard form yields

$$[Z_1 + Z_2 + Z_3]\mathbf{I}_A - [Z_2]\mathbf{I}_B - [Z_3]\mathbf{I}_C = \mathbf{V}_{S1} - \mathbf{V}_{S2}$$

This equation also displays a familiar pattern. The unknowns $\mathbf{I}_A$, $\mathbf{I}_B$, and $\mathbf{I}_C$ are mesh-current phasors. The coefficient $[Z_1 + Z_2 + Z_3]$ of $\mathbf{I}_A$ is the sum of the impedances in mesh A. The coefficient $[Z_2]$ of $\mathbf{I}_B$ is the impedance in both mesh A and mesh B, while $[Z_3]$ is the impedance common to meshes A and C. Finally, $\mathbf{V}_{S1}$ and $\mathbf{V}_{S2}$ are the phasor voltage sources in mesh A. These observations allow us to write mesh-current equations for phasor circuits by inspection.

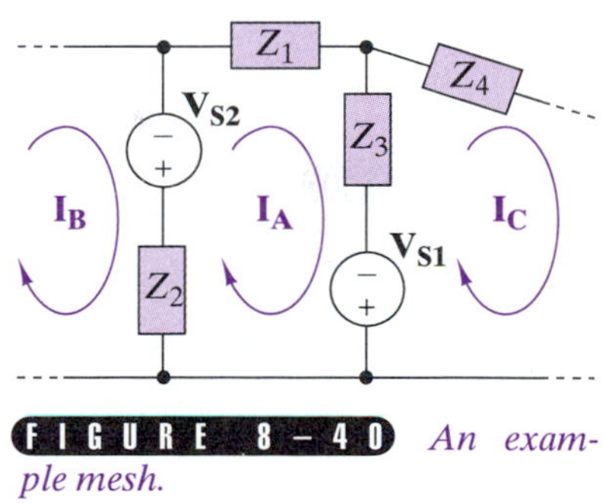

FIGURE 8–40 *An example mesh.*

The preceding discussion assumes that the circuit contains only current sources in the case of node analysis and voltage sources in mesh analysis. If there is a mixture of sources, we may be able to use the source transformations discussed in Sect. 8–4 to convert from voltage to current sources, or vice versa. A source transformation is possible only when there is an impedance connected in series with a voltage source or an admittance in parallel with a current source. When a source transformation is not possible, we use the phasor version of the modified node- and mesh-analysis methods described in Chapter 3.

Formulating a set of equilibrium equations in phasor form is a straightforward process involving concepts that we have used before in Chapters 3 and 4. Once formulated, we use Cramer's rule or Gaussian reduction to solve these equations for phasor responses, although this requires manipulating linear equations with complex coefficients. In principle, the solution process can be done by hand, but as a practical matter circuits with more than three nodes or meshes are best handled using computer tools. Modern hand-held scientific calculators and math analysis program like Mathcad can deal with sets of linear equations with complex coefficients. Circuit analysis programs such as SPICE or MICRO-CAP have ac analysis options that handle steady-state circuit analysis problems.

If computer tools are required for all but the simplest circuits, why bother with the hand solution at all? Why not always use SPICE or Mathcad? The answer is that hand analysis and computer-aided analysis are complementary rather than competitive. Computer-aided analysis excels at generating numerical responses when numerical values of circuit parameters are given. With hand analysis we can generate responses in symbolic form for all possible element values and input frequency. The symbolic solutions for simple circuits give us the insight needed to intelligently use the numerical profusion generated by computer-aided analysis of large-scale circuits.

EXAMPLE 8–20

Use node analysis to find the node voltages $\mathbf{V}_A$ and $\mathbf{V}_B$ in Figure 8–41(a).

FIGURE 8–41

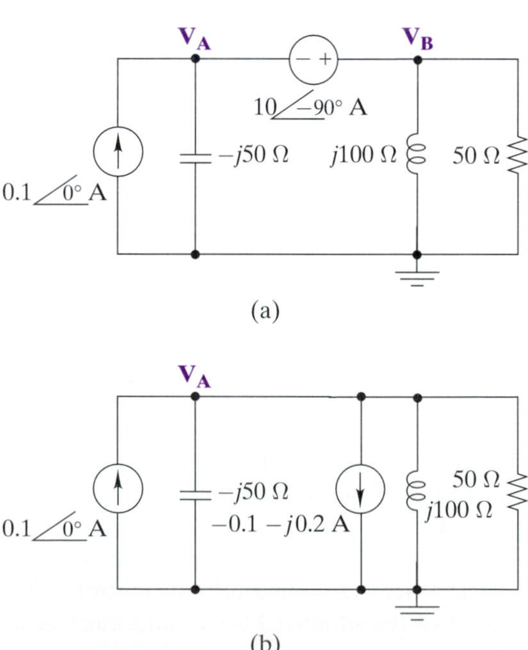

SOLUTION:

The voltage source in Figure 8–41(a) is connected in series with an impedance consisting of a resistor and inductor connected in parallel. The equivalent impedance of this parallel combination is

$$Z_{\text{EQ}} = \frac{1}{\dfrac{1}{50} + \dfrac{1}{j100}} = 40 + j20\ \Omega$$

Applying a source transformation produces an equivalent current source of

$$\mathbf{I}_{\text{EQ}} = \frac{10\angle -90^\circ}{40 + j20} = -0.1 - j0.2\ \text{A}$$

Figure 8–41(b) shows the circuit produced by the source transformation. Note that the transformation eliminates node B. The node-voltage equation at the remaining nonreference node in Figure 8–41(b) is

$$\left(\frac{1}{-j50} + \frac{1}{j100} + \frac{1}{50}\right)\mathbf{V}_{\text{A}} = 0.1\angle 0^\circ - (-0.1 - j0.2)$$

Solving for $\mathbf{V}_{\text{A}}$ yields

$$\mathbf{V}_{\text{A}} = \frac{0.2 + j0.2}{0.02 + j0.01} = 12 + j4 = 12.6\angle 18.4^\circ\ \text{V}$$

Referring to Figure 8–41(a), we see that KVL requires $\mathbf{V}_{\text{B}} = \mathbf{V}_{\text{A}} + 10\angle{-90^\circ}$. Therefore, $\mathbf{V}_{\text{B}}$ is found to be

$$\mathbf{V}_{\text{B}} = (12 + j4) + 10\angle -90^\circ = 12 - j6 = 13.4\angle -26.6^\circ\ \text{V}$$

■

EXAMPLE 8–21

Use node analysis to find the current $\mathbf{I}_{\text{X}}$ in Figure 8–42.

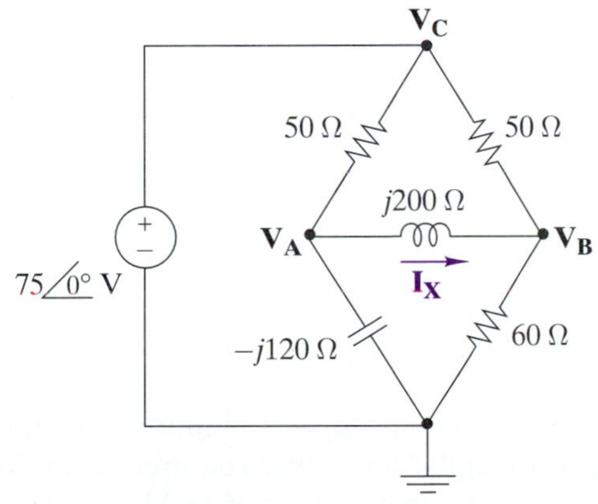

FIGURE 8–42

SOLUTION:

In this example we use node analysis on a problem solved in Example 8–12 using a Δ-to-Y transformation and solved again in Example 8–18 using a Thévenin equivalent circuit. The voltage source cannot be replaced by source transformation because it is not connected in series with an impedance. By inspection, the node equations at nodes A and B are

$$\text{Node A: } \frac{\mathbf{V}_A}{-j120} + \frac{\mathbf{V}_A - \mathbf{V}_B}{j200} + \frac{\mathbf{V}_A - \mathbf{V}_C}{50} = 0$$

$$\text{Node B: } \frac{\mathbf{V}_B}{60} + \frac{\mathbf{V}_B - \mathbf{V}_A}{j200} + \frac{\mathbf{V}_B - \mathbf{V}_C}{50} = 0$$

A node equation at node C is not required because the voltage source forces the condition $\mathbf{V}_C = 75\angle 0°$. Substituting this constraint into the equations of nodes A and B and arranging the equations in standard form yields two equations in two unknowns:

$$\text{Node A: } \left(\frac{1}{50} + \frac{1}{-j120} + \frac{1}{j200}\right)\mathbf{V}_A - \left(\frac{1}{j200}\right)\mathbf{V}_B = \left(\frac{75\angle 0°}{50}\right)$$

$$\text{Node B: } -\left(\frac{1}{j200}\right)\mathbf{V}_A + \left(\frac{1}{50} + \frac{1}{60} + \frac{1}{j200}\right)\mathbf{V}_B = \left(\frac{75\angle 0°}{50}\right)$$

Solving these equations for $\mathbf{V}_A$ and $\mathbf{V}_B$ yields

$$\mathbf{V}_A = 70.4 - j21.4 \text{ V}$$

$$\mathbf{V}_B = 38.6 - j4.33 \text{ V}$$

Using these values for $\mathbf{V}_A$ and $\mathbf{V}_B$, the unknown current is found to be

$$\mathbf{I}_X = \frac{\mathbf{V}_A - \mathbf{V}_B}{j200} = \frac{31.8 - j17.1}{j200} = 0.180\angle -118° \text{ A}$$

This value of $\mathbf{I}_X$ is the same as the answer obtained in Example 8–12 and again in Example 8–18. Review these three examples together to gain perspective on different approaches to phasor circuit analysis. ■

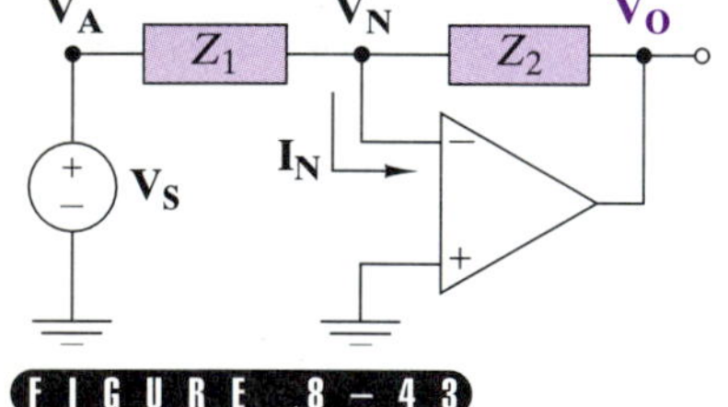

FIGURE 8–43

EXAMPLE 8–22

Use node-voltage analysis to determine the phasor input–output relationship of the OP AMP circuit in Figure 8–43.

SOLUTION:

In the sinusoidal steady state the sum of currents leaving the inverting input node is

$$\frac{\mathbf{V}_N - \mathbf{V}_S}{Z_1} + \frac{\mathbf{V}_N - \mathbf{V}_O}{Z_2} + \mathbf{I}_N = 0$$

This is the only required node equation, since input source forces the condition $\mathbf{V}_A = \mathbf{V}_S$ and no node equation is ever required at an OP AMP output. In the time domain the i–v relationships of an ideal OP AMP are $v_P(t) = v_N(t)$ and $i_P(t) = i_N(t) = 0$. In the sinusoidal steady state these equations are written in phasor form as $\mathbf{V}_P = \mathbf{V}_N$ and $\mathbf{I}_P = \mathbf{I}_N = 0$. In the present case this means $\mathbf{V}_N = 0$ since the noninverting input is grounded. When the ideal

OP AMP constraints are inserted in the node equation, we can solve for the OP AMP input-output relationship as

$$\mathbf{V}_O = -\frac{Z_2}{Z_1}\mathbf{V}_S$$

This result is the phasor domain version of the inverting amplifier configuration. In the phasor domain, the "gain" $K = -Z_2/Z_1$ is determined by a ratio of impedances rather than resistances. Thus, the gain affects both the amplitude and the phase angle of the steady-state output. ■

D DESIGN AND EVALUATION EXAMPLE

Design of an Inverting Amplifier

(a) Use the inverting amplifier circuit in Figure 8–43 to design an OP AMP circuit that produces a steady-state output $v_O(t) = 2\sin(2000t)$ when the input is $v_S(t) = 15\cos(2000t)$. Use only resistors and capacitors in Z_1 and Z_2.

(b) Compare the OP AMP circuit design in this example with the passive *RLC* circuit design developed in Example 8–7.

SOLUTION:

(a) The phasor representation of the input voltage is $\mathbf{V}_S = 15\angle 0 = 15 + j0$. Using the identity $\cos(x - 90°) = \sin x$, we write the required output phasor as $\mathbf{V}_O = 2\angle{-90°} = 0 - j2$. The design problem is to select the impedances Z_1 and Z_2 so that

$$0 - j2 = -\frac{Z_2}{Z_1}(15 + j0)$$

Solving for Z_1 yields $Z_1 = -j7.5 \times Z_2$. Selecting a value for Z_2 determines Z_1. The design problem statement limits us to resistors and capacitors. If we choose $Z_2 = 10^4$ (a 10-kΩ resistor) then $Z_1 = -j7.5 \times 10^4$, which is a capacitive reactance. Since $X_C = -(\omega C)^{-1}$, the required capacitance is $C = (7.5 \times 10^4 \times 2000) = 6.67$ nF. Figure 8–44 shows the OP AMP circuit design, which we recognize as the differentiating circuit from Chapter 6.

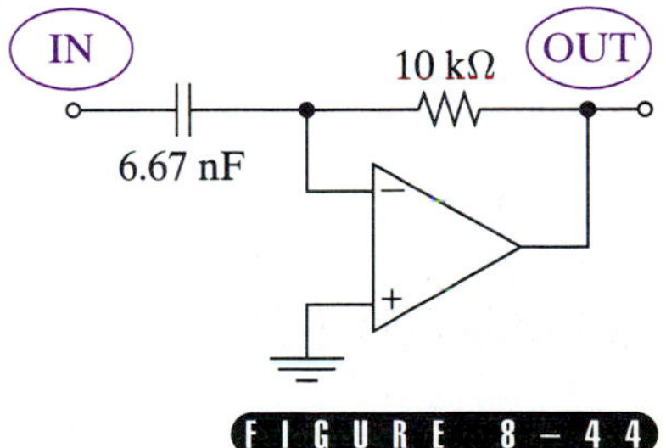

FIGURE 8–44

(b) The passive voltage divider designed in Example 8–7 meets the same design requirements used in this example. The two designs are summarized as follows:

EXAMPLE	FIGURE	DESCRIPTION	R	L	C	OP AMP
8–7	8–14	*RLC* voltage divider	1	1	1	0
8–16	8–44	*RC* inverting amplifier	1	0	1	1

Selecting a final design involves evaluation using additional factors, such as the cost of the power supply required by the OP AMP circuit versus the fact that it can drive reasonable loads. ■

EXAMPLE 8–24

The circuit in Figure 8–45 is an equivalent circuit of an ac induction motor. The current $\mathbf{I}_S$ is called the stator current, $\mathbf{I}_R$ the rotor current, and $\mathbf{I}_M$ the magnetizing current. Use the mesh-current method to solve for the branch currents $\mathbf{I}_S$, $\mathbf{I}_R$, and $\mathbf{I}_M$.

FIGURE 8–45

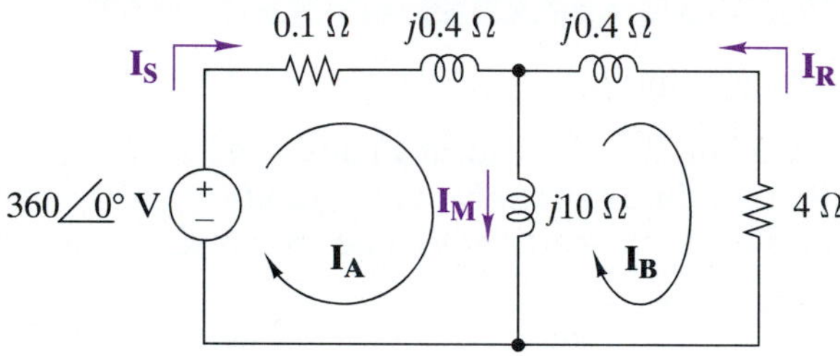

SOLUTION:

Applying KVL to the sum of voltages around each mesh in Figure 8–45 yields

$$\text{Mesh A:} \quad -360\angle 0° + [0.1 + j0.4]\mathbf{I}_A + j10(\mathbf{I}_A - \mathbf{I}_B] = 0$$

$$\text{Mesh B:} \quad j10(\mathbf{I}_B - \mathbf{I}_A) + [4 + j0.4]\mathbf{I}_B \qquad = 0$$

Arranging these equations in standard form yields

$$(0.1 + j10.4)\mathbf{I}_A - (j10)\mathbf{I}_B = 360\angle 0°$$

$$-(j10)\mathbf{I}_A + (4 + j10.4)\mathbf{I}_B = 0$$

Solving these equations for $\mathbf{I}_A$ and $\mathbf{I}_B$ produces

$$\mathbf{I}_A = 79.0 - j48.2 \text{ A}$$

$$\mathbf{I}_B = 81.7 - j14.9 \text{ A}$$

The required stator, rotor, and magnetizing currents are related to these mesh current, as follows:

$$\mathbf{I}_S = \mathbf{I}_A = 92.5\angle -31.4° \text{ A}$$

$$\mathbf{I}_R = -\mathbf{I}_B = -81.8 + j14.7 = 83.0\angle 170° \text{ A}$$

$$\mathbf{I}_M = \mathbf{I}_A - \mathbf{I}_B = -2.68 - j33.3 = 33.4\angle -94.6° \text{ A}$$

■

EXAMPLE 8–25

Use the mesh-current method to solve for output voltage $\mathbf{V}_2$ and input impedance Z_{IN} of the circuit in Figure 8–46.

FIGURE 8–46

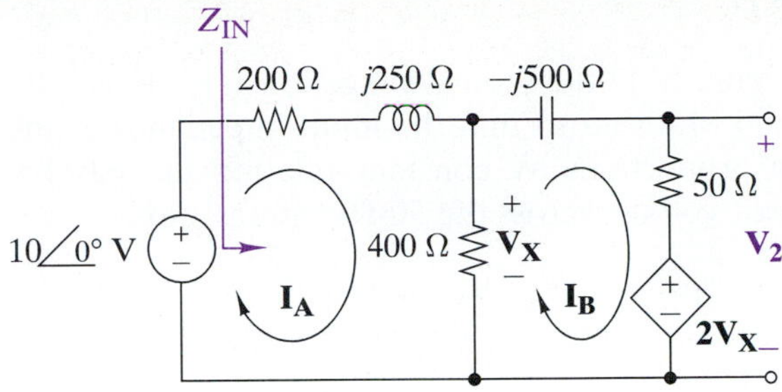

SOLUTION:

The circuit contains a voltage-controlled voltage source. We initially treat the dependent source as an independent source and use KCL to write the sum of voltages around each mesh:

$$\text{Mesh A:}\ -10\angle 0° + [200 + j250]\mathbf{I}_A + 400(\mathbf{I}_A - \mathbf{I}_B) = 0$$

$$\text{Mesh B:}\ 400(\mathbf{I}_B - \mathbf{I}_A) + [50 - j500]\mathbf{I}_B + 2\mathbf{V}_X = 0$$

Arranging these equations in standard form produces

$$\text{Mesh A:}\ (600 + j250)\mathbf{I}_A - 400\mathbf{I}_B = 10\angle 0°$$

$$\text{Mesh B:}\ -400\mathbf{I}_A + (450 - j500)\mathbf{I}_B = -2\mathbf{V}_X$$

Using Ohm's law, the control voltage $\mathbf{V}_X$ is

$$\mathbf{V}_X = 400(\mathbf{I}_A - \mathbf{I}_B)$$

Eliminating $\mathbf{V}_X$ from the mesh equations yields

$$\text{Mesh A:}\ (600 + j250)\mathbf{I}_A - 400\mathbf{I}_B = 10\angle 0°$$

$$\text{Mesh B:}\ 400\mathbf{I}_A + (-350 - j500)\mathbf{I}_B = 0$$

Solving for the two mesh currents produces

$$\mathbf{I}_A = 10.8 - j11.1 \text{ mA}$$

$$\mathbf{I}_B = -1.93 - j9.95 \text{ mA}$$

Using these values of the mesh currents, the output voltage and input impedance are

$$\mathbf{V}_2 = 2\mathbf{V}_X + 50\mathbf{I}_B = 800(\mathbf{I}_A - \mathbf{I}_B) + 50\mathbf{I}_B$$

$$= 800\mathbf{I}_A - 750\mathbf{I}_B = 10.1 - j1.42$$

$$= 10.2\angle -8.00° \text{ V}$$

$$Z_{IN} = \frac{10\angle 0°}{\mathbf{I}_A} = \frac{10\angle 0°}{0.0108 - j0.0111} = 450 + j463\ \Omega$$ ■

EXAMPLE 8–26

In the circuit in Figure 8–47 the input voltage is $v_S(t) = 10 \cos 10^5 t$. Use mesh equations and Mathcad to find the input impedance at the input interface and the proportionality constant relating the input voltage phasor to the phasor voltage across the 50-Ω load resistor.

FIGURE 8–47

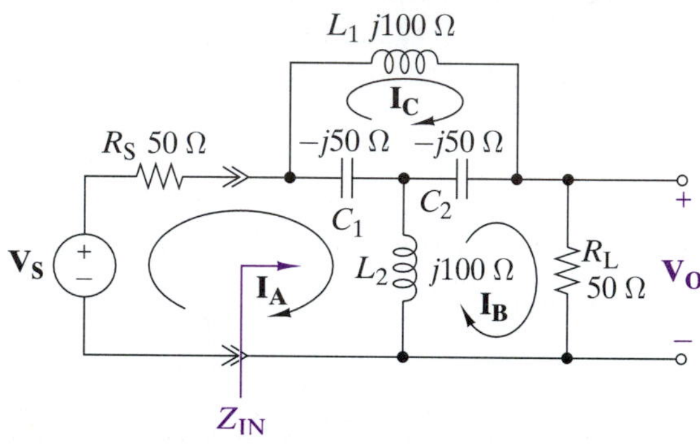

SOLUTION:

Figure 8–48 shows a Mathcad worksheet that implements a solution to this problem. The first two lines define circuit parameters and impedances. The third line lists initial guesses for the mesh-current equation solve block.

FIGURE 8–48

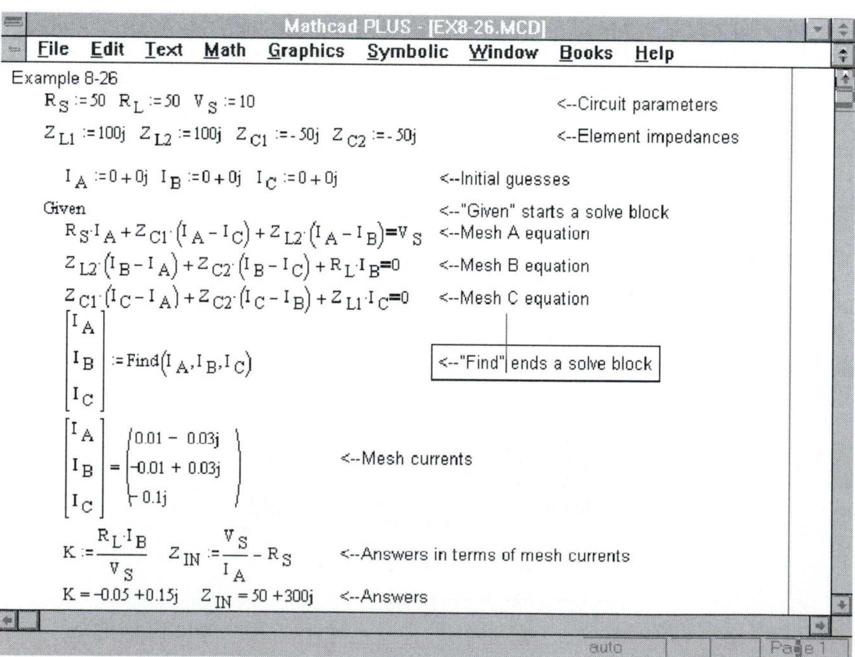

The initial guesses are complex numbers $(0 + j0)$ to let Mathcad know that the unknowns in the solve block are complex. The block starts with the reserve word **"Given"** and ends with the reserve word **"Find."** Each mesh current equation within the solve block is written as a sum of voltages around the mesh. Mathcad solves these equations iteratively using the initial guesses as a starting point. The 3×1 vector listing the mesh current solutions follows the solve block. The required circuit parameters K and Z_{IN} are then written in terms of the mesh currents and their numerical values are displayed. Note that $\mathbf{V}_S/\mathbf{I}_A$ is the impedance seen by the voltage source. To obtain the input impedance at the interface, we must "subtract out" the 50-Ω source resistor. ■

Exercise 8–16

Use the mesh-current or node-voltage method to find the branch currents $\mathbf{I}_1$, $\mathbf{I}_2$, and $\mathbf{I}_3$ in Figure 8–49.

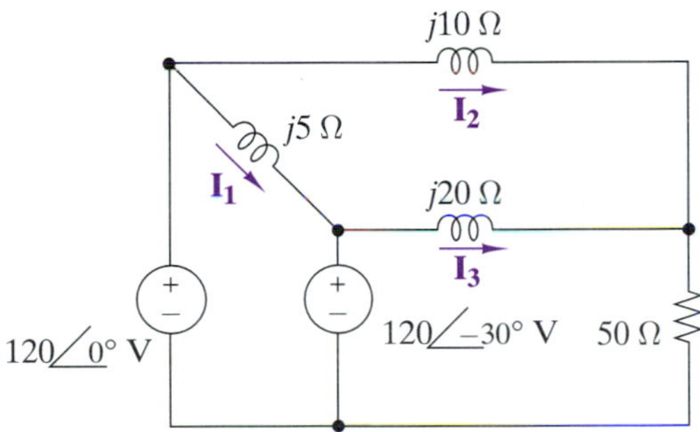

FIGURE 8–49

Answer:

$\mathbf{I}_1 = 12.4\angle{-15°}$ A, $\mathbf{I}_2 = 3.61\angle{-16.1°}$ A, $\mathbf{I}_3 = 1.31\angle 166°$ A

Exercise 8–17

Use the mesh-current or node-voltage method to find the output voltage $\mathbf{V}_2$ and input impedance Z_{IN} in Figure 8–50.

FIGURE 8–50

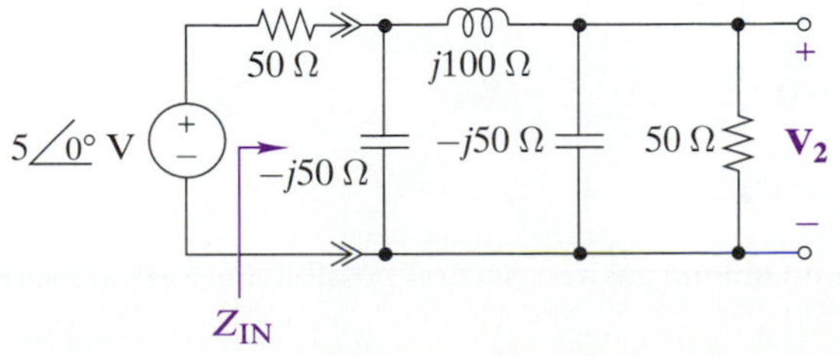

50 Ω
j100 Ω
5∠0° V
−j50 Ω
−j50 Ω
50 Ω
$\mathbf{V}_2$
Z_{IN}

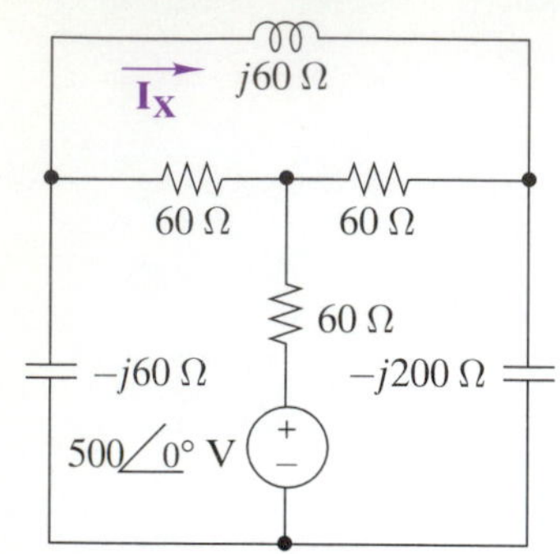

FIGURE 8–51

Answer:

$$\mathbf{V}_2 = 1.77\angle{-135°}\text{ V},\ Z_{IN} = 100 - j100\ \Omega$$

Exercise 8–18

Use the mesh-current or node-voltage method to find the current $\mathbf{I}_X$ in Figure 8–51.

Answer:

$$\mathbf{I}_X = 1.44\angle 171°\text{ mA}$$

Exercise 8–19

Use the mesh-current or node-voltage method to find the current $\mathbf{I}_X$ in Figure 8–34.

Answer:

$$\mathbf{I}_X = 0.206\angle{-158.2°}\text{ A}$$

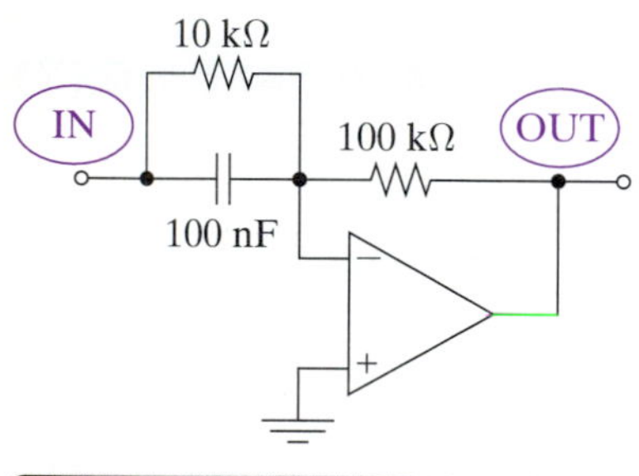

FIGURE 8–52

Exercise 8–20

Find the gain of the inverting OP AMP circuit in Figure 8–52 at $\omega = 1000$ rad/s.

Answer:

$$K = -10 + j10$$

D DESIGN EXERCISE: 8–21

Design a circuit whose phasor input is $\mathbf{V}_S = 10 + j0$ and whose phasor output is $\mathbf{V}_O = 5 - j5$.

FIGURE 8–53

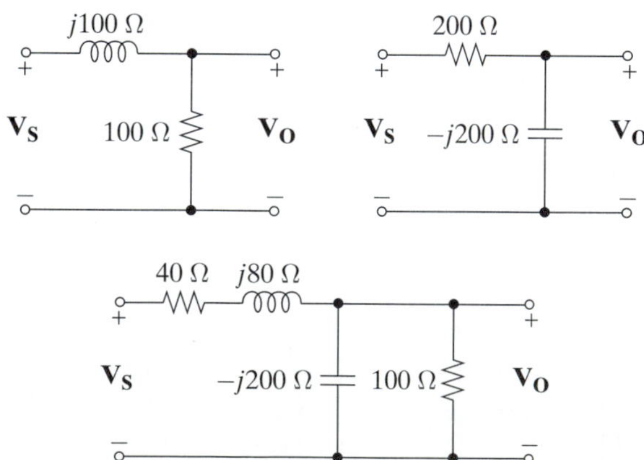

Answer: There is no unique answer. Several possible answers are shown in Figure 8–53.

8–6 THE LINEAR TRANSFORMER

A linear transformer is a circuit element based on the mutual inductance coupling between two coils. In Chapter 6 we introduced the transformer using an ideal model that assumes perfect coupling between the coils. In this section we study the sinusoidal steady-state response of transformers using a model that does not assume perfect coupling.

The element equations for a pair of coupled coils are derived in the time domain in Chapter 6.

$$\text{Coil 1: } v_1(t) = L_1\frac{di_1(t)}{dt} \pm M\frac{di_2(t)}{dt}$$

$$\text{Coil 2: } v_2(t) = \pm M\frac{di_1(t)}{dt} + L_2\frac{di_2(t)}{dt}$$

Transforming these equations into the phasor domain involves replacing waveforms by phasors using the derivative property to obtain the phasors for di_1/dt and di_2/dt:

$$\begin{aligned}\text{Coil 1: } \mathbf{V}_1 &= j\omega L_1\mathbf{I}_1 \pm j\omega M\mathbf{I}_2 \\ \text{Coil 2: } \mathbf{V}_2 &= \pm j\omega M\mathbf{I}_1 + j\omega L_1\mathbf{I}_2\end{aligned} \qquad (8-30)$$

where

1. $\mathbf{V}_1$, $\mathbf{I}_1$, and L_1 are the voltage, current, and self-inductance of coil 1.
2. $\mathbf{V}_2$ $\mathbf{I}_2$, and L_2 are the voltage, current, and self-inductance of coil 2.
3. M is the mutual inductance of the pair of coils.

The ± signs in Eqs. (8–30) remind us that mutual inductance coupling can be either additive (the + sign) or subtractive (the – sign). The appropriate sign depends on the orientation of the reference marks assigned to the voltages and currents relative to dots indicating the spacial orientation of the two coils. Figure 8–54 shows a given pair of coil dots and all possible reference mark assignments for the passive sign convention. The dot convention (see Chapter 6) states that mutual coupling is additive when the current reference marks both enter or both leave a dotted terminal; otherwise, the coupling is subtractive. When using this rule, remember that the coil dots cannot be changed because they describe the physical orientation of the coils. The reference marks for voltage and current can be changed but must adhere to the passive sign convention.

The two self-inductances relate voltage and current at the same pair of terminals, while the mutual inductance relates voltage at one pair of terminals to the current at the other pair. The degree of coupling between coils is specified by the coupling coefficient k defined as

$$k = \frac{M}{\sqrt{L_1L_2}}$$

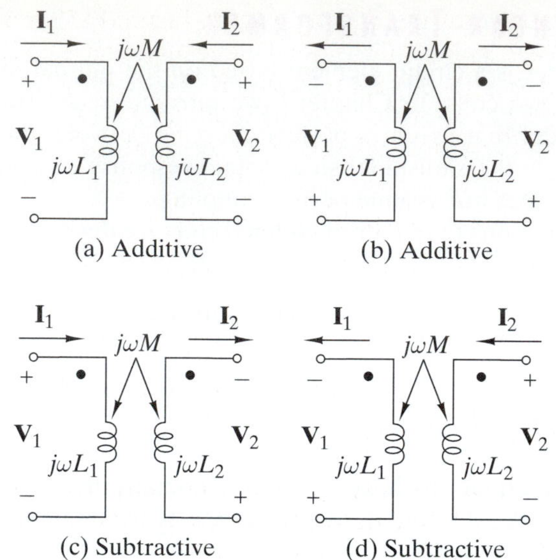

FIGURE 8–54 *Voltage and current reference assignments for a pair of coupled coils.*

Based on energy considerations, we know that $0 \le k \le 1$. The ideal transformer element developed in Chapter 6 assumes that $k = 1$. In this chapter we use the coupled-coil model of the transformer with a coupling coefficient less than 1.

Figure 8–55 shows a phasor-domain model for transformer coupling between a source and a load. The coil connected to the source is called the **primary winding** and the coil connected to the load is called the **secondary winding**. We think of signal transfer passing from the primary to the secondary winding, although signals can travel in either direction.

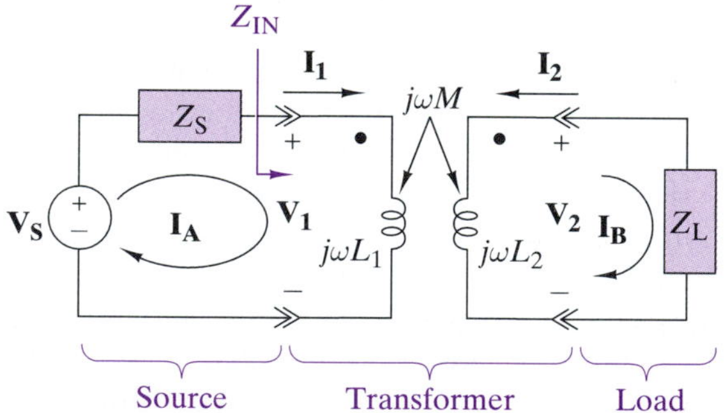

FIGURE 8–55 *Phasor circuit model of transformer coupling.*

Our immediate objective is to write circuit equations for the transformer using the mesh currents $\mathbf{I}_A$ and $\mathbf{I}_B$ in Figure 8–55. Applying KVL around the primary circuit (mesh A) and secondary circuit (mesh B), we obtain the following equations:

$$\begin{aligned} &\text{Mesh A:} \quad Z_S\mathbf{I}_A + \mathbf{V}_1 = \mathbf{V}_S \\ &\text{Mesh B:} \quad -\mathbf{V}_2 + Z_L\mathbf{I}_B = 0 \end{aligned} \tag{8–31}$$

The reference directions for the coil currents in Figure 8–55 are both directed in at dotted terminals, so the mutual inductance coupling is additive and the plus signs in Eq. (8–30) apply. Using KCL, we see that the reference directions for the currents lead to the relations $\mathbf{I}_1 = \mathbf{I}_A$ and $\mathbf{I}_2 = -\mathbf{I}_B$. The **I–V** relationships of the coupled coils in terms of the mesh currents are

$$\begin{aligned} \mathbf{V}_1 &= +j\omega L_1\mathbf{I}_A + j\omega M(-\mathbf{I}_B) \\ \mathbf{V}_2 &= +j\omega M\mathbf{I}_A + j\omega L_2(-\mathbf{I}_B) \end{aligned} \quad (8-32)$$

Substituting the coil voltages from Eq. (8–32) into the KVL equations in Eq. (8–31) yields

$$\begin{aligned} &\text{Mesh A:}\ (Z_S + j\omega L_1)\mathbf{I}_A - j\omega M\mathbf{I}_B = \mathbf{V}_S \\ &\text{Mesh B:}\ -j\omega M\mathbf{I}_A + (Z_L + j\omega L_2)\mathbf{I}_B = 0 \end{aligned} \quad (8-33)$$

This set of mesh equations provides a complete description of the circuit response. Once we solve for the mesh currents, we can calculate every voltage and current using Kirchhoff's laws and element equations.

The method used to develop Eqs. (8–33) illustrates a general approach to the analysis of transformer circuits. The steps in the method are as follows:

STEP 1: Write KVL equations around the primary and secondary circuits using assigned mesh currents, source voltages, and coil voltages.

STEP 2: Write the **I–V** characteristics of the coupled coils in terms of the mesh currents using the dot convention to determine whether the coupling is additive or subtractive.

STEP 3: Use the **I–V** relationships from step 2 to eliminate the coil voltages from the KVL equations obtained in step 1 to obtain mesh-current equations.

The next two examples illustrate this method of formulating mesh equations.

EXAMPLE 8–27

The source circuit in Figure 8–55 has $Z_S = 600 + j800\ \Omega$ and $\mathbf{V}_S = 25\angle 0°$ at $\omega = 1$ krad/s. The transformer has $L_1 = 450$ mH, $L_2 = 50$ mH, and $M = 100$ mH. The load is a 60-Ω resistor in series with a 5-μF capacitor. Find $\mathbf{I}_A$, $\mathbf{I}_B$, $\mathbf{V}_1$, $\mathbf{V}_2$, and the input impedance Z_{IN} seen by the source circuit.

SOLUTION:

The transformer and load impedances are

$$\begin{aligned} j\omega L_1 &= j1000 \times 0.45 = j450\ \Omega \\ j\omega L_2 &= j1000 \times 0.05 = j50\ \Omega \\ j\omega M &= j1000 \times 0.1 = j100\ \Omega \end{aligned}$$

$$Z_L = 60 - j\frac{1}{1000 \times 5 \times 10^{-6}} = 60 - j200\ \Omega$$

Using these impedances in Eq. (8–33) yields the following mesh equations:

$$\text{Mesh A: } (600 + j800 + j450)\mathbf{I}_A - j100\mathbf{I}_B = 25\angle 0^\circ$$

$$\text{Mesh B: } -j100\mathbf{I}_A + (60 - j200 + j50)\mathbf{I}_B = 0$$

Solving these equations for the mesh currents yields

$$\mathbf{I}_A = 7.425 \times 10^{-3} - j15.6 \times 10^{-3} = 17.3\angle -64.5^\circ \text{ mA}$$

$$\mathbf{I}_B = -0.685 \times 10^{-3} + j10.7 \times 10^{-3} = 10.7\angle 93.7^\circ \text{ mA}$$

The coil voltages are found to be

$$\mathbf{V}_1 = \mathbf{V}_S - Z_S\mathbf{I}_A = 8.08 + j3.41 = 8.77\angle 22.9^\circ \text{ V}$$

$$\mathbf{V}_2 = Z_L\mathbf{I}_B = 2.10 + j0.779 = 2.24\angle 20.4^\circ \text{ V}$$

The input impedance seen by the source circuit is

$$Z_{IN} = \frac{\mathbf{V}_1}{\mathbf{I}_A} = \frac{8.08 + j3.41}{(7.43 - j15.6) \times 10^{-3}} = 23.0 + j507.5\ \Omega$$

Exercise 8–22

Repeat Example 8–27 when the dot on the secondary coil in Figure 8–55 is moved to the bottom terminal and all other reference marks stay the same.

Answers:

$\mathbf{I}_A = 17.3\angle -64.5^\circ$ mA; $\mathbf{I}_B = 10.7\angle -86.3^\circ$ mA

$\mathbf{V}_1 = 8.77\angle 22.9^\circ$ V; $\mathbf{V}_2 = 2.23\angle 159.6^\circ$ V; $Z_{IN} = 23.0 + j\,507\ \Omega$

EXAMPLE 8–28

Find $\mathbf{I}_A$, $\mathbf{I}_B$, $\mathbf{V}_1$, $\mathbf{V}_2$, and the impedance Z_{IN} seen by the source circuit in Figure 8–56.

FIGURE 8–56

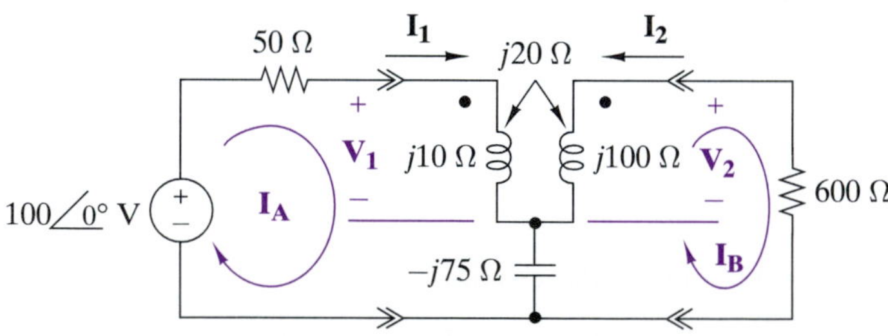

SOLUTION:

The KVL equations around meshes A and B are

$$\text{Mesh A: } (50 - j75)\mathbf{I}_A - (-j75)\mathbf{I}_B + \mathbf{V}_1 = 100\angle 0^\circ$$

$$\text{Mesh B: } -(-j75)\mathbf{I}_A + (600 - j75)\mathbf{I}_B - \mathbf{V}_2 = 0$$

For the assigned reference directions, the mutual coupling is additive and $\mathbf{I}_1 = \mathbf{I}_A$ and $\mathbf{I}_2 = -\mathbf{I}_B$. The coil i–v relations in terms of the mesh currents are

$$\mathbf{V}_1 = j10\mathbf{I}_A + j20(-\mathbf{I}_B)$$
$$\mathbf{V}_2 = j20\mathbf{I}_A + j100(-\mathbf{I}_B)$$

Using these equations to eliminate the coil voltages from the KVL equations yields the following mesh equations:

$$\text{Mesh A: } (50 - j75 + j10)\mathbf{I}_A + (j75 - j20)\mathbf{I}_B = 100\angle 0^\circ$$
$$\text{Mesh B: } (j75 - j20)\mathbf{I}_A + (600 - j75 + j100)\mathbf{I}_B = 0$$

Solving these equations for the mesh currents produces

$$\mathbf{I}_A = 0.756 + j0.896 = 1.17\angle 49.8^\circ \quad \text{A}$$
$$\mathbf{I}_B = 0.0791 - j0.0726 = 0.107\angle -42.5^\circ \quad \text{A}$$

Given the mesh currents, we find the coil voltages from the i–v relations:

$$\mathbf{V}_1 = j10\mathbf{I}_A - j20\mathbf{I}_B = -10.4 + j5.98 = 12.0\angle 150^\circ \quad \text{V}$$
$$\mathbf{V}_2 = j20\mathbf{I}_A - j100\mathbf{I}_B = -25.2 + j7.21 = 25.8\angle 164^\circ \quad \text{V}$$

Finally, the impedance seen looking into the input interface is

$$Z_{IN} = \frac{\mathbf{V}_S - 50\mathbf{I}_A}{\mathbf{I}_A} = 5.06 - j65.2 \quad \Omega$$

■

Exercise 8–23

Find $\mathbf{V}_L$, $\mathbf{V}_1$, $\mathbf{V}_2$, and Z_{IN} in the circuit shown in Figure 8–57.

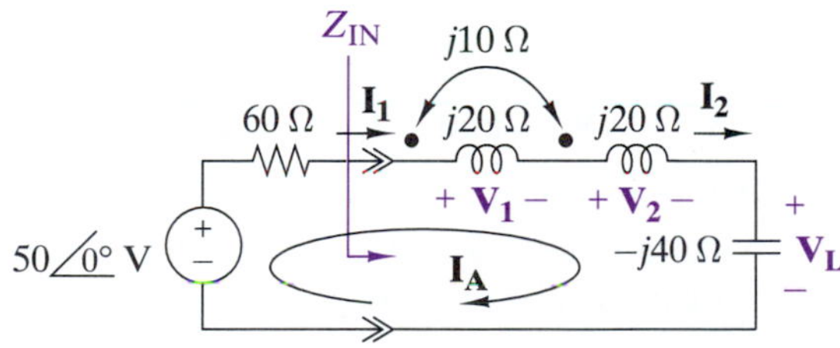

FIGURE 8–57

Answers:

$\mathbf{V}_L = 31.6\angle{-108^\circ}$ V, $\mathbf{V}_1 = 23.7\angle 71.6^\circ$ V, $\mathbf{V}_2 = 23.7\angle 71.6^\circ$ V, $Z_{IN} = 0 + j20\ \Omega$

EQUIVALENT CIRCUITS

Sometimes it is advantageous to replace a pair of coupled coils by an equivalent circuit that does not involve mutual inductance. Two circuits are equivalent if they have the same **I–V** characteristics at specified terminal pairs. Since coupled coils involve two terminal pairs, equivalence requires identical characteristics at both pairs. Although there are many equivalent circuits for coupled coils, we only treat two to illustrate the process.

The element equations for a pair of coupled coils with additive coupling are

$$\mathbf{V}_1 = +j\omega L_1\mathbf{I}_1 + j\omega M\mathbf{I}_2 \qquad (8\text{–}34)$$
$$\mathbf{V}_2 = +j\omega M\mathbf{I}_1 + j\omega L_2\mathbf{I}_2$$

Solving the first of these equations for $\mathbf{I}_1$ yields

$$\mathbf{I}_1 = \frac{\mathbf{V}_1}{j\omega L_1} - \frac{M}{L_1}\mathbf{I}_2 \qquad (8\text{–}35)$$

Using this result to eliminate $\mathbf{I}_1$ from the second equation in Eq. (8–34) produces

$$\mathbf{V}_2 = \frac{M}{L_1}\mathbf{V}_1 + j\omega L_2\left(1 - \frac{M^2}{L_1L_2}\right)\mathbf{I}_2 \qquad (8\text{–}36)$$

Defining a real parameter $n = M/L_1$ and recognizing that the term M^2/L_1L_2 is the square of the coupling coefficient (k^2) allows us to write the **I–V** characteristics of the coupled coils as

$$\mathbf{I}_1 = \frac{\mathbf{V}_1}{j\omega L_1} - n\mathbf{I}_2 \qquad (8\text{–}37)$$
$$\mathbf{V}_2 = n\mathbf{V}_1 + j\omega L_2(1 - k^2)\mathbf{I}_2$$

The first of these two equations is a KCL constraint in the primary circuit and the second is a KVL constraint in the secondary circuit. Taken together, these two equations describe an equivalent circuit shown in Figure 8–58, where the element within the box is an ideal transformer whose element equations are

$$\mathbf{V}_2' = n\mathbf{V}_1' \quad \text{and} \quad \mathbf{I}_1' = -n\mathbf{I}_2' \qquad (8\text{–}38)$$

However, applying KVL in the primary circuit yields $\mathbf{V}_1 = \mathbf{V}'_1$ and applying KCL in the secondary circuit yields $\mathbf{I}_2 = \mathbf{I}_2'$. Hence, the element equations of the ideal transformer can also be expressed as

$$\mathbf{V}_2' = n\mathbf{V}_1 \quad \text{and} \quad \mathbf{I}_1' = -n\mathbf{I}_2 \qquad (8\text{–}39)$$

which is the form required to relate the two equations Eq. (8–37) to the equivalent circuit in Figure 8–58.

The equivalent circuit in Figure 8–58 illustrates that an ideal transformer in combination with two uncoupled inductances can represent a pair of coupled coils. In this equivalent circuit the self-inductance of the primary coil is connected in the parallel across the input. For dc signals this inductance acts like a short circuit that blocks signal passage in either direction. In other words, a transformer cannot pass dc signals. In Figure 8–58 the self-inductance of the secondary coil leads to an impedance $j\omega L_2(1 - k^2)$ connected in series with the load impedance. With perfect

CIRCUITS I 02/03/00

1.) P1.12 (LAMP COST)

2.) P1.13 (BATTERY LIFE)

3.) P1.23 (POWER ABSORPTION)

(4.) P2.20(C4) (SOURCE TRANSFORMATION)

5.) P2.22 (KCL & KVL)

6.) P2.31 (EQUIVALENT CIRCUIT)

7.) P2.51 (CIRCUIT REDUCTION)

8.) P2.54 (CIRCUIT REDUCTION)

			HOMEWORK:	
WED	03/15	4-13		
THURS	03/16	EXERCISE 4-10	DUE 03/27/00	
MON	03/20	4-23	4-25	4-22
WED	03/22	4-27	4-31	4-20(a) & (b) & (c)
THURS	03/23	4-41		4-24

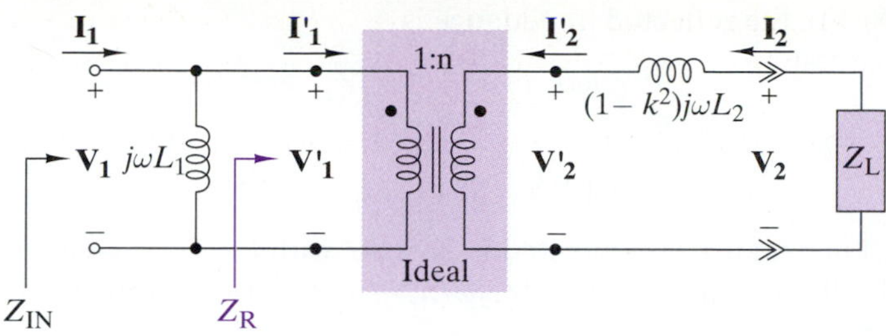

FIGURE 8–58 *Equivalent circuit with ideal transformer when* n = M/L*1*.

coupling ($k = 1$) this impedance is zero and the voltage across the load becomes $\mathbf{V}_2 = \mathbf{V}'_2 = n\mathbf{V}_1$. In other words, in a transformer with perfect or nearly perfect ($k \approx 1$) coupling the secondary voltage is equal to the turns ratio times the primary voltage.

The impedance seen looking into the primary side of the ideal transformer in Figure 8–58 is called the **reflected impedance** Z_R. In Chapter 6 we showed that the input resistance of an ideal transformer with turns ratio n is R_L/n^2, where R_L is the total resistance connected to the secondary winding. Clearly the same concept applies in the phasor domain, where the load is represented by impedance. The total impedance connected to the secondary of the ideal transformer in Figure 8–58 is $j\omega L_2(1 - k^2) + Z_L$, so the reflected impedance seen on the primary side of the ideal transformer is

$$Z_R = \frac{j\omega L_2(1 - k^2) + Z_L}{n^2} \qquad (8\text{–}40)$$

For perfect or nearly perfect coupling ($k \approx 1$) the reflected impedance is Z_L/n^2.

The reflected impedance in Eq. (8–40) is connected in parallel with the impedance of the self-inductance of the primary winding. Consequently, the input impedance in Figure 8–58 is

$$Z_{IN} = (j\omega L_1)\|Z_R = \frac{1}{\dfrac{1}{j\omega L_1} + \dfrac{n^2}{j\omega L_2(1 - k^2) + Z_L}} \qquad (8\text{–}41)$$

The next example applies these results.

EXAMPLE 8–29

Use the equivalent circuit in Figure 8–58 to find the reflected impedance and the input impedance of the coupled coil circuit in Figure 8–55 for $L_1 = 450$ mH, $L_2 = 50$ mH, $M = 100$ mH, $\omega = 1000$ rad/s, and $Z_L = 60 - j200\ \Omega$.

SOLUTION:

The parameters for the transformer are

$$k^2 = \frac{M^2}{L_1L_2} = \frac{4}{9} \quad \text{and} \quad n = \frac{M}{L_1} = \frac{2}{9}$$

Using Eq. (8–40), the reflected impedance is

$$Z_R = \frac{j\omega L_2(1 - k^2) + Z_L}{n^2}$$
$$= 1215 - j3487\ \Omega$$

The reflected impedance is connected in parallel with the impedance of the primary coil self-inductance—namely, $j\omega L_1 = j1000 \times 0.45 = j450\ \Omega$. Hence, the input impedance is

$$Z_{IN} = \frac{1}{\dfrac{1}{j450} + \dfrac{1}{1215 - j3487}} = 23.0 + j507.5\quad \Omega$$

This result agrees with the answer in Example 8–27, where the input impedance was found using mesh-current analysis. ■

Exercise 8–24

Find the coupling coefficient, turns ratio, and reflected impedance of the equivalent circuit in Figure 8–58 for $L_1 = 20$ mH, $L_2 = 100$ mH, $M = 44$ mH, $\omega = 2500$ rad/s, and $Z_L = 250 + j0\ \Omega$.

Answers:

$k = 0.984$, $n = 11/5$, and $Z_R = 51.65 + j1.65\ \Omega$

Figure 8–59 shows a T-circuit consisting of three uncoupled inductances. Using the mesh currents $\mathbf{I}_A$ and $\mathbf{I}_B$, we can write mesh equations for the T-circuit as

$$\mathbf{V}_1 = [j\omega(L_1 \mp M) \pm j\omega M]\mathbf{I}_A - (\pm j\omega M)\mathbf{I}_B$$
$$-\mathbf{V}_2 = -(\pm j\omega M)\mathbf{I}_A + [j\omega(L_2 \mp M) \pm j\omega M]\mathbf{I}_B$$

FIGURE 8–59 T-equivalent circuit.

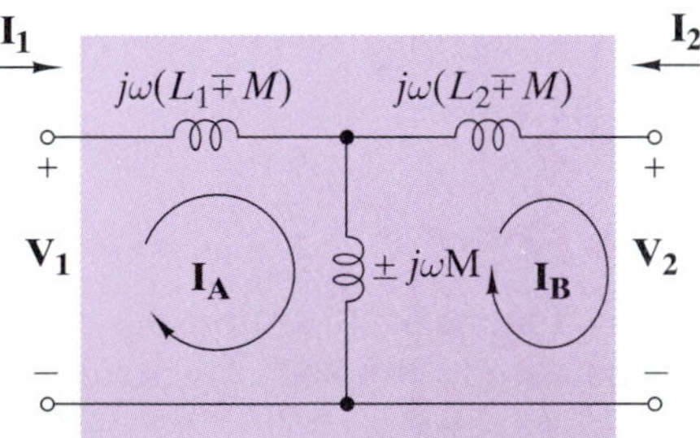

But the coil currents $\mathbf{I}_1$ and $\mathbf{I}_2$ in Figure 8–59 are related to the mesh currents as $\mathbf{I}_1 = \mathbf{I}_A$ and $\mathbf{I}_2 = -\mathbf{I}_B$, and so these mesh equations reduce to

$$\mathbf{V}_1 = j\omega L_1\mathbf{I}_1 \pm j\omega M\mathbf{I}_2$$
$$\mathbf{V}_2 = \pm j\omega M\mathbf{I}_1 + j\omega L_2\mathbf{I}_2$$

These equations are the same as the coupled-coil relations in Eqs. (8–30). Hence, the T-circuit in Figure 8–59 is equivalent to a pair of coupled coils with additive (plus sign) or subtractive (minus sign) coupling.

For additive coupling, the equivalent T-circuit involves three uncoupled inductances whose values are $L_1 - M$, $L_2 - M$, and M. For subtractive coupling the three inductances are $L_1 + M$, $L_2 + M$, and $-M$. In both cases, one of the inductances in the equivalent T-circuit is negative. Negative inductances can be used in circuit analysis even though they are not physically realizable using passive elements.

EXAMPLE 8–30

Use the equivalent T-circuit in Figure 8–59 to find the input impedance of the coupled coil circuit in Figure 8–55 for $L_1 = 450$ mH, $L_2 = 50$ mH, $M = 100$ mH, $\omega = 1000$ rad/s, and $Z_L = 60 - j200\ \Omega$.

SOLUTION:

The coils in Figure 8–55 have additive coupling, so the three impedances in the equivalent T-circuit are

$$j\omega(L_1 - M) = j250\ \Omega$$
$$j\omega(L_2 - M) = -j50\ \Omega$$
$$j\omega M = j100\ \Omega$$

Note that $L_2 - M = -50$ mH is a negative inductance. Figure 8–60 shows the equivalent T-circuit together with the load. The input impedance to this circuit is

$$\begin{aligned} Z_{IN} &= j350 + j100 \| (-j50 + Z_L) \\ &= j350 + \cfrac{1}{\cfrac{1}{j100} + \cfrac{1}{60 - j250}} \\ &= 22.0 + j507.5\ \Omega \end{aligned}$$

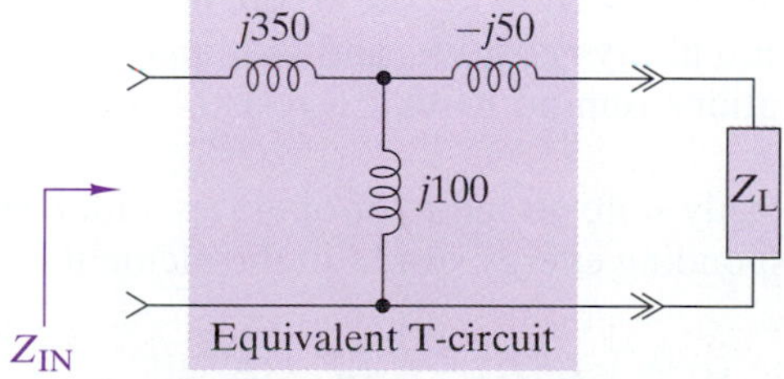

FIGURE 8–60

This result agrees with the answer in Example 8–29, where the input impedance was found using a different equivalent circuit. ■

Exercise 8–25

Use an equivalent T-circuit to find the input impedance of a pair of coils with subtractive coupling and $L_1 = 20$ mH, $L_2 = 250$ mH, $M = 70$ mH, $\omega = 2000$ rad/s, and $Z_L = 500 + j100\ \Omega$.

Answer:

$$16.1 + j20.7\ \Omega$$

8–7 ENERGY AND POWER

In the sinusoidal steady state, ac power is transferred from sources to various loads. To study the transfer process, we must calculate the power delivered in the sinusoidal steady state to any specified load. It turns out that there is an upper bound on the available load power; hence, we need to understand how to adjust the load to extract the maximum power from the rest of the circuit. In this section the load is assumed to be made up of passive resistance, inductance, and capacitance. To reach our objectives, we must first study the power and energy delivered to these passive elements in the sinusoidal steady state.

In the sinusoidal steady state the current through a resistor can be expressed as $i_R(t) = I_A \cos(\omega t)$. The instantaneous power delivered to the resistor is

$$\begin{aligned} p_R(t) &= Ri_R^2(t) = RI_A^2 \cos^2(\omega t) \\ &= \frac{RI_A^2}{2}[1 + \cos(2\omega t)] \end{aligned} \tag{8-42}$$

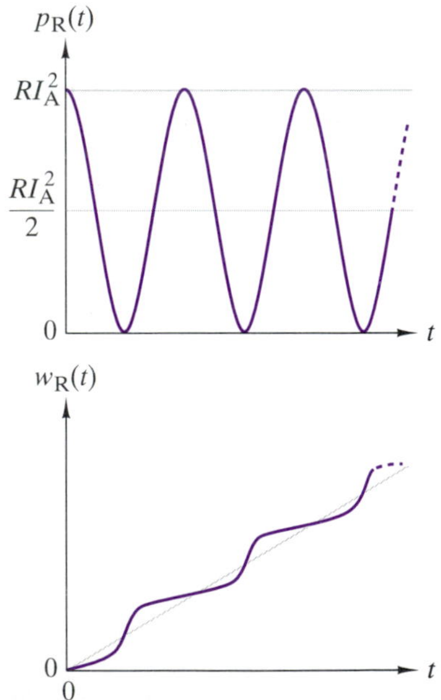

FIGURE 8–61 *Resistor power and energy in the sinusoidal steady state.*

where the identity $\cos^2(x) = ½[1 + \cos(2x)]$ is used to obtain the last line in Eq. (8–42). The energy delivered for $t \geq 0$ is found to be

$$\begin{aligned} w_R(t) &= \int_0^t p_R(x)dx = \frac{RI_A^2}{2}\int_0^t dx + \frac{RI_A^2}{2}\int_0^t \cos 2\omega x\, dx \\ &= \frac{RI_A^2}{2}t + \frac{RI_A^2}{4\omega}\sin 2\omega t \end{aligned}$$

Figure 8–61 shows the time variation of $p_R(t)$ and $w_R(t)$. Note that the power is a periodic function with twice the frequency of the current, that both $p_R(t)$ and $w_R(t)$ are always positive, and that $w_R(t)$ increases without bound. These observations remind us that a resistor is a passive element that dissipates energy.

In the sinusoidal steady state an inductor operates with a current $i_L(t) = I_A \cos(\omega t)$. The corresponding energy stored in the element is

$$\begin{aligned} w_L(t) &= \frac{1}{2}Li_L^2(t) = \frac{1}{2}LI_A^2\cos^2\omega t \\ &= \frac{1}{4}LI_A^2(1 + \cos 2\omega t) \end{aligned}$$

where the identity $\cos^2(x) = ½\,[1 + \cos(2x)]$ is again used to produce the last line. The instantaneous power delivered to the inductor is

$$p_L(t) = \frac{dw_L}{dt} = -\frac{\omega L I_A^2}{2}\sin(2\omega t) \qquad (8\text{–}43)$$

Figure 8–62 shows the time variation of $p_L(t)$ and $w_L(t)$. Observe that both $p_L(t)$ and $w_L(t)$ are periodic functions at twice the frequency of the ac current, that $p_L(t)$ is alternately positive and negative, and that $w_L(t)$ is never negative. Since $w_L(t) \geq 0$, the inductor does not deliver net energy to the rest of the circuit. Unlike the resistor's energy in Figure 8–61, the energy in the inductor is bounded by $½\, LI_A^2 \geq w_L(t)$, which means that the inductor does not dissipate energy. Finally, since $p_L(t)$ alternates signs, we see that the inductor stores energy during a positive half cycle and then returns the energy undiminished during the next negative half cycle. Thus, in the sinusoidal steady state there is a lossless interchange of energy between an inductor and the rest of the circuit.

In the sinusoidal steady state the voltage across a capacitor is $v_C(t) = V_A\cos(\omega t)$. The energy stored in the element is

$$\begin{aligned} w_C(t) &= \frac{1}{2}Cv_C^2(t) = \frac{1}{2}CV_A^2\cos^2\omega t \\ &= \frac{1}{4}CV_A^2(1 + \cos 2\omega t) \end{aligned}$$

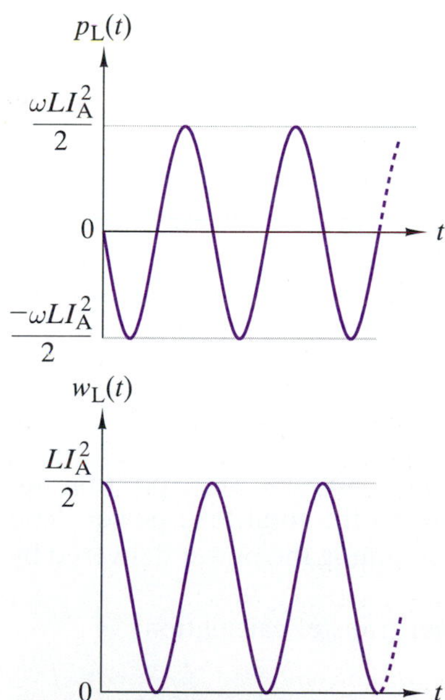

FIGURE 8–62 *Inductor power and energy in the sinusoidal steady state.*

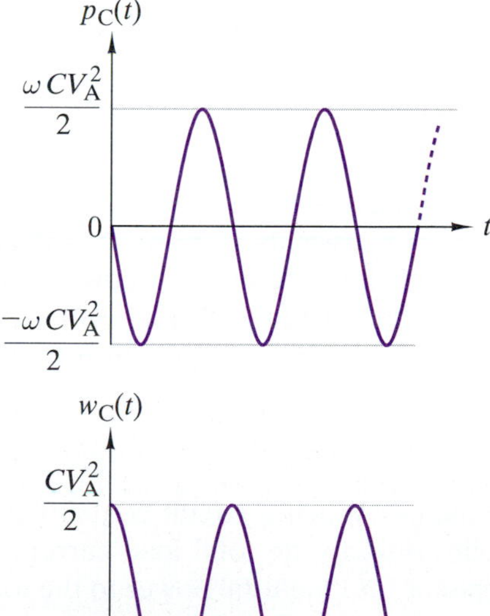

FIGURE 8–63 *Capacitor power and energy in the sinusoidal steady state.*

The instantaneous power delivered to the capacitor is

$$p_C(t) = \frac{dw_C}{dt} = -\frac{\omega C V_A^2}{2}\sin(2\omega t) \tag{8-44}$$

Figure 8–63 shows the time variation of $p_C(t)$ and $w_C(t)$. Observe that these relationships are the duals of those found for the inductor. Thus, in the sinusoidal steady state the element power is sinusoidal and there is a lossless interchange of energy between the capacitor and the rest of the circuit.

AVERAGE POWER

We are now in a position to calculate the average power delivered to various loads. The instantaneous power delivered to any of the three passive elements is a periodic function that can be described by an average value. The **average power** in the sinusoidal steady state is defined as

$$P = \frac{1}{T_0}\int_0^{T_0} p(t)dt$$

The power variation of the inductor in Eq. (8–43) and capacitor in Eq. (8–44) have the same sinusoidal form. The average value of any sinusoid is zero since the areas under alternate cycles cancel. Hence, the average power delivered to an inductor or capacitor is zero:

$$\text{Inductor: } P_L = 0$$

$$\text{Capacitor: } P_C = 0$$

The resistor power in Eq. (8–42) has both a sinusoidal ac component and a constant dc component $\frac{1}{2}RI_A^2$. The average value of the ac component is zero, but the dc component yields

$$\text{Resistor: } P_R = \frac{1}{2}RI_A^2$$

To calculate the average power delivered to an arbitrary load $Z_L = R_L + jX_L$, we use phasor circuit analysis to find the phasor current $\mathbf{I}_L$ through Z_L. The average power delivered to the load is dissipated in R_L, since the reactance X_L represents the net inductance or capacitance of the load. Hence the average power to the load is

$$P = \frac{1}{2}R_L|\mathbf{I}_L|^2 \tag{8-45}$$

Caution: When a circuit contains two or more sources, superposition applies only to the total load current and not to the total load power. You cannot find the total power to the load by summing the power delivered by each source acting alone.

The following example illustrates a power transfer calculation.

EXAMPLE 8–31

Find the average power delivered to the load to the right of the interface in Figure 8–64.

FIGURE 8–64

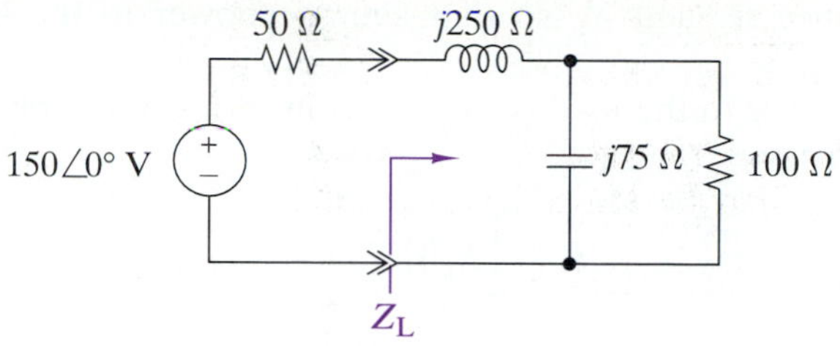

50 Ω
j250 Ω
150∠0° V
j75 Ω
100 Ω
Z_L

SOLUTION:

The equivalent impedance to the right of the interface is

$$Z_L = j250 + \frac{1}{\dfrac{1}{-j75} + \dfrac{1}{100}} = 36 + j202 \quad \Omega$$

The current delivered to the load is

$$\mathbf{I}_L = \frac{150\angle 0^\circ}{50 + Z_L} = 0.683\angle -66.9^\circ \quad \text{A}$$

Hence the average power delivered across the interface is

$$P = \frac{1}{2} R_L |\mathbf{I}_L|^2 = \frac{36}{2}|0.683|^2 = 8.40 \quad \text{W}$$

Note: All of this power goes into the 100-Ω resistor since the inductor and capacitor do not absorb average power. ■

Exercise 8–26

Find the average power delivered to the 25-Ω load resistor in Figure 8–65.

Answer: 234 W

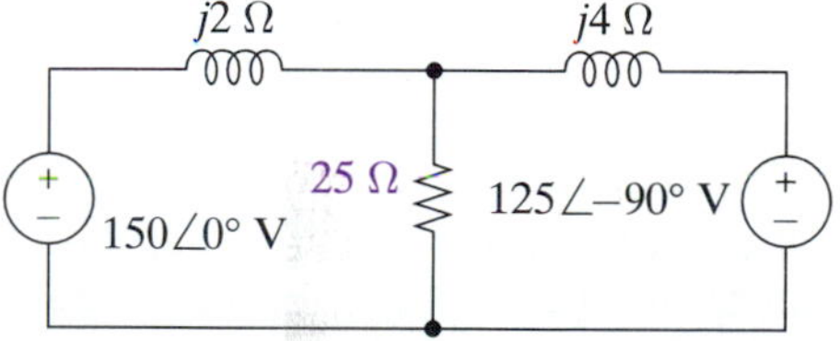

FIGURE 8–65

MAXIMUM POWER

To address the maximum power transfer problem, we model the source/load interface as shown in Figure 8–66. The source circuit is represented by a Thévenin equivalent circuit with source voltage $\mathbf{V}_T$ and source impedance $Z_T = R_T + jX_T$. The load circuit is represented by an equivalent impedance $Z_L = R_L + jX_L$. In the maximum power transfer problem the source parameters $\mathbf{V}_T$, R_T, and X_T are given, and the objective is to adjust

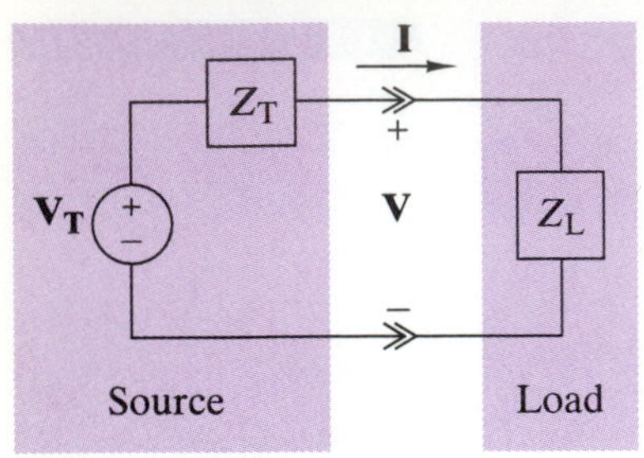

FIGURE 8–66 *A source-load interface in the sinusoidal steady state.*

the load impedance R_L and X_L so that average power to the load is a maximum.

The average power to the load is expressed in terms of the phasor current and load resistance:

$$P = \frac{1}{2}R_L|\mathbf{I}|^2$$

Then, using series equivalence, we express the magnitude of the interface current as

$$|\mathbf{I}| = \left|\frac{\mathbf{V}_T}{Z_T + Z_L}\right| = \frac{|\mathbf{V}_T|}{|(R_T + R_L) + j(X_T + X_L)|}$$
$$= \frac{|\mathbf{V}_T|}{\sqrt{(R_T + R_L)^2 + (X_T + X_L)^2}}$$

Combining the last two equations yields the average power delivered across the interface:

$$P = \frac{1}{2}\frac{R_L|\mathbf{V}_T|^2}{(R_T + R_L)^2 + (X_T + X_L)^2} \tag{8–46}$$

The quantities $|\mathbf{V}_T|$, R_T, and X_T in Eq. (8–46) are fixed. Our problem is to select R_L and X_L to maximize P.

Clearly, for every value of R_L the denominator in Eq. (8–46) is minimized and P maximized when $X_L = -X_T$. This choice of X_L is possible because a reactance can be positive or negative. When the source Thévenin equivalent has an inductive reactance ($X_T > 0$), we modify the load to have a capacitive reactance of the same magnitude, and vice versa. This step reduces the net reactance of the series connection in Figure 8–66 to zero, creating a condition in which the net impedance seen by the Thévenin voltage source is purely resistive.

When the source and load reactances cancel out, the expression for average power in Eq. (8–46) reduces to

$$P = \frac{1}{2}\frac{R_L|\mathbf{V}_T|^2}{(R_T + R_L)^2} \tag{8–47}$$

This equation has the same form encountered in Chapter 3 in dealing with maximum power transfer in resistive circuits. From the derivation in Sect. 3-5, we know P is maximized when $R_L = R_T$. In summary, to obtain maximum power transfer in the sinusoidal steady state, we select the load resistance and reactance so that

$$R_L = R_T \quad \text{and} \quad X_L = -X_T \tag{8–48}$$

These conditions can be compactly expressed in the following way:

$$Z_L = Z_T^* \tag{8–49}$$

The condition for maximum power transfer is called a **conjugate match**, since the load impedance is the conjugate of the source impedance. When the conjugate-match conditions are inserted into Eq. (8–46), we find that the maximum average power available from the source circuit is

$$P_{MAX} = \frac{|\mathbf{V}_T|^2}{8R_T} \quad (8-50)$$

where $|\mathbf{V}_T|$ is the peak amplitude of the Thévenin equivalent voltage.

It is important to remember that conjugate matching applies when the source is fixed and the load is adjustable. These conditions arise frequently in power-limited communication systems. However, as we will see in Chapter 14, conjugate matching does not apply to electrical power systems because the power transfer constraints are different.

EXAMPLE 8–32

(a) Calculate the average power delivered to the load in the circuit shown in Figure 8–67 for $v_S(t) = 5 \cos 10^6 t$, $R = 200\ \Omega$, $R_L = 200\ \Omega$, and $C = 10$ nF.
(b) Calculate the maximum average power available at the interface and specify the load required to draw the maximum power.

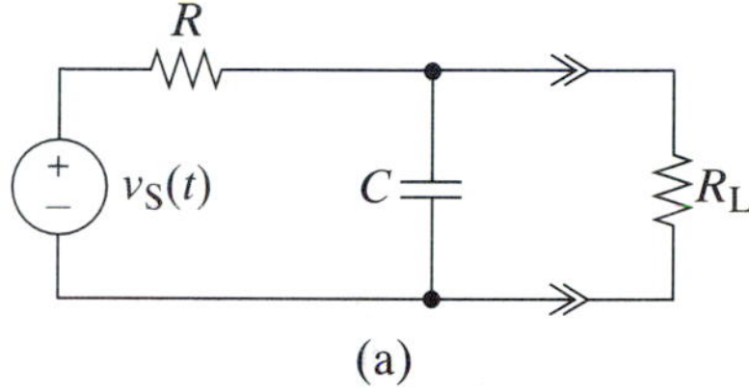

(a)

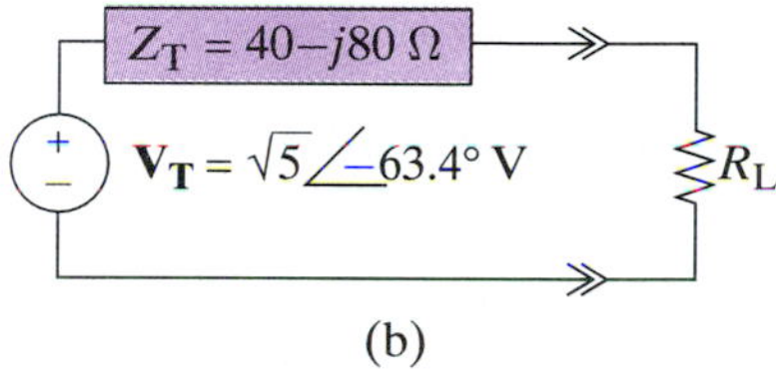

(b)

FIGURE 8–67

SOLUTION:

(a) To find the power delivered to the 200-Ω load resistor, we use a Thévenin equivalent circuit. By voltage division, the open-circuit voltage at the interface is

$$\mathbf{V}_T = \frac{Z_C}{Z_R + Z_C}\mathbf{V}_S = \frac{-j100}{200 - j100}5\angle 0°$$
$$= 1 - j2 = \sqrt{5}\angle -63.4° \text{ V}$$

By inspection, the short-circuit current at the interface is

$$\mathbf{I}_N = \frac{5\angle 0°}{200} = 0.025 + j0 \text{ A}$$

Given $\mathbf{V}_T$ and $\mathbf{I}_N$, we calculate the Thévenin source impedance.

$$Z_T = \frac{\mathbf{V}_T}{\mathbf{I}_N} = \frac{1 - j2}{0.025} = 40 - j80 \ \ \Omega$$

Using the Thévenin equivalent shown in Figure 8–67(b), we find that the current through the 200-Ω resistor is

$$\mathbf{I} = \frac{\mathbf{V}_T}{Z_T + Z_L} = \frac{\sqrt{5}\angle -63.4°}{40 - j80 + 200} = 8.84\angle -45° \text{ mA}$$

and the average power delivered to the load resistor is

$$P = \frac{1}{2}R_L|\mathbf{I}|^2 = 100(8.84 \times 10^{-3})^2 = 7.81 \text{ mW}$$

(b) Using Eq. (8–50), the maximum average power available at the interface is

$$P_{MAX} = \frac{|\mathbf{V}_T|^2}{8R_T} = \frac{(\sqrt{5})^2}{(8)(40)} = 15.6 \text{ mW}$$

The 200-Ω load resistor in part (a) draws about half of the maximum available power. To extract maximum power, the load impedance must be

$$Z_L = Z_T^* = 40 + j80 \ \Omega$$

This impedance can be obtained using a 40-Ω resistor in series with a reactance of +80 Ω. The required reactance is inductive (positive) and can be produced by an inductance of

$$L = \frac{|X_T|}{\omega} = \frac{80}{10^6} = 80 \ \mu\text{H}$$ ■

EXAMPLE 8–33

(a) Find the maximum average power available at the output interface of the transformer circuit in Figure 8–68.
(b) Compare the result in part (a) with the average power delivered for $Z_L = 400 \ \Omega$.

FIGURE 8–68

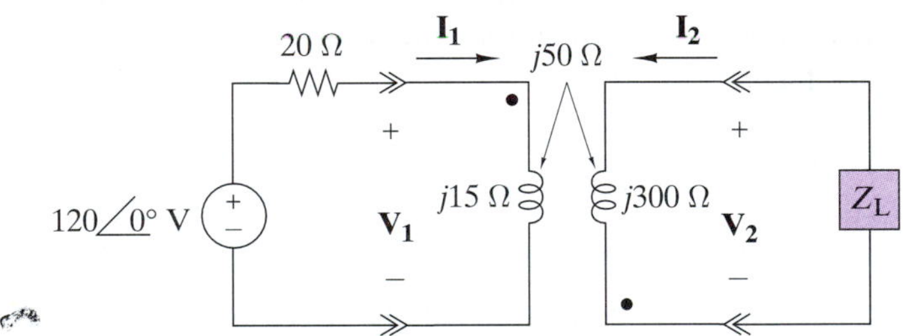

SOLUTION:

(a) To obtain the Thévenin equivalent seen by the load in Figure 8–68, we need the open-circuit voltage and short-circuit current at the output interface. Given the reference directions in the figure, the coupling is subtractive and the coupled coil element equations are

$$\mathbf{V}_1 = j15\mathbf{I}_1 - j50\mathbf{I}_2$$

$$\mathbf{V}_2 = -j50\mathbf{I}_1 + j300\mathbf{I}_2$$

The KVL equation around the primary circuit is

$$120\angle 0° = 20\mathbf{I}_1 + \mathbf{V}_1$$

Given these KVL and element equations, we can now determine the open-circuit voltage and short-circuit current.

With an open circuit at the output, $\mathbf{I}_2 = 0$ and the first element equation yields $\mathbf{V}_1 = j15\mathbf{I}_1$. When this result is substituted into the KVL equation, we can solve for $\mathbf{I}_1$:

$$\mathbf{I}_1 = \frac{120\angle 0^\circ}{20 + j15} = 4.80\angle -36.9^\circ$$

Inserting this value into the second element equation yields the open-circuit voltage.

$$\mathbf{V}_T = \mathbf{V}_2 = -j50\mathbf{I}_1 = 240\angle -126.9^\circ \text{ V}$$

With a short circuit at the output $\mathbf{V}_2 = 0$ and the second element equation yields $\mathbf{I}_1 = 6\mathbf{I}_2$. When this relationship for $\mathbf{I}_1$ is substituted into the first element equation, we obtain

$$\mathbf{V}_1 = j15(6\mathbf{I}_2) = j50\mathbf{I}_2 = j40\mathbf{I}_2$$

Inserting $\mathbf{V}_1 = j40\mathbf{I}_2$ and $\mathbf{I}_1 = 6\mathbf{I}_2$ into the KVL equation allows us to solve for the short-circuit current:

$$\mathbf{I}_N = -\mathbf{I}_2 = -\frac{120\angle 0^\circ}{120 + j40} = -0.9 + j0.3$$

Given the open-circuit voltage and short-circuit current, the Thévenin impedance is

$$Z_T = \frac{\mathbf{V}_T}{\mathbf{I}_N} = \frac{240\angle -126.9^\circ}{-0.9 + j0.3} = 80 + j240 \ \Omega$$

Finally, given the Thévenin voltage and impedance, we calculate the maximum average power available at the load:

$$P_{\text{MAX}} = \frac{|\mathbf{V}_T|^2}{8R_T} = \frac{(240)^2}{8 \times 80} = 90 \text{ W}$$

(b) For $Z_L = 400\ \Omega$, the current through the load is

$$\mathbf{I}_L = \frac{\mathbf{V}_T}{400 + Z_T} = \frac{240\angle -126.9^\circ}{480 + j240} = 0.447\angle -153.4^\circ \text{ A}$$

The average power delivered to a 400-Ω load resistance is

$$P = \frac{1}{2}R_L|\mathbf{I}_L|^2 = 200\,(0.447)^2 = 39.96 \text{ W}$$ ■

Exercise 8–27

Calculate the maximum average power available at the interface in Figure 8–69.

Answer: 125 mW.

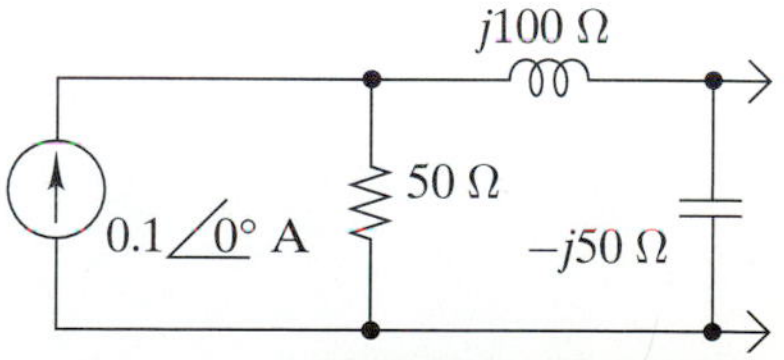

j100 Ω
50 Ω
0.1∠0° A
−j50 Ω

FIGURE 8–69

SUMMARY

- A phasor is a complex number representing a sinusoidal waveform. The magnitude and angle of the phasor correspond to the amplitude and phase angle of the sinusoid. The phasor does not provide frequency information.

- The additive property states that adding phasors is equivalent to adding sinusoids of the same frequency. The derivative property states that multiplying a phasor by $j\omega$ is equivalent to differentiating the corresponding sinusoid.
- In the sinusoidal steady state, phasor currents and voltages obey Kirchhoff's laws and the element i–v relationships are written in terms of impedances. Impedance can be defined as the ratio of phasor voltage over phasor current. The device and connection constraints for phasor circuit analysis have the same form as resistance circuits.
- Phasor circuit analysis techniques include series equivalence, parallel equivalence, Y-Δ transformations, circuit reduction, Thévenin's and Norton's theorems, unit output method, superposition, node-voltage analysis, and mesh-current analysis.
- In the sinusoidal steady state the equivalent impedance at a pair of terminals is $Z(j\omega) = R(\omega) + jX(\omega)$, where $R(\omega)$ is called resistance and $X(\omega)$ is called reactance. A frequency at which an equivalent impedance is purely real is called a resonant frequency. Admittance is the reciprocal of impedance.
- A linear transformer is a two-port circuit element based on the mutual inductance coupling between two coils. Linear transformers can be analyzed using a mesh-current approach and have several different equivalent circuits.
- In the sinusoidal steady state the instantaneous power to a passive element is a periodic function at twice the frequency of the driving force. The average power delivered to an inductor or capacitor is zero. The average power delivered to a resistor is $\frac{1}{2}R|\mathbf{I}_R|^2$. The maximum average power is delivered by a fixed source to an adjustable load when the source and load impedances are conjugates.

EN ROUTE OBJECTIVES AND ASSOCIATED PROBLEMS

ERO 8–1 SINUSOIDS AND PHASORS (SECT. 8–1)

Use the additive and derivative properties of phasors to convert sinusoidal waveforms into phasors and vice versa.

8–1 Transform the following sinusoids into phasor form. Use the additive property of phasors to find $v_1(t) + v_2(t)$. Construct a phasor diagram showing these voltages.

$$\text{(a) } v_1(t) = 100\cos(\omega t + 45°)$$

$$\text{(b) } v_2(t) = 150\cos\omega t + 200\sin\omega t$$

8–2 Transform the following sinusoids into phasor form. Use the additive property of phasors to find $i_1(t) + i_2(t)$. Construct the phasor diagram showing these currents.

(a) $i_1(t) = 6 \sin \omega t$

(b) $i_2(t) = 3 \cos(\omega t - 90°)$

8–3 Convert the following phasors into sinusoidal waveforms at a frequency of 10 krad/s:

(a) $\mathbf{V}_1 = 10e^{-j30°}$ (b) $\mathbf{V}_2 = 60e^{-j220°}$

(c) $\mathbf{I}_1 = 5e^{j90°}$ (d) $\mathbf{I}_2 = 2e^{j270°}$

8–4 Use the additive property on the phasors in Problem 8–3 to find $v_1(t) + v_2(t)$ and $i_1(t) + i_2(t)$. Construct phasor diagrams for the phasors and the sums.

8–5 Use the derivative property on the phasors in Problem 8–3 to find the time derivatives of $v_1(t)$ and $v_2(t)$.

8–6 Convert the following phasors into sinusoids at a frequency of 200 rad/s.

(a) $\mathbf{V}_1 = \dfrac{10 + j10}{2 - j3}$ (b) $\mathbf{V}_2 = (3 - j8)5e^{-j60°}$

(c) $\mathbf{I}_1 = \dfrac{10}{1 + j3}$ (d) $\mathbf{I}_2 = \dfrac{1 + j3}{1 - j3}$

8–7 Use the additive and derivative properties of phasors to find the $v(t)$ that meets the condition

$$\frac{dv(t)}{dt} + 100v(t) = \sin 50t$$

8–8 Given the sinusoids

$$v_1(t) = 50 \cos(\omega t - 45°) \quad \text{and} \quad v_2(t) = 25 \sin \omega t$$

use the additive property of phasors to find $v_3(t)$ such that $v_1 + v_2 + v_3 = 0$.

8–9 The phasor $\mathbf{V}_1 = 4 + j6$ is rotated clockwise by 70°. Express the resulting phasor in rectangular form.

8–10 Given a phasor $\mathbf{V}_1 = -3 + j4$, use phasor methods to find a voltage $v_2(t)$ that leads $v_1(t)$ by 90° and has an amplitude of 10 V.

ERO 8–2 EQUIVALENT IMPEDANCE (SECTS. 8–2, 8–3)

Given a linear circuit, use series and parallel equivalence to find the equivalent impedance at a specified pair of terminal.

8–11 Express the equivalent impedance of the following circuits in rectangular and polar form:

(a) A 50-Ω resistor in series with a 20-mH inductor at $\omega = 2000$ rad/s

(b) A 50-Ω resistor in parallel with a 20-μF capacitor at $\omega = 2000$ rad/s

(c) The circuit formed by connecting the circuits in (a) and (b) in parallel.

(d) Repeat (c) at $\omega = 4000$ rad/s.

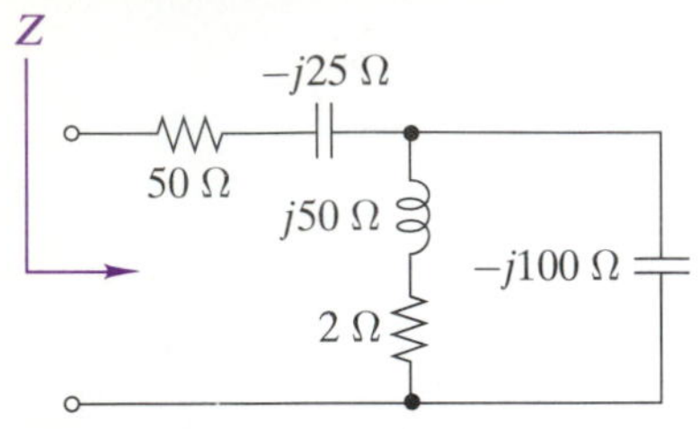

FIGURE P8-12

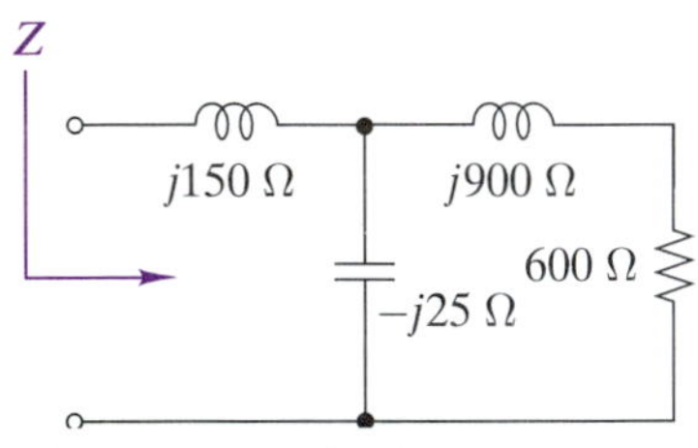

FIGURE P8-14

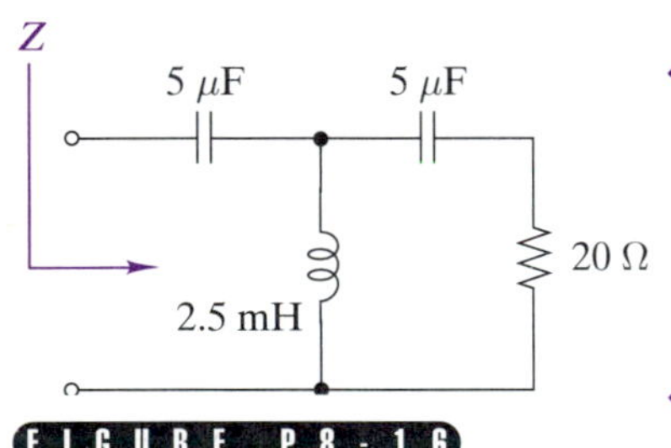

FIGURE P8-16

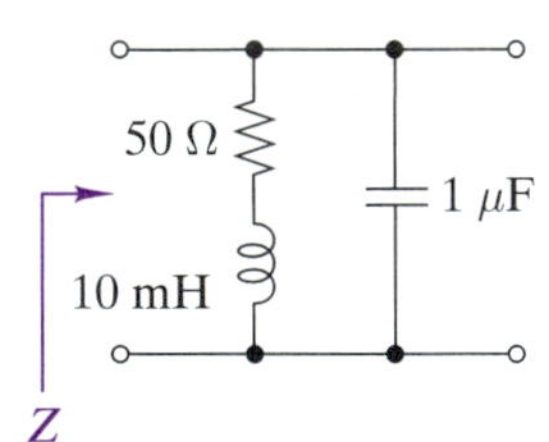

FIGURE P8-18

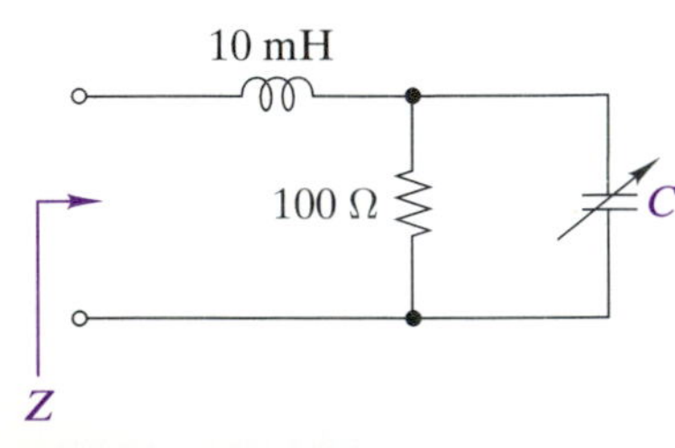

FIGURE P8-20

8–12 Find the equivalent impedance Z in Figure P8–12. Express the result in both polar and rectangular form:

8–13 Express the equivalent impedance of the following circuits in rectangular and polar form:

- **(a)** A 100-mH inductor in series with a 1-μF capacitor at $\omega = 4000$ rad/s
- **(b)** A 30-mH inductor in parallel with 60-Ω resistor at $\omega = 4000$ rad/s
- **(c)** The circuit formed by connecting the circuits in (a) and (b) in series
- **(d)** Repeat (c) at $\omega = 2000$ rad/s.

8–14 Find the equivalent impedance Z in Figure P8–14. Express the result in both polar and rectangular form.

8–15 The voltage applied at the input to a linear circuit is $v(t) = 200 \cos(1000t - 45°)$ V. In the sinusoidal steady state the input current is observed to be $i(t) = 20 \sin 1000t$ mA.

- **(a)** Find the equivalent impedance at the input.
- **(b)** Find the steady-state current $i(t)$ for $v(t) = 150 \sin(1000t - 270°)$ V.

8–16 The circuit in Figure P8–16 is operating in the sinusoidal steady state with $\omega = 500$ rad/s. Find the equivalent impedance Z. Which element dominates the equivalent impedance? Repeat for $\omega = 500$ krad/s.

8–17 **D** An inductor L is connected in parallel with a 600-Ω resistor. The parallel combination is then connected in series with a capacitor C. Select the values of L and C so that the equivalent impedance of the combination is $50 + j0$ Ω at $\omega = 100$ krad/s.

8–18 The circuit in Figure P8–18 is operating in the sinusoidal steady state with $\omega = 10$ krad/s. Find the equivalent impedance Z.

8–19 **D** A capacitor C is connected in series with a 50-Ω resistor. The series combination is then connected in parallel with an inductor L. Select the values of L and C so that the equivalent impedance of the combination is $600 + j0$ Ω at $\omega = 1$ Mrad/s.

8–20 **D** The circuit in Figure P8–20 is operating in the sinusoidal steady state with $\omega = 5$ krad/s.

- **(a)** Find the value of capacitance C that causes the input impedance Z to be purely resistive.
- **(b)** Find the input resistance for this value of C.

ERO 8–3 BASIC PHASOR CIRCUIT ANALYSIS (SECTS. 8–2, 8–3, 8–4)

Given a linear circuit operating in the sinusoidal steady state, find phasor responses using basic analysis methods such as series and parallel equivalence, voltage and current division, circuit reduction, Thévenin or Norton equivalent circuits, and proportionality or superposition.

8–21 A voltage $v(t) = 10 \cos 2500t$ V is applied across a series connection of a 100-Ω resistor and 40-mH inductor. Find the steady-state current $i(t)$ through the series connection. Draw a phasor diagram showing **V** and **I**.

8–22 The circuit in Figure P8–22 is operating in the sinusoidal steady state with $v_S(t) = V_A \cos \omega t$ V. Use phasor circuit reduction to derive a general expression for the steady-state response $i_L(t)$.

8–23 A current source delivering $i(t) = 300 \cos 377t$ mA is connected across a parallel combination of a 100-kΩ resistor and a 50-nF capacitor. Find the steady-state current $i_R(t)$ through the resistor and the steady-state current $i_C(t)$ through the capacitor. Draw a phasor diagram showing **I**, $\mathbf{I}_C$, and $\mathbf{I}_R$.

8–24 The circuit in Figure P8–24 is operating in the sinusoidal steady state with $i_S(t) = I_A \cos \omega t$ A. Use phasor circuit reduction to derive a general expression for the steady-state response $v_R(t)$.

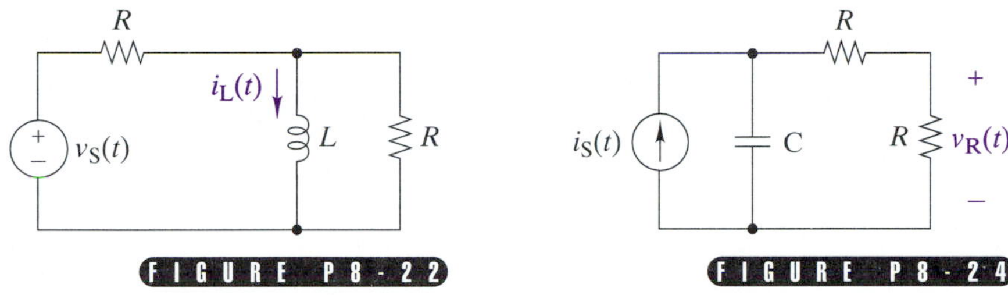

FIGURE P8-22

FIGURE P8-24

8–25 A voltage $v(t) = 50 \cos(1000t + 45°)$ V is applied across a parallel connection of a 5-kΩ resistor and a 200-nF capacitor. Find the steady-state current $i_C(t)$ through the capacitor and the steady-state current $i_R(t)$ through the resistor. Draw a phasor diagram showing **V**, $\mathbf{I}_C$, and $\mathbf{I}_R$.

8–26 The circuit in Figure P8–26 is operating in the sinusoidal steady state. Use circuit reduction to find the input impedance seen by the voltage source and the steady-state response $v_X(t)$.

8–27 The circuit in Figure P8–27 is operating in the sinusoidal steady state. Use circuit reduction to find the input impedance seen by the current source and steady-state response $v_X(t)$.

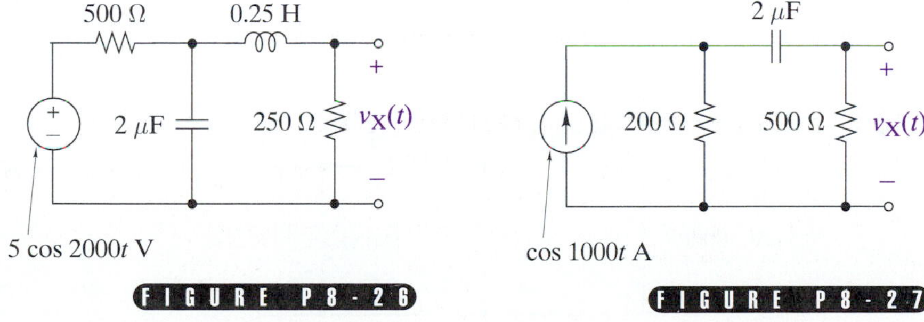

FIGURE P8-26

FIGURE P8-27

8–28 The circuit in Figure P8–28 is operating in the sinusoidal steady state. Use circuit reduction to find the input impedance seen by the voltage source and the steady-state phasor response $\mathbf{V}_X$.

FIGURE P8-28

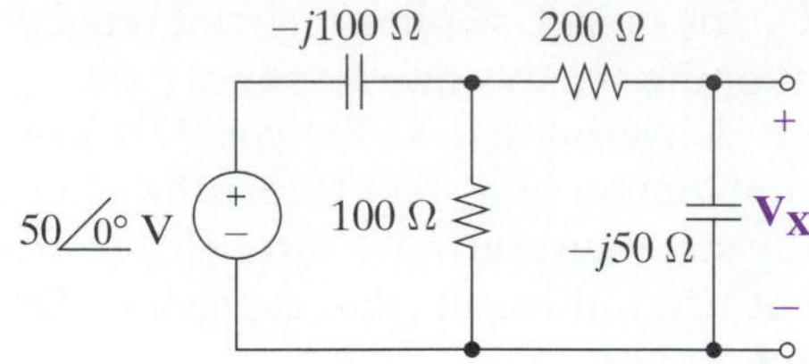

8–29 The circuit in Figure P8–29 is operating in the sinusoidal steady state. Use superposition to find the phasor response $\mathbf{I}_X$.

FIGURE P8-29

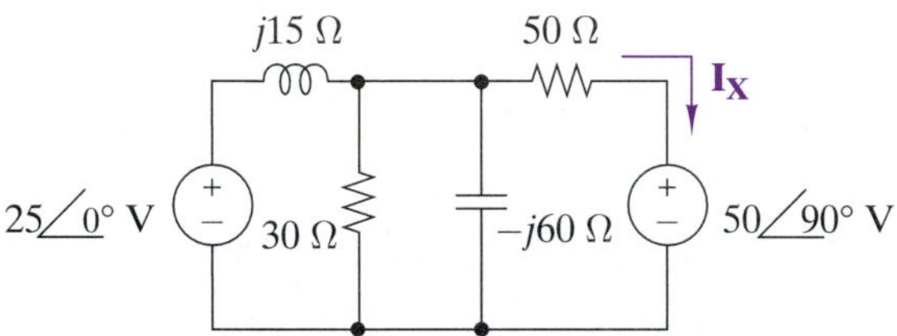

8–30 The circuit in Figure P8–30 is operating in the sinusoidal steady state. Use superposition to find the phasor response $\mathbf{V}_X$.

FIGURE P8-30

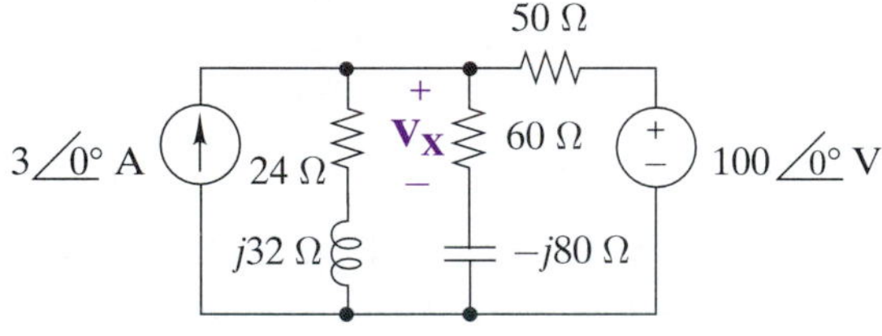

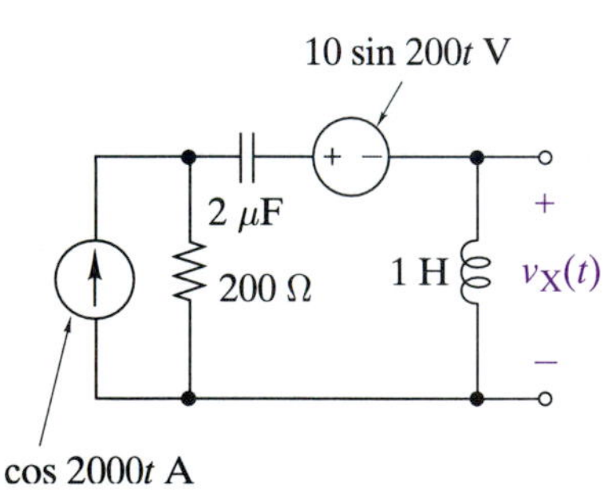

FIGURE P8-31

8–31 The circuit in Figure P8–31 is operating in the sinusoidal steady state. Use superposition to find the response $v_X(t)$. *Note:* The sources do not have the same frequency.

8–32 The circuit in Figure P8–32 is operating in the sinusoidal steady state. Use the unit output method to find the input impedance seen by the voltage source and the steady-state response $v_X(t)$.

FIGURE P8-32

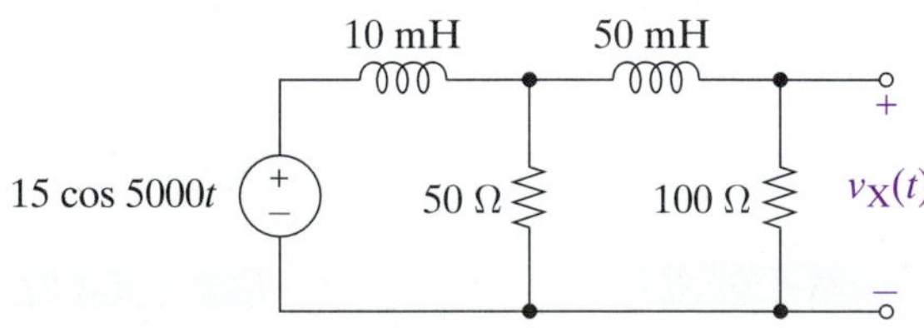

8–33 The circuit in Figure P8–33 is operating in the sinusoidal steady state. Use the unit output method to find the input impedance seen by the voltage source and the phasor response $\mathbf{V}_X$.

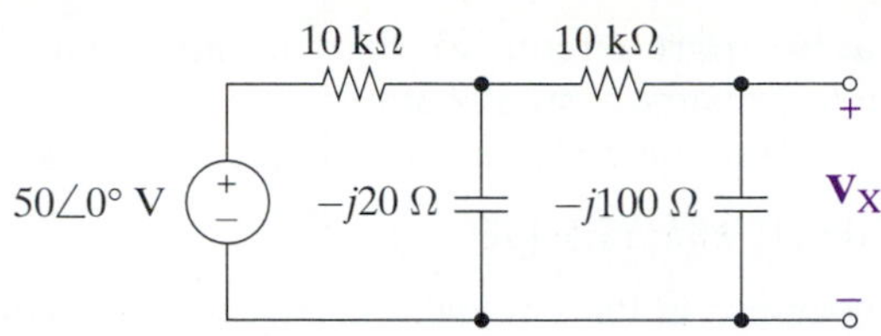

FIGURE P8-33

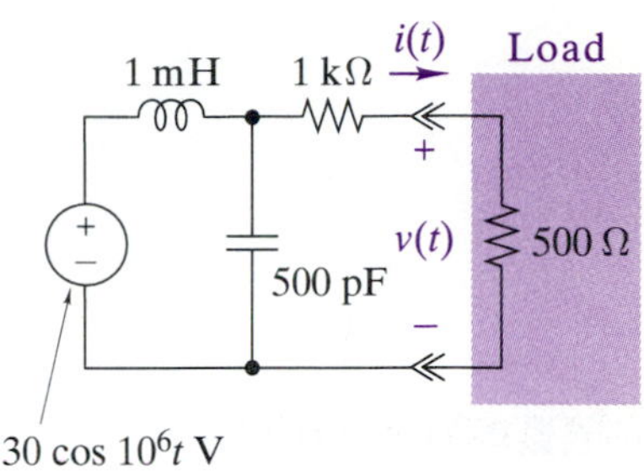

FIGURE P8-34

8–34 Find the phasor Thévenin equivalent of the source circuit to the left of the interface in Figure P8–34. Then use the equivalent circuit to find the steady-state voltage $v(t)$ and current $i(t)$ delivered to the load.

8–35 Find the phasor Thévenin equivalent of the source circuit to the left of the interface in Figure P8–35. Then use the equivalent circuit to find the phasor voltage **V** and current **I** delivered to the load.

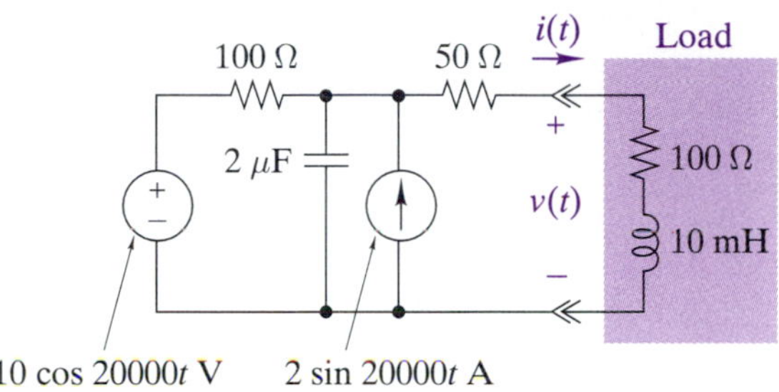

FIGURE P8-35

8–36 The circuit in Figure P8–36 is operating in the sinusoidal steady state. When $Z_L = 0$ the phasor current at the interface is $\mathbf{I} = 3.6 - j4.8$ mA. When $Z_L = -j40$ kΩ the phasor interface current is $\mathbf{I} = 10 + j0$ mA. Find the Thévenin equivalent of the source circuit.

8–37 Derive an expression for the equivalent impedance of the circuit in Figure P8–37. Arrange the result in the form $Z = R + jX$. Derive an expression for the resonance frequency ω_0 at which the reactance is zero.

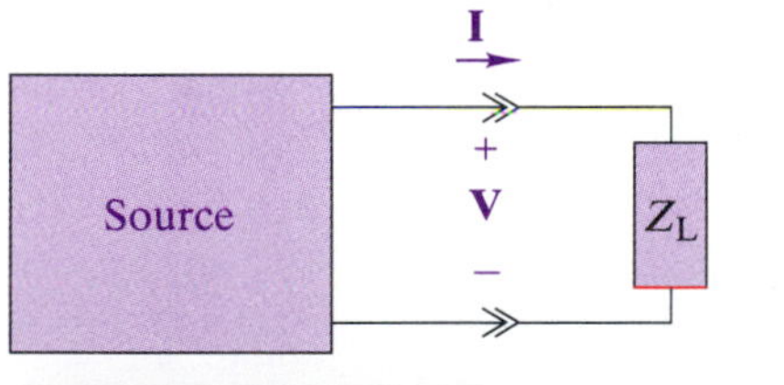

FIGURE P8-36

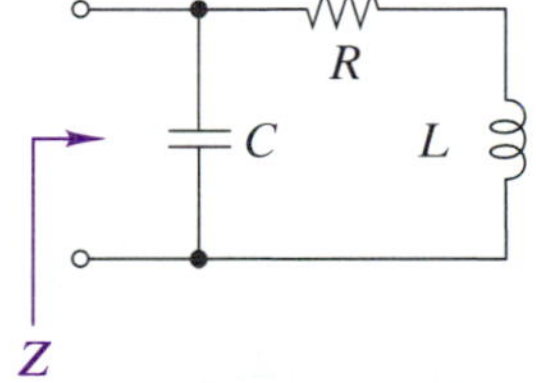

FIGURE P8-37

8–38 **D** Design a two-port circuit so that an input voltage $v_S(t) = 10\cos(2000t)$ V produces a steady-state output voltage of $v_O(t) = 5\cos(2000t + 45°)$ V.

8–39 **D** Design a two-port circuit so that an input voltage $v_S(t) = 100\cos(10^4 t)$ V delivers a steady-state output current of $i_O(t) = 10\cos(10^4 t - 35°)$ mA to a 600-Ω resistive load.

8–40 **D** Design a two-port circuit so that an input current $i_S(t) = 25\cos(5000t)$ mA delivers a steady-state output voltage of $v_O(t) = 50\cos(10^4 t + 45°)$ V and has an input impedance $|Z| > 10$ kΩ.

ERO 8–4 GENERAL CIRCUIT ANALYSIS (SECT. 8–5)

Given a linear circuit operating in the sinusoidal steady-state, find equivalent impedances and phasor responses using node-voltage or mesh-current analysis.

8–41 Use node-voltage analysis to find the sinusoidal steady-state response $v_X(t)$ in the circuit shown in Figure P8–41.

FIGURE P8-41

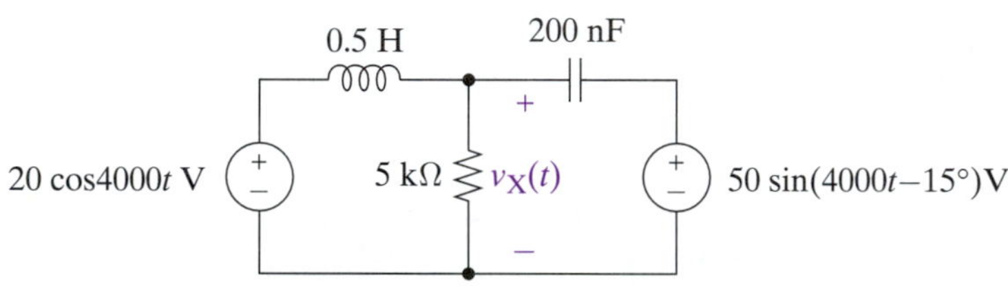

8–42 Use node-voltage analysis to find the steady-state phasor response $\mathbf{V}_O$ in the circuit shown in Figure P8–42.

FIGURE P8-42

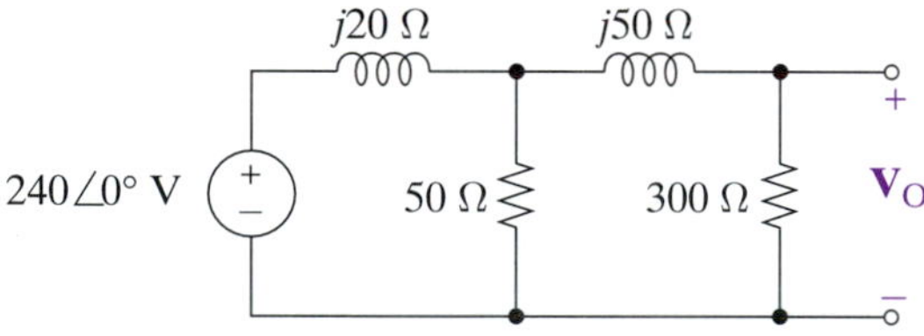

8–43 Use node-voltage analysis to find the input impedance Z_{IN} and gain $K = \mathbf{V}_O/\mathbf{V}_S$ of the circuit shown in Figure P8–43 with $\mu = 100$.

FIGURE P8-43

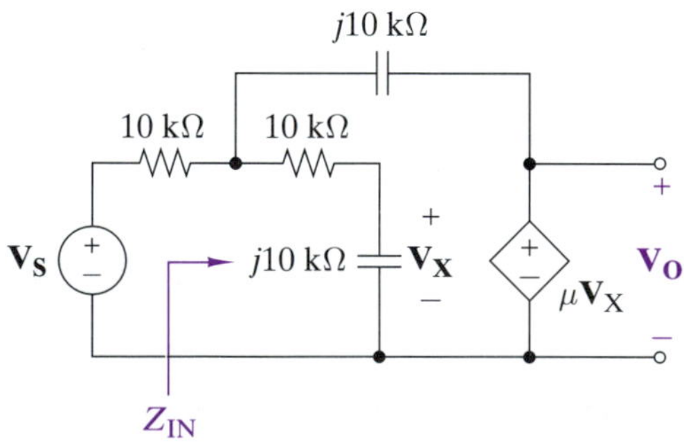

8–44 Use mesh-current analysis to find the phasor branch currents $\mathbf{I}_1$, $\mathbf{I}_2$, and $\mathbf{I}_3$ in the circuit shown in Figure P8–44.

FIGURE P8-44

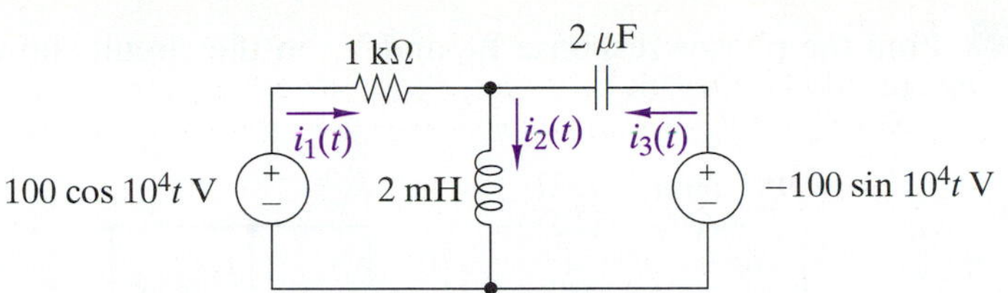

8–45 Use mesh-current analysis to find the phasor response $\mathbf{V}_Y$ and $\mathbf{I}_X$ in the circuit shown in Figure P8–45.

FIGURE P8-45

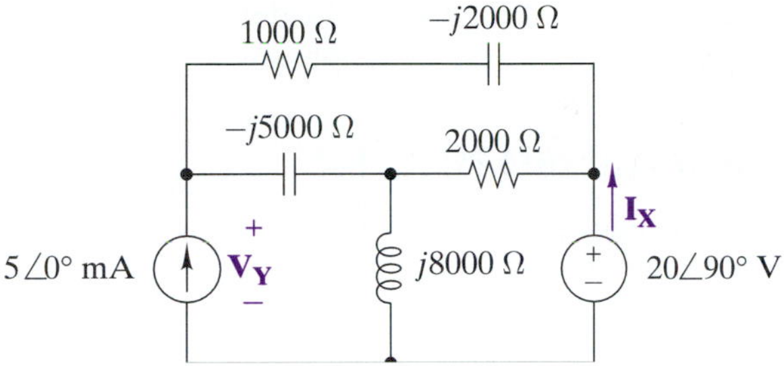

8–46 Use mesh-current analysis to find the input impedance Z_{IN} and gain $K = \mathbf{V}_O/\mathbf{V}_S$ of the circuit shown in Figure P8–46.

FIGURE P8-46

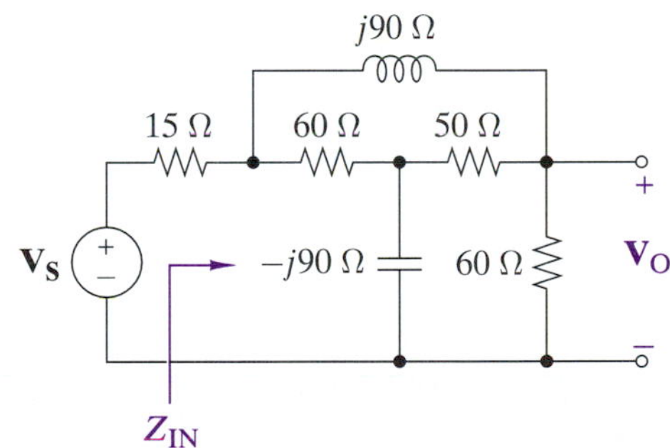

8–47 Find the input impedance Z_{IN} and gain $K = \mathbf{V}_O/\mathbf{V}_S$ of the circuit shown in Figure P8–47.

8–48 Find the sinusoidal steady-state response $v_O(t)$ in the circuit shown in Figure P8–48. The element values are $\omega = 500$ rad/s, $\mathbf{V}_S = 80$ mV, $R_1 = 10$ kΩ, $R_P = 1$ kΩ, $R_F = 1$ MΩ, $R_C = 20$ kΩ, $R_L = 100$ kΩ, $C = 0.25$ nF, and $\beta = 100$.

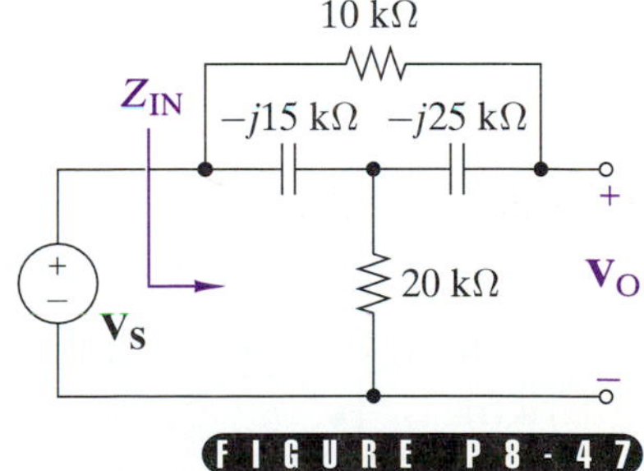

FIGURE P8-47

FIGURE P8-48

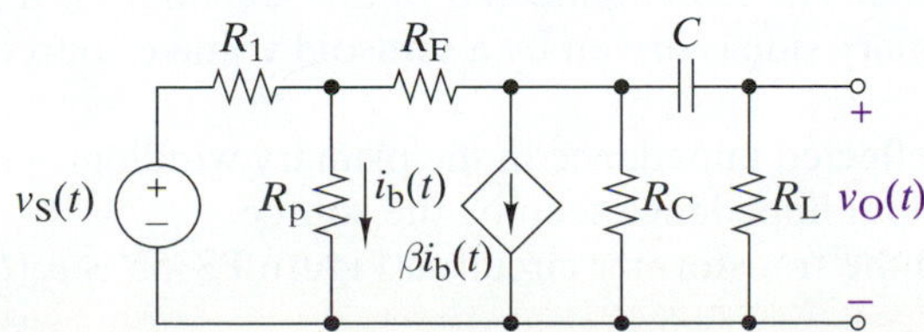

8–49 Find the phasor response $\mathbf{I}_{IN}$ and $\mathbf{V}_O$ in the circuit shown in Figure P8–49.

FIGURE P8-49

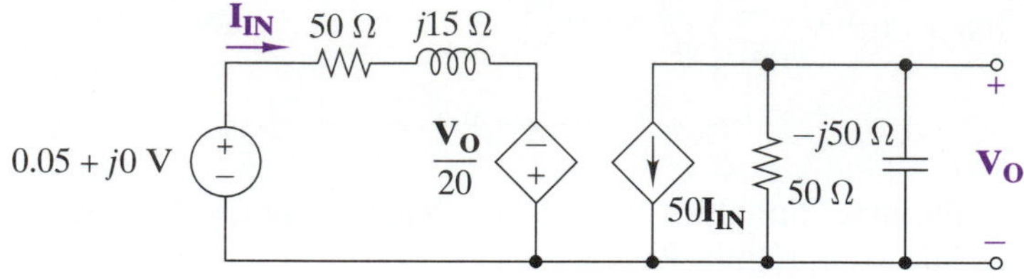

Vs
Z2
Z1
VO

FIGURE P8-50

8–50 For the OP AMP circuit in Figure P8–50, derive an expression relating the output phasor $\mathbf{V}_O$ and the input phasor $\mathbf{V}_S$ in terms of the impedance Z_1 and Z_2.

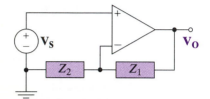

ERO 8–5 THE LINEAR TRANSFORMER (SECT. 8–6)

Given two coupled coils in a linear circuit operating in the sinusoidal steady state, find circuit responses and equivalent impedances.

8–51 The input voltage to the transformer in Figure P8–51 is a sinusoid $v_1(t) = 10 \cos 2000t$. Use mesh-current analysis to find the steady-state output voltage $v_2(t)$ and the equivalent impedance seen by the input source.

FIGURE P8-51

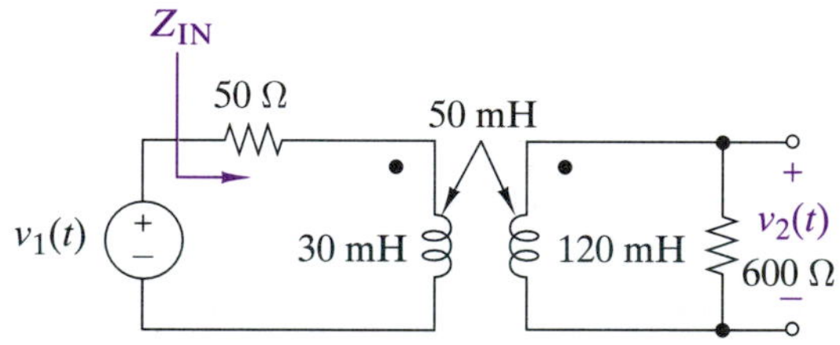

8–52 A sinusoidal voltage source is connected to the primary of a linear transformer with $L_1 = 20$ mH, $L_2 = 45$ mH, and $k = 0.75$. The source has a peak amplitude of 90 V and a frequency of 4 krad/s. The load connected to the secondary of the transformer is a 125-Ω resistor in series with 1-μF capacitor. Assume additive coupling.

(a) Find the phasor responses $\mathbf{I}_1$, $\mathbf{I}_2$, $\mathbf{V}_1$, and $\mathbf{V}_2$.

(b) Find the input impedance seen by the source.

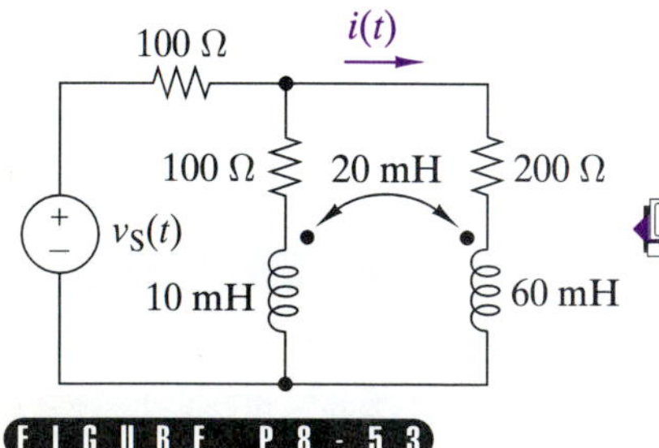

FIGURE P8-53

8–53 The input voltage in Figure P8–53 is a sinusoid $v_S(t) = 20 \cos 20000t$. Find the steady-state response of $i(t)$.

8–54 The inductances of a transformer are $L_1 = 800$ mH, $L_2 = 500$ mH, and $M = 600$ mH. The load connected to the secondary is a 300-Ω resistor. The primary side is driven by a sinusoid voltage source with $\omega = 800$ rad/s.

(a) Find the reflected impedance in the primary winding.

(b) Find the input impedance seen by the source.

8–55 The input to the transformer circuit in Figure P8–55 is $v_S(t) = 10 \sin 4000t$ V.

(a) Find the impedance reflected into the primary circuit of the transformer.

(b) Use the reflected impedance in part (a) to find the input current $i(t)$.

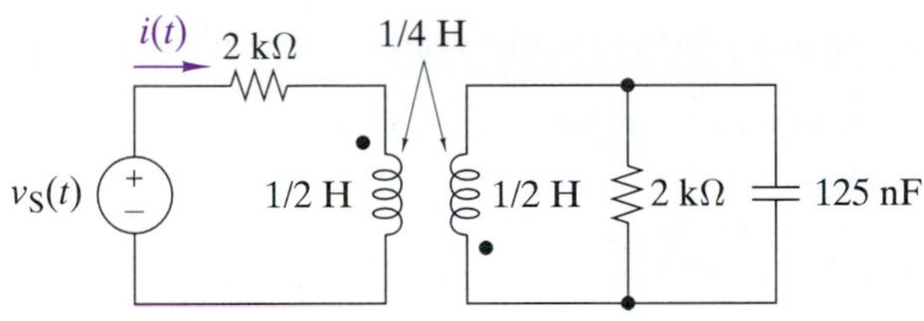

FIGURE P8-55

8–56 Replace the coupled coils in Figure P8–55 by their T-equivalent circuit.

(a) Use circuit reduction to find the equivalent impedance seen by the voltage source $v_S(t) = 10 \sin 4000t$ V.

(b) Use the equivalent impedance in part (a) to find the input current $i(t)$.

8–57 The voltage source in Figure P8–57 generates $v_S(t) = 35 \cos 5000t$ V. The resistors in series with the coils simulate winding resistances.

(a) Find the input impedance seen at the input interface.

(b) Find the phasor voltage delivered at the input interface.

(c) Find the phasor voltage delivered at the output interface.

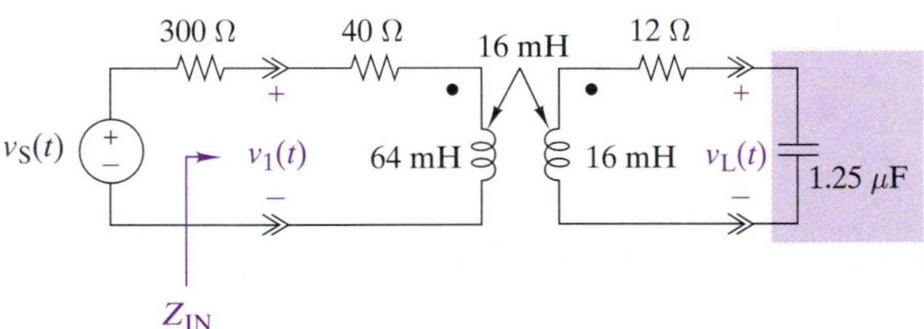

FIGURE P8-57

8–58 The frequency of the voltage source in Figure P8–57 is adjustable. Find the frequency at which the impedance seen at the input interface is purely real.

8–59 The impedance looking into the primary winding of a transformer with the secondary winding connected to an open circuit is $j200\ \Omega$. The impedance looking into the primary winding with the secondary winding short circuited is $j150\ \Omega$. The impedance looking into the secondary winding with the primary connected to an open circuit is $j200\ \Omega$. Find the coupling coefficient of the transformer.

8–60 The magnitudes of the steady-state ac voltages and currents in a transformer are measured with the secondary open circuited and short circuited. The following data summarize the results. All measurements were made at $f = 400$ Hz. Find L_1, L_2, and M.

SECONDARY	$\lvert V_1 \rvert$ <V>	$\lvert I_1 \rvert$ <MA>	$\lvert V_2 \rvert$ <V>	$\lvert I_2 \rvert$ <MA>
Open Circuit	10	12	44	0
Short Circuit	—	10	0	2.2

ERO 8–6 AVERAGE POWER AND MAXIMUM POWER TRANSFER (SECT. 8–7)

Given a linear circuit operating in the sinusoidal steady-state,

(a) Find the average power delivered at a specified interface.
(b) Find the maximum average power available at a specified interface.
(c) Find the load impedance required to draw the maximum available power.

8–61 A load consisting of a 50-Ω resistor in parallel with a 100-mH inductor is connected across a voltage source $v_S(t) = 35 \cos 500t$ V. Find the phasor voltage, current, and average power delivered to the load.

8–62 A load consisting of a 100-Ω resistor in parallel with a 40-μF capacitor is connected across a voltage source $v_S(t) = 50 \cos 2500t$ V. Find the phasor voltage, current, and average power delivered to the load.

8–63 A load consisting of a resistor and capacitor connected in parallel draws an average power of 100 mW and a peak current of 44 mA when connected to voltage source $v_S(t) = 16 \cos 2500t$ V. Find the values of R and C.

8–64 A load consists of a 400-Ω resistor in parallel with an inductor whose reactance is 800 Ω is connected to a current source whose peak amplitude is 26 mA. Find the average power delivered to the load.

8–65 (a) Find the average power delivered to the load in Figure P8–65.
(b) Find the maximum available average power at the interface shown in Figure P8–65.
(c) Specify the load required to extract the maximum average power.

FIGURE P8-65

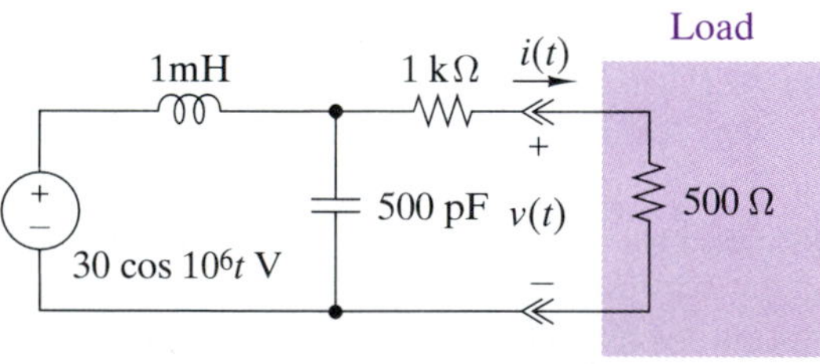

8–66 **(a)** Find the average power delivered to the load in Figure P8–66.
(b) Find the maximum available average power at the interface shown in Figure P8–66.
(c) Specify the load required to extract the maximum average power.

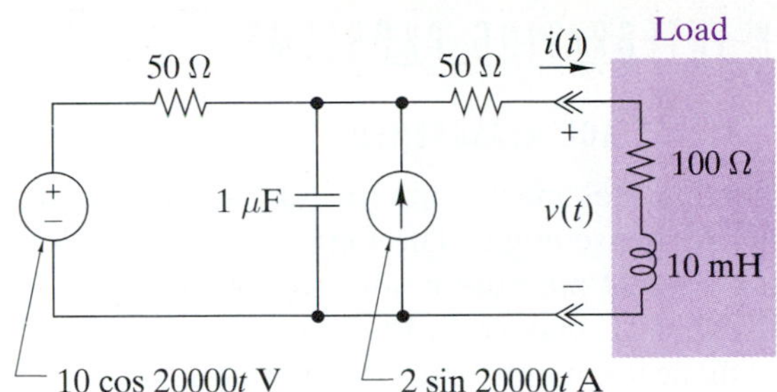

FIGURE P8-66

8–67 **(a)** Find the maximum average power available at the interface in Figure P8–67.

(b) Specify the values of R and C that will extract the maximum power from the source circuit.

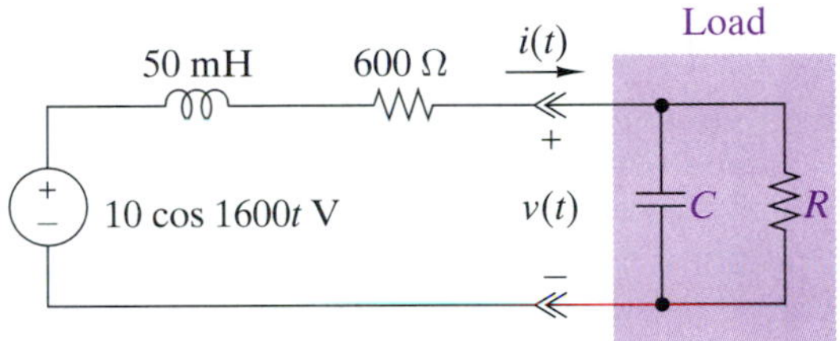

FIGURE P8-67

8–68 The steady-state open-circuit voltage at the output interface of a source circuit is $10\angle 0^{\circ}$ V. When a 50-Ω resistor is connected across the interface, the steady-state output voltage is $4.68\angle{-20.56^{\circ}}$ V. Find the maximum average power available at the interface and the resistance and reactance required to extract the maximum power.

8–69 The phasor Thévenin voltage of a certain source is $\mathbf{V}_T = 10 + j0$ V and the Thévenin impedance is $Z_T = 50 + j100$ Ω. The problem is to extract as much average power as possible from this source using only one standard value resistor as the load. The values of resistance available are 1.0, 1.5, 2.2, 3.3, 4.7,6.8, and multiples of 10 times these values.

(a) Find the maximum available average power from the source.

(b) Find the standard load resistor that extracts the most average power.

8–70 The source circuit with $\omega = 10^6$ rad/s has a phasor Thévenin equivalent circuit with $\mathbf{V}_T = 125 + j0$ V and is $Z_T = 50 + j300$ Ω. This source powers a load whose impedance is $600 + j0$ Ω.

(a) Find the maximum available power available from the source.

(b) Place a capacitor C in parallel with the load. Calculate the average power delivered to the device as a function of C, and then select the value of C that maximizes the average power.

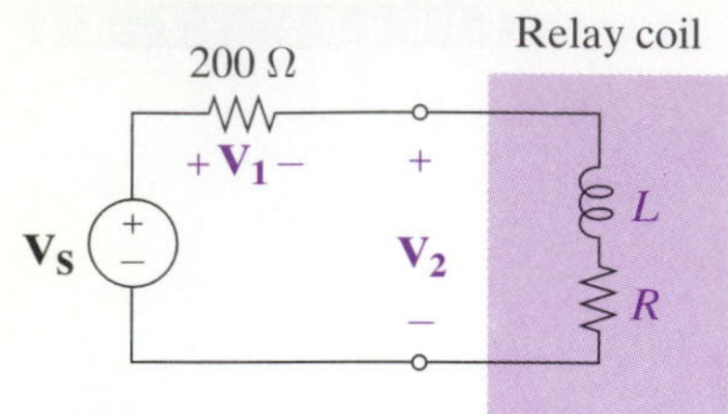

FIGURE P8-71

CHAPTER-INTEGRATING PROBLEMS

8–71 A AC VOLTAGE MEASUREMENT

An ac voltmeter measurement indicates the amplitude of a sinusoid and not its phase angle. The magnitude and phase can be inferred by making several measurements and using KVL. For example, Figure P8–71 shows a relay coil of unknown resistance and inductance. The following ac voltmeter readings are taken with the circuit operating in the sinusoidal steady state at $f = 1$ kHz: $|\mathbf{V}_S| = 10$ V, $|\mathbf{V}_1| = 4$ V, and $|\mathbf{V}_2| = 8$ V.

(a) Use these voltage magnitude measurements to solve for R and L.

(b) Determine the phasor voltage across each element and show that they satisfy KVL.

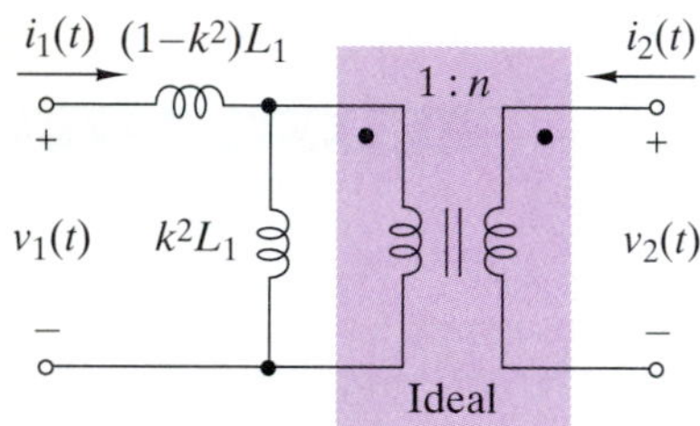

FIGURE P8-72

8–72 A TRANSFORMER EQUIVALENT CIRCUIT

The circuit in Figure P8–72 is equivalent to two coupled coils with the inductances L_1, L_2, and M. The equivalent circuit consists of uncoupled inductances $(1-k^2)L_1$ and k^2L_1, where k is the coupling coefficient and an ideal transformer whose turns ratio is $n = L_2/M$.

(a) Verify that this circuit is equivalent to two coupled coils with additive coupling.

(b) Use the model to explain why perfect coupling produces $v_2(t) = nv_1(t)$ but not $i_1(t) = -ni_2(t)$.

(c) Use the model to explain why an ideal transformer has perfect coupling and infinite self-inductance.

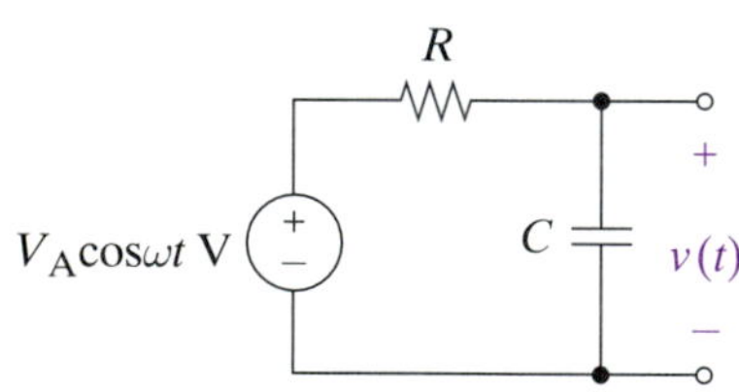

FIGURE P8-73

8–73 A CIRCUIT FORCED RESPONSE

The purpose of this problem is to demonstrate that the steady-state response obtained using phasor circuit analysis is the forced component of the solution of the circuit differential equation.

(a) Transform the circuit in Figure P8–73 into the phasor domain and use voltage division to solve for phasor output **V**.

(b) Convert the phasor found in (a) into a sinusoid of the form $v(t) = a \cos \omega t + b \sin \omega t$.

(c) Formulate the circuit differential equation in the capacitor voltage $v(t)$.

(d) Show that the $v(t)$ found in part (b) satisfies the differential equation in (c).

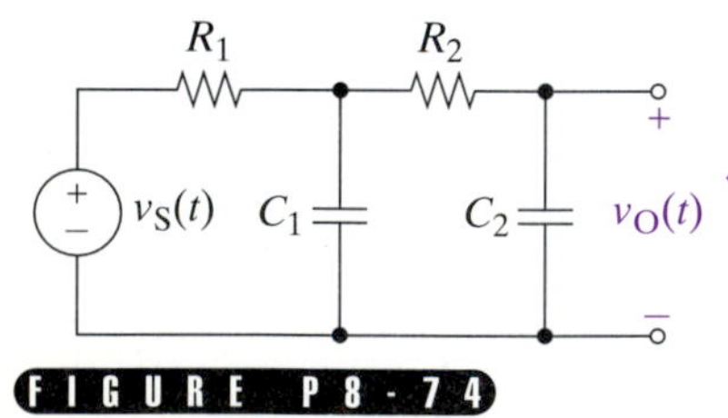

FIGURE P8-74

8–74 D AC CIRCUIT DESIGN

Select the element values in the circuit shown in Figure P8–74 so that an input $v_S(t) = 15 \cos 2000t$ V produces and output $v_O(t) = 2 \sin 2000t$.

8–75 D AC CIRCUIT DESIGN

Select values for the reactances X_1 and X_2 in Figure P8–75 so that the input voltage source sees an equivalent impedance of $50 + j0\ \Omega$ and the 600-Ω load resistor sees an equivalent source impedance of $600 + j0\ \Omega$. Select values of inductance and capacitance to produce these reactances when the frequency is $\omega = 10^6$ rad/s.

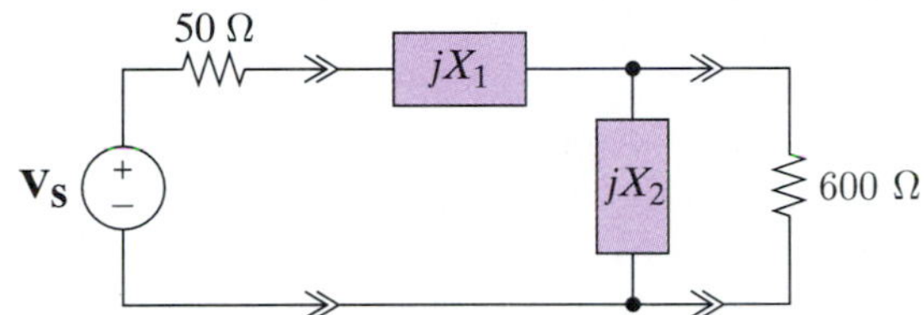

FIGURE P8-75

Laplace Transforms

My method starts with a complex integral; I fear this sounds rather formidable; but it is really quite simple . . . I am afraid that no physical people will ever try to make out my method: but I am hoping that it may give them confidence to try your methods.

Thomas John Bromwich, 1915,
British Mathematician

Laplace transforms have their roots in the pioneering work of the eccentric British engineer Oliver Heaviside (1850–1925). His operational calculus was essentially a collection of intuitive rules that allowed him to formulate and solve a number of the important technical problems of his day. Heaviside was a practical man with no interest in mathematical elegance. His intuitive approach drew bitter criticism from the mathematicians of his day. However, mathematicians like John Bromwich and others eventually recognized the importance of Heaviside's methods and began to supply the necessary mathematical foundations. The foregoing quotation is taken from a 1915 letter from Bromwich to Heaviside in which he described what we now call the Laplace transformation. The transformation is named for Laplace because a complete mathematical development of Heaviside's methods was eventually found in the 1780 writings of the French mathematician Pierre Simon Laplace.

The Laplace transformation provides a new and important method of representing circuits and signals. The transform approach offers a viewpoint and terminology that pervades electrical engineering, particularly in linear circuit analysis and design. The first two sections of this chapter present the basic properties of the Laplace transformation and the concept of converting signals from the time domain to the frequency domain. The third section introduces frequency domain signal description via the pole-zero diagram. The fourth and fifth sections treat the inverse procedure for transforming signals from the frequency domain back into the time domain. In the sixth section, transform methods are used to solve differential equations that describe the response of linear dynamic circuits. The last two sections treat additional properties of the Laplace transformation that provide important insights into the relationship between the time and frequency domains.

9–1 SIGNAL WAVEFORMS AND TRANSFORMS

A mathematical transformation employs rules to change the form of data without altering its meaning. An example of a transformation is the conversion of numerical data from decimal to binary form. In engineering circuit analysis, transformations are used to obtain alternative representations of circuits and signals. These alternate forms provide a different perspective that can be quite useful or even essential. Examples of the transformations used in circuit analysis are the Fourier transformation, the Z-transformation, and the Laplace transformation. These methods all involve specific transformation rules, make certain analysis techniques more manageable, and provide a useful viewpoint for circuit and system design.

This chapter deals with the Laplace transformation. The discussion of the Laplace transformation follows the path shown in Figure 9–1 by the solid arrow. The process begins with a linear circuit. We derive a differential equation describing the circuit response and then transform this equation into the frequency domain, where it becomes an algebraic equation. Algebraic techniques are then used to solve the transformed equation for the circuit response. The inverse Laplace transformation then changes the frequency domain response into the response waveform in the time domain. The dashed arrow in Figure 9–1 shows that there is another route to the time domain response using the classical techniques discussed in Chapter 8. The classical approach appears to be more direct, but the advantage of the Laplace transformation is that solving a differential equation becomes an algebraic process.

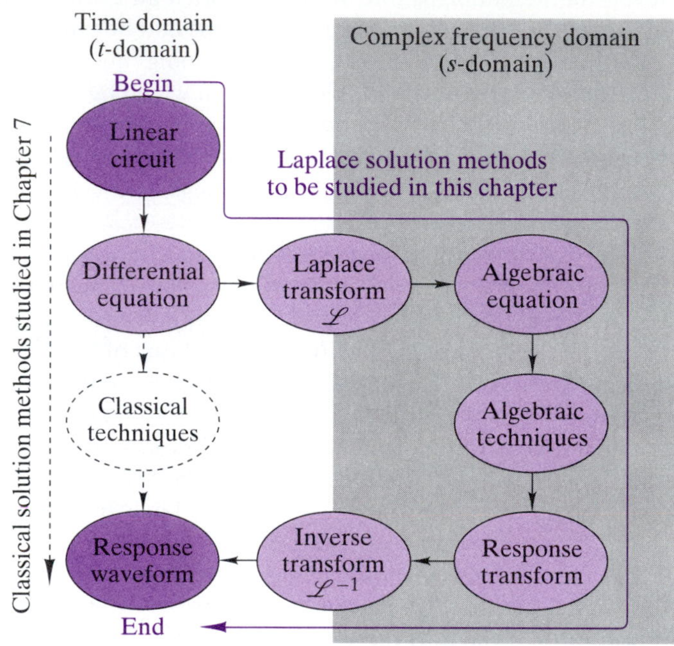

FIGURE 9–1 *Flow diagram dynamic circuit analysis with Laplace transforms.*

Symbolically, we represent the Laplace transformation as

$$\mathcal{L}\{f(t)\} = F(s) \tag{9-1}$$

This expression states that $F(s)$ is the Laplace transform of the waveform $f(t)$. The transformation operation involves two domains: (1) the time domain, in which the signal is characterized by its **waveform** $f(t)$, and (2) the complex frequency domain, in which the signal is represented by its **transform** $F(s)$.

The symbol s stands for the complex frequency variable, a notation we first introduced in Chapter 7 in connection with the zero-state response of linear circuits. The variable s has the dimensions of reciprocal time, or frequency, and is expressed in units of radians per second. In this chapter the complex frequency variable is written as $s = \sigma + j\omega$, where $\sigma = \text{Re}\{s\}$ is the real part and $\omega = \text{Im}\{s\}$ is the imaginary part. This variable is the independent variable in the s-domain, just as t is the independent variable in the time domain. Although we cannot physically measure complex frequency in the same sense that we measure time, it is an extremely useful concept that pervades the analysis and design of linear systems.

A signal can be expressed as a waveform or a transform. Collectively, $f(t)$ and $F(s)$ are called a **transform pair**, where the pair involves two representations of the signal. To distinguish between the two forms, a lowercase letter denotes a waveform and an uppercase a transform. For electrical waveforms such as current $i(t)$ or voltage $v(t)$, the corresponding transforms are denoted $I(s)$ and $V(s)$. In this chapter we will use $f(t)$ and $F(s)$ to stand for signal waveforms and transforms in general.

The **Laplace transformation** is defined by the integral

$$F(s) = \int_{0-}^{\infty} f(t)e^{-st}dt \qquad (9-2)$$

Since the definition involves an improper integral (the upper limit is infinite), we must discuss the conditions under which the integral exists (converges). The integral exists if the waveform $f(t)$ is piecewise continuous and of exponential order. **Piecewise continuous** means that $f(t)$ has a finite number of steplike discontinuities in any finite interval. **Exponential order** means that constants K and b exist such that $|f(t)| < Ke^{bt}$ for all $t > 0$. As a practical matter, the signals encountered in engineering applications meet these conditions.

From the integral definition of the Laplace transformation, we see that when a voltage waveform $v(t)$ has units of volts (V) the corresponding voltage transform $V(s)$ has units of volt-seconds (V-s). Similarly, when a current waveform $i(t)$ has units of amperes (A), the corresponding current transform $I(s)$ has units of ampere-seconds (A-s). Thus, waveforms and transforms do not have the same units. Even so, we often refer to both $V(s)$ and $v(t)$ as voltages and both $I(s)$ and $i(t)$ as currents despite the fact that they have different units. The reason is simply that it is awkward to keep adding the words *waveform* and *transform* to statements when the distinction is clear from the context.

Equation (9–2) uses a lower limit denoted $t = 0-$ to indicate a time just a whisker before $t = 0$. We use $t = 0-$ because in circuit analysis $t = 0$ is defined by a discrete event, such as closing a switch. Such an event may cause a discontinuity in $f(t)$ at $t = 0$. To capture this discontinuity, we set the lower limit at $t = 0-$, just prior to the event. Fortunately, in many situations there is no discontinuity so we will not distinguish between $t = 0-$ and $t = 0$ unless it is crucial.

Equally fortunate is the fact that the number of different waveforms encountered in linear circuits is relatively small. The list includes the three basic waveforms from Chapter 5 (the step, exponential, and sinusoid), as well as composite waveforms such as the impulse, ramp, damped ramp, and damped sinusoid. Since the number of waveforms of interest is relatively small, we do not often use the integral definition in Eq. (9–2) to find Laplace transforms. Once a transform pair has been found, it can be cataloged in a table for future reference and use. Tables 9–2 and 9–3 in this chapter are sufficient for our purposes.

EXAMPLE 9–1

Show that the Laplace transform of the unit step function $f(t) = u(t)$ is $F(s) = 1/s$.

SOLUTION:
Applying Eq. (9–2) yields

$$F(s) = \int_0^{\infty} u(t)e^{-st}dt$$

Since $u(t) = 1$ throughout the range of integration this integral becomes

$$F(s) = \int_{0-}^{\infty} e^{-st}dt = -\left.\frac{e^{-st}}{s}\right|_{0-}^{\infty} = -\left.\frac{e^{-(\sigma+j\omega)t}}{\sigma + j\omega}\right|_{0-}^{\infty}$$

The last expression on the right side vanishes at the upper limit since e^{-st} goes to zero as t approaches infinity provided that $\sigma > 0$. At the lower limit the expression reduces to $1/s$. The integral used to calculate $F(s)$ is only valid in the region for which $\sigma > 0$. However, once evaluated, the result $F(s) = 1/s$ can be extended to neighboring regions provided that we avoid the point at $s = 0$ where the function blows up. ■

EXAMPLE 9–2

Show that the Laplace transform $f(t) = [e^{-\alpha t}]u(t)$ is $F(s) = 1/(s + \alpha)$.

SOLUTION:
Applying Eq. (9–2) yields

$$F(s) = \int_0^{\infty} e^{-\alpha t}e^{-st}\,dt = \int_0^{\infty} e^{-(s+\alpha)t}dt = \left.\frac{e^{-(s+\alpha)t}}{-(s+\alpha)}\right|_0^{\infty}$$

The last term on the right side vanishes at the upper limit since $e^{-(s+\alpha)t}$ vanishes as t approaches infinity provided that $\sigma > \alpha$. At the lower limit the last term reduces to $1/(s + \alpha)$. Again, the integral is only valid for a limited region, but the result $F(s) = 1/(s + \alpha)$ can be extended outside this region if we avoid the point at $s = -\alpha$. ■

EXAMPLE 9–3

Show that the Laplace transform of the impulse function $f(t) = \delta(t)$ is $F(s) = 1$.

SOLUTION:
Applying Eq. (9–2) yields

$$F(s) = \int_{0-}^{\infty} \delta(t)e^{-st}\,dt = \int_{0-}^{0+} \delta(t)e^{-st}\,dt = \int_{0-}^{0+} \delta(t)dt = 1$$

The difference between $t = 0-$ and $t = 0$ is important since the impulse is zero everywhere except at $t = 0$. To capture the impulse in the integration, we take a lower limit at $t = 0-$ and an upper limit at $t = 0+$. Since $e^{-st} = 1$ and $\int \delta(t)dt = 1$ on this integration interval, we find that $F(s) = 1$. ■

INVERSE TRANSFORMATION

So far we have used the direct transformation to convert waveforms into transforms. But Figure 9–1 points out the need to perform the inverse transformation to convert transforms into waveforms. Symbolically, we represent the inverse process as

$$\mathcal{L}^{-1}\{F(s)\} = f(t) \qquad (9-3)$$

This equation states that $f(t)$ is the inverse Laplace transform of $F(s)$. The **inverse Laplace transformation** is defined by the complex inversion integral

$$f(t) = \frac{1}{2\pi j}\int_{\alpha - j\infty}^{\alpha + j\infty} F(s)e^{st}\,ds \qquad (9-4)$$

The Laplace transformation is an integral transformation since both the direct process in Eq. (9–2) and the inverse process in Eq. (9–4) involve integrations. The Fourier transformation treated in Chapter 16 is another example of an integral transformation.

Happily, formal evaluation of the complex inversion integral is not necessary because of the uniqueness property of the Laplace transformation. A symbolical statement of the **uniqueness property** is

$$\text{IF } \mathcal{L}\{f(t)\} = F(s) \text{ THEN } \mathcal{L}^{-1}\{F(s)\}(=)u(t)f(t)$$

The mathematical justification for this statement is beyond the scope of our treatment.[1] However, the notation (=) means "equal almost everywhere." The only points where equality may not hold is at the discontinuities of $f(t)$.

If we just look an the definition of the direct transformation in Eq. (9–2), we could conclude that $F(s)$ is not affected by the values of $f(t)$ for $t < 0$. However, when we use Eq. (9–2) we are not just looking for the Laplace transform of $f(t)$, but a Laplace transform pair such that $\mathcal{L}\{f(t)\} = F(s)$ and $\mathcal{L}^{-1}\{F(s)\} = f(t)$. The inverse Laplace transformation in Eq. (9–4) always produces a causal waveform, one that is zero for $t < 0$. Hence a transform pair $[f(t) \leftrightarrow F(s)]$ is unique if and only if $f(t)$ is causal. For instance, in Example 9–1 we show that $\mathcal{L}\{u(t)\} = 1/s$; hence by the uniqueness property we know that $\mathcal{L}^{-1}\{1/s)\}$ (=) $u(t)$.

For this reason Laplace transform–related waveforms are written as $[f(t)]u(t)$ to make their causality visible. For example, in the next section we find the Laplace transform of the sinusoid waveform $\cos \beta t$. In the context of Laplace transforms this signal is not an eternal sinusoid but a causal waveform $f(t) = [\cos \beta t]u(t)$. It is important to remember that causality and Laplace transforms go hand in hand when interpreting the results of circuit analysis.

---

1 See Wilber R. LePage, *Complex Variables and Laplace Transform for Engineering*, Dover Publishing Co., New York, 1980, p. 318.

9–2 BASIC PROPERTIES AND PAIRS

The previous section gave the definition of the Laplace transformation and showed that the transforms of some basic signals can be found using the integral definition. In this section we develop the basic properties of the Laplace transformation and show how these properties can be used to obtain additional transform pairs.

The **linearity** property of the Laplace transformation states that

$$\mathcal{L}\{Af_1(t) + Bf_2(t)\} = AF_1(s) + BF_2(s) \tag{9–5}$$

where A and B are constants. This property is easily established using the integral definition in Eq. (9–2):

$$\begin{aligned}\mathcal{L}\{Af_1(t) + Bf_2(t)\} &= \int_0^{\infty} [Af_1(t) + Bf_2(t)]e^{-st}dt \\ &= A\int_0^{\infty} f_1(t)e^{-st}dt + B\int_0^{\infty} f_2(t)e^{-st}dt \\ &= AF_1(s) + BF_2(s)\end{aligned}$$

The integral definition of the inverse transformation in Eq. (9–4) is also a linear operations, so it follows that

$$\mathcal{L}^{-1}\{AF_1(s) + BF_2(s)\} = Af_1(t) + Bf_2(t) \tag{9–6}$$

An important consequence of linearity is that for any constant K

$$\mathcal{L}\{Kf(t)\} = KF(s) \text{ and } \mathcal{L}^{-1}\{KF(s)\} = Kf(t) \tag{9–7}$$

The linearity property is an extremely important feature that we will use many times in this and subsequent chapters. The next two examples show how this property can be used to obtain the transform of the exponential rise waveform and a sinusoidal waveform.

EXAMPLE 9–4

Show that the Laplace transform of $f(t) = A(1 - e^{-\alpha t})u(t)$ is

$$F(s) = \frac{A\alpha}{s(s + \alpha)}$$

SOLUTION:

This waveform is the difference between a step function and an exponential. We can use the linearity property of Laplace transforms to write

$$\mathcal{L}\{A(1 - e^{-\alpha t})u(t)\} = A\mathcal{L}\{u(t)\} - A\mathcal{L}\{e^{-\alpha t}u(t)\}$$

The transforms of the step and exponential functions were found in Examples 9–1 and 9–2. Using linearity, we find that the transform of the exponential rise is

$$F(s) = \frac{A}{s} - \frac{A}{s + \alpha} = \frac{A\alpha}{s(s + \alpha)}$$

■

EXAMPLE 9–5

Show that the Laplace transform of the sinusoid $f(t) = A[\sin(\beta t)]u(t)$ is $F(s) = A\beta/(s^2 + \beta^2)$.

SOLUTION:

Using Euler's relationship, we can express the sinusoid as a sum of exponentials.

$$e^{+j\beta t} = \cos\beta t + j\sin\beta t$$

$$e^{-j\beta t} = \cos\beta t - j\sin\beta t$$

Subtracting the second equation from the first yields

$$f(t) = A\sin\beta t = \frac{A(e^{j\beta t} - e^{-j\beta t})}{2j} = \frac{A}{2j}e^{j\beta t} - \frac{A}{2j}e^{-j\beta t}$$

The transform pair $\mathcal{L}\{e^{-\alpha t}\} = 1/(s + \alpha)$ in Example 9–2 is valid even if the exponent α is complex. Using this fact and the linearity property, we obtain the transform of the sinusoid as

$$\mathcal{L}\{A\sin\beta t\} = \frac{A}{2j}\mathcal{L}\{e^{j\beta t}\} - \frac{A}{2}\mathcal{L}\{e^{-j\beta t}\}$$

$$= \frac{A}{2j}\left[\frac{1}{s - j\beta} - \frac{1}{s + j\beta}\right]$$

$$= \frac{A\beta}{s^2 + \beta^2}$$

■

INTEGRATION PROPERTY

In the time domain the *i–v* relationships for capacitors and inductors involve integration and differentiation. Since we will be working in the *s* domain, it is important to establish the *s*-domain equivalents of these mathematical operations. Applying the integral definition of the Laplace transformation to a time-domain integration yields

$$\mathcal{L}\left[\int_0^t f(\tau)d\tau\right] = \int_0^\infty \left[\int_0^t f(\tau)d\tau\right]e^{-st}\,dt \qquad (9-8)$$

The right side of this expression can be integrated by parts using

$$y = \int_0^t f(\tau)d\tau \quad \text{and} \quad dx = e^{-st}\,dt$$

These definitions result in

$$dy = f(t) \quad \text{and} \quad x = \frac{-e^{-st}}{s}$$

Using these factors reduces the right side of Eq. (9–8) to

$$\mathcal{L}\left[\int_0^t f(\tau)d\tau\right] = \left[\frac{-e^{-st}}{s}\int_0^t f(\tau)d\tau\right]_0^\infty + \frac{1}{s}\int_0^\infty f(t)e^{-st}\,dt \quad (9-9)$$

The first term on the right in Eq. (9–9) vanishes at the lower limit because the integral over a zero-length interval is zero provided that $f(t)$ is finite at $t = 0$. It vanishes at the upper limit because e^{-st} approaches zero as t goes to infinity for $\sigma > 0$. By the definition of the Laplace transformation, the second term on the right is $F(s)/s$. We conclude that

$$\mathcal{L}\left[\int_0^t f(\tau)d\tau\right] = \frac{F(s)}{s} \quad (9-10)$$

The **integration property** states that time-domain integration of a waveform $f(t)$ can be accomplished in the s domain by the algebraic process of dividing its transform $F(s)$ by s. The next example applies the integration property to obtain the transform of the ramp function.

EXAMPLE 9–6

Show that the Laplace transform of the ramp function $r(t) = tu(t)$ is $1/s^2$.

SOLUTION:

From our study of signals, we know that the ramp waveform can be obtained from $u(t)$ by integration.

$$r(t) = \int_0^t u(\tau)\,d\tau$$

In Example 9–1 we found $\mathcal{L}\{u(t)\} = 1/s$. Using these facts and the integration property of Laplace transforms, we obtain

$$\mathcal{L}\{r(t)\} = \mathcal{L}\left[\int_0^t u(\tau)\,d\tau\right] = \frac{1}{s}\mathcal{L}\{u(t)\} = \frac{1}{s^2}$$ ■

DIFFERENTIATION PROPERTY

The time-domain differentiation operation transforms into the s domain as follows:

$$\mathcal{L}\left[\frac{df(t)}{dt}\right] = \int_0^\infty \left[\frac{df(t)}{dt}\right]e^{-st}\,dt \quad (9-11)$$

The right side of this equation can be integrated by parts using

$$y = e^{-st} \text{ and } dx = \frac{df(t)}{dt}\,dt$$

These definitions result in

$$dy = -se^{-st}\,dt \quad \text{and} \quad x = f(t)$$

Inserting these factors reduces the right side of Eq. (9–11) to

$$\mathcal{L}\left[\frac{df(t)}{dt}\right] = f(t)e^{-st}\Big|_{0-}^{\infty} + s\int_{0-}^{\infty} f(t)e^{-st}\,dt \tag{9-12}$$

For $\sigma > 0$ the first term on the right side of Eq. (9–12) is zero at the upper limit because e^{-st} approaches zero as t goes to infinity. At the lower limit it reduces to $-f(0-)$. By the definition of the Laplace transform, the second term on the right side is $sF(s)$. We conclude that

$$\mathcal{L}\left[\frac{df(t)}{dt}\right] = sF(s) - f(0-) \tag{9-13}$$

The **differentiation property** states that time-domain differentiation of a waveform $f(t)$ is accomplished in the s-domain by the algebraic process of multiplying the transform $F(s)$ by s and subtracting the constant $f(0-)$. Note that the constant $f(0-)$ is the value of $f(t)$ at $t = 0-$ just prior to $t = 0$.

The s-domain equivalent of a second derivative is obtained by repeated application of Eq. (9–13). We first define a waveform $g(t)$ as

$$g(t) = \frac{df(t)}{dt} \quad \text{hence} \quad \frac{d^2f(t)}{dt^2} = \frac{dg(t)}{dt}$$

Applying the differentiation rule to these two equations yields

$$G(s) = sF(s) - f(0-) \text{ and } \mathcal{L}\left[\frac{d^2f(t)}{dt^2}\right] = sG(s) - g(0-)$$

Substituting the first of these equations into the second results in

$$\mathcal{L}\left[\frac{d^2f(t)}{dt^2}\right] = s^2F(s) - sf(0-) - f'(0-)$$

where

$$f'(0-) = \frac{df}{dt}\Big|_{t=0-}$$

Repeated application of this procedure produces the nth derivative:

$$\mathcal{L}\left[\frac{d^nf(t)}{dt^n}\right] = s^nF(s) - s^{n-1}f(0-) - s^{n-2}f'(0-)\ldots f^{(n)}(0-) \tag{9-14}$$

where $f^{(n)}(0-)$ is the nth derivative of $f(t)$ evaluated at $t = 0-$.

A hallmark feature of the Laplace transformation is the fact that time integration and differentiation change into algebraic operations in the s domain. This observation gives us our first hint as to why it is often easier to work with circuits and signals in the s domain. The next example shows how the differentiation rule can be used to obtain additional transform pairs.

EXAMPLE 9–7

Show that the Laplace transform of $f(t) = [\cos \beta t]u(t)$ is $F(s) = s/(s^2 + \beta^2)$.

SOLUTION:

We can express $\cos \beta t$ in terms of the derivative of $\sin \beta t$ as

$$\cos \beta t = \frac{1}{\beta}\frac{d}{dt}\sin \beta t$$

In Example 9–5 we found $\mathscr{L}\{\sin \beta t\} = \beta/(s^2 + \beta^2)$. Using these facts and the differentiation rule, we can find the Laplace transform of $\cos \beta t$ as follows:

$$\mathscr{L}\{\cos \beta t\} = \frac{1}{\beta}\mathscr{L}\left\{\frac{d}{dt}\sin \beta t\right\} = \frac{1}{\beta}\left[s\left(\frac{\beta}{s^2+\beta^2}\right) - \sin(0-)\right]$$

$$= \frac{s}{s^2+\beta^2}$$ ■

In this section we derived the basic transform properties listed in Table 9–1.

TABLE 9–1 BASIC LAPLACE TRANSFORMATION PROPERTIES

PROPERTIES	TIME DOMAIN	FREQUENCY DOMAIN
Independent variable	t	s
Signal representation	$f(t)$	$F(s)$
Uniqueness	$\mathscr{L}^{-1}\{F(s)\} \,(=)\, [f(t)]u(t)$	$\mathscr{L}\{f(t)\} = F(s)$
Linearity	$Af_1(t) + Bf_2(t)$	$AF_1(s) + BF_2(s)$
Integration	$\int_0^t f(\tau)\, d\tau$	$\frac{F(s)}{s}$
Differentiation	$\frac{df(t)}{dt}$	$sF(s) - f(0-)$
	$\frac{d^2f(t)}{dt^2}$	$s^2F(s) - sf(0-) - f'(0-)$
	$\frac{d^3f(t)}{dt^3}$	$s^3F(s) - s^2f(0-) - sf'(0-) - f''(0-)$

The Laplace transformation has other properties that are useful in signal-processing applications. We treat some of these properties in the last three sections of this chapter. However, the basic properties in Table 9–1 are used frequently in circuit analysis and are sufficient for nearly all of the applications in this book.

Similarly, Table 9–2 lists a basic set of Laplace transform pairs that is sufficient for most of the applications in this book. All of these pairs were derived in the preceding two sections, except for the damped ramp,

TABLE 9–2 BASIC LAPLACE TRANSFORM PAIRS

SIGNAL	WAVEFORM $f(t)$	TRANSFORM $F(s)$
Impulse	$\delta(t)$	1
Step function	$u(t)$	$\frac{1}{s}$
Ramp	$tu(t)$	$\frac{1}{s^2}$
Exponential	$[e^{-\alpha t}]u(t)$	$\frac{1}{s+\alpha}$
Damped ramp	$[te^{-\alpha t}]u(t)$	$\frac{1}{(s+\alpha)^2}$
Sine	$[\sin \beta t]u(t)$	$\frac{\beta}{s^2+\beta^2}$
Cosine	$[\cos \beta t]u(t)$	$\frac{s}{s^2+\beta^2}$
Damped sine	$[e^{-\alpha t} \sin \beta t]u(t)$	$\frac{\beta}{(s+\alpha)^2+\beta^2}$
Damped cosine	$[e^{-\alpha t} \cos \beta t]u(t)$	$\frac{(s+\alpha)}{(s+\alpha)^2+\beta^2}$

damped sine, and damped cosine. The Laplace transforms of these damped waveforms are listed in Table 9–2 but are derived in Sect. 9–7.

All of the waveforms in Table 9–2 are causal. As a result, the Laplace transform pairs are unique and we can use the table in either direction. That is, given an $f(t)$ in the waveform column we find its Laplace transform in the right column, or given an $F(s)$ in the right column we find its inverse transform in the waveform column.

The last example in this section shows how to use the properties and pairs in Tables 9–1 and 9–2 to obtain the transform of a waveform not listed in the tables.

EXAMPLE 9–8

Find the Laplace transform of the waveform

$$f(t) = 2u(t) - 5[e^{-2t}]u(t) + 3[\cos 2t]u(t) + 3\,[\sin 2t]u(t)$$

SOLUTION:

Using the linearity property, we write the transform of $f(t)$ in the form

$$\mathcal{L}\{f(t)\} = 2\mathcal{L}\{u(t)\} - 5\mathcal{L}\{[e^{-2t}u(t)\} + 3\mathcal{L}\{[\cos 2t]u(t)\} + 3\mathcal{L}\{[\sin 2t]u(t)\}$$

The transforms of each term in this sum are listed in Table 9–2:

$$F(s) = \frac{2}{s} - \frac{5}{s+2} + \frac{3s}{s^2+4} + \frac{6}{s^2+4}$$

Normally, a Laplace transform is written as a quotient of polynomials rather than as a sum of terms. Rationalizing the preceding sum yields

$$F(s) = \frac{16(s^2+1)}{s(s+2)(s^2+4)}$$ ■

Exercise 9–1

Find the Laplace transforms of the following waveforms:

$$\text{(a) } f(t) = [e^{-2t}]u(t) + 4tu(t) - u(t)$$

$$\text{(b) } f(t) = [2 + 2\sin 2t - 2\cos 2t]u(t)$$

Answers:

$$\text{(a) } F(s) = \frac{2(s+4)}{s^2(s+2)}$$

$$\text{(b) } F(s) = \frac{4(s+2)}{s(s^2+4)}$$

Exercise 9–2

Find the Laplace transforms of the following waveforms:

$$\text{(a) } f(t) = [e^{-4t}]u(t) + 5\int_0^t \sin 4x\, dx$$

$$\text{(b) } f(t) = 5[e^{-40t}]u(t) + \frac{d[5te^{-40t}]u(t)}{dt}$$

Answers:

$$\text{(a) } F(s) = \frac{s^3 + 36s + 80}{s(s+4)(s^2+16)}$$

$$\text{(b) } F(s) = \frac{10s + 200}{(s+40)^2}$$

Exercise 9–3

Find the Laplace transforms of the following waveforms:

$$\text{(a) } f(t) = A[\cos(\beta t - \phi)]u(t)$$

$$\text{(b) } f(t) = A[e^{-\alpha t}\cos(\beta t - \phi)]u(t)$$

Answers:

$$\text{(a) } F(s) = A\cos\phi\left[\frac{s + \beta\tan\phi}{s^2 + \beta^2}\right]$$

$$\text{(b) } F(s) = A\cos\phi\left[\frac{s + \alpha + \beta\tan\phi}{(s + \alpha)^2 + \beta^2}\right]$$

Exercise 9–4

Find the waveforms corresponding to the following Laplace transforms:

$$\text{(a) } F(s) = \frac{10s}{s^2 + 25} - \frac{5}{s + 10} + 2$$

$$\text{(b) } F(s) = 2\frac{s + 20}{(s + 20)^2 + 20^2} + \frac{4}{s^2}$$

Answers:

$$\text{(a) } f(t) = [10\cos 5t - 5e^{-10t}]u(t) + 2\delta(t)$$

$$\text{(b) } f(t) = [2e^{-20t}\cos 20t + 4t]u(t)$$

9–3 POLE-ZERO DIAGRAMS

The transforms for signals in Table 9–2 are ratios of polynomials in the complex frequency variable s. Likewise, the transform found in Example 9–8 takes the form of a ratio of two polynomials in s. These results illustrate that the signal transforms of greatest interest to us usually have the form

$$F(s) = \frac{b_m s^m + b_{m-1}s^{m-1} + \ldots + b_1 s + b_0}{a_n s^n + a_{n-1}s^{n-1} + \ldots + a_1 s + a_0} \tag{9-15}$$

If numerator and denominator polynomials are expressed in factored form, then $F(s)$ is written as

$$F(s) = K\frac{(s - z_1)(s - z_2)\ldots(s - z_m)}{(s - p_1)(s - p_2)\ldots(s - p_n)} \tag{9-16}$$

where the constant $K = b_m/a_n$ is called the **scale factor.**

The roots of the numerator and denominator polynomials, together with the scale factor K, uniquely define a transform $F(s)$. The denominator roots are called **poles** because for $s = p_i$ $(i = 1, 2, \ldots n)$ the denominator vanishes and $F(s)$ becomes infinite. The roots of the numerator polynomial are called **zeros** because the transform $F(s)$ vanishes for $s = z_i$ $(i = 1, 2, \ldots m)$. Collectively the poles and zeros are called **critical frequencies** because they are values of s at which $F(s)$ does dramatic things, like vanish or blow up.

In the s-domain we can specify a signal transform by listing the location of its critical frequencies together with the scale factor K. That is, in the frequency domain we describe signals in terms of poles and zeros. The description takes the form of a **pole-zero diagram**, which shows the location of poles and zeros in the complex s-plane. The pole locations in such plots are indicated by an × and the zeros by an ○. The independent variable in the frequency domain is complex frequency, so the poles or zeros can be complex as well. In the *s*-plane we use a horizontal axis to plot the value of the real part of *s* and a vertical *j*-axis to plot the imaginary part. The *j*-axis is an important boundary in the frequency domain because it divides the *s* plane into two distinct half planes. The real part of *s* is negative in the left half plane and positive in the right half plane. As we will soon see, the sign of the real part of a pole has a profound effect on the form of the corresponding waveform.

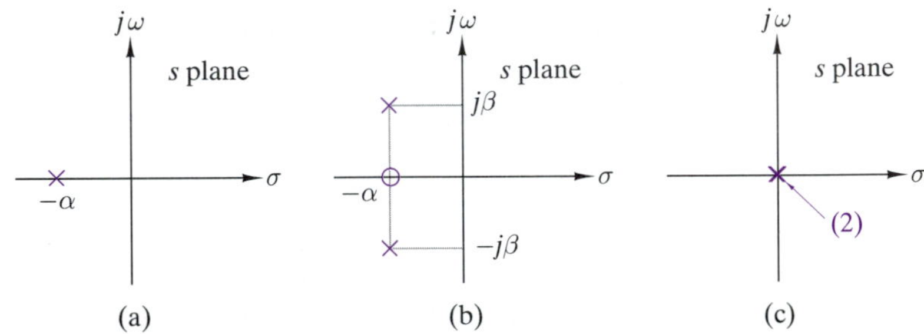

FIGURE 9–2 *Pole-zero diagrams in the s-plane.*

For example, Table 9–2 shows that the transform of the exponential waveform $f(t) = e^{-\alpha t}u(t)$ is $F(s) = 1/(s + \alpha)$. The exponential signal has a single pole at $s = -\alpha$ and no finite zeros. The pole-zero diagram in Figure 9–2(a) is the *s*-domain portrayal of the exponential signal. In this diagram the × identifies the pole located at $s = -\alpha + j0$, a point on the negative real axis in the left half plane.

The damped sinusoid $f(t) = [A\, e^{-\alpha t} \cos \beta t]u(t)$ is an example of a signal with complex poles. From Table 9–2 the corresponding transform is

$$F(s) = \frac{A(s + \alpha)}{(s + \alpha)^2 + \beta^2}$$

The transform $F(s)$ has a finite zero on the real axis at $s = -\alpha$. The roots of the denominator polynomial are $s = -\alpha \pm j\beta$. The resulting pole-zero diagram is shown in Figure 9–2(b). The poles of the damped cosine do not lie on either axis in the *s*-plane because neither the real nor imaginary parts are zero.

Finally, the transform of a unit ramp $f(t) = tu(t)$ is $F(s) = 1/s^2$. This transform has no finite zeros and two poles at the origin ($s = 0 + j0$) in the *s*-plane as shown in Figure 9–2(c). The poles in all of the diagrams of Figure 9–2 lie in the left half plane or on the *j*-axis boundary.

The diagrams in Figure 9–2 show the poles and zeros in the finite part of the *s*-plane. Signal transforms may have poles or zeros at infinity as well. For example, the step function has a zero at infinity since $F(s) = 1/s$ approaches zero as $s \to \infty$. In general, a transform $F(s)$ given by Eq. 9–16 has a zero of order $n - m$ at infinity if $n > m$ and a pole of order $m - n$ at infinity if $n < m$. Thus, the number of zeros equals the number of poles if we include those at infinity.

The pole-zero diagram is the *s*-domain portrayal of the signal, just as a plot of the waveform versus time depicts the signal in the *t*-domain. The utility of a pole-zero diagram as a description of circuits and signals will become clearer as we develop additional *s*-domain analysis and design concepts.

EXAMPLE 9–9

Find the poles and zeros of the waveform

$$f(t) = [e^{-2t} + \cos 2t - \sin 2t]u(t)$$

SOLUTION:

Using the linearity property and the basic pairs in Table 9–2, we write the transform in the form

$$F(s) = \frac{1}{s+2} + \frac{s}{s^2+4} - \frac{2}{s^2+4}$$

Rationalizing this expression yields $F(s)$.

$$F(s) = \frac{2s^2}{(s+2)(s^2+4)} = \frac{2s^2}{(s+2)(s+j2)(s-j2)}$$

This transform has three zeros and three poles. There are two zeros at $s = 0$ and one at $s = \infty$. There is a pole on the negative real axis at $s = -2 + j0$, and two poles on the imaginary axis at $s = \pm j2$. The resulting pole-zero diagram is shown in Figure 9–3. Reviewing the analysis, we can trace the poles to the components of $f(t)$. The pole on the real axis at $s = -2$ came from the exponential e^{-2t}, while the complex conjugate poles on the j-axis came from the sinusoid $\cos 2t - \sin 2t$. The zeros, however, are not traceable to specific components. Their locations depend on all three components. ■

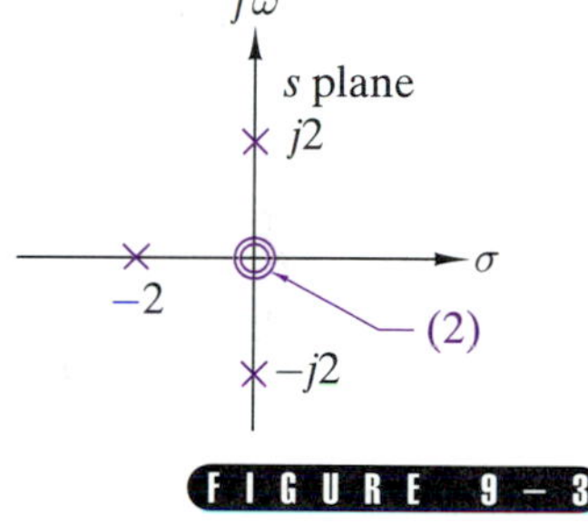

FIGURE 9–3

EXAMPLE 9–10

Use a math analysis program to find the transform of the waveform

$$f(t) = [200te^{-25t} + 10e^{-50t} \sin(25t)]u(t)$$

and construct a pole-zero map of $F(s)$.

SOLUTION:

Programs like Mathcad have symbolic operating modes in which they can, among other things, calculate Laplace transforms. The Mathcad worksheet in Figure 9–4 demonstrates this capability. The first line is the waveform $f(t)$ given previously, which consists of a damped ramp $200te^{-25t}$ and a damped sine $10e^{-50t} \sin 40t$. To obtain the Laplace transform of this expression, we first highlight (click on) one of the "t's" in the expression to identify the independent variable. Then selecting **Symbolic, Transforms, Laplace Transform** from the menu bar causes Mathcad to generate the Laplace transform shown in the second line. This transform has the four poles shown in the third line. The double pole at $s = -25$ is due to the damped ramp, and the pair of complex poles at $s = -50 \pm j40$ is due to the damped sine. The transform numerator polynomial has a pair of complex roots, as shown in the fourth line, leading to the zero locations given in the fifth line. The pole index ($i = 1,2,3,4$) and zero index ($k = 1,2$) then generate the pole-zero diagram. The double pole at $s = -25$ appears to generate

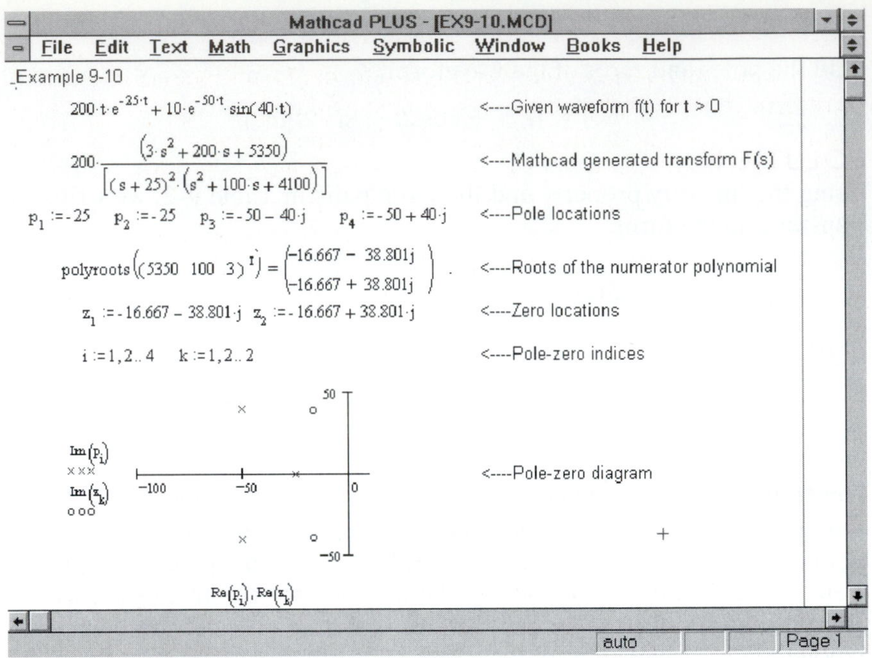

FIGURE 9–4

only a single X in the pole-zero diagram since the plotting routine places one pole symbol directly on top of the other. ■

Exercise 9–5

Find the poles and zeros of transforms of each of the following waveforms:

$$\text{(a) } f(t) = [-2e^{-t} - t + 2]u(t)$$

$$\text{(b) } f(t) = [4 - 3\cos\beta t]u(t)$$

$$\text{(c) } f(t) = [e^{-\alpha t}\cos\beta t + (\alpha/\beta)\, e^{-\alpha t}\sin\beta t]u(t)$$

Answers:

(a) Zeros: $s = 1$, $s = \infty$ (2); poles: $s = 0$ (2), $s = -1$
(b) Zeros: $s = \pm j2\beta$, $s = \infty$; poles: $s = 0$, $s = \pm j\beta$
(c) Zeros: $s = -2\alpha$, $s = \infty$; poles: $s = -\alpha \pm j\beta$

Exercise 9–6

A transform has poles at $s = -3 \pm j6$ and $s = -2$ and finite zeros at $s = 0$ and $s = -1$. Write $F(s)$ as a quotient of polynomials in s.

Answer:

$$F(s) = K\frac{s^2 + s}{s^3 + 8s^2 + 57s + 90}$$

9–4 INVERSE LAPLACE TRANSFORMS

The inverse transformation converts a transform $F(s)$ into the corresponding waveform $f(t)$. Applying the inverse transformation in Eq. (9–4) requires knowledge of a branch of mathematics called the complex variable. Fortunately, we do not need Eq. (9–4) because the uniqueness of the Laplace transform pairs in Table 9–2 allows us to go from a transform to a waveform. This may not seem like much help since it does not take a very complicated circuit or signal before we exceed the listing in Table 9–2, or even the more extensive tables that are available. However, there is a general method of expanding $F(s)$ into a sum of terms that are listed in Table 9–2.

For linear circuits the transforms of interest are ratios of polynomials in s. In mathematics such functions are called **rational functions**. To perform the inverse transformation, we must find the waveform corresponding to rational functions of the form

$$F(s) = K\frac{(s - z_1)(s - z_2)\ldots(s - z_m)}{(s - p_1)(s - p_2)\ldots(s - p_n)} \tag{9–17}$$

where the K is the scale factor, z_i $(i = 1, 2, \ldots m)$ are the zeros, and p_i $(i = 1, 2, \ldots n)$ are the poles of $F(s)$.

If there are more finite poles than finite zeros $(n > m)$, then $F(s)$ is called a **proper rational function**. If the denominator in Eq. (9–17) has no repeated roots $(p_i \neq p_j$ for $i \neq j)$, then $F(s)$ is said to have **simple poles**. In this section we treat the problem of finding the inverse transform of proper rational functions with simple poles. The problem of improper rational functions and multiple poles is covered in the next section.

If a proper rational function has only simple poles, then it can be decomposed into a partial fraction expansion of the form

$$F(s) = \frac{k_1}{s - p_1} + \frac{k_2}{s - p_2} + \ldots + \frac{k_n}{s - p_n} \tag{9–18}$$

In this case, $F(s)$ can be expressed as a linear combination of terms with one term for each of its n simple poles. The k's associated with each term are called **residues**.

Each term in the partial fraction decomposition has the form of the transform of an exponential signal. That is, we recognize that $\mathcal{L}^{-1}\{k/(s + \alpha)\} = [ke^{-\alpha t}]u(t)$. We can now write the corresponding waveform using the linearity property

$$f(t) = [k_1e^{p_1t} + k_2e^{p_2t} + \ldots + k_ne^{p_nt}]u(t) \tag{9–19}$$

In the time domain, the s-domain poles appear in the exponents of exponential waveforms and the residues at the poles become the amplitudes.

Given the poles of $F(s)$, finding the inverse transform $f(t)$ reduces to finding the residues. To illustrate the procedure, consider a case in which $F(s)$ has three simple poles and one finite zero.

$$F(s) = K\frac{(s - z_1)}{(s - p_1)(s - p_2)(s - p_3)} = \frac{k_1}{s - p_1} + \frac{k_2}{s - p_2} + \frac{k_3}{s - p_3}$$

We find the residue k_1 by first multiplying this equation through by the factor $(s - p_1)$:

$$(s - p_1)F(s) = K\frac{(s - z_1)}{(s - p_2)(s - p_3)} = k_1 + \frac{k_2(s - p_1)}{s - p_2} + \frac{k_3(s - p_1)}{s - p_3}$$

If we now set $s = p_1$, the last two terms on the right vanish, leaving

$$k_1 = (s - p_1)F(s)\big|_{s=p_1} = K\frac{(s - z_1)}{(s - p_2)(s - p_3)}\bigg|_{s=p_1}$$

Using the same approach for k_2 yields

$$k_2 = (s - p_2)F(s)\big|_{s=p_2} = K\frac{(s - z_1)}{(s - p_1)(s - p_3)}\bigg|_{s=p_2}$$

The technique generalizes so that the residue at any simple pole p_i is

$$k_i = (s - p_i)F(s)\big|_{s=p_i} \tag{9-20}$$

The process of determining the residue at any simple pole is sometimes called the **cover-up algorithm** because we temporarily remove (cover up) the factor $(s - p_i)$ in $F(s)$ and then evaluate the remainder at $s = p_i$.

EXAMPLE 9–11

Find the waveform corresponding to the transform

$$F(s) = 2\frac{(s + 3)}{s(s + 1)(s + 2)}$$

SOLUTION:

$F(s)$ is a proper rational function and has simple poles at $s = 0$, $s = -1$, $s = -2$. Its partial fraction expansion is

$$F(s) = \frac{k_1}{s} + \frac{k_2}{s + 1} + \frac{k_3}{s + 2}$$

The cover-up algorithm yields the residues as

$$k_1 = sF(s)\big|_{s=0} = \frac{2(s + 3)}{(s + 1)(s + 2)}\bigg|_{s=0} = 3$$

$$k_2 = (s + 1)F(s)\big|_{s=-1} = \frac{2(s + 3)}{s(s + 2)}\bigg|_{s=-1} = -4$$

$$k_3 = (s + 2)F(s)\big|_{s=-2} = \frac{2(s + 3)}{s(s + 1)}\bigg|_{s=-2} = 1$$

The inverse transform $f(t)$ is

$$f(t) = [3 - 4e^{-t} + e^{-2t}]u(t)$$ ■

Exercise 9–7

Find the waveforms corresponding to the following transforms:

$$\text{(a) } F(s) = \frac{4}{(s+1)(s+3)}$$

$$\text{(b) } F(s) = \frac{4(s+2)}{(s+1)(s+3)}$$

Answers:

$$\text{(a) } f(t) = [2e^{-t} - 2e^{-3t}]u(t)$$

$$\text{(b) } f(t) = [2e^{-t} + 2e^{-3t}]u(t)$$

Exercise 9–8

Find the waveforms corresponding to the following transforms:

$$\text{(a) } F(s) = \frac{6(s+2)}{s(s+1)(s+4)}$$

$$\text{(b) } F(s) = \frac{4(s+1)}{s(s+1)(s+4)}$$

Answers:

$$\text{(a) } f(t) = [3 - 2e^{-t} - e^{-4t}]u(t)$$

$$\text{(b) } f(t) = [1 - e^{-4t}]u(t)$$

COMPLEX POLES

Special treatment is necessary when $F(s)$ has a complex pole. In physical situations the function $F(s)$ is a ratio of polynomials with real coefficients. If $F(s)$ has a complex pole $p = -\alpha + j\beta$, then it must also have a pole $p^* = -\alpha - j\beta$; otherwise the coefficients of the denominator polynomial would not be real. In other words, for physical signals the complex poles of $F(s)$ must occur in conjugate pairs. As a consequence, the partial fraction decomposition of $F(s)$ will contain two terms of the form

$$F(s) = \ldots + \frac{k}{s + \alpha - j\beta} + \frac{k^*}{s + \alpha + j\beta} + \ldots \quad (9-21)$$

The residues k and k^* at the conjugate poles are themselves conjugates because $F(s)$ is a rational function with real coefficients. These residues can be calculated using the cover-up algorithm and, in general, they turn out to be complex numbers. If the complex residues are written in polar form as

$$k = |k|e^{j\theta} \text{ and } k^* = |k|e^{-j\theta}$$

then the waveform corresponding to the two terms in Eq. (9–21) is

$$f(t) = [\ldots + |k|e^{j\theta}e^{(-\alpha + j\beta)t} + |k|e^{-j\theta}e^{(-\alpha - j\beta)t} + \ldots]u(t)$$

This equation can be rearranged in the form

$$f(t) = \left[\ldots + 2|k|e^{-\alpha t}\left\{\frac{e^{+j(\beta t+\theta)} + e^{-j(\beta t+\theta)}}{2}\right\} + \ldots\right]u(t) \quad (9-22)$$

The expression inside the brackets is of the form

$$\cos x = \left\{\frac{e^{+jx} + e^{-jx}}{2}\right\}$$

Consequently, we combine terms inside the braces as a cosine function with a phase angle:

$$f(t) = [\ldots + 2|k|e^{-\alpha t}\cos(\beta t + \theta) + \ldots]u(t) \quad (9-23)$$

In summary, if $F(s)$ has a complex pole, then in physical applications there must be an accompanying conjugate complex pole. The inverse transformation combines the two poles to produce a damped cosine waveform. We only need to compute the residue at one of these poles because the residues at conjugate poles must be conjugates. Normally, we calculate the residue for the pole at $s = -\alpha + j\beta$ because its angle equals the phase angle of the damped cosine. Note that the imaginary part of this pole is positive, which means that the pole lies in the upper half of the s-plane.

The inverse transform of a proper rational function with simple poles can be found by the partial fraction expansion method. The residues k at the simple poles can be found using the cover-up algorithm. The resulting waveform is a sum of terms of the form $[ke^{-\alpha t}]u(t)$ for real poles and $[2|k|e^{-\alpha t}\cos(\beta t + \theta)]u(t)$ for a pair of complex conjugate poles. The partial fraction expansion of the transform contains all of the data needed to construct the corresponding waveform.

EXAMPLE 9–12

Find the inverse transform of

$$F(s) = \frac{20(s + 3)}{(s + 1)(s^2 + 2s + 5)}$$

SOLUTION:

$F(s)$ has a simple pole at $s = -1$ and a pair of conjugate complex poles located at the roots of the quadratic factor

$$(s^2 + 2s + 5) = (s + 1 - j2)(s + 1 + j2)$$

The partial fraction expansion of $F(s)$ is

$$F(s) = \frac{k_1}{s + 1} + \frac{k_2}{s + 1 - j2} + \frac{k_2^*}{s + 1 + j2}$$

The residues at the poles are found from the cover-up algorithm.

$$k_1 = \left.\frac{20(s + 3)}{s^2 + 2s + 5}\right|_{s=-1} = 10$$

$$k_2 = \left.\frac{20(2 + 3)}{(s + 1)(s + 1 + j2)}\right|_{s=-1+j2} = -5 - j5 = 5\sqrt{2}e^{+j5\pi/4}$$

We now have all of the data needed to construct the inverse transform.

$$f(t) = [10e^{-t} + 10\sqrt{2}e^{-t}\cos(2t + 5\pi/4)]u(t)$$

In this example we used k_2 to obtain the amplitude and phase angle of the damped cosine term. The residue k_2^* is not needed, but to illustrate a point we note that its value is

$$k_2^* = (-5 - j5)^* = -5 + j5 = 5\sqrt{2}e^{-j5\pi/4}$$

If k_2^* is used instead, we get the same amplitude for the damped sine but the wrong phase angle. *Caution:* Remember that Eq. (9–23) uses the residue at the complex pole with a positive imaginary part. In this example this is the pole at $s = -1 + j2$, not the pole at $s = -1 - j2$.

Exercise 9–9

Find the inverse transforms of the following rational functions:

$$\text{(a) } F(s) = \frac{16}{(s + 2)(s^2 + 4)}$$

$$\text{(b) } F(s) = \frac{2(s + 2)}{s(s^2 + 4)}$$

Answers:

$$\text{(a) } f(t) = [2e^{-2t} + 2\sqrt{2}\cos(2t - 3\pi/4)]u(t)$$

$$\text{(b) } f(t) = [1 + \sqrt{2}\cos(2t - 3\pi/4)]u(t)$$

Exercise 9–10

Find the inverse transforms of the following rational functions:

$$\text{(a) } F(s) = \frac{8}{s(s^2 + 4s + 8)}$$

$$\text{(b) } F(s) = \frac{4s}{s^2 + 4s + 8)}$$

Answers:

$$(a)\ f(t) = [1 + \sqrt{2}e^{-2t}\cos(2t + 3\pi/4)]u(t)$$
$$(b)\ f(t) = [4\sqrt{2}e^{-2t}\cos(2t + \pi/4)]u(t)$$

SUMS OF RESIDUES

The sum of the residues of a proper rational function are subject to certain conditions that are useful for checking the calculations in a partial fraction expansion. To derive these conditions, we multiply Eqs. (9–17) and (9–18) by s and take the limit as $s \to \infty$. These operations yield

$$\lim_{s\to\infty} sF(s) = \lim_{s\to\infty} \frac{Ks^{m+1}}{s^n} = \lim_{s\to\infty}\left(\frac{k_1 s}{s+p_1} + \ldots + \frac{k_n s}{s+p_n}\right)$$

In the limit this equation reduces to

$$K\left[\lim_{s\to\infty}\frac{s^{m+1}}{s^n}\right] = k_1 + k_2 + \ldots + k_n$$

Since $F(s)$ is a proper rational function with $n > m$, the limit process in this equation yields to following conditions:

$$k_1 + k_2 + \ldots + k_n = \begin{cases} 0 \text{ if } n > m \\ K \text{ if } n = m \end{cases} \quad (9-24)$$

For a proper rational function with simple poles, the sum of residues is either zero or else equal to the transform scale factor K.

Exercise 9–11

Use the sum of residues to find the unknown residue in the following expansions:

$$(a)\ \frac{21\,(s+5)}{(s+3)(s+10)} = \frac{6}{s+3} + \frac{k}{s+10}$$
$$(b)\ \frac{58s}{(s+2)(s^2+25)} = \frac{k}{s+2} + \frac{2+j5}{s+j5} + \frac{2-j5}{s-j5}$$

Answers:

(a) $k = 15$
(b) $k = -4$

9–5 SOME SPECIAL CASES

Most of the transforms encountered in physical applications are proper rational functions with simple poles. The inverse transforms of such functions can be handled by the partial fraction expansion method developed in the previous section. This section covers the problem of finding the inverse transform when $F(s)$ is an improper rational function or has multiple poles. These matters are treated as special cases because they only occur for certain discrete values of circuit or signal parameters. However, some of these special cases are important, so we need to learn how to handle improper rational functions and multiple poles.

$F(s)$ is an **improper rational function** when the order of the numerator polynomial equals or exceeds the order of the denominator ($m \geq n$). For example, the transform

$$F(s) = \frac{s^3 + 6s^2 + 12s + 8}{s^2 + 4s + 3} \tag{9–25}$$

is improper because $m = 3$ and $n = 2$. This function can be reduced to a quotient and a remainder, which is a proper function using long division as follows:

$$\begin{array}{r} s + 2 \\ s^2 + 4s + 3 \overline{) s^3 + 6s^2 + 12s + 8} \\ \underline{s^3 + 4s^2 + 3s} \\ 2s^2 + 9s + 8 \\ \underline{2s^2 + 8s + 6} \\ s + 2 \end{array}$$

which yields

$$\begin{aligned} F(s) &= s + 2 + \frac{s + 2}{s^2 + 4s + 3} \\ &= \text{Quotient} + \text{Remainder} \end{aligned}$$

The remainder is a proper rational function, which can be expanded by partial fractions to produce

$$F(s) = s + 2 + \frac{1/2}{s + 1} + \frac{1/2}{s + 3}$$

All of the terms in this expansion are listed in Table 9–2 except the first term. The inverse transform of the first term is found using the transform of an impulse and the differentiation property. The Laplace transform of the derivative of an impulse is

$$\mathcal{L}\left[\frac{d\delta(t)}{dt}\right] = s\mathcal{L}[\delta(t)] - \delta(0-) = s$$

since $\mathcal{L}\{\delta(t)\} = 1$ and $\delta(0-) = 0$. By the uniqueness property of the Laplace transformation, we have $\mathcal{L}^{-1}\{s\} = d\delta(t)/dt$. The first derivative of an impulse is called a doublet. The inverse transform of the improper rational function in Eq. (9–25) is

$$f(t) = \frac{d\delta(t)}{dt} + 2\delta(t) + \left[\frac{1}{2}e^{-t} + \frac{1}{2}e^{-3t}\right]u(t)$$

The method illustrated by this example generalizes in the following way. When $m = n$, long division produces a quotient K plus a proper rational function remainder. The constant K corresponds to an impulse $K\delta(t)$, and the remainder can be expanded by partial fractions to find the corresponding waveform. If $m > n$, then long division yields a quotient with terms like $s, s^2, \ldots s^{m-n}$ before a proper remainder function is obtained. These higher powers of s correspond to derivatives of the impulse. These pathological waveforms are theoretically interesting, but they do not actually occur in real circuits.

Improper rational functions can arise during mathematical manipulation of signal transforms. When $F(s)$ is improper, it is essential to reduce it by long division prior to expansion; otherwise the resulting partial fraction expansion will be incomplete.

Exercise 9–12

Find the inverse transforms of the following functions:

$$\text{(a) } F(s) = \frac{s^2 + 4s + 5}{s^2 + 4s + 3}$$

$$\text{(b) } F(s) = \frac{s^2 - 4}{s^2 + 4}$$

Answers:

$$\text{(a) } f(t) = \delta(t) + [e^{-t} - e^{-3t}]u(t)$$

$$\text{(b) } f(t) = \delta(t) - [4\sin(2t)]u(t)$$

Exercise 9–13

Find the inverse transforms of the following functions:

$$\text{(a) } F(s) = \frac{2s^2 + 3s + 5}{s}$$

$$\text{(b) } F(s) = \frac{s^3 + 2s^2 + s + 3}{s + 2}$$

Answers:

$$\text{(a) } f(t) = 2\frac{d\delta(t)}{dt} + 3\delta(t) + 5u(t)$$

$$\text{(b) } f(t) = \frac{d^2\delta(t)}{dt^2} + \delta(t) + [e^{-2t}]u(t)$$

MULTIPLE POLES

Under certain special conditions, transforms can have multiple poles. For example, the transform

$$F(s) = \frac{K(s - z_1)}{(s - p_1)(s - p_2)^2} \qquad (9-26)$$

has a simple pole at $s = p_1$ and a pole of order 2 at $s = p_2$. Finding the inverse transform of this function requires special treatment of the multiple pole. We first factor out one of the two multiple poles.

$$F(s) = \frac{1}{s - p_2}\left[\frac{K(s - z_1)}{(s - p_1)(s - p_2)}\right] \tag{9-27}$$

The quantity inside the brackets is a proper rational function with only simple poles and can be expanded by partial fractions using the method of the previous section.

$$F(s) = \frac{1}{s - p_2}\left[\frac{c_1}{s - p_1} + \frac{k_{22}}{s - p_2}\right]$$

We now multiply through by the pole factored out in the first step to obtain

$$F(s) = \frac{c_1}{(s - p_1)(s - p_2)} + \frac{k_{22}}{(s - p_2)^2}$$

The first term on the right is a proper rational function with only simple poles, so it too can be expanded by partial fractions as

$$F(s) = \frac{k_1}{s - p_1} + \frac{k_{21}}{s - p_2} + \frac{k_{22}}{(s - p_2)^2}$$

After two partial fraction expansions, we have an expression in which every term is available in Table 9–2. The first two terms are simple poles that lead to exponential waveforms. The third term is of the form $k/(s + \alpha)^2$, which is the transform of a damped ramp waveform $[kt\ e^{-\alpha t}]u(t)$. Therefore, the inverse transform of $F(s)$ in Eq. (9–26) is

$$f(t) = [k_1e^{p_1t} + k_{12}e^{p_2t} + k_{22}te^{p_2t}]u(t) \tag{9-28}$$

Caution: If $F(s)$ in Eq. (9–26) had another finite zero, then the term in the brackets in Eq. (9–27) would be an improper rational function. When this occurs, long division must be used to reduce the improper rational function before proceeding to the partial-fraction expansion in the next step.

As with simple poles, the *s*-domain location of multiple poles determines the exponents of the exponential waveforms. The residues at the poles are the amplitudes of the waveforms. The only difference here is that the double pole leads to two terms rather than a single waveform. The first term is an exponential of the form e^{pt}, and the second term is a damped ramp of the form te^{pt}.

EXAMPLE 9–13

Find the inverse transform of

$$F(s) = \frac{4(s + 3)}{s(s + 2)^2}$$

SOLUTION:

The given transform has a simple pole at $s = 0$ and a double pole at $s = -2$. Factoring out one of the multiple poles and expanding the remainder by partial fractions yields

$$F(s) = \frac{1}{s+2}\left[\frac{4(s+3)}{s(s+2)}\right] = \frac{1}{s+2}\left[\frac{6}{s} - \frac{2}{s+2}\right]$$

Multiplying through by the removed factor and expanding again by partial fractions produces

$$F(s) = \frac{6}{s(s+2)} - \frac{2}{(s+2)^2} = \frac{3}{s} - \frac{3}{s+2} - \frac{2}{(s+2)^2}$$

The last expansion on the right yields the inverse transform as

$$f(t) = [3 - 3e^{-2t} - 2te^{-2t}]u(t)$$ ■

In principle, the procedure illustrated in this example can be applied to higher-order poles, although the process rapidly becomes quite tedious. For example, an nth-order pole would require n partial-fraction expansions, which is not an idea with irresistible appeal. Mathematics offers other methods of determining multiple pole residues that reduce the computational burden somewhat. But fortunately, pole multiplicities with $n > 2$ require unique circumstances that only rarely occur in real circuits.

Thus, for practical reasons our interest in multiple pole transforms is limited to two possibilities. First, a double pole on the negative real axis leads to the damped ramp:

$$\mathcal{L}^{-1}\left[\frac{k}{(s+\alpha)^2}\right] = [kte^{-\alpha t}]u(t) \tag{9–29}$$

Second, a pair of double, complex poles leads to the damped cosine ramp:

$$\mathcal{L}^{-1}\left[\frac{k}{(s+\alpha-j\beta)^2} + \frac{k^*}{(s+\alpha+j\beta)^2}\right] = [2\,|k|\,te^{-\alpha t}\cos(\beta t + \angle k)]u(t) \tag{9–30}$$

These two cases illustrate a general principle: When a simple pole leads to a waveform $f(t)$, then a double pole at the same location leads in a waveform $tf(t)$. Multiplying a waveform by t tends to cause the waveform to increase without bound unless exponential damping term is present. The following example illustrates a case in which the damping term is not present.

EXAMPLE 9–14

Use a math analysis program to find the waveform corresponding to a transform with a zero at $s = -400$, a simple pole at $s = -1000$, a double pole at $s = j400$, a double pole at $s = -j400$, and a value at $s = 0$ of $F(0) = 2 \times 10^{-4}$. Plot the resulting waveform $f(t)$.

SOLUTION:

The symbolic analysis capability of Mathcad includes inverse Laplace transforms. Figure 9–5 is a worksheet demonstrating this capability. The specified critical frequencies define the $F(s)$ shown in the first line. The specified value at $s = 0$ allows us to evaluate the unknown scale factor K as

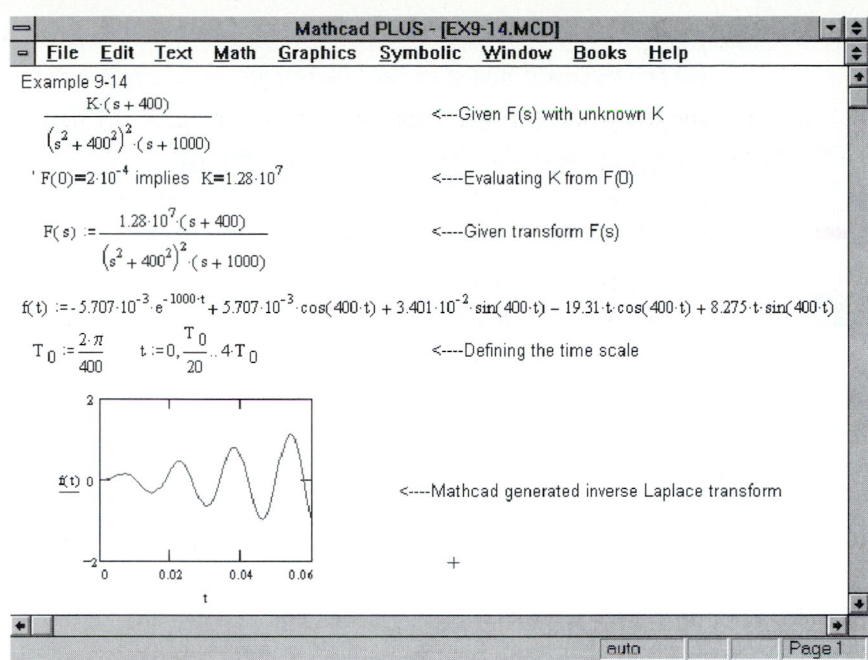

Mathcad PLUS - [EX9-14.MCD]
File Edit Text Math Graphics Symbolic Window Books Help
Example 9-14
$\frac{K\cdot(s+400)}{(s^2+400^2)^2\cdot(s+1000)}$
<---Given F(s) with unknown K
' F(0)=2·10^-4 implies K=1.28·10^7
<----Evaluating K from F(0)
$F(s) := \frac{1.28\cdot 10^7\cdot(s+400)}{(s^2+400^2)^2\cdot(s+1000)}$
<----Given transform F(s)
$f(t) := -5.707\cdot 10^{-3}\cdot e^{-1000\cdot t} + 5.707\cdot 10^{-3}\cdot\cos(400\cdot t) + 3.401\cdot 10^{-2}\cdot\sin(400\cdot t) - 19.31\cdot t\cdot\cos(400\cdot t) + 8.275\cdot t\cdot\sin(400\cdot t)$
$T_0 := \frac{2\cdot\pi}{400}$ $t := 0, \frac{T_0}{20} .. 4\cdot T_0$
<----Defining the time scale
<----Mathcad generated inverse Laplace transform
auto
Page 1

FIGURE 9–5

shown in the second line. This leads directly to the transform in the third line. After highlighting (clicking on) an "s" in $F(s)$ to identify the independent variable, we select **Symbolic, Transforms, Inverse Laplace Transform** from the menu bar. Mathcad responds by producing the $f(t)$ shown in the figure. This waveform contains five terms: The exponential e^{-1000t} came from the simple pole at $s = -1000$, and the four sinusoidal terms $\cos(400t)$, $\sin(400t)$, $t \times \cos(400t)$, and $t \times \sin(400t)$ all came from the double poles at $s = \pm j400$. As time increases, the terms $t \times \cos(400t)$ and $t \times \sin(400t)$ increase without bound, leading to the linearly increasing amplitude shown in the waveform plot. A key point to remember is that poles on the j-axis lead to sustained waveforms, like the step function and sinusoid, that do not decay. Consequently, double poles on the j-axis lead to $tf(t)$ waveforms whose amplitudes increase without bound.

Exercise 9–14

Find the inverse transforms of the following functions:

$$\text{(a) } F(s) = \frac{s}{(s+1)(s+2)^2}$$

$$\text{(b) } F(s) = \frac{16}{s^2(s+4)}$$

$$\text{(c) } F(s) = \frac{800\, s(s+1)}{(s+2)(s+10)^2}$$

Answers:

$$(a)\ f(t) = [-e^{-t} + e^{-2t} + 2te^{-2t}]u(t)$$

$$(b)\ f(t) = [4t - 1 + e^{-4t}]u(t)$$

$$(c)\ f(t) = [25e^{-2t} + 775e^{-10t} - 9000te^{-10t}]u(t)$$

9–6 CIRCUIT RESPONSE USING LAPLACE TRANSFORMS

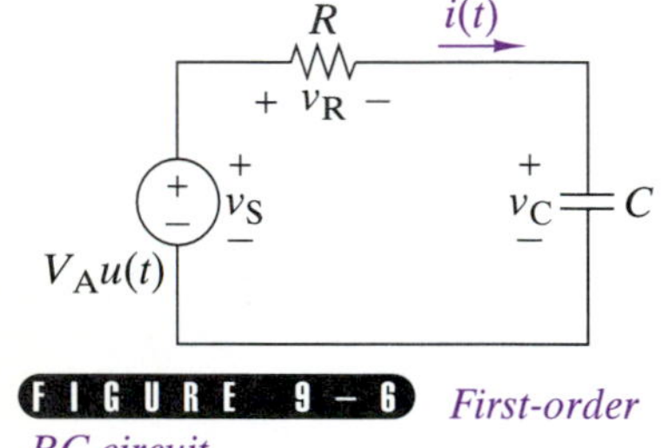

FIGURE 9–6 First-order *RC* circuit.

The payoff for learning about the Laplace transformation comes when we use it to find the response of dynamic circuits. The pattern for circuit analysis is shown by the solid line in Figure 9–1. The basic analysis steps are as follows:

STEP 1: Develop the circuit differential equation in the time domain.

STEP 2: Transform this equation into the *s*-domain and algebraically solve for the response transform.

STEP 3: Apply the inverse transformation to this transform to produce the response waveform.

The first-order *RC* circuit in Figure 9–6 will be used to illustrate these steps.

STEP 1

The KVL equation around the loop and the element i–v relationship or element equations are

$$\text{KVL:}\ -v_S(t) + v_R(t) + v_C(t) = 0$$

$$\text{Source:}\ v_S(t) = V_A u(t)$$

$$\text{Resistor:}\ v_R(t) = i(t)R$$

$$\text{Capacitor:}\ i(t) = C\frac{dv_C(t)}{dt}$$

Substituting the i–v relationships into the KVL equation and rearranging terms produces a first-order differential equation

$$RC\frac{dv_C(t)}{dt} + v_C(t) = V_A u(t) \tag{9–31}$$

with an initial condition $v_C(0-) = V_0$ V.

STEP 2

The analysis objective is to use Laplace transforms to find the waveform $v_C(t)$ that satisfies this differential equation and the initial condition. We first apply the Laplace transformation to both sides of Eq. (9–31):

$$\mathcal{L}\left[RC\frac{dv_C(t)}{dt} + v_C(t)\right] = \mathcal{L}[V_A u(t)]$$

Using the linearity property leads to

$$RC\mathcal{L}\left[\frac{dv_C(t)}{dt}\right] + \mathcal{L}[v_C(t)] = V_A\mathcal{L}[u(t)]$$

Using the differentiation property and the transform of a unit step function produces

$$RC[sV_C(s) - V_0] + V_C(s) = V_A\frac{1}{s} \tag{9–32}$$

This result is an algebraic equation in $V_C(s)$, which is the transform of the response we seek. We rearrange Eq. (9–32) in the form

$$(s + 1/RC)V_C(s) = \frac{V_A/RC}{s} + V_0$$

and algebraically solve for $V_C(s)$.

$$V_C(s) = \frac{V_A/RC}{s(s + 1/RC)} + \frac{V_0}{s + 1/RC} \quad \text{V-s} \tag{9–33}$$

The function $V_C(s)$ is the transform of the waveform $v_C(t)$ that satisfies the differential equation and the initial condition. The initial condition appears explicitly in this equation as a result of applying the differentiation rule to obtain Eq. (9–32).

STEP 3

To obtain the waveform $v_C(t)$, we find the inverse transform of the right side of Eq. (9–33). The first term on the right is a proper rational function with two simple poles on the real axis in the s-plane. The pole at the origin was introduced by the step function input. The pole at $s = -1/RC$ came from the circuit. The partial fraction expansion of the first term in Eq. (9–33) is

$$\frac{V_A/RC}{s(s + 1/RC)} = \frac{k_1}{s} + \frac{k_2}{s + 1/RC}$$

The residues k_1 and k_2 are found using the cover-up algorithm.

$$k_1 = \left.\frac{V_A/RC}{s + 1/RC}\right|_{s=0} = V_A \quad \text{and} \quad k_2 = \left.\frac{V_A/RC}{s}\right|_{s=-1/RC} = -V_A$$

Using these residues, we expand Eq. 9–(33) by partial fractions as

$$V_C(s) = \frac{V_A}{s} - \frac{V_A}{s + 1/RC} + \frac{V_0}{s + 1/RC} \tag{9–34}$$

Each term in this expansion is recognizable: The first is a step function and the next two are exponentials. Taking the inverse transform of Eq. (9–34) gives

$$v_C(t) = [V_A - V_A e^{-t/RC} + V_0 e^{-t/RC}]u(t)$$
$$= [V_A + (V_0 - V_A)e^{-t/RC}]u(t) \quad \text{V} \qquad (9-35)$$

The waveform $v_C(t)$ satisfies the differential equation in Eq. (9–31) and the initial condition $v_C(0-) = V_0$. The term $V_A u(t)$ is the forced response due to the step function input, and the term $[(V_0 - V_A)e^{t/RC}]u(t)$ is the natural response. The complete response depends on three parameters: the input amplitude V_A, the circuit time constant RC, and the initial condition V_0.

These results are identical to those found using the classical methods in Chapter 7. The outcome is the same, but the method is quite different. The Laplace transformation yields the complete response (forced and natural) by an algebraic process that inherently accounts for the initial conditions. The solid arrow in Figure 9–1 shows the overall procedure. Begin with Eq. (9–31) and relate each step leading to Eq. (9–35) to steps in Figure 9–1.

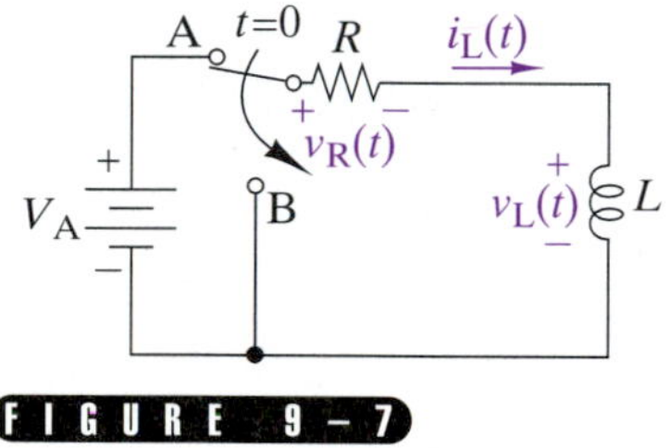

FIGURE 9–7

EXAMPLE 9–15

The switch in Figure 9–7 has been in position A for a long time. At $t = 0$ it is moved to position B. Find $i_L(t)$ for $t \geq 0$.

SOLUTION:

Step 1: The circuit differential equation is found by combining the KVL equation and element equations with the switch in position B.

$$\text{KVL: } v_R(t) + v_L(t) = 0$$
$$\text{Resistor: } v_R(t) = i_L(t)R$$
$$\text{Inductor: } v_L(t) = L\frac{di_L(t)}{dt}$$

Substituting the element equations into the KVL equation yields

$$L\frac{di_L(t)}{dt} + Ri_L(t) = 0$$

Prior to $t = 0$, the circuit was in a dc steady-state condition with the switch in position A. Under dc conditions the inductor acts like a short circuit, and the inductor current just prior to moving the switch is $i_L(0-) = I_0 = V_A/R$.

Step 2: Using the linearity and differentiation properties, we transform the circuit differential equation into the s-domain as

$$L[sI_L(s) - I_0] + RI_L(s) = 0$$

Solving algebraically for $I_L(s)$ yields

$$I_L(s) = \frac{I_0}{s + R/L} \quad \text{A-s}$$

Step 3: The inverse transform of $I_L(s)$ is an exponential waveform:

$$i_L(t) = [I_0 e^{-Rt/L}]u(t) \quad \text{A}$$

where $I_0 = V_A/R$. Substituting $i_L(t)$ back into the differential equation yields

$$L\frac{di_L(t)}{dt} + Ri_L(t) = -RI_0 e^{-Rt/L} + RI_0 e^{-Rt/L} = 0$$

The waveform found using Laplace transforms does indeed satisfy the circuit differential equation and the initial condition. ■

EXAMPLE 9–16

The switch in Figure 9–8 has been open for a long time. At $t = 0$ the switch is closed. Find $i(t)$ for $t \geq 0$.

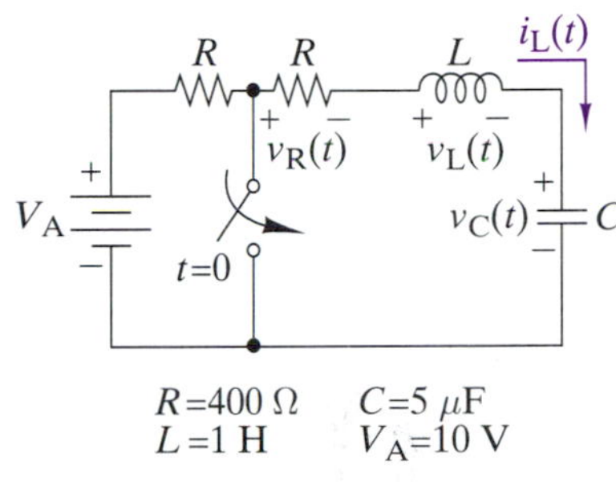

FIGURE 9–8

SOLUTION:

The governing equation for the second-order circuit in Figure 9–8 is found by combining the element equations and a KVL equation around the loop with the switch closed:

$$\text{KVL: } v_R(t) + v_L(t) + v_C(t) = 0$$

$$\text{Resistor: } v_R(t) = Ri(t)$$

$$\text{Inductor: } v_L(t) = L\frac{di(t)}{dt}$$

$$\text{Capacitor: } v_C(t) = \frac{1}{C}\int_0^t i(\tau)d\tau + v_C(0)$$

Substituting the element equations into the KVL equation yields

$$L\frac{di(t)}{dt} + Ri(t) + \frac{1}{C}\int_0^t i(\tau)d\tau + v_C(0) = 0$$

Using the linearity property, the differentiation property, and the integration property, we transform this second-order integro-differential equation into the s domain as

$$L[sI(s) - i_L(0)] + RI(s) + \frac{1}{C}\frac{I(s)}{s} + v_C(0)\frac{1}{s} = 0$$

Solving for $I(s)$ results in

$$I(s) = \frac{si_L(0) - v_C(0)/L}{s^2 + \frac{R}{L}s + \frac{1}{LC}} \quad \text{A-s}$$

Prior to $t = 0$, the circuit was in a dc steady-state condition with the switch open. In dc steady state, the inductor acts like a short circuit and the capacitor like an open circuit, so the initial conditions are $i_L(0-) = 0$ A and $v_C(0-) = V_A = 10$ V. Inserting the initial conditions and the numerical values of the circuit parameters into the equation for $I(s)$ gives

$$I(s) = -\frac{10}{s^2 + 400s + 2 \times 10^5} \quad \text{A-s}$$

The denominator quadratic can be factored as $(s + 200)^2 + 400^2$ and $I(s)$ written in the following form:

$$I(s) = -\frac{10}{400}\left[\frac{400}{(s + 200)^2 + (400)^2}\right] \quad \text{A-s}$$

Comparing the quantity inside the brackets with the entries in the $F(s)$ column of Table 9–2, we find that $I(s)$ is a damped sine with $\alpha = 200$ and $\beta = 400$. By linearity, the quantity outside the brackets is the amplitude of the damped sine. The inverse transform is

$$i(t) = [-0.025\, e^{-200t} \sin 400t]u(t) \text{ A}$$

Substituting this result back into the circuit integro-differential equation yields the following term-by-term tabulation:

$$L\frac{di(t)}{dt} = +5e^{-200t} \sin 400t - 10e^{-200t} \cos 400t$$

$$Ri(t) = -10e^{-200t} \sin 400t$$

$$\frac{1}{C}\int_0^t i(\tau)d\tau = +5e^{-200t} \sin 400t + 10e^{-200t} \cos 400t - 10$$

$$v_C(0) = +10$$

The sum of the right-hand sides of these equations is zero. This result shows that the waveform $i(t)$ found using Laplace transforms does indeed satisfy the circuit integro-differential equation and the initial conditions. ■

Exercise 9–15

Find the transform $V(s)$ that satisfies the following differential equations and the initial conditions:

$$\text{(a)}\ \frac{dv(t)}{dt} + 6v(t) = 4u(t) \qquad v(0-) = -3$$

$$\text{(b)}\ 4\frac{dv(t)}{dt} + 12v(t) = 16 \cos 3t, \qquad v(0-) = 2$$

Answers:

$$\text{(a)}\ V(s) = \frac{4}{s(s + 6)} - \frac{3}{s + 6} \quad \text{V-s}$$

$$\text{(b)}\ V(s) = \frac{4s}{(s^2 + 9)(s + 3)} + \frac{2}{s + 3} \quad \text{V-s}$$

Exercise 9–16

Find the $V(s)$ that satisfies the following equations:

(a) $\int_0^t v(\tau)d\tau + 10v(t) = 10u(t)$

(b) $\dfrac{d^2v(t)}{dt^2} + 4\dfrac{dv(t)}{dt} + 3v(t) = 5e^{-2t} \qquad v'(0-) = 2 \qquad v(0-) = -2$

Answers:

(a) $V(s) = \dfrac{1}{s + 0.1}$ V-s

(b) $V(s) = \dfrac{5}{(s + 1)(s + 2)(s + 3)} - \dfrac{2}{s + 1}$ V-s

CIRCUIT RESPONSE WITH TIME-VARYING INPUTS

It is encouraging to find that the Laplace transformation yields results that agree with those obtained by classical methods. The transform method reduces solving circuit differential equations to an algebraic process that includes the initial conditions. However, before being overcome with euphoria we must remember that the Laplace transform method begins with the circuit differential equation and the initial conditions. It does not provide these quantities to us. The transform method simplifies the solution process, but it does not substitute for understanding how to formulate circuit equations.

The Laplace transform method is especially usefully when the circuit is driven by time-varying inputs. To illustrate, we return to the *RC* circuit in Figure 9–6 and replace the step function input by a general input signal denoted $v_S(t)$. The right side of the circuit differential equation in Eq. (9–31) changes to accommodate the new input by taking the form

$$RC\frac{dv_C(t)}{dt} + v_C(t) = v_S(t) \tag{9-36}$$

with an initial condition $v_C(0) = V_0$ V.

The only change here is that the driving force on the right side of the differential equation is a general time-varying waveform $v_S(t)$. The objective is to find the capacitor voltage $v_C(t)$ that satisfies the differential equation and the initial conditions. The classical methods of solving for the forced response depend on the form of $v_S(t)$. However, with the Laplace transform method we can proceed without actually specifying the form of the input signal.

We first transform Eq. (9–36) into the s-domain:

$$RC[sV_C(s) - V_0] + V_C(s) = V_S(s)$$

The only assumption here is that the input waveform is Laplace transformable, a condition met by all causal signals of engineering interest. We now algebraically solve for the response $V_C(s)$:

$$V_C(s) = \frac{V_S(s)/RC}{s + 1/RC} + \frac{V_0}{s + 1/RC} \quad \text{V-s} \tag{9-37}$$

The function $V_C(s)$ is the transform of the response of the *RC* circuit in Figure 9–6 due to a general input signal $v_S(t)$. We have gotten this far without specifying the form of the input signal. In a sense, we have found the general solution in the *s* domain of the differential equation in Eq. (9–36) for any casual input signal.

All of the necessary ingredients are present in Eq. (9–37):

1. The transform $V_S(s)$ represents the applied input signal.
2. The pole at $s = -1/RC$ defines the circuit time constant.
3. The initial value $v_C(0-) = V_0$ summarizes all events prior to $t = 0$.

However, we must have a particular input in mind to solve for the waveform $v_C(t)$. The following examples illustrate the procedure for different input driving forces.

EXAMPLE 9–17

Find $v_C(t)$ in the *RC* circuit in Figure 9–6 when the input is the waveform $v_S(t) = [V_A e^{-\alpha t}]u(t)$.

SOLUTION:

The transform of the input is $V_S(s) = V_A/(s + \alpha)$. For the exponential input the response transform in Eq. (9–37) becomes

$$V_C(s) = \frac{V_A/RC}{(s + \alpha)(s + 1/RC)} + \frac{V_0}{s + 1/RC} \quad \text{V-s} \tag{9-38}$$

If $\alpha \neq 1/RC$ then the first term on the right is a proper rational function with two simple poles. The pole at $s = -\alpha$ came from the input and the pole at $s = -1/RC$ from the circuit. A partial fraction expansion of the first term has the form

$$\frac{V_A/RC}{(s + \alpha)(s + 1/RC)} = \frac{k_1}{s + \alpha} + \frac{k_2}{s + 1/RC}$$

The residues in this expansion are

$$k_1 = \left.\frac{V_A/RC}{s + 1/RC}\right|_{s=-\alpha} = \frac{V_A}{1 - \alpha RC}$$

$$k_2 = \left.\frac{V_A/RC}{s + \alpha}\right|_{s=-1/RC} = \frac{V_A}{\alpha RC - 1}$$

The expansion of the response transform $V_C(s)$ is

$$V_C(s) = \frac{V_A/(1-\alpha RC)}{s+\alpha} + \frac{V_A/(\alpha RC - 1)}{s + 1/RC} + \frac{V_0}{s+1/RC} \quad \text{V-s}$$

The inverse transform of $V_C(s)$ is

$$v_C(t) = \left[\frac{V_A}{1-\alpha RC}e^{-\alpha t} + \frac{V_A}{\alpha RC - 1}e^{-t/RC} + V_0 e^{-t/RC}\right]u(t) \quad \text{V}$$

The first term is the forced response, and the last two terms are the natural response. The forced response is an exponential because the input introduced a pole at $s = -\alpha$. The natural response is also an exponential, but its time constant depends on the circuit's pole at $s = -1/RC$. In this case the forced and natural responses are both exponential signals with poles on the real axis. However, the forced response comes from the pole introduced by the input, while the natural response depends on the circuit's pole.

If $\alpha = 1/RC$, then the response just given is no longer valid (k_1 and k_2 become infinite). To find the response for this condition, we return to Eq. (9–38) and replace α by $1/RC$:

$$V_C(s) = \frac{V_A/RC}{(s+1/RC)^2} + \frac{V_0}{s+1/RC} \quad \text{V-s}$$

We now have a double pole at $s = -1/RC = -\alpha$. The double pole term is the transform of a damped ramp, so the inverse transform is

$$v_C(t) = \left[V_A\frac{t}{RC}e^{-t/RC} + V_0 e^{-t/RC}\right]u(t) \quad \text{V}$$

When $\alpha = 1/RC$ the s-domain poles of the input and the circuit coincide and the zero-state ($V_0 = 0$) response has the form $\alpha te^{-\alpha t}$. We cannot separate this response into forced and natural components since the input and circuit poles coincide. ■

EXAMPLE 9–18

Find $v_C(t)$ when the input to the RC circuit in Figure 9–6 is $v_S(t) = [V_A \cos \beta t]u(t)$.

SOLUTION:

The transform of the input is $V_S(s) = V_A s/(s^2 + \beta^2)$. For a cosine input the response transform in Eq. (9–37) becomes

$$V_C(s) = \frac{sV_A/RC}{(s^2+\beta^2)(s+1/RC)} + \frac{V_0}{s+1/RC} \quad \text{V-s}$$

The sinusoidal input introduces a pair of poles located at $s = \pm j\beta$. The first term on the right is a proper rational function with three simple poles. The partial fraction expansion of the first term is

$$\frac{sV_A/RC}{(s - j\beta)(s + j\beta)(s + 1/RC)} = \frac{k_1}{s - j\beta} + \frac{k_1^*}{s + j\beta} + \frac{k_2}{s + 1/RC}$$

To find the response, we need to find the residues k_1 and k_2:

$$k_1 = \left.\frac{sV_A/RC}{(s + j\beta)(s + 1/RC)}\right|_{s=j\beta} = \frac{V_A/2}{1 + j\beta RC} = |k_1|e^{j\theta}$$

where

$$|k_1| = \frac{V_A/2}{\sqrt{1 + (\beta RC)^2}} \quad \text{and} \quad \theta = -\tan^{-1}(\beta RC)$$

The residue k_2 at the circuit pole is

$$k_2 = \left.\frac{sV_A/RC}{s^2 + \beta^2}\right|_{s=-1/RC} = -\frac{V_A}{1 + (\beta RC)^2}$$

We now perform the inverse transform to obtain the response waveform:

$$v_C(t) = [2|k_1|\cos(\beta t + \theta) + k_2 e^{-t/RC} + V_0 e^{-t/RC}]u(t)$$

$$= \left[\frac{V_A}{\sqrt{1 + (\beta RC)^2}}\cos(\beta t + \theta) - \frac{V_A}{1 + (\beta RC)^2}e^{-t/RC} + V_0 e^{-t/RC}\right]u(t) \quad \text{V}$$

The first term is the forced response, and the remaining two are the natural response. The forced response is sinusoidal because the input introduces poles at $s = \pm j\beta$. The natural response is an exponential with a time constant determined by the location of the circuit's pole at $s = -1/RC$. ■

Exercise 9–17

Find $v_C(t)$ for the *RC* circuit in Figure 9–6 when the input is

(a) A ramp $v_S(t) = [V_A t/T]u(t)$
(b) A sinusoid $v_S(t) = [V_A \sin \beta t]u(t)$.

Answers:

(a) $v_C(t) = [V_A t/T - V_A RC/T + (V_0 + V_A RC/T)e^{-t/RC}]u(t) \quad \text{V}$

(b) $v_C(t) = \left[\frac{V_A}{\sqrt{1 + (\beta RC)^2}}\cos(\beta t + \theta) + \left(\frac{\beta RC V_A}{1 + (\beta RC)^2} + V_0\right)e^{-t/RC}\right]u(t) \quad \text{V}$

where

$$\theta = -\pi/2 - \tan^{-1}(\beta RC)$$

9–7 TRANSLATION AND SCALING PROPERTIES

The four basic properties of the Laplace transformation are uniqueness, linearity, time integration, and time differentiation. These essential features are sufficient to cover most applications of Laplace transforms in circuit analysis and design. In the next three sections we introduce additional properties of the Laplace transformation that give further insight into the relationship between the time and frequency domains. We begin with properties that relate the origin and scale factors of the time and s-domains.

TIME-DOMAIN TRANSLATION PROPERTY

The ***t*-domain translation property** of the Laplace transformation is

$$\text{IF } \mathcal{L}\{f(t)\} = F(s) \text{ THEN for } a > 0 \ \mathcal{L}\{f(t-a)u(t-a)\} = e^{-as}F(s) \tag{9-39}$$

The theorem states that multiplying $F(s)$ by e^{-as} is equivalent to shifting $f(t)$ to the right in the t-domain—that is, delaying $f(t)$ in time by an amount $a > 0$. Proof of this property follows from the definition of the Laplace transformation.

$$\mathcal{L}\{f(t-a)u(t-a)\} = \int_{0-}^{\infty} f(t-a)u(t-a)e^{-st}\,dt = \int_{a}^{\infty} f(t-a)e^{-st}\,dt \tag{9-40}$$

In this equation we have used the fact that $u(t - a)$ is zero for $t < a$ and is unity for $t \geq a$. We now change the integration variable from t to $\tau = t - a$. With this change of variable the last integral in Eq. (9–40) takes the form

$$\begin{aligned}\mathcal{L}\{f(t-a)u(t-a)\} &= \int_{0}^{\infty} f(\tau)e^{-st}e^{-as}\,d\tau \\ &= e^{-as}\int_{0}^{\infty} f(\tau)e^{-st}\,d\tau \\ &= e^{-as}F(s)\end{aligned}$$

The last line in this result confirms the statement in Eq. (9–39).

The rectangular pulse waveform in Figure 9–9 provides an application of the time translation property. Our previous study of waveform synthesis showed that the rectangular pulse can be generated as the difference of a step function and a delayed step function:

$$f(t) = Au(t) - Au(t-a)$$

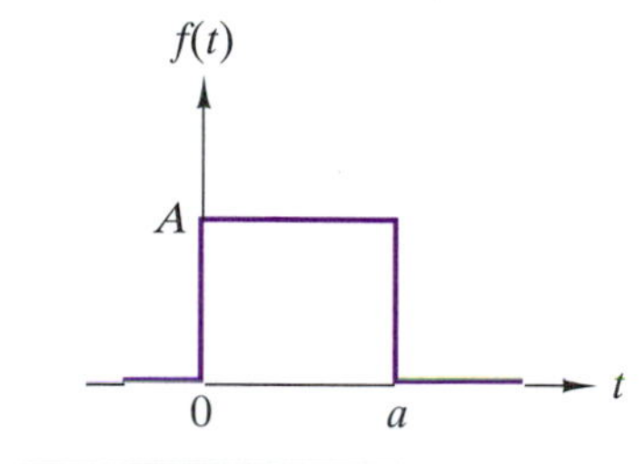

FIGURE 9–9 *Rectangular pulse waveform.*

The t-domain translation property yields the transform of a rectangular pulse:

$$\begin{aligned}F(s) &= A\mathcal{L}\{u(t)\} - A\mathcal{L}\{u(t-a)\} \\ &= A\frac{1}{s} - Ae^{-as}\frac{1}{s} \\ &= \frac{A(1-e^{-as})}{s}\end{aligned}$$

The fact that the pulse transform is not a rational function does not cause any particular problem. Multiplying a rational function $F(s)$ by e^{-as} means that the waveform $g(t) = \mathcal{L}^{-1}\{e^{-as}F(s)\}$ is a delayed version of $f(t) = \mathcal{L}^{-1}\{F(s)\}$.

The next example shows how to find circuit responses using delayed waveforms.

EXAMPLE 9–19

Find $v_C(t)$ in the RC circuit of Figure 9–6 when the input is a rectangular pulse

$$v_S(t) = V_A u(t) - V_A u(t-a) \quad \text{V}$$

SOLUTION:

The input is a rectangular pulse that begins at $t = 0$ and ends at $t = a$. Using the t-domain translation property, the transform of the input is

$$V_S(s) = \frac{V_A(1 - e^{-as})}{s} \quad \text{V-s}$$

Using the rectangular pulse input, the circuit response transform in Eq. (9–37) becomes

$$V_C(s) = V_A\left[\frac{1/RC}{s(s + 1/RC)}\right] - V_A e^{-as}\left[\frac{1/RC}{s(s + 1/RC)}\right] + \frac{V_0}{s + 1/RC} \quad \text{V-s}$$

The rational functions inside the brackets can be expanded by partial fractions.

$$V_C(s) = V_A\left[\frac{1}{s} - \frac{1}{s + 1/RC}\right] - V_A e^{-as}\left[\frac{1}{s} - \frac{1}{s + 1/RC}\right] + \frac{V_0}{s + 1/RC} \quad \text{V-s}$$

The two rational functions have the same expansion whose inverse transform is

$$f(t) = [1 - e^{-t/RC}]u(t) \quad \text{V}$$

The factor e^{-as} multiplying the second expansion means that the corresponding waveform is delayed by a factor $t = a$. Using the t-domain translation property, the response waveform for a rectangular pulse input is

$$v_C(t) = V_A[1 - e^{-t/RC}]u(t) + V_A[1 - e^{-(t-a)/RC}]u(t-a) + V_0 e^{-t/RC}u(t) \quad \text{V}$$

The first factor is caused by the step function at $t = 0$ and the second by the step at $t = a$. The last term is the effect of the initial capacitor voltage at $t = 0$. Two plots of this response are shown in Figure 9–10 for $V_0 = 0$. For the short pulse, $a = RC$ and the negative step function at $t = a$ occurs before the circuit has fully responded to the positive step function at $t = 0$. For the long pulse, $a = 8RC$ and the step function at $t = a$ occurs after the circuit has reached a steady-state condition due to the step at $t = 0$. ■

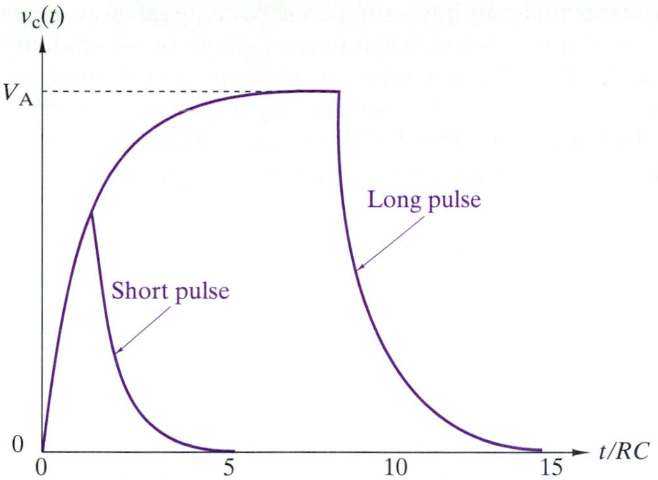

FIGURE 9–10

Exercise 9–18

Find the Laplace transforms of the waveforms in Figure 9–11.

Answers:

$$\text{(a) } F(s) = A\frac{(1 - e^{-\frac{sT}{2}})^2}{s}$$

$$\text{(b) } F(s) = A\frac{(Ts - 1 + e^{-sT})}{Ts^2}$$

Exercise 9–19

Find the waveform corresponding to the following Laplace transforms:

$$\text{(a) } F(s) = e^{-2s}\frac{2(s+2)}{s^2 + 4s + 3}$$

$$\text{(b) } F(s) = \frac{4\pi}{T}\frac{(1 - e^{-Ts})}{s^2 + (2\pi/T)^2}$$

Answers:

$$\text{(a) } f(t) = [e^{-(t-2)} + e^{-3(t-2)}]u(t-2)$$

$$\text{(b) } f(t) = 2\left[\sin\left(\frac{2\pi t}{T}\right)\right]u(t) - 2\left[\sin\left(\frac{2\pi(t-T)}{T}\right)\right]u(t-T)$$

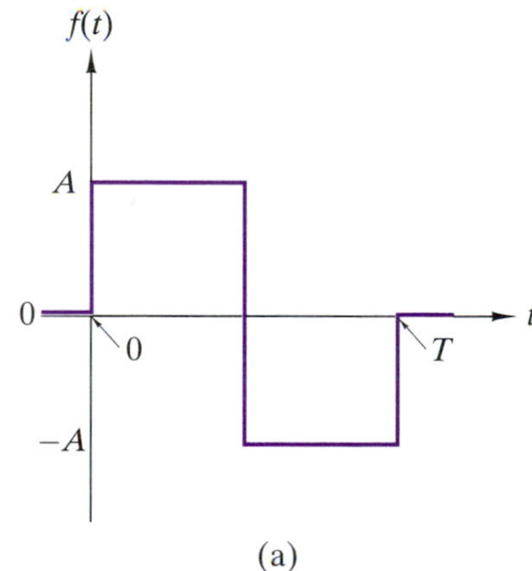

(a)

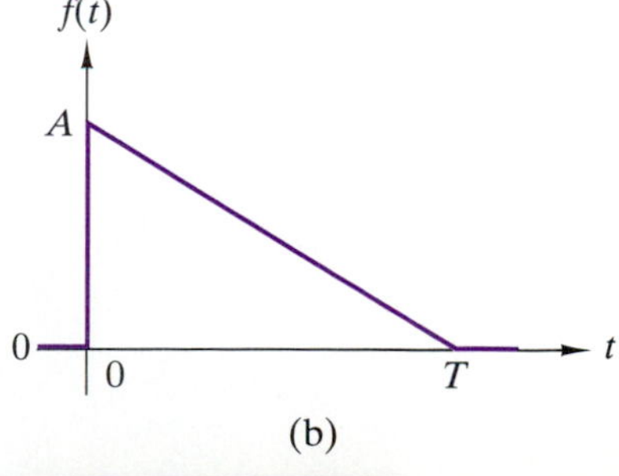

(b)

FIGURE 9–11

FREQUENCY-DOMAIN TRANSLATION PROPERTY

The ***s*-domain translation property** of the Laplace transformation is

$$\text{IF } \mathscr{L}\{f(t)\} = F(s) \text{ THEN } \mathscr{L}\{e^{-\alpha t}f(t)\} = F(s+\alpha) \quad (9\text{–}41)$$

This theorem states that multiplying $f(t)$ by $e^{-\alpha t}$ is equivalent to replacing s by $s + \alpha$ (that is, translating the origin in the s-plane by an amount α). In engineering applications the parameter α. is always a real number, but it can be either positive or negative so the origin in the s-domain can be translated to the left or right. Proof of the theorem follows almost immediately from the definition of the Laplace transformation:

$$\begin{aligned}\mathcal{L}\{e^{-\alpha t}f(t)\} &= \int_0^\infty e^{-\alpha t}f(t)e^{-st}\,dt \\ &= \int_0^\infty f(t)e^{-(s+\alpha)t}\,dt \\ &= F(s+\alpha)\end{aligned}$$

The s-domain translation property can be used to derive transforms of damped waveforms from undamped prototypes. For instance, the Laplace transform of the ramp, cosine, and sine functions are

$$\begin{aligned}\mathcal{L}\{tu(t)\} &= \frac{1}{s^2} \\ \mathcal{L}\{[\cos \beta t]u(t)\} &= \frac{s}{s^2+\beta^2} \\ \mathcal{L}\{[\sin \beta t]u(t)\} &= \frac{\beta}{s^2+\beta^2}\end{aligned}$$

To obtain the damped ramp, damped cosine, and damped sine functions, we multiply each waveform by $e^{-\alpha t}$. Using the s-domain translation property, we replace s by $s + \alpha$ to obtain transforms of the damped waveforms.

$$\begin{aligned}\mathcal{L}\{te^{-\alpha t}u(t)\} &= \frac{1}{(s+\alpha)^2} \\ \mathcal{L}\{[e^{-\alpha t}\cos \beta t]u(t)] &= \frac{s+\alpha}{(s+\alpha)^2+\beta^2} \\ \mathcal{L}\{[e^{-\alpha t}\sin \beta t]u(t)] &= \frac{\beta}{(s+\alpha)^2+\beta^2}\end{aligned}$$

This completes the derivation of all the transform pairs in Table 9–2.

The s-domain translation property highlights the relationship between waveform damping and the location of poles in the s domain. Figure 9–12 shows several damped cosine waveforms and the corresponding pole-zero diagram for several values of α. For $\alpha = 0$ the poles lie on the j-axis and the waveform is a sustained oscillation that neither decays nor grows. For $\alpha > 0$ the poles shift horizontally into the left half plane and the waveform decays exponentially to zero. For $\alpha < 0$ the poles shift horizontally into the right half plane and the waveform grows exponentially without bound (blows up).

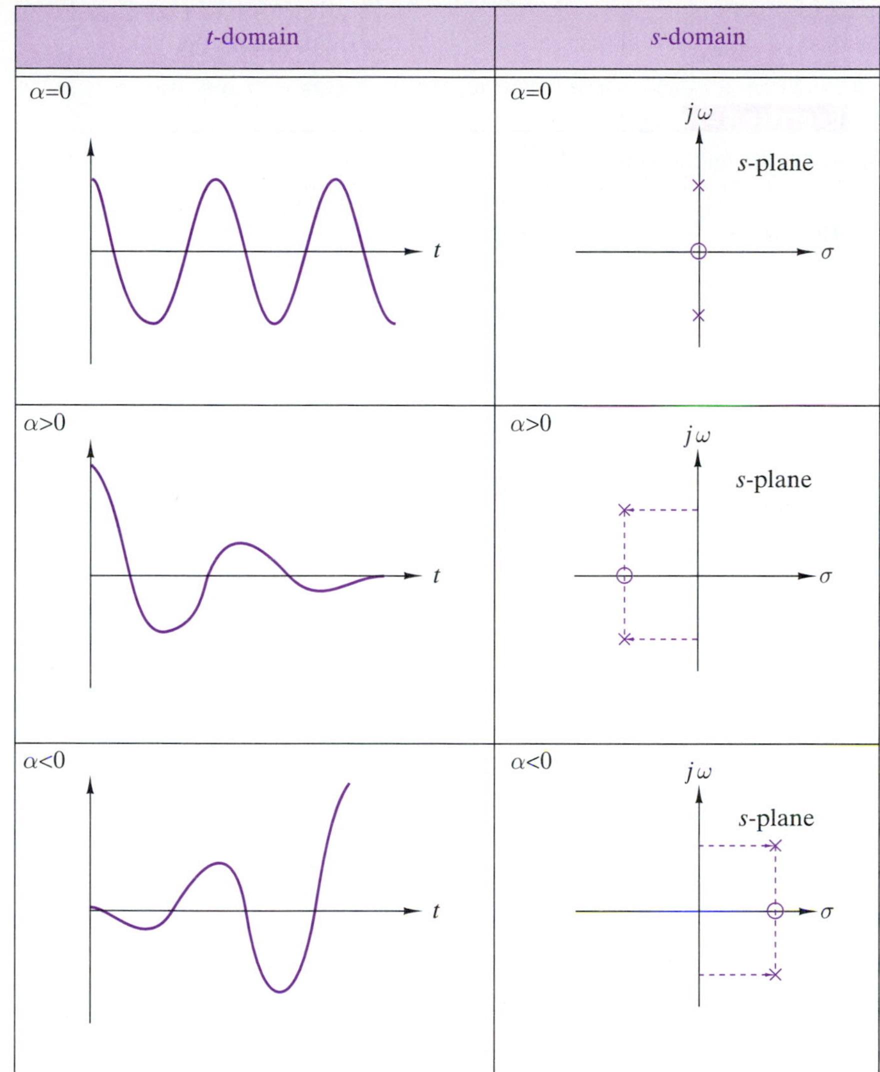

FIGURE 9–12 *Effect of* s*-domain translation on time-domain waveforms.*

Replacing s by $s + \alpha$ shifts the critical frequencies of $F(s)$ to the left in the s plane if $\alpha > 0$, and to the right if $\alpha < 0$. Shifting poles to the left in the s plane increases waveform damping in the time domain, while shifting to the right decreases the damping. Whether s-domain translation causes the waveforms to decay or blow up depends on whether the poles end up in the left half plane or right half plane.

The j-axis is an important boundary in the s plane since it divides signals into two distinct classes. Signals with all of their poles in the left half plane have waveforms that decay to zero as $t \to \infty$. Those with one or more poles in the right half plane do not decay and become unbounded as $t \to \infty$. Half-plane location is revealed by the sign of the real part of the pole. If the real part of a pole is negative, then it is located in the left half plane; and conversely, a positive real part means it is in the right half plane.

Exercise 9–20

Consider the following transforms:

(a) $F(s) = \dfrac{s-1}{s^2+4s+3}$ (b) $F(s) = \dfrac{-2(s+7)}{s^2-2s+10}$

(c) $F(s) = \dfrac{s}{s^2+4}$ (d) $F(s) = \dfrac{s}{s^2-4}$ (e) $F(s) = \dfrac{s+2}{s^2+4s+4}$

(1) Classify them according to the half-plane location of their poles.
(2) Classify them as to whether the corresponding waveforms are bounded or unbounded.

Answers:

(1) The transforms in (a) and (e) have all their poles in the left half of the s-plane. The transform in (d) has one pole in the right half plane and one in the left half. The transform in (b) has both poles in the right half plane. The transform is (c) has poles on the j-axis.
(2) Waveforms corresponding to (a), (c), and (e) are bounded. Waveforms corresponding to (b) and (d) are unbounded.

SCALING

The **scaling property** is

$$\text{IF } \mathscr{L}\{f(t)\} = F(s) \text{ THEN for } a > 0 \ \mathscr{L}\{f(at)\} = \frac{1}{a}F\left(\frac{s}{a}\right) \tag{9-42}$$

The scaling property states that if t is replaced by at, then s is replaced by s/a and $F(s)$ is divided by a. Proof follows directly from the integral definition of the Laplace transformation.

$$\begin{aligned}\mathscr{L}\{f(at)\} &= \int_0^{\infty} f(at)e^{-st}\,dt \\ &= \frac{1}{a}\int_0^{\infty} f(\tau)e^{-\tau s/a}\,d\tau \\ &= \frac{1}{a}F\left(\frac{s}{a}\right)\end{aligned}$$

The second integral in this equation is obtained by changing the integration variable from t to $\tau = at$.

The scaling property is important in situations where a unity parameter prototype is adjusted to cover a large number of applications—for example, the transform of a cosine waveform with unity frequency is $\mathscr{L}\{\cos t\} = s/(s^2+1)$. The scaling property allows us to adjust this prototype to produce the transform at any frequency β as

$$\mathscr{L}\{\cos \beta t\} = \frac{1}{\beta} \frac{s/\beta}{(s/\beta)^2 + 1} = \frac{s}{s^2 + \beta^2}$$

The scaling property highlights the reciprocal spreading relationship between the t-domain and s-domain. If the time scale is compressed ($a < 1$), then scale of the s plane expands, and vice versa. Figure 9–13 shows damped cosine waveforms and pole-zero maps for different scale factors. As the figure shows, increasing a compresses the waveform in the t domain and expands the critical frequencies radially outward in the s domain. The reciprocal spreading concept is important to understanding the relationship of s-plane geometry to t-domain waveforms.

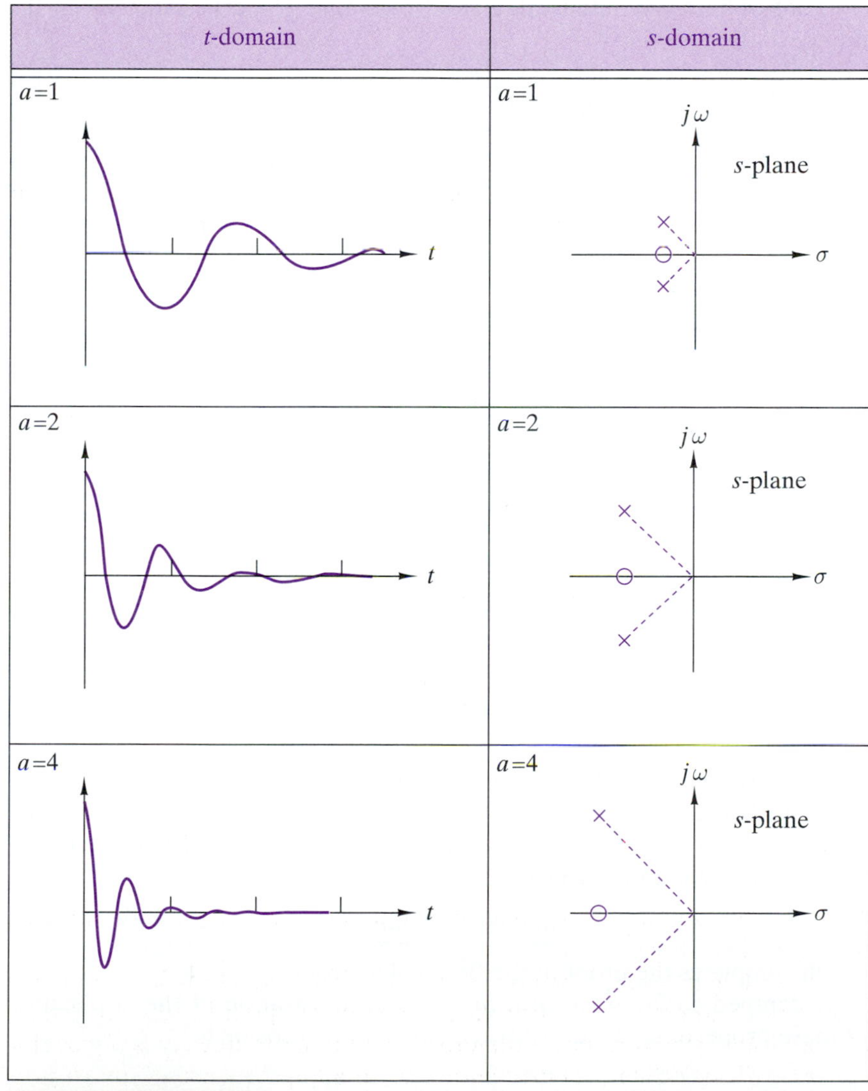

FIGURE 9–13 *Effect of* s*-domain scaling on time-domain waveforms.*

9–8 INITIAL VALUE AND FINAL VALUE PROPERTIES

The **initial value** and **final value properties** can be stated as follows:

$$\text{Initial value: } \lim_{t\to 0+} f(t) = \lim_{s\to\infty} sF(s) \qquad (9-43)$$
$$\text{Final value: } \lim_{t\to\infty} f(t) = \lim_{s\to 0} sF(s)$$

These properties display the relationship between the origin and infinity in the time and frequency domains. The value of $f(t)$ at $t = 0+$ in the time domain (initial value) is the same as the value of $sF(s)$ at infinity in the s-plane. Conversely, the value of $f(t)$ as $t \to \infty$ (final value) is the same as the value of $sF(s)$ at the origin in the s-plane.

Proof of both the initial value and final value properties starts with the differentiation property:

$$sF(s) - f(0-) = \int_{0-}^{\infty} \frac{df}{dt} e^{-st}\, dt \qquad (9-44)$$

To establish the initial value property, we rewrite the integral on the right side of this equation and take the limit of both sides as $s \to \infty$.

$$\lim_{s\to\infty} [sF(s) - f(0-)] = \lim_{s\to\infty} \int_{0-}^{0+} \frac{df}{dt} e^{-st} dt + \lim_{s\to\infty} \int_{0+}^{\infty} \frac{df}{dt} e^{-st}\, dt \qquad (9-45)$$

The first integral on the right side reduces to $f(0+) - f(0-)$ since e^{-st} is unity on the interval from $t = 0-$ to $t = 0+$. The second integral vanishes because e^{-st} goes to zero as $s \to \infty$. In addition, on the left side of Eq. (9–45) the $f(0-)$ is independent of s and can be taken outside the limiting process. Inserting all of these considerations reduces Eq. (9–45) to

$$\lim_{s\to\infty} sF(s) = \lim_{t\to 0+} f(t) \qquad (9-45)$$

which completes the proof of the initial-value property.

Proof of the final value theorem begins by taking the limit of both sides of Eq. (9–44) as $s \to 0$:

$$\lim_{s\to 0} [sF(s) - f(0-)] = \lim_{s\to 0} \int_{0-}^{\infty} \frac{dt}{dt} e^{-st}\, dt \qquad (9-47)$$

The integral on the right side of this equation reduces to $f(\infty) - f(0-)$ because e^{-st} becomes unity as $s \to 0$. Again, the $f(0-)$ on the left side is independent of s and can be taken outside of the limiting process. Inserting all of these considerations reduces Eq. (9–47) to

$$\lim_{s\to 0} sF(s) = \lim_{t\to\infty} f(t) \qquad (9-48)$$

which completes the proof of the final value property.

A damped cosine waveform provides an illustration of the application of these properties. The transform of the damped cosine is

$$\mathcal{L}\{[Ae^{-\alpha t} \cos \beta t]u(t)\} = \frac{A(s + \alpha)}{(s + \alpha)^2 + \beta^2}$$

Applying the initial and final value limits, we obtain

$$\text{Initial value: } \lim_{t\to 0} f(t) = \lim_{t\to 0} Ae^{-\alpha t}\cos\beta t = A$$

$$\lim_{s\to\infty} sF(s) = \lim_{s\to\infty} \frac{sA\,(s+\alpha)}{(s+\alpha)^2+\beta^2} = A$$

$$\text{Final value: } \lim_{t\to\infty} f(t) = \lim_{t\to\infty} Ae^{-\alpha t}\cos\beta t = 0$$

$$\lim_{s\to 0} sF(s) = \lim_{s\to 0} \frac{sA\,(s+\alpha)}{(s+\alpha)^2+\beta^2} = 0$$

Note the agreement between the t-domain and s-domain limits in both cases.

There are restrictions on the initial and final value properties. The initial value property is valid when $F(s)$ is a proper rational function or, equivalently, when $f(t)$ does not have an impulse at $t = 0$. The final value property is valid when the poles of $sF(s)$ are in the left half plane or, equivalently, when $f(t)$ is a waveform that approaches a final value at $t \to \infty$. Note that the final value restriction allows $F(s)$ to have a simple pole at the origin since the limitation is on the poles of $sF(s)$.

Caution: The initial and final value properties will appear to work when the aforementioned restrictions are not met. In other words, these properties do not tell you they are giving nonsense answers when you violate their limitations. You must always check the restrictions on $F(s)$ before applying either of these properties.

For example, applying the final value property to a cosine waveform yields

$$\lim_{t\to\infty} \cos\beta t = \lim_{s\to 0} s\left[\frac{s}{s^2+\beta^2}\right] = 0$$

The final value property appears to say that $\cos\beta t$ approaches zero as $t \to \infty$. This conclusion is incorrect since the waveform oscillates between ± 1. The problem is that the final value property does not apply to cosine waveform because $sF(s)$ has poles on the j-axis at $s = \pm j\beta$.

EXAMPLE 9–20

Find initial and final values of $v_C(t)$ in the RC circuit of Figure 9–6 when the input is a step function $v_S(t) = V_A\,u(t)$.

SOLUTION:

The input transform is V_A/s and the circuit response transform in Eq. (9–37) becomes

$$V_C(s) = \frac{V_A/RC}{s(s+1/RC)} + \frac{V_0}{s+1/RC} \quad \text{V}$$

The initial value property applies because $V_C(s)$ is a proper rational function. The initial value is

$$\lim_{t\to 0} v_C(t) = \lim_{s\to\infty} sV_C(s)$$

$$= \lim_{s\to\infty}\left[\frac{V_A/RC}{s+1/RC}\right] + \lim_{s\to\infty}\left[\frac{sV_0}{s+1/RC}\right]$$

$$= 0 + V_0 = v_C(0) \quad \text{V}$$

which is true by definition. The final value property applies since the pole of $sF(s)$ is located at $s = -1/RC$, which is in the left half plane. The final value is

$$\lim_{t\to\infty} v_C(t) = \lim_{s\to 0} sV_C(s)$$

$$= \lim_{s\to 0}\left[\frac{V_A/RC}{s+1/RC}\right] + \lim_{s\to 0}\left[\frac{sV_0}{s+1/RC}\right]$$

$$= V_A \quad \text{V}$$

A step function of amplitude V_A drives the circuit response from an initial value $v_C(0)$ to a final value V_A. ■

Exercise 9–21

Find the initial value at $t = 0+$ and final value of the waveforms corresponding to the transforms in Exercise 9–20.

Answers:

(a) Initial value = 1, final value = 0
(b) Initial value = –2, final value does not exist
(c) Initial value = 1, final value does not exist
(d) Initial value = 1, final value does not exist
(e) Initial value = 1, final value = 0

Exercise 9–22

Find the initial and final values of the waveforms corresponding to the following transforms:

$$\text{(a) } F(s) = 100\frac{s+3}{s(s+5)(s+20)}$$

$$\text{(b) } F(s) = e^{-10s}\frac{s(s+2)}{(s+1)(s+4)}$$

Answers:

(a) Initial value = 0, final value = 3
(b) Initial value = final value = 0

Table 9–3 summarizes the additional Laplace transform properties we have developed beyond the basic properties given in Table 9–1.

TABLE 9–3 ADDITIONAL LAPLACE TRANSFORM PROPERTIES AND PAIRS

FEATURE	TIME DOMAIN	FREQUENCY DOMAIN
Simple complex poles	$[2\|k\|e^{-\alpha t}\cos(\beta t + \angle k)]u(t)$	$\dfrac{k}{s+\alpha-j\beta} + \dfrac{k^*}{s+\alpha+j\beta}$
Double complex poles	$[2\|k\|te^{-\alpha t}\cos(\beta t + \angle k)]u(t)$	$\dfrac{k}{(s+\alpha-j\beta)^2} + \dfrac{k^*}{(s+\alpha+j\beta)^2}$
Time-domain translation	$[f(t-a)]u(t-a)$	$e^{-as}F(s)$
s-Domain translation	$e^{-\alpha t}f(t)$	$F(s+\alpha)$
Scaling	$f(at)$	$\dfrac{1}{a}F\left(\dfrac{s}{a}\right)$
Initial value	$\lim_{t\to 0+} f(t)$	$\lim_{s\to\infty} sF(s)$
Final value	$\lim_{t\to\infty} f(t)$	$\lim_{s\to 0} sF(s)$

SUMMARY

- The Laplace transformation converts waveforms in the time domain to transforms in the s-domain. The inverse transformation converts transforms into causal waveforms. A transform pair is unique if and only if $f(t)$ is casual.
- The Laplace transforms of basic signals like the step function, exponential, and sinusoid are easily derived from the integral definition. Other transform pairs can be derived using basic signal transforms and the uniqueness, linearity, time integration, and time differentiation properties of the Laplace transformation.
- Proper rational functions with simple poles can be expanded by partial fraction to obtain inverse Laplace transforms. Simple real poles lead to exponential waveforms and simple complex poles to damped sinusoids. Partial-fraction expansions of improper rational functions and functions with multiple poles require special treatment.
- Using Laplace transforms to find the response of a linear circuit involves transforming the circuit differential equation into the s domain, algebraically solving for the response transform, and performing the inverse transformation to obtain the response waveform.
- The translation and scaling properties display the reciprocal relationships between t-domain waveforms and s-domain transforms.
- The initial and final value properties determine the initial and final values of a waveform $f(t)$ from the value of $sF(s)$ at $s \to \infty$ and $s = 0$, respectively. The initial value property applies if $F(s)$ is a proper rational func-

tion. The final value property applies if all of the poles of $sF(s)$ are in the left half plane.

EN ROUTE OBJECTIVES AND ASSOCIATED PROBLEMS

ERO 9–1 LAPLACE TRANSFORM (SECTS. 9–1, 9–2, 9–3)

Given a signal waveform, use the integral definition of the Laplace transformation or its basic properties and pairs to find the Laplace transform. Construct pole-zero diagrams.

9–1 Find the Laplace transforms of the following functions and plot their pole-zero diagrams for $\alpha > 0$.

$$\text{(a) } f(t) = A[2e^{-\alpha t} - 1]u(t) \quad \text{(b) } f(t) = A[(1 - 2\alpha t)e^{-\alpha t}]u(t)$$

9–2 Find the Laplace transform of $f(t) = A[\alpha e^{-\alpha t} - \gamma e^{-\gamma t}]u(t)$ and plot its pole-zero diagram for $\alpha > \gamma > 0$.

9–3 Find the Laplace transform of $f(t) = A[2 \sin(\beta t) - 1]u(t)$ for $\beta > 0$. Show that $F(s)$ has poles at $s = 0$ and $s = \pm j\beta$, and a double zero at $s = \beta$.

9–4 Find the Laplace transform of $f(t) = A[e^{-\beta t} - \sin \beta t]u(t)$ for $\beta > 0$. Show that $F(s)$ has poles at $s = -\beta$ and $s = \pm j\beta$, and zeros at $s = 0$ and $s = \beta$.

9–5 Find the Laplace transform of $f(t) = A\delta(t) - A\beta e^{-\alpha t} \sin(\beta t)u(t)$ for $\alpha > 0$ and $\beta > 0$. Show that $F(s)$ has poles $s = -\alpha \pm j\beta$ and a double zero at $s = -\alpha$.

9–6 Use the integral definition of the Laplace transformation to find the transform of a rectangular pulse $p(t) = Au(t) - Au(t - T)$.

9–7 Find the Laplace transforms of the following functions and plot their pole-zero diagrams.

$$\text{(a) } f(t) = [5e^{-10t} - 10e^{-20t}]u(t) \quad \text{(b) } f(t) = 15\,[\cos(100t) - \cos(200t)]u(t)$$

9–8 Find the Laplace transforms of the following functions and plot their pole-zero diagrams:

$$\text{(a) } f(t) = \delta(t) + [5e^{-50t} - 5e^{-20t}]u(t) \quad \text{(b) } f(t) = [25 - 25\cos(500t)]u(t)$$

9–9 Find the Laplace transforms of the following function and plot its pole-zero diagram:

$$f(t) = \delta(t) + [5e^{-50t} - 250te^{-50t}]u(t)$$

9–10 Find the Laplace transforms of the following function and plot its pole-zero diagrams:

$$f(t) = \delta(t) + [5e^{-50t} - 250t + 10\cos(200t)]u(t)$$

9–11 The Laplace transform of $f(t) = A[\alpha te^{-\alpha t}]u(t)$ is $F(s) = A\alpha/(s + \text{a})^2$.

(a) Use the differentiation property of Laplace transforms to obtain the transform $G(s) = \mathscr{L}\{df(t)/dt\}$.

(b) Check your result by first differentiating $f(t)$ and then transforming the resulting waveform $g(t)$.

(c) Are there any poles or zeros in $G(s)$ that are not in $F(s)$? Explain.

9–12 The Laplace transform of $f(t) = 5[e^{-t} \sin 4t]u(t)$ is $F(s) = 20/(s^2 + 2s + 17)$.

(a) Use the differentiation property of Laplace transforms to obtain the transform $G(s) = \mathcal{L}\{df(t)/dt\}$.

(b) Check your result by first differentiating $f(t)$ and then transforming the resulting waveform $g(t)$.

(c) Are there any poles or zeros in $G(s)$ that are not in $F(s)$? Explain.

9–13 The Laplace transform of $f(t) = A[\sin \beta t]u(t)$ is $F(s) = A\beta/(s^2 + \beta^2)$.

(a) Use the integration property of Laplace transforms to obtain the transform $G(s) = \mathcal{L}\{\int_0^t f(x)dx\}$.

(b) Check your result by first integrating $f(t)$ and then transforming the resulting waveform $g(t)$.

(c) Are there any poles or zeros in $G(s)$ that are not in $F(s)$? Explain.

9–14 Find the Laplace transform of

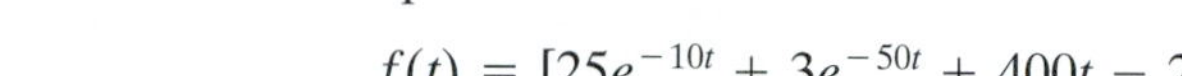

$$f(t) = [25e^{-10t} + 3e^{-50t} + 400t - 2]u(t)$$

Locate the poles and zeros of $F(s)$.

9–15 Find the Laplace transform of

$$f(t) = [-e^{-10t} + 10 - 2\sin(5t) - 9\cos(5t)]u(t)$$

Locate the poles and zeros of $F(s)$.

ERO 9–2 INVERSE TRANSFORMS (SECTS. 9–4, 9–5)

Given a rational signal transform, plot its pole-zero map, find the inverse transform, and sketch its waveform.

9–16 Find the inverse Laplace transforms of the following functions and sketch their waveforms for $\beta > \alpha > 0$:

$$\text{(a) } F_1(s) = \frac{s}{(s+\alpha)(s+\beta)} \qquad \text{(b) } F_2(s) = \frac{s+\alpha}{s(s+\beta)}$$

9–17 Find the inverse transforms of the following functions and sketch their waveforms for $\alpha > 0$. Comment on the effect of adding zeros at the origin.

$$\text{(a) } F_1(s) = \frac{1}{(s+\alpha)^2} \qquad \text{(b) } F_2(s) = sF_1(s) \qquad \text{(c) } F_3(s) = s^2F_1(s)$$

9–18 Find the inverse transforms of the following functions and sketch their waveforms for $\alpha > 0$. Comment on the effect of adding poles at the origin.

$$\text{(a) } F_1(s) = \frac{1}{s+\alpha} \qquad \text{(b) } F_2(s) = \frac{F_1(s)}{s} \qquad \text{(c) } F_3(s) = \frac{F_1(s)}{s^2}$$

9–19 Find the inverse Laplace transforms of the following functions and sketch their waveforms for $\alpha > 0$. Comment on the effect of adding zeros at $s = -\alpha$.

$$\text{(a) } F_1(s) = \frac{1}{(s+\alpha)^2} \qquad \text{(b) } F_2(s) = (s+\alpha)F_1(s) \qquad \text{(c) } F_3(s) = (s+\alpha)^2F_1(s)$$

9–20 Find the inverse Laplace transforms of the following functions and sketch their waveforms for $\alpha > 0$. Comment on the effect of adding poles at $s = -\alpha$.

$$\text{(a) } F_1(s) = 1 \quad \text{(b) } F_2(s) = \frac{F_1(s)}{s + \alpha} \quad \text{(c) } F_3(s) = \frac{F_1(s)}{(s + \alpha)^2}$$

9–21 Plot the pole-zero diagrams of the following transforms, find the corresponding inverse transforms, and sketch their waveforms.

$$\text{(a) } F_1(s) = \frac{900}{s^2 + 65s + 900}$$

$$\text{(b) } F_2(s) = \frac{900}{s^2 + 60s + 900}$$

$$\text{(c) } F_3(s) = \frac{900}{s^2 + 36s + 900}$$

9–22 Verify that the following partial-fraction expansions are correct. Find the unknown residue(s) and find $f(t)$.

$$\text{(a) } F(s) = \frac{6s^2 + 24s + 18}{(s + 2)(s + 4)(s + 5)} = \frac{-1}{s + 2} + \frac{K}{s + 4} + \frac{16}{s + 5}$$

$$\text{(b) } F(s) = \frac{s^2 + 5s + 6}{(s + 2)(s + 4)(s + 5)} = \frac{K}{s + 2} + \frac{-1}{s + 4} + \frac{2}{s + 5}$$

$$\text{(c) } F(s) = \frac{8s + 16}{s(s^2 + 4s + 8)} = \frac{2}{s} + \frac{K}{s + 2 - j2} + \frac{-1 + j}{s + 2 + j2}$$

$$\text{(d) } F(s) = \frac{4}{(s + 1)^2(s^2 + 1)} = \frac{A}{s + 1} + \frac{2}{(s + 1)^2} + \frac{-1}{s - j} + \frac{B}{s + j}$$

$$\text{(e) } F(s) = \frac{8(s^2 + 1)}{s(s^2 + 4)} = \frac{2}{s} + \frac{A}{s - j2} + \frac{B}{s + j2}$$

9–23 Find the inverse transforms for the following transforms:

$$\text{(a) } F_1(s) = \frac{(s + 4)(s + 8)}{s(s + 2)(s + 6)} \quad \text{(b) } F_2(s) = \frac{(s^2 + 20)(s^2 + 60)}{s(s^2 + 45)(s^2 + 80)}$$

9–24 Find $f(t)$ for each of the following transforms:

$$\text{(a) } F(s) = \frac{(s + 2)}{s(s^2 + 2s + 1)(s + 3)} \quad \text{(b) } F(s) = \frac{(s + 2)}{s^3 + 2s^2 + 2s + 1}$$

9–25 Find $f(t)$ for each of the following transforms:

$$\text{(a) } F(s) = \frac{(s + 3)(s + 12)}{s^2(s^2 + 6s + 36)} \quad \text{(b) } F(s) = \frac{10(s + 13)(s + 18)}{s(s^2 + 20s + 100)}$$

9–26 Find $f(t)$ for each of the following transforms:

$$\text{(a) } F(s) = \frac{(s + 10)(s + 200)}{(s + 20)(s + 100)} \quad \text{(b) } F(s) = \frac{10(s + 2)}{s^3 + 1}$$

9–27 A certain transform has a simple pole at $s = -30$ and a simple zero at $s = -\gamma$. The value of the transform at $s = 0$ is $F(0) = K$. Select values for K and γ so the inverse transform is
(a) $f(t) = \delta(t) - 10e^{-30t}$ (b) $f(t) = \delta(t)$ (c) $f(t) = \delta(t) + 10e^{-30t}$

9–28 A transform has the form

$$F(s) = K\frac{(s^2 + b_1 s + b_0)}{(s^2 + 400)(s + 10)^2}$$

where the parameters K, b_1, and b_0 are real numbers. Select the values for K, b_1, and b_0 so that the inverse transform is
(a) $f(t) = [10te^{-10t}]u(t)$
(b) $f(t) = [10\sin(20t)]u(t)$
(c) $f(t) = [10e^{-10t} + 10\sin(20t) - 10\cos(20t)]u(t)$

9–29 Use Mathcad to find the inverse transform of the following function:

$$F(s) = 5\frac{(s^2 + 7s + 12)(s^2 + 3s + 6)}{(s + 4)(s^3 + 3s^2 + 6s + 4)}$$

9–30 Use Mathcad to find the inverse transform of the following function:

$$F(s) = 10\frac{(s^2 + s + 1)}{(s + 4)(s^3 + 6s^2 + 11s + 6)}$$

ERO 9–3 CIRCUIT RESPONSE USING LAPLACE TRANSFORMS (SECT. 9–6)

Given a first- or second-order circuit,

(a) Determine the circuit differential equation and the initial conditions (if not given).
(b) Transform the differential equation into the s domain and solve for the response transform.
(c) Use the inverse transformation to find the response waveform.
(d) Identify the forced and natural components in the waveform and transform.

9–31 Use the Laplace transformation to find the $y(t)$ that satisfies the following first-order differential equations:

$$\text{(a)}\ \frac{dy}{dt} + 10y = 0, \quad y(0-) = 5$$

$$\text{(b)}\ 10^{-4}\frac{dy}{dt} + y = 10u(t), \quad y(0-) = -10$$

9–32 Use the Laplace transformation to find the $y(t)$ that satisfies the following first-order differential equations:

$$10^{-2}\frac{dy}{dt} + y = 5[\cos(100t)]u(t), \quad y(0-) = 0$$

9–33 The switch in Figure P9–33 has been open for a long time and is closed at $t = 0$.

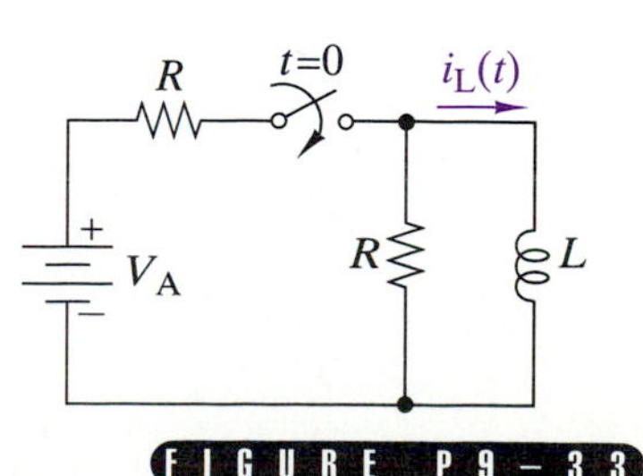

FIGURE P9–33

(a) Find the differential equation and initial condition for the inductor current $i_L(t)$.
(b) Solve for $i_L(t)$ using the Laplace transformation.
(c) Identify the forced and natural components in the response waveform and transform.

9–34 The switch in Figure P9–33 has been closed for a long time and is opened at $t = 0$.
(a) Find the differential equation and initial condition for the inductor current $i_L(t)$.
(b) Solve for $i_L(t)$ using the Laplace transformation.
(c) Identify the forced and natural components in the response waveform and transform.

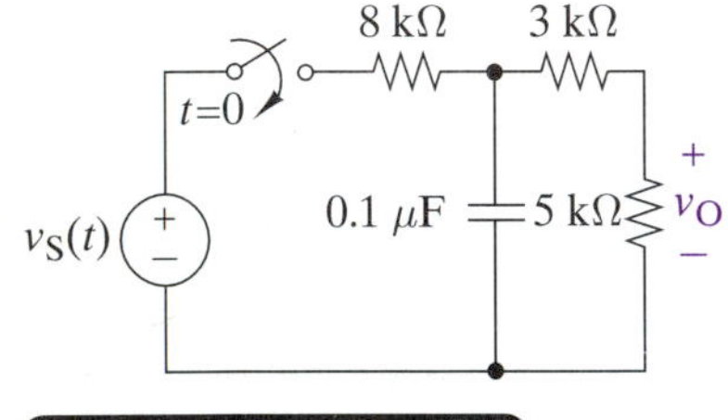

FIGURE P9–35

9–35 The switch in Figure P9–35 has been open for a long time. At $t = 0$ the switch is closed.
(a) Find the differential equation for the circuit and initial condition.
(b) Find $v_O(t)$ using the Laplace transformation for $v_S(t) = 10[e^{-1000t}]u(t)$.
(c) Identify the forced and natural components in the response waveform and transform.

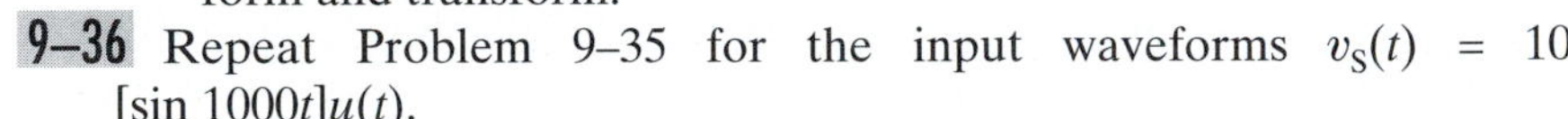
9–36 Repeat Problem 9–35 for the input waveforms $v_S(t) = 10[\sin 1000t]u(t)$.

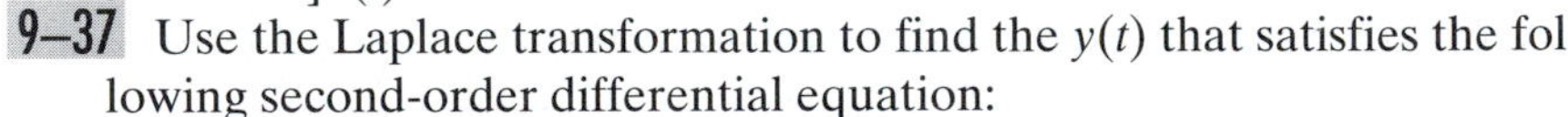
9–37 Use the Laplace transformation to find the $y(t)$ that satisfies the following second-order differential equation:

$$\frac{d^2y}{dt^2} + 21\frac{dy}{dt} + 90y = 0, \quad y(0-) = 0, \quad y'(0-) = 50$$

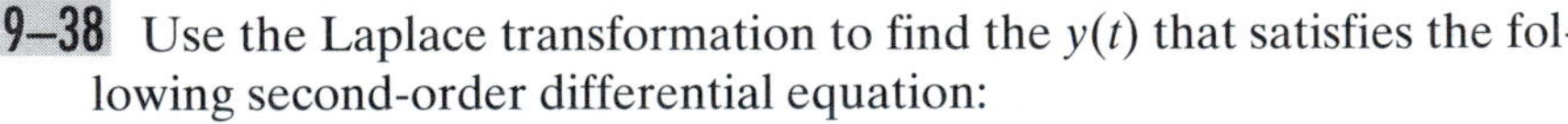
9–38 Use the Laplace transformation to find the $y(t)$ that satisfies the following second-order differential equation:

$$\frac{d^2y}{dt^2} + 11\frac{dy}{dt} + 10y = 100u(t), \quad y(0-) = 0, \quad y'(0-) = 0$$

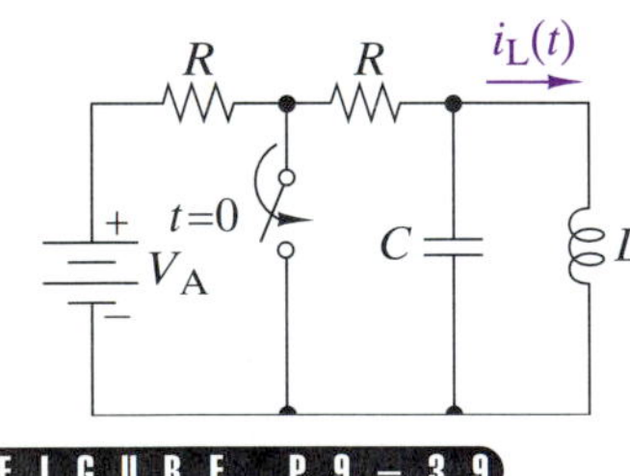

FIGURE P9–39

9–39 The switch in Figure P9–39 has been open for a long time and is closed at $t = 0$. The circuit parameters are $R = 1$ kΩ, $L = 200$ mH, $C = 0.5$ μF, and $V_A = 10$ V.
(a) Find the differential equation for the circuit and the initial conditions.
(b) Use Laplace transforms to solve for the $i_L(t)$ for $t \geq 0$.

9–40 The switch in Figure P9–39 has been closed for a long time and is opened at $t = 0$. The circuit parameters are $R = 5$ kΩ, $L = 10$ mH, $C = 100$ nF, and $V_A = 10$ V.
(a) Find the differential equation for the circuit and the initial conditions.
(b) Use Laplace transforms to solve for the $i_L(t)$ for $t \geq 0$.

ERO 9–4 LAPLACE TRANSFORMATION PROPERTIES (SECTS. 9–7, 9–8, 9–9)

(a) Use the translation properties to relate waveforms and transforms.
(b) Use transforms and the initial and final value properties to find the initial and final value of waveforms.

9–41 **(a)** Write an expression for the waveform $f(t)$ in Figure P9–41 using only step functions and ramps.
(b) Use the time-domain translation property to find the Laplace transform of the waveform found in part (a).
(c) Verify your answer in a using the integral definition of the Laplace transformation.

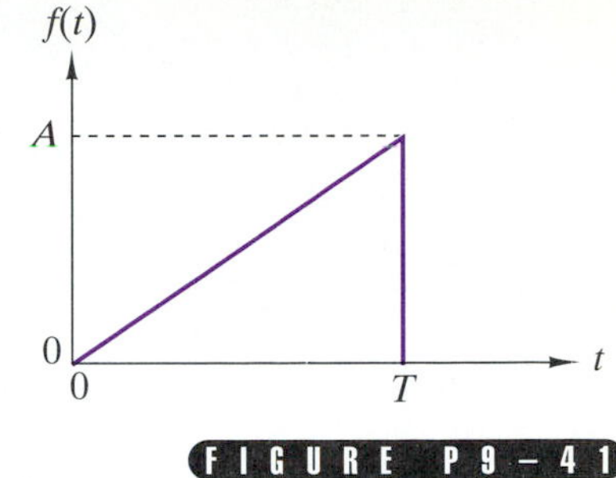

FIGURE P9–41

9–42 **(a)** Write an expression for the waveform $f(t)$ in Figure P9–42 using only step functions and ramps.
(b) Use the time-domain translation property to find the Laplace transform of the waveform found in part (a).
(c) Verify your answer in a using the integral definition of the Laplace transformation.

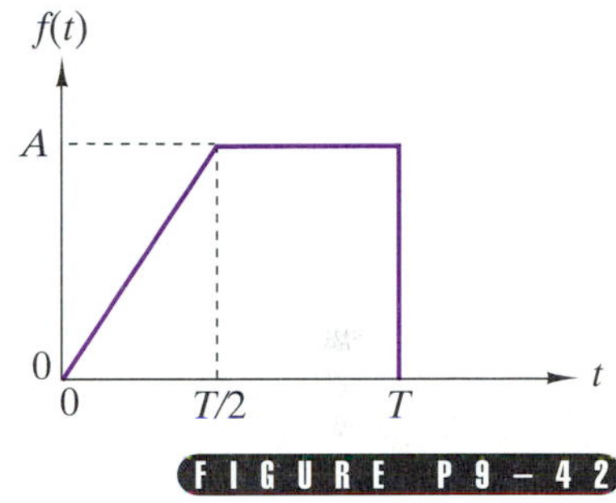

FIGURE P9–42

9–43 There is no initial energy storage in the circuit in Figure P9–43. Use Laplace transforms to find the current $i(t)$ when input is $v_S(t) = V_A\,u(t) - V_A\,u(t - T)$.

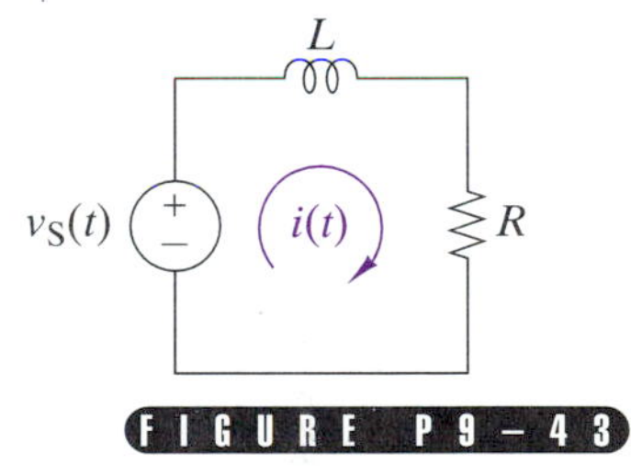

FIGURE P9–43

9–44 Find $f(t)$ for the following transforms:

$$\text{(a) } F_1(s) = e^{-2s}\frac{10(s+2)}{s(s+5)} \qquad \text{(b) } F_2(s) = \frac{1}{s+4} + e^{-5s}\frac{20}{s^2+4s+8}$$

9–45 Given that $\mathscr{L}\{tu(t)\} = 1/s^2$, use the s-domain translation property to derive the Laplace transform of the damped ramp $f(t) = [te^{-\alpha t}]u(t)$.

9–46 Use the initial and final value properties to find the initial and final values of the waveform corresponding to the following transforms. If either property is not applicable, explain why.

$$\text{(a) } F_1(s) = \frac{(s+4)(s+8)}{(s+2)(s+6)} \qquad \text{(b) } F_2(s) = \frac{(s^2+20)(s^2+60)}{s(s^2+45)(s^2+80)}$$

9–47 Use the initial and final value properties to find the initial and final values of the waveform corresponding to the following transforms. If either property is not applicable, explain why.

$$\text{(a) } F_1(s) = \frac{(s+2)}{s(s^2+2s+1)(s+3)} \qquad \text{(b) } F_2(s) = \frac{(s+2)}{s^3+2s^2+2s+1}$$

9–48 Use the initial and final value properties to find the initial and final values of the waveform corresponding to the following transforms. If either property is not applicable, explain why.

$$\text{(a) } F_1(s) = \frac{(s^2+15s+36)}{s^2(s^2+6s+36)} \qquad \text{(b) } F_2(s) = \frac{10(s^2+10s-20)}{s(s^2+20s+100)}$$

9–49 Use the initial and final value properties to find the initial and final values of the waveform corresponding to the transforms in Problem 9–25. If either property is not applicable, explain why.

9–50 Use the initial and final value properties to find the initial and final values of the waveform corresponding to the transforms in Problem 9–26. If either property is not applicable, explain why.

CHAPTER-INTEGRATING PROBLEMS

9–51 A THE DOMINANT POLE APPROXIMATION

When a transform $F(s)$ has widely separated poles, then those closest to the j-axis tend to dominate the response because they have less damping. An approximation to the waveform can be obtained by ignoring the contributions of all except the dominant poles. We can ignore the nondominant poles by simply discarding their terms in the partial fraction expansion of $F(s)$. The purpose of this example is to examine a dominant pole approximation. Consider the transform

$$F(s) = 10^6 \frac{s + 1000}{(s + 5000)[(s + 20)^2 + 50^2]}$$

(a) Construct a partial fraction expansion of $F(s)$ and find $f(t)$.
(b) Construct a pole-zero diagram of $F(s)$ and identify the dominant poles.
(c) Construct a dominant pole approximation $g(t)$ by discarding the nondominant poles in the partial-fraction expansion in (a).
(d) Plot $f(t)$ and $g(t)$ and comment on the accuracy of the approximation.

9–52 A FIRST-ORDER CIRCUIT STEP RESPONSE

In Chapter 7 we found that the step response of a first-order circuit can be written as

$$f(t) = f(\infty) + [f(0) - f(\infty)]e^{-t/T_C}$$

where $f(0)$ is the initial value, $f(\infty)$ is the final value, and T_C is the time constant. Show that the corresponding transform has the form

$$F(s) = K\left[\frac{s + \gamma}{s(s + \alpha)}\right]$$

and relate the time domain parameters $f(0)$, $f(\infty)$, and T_C to the s-domain parameters K, γ, and α.

9–53 A ACTIVE RC CIRCUIT RESPONSE

The purpose of this problem is to use Laplace transforms to analyze the OP AMP circuit in Figure P9–53.

(a) Formulate the circuit differential equation in terms of the output $v_O(t)$.
(b) For $v_O(0-) = 0$ and $v_S(t) = V_A\, u(t)$, transform the differential equation in (a) into the s-domain and solve for the response transform $V_O(s)$. Identify the forced and natural poles in $V_O(s)$. Is the circuit stable or unstable?
(c) Perform the inverse Laplace transformation to obtain $v_O(t)$.
(d) Specify a limit on the amplitude V_A so that neither OP AMP saturates. Assume that the OP AMP saturates at $\pm V_{CC}$.

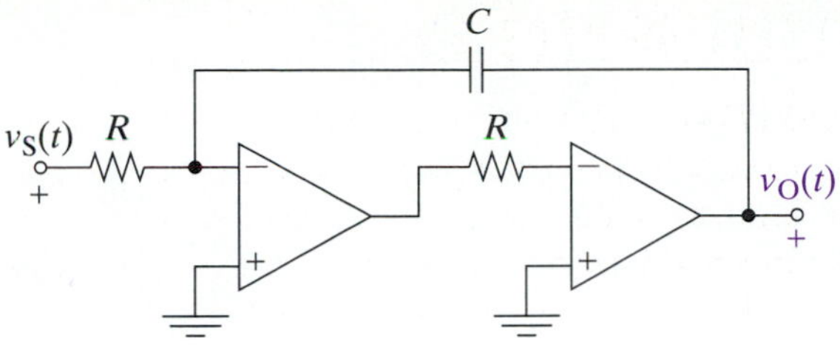

9–54 A LAPLACE TRANSFORMS AND PHASORS

In Chapter 8 we used phasors to solve for the sinusoidal steady-state response of a circuit. In this chapter we used Laplace transforms to solve for both the transient and the steady-state response. The purpose of this problem is to explore the connection between transforms and phasors. When a certain circuit is driven by a sinusoidal input, the Laplace transform of the output is found to be

$$V_0(s) = 10^6 \frac{s + 500}{(s^2 + 200s + 50{,}000)(s^2 + 62{,}500)}$$

Find the phasor representation of the sinusoidal steady-state output.

9–55 A DAMPING RATIO AND POLE LOCATIONS

In Chapter 7 we found that the damping ratio ζ and the undamped natural frequency ω_0 describe the natural frequencies of a second-order circuit. Consider the transform

$$F(s) = K \frac{\omega_0^2}{s^2 + 2\zeta\omega_0 s + \omega_0^2}$$

Plot the locus of the poles $F(s)$ as the damping ratio varies over the range $0 \leq \zeta \leq 2$. Discuss the effect of the damping ratio on the pole locations.

CHAPTER 10

s-DOMAIN CIRCUIT ANALYSIS

The resistance operator Z *is a function of the electrical constants of the circuit components and of* d/dt, *the operator of time-differentiation, which will in the following be denoted by* p *simply.*

Oliver Heaviside, 1887,
British Engineer

The Laplace transform techniques in this chapter have their roots in the works of Oliver Heaviside (1850–1925). The preceding quotation was taken from his book *Electrical Papers* originally published in 1887. His resistance operator Z, which he later called impedance, is a central theme for much of electrical engineering. Heaviside does not often receive the recognition he deserves because his intuitive approach to mathematics was not accepted by most Victorian scientists of his day. Mathematical justification for his methods was eventually supplied by John Bromwich and others. However, no important errors were found in Heaviside's results.

In this chapter we transform circuits directly from the time domain into the s domain without first developing a circuit differential equation. The process begins in the first section, where we find that the transformed circuit obeys Kirchhoff's laws and that the passive element i–v characteristics become linear algebraic equations in transform variables. The algebraic form of the element constraints leads to the concept of s-domain impedance as a generalization of resistance. In the s-domain the underlying element and connection constraints are similar to those for resistance circuits. As a result, s-domain circuit analysis uses techniques like equivalence, superposition, and Thévenin's theorem, which parallel those developed for resistance circuit. Most of this chapter is devoted to extending resistance circuit analysis methods to cover dynamic circuits in the s-domain. The basic analysis tools and circuit theorems are discussed in the second and third sections. The fourth and fifth sections develop general methods of circuit analysis using node voltages and mesh currents.

10–1 TRANSFORMED CIRCUITS

So far we have used the Laplace transformation to change waveforms into transforms and convert circuit differential equations into algebraic equations. These operations provide a useful introduction to the s domain. However, the real power of the Laplace transformation emerges when we transform the circuit itself and study its behavior directly in the s domain.

The solid arrow in Figure 10–1 indicates the analysis path we will be following in this chapter. The process begins with a linear circuit in the time domain. We transform the circuit into the s-domain, write the circuit equations directly in that domain, and then solve these algebraic equations for response transform. The inverse Laplace transformation then produces the response waveform. However, the s-domain approach is not just another way to derive response waveforms. This approach allows us to work directly with the circuit model using analysis tools such as voltage division and equivalence. By working directly with the circuit model, we gain insights into the interaction between circuits and signals that cannot be obtained using the classical approach indicated by the dotted path in Figure 10–1.

How are we to transform a circuit? We have seen several times that circuit analysis is based on device and connection constraints. The connection

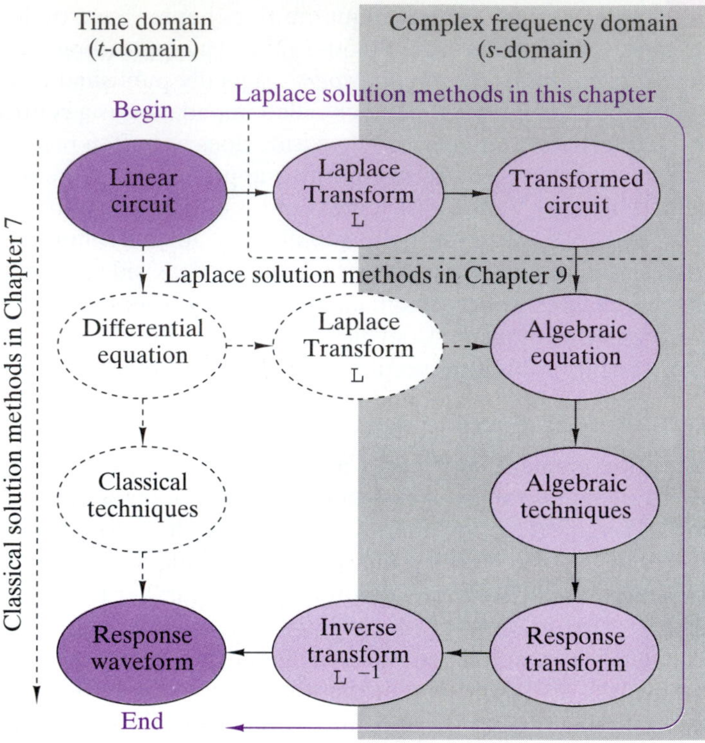

FIGURE 10–1 *Flow diagram for s-domain circuit analysis*

constraints are derived from Kirchhoff's laws and the device constraints from the i–v relationships used to model the physical devices in the circuit. To transform circuits, we must see how these two types of constraints are altered by the Laplace transformation.

CONNECTION CONSTRAINTS IN THE *S* DOMAIN

A typical KCL connection constraint could be written as

$$i_1(t) + i_2(t) - i_3(t) + i_4(t) = 0$$

This connection constraint requires the sum of the current waveforms at a node be zero for all times t. Using the linearity property, the Laplace transformation of this equation is

$$I_1(s) + I_2(s) - I_3(s) + I_4(s) = 0$$

In the s-domain the KCL connection constraint requires that the sum of the current transforms be zero for all values of s. This idea generalizes to any number of currents at a node and any number of nodes. In addition, this idea obviously applies to Kirchhoff's voltage law as well. The form of the connection constraints do not change because they are linear equations and the Laplace transformation is a linear operation. In summary, KCL and KVL apply to waveforms in the t-domain and to transforms in the s-domain.

ELEMENT CONSTRAINTS IN THE S DOMAIN

Turning now to the element constraints, we first deal with the independent signal sources shown in Figure 10–2. The i–v relationships for these elements are

$$\begin{aligned} \text{Voltage source: } v(t) &= v_S(t) \\ i(t) &= \text{Depends on Circuit} \\ \text{Current source: } i(t) &= i_S(t) \\ v(t) &= \text{Depends on Circuit} \end{aligned} \tag{10-1}$$

Independent sources are two-terminal elements. In the t domain they constrain the waveform of one signal variable and adjust the unconstrained variable to meet the demands of the external circuit. We think of an independent source as a generator of a specified voltage or current waveform. The Laplace transformation of the expressions in Eq. (10–1) yields

$$\begin{aligned} \text{Voltage source: } V(s) &= V_S(s) \\ I(s) &= \text{Depends on Circuit} \\ \text{Current source: } I(s) &= I_S(s) \\ V(s) &= \text{Depends on Circuit} \end{aligned} \tag{10-2}$$

In the s-domain independent sources function the same way as in the t domain, except that we think of them as generating voltage or current transforms rather than waveforms.

Next we consider the active elements in Figure 10–3. In the time domain the element constraints for linear dependent sources are linear algebraic equations. Because of the linearity property of the Laplace transformation,

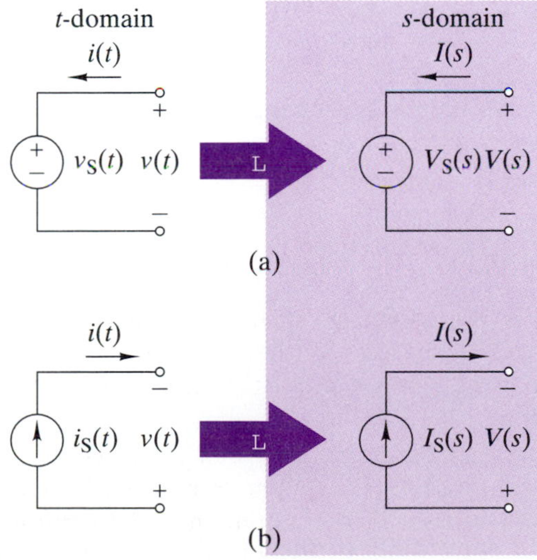

FIGURE 10–2 *s-Domain models of independent sources.*

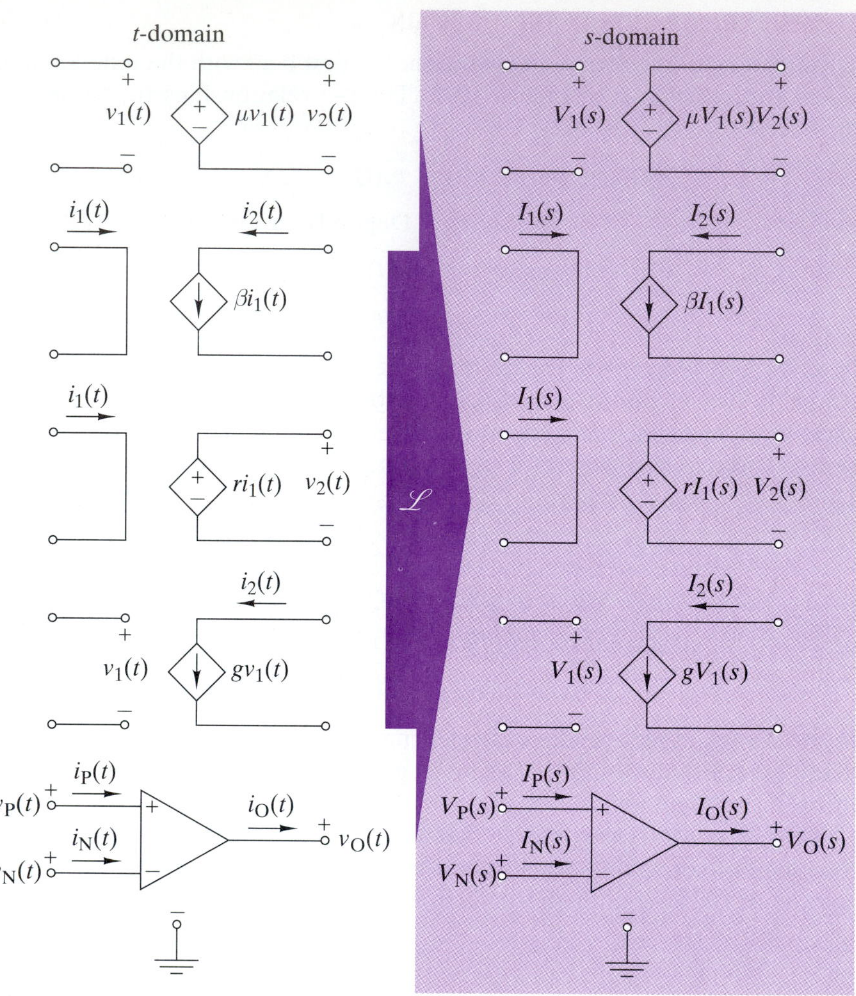

FIGURE 10–3 *s-Domain models of dependent sources and OP AMPs.*

the forms of these constraints are unchanged when they are transformed into the *s* domain:

	t domain	s domain
Voltage-controlled voltage source	$v_2(t) = \mu v_1(t)$	$V_2(s) = \mu V_1(s)$
Current-controlled current source	$i_2(t) = \beta i_1(t)$	$I_2(s) = \beta I_1(s)$
Current-controlled voltage source	$v_2(t) = ri_1(t)$	$V_2(s) = rI_1(s)$
Voltage-controlled current source	$i_2(t) = gv_1(t)$	$I_2(s) = gV_1(s)$

(10–3)

Similarly, the element constraints of the ideal OP AMP are linear algebraic equations that are unchanged in form by the Laplace transformation:

t domain	s domain	
$v_P(t) = v_N(t)$	$V_P(s) = V_N(s)$	
$i_N(t) = 0$	$I_N(s) = 0$	(10–4)
$i_P(t) = 0$	$I_P(s) = 0$	

Thus, for linear active devices the only difference is that in the s domain the ideal element constraints apply to transforms rather than waveforms.

Finally, we consider the two-terminal passive circuit elements shown in Figure 10–4. In the time domain their i–v relationships are

$$\text{Resistor: } v_R(t) = R\, i_R(t)$$

$$\text{Inductor: } v_L(t) = L\frac{di_L(t)}{dt} \qquad (10\text{–}5)$$

$$\text{Capacitor: } v_C(t) = \frac{1}{C}\int_0^t i_C(\tau)d\tau + v_C(0)$$

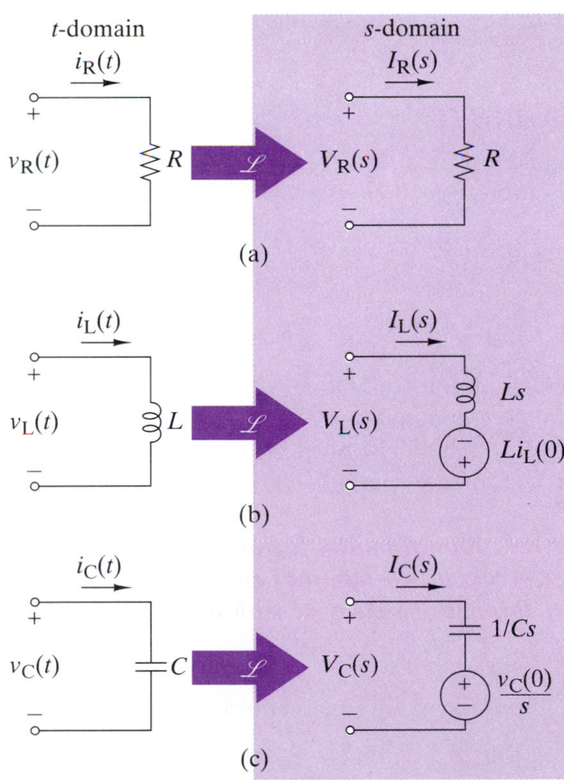

FIGURE 10–4 *s-Domain models of passive elements using voltage sources for initial conditions.*

These element constraints are transformed into the s domain by taking the Laplace transform of both sides of each equation using the linearity, differentiation, and integration properties.

$$\text{Resistor: } V_R(s) = R\, I_R(s)$$
$$\text{Inductor: } V_L(s) = LsI_L(s) - Li_L(0) \tag{10–6}$$
$$\text{Capacitor: } V_C(s) = \frac{1}{Cs} I_C(s) + \frac{v_C(0)}{s}$$

As expected, the element relationships are algebraic equations in the s domain. For the linear resistor the s domain version of Ohm's law says that the voltage transform $V_R(s)$ is proportional to the current transform $I_R(s)$. The element constraints for the inductor and capacitor also involve a proportionality between voltage and current, but include a term for the initial conditions as well.

The element constraints in Eq. (10–6) lead to the s-domain circuit models shown on the right side of Figure 10–4. The t-domain parameters L and C are replaced by proportionality factors Ls and $1/Cs$ in the s domain. The initial conditions associated with the inductor and capacitor are modeled as voltage sources in series with these elements. The polarities of these sources are determined by the sign of the corresponding initial condition terms in Eq. (10–6). These initial condition voltage sources must be included when using these models to calculate the voltage transforms $V_L(s)$ or $V_C(s)$.

IMPEDANCE AND ADMITTANCE

The concept of impedance is a basic feature of s-domain circuit analysis. For zero initial conditions the element constraints in Eq. (10–6) reduce to

$$\text{Resistor: } V_R(s) = (R)\, I_R(s)$$
$$\text{Inductor: } V_L(s) = (Ls)I_L(s) \tag{10–7}$$
$$\text{Capacitor: } V_C(s) = (1/Cs)\, I_C(s)$$

In each case the element constraints are all of the form $V(s) = Z(s)I(s)$, which means that in the s-domain the voltage across the element is proportional to the current through it. The proportionality factor is called the element **impedance** $Z(s)$. Stated formally,

> **Impedance** ***is the proportionality factor relating the transform of the voltage across a two-terminal element to the transform of the current through the element with all initial conditions set to zero.***

The impedances of the three passive elements are

$$\text{Resistor: } Z_R(s) = R$$
$$\text{Inductor: } Z_L(s) = (Ls) \qquad \text{with } i_L(0) = 0 \tag{10–8}$$
$$\text{Capacitor: } Z_C(s) = (1/Cs) \qquad \text{with } v_C(0) = 0$$

It is important to remember that part of the definition of s-domain impedance is that the initial conditions are zero.

The s-domain impedance is a generalization of the t-domain concept of resistance. The impedance of a resistor is its resistance R. The impedance of the inductor and capacitor depend on the inductance L and capacitance C and the complex frequency variable s. Since a voltage transform has units of V-s and current transform has units of A-s, it follows that impedance has units of ohms since (V-s)/(A-s) = V/A = Ω.

Algebraically solving Eqs. (10–6) for the element currents in terms of the voltages produces alternative s-domain models.

$$\begin{aligned}\text{Resistor: } I_R(s) &= \frac{1}{R}V_R(s)\\ \text{Inductor: } I_L(s) &= \frac{1}{Ls}V_L(s) + \frac{i_L(0)}{s}\\ \text{Capacitor: } I_C(s) &= Cs\,V_C(s) - C\,v_C(0)\end{aligned} \tag{10-9}$$

In this form, the i–v relations lead to the s-domain models shown in the Figure 10–5. The reference directions for the initial condition current sources are determined by the sign of the corresponding terms in Eqs. (10–9). The initial condition sources are in parallel with what is called the element admittance.

Admittance $Y(s)$ is the s-domain generalization of the t-domain concept of conductance and can be defined as the reciprocal of impedance.

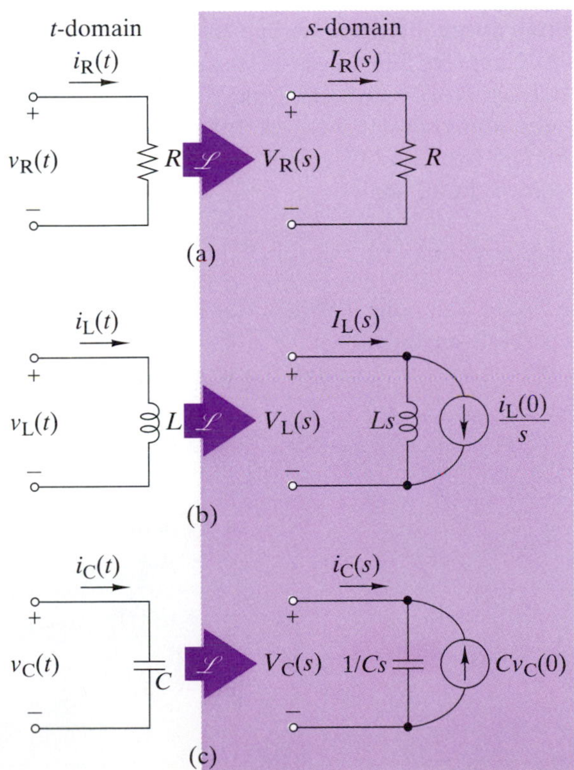

FIGURE 10–5 *s-Domain models of passive elements using current sources for initial conditions.*

$$Y(s) = \frac{1}{Z(s)} \tag{10-10}$$

Using this definition, the admittances of the three passive elements are

$$\text{Resistor: } Y_R(s) = \frac{1}{Z_R(s)} = \frac{1}{R} = G$$

$$\text{Inductor: } Y_L(s) = \frac{1}{Z_L(s)} = \frac{1}{Ls} \quad \text{with } i_L(0) = 0 \tag{10-11}$$

$$\text{Capacitor: } Y_C(s) = \frac{1}{Z_C(s)} = Cs \quad \text{with } v_C(0) = 0$$

Since $Y(s)$ is the reciprocal of impedance, its units are siemens since $\Omega^{-1} = \text{A/V} = \text{S}$.

In summary, to transform a circuit into the s domain we replace each element by an s-domain model. For independent sources, dependent sources, OP AMPs, and resistors, the only change is that these elements now constrain transforms rather than waveforms. For inductors and capacitors, we can use either the impedance model with a series initial condition voltage source (Figure 10–4), or the admittance model with a parallel initial condition current source (Figure 10–5). However, to avoid possible confusion we will always write the inductor impedance Ls and capacitor impedance $1/Cs$ beside the transformed element regardless of which initial condition source is used.

To analyze the transformed circuit, we can use the tools developed for resistance circuits in Chapters 2 through 4. These tools are applicable because KVL and KCL apply to transforms, and the s-domain element constraints are linear equations similar to those for resistance circuits. These features make s-domain analysis of dynamic circuits an algebraic process that is akin to resistance circuit analysis.

EXAMPLE 10–1

(a) Transform the circuit in Figure 10–6(a) into the s-domain.
(b) Solve for the current transform $I(s)$.
(c) Perform the inverse transformation to the waveform $i(t)$.

FIGURE 10–6

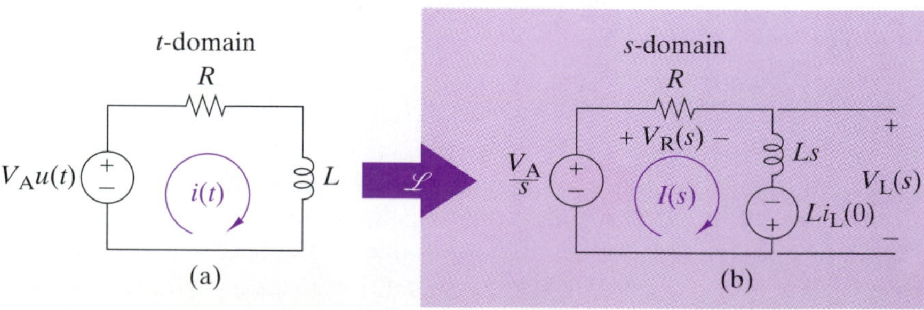

SOLUTION:

(a) Figure 10–6(b) shows the transformed circuit using a series voltage source $Li_L(0)$ to represent the inductor initial condition. The impedances of the two passive elements are R and Ls. The independent source voltage $V_A u(t)$ transforms as V_A/s.

(b) By KVL, the sum of voltage transforms around the loop is

$$-\frac{V_A}{s} + V_R(s) + V_L(s) = 0$$

Using the impedance models, the s-domain element constraints are

$$\text{Resistor: } V_R(s) = RI(s)$$
$$\text{Inductor: } V_L(s) = LsI(s) - Li_L(0)$$

Substituting the element constraints into the KVL constraint and collecting terms yields

$$-\frac{V_A}{s} + (R + Ls)I(s) - Li_L(0) = 0$$

Solving for $I(s)$ produces

$$I(s) = \frac{V_A/L}{s(s + R/L)} + \frac{i_L(0)}{s + R/L} \quad \text{A-s}$$

The current $I(s)$ is the transform of the circuit response for a step function input. $I(s)$ is a rational function with simple poles at $s = 0$ and $s = -R/L$.

(c) To perform the inverse transformation, we expand $I(s)$ by partial fractions:

$$I(s) = \overbrace{\frac{V_A/R}{s}}^{\text{Forced}} \overbrace{- \frac{V_A/R}{s + R/L} + \frac{i_L(0)}{s + R/L}}^{\text{Natural}} \quad \text{A-s}$$

Taking the inverse transform of each term in this expansion gives

$$i(t) = \Bigg[\overbrace{\frac{V_A}{R}}^{\text{Forced}} \overbrace{- \frac{V_A}{R} e^{-Rt/L} + i_L(0)\, e^{-Rt/L}}^{\text{Natural}}\Bigg] u(t) \quad \text{A}$$

The forced response is caused by the step function input. The exponential terms in the natural response depend on the circuit time constant L/R. The step function and exponential components in $i(t)$ are directly related to the terms in the partial-fraction expansion of $I(s)$. The pole at the origin came from the step function input and leads to the forced response. The pole at $s = -R/L$ came from the circuit and leads to the natural response. Thus, in the s-domain the forced response is that part of the total response that has the same poles as the input excitation. The natural response is that part of the total response whose poles came from the circuit. We say that the circuit contributes the natural poles because their locations depend on circuit parameters and not on the input. In other words, poles in the response do not occur by accident. They are present because the physical response depends on two things—(1) the input and (2) the circuit. ■

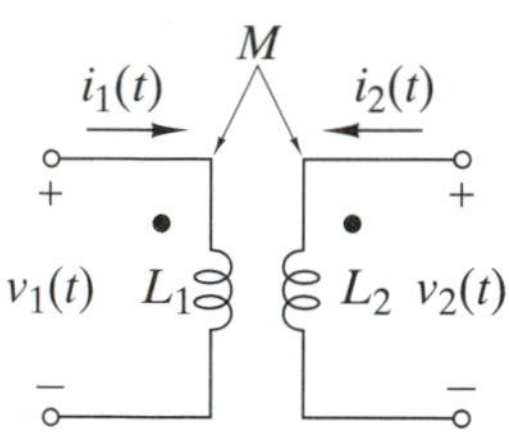

FIGURE 10–7

EXAMPLE 10–2

Develop an s-domain model for the coupled coils in Figure 10–7.

SOLUTION:

For the given reference marks, the element i–v relationships are

$$v_1(t) = L_1 \frac{di_1(t)}{dt} + M \frac{di_2(t)}{dt}$$

$$v_2(t) = M \frac{di_1(t)}{dt} + L_2 \frac{di_2(t)}{dt}$$

These equations are transformed into the s domain using the linearity and differentiation properties of the Laplace transformation:

$$V_1(s) = L_1 s I_1(s) - L_1 i_1(0) + M s I_2(s) - M i_2(0)$$

$$V_2(s) = M s I_1(s) - M i_1(0) + L_2 s I_2(s) - L_2 i_2(0)$$

Collecting related terms rearranges these equations as follows:

$$V_1(s) = L_1 s I_1(s) + M s I_2(s) - L_1 i_1(0) - M i_2(0)$$

$$V_2(s) = M s I_1(s) + L_2 s I_2(s) - M i_1(0) - L_2 i_2(0)$$

The factors $L_1 s$ and $L_2 s$ are the impedance of the self-inductance of primary and secondary windings, respectively. The factor Ms is the coupling impedance caused by mutual inductance coupling. A mutual initial condition term for the secondary (primary) current appears in the equation for the primary (secondary) because mutual inductance couples the two windings. These equations lead to the s-domain model of coupled coils shown in Figure 10–8(a).

An alternative s-domain model is obtained by rearranging the element equations in the form

$$V_1(s) = L_1 s \underbrace{\left[I_1(s) - \frac{i_1(0)}{s} \right]}_{I_A(s)} + Ms \underbrace{\left[I_2(s) - \frac{i_2(0)}{s} \right]}_{I_B(s)}$$

$$V_2(s) = Ms \overbrace{\left[I_1(s) - \frac{i_1(0)}{s} \right]} + L_2 s \overbrace{\left[I_2(s) - \frac{i_2(0)}{s} \right]}$$

In this form we see that the currents $I_A(s)$ and $I_B(s)$ together with the impedances $L_1 s$, $L_2 s$, and Ms determine the terminal voltages $V_1(s)$ and $V_2(s)$.

FIGURE 10–8

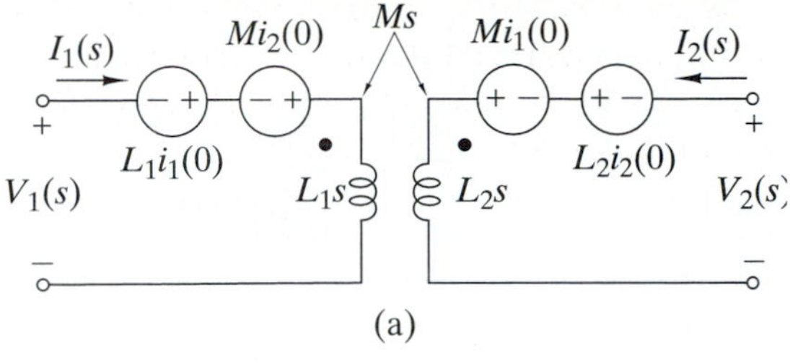

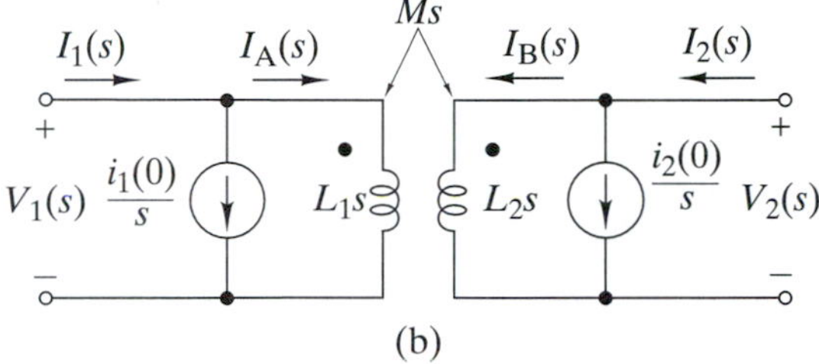

Inserting initial condition current sources as shown in Figure 10–8(b) ensures that the terminal currents $I_1(s)$ and $I_2(s)$ are correct and produces an alternative s-domain model of a pair of coupled coils. ■

10–2 BASIC CIRCUIT ANALYSIS IN THE S DOMAIN

In this section we develop the s-domain versions of series and parallel equivalence, and voltage and current division. These analysis techniques are the basic tools in s-domain circuit analysis, just as they are for resistance circuit analysis. These methods apply to circuits with elements connected in series or parallel. General analysis methods using node-voltage or mesh-current equations are covered later in Sects. 10–4 and 10–5.

SERIES EQUIVALENCE AND VOLTAGE DIVISION

The concept of a series connection applies in the s domain because Kirchhoff's laws do not change under the Laplace transformation. In Figure 10–9 the two-terminal elements are connected in series; hence by KCL the same current $I(s)$ exists in impedances $Z_1(s)$, $Z_2(s)$, . . . $Z_N(s)$. Using KVL and the element constraints, the voltage across the series connection can be written as

$$\begin{aligned} V(s) &= V_1(s) + V_2(s) + \cdots + V_N(s) \\ &= Z_1(s)I(s) + Z_2(s)I(s) + \cdots + Z_N(s)I(s) \qquad (10\text{–}12) \\ &= [Z_1(s) + Z_2(s) + \cdots + Z_N(s)]\, I(s) \end{aligned}$$

The last line in this equation points out that the responses $V(s)$ and $I(s)$ do not change when the series-connected elements are replaced by an **equivalent impedance**:

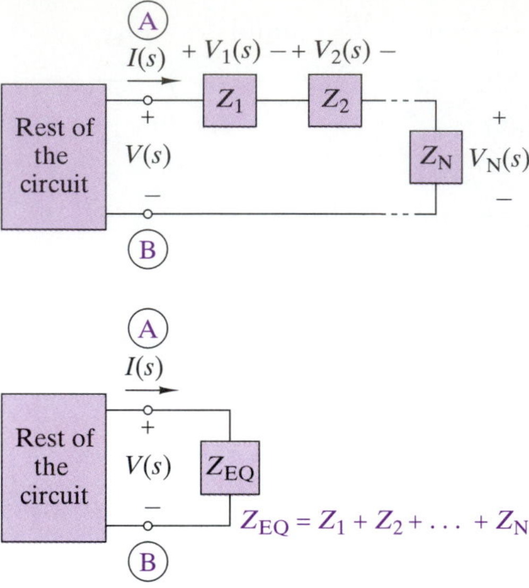

FIGURE 10–9 *Series equivalence in the s-domain.*

$$Z_{\text{EQ}}(s) = Z_1(s) + Z_2(s) + \cdots + Z_{\text{N}}(s) \qquad (10\text{–}13)$$

In general, the equivalent impedance $Z_{\text{EQ}}(s)$ is a quotient of polynomials in the complex frequency variable of the form

$$Z_{\text{EQ}}(s) = \frac{b_m s^m + b_{m-1} s^{m-1} + \cdots + b_1 s + b_0}{a_n s^n + a_{n-1} s^{n-1} + \cdots + a_1 s + a_0} \qquad (10\text{–}14)$$

The roots of the numerator polynomial are the zeros of $Z_{\text{EQ}}(s)$, while the roots of the denominator are the poles.

Combining Eqs. (10–12) and (10–13), we can write the element voltages in the form

$$V_1(s) = \frac{Z_1(s)}{Z_{\text{EQ}}(s)} V(s) \quad V_2(s) = \frac{Z_2(s)}{Z_{\text{EQ}}(s)} V(s) \cdots V_{\text{N}}(s) = \frac{Z_{\text{N}}(s)}{Z_{\text{EQ}}(s)} V(s)$$

$$(10\text{–}15)$$

These equations are the s-domain **voltage division principle**:

> ***Every element voltage in a series connection is equal to its impedance divided by the equivalent impedance of the connection times the voltage across the series circuit.***

This statement parallels the corresponding rule for resistance circuits given in Chapter 4.

PARALLEL EQUIVALENCE AND CURRENT DIVISION

The parallel circuit in Figure 10–10 is the dual of the series circuit discussed previously. In this circuit the two-terminal elements are connected in parallel; hence by KVL the same voltage $V(s)$ appears across admit-

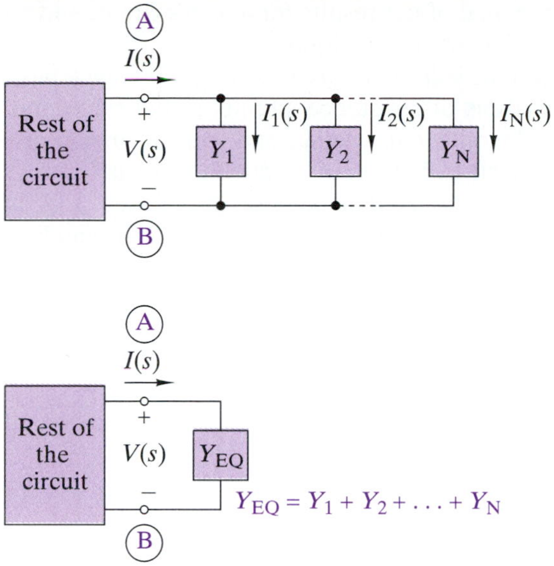

FIGURE 10–10 *Parallel equivalence in the s-domain.*

tances $Y_1(s)$, $Y_2(s)$, . . . $Y_N(s)$. Using KCL and the element constraints, the current into the parallel connection can be written as

$$\begin{aligned} I(s) &= I_1(s) + I_2(s) + \cdots + I_N(s) \\ &= Y_1(s)V(s) + Y_2(s)V(s) + \cdots + Y_N(s)V(s) \\ &= [Y_1(s) + Y_2(s) + \cdots + Y_N(s)]V(s) \end{aligned} \quad (10\text{–}16)$$

The last line in this equation points out that the responses $V(s)$ and $I(s)$ do not change when the parallel connected elements are replaced by an **equivalent admittance**:

$$Y_{EQ}(s) = Y_1(s) + Y_2(s) + \cdots + Y_N(s) \quad (10\text{–}17)$$

In general, the equivalent admittance $Y_{EQ}(s)$ is a quotient of polynomials in the complex frequency variable s. Since impedance and admittance are reciprocals, it turns out that if $Y_{EQ}(s) = p(s)/q(s)$, then the equivalent impedance at the same pair of terminals has the form $Z_{EQ}(s) = 1/Y_{EQ}(s) = q(s)/p(s)$. That is, at a given pair of terminals the poles of $Z_{EQ}(s)$ are zeros of $Y_{EQ}(s)$, and vice versa.

Combining Eqs. (10–16) and (10–17), we can write the element currents in the form

$$I_1(s) = \frac{Y_1(s)}{Y_{EQ}(s)}I(s) \quad I_2(s) = \frac{Y_2(s)}{Y_{EQ}(s)}I(s) \cdots I_N(s) = \frac{Y_N(s)}{Y_{EQ}(s)}I(s) \quad (10\text{–}18)$$

These equations are the s-domain **current division principle**:

Every element current in a parallel connection is equal to its admittance divided by the equivalent admittance of the connection times the current into the parallel circuit.

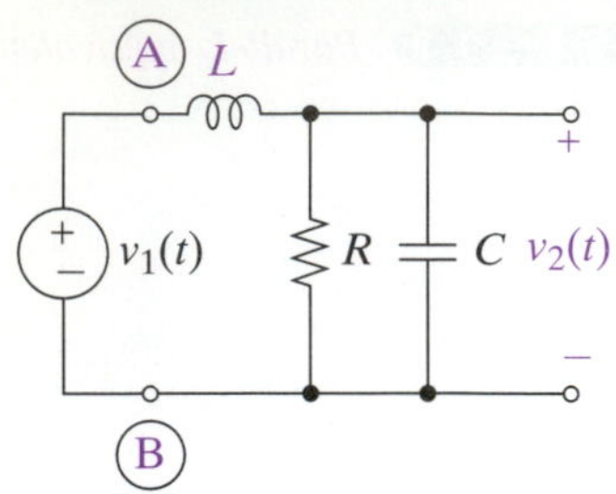

FIGURE 10–11

This statement is the dual of the results for a series circuit and parallels the current division rule for resistance circuits.

We begin to see that s-domain circuit analysis involves basic concepts that parallel the analysis of resistance circuits in the t domain. Repeated application of series/parallel equivalence and voltage/current division leads to an analysis approach called circuit reduction, discussed in Chapter 2. The major difference here is that we use impedance and admittances rather than resistance and conductance, and the analysis yields voltage and current transforms rather than waveforms.

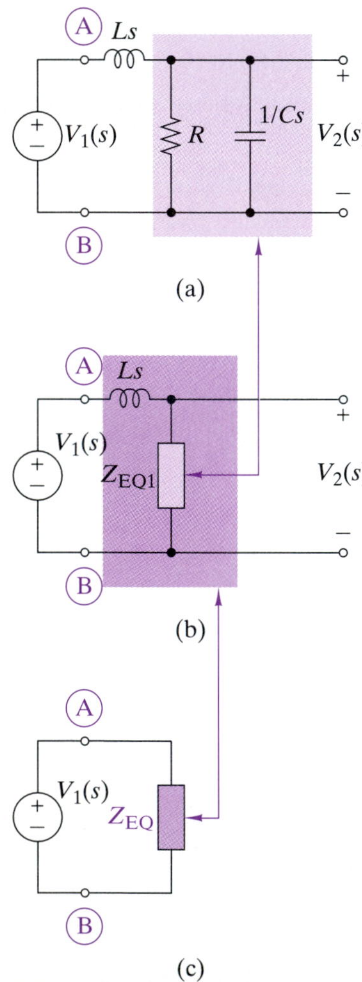

FIGURE 10–12

EXAMPLE 10–3

The inductor current and capacitor voltage in Figure 10–11 are zero at $t = 0$.

(a) Transform the circuit into the s domain and find the equivalent impedance between terminals A and B.
(b) Use voltage division to solve for the output voltage transform $V_2(s)$.

SOLUTION:

(a) Figure 10–12(a) shows the circuit in Figure 10–11 transformed into the s domain. As a first step we use parallel equivalence to find the equivalent impedance of the parallel resistor and capacitor.

$$Z_{EQ1}(s) = \frac{1}{Y_{EQ1}(s)} = \frac{1}{\dfrac{1}{R} + Cs} = \frac{R}{RCs + 1}$$

Figure 10–12(b) shows that the equivalent impedance $Z_{EQ1}(s)$ is connected in series with the inductor. This series combination can be replaced by an equivalent impedance

$$Z_{EQ}(s) = Ls + Z_{EQ1}(s) = Ls + \frac{R}{RCs + 1}$$

$$= \frac{RLCs^2 + Ls + R}{RCs + 1} \quad \Omega$$

as shown in Figure 10–12(c). The rational function $Z_{EQ}(s)$ is the impedance seen between terminals A and B in Figure 10–12(a).

(b) Using voltage division in Figure 10–12(b), we find $V_2(s)$ as

$$V_2(s) = \left[\frac{Z_{EQ1}(s)}{Z_{EQ}(s)}\right] V_1(s) = \left[\frac{R}{RLCs^2 + Ls + R}\right] V_1(s)$$

Note that $Z_{EQ}(s)$ and $V_2(s)$ are rational functions of the complex frequency variable s. ■

D **EXAMPLE 10–4**

In a circuit analysis problem we are required to find the poles and zeros of a circuit. In circuit design we are required to adjust circuit parameters to place the poles and zeros at specified s-plane locations. This example is a simple pole-placement design problem.

(a) Transform the circuit in Figure 10–13(a) into the s domain and find the equivalent impedance between terminals A and B.
(b) Select the values of R and C such that $Z_{EQ}(s)$ has a zero at $s = -5000$ rad/s.

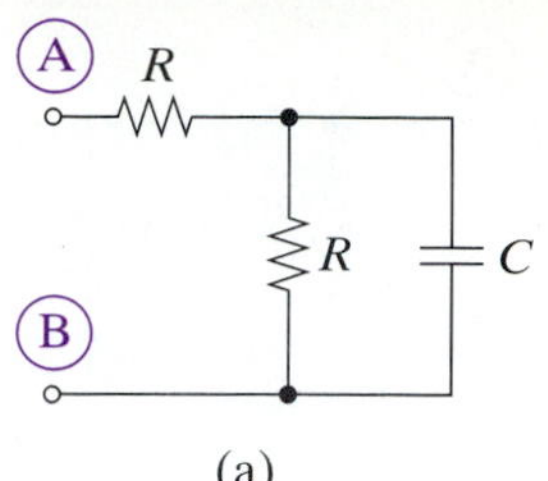

(a)

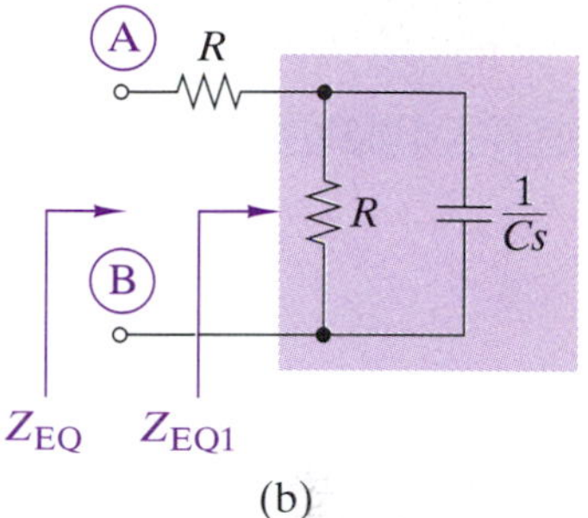

(b)

FIGURE 10–13

SOLUTION:

(a) Figure 10–13(b) shows the circuit transformed to the s domain. The equivalent impedance $Z_{EQ1}(s)$ is

$$Z_{EQ1}(s) = \frac{1}{Y_R + Y_C} = \frac{1}{\frac{1}{R} + Cs}$$

$$= \frac{R}{RCs + 1}$$

Hence the equivalent impedance between terminals A and B is

$$Z_{EQ}(s) = R + Z_{EQ1}(s) = R + \frac{R}{RCs + 1}$$

$$= R\frac{RCs + 2}{RCs + 1} \quad \Omega$$

(b) For $Z_{EQ}(s)$ to have a zero at $s = -5000$ requires $2/RC = 5000$ or $RC = 4 \times 10^{-4}$. Selecting a standard value for the resistor $R = 10$ kΩ in turn requires $C = 40$ nF. ■

Exercise 10–1

The inductor current and capacitor voltage in Figure 10–14 are zero at $t = 0$.

(a) Transform the circuit into the s domain and find the equivalent admittance between terminals A and B.
(b) Solve for the output current transform $I_2(s)$ in terms of the input current $I_1(s)$.

Answers:

$$\text{(a) } Y_{EQ}(s) = \frac{LCs^2 + RCs + 1}{Ls(RCs + 1)}$$

$$\text{(b) } I_2(s) = \left[\frac{LCs^2}{LCs^2 + RCs + 1}\right] I_1(s)$$

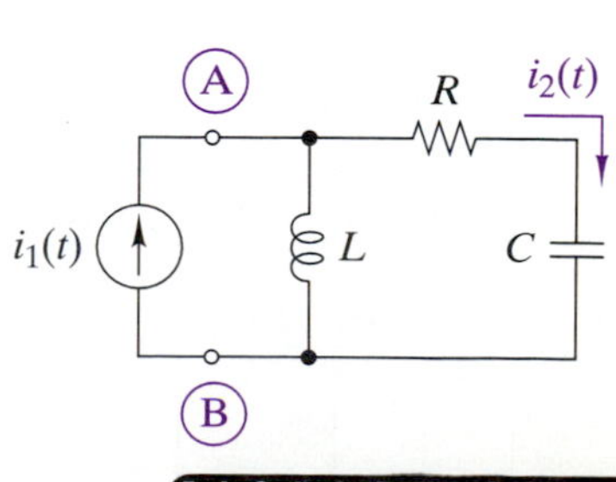

FIGURE 10–14

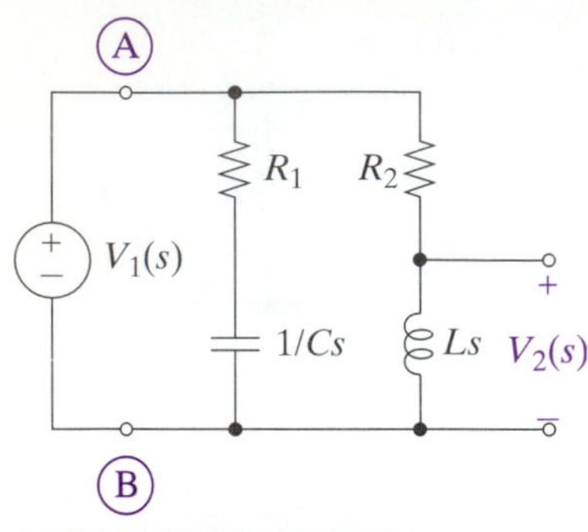

FIGURE 10–15

Exercise 10–2

The inductor current and capacitor voltage in Figure 10–15 are zero at $t = 0$.

(a) Transform the circuit into the s domain and find the equivalent impedance between terminals A and B.
(b) Solve for the output voltage transform $V_2(s)$ in terms of the input voltage $V_1(s)$.

Answers:

$$\text{(a) } Z_{EQ}(s) = \frac{(R_1Cs + 1)(Ls + R_2)}{LCs^2 + (R_1 + R_2)Cs + 1}$$

$$\text{(b) } V_2(s) = \left[\frac{Ls}{Ls + R_2}\right] V_1(s)$$

10–3 CIRCUIT THEOREMS IN THE s DOMAIN

In this section we study the s-domain versions of proportionality, superposition, and Thévenin/Norton equivalent circuits. These theorems define fundamental properties that provide conceptual tools for the analysis and design of linear circuits. With some modifications, all of the theorems studied in Chapter 3 apply to linear dynamic circuits in the s domain.

PROPORTIONALITY

For linear resistance circuits the **proportionality theorem** states that any output y is proportional to the input x:

$$y = Kx \tag{10–19}$$

The same concept applies to linear dynamic circuits in the s domain except that the proportionality factor K is a rational function of s rather than a constant. For instance, in Example 10–3 we found the output voltage $V_2(s)$ to be

$$V_2(s) = \left[\frac{R}{RLCs^2 + Ls + R}\right] V_1(s) \tag{10–20}$$

where $V_1(s)$ is the transform of the input voltage. The quantity inside the brackets is a rational function that serves as the proportionality factor between the input and output transforms.

In the s-domain rational functions that relate inputs and outputs are called **network functions**. We begin the formal study network functions in Chapter 11. In this chapter we will simply illustrate network functions by an example.

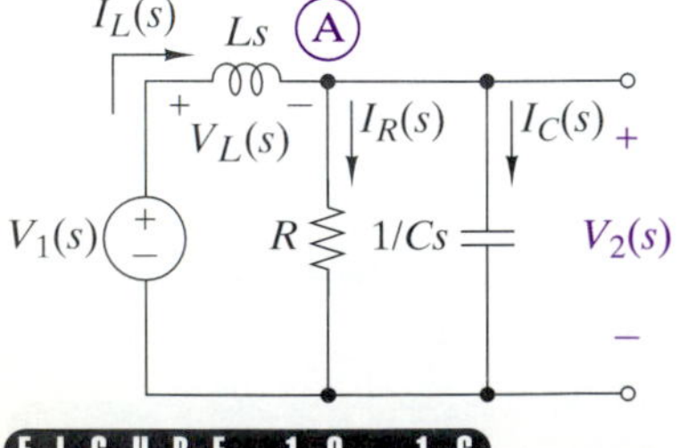

FIGURE 10–16

EXAMPLE 10–5

There is no initial energy stored in the circuit in Figure 10–16. Find the network functions relating $I_R(s)$ to $V_1(s)$ and $I_C(s)$ to $V_1(s)$.

SOLUTION:

The equivalent impedance seen by the voltage source is

$$Z_{EQ} = Ls + \frac{1}{\dfrac{1}{R} + Cs} = \frac{RLCs^2 + Ls + R}{RCs + 1}$$

Hence we can relate the $I_L(s)$ and $V_1(s)$ as

$$I_L(s) = \frac{V_1(s)}{Z_{EQ}(s)} = \left[\frac{RCs + 1}{RLCs^2 + Ls + R}\right] V_1(s)$$

Using s-domain current division, we can relate $I_R(s)$ and $I_C(s)$ to $I_L(s)$ as

$$I_R(s) = \frac{\dfrac{1}{R}}{\dfrac{1}{R} + Cs} I_L(s) = \left[\frac{1}{RCs + 1}\right] I_L(s)$$

$$I_C(s) = \frac{Cs}{\dfrac{1}{R} + Cs} I_L(s) = \left[\frac{RCs}{RCs + 1}\right] I_L(s)$$

Finally, using these relationships plus the relationship between $I_L(s)$ and $V_1(s)$ derived previously, we obtain the required network functions.

$$I_R(s) = \left[\frac{1}{RLCs^2 + Ls + R}\right] V_1(s)$$

$$I_C(s) = \left[\frac{RCs}{RLCs^2 + Ls + R}\right] V_1(s)$$

■

Exercise 10–3

In Figure 10–17 find the network function relating the output $V_2(s)$ to the input $I_1(s)$.

Answer:

$$V_2(s) = \left[\frac{R}{LCs^2 + RCs + 1}\right] I_1(s)$$

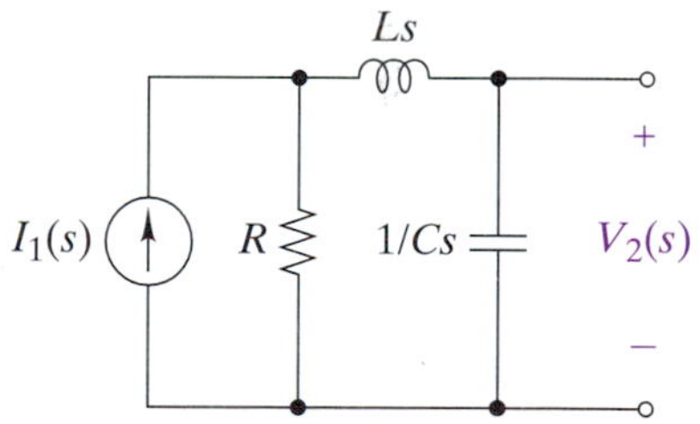

FIGURE 10–17

SUPERPOSITION

For linear resistance circuits the **superposition theorem** states that any output y of a linear circuit can be written as

$$y = K_1x_1 + K_2x_2 + K_3x_3 + \cdots \qquad (10\text{–}21)$$

where $x_1, x_2, x_3, \ldots$ are circuit inputs and $K_1, K_2. K_3, \ldots$ are weighting factors that depend on the circuit. The same concept applies to linear dynamic circuits in the s-domain except that the weighting factors are rational functions of s rather than constants.

Superposition is usually thought of as a way to find the circuit response by adding the individual responses caused by each input acting alone.

However, the principle applies to groups of sources as well. In particular, in the s domain there are two types of independent sources: (1) voltage and current sources representing the external driving forces for $t \geq 0$ and (2) initial condition voltage and current sources representing the energy stored at $t = 0$. As a result, the superposition principle states that the s-domain response can be found as the sum of two components: (1) the **zero-input response** caused by the initial condition sources with the external inputs turned off; or (2) the **zero-state response** caused by the external inputs with the initial condition sources turned off. Turning a source off means replacing voltage sources by short circuits $[V_S(s) = 0]$ and current sources by open circuits $[I_S(s) = 0]$.

The zero-input response is the response of a circuit to its initial conditions when the input excitations are set to zero. The zero-state response is the response of a circuit to its input excitations when all of the initial conditions are set to zero. The term *zero input* is self-explanatory. The term *zero state* is used because there is no energy stored in the circuit at $t = 0$.

The result is that voltage and current transform in a linear circuit can be found as the sum of two components of the form

$$V(s) = V_{zs}(s) + V_{zi}(s) \qquad I(s) = I_{zs}(s) + I_{zi}(s) \qquad (10-22)$$

where the subscript zs stands for zero state and zi for zero input. An important corollary is that the time-domain response can also be partitioned into zero-state and zero-input components because the inverse Laplace transformation is a linear operation.

We analyze the circuit treated in Example 10–1 to illustrate the superposition of zero-state and zero-input responses. The transformed circuit in Figure 10–18 has two independent voltage sources: (1) an input voltage source and (2) a voltage source representing the initial inductor current. The resistor and inductor are in series, so these two elements can be replaced by an impedance $Z_{EQ}(s) = Ls + R$.

First we turn off the initial condition source and replace its voltage source by a short circuit. Using the resulting zero-state circuit shown in Figure 10–18, we obtain the zero-state response:

$$I_{zs}(s) = \frac{V_A/s}{Z_{EQ}(s)} = \frac{V_A/L}{s(s + R/L)} \qquad (10-23)$$

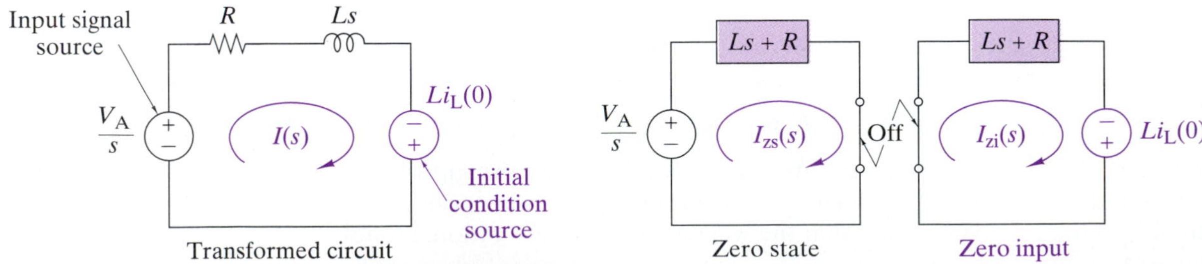

FIGURE 10–18 *Using superposition to find the zero-state and zero-input responses.*

The pole at $s = 0$ comes from the input source and the pole at $s = -R/L$ comes from the circuit. Next, we turn off the input source and use the zero-input circuit shown in Figure 10–18 to obtain the zero-input response:

$$I_{zi}(s) = \frac{Li_L(0)}{Z_{EQ}(s)} = \frac{i_L(0)}{s + R/L} \quad (10-24)$$

The pole at $s = -R/L$ comes from the circuit. The zero-input response does not have a pole at $s = 0$ because the step function input is turned off.

Superposition states that the total response is the sum of the zero-state component in Eqs. (10–23) and the zero-input component in Eq. (10–24).

$$I(s) = I_{zs}(s) + I_{zi}(s) = \frac{V_A/L}{s(s + R/L)} + \frac{i_L(0)}{s + R/L} \quad (10-25)$$

The transform $I(s)$ in this equation is the same as found in Example 10–1. To derive the time-domain response, we expand $I(s)$ by partial fractions:

$$I(s) = \underbrace{\frac{V_A/R}{s} - \frac{V_A/R}{s + R/L}}_{\text{Zero State}} + \underbrace{\frac{i_L(0)}{s + R/L}}_{\text{Zero Input}} \quad (10-26)$$

Performing the inverse transformation on each term yields

$$i(t) = \Bigg[\overbrace{\frac{V_A}{R}}^{\text{Forced}} - \frac{V_A}{R} e^{-Rt/L} + i_L(0)\, e^{-Rt/L}\Bigg] u(t) \quad \text{A} \quad (10-27)$$

(Natural: $-\frac{V_A}{R} e^{-Rt/L} + i_L(0)\, e^{-Rt/L}$; Zero State: $\frac{V_A}{R} - \frac{V_A}{R} e^{-Rt/L}$; Zero Input: $i_L(0)\, e^{-Rt/L}$)

Using superposition to partition the waveform into zero-state and zero-input components produces the same result as Example 10–1. The zero-state component contains the forced response. The zero-state and zero-input components both contain an exponential term due to the natural pole at $s = -R/L$ because both the external driving force and the initial condition source excite the circuit's natural response.

The superposition theorem helps us understand the response of circuits with multiple inputs, including initial conditions. It is a conceptual tool that helps us organize our thinking about s-domain circuits in general. It is not necessarily the most efficient analysis tool for finding the response of a specific multiple-input circuit.

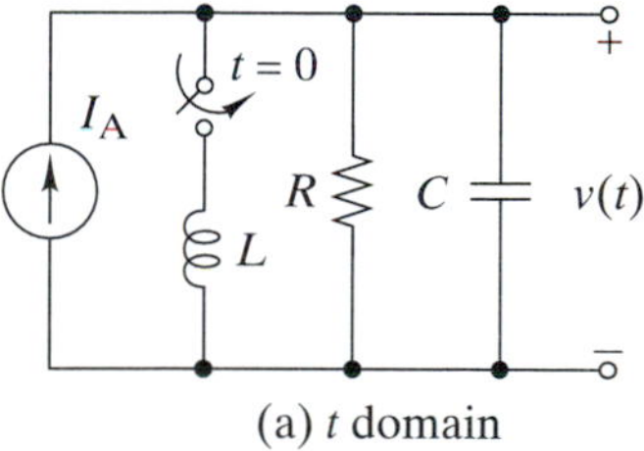

(a) t domain

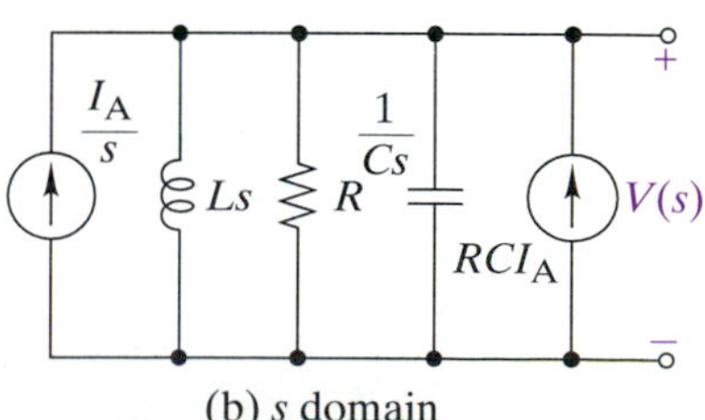

(b) s domain

FIGURE 10–19

EXAMPLE 10–6

The switch in Figure 10–19(a) has been open for a long time and is closed at $t = 0$.

(a) Transform the circuit into the s domain.
(b) Find the zero-state and zero-input components of $V(s)$.
(c) Find $v(t)$ for $I_A = 1$ mA, $L = 2$ H, $R = 1.5$ kΩ, and $C = 1/6$ μF.

SOLUTION:

(a) To transform the circuit into the s domain, we must find the initial inductor current and capacitor voltage. For $t < 0$ the circuit is in a dc steady-state condition with the switch open. The inductor acts like a short circuit, and the capacitor acts like an open circuit. By inspection, the initial conditions at $t = 0-$ are $i_L(0) = 0$ and $v_C(0) = I_A R$. Figure 10–19(b) shows the s-domain circuit for these initial conditions. The current source version for the capacitor's initial condition is used here because the circuit elements are connected in parallel. The switch and constant current source combine to produce a step function $I_A u(t)$ whose transforms is I_A/s.

(b) The resistor, capacitor, and inductor can be replaced by an equivalent impedance

$$Z_{EQ} = \frac{1}{Y_{EQ}} = \frac{1}{\dfrac{1}{Ls} + \dfrac{1}{R} + Cs}$$

$$= \frac{RLs}{RLCs^2 + Ls + R}$$

The zero-state response is found with the capacitor initial condition source replaced by an open circuit and the step function input source on:

$$V_{zs}(s) = Z_{EQ}(s)\frac{I_A}{s} = \left[\frac{RLs}{RLCs^2 + Ls + R}\right]\frac{I_A}{s} = \frac{I_A/C}{s^2 + \dfrac{s}{RC} + \dfrac{1}{LC}}$$

The pole in the input at $s = 0$ is canceled by the zero at the origin in $Z_{EQ}(s)$. As a result, the zero-state response does not have a forced pole at $s = 0$. The zero-input response is found by replacing the input source by an open circuit and turning the capacitor initial condition source on:

$$V_{zi}(s) = [Z_{EQ}(s)]\,[CRI_A] = \frac{RI_A s}{s^2 + \dfrac{s}{RC} + \dfrac{1}{LC}}$$

(c) Inserting the given numerical values of the circuit parameters and expanding the zero-state and zero-input response transforms by partial fractions yields

$$V_{zs} = \frac{6000}{(s + 1000)\,(s + 3000)} = \frac{3}{s + 1000} + \frac{-3}{s + 3000} \quad \text{V-s}$$

$$V_{zi}(s) = \frac{1.5\,s}{(s + 1000)\,(s + 3000)} = \frac{-0.75}{s + 1000} + \frac{2.25}{s + 3000} \quad \text{V-s}$$

The inverse transforms of these expansions are

$$v_{zs}(t) = [3e^{-1000t} - 3e^{-3000t}]\,u(t) \quad \text{V}$$

$$v_{zi}(t) = [-0.75e^{-1000t} + 2.25e^{-3000t}]\,u(t) \quad \text{V}$$

Note that the circuit responses contain only transient terms that decay to zero. There is no forced response because in the dc steady state the inductor acts like a short circuit, forcing $v(t)$ to zero for $t \to \infty$. From an s domain viewpoint there is no forced response because the forced pole at $s = 0$ is canceled by a zero in the network function. ■

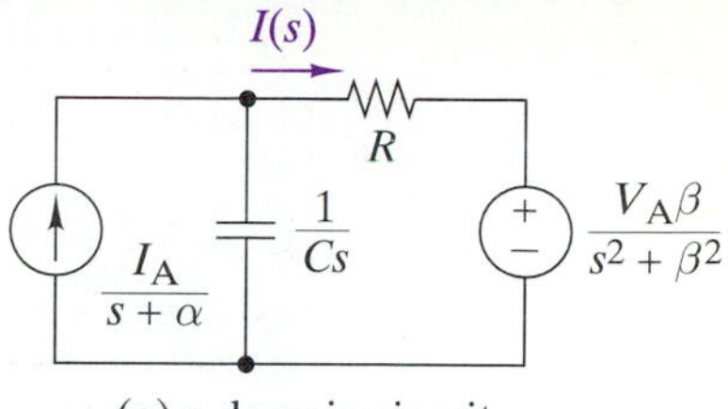

(a) s-domain circuit

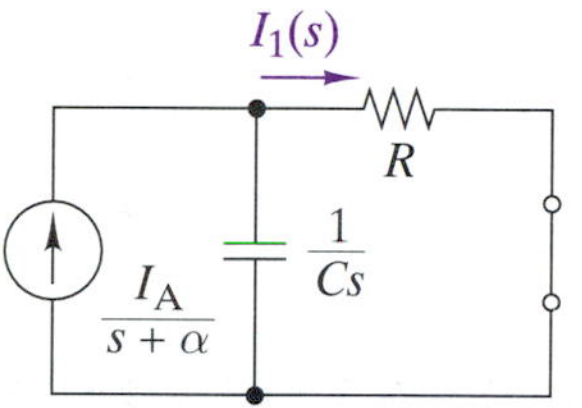

(b) Voltage source OFF

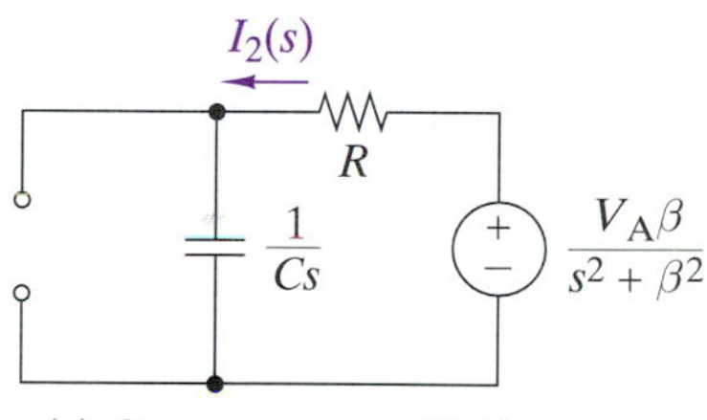

(c) Current source OFF

FIGURE 10–20

EXAMPLE 10–7

Use superposition to find the zero-state component of $I(s)$ in the s-domain circuit shown in Figure 10–20(a).

SOLUTION:

Turning the voltage source off produces the circuit in Figure 10–20(b). In this circuit the resistor and capacitor are connected in parallel, so current division yields $I_1(s)$ in the form

$$I_1(s) = \frac{Y_R}{Y_C + Y_R}\frac{I_A}{(s+\alpha)} = \frac{I_A}{(RCs+1)(s+\alpha)}$$

Turning the voltage source on and the current source off produces the circuit in Figure 10–20(c). In this case the resistor and capacitor are connected in series, and series equivalence gives the current $I_2(s)$ as

$$I_2(s) = \frac{1}{Z_R + Z_C}\frac{V_A\beta}{s^2+\beta^2} = \frac{CsV_A\beta}{(RCs+1)(s^2+\beta^2)}$$

Using superposition, the total zero-state response is

$$\begin{aligned} I_{zs}(s) &= I_1(s) - I_2(s) \\ &= \frac{I_A}{(RCs+1)(s+\alpha)} - \frac{CsV_A\beta}{(RCs+1)(s^2+\beta^2)} \end{aligned}$$

There is a minus in this equation because $I_1(s)$ and $I_2(s)$ were assigned opposite reference directions in Figures 10–20(b) and 10–20(c). The total zero-state response has four poles. The natural pole at $s = -1/RC$ came from the circuit. The forced pole at $s = -\alpha$ came from the current source, and the two forced poles at $s = \pm j\beta$ came from the voltage source.

In this example the time-domain response would have a transient component $Ke^{-t/RC}$ due to the natural pole, a forced component $Ke^{-\alpha t}$ due to the current source, and a forced component of the form $K_A \cos \beta t + K_B \sin \beta t$ due to the voltage source. We can infer these general conclusions regarding the time-domain response by simply examining the poles of the s-domain response. ■

Exercise 10–4

The initial conditions for the circuit in Figure 10–21 are $v_C(0-) = 0$ and $i_L(0-) = I_0$. Transform the circuit into the s domain and find the zero-state and zero-input components of $V(s)$.

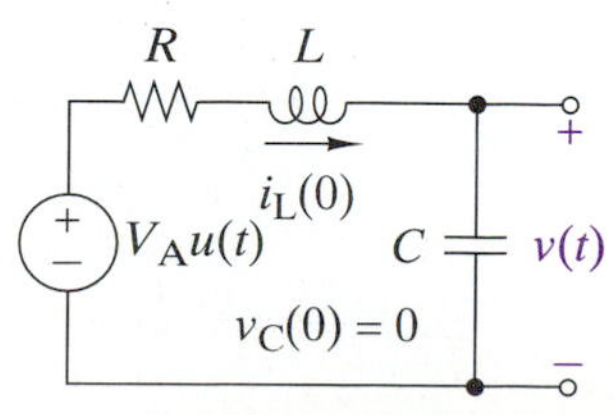

FIGURE 10–21

Answers:

$$V_{zs}(s) = \left[\frac{1}{LCs^2 + RCs + 1}\right]\frac{V_A}{s}$$

$$V_{zi}(s) = \frac{LI_0}{LCs^2 + RCs + 1}$$

Exercise 10–5

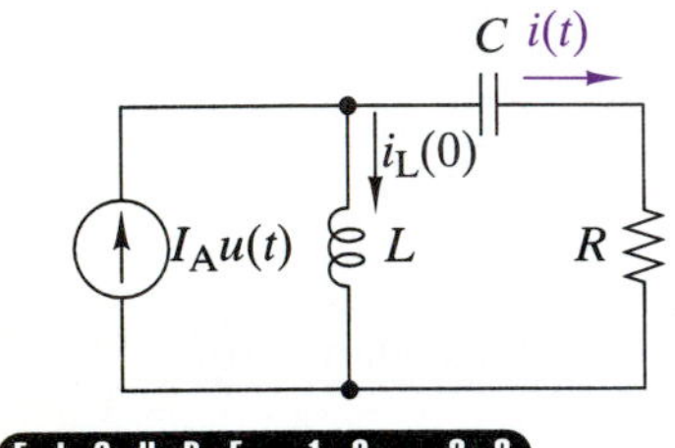

FIGURE 10–22

The initial conditions for the circuit in Figure 10–22 are $v_C(0-) = 0$ and $i_L(0-) = I_0$. Transform the circuit into the s domain and find the zero-state and zero-input components of $I(s)$.

Answers:

$$I_{zs}(s) = \left[\frac{LC\,s^2}{LCs^2 + RCs + 1}\right]\frac{I_A}{s}$$

$$I_{zi}(s) = \left[\frac{LC\,s^2}{LCs^2 + RCs + 1}\right]\frac{I_0}{s}$$

THÉVENIN AND NORTON EQUIVALENT CIRCUITS AND SOURCE TRANSFORMATIONS

When the source circuit in Figure 10–23(a) contains only independent sources and linear elements, it can be replaced by the Thévenin equivalent circuit in Figure 10–23(b) or the Norton equivalent circuit in Figure 10–23(c). In the s domain the methods of finding and using Thévenin or Norton equivalent circuits are similar to those for resistive circuits. The important differences are that the signals are transforms rather than waveforms and the circuit elements are impedances rather than resistances.

The open-circuit voltage and short-circuit current at the interface provided enough information to define the Thévenin and Norton equivalent circuits. With an open-circuit load connected in Figures 10–23(b) and 10–23(c), we see that the interface voltage is

$$V(s) = V_{OC}(s) = I_N(s)Z_N(s) = V_T(s) \qquad (10-28)$$

With a short-circuit load connected, the interface currents is

$$I(s) = I_{SC}(s) = V_T(s)/Z_T(s) = I_N(s) \qquad (10-29)$$

Taken together, Eqs. (10–28) and (10–29) yield the conditions

$$V_T(s) = V_{OC}(s) \quad I_N(s) = I_{SC}(s) \qquad Z_T(s) = Z_N(s) = \frac{V_{OC}(s)}{I_{SC}(s)} \qquad (10-30)$$

Algebraically, the results in Eq. (10–30) are identical to the corresponding equations for resistance circuits. The important difference, as noted previously, is that these equations involve transforms and impedances

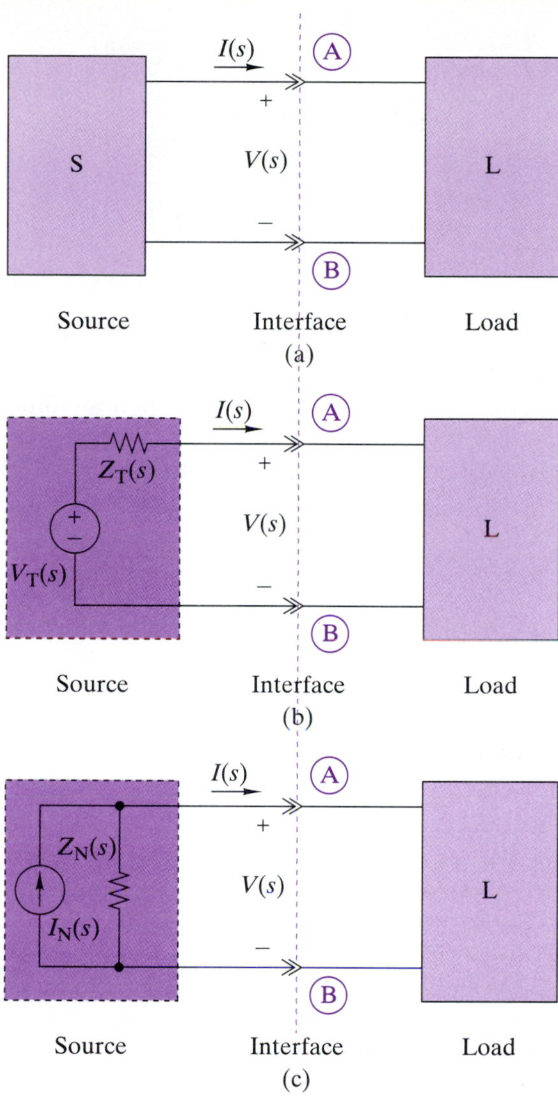

FIGURE 10–23 *Thévenin and Norton equivalent circuits in the s-domain.*

rather than waveforms and resistances. In any case, the equations point out that the open-circuit voltage and short-circuit current are sufficient to define either equivalent circuit.

The Thévenin and Norton equivalent circuits are related by an s-domain source transformation. The s-domain **source transformation** relations in Eq. (10–30) allow us to transform a voltage source in series with an impedance into a current source in parallel with the same impedance, and vice versa. We use these source transformations when formulating node-voltage and mesh-current equations in the s domain.

Consider the interface shown in Figure 10–24. The source circuit is given in the s domain with zero initial voltage on the capacitor. The open-circuit voltage at the interface is found by voltage division:

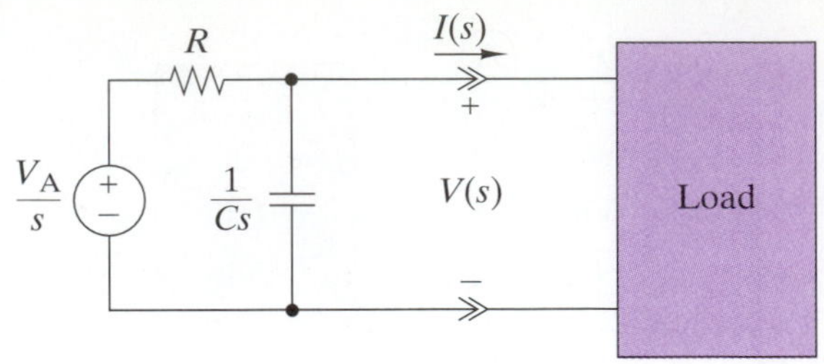

FIGURE 10–24 *A source-load interface in the s-domain.*

$$V_{OC}(s) = \frac{1/Cs}{R + 1/Cs}\frac{V_A}{s} = \frac{V_A}{s(RCs + 1)} \quad (10\text{–}31)$$

The pole in $V_{OC}(s)$ at $s = 0$ comes from the step function voltage source and the pole at $s = -1/RC$ from the RC circuit. Connecting a short circuit at the interface effectively removes the capacitor from the circuit. The short-circuit current is

$$I_{SC}(s) = \frac{1}{R}\frac{V_A}{s} \quad (10\text{–}32)$$

This current does not have a pole at $s = -1/RC$ because the capacitor is shorted out. Taking the ratio of Eqs. (10–31) and (10–32) yields the Thévenin impedance:

$$Z_T(s) = \frac{V_{OC}(s)}{I_{SC}(s)} = \frac{R}{RCs + 1} \quad (10\text{–}33)$$

When there are no dependent sources present, the Thévenin impedance can be found using the lookback method from Chapter 3. That is, the Thévenin impedance is the equivalent impedance seen looking back into the source circuit with the independent sources (external inputs and initial conditions) turned off. Replacing the voltage source in Figure 10–24 by a short circuit reduces the source circuit to a parallel combination of a resistor and capacitor. The equivalent lookback impedance of the combination is

$$Z_T(s) = \frac{1}{Y_R + Y_C} = \frac{1}{\dfrac{1}{R} + Cs} = \frac{R}{RCs + 1} \quad (10\text{–}34)$$

which is the same result as Eq. (10–33).

This example illustrates that in the s domain, Thévenin or Norton theorems involve concepts similar to those discussed in Chapter 3. At a given interface these equivalent circuits are defined by any two of the following: (1) the open-circuit voltage, (2) the short-circuit current, or (3) the lookback impedance (when no dependent sources are involved). Thévenin and Norton equivalent circuits are useful tools that help us understand the operation of a circuit, especially when we must evaluate the circuit performance with different loads or parameter variations at an interface. They are not, in general, a way to reduce the computational burden of finding the response of a fixed circuit.

EXAMPLE 10–8

Find the interface voltage $v(t)$ in Figure 10–24 when the load is (a) a resistance R and (b) a capacitance C.

SOLUTION:

Figure 10–25 shows the *s*-domain circuit model of the source-load interface. The parameters of the Thévenin equivalent are given in Eqs. (10–31) and (10–33) as

$$V_T(s) = \frac{V_A}{s(RCs + 1)} \quad \text{and} \quad Z_T(s) = \frac{R}{RCs + 1}$$

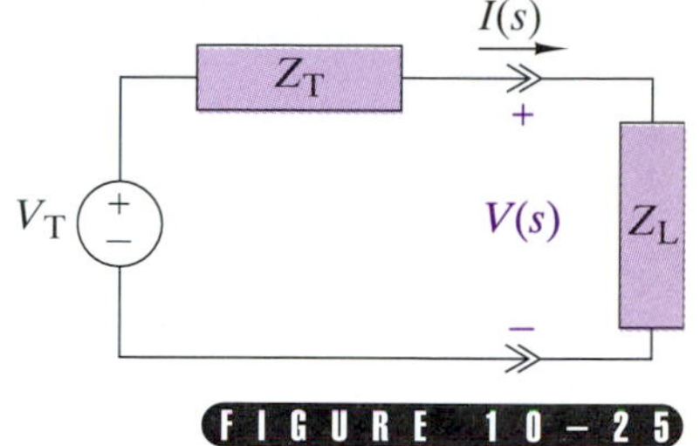

FIGURE 10–25

(a) For a resistance load, $Z_L(s) = R$ and the interface voltage is found by voltage division:

$$V(s) = \frac{Z_L(s)}{Z_T(s) + Z_L(s)} V_T(s)$$

$$= \left(\frac{R}{\dfrac{R}{RCs + 1} + R} \right) \frac{V_A}{s(RCs + 1)}$$

$$= \frac{V_A/RC}{s(s + 2/RC)} \quad \text{V-s}$$

The partial fraction expansion of $V(s)$ is

$$V(s) = \frac{V_A/2}{s} - \frac{V_A/2}{s + 2/RC}$$

Applying the inverse transform yields the interface voltage waveform as

$$v(t) = \frac{V_A}{2}[1 - e^{-2t/RC}]\, u(t) \quad \text{V}$$

(b) For a capacitance load, $Z_L(s) = 1/Cs$ and the interface voltage transform is

$$V(s) = \frac{Z_L(s)}{Z_T(s) + Z_L(s)} V_T(s) = \left(\frac{\dfrac{1}{Cs}}{\dfrac{R}{RCs + 1} + \dfrac{1}{Cs}} \right) \frac{V_A}{s(RCs + 1)}$$

$$= \frac{V_A/2RC}{s(s + 1/2\,RC)} \quad \text{V-s}$$

The partial fraction expansion of $V(s)$ is

$$V(s) = \frac{V_A}{s} - \frac{V_A}{s + 2/RC}$$

Applying the inverse transform to each term yields the interface voltage waveform for the capacitance load as

$$v(t) = V_A[1 - e^{-t/2RC}]\,u(t) \quad \text{V}$$

This example illustrates an important difference between resistive circuits and dynamic circuits. In a resistive circuit the load affects the amplitude but not the waveshape of the interface signals. In a dynamic circuit the load can change both amplitude and the waveshape. ■

D DESIGN EXAMPLE 10–9

Real Pole Placement Design

The circuit in Figure 10–26(a) is a low-frequency model of a transistor circuit. Select the value of C_E so that the circuit has a pole at $s = -300$ rad/s.

FIGURE 10–26

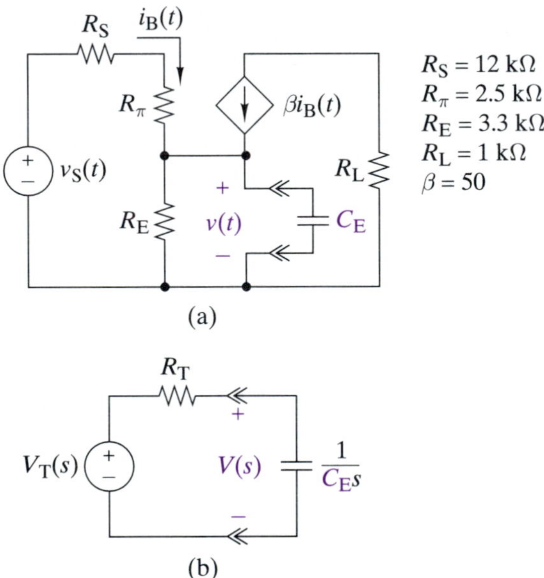

SOLUTION:

Figure 10–26(b) shows the Thévenin equivalent seen by the capacitor C_E. In this circuit the voltage across the capacitor is

$$V_C(s) = \frac{1/C_E s}{R_T + 1/C_E s} V_T(s) = \frac{1}{R_T C_E s + 1} V_T(s)$$

The circuit has a simple pole at $s = -1/R_T C_E$, where R_T is the Thévenin equivalent resistance seen by the capacitor. To place the circuit pole at $s = -300$, we must select $C_E = 1/300R_T$. Hence the problem reduces to finding the Thévenin equivalent resistance seen by the capacitor. With the capacitor in Figure 10–26(a) replaced by a short circuit, we find

$$i_{SC}(t) = \beta i_B(t) + i_B(t) = (\beta + 1)\left[\frac{v_S(t)}{R_S + R_\pi}\right]$$

$$= 3.52 v_S(t) \quad \text{mA}$$

Next, replacing the capacitor by an open circuit yields

$$v_{OC}(t) = i_B(t)R_E + \beta i_B(t)R_E$$

$$= (\beta + 1)R_E\left[\frac{v_S(t) - v_{OC}(t)}{R_S + R_\pi}\right]$$

Solving this expression for $v_{OC}(t)$, we obtain

$$v_{OC}(t) = \frac{(\beta + 1)R_E}{R_S + R_\pi + (\beta + 1)R_E} v_S(t)$$

$$= 0.921 v_S(t) \quad \text{V}$$

The Thévenin equivalent resistance seen by the capacitor is $R_T = v_{OC}/i_{SC} = 262\ \Omega$, and the required value of capacitance is $C_E = 12.7\ \mu\text{F}$. This example illustrates the general principle that we can select element values to position a circuit's poles at specified locations. ■

Exercise 10–6

Find the Norton equivalent of the *s*-domain circuits in Figure 10–27.

Answers:

(a) $I_N(s) = \dfrac{I_A}{(RCs + 1)(s + \alpha)} \qquad Z_N(s) = \dfrac{RCs + 1}{Cs}$

(b) $I_N(s) = \dfrac{RI_A}{(Ls + R)(s + \alpha)} \qquad Z_N(s) = \dfrac{Ls + R}{LCs^2 + RCs + 1}$

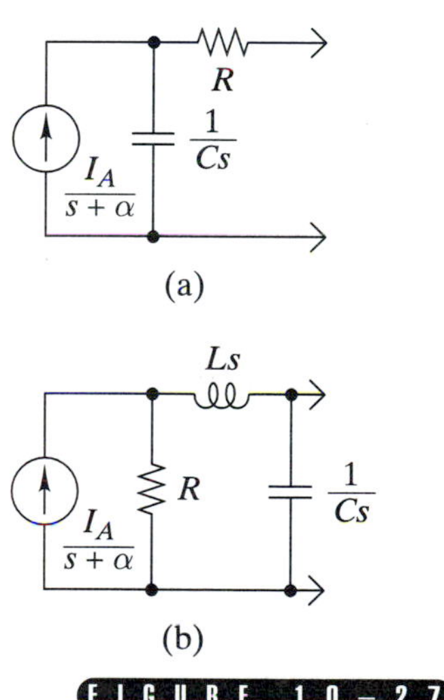

FIGURE 10–27

10–4 NODE-VOLTAGE ANALYSIS IN THE S DOMAIN

The previous sections deal with basic analysis methods using equivalence, reduction, and circuit theorems. These methods are valuable because we work directly with the element impedances and thereby gain insight into *s*-domain circuit behavior. We also need general methods to deal with more complicated circuits that these basic methods cannot easily handle.

FORMULATING NODE-VOLTAGE EQUATIONS

Formulating node-voltage equations involves selecting a reference node and assigning a node-to-datum voltage to each of the remaining nonreference nodes. Because of KVL, the voltage across any two-terminal element

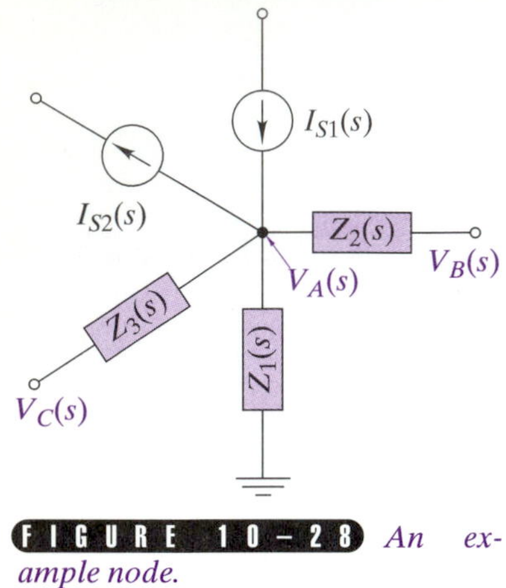

FIGURE 10–28 *An example node.*

is equal to the difference of two node voltages. This fundamental property of node voltages, together with element impedances, allows us to write KCL constraints at each of the nonreference nodes.

For example, consider the *s*-domain circuit in Figure 10–28. The sum of currents leaving node A can be written as

$$I_{S2}(s) - I_{S1}(s) + \frac{V_A(s)}{Z_1(s)} + \frac{V_A(s) - V_B(s)}{Z_2(s)} + \frac{V_A(s) - V_C(s)}{Z_3(s)} = 0$$

Rewriting this equation with unknown node voltages grouped on the left and inputs on the right yields

$$\left[\frac{1}{Z_1(s)} + \frac{1}{Z_2(s)} + \frac{1}{Z_3(s)}\right] V_A(s) - \frac{1}{Z_2(s)} V_B(s) - \frac{1}{Z_3(s)} V_C(s) = I_{S1}(s) - I_{S2}(s)$$

Expressing this result in terms of admittances produces the following equation:

$$\begin{aligned}[Y_1(s) + Y_2(s) + Y_3(s)]\, V_A(s) - [Y_2(s)]\, V_B(s)\\ - [Y_3(s)]V_C(s) = I_{S1}(s) - I_{S2}(s)\end{aligned}$$

This equation has a familiar pattern. The unknowns are the node-voltage transforms $V_A(s)$, $V_B(s)$, and $V_C(s)$. The coefficient $[Y_1(s) + Y_2(s) + Y_3(s)]$ of $V_A(s)$ is the sum of the admittances of the elements connected to node A. The coefficient $[Y_2(s)]$ of $V_B(s)$ is the admittance of the elements connected between nodes A and B, while $[Y_3(s)]$ is the admittance of the elements connected between nodes A and C. Finally, $I_{S1}(s) - I_{S2}(s)$ is the sum of the source currents directed into node A. These observations suggest that we can write node-voltage equations for *s*-domain circuits by inspection, just as we did with resistive circuits.

The formulation method just outlined assumes that there are no voltage sources in the circuit. When transforming the circuit we can always select the current source models to represent the initial conditions. However, the circuit may contain dependent or independent voltage sources. If so, they can be treated using the following methods:

Method 1: If there is an impedance in series with the voltage source, use a source transformation to convert it into an equivalent current source.

Method 2: Select the reference node so that one terminal of one or more of the voltage sources is connected to ground. The source voltage then determines the node voltage at the other source terminal, thereby eliminating an unknown.

Method 3: Create a supernode surrounding any voltage source that cannot be handled by method 1 or 2.

Some circuits may require more than one of these methods.

Formulating a set of equilibrium equations in the *s*-domain is a straightforward process involving concepts developed in Chapters 3 and 4 for resistance circuits. The following example illustrates the formulation process.

EXAMPLE 10–10

Formulate s-domain node-voltage equations for the circuit in Figure 10–29(a).

FIGURE 10–29

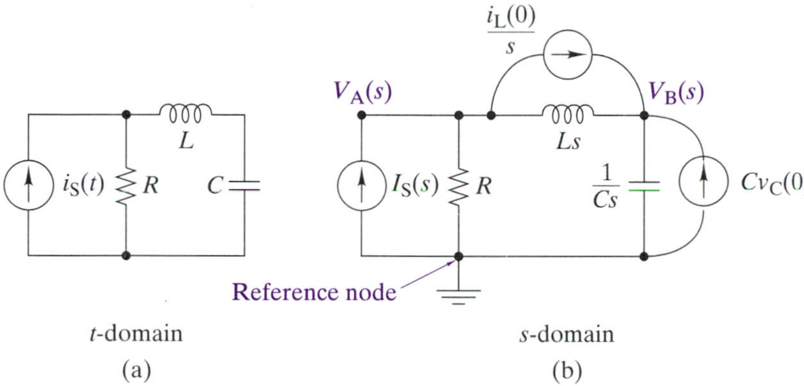

t-domain
(a)

s-domain
(b)

SOLUTION:

Figure 10–29(b) shows the circuit in the s domain. In transforming the circuit, we use current sources to represent the inductor and capacitor initial conditions. This choice facilitates writing node equations since the resulting s-domain circuit contains only current sources. The sum of currents leaving nodes A and B can be written as

$$\text{Node A: } \frac{V_A(s)}{R} + \frac{V_A(s) - V_B(s)}{Ls} - I_S(s) + \frac{i_L(0)}{s} = 0$$

$$\text{Node B: } \frac{V_B(s)}{1/Cs} + \frac{V_B(s) - V_A(s)}{Ls} - \frac{i_L(0)}{s} - Cv_C(0) = 0$$

Rearranging these equations in the standard format with the unknowns on the left and the inputs on the right yields

$$\text{Node A: } \left(G + \frac{1}{Ls}\right) V_A(s) - \left(\frac{1}{Ls}\right) V_B(s) = I_S(s) - \frac{i_L(0)}{s}$$

$$\text{Node B: } -\left(\frac{1}{Ls}\right) V_A(s) + \left(\frac{1}{Ls} + Cs\right) V_B(s) = Cv_C(0) + \frac{i_L(0)}{s}$$

where $G = 1/R$ is the conductance of the resistor. Note that $(G + 1/Ls)$ is the sum of the admittance connected to node A, $(1/Ls + Cs)$ is the sum of the admittances connected to node B, and $1/Ls$ is the admittance connected between nodes A and B. The circuit is driven by an independent current source $I_S(s)$ and two initial condition sources $Cv_C(0)$ and $i_L(0)/s$. The terms on the right side of these equations are the sum of source currents directed into each node. With practice, we learn to write these equations by inspection. ■

EXAMPLE 10–11

Formulate node-voltage equations for the circuit in Figure 10–30(a).

FIGURE 10–30

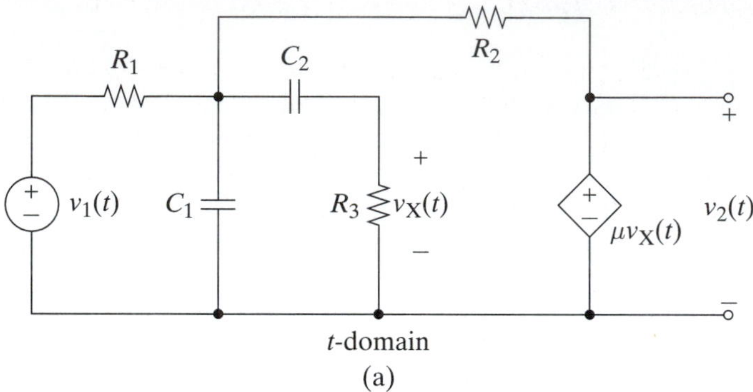

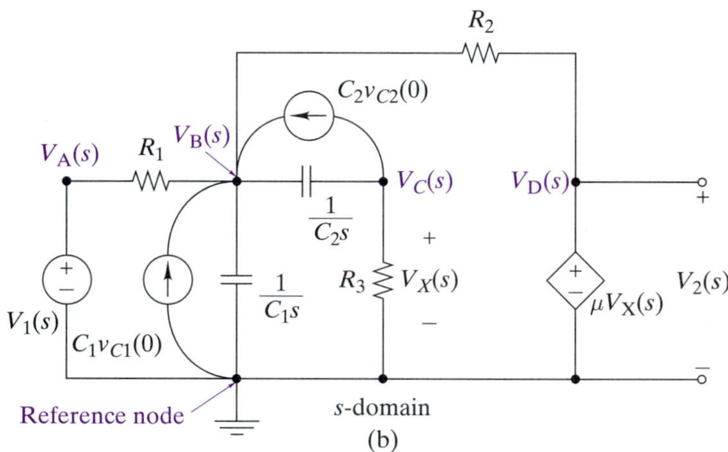

SOLUTION:

Figure 10–30(b) shows the circuit in the s domain using current sources for the two capacitor initial conditions. The indicated reference node was selected so that the two voltage sources are connected to ground. As a result, the voltage sources determine the voltages at nodes A and D. The only unknowns are the voltages at nodes B and C. The sums of currents leaving nodes B and C are

$$\text{Node B: } \frac{V_B(s) - V_A(s)}{R_1} + \frac{V_B(s) - V_D(s)}{R_2} + \frac{V_B(s)}{1/C_1s} + \frac{V_B(s) - V_C(s)}{1/C_2s} - C_1v_{C_1}(0) - C_2v_{C_2}(0) = 0$$

$$\text{Node C: } \frac{V_C(s)}{R_3} + \frac{V_C(s) - V_B(s)}{1/C_2s} + C_2v_{C_2}(0) = 0$$

Writing these equations with node voltages on the left and the source terms on the right yields

$$\text{Node B: } -G_1V_A(s) + [C_1s + C_2s + G_1 + G_2]\,V_B(s) - C_2sV_C(s) - G_2V_D(s) = C_1v_{C_1}(0) + C_2v_{C_2}(0)$$

$$\text{Node C: } -C_2sV_B(s) + [C_2s + G_3]\,V_C(s) = -C_2v_{C_2}(0)$$

where $G_1 = 1/R_1$, $G_2 = 1/R_2$, and $G_3 = 1/R_3$ are the conductances of the three resistors. In the node B equation the coefficient in the term $[C_1s + C_2s + G_1 + G_2]V_B(s)$ is the sum of the admittances connected to node B. The coefficients of the other terms in the same equation are the admittances connected between node B and the other nodes. The same pattern exists in the node B equation. Once we recognize this pattern, we can learn to write the foregoing node equations by inspection.

For the selected reference node, $V_A(s) = V_1(s)$ and $V_D(s) = \mu V_X(s) = \mu V_C(s)$. Substituting these relations into the foregoing node equations and arranging the result in standard form yields

$$\text{Node B: } (C_1s + C_2s + G_1 + G_2)\,V_B(s) - (C_2s + \mu G_2)\,V_C(s) = G_1V_1(s) + C_1v_{C_1}(0) + C_2v_{C_2}(0)$$

$$\text{Node C: } -C_2sV_B(s) + (C_2s + G_3)\,V_C(s) = -C_2v_{C_2}(0)$$

We now have two equations in the two unknown node voltages $V_B(s)$ and $V_C(s)$. The final node equations are not symmetrical because the dependent source is not a bilateral element like resistors, capacitors, and inductors. ■

Exercise 10–7

Formulate node-voltage equations for the circuit in Figure 10–31. Assume that the initial conditions are zero.

Answer:

$$\left(G_1 + G_2 + \frac{1}{Ls}\right)V_B(s) - G_2V_C(s) = G_1V_S(s)$$

$$-G_2V_B(s) + (G_2 + C_S)V_C(s) = CsV_S(s)$$

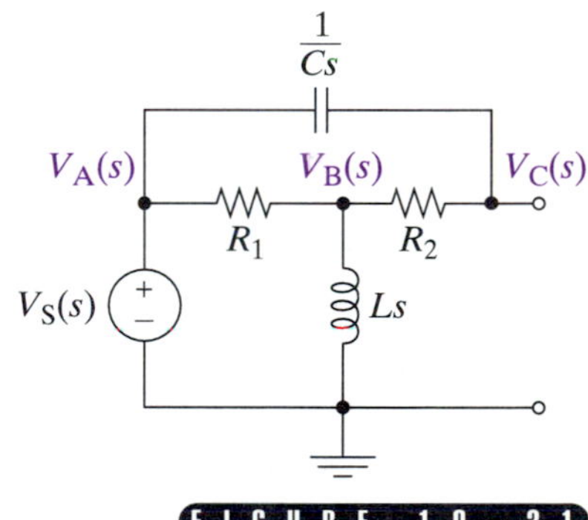

FIGURE 10–31

Exercise 10–8

Formulate node-voltage equations for the circuit in Figure 10–31 when the initial conditions are not zero and a resistor R_3 is connected between nodes A and C.

Answer:

$$\left(G_1 + G_2 + \frac{1}{Ls}\right)V_B(s) - G_2V_C(s) = G_1V_S(s) - \frac{i_L(0)}{s}$$

$$-G_2V_B(s) + (G_2 + G_3 + Cs)V_C(s) = (G_3 + Cs)V_S(s) - Cv_C(0)$$

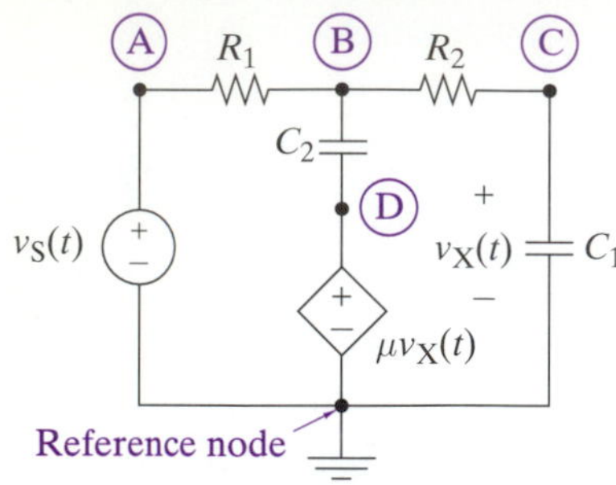

FIGURE 10–32

Exercise 10–9

Formulate node-voltage equations for the circuit in Figure 10–32. Assume that the initial conditions are zero.

Answer:

$$(G_1 + G_2 + C_2 s)V_B(s) - (G_2 + \mu C_2 s)V_C(s) = G_1 V_S(s)$$
$$-G_2 V_B(s) + (G_2 + C_1 s)V_C(s) = 0$$

Exercise 10–10

Formulate node-voltage equations for the circuit in Figure 10–32 when a resistor R_3 is connected between nodes A and C. Assume that initial conditions are zero.

Answer:

$$(G_1 + G_2 + C_2 s)V_B(s) - (G_2 + \mu C_2 s)V_C(s) = G_1 V_S(s)$$
$$-G_2 V_B(s) + (G_2 + G_3 + C_1 s)V_C(s) = G_3 V_S(s)$$

SOLVING S-DOMAIN CIRCUIT EQUATIONS

Examples 10–10 and 10–11 show that node-voltage equations are linear algebraic equations in the unknown node voltages. In theory, solving these node equations is accomplished using techniques such as Cramer's rule or perhaps Gaussian reduction. In practice, we quickly lose interest in Gaussian reduction since coefficients in the equations are polynomials, making the algebra rather complicated. For hand analysis Cramer's rule is the better approach, especially when the element parameters are in symbolic form. For computer aided analysis we use the symbolic analysis capability of programs like Mathcad and others to solve these linear equations.

We will illustrate the Cramer's rule solution process using an example from earlier in this section. In Example 10–10 we formulated the following node-voltage equations for the circuit in Figure 10–29:

$$\left(G + \frac{1}{Ls}\right) V_A(s) - \frac{1}{Ls} V_B(s) = I_S(s) - \frac{i_L(0)}{s}$$

$$-\frac{1}{Ls} V_A(s) + \left(Cs + \frac{1}{Ls}\right) V_B(s) = \frac{i_L(0)}{s} + Cv_C(0)$$

When using Cramer's rule, it is convenient first to find the determinant of these equations:

$$\Delta(s) = \begin{vmatrix} G + 1/Ls & -1/Ls \\ -1/Ls & Cs + 1/Ls \end{vmatrix}$$
$$= (G + 1/Ls)(Cs + 1/Ls) - (1/Ls)^2$$
$$= \frac{GLCs^2 + Cs + G}{Ls}$$

We call $\Delta(s)$ the **circuit determinant** because it only depends on the element parameters L, C, and $G = 1/R$. The determinant $\Delta(s)$ characterizes the circuit and does not depend on the input driving forces or initial conditions.

The node voltage $V_A(s)$ is found using Cramer's rule.

$$V_A(s) = \frac{\Delta_A(s)}{\Delta(s)} = \frac{\begin{vmatrix} I_S(s) - \dfrac{i_L(0)}{s} & -\dfrac{1}{Ls} \\ \dfrac{i_L(0)}{s} + Cv_C(0) & Cs + \dfrac{1}{Ls} \end{vmatrix}}{\Delta(s)} \quad (10\text{–}35)$$

$$= \underbrace{\frac{(LCs^2 + 1)\, I_S(s)}{GLC\, s^2 + Cs + G}}_{\text{Zero State}} + \underbrace{\frac{-LCsi_L(0) + Cv_C(0)}{GLC\, s^2 + Cs + G}}_{\text{Zero Input}}$$

Solving for the other node voltage $V_B(s)$ yields

$$V_B(s) = \frac{\Delta_B(s)}{\Delta(s)} = \frac{\begin{vmatrix} G + \dfrac{1}{Ls} & I_S(s) - \dfrac{i_L(0)}{s} \\ -\dfrac{1}{Ls} & \dfrac{i_L(0)}{s} + Cv_C(0) \end{vmatrix}}{\Delta(s)} \quad (10\text{–}36)$$

$$= \underbrace{\frac{I_S(s)}{GLCs^2 + Cs + G}}_{\text{Zero State}} + \underbrace{\frac{GLi_L(0) + (GLs + 1)Cv_C(0)}{GLCs^2 + Cs + G}}_{\text{Zero Input}}$$

Cramer's rule gives both the zero-input and zero-state components of the response transforms $V_A(s)$ and $V_B(s)$.

Cramer's rule yields the node voltages as a ratio of determinants of the form

$$V_X(s) = \frac{\Delta_X(s)}{\Delta(s)} \quad (10\text{–}37)$$

The response transform is a rational function of s whose poles are either zeros of the circuit determinant or poles of the determinant $\Delta_X(s)$. That is, $V_X(s)$ in Eq. (10–37) has poles when $\Delta(s) = 0$ or $\Delta_X(s) \to \infty$. The partial-fraction expansion of $V_X(s)$ will contain terms for each of these poles. We call the zeros of $\Delta(s)$ the **natural poles** because they depend only on the circuit and give rise to the natural response terms in the partial-fraction expansion. We call the poles of $\Delta_X(s)$ the **forced poles** because they depend on the form of the input signal and give rise to the forced response terms in the partial-fraction expansion.

EXAMPLE 10–12

Use computer-aided circuit analysis to solve the *s*-domain node equations for the circuit in Figure 10–29.

SOLUTION:

The node equations were formulated in Example 10–10 as

$$\text{Node A: } \left(G + \frac{1}{Ls}\right) V_A(s) - \left(\frac{1}{Ls}\right) V_B(s) = I_S(s) - \frac{i_L(0)}{s}$$

$$\text{Node B: } -\left(\frac{1}{Ls}\right) V_A(s) + \left(Cs + \frac{1}{Ls}\right) V_B(s) = \frac{i_L(0)}{s} + Cv_C(0)$$

In matrix form these equations are written as follows:

$$\begin{bmatrix} G + \dfrac{1}{Ls} & -\dfrac{1}{Ls} \\ -\dfrac{1}{Ls} & Cs + \dfrac{1}{Ls} \end{bmatrix} \begin{bmatrix} V_A(s) \\ V_B(s) \end{bmatrix} = \begin{bmatrix} I_S(s) - \dfrac{i_L(0)}{s} \\ \dfrac{i_L(0)}{s} + Cv_C(0) \end{bmatrix}$$

This matrix equation is of the form **YV** = **I**, where **Y** is a two-by-two matrix of admittances, **V** is a column vector containing the unknown node voltages, and **I** is a column vector containing the input driving forces and initial conditions. The matrix equation is solved by left multiplying both sides by $\mathbf{Y}^{-1}$ (the inverse of the admittance matrix) to obtain $\mathbf{V} = \mathbf{Y}^{-1}\mathbf{I}$.

Figure 10–33 shows a Mathcad worksheet that implements the matrix solution. The first line shows the node equation in matrix form. We solve this matrix equation by first highlighting the admittance matrix **Y** and then selecting the **Symbolic/MatrixOperation/InvertMatrix** command followed by a **Symbolic/Simplify command**. Selecting these commands from the menu bar causes Mathcad to produce the inverse shown in the second line of Figure 10–33. Using standard cut-and-paste operations, we form the ma-

FIGURE 10–33

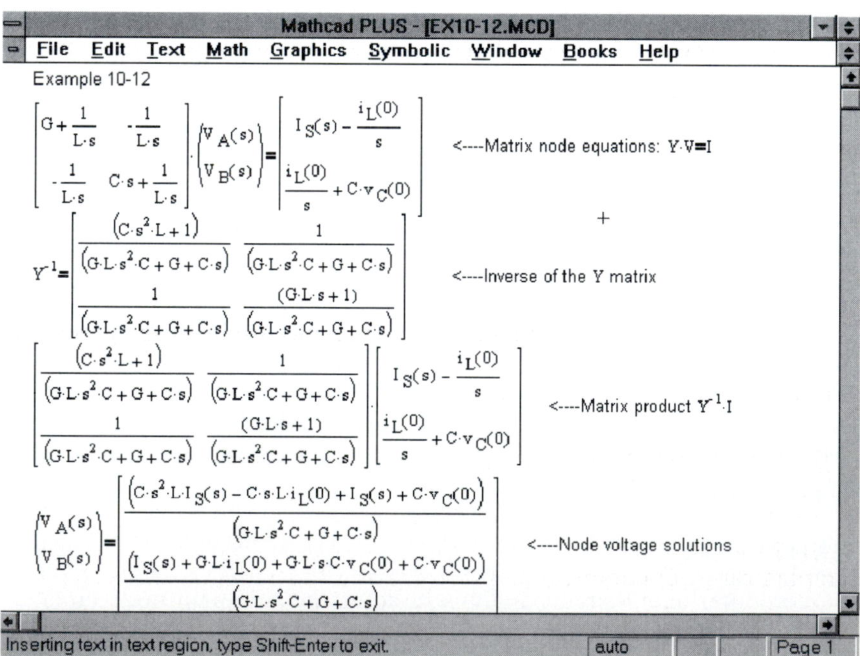

trix product $\mathbf{Y}^{-1}\mathbf{I}$ shown in the third line. Highlighting this matrix product and selecting a **Symbolic/Evaluate** followed by a **Symbolic/Simplify** command produces the matrix solution for $V_A(s)$ and $V_B(s)$ in the last line. Note that the Mathcad's matrix solution agrees with the Cramer's rule results given in Eqs. (10–35) and (10–36). ■

EXAMPLE 10–13

Find the zero-state component for $v_B(t)$ in Eq. (10–36) for $R = 1\ \text{k}\Omega$, $L = 0.5$ H, $C = 1\ \mu$F, and $i_S(t) = 10u(t)$ mA.

SOLUTION:

To find the required response, we insert $I_S(s) = 10^{-2}/s$ and the numerical values of circuit parameters in the zero-state component in Eq. (10–36):

$$V_B(s) = \frac{10^{-2}/s}{5 \times 10^{-10}s^2 + 10^{-6}s + 10^{-3}} = \frac{2 \times 10^7}{s(s^2 + 2 \times 10^3 s + 2 \times 10^6)}$$

$$= \frac{2 \times 10^7}{s(s + 1000 - j1000)(s + 1000 + j1000)} \quad \text{V-s}$$

The response transform has three poles: a forced pole at $s = 0$ and two natural poles at $s = -1000 \pm j1000$. The forced pole comes from the step function input, and the two natural poles are zeros of the circuit determinant. Expanding this rational function into partial fractions yields

$$V_B(s) = \frac{10}{s} + \frac{(10/\sqrt{2})\,e^{+j135°}}{s + 1000 - j1000} + \frac{(10/\sqrt{2})\,e^{-j135°}}{s + 1000 + j1000}$$

Taking the inverse transforms of each term from Tables 9–2 and 9–3 yields the required zero-state response waveform:

$$v_B(t) = 10\,u(t) + [10\sqrt{2}\,e^{-1000t}\cos(1000t + 135°)]u(t) \quad \text{V}$$

The step function in $v_B(t)$ is the forced response caused by the forced pole at $s = 0$. The damped cosine is the natural response determined by the natural poles in $V_B(s)$.

Figure 10–34 shows a portion of a Quattro Pro spreadsheet that produces a plot of $v_B(t)$. Spreadsheets are useful for generating graphs, especially when we wish to compare experimental and analytical results. In Figure 10–34 we compare the foregoing analytical result with the results from a PSpice simulation of the circuit. The two results are in close agreement, as can be seen from the numerical data in columns B and C, or the overlay of PSpice data on the analytical curve.

APPLICATION NOTE: EXAMPLE 10–14

In s-domain circuit analysis and design, the location of complex poles is often specified in terms of the undamped natural frequency (ω_0) and damping ratio (ζ) parameters introduced in Chapter 7. Using these parameters, the standard form of a second-order factor is $s^2 + 2\,\zeta\,\omega_0 s + \omega_0^2$, which locates the poles at

FIGURE 10–34

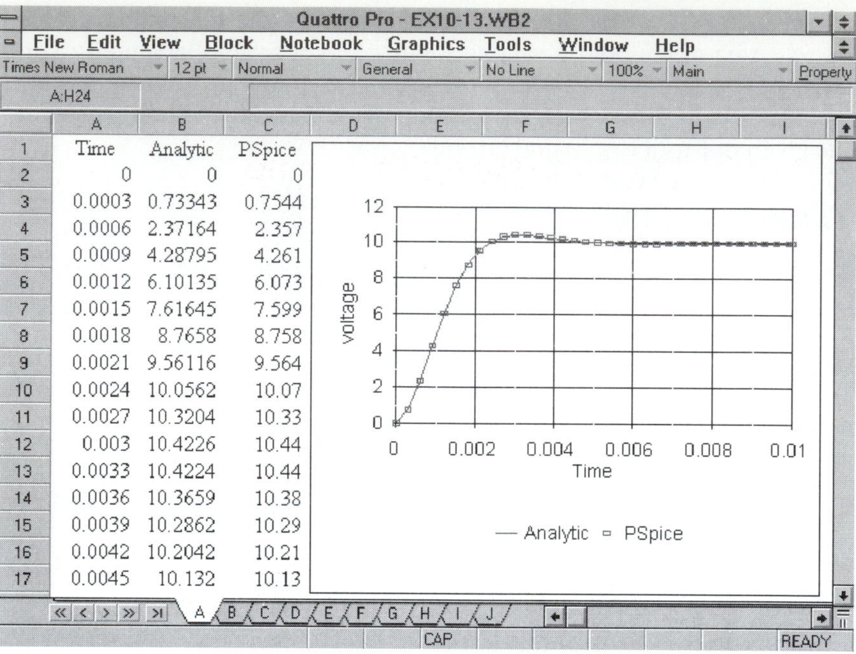

	A	B	C
1	Time	Analytic	PSpice
2	0	0	0
3	0.0003	0.73343	0.7544
4	0.0006	2.37164	2.357
5	0.0009	4.28795	4.261
6	0.0012	6.10135	6.073
7	0.0015	7.61645	7.599
8	0.0018	8.7658	8.758
9	0.0021	9.56116	9.564
10	0.0024	10.0562	10.07
11	0.0027	10.3204	10.33
12	0.003	10.4226	10.44
13	0.0033	10.4224	10.44
14	0.0036	10.3659	10.38
15	0.0039	10.2862	10.29
16	0.0042	10.2042	10.21
17	0.0045	10.132	10.13

$$s_{1,2} = \omega_0(-\zeta \pm \sqrt{\zeta^2 - 1})$$

The quantity under the radical depends only on the damping ratio ζ. When $\zeta > 1$ the quantity is positive and the two poles are real and distinct, and the second-order factor becomes the product of two first-order terms. If $\zeta = 1$ the quantity under the radical vanishes and there is a double pole as $s = -\omega_0$. If $\zeta < 1$ the quantity under the radical is negative and the two roots are complex conjugates.

The location of complex poles is also defined in terms of the two natural frequency parameters α and β. Using these parameters, the poles are at $s_{1,2} = -\alpha \pm j\beta$, and the standard form of a second-order factor is $(s + \alpha)^2 + \beta^2$.

In s-domain circuit design, we often need to convert from one set of parameters to the other. First, equating their standard forms

$$s^2 + 2\alpha s + \alpha^2 + \beta^2 = s^2 + 2\zeta\omega_0 s + \omega_0^2$$

and then equating the coefficients of like powers of s yields

$$\omega_0 = \sqrt{\alpha^2 + \beta^2} \quad \text{and} \quad \zeta = \frac{\alpha}{\sqrt{\alpha^2 + \beta^2}}$$

and conversely

$$\alpha = \zeta\omega_0 \quad \text{and} \quad \beta = \omega_0\sqrt{1 - \zeta^2}$$

Figure 10–35 shows how these parameters define the locations of complex poles in the s plane. The natural frequency parameters α and β define the rectangular coordinates of the poles. In a sense, the parameters

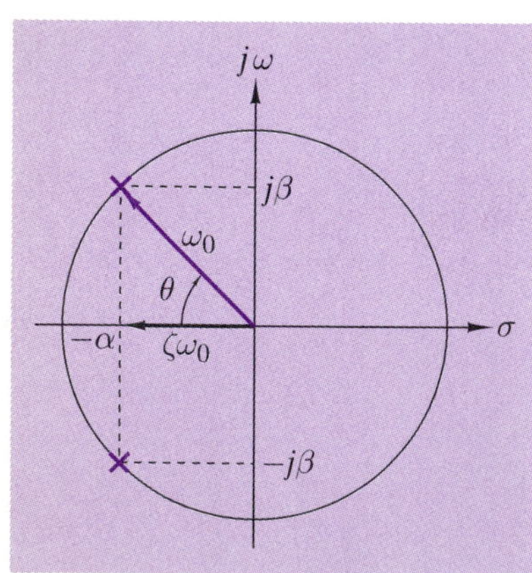

FIGURE 10–35 *s-Plane geometry relating α and β to ζ and ω_0.*

ω_0 and ζ define the corresponding polar coordinates. The parameter ω_0 is the radial distance from the origin to the poles. The angle θ is determined by the damping ratio ζ alone, since $\theta = \cos^{-1}\zeta$.

D DESIGN EXAMPLE 10–15

Complex Pole Placement Design

The circuit in Figure 10–36 is designed to produce a pair of complex poles. To simplify production, the final design must have equal element values $R_1 = R_2 = R_3 = R$ and $C_1 = C_2 = C$. Select the values of R, C, and the gain μ so that the circuit has natural poles defined by $\zeta = 0.5$ and $\omega_0 = 1000$ rad/s.

FIGURE 10–36

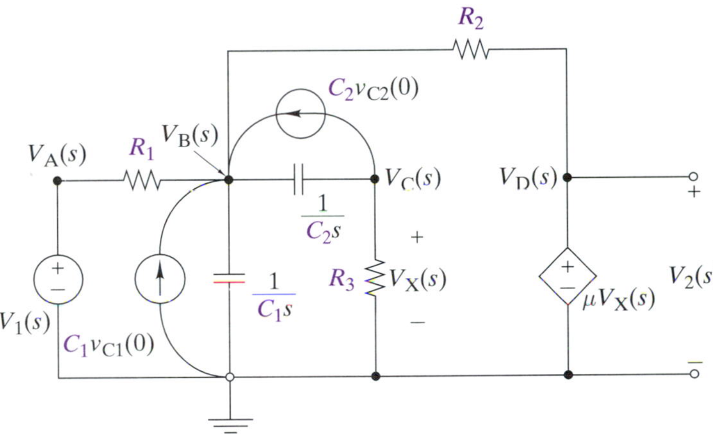

SOLUTION:

In Example 10–11 we formulated the following node-voltage equations for this circuit:

$$(C_1s + C_2s + G_1 + G_2)V_B(s) - (C_2s + \mu G_2)\,V_C(s)$$
$$= G_1V_1(s) + C_1v_{C_1}(0) + C_2v_{C_2}(0)$$
$$-C_2sV_B(s) + (C_2s + G_3)\,V_C(s) = -C_2v_{C_2}(0)$$

The natural poles are zeros of the circuit determinant:

$$\Delta(s) = \begin{vmatrix} C_1s + C_2s + G_1 + G_2 & -C_2s - \mu G_2 \\ -C_2s & C_2s + G_3 \end{vmatrix}$$
$$= C_1\,C_2s^2 + (C_1G_3 + C_2G_1 + C_2G_2 + C_2G_3 - \mu G_2C_2)s$$
$$+ G_1G_3 + G_2G_3$$

For equal resistances $R_1 = R_2 = R_3 = R$ and equal capacitances $C_1 = C_2 = C$, the circuit determinant reduces to

$$\frac{\Delta(s)}{C^2} = s^2 + \frac{4-\mu}{RC}s + \frac{2}{(RC)^2}$$

Comparing this second-order factor to the standard form $s^2 + 2\zeta\,\omega_0 s + \omega_0^2$ yields the following design constraints:

$$\omega_0 = \frac{\sqrt{2}}{RC} = 1000 \quad \text{and} \quad \zeta = \frac{4 - \mu}{\sqrt{2}} = 0.5$$

These constraints yield $RC = \sqrt{2} \times 10^{-3}$ and $\mu = 4 - \sqrt{2} = 2.586$. Selecing $R = 10\ \text{k}\Omega$ makes $C = 141.4\ \text{nF}$. ■

Exercise 10–11

(a) Solve for the determinant of the circuit in Figure 10–31 using the node equations in Exercise 10–7.
(b) Solve for the zero-state component of $V_B(s)$.

Answers:

$$\text{(a) } \Delta(s) = \frac{(G_1 + G_2)\,LCs^2 + (G_1G_2L + C)s + G_2}{Ls}$$

$$\text{(b) } V_B(s) = \left[\frac{(G_1 + G_2)LCs^2 + G_1G_2Ls}{(G_1 + G_2)LCs^2 + (G_1G_2L + C)s + G_2}\right] V_S(s)$$

Exercise 10–12

(a) Solve for the determinant of the circuit in Figure 10–32 using the node equations in Exercise 10–9.
(b) Solve for the zero-state component of $V_D(s)$.

Answers:

$$\text{(a) } \Delta(s) = C_1C_2s^2 + (G_1C_1 + G_2C_1 + G_2C_2 - \mu G_2C_2)s + G_1G_2$$

$$\text{(b) } V_D(s) = \left[\frac{\mu G_1G_2}{C_1C_2s^2 + (G_1C_1 + G_2C_1 + G_2C_2 - \mu G_2C_2)s + G_1G_2}\right] V_S(s)$$

EXAMPLE 10–16

(a) Formulate s-domain node-voltage equations for the OP AMP circuit in Figure 10–37(a).
(b) Solve for the s-domain input-output relationship between the input $V_S(s)$ and the zero-state component of the output $V_O(s)$
(c) Solve for the zero-state output $v_O(t)$ when the input is a unit step function $v_S(t) = u(t)$.

SOLUTION:

(a) Figure 10–37(b) shows the transformed circuit in the s-domain. Node equations are not required at nodes A and D because the selected reference node makes $V_A(s) = V_S(s)$ and $V_D(s)$ is the OP AMP output. By inspection, the equations at nodes B and C are

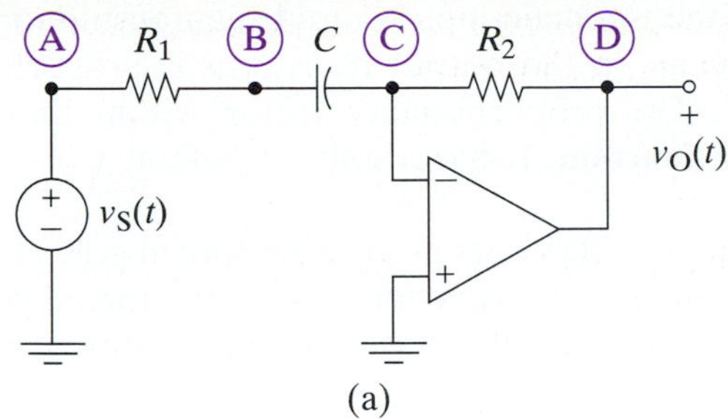

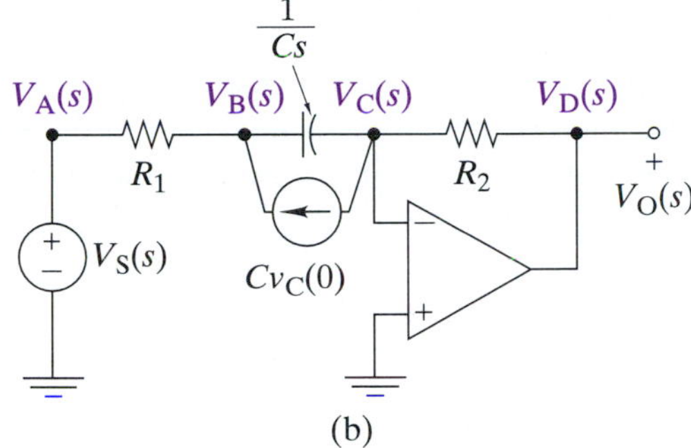

FIGURE 10–37

$$\text{Node B:} \quad -G_1V_A(s) + (G_1 + Cs)V_B(s) - CsV_C(s) = Cv_C(0)$$

$$\text{Node C:} \quad -CsV_B(s) + (G_2 + Cs)V_C(s) - G_2V_D(s) = -Cv_C(0)$$

where $G_1 = 1/R_1$ and $G_2 = 1/R_2$. The preceding result yields two node equations in four node voltages. However, as noted previously, $V_A(s) = V_S(s)$ and $V_D(s) = V_O(s)$. The OP AMP voltage constraint requires $V_C(s) = 0$ since the noninverting input is grounded. Inserting the conditions $V_A(s) = V_S(s)$ and $V_C(s) = 0$ reduces node-voltage equations to the following form:

$$\text{Node B:} \quad (G_1 + Cs)V_B(s) = Cv_C(0) + G_1V_S(s)$$

$$\text{Node C:} \quad -CsV_B(s) - G_2V_O(s) = -Cv_C(0)$$

We now have two equations in two unknowns $V_B(s)$ and $V_O(s)$.

(b) For the zero-state response the initial condition $v_C(0) = 0$. Solving the node B equation for $V_B(s)$ in terms of $V_S(s)$,

$$V_B(s) = \left[\frac{G_1}{G_1 + Cs}\right] V_S(s)$$

Substituting this results into the node C equation and solving for $V_O(s)$ yields

$$V_O(s) = \left[\frac{G_1Cs/G_2}{G_1 + Cs}\right] V_S(s)$$

$$= -\left[\frac{R_2}{R_1}\frac{s}{s + 1/R_1C}\right] V_S(s) \quad \text{V-s}$$

This equation is the s-domain input-output relationship for the circuit. The circuit is linear, so the output transform is proportional to the input transform. The proportionality factor within the brackets is called a **network function**. It has a natural pole at $s = -1/R_1C$ and a zero at $s = 0$.

(c) A step function input $V_S(s) = 1/s$ produces a forced pole at $s = 0$. However, the zero in the network function cancels the forced pole. The net result is that the zero-state output contains only a natural pole and has the form

$$v_O(t) = \mathscr{L}^{-1}\left\{-\frac{R_2}{R_1}\frac{1}{s + 1/R_1C}\right\} = -\left[\frac{R_2}{R_1}e^{-t/R_1C}\right]u(t) \quad \text{V}$$

The general principle is that the forced response of a circuit can be zero even when the input driving force is not zero. In the s domain this occurs when the network function has a zero at the same location as the forced pole. ■

10–5 MESH-CURRENT ANALYSIS IN THE S DOMAIN

We can use the mesh-current method only when the circuit can be drawn on a flat surface without crossovers. Such planar circuits have special loops called meshes that are defined as closed paths that do not enclose any elements. The mesh-current variables are the loop currents assigned to each mesh in a planar circuit. Because of KCL the current through any two-terminal element can be expressed as the difference of two adjacent mesh currents. This fundamental property of mesh currents, together with the element impedances, allows us to write KVL constraints around each of the meshes.

For example, in Figure 10–38 the sum of voltages around mesh A can be written as

$$Z_1(s)I_A(s) + Z_3[I_A(s) - I_C(s)] - V_{S1}(s) + Z_2[I_A(s) - I_B(s)] + V_{S2}(s) = 0$$

Rewriting this equation with unknown mesh currents grouped on the left and inputs on the right yields

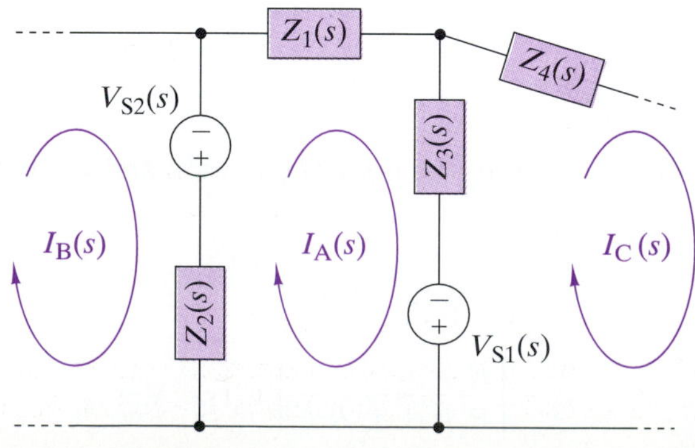

FIGURE 10–38 An example mesh.

$$(Z_1 + Z_2 + Z_3)I_A(s) - Z_2I_B(s) - Z_3I_C(s) = V_{S1}(s) - V_{S2}(s)$$

This equation displays the following pattern. The unknowns are the mesh-current transforms $I_A(s)$, $I_B(s)$, and $I_C(s)$. The coefficient $[Z_1(s) + Z_2(s) + Z_3(s)]$ of $I_A(s)$ is the sum of the impedances of the elements in mesh A. The coefficients $[Z_2(s)]$ of $I_B(s)$ and $[Z_3(s)]$ of $I_C(s)$ are the impedances common to mesh A and the other meshes. Finally, $V_{S1}(s) - V_{S2}(s)$ is the sum of the source voltages around mesh A. These observations suggest that we can write node-voltage equations for *s*-domain circuits by inspection, just as we did with resistive circuits.

The formulation approach just outlined assumes that there are no current sources in the circuit. When writing mesh-current equations, we select the voltage source model to represent the initial conditions. If the circuit contains dependent or independent current sources, they can be treated using the following methods:

Method 1: If there is an admittance in parallel with the current source, use a source transformation to convert it into an equivalent voltage source.

Method 2: Draw the circuit diagram so that only one mesh current circulates through the current source. This mesh current is then determined by the source current.

Method 3: Create a supermesh for any current source that cannot be handled by methods 1 or 2.

Some circuits may require more than one of these methods.

The following examples illustrate the mesh-current method of *s*-domain circuit analysis.

EXAMPLE 10–17

(a) Formulate mesh-current equations for the circuit in Figure 10–39(a).
(b) Solve for the zero-input component of $I_A(s)$ and $I_B(s)$.
(c) Find the zero-input responses $i_A(t)$ and $i_B(t)$ for $R_1 = 200\ \Omega$, $R_2 = 300\ \Omega$, $L_1 = 50$ mH, and $L_2 = 100$ mH.

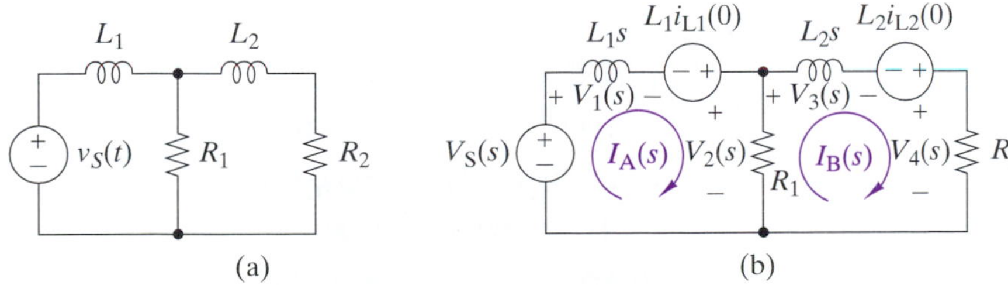

FIGURE 10–39

SOLUTION:

(a) Figure 10–39(b) shows the circuit transformed into the *s* domain. In transforming the circuit we used the voltage source model for the initial conditions. The net result is that the transformed circuit contains only voltage sources. The sum of voltages around meshes A and B can be written as

$$\text{Mesh A:}\ -V_S(s) + L_1 s I_A(s) - L_1 i_{L_1}(0) + R_1[I_A(s) - I_B(s)] = 0$$

$$\text{Mesh B:}\ R_1[I_B(s) - I_A(s)] + L_2 s I_B(s) - L_2 i_{L_2}(0) + R_2 I_B(s) = 0$$

Rearranging these equation in standard form yields

$$\text{Mesh A:}\qquad (L_1 s + R_1)I_A(s) - R_1 I_B(s) = V_S(s) + L_1 i_{L_1}(0)$$

$$\text{Mesh B:}\ -R_1 I_A(s) + (L_2 s + R_1 + R_2)I_B(s) = L_2 i_{L_2}(0)$$

These s-domain circuit equations are two linear algebraic equations in the two unknown mesh currents $I_A(s)$ and $I_B(s)$.

(b) To solve for the mesh equations, we first find the circuit determinant:

$$\Delta(s) = \begin{vmatrix} L_1 s + R_1 & -R_1 \\ -R_1 & L_2 s + R_1 + R_2 \end{vmatrix}$$

$$= L_1 L_2 s^2 + (R_1 L_2 + R_1 L_1 + R_2 L_1)s + R_1 R_2$$

To find the zero-input component of $I_A(s)$, we let $V_S(s) = 0$ and use Cramer's rule:

$$I_A(s) = \frac{\begin{vmatrix} L_1 i_{L_1}(0) & -R_1 \\ L_2 i_{L_2}(0) & L_2 s + R_1 + R_2 \end{vmatrix}}{\Delta(s)}$$

$$= \frac{(L_2 s + R_1 + R_2)L_1 i_{L_1}(0) + R_1 L_2 i_{L_2}(0)}{L_1 L_2 s^2 + (R_1 L_2 + R_1 L_1 + R_2 L_1)s + R_1 R_2}$$

Similarly, the zero-input component in $I_B(s)$ is

$$I_B = \frac{\begin{vmatrix} L_1 s + R_1 & L_1 i_{L_1}(0) \\ -R_1 & L_2 i_{L_2}(0) \end{vmatrix}}{\Delta(s)}$$

$$= \frac{(L_1 s + R_1)L_2 i_{L_2}(0) + R_1 L_1 i_{L_1}(0)}{L_1 L_2 s^2 + (R_1 L_2 + R_1 L_1 + R_2 L_1)s + R_1 R_2}$$

(c) To find the time-domain response, we insert the numerical parameters into the preceding expressions to obtain

$$I_A(s) = \frac{(0.005s + 15)i_{L_1}(0) + 10 i_{L_2}(0)}{0.005s^2 + 250s + 20{,}000}$$

$$= \frac{(s + 3000)i_{L_1}(0) + 2000\, i_{L_2}(0)}{(s + 1000)\,(s + 4000)}$$

$$I_B(s) = \frac{(0.005s + 100)i_{L_2}(0) + 5 i_{L_1}(0)}{0.005s^2 + 250s + 20{,}000}$$

$$= \frac{(s + 2000)i_{L_2}(0) + 1000 i_{L_1}(0)}{(s + 1000)\,(s + 4000)}$$

The circuit has natural poles at $s = -1000$ and -4000 rad/s. Expanding by partial fractions yields

$$I_A(s) = \frac{2}{3} \times \frac{i_{L_1}(0) + i_{L_2}(0)}{s + 1000} + \frac{1}{3} \times \frac{i_{L_1}(0) - 2i_{L_2}(0)}{s + 4000} \quad \text{A-s}$$

$$I_B(s) = \frac{1}{3} \times \frac{i_{L_1}(0) + i_{L_2}(0)}{s + 1000} - \frac{1}{3} \times \frac{i_{L_1}(0) - 2i_{L_2}(0)}{s + 4000} \quad \text{A-s}$$

The inverse transforms of these expansions are the required zero-state response waveforms:

$$i_A(t) = \left[\frac{2}{3}[i_{L_1}(0) + i_{L_2}(0)]e^{-1000t} + \frac{1}{3}[i_{L_1}(0) - 2i_{L_2}(0)]e^{-4000t}\right] u(t) \quad \text{A}$$

$$i_B(t) = \left[\frac{1}{3}[i_{L_1}(0) + i_{L_2}(0)]e^{-1000t} - \frac{1}{3}[i_{L_1}(0) - 2i_{L_2}(0)]e^{-4000t}\right] u(t) \quad \text{A}$$

Notice that if the initial conditions are $i_{L1}(0) = -i_{L2}(0)$, then both $I_A(s)$ and $I_B(s)$ have a zero at $s = -1000$. This zero effectively cancels the natural pole at $s = -1000$. As a result, this pole has zero residue in both partial fraction expansions, and the corresponding terms disappear from the time-domain responses. Likewise, if the initial conditions are $i_{L_1}(0) = 2i_{L_2}(0)$, then both $I_A(s)$ and $I_B(s)$ have a zero at $s = -4000$, and the natural pole at $s = -4000$ disappears in the s-domain responses. The general principle is that all of the circuit's natural poles may not be present in a given response. When this happens the response transform has a zero at the same location as a natural pole, and we say that the natural pole is not observable in the specified response.

EXAMPLE 10–18

(a) Formulate mesh-current equations for the circuit in Figure 10–40(a).
(b) Solve for the zero-input component of $i_A(t)$ for $i_L(0) = 0$, $v_C(0) = 10$ V, $L = 250$ mH, $C = 1$ μF and $R = 1$ kΩ.

SOLUTION:

(a) Figure 10–40(a) is the s-domain circuit used in Example 10–10 to develop node equations. In this circuit each current source is connected in parallel with an impedance. Source transformations convert these current sources into the equivalent voltage sources shown in Figure 10–40(b). The circuit in Figure 10–40(b) is a series RLC circuit of the type treated in Chapter 7. By inspection, the KVL equation for the single mesh in this circuit is

$$\left[R + Ls + \frac{1}{Cs}\right] I_A(s) = RI_S(s) + Li_L(0) - \frac{v_C(0)}{s}$$

The circuit determinant is the factor $R + Ls + 1/Cs = (LCs^2 + RCs + 1)/Cs$. The zeros of the circuit determinant are roots of the quadratic equation $LCs^2 + RCs + 1 = 0$, which we recognize as the characteristic equation of

FIGURE 10–40

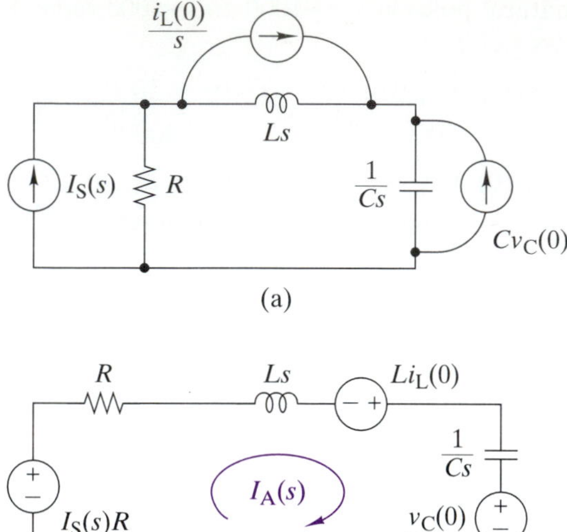

a series RLC circuit. In Chapter 7 we called these roots natural frequencies. Thus, the natural poles of the circuit are its natural frequencies.

(b) Solving the mesh equation for the zero-input component yields

$$I_A(s) = \frac{LCsi_L(0) - Cv_C(0)}{LCs^2 + RCs + 1} \quad \text{A-s}$$

Inserting the given numerical values produces

$$I_A(s) = -\frac{10^{-5}}{0.25 \times 10^{-6}s^2 + 10^{-3}s + 1} = -\frac{40}{s^2 + 4 \times 10^3 s + 4 \times 10^6}$$

$$= -\frac{40}{(s + 2000)^2} \quad \text{A}$$

The zero-state response has two natural poles, both located at $s = -2000$. The inverse transform of $I_A(s)$ is a damped ramp waveform:

$$i_A(t) = -[40te^{-2000t}]\, u(t) \quad \text{A}$$

The damped ramp response indicates a critically damped second-order circuit. The minus sign means the direction of the actual current is opposite to the reference mark assigned to $I_A(s)$ in Figure 10–40. This sign makes sense physically since the capacitor initial condition source in Figure 10–40(b) tends to drive current in a direction opposite to the assigned reference mark. ■

EXAMPLE 10–19

(a) Formulate mesh-current equations for the coupled coil circuit in Figure 10–41(a).

(b) Find the input impedance seen by the voltage source $V_1(s)$ in Figure 10–41(b).

FIGURE 10–41

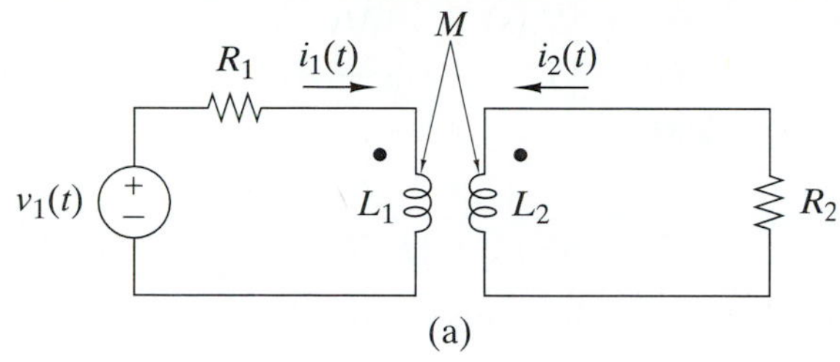

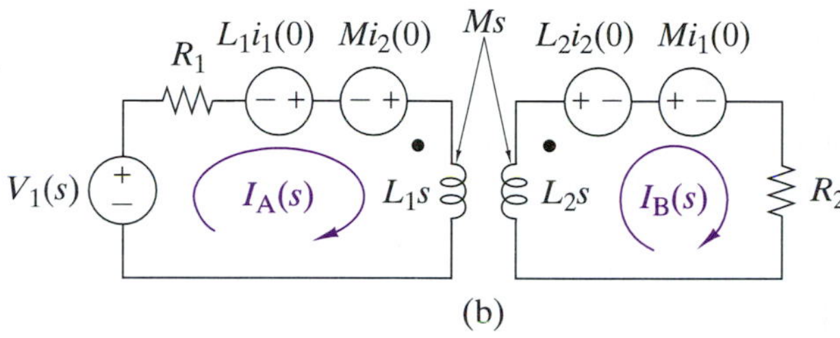

SOLUTION:

(a) The transformed circuit in Figure 10–41(b) uses the s-domain model developed in Example 10–2. This circuit contains only voltage sources, so we proceed directly to formulating the mesh equations. The total impedances in meshes A and B are $R_1 + L_1s$ and $R_2 + L_2s$, respectively. The impedance common to meshes A and B is the mutual inductance Ms. By inspection, the mesh equations are

$$(L_1s + R_1)I_A(s) - MsI_B(s) = V_1(s) + L_1i_1(0) + Mi_2(0)$$
$$-MsI_A(s) + (L_2s + R_2)I_B(s) = -L_2i_2(0) - Mi_1(0)$$

The negative sign on the mutual inductance term follows the dot convention discussed in Chapter 6. The negative sign is proper because reference direction for the mesh current $I_A(s)$ is directed toward a dot while reference direction for $I_B(s)$ is directed away from a dot. The signs of the initial condition terms depend on the reference directions originally assigned to $i_1(t)$ and $i_2(t)$ in Figure 10–40(a).

(b) We first find the circuit determinant:

$$\Delta(s) = \begin{vmatrix} L_1s + R_1 & -Ms \\ -Ms & L_2s + R_2 \end{vmatrix}$$

$$= (L_1L_2 - M^2)s^2 + (L_1R_2 + L_2R_1)s + R_1R_2$$

In general, impedance is the proportionality factor relating transform voltage and transform current when all initial conditions are zero. Hence to find the input impedance the circuit must be in the zero state. Using Cramer's rule to find the zero-state component of $I_A(s)$,

$$I_A(s) = \frac{\Delta_A(s)}{\Delta(s)} = \frac{\begin{vmatrix} V_1(s) & -Ms \\ 0 & L_2s + R_2 \end{vmatrix}}{\Delta(s)}$$

$$= \frac{(L_2s + R_2)V_1(s)}{(L_1L_2 - M^2)s^2 + (L_1R_2 + L_2R_1)s + R_1R_2}$$

The input impedance of the coupled coil circuit is

$$Z_{IN}(s) = \frac{V_1(s)}{I_A(s)} = \frac{(L_1L_2 - M^2)s^2 + (L_1R_2 + L_2R_1)s + R_1R_2}{L_2s + R_2} \quad \Omega$$

In Chapter 6 we showed that perfect coupling occurs when the coupling coefficient $k^2 = M^2/L_1L_2$ is unity. Perfect coupling means that $M^2 = L_1L_2$ and the input impedance reduces to

$$Z_{IN}(s) = \frac{(L_1R_2 + L_2R_1)s + R_1R_2}{L_2s + R_2} \quad \Omega$$

■

D DESIGN EXAMPLE 10–20

Triple Pole Placement Design

Select the element values in Figure 10–42 so that the circuit has a real natural pole at $s = -20$ krad/s and a pair of complex poles with $\zeta = 0.5$ and $\omega_0 = 20$ krad/s.

FIGURE 10–42

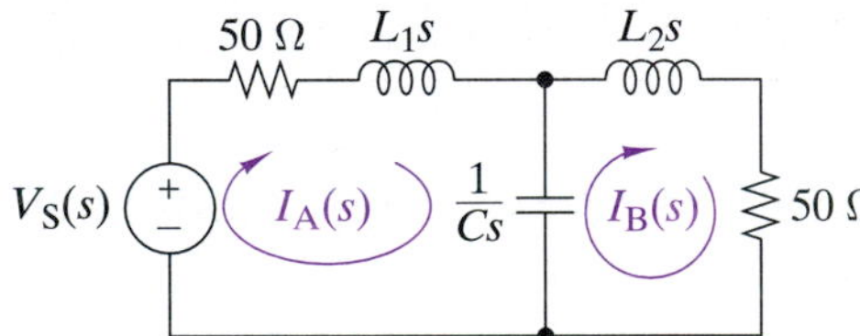

SOLUTION:

To locate the circuit poles, we first write two mesh equations:

$$\text{Mesh A:} \quad \left(50 + \frac{1}{Cs} + L_1s\right) I_A(s) - \frac{1}{Cs} I_B(s) = V_S(s)$$

$$\text{Mesh B:} \quad -\frac{1}{Cs} I_A(s) + \left(50 + \frac{1}{Cs} + L_2s\right) I_B(s) = 0$$

The circuit determinant is

$$\Delta(s) = \left(50 + \frac{1}{Cs} + L_1s\right)\left(50 + \frac{1}{Cs} + L_2s\right) - \left(\frac{1}{Cs}\right)^2$$

$$= \frac{L_1L_2Cs^3 + (50L_1C + 50\,L_2C)s^2 + (L_1 + L_2 + 2500\,C)s + 100}{Cs}$$

The circuit characteristic equation in the numerator of $\Delta(s)$ can be placed in the following form:

$$q(s) = s^3 + \frac{(50L_1 + 50L_2)}{L_1L_2}s^2 + \frac{(L_1 + L_2 + 2500C)}{L_1L_2C}s + \frac{100}{L_1L_2C}$$

To have the required pole positions, the circuit characteristic equation must have the form

$$q(s) = (s + 20{,}000)\,(s^2 + 20{,}000s + 20{,}000^2)$$
$$= s^3 + 4 \times 10^4 s^2 + 8 \times 10^8 s + 8 \times 10^{12}$$

Comparing the circuit's symbolic equation with the required polynomial leads to the following design constraints:

$$\frac{50L_1 + 50L_2}{L_1L_2} = 4 \times 10^4 \qquad \frac{L_1 + L_2 + 2500C}{L_1L_2C} = 8 \times 10^8$$

$$\frac{100}{L_1L_2C} = 8 \times 10^{12}$$

Figure 10–43 shows a Mathcad worksheet that solves these three nonlinear equations for required element values. To two significant figures these values are $L_1 = L_2 = 2.5$ mH and $C = 2$ μF. In this example we can adjust the circuit parameters to achieve the specified pole locations. This may not always be possible. ■

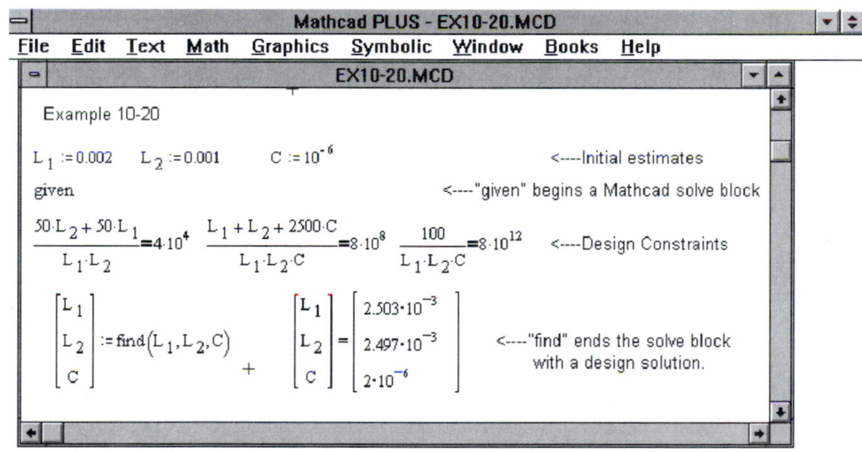

Exercise 10–13

(a) Formulate mesh-current equations for the circuit in Figure 10–44. Assume that the initial conditions are zero.

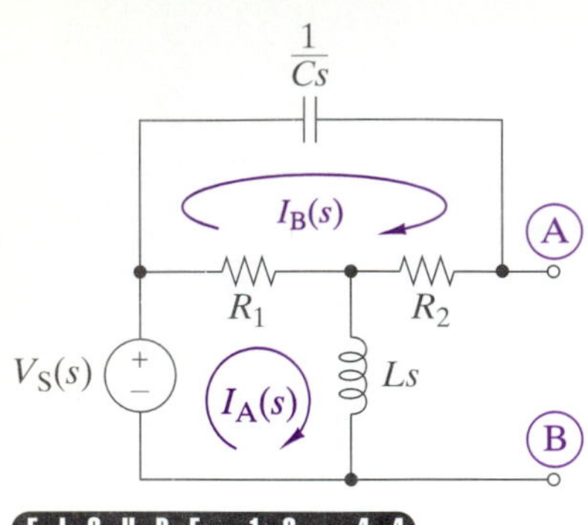

FIGURE 10–44

(b) Find the circuit determinant.
(c) Solve for the zero-state component of $I_B(s)$.

Answers:

(a) $$\begin{cases} (R_1 + Ls)I_A(s) - R_1 I_B(s) = V_S(s) \\ -R_1 I_A(s) + (R_1 + R_2 + 1/Cs)I_B(s) = 0 \end{cases}$$

(b) $$\Delta(s) = \frac{(R_1 + R_2)LCs^2 + (R_1R_2C + L)s + R_1}{Cs}$$

(c) $$I_B(s) = \frac{R_1 Cs V_S(s)}{(R_1 + R_2)LCs^2 + (R_1R_2C + L)s + R_1}$$

Exercise 10–14

Formulate mesh-current equations for the circuit in Figure 10–44 when a resistor R_3 is connected between nodes A and B. Assume that the initial conditions are zero.

Answer:

$$(R_1 + Ls)I_A(s) - R_1 I_B(s) - LsI_C(s) = V_S(s)$$

$$-R_1 I_A(s) + \left(R_1 + R_2 + \frac{1}{Cs}\right)I_B(s) - R_2 I_C(s) = 0$$

$$-LsI_A(s) - R_2 I_B(s) + (R_2 + R_3 + Ls)I_C(s) = 0$$

10–6 SUMMARY OF s-DOMAIN CIRCUIT ANALYSIS

At this point we review our progress and put *s*-domain circuit analysis into perspective. We have shown that linear circuits can be transformed from the time domain into the *s* domain. In this domain KCL and KVL apply to transforms and the passive element *i*–*v* characteristics become impedances with series or parallel initial condition sources. In relatively simple circuits we can use basic analysis methods, such as reduction, superposition, and voltage/current division. For more complicated circuits we use systematic procedures, such as the node-voltage or mesh-current methods, to solve for the circuit response.

In theory, we can perform *s*-domain analysis on circuits of any complexity. In practice, the algebraic burden of hand computations gets out of hand for circuits with more than three or four nodes or meshes. Of what practical use is an analysis method that becomes impractical at such a modest level of circuit complexity? Why not just appeal to computer-aided analysis tools like PSpice or MICRO-CAP in the first place?

Unquestionably, large-scale circuits are best handled by computer-aided analysis. Computer-aided analysis is probably the right approach even for small-scale circuits when numerical values for all circuit parameters are known and the desired end product is a plot or numerical listing of the response waveform. Simply put, s-domain circuit analysis is not a particularly efficient algorithm for generating numerical response data.

The purpose of s-domain circuit analysis is to gain insight into circuit behavior, not to grind out particular response waveforms. In this regard s-domain circuit analysis complements programs like PSpice. It offers a way of characterizing circuits in very general terms. It provides guidelines that allow us to use computer-aided analysis tools intelligently. Some of the useful general principles derived in this chapter are the following.

The response transform $Y(s)$[1] is a rational function whose partial fraction expansion leads directly to a response waveform of the form

$$y(t) = \sum_{j=1}^{\text{number of poles}} k_j e^{p_j t}$$

where k_j is the residue of the pole in $Y(s)$ located at $s = -p_j$. The location of the poles tells us a great deal about the form of the response. The pair of conjugate complex poles in Example 10–13 produced a damped sine waveform, the two distinct real poles in Example 10–17 produced exponential waveforms, and the double pole in Example 10–18 led to a damped ramp waveform. The general principle illustrated is as follows:

The poles of* Y(s) *are either real or complex conjugates. Simple real poles lead to exponentials, double real poles lead to a damped ramp, and complex conjugate poles lead to damped sinusoids.

The poles in $Y(s)$ are introduced either by the circuit itself (natural poles) or by the input driving force (forced poles).

The natural poles are zeros of the circuit determinant and lead to the natural response. The forced poles are poles of the input* X(s) *and lead to the forced response.

Figure 10–45 shows the waveforms corresponding to different pole locations in the s plane. Poles in the right half of the s-plane produce waveforms whose amplitudes increase without bound, poles on the j-axis produce waveforms with constant amplitudes, and poles in the left half plane have amplitudes that decay to zero. A linear circuit is said to be stable if its natural response decays to zero as time marches on. As a result, we say that

A circuit is stable if all of its natural poles are located in the left half of the* s *plane.

Some natural poles may be canceled by zeros in $Y(s)$, and the corresponding waveforms do not appear in the waveform $y(t)$.

---

1 In this context $Y(s)$ is not an admittance but the Laplace transform of the circuit output $y(t)$.

FIGURE 10–45 *Form of the natural response corresponding to different pole locations.*

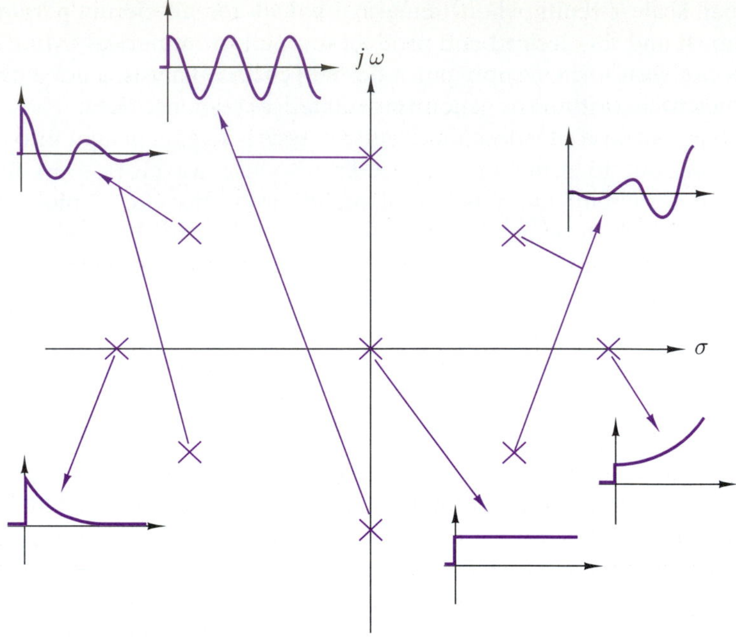

Natural poles of a circuit that are not present in* Y(s) *are said to be not observable.

Since natural poles play such a key role, we would like to find out how many to expect by simply examining the circuit. The following summary of this chapter's examples offers a hint:

EXAMPLE	NUMBER OF NATURAL POLES	NUMBER OF CAPACITORS	NUMBER OF INDUCTORS
10–5	1	0	1
10–9	1	1	0
10–13	2	1	1
10–14	2	2	0
10–16	2	0	2
10–19	3	1	2

These results suggest that the number of natural poles is equal to the number of energy storage elements in the circuit. This rule is a useful general guideline. There are exceptions, however, such as capacitors connected in parallel. As a result, the most we can say is that

The number of natural poles does not exceed the number of energy storage elements in a circuit.

In Design Examples 10–9, 10–14, and 10–19, we found that the parameters of a given circuit could be adjusted to produce specified locations for natural poles. This may not always be possible. That is, a given circuit may not be able to produce the specified pole locations no matter what element values we try. The general principle is as follows:

> ***The general s-domain circuit design problem is to create a circuit arrangement that produces specified natural poles.***

We address this type of design problem in the next chapter.

SUMMARY

- Kirchhoff's laws apply to voltage and current waveforms in the time domain and to the corresponding transforms in the s domain.
- The s-domain models for the passive elements include initial condition sources and the element impedance or admittance. Impedance is the proportionality factor in the expression $V(s) = Z(s)I(s)$ relating the voltage and current transforms. Admittance is the reciprocal of impedance.
- The impedances of the three passive elements are $Z_R(s) = R$, $Z_L(s) = Ls$, and $Z_C(s) = 1/Cs$.
- The s-domain circuit analysis techniques closely parallel the analysis methods developed for resistance circuits. Basic analysis techniques, such as circuit reduction, Thévenin's and Norton's theorems, the unit output method, or superposition, can be used in simple circuits. More complicated networks require a general approach, such as the node-voltage or mesh-current methods.
- Response transforms are rational functions whose poles are zeros of the circuit determinant or poles of the transform of the input driving forces. Poles introduced by the circuit determinant are called natural poles and lead to the natural response. Poles introduced by the input are called forced poles and lead to the forced response.
- In linear circuits, response transforms and waveforms can be separated into zero-state and zero-input components. The zero-state component is found by setting the initial capacitor voltages and inductor currents to zero. The zero-input component is found by setting all input driving forces to zero.
- The main purpose of s-domain circuit analysis is to gain insight into circuit performance without necessarily finding the time-domain response. The natural poles reveal the form, stability, and observability of the circuit's response. The number of natural poles is never greater than the number of energy storage elements in the circuit.
- The locations of the natural poles can be altered by adjusting circuit parameters. In some circuits there are limitations on the natural pole configuration that can be achieved by adjusting circuit parameters.

EN ROUTE OBJECTIVES AND ASSOCIATED PROBLEMS

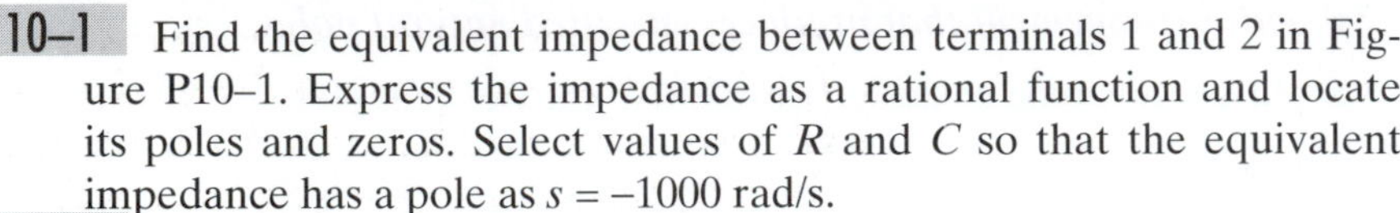

ERO 10–1 EQUIVALENT IMPEDANCE (SECTS. 10–1, 10–2)

Given a linear circuit, use series and parallel equivalence to find the equivalent impedance at a specified terminal pair. Select element values to obtain specified pole locations.

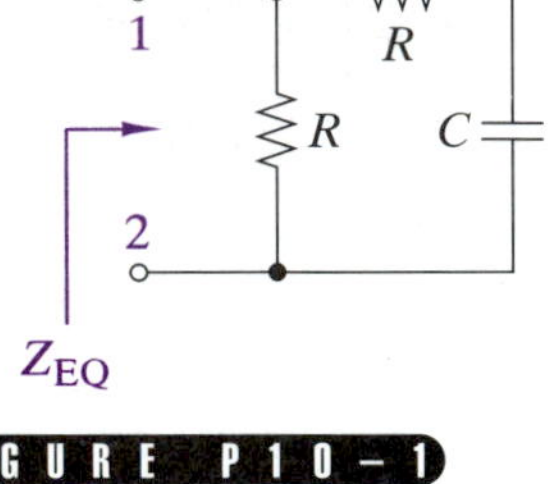

FIGURE P10–1

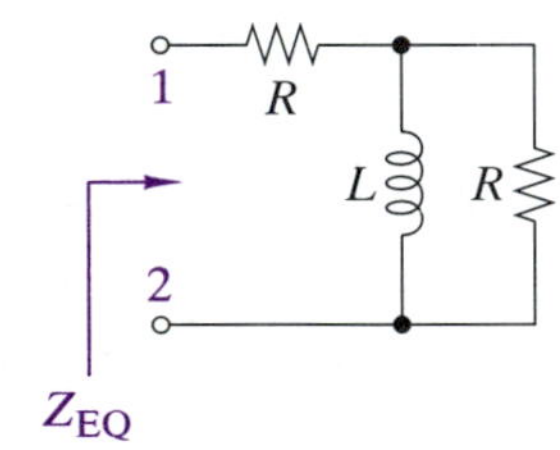

FIGURE P10–4

10–1 Find the equivalent impedance between terminals 1 and 2 in Figure P10–1. Express the impedance as a rational function and locate its poles and zeros. Select values of R and C so that the equivalent impedance has a pole as $s = -1000$ rad/s.

10–2 A 2-kΩ resistor and a 0.5-H inductor are connected in series. The series combination is connected in parallel with a 0.1-μF capacitor. Find the equivalent impedance of the combination. Express the impedance as a rational function and locate its poles and zeros.

10–3 A 100-nF capacitor and a 0.5-H inductor are connected in series. The series combination is connected in parallel with a 5-kΩ resistor. Find the equivalent impedance of the combination. Express the impedance as a rational function and locate its poles and zeros.

10–4 Find the equivalent impedance between terminals 1 and 2 in Figure P10–4. Express the impedance as a rational function and locate its poles and zeros. Select values of R and L so that the impedance has a pole at $s = -1000$ rad/s and $Z_{EQ}(0) = 5$ kΩ.

10–5 A 1-kΩ resistor and a 500-mH inductor are connected in parallel. The parallel combination is connected in series with a 0.25-μF capacitor. Find the equivalent impedance of the combination. Express the impedance as a rational function and locate its poles and zeros.

10–6 Find the equivalent impedance between terminals 1 and 2 in the circuit of Figure P10–6. Express the impedance as a rational function and locate its poles and zeros. Evaluate $Z_{EQ}(s)$ at $s = 0$ and $s = \infty$. Explain your results in terms of the impedances of the inductor and capacitor.

10–7 Find the equivalent impedance between terminals 1 and 2 in the circuit of Figure P10–7. Express the impedance as a rational function and locate its poles and zeros.

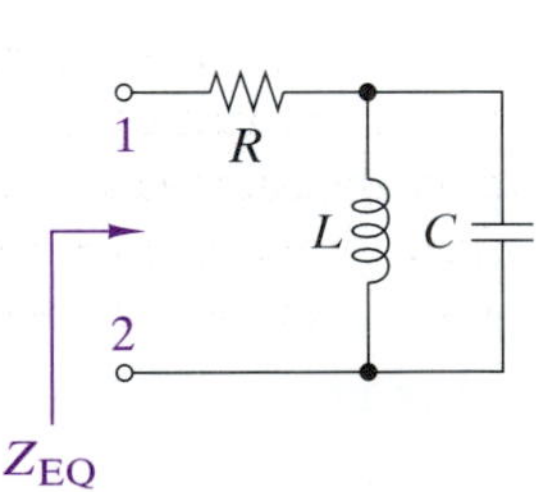

FIGURE P10–6

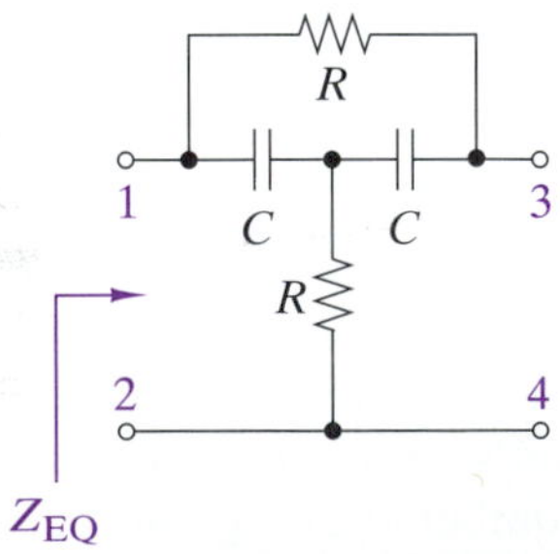

FIGURE P10–7

10–8 Find the equivalent impedance between terminals 1 and 2 in the circuit of Figure P10–7 when a short circuit is connected between terminals 3 and 4. Express the impedance as a rational function and locate its poles and zeros.

10–9 Find the equivalent impedance between terminals 1 and 2 in the circuit of Figure P10–9. Select values of R and C so that Z_{EQ} has a pole at $s = -1000$ rad/s. Identify the location of the other poles and zeros of Z_{EQ} for your values of R and C.

10–10 Find the equivalent impedance between terminals 1 and 2 in the circuit of Figure P10–10. Select values of R and L so that Z_{EQ} has a pole at $s = -1000$ rad/s. Identify the location of the zeros of Z_{EQ} for your values of R and L.

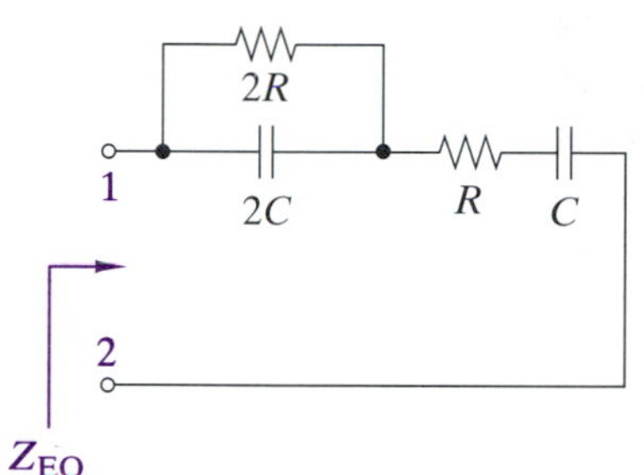

FIGURE P10–9

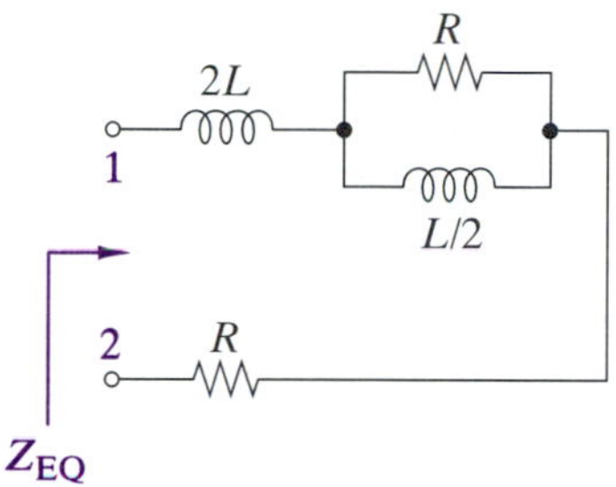

FIGURE P10–10

ERO 10–2 BASIC CIRCUIT ANALYSIS TECHNIQUES (SECTS. 10–2, 10–3)

Given a linear circuit,

(a) Determine the initial conditions (if not given) and transform the circuit into the s-domain.
(b) Solve for zero-state and/or zero-input response transforms and waveforms using basic analysis methods such as circuit reduction, unit output, Thévenin/Norton equivalent circuits, or superposition.
(c) Identify the forced and natural poles or adjust circuit parameters to place the natural poles at specified locations.

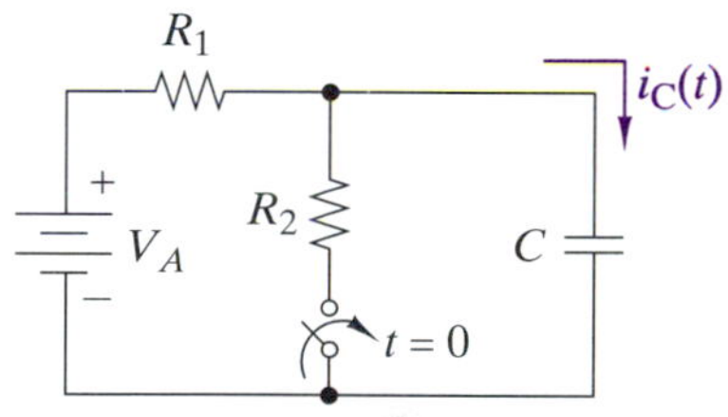

FIGURE P10–11

10–11 The switch in Figure P10–11 has been open for a long time and is closed at $t = 0$. Transform the circuit into the s domain and solve for $I_C(s)$ and $i_C(t)$ in symbolic form.

10–12 The switch in Figure P10–11 has been closed for a long time and is opened at $t = 0$. Transform the circuit into the s-domain and solve for $I_C(s)$ and $i_C(t)$ in symbolic form.

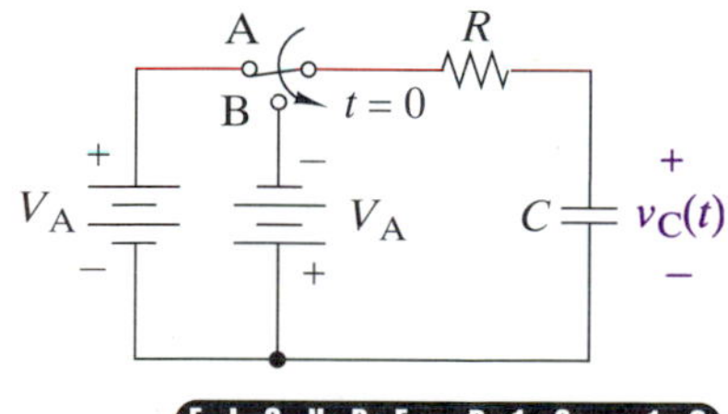

FIGURE P10–13

10–13 The switch in Figure P10–13 has been in position A for a long time and is moved to position B at $t = 0$. Transform the circuit into the s domain and solve for $V_C(s)$ and $v_C(t)$ in symbolic form.

10–14 The switch in Figure P10–13 has been in position B for a long time and is moved to position A at $t = 0$. Transform the circuit into the s domain and solve for $V_C(s)$ and $v_C(t)$ in symbolic form.

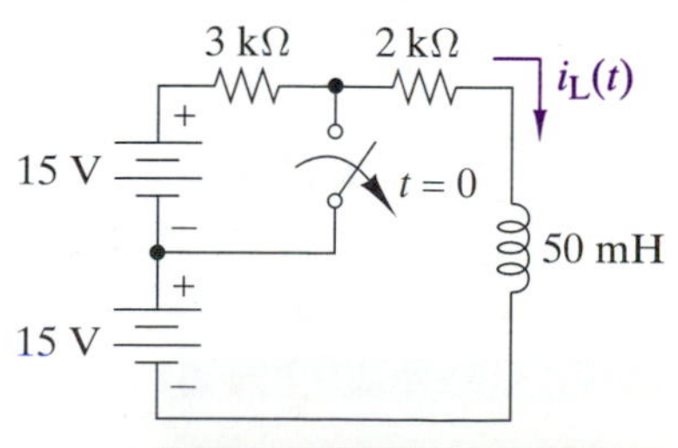

FIGURE P10–15

10–15 The switch in Figure P10–15 has been closed for a long time and is opened at $t = 0$. Transform the circuit into the s domain and solve for $I_L(s)$ and $i_L(t)$.

10–16 The switch in Figure P10–15 has been open for a long time and is closed at $t = 0$. Transform the circuit into the s domain and solve for $I_L(s)$ and $i_L(t)$.

10–17 The switch in Figure P10–17 has been in position A for a long time and is moved to position B at $t = 0$.

(a) Transform the circuit into the s domain and solve for $V_C(s)$ and $I_L(s)$ in symbolic form.

(b) Find $v_C(t)$ and $i_L(t)$ for $R_1 = R_2 = 500\ \Omega$, $L = 500$ mH, $C = 1\ \mu$F, and $V_A = 15$ V.

FIGURE P10–17

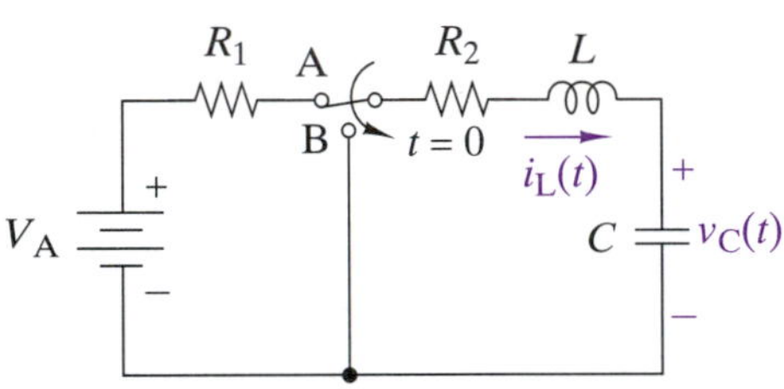

10–18 The switch in Figure P10–17 has been in position B for a long time and is moved to position A at $t = 0$.

(a) Transform the circuit into the s domain and solve for $V_C(s)$ and $I_L(s)$ in symbolic form.

(b) Find $v_C(t)$ and $i_L(t)$ for $R_1 = R_2 = 750\ \Omega$, $L = 500$ mH, $C = 1\ \mu$F, and $V_A = 15$ V.

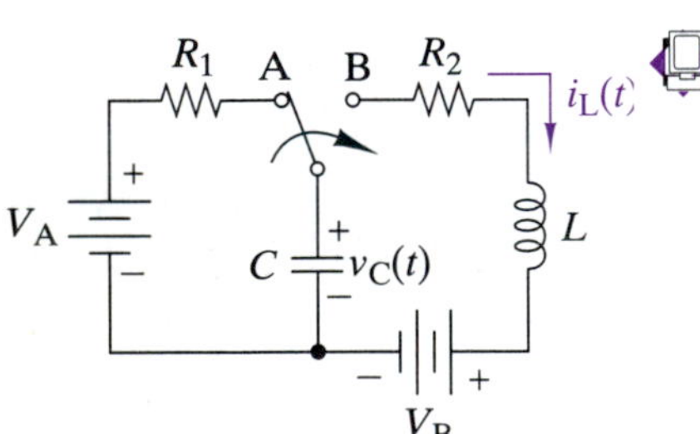

FIGURE P10–19

10–19 The switch in Figure P10–19 has been in position A for a long time and is moved to position B at $t = 0$.

(a) Transform the circuit into the s domain and solve for $V_C(s)$ and $I_L(s)$ in symbolic form.

(b) Find $v_C(t)$ and $i_L(t)$ for $R_1 = 5$ kΩ, $R_2 = 2$ kΩ, $L = 1$ H, $C = 1\ \mu$F, $V_A = 10$ V, and $V_B = 5$ V.

10–20 The switch in Figure P10–19 has been in position B for a long time and is moved to position A at $t = 0$.

(a) Transform the circuit into the s domain and solve for $V_C(s)$ and $I_L(s)$ in symbolic form.

(b) Find $v_C(t)$ and $i_L(t)$ for $R_1 = 5$ kΩ, $R_2 = 2$ kΩ, $L = 1$ H, $C = 1\ \mu$F, $V_A = 10$ V, and $V_B = 5$ V.

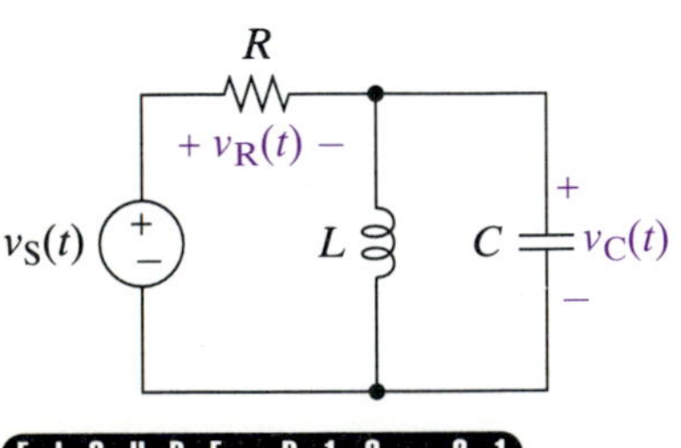

FIGURE P10–21

10–21 There is no initial energy stored in the circuit in Figure P10–21.

(a) Transform the circuit into the s domain and use voltage division to solve for $V_C(s)$.

(b) Identify the forced and natural poles in $V_C(s)$ when $v_S = 100\ u(t)$ V, $L = 50$ mH, $C = 0.05\ \mu$F, and $R = 5$ kΩ.

10–22 There is no initial energy stored in the circuit in Figure P10–21.

(a) Transform the circuit into the s domain and use voltage division to solve for $V_R(s)$.

(b) Identify the forced and natural poles in $V_R(s)$ when $v_S(t) = [10 \cos 20000t]u(t)$ V, $L = 50$ mH, $C = 0.05\ \mu$F, and $R = 500\ \Omega$.

10–23 There is no energy stored in the capacitor in Figure P10–23 at $t = 0$. Transform the circuit into the s domain and use current division to find $v_O(t)$ when the input is $i_S(t) = 0.1e^{-100t}u(t)$ A. Identify the forced and natural poles in $V_O(s)$.

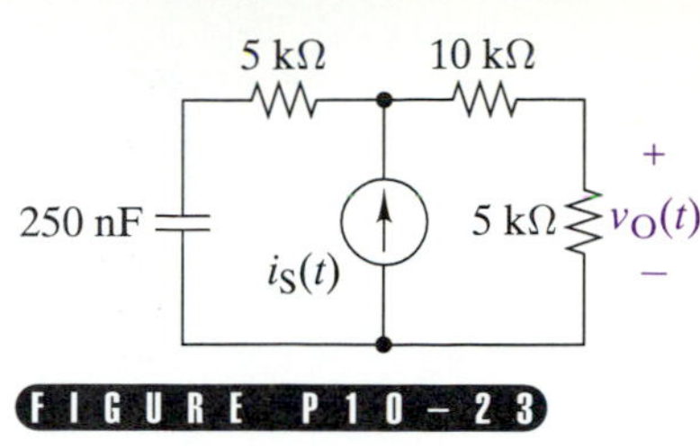

FIGURE P10–23

10–24 Repeat Problem 10–23 when $i_S(t) = 0.1e^{-200t}u(t)$ A.

10–25 The initial capacitor voltage in Figure P10–25 is V_0.

(a) Transform the circuit into the s domain and find the Thévenin equivalent at the interface shown in the figure.

(b) Use the Thévenin equivalent to determine the zero-state and zero-input components of $I(s)$ when $i_S(t) = I_A\, u(t)$.

10–26 Repeat Problem 10–25 when the current source delivers $i_S(t) = I_A\,[\cos \beta t]u(t)$.

10–27 Adjust the value of C in Figure P10–27 so that the circuit has a natural pole at $s = -10$ Mrad/s when $R_S = 550\ \Omega$, $R_L = 2$ kΩ, and $g = 40$ mS.

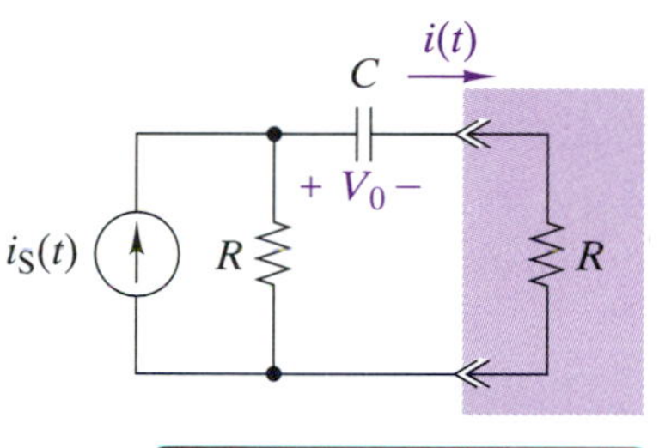

FIGURE P10–25

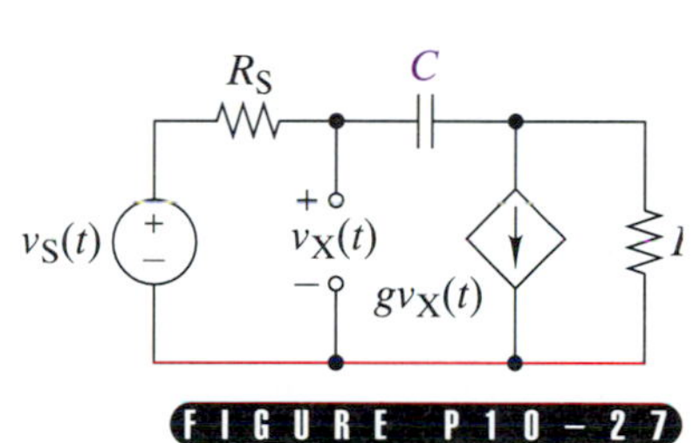

FIGURE P10–27

10–28 There is no initial energy stored in the circuit in Figure P10–28. Transform the circuit into the s domain and solve for the zero-state component of $V(s)$. Identify the forced and natural poles in $V(s)$.

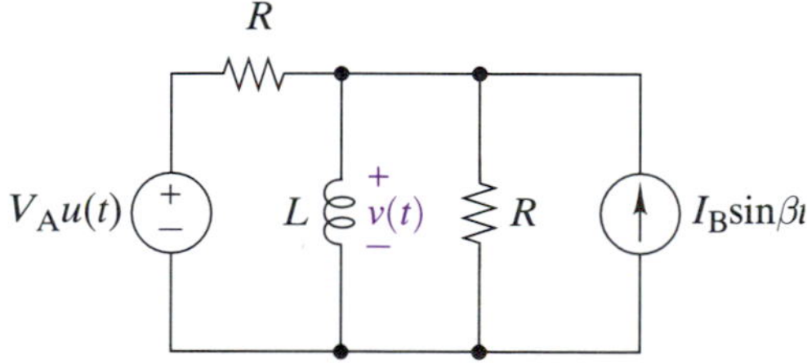

FIGURE P10–28

10–29 A series connection of a resistor and capacitor are connected across a voltage source with $v_S(t) = [10e^{-2000t}]u(t)$ V. The circuit response is observed to be $v_C(t) = [5e^{-2000t} - 2e^{-4000t}]u(t)$ V.

(a) Find the zero-state and zero-input components of $v_C(t)$.

(b) Identify the forced and natural poles in $V_C(s)$.

(c) Find $v_C(t)$ when the input voltage is changed to $v_S(t) = [20e^{-2000t}]u(t)$ V.

10–30 There is no initial energy stored in the circuit in Figure P10–30. Use circuit reduction to find the output voltage $V_2(s)$ in terms of the input voltage $V_1(s)$.

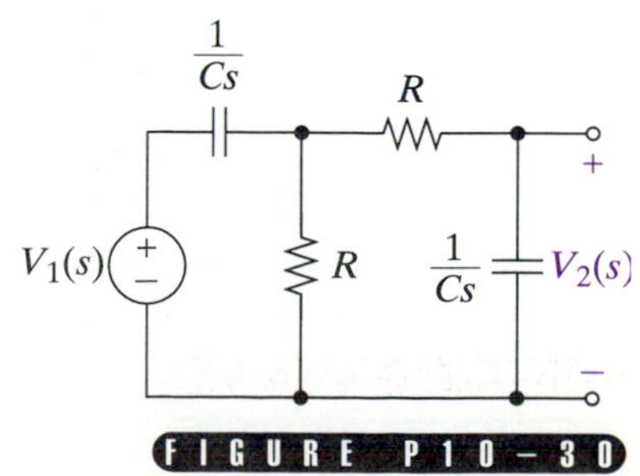

FIGURE P10–30

ERO 10–3 GENERAL CIRCUIT ANALYSIS (SECTS. 10–4, 10–5, 10–6)

Given a linear circuit,

(a) Determine the initial conditions (if not given) and transform the circuit into the s domain.
(b) Solve for zero-state and/or zero-input response transforms and waveforms using node-voltage or mesh-current methods.
(c) Identify the forced and natural poles or adjust circuit parameters to place the natural poles at specified locations.

10–31 There is no initial energy stored in the circuit in Figure P10–31.

(a) Transform the circuit into the s domain and formulate node-voltage equations.

(b) Use these equations to find $V_2(s)$ and $I_2(s)$ in symbolic form.

(c) Find $i_2(t)$ for $v_1(t) = 10u(t)$, $R_1 = 10\ \text{k}\Omega$, $R_2 = 2.2\ \text{k}\Omega$, $L = 100$ mH, and $C = 40$ nF.

10–32 Repeat Problem 10–31 using mesh-current equations.

10–33 There is no initial energy stored in the circuit in Figure P10–33.

(a) Transform the circuit into the s domain and formulate node-voltage equations.

(b) Use these equations to find $V_2(s)$ and $I_2(s)$ in symbolic form.

(c) Find $v_2(t)$ for $v_1(t) = 10u(t)$, $R_1 = 10\ \text{k}\Omega$, $R_2 = 36\ \text{k}\Omega$, $C_1 = 550$ nF, and $C_2 = 400$ nF.

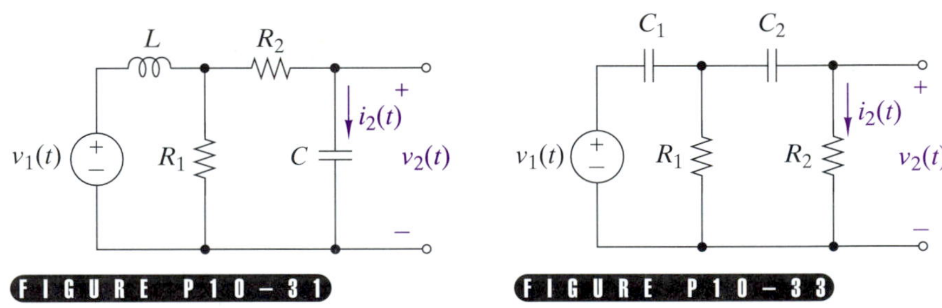

FIGURE P10–31

FIGURE P10–33

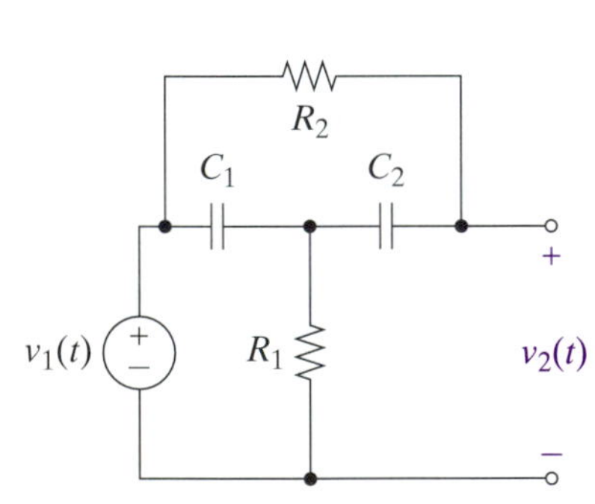

FIGURE P10–36

FIGURE P10–37

10–34 Repeat Problem 10–33 using mesh-current equations.

10–35 In Figure P10–33 the input $v_1(t)$ is set to zero and the initial conditions $v_{C1}(0)$ and $v_{C2}(0)$ are not zero.

(a) Transform the circuit into the s domain and formulate mesh-current or node-voltage equations.

(b) Solve these equations for $V_2(s)$ and $I_2(s)$.

10–36 The circuit in Figure P10–36 is called a bridged-T.

(a) Transform the circuit into the s domain and formulate either node-voltage or mesh-current equations.

(b) Show that the zero-state component of $V_2(s)$ has a double zero at $s = -1/RC$ when $R_1 = R_2 = R$ and $C_1 = C_2 = C$.

(c) Select values of R and C so that $v_2(t)$ does not contain a forced component when the input voltage is $v_1(t) = V_A\, e^{-2000t}$. Locate the natural poles of the circuit for your values of R and C.

10–37 The circuit in Figure P10–37 is an active RC filter with an OP AMP voltage follower.

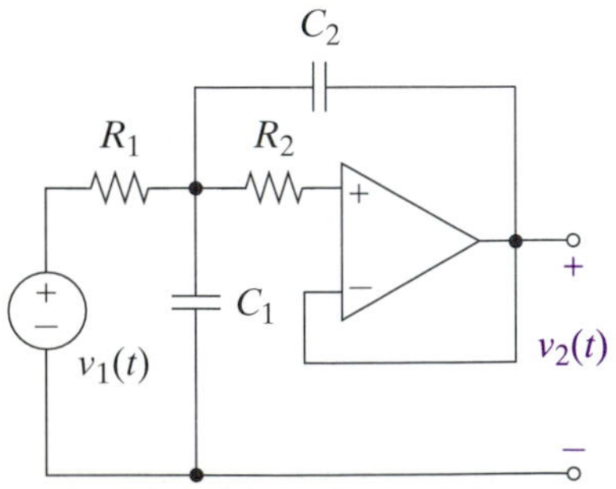

(a) Transform the circuit into the s domain and solve for the zero-state component of the output voltage $V_2(s)$ in terms of input voltage $V_1(s)$.

(b) The circuit has two capacitors, yet $V_2(s)$ has only one natural pole. The capacitor C_2 does not introduce a natural pole. Explain why.

10–38 The circuit in Figure P10–38 is an active RC filter with two feedback paths to the OP AMP's inverting input. Transform the circuit into the s domain and show that when $R_1 = R_2 = R_3 = R$ and $C_1 = C_2 = C$, the circuit's natural poles are complex. Select values of R and C so that the natural poles are located at $s_{1,2} = -1000 \pm j1000$ rad/s.

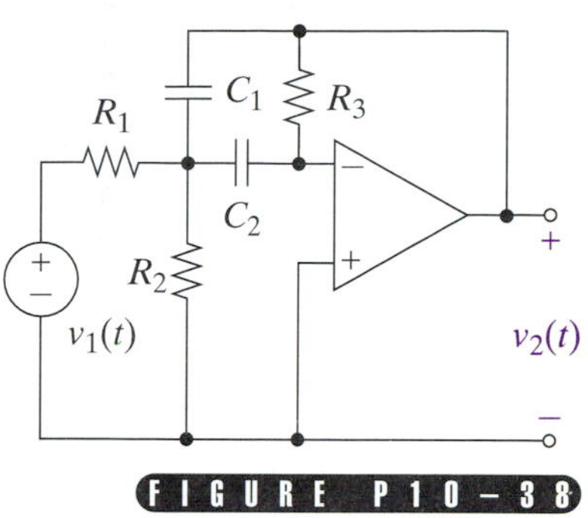

FIGURE P10–38

10–39 D The circuit in Figure P10–39 represents an active RC highpass filter originally proposed by R. P. Sallen and E. K. Key in 1955.

(a) Transform the circuit into the s domain and find the circuit determinant.

(b) Select values of R, C, and μ so the circuit has natural poles at $s = \pm j5000$ rad/s.

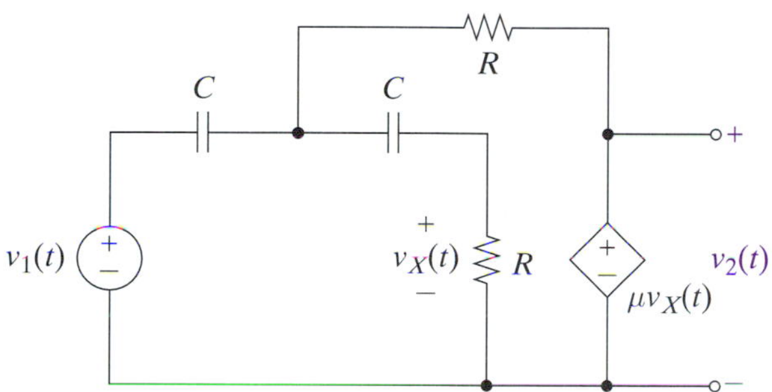

FIGURE P10–39

10–40 D The circuit in Figure P10–40 represents an active RC bandpass filter proposed by J. J. Friend in 1970.

(a) Transform the circuit into the s domain and find the circuit determinant.

(b) Locate the natural poles when $R_1 = 10$ kΩ, $R_2 = 40$ kΩ, $C_1 = C_2 = 10$ nF, and $\mu = 4$.

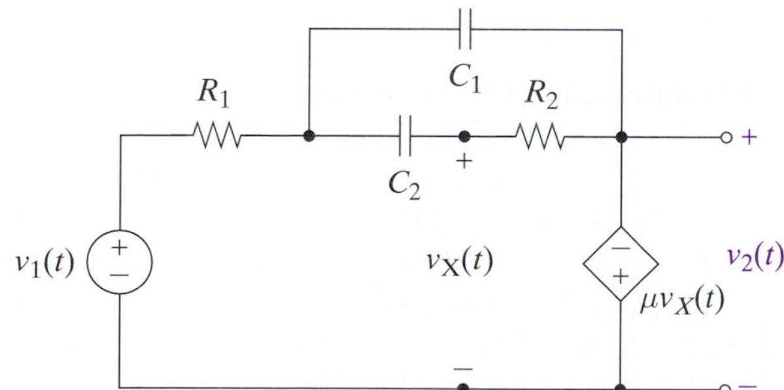

FIGURE P10–40

10–41 The circuit in Figure P10–41 is a low-frequency model of a transistor in the common emitter configuration.

FIGURE P10–41

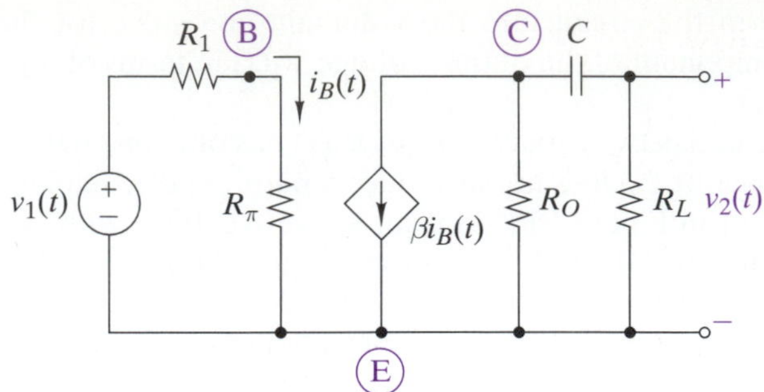

(a) Transform the circuit into the s domain and solve for the zero-state output voltage $V_2(s)$ in terms of the input $V_1(s)$.

(b) Find the zero-state response $v_2(t)$ for $v_1(t) = 10u(t)$ mV, $R_1 = 10$ kΩ, $R_\pi = 1$ kΩ, β = 100, $R_O = 10$ kΩ, $C = 0.1$ μF, and $R_L = 100$ kΩ.

10–42 The circuit in Figure P10–41 is a low-frequency model of a transistor in the common emitter configuration. For $R_O = R_L = 20$ kΩ, select the value of C so the circuit has a natural pole at $s = -100$ rad/s.

10–43 There is no initial energy stored in the circuit in Figure P10–43.

(a) Transform the circuit into the s domain and formulate mesh-current equations.

(b) Solve the mesh-current equations for $I_A(s)$ and $I_B(s)$ in terms of V_A.

(c) Find $i_A(t)$ and $i_B(t)$ for $V_A = 50$ V, $R_1 = 50$ Ω, $R_2 = 80$ Ω, $L_1 = 0.75$ mH, $L_2 = 1$ mH, and $M = 0.8$ mH.

FIGURE P10–43

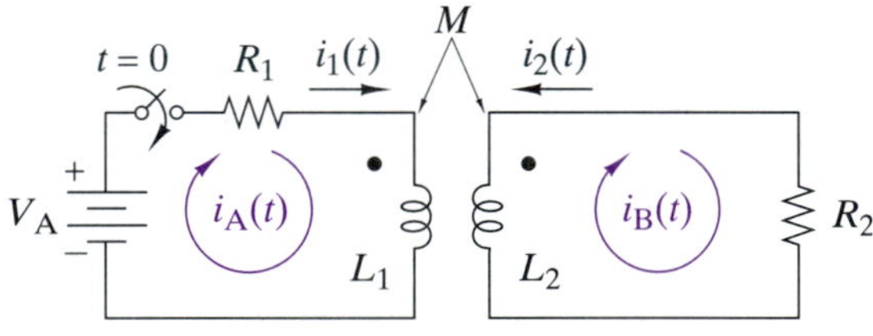

10–44 The switch in Figure P10–44 has been in position A for a long time and is moved to position B at $t = 0$. Solve for $V_C(s)$ and $v_C(t)$.

FIGURE P10–44

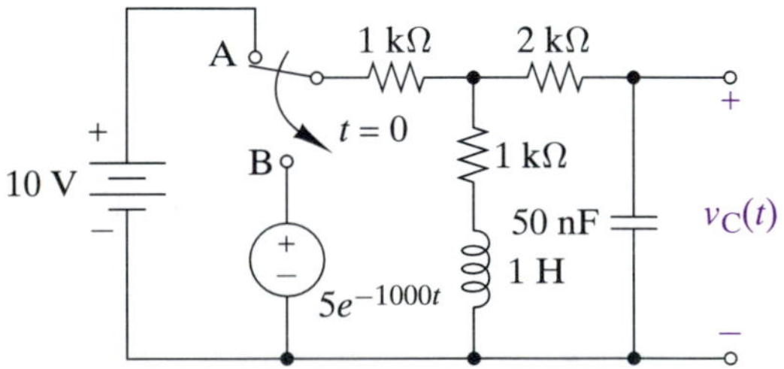

10–45 There is no energy stored in the circuit in Figure P10–45 at $t = 0-$. Transform the circuit into the s domain and solve for $V_O(s)$ and $v_O(t)$.

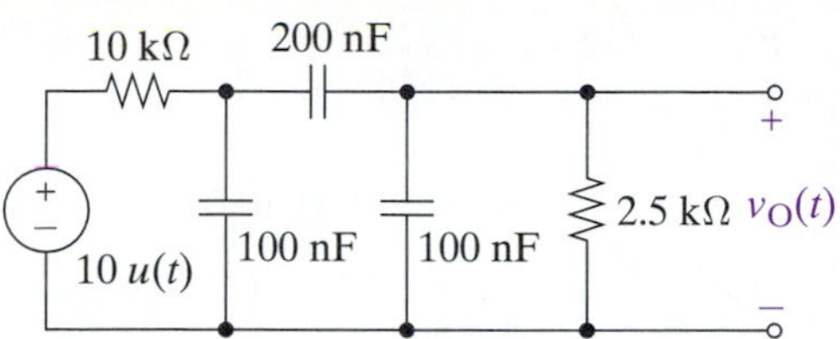

FIGURE P10–45

10–46 The switch in Figure P10–46 has been open for a long time and is closed at $t = 0$. Transform the circuit into the s domain and solve for $I_O(s)$ and $i_O(t)$.

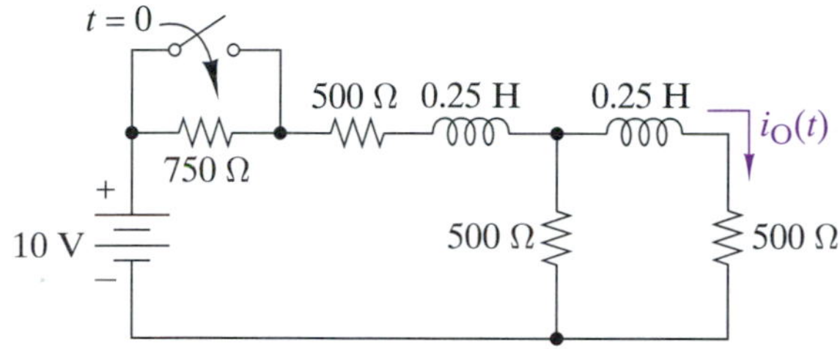

FIGURE P10–46

10–47 There is no initial energy stored in the circuit in Figure P10–47.

(a) Transform the circuit into the s domain and solve for $V_O(s)$ in symbolic form.

(b) Find $v_O(t)$ when $v_S(t) = 10^4 tu(t)$ V, $R_1 = R_2 = 200\ \Omega$, $C = 1\ \mu$F, and $L = 40$ mH.

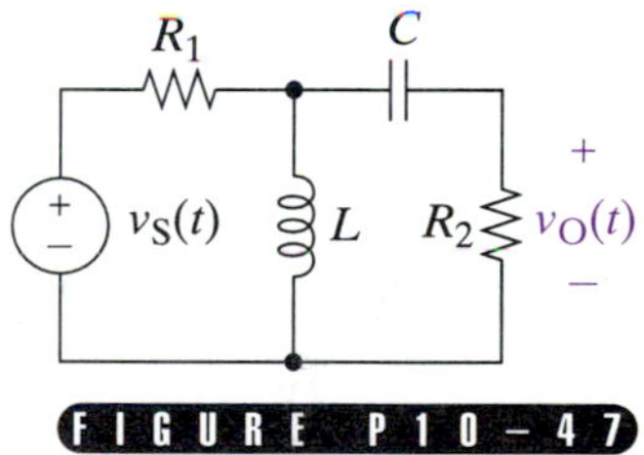

FIGURE P10–47

10–48 There is no initial energy stored in the circuit in Figure P10–48.

(a) Show that the circuit has natural poles at $s = -1000$ rad/s and $s = -2000$ rad/s when $R_1 = 10$ kΩ, $C_1 = 100$ nF, $R_2 = 10$ kΩ, and $C_2 = 50$ nF.

(b) When the input is $v_S(t) = 10u(t)$ V, show that $V_1(s)$ has a forced pole at $s = 0$ but only one natural pole at $s = -1000$ rad/s.

(c) For the input in (b), show that $V_2(s)$ has both of the circuit's natural poles but does not have a forced pole at $s = 0$.

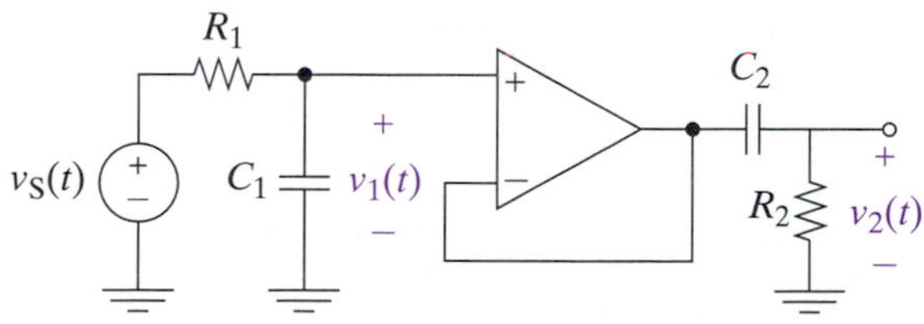

FIGURE P10–48

10–49 The circuit in Figure P10–49 is a third-order lowpass filter. Show that the circuit has natural poles at $s = -2/RC$ and $s = (-1 \pm j)/RC$ when $L = R^2C$.

FIGURE P10–49

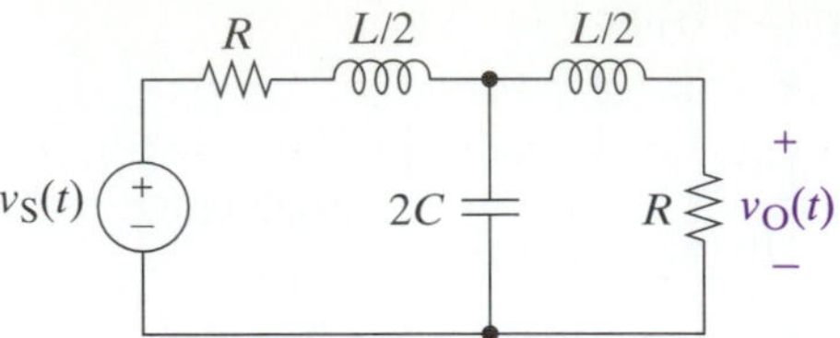

10–50 **D** Select values of R_1, R_2, C_1, and C_2 such that the circuit in Figure P10–50 has natural poles located at $s = -100$ rad/s and $s = -500$ rad/s.

FIGURE P10–50

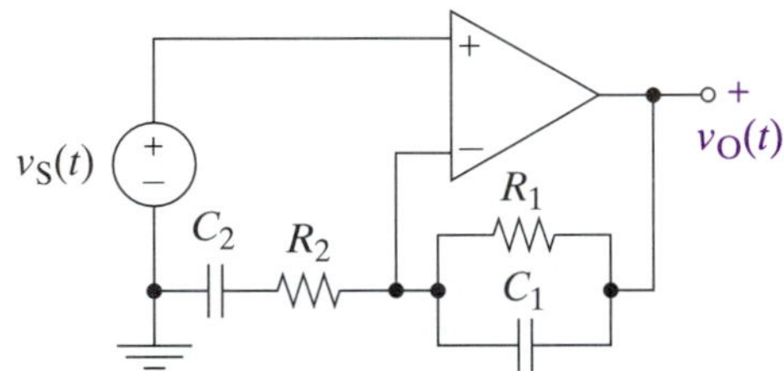

CHAPTER-INTEGRATING PROBLEMS

10–51 A THÉVENIN'S THEOREM FROM TIME-DOMAIN DATA

A black box containing a linear circuit has an on-off switch and a pair of external terminals. When the switch is turned on, the open-circuit voltage between the external terminals is observed to be a sinewave with a period of 10 ms and a peak-to-peak amplitude of 20 V. When a short circuit is connected to the external terminals and the switch again turned on, the current is observed to be a steady 10 mA. Predict the current the box would deliver to a 50-Ω resistive load.

10–52 A IMPEDANCE FROM TIME-DOMAIN DATA

A current of $u(t)$ amperes is injected at a two-terminal interface and the interface voltage is observed to be $[10 + 20 \sin 1000t]u(t)$ V. Find the waveform of the interface current when a unit-step function voltage is applied across the same pair of terminals.

10–53 A THÉVENIN EQUIVALENT OF A TRANSFORMER

(a) Find the Thévenin equivalent circuit seen by the load impedance in Figure P10–53.

(b) Show that the Thévenin impedance found in (a) reduces to zero when the coils are perfectly coupled.

FIGURE P10–53

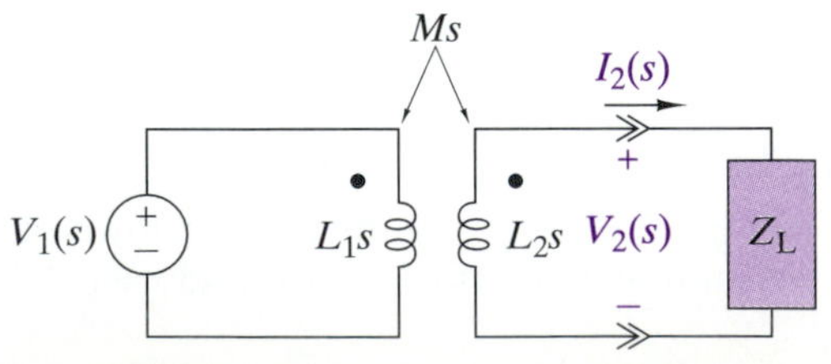

10–54 A D LIGHTNING PULSER DESIGN

The circuit in Figure P10–54 is a simplified circuit diagram of a pulser that is used to test equipment against lightning-induced transients. Select the values of V_0, R_1, R_2, C_1, and C_2 so that the pulser delivers an output pulse

$$v_O(t) = 750(e^{-1000t} - e^{-80000t})\ \text{V}$$

The pulser is completely discharged prior to delivering a pulse.

FIGURE P10–54

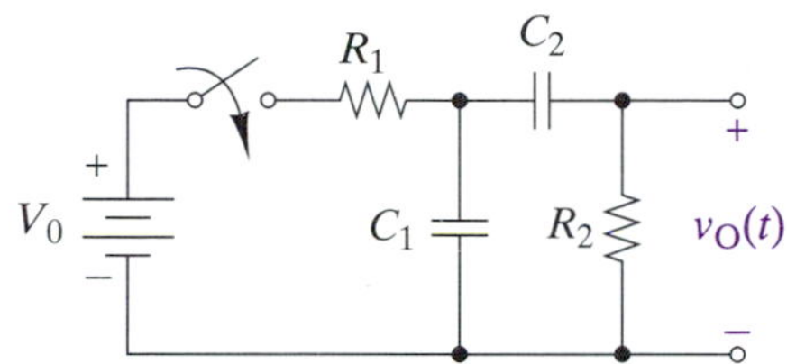

10–55 E PULSE CONVERSION CIRCUIT

The purpose of the test setup in Figure P10–55 is to deliver damped sine pulses to the test load. The excitation comes from a 1-Hz square wave generator. The pulse conversion circuit must deliver damped sine waveforms with $\zeta < 0.5$ and $\omega_0 > 10$ krad/s to 50-Ω and 600-Ω loads. The recommended values for the pulse conversion circuit are $L = 10$ mH and $C = 100$ nF. Verify that the test setup meets the specifications. If you find it does not meet the requirements, suggest a simple modification that will bring it within the specification limits.

FIGURE P10–55

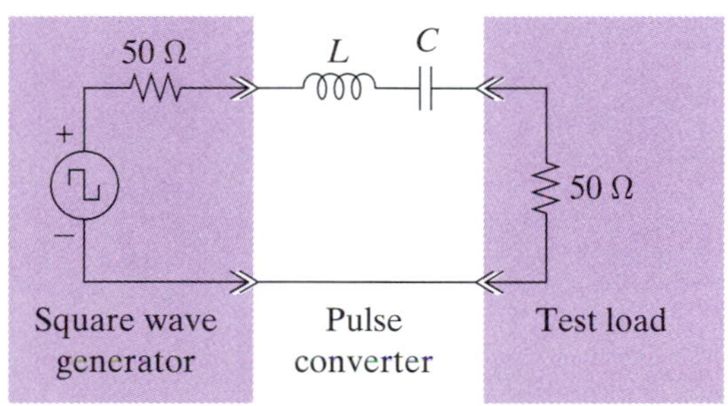

NETWORK FUNCTIONS

The driving-point impedance of a network is the ratio of an impressed electromotive force at a point in a branch of the network to the resulting current at the same point.

Ronald M. Foster, 1924,
American Engineer

The concept of network functions emerged in the 1920s during the development of systematic methods of designing electric filters for long-distance telephone systems. The filter design effort eventually evolved into a formal realizability theory that came to be known as network synthesis. The objective of network synthesis is to design one or more networks that accomplish or realize a given network function. The foregoing quotation is taken from one of the first papers to approach network design from a synthesis viewpoint.[1] Ronald Foster, along with Sidney Darlington, Hendrik Bode, Wilhelm Cauer, and Otto Brune are generally considered the founders of the field of network synthesis. The classical synthesis methods they developed emphasized passive realizations using only resistors, capacitors, and inductors because the active elements of their era were costly and unreliable vacuum tubes. With the advent of semiconductor electronics, emphasis shifted to realizations using resistors, capacitors, and active devices such as transistors and OP AMPs.

In the last chapter we found that the transform of the zero-state output of a linear circuit is proportional to the transform of the input signal. In the s-domain the proportionality factor is a rational function of s called a network function. The network function concept is used extensively in linear circuit analysis and design. This chapter begins a study of the properties of these functions that continues throughout the rest of this book.

The first two sections of this chapter show how to define and calculate network functions for different types of circuits. The next three sections discuss how to use network functions to obtain the impulse response, step response, and sinusoidal steady-state responses of a circuit. The sixth section uses convolution to show that a network function contains sufficient information to obtain the response to any causal input. The final section treats some basic methods of synthesizing circuits that realize a specified network function.

11-1 DEFINITION OF A NETWORK FUNCTION

The proportionality property of linear circuits states that the output is proportional to the input. In Chapter 10 we noted that in the s domain the proportionality factor is a rational function of s called a network function. More formally, a network function is defined as the ratio of a zero-state response transform (output) to the excitation (input) transform.

$$\text{Network Function} = \frac{\text{Zero-state Response Transform}}{\text{Input Signal Transform}} \quad (11-1)$$

Note carefully that this definition specifies zero initial conditions and implies only one input.

To study the role of network functions in determining circuit responses, we write the s-domain input-output relationship as

1 R. M. Foster, "A Reactance Theorem," *Bell System Technical Journal,* No. 3, pp. 259–267, 1924.

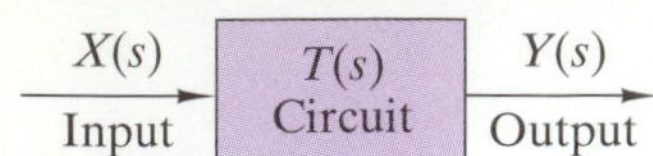

FIGURE 11–1 *Block diagram for an s-domain input-output relationship.*

$$Y(s) = T(s)X(s) \tag{11–2}$$

where $T(s)$ is a network function, $X(s)$ is the input signal transform, and $Y(s)$ is a zero-state response or output.[2] Figure 11–1 shows a block diagram representation of the s-domain input–output relationship in Eq. (11–2).

In an analysis problem, the circuit and input [$X(s)$ or $x(t)$] are specified. We determine $T(s)$ from the circuit, use Eq. (11–2) to find the response transform $Y(s)$, and use the inverse transformation to obtain the response waveform $y(t)$. In a design problem the circuit is unknown. The input and output are specified, or their ratio $T(s) = Y(s)/X(s)$ is given. The objective is to devise a circuit that realizes the specified input-output relationship. A linear circuit analysis problem has a unique solution, but a design problem may have one, many, or even no solutions.

Equation (11–2) points out that the poles of the response $Y(s)$ come from either the network function $T(s)$ or the input signal $X(s)$. When there are no repeated poles, the partial-fraction expansion of the right side of Eq. (11–2) takes the form

$$Y(s) = \underbrace{\sum_{j=1}^{N} \frac{k_j}{s - p_j}}_{\substack{\text{Natural}\\ \text{Poles}}} + \underbrace{\sum_{\ell=1}^{M} \frac{k_\ell}{s - p_\ell}}_{\substack{\text{Forced}\\ \text{Poles}}} \tag{11–3}$$

where p_j ($j = 1, 2, \ldots N$) are the poles of $T(s)$ and $s = p_\ell$ ($\ell = 1, 2, \ldots M$) are the poles of $X(s)$. The inverse transform of this expansion is

$$y(t) = \underbrace{\sum_{j=1}^{N} k_j e^{p_j t}}_{\substack{\text{Natural}\\ \text{Response}}} + \underbrace{\sum_{\ell=1}^{M} k_\ell e^{p_\ell t}}_{\substack{\text{Forced}\\ \text{Response}}} \tag{11–4}$$

The poles of $T(s)$ lead to the natural response. In a stable circuit, the natural poles are all in the left half of the s plane, and all of the exponential terms in the natural response eventually decay to zero. The poles of $X(s)$ lead to the forced response. In a stable circuit, those elements in the forced response that do not decay to zero are called the **steady-state response**.

It is important to remember that the complex frequencies in the natural response are determined by the circuit and do not depend on input. Conversely, the complex frequencies in the forced response are determined by the input and do not depend on the circuit. However, the amplitude of each part of the response depend on the residues in the partial fraction expansion in Eq. (11–3). These residues are influenced by all of the poles and zeros, whether forced or natural. Thus, the amplitudes of the forced and natural responses depend on an interaction between the poles and zeros of $T(s)$ and $X(s)$.

The following example illustrates this discussion.

---

2 In this context $Y(s)$ is not an admittance, but the transform of the output waveform $y(t)$.

EXAMPLE 11–1

The transfer function of a circuit is

$$T(s) = \frac{V_2(s)}{V_1(s)} = \frac{2000\,(s + 2000)}{(s + 1000)\,(s + 4000)}$$

Find the zero-state response $v_2(t)$ when the input waveform is $v_1(t) = [20 + 15e^{-5000t}]u(t)$.

SOLUTION:

(a) The transform of the input waveform is

$$V_1(s) = \frac{20}{s} + \frac{15}{s + 5000} = \frac{35\,s + 10^5}{s(s + 5000)}$$

Using the s-domain input-output relationship in Eq. (11–2), the transform of the response is

$$V_2(s) = \frac{10^4(s + 2000)\,(7s + 20000)}{(s + 1000)\,(s + 4000)s(s + 5000)}$$

Expanding by partial fractions,

$$V_2(s) = \underbrace{\frac{k_1}{s + 1000} + \frac{k_2}{s + 4000}}_{\text{Natural Poles}} + \underbrace{\frac{k_3}{s} + \frac{k_4}{s + 5000}}_{\text{Forced Poles}}$$

The two natural poles came from the circuit via the network function $T(s)$. The forced poles came from the step function and exponential inputs. Using the cover-up method to evaluate the residues yields

$$k_1 = \left.\frac{10^4(s + 2000)\,(7s + 20000)}{(s + 4000)s(s + 5000)}\right|_{s=-1000} = -\frac{65}{6}$$

$$k_2 = \left.\frac{10^4(s + 2000)\,(7s + 20000)}{(s + 1000)s(s + 5000)}\right|_{s=-4000} = \frac{40}{3}$$

$$k_3 = \left.\frac{10^4(s + 2000)\,(7s + 20000)}{(s + 1000)\,(s + 4000)\,(s + 5000)}\right|_{s=0} = 20$$

$$k_4 = \left.\frac{10^4(s + 2000)\,(7s + 20000)}{(s + 1000)\,(s + 4000)s}\right|_{s=-5000} = -\frac{45}{2}$$

Collectively the residues depend on all of the poles and zeros. The inverse transform yields the zero-state response as

$$v_2(t) = \Bigg[\underbrace{-\frac{65}{6}e^{-1000t} + \frac{40}{3}e^{-4000t}}_{\text{Natural Response}} + \underbrace{20 - \frac{45}{2}e^{-5000t}}_{\text{Forced Response}}\Bigg]u(t)$$

The natural poles as $s = -1000$ and $s = -4000$ are in the left half of the s plane, so the natural response decays to zero. The forced pole as $s =$

−5000 leads to an exponential term that also decays to zero, leaving a steady-state response of $20u(t)$. ■

11–2 NETWORK FUNCTIONS OF ONE- AND TWO-PORT CIRCUITS

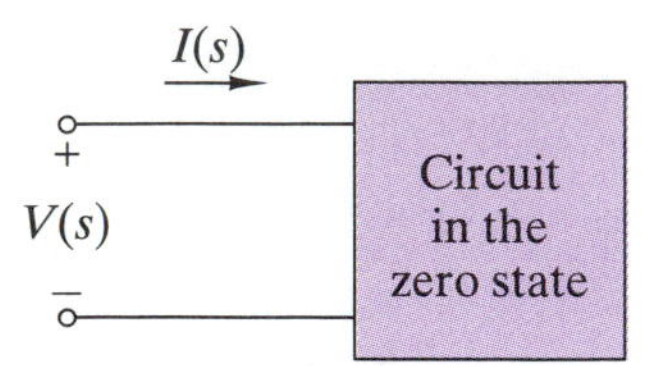

FIGURE 11–2 *One-port circuit and driving-point impedance.*

The two major types of network functions are driving-point impedance and transfer functions. A **driving-point impedance** relates the voltage and current at a pair of terminals called a port. The driving-point impedance $Z(s)$ of the one-port circuit in Figure 11–2 is defined as

$$Z(s) = \frac{V(s)}{I(s)} \tag{11-5}$$

When the one port is driven by a current source the response is $V(s) = Z(s)I(s)$ and the natural frequencies in the response are the poles of impedance $Z(s)$. On the other hand, when the one port is driven by a voltage source the response is $I(s) = [Z(s)]^{-1}V(s)$ and the natural frequencies in the response are the poles of $1/Z(s)$; that is, the zeros of $Z(s)$. In other words, the driving-point impedance is a network function whether upside down or right side up.

The term *driving point* means that the circuit is driven at one port and the response is observed at the same port. The element impedances defined in Sect. 10–1 are elementary examples of driving-point impedances. The equivalent impedances found by combining elements in series and parallel are also driving-point impedances. Driving-point functions are the s-domain generalization of the concept of the input resistance. The terms *driving-point impedance*, *input impedance*, and *equivalent impedance* are synonymous.

Transfer functions are usually of greater interest in signal-processing applications than driving-point impedances because they describe how a signal is modified by passing through a circuit. A **transfer function** relates an input and response (or output) at different ports in the circuit. Figure 11–3 shows the possible input-output configurations for a two-port circuit. Since the input and output signals can be either a current or a voltage, we can define four kinds of transfer function:

FIGURE 11–3 *Two-port circuits and transfer functions.*

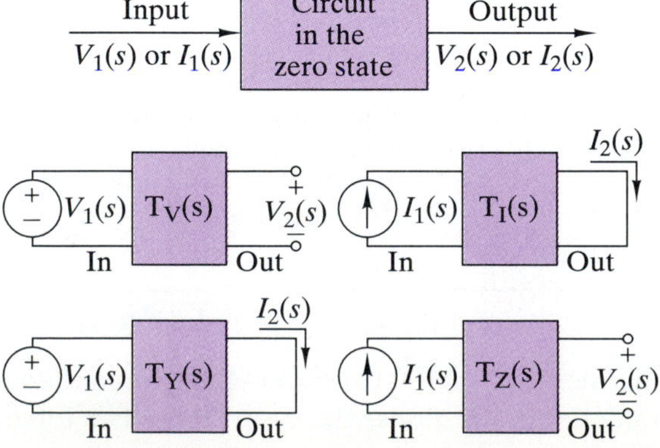

$$T_V(s) = \text{Voltage Transfer Function} = \frac{V_2(s)}{V_1(s)}$$

$$T_I(s) = \text{Current Transfer Function} = \frac{I_2(s)}{I_1(s)} \qquad (11\text{–}6)$$

$$T_Y(s) = \text{Transfer Admittance} = \frac{I_2(s)}{V_1(s)}$$

$$T_Z(s) = \text{Transfer Impedance} = \frac{V_2(s)}{I_1(s)}$$

The functions $T_V(s)$ and $T_I(s)$ are dimensionless since the input and output signals have the same units. The function $T_Z(s)$ has units of ohms and $T_Y(s)$ has units of siemens.

The functions in Eq. (11–6) are sometimes called forward transfer functions because they relate inputs applied at port 1 to outputs occurring at port 2. There are, of course, reverse transfer functions that relate inputs at port 2 to outputs at port 1. It is important to realize that a transfer function is only valid for a specified input port and output port. For example, the voltage transfer function $T_V(s) = V_2(s)/V_1(s)$ relates the input voltage applied at port 1 in Figure 11–3 to the voltage response observed at the output port. The reverse voltage transfer function for signal transmission from output to input is *not* $1/T_V(s)$. Unlike driving-point impedance, transfer functions are not network functions when they are turned upside down.

DETERMINING NETWORK FUNCTIONS

The rest of this section illustrates analysis techniques for deriving network functions. The application of network functions in circuit analysis and design begins in the next section and continues throughout the rest of this book. But first, we illustrate ways to find the network functions of a given circuit.

The divider circuits in Figure 11–4 occur so frequently that it is worth taking time to develop their transfer functions in general terms. Using s-domain voltage division in Figure 11–4(a), we can write

$$V_2(s) = \left[\frac{Z_2(s)}{Z_1(s) + Z_2(s)}\right] V_1(s)$$

Therefore, the voltage transfer function of a voltage divider circuit is

$$T_V(s) = \frac{V_2(s)}{V_1(s)} = \frac{Z_2(s)}{Z_1(s) + Z_2(s)} \qquad (11\text{–}7)$$

Similarly, using s-domain current division in Figure 11–4(b) yields the transfer function of a current divider circuit as

$$T_I(s) = \frac{I_2(s)}{I_1(s)} = \frac{Y_2(s)}{Y_1(s) + Y_2(s)} \qquad (11\text{–}8)$$

By series equivalence, the driving-point impedance at the input of the voltage divider is $Z_{EQ}(s) = Z_1(s) + Z_2(s)$. By parallel equivalence the driving-

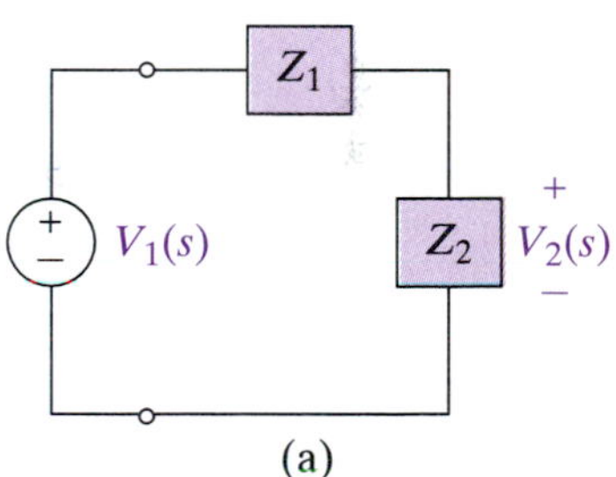

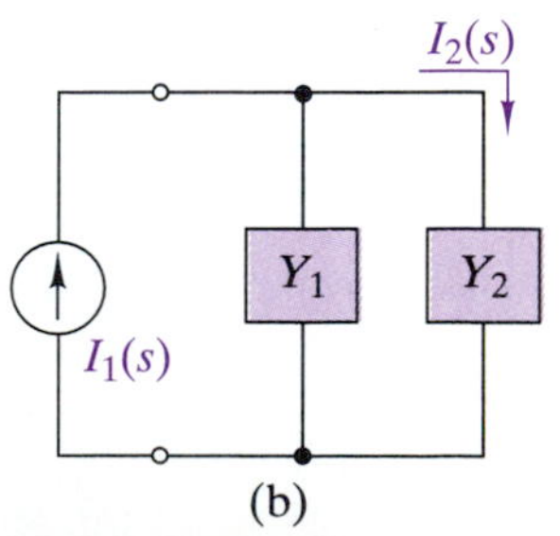

FIGURE 11–4
Basic divider circuits. (a) Voltage divider. (b) Current divider.

point impedance at the input of the current divider is $Z_{EQ}(s) = 1/(Y_1(s) + Y_2(s))$.

Two other useful circuits are the inverting and noninverting OP AMP configurations shown in Figure 11–5. To determine the voltage transfer function of the inverting circuit in Figure 11–5(a), we write the sum of currents leaving node B:

$$\frac{V_B(s) - V_A(s)}{Z_1(s)} + \frac{V_B(s) - V_C(s)}{Z_2(s)} - I_N(s) = 0$$

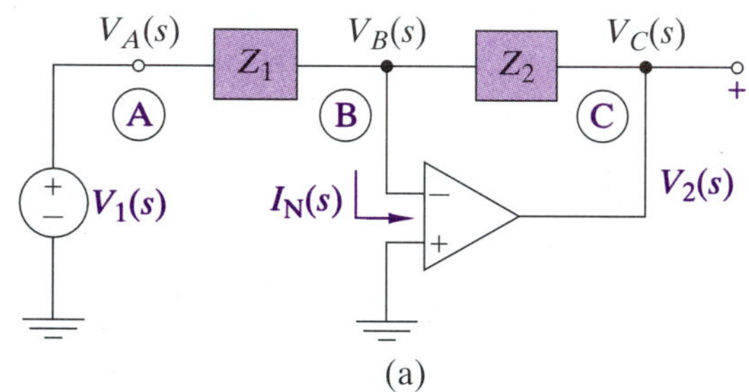

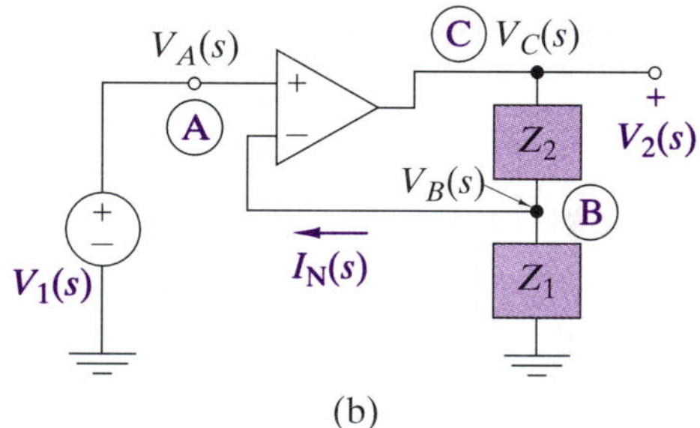

FIGURE 11–5 *Basic OP AMP circuits. (a) Inverting amplifier. (b) Noninverting amplifier.*

But the ideal OP AMP constraints require that $I_N(s) = 0$ and $V_B(s) = 0$ since the noninverting input is grounded. By definition, the output voltage $V_2(s)$ equals node voltage $V_C(s)$ and the voltage source forces $V_A(s)$ to equal the input voltage $V_1(s)$. Inserting all of these considerations into the node equations and solving for the voltage transfer function yields

$$T_V(s) = \frac{V_2(s)}{V_1(s)} = -\frac{Z_2(s)}{Z_1(s)} \tag{11–9}$$

From the study of OP AMP circuits in Chapter 4, you should recognize Eq. (11–9) as the s-domain generalization of the inverting OP AMP circuit gain equation, $K = -R_2/R_1$.

The driving-point impedance at the input to the inverting circuit is

$$Z_{IN}(s) = \frac{V_S(s)}{[V_A(s) - V_B(s)]/Z_1(s)}$$

But $V_A(s) = V_S(s)$ and $V_B(s) = 0$; hence the input impedance is $Z_{IN}(s) = Z_1(s)$.

For the noninverting circuit in Figure 11–4(b), the sum of currents leaving node B is

$$\frac{V_B(s) - V_C(s)}{Z_1(s)} + \frac{V_B(s)}{Z_2(s)} - I_N(s) = 0$$

In the noninverting configuration the ideal OP AMP constraints require that $I_N(s) = 0$ and $V_B(s) = V_1(s)$. By definition, the output voltage $V_2(s)$ equals node voltage $V_C(s)$. Combining all of these considerations and solving for the voltage transfer function yields

$$T_V(s) = \frac{V_2(s)}{V_1(s)} = \frac{Z_1(s) + Z_2(s)}{Z_1(s)} \tag{11-10}$$

Equation (11–10) is the s-domain version of the noninverting amplifier gain equation, $K = (R_1 + R_2)/R_1$. The transfer function of the noninverting configuration is the reciprocal of the transfer function of the voltage divider in the feedback path. The ideal OP AMP draws no current at its input terminals, so theoretically the input impedance of the noninverting circuit is infinite.

The transfer functions of divider circuits and the basic OP AMP configurations are useful analysis and design tools in many practical situations. However, a general method is needed to handle circuits of greater complexity. One general approach is to formulate either node-voltage or mesh-current equations with all initial conditions set to zero. These equations are then solved for network functions using Cramer's rule for hand calculations or symbolic math analysis programs such as Mathcad. The algebra involved can be a bit tedious at times, even with Mathcad. But the tedium is reduced somewhat because we only need the zero-state response for a single input source.

The following examples illustrate methods of calculating network functions.

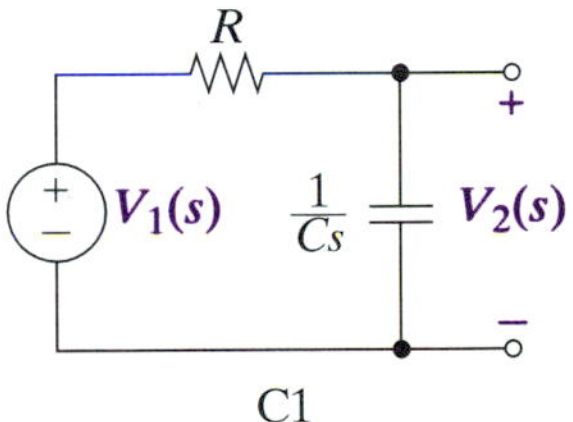

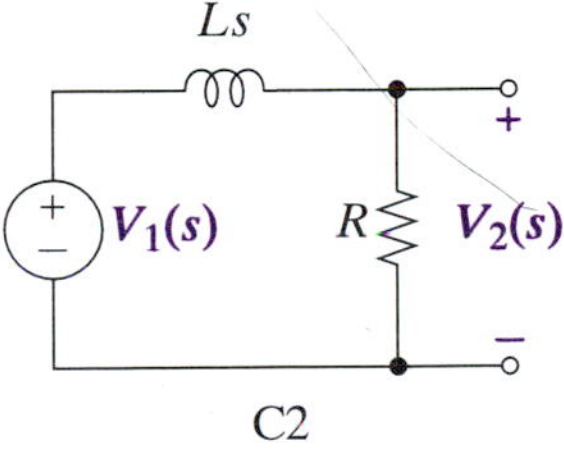

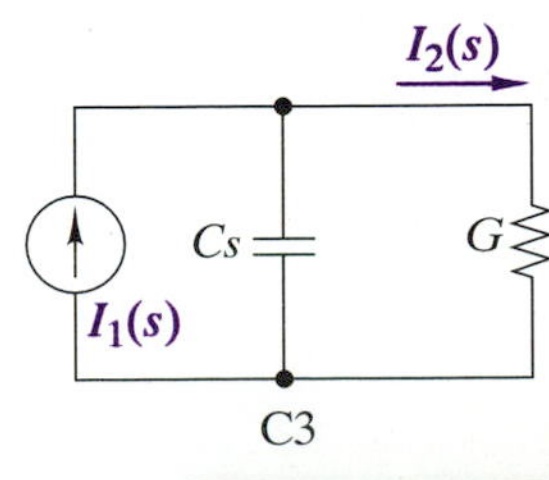

FIGURE 11–6

EXAMPLE 11–2

(a) Find the transfer functions of the circuits in Figure 11–6.
(b) Find the driving-point impedances seen by the input sources in these circuits.

SOLUTION:

(a) These are all divider circuits, so the required transfer functions can be obtained using Eq. (11–7) or (11–8).

For Circuit C1: $Z_1 = R$, $Z_2 = 1/Cs$, and $T_V(s) = 1/(RCs + 1)$

For Circuit C2: $Z_1 = Ls$, $Z_2 = R$, and $T_V(s) = 1/(GLs + 1)$

For Circuit C3: $Y_1 = Cs$, $Y_2 = G$, and $T_I(s) = 1/(RCs + 1)$

These transfer functions are all of the form $1/(\tau s + 1)$, where τ is the circuit time constant.

b) The driving-point impedances are found by series or parallel equivalence.

For circuit C1: $Z(s) = Z_1 + Z_2 = (RCs + 1)/Cs$

For circuit C2: $Z(s) = Z_1 + Z_2 = Ls + R$

For circuit C3: $Z(s)= 1/(Y_1 + Y_2) = 1/(Cs + G) = R/(RCs + 1)$

The three circuits have different driving-point impedances even though they have the same transfer functions.

The general principle illustrated here is that several different circuits can have the same transfer function. Put differently, a desired transfer function can be realized by several different circuits. This fact is important in design because circuits that produce the same transfer function offer alternatives that may differ in other features. In this example, they all have different input impedances. ■

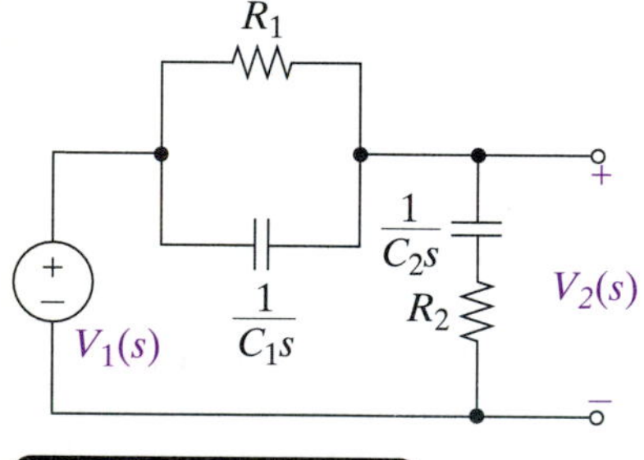

FIGURE 11–7

EXAMPLE 11–3

(a) Find the input impedance seen by the voltage source in Figure 11–7.
(b) Find the voltage transfer function $T_V(s) = V_2(s)/V_1(s)$ of the circuit.

SOLUTION:

(a) The circuit is a voltage divider. We first calculate the equivalent impedances of the two legs of the divider. The two elements in parallel combine to produce the series leg impedance $Z_1(s)$ as

$$Z_1(s) = \frac{1}{C_1s + 1/R_1} = \frac{R_1}{R_1C_1s + 1}$$

The two elements in series combine to produce shunt leg impedance $Z_2(s)$:

$$Z_2(s) = R_2 + 1/C_2s = \frac{R_2C_2s + 1}{C_2s}$$

Using series equivalence, the driving-point impedance seen at the input is

$$\begin{aligned} Z_{EQ}(s) &= Z_1(s) + Z_2(s) \\ &= \frac{R_1C_1R_2C_2s^2 + (R_1C_1 + R_2C_2 + R_1C_2)s + 1}{C_2s(R_1C_1s + 1)} \end{aligned}$$

(b) Using voltage division, the voltage transfer function is

$$T_V(s) = \frac{Z_2(s)}{Z_{EQ}(s)} = \frac{(R_1C_1s + 1)(R_2C_2s + 1)}{R_1C_1R_2C_2s^2 + (R_1C_1 + R_2C_2 + R_1C_2)s + 1}$$ ■

EXAMPLE 11–4

Find the driving-point impedance seen by the voltage source in Figure 11–8. Find the voltage transfer function $T_V(s) = V_2(s)/V_1(s)$ of the circuit.

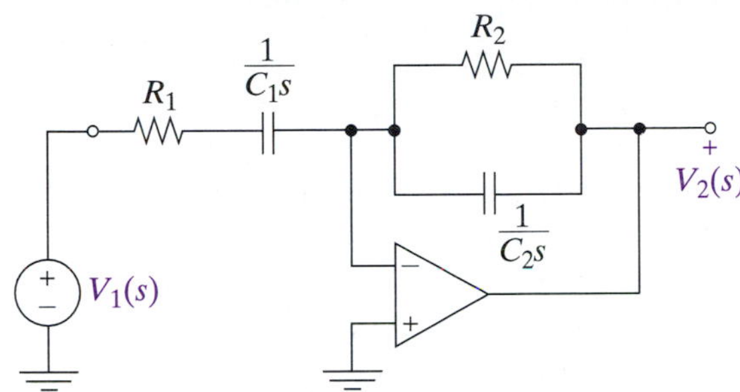

FIGURE 11–8

SOLUTION:
The circuit is an inverting OP AMP configuration of the form in Figure 11–5(a). The input impedance of this circuit is

$$Z_1(s) = R_1 + \frac{1}{C_1 s} = \frac{R_1 C_1 s + 1}{C_1 s}$$

The impedance Z_2 in the feedback path is

$$Z_2(s) = \frac{1}{C_2 s + 1/R_2} = \frac{R_2}{R_2 C_2 s + 1}$$

and the voltage transfer function is

$$T_V(s) = -\frac{Z_2(s)}{Z_1(s)} = -\frac{R_2 C_1 s}{(R_1 C_1 s + 1)(R_2 C_2 s + 1)}$$

EXAMPLE 11–5

For the circuit in Figure 11–9 find the input impedance $Z(s) = V_1(s)/I_1(s)$, the transfer impedance $T_Z(s) = V_2(s)/I_1(s)$, and the voltage transfer function $T_V(s) = V_2(s)/V_1(s)$.

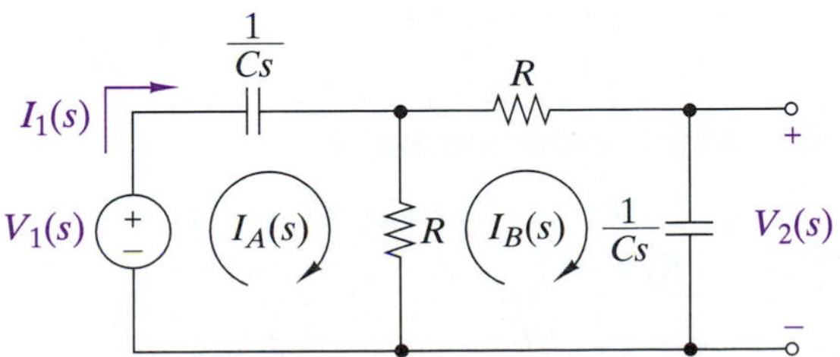

FIGURE 11–9

SOLUTION:

The circuit is not a divider, so we use mesh-current equations to illustrate the general approach to finding network functions. By inspection, the mesh-current equations for this ladder circuit are

$$\left(R + \frac{1}{Cs}\right) I_A(s) - RI_B(s) = V_1(s)$$

$$-RI_A(s) + \left(2R + \frac{1}{Cs}\right) I_B(s) = 0$$

In terms of the mesh current, the input impedance is $Z(s) = V_1(s)/I_A(s)$. Using Cramer's rule to solve for $I_A(s)$ yields

$$I_A(s) = \frac{\Delta_A}{\Delta} = \frac{\begin{vmatrix} V_1(s) & -R \\ 0 & 2R + \dfrac{1}{Cs} \end{vmatrix}}{\begin{vmatrix} R + \dfrac{1}{Cs} & -R \\ -R & 2R + \dfrac{1}{Cs} \end{vmatrix}} = \frac{Cs(2RCs + 1)}{(RCs)^2 + 3RCs + 1} V_1(s)$$

The input impedance of the circuit is

$$Z(s) = \frac{V_1(s)}{I_A(s)} = \frac{(RCs)^2 + 3RCs + 1}{Cs(2RCs + 1)}$$

In terms of mesh current, the transfer impedance is $T_Z(s) = V_2(s)/I_A(s)$. The mesh-current equations do not yield the output voltage directly. But since $V_2(s) = I_B(s)Z_C(s)$, we can solve the second mesh equation for $I_B(s)$ in terms of as $I_A(s)$ as

$$I_B(s) = \frac{RCs}{2RCs + 1} I_A(s)$$

and obtain the specified transfer impedance as

$$T_Z(s) = \frac{I_B(s)[1/Cs]}{I_A(s)} = \frac{R}{2RCs + 1}$$

To obtain the specified voltage transfer function, we could use Cramer's rule to solve for $I_B(s)$ in terms of as $V_1(s)$ and then use the fact that $V_2(s) = I_B(s)Z_C(s)$. But a moment's reflection reveals that

$$T_V(s) = \frac{V_2(s)}{V_1(s)} = \left[\frac{V_2(s)}{I_1(s)}\right]\left[\frac{I_1(s)}{V_1(s)}\right] = T_Z(s) \times \frac{1}{Z(s)}$$

Hence the specified voltage transfer function is

$$T_V(s) = \frac{R}{2RCs + 1} \times \frac{Cs(2RCs + 1)}{(RCs)^2 + 3RCs + 1}$$

$$= \frac{RCs}{(RCs)^2 + 3RCs + 1}$$

■

EXAMPLE 11–6

Find the voltage transfer function $T_V(s) = V_2(s)/V_1(s)$ of the circuit in Figure 11–10.

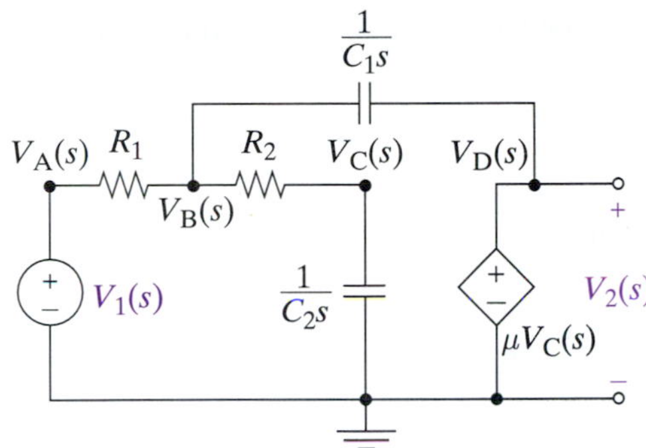

FIGURE 11–10

SOLUTION:

The voltage-controlled voltage source make this an active RC circuit. We use node-voltage equations in this problem because the required output is a voltage. The circuit contains two voltage sources connected at a common node. Selecting this common node as the reference eliminates two unknowns since $V_A(s) = V_1(s)$ and $V_D(s) = \mu V_C(s) = V_2(s)$. The sums of currents leaving nodes B and C are

$$\text{Node B: } \frac{V_B(s) - V_1(s)}{R_1} + \frac{V_B(s) - V_C(s)}{R_2} + \frac{V_B(s) - \mu V_C(s)}{1/C_1(s)} = 0$$

$$\text{Node C: } \frac{V_C(s) - V_B(s)}{R_2} + \frac{V_C(s)}{1/C_2 s} = 0$$

Multiplying both equations by R_1R_2 and rearranging terms produces

$$\text{Node B: } (R_1 + R_2 + R_1R_2C_1s)V_B(s) - (R_1 + \mu R_1R_2C_1s)V_C(s) = R_2V_1(s)$$

$$\text{Node C: } -V_B(s) + (1 + R_2C_2s)V_C(s) = 0$$

Using the node C equation to eliminate $V_B(s)$ from the node B equation leaves

$$(R_1 + R_2 + R_1R_2C_1s)(1 + R_2C_2s)V_C(s)$$
$$- (R_1 + \mu R_1R_2C_1s)V_C(s) = R_2V_1(s)$$

Since the output $V_2(s) = \mu V_C(s)$, the required transfer function is

$$T_V(s) = \frac{V_2(s)}{V_1(s)} = \frac{\mu}{R_1R_2C_1C_2s^2 + (R_1C_1 + R_1C_2 + R_2C_2 - \mu R_1C_1)s + 1}$$

This circuit is used in filter design with $R_1 = R_2 = R$ and $C_1 = C_2 = C$, in which case the transfer function reduces to

$$T_V(s) = \frac{\mu}{(RCs)^2 + (3 - \mu)RCs + 1}$$

We will encounter this result again in later chapters.

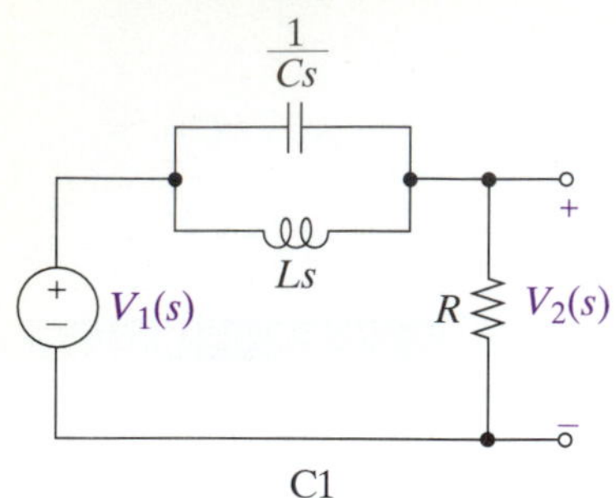

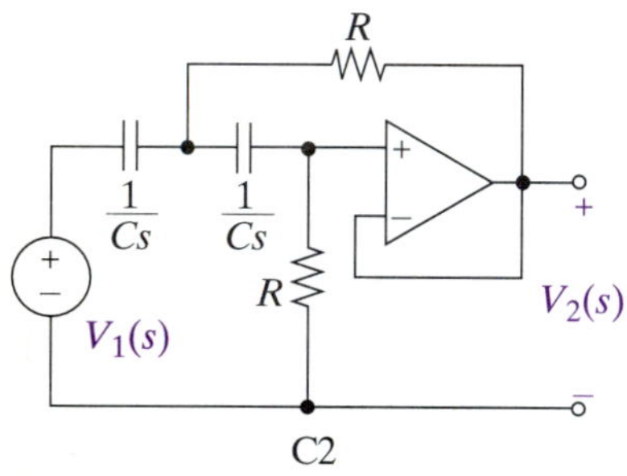

FIGURE 11–11

Exercise 11–1

Find the driving-point impedance seen by each of the voltage sources in Figure 11–11.

Answers:

$$\text{Circuit C1: } Z(s) = \frac{RLCs^2 + Ls + R}{LCs^2 + 1}$$

$$\text{Circuit C2: } Z(s) = \frac{RCs + 1}{Cs}$$

Exercise 11–2

Find the voltage transfer functions $T_V(s) = V_2(s)/V_1(s)$ of each of the circuits in Figure 11–11.

Answers:

$$\text{Circuit C1: } T_V(s) = \frac{LCs^2 + 1}{LCs^2 + GLs + 1}$$

$$\text{Circuit C2: } T_V(s) = \frac{(RCs)^2}{(RCs + 1)^2}$$

THE CASCADE CONNECTION AND THE CHAIN RULE

Signal-processing circuits often involve a **cascade connection** in which the output voltage of one circuit serves as the input to the next stage. In some cases, the overall voltage transfer function of the cascade can be related to the transfer functions of the individual stages by a **chain rule**

$$T_V(s) = T_{V1}(s)T_{V2}(s) \cdots T_{Vk}(s) \qquad (11\text{–}11)$$

where T_{V1}, T_{V2}, . . . and T_{Vk} are the voltage transfer functions of the individual stages when operated separately. It is important to understand when the chain rule applies since it greatly simplifies the analysis and design of cascade circuits.

The chain rule in Eq. (11–11) applies if connecting the stages in cascade does not load (change) the output of any stage in the cascade. At any given stage, interface loading does not occur if (1) the Thévenin impedance of the source stage is zero or (2) the input impedance of the load stage is infinite. As a practical matter, however, the chain rule yields acceptable results when the Thévenin impedance of the source is simply much smaller than the input impedance of the load.

To illustrate the effect of loading, consider the two RC circuits or stages in Figure 11–12. When disconnected and operated separately, the transfer functions of each stage are easily found using voltage division as follows:

$$T_{V1}(s) = \frac{R}{R + 1/Cs} = \frac{RCs}{RCs + 1}$$

$$T_{V2}(s) = \frac{1/Cs}{R + 1/Cs} = \frac{1}{RCs + 1}$$

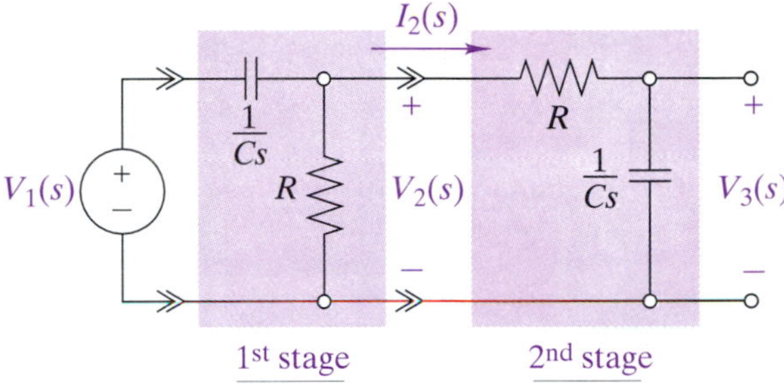

FIGURE 11–12 Two-port circuits connected in cascade.

When connected in cascade, the output of the first stage serves as the input to the second stage. If the chain rule applies, we would obtain the overall transfer function as

$$T_V(s) = \frac{V_3(s)}{V_1(s)} = \left(\frac{V_2(s)}{V_1(s)}\right)\left(\frac{V_3(s)}{V_2(s)}\right) = (T_{V1}(s))\,(T_{V2}(s)) \tag{11-12}$$

$$= \underbrace{\left(\frac{RCs}{RCs + 1}\right)}_{\text{First Stage}}\underbrace{\left(\frac{1}{RCs + 1}\right)}_{\text{Second Stage}} = \underbrace{\frac{RCs}{(RCs)^2 + 2RCs + 1}}_{\text{Overall}}$$

However, in Example 11–5, the overall transfer function of this circuit was found to be

$$T_V(s) = \frac{RCs}{(RCs)^2 + 3RCs + 1} \tag{11-13}$$

which disagrees with the chain rule result in Eq. (11–12).

The reason for the discrepancy is that when they are connected in cascade, the second circuit "loads" the first circuit. That is, the voltage-divider rule requires that the interface current $I_2(s)$ in Figure 11–12 be zero. The no-load condition $I_2(s) = 0$ applies when the stages operate separately, but when connected in cascade, the interface current is not zero. The chain rule does not apply here because loading caused by the second stage changes the transfer function of the first stage.

However, Figure 11–13 shows how the loading problem goes away when OP AMP voltage follower is inserted between the *RC* circuit stages. The follower does not draw any current from the first *RC* circuit [$I_2(s) = 0$] and applies $V_2(s)$ directly across the input of the second *RC* circuit. With this modification the chain rule in Eq. (11–11) applies because the voltage follower isolates the two circuits, thereby solving the loading problem.

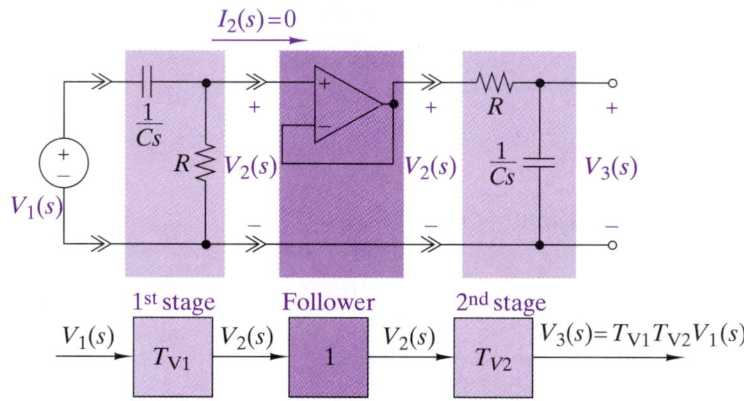

FIGURE 11–13 *Cascade connection with voltage-follower isolation.*

Thus, loading can be avoided by connecting an OP AMP voltage follower between stages, as in Figure 11–13. More important, loading does not occur if the output of the driving stage is the output of an OP AMP or controlled source. These elements act like ideal voltage sources whose outputs are unchanged by connecting the subsequent stage.

For example, the two circuits in Figure 11–14 are connected in a cascade, with circuit C1 appearing first in the cascade followed by circuit C2. The chain rule applies to this configuration because the Thévenin impedance of the OP AMP circuit is essentially zero so that circuit C1 drives the input impedance presented by circuit C2. On the other hand, if the stages are interchanged so that circuit C2 drives circuit C1 in the cascade, then the chain rule does not apply because the input impedance of circuit C1 would load the output of circuit C2.

EXAMPLE 11–7

Find the voltage transfer function of the cascade connection in Figure 11–14 for a cascade connection in which circuit C1 is followed by circuit C2.

SOLUTION:

The chain rule applies to this configuration, since the output of circuit C1 is an OP AMP. Circuit C1 is an inverting OP AMP circuit and its transfer function is found from Eq. (11–9) as

$$T_{V1}(s) = -\frac{Z_2(s)}{Z_1(s)} = -\frac{R_2}{R_1 + 1/C_1 s} = -\frac{R_2 C_1 s}{R_1 C_1 s + 1}$$

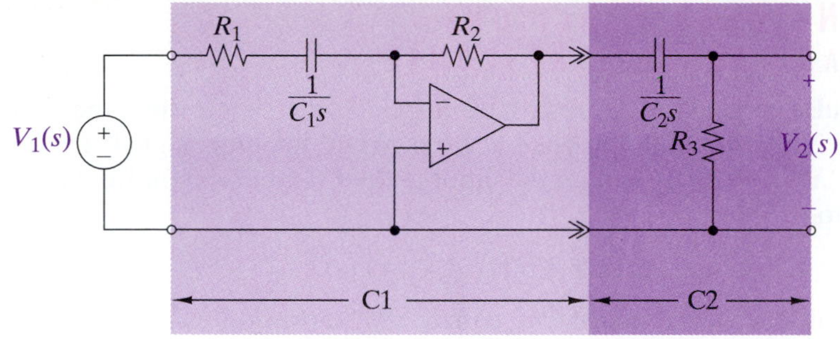

FIGURE 11–14

Circuit C2 is a voltage divider whose voltage transfer function is given by the voltage-divider rule as

$$T_{V2}(s) = \frac{Z_2(s)}{Z_2(s) + Z_1(s)} = \frac{R_3}{R_3 + 1/C_2s} = \frac{R_3C_2s}{R_3C_2s + 1}$$

Applying the chain rule in Eq. (11–11) yields the overall transfer function as

$$T_V(s) = T_{V1}(s)T_{V2}(s) = -\frac{R_2C_1R_3C_2s^2}{(R_1C_1s + 1)(R_3C_2s + 1)}$$ ■

Exercise 11–3

Find the voltage transfer function when the positions of circuits C1 and C2 in Figure 11–14 are reversed. That is, circuit C2 is the first stage in the cascade connection and circuit C1 is the second stage.

Answer:

$$T_V(s) = -\frac{R_2C_1R_3C_2s^2}{R_1C_1R_3C_2s^2 + (R_1C_1 + R_3C_2 + R_3C_1)s + 1}$$

Note that this is not the same answer obtained in Example 11–7, where the chain rule applied.

Exercise 11–4

The transfer functions of the circuits in Figure 11–11 are

$$\text{Circuit C1: } T_V(s) = \frac{LCs^2 + 1}{LCs^2 + GLs + 1}$$

$$\text{Circuit C2: } T_V(s) = \frac{(RCs)^2}{(RCs + 1)^2}$$

Find the overall transfer function of a cascade connection in which circuit C2 is the first stage and circuit C1 is the second stage.

Answer:

$$T_V(s) = \frac{(RCs)^2(LCs^2 + 1)}{(RCs + 1)^2\,(LCs^2 + GLs + 1)}$$

11–3 NETWORK FUNCTIONS AND IMPULSE RESPONSE

The **impulse response** is the zero-state response of a circuit when the driving force is a unit impulse applied at $t = 0$. When the input signal is $x(t) = \delta(t)$ then $X(s) = \mathscr{L}\{\delta(t)\} = 1$ and the input–output relationship in Eq. (11–2) reduces to

$$Y(s) = T(s) \times 1 = T(s)$$

The impulse response transform equals the network function, and we could treat $T(s)$ as if it is a signal transform. However, to avoid possible confusion between a network function (description of a circuit) and a transform (description of a signal), we denote the impulse response transform as $H(s)$ and use $h(t)$ to denote the corresponding waveform.[3] That is,

Impulse Response

$$\begin{array}{cc} \text{Transform} & \text{Waveform} \\ H(s) = T(s) \times 1 & h(t) = \mathscr{L}^{-1}\{H(s)\} \end{array} \qquad (11\text{–}14)$$

When there are no repeated poles, the partial fraction expansion of $H(s)$ is

$$H(s) = \underbrace{\frac{k_1}{s - p_1} + \frac{k_2}{s - p_2} + \cdots + \frac{k_N}{s - p_N}}_{\text{Natural Poles}}$$

where $p_1, p_2, \ldots p_N$ are the natural poles in the denominator of the transfer function $T(s)$. All of the poles of $H(s)$ are natural poles since the impulse excitation does not introduce any forced poles. The inverse transform gives the impulse response waveform as

$$h(t) = \underbrace{[k_1 e^{p_1 t} + k_2 e^{p_2 t} + \cdots + k_N e^{p_N t}]}_{\text{Natural Response}} u(t)$$

When the circuit is stable, all of the natural poles are in the left half plane and the impulse response waveform $h(t)$ decays to zero as $t \to \infty$. A linear circuit whose impulse response ultimately returns to zero is said to be **asymptotically stable**. Asymptotic stability means that the impulse response has a finite time duration. That is, for every $\varepsilon > 0$ there exists a finite time duration T_D such that $|h(t)| < \varepsilon$ for all $t > T_D$.

It is important to note that the impulse response $h(t)$ contains all the information needed to determine the circuit response to any other input. That is, since $\mathscr{L}\{h(t)\} = T(s)$, we can calculate the output $y(t)$ for any Laplace transformable input $x(t)$ as

$$y(t) = \mathscr{L}^{-1}\{H(s)X(s)\}$$

3 Not all books make this distinction. Books on signals and circuits often use $H(s)$ to represent both a transfer function and the impulse response transform.

Since calculating the impulse response $h(t)$ is obviously important, we discuss three methods of doing so. The first method simply involves finding the circuit transfer function and then performing the inverse Laplace transformation. The following example illustrates this method.

EXAMPLE 11–8

Find the response $v_2(t)$ in Figure 11–15 when the input is $v_1(t) = \delta(t)$. Use the element values $R_1 = 10\ \text{k}\Omega$, $R_2 = 12.5\ \text{k}\Omega$, $C_1 = 1\ \mu\text{F}$, and $C_2 = 2\ \mu\text{F}$.

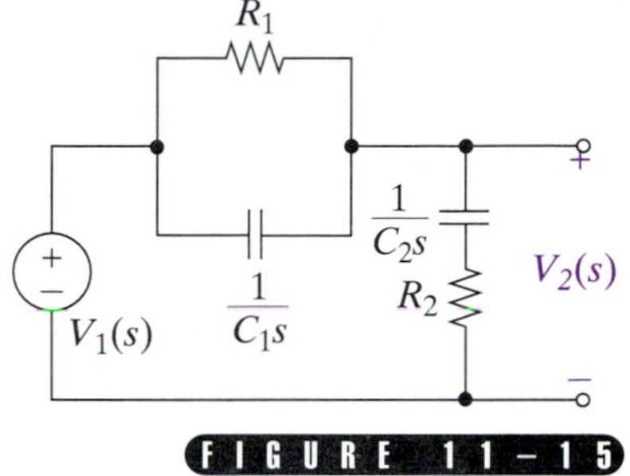

FIGURE 11–15

SOLUTION:

In Example 11–3, the transfer function of this circuit was found to be

$$T_V(s) = \frac{V_2(s)}{V_1(s)} = \frac{(R_1C_1s + 1)(R_2C_2s + 1)}{R_1C_1R_2C_2s^2 + (R_1C_1 + R_2C_2 + R_1C_2)s + 1}$$

For the given element values, the impulse response transform is

$$H(s) = \frac{(s + 100)\,(s + 40)}{s^2 + 220s + 4000} = \frac{(s + 100)\,(s + 40)}{(s + 20)\,(s + 200)}$$

This $H(s)$ is not a proper rational function, so we use one step of a long division plus a partial-fraction expansion to obtain

$$H(s) = 1 + \frac{80/9}{s + 20} - \frac{800/9}{s + 200}$$

and the impulse response is

$$h(t) = \delta(t) + \frac{80}{9}[e^{-20t} - 10e^{-200t}]u(t)$$

In this case, the impulse response contains an impulse because the network function is not a proper rational function. ■

The second method involves approximating the impulse by a short pulse. If we drive a linear circuit with an input $x(t) = A\delta(t)$, then because of proportionality the response is $y(t) = Ah(t)$. In this case, the area under the input is

$$\int_{-\infty}^{\infty} x(t)dt = A\int_{-\infty}^{\infty} \delta(t)dt = A$$

This results points out that the circuit response $Ah(t)$ is proportional to the area under the impulsive input. This area proportionality is approximately true for short pulse excitations in general. When the input is a pulse $p(t)$ whose duration is short compared to the duration of $h(t)$, then the response is approximately $y(t) \approx Ah(t)$, where A is the area under $p(t)$. To approximate a unit impulse, a short pulse $p(t)$ must be zero everywhere outside of a time interval $(0, T)$ and the area under $p(t)$ must be 1; that is,

$$\int_0^T p(t)dt = 1$$

To qualify as a short pulse, the time interval $(0, T)$ must be short compared to the duration of $h(t)$.

We refer to this method of calculating the impulse response as the **short pulse approximation**. The following example illustrates this method.

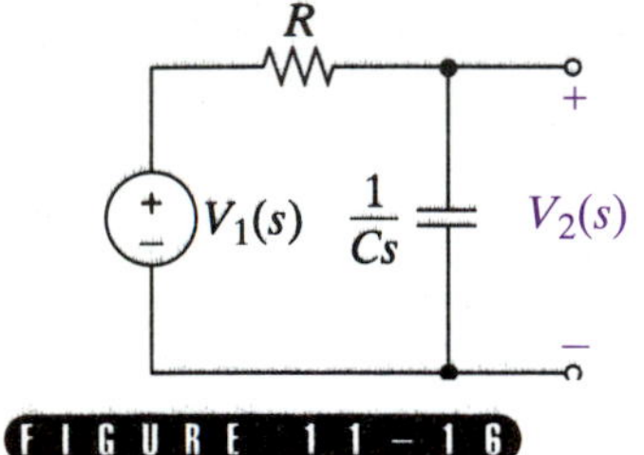

FIGURE 11–16

EXAMPLE 11–9

Circuit analysis programs like SPICE and MICRO-CAP do not simulate the theoretical impulse waveform. However, the short pulse approximation allows these programs to generate useful substitutes for an impulse response. The purpose of this example is to demonstrate this capability using MicroSim Design Center to find the impulse response of $v_2(t)$ in Figure 11–16 for $R = 10$ kΩ and $C = 1$ μF.

SOLUTION:

In Example 11–2 the transfer function of this circuit is shown to be $T_V(s) = 1/(RCs + 1)$. For the given element values the impulse response is

$$v_2(t) = h(t) = \mathscr{L}^{-1}\left\{\frac{100}{s + 100}\right\} = [100e^{-100t}]u(t)$$

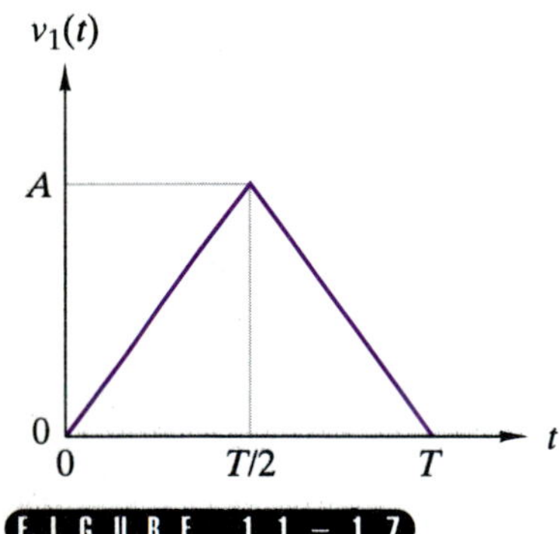

FIGURE 11–17

The circuit has a time constant of $T_C = 10$ ms. We use the triangular pulse in Figure 11–17 to simulate an impulse with MicroSim PSpice. For this waveform an area of unity requires $AT = 2$ and a "short" duration requires $T << T_C$. Choosing $T = 0.2$ ms means that $A = 10$ kV.

Figure 11–18 shows the key screens in the MicroSim Design Center simulation of this circuit. The voltage source V_1 is the piecewise linear voltage source (**VPWL**) found in the source library. Selecting (double clicking) the source brings up the **VPWL** parameter menu shown in the figure. The **VPWL** source produces its waveform by connecting straight lines between a sequence of time/voltage pairs $\{T_k, V_k\}k = 1, 2, \ldots n$. The **VPWL** parameter menu in the figure shows that we delay the start of the pulse for 1 ms, so the pairs $\{T_2 = 1 \text{ ms}, V_2 = 0\}$, $\{T_3 = 1.1 \text{ ms}, V_3 = 10 \text{ kV}\}$, and $\{T_3 = 1.2 \text{ ms}, V_2 = 0\}$ generate a time-shifted triangular waveform whose area is 1.

Impulse response is a zero-state response. To ensure a zero-state condition, we set the capacitor initial condition to zero (**IC = 0** in the component dialog box) and then select **Analysis/Set-up/Transient** and put a check mark in the **Use Initial Conditions** box. If this box is not checked, PSpice will recalculate the initial conditions prior to running a transient response calculation. Selecting the **Analysis/Simulate** command from the menu bar causes MicroSim PSpice to calculate the zero-state response for the triangular pulse input.

The MicroSim Probe plots in Figure 11–18 show the input pulse and the resulting pulse response. The following data compare the MicroSim PSpice results to the delayed impulse response $h(t - 0.001)$. For $t > 0.002$ s (the end of the simulated impulse) the PSpice results and the theoretical value of $h(t - 0.001)$ generally agree to three significant figures. They do not agree at all at $t = 0.001$ s (the start of the simulated impulse) because the triangular pulse in the simulation cannot produce an instantaneous jump in the voltage across a capacitor.

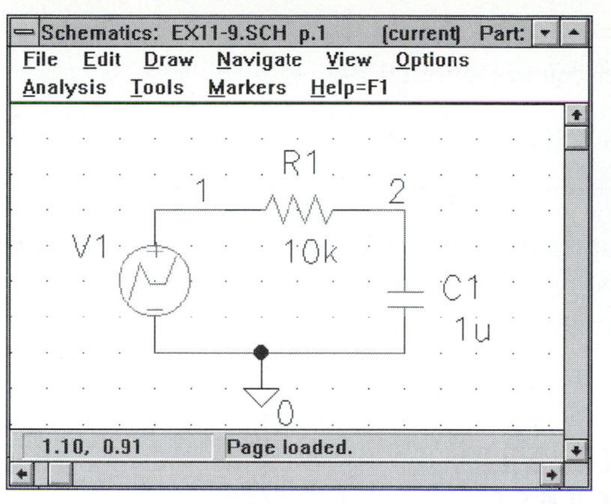

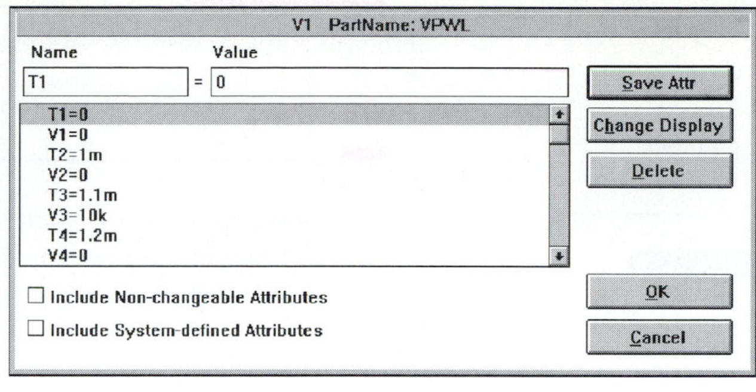

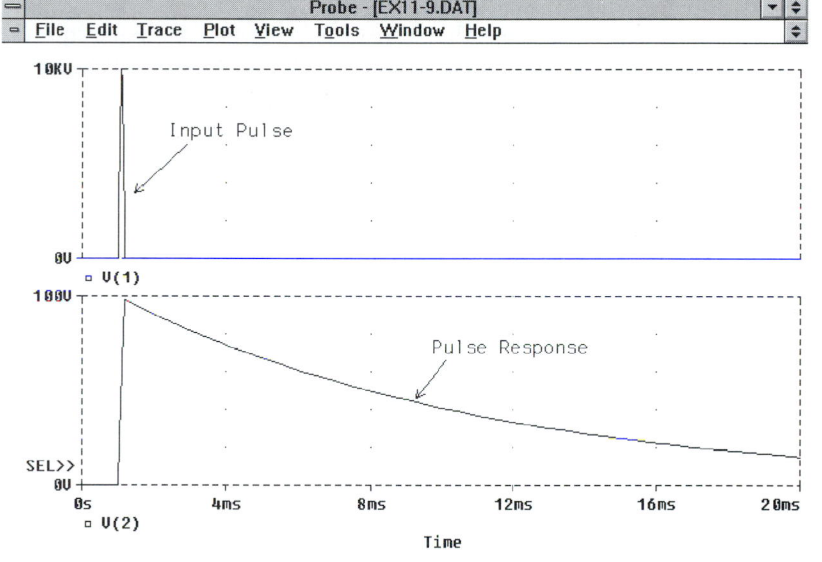

FIGURE 11–18

TIME	PSPICE	$h(t-0.001)$	TIME	PSPICE	$h(t-0.001)$	TIME	PSPICE	$h(t-0.001)$
0.001	0	100	0.006	60.75	60.65	0.011	36.84	36.79
0.002	90.63	90.48	0.007	54.96	54.88	0.012	33.34	33.29
0.003	81.99	81.87	0.008	49.74	49.66	0.013	30.16	30.12
0.004	74.20	74.08	0.009	45.00	44.93	0.014	27.29	27.25
0.005	67.13	67.03	0.01	40.72	40.66	0.015	24.69	24.66

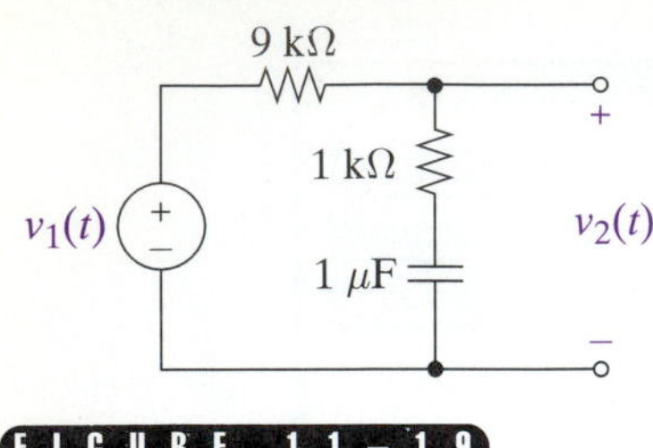

FIGURE 11–19

Exercise 11–5

Find the impulse response of the circuit in Figure 11–19.

Answer: $h(t) = 0.1\delta(t) + [90e^{-100t}]u(t)$

The third method of calculating the impulse response of a linear circuit is to establish a relationship between the impulse and the step response. This method is developed in the next section.

11–4 NETWORK FUNCTIONS AND STEP RESPONSE

The **step response** is the zero-state response of the circuit output when the driving force is a unit step function applied at $t = 0$. When the input is $x(t) = u(t)$, then $X(s) = \mathscr{L}\{u(t)\} = 1/s$ and the s-domain input-output relationship in Eq. (11–2) yields $Y(s) = T(s)/s$. The step response transform and waveform will be denoted by $G(s)$ and $g(t)$, respectively. That is,

Step Response

Transform	Waveform
$G(s) = \dfrac{T(s)}{s}$	$g(t) = \mathscr{L}^{-1}\{G(s)\}$

(11–15)

The poles of $G(s)$ are the natural poles contributed by the network function $T(s)$ and a forced pole at $s = 0$ introduced by the step function input. The partial fraction expansion of $G(s)$ takes the form

$$G(s) = \underbrace{\frac{k_0}{s}}_{\text{Forced Pole}} + \underbrace{\frac{k_1}{s-p_1} + \frac{k_2}{s-p_2} + \cdots + \frac{k_N}{s-p_N}}_{\text{Natural Poles}}$$

where $p_1, p_2, \ldots p_N$ are the natural poles in $T(s)$. The inverse transformation gives the step response waveform as

$$g(t) = \underbrace{k_0 u(t)}_{\text{Forced Response}} + \underbrace{[k_1 e^{p_1 t} + k_2 e^{p_2 t} + \cdots + k_N e^{p_N t}]u(t)}_{\text{Natural Response}}$$

When the circuit is stable, the natural response decays to zero, leaving a forced component called the **dc steady-state response**. The amplitude of the steady-state response is the residue in the partial-fraction expansion of the forced pole at $s = 0$. By the cover-up method, this residue is

$$k_0 = sG(s)|_{s=0} = T(0)$$

For a unit step input the amplitude of the dc steady-state response equals the value of the transfer function at $s = 0$. By linearity, the general principle is that an input $Au(t)$ produces a dc steady-state output whose amplitude is $AT(0)$.

We next show the relationship between the impulse and step responses. First, combining Eqs. (11–14) and (11–15) gives

$$G(s) = \frac{H(s)}{s}$$

The step response transform is the impulse response transform divided by s. The integration property of the Laplace transform tells us that division by s in the s domain corresponds to integration in the time domain. Therefore, in the time domain, we can relate the impulse and step response waveforms by integration:

$$g(t) = \int_0^t h(\tau)d\tau \qquad (11\text{–}16)$$

Using the fundamental theorem of calculus, the impulse response waveform is expressed in terms of the step response waveform

$$h(t)(=)\frac{dg(t)}{dt} \qquad (11\text{–}17)$$

where the symbol (=) means equal almost everywhere, a condition that excludes those points at which $g(t)$ has a discontinuity. In the time domain, the step response waveform is the integral of the impulse response waveform. Conversely, the impulse response waveform is (almost everywhere) the derivative of the step response waveform.

The key idea is that there are relationships between the network function $T(s)$ and the responses $H(s)$, $h(t)$, $G(s)$, and $g(t)$. If any one of these quantities is known, we can obtain any of the other four using relatively simple mathematical operations.

EXAMPLE 11–10

Find $g(t)$ and $h(t)$ for the circuit in Figure 11–20.

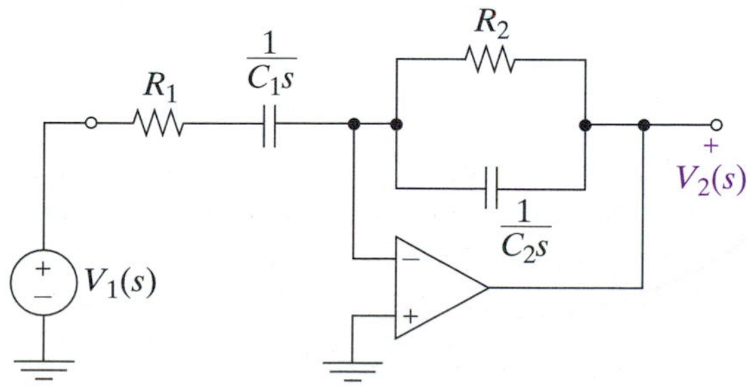

FIGURE 11–20

SOLUTION:
In Example 11–4, the transfer function of this circuit is shown to be

$$T_V(s) = \frac{V_2(s)}{V_1(s)} = -\frac{R_2C_1s}{(R_1C_1s + 1)(R_2C_2s + 1)}$$

For a unit step function input $V_1(s) = 1/s$ and the step response transform is

$$G(s) = \frac{T_V(s)}{s} = -\frac{R_2C_1}{(R_1C_1s + 1)(R_2C_2s + 1)}$$

In this case the forced pole at $s = 0$ is canceled by a zero of $T_V(s)$. In other words, $T_V(0) = 0$ and the dc steady-state output of the circuit is zero. Recall from Chapter 6 that in the dc steady state capacitors can be replaced by open circuits. Replacing C_1 in Figure 11–20 by an open circuit disconnects the input source from the OP AMP, so no dc signal can be transferred through the circuit. When a series capacitor is included in a circuit to prevent the passage of dc signals, it is commonly called a blocking capacitor. Expanding $G(s)$ by partial fractions,

$$G(s) = \left[\frac{R_2C_1}{R_1C_1 - R_2C_2}\right]\left[\frac{1}{s + 1/R_1C_1} - \frac{1}{s + 1/R_2C_2}\right]$$

The inverse transform yields

$$g(t) = \frac{R_2C_1}{R_1C_1 - R_2C_2}[e^{-t/R_1C_1} - e^{-t/R_2C_2}]u(t)$$

Differentiating $g(t)$ yields the impulse response as

$$h(t) = \frac{dg(t)}{dt} = \frac{1}{R_1C_1 - R_2C_2}\left[-\frac{R_2}{R_1}e^{-t/R_1C_1} + \frac{C_1}{C_2}e^{-t/R_2C_2}\right]u(t)$$ ■

EXAMPLE 11–11

The purpose of this example is to show that the s-domain transfer function can be determined from a t-domain graph of the step response. Figure 11–21 shows a graph of the step response of a first-order circuit. Find $T(s)$.

FIGURE 11–21

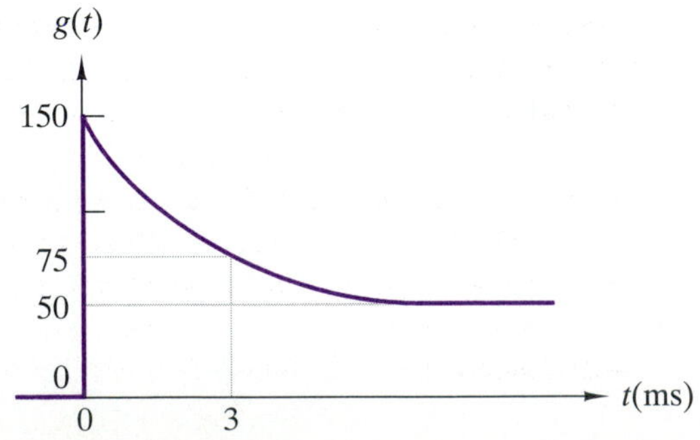

SOLUTION:

The step response of a first-order circuit has the form

$$g(t) = [B + (A - B)e^{-\alpha t}]u(t)$$

where A is the value of $g(t)$ at $t = 0$ and B is the dc steady-state output. Inspecting the graph, we find that $A = 150$ V and $B = 50$ V; hence, $g(t)$ has the form $g(t) = [50 + 100e^{-\alpha t}]u(t)$. In Figure 11–21 $g(t)$ passes through 75 V at $t = 0.003$ s. This condition requires that $e^{-0.003\alpha} = 0.25$. Solving for α yields $\alpha = \ln(4)/0.003 = 462$ rad/s. All of the parameters defining the step response waveform are now available. The Laplace transform of $g(t)$ is

$$G(s) = \frac{50}{s} + \frac{100}{s + 462} = 50\left[\frac{3s + 462}{s(s + 462)}\right]$$

and the circuit transfer function is found to be

$$T(s) = sG(s) = 50\left[\frac{3s + 462}{s + 462}\right]$$ ■

Exercise 11–6

Find $g(t)$ for the circuit in Exercise 11–5 (Figure 11–19).

Answer: $g(t) = [1 - 0.9e^{-1000t}]u(t)$

Exercise 11–7

The step response of a linear circuit is $g(t) = 5[e^{-1000t}\sin(2000t)]u(t)$. Find the circuit transfer function $T(s)$.

Answer:

$$T(s) = \frac{10^4 s}{s^2 + 2000s + 5 \times 10^6}$$

11–5 NETWORK FUNCTIONS AND SINUSOIDAL STEADY-STATE RESPONSE

When a stable, linear circuit is driven by a sinusoidal input, the output contains a steady-state component that is a sinusoid of the same frequency as the input. This section deals with using the circuit transfer function to find the amplitude and phase angle of the sinusoidal steady-state response. To begin, we write a general sinusoidal input in the form

$$x(t) = X_A \cos(\omega t + \phi) \qquad (11-18)$$

which can be expanded as

$$x(t) = X_A(\cos \omega t \cos \phi - \sin \omega t \sin \phi)$$

The waveforms cos ωt and sin ωt are basic signals whose transforms are given in Table 9–2 as $\mathcal{L}\{\cos \omega t\} = s/(s^2 + \omega^2)$ and $\mathcal{L}\{\sin \omega t\} = \omega/(s^2 + \omega^2)$. Therefore, the input transform is

$$\begin{aligned} X(s) &= X_A\left[\frac{s}{s^2+\omega^2}\cos\phi - \frac{\omega}{s^2+\omega^2}\sin\phi\right] \\ &= X_A\left[\frac{s\cos\phi - \omega\sin\phi}{s^2+\omega^2}\right] \end{aligned} \tag{11-19}$$

Equation (11–19) is the Laplace transform of the general sinusoidal waveform in Eq. (11–18).

Using Eq. (11–2), we obtain the response transform for a general sinusoidal input:

$$Y(s) = X_A\left[\frac{s\cos\phi - \omega\sin\phi}{(s-j\omega)\,(s+j\omega)}\right]T(s) \tag{11-20}$$

The response transform contains forced poles at $s = \pm j\omega$ because the input is a sinusoid. Expanding Eq. (11–20) by partial fractions,

$$Y(s) = \underbrace{\frac{k}{s-j\omega} + \frac{k^*}{s+j\omega}}_{\text{Forced Poles}} + \underbrace{\frac{k_1}{s-p_1} + \frac{k_2}{s-p_2} + \cdots + \frac{k_N}{s-p_N}}_{\text{Natural Poles}}$$

where $p_1, p_2, \ldots p_N$ are the natural poles contributed by the transfer function $T(s)$. To obtain the response waveform, we perform the inverse transformation:

$$y(t) = \underbrace{ke^{j\omega t} + k^*e^{-j\omega t}}_{\text{Forced Response}} + \underbrace{k_1e^{p_1 t} + k_2e^{p_2 t} + \cdots + k_N e^{p_N t}}_{\text{Natural Response}}$$

When the circuit is stable, the natural response decays to zero, leaving a sinusoidal steady-state response due to the forced poles as $s = \pm j\omega$. The steady-state response is

$$y_{SS}(t) = ke^{j\omega t} + k^*e^{-j\omega t}$$

where the subscript SS identifies a steady-state condition.

To determine the amplitude and phase of the steady-state response, we must find the residue k. Using the cover-up method from Chapter 9, we find k to be

$$\begin{aligned} k &= (s-j\omega)X_A\left[\frac{s\cos\phi - \omega\sin\phi}{(s-j\omega)(s+j\omega)}\right]T(s)\bigg|_{s=j\omega} \\ &= X_A\left[\frac{j\omega\cos\phi - \omega\sin\phi}{2j\omega}\right]T(j\omega) \\ &= X_A\left[\frac{\cos\phi + j\sin\phi}{2}\right]T(j\omega) = \frac{1}{2}X_A e^{j\phi}T(j\omega) \end{aligned}$$

The complex quantity $T(j\omega)$ can be written in magnitude and angle form as $|T(j\omega)|e^{j\theta}$. Using these results, the residue becomes

$$k = \left[\frac{1}{2}X_A e^{j\phi}\right]\left|T(j\omega)\right|e^{j\theta}$$
$$= \frac{1}{2}X_A\left|T(j\omega)\right|e^{j(\phi+\theta)}$$

The inverse transform yields the steady-state response in the form

$$y_{SS}(t) = 2|k|\cos(\omega t + \phi + \angle k)$$
$$= \underbrace{X_A|T(j\omega)|}_{\text{Amplitude}}\cos(\omega t + \underbrace{\phi + \theta}_{\text{Phase}}) \qquad (11\text{–}21)$$

The steady-state response is a sinusoid with the same frequency as the input but with a different amplitude and phase angle. The relationships between the input and output sinusoids can be summarized in the following statements:

$$\text{Output Amplitude} = (\text{Input Amplitude}) \times (\text{Magnitude of } T(j\omega))$$
$$\text{Output Phase} = (\text{Input Phase}) + (\text{Angle of } T(j\omega))$$

Alternatively, we can express the transfer function in terms of the input and output sinusoids as

$$\text{Magnitude of } T(j\omega) = \frac{\text{Output Amplitude}}{\text{Input Amplitude}}$$
$$\text{Angle of } T(j\omega) = \text{Output Phase} - \text{Input Phase}$$

The next two examples use these results to obtain the sinusoidal steady-state responses from a transfer function.

EXAMPLE 11–12

Find the steady-state output in Figure 11–22 for a general input $v_1(t) = V_A\cos(\omega t + \phi)$.

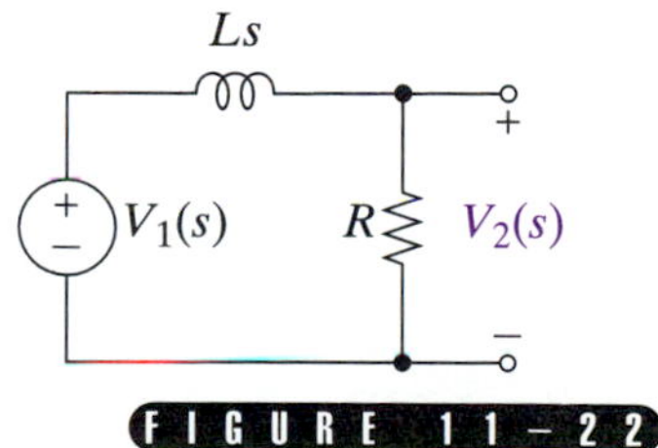

FIGURE 11–22

SOLUTION:

In Example 11–2, the circuit transfer function is shown to be

$$T(s) = \frac{R}{Ls + R}$$

The magnitude and angle of $T(j\omega)$ are

$$|T(j\omega)| = \frac{R}{\sqrt{R^2 + (\omega L)^2}}$$

$$\theta(\omega) = -\tan^{-1}\left(\frac{\omega L}{R}\right)$$

Using Eq. (11–21), the sinusoidal steady-state output is

$$v_{2SS}(t) = \frac{V_A R}{\sqrt{R^2 + (\omega L)^2}} \cos[\omega t + \phi - \tan^{-1}(\omega L/R)]$$

Note that both the amplitude and phase angle of the steady-state response depend on the frequency of the input sinusoid. ■

EXAMPLE 11–13

The step response of a linear circuit is $g(t) = 5[e^{-1000t} \sin 2000t]u(t)$.
(a) Find the sinusoidal steady-state response when $x(t) = 5 \cos 1000t$.
(b) Repeat part (a) when $x(t) = 5 \cos 3000t$.

SOLUTION:

The transfer function corresponding to $g(t)$ is

$$\begin{aligned} T(s) &= sG(s) = s\mathscr{L}\{g(t)\} \\ &= s\left[5\,\frac{2000}{(s+1000)^2 + (2000)^2}\right] \\ &= \frac{10^4 s}{s^2 + 2000s + 5\times 10^6} \end{aligned}$$

(a) At $\omega = 1000$ rad/s, the value of $T(j\omega)$ is

$$\begin{aligned} T(j1000) &= \frac{10^4(j1000)}{(j1000)^2 + 2000\,(j1000) + 5\times 10^6} \\ &= \frac{j10^7}{(5\times 10^6 - 10^6) + j2\times 10^6} = \frac{j10}{4 + j2} \\ &= \frac{10\,e^{j90^\circ}}{\sqrt{20}e^{j26.6^\circ}} = 2.24\,e^{j63.4^\circ} \end{aligned}$$

and the steady-state response for $x(t) = 5 \cos 1000t$ is

$$\begin{aligned} y_{SS}(t) &= 5\times 2.24 \cos(1000t + 0^\circ + 63.4^\circ) \\ &= 11.2 \cos(1000t + 63.4^\circ) \end{aligned}$$

(b) At $\omega = 3000$ rad/s, the value of $T(j\omega)$ is

$$\begin{aligned} T(j3000) &= \frac{10^4(j3000)}{(j3000)^2 + 2000\,(j3000) + 5\times 10^6} \\ &= \frac{j3\times 10^7}{5\times 10^6 - 9\times 10^6 + j6\times 10^6} \\ &= \frac{j30}{-4 + j6} = \frac{30\,e^{j90^\circ}}{\sqrt{52}e^{j123.7^\circ}} = 4.16\,e^{-j33.7^\circ} \end{aligned}$$

and the steady-state response for $x(t) = 5 \cos 3000t$ is

$$y_{SS}(t) = 5 \times 4.16 \cos(3000t + 0° - 33.7°)$$
$$= 20.8 \cos(3000t - 33.7°)$$

Again note that the amplitude and phase angle of the steady-state response depend on the input frequency. ■

Exercise 11–8

The transfer function of a linear circuit is $T(s) = 5(s + 100)/(s + 500)$. Find the steady-state output for
(a) $x(t) = 3 \cos 100t$
(b) $x(t) = 2 \sin 500t$.

Answers:
(a) $y_{SS}(t) = 4.16 \cos(100t + 33.7°)$
(b) $y_{SS}(t) = 7.21 \cos(500t - 56.3°)$

Exercise 11–9

The impulse response of a linear circuit is $h(t) = \delta(t) - 100[e^{-100t}]u(t)$. Find the steady-state output for
(a) $x(t) = 25 \cos 100t$
(b) $x(t) = 50 \sin 100t$.

Answers:
(a) $y_{SS}(t) = 17.7 \cos(100t + 45°)$
(b) $y_{SS}(t) = 35.4 \cos(100t - 45°)$

NETWORK FUNCTIONS AND PHASOR CIRCUIT ANALYSIS

We have two methods of calculating the steady-state response $y_{SS}(t)$ when the input is a sinusoid of the form

$$x(t) = X_A \cos(\omega t + \phi)$$

The first method requires that we convert the input sinusoid into a phasor, calculate the impedance of the circuit elements at the frequency of the input, and then use the phasor circuit analysis methods developed in Chapter 8 to find the phasor response. The phasor response must then be converted into a waveform to obtain $y_{SS}(t)$. The method developed in this section requires that we find the network function $T(s)$ relating input and output, evaluate $T(j\omega)$ (where ω is the frequency of the input sinusoid), and then use Eq. (11–21) to find $y_{SS}(t)$. Under what conditions is one method preferable to the other?

Phasor circuit analysis works best when the circuit is driven at a single frequency and we need to find several voltages and currents, or perhaps average and maximum available power. The network function method works best when the circuit is driven at several frequencies and we only need to find a single response called the output. The network function is also the only method available when all we know about the circuit is its impulse or step response waveform. Thus, the preferred method depends on how the circuit is driven (single or multiple frequency) and what we need to find out (single or multiple response).

11–6 NETWORK FUNCTIONS AND CONVOLUTION

In the s domain, the circuit transfer function $T(s)$ relates the input and output signals, and the input-output relationship $Y(s) = T(s)X(s)$ allows us to calculate the zero-state output for any input. The purpose of this section is to show that there is a time-domain method of calculating the zero-state response using the circuit impulse response.

DERIVATION OF THE CONVOLUTION INTEGRAL

Our derivation begins using the integral definition of the Laplace transformation to write the input transform as

$$X(s) = \int_0^\infty x(\tau)e^{-s\tau}\, d\tau$$

where τ is a dummy variable of integration. Recognizing that $T(s) = H(s)$, we use this expression to write the s-domain input-output relationship in the following way:

$$Y(s) = H(s)\left[\int_0^\infty x(\tau)e^{-s\tau}\, d\tau\right]$$

The impulse response transform $H(s)$ can be moved inside the integration since the integration variable is the dummy variable τ:

$$Y(s) = \int_0^\infty x(\tau)[H(s)e^{-s\tau}]d\tau$$

The time translation property discussed in Chapter 9 shows that the quantity inside the brackets on the right side of this equation is $\mathcal{L}\{[h(t-\tau)]u(t-\tau)\}$. Using the integral definition of the Laplace transformation and the time translation property, we can write this equation as

$$Y(s) = \int_0^\infty x(\tau)\left[\int_0^\infty h(t-\tau)u(t-\tau)e^{-st}\, dt\right]d\tau$$

Interchanging the order of integration, we express this result in the form

$$Y(s) = \int_0^\infty\left[\int_0^t x(\tau)\, h(t-\tau)d\tau\right]e^{-st}\, dt$$

The integration with respect to τ within the brackets only extends from 0 to t since the integral vanishes for $\tau > t$ since $u(t-\tau) = 0$ for $\tau > t$. By definition, the outer integration in this equation is the Laplace transform of the quantity inside the brackets. That is,

$$Y(s) = \mathscr{L}\left[\int_0^t x(\tau)\, h(t - \tau)\, d\tau\right]$$

Finally, applying the inverse Laplace transformation to both sides of this equations produces

$$y(t) = \int_0^t x(\tau)\, h(t - \tau) d\tau \qquad (11\text{–}22a)$$

The expression in Eq. (11–22a) is called the **convolution integral**. Another equivalent form of the convolution integral can be derived by interchanging $X(s)$ and $H(s)$ in the preceding derivation to obtain

$$y(t) = \int_0^t h(\tau) x(t - \tau) d\tau \qquad (11\text{–}22b)$$

The integrals in Eqs. (11–22a) and (22b) are equivalent, and we can use either one as may suit our fancy. The shorthand notation for the first integral is $y(t) = x(t)*h(t)$ and for the second $y(t) = h(t)*x(t)$. The asterisk indicates convolution, not multiplication. The expression $y(t) = h(t)*x(t)$ reads "$h(t)$ convolved with $x(t)$."

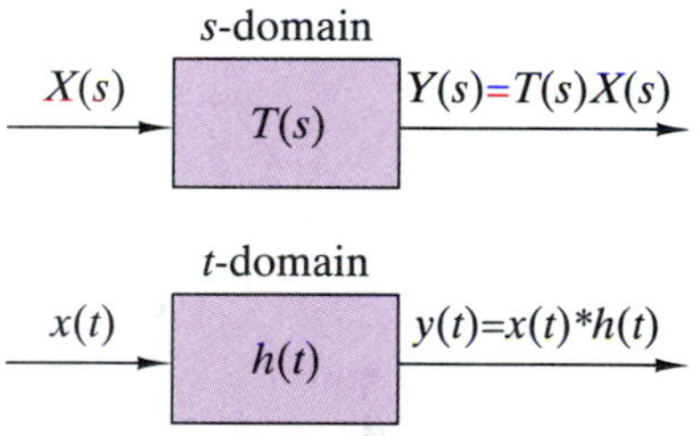

s-domain

X(s) → T(s) → Y(s)=T(s)X(s)

t-domain

x(t) → h(t) → y(t)=x(t)*h(t)

FIGURE 11–23 *Input-output relationships in the* s*-domain and* t*-domain.*

APPLICATIONS OF CONVOLUTION

The convolution integral yields the zero-state response $y(t)$ of a linear circuit with a casual input $x(t)$ and a casual impulse response $h(t)$. Figure 11–23 indicates the parallelism between the input-output relationships in the s domain and t domain. In the s domain path the transfer $T(s)$ relates the input and output transforms. The t domain route uses the impulse response $h(t)$ and convolution to relate the input and output waveforms. The next example uses both methods.

EXAMPLE 11–14

(a) Use convolution to find the output of the circuit in Figure 11–24 when the input is $v_1(t) = tu(t)$.
(b) Use s-domain analysis to find the circuit output for the same input.

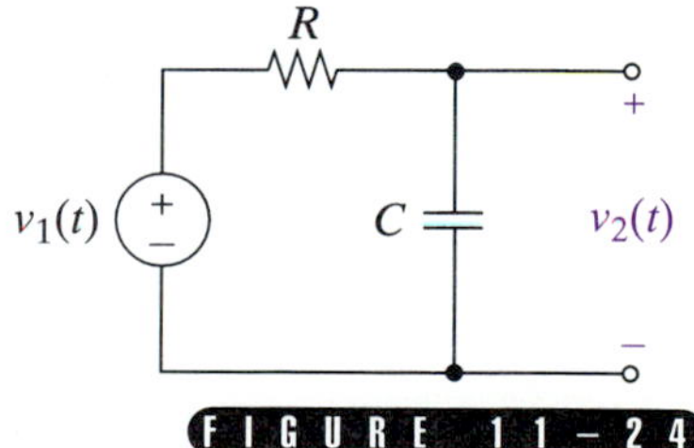

FIGURE 11–24

SOLUTION:

(a) In Example 11–2 the transfer function of this circuit is shown to be $T_V(s) = 1/(RCs + 1)$. Hence the circuit's impulse response is

$$h(t) = \mathscr{L}^{-1}\left[\frac{1/RC}{s + 1/RC}\right] = \left[\frac{e^{-t/RC}}{RC}\right]u(t)$$

For this $h(t)$ and the input $v_1(t) = x(t) = tu(t)$, the version of the convolution integral in Eq. (11–22a) yields the output $y(t)$ in the form

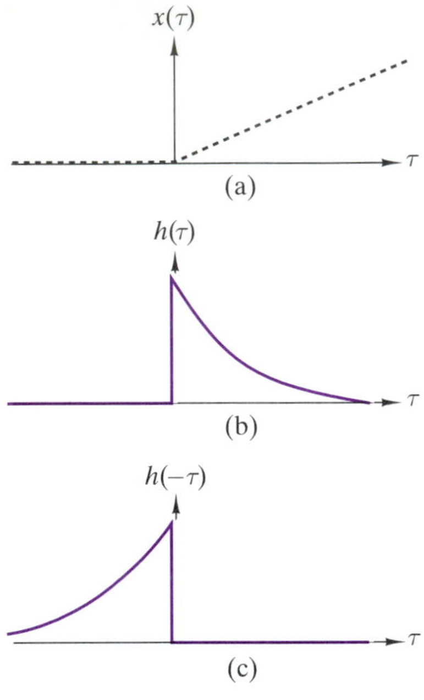

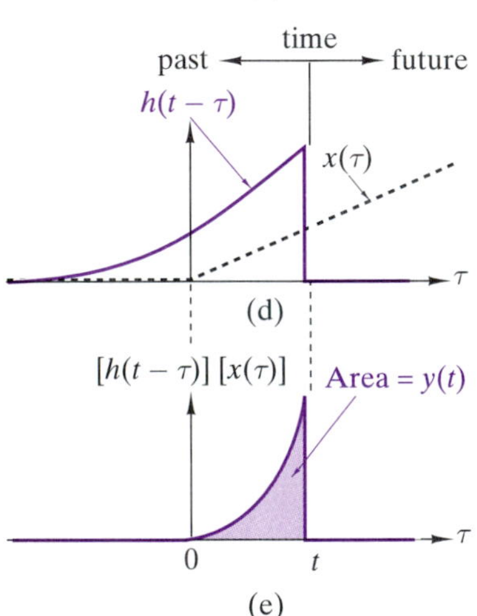

FIGURE 11–25 Graphical interpretation of convolution.

$$y(t) = \int_0^t \frac{e^{-(t-\tau)/RC}}{RC}\tau\, d\tau = \frac{e^{-t/RC}}{RC}\int_0^t \tau e^{\tau/RC}\, d\tau$$

$$= \frac{e^{-t/RC}}{RC}[RCe^{\tau/RC}(\tau - RC)]_0^t$$

$$= t - RC + RCe^{-t/RC} \qquad \text{for} \quad t \geqslant 0$$

Convolution supplies the complete response, including both the forced and natural components.

(b) To obtain the response via the s-domain, we first transform the input as $\mathscr{L}\{tu(t)\} = 1/s^2$ and write the response transform in the form

$$Y(s) = \left[\frac{1/RC}{s + 1/RC}\right]\frac{1}{s^2} = \frac{1}{s^2} - \frac{RC}{s} + \frac{RC}{s + 1/RC}$$

Performing the inverse transform yields

$$y(t) = [t - RC + RCe^{-t/RC}]u(t)$$

The two methods produce the same result, of course. The difference is that convolution is carried out entirely in the time domain. ■

Exercise 11–10

Use convolution to find the output of the circuit in Figure 11–24 when the input is $v_1(t) = [V_A e^{-\alpha t}]u(t)$. Assume that $\alpha RC \neq 1$.

Answer:

$$v_2(t) = \frac{V_A}{1 - RC\alpha}[e^{-\alpha t} - e^{-t/RC}]u(t)$$

We can use the waveforms in Example 11–14 to illustrate a geometric interpretation of convolution. The process begins in Figures 11–25(a) and 11–25(b), where the input and impulse response waveforms are plotted against the dummy integration variable τ. Generating $h(-\tau)$ reflects or folds the impulse response about the $\tau = 0$ axis as shown in Figure 11–25(c). Forming $h(t - \tau)$ advances the reflected waveform by t seconds, as shown in Figure 11–25(d). The product $h(t - \tau) \times x(\tau)$ is shown in Figure 11–25(e). The integral

$$\int_0^t h(t - \tau) \times x(\tau) d\tau$$

is the area under this product and yields the value of the output $y(t)$ at time t. Advancing in time t drags the function $h(t - \tau)$ further to the right, creating a new product $h(t - \tau) \times x(\tau)$, whose area gives a new value of $y(t)$.

Geometrically, we visualize convolution as a process that reflects the impulse response across the origin and then drags it across the input $x(\tau)$ as t increases. At any time t, the output is the area shown in Figure 11–25(e). In this process, we can think of the impulse response as a weighting function. The output at any time t is a function of the input at that instant and previous values of the input. The importance of, and hence weight assigned to, different portions of the input waveform is determined by the amplitude of the impulse response waveform.

For example, the impulse response in Figure 11–25 is an exponential with a time constant of $T_C = RC$. Values of $x(\tau)$ for which $t - \tau > 5T_C$ will receive almost no weight in determining $y(t)$, because $h(t - \tau)$ is negligibly small in that range. Only those values of $x(\tau)$ that are in the window $0 < t - \tau < 5T_C$ have any significant impact on the value of $y(t)$. In effect, the circuit ignores (forgets) inputs outside of this window. In other words, a stable dynamic circuit has a **memory time** defined by the duration of its impulse response.

EXAMPLE 11–15

A certain circuit has an impulse response $h(t) = [200e^{-100t}]u(t)$. Use convolution to find the circuit response for $x(t) = 5[u(t) - u(t - 0.02)]$.

SOLUTION:

To apply convolution, we divide the process into the three situations shown in Figure 11–26. For $t < 0$ in Figure 11–26(a), the folded impulse response $h(t - \tau)$ and the input $x(\tau)$ do not overlap and the area under their product is zero. Hence $y(t) = 0$ for $t < 0$. This simply says that a causal impulse response and a causal input produce a causal output. For $0 < t < 0.02$ the folded impulse response and input overlap, as shown in Figure 11–25(b). During this interval the area under the product $h(t - \tau) \times x(\tau)$ is confined between $\tau = 0$ and $\tau = t$. Hence we evaluate the convolution integral as

$$\begin{aligned} y(t) &= \int_0^t [2000\, e^{-100(t-\tau)}]\,[5]d\tau \\ &= 1000\, e^{-100t} \int_0^t e^{100\tau}\, d\tau \\ &= 10(1 - e^{-100t}) \qquad \text{for} \quad 0 < t < 0.02 \text{ s} \end{aligned}$$

For $0.02 < t$ the folded impulse response and input overlap, as shown in Figure 11–25(c). In this case, the overlap is confined to the interval $0 < \tau < 0.02$ since the input $x(\tau)$ is zero everywhere outside of this interval. To find the area under the product $h(t - \tau) \times x(\tau)$ during this interval, the limits of integration are $\tau = 0$ and $\tau = 0.02$, and the convolution integral is

$$\begin{aligned} y(t) &= \int_0^{0.02} [200e^{-100(t-\tau)}]\,[5]d\tau \\ &= 1000\, e^{-100t} \int_0^{0.02} e^{100\tau}\, d\tau \\ &= 10\, e^{-100t}(e^2 - 1) \qquad \text{for} \quad 0.02 \text{ s} < t \end{aligned}$$

FIGURE 11–26

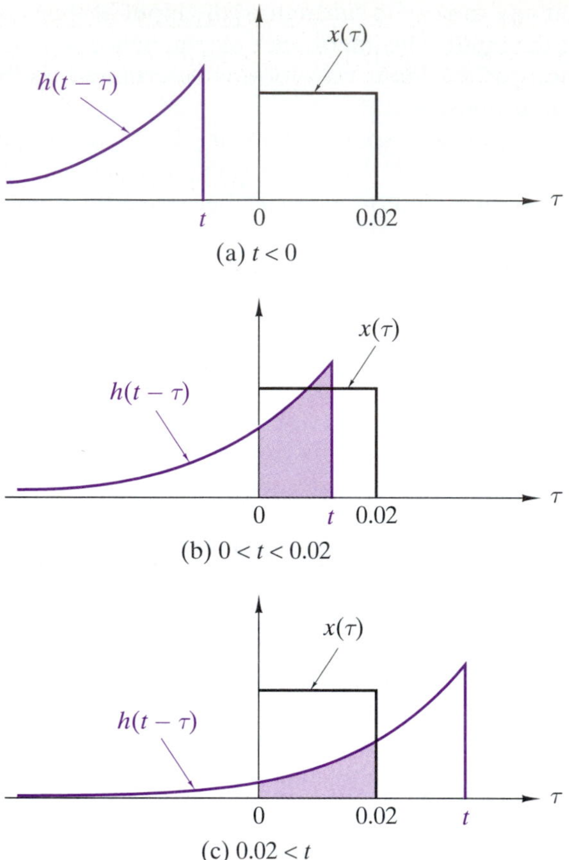

Our analysis approach is guided by the geometric interpretation of convolution in Figure 11–26 and leads to a solution that defines $y(t)$ on three intervals. Figure 11–27 is a Mathcad worksheet showing how the three solutions combine to produce the waveform of $y(t)$. ■

APPLICATION NOTE: EXAMPLE 11–16

One of the practical difficulties with convolution is that laboratory equipment and computer circuit analysis programs cannot produce the theoretical impulse waveform needed to generate the impulse response. In Sect. 11–3, we found that a short pulse approximation allowed us to get a good approximation to the impulse response using PSpice. In general, we can get a useful approximation to the impulse response by driving a circuit with a pulse whose duration is very short compared to the circuit's natural response. It is important to see what convolution has to say about this short pulse approximation.

The previous example showed that applying convolution with pulse excitation involves three situations: Figure 11–26(a) no overlap, Figure

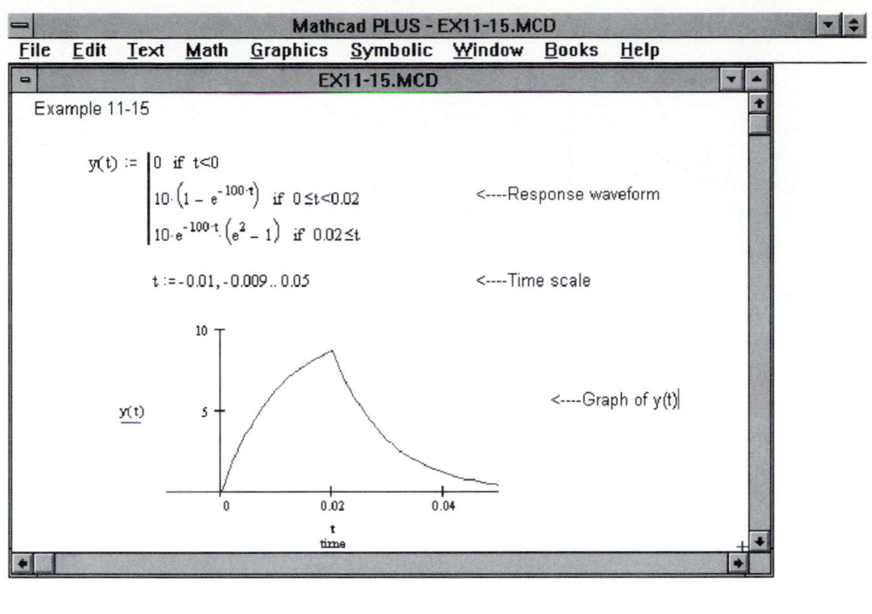

FIGURE 11–27

11–26(b) partial overlap, and Figure 11–26(c) complete overlap. When the pulse duration is very short compared to the duration of the impulse response, then almost all of the response is due to the third situation. Figure 11–28 shows the geometric interpretation of convolution for this case. The overlap between $h(t - \tau)$ and the input $x(\tau)$ is confined to a narrow range from $\tau = 0$ to $\tau = a$, where a is the pulse duration. By convolution, the response for $t > a$ is

$$y(t) = \int_0^a h(t - \tau)\, x(\tau) d\tau$$

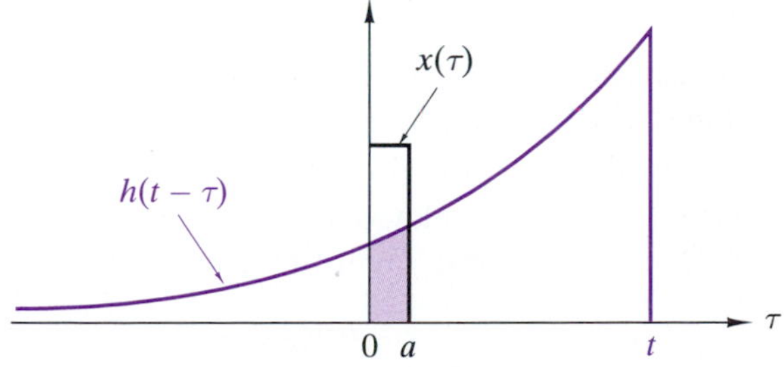

FIGURE 11–28

But on this integration interval Figure 11–28 shows that $h(t - \tau)$ is essentially constant. The nearly constant value is approximately $h(t)$ since

$\tau \approx 0$. Hence the impulse response can be taken outside the integration to yield

$$y(t) = h(t)\int_0^a x(\tau)d\tau$$

The integral in this expression is none other than the area under the input pulse. Thus, convolution confirms that when the input is a pulse whose duration is very short compared to the memory time of the circuit, then a good approximation for the response is $Ah(t)$, where A is the area under the pulse.

11–7 NETWORK FUNCTION DESIGN

Finding and using a network function of a given circuit is an s-domain **analysis** problem. An s-domain **synthesis** problem involves finding a circuit that realizes a given network function. For linear circuits an analysis problem always has a unique solution. In contrast, a synthesis problem may have many solutions because different circuits can have the same network function. A transfer function design problem involves synthesizing several circuits that realize a given function and evaluating the alternative designs, using criteria such as input impedance, cost, and power consumption.

In this section we develop methods of synthesizing first-order and second-order transfer functions using the circuits shown in Figure 11–29. In an analysis problem we start with a circuit diagram and transform the circuit into the s domain and the transfer function using the appropriate relationship in Figure 11–29. The analysis process proceeds from a circuit diagram to a network function and always has a unique solution.

The synthesis process proceeds in the opposite direction. We start with a transfer function, select one of the configurations in Figure 11–29, assign values to the impedances $Z_1(s)$ and $Z_2(s)$, and then draw the circuit diagram as the final step. In some cases it may not be possible to realize the given transfer function using the selected circuit configuration. In other cases, restrictions on the transfer function may be needed to ensure that $Z_1(s)$ and $Z_2(s)$ are physically realizable. In any event, the synthesis process proceeds from a network function to a circuit diagram and may have many solutions or possibly no solutions.

FIRST-ORDER VOLTAGE-DIVIDER CIRCUIT DESIGN

We begin our study of transfer function design by developing a voltage-divider realization of a first-order transfer function of the form $K/(s + \alpha)$. The impedances $Z_1(s)$ and $Z_2(s)$ are related to the given transfer function using the voltage-divider relationship in Figure 11–29:

$$T_V(s) = \frac{K}{s + \alpha} = \frac{Z_2(s)}{Z_1(s) + Z_2(s)} \qquad (11-23)$$

To obtain a circuit realization, we must assign part of the given $T_V(s)$ to $Z_2(s)$ and the remainder to $Z_1(s)$. There are many possible realizations of $Z_1(s)$ and $Z_2(s)$ because there is no unique way to make this assignment.

Circuit	Transfer Function
Voltage divider	$T_v(s) = \frac{Z_2(s)}{Z_1(s)+Z_2(s)}$
Inverting OP AMP	$T_v(s) = -\frac{Z_2(s)}{Z_1(s)}$
Noninverting OP AMP	$T_v(s) = \frac{Z_1(s)+Z_2(s)}{Z_1(s)}$

FIGURE 11–29 *Voltage divider and OP AMP circuit building blocks*

For example, simply equating the numerators and denominators in Eq. (11–23) yields

$$Z_2(s) = K \quad \text{and} \quad Z_1(s) = s + \alpha - Z_2(s) = s + \alpha - K \qquad (11\text{–}24)$$

Inspecting this result, we see that $Z_2(s)$ is realizable as a resistance ($R_2 = K\ \Omega$) and $Z_1(s)$ as an inductance ($L_1 = 1$ H) in series with a resistance [$R_1 = (\alpha - K)\ \Omega$]. The resulting circuit diagram is shown in Figure 11–30(a). For $K = \alpha$ the resistance R_1 can be replace by a short circuit because its resistance is zero. A gain restriction $K \leq \alpha$ is necessary because a negative R_1 is not physically realizable as a single component.

An alternative synthesis approach involves factoring s out of the denominator of the given transfer function. In this case Eq. (11–23) is rewritten in the form

$$T_V(s) = \frac{K/s}{1 + \alpha/s} = \frac{Z_2(s)}{Z_1(s) + Z_2(s)} \qquad (11\text{–}25)$$

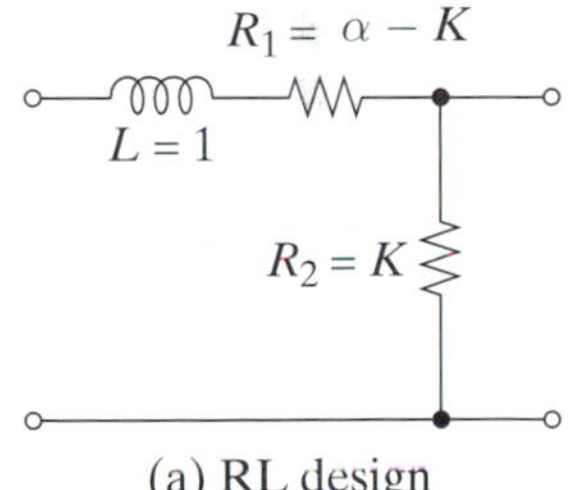

(a) RL design

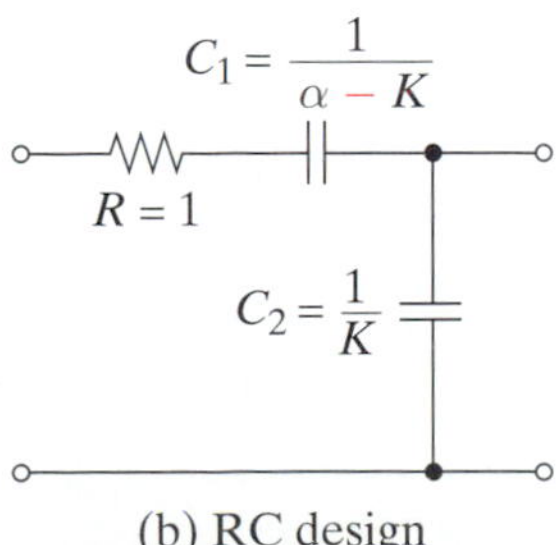

(b) RC design

FIGURE 11–30 *Circuit realizations of* $T(s) = K/(s + \alpha)$ *for* $K \leq \alpha$.

Equating numerators and denominators yields the branch impedances

$$Z_2(s) = \frac{K}{s} \quad \text{and} \quad Z_1(s) = 1 + \frac{\alpha}{s} - Z_2(s) = 1 + \frac{\alpha - K}{s} \tag{11-26}$$

In this case we see that $Z_2(s)$ is realizable as a capacitance ($C_2 = 1/K$ F) and $Z_1(s)$ as a resistance ($R_1 = 1\ \Omega$) in series with a capacitance [$C_1 = 1/(\alpha - K)$ F]. The resulting circuit diagram is shown in Figure 11–30(b). For $K = \alpha$ the capacitance C_1 can be replaced by a short circuit because its capacitance is infinite. A gain restriction $K \leq \alpha$ is required to keep C_1 from being negative.

As a second design example, consider a voltage-divider realization of the transfer function $Ks/(s + \alpha)$. We can find two voltage-divider realizations by writing the specified transfer function in the following two ways:

$$T(s) = \frac{Ks}{s + \alpha} = \frac{Z_2(s)}{Z_1(s) + Z_2(s)} \tag{11-27a}$$

$$T(s) = \frac{K}{1 + \alpha/s} = \frac{Z_2(s)}{Z_1(s) + Z_2(s)} \tag{11-27b}$$

Equation (11–27a) uses the transfer function as given, while Eq. (11–27b) factors s out of the numerator and denominator. Equating the numerators and denominators in Eqs. (11–27a) and (11–27b) yields two possible impedance assignments:

$$\text{Using Eq. (11–27a): } Z_2 = Ks \quad \text{and} \quad Z_1 = s + \alpha - Z_2 = (1 - K)s + \alpha \tag{11-28a}$$

$$\text{Using Eq. (11–27b): } Z_2 = K \quad \text{and} \quad Z_1 = 1 + \frac{\alpha}{s} - Z_2 = (1 - K) + \frac{\alpha}{s} \tag{11-28b}$$

The assignment in Eq. (11–28a) yields $Z_2(s)$ as an inductance ($L_2 = K$ H) and $Z_1(s)$ as an inductance [$L_1 = (1 - K)$ H] in series with a resistance ($R_1 = \alpha\ \Omega$). The assignment in Eq. (11–28b) yields $Z_2(s)$ as a resistance ($R_2 = K$) and $Z_1(s)$ as a resistance [$R_1 = (1 - K)\ \Omega$] in series with a capacitance ($C_1 = 1/\alpha$ F). The two realizations are shown in Figure 11–31. Both realizations require $K \leq 1$ for the branch impedances to be realizable and both simplify when $K = 1$.

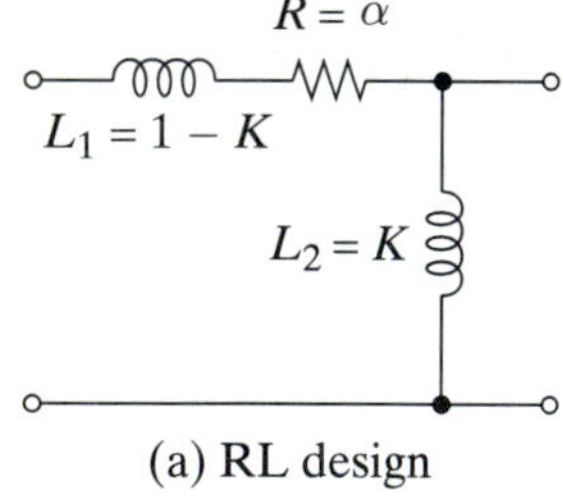

(a) RL design

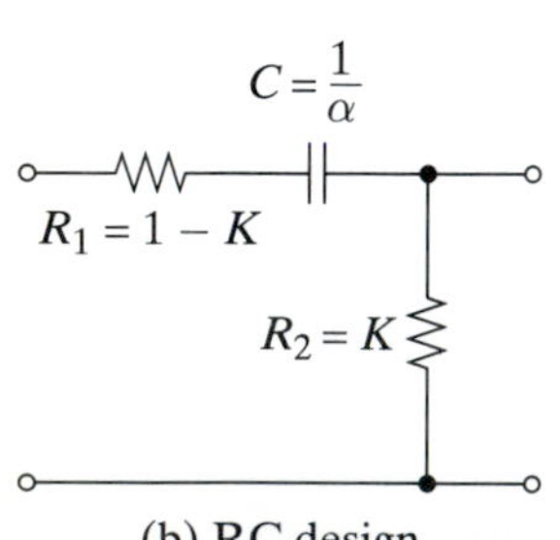

(b) RC design

FIGURE 11–31 *Circuit realizations of* $T(s) = Ks/(s + \alpha)$ *for* $K \leq 1$.

VOLTAGE-DIVIDER AND OP AMP CASCADE CIRCUIT DESIGN

The examples in Figures 11–30 and 11–31 illustrate an important feature of voltage-divider realizations. In general, we can write a transfer function as a quotient of polynomials $T(s) = r(s)/q(s)$. A voltage-divider realization requires the impedances $Z_2(s) = r(s)$ and $Z_1(s) = q(s) - r(s)$ to be physically realizable. A voltage-divider circuit usually places limitations on the gain K. This gain limitation can be overcome by using an OP AMP circuit in cascade with divider circuit.

For example, a voltage-divider realization of the transfer function in Eq. (11–23) requires $K \leq \alpha$. When $K > \alpha$, then $T(s)$ is not realizable as a simple voltage divider, since $Z_2(s) = s + \alpha - K$ requires a negative resistance. However, the given transfer function can be written as a two-stage product:

$$T_V(s) = \frac{K}{s+\alpha} = \underbrace{\left[\frac{K}{\alpha}\right]}_{\substack{\text{First} \\ \text{Stage}}} \underbrace{\left[\frac{\alpha}{s+\alpha}\right]}_{\substack{\text{Second} \\ \text{Stage}}} \tag{11–29}$$

When $K > \alpha$, the first stage is a positive gain greater than unity and can be realized using the noninverting OP AMP configuration. Using the transfer function from Figure 11–29 for this circuit yields

$$\frac{Z_1(s) + Z_2(s)}{Z_1(s)} = \frac{K}{\alpha} \tag{11–30}$$

Arbitrarily choosing $Z_1(s) = R_1 = 1\ \Omega$, we solve for $Z_2(s)$ and find $R_2 = K/(\alpha - 1)$. The second stage in Eq. (11–29) is realizable as a voltage divider because $q(s) - r(s) = s$ is realizable as an inductance.

Alternatively, factoring s out of the second-stage transfer function yields a different RC divider realization:

$$\frac{\alpha/s}{1 + \alpha/s} = \frac{Z_2(s)}{Z_1(s) + Z_2(s)} \tag{11–31}$$

Equating numerators and denominators yields $Z_2(s) = \alpha/s$ and $Z_1(s) = 1$. Figure 11–32 shows a cascade connection of a noninverting first stage and the RC divider second stage. The chain rule applies to this circuit, since the first stage has an OP-AMP output. The cascade circuit in Figure 11–32 realizes the first-order transfer function $K/(s + \alpha)$ for $K > \alpha$, a gain requirement that cannot be met by the divider circuit alone.

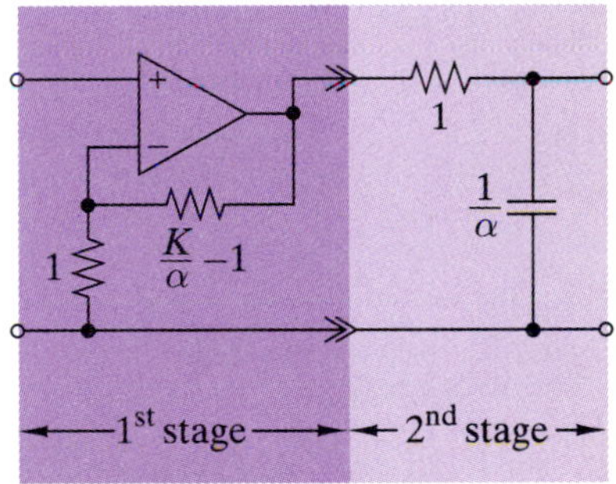

FIGURE 11–32 *Circuit realization of* $T(s) = K/(s + \alpha)$ *for* $K > \alpha$.

D DESIGN EXAMPLE: 11–17

Transfer Function Design

Design a circuit to realize the following transfer function using only resistors, capacitors, and OP AMPs:

$$T_V(s) = \frac{3000s}{(s + 1000)(s + 4000)}$$

SOLUTION:

The given transfer function can be written as a three-stage product.

$$T_V(s) = \underbrace{\left[\frac{K_1}{s+1000}\right]}_{\substack{\text{First} \\ \text{Stage}}} \underbrace{[K_2]}_{\substack{\text{Second} \\ \text{Stage}}} \underbrace{\left[\frac{K_3 s}{s+4000}\right]}_{\substack{\text{Third} \\ \text{Stage}}}$$

where the stage gains K_1, K_2, and K_3 have yet to be selected. Factoring s out of the denominator of the first-stage transfer function leads to an RC divider realization:

$$\frac{K_1/s}{1 + 1000/s} = \frac{Z_2(s)}{Z_1(s) + Z_2(s)}$$

Equating numerators and denominators yields

$$Z_2(s) = K_1/s \text{ and } Z_1(s) = 1 + (1000 - K_1)/s$$

The first stage $Z_1(s)$ is simpler when we select $K_1 = 1000$. Factoring s out of the denominator of the third-stage transfer function leads to an RC divider realization:

$$\frac{K_3}{1 + 4000/s} = \frac{Z_2(s)}{Z_1(s) + Z_2(s)}$$

Equating numerators and denominators yields

$$Z_2(s) = K_3 \text{ and } Z_1(s) = 1 - K_3 + 4000/s$$

The third stage $Z_1(s)$ is simpler when we select $K_3 = 1$. The stage gains must meet the constraint $K_1 \times K_2 \times K_3 = 3000$ since the overall gain of the given transfer function is 3000. We have selected $K_1 = 1000$ and $K_3 = 1$, which requires $K_2 = 3$. The second stage must have a positive gain greater than 1 and can be realized using a noninverting amplifier with $K_2 = (R_1 + R_2)/R_1 = 3$. Selecting $R_1 = 1\ \Omega$ requires that $R_2 = 2\ \Omega$.

Figure 11–33 shows the three stages connected in cascade. The chain rule applies to this cascade connection because the OP AMP in the second stage isolates the *RC* voltage-divider circuits in the first and third stages. The circuit in Figure 11–33 realizes the given transfer function but is not a realistic design because the values of resistance and capacitance are impractical. For this reason we call this circuit a **prototype** design. We will shortly discuss how to scale a prototype to obtain practical element values. ■

FIGURE 11–33

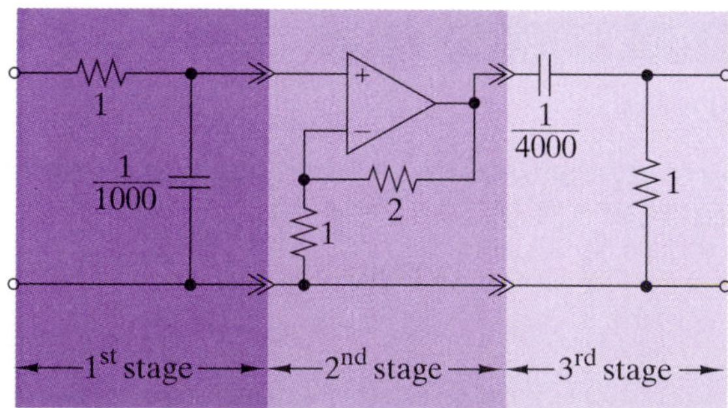

INVERTING OP AMP CIRCUIT DESIGN

The inverting OP AMP circuit is more versatile than the voltage divider because it places fewer restrictions on the form of the transfer function. There are at least four different inverting OP AMP circuit designs for a general first-order transfer function of the form

$$T_V(s) = -K\frac{s+\gamma}{s+\alpha}$$

The first realization results from equating $T_V(s)$ to the inverting OP AMP relationship in Figure 11–29:

$$-\frac{Ks + K\gamma}{s+\alpha} = -\frac{Z_2(s)}{Z_1(s)} \qquad (11-32)$$

Equating numerators and denominators yields the impedance $Z_1(s) = s + \alpha$ and $Z_2(s) = Ks + K\gamma$. Both of these impedances are of the form $Ls + R$ and can be realized by an inductance in series with a resistor. These impedance identifications produce the *RL* circuit in Figure 11–34(a).

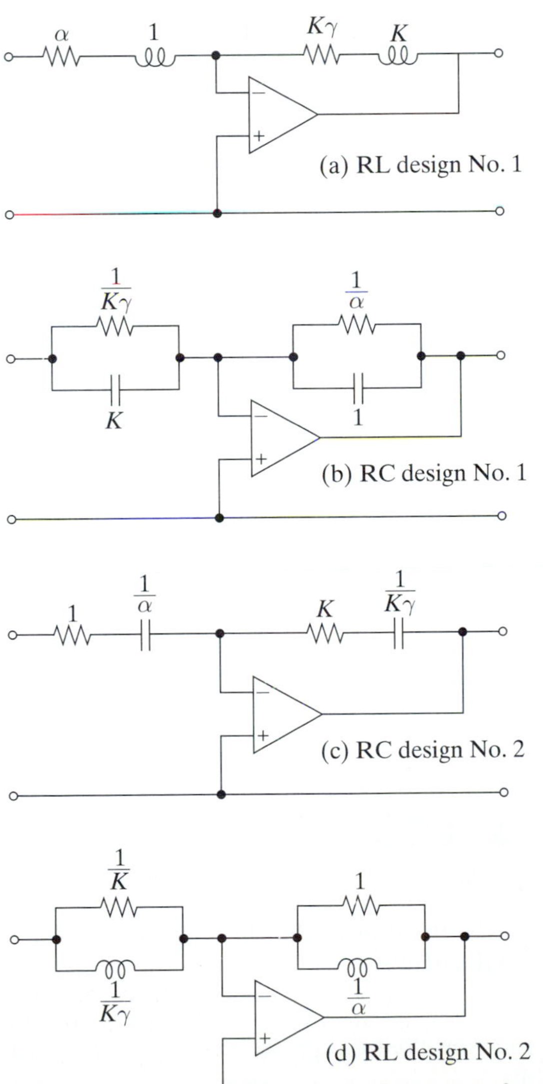

FIGURE 11–34 *Inverting OP AMP circuit realizations of* $T(s) = K(s+\gamma)/(s+\alpha)$.

A second inverting OP AMP realization is obtained by equating $Z_2(s)$ in Eq. (11–32) to the reciprocal of the denominator and equating $Z_1(s)$ to the reciprocal of the numerator. This assignment yields the impedances $Z_1(s) = 1/(Ks + K\gamma)$ and $Z_2(s) = 1/(s + \alpha)$. Both of these impedances are of the form $1/(Cs + G)$, where Cs is the admittance of a capacitor and G is the admittance of a resistor. Both impedances can be realized by a capacitance in parallel with a resistance. These impedance identifications produce the *RC* circuit in Figure 11–34(b).

Two more inverting realizations are obtained by factoring s out of the denominator of Eq. (11–32):

$$-\frac{K + K\gamma/s}{1 + \alpha/s} = -\frac{Z_2(s)}{Z_1(s)} \tag{11–33}$$

Equating numerators and denominators yields $Z_2(s) = K + K\gamma/s$ and $Z_1(s) = 1 + \alpha/s$. Both of these impedances are realizable as a resistance in series with a capacitance and lead to the *RC* circuit in Figure 11–34(c). When we equate $Z_2(s)$ in Eq. (11–33) to the reciprocal of the denominator and $Z_1(s)$ to the reciprocal of the numerator, we find

$$Z_2(s) = \frac{1}{1 + \alpha/s} \quad \text{and} \quad Z_1(s) = \frac{1}{K + K\gamma/s} \tag{11–34}$$

Both of these impedances are of the form $1/(G + 1/Ls)$, where G is the admittance of a resistor and $1/Ls$ is the admittance of an inductor. As a result, both are realizable by a resistor in parallel with an inductor, as shown by the *RL* circuit in Figure 11–34(d).

The four circuits in Figure 11–34 show that there are several ways to partition a transfer function into realizable input and feedback impedances for an inverting OP AMP circuit. For a first-order circuit the only limitation is that the parameters K, γ, and α must be positive. These conditions are less restrictive than the gain restrictions for the voltage-divider circuit.

Because it has fewer restrictions, it is often easier to realize transfer functions using the inverting OP AMP circuit. To use inverting circuits, the given transfer function must require an inversion or be realized using an even number of inverting stages. In some cases, the sign in front of the transfer function is immaterial and the required transfer function is specified as $\pm T_V(s)$.

D DESIGN EXAMPLE: 11–18

Transfer Function Design

Design a circuit to realize the transfer function given in Example 11–17 using inverting OP AMP circuits.

SOLUTION:

The given transfer function can be expressed as the product of two inverting transfer functions:

$$T_V(s) = \frac{3000s}{(s+1000)(s+4000)} = \underbrace{\left[-\frac{K_1}{s+1000}\right]}_{\text{First Stage}}\underbrace{\left[-\frac{K_2 s}{s+4000}\right]}_{\text{Second Stage}}$$

where the stage gains K_1 and K_2 have yet to be selected. The first stage can be realized in an inverting OP AMP circuit since

$$-\frac{K_1}{s+1000} = -\frac{K_1/1000}{1+s/1000} = -\frac{Z_2(s)}{Z_1(s)}$$

Equating the $Z_2(s)$ to the reciprocal of the denominator and $Z_1(s)$ to the reciprocal of the numerator yields

$$Z_2 = \frac{1}{1+s/1000} \quad \text{and} \quad Z_1 = 1000/K_1$$

The impedance $Z_2(s)$ is realizable as a capacitance ($C_2 = 1/1000$ F) in parallel with a resistance ($R_2 = 1\ \Omega$) and $Z_1(s)$ as a resistance ($R_1 = 1000/K_1\ \Omega$). We select $K_1 = 1000$ so that the two resistances in the first stage are equal. Since the overall gain requires $K_1 \times K_2 = 3000$, this means that $K_2 = 3$. The second-stage transfer function can also be produced using an inverting OP AMP circuit:

$$-\frac{3s}{s+4000} = -\frac{3}{1+4000/s} = -\frac{Z_2(s)}{Z_1(s)}$$

Equating numerators and denominators yields $Z_2(s) = R_2 = 3$ and $Z_1(s) = R_1 + 1/C_1 s = 1 + 4000/s$.

Figure 11–35 shows the cascade connection of the two *RC* OP AMP circuits that realize each stage. The overall transfer function is noninverting because the cascade uses an even number of inverting stages. The chain rule applies here since the first stage has an OP AMP output. The circuit in Figure 11–35 is a prototype design because the values of resistance and capacitance are impractical. ■

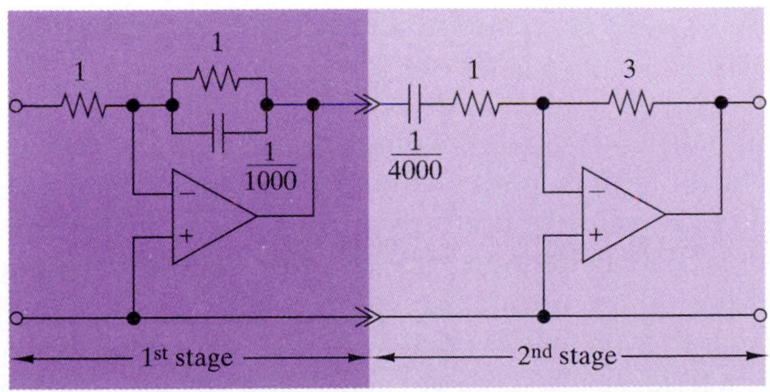

FIGURE 11–35

MAGNITUDE SCALING

The circuits obtained in Examples 11–17 and 11–18 are called prototype designs because the element values are outside of practical ranges. The allowable ranges depend on the fabrication technology used to construct the circuits. For example, monolithic integrated circuit technology limits capacitances to a few hundred picofarads. An OP AMP circuit should have a feedback resistance greater than around 10 kΩ to keep the output current demand within the capabilities of general-purpose OP AMP devices. Other technologies and applications place different constraints on element values.

There are no hard and fast rules here, but, roughly speaking, a circuit is probably realizable by some means if its passive element values fall in the following ranges:

Capacitors: 1 pF to 100 μF

Inductors: 10 μH to 100 mH

Resistors: 10 Ω to 100 MΩ.

The important idea here is that circuit designs like Figure 11–35 are impractical because 1-Ω resistors and 1-mF capacitors are unrealistic values.

It is often possible to scale the magnitude of circuit impedances so that the element values fall into practical ranges. The key is to scale the element values in a way that does not change the transfer function of the circuit. Multiplying the numerator and denominator of the transfer function of a voltage-divider circuit by a scale factor k_m yields

$$T_V(s) = \frac{k_m}{k_m}\frac{Z_2(s)}{Z_1(s) + Z_2(s)} = \frac{k_m Z_2(s)}{k_m Z_1(s) + k_m Z_2(s)} \tag{11-35}$$

Clearly, this modification does not change the transfer function, but scales each impedance by a factor of k_m and changes the element values in the following way:

$$R_{after} = k_m R_{before} \quad L_{after} = k_m L_{before} \quad C_{after} = \frac{C_{before}}{k_m} \tag{11-36}$$

Equation (11–36) was derived using the transfer function of a voltage-divider circuit. It is easy to show that we would reach the same conclusion if we had used the transfer functions of inverting or noninverting OP AMP circuits in Figure 11–29.

In general, a circuit is magnitude scaled by multiplying all resistances, multiplying all inductances, and dividing all capacitances by a scale factor k_m. The scale factor must be positive, but can be greater than or less than 1. Different scale factors can be used for each stage of a cascade design, but only one scale factor can be used for each stage. These scaling operations do not change the voltage transfer function realized by the circuit.

Our design strategy is first to create a prototype circuit whose element values may be unrealistically large or small. Applying magnitude scaling to the prototype produces a design with practical element values. Sometimes there may be no scale factor that brings the prototype element values into a practical range. When this happens, we must seek alternative realizations because the scaling process is telling us that the prototype is not a viable candidate.

EXAMPLE 11–19

Magnitude scale the circuit in Figure 11–35 so all resistances are at least 10 kΩ and all capacitances are less than 1 μF.

SOLUTION:

The resistance constraint requires $k_m R \geq 10^4\ \Omega$. The smallest resistance in the prototype circuit is 1 Ω; therefore, the resistance constraint requires $k_m \geq 10^4$. The capacitance constraint requires $C/k_m \leq 10^{-6}$ F. The largest capacitance in the prototype is 10^{-3} F; therefore, the capacitance constraint requires $k_m \geq 10^3$. The resistance condition on k_m dominates the two constraints. Selecting $k_m = 10^4$ produces the scaled design in Figure 11–36. This circuit realizes the same transfer function as the prototype in Figure 11–35, but uses practical element values.

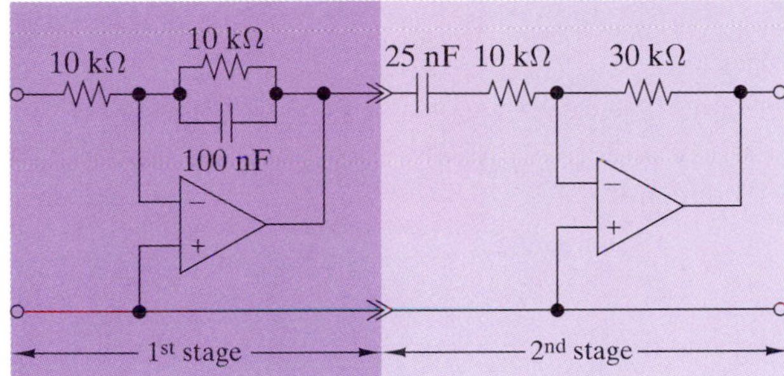

FIGURE 11–36

Exercise 11–11

Select a magnitude scale factor for each stage in Figure 11–33 so that both capacitances are 10 nF and all resistances are greater than 10 kΩ.

Answer: $k_m = 10^5$ for the first stage, $k_m = 10^4$ for the second stage, and $k_m = 0.25 \times 10^5$ for the third stage.

SECOND-ORDER CIRCUIT DESIGN

The voltage divider in Figure 11–29 can also be used to realize second-order transfer functions. For example, the transfer function

$$T_V(s) = \frac{K}{s^2 + 2\zeta\omega_0 s + \omega_0^2}$$

can be realized by factoring s out of the denominator and equating the result to the voltage-divider input–output relationship:

$$T_V(s) = \frac{K/s}{s + 2\zeta\omega_0 + \omega_0^2/s} = \frac{Z_2(s)}{Z_1(s) + Z_2(s)} \quad (11-37)$$

Equating numerators and denominators yields

$$Z_2(s) = \frac{K}{s} \text{ and } Z_1(s) = s + 2\zeta\omega_0 + \frac{\omega_0^2 - K}{s} \tag{11-38}$$

The impedance $Z_2(s)$ is realizable as a capacitance ($C_2 = 1/K$ F) and $Z_1(s)$ as a series connection of an inductance ($L_1 = 1$ H), resistance ($R_1 = 2\zeta\omega_0\ \Omega$), and capacitance [$C_1 = 1/(\omega_0^2 - K)$ F]. The resulting voltage-divider circuit is shown in Figure 11–37(a). The impedances in this circuit are physically realizable when $K \leq \omega_0^2$. Note that the resistance controls the damping ratio ζ because it is the element that dissipates energy in the circuit.

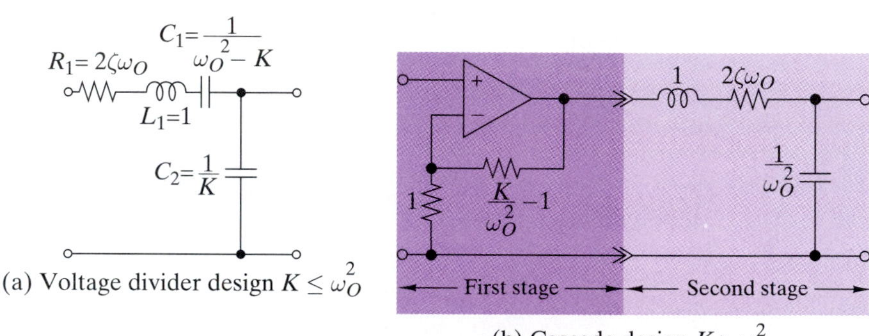

(a) Voltage divider design $K \leq \omega_O^2$

(b) Cascade design $K > \omega_O^2$

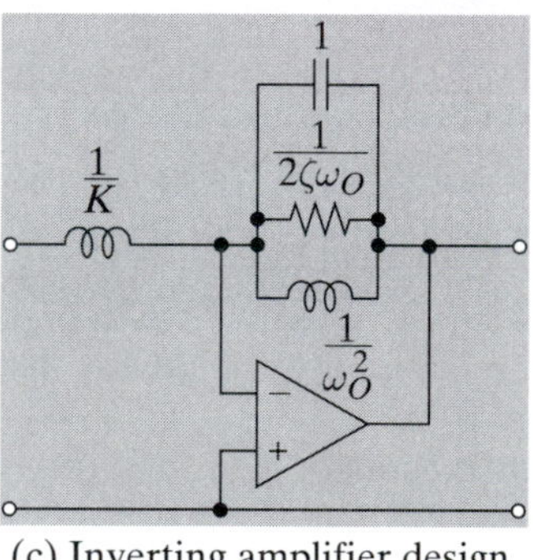

(c) Inverting amplifier design

FIGURE 11–37 *Second-order circuit realizations.*

When $K > \omega_0^2$, we can partition the transfer function into a two-stage cascade of the form

$$T_V(s) = \underbrace{\left[\frac{K}{\omega_0^2}\right]}_{\text{First Stage}} \underbrace{\left[\frac{\omega_0^2/s}{s + 2\zeta\omega_0 + \omega_0^2/s}\right]}_{\text{Second Stage}} \tag{11-39}$$

The first stage requires a positive gain greater than unity and can be realized using a noninverting OP AMP circuit. The second stage can be realized as a voltage divider with $Z_2(s) = \omega_0^2/s$ and $Z_1(s) = s + 2\zeta\omega_0$. The resulting cascade circuit is shown in Figure 11–37(b).

An inverting OP-AMP design of the second-order function also is possible provided that the given transfer function requires inversion or its sign is not specified. For example, starting with

$$T_V(s) = -\frac{K}{s^2 + 2\zeta\omega_0 s + \omega_0^2}$$

we factor s out of the denominator and equate the result to the inverting OP AMP transfer function:

$$T_V(s) = -\frac{K/s}{s + 2\zeta\omega_0 + \omega_0^2/s} = -\frac{Z_2(s)}{Z_1(s)} \tag{11-40}$$

Equating $Z_2(s)$ to the reciprocal of the denominator and $Z_1(s)$ to the reciprocal of the numerator yields

$$Z_1(s) = \frac{s}{K} \quad \text{and} \quad Z_2(s) = \frac{1}{s + 2\zeta\omega_0 + \omega_0^2/s} \tag{11-41}$$

The impedance $Z_1(s)$ is realizable as an inductance ($L_1 = 1/K$ H) and the impedance $Z_2(s)$ as the parallel connection of a capacitance ($C_2 = 1$ F), resistance [$R_2 = 1/(2\zeta\omega_0)\ \Omega$], and inductance ($L_2 = 1/\omega_0^2$ H). The resulting inverting OP AMP realization is shown in Figure 11–37(c).

The examples in Figure 11–37 illustrate a general approach to designing prototype circuits for second-order transfer functions. The approach begins by factoring s out of the denominator. A voltage-divider realization is possible when the resulting denominator minus the numerator is a realizable impedance. When it is not realizable, either a cascade design with a noninverting gain stage or an inverting OP AMP realization can be used. Realizing a second-order transfer function requires resistors, inductors, and capacitors because factoring out an s leaves the denominator of the transfer function in the form

$$s + 2\zeta\omega_0 + \omega_0^2/s = Ls + R + 1/Cs$$

We can use this approach for any value of $\zeta > 0$. However, when $\zeta \geq 1$ the second-order transfer function can be factored into a product of two first-order transfer functions and realized as a cascade connection. Conversely, a transfer function consisting of the product of two first-order functions can be realized as a single second-order stage.

D DESIGN EXAMPLE 11–20

Transfer Function Design

Find a second-order realization of the transfer function given in Example 11–17.

SOLUTION:

The given transfer function can be written as

$$T_V(s) = \frac{3000s}{(s + 1000)(s + 4000)} = \frac{3000s}{s^2 + 5000s + 4 \times 10^6}$$

Factoring s out of the denominator and equating the result to the transfer function of a voltage divider gives

$$\frac{3000}{s + 5000 + 4 \times 10^6/s} = \frac{Z_2(s)}{Z_1(s) + Z_2(s)}$$

Equating the numerators and denominators yields

$$Z_2(s) = 3000 \quad \text{and} \quad Z_1(s) = s + 2000 + 4 \times 10^6/s$$

Both of these impedances are realizable, so a single-stage voltage-divider design is possible. The prototype impedance $Z_1(s)$ requires a 1-H inductor, which is a bit large. A more practical value is obtained using a scale factor of $k_m = 0.1$. The resulting scaled voltage divider circuit is shown in Figure 11–38. ■

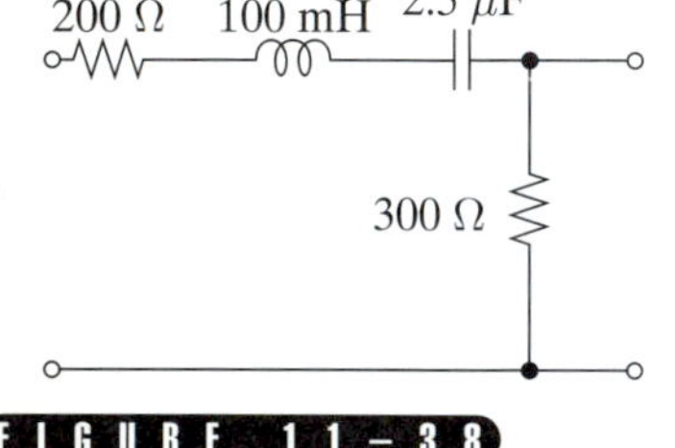

FIGURE 11–38

DESIGN EVALUATION SUMMARY

Examples 11–17, 11–18, and, 11–20 show that there are several ways to realize a given transfer function, as summarized here:

EXAMPLE	FIGURE	DESCRIPTION	NUMBER OF R	L	C	OP AMP
11–17	11–33	*RC* voltage-divider cascade	4	0	2	1
11–18	11–35	*RC* inverting cascade	4	0	2	2
11–20	11–38	*RLC* voltage divider	2	1	1	0

Selecting a final design from among these alternatives involves evaluation of each circuit using additional criteria. For example, inductors are heavy and lossy in low-frequency applications. These applications favor the first two circuits since they are "inductorless" realizations. However, the two *RC* circuits contain OP AMPs, which require a dc power supply. The *RC* voltage-divider cascade uses only one OP AMP, requiring less dc power than the *RC* inverting cascade, which uses two OP AMPs. On the other hand, the inverting circuit has an OP AMP output, so it could drive reasonable load impedances without changing the transfer function. Finally, in some applications, the fact that the passive *RLC* voltage divider does not require a dc power supply could outweigh the disadvantage of the inductor.

A design problem involves more than simply finding a prototype that realizes a given transfer function. In general, the first step in a design problem involves determining an acceptable transfer function, one that meets performance requirements such as the characteristics of the transient or frequency response. In other words, we must first design the transfer function and then design several circuits that realize the transfer function. To deal with transfer function design we must understand how performance characteristics are related to transfer functions. The next two chapters provide some background on this issue.

D E DESIGN AND EVALUATION EXAMPLE: 11–21

Step Response Design

Given the step response $g(t) = [1 + 4e^{-500t}]u(t)$,

(a) Find the transfer function $T(s)$.
(b) Design two *RC* OP AMP circuits that realize the $T(s)$ found in part (a).
(c) Compare the two designs on the basis of element count, input impedance, output impedance.

SOLUTION:

(a) The transform of the step response is

$$G(s) = \mathscr{L}\{[1 + 4e^{-500t}]u(t)\} = \frac{1}{s} + \frac{4}{s + 500} = \frac{5s + 500}{s(s + 500)}$$

and the required transfer function is

$$T(s) = H(s) = sG(s) = \frac{5s + 500}{s + 500}$$

(b) For the first design we partition $T(s)$ as

$$T(s) = \underbrace{[5]}_{\text{First Stage}} \times \underbrace{\left[\frac{s + 100}{s + 500}\right]}_{\text{Second Stage}}$$

The first stage has a positive gain greater than 1 and can be realized by a noninverting OP AMP configuration with $R_2 = 4R_1$. The second stage can be realized as a voltage divider. Equating the second-stage transfer function to the voltage-divider transfer function expressed in terms of admittances gives

$$\frac{s + 100}{s + 500} = \frac{Y_1(s)}{Y_1(s) + Y_2(s)} = \frac{Z_2(s)}{Z_1(s) + Z_2(s)}$$

Equating numerators and denominators yields

$$Y_1(s) = s + 100 \quad \text{and} \quad Y_2(s) = s + 500 - Y_1(s) = 400$$

The admittance $Y_1(s)$ is realizable as a capacitance ($C_1 = 1$ F) in parallel with a resistor ($G_1 = 100$ S) and $Y_2(s)$ as a resistance ($G_2 = 400$ S). Using a scale factor of $k_m = 10^6$ produces circuit C1 in Figure 11–39.

A second prototype is obtained by factoring s out of the denominator of $T(s)$ and equating the result to the transfer function of the noninverting OP AMP circuit in Figure 11–29:

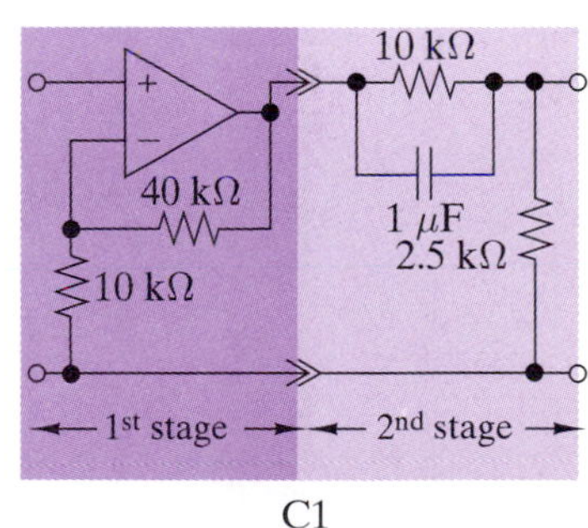

C1

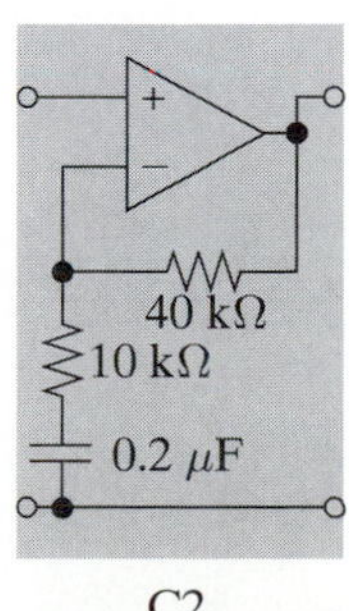

C2

FIGURE 11–39

$$\frac{5 + 500/s}{1 + 500/s} = \frac{Z_1(s) + Z_2(s)}{Z_1(s)}$$

Equating numerators and denominators yields

$$Z_1(s) = 1 + \frac{500}{s} \quad \text{and} \quad Z_2(s) = 5 + \frac{500}{s} - Z_1(s) = 4$$

The impedance $Z_1(s)$ is realizable as a resistance ($R_1 = 1\ \Omega$) in series with a capacitance ($C_1 = 1/500$ F) and $Z_2(s)$ as a resistance ($R_2 = 4\ \Omega$). Using a scale factor of $k_m = 10^4$ produces circuit C2 in Figure 11–39.

(c) Circuit C1 uses two more resistors than circuit C2. Both circuits have infinite input impedance, since their inputs are connected to the noninverting terminal of an OP AMP. Circuit C2 has zero output impedance, while circuit C1 has an output Thévenin impedance of

$$Z_T = \frac{1}{\dfrac{1}{10^4} + \dfrac{1}{2.5 \times 10^3} + \dfrac{s}{10^6}} = \frac{10^6}{s + 500}$$

This output impedance limits the loads that circuit C1 can drive without changing its transfer function. ■

D DESIGN EXAMPLE 11–22

Design Verification

Verify that circuit C2 in Figure 11–39 meets its design requirements.

SOLUTION:

One of the important uses of computer-aided analysis is to verify that a proposed design meets the performance specifications. The circuits in Example 11–21 are designed to produce a specified step response $g(t)$. This example involves verifying that the circuit C2 meets the design specification.

Figure 11–40 shows circuit C2 as drawn in MicroSim Schematics. The input step function is generated by a piecewise linear voltage source (**VPWL**) found in the source library. The required input is obtained by selecting (double clicking) the source symbol to bring up the source parameter menu. To get a unit step function, we assign values to the time/voltage pair as shown in the figure. Step response is a zero-state response. To ensure a zero-state condition, we set the capacitor initial condition to zero (**IC = 0** in the component dialog box) and then select **Analysis/Setup/Transient** and put a check mark in the **Use Initial Conditions** box. If this box is not checked, PSpice will recalculate the initial conditions prior to running a transient response calculation. Selecting the **Analysis/Simulate** command from the menu bar causes MicroSim PSpice to calculate the zero-state response for a unit step function input.

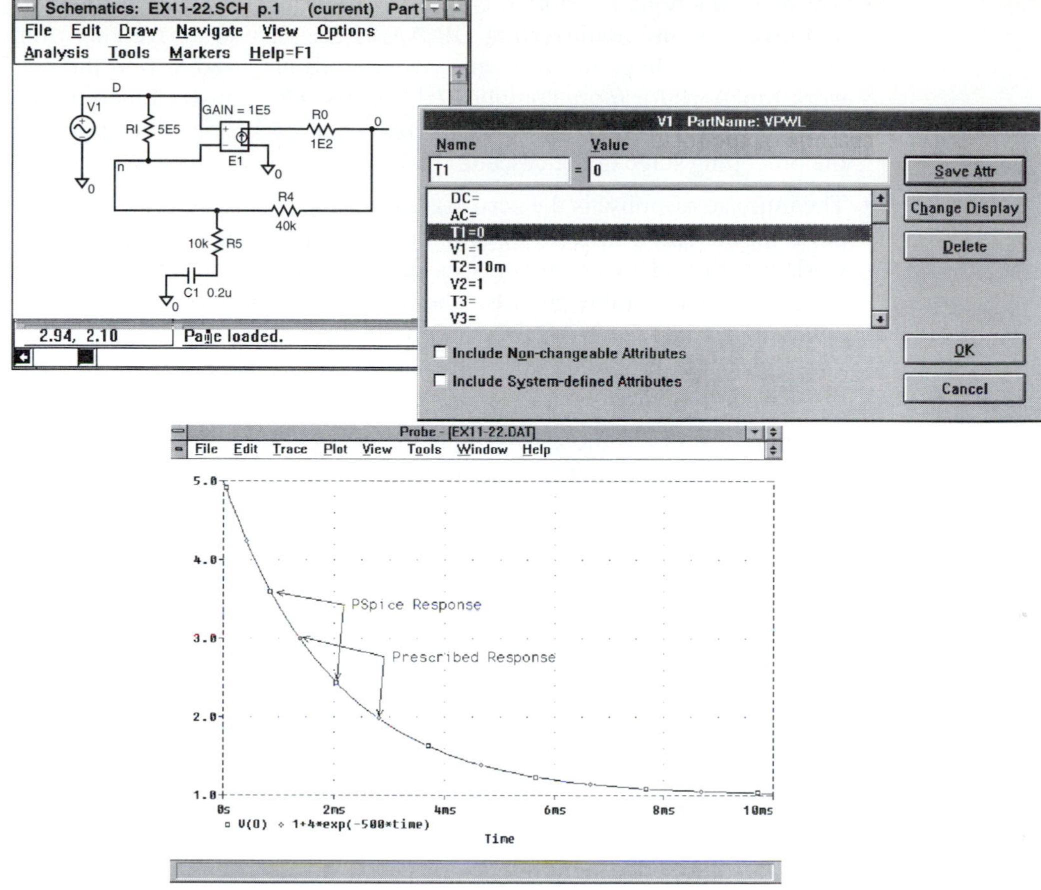

FIGURE 11–40

Figure 11–40 shows the MicroSim Probe plot of the step response calculated by PSpice compared to a plot of the analytical expression for the prescribed $g(t)$. The two plots are essentially identical, thus verifying that circuit C2 meets the design specification. One final note: In Example 11–21 circuit C2 is designed to produce a transfer function $T_V(s)$ that is analytically derived from the specified $g(t)$. Analyzing the circuit to see if it produces $T_V(s)$ does not provide a complete design verification since we may have erred in going from $g(t)$ to $T_V(s)$. Thus, we must return to the specification on $g(t)$ to verify the overall design process. ■

SUMMARY

- A network function is defined as the ratio of the zero-state response transform to the input transform. Network functions are either driving-point functions or transfer functions. Network functions are rational functions of s with real coefficients whose complex poles and zeros occur in conjugate pairs.

- Network functions for simple circuits like voltage and current dividers and inverting and noninverting OP AMPs are easy to derive and often useful. Node-voltage or mesh-current methods are used to find the network functions for more complicated circuits. The transfer function of a cascade connection obeys the chain rule when each stage does not load the preceding stage in the cascade.
- The impulse response is the zero-state response of a circuit for a unit impulse input. The transform of the impulse response is equal to the network function. The impulse response contains only natural poles and decays to zero in stable circuits. The impulse response of a linear, time-invariant circuit obeys the proportionality and time-shifting properties. The short pulse approximation is a useful way to simulate the impulse response in practical situations.
- The step response is the zero-state response of a circuit when the input is a unit step function. The transform of the step response transform is equal to the network function times $1/s$. The step response contains natural poles and a forced pole at $s = 0$ that leads to a dc steady-state response in stable circuits. The amplitude of the dc steady-state response can be found by evaluating the network function at $s = 0$. The step response waveform can also be found by integrating the impulse response waveform.
- The sinusoidal steady-state response is the forced response of a stable circuit for a sinusoidal input. With a sinusoidal input the response transform contains natural poles and forced poles at $s = \pm j\omega$ that lead to a sinusoidal steady-state response in stable circuits. The amplitude and phase angle of the sinusoidal steady-state response can be found by evaluating the network function at $s = j\omega$.
- The sinusoidal steady-state response can be found using phasor circuit analysis or directly from the transfer function. Phasor circuit analysis works best when the circuit is driven at only one frequency and several responses are needed. The network function method works best when the circuit is driven at several frequencies and only one response is needed.
- A convolution integral provides a t-domain relationship between the output waveform $y(t)$, the circuit impulse response $h(t)$, and the input waveform $x(t)$. In the t domain the impulse response $h(t)$ plays the same role as the network function in the s domain. Geometrically, we visualize convolution as an integration process that reflects the impulse response across the origin and then drags it through the input $x(\tau)$ as t increases.
- First- and second-order transfer functions can be designed using voltage dividers and inverting or noninverting OP AMP circuits. Higher-order transfer functions can be realized using a cascade connection of first- and second-order circuits. Prototype designs usually require magnitude scaling to obtain practical element values.

EN ROUTE OBJECTIVES AND ASSOCIATED PROBLEMS

ERO 11–1 NETWORK FUNCTIONS (SECTS. 11–1, 11–2)

Given a linear circuit in the zero state, find specified network functions and locate their poles and zeros.

11–1 Connect a voltage source $v_1(t)$ at the input port and an open circuit at the output port of the circuit in Figure P11–1.

(a) Transform the circuit into the s domain and find the driving-point impedance $Z(s) = V_1(s)/I_1(s)$ and the transfer function $T_V(s) = V_2(s)/V_1(s)$.

(b) Find the poles and zeros of $Z(s)$ and $T_V(s)$ for $R_1 = R_2 = 2\ \text{k}\Omega$, $L = 100\ \text{mH}$, $C = 250\ \text{nF}$.

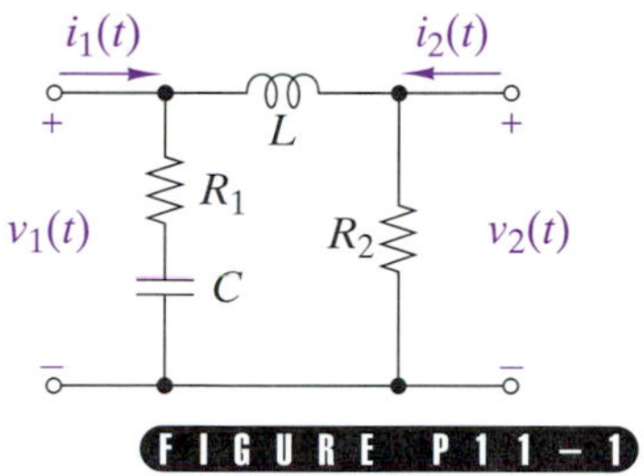

FIGURE P11–1

11–2 Connect a current source $i_1(t)$ at the input port and a short circuit at the output port of the circuit in Figure P11–1.

(a) Transform the circuit into the s domain and find the input impedance $Z(s) = V_1(s)/I_1(s)$ and the transfer function $T_I(s) = I_2(s)/I_1(s)$.

(b) Find the poles and zeros of $Z(s)$ and $T_Y(s)$ for $R_1 = 1\ \text{k}\Omega$, $L = 0.5\ \text{H}$, $C = 1\ \mu\text{F}$.

11–3 Connect a voltage source $v_1(t)$ at the input port and a short circuit at the output port of the circuit in Figure P11–3.

(a) Transform the circuit into the s domain and find the driving-point impedance $Z(s) = V_1(s)/I_1(s)$ and the transfer function $T_Y(s) = V_2(s)/V_1(s)$.

(b) Find the poles and zero of $Z(s)$ and $T_Y(s)$ for $R_1 = 100\ \Omega$, $R_2 = 50\ \Omega$, $L_1 = 0.5\ \text{H}$, and $L_2 = 0.25\ \text{H}$.

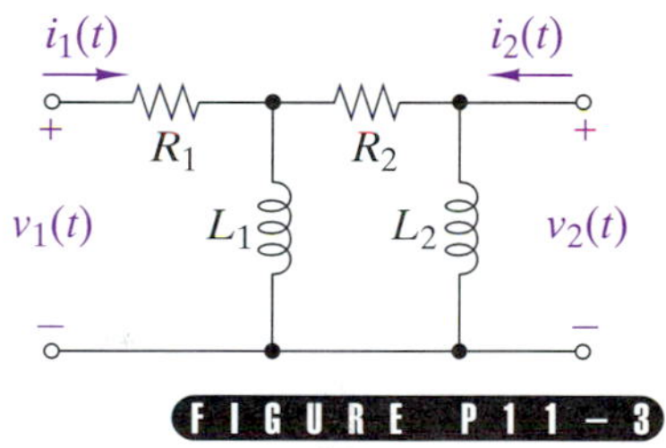

FIGURE P11–3

11–4 Connect a current source $i_1(t)$ at the input port and an open circuit at the output port of the circuit in Figure P11–3.

(a) Transform the circuit into the s-domain and find the driving-point impedance $Z(s) = V_1(s)/I_1(s)$ and the transfer impedance $T_Z(s) = V_2(s)/I_1(s)$.

(b) Find the poles and zero of $Z(s)$ and $T_Z(s)$ for $R_1 = 300\ \Omega$, $R_2 = 2500\ \Omega$, $L_1 = 0.4\ \text{H}$, and $L_2 = 0.1\ \text{H}$.

11–5 Transform the circuit in Figure P11–5 into the s domain and show that

$$T_V(s) = \frac{V_2(s)}{V_1(s)} = \frac{R_1C_1R_2C_2s^2 + (R_1C_1 + R_1C_2)s + 1}{R_1C_1R_2C_2s^2 + (R_1C_1 + R_2C_2 + R_1C_2)s + 1}$$

Locate the poles and zeros of $T_V(s)$ for $R_1 = R_2 = 20\ \text{k}\Omega$, $C_1 = C_2 = 20\ \text{nF}$.

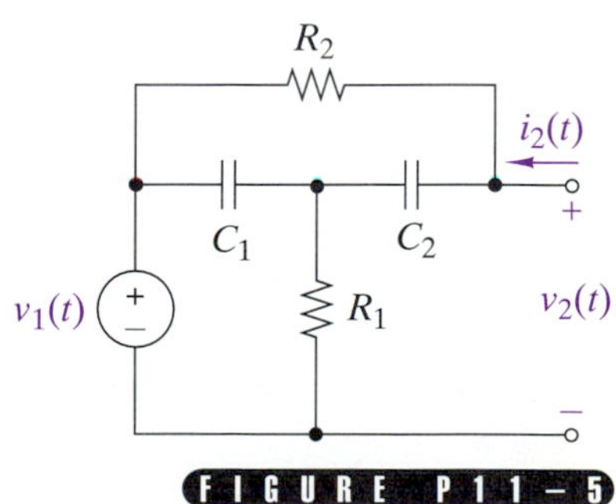

FIGURE P11–5

11–6 Replace the voltage source in Figure P11–5 by a current source $i_1(t)$ and connect a short circuit across the output port. Transform this circuit into the s-domain and show that

$$T_I(s) = \frac{I_2(s)}{I_1(s)} = -\frac{R_1C_1R_2C_2s^2 + (R_1C_1 + R_1C_2)s + 1}{R_1C_1R_2C_2s^2 + (R_1C_1 + R_2C_2 + R_2C_1)s + 1}$$

Locate the poles and zeros of $T_I(s)$ for $R_1 = 5$ kΩ, $R_2 = 10$ kΩ, $C_1 = 0.5$ μF, and $C_2 = 0.4$ μF.

11–7 Transform the circuit in Figure P11–7 into the s domain and solve for the transfer function $T_V(s) = V_2(s)/V_1(s)$. Locate the poles and zeros of the transfer function.

11–8 Transform the circuit in Figure P11–8 into the s domain and solve for the transfer function $T_V(s) = V_2(s)/V_1(s)$. Locate the poles and zeros of the transfer function.

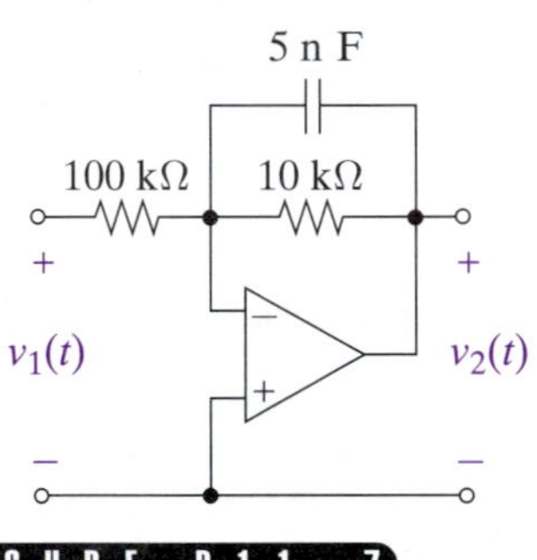

FIGURE P11–7

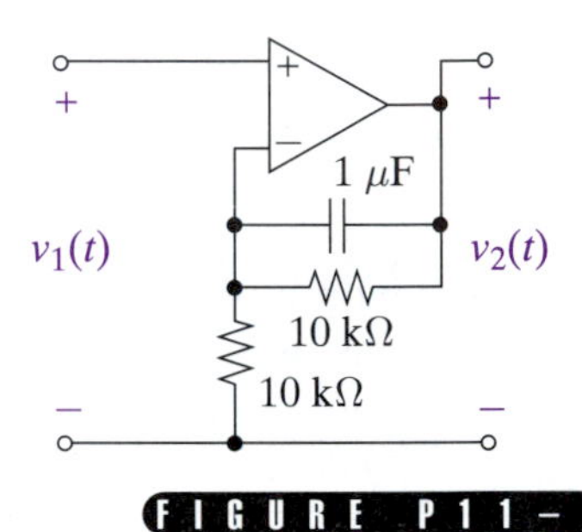

FIGURE P11–8

11–9 Transform the circuit in Figure P11–9 into the s-domain and solve for the transfer function $T_V(s) = V_2(s)/V_1(s)$. Locate the poles and zeros of the transfer function.

FIGURE P11–9

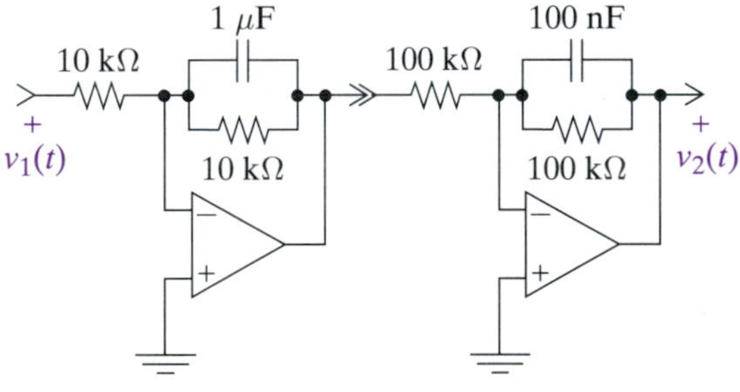

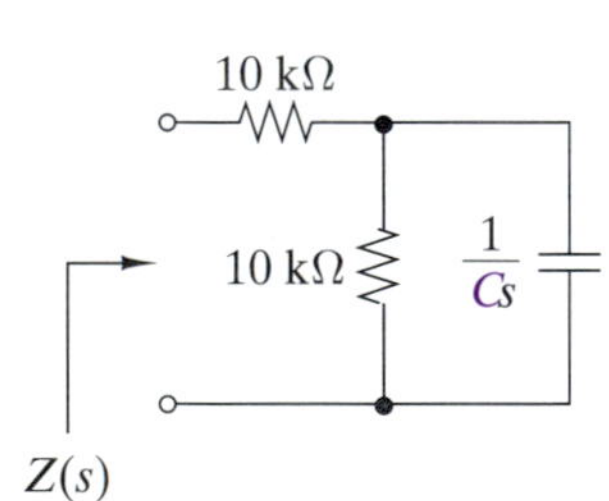

FIGURE P11–10

11–10 The input impedance of the circuit in Figure P11–10 is $Z(s) = 10^4(s + 200)/(s + 100)$ Ω. Find the value of C.

ERO 11–2 NETWORK FUNCTIONS AND IMPULSE RESPONSE (SECT. 11–3)

(a) Given a first- or second-order linear circuit, find its impulse response.
(b) Given the impulse responses of a linear circuit, find the network functions.

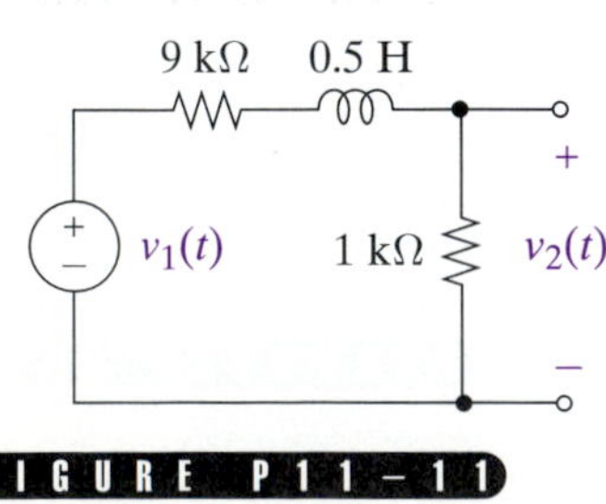

FIGURE P11–11

11–11 Find the transfer function $T_V(s) = V_2(s)/V_1(s)$ of the circuit in Figure P11–11. Find $v_2(t)$ when the input $v_1(t)$ is a unit impulse.

11–12 Find the transfer function $T_V(s) = V_2(s)/V_1(s)$ of the circuit in Figure P11–12. Find $v_2(t)$ when the input $v_1(t)$ is a unit impulse.

11–13 Find the transfer function $T_V(s) = V_2(s)/V_1(s)$ of the circuit in Figure P11–13. Find $v_2(t)$ when the input $v_1(t)$ is a unit impulse.

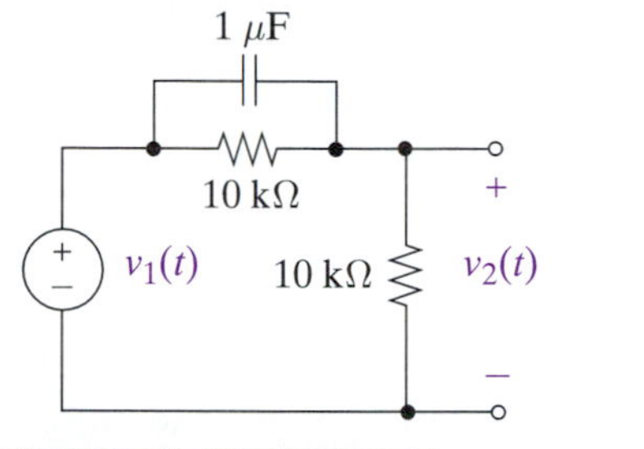

FIGURE P11–12

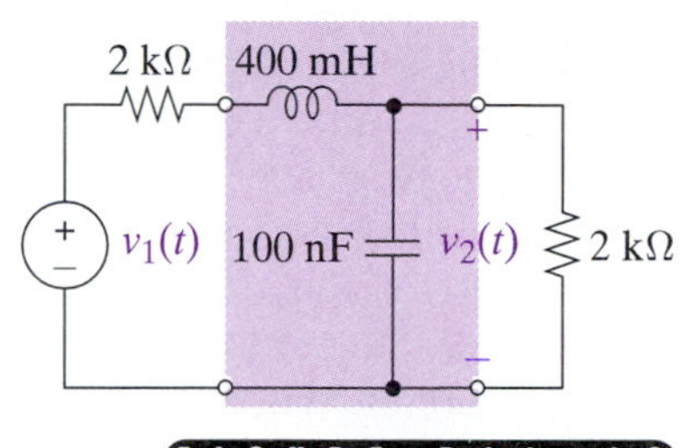

FIGURE P11–13

11–14 Find the transfer function $T_V(s) = V_2(s)/V_1(s)$ of the circuit in Figure P11–14. Find $v_2(t)$ when the input $v_1(t)$ is a unit impulse.

11–15 Find the transfer function $T_V(s) = V_2(s)/V_1(s)$ of the circuit in Figure P11–15. Find $v_2(t)$ when the input $v_1(t)$ is a unit impulse.

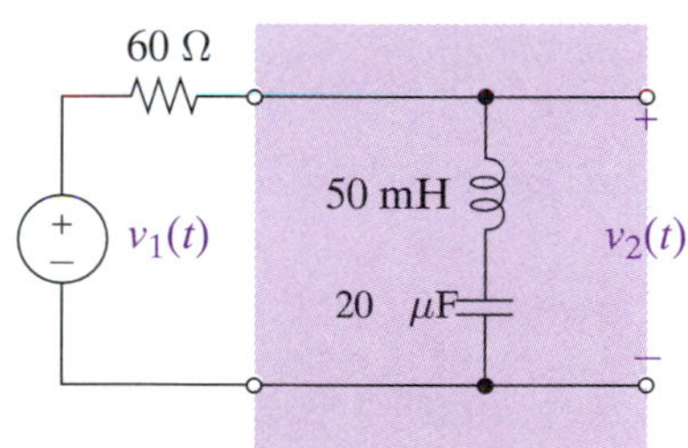

FIGURE P11–14

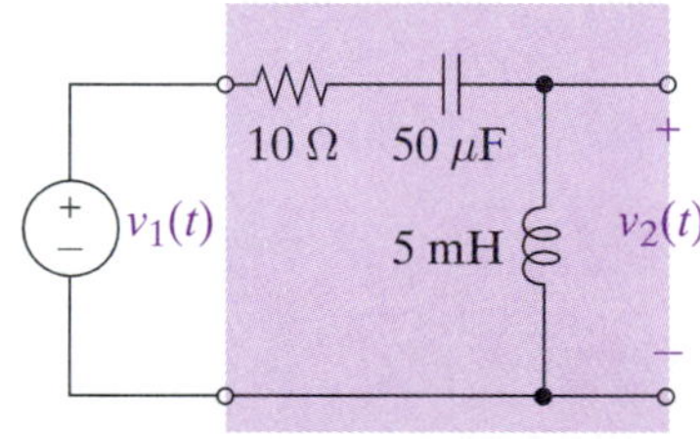

FIGURE P11–15

11–16 Find the network functions $Z(s) = V_1(s)/I_1(s)$ and $T_I(s) = I_2(s)/I_1(s)$ for the circuit in Figure P11–16. Find $v_1(t)$ and $i_2(t)$ when the input $i_1(t) = \delta(t)$, $R_1 = 100\ \Omega$, $R_2 = 200\ \Omega$, and $L = 100$ mH.

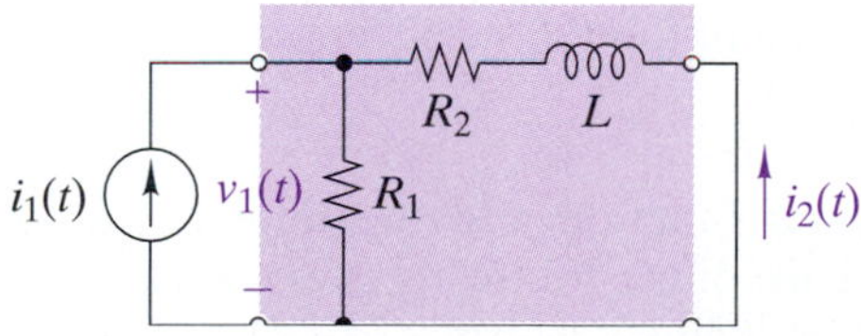

FIGURE P11–16

11–17 Find the network functions $Z(s) = V_1(s)/I_1(s)$ and $T_I(s) = I_2(s)/I_1(s)$ for the circuit in Figure P11–17. Find $v_1(t)$ and $i_2(t)$ when $i_1(t) = \delta(t)$, $R = 1\ \text{k}\Omega$, L = 400 mH, and C = 500 nF.

FIGURE P11–17

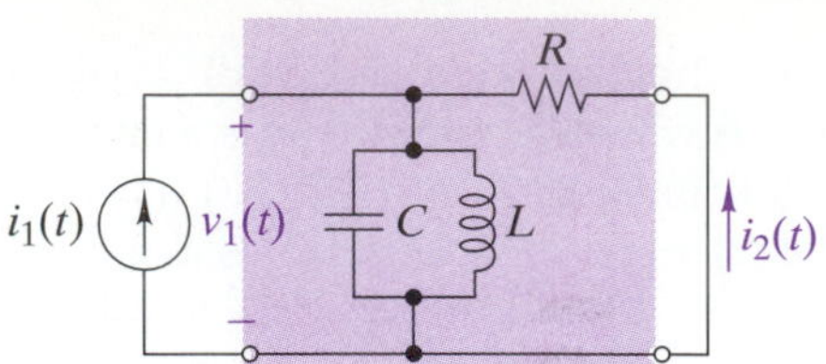

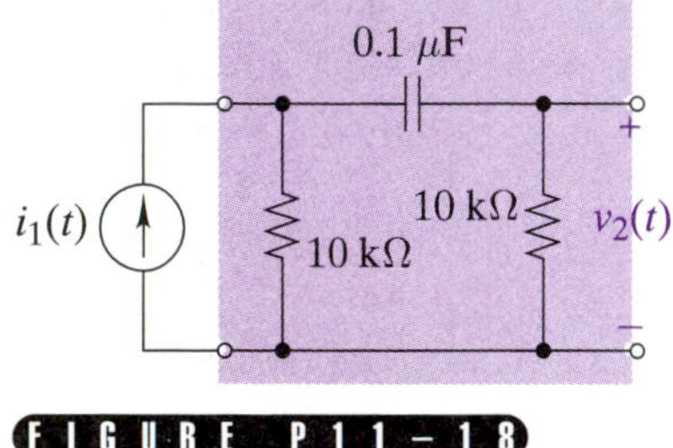

FIGURE P11–18

11–18 The input $i_1(t)$ in Figure P11–18 is a unit impulse $\delta(t)$. Find $v_2(t)$.

11–19 A one-port circuit is driven by a unit impulse of current and the voltage response is found to be $v(t) = \delta(t) + (e^{-100t} + e^{-200t})u(t)$ V. Find the current response when the one-port circuit is driven by a unit impulse of voltage.

11–20 A voltage source delivers a rectangular pulse to the input of a two-port circuit. When the pulse amplitude is set to 10 V and the pulse duration to 2 μs, the voltage response at the output port is found to be $v_2(t) = 2e^{-100t}$ mV. Find the impulse response of the two-port circuit.

ERO 11–3 NETWORK FUNCTIONS AND STEP RESPONSE (SECT. 11–4)

(a) Given a first- or second-order linear circuit, find its step response.
(b) Given one of the responses $H(s)$, $h(t)$, $G(s)$, or $g(t)$, find any of the other three responses.

11–21 In Figure P11–11 the input is $v_1(t) = u(t)$. Find $T_V(s) = V_2(s)/V_1(s)$ and $v_2(t)$.

11–22 In Figure P11–12 the input is $v_1(t) = u(t)$. Find $T_V(s) = V_2(s)/V_1(s)$ and $v_2(t)$.

11–23 In Figure P11–13 the input is $v_1(t) = u(t)$. Find $T_V(s) = V_2(s)/V_1(s)$ and $v_2(t)$.

11–24 In Figure P11–14 the input is $v_1(t) = u(t)$. Find $T_V(s) = V_2(s)/V_1(s)$ and $v_2(t)$.

11–25 In Figure P11–15 the input is $v_1(t) = u(t)$. Find $T_V(s) = V_2(s)/V_1(s)$ and $v_2(t)$.

11–26 Find the transfer function and step response waveform corresponding to each of the following impulse responses:
(a) $h(t) = -1000[e^{-1000t}]u(t)$
(b) $h(t) = \delta(t) - 1000[e^{-1000t}]u(t)$

11–27 Find the transfer function and the impulse response waveform corresponding to each of the following step responses:
(a) $g(t) = [-e^{-2000t}]u(t)$
(b) $g(t) = [1 - e^{-2000t}]u(t)$

11–28 Find the transfer function and the impulse response waveform corresponding to each of the following step responses:
(a) $g(t) = [-1 + 0.8e^{-2000t}]u(t)$
(b) $g(t) = [-1 + 2e^{-2000t}]u(t)$

11–29 Find the transfer function and step response waveform corresponding to each of the following impulse responses:
(a) $h(t) = 1000[e^{-1000t} \sin 2000t]u(t)$
(b) $h(t) = 2000[e^{-1000t} \cos 2000t]u(t)$

11–30 Find the transfer function and the impulse response waveform corresponding to each of the following step responses:
(a) $g(t) = 20[e^{-1000t} \sin 2000t]u(t)$
(b) $g(t) = [e^{-100t} - e^{-2000t}]u(t)$

ERO 11–4 NETWORK FUNCTIONS AND SINUSOIDAL STEADY-STATE RESPONSE (SECT. 11–5)

(a) Given a first- or second-order linear circuit with a specified input sinusoid, find the amplitude and phase angle of the sinusoidal steady-state response.
(b) Given one of the responses $H(s)$, $h(t)$, $G(s)$, or $g(t)$, find the sinusoidal steady-state response for a specified input sinusoid.

11–31 Find the amplitude and phase angle of the steady-state output $v_{2SS}(t)$ of the circuit in Figure P11–7 for $v_1(t) = 5 \cos 10^5 t$. Repeat for $v_1(t) = 10 \sin 10^3 t$.

11–32 Find the amplitude and phase angle of the steady-state output $v_{2SS}(t)$ of the circuit in Figure P11–8 for $v_1(t) = 10 \sin 100t$. Repeat for $v_1(t) = 3 \cos 200t$.

11–33 Find the amplitude and phase angle of the steady-state output $v_{2SS}(t)$ of the circuit in Figure P11–11 for $v_1(t) = 5 \cos 10^4 t$. Repeat for $v_1(t) = 10 \sin 10^3 t$.

11–34 Find the amplitude and phase angle of the steady-state output $v_{2SS}(t)$ of the circuit in Figure P11–12 for $v_1(t) = 10 \sin 100t$. Repeat for $v_1(t) = 3 \cos 200t$.

11–35 Find the amplitude and phase angle of the steady-state output $v_{2SS}(t)$ of the circuit in Figure P11–13 for $v_1(t) = 10 \cos 5000t$. Repeat for $v_1(t) = 5 \cos 2000t$.

11–36 Find the amplitude and phase angle of the steady-state output $v_{2SS}(t)$ of the circuit in Figure P11–14 for $v_1(t) = 15 \cos 10^3 t$. Repeat for $v_1(t) = 5 \cos 2 \times 10^3 t$.

The next series of problems give the time-domain impulse or step response of a linear circuit and a sinusoidal input. Find the amplitude and phase angle of the sinusoidal steady-state output for the sinusoidal input listed.

PROBLEM	IMPULSE OR STEP RESPONSE	INPUT
11–37	$g(t) = [e^{-2000t}]u(t)$	$x(t) = 5 \cos 1000t$
11–38	$g(t) = [-1 + 0.8e^{-1000t}]u(t)$	$x(t) = 4 \cos 1000t$
11–39	$h(t) = [2000e^{-1000t} \sin 1000t]u(t)$	$x(t) = 3 \sin 4000t$
11–40	$h(t) = 400[e^{-100t} - e^{-5000t}]u(t)$	$x(t) = 5 \cos 1000t$

ERO 11–5 NETWORK FUNCTIONS AND CONVOLUTION (SECT. 11–6)

Given the impulse or step response of a linear circuit, use a convolution integral to find the response due to a specified input.

11–41 Use convolution to find the output $v_2(t)$ of the circuit in Figure P11–11 when the input is $v_1(t) = 5tu(t)$.

11–42 Use convolution to find the output $v_2(t)$ of the circuit in Figure P11–13 when the input is $v_1(t) = 5tu(t)$ V.

11–43 The impulse response of a linear circuit is $h(t) = 20[u(t) - u(t-5)]$. Use convolution to find the response due to an input $x(t) = tu(t)$.

11–44 Repeat Problem 11–43 for $x(t) = 5e^{-1000t}u(t)$. Use the short pulse approximation if applicable.

11–45 The impulse response of a linear circuit is $h(t) = u(t) - u(t - 10)$. Use convolution to find the response due to an input $x(t) = tu(t)$.

11–46 The impulse response of a linear circuit is $h(t) = [200e^{-200t}]u(t)$. Use convolution to the find the response due to an input $x(t) = 5tu(t)$.

11–47 Repeat Problem 11–46 for $x(t) = 10u(t) - 10u(t - 0.1)$. Use the short pulse approximation if applicable.

11–48 The impulse response of a linear circuit is $h(t) = -1000[e^{-1000t}]u(t)$. Use convolution to find the response due to an input $x(t) = 10tu(t) + 10\delta(t)$.

11–49 The impulse response of a linear circuit is $h(t) = 10[e^{-1000t} \sin 2000t]u(t)$.
Use convolution to find the circuit response for an input $x(t) = 10tu(t)$.

11–50 The impulse response of a memoryless circuit is $h(t) = K\,\delta(t)$. Use convolution to show that the output for any input is $y(t) = Kx(t)$.

ERO 11–6 NETWORK FUNCTION DESIGN (SECT. 11–7)

Given a transfer function $T(s)$,
(a) Design a prototype circuit that realizes $T(s)$ and meets stated constraints on the available elements.
(b) Magnitude scale the prototype to obtain practical element values.

11–51 D Design a circuit to realize the following transfer function using only resistors, capacitors, and OP AMPs. Scale the circuit so that all resistors are greater than 10 kΩ and all capacitors are less than 1 μF.

$$T_V(s) = \pm\frac{10^5}{(s + 200)(s + 4000)}$$

11–52 D Design a circuit to realize the following transfer function using only resistors, capacitors, and not more than one OP AMP. Scale the circuit so that all capacitors are exactly 100 nF.

$$T_V(s) = \pm\frac{100(s + 500)}{(s + 200)(s + 4000)}$$

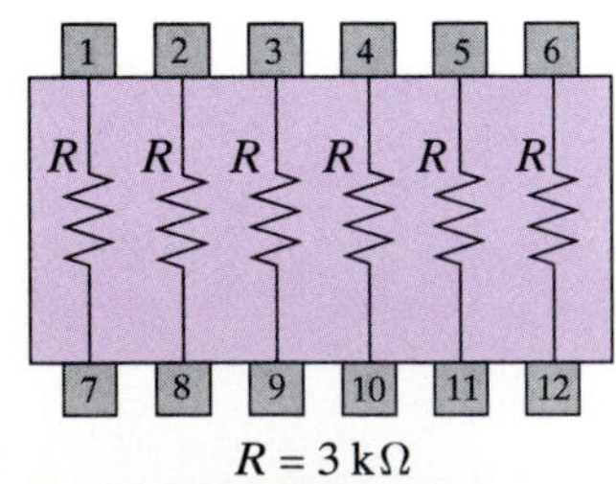

FIGURE P11–53

11–53 D Design a circuit to realize the following transfer function using only resistors, capacitors and no more than one OP AMP. Scale the circuit so that all of the resistors needed can be supplied using one or more of the resistor array packages in Figure P11–53. *Hint*: Series and parallel resistor combinations can be used.

$$T_V(s) = \pm\frac{1000s}{(s + 50)(s + 2000)}$$

11–54 **D** Design a circuit to realize the following transfer function using only resistors, capacitors, and inductors (no OP AMPs allowed). Scale the circuit so that all inductors are 100 mH or less.

$$T_V(s) = \frac{s^2}{(s + 1000)(s + 4000)}$$

11–55 **D** Design a circuit to realize the following transfer function using only resistors, capacitors, and not more than one OP AMP. Scale the circuit so that all resistors are greater than 10 kΩ and all capacitors are less than 1 μF.

$$T_V(s) = \pm\frac{(s + 100)(s + 1000)}{(s + 200)(s + 500)}$$

11–56 **D** Design a circuit to realize the following transfer function using only resistors, capacitors, and OP AMPs. Scale the circuit so that all capacitors are exactly 100 nF.

$$T_V(s) = -\frac{100(s + 400)}{s(s + 200)}$$

11–57 **D** Design a circuit to realize the following transfer function using practical element values.

$$T_V(s) = \pm\frac{10^6}{s^2 + 1000s + 10^6}$$

11–58 **D** Design a circuit to realize the following transfer below using practical element values.

$$T_V(s) = -\frac{s^2}{s^2 + 2000s + 2 \times 10^6}$$

11–59 **D** Design a circuit that produces the following step response:

$$g(t) = [10 + 20e^{-50t}]u(t)$$

11–60 **D** Design a circuit that produces the following step response:

$$g(t) = [1 - e^{-50t} - 50te^{-50t}]u(t)$$

CHAPTER-INTEGRATING PROBLEMS

11–61 **A** CIRCUIT OUTPUT RESPONSES

A circuit has a transfer function

$$T(s) = \frac{s}{(s + 1)(s + 2)}$$

(a) A certain input produced a zero-state output $y(t) = [-e^{-t} + \cos t + \sin t]u(t)$. What was the input waveform?

(b) A step function input produced $y(t) = [e^{-t} + e^{-2t}]u(t)$ as the output. Was the circuit in the zero state?

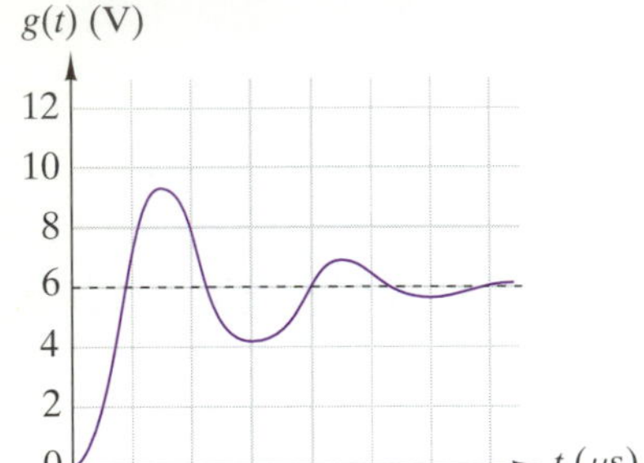

FIGURE P11–62

(c) An output $y(t) = [e^{-6t} + e^{-3t}]u(t)$ is observed. Is this a zero-input response?

(d) An output $y(t) = [e^{-t} + 2e^{-2t}]u(t)$ is observed. Was the input an impulse?

11–62 A D SECOND-ORDER CIRCUIT STEP RESPONSE

The step response in Figure P11–62 is of the form

$$g(t) = \frac{K}{\alpha^2 + \beta^2}\left[1 - e^{-\alpha t}\cos\beta t - \frac{\alpha}{\beta}e^{-\alpha t}\sin\beta t\right]u(t)$$

(a) **A** Estimate values for the parameters K, α, and β from the plot of $g(t)$.

(b) **A** Find the transfer function $T(s)$ corresponding to $g(t)$.

(c) **D** Design a circuit that realizes the $T(s)$ found in (b).

(d) **D** Use computer-aided circuit analysis to verify your design.

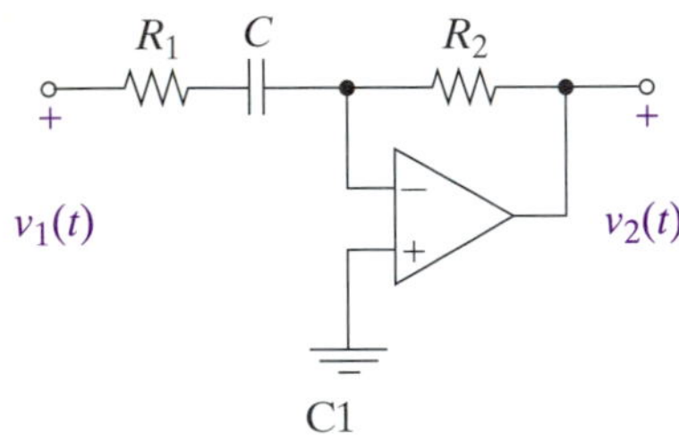

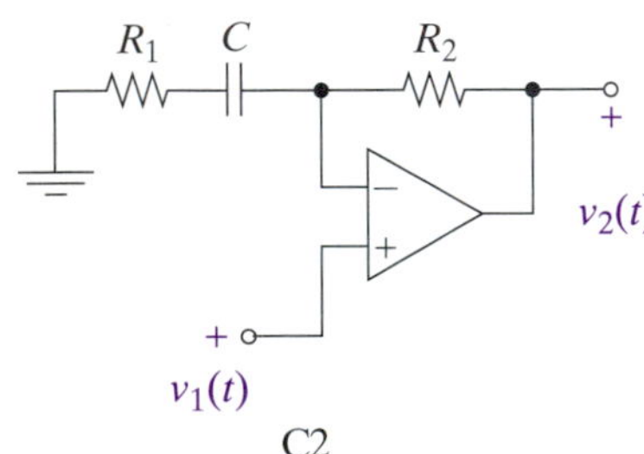

FIGURE P11–63

11–63 A D E RC OP AMP CIRCUIT DESIGN EVALUATION

This problem uses circuits C1 and C2 in Figure P11–63.

(a) **A** Determine the transfer functions $T_V(s) = V_2(s)/V_1(s)$ for each circuit. Locate the poles and zeros for each function and relate their locations to circuit parameters.

(b) **D** Use a cascade connection of one or more of these circuits to realize the following transfer functions. *Hint:* A circuit may be used more than once.

$$T_1(s) = \frac{s^2}{(s+100)(s+400)} \quad \text{and} \quad T_2(s) = \frac{s(s+200)}{(s+100)(s+400)}$$

(c) **E** Show that a cascade connection of these circuits *cannot* realize the following transfer function and explain why in terms of poles and zeros:

$$T_3(s) = \frac{s(s+500)}{(s+100)(s+400)}$$

(d) **E** Develop a design rule that restricts the locations of the poles and zeros of $T(s)$ to ensure that $T(s)$ can be realized using a cascade connection of these circuits.

11–64 A RC OP AMP INTEGRATOR CIRCUITS

(a) In Chapter 6 the input-output relationship of the OP AMP integrator was shown to be

$$v_O(t) = -\frac{1}{RC}\int_0^t v_S(\tau)d\tau$$

Find the voltage transfer function of the integrator. Is the circuit stable or unstable?

(b) Find the impulse and step responses of the OP AMP integrator. Is the impulse consistent with your answers in part (a)?

(c) What is the voltage transfer function of a cascade connection of two OP AMP integrators? Does the chain rule apply in this case? Is the cascade circuit stable or unstable?

(d) Figure P11–64 shows an OP AMP summer and two OP AMP integrators connected in cascade with a feedback path from output to input. Find the voltage transfer function of this circuit. Is this circuit stable or unstable?

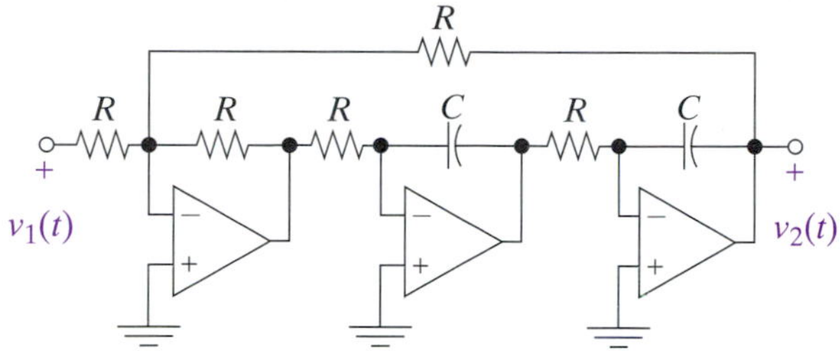

FIGURE P11–64

11–65 A IMPULSE RESPONSE IN THE TIME DOMAIN

In this chapter a circuit impulse response $h(t)$ is found using the inverse Laplace transform of a network function. Since convolution works entirely in the time domain, it would be handy to have a way to find $h(t)$ without resorting to s-domain analysis. In Chapter 7 we used time-domain methods to find the step response from the circuit differential equation. Since impulse response is the derivative of step response, we can derive $h(t)$ from the step response found by the classical methods in Chapter 7.

(a) Find the impulse response of the circuits described by the following differential equations without using Laplace transforms. Remember that impulse and step response are zero-state responses.

$$(1) \quad 10^{-3}\frac{dy}{dt} + y(t) = x(t)$$

$$(2) \frac{d^2y}{dt^2} + 4\frac{dy}{dt} + 4y = 2x(t)$$

(b) Transform these differential equations into the s-domain and solve for the transfer functions relating $X(s)$ and $Y(s)$.

(c) Take the inverse Laplace transforms of the transfer functions found in (b) and check to see if they agree with the impulse responses found in (a).

PART 2

DYNAMIC CIRCUITS

COURSE-INTEGRATING PROBLEMS
COURSE OBJECTIVES

A Analysis Given a dynamic circuit with time-varying input signals, select an analysis technique and find the circuit's response in terms of output signal waveforms, phasors, or transforms.

D Design Given a specified dynamic signal or power processing function stated in terms of output signal waveforms, phasors, or transforms, design one or more circuits that implement the specified function within stated constraints.

E Evaluation Given several dynamic circuits that reportedly perform the same dynamic signal- or power-processing function, verify the claim and rank order the circuits using stated evaluation criteria.

I-11 A D RC CIRCUIT ANALYSIS AND DESIGN

The *RC* circuit in Figure PI-11 is driven by the exponential voltage shown.

(a) A Determine the zero-state response $v_O(t)$ for $C = 200$ nF. Identify the forced response and the natural responses.

(b) A For $C = 200$ nF, determine the initial condition $v_C(0)$ such that the natural response in $v_O(t)$ is identically zero.

(c) D Adjust the value of C until the zero-state response is of the form $Kte^{-\alpha t}$. What are the values of K and α?

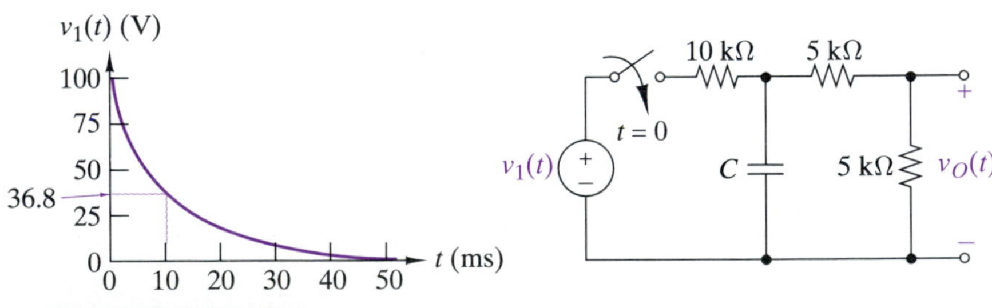

FIGURE PI–11

I-12 A AC CIRCUIT ANALYSIS

Ten years after graduating with a B.S.E.E., you decide to go to graduate school for a master's degree. In desperate need of income, you agree to sign on as a grader in the basic circuit analysis course. One of the problems asks the students to find $v(t)$ in Figure PI-12 when the circuit operates in the sinusoidal steady state. One of the students offers the following solution:

$$\begin{aligned} v(t) &= (R + j\omega L) \times i(t) \\ &= (20 + j20) \times 0.5 \cos 200t \\ &= 10 \cos 200t + j10 \cos 200t \\ &= 10\sqrt{2} \cos(200t + 45°) \end{aligned}$$

Is the answer correct? If not, what grade would you give the student? If correct, what comments would you give the student about the method of solution?

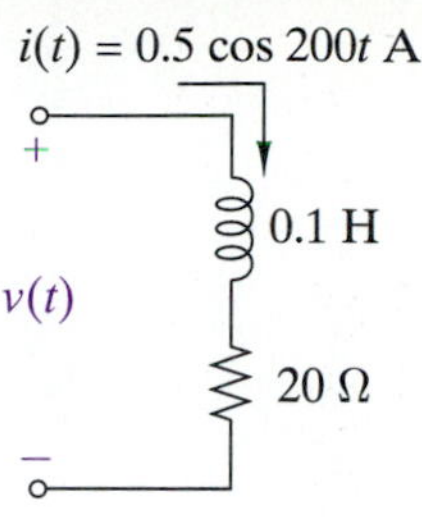

FIGURE PI-12

I-13 D E NETWORK FUNCTIONS AND PHASE SHIFT

In the sinusoidal steady state the transfer function $T(j\omega)$ relates the input and output sinusoids. The angle of $T(j\omega)$ is called the phase shift through the circuit and indicates the amount by which the input and output sinusoids are out of phase.

(a) D Select the element values of circuit C1 in Figure PI-13 so that $v_2(t)$ and $v_3(t)$ are 90° out of phase at $\omega = 2$ krad/s.

(b) E It is claimed that in the sinusoidal steady state the voltages $v_2(t)$ and $v_3(t)$ in circuit C2 are always 90° out of phase regardless of frequency. Prove or disprove this claim.

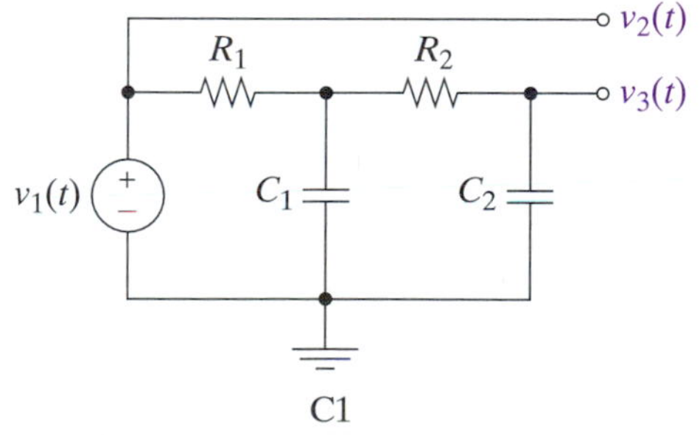

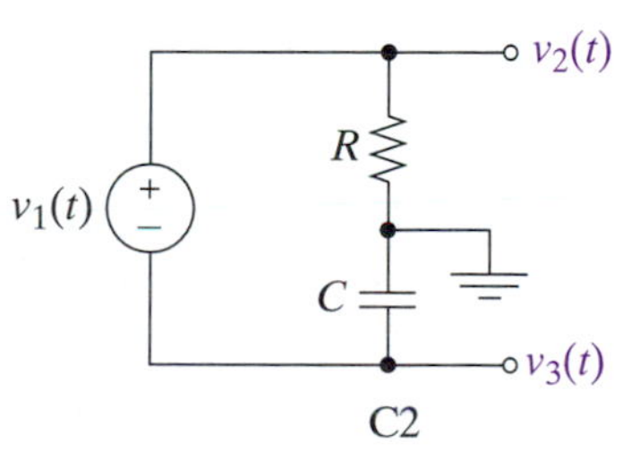

FIGURE PI-13

I-14 A D E EVALUATING ACTIVE AND PASSIVE CIRCUIT DESIGN OPTIONS

Figure PI-14 shows an RLC voltage divider and an RC OP-AMP circuit.

(a) A Show that both circuits have a transfer function of the form

$$T_V(s) = \frac{V_2(s)}{V_1(s)} = \frac{s^2}{s^2 + 2\zeta\omega_0 s + \omega_0^2}$$

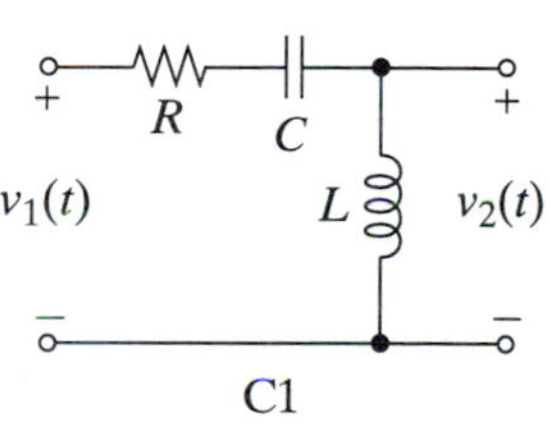

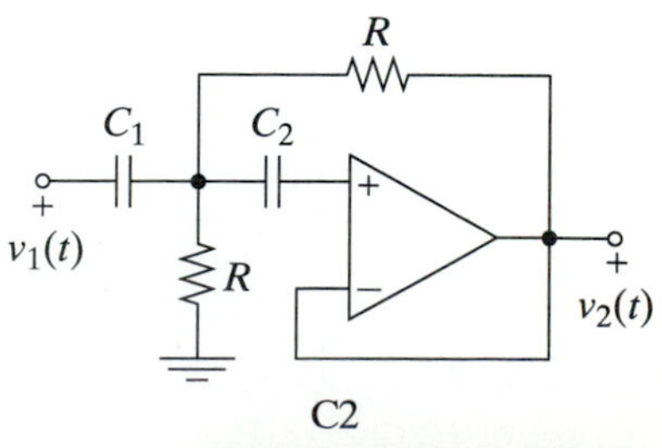

FIGURE PI-14

(b) **D** If possible, select element values so that $\omega_0 = 10^6$ rad/s and $\zeta = 0.5$. Which circuit best meets these requirements?

(c) **D** If possible, select element values so that $\omega_0 = 10^2$ rad/s and $\zeta = 2$. Which circuit best meets these requirements?

I-15 A SINUSOIDAL-STEADY STATE RESPONSE

The input to the RL circuit in Figure PI-15 is $v_1(t) = V_A \cos \omega t$.

(a) Use the s-domain network function method in Chapter 11 to find the sinusoidal steady-state response $i_{SS}(t)$.

(b) Use the phasor circuit analysis method of Chapter 8 to find sinusoidal current response.

(c) Formulate the circuit differential equation and use the classical methods of Chapter 7 to find the forced component of $i(t)$.

(d) The responses found in (a), (b), and (c) should be identical. Which method do you think is easiest to apply? Discuss.

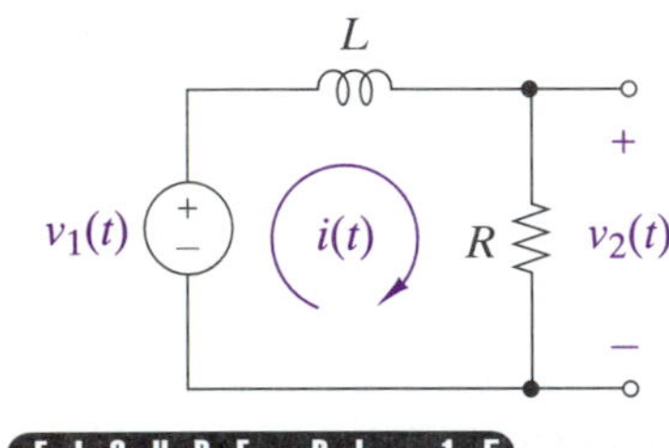

FIGURE PI-15

I-16 A E NEW PRODUCT EVALUATION

The New Products Division of the RonAl Corporation (founded by two well-known authors) has announced the availability of an integrated circuit package called the Universal Single-Pole Transfer Function Synthesizer (USPTS). Figure PI-16 shows the first page of the data sheets on this new device. Unfortunately, the second page, which describes how to interconnect the circuit pins to obtain each transfer function, has been lost in the mail.

(a) **A** Reconstruct the missing second page by showing how to interconnect the circuit pins to obtain each transfer function listed. All connections are short circuits from pin to pin, pin to ground, or pin to power. No external components other than the power supply are required. *Hint:* The output is always pin 7.

(b) **E** Explain why the transfer functions are independent of the load provided that $R_L > 2$ kΩ.

(c) **E** Explain why the RC products are controlled to ± 1% whereas the OP AMP gain is only controlled to within a factor of 10.

I-17 A E NEW PRODUCT EVALUATION

The RonAl Corporation has issued Application Note No. 1 on the USPTS integrated circuit described in Problem I-16. The note claims that interconnecting two circuits as shown in Figure PI-17 produces a pair of complex poles with $\zeta = \sqrt{2}/2$ and $\omega_0 = \sqrt{2}/RC$.

(a) Verify or disprove the claim.

(b) The Application Note further claims that interchanging the connections at pins 2 and 3 on both circuits adds a zero at the origin in the s-plane but does not change the poles. Verify or disprove this claim.

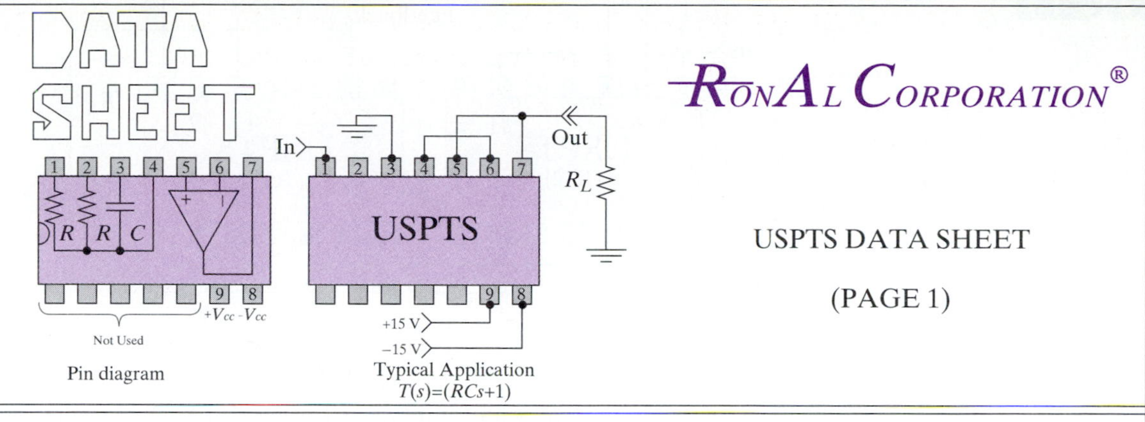

PERFORMANCE CHARACTERISTICS

1. OP AMP: For $V_{CC} = 15$ V gain (MIN) = 50 V/mV; output voltage swing = ±14 V gain (MAX)= 500 V/mV; output current (MAX)= 20 mA

2. For $R_L > 2$ kΩ the available transfer functions are:

ALL POLE TYPE

$$\frac{1}{RCs+1},\quad \frac{2}{RCs+2},\quad \frac{1}{RCs+2},\quad -\frac{1}{RCs+1},\quad -\frac{1}{RCs},\quad -\frac{2}{RCs}$$

ALL ZEROTYPE

$$RCs+1,\quad \tfrac{1}{2}(RCs+2),\quad RCs+2,\quad -(RCs+1),\quad -RCs,\quad -\tfrac{1}{2}RCs$$

POLE-ZERO TYPE

$$\frac{RCs}{RCs+1},\quad \frac{RCs}{RCs+2},\quad \frac{RCs+1}{RCs+2},\quad \frac{RCs+1}{RCs},\quad \frac{RCs+2}{RCs},\quad \frac{RCs+2}{RCs+1}$$

3. To obtain different pole-zero locations order from standard models or order custom models in lots of 1000 or more.

Model	*RC(ms)*	*Tolerance*
USPTS - 0.1	0.1	±1%
USPTS - 0.3	0.3	±1%
USPTS - 1.0	1.0	±1%
USPTS - 3.0	3.0	±1%
USPTS - 10.0	10.0	±1%

FIGURE PI–16

FIGURE PI-17

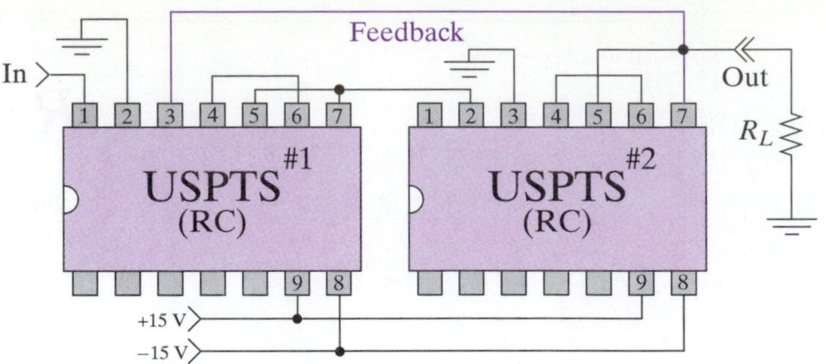

I-18 A NONLINEAR DYNAMIC CIRCUIT ANALYSIS

The inverting amplifier and integrator in Figure PI-18 have the same input. Their outputs drive the inputs of a comparator. The comparator has an output $+V_{CC}$ when $v_P > v_N$ and an output $-V_{CC}$ when $v_P < v_N$. Assume that there is no initial voltage on the capacitor at $t = 0$.

(a) Show that when an input $v_1 = +V_{CC}$ is applied at $t = 0$, the comparator output is $+V_{CC}$ until $t = RC$ and is $-V_{CC}$ thereafter.

(b) Show that when an input $v_1 = -V_{CC}$ is applied at $t = 0$, the comparator output is $-V_{CC}$ until $t = RC$ and is $+V_{CC}$ thereafter.

(c) Now force the condition $v_1 = v_O$ by making a feedback connection from the comparator output to the input. Assume that the initial comparator output is $+V_{CC}$. Show that the comparator output is a square wave with a period of $4RC$ and the integrator output is a triangular wave with the same period.

FIGURE PI-18

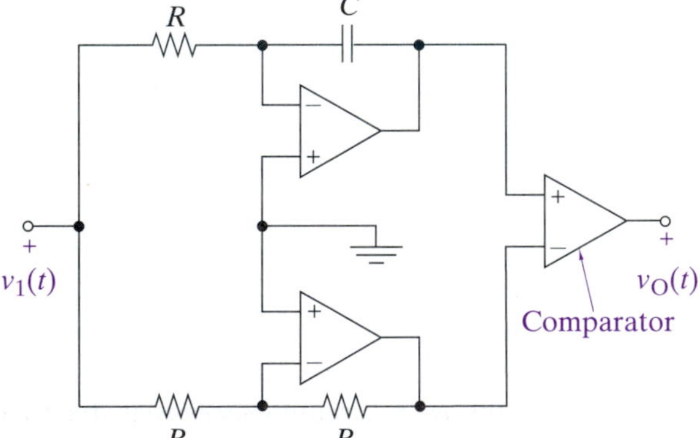

I-19 A INDUCTOR SIMULATION CIRCUIT

Inductors based on magnetic effects are difficult or impossible to fabricate using integrated circuit technology. However, it is possible to fabricate circuits using resistors, capacitors, and OP AMPs that simulate the characteristics of inductance. One such circuit is shown in Figure PI–19.

(a) Show that the i–v relationship at the input port of the circuit in Figure PI-19 is

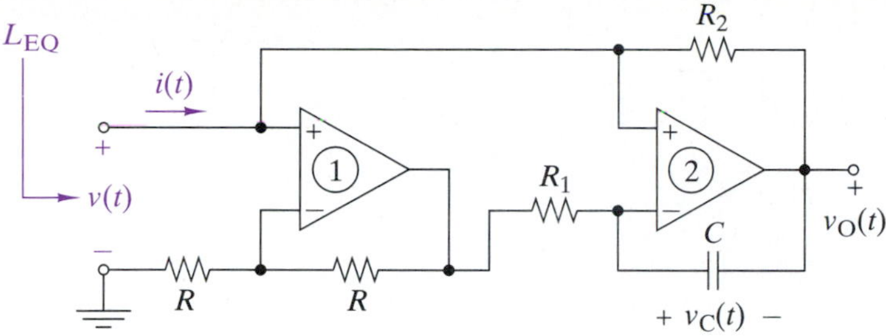

FIGURE PI-19

$$i(t) = \frac{1}{L_{EQ}} \int_0^t v\,dt \qquad \text{where} \qquad L_{EQ} = R_1 R_2 C$$

(b) For $R_1 = 10$ kΩ, $R_2 = 10$ kΩ, $C = 1$ μF, and $v(t) = 10u(t)$ V, derive expressions for $v_C(t)$ and $v_O(t)$. For $V_{CC} = \pm 15$ V, find the time at which OP AMP no. 2 saturates. Assume that $v_C(0) = 0$.

(c) For the conditions given in (b), find the energy stored on the capacitor at the time OP AMP no. 2 saturates.

(d) For the conditions given in (b), find the energy stored in the simulated inductor at the time OP AMP no. 2 saturates. Should there be any relationship between the energy found in (c) and the energy found in (d)? Discuss.

I-20 A FREQUENCY DEPENDENT NEGATIVE RESISTOR

The frequency-dependent negative resistor (FDNR) is an integrated circuit device whose circuit symbol is shown in Figure PI-20(a). Using the passive sign convention, the i–v relationship of the element modeling the device is

$$i(t) = D\frac{d^2v(t)}{dt^2} \qquad \text{with} \qquad D > 0$$

(a) Find the element impedance $Z(s) = V(s)/I(s)$. Evaluate $Z(j\omega)$ and discuss any reasons you see for the device's name.

(b) In the sinusoidal steady state the voltage across an FDNR is $v(t) = V_A \cos \omega t$. Find the instantaneous power delivered to the element. Is the FDNR active or passive?

(c) FDNR devices are used to produce inductorless circuits with transfer functions like RLC circuits. Show that the RLC circuit in Figure PI-20(b) and the RDC circuit in Figure PI–20(c) have the same transfer function $T(s) = V_2(s)/V_1(s)$ when $DR_2 = L_1C_1$ and $D/C_2 = R_1C_1$.

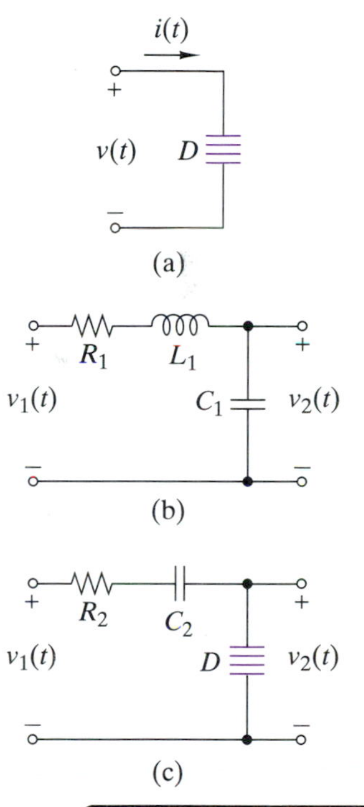

FIGURE PI-20

PART 3

APPLICATIONS

COURSE OBJECTIVES

A Analysis Given a dynamic circuit with sinusoidal input signals, select an analysis technique and find the circuit's response in terms of complex power flow, frequency response, harmonic response, or spectral response.

D Design Given a specified ac signal or power processing function stated in terms of frequency response, complex power flow, harmonic response, or spectral response, design one or more circuits that implement the stated function within given constraints.

E Evaluation Given several dynamic circuits that reportedly perform the same ac signal- or power-processing function, verify the claim and rank order the circuits using stated evaluation criteria.

Frequency Response

The advantage of the straight-line approximation is, of course, that it reduces the complete characteristics to a sum of elementary characteristics.

Hendrik W. Bode, 1945,
American Engineer

In the sinusoidal steady state, both the input and the output of a stable linear circuit are sinusoids of the same frequency. The term *frequency response* refers to the frequency-dependent relation, in both gain and phase, between a sinusoidal input and the resulting sinusoidal steady-state output. The gain and phase relationships can be presented as equations or graphs. When presented as separate graphs of gain and phase versus logarithmic frequency, the result is commonly called a **Bode diagram**.

Hendrick Bode (pronounced Bow Dee) spent most of his distinguished career as a member of the technical staff of the Bell Telephone Laboratories. In the 1930s Bode made major contributions to circuit and feedback amplifier theory as part of the effort to develop the precise frequency-selective amplifiers required by long-distance telephone systems. In describing his work Bode used straight-line approximations as an aid to understanding and simplifying the slide rule calculations required in his day. With the advent of digital computers, the computational benefits of Bode diagrams are no longer important. His straight-line method is still useful today, however, because it allows us to quickly visualize how the poles and zeros of a transfer function affect the frequency response of a circuit. Thus, Bode diagrams are a conceptual tool that simplifies the analysis and design of circuits and systems, just as they did in Bode's day.

The first section of this chapter defines the parameters used to characterize the frequency response. The frequency response of first- and second-order circuits is discussed in the following two sections. The fourth section describes how the frequency-response characteristics of series and parallel *RLC* circuits can be traced to variation in the impedance of specific elements in the circuit. The formal treatment of Bode diagrams in the fifth and sixth sections generalizes the results obtained using basic first- and second-order circuits. The final section discusses the relationship between frequency response and the time-domain step response.

12–1 FREQUENCY-RESPONSE DESCRIPTORS

In Chapter 11, we found that replacing s by $j\omega$ allows us to find the steady-state response of a stable circuit directly from its transfer function. The circuit transfer function influences the sinusoidal steady-state response through the **gain** function $|T(j\omega)|$ and **phase** function $\theta(\omega)$.

$$\text{Output Amplitude} = |T(j\omega)| \times (\text{Input Amplitude})$$

$$\text{Output Phase} = \text{Input Phase} + \theta(\omega)$$

Taken together, the gain and phase functions show how the circuit modifies the input amplitude and phase angle to produce the output sinusoid. These two functions define the **frequency response** of the circuit since they are frequency-dependent functions that relate the sinusoidal steady-state input and output. The gain and phase functions can be expressed mathematically or presented graphically as the frequency response plots in Figure 12–1.

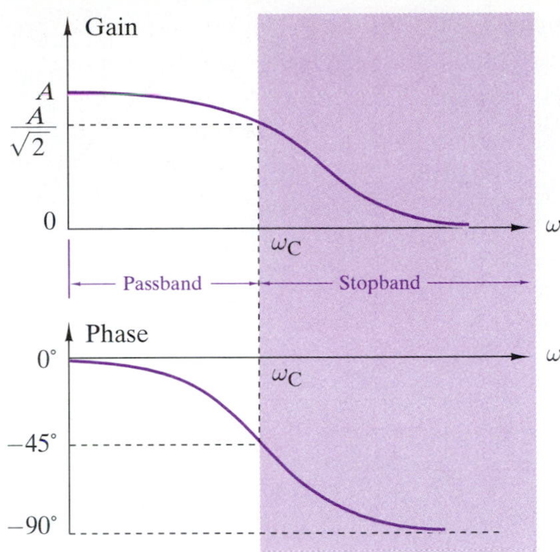

FIGURE 12–1 *Frequency-response plots.*

The terminology used to describe the frequency response of circuits and systems is based on the form of the gain plot. For example, at high frequencies the gain in Figure 12–1 falls off so that output signals in this frequency range are reduced in amplitude. The range of frequencies over which the output is significantly attenuated is called the **stopband**. At low frequencies the gain is essentially constant and there is relatively little attenuation. The frequency range over which there is little attenuation is called a **passband**. The frequency associated with the boundary between a passband and an adjacent stopband is called the **cutoff frequency** ($\omega_C = 2\pi f_C$). In general, the transition from the passband to the stopband is gradual, so the precise location of the cutoff frequency is a matter of definition. The most widely used definition specifies the cutoff frequency to be the frequency at which the gain has decreased by a factor of $1/\sqrt{2} = 0.707$ from its maximum value in the passband.

Again this definition is arbitrary, since there is no sharp boundary between a passband and an adjacent stopband. However, the definition is motivated by the fact that the power delivered to a resistance by a sinusoidal current or voltage waveform is proportional to the square of its amplitude. At a cutoff frequency the gain is reduced by a factor of $1/\sqrt{2}$ and the square of the output amplitude is reduced by a factor of one-half. For this reason the cutoff frequency is also called the **half-power frequency**.

When the gain response is plotted on log-log scales, we obtain the four prototype gain characteristics shown in Figure 12–2. A **low-pass** gain characteristic has a single passband extending from zero frequency (dc) to the cutoff frequency. A **high-pass** gain characteristic has a single passband extending from the cutoff frequency to infinite frequency. A **bandpass** gain has a single passband with two cutoff frequencies, neither of which is zero or infinite. Finally, the **bandstop** gain has a single stopband with two cutoff frequencies, neither of which is zero or infinite.

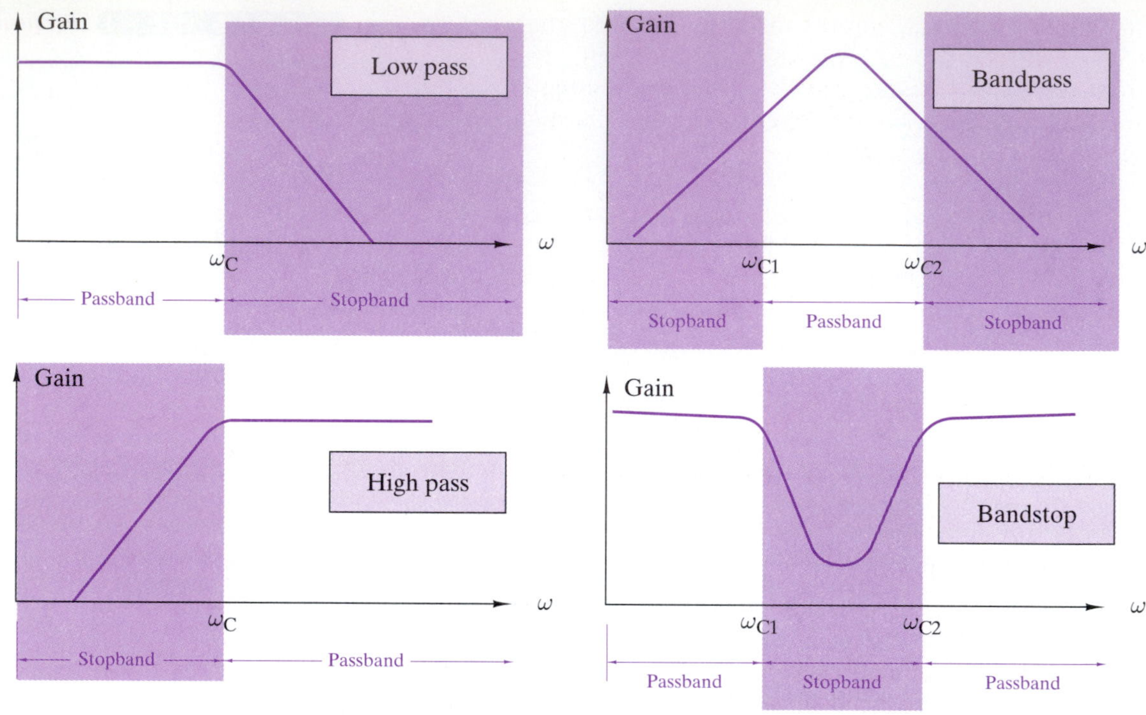

FIGURE 12–2 *Prototype gain responses.*

The **bandwidth** of a gain characteristic is defined as the frequency range spanned by its passband. The bandwidth of a low-pass circuit is equal to its cutoff frequency ($B = \omega_C$). The bandwidth of a high-pass characteristic is infinite since passband extends to infinity. For the bandpass and bandstop cases in Figure 12–2, the bandwidth is the difference in the two cutoff frequencies:

$$B = \omega_{C2} - \omega_{C1} \tag{12–1}$$

For the bandstop case Eq. (12–1) defines the width of the stopband rather than the passbands.

The gain responses in Figure 12–2 have different characteristics at zero and infinite frequency—namely,

	GAIN AT	
	$\omega = 0$	$\omega = \infty$
Low pass	Finite	0
High pass	0	Finite
Bandpass	0	0
Bandstop	Finite	Finite

Since these extreme values form a unique pattern, the type of gain response can be inferred from the values of $|T(0)|$ and $|T(\infty)|$. These end-point values, in turn, are usually determined by the impedance of capacitors and inductors in the circuit. In the sinusoidal steady state the impedances of these elements are

$$Z_C(j\omega) = \frac{1}{j\omega C} \quad \text{and} \quad Z_L(j\omega) = j\omega L \qquad (12-2)$$

These impedances form a unique pattern at zero and infinite frequency—namely,

	IMPEDANCE AT $\omega = 0$	$\omega = \infty$
Capacitor	Infinite	0
Inductor	0	Infinite

Thus, the capacitor acts like an open circuit at zero frequency and a short circuit at infinite frequency, while the inductor acts like a short circuit at dc and an open circuit at infinite frequency. These observations often allow us to infer the type of gain response directly from the circuit itself without finding the transfer function.

When frequency-response plots use logarithmic scales for the frequency variable, they are normally referred to as **Bode diagrams**. Logarithmic scales are used to compress the data range because the frequency ranges of interest often span several orders of magnitude. The use of a logarithmic frequency scale involves some special terminology. Any frequency range whose end points have a 2:1 ratio is called an **octave**. Any range whose end points have a 10:1 ratio is called a **decade**. For example, the frequency range from 10 Hz to 20 Hz is one octave, as is the range from 20 MHz to 40 MHz. The standard UHF (ultra high frequency) band spans one decade from 0.3 to 3 GHz.

In Bode diagrams the gain $|T(j\omega)|$ is usually expressed in **decibels** (dB), defined as

$$|T(j\omega)|_{dB} = 20 \log_{10}|T(j\omega)| \qquad (12-3)$$

To construct and interpret frequency-response plots, you must have some familiarity with gains expressed in decibels. First note that the gain in dB can be either positive, negative, or zero. A gain of zero dB means that $|T(j\omega)| = 1$ (i.e., the input and output amplitudes are equal). When $|T(j\omega)| > 1$ the output amplitude exceeds the input and $|T(j\omega)|_{dB} > 0$. When $|T(j\omega)| < 1$ the output amplitude is less than the input and $|T(j\omega)|_{dB} < 0$. A cutoff frequency occurs when the gain is reduced from its maximum passband value by a factor $1/\sqrt{2}$. Expressed in dB, this is a gain reduction of

$$20\log_{10}\left(\frac{1}{\sqrt{2}}|T|_{\text{MAX}}\right) = 20\log_{10}|T_{\text{MAX}}| - 20\log_{10}\sqrt{2}$$
$$\approx |T|_{\text{MAX, dB}} - 3\text{ dB}$$

That is, cutoff occurs when the dB gain is reduced by about 3 dB. For this reason the cutoff is also called the **3-dB down frequency**.

The generalization of this idea is that multiplying $|T(j\omega)|$ by a factor K means $20 \times \log|K|T(j\omega) = |T(j\omega)|_{\text{dB}} + 20\log(K)$. That is, multiplying the gain by K changes the gain in dB by an additive factor K_{dB}. Some multiplicative factors whose dB equivalents are worth remembering are as follows:

- A multiplicative factor $K = 1$ changes $|T(j\omega)|_{\text{dB}}$ by 0 dB.
- A multiplicative factor $K = (1/\sqrt{2})$ changes $|T(j\omega)|_{\text{dB}}$ by about +3 dB (–3 dB).
- A multiplicative factor $K = 2$ (1/2) changes $|T(j\omega)|_{\text{dB}}$ by about +6 dB (–6 dB).
- A multiplicative factor $K = 10$ (1/10) changes $|T(j\omega)|_{\text{dB}}$ by +20 dB (–20 dB).
- A multiplicative factor $K = 30$ (1/30) changes $|T(j\omega)|_{\text{dB}}$ by about +30 dB (–30 dB).
- A multiplicative factor $K = 100$ (1/100) changes $|T(j\omega)|_{\text{dB}}$ by +40 dB (–40 dB).
- A multiplicative factor $K = 1000$ (1/1000) + 60 dB changes $|T(j\omega)|_{\text{dB}}$ by +60 dB (–60 dB).

In summary, Bode diagrams use logarithmic frequency scales and linear scales for the gain (in dB) and phase (in radians or degrees). Both plots are semilog graphs, although in effect the gain plot is log/log because of the logarithmic definition of $|T(j\omega)|_{\text{dB}}$. To create frequency-response plots we must calculate $|T(j\omega)|$ and $\theta(\omega)$ at a sufficient number of frequencies to define adequately the stop and passband characteristics. The most efficient way to generate accurate plots is to use one of the many computer-aided analysis tools. Spreadsheets and math analysis programs like Mathcad can be used to calculate and plot frequency-response curves. Circuit analysis programs such as SPICE and MICRO-CAP have ac analysis options that generate the frequency-response plots. We will illustrate the use of these tools in several examples in this chapter.

As always, some knowledge of the expected response is required to use computer-aided circuit analysis tools effectively. Using computer tools to generate frequency-response plots requires at least some preliminary analysis or a rough sketch of the expected response. To develop the required insight, we treat first- and second-order circuits and then use Bode plots to show how these building blocks combine to produce the frequency response of more complicated circuits.

APPLICATION NOTE: EXAMPLE 12–1

The use of the decibel as a measure of performance pervades the literature and folklore of electrical engineering. The decibel originally came from the definition of power ratios in **bels**.[1]

$$\text{Number of bels} = \log_{10}\frac{P_{\text{OUT}}}{P_{\text{IN}}}$$

The decibel (dB) is a more commonly used in practice. The number of decibels is 10 times the number of bels:

$$\text{Number of dB} = 10 \times (\text{Number of bels}) = 10\log_{10}\frac{P_{\text{OUT}}}{P_{\text{IN}}}$$

When the input and output powers are delivered to equal input and output resistances R, then the power ratio can be expressed in terms of voltages across the resistances.

$$\text{Number of dB} = 10\log_{10}\frac{v_{\text{OUT}}^2/R}{v_{\text{IN}}^2/R} = 20\log_{10}\frac{v_{\text{OUT}}}{v_{\text{IN}}}$$

or in terms of currents through the resistances:

$$\text{Number of dB} = 10\log_{10}\frac{i_{\text{OUT}}^2 \times R}{i_{\text{IN}}^2 \times R} = 20\log_{10}\frac{i_{\text{OUT}}}{i_{\text{IN}}}$$

The definition of gain in dB in Eq. (12–3) is consistent with these results, since in the sinusoidal steady state the transfer function equals the ratio of output amplitude to input amplitude. The preceding discussion is not a derivation of Eq. (12–3) but simply a summary of its historical origin. In practice Eq. (12–3) is applied when the input and output are not measured across resistances of equal value.

When the chain rule applies to a cascade connection, the overall transfer function is a product

$$T(j\omega) = T_1 \times T_2 \times \ldots T_{\text{N}}$$

where $T_1, T_2, \ldots T_{\text{N}}$ are the transfer functions of the individual stages in the cascade. Expressed in dB, the overall gain is

$$\begin{aligned}|T(j\omega)|_{\text{dB}} &= 20\log_{10}(|T_1| \times |T_2| \times \ldots |T_{\text{N}}|)\\ &= 20\log_{10}|T_1| + 20\log_{10}|T_2| + \ldots + 20\log_{10}|T_{\text{N}}|\\ &= |T_1|_{\text{dB}} + |T_2|_{\text{dB}} + \ldots + |T_{\text{N}}|_{\text{dB}}\end{aligned}$$

Because of the logarithmic definition, the overall gain (in dB) is the sum of the gains (in dB) of the individual stages in a cascade connection. The effect of altering a stage or adding an additional stage can be calculated by simply adding or subtracting the change in dB. Since summation is simpler than multiplication, the enduring popularity of the dB comes from its logarithmic definition and not its somewhat tenuous relationship to power ratios.

1 The name of the unit honors Alexander Graham Bell (1847–1922), the inventor of the telephone.

12–2 FIRST-ORDER CIRCUIT FREQUENCY RESPONSE

FIRST-ORDER LOW PASS RESPONSE

We begin the study of frequency response with the first-order low-pass transfer function:

$$T(s) = \frac{K}{s + \alpha} \tag{12-4}$$

The constants K and α are real. The constant K can be positive or negative, but α must be positive so that the natural pole at $s = -\alpha$ is in the left half of the s plane to ensure that the circuit is stable. Remember, the concepts of sinusoidal steady state and frequency response do not apply to unstable circuits that have poles in the right half of the s plane or on the j-axis.

To describe the frequency response of the low pass transfer function, we replace s by $j\omega$ in Eq. (12–4)

$$T(j\omega) = \frac{K}{\alpha + j\omega} \tag{12-5}$$

and express the gain and phase functions as

$$|T(j\omega)| = \frac{|K|}{\sqrt{\omega^2 + \alpha^2}}$$
$$\theta(\omega) = \angle K - \tan^{-1}(\omega/\alpha) \tag{12-6}$$

The gain function is a positive number. Since K is real, the angle of K ($\angle K$) is either 0° when $K > 0$ or ±180° when $K < 0$. An example of a negative K occurs in an inverting OP AMP configuration where $T(s) = -Z_2(s)/Z_1(s)$.

Figure 12–3 shows the gain and phase functions plotted versus normalized frequency ω/α. In the gain plot the left vertical scale is a log scale for $|T(j\omega)|$ and the right scale is the equivalent linear scale for $|T(j\omega)|_{\text{dB}}$. The maximum passband gain occurs at $\omega = 0$ where $|T(0)| = |K|/\alpha$. As frequency increases the gain gradually decreases until at $\omega = \alpha$

$$|T(j\alpha)| = \frac{|K|}{\sqrt{\alpha^2 + \alpha^2}} = \frac{|K|/\alpha}{\sqrt{2}} = \frac{|T(0)|}{\sqrt{2}} \tag{12-7}$$

That is, the cutoff frequency of the first-order low-pass transfer function is $\omega_C = \alpha$. The graph of the gain function in Figure 12–3 displays a low-pass characteristic with a finite dc gain and zero infinite frequency gain.

The low- and high-frequency gain asymptotes shown in Figure 12–3 are especially important. The low-frequency asymptote is the horizontal line and the high-frequency asymptote is the sloped line. At low frequencies ($\omega << \alpha$) the gain approaches $|T(j\omega)| \rightarrow |K|/\alpha$. At high frequencies ($\omega >> \alpha$) the gain approaches $|T(j\omega)| \rightarrow |K|/\omega$. The intersection of the two asymptotes occurs when $|K|/\alpha = |K|/\omega$. The intersection forms a "corner" at $\omega = \alpha$, so the cutoff frequency is also called the **corner frequency**.

The high-frequency gain asymptote decreases by a factor of 10 (–20 dB) whenever the frequency increases by a factor of 10 (one decade). As a re-

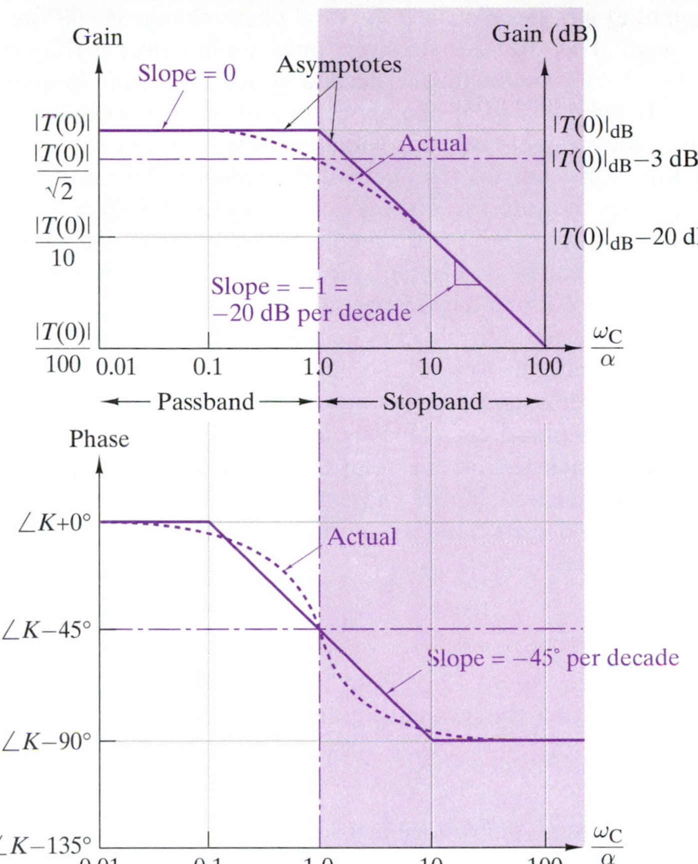

FIGURE 12–3 *First-order low-pass frequency-response plots.*

sult, the high-frequency asymptote has a slope of –1 or –20 dB per decade and the low-frequency asymptote has a slope of 0 or 0 dB/decade. These two asymptotes provide a straight-line approximation to the gain response that differs from the true response by a maximum of 3 dB at the corner frequency.

The semilog plot of the phase shift of the first-order low-pass transfer function is shown in Figure 12–3. At $\omega = \alpha$ the phase angle in Eq. (12–12) is

$$\begin{aligned}\theta(\omega_C) &= \angle K - \tan^{-1}\left(\frac{\alpha}{\alpha}\right)\\ &= \angle K - 45^\circ\end{aligned}$$

At low frequency ($\omega << \alpha$) the phase angle approaches $\angle K$ and at high frequencies ($\omega >> \alpha$) the phase approaches $\angle K - 90^\circ$. Almost all of the -90° phase change occurs in the two-decade range from $\omega/\alpha = 0.1$ to $\omega/\alpha = 10$. The straight-line segments in Figure 12–3 provide an approximation of the phase response. The phase approximation below $\omega/\alpha = 0.1$ is $\theta = \angle K$ and above $\omega/\alpha = 10$ is $\theta = \angle K - 90^\circ$. Between these values the phase approximation is a straight line that begins at $\theta = \angle K$, passes through $\theta = \angle K - 45^\circ$ at the cutoff frequency, and reaches $\theta = \angle K - 90^\circ$ at $\omega/\alpha = 10$. The slope of this line segment is –45°/decade since the total phase change is –90° over a two-decade range. The –45°/decade slope only applies over a frequency range from one decade below to one decade above the cutoff frequency. Outside of this range the straight-line approximation has zero slope.

To construct the straight-line approximations for a first-order low-pass transfer function, we need two parameters, the value of $T(0)$ and α. The parameter α defines the cutoff frequency and the value of $T(0)$ defines the passband gain $|T(0)|$ and the low-frequency phase $\angle T(0)$. The required quantities $T(0)$ and α can be determined directly from the transfer function $T(s)$ and can often be estimated by inspecting the circuit itself.

Using logarithmic scales in frequency-response plots allows us to make straight-line approximations to both the gain and phase responses. These approximations provide a useful way of visualizing a circuit's frequency response. Often such graphical estimates are adequate for developing analysis and design approaches. For example, the frequency response of the first-order low-pass function can be characterized by calculating the gain and phase over a two-decade band from one decade below to one decade above the cutoff frequency.

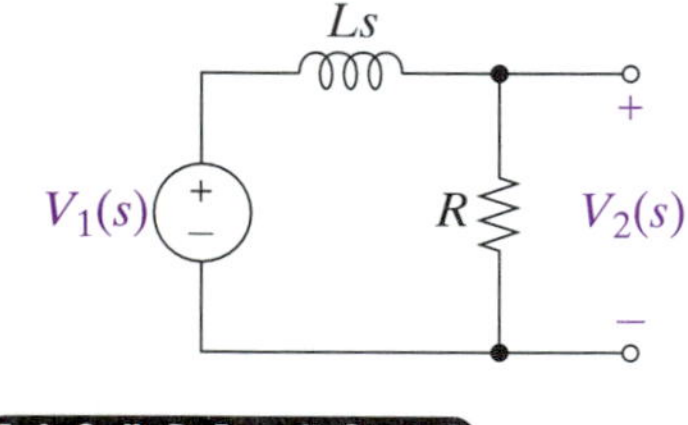

FIGURE 12–4

EXAMPLE 12–2

Consider the circuit in Figure 12–4. Find the transfer function $T(s) = V_2(s)/V_1(s)$ and construct the straight-line approximations to the gain and phase responses.

SOLUTION:

Applying voltage division, the voltage transfer function for the circuit is

$$T(s) = \frac{R}{Ls + R} = \frac{R/L}{s + R/L}$$

Comparing this with Eq. (12–4), we see that the circuit has a low-pass gain response with $\alpha = R/L$ and $T(0) = 1$. Therefore, $|T(0)|_{dB} = 0$ dB, $\omega_C = R/L$, and $\angle K = 0°$. Given these quantities, we construct the straight-line approximations shown in Figure 12–5. Note that the frequency scale in Figure 12–5 is normalized by multiplying ω by $L/R = 1/\alpha$.

Circuit Interpretation: The low-pass response in Figure 12–5 can be explained in terms of circuit behavior. At zero frequency the inductor acts like a short circuit that directly connects the input port to the output port to produce a passband gain 1 (or 0 dB). At infinite frequency the inductor acts like an open circuit, effectively disconnecting the input and output ports and leading to a gain of zero. Between these two extremes the impedance of the inductor gradually increases, causing the circuit gain to decrease. In particular, at the cutoff frequency we have $\omega L = R$, the impedance of the inductor is $j\omega L = jR$, and the transfer function reduces to

$$T(j\omega_C) = \frac{R}{R + jR} = \frac{1}{\sqrt{2}}\angle -45°$$

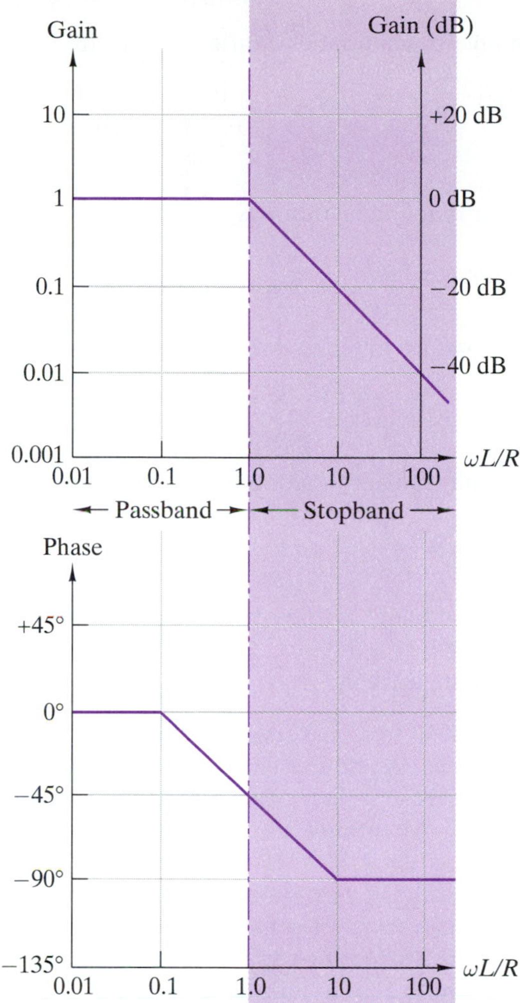

FIGURE 12-5

In other words, at the cutoff frequency the gain is –3 dB and the phase shift –45°. Obviously, the changing impedance of the inductor gives the circuit its low-pass gain features. ■

D DESIGN EXAMPLE 12–3

First-Order Low Pass Filter Design

(a) Show that the transfer function $T(s) = V_2(s)/V_1(s)$ in Figure 12–6 has a low-pass gain characteristic.
(b) Select element values so the passband gain is 4 and the cutoff frequency is 100 rad/s.

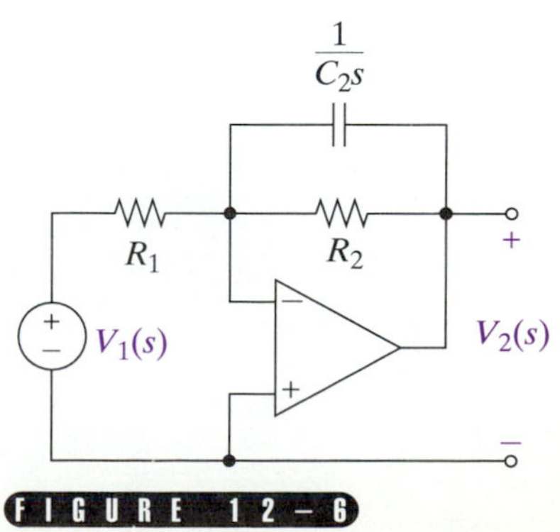

FIGURE 12-6

SOLUTION:

(a) The circuit is an inverting amplifier configuration with

$$Z_1(s) = R_1 \quad \text{and} \quad Z_2(s) = \frac{1}{C_2 s + \dfrac{1}{R_2}} = \frac{R_2}{R_2 C_2 s + 1}$$

The circuit transfer function is found as

$$T(s) = -\frac{Z_2(s)}{Z_1(s)} = -\frac{R_2}{R_1} \times \frac{1}{R_2 C_2 s + 1}$$

Rearranging the standard low-pass form in Eq. (12–4) as

$$T(s) = \frac{K/\alpha}{s/\alpha + 1}$$

shows that the circuit transfer function has a low-pass form with

$$\omega_C = \alpha = \frac{1}{R_2 C_2} \quad \text{and} \quad T(0) = -\frac{R_2}{R_1}$$

This is an inverting circuit, so the –90° phase swing of the low-pass form runs from $\angle T(0) = -180°$ to $\angle T(\infty) = -270°$, passing through $\angle T(j\omega_C) = -225°$ along the way.

Circuit Interpretation: The low-pass response is easily deduced from known circuit performance. At dc the capacitor acts like an open circuit and the circuit in Figure 12–6 reduces to a resistance inverting amplifier with $K = T(0) = -R_2/R_1$. At infinite frequency the capacitor acts like a short circuit that connects the OP AMP output directly to the inverting input. This connection results in zero output since the node voltage at the inverting input is necessarily zero. In between these two extremes the gain gradually decreases as the decreasing capacitor impedance gradually pulls the OP AMP output down to zero at infinite frequency.

(b) The design constraints require that $\omega_C = 1/R_2C_2 = 100$ and $|T(0)| = R_2/R_1 = 4$. Selecting $R_1 = 10$ kΩ implies that $R_2 = 40$ kΩ and $C_2 = 250$ nF.

APPLICATION NOTE: GAIN-BANDWIDTH PRODUCT EXAMPLE 12–4

In terms of frequency response, the ideal OP AMP model introduced in Chapter 4 assumes that the device has an infinite gain and an infinite bandwidth. A more realistic model of the device is shown in Figure 12–7(a). The controlled source gain in Figure 12–7(a) is a low-pass transfer function with a dc gain of μ and a cutoff frequency ω_C. The straight-line asymptotes of controlled source gain are shown in Figure 12–7(b). The **gain-bandwidth product** ($G = \mu\omega_C$) is the basic performance parameter of this model.

With no feedback the OP AMP transfer function is the same as the controlled-source transfer function. The gain-bandwidth product of the open-loop transfer function is

FIGURE 12–7

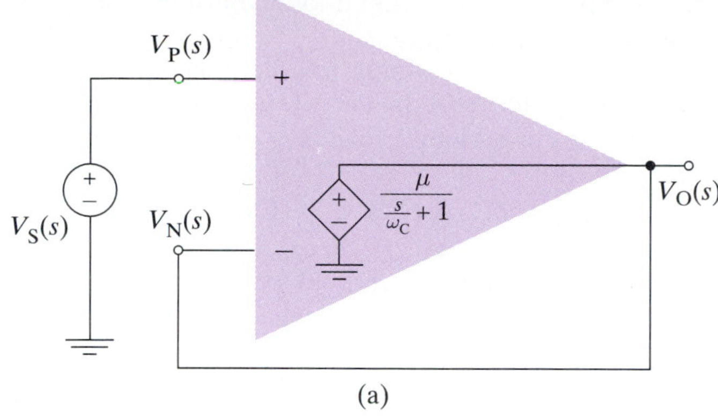

(a)

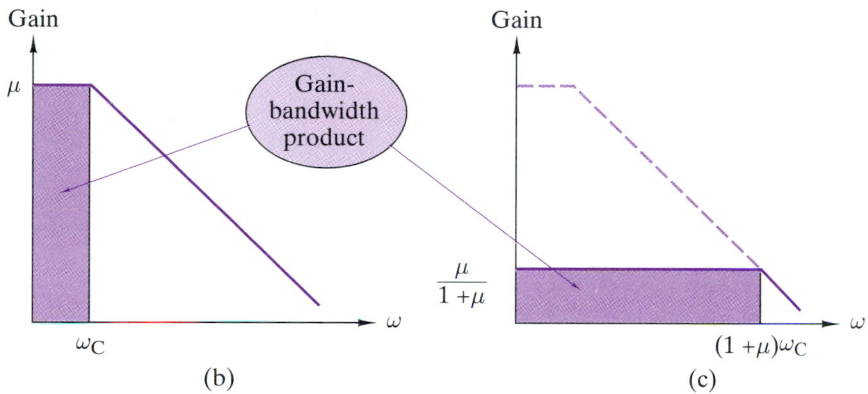

(b) (c)

$$G = \mu\omega_C \quad \text{(Open Loop)}$$

The closed-loop transfer function of the circuit in Figure 12–7(a) is found by writing the following device and connection equations:

$$\begin{aligned} \text{Device Equation: } V_O &= \frac{\mu}{s/\omega_C + 1}(V_P - V_N) \\ \text{Input Connection: } V_P &= V_S \\ \text{Feedback Connection: } V_N &= V_O \end{aligned}$$

Substituting the connection equations into the OP AMP device equation yields

$$V_O(s) = \frac{\mu}{s/\omega_C + 1}(V_S(s) - V_O(s))$$

Solving for the closed-loop transfer function produces

$$T(s) = \frac{V_O(s)}{V_S(s)} = \frac{\mu}{\mu + 1}\left[\frac{1}{\dfrac{s}{(\mu + 1)\omega_C} + 1}\right]$$

The straight-line asymptotes of the closed-loop transfer function are shown in Figure 12–7(c).

The closed-loop circuit has a low-pass transfer function with a dc gain of $\mu/(\mu + 1)$ and a cutoff frequency of $(\mu + 1)\omega_C$. The gain-bandwidth product of the closed-loop circuit is

$$G = \left[\frac{\mu}{\mu + 1}\right][(\mu + 1)\omega_C] = \mu\omega_C \quad \text{(Closed Loop)}$$

which is the same as the open-loop case. In other words, the gain-bandwidth product is invariant and is not changed by feedback. It can be shown that this result is a general one that applies to all linear OP AMP circuits, regardless of the circuit configuration.

Gain-bandwidth product is a fundamental parameter that limits the frequency response of OP AMP circuits. For example, an OP AMP with a gain-bandwidth product of $G = 10^6$ Hz is connected as a noninverting amplifier with a closed–loop gain of 20. The frequency response of the resulting closed-loop circuit has a low pass characteristic with a passband gain of 20 and a cutoff frequency of

$$f_C = \frac{10^6}{20} = 50 \text{ kHz}$$

FIRST-ORDER HIGH-PASS RESPONSE

We next treat the first-order high-pass transfer function

$$T(s) = \frac{Ks}{s + \alpha} \tag{12–8}$$

The high-pass function differs from the low pass case by the introduction of a zero at $s = 0$. Replacing s by $j\omega$ in $T(s)$ and solving for the gain and phase functions yields

$$|T(j\omega)| = \frac{|K|\omega}{\sqrt{\omega^2 + \alpha^2}}$$
$$\theta(\omega) = \angle K + 90° - \tan^{-1}(\omega/\alpha) \tag{12–9}$$

Figure 12–8 shows the gain and phase functions versus normalized frequency ω/α. The maximum gain occurs at high frequency ($\omega >> \alpha$) where $|T(j\omega)| \to |K|$. At low frequency ($\omega << \alpha$) the gain approaches $|K|\omega/\alpha$. At $\omega = \alpha$ the gain is

$$|T(j\alpha)| = \frac{|K|\alpha}{\sqrt{\alpha^2 + \alpha^2}} = \frac{|K|}{\sqrt{2}} \tag{12–10}$$

which means the cutoff frequency is $\omega_C = \alpha$. The gain response plot in Figure 12–8 displays a high-pass characteristic with a passband extending from $\omega = \alpha$ to infinity and a stopband between zero frequency and $\omega = \alpha$.

The low- and high-frequency gain asymptotes approximate the gain response in Figure 12–8. The high-frequency asymptote ($\omega >> \alpha$) is the horizontal line whose ordinate is $|K|$ (slope = 0 or 0 dB/decade). The low-

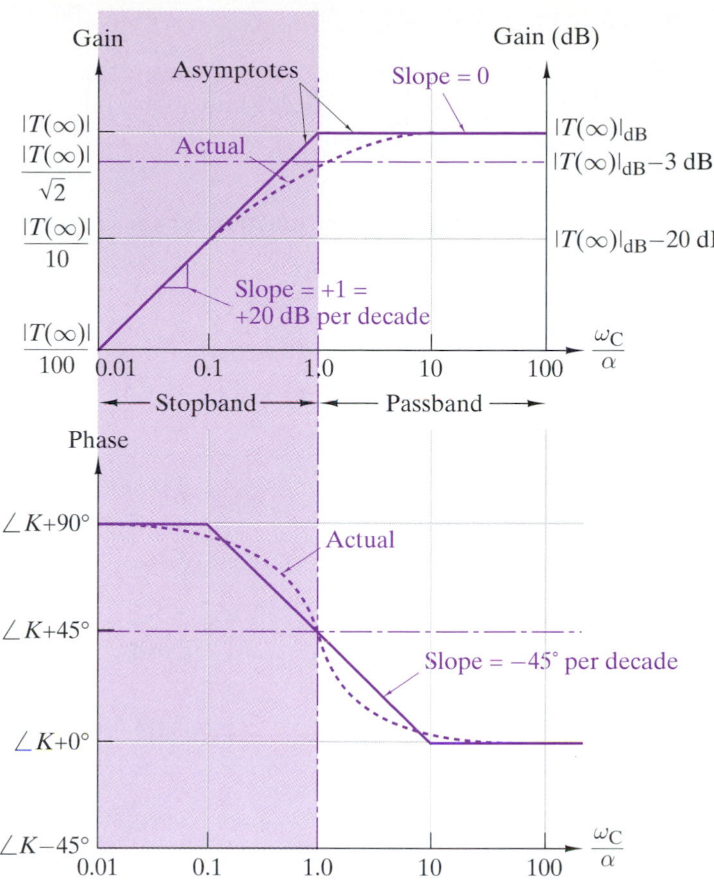

FIGURE 12–8

First-order high-pass frequency-response plots.

frequency asymptote ($\omega << \alpha$) is a line of the form $|K|\omega/\alpha$ (slope = +1 or +20 dB/decade). The intersection of these two asymptotes occurs when $|K| = |K|\omega/\alpha$, which defines a corner frequency at $\omega = \alpha$.

The semilog plot of the phase shift of the first-order high-pass function is shown in Figure 12–8. The phase shift approaches $\angle K$ at high frequency, passes through $\angle K + 45°$ at the cutoff frequency, and approaches $\angle K + 90°$ at low frequency. Most of the 90° phase change occurs over the two-decade range centered on the cutoff frequency. The phase shift can be approximated by the straight-line segments shown in the Figure 12–8. As in the low-pass case, $\angle K$ is 0° when K is positive and ±180° when K is negative.

Like the low-pass function, the first-order high-pass frequency response can be approximated by straight-line segments. To construct these lines we need two parameters, $T(\infty)$ and α. The parameter α defines the cutoff frequency, and the quantity $T(\infty)$ gives the passband gain $|T(\infty)|$ and the high-frequency phase angle $\angle T(\infty)$. The quantities $T(\infty)$ and α can be determined directly from the transfer function or estimated directly from the circuit in some cases. The straight line shows that the first-order high-pass response can be characterized by calculating the gain and phase over a two-decade band from one decade below to one decade above the cutoff frequency.

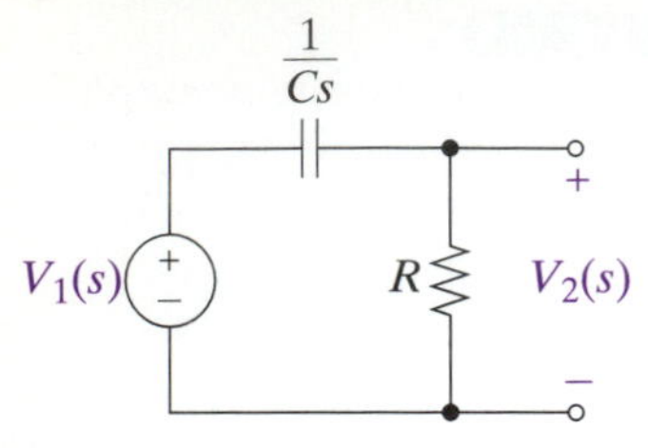

FIGURE 12–9

EXAMPLE 12–5

Show that the transfer function $T(s) = V_2(s)/V_1(s)$ in Figure 12–9 has a high-pass gain characteristic. Construct the straight-line approximations to the gain and phase responses of the circuit.

SOLUTION:

Applying voltage division, the voltage transfer function for the circuit is

$$T(s) = \frac{R}{R + 1/Cs} = \frac{RCs}{RCs + 1}$$

Rearranging Eq. (12–8) as

$$T(s) = \frac{K(s/\alpha)}{s/\alpha + 1}$$

FIGURE 12–10

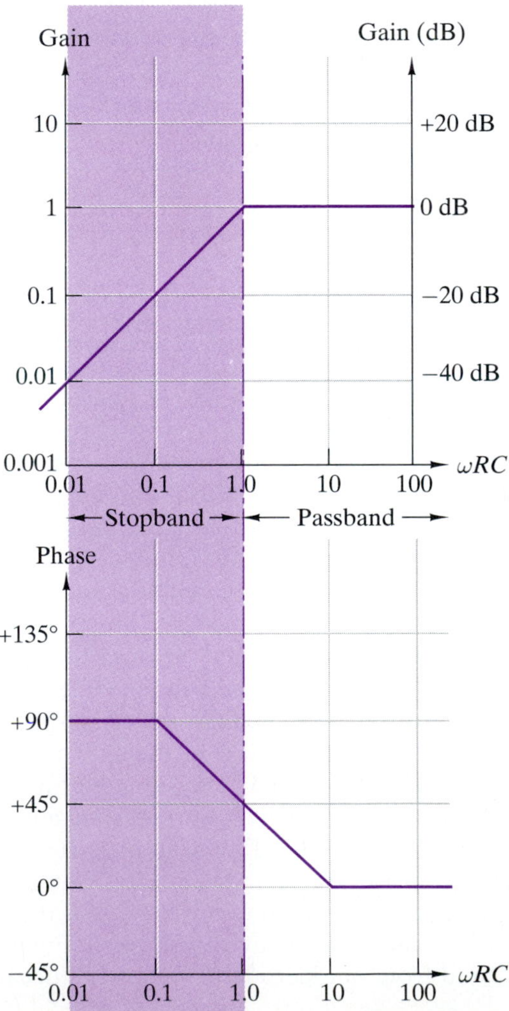

shows that the circuit has a high-pass gain characteristic with $\alpha = RC$ and $T(\infty) = 1$. Therefore, $|T(\infty)|_{dB} = 0$ dB, $\omega_C = 1/RC$, and $\angle T(\infty) = 0°$. Given these quantities, we construct the straight-line gain and phase approximations in Figure 12–10. The frequency scale in Figure 12–10 is normalized by multiplying ω by $RC = 1/\alpha$.

Circuit Interpretation: The high-pass response in Figure 12–10 can be understood in terms of known circuit behavior. At zero frequency the capacitor acts like an open circuit that effectively disconnects the input signal source, leading to zero gain. At infinite frequency the capacitor acts like a short circuit that directly connects the input to the output, leading to a passband gain of 1(or 0 dB). Between these two extremes the impedance of the capacitor gradually decreases, causing the gain to increase. In particular, at the cutoff frequency we have $1/\omega C = R$, the impedance of the capacitor is $1/j\omega C = -jR$, and the transfer function is

$$T(j\omega_C) = \frac{R}{R - jR} = \frac{1}{\sqrt{2}}\angle + 45°$$

In other words, at the cutoff frequency the gain is –3 dB and the phase shift +45°. Obviously, the decreasing impedance of the capacitor gives the circuit its high-pass gain characteristics. ■

DESIGN EXAMPLE 12–6

First-Order High Pass Filter Design

(a) Show that the transfer function $T(s) = V_2(s)/V_1(s)$ of the circuit in Figure 12–11 has a high-pass gain characteristic.

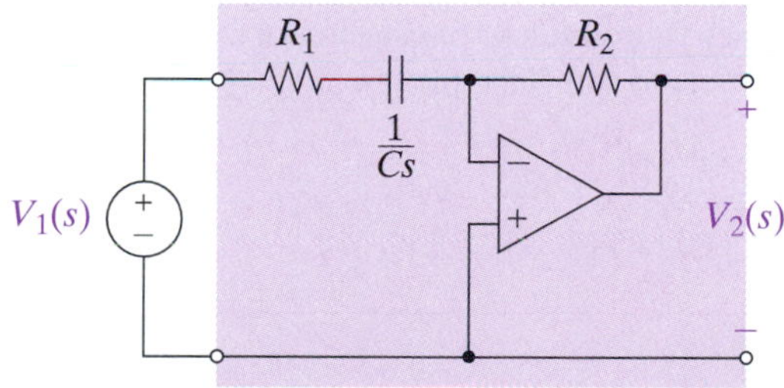

FIGURE 12–11

(b) Select the element values to produce a passband gain of 4 and a cutoff frequency of 40 krad/s.

SOLUTION:

(a) The branch impedances of the inverting OP AMP configuration in Figure 12–11 are

$$Z_1(s) = R_1 + \frac{1}{Cs} = \frac{R_1Cs + 1}{Cs} \quad \text{and} \quad Z_2(s) = R_2$$

and the voltage transfer function is

$$T(s) = -\frac{Z_2(s)}{Z_1(s)} = -\frac{R_2Cs}{R_1Cs + 1} = \frac{(-R_2/R_1)s}{s + 1/R_1C}$$

This results in a high-pass transfer function of the form $Ks/(s + \alpha)$ with $K = -R_2/R_1$ and $\alpha = \omega_C = 1/R_1C$.

Circuit Interpretation: The high-pass response of this circuit is easily understood in terms of element impedances. At dc the capacitor in Figure 12–11 acts like an open circuit that effectively disconnects the input source, resulting in zero gain. At infinite frequency the capacitor acts like a short circuit that reduces the circuit to an inverting amplifier with $K = T(\infty) = -R_2/R_1$. As the frequency varies from zero to infinity, the gain gradually increases as the capacitor impedance decreases.

(b) The design requirements specify that $1/R_1C = 4 \times 10^4$ and $R_2/R_1 = 4$. Selecting $R_1 = 10$ kΩ requires $R_2 = 40$ kΩ and $C = 2.5$ nF. ■

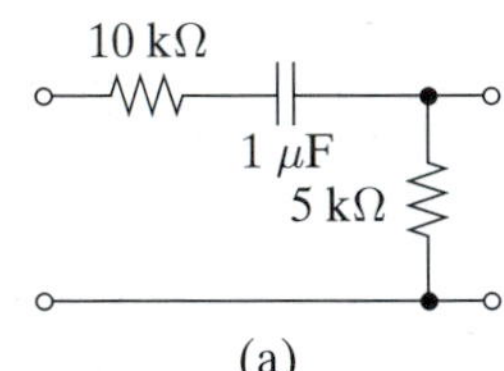

(a)

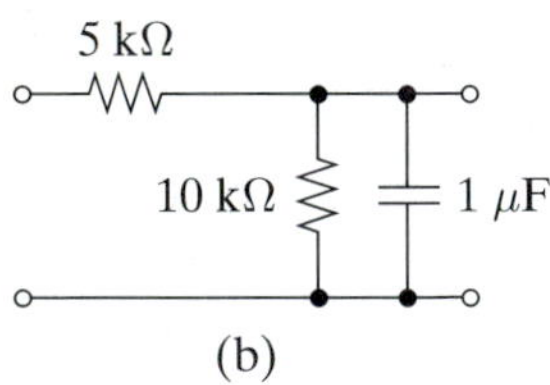

(b)

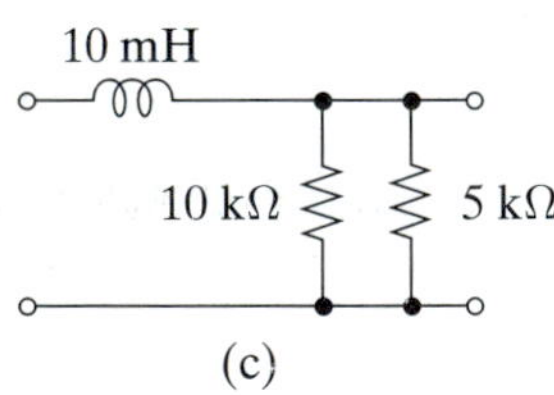

(c)

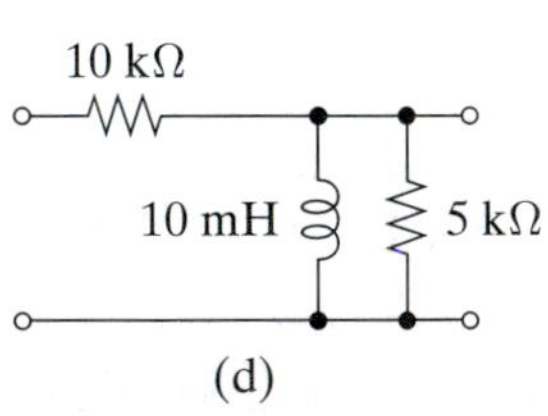

(d)

FIGURE 12–12

Exercise 12–1

For each circuit in Figure 12–12 identify whether the gain response has low-pass or high-pass characteristics and find the passband gain and cutoff frequency.

Answers:
(a) High pass, $|T(\infty)| = 1/3$, $\omega_C = 66.7$ rad/s
(b) Low pass, $|T(0)| = 2/3$, $\omega_C = 300$ rad/s
(c) Low pass, $|T(0)| = 1$, $\omega_C = 333$ krad/s
(d) High pass, $|T(\infty)| = 1/3$, $\omega_C = 333$ krad/s

Exercise 12–2

A first-order circuit has a step response $g(t) = 5[e^{-2000t}]u(t)$.
(a) Is the circuit frequency response low-pass or high-pass?
(b) Find the passband gain and cutoff frequency.

Answers:
(a) High-pass
(b) $|T(\infty)| = 5$ and $\omega_C = 2000$ rad/s

BANDPASS AND BANDSTOP RESPONSES USING FIRST-ORDER CIRCUITS

The first-order high-pass and low-pass circuits can be used in a building block fashion to produce circuits with bandpass or bandstop responses. Figure 12–13 shows a cascade connection of first-order high-pass and low-

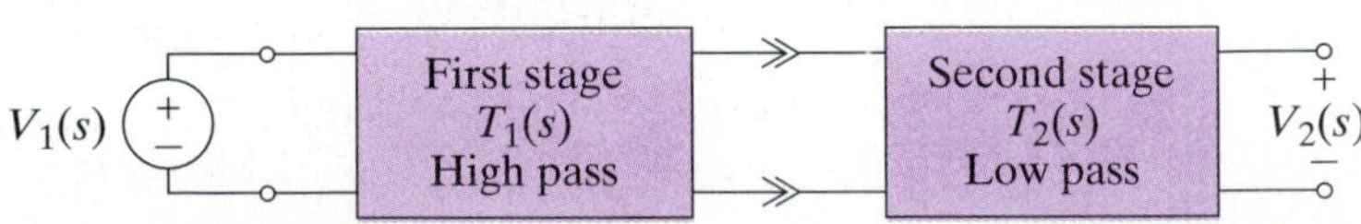

FIGURE 12–13 *Cascade connection of high-pass and low-pass circuits.*

pass circuits. When the second stage does not load the first, the overall transfer function can be found by the chain rule:

$$T(s) = T_1(s) \times T_2(s) = \underbrace{\left(\frac{K_1 s}{s + \alpha_1}\right)}_{\text{High Pass}} \underbrace{\left(\frac{K_2}{s + \alpha_2}\right)}_{\text{Low Pass}} \tag{12–11}$$

Replacing s by $j\omega$ in Eq. (12–11) and solving for the gain response yields

$$|T(j\omega)| = \underbrace{\left(\frac{|K_1|\omega}{\sqrt{\omega^2 + \alpha_1^2}}\right)}_{\text{High Pass}} \underbrace{\left(\frac{|K_2|}{\sqrt{\omega^2 + \alpha_2^2}}\right)}_{\text{Low Pass}} \tag{12–12}$$

Note that the gain of the cascade is zero at $\omega = 0$ and at infinite frequency.

When $\alpha_1 << \alpha_2$ the high-pass cutoff frequency is much lower than the low-pass cutoff frequency, and the overall transfer function has a bandpass characteristic. At low frequencies ($\omega << \alpha_1 << \alpha_2$) the gain approaches $|T(j\omega)| \to |K_1K_2|\omega/\alpha_1\alpha_2$. At mid frequencies ($\alpha_1 << \omega << \alpha_2$) the gain approaches $|T(j\omega)| \to |K_1K_2|/\alpha_2$. The low- and mid-frequency asymptotes intersect when $|K_1K_2|\omega/\alpha_1\alpha_2 = |K_1K_2|/\alpha_2$ at $\omega = \alpha_1$ (that is, at the cutoff frequency of the high-pass stage). At high frequencies ($\alpha_1 << \alpha_2 << \omega$) the gain approaches $|T(j\omega)| \to |K_1K_2|/\omega$. The high- and mid-frequency asymptotes intersect when $|K_1K_2|/\omega = |K_1K_2|/\alpha_2$ at $\omega = \alpha_2$ (that is, at the cutoff frequency of the low-pass stage). The plot of these asymptotes in Figure 12–14 shows that the asymptotic gain exhibits a passband between α_1 and α_2. Input sinusoids whose frequencies are outside of this range fall in one of the two stopbands.

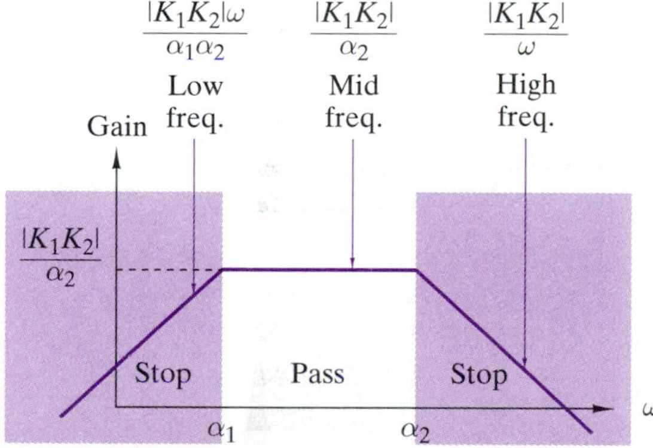

FIGURE 12–14 *Asymptotic gain of a bandpass characteristic.*

In the bandpass cascade connection the input signal must pass both a low- and a high-pass stage to reach the output. In the parallel connection in Figure 12–15 the input can reach the output via either a low- or a high-pass path. The overall transfer function is the sum of the low- and high-pass transfer functions

$$|T(j\omega)| = \underbrace{\left(\frac{|K_1|\omega}{\sqrt{\omega^2 + \alpha_1^2}}\right)}_{\text{High Pass}} + \underbrace{\left(\frac{|K_2|}{\sqrt{\omega^2 + \alpha_2^2}}\right)}_{\text{Low Pass}} \tag{12–13}$$

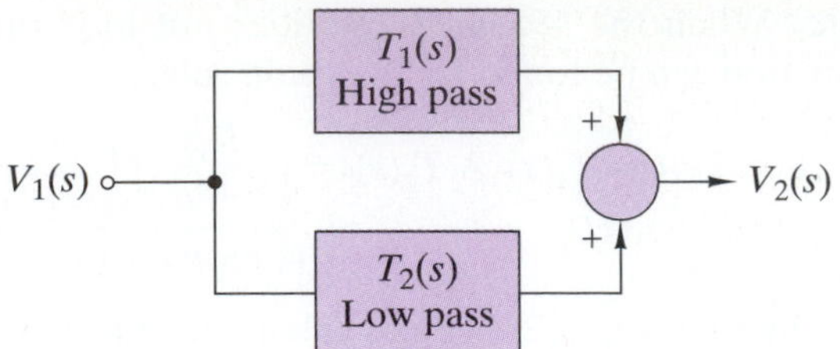

FIGURE 12–15 *Parallel connection of high-pass and low-pass circuits.*

Any sinusoid whose frequency falls in either passband will find its way to the output unscathed. An input sinusoid whose frequency falls in both stopbands will be attenuated.

When $\alpha_1 >> \alpha_2$ the high-pass cutoff frequency is much higher than the low-pass cutoff frequency, and the overall transfer function has a bandstop gain response as shown in Figure 12–16. At low frequencies ($\omega << \alpha_2 << \alpha_1$) the high-pass gain is negligible and the over asymptote approaches the passband gain of the low-pass function $|T(j\omega)| \rightarrow |K_2|/\alpha_2$. At high frequencies ($\alpha_2 << \alpha_1 << \omega$) the low-pass gain is negligible and the overall gain approaches the bandpass gain of the high-pass function $|T(j\omega)| \rightarrow |K_1|$. With a bandstop function the two passbands normally have the same gain, hence $|K_1| = |K_2|/\alpha_2$. Between these two passbands there is a stopband. For $\omega > \alpha_2$ the low-pass asymptote is $|K_2|/\omega$ and for $\omega < \alpha_1$ the high-pass asymptote is $|K_1|\omega/\alpha_1$. The asymptotes intersect at $\omega^2 = \alpha_1|K_2|/|K_1|$. But equal gains in the two passband frequencies require $|K_1| = |K_2|/\alpha_2$, so the intersection frequency is $\omega = \sqrt{\alpha_1\alpha_2}$. Below this frequency the stopband attenuation is determined by the low-pass function, and above this frequency the attenuation is governed by the high-pass function.

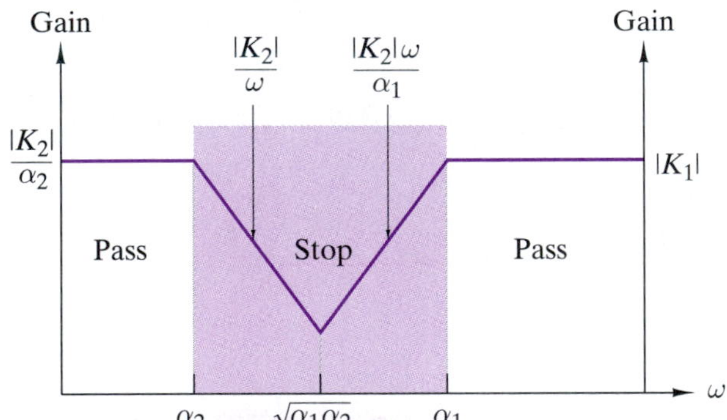

FIGURE 12–16 *Asymptotic gain of a bandstop characteristic.*

The analysis of the bandpass and bandstop transfer functions in Eqs. (12–12) and (12–13) illustrates that the asymptotic gain plots of first-order functions can help us understand and describe other types of gain response as well. The asymptotic responses in Figures 12–14 and 12–16 are a reasonably good approximation as long as the two first-order cutoff frequencies are widely separated. The straight-line approximation shows us that the frequency range of interest extends from a decade below the lowest cutoff frequency to a decade above the highest. This range could be a very wide indeed, since the two cutoff frequencies may be separated by several decades.

DESIGN EXAMPLE 12–7

First-Order Cascade Bandpass Design

Design a bandpass circuit with a passband gain of 10 and cutoff frequencies at 20 Hz and 20 kHz.

SOLUTION:

Our design uses a cascade connection of first-order low- and high-pass building blocks. The required transfer function has the form

$$T(s) = \left(\frac{K_1 s}{s + \alpha_1}\right)\left(\frac{K_2}{s + \alpha_2}\right)$$

with the following constraints:

$$\text{Lower Cutoff Frequency: } \alpha_1 = 2\pi(20) = 40\pi \quad \text{rad}/s$$

$$\text{Upper Cutoff Frequency: } \alpha_2 = 2\pi(20 \times 10^3) = 4\pi \times 10^4 \quad \text{rad/s}$$

$$\text{Midband Gain: } \frac{|K_1 K_2|}{\alpha_2} = 10$$

With numerical values inserted, the required transfer function is

$$T(s) = \underbrace{\frac{s}{s + 40\pi}}_{\text{High Pass}} \times \underbrace{10}_{\text{Gain}} \times \underbrace{\frac{4\pi \times 10^4}{s + 4\pi \times 10^4}}_{\text{Low Pass}}$$

This transfer function can be realized using the high-pass/low-pass cascade circuit in Figure 12–17. The first stage is the RC high-pass circuit from Example 12–5 and the third stage is the RL low-pass circuit from Example 12–2.

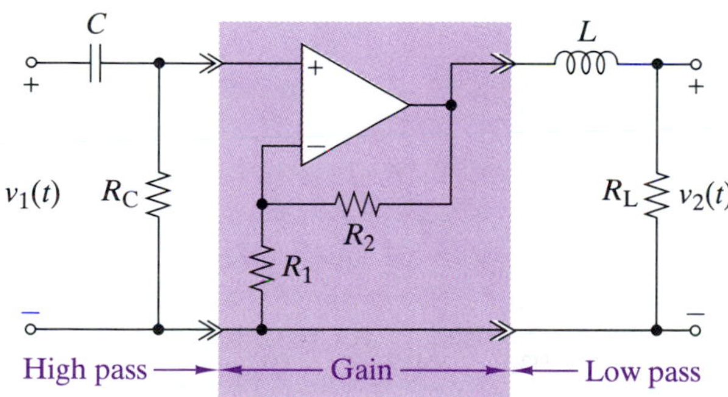

FIGURE 12–17

The noninverting OP AMP second stage serves two purposes: (1) It isolates the first and third stages, so the chain rule applies, and (2) it supplies the midband gain. Using the chain rule, the transfer function of this circuit is

$$T(s) = \underbrace{\left[\frac{s}{s + 1/R_C C}\right]}_{\text{High pass}} \underbrace{\left[\frac{R_1 + R_2}{R_1}\right]}_{\text{Gain}} \underbrace{\left[\frac{R_L/L}{s + R_L/L}\right]}_{\text{Low pass}}$$

Comparing this to the required transfer function leads to the following design constraints:

High-pass Stage: $R_C C = 1/40\pi$ Let $R_C = 100$ kΩ Then $C = 79.6$ nF

Gain Stage: $(R_1 + R_2)/R_1 = 10$ Let $R_1 = 10$ kΩ Then $R_2 = 90$ kΩ

Low-pass Stage: $R_L/L = 40000\pi$ Let $R_L = 200$ kΩ Then $L = 0.628$ H

EXAMPLE 12–8

Use computer-aided analysis to show that the circuit in Figure 12–18 implements a bandstop gain response.

FIGURE 12–18

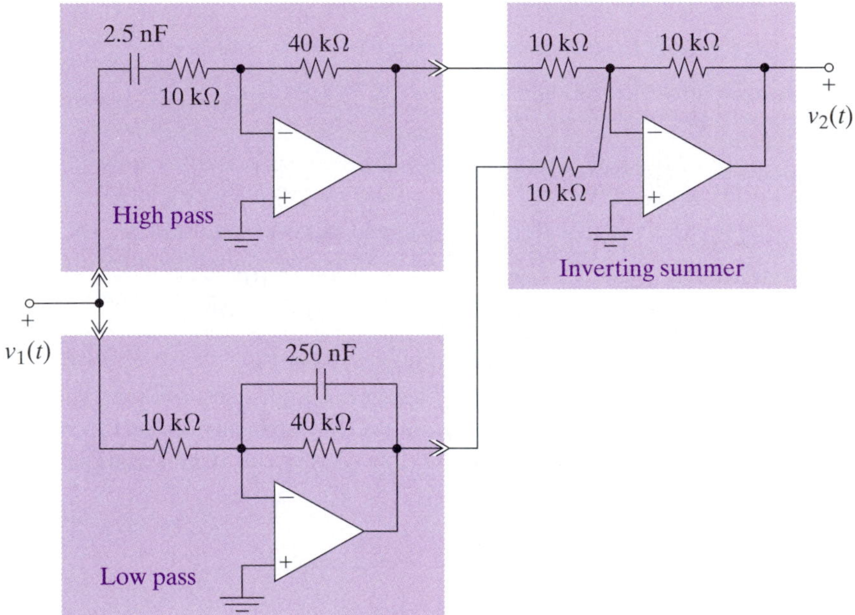

SOLUTION:

This circuit implements the block diagram in Figure 12–15. The two first-order circuits have the same input. The upper circuit is the high-pass OP AMP circuit designed in Example 12–6 to have a passband gain of 4 and a cutoff frequency $\alpha_1 = 40$ krad/s. The lower path is the low-pass OP AMP circuit designed in Example 12–3 to have a passband gain of 4 and a cutoff frequency $\alpha_2 = 100$ rad/s. The inverting summer at the far right implements the summing point function in Figure 12–15. Since the cutoff frequency of the low pass circuit is much lower than the cutoff frequency of the high-pass circuit, we expect to see two passbands on either side of a stopband centered at

$$\omega = \sqrt{\alpha_1 \alpha_2} = \sqrt{100 \times 4 \times 10^4} = 2000 \text{ rad}/s$$

Figure 12–19 shows the circuit as drawn using MicroSim Schematics. The input voltage source V1 is set to produce 1-V ac, so the ac voltage at the node labeled "out" is the circuit gain. To obtain the circuit's frequency

FIGURE 12–19

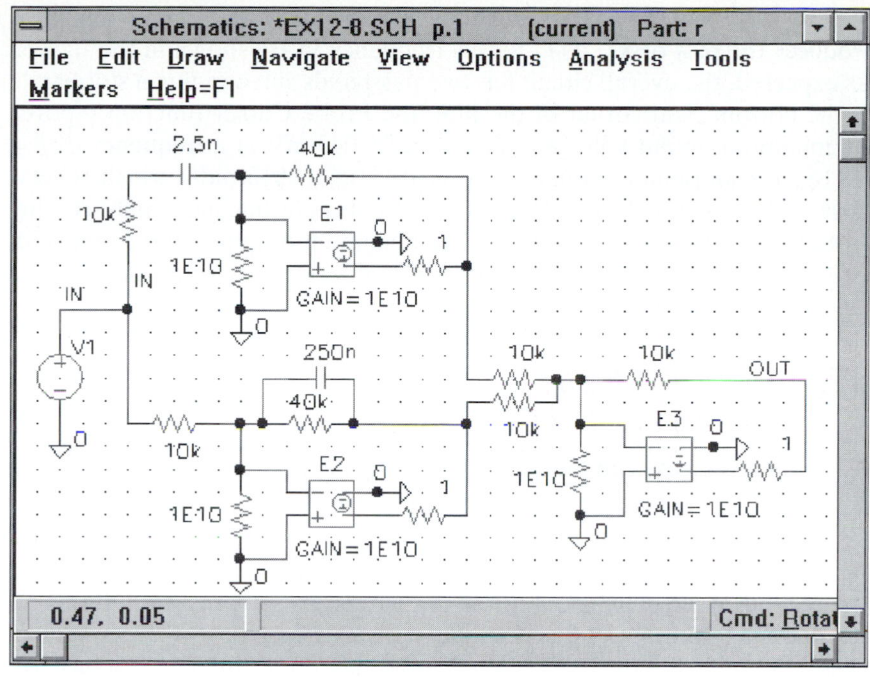

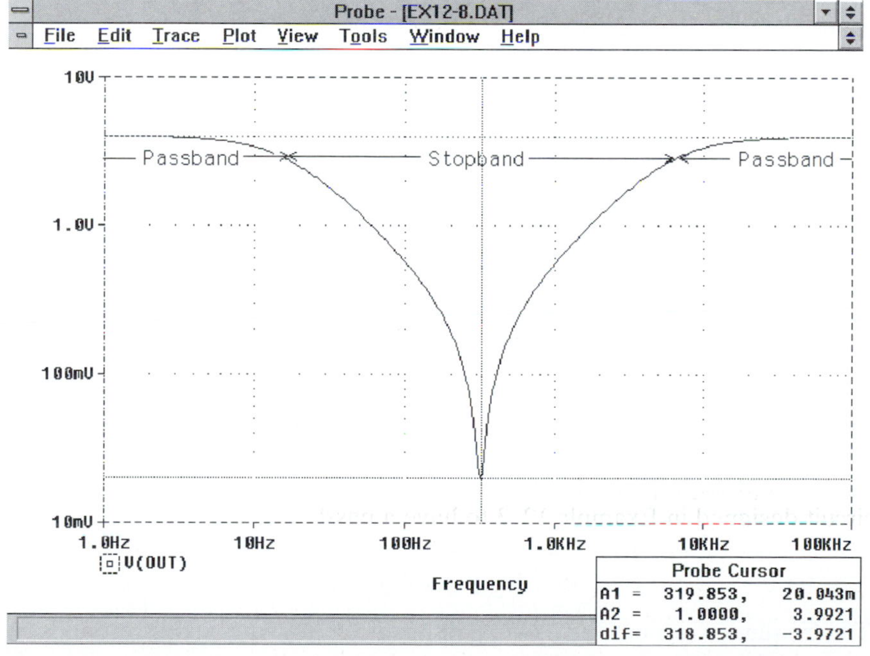

response, we select **Analysis/Set Up** and enable the **AC Sweep** option. The simulation frequency range should extend from at least a decade below the lowest cutoff frequency ($\alpha_2/2\pi = 16$ Hz) to at least a decade above the highest cutoff frequency ($\alpha_1/2\pi = 6.4$ kHz). To span this range we select a **decade sweep** with a **start freq.** of 1 Hz and an **end freq.** of 100 kHz.

After a PSpice ac analysis run, the MicroSim Probe graphic analyzer produces the plot of V(OUT) versus frequency in Hz shown in the figure. As expected, the overall circuit has two passbands surrounding a stopband. In the bottom right corner of the plot, the Probe Cursor function reports the minimum output voltage (gain) to be 20.043 mV at a frequency of f = 319.853 Hz. In radian frequency this is $\omega = 2\pi f = 2010$ rad/s, which is very close to the value of 2000 rad/s predicted by straight-line gain analysis. The Probe Cursor function also reports the maximum output voltage (gain) to be 3.9921 V at f = 1 Hz. This confirms that the two passbands have gain = 4, as straight-line analysis predicts.

12–3 SECOND-ORDER CIRCUIT FREQUENCY RESPONSE

We begin our study with the second-order bandpass transfer function:

$$T(s) = \frac{Ks}{s^2 + 2\zeta\omega_0 s + \omega_0^2} \tag{12–14}$$

The second-order polynomial in the denominator is expressed in terms of the damping ratio ζ and undamped natural frequency ω_0 parameters. These parameters play a key role in describing the frequency response of second-order circuits. When the damping ratio is less than 1, the complex poles of $T(s)$ dramatically influence the frequency response.

To gain a qualitative understanding of the effect of complex poles, we write Eq. (12–14) in factored form:

$$T(s) = \frac{Ks}{(s - p_1)(s - p_2)} \tag{12–15}$$

where p_1 and p_2 are the complex poles of $T(s)$. The frequency-response gain function is

$$|T(j\omega)| = \frac{|K|\omega}{|j\omega - p_1|\,|j\omega - p_2|} = \frac{|K|\omega}{M_1 M_2} \tag{12–16}$$

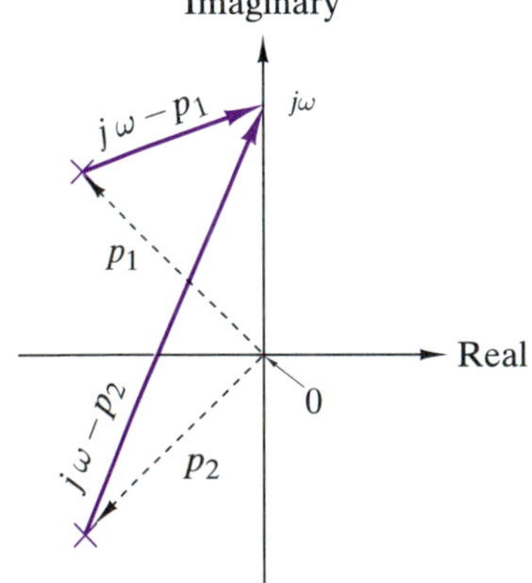

FIGURE 12–20 *s-Plane vectors defining* $|T(j\omega)|$.

As shown in Figure 12–20, the factors $(j\omega - p_1)$ and $(j\omega - p_2)$ can be interpreted as vectors from the natural poles at $s = p_1$ and $s = p_2$ to the point $s = j\omega$, where ω is the frequency at which the gain is being calculated. The lengths of these vectors are

$$M_1 = |j\omega - p_1|$$
$$M_2 = |j\omega - p_2|$$

The frequency response of a circuit depends on how the circuit responds to sinusoidal inputs of constant amplitude by changing frequencies. The sinusoidal input produces two forced poles on the j-axis whose location depends of the frequency of the input. Changing the input frequency causes the forced pole at $s = j\omega$ to slide up or down the imaginary axis. This, in turn, changes the lengths M_1 and M_2, since the tips of the vectors $j\omega - p_1$ and $j\omega - p_2$ move up or down the j-axis while the tails remain fixed at the location of the natural poles. The length M_1 reaches a minimum when the forced pole at $s = j\omega$ is close to the natural pole at $s = p_1$. Since M_1 appears in the denominator of Eq. (12–16), this minimum tends to produce a maximum or peak in the gain response.

Figure 12–21 shows how different input frequencies change the lengths M_1 and M_2 to produce the gain response curve. The lengths M_1 and M_2 are approximately equal at low frequencies ($\omega << \omega_1$) and again at high frequencies ($\omega >> \omega_3$). At intermediate frequencies ($\omega_1 < \omega < \omega_3$) the lengths differ, especially in the neighborhood of ω_2, where length M_1 reaches a minimum and is very small compared with length M_2. The small value of the length M_1 produces a maximum in the gain response indicative of a phenomenon called resonance. **Resonance** is the increased response observed when the frequency of a periodic driving force like a sinusoid is close to a natural frequency of the circuit. In terms of s-plane geometry, resonance occurs when the point at $s = j\omega$ and the natural pole at $s = p_1$ are close together so the length M_1 is small.

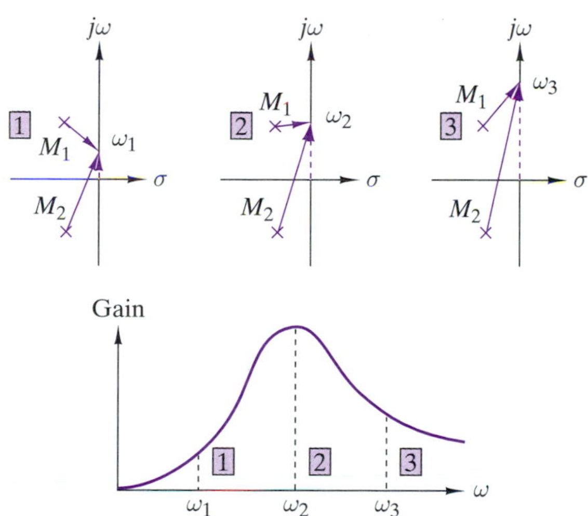

FIGURE 12–21 *Gain-response resonance from s-plane geometry.*

The resonant peak decreases when p_1 and p_2 are shifted to the left in the s plane. Replacing s by $s + \alpha$ produces such a shift. The s-domain translation property

$$\mathcal{L}^{-1}\{F(s + \alpha)\} = e^{-\alpha t}f(t)$$

then shows that shifting the poles of $F(s)$ to the left increases the damping in the time domain. Qualitatively, we expect resonant peaks in the frequency response to be less pronounced when circuit damping increases and more pronounced when it decreases.

SECOND-ORDER BANDPASS CIRCUITS

To develop a quantitative understanding of resonance, we replace s by $j\omega$ in Eq. (12–14) to produce

$$T(j\omega) = \frac{Kj\omega}{-\omega^2 + 2\zeta\omega_0 j\omega + \omega_0^2} \tag{12-17}$$

At low frequencies ($\omega << \omega_0$) the gain approaches $|T(j\omega)| \to |K|\omega/\omega_0^2$. At high frequencies ($\omega >> \omega_0$) the gain approaches $|T(j\omega)| \to |K|/\omega$. The low-frequency asymptote is directly proportional to frequency (slope = +1 or +20 dB/decade), while the high-frequency asymptote is inversely proportional to frequency (slope = −1 or −20 dB/decade). As shown in Figure 12–22, the two asymptotes intersect at $\omega = \omega_0$. At this intersection the gain is $|K|/\omega_0$. Note that the frequency scale in Figure 12–16 is logarithmic and normalized by dividing ω by the undamped natural frequency ω_0.

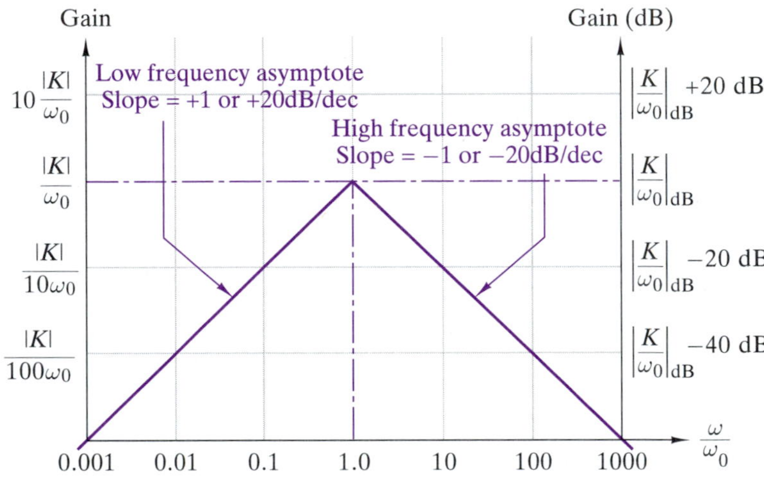

FIGURE 12–22 *Asymptotic gain of a second-order bandpass response.*

The two asymptotes display the characteristics of a bandpass response located around ω_0. For this reason, in a second-order bandpass circuit ω_0 is also called the **center frequency**. To examine the gain response in more detail, we must consider the effect of circuit damping. Factoring $j\omega\omega_0$ out of the denominator of Eq. (12–17) produces

$$T(j\omega) = \frac{K/\omega_0}{2\zeta + j\left(\dfrac{\omega}{\omega_0} - \dfrac{\omega_0}{\omega}\right)} \tag{12-18}$$

Arranging the transfer function in this form shows that only the imaginary part in the denominator varies with frequency. Clearly, the maximum gain occurs when the imaginary part in the denominator of Eq. (12–18) vanishes at $\omega = \omega_0$. The maximum gain is

$$|T(j\omega)|_{MAX} = \frac{|K|/\omega_0}{2\zeta} \tag{12-19}$$

Since the maximum gain is inversely proportional to the damping ratio, the resonant peak will increase as circuit damping decreases, and vice versa. The quantity $|K|/\omega_0$ in the numerator of Eq. (12–19) is the gain at the point in Figure 12–22 where the low- and high-frequency asymptotes intersect.

Figure 12–23 shows plots of the gain of the bandpass function for several values of the damping ratio ζ. For $\zeta < 0.5$ the gain curve lies above the asymptotes and has a narrow resonant peak at ω_0. For $\zeta > 0.5$ the gain curve flattens out and lies below the asymptotes. When $\zeta = 0.5$ the gain curve remains fairly close to the asymptotes.

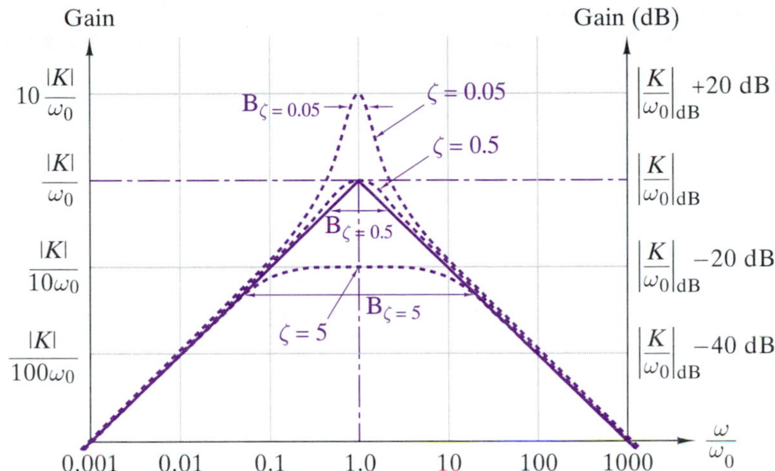

FIGURE 12–23 *Second-order bandpass gain responses.*

The gain response has a bandpass characteristic regardless of the value of the damping ratio. The passband is defined by a cutoff frequency on either side of the center frequency ω_0. To locate the two cutoff frequencies, we must find the values of ω at which the gain is $|T(j\omega)|_{MAX}/\sqrt{2}$, where the maximum gain is given in Eq. (12–19). We note that when the imaginary part in the denominator of Eq. (12–18) equals $\pm 2\zeta$, the gain is

$$|T(j\omega)| = \frac{|K|/\omega_0}{|2\zeta \pm j2\zeta|} = \frac{\dfrac{|K|/\omega_0}{2\zeta}}{\sqrt{2}} = \frac{|T(j\omega)|_{MAX}}{\sqrt{2}} \qquad (12\text{–}20)$$

The values of frequency ω that cause the imaginary part to be $\pm j2\zeta$ are the cutoff frequencies because at these points the gain is reduced by a factor of $1/\sqrt{2}$ from its maximum value at $\omega = \omega_0$.

To find the cutoff frequencies, we set the imaginary part in the denominator in Eq. (12–18) equal to $\pm 2\zeta$:

$$\frac{\omega}{\omega_0} - \frac{\omega_0}{\omega} = \pm 2\zeta \qquad (12\text{–}21)$$

which yields the quadratic equation

$$\omega^2 \mp 2\zeta\omega_0\omega - \omega_0 = 0 \qquad (12\text{–}22)$$

Because of the $\mp$ sign this quadratic has four roots:

$$\omega_{C1}, \omega_{C2} = \omega_0(\pm \zeta \pm \sqrt{1 + \zeta^2}) \qquad (12\text{–}23)$$

Only the two positive roots have physical significance. Since $\sqrt{1 + \zeta^2} > \zeta$, the two positive roots are

$$\omega_{C1} = \omega_0(-\zeta + \sqrt{1 + \zeta^2})$$
$$\omega_{C2} = \omega_0(+\zeta + \sqrt{1 + \zeta^2}) \qquad (12\text{–}24)$$

Since $\zeta > 0$, these equations show that $\omega_{C1} < \omega_0$ is the lower cutoff frequency, while $\omega_{C2} > \omega_0$ is the upper cutoff frequency. Multiplying ω_{C1} times ω_{C2} produces

$$\omega_0^2 = \omega_{C1}\omega_{C2} \qquad (12\text{–}25)$$

This result means that the center frequency ω_0 is the geometric mean of the two cutoff frequencies. The **bandwidth (B)** of the passband is found by subtracting ω_{C1} from ω_{C2}:

$$B = \omega_{C2} - \omega_{C1} = 2\zeta\omega_0 \qquad (12\text{–}26)$$

The bandwidth is proportional to the product of the damping ratio and the natural frequency. When $\zeta < 0.5$ then $B < \omega_0$ and when $\zeta > 0.5$ then $B > \omega_0$.

We can think of $\zeta = 0.5$ as the boundary between two extreme cases. In the **narrowband** case ($\zeta << 0.5$) the complex natural poles are close to the j-axis and the gain response has a resonant peak that produces a bandwidth that is small compared to the circuit's natural frequency. In the **wideband** case ($\zeta >> 0.5$) the gain response is relatively flat because the natural poles are farther from the j-axis because the circuit has more damping. The narrowband response is highly selective, passing only a very restricted range of frequencies, often less than one octave. In contrast, the wideband response usually encompasses several decades within its passband. Both cases are widely used in applications.

The narrow and broadband cases also show up in the phase response. From Eq. (12–18) the phase angle is

$$\theta(\omega) = \angle K - \tan^{-1}\left[\frac{\omega/\omega_0 - \omega_0/\omega}{2\zeta}\right] \qquad (12\text{–}27)$$

At low frequency ($\omega << \omega_0$) the phase angle approaches $\theta(\omega) \to \angle K + 90°$. At the center frequency ($\omega = \omega_0$) the phase reduces to $\theta(\omega_0) = \angle K$. Finally, at high frequencies ($\omega >> \omega_0$) the phase approaches $\theta(\omega) \to \angle K - 90°$. Graphs of the phase response for several values of damping are shown in Figure 12–24. The phase shift at the center frequency is 90° and the total phase change is –180° regardless of the damping ratio. However, the transition from +90° to –90° is very abrupt for the narrowband case ($\zeta = 0.05$) and more gradual for the wideband case ($\zeta = 5$).

EXAMPLE 12–9

(a) Show that the transfer function $T(s) = V_2(s)/V_1(s)$ of the circuit in Figure 12–25 has a bandpass characteristic.
(b) Select the element values to obtain a center frequency of 455 kHz and a bandwidth of 10 kHz.[2]
(c) Calculate the cutoff frequencies for the values selected in (b).

---

2 These values are typical of the bandpass filters in a conventional AM radio receiver.

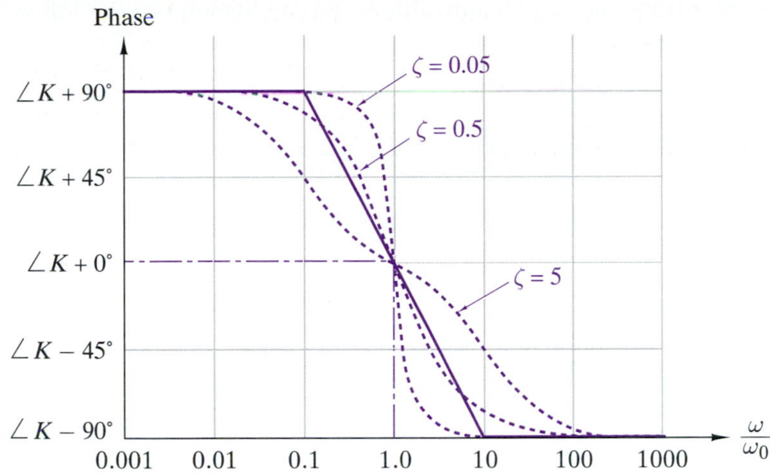

FIGURE 12-24 *Second-order bandpass phase responses.*

SOLUTION:

(a) The given circuit is a voltage divider with branch impedances

$$Z_1 = R$$

$$Z_2 = \frac{1}{Cs + \dfrac{1}{Ls}} = \frac{Ls}{LCs^2 + 1}$$

By voltage division, the transfer function is

$$T(s) = \frac{Z_2}{Z_1 + Z_2} = \frac{Ls}{RLCs^2 + Ls + R}$$

$$= \frac{s/RC}{s^2 + s/RC + 1/LC}$$

This transfer function is of the standard bandpass form $Ks/(s^2 + 2\zeta\omega_0 s + \omega_0^2)$.

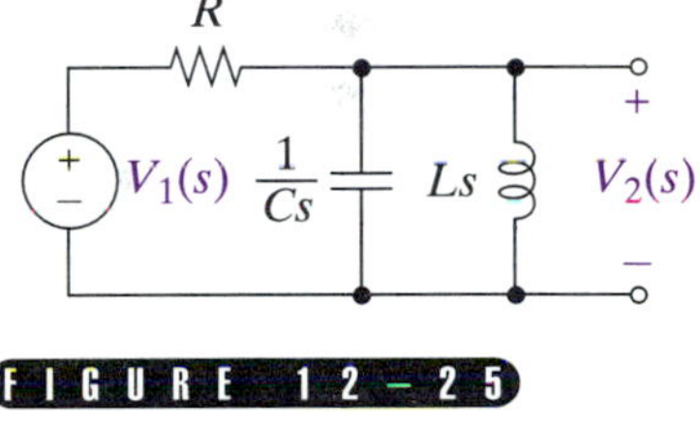

FIGURE 12-25

Circuit Interpretation: The circuit's bandpass response is easily explained by the element impedances at zero and infinite frequency. At zero frequency the inductor acts like a short circuit that forces the output down to zero. At infinite frequency the capacitor is a short circuit again, forcing the output to zero. Thus, the circuit has zero gain at dc and zero gain at infinite frequency, which is the characteristic pattern of a bandpass response.

(b) Comparing the circuit's transfer function with the standard form yields the following relationships:

$$\omega_0^2 = \frac{1}{LC}$$

$$\zeta = \frac{\sqrt{L/C}}{2R}$$

The center frequency and bandwidth requirements impose the following numerical values:

$$\omega_0 = 2\pi \times 455 \times 10^3 = 2.86 \times 10^6 \text{ rad/s}$$

$$\zeta = \frac{B}{2\omega_O} = \frac{2\pi \times 10 \times 10^3}{2(2\pi \times 455 \times 10^3)} = 0.0110$$

and the resulting design constraints on the element values are

$$LC = \frac{1}{\omega_0^2} = 1.22 \times 10^{-13} \quad \text{and} \quad \frac{\sqrt{L/C}}{2R} = \zeta = 0.011$$

Selecting $C = 10$ nF yields $L = 12.2$ μH and $R = 1.59$ kΩ.

(c) Using Eq. (12–24), the cutoff frequencies are

$$f_{C1} = \frac{\omega_0(-\zeta + \sqrt{1 + \zeta^2})}{2\pi} = 450.2 \text{ kHz}$$

$$f_{C2} = \frac{\omega_0(+\zeta + \sqrt{1 + \zeta^2})}{2\pi} = 460.2 \text{ kHz}$$

Since the damping ratio is very small, the natural poles are quite close to the j-axis, producing a very narrow resonant peak at 455 kHz. ■

Exercise 12–3

Find the natural frequency, damping ratio, cutoff frequencies, bandwidth, and maximum gain of the following bandpass transfer functions:

$$\text{(a) } T(s) = \frac{500s}{s^2 + 200s + 10^6}$$

$$\text{(b) } T(s) = \frac{5 \times 10^{-3} s}{2.5 \times 10^{-5} s^2 + 5 \times 10^{-3} s + 1}$$

Answers:

	ω_0(rad/s)	ζ	ω_{C1}(rad/s)	ω_{C2}(rad/s)	B(rad/s)	$\lvert T(j\omega)\rvert_{MAX}$
(a)	1000	0.1	905	1105	200	2.5
(b)	200	0.5	123.6	323.6	200	1

Exercise 12–4

A bandpass circuit has a center frequency of $\omega_0 = 1$ krad/s and a bandwidth of $B = 10$ krad/s.

Find the damping ratio ζ and cutoff frequencies. Is this a narrowband or broadband circuit?

Answers:

$\zeta = 5$, $\omega_{C1} = 99.02$ rad/s, $\omega_{C2} = 10.099$ krad/s, broadband

Exercise 12–5

A bandpass circuit has cutoff frequencies at $\omega_{C1} = 20$ krad/s and $\omega_{C2} = 50$ krad/s. Find the center frequency ω_0, damping ratio ζ, and bandwidth B.

Answers:
$\omega_0 = 31.6$ krad/s, $\zeta = 0.474$, $B = 30$ krad/s

SECOND-ORDER LOW-PASS CIRCUITS

The transfer function of a second-order low-pass prototype has the form

$$T(s) = \frac{K}{s^2 + 2\zeta\omega_0 s + \omega_0^2} \tag{12-28}$$

The frequency response is found by replacing s by $j\omega$.

$$T(j\omega) = \frac{K}{\omega_0^2 - \omega^2 + j2\zeta\omega_0\omega} \tag{12-29}$$

At low frequencies ($\omega << \omega_0$) the gain approaches $|T(j\omega)| \to |K|/\omega_0^2 = |T(0)|$. At high frequencies ($\omega >> \omega_0$) the gain approaches $|T(j\omega)| \to |K|/\omega^2$. The low-frequency asymptote is a constant equal to the zero frequency or dc gain. The high-frequency asymptote is inversely proportional to the square of the frequency. As a result, the high-frequency gain asymptote has a slope of –40 dB/decade (slope = –2). The two asymptotes intersect to form a corner at $\omega = \omega_0$, as indicated in Figure 12–26. The two asymptotes display a low-pass gain characteristic with a passband below ω_0, and a stopband above ω_0. The passband gain is the dc gain $|T(0)|$ and the slope of the gain asymptote in the stopband is –40 dB/decade.

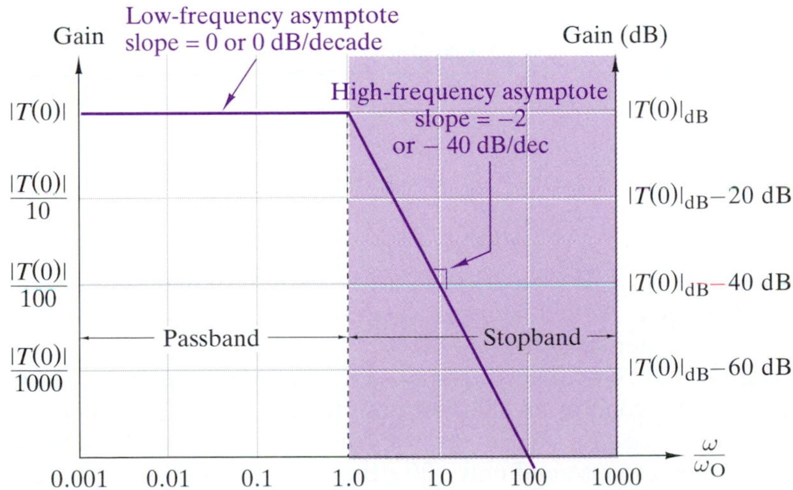

FIGURE 12–26 *Asymptotic gain of a second-order low-pass response.*

The influence of the damping ratio on the gain response can be illustrated by evaluating the gain at $\omega = \omega_0$:

$$|T(j\omega_0)| = \frac{|K|/\omega_0^2}{2\zeta} = \frac{|T(0)|}{2\zeta} \qquad (12\text{–}30)$$

This result and the plots in Figure 12–27 show that the actual gain curve lies above the asymptotes when $\zeta < 0.5$, below the asymptotes when $\zeta > 0.5$, and close to the asymptotes when $\zeta = 0.5$. When $\zeta = 1/\sqrt{2}$ then the gain at $\omega = \omega_0$ is

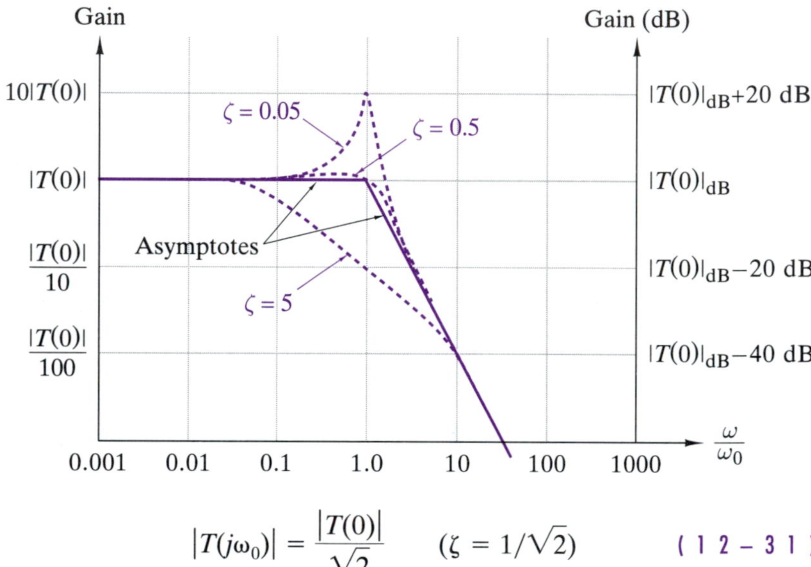

FIGURE 12–27 *Second-order low-pass gain responses.*

$$|T(j\omega_0)| = \frac{|T(0)|}{\sqrt{2}} \qquad (\zeta = 1/\sqrt{2}) \qquad (12\text{–}31)$$

Since the passband gain is $|T(0)|$, this result means that the cutoff frequency is equal to ω_0 when $\zeta = 1/\sqrt{2}$

The distinctive feature of the low-pass case is a narrow resonant peak in the neighborhood of ω_0 for lightly damped circuits. The actual maximum gain of a second-order low-pass response is

$$|T(j\omega)|_{MAX} = \frac{|T(0)|}{2\zeta\sqrt{1-\zeta^2}} \qquad (12\text{–}32)$$

and occurs at

$$\omega_{MAX} = \omega_0\sqrt{1-2\zeta^2} \qquad (12\text{–}33)$$

Note that the ω_{MAX} is always less than the natural frequency ω_0. Deriving Eqs. (12–32) and (12–33) is straightforward and is left as a problem at the end of this chapter (Problem 12–20).

Figure 12–28 compares the response of the first-order low-pass prototype with the second-order gain response for $\zeta = 1/\sqrt{2}$. The important difference is that the gain slope in the stopband is –2 or –40 dB/decade for the second-order response and only –20 dB/decade for the first-order circuit. The two poles in the second-order case produce a steeper slope because the high-frequency response decreases as $1/\omega^2$, rather than $1/\omega$ as in the first-order case. The generalization is that the high-frequency gain asymptote of an n-pole low-pass function has a slope of $-n$ or –20n dB/decade.

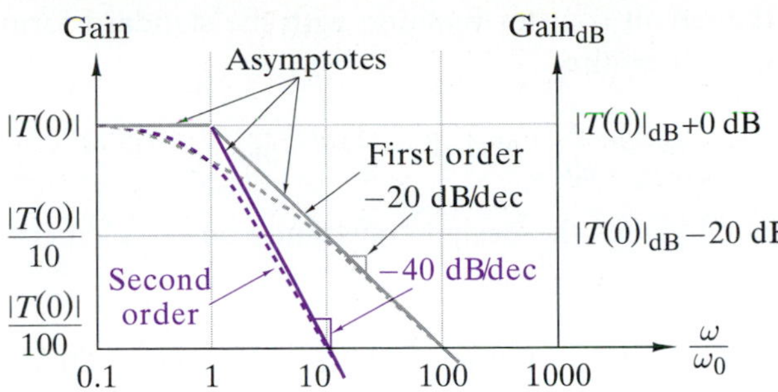

FIGURE 12–28 *Comparison of first- and second-order gain responses.*

EXAMPLE 12–10

(a) Show that the transfer function $T(s) = V_2(s)/V_1(s)$ of the circuit in Figure 12–29 has a low-pass gain characteristic.

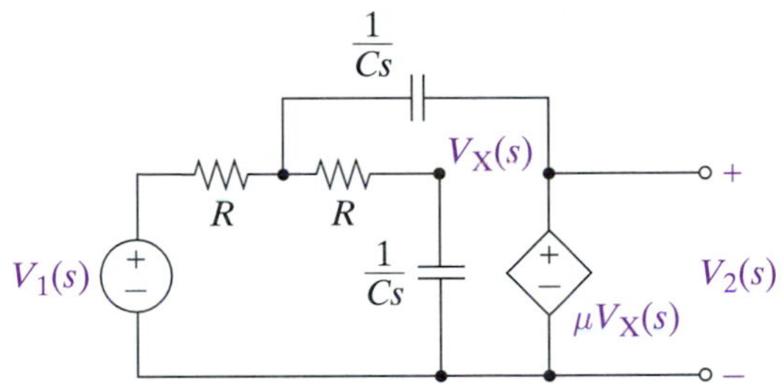

FIGURE 12–29

(b) Derive expressions relating the damping ratio ζ and undamped natural frequency ω_0 to the circuit element values. Use these relationships to select the element values to produce $\zeta = 0.1$ and $\omega_0 =$ 5 krad/s.

SOLUTION:

(a) The transfer function of this circuit is found in Example 11-6 using node-voltage analysis.

$$T(s) = \frac{V_2(s)}{V_1(s)} = \frac{\mu}{(RCs)^2 + (3 - \mu)RCs + 1}$$

This is a second-order low-pass transfer function of the form $K/(s^2/\omega_0^2 + 2\zeta s/\omega_0 + 1)$.

Circuit Interpretation: At zero frequency both capacitors in Figure 12–29 act like open circuits and the control voltage $V_X(s) = V_1(s)$ since there is no voltage drop across either resistor. As a result, the dc output voltage is $V_2(s) = \mu V_X(s) = \mu V_1$. In other words, the dc gain of the circuit is $T(0) = \mu$. At infinite frequency both capacitors act like short circuits. The shunt capacitor shorts the control node X to ground so that $V_X = 0$, the dependent voltage source μV_X is turned off, and the output voltage is zero. The circuit has a finite gain at dc and zero gain at infinite frequency, which is the characteristic pattern of a low-pass response.

(b) Comparing the circuit transfer function with the standard form yields the following relationships:

$$\omega_0 = \frac{1}{RC} \quad \text{and} \quad \zeta = \frac{1}{2}(3 - \mu)$$

For the specified values the design constraints on the element values are

$$RC = \frac{1}{\omega_0} = 2 \times 10^{-4} \qquad \text{Let } R = 10\text{ k}\Omega \qquad \text{Then } C = 20\text{ nF}$$

$$\mu = 3 - 2\zeta = 2.8$$

The maximum gain for these conditions is

$$|T(j\omega)|_{\text{MAX}} = \frac{|T(0)|}{2\zeta\sqrt{1 - \zeta^2}} = 5.03 \times |T(0)|$$

The peak gain is five times as large as the dc gain. Thus, lightly damped second-order circuits of all types have strong resonant peaks in their gain response. ■

Exercise 12–6

Find the natural frequency ω_0 damping ratio ζ, dc gain $T(0)$, and maximum gain of the following second-order low-pass transfer functions:

(a) $$T(s) = \frac{(4000)^2}{(s + 3000)^2 + (4000)^2}$$

(b) $$T(s) = \frac{5}{0.25 \times 10^{-4}s^2 + 10^{-2}s + 1}$$

Answers:

(a) $\omega_0 = 5$ krad/s, $\zeta = 0.6$, $T(0) = 0.64$, $T_{\text{MAX}} = 0.667$

(b) $\omega_0 = 200$ rad/s, $\zeta = 1.00$, $T(0) = 5$, $T_{\text{MAX}} = T(0)$

Exercise 12–7

The impulse response of a second-order low-pass circuit is

$$h(t) = 2000[e^{-1000t} \sin 1000t]u(t)$$

Find the natural frequency ω_0, damping ratio ζ, dc gain $T(0)$, and maximum gain.

Answers:

$\omega_0 = 1414$ rad/s, $\zeta = 0.707$, $T(0) = T_{\text{MAX}} = 1$

SECOND-ORDER HIGH-PASS CIRCUITS

To complete the study of second-order circuits, we treat the high-pass case.

$$T(s) = \frac{Ks^2}{s^2 + 2\zeta\omega_0 s + \omega_0^2} \tag{12-34}$$

The high-pass frequency response is a mirror image of the low-pass case reflected about $\omega = \omega_0$. At low frequencies ($\omega << \omega_0$) the gain approaches $|T(j\omega)| \to |K|\omega^2/\omega_0^2$. At high frequencies ($\omega >> \omega_0$) the gain approaches $|T(j\omega)| \to |K| = |T(\infty)|$. The high-frequency gain is a constant $|T(\infty)|$ called the infinite frequency gain. The low-frequency asymptote is inversely proportional to the square of the frequency (slope = +2 or +40 dB/decade). The two asymptotes intersect at the natural frequency ω_0, as shown in Figure 12–30. The asymptotes display a high-pass gain response with a passband above ω_0 and a stopband below ω_0. The passband gain is $|T(\infty)|$ and the slope of the gain asymptote in the stopband is +2 or +40 dB/decade.

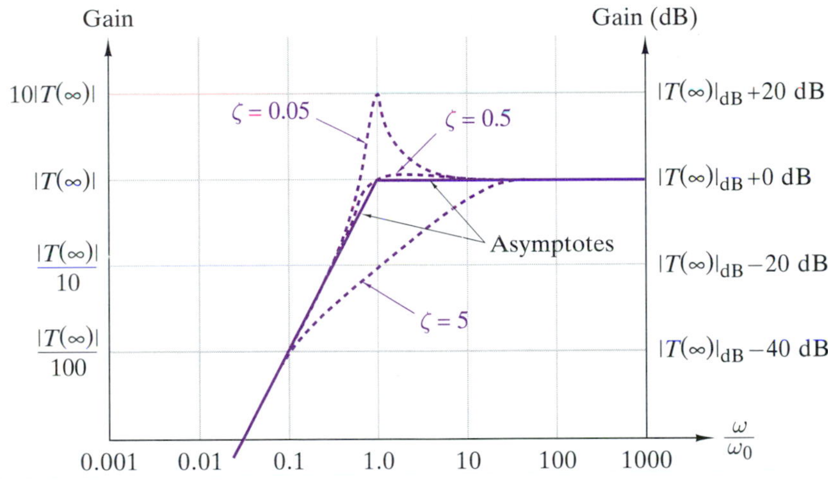

FIGURE 12–30 *Second-order high-pass gain responses.*

Figure 12–30 also shows the effect of the damping ratio on the actual gain curve. Evaluating the gain response at $\omega = \omega_0$ produces

$$|T(j\omega_0)| = \frac{|K|}{2\zeta} = \frac{|T(\infty)|}{2\zeta} \tag{12-35}$$

This result and the plots in Figure 12–30 show that the gain response will be above the asymptotes for $\zeta < 0.5$, below for $\zeta > 0.5$, and close to the asymptotes for $\zeta = 0.5$. When $\zeta = 1/\sqrt{2}$ the gain in Eq. (12–35) is $|T(\infty)|/\sqrt{2}$. That is, ω_0 is the cutoff frequency when $\zeta = 1/\sqrt{2}$.

Again, the distinctive feature of the second-order response is the peak in the neighborhood of ω_0 for lightly damped circuits with $\zeta << 0.5$. For the second-order high-pass function the maximum gain is

$$|T(j\omega)|_{MAX} = \frac{|T(\infty)|}{2\zeta\sqrt{1-\zeta^2}} \tag{12-36}$$

and occurs at

$$\omega_{MAX} = \frac{\omega_0}{\sqrt{1 - 2\zeta^2}} \tag{12-37}$$

The frequency at which the gain maximum occurs is always above ω_0. Deriving Eqs. (12–36) and (12–37) is straightforward and is similar to the low-pass case.

EXAMPLE 12–11

(a) Show that the transfer function $T(s) = V_2(s)/V_1(s)$ of the circuit in Figure 12–31 has a high-pass characteristic.

FIGURE 12–31

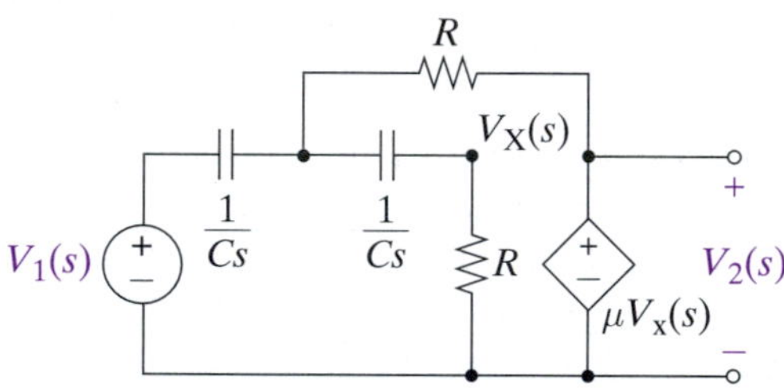

(b) Derive expressions relating the damping ratio ζ and undamped natural frequency ω_0 to the circuit element values.

SOLUTION:

This high-pass circuit is obtained from the low-pass circuit in Figure 12–29 by interchanging the positions of the resistors and capacitors. This interchange is an example of a transformation that converts any low-pass *RC* circuit into a high-pass *RC* circuit. The *CR-RC* transformation is carried out by:

1. Replacing every impedance R by an impedance $1/Cs$, and
2. Replacing every impedance $1/Cs$ by an impedance R.

Applying this transformation at the circuit level converts the low-pass circuit in Figure 12–29 into the high-pass circuit in Figure 12–31. The transformation can also be applied at the transfer function level. The transfer function of the low-pass prototype is given in Example 12–10 as

$$T_{LP}(s) = \frac{\mu}{(RCs)^2 + (3 - \mu)RCs + 1}$$

$$= \frac{\mu}{(R)^2\left(\frac{Cs}{1}\right)^2 + (3 - \mu)(R)\left(\frac{Cs}{1}\right) + 1}$$

Performing the *CR-RC* transformation defined previously on the second expression yields

$$T_{HP}(s) = \frac{\mu}{\left(\frac{1}{Cs}\right)^2\left(\frac{1}{R}\right)^2 + (3-\mu)\left(\frac{1}{Cs}\right)\left(\frac{1}{R}\right) + 1}$$

$$= \frac{\mu(RCs)^2}{(RCs)^2 + (3-\mu)RCs + 1}$$

The low-pass transfer function is converted into a high-pass form with an infinite frequency gain of $|T(\infty)| = \mu$. Comparing the denominator of $T_{HP}(s)$ with the standard second-order form yields

$$\omega_0 = \frac{1}{RC} \quad \text{and} \quad \zeta = \frac{3-\mu}{2}$$

These are the same relationships we obtained for the low-pass prototype in Example 12–10. Note that the *CR-RC* transformation only affects the resistors and capacitors and does not change the dependent source.

Circuit Interpretation: It is not hard to see why the circuit in Figure 12–31 has a high-pass response with zero gain at dc and finite gain at infinite frequency. At zero frequency both capacitors act like open circuits that disconnect the input source, leading to zero output and zero gain. At infinite frequency the capacitors act like short circuits that directly connect the input source to the control voltage node, forcing the condition $V_X(s) = V_1(s)$. As a result, the output is $V_2(s) = \mu V_1(s)$, which means the infinite frequency gain is μ. ■

Exercise 12–8

The transfer function of a high-pass circuit is $T(s) = 0.2s^2/(s^2 + 10^4 s + 10^6)$. Find the undamped natural frequency ω_0, damping ratio ζ, high-frequency gain $T(\infty)$, and maximum gain of the transfer function.

Answers:
$\omega_0 = 10^3$ rad/s, $\zeta = 5$, $T(\infty) = 0.2$, $T_{MAX} = T(\infty)$

Exercise 12–9

The step response of a second-order high-pass circuit is

$$g(t) = [e^{-1000t}\cos 2000t - 0.5e^{-1000t}\sin 2000t]u(t)$$

Find the natural frequency ω_0, damping ratio ζ, high-frequency gain $T(\infty)$, and maximum gain of the circuit.

Answers:
$\omega_0 = 2236$ rad/s, $\zeta = 0.447$, $T(\infty) = 1$, $T_{MAX} = 1.25$

12–4 THE FREQUENCY RESPONSE OF *RLC* CIRCUITS

The series *RLC* circuit and the parallel *RLC* circuit are canonical examples traditionally used in electrical engineering to illustrate the response of

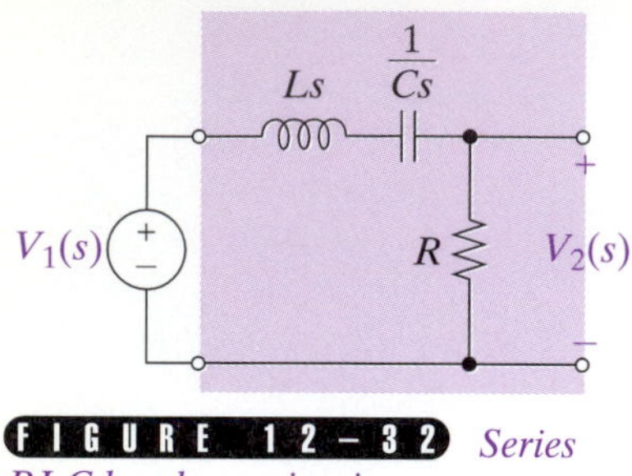

FIGURE 12–32 Series RLC bandpass circuit.

second-order circuits. These circuits give us a special insight because the form of a response is easily related to the circuit elements. We first encountered these circuits in Chapter 7, where they served as vehicles for studying the solution of second-order differential equations. In this section we concentrate on the frequency response of the traditional *RLC* circuits starting with the series circuit in Figure 12–32.

By voltage division, the transfer function of the series *RLC* circuit in Figure 12–32 is

$$T(s) = \frac{R}{Ls + 1/Cs + R} = \frac{\frac{R}{L}s}{s^2 + \frac{R}{L}s + \frac{1}{LC}} \tag{12–38}$$

Comparing this result with the standard bandpass in Eq. (12–14), we conclude that the circuit has a bandpass response with

$$K = \frac{R}{L}$$
$$\omega_0 = \frac{1}{\sqrt{LC}} \tag{12–39}$$
$$2\zeta\omega_0 = \frac{R}{L}$$

Inserting these conclusions into Eqs. (12–19), (12–24), and (12–26), we find the descriptive parameters of the passband to be

$$|T(j\omega)|_{\text{MAX}} = \frac{K}{2\zeta\omega_0} = 1$$
$$B = 2\zeta\omega_0 = \frac{R}{L} \tag{12–40}$$

and

$$\omega_{C1} = -\frac{R}{2L} + \sqrt{\left(\frac{R}{2L}\right)^2 + \frac{1}{LC}}$$
$$\omega_{C2} = +\frac{R}{2L} + \sqrt{\left(\frac{R}{2L}\right)^2 + \frac{1}{LC}} \tag{12–41}$$

For historical reasons, it is traditional to add a fifth descriptive parameter called the **quality factor** Q.[3] We can define the quality factor of any bandpass filter as $Q = \omega_0/B$. In general, this means that for a second-order circuit, $Q = 1/2\zeta$. In the particular case of the series *RLC* circuit, this requires

3 Q was originally defined as a measure of the quality of lossy inductors. In modern usage it is a substitute parameter for the damping ratio of a second-order factor. The relationship between the two parameters is $2\zeta = 1/Q$. Since the two are reciprocally related, their comparative adjectives are reversed; that is, high Q means low damping and low Q means high damping.

$$Q = \frac{1/\sqrt{LC}}{R/L} = \frac{\sqrt{L/C}}{R} \quad (12\text{–}42)$$

The consequences of these results are illustrated graphically in Figure 12–33. The maximum gain is always 1 (or 0 dB) regardless of the bandwidth. The bandwidth is directly proportional to the resistance, so ω_{C1} decreases and ω_{C2} increases as R increases. The boundary between broadband and narrowband occurs when $\zeta = 0.5$, which requires that $Q = 1$. Figure 12–33 shows the response for values of Q one decade above and one decade below this boundary value. Increasing Q causes the passband to shrink into a high-Q, narrowband response. Conversely, decreasing Q expands the passband into a low-Q, broadband response. But regardless of the value of Q, the maximum gain remains anchored at $\omega = \omega_0$ with a value of 1.

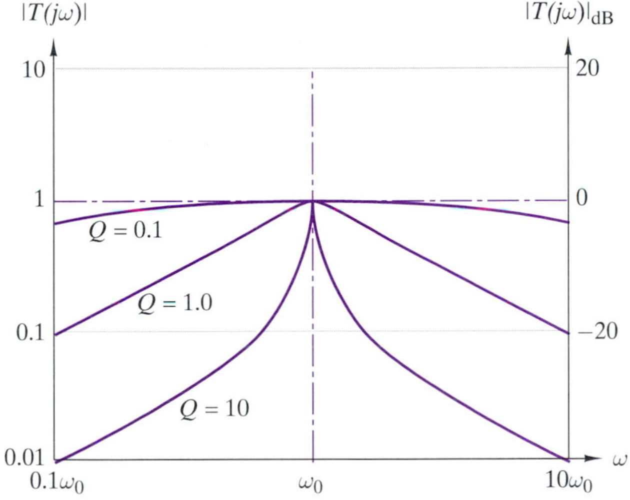

FIGURE 12–33 *Effect of Q on the series RLC bandpass response.*

What is interesting, and worth remembering, about this circuit is the way the impedances of the inductor and capacitor combine to produce the bandpass response. Again, using voltage division in Figure 12–32, we write the transfer function in the form

$$T(j\omega) = \frac{R}{R + Z_{LC}(j\omega)}$$

where

$$Z_{LC}(j\omega) = j\omega L + \frac{1}{j\omega C} = j\left(\omega L - \frac{1}{\omega C}\right)$$

is the impedance of inductor and capacitor in the series leg of the voltage divider. The variation of this impedance affects the gain response as follows:

- At $\omega = 0$ the impedance $Z_{LC}(j\omega)$ is infinite since the capacitor acts like an open circuit. The open circuit disconnects the input source, leading to zero output and $|T(0)| = 0$.

- At $\omega = \infty$ the impedance $Z_{LC}(j\omega)$ is infinite since the inductor acts like an open circuit. The open circuit disconnects the input source, leading to zero output and $|T(\infty)| = 0$.
- At $\omega = \omega_0$ the impedance $Z_{LC}(j\omega)$ is zero since

$$Z_{LC}(j\omega_0) = j\left(\omega_0 L - \frac{1}{\omega_0 C}\right) = j\left(\sqrt{\frac{L}{C}} - \sqrt{\frac{L}{C}}\right) = 0$$

The inductor and capacitor together act like a short circuit that directly connects the input across the output, leading to $|T(j\omega_0)| = 1$.

- At $\omega = \omega_{C1}$ the impedance $Z_{LC}(j\omega) = -jR$ since this value yields

$$T(j\omega_{C1}) = \frac{R}{R - jR} = \frac{1}{\sqrt{2}}\angle + 45°$$

The inductor and capacitor together act like an impedance $-jR$ with the result that the the gain at the lower cutoff frequency is $|T(j\omega_{C1})| = 1/\sqrt{2}$ as required.

- At $\omega = \omega_{C2}$ the impedance $Z_{LC}(j\omega) = +jR$ since this value yields

$$|T(j\omega_{C2})| = \frac{R}{R + jR} = \frac{1}{\sqrt{2}}\angle - 45°$$

The inductor and capacitor together act like an impedance $+jR$ with the result that the the gain at the upper cutoff frequency is $|T(j\omega_{C2})| = 1/\sqrt{2}$ as required.

Figure 12–34 summarizes these observations graphically and shows how the impedance $Z_{LC}(j\omega)$ controls the gain response of the circuit. Knowing this impedance at five frequencies is enough to describe the bandpass characteristics.

EXAMPLE 12–12

A series RLC circuit has a resonant frequency of $\omega_0 = 20$ krad/s, $Q = 5$, and a resistance of 50 Ω. Find the values of L, C, B, ω_{C1}, and ω_{C2}.

SOLUTION:

From the definition of Q, we have $B = \omega_0/Q = 4000$ rad/s. For the series RLC circuit, $B = R/L$; hence we can calculate the inductance as $L = R/B =$ 12.5 mH and the capacitance as $C = 1/\omega_0^2 L = 0.2$ μF. Inserting these results into Eq. (12–41) yields the cutoff frequencies as

$$\omega_{C1} = -\frac{4000}{2} + \sqrt{\left(\frac{4000}{2}\right)^2 + 20{,}000^2} = 18.1 \text{ krad/s}$$

$$\omega_{C2} = +\frac{4000}{2} + \sqrt{\left(\frac{4000}{2}\right)^2 + 20{,}000^2} = 22.1 \text{ krad/s}$$ ■

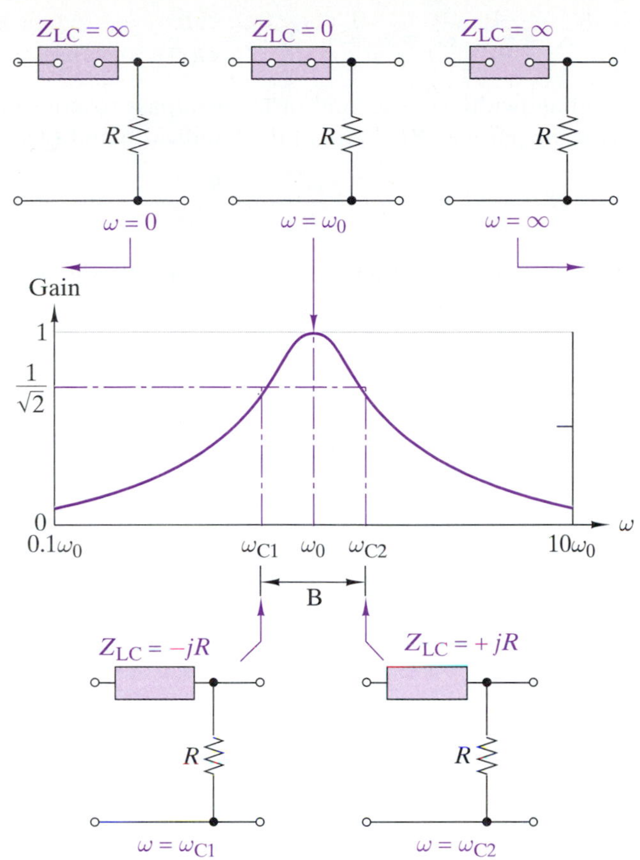

FIGURE 12-34 *Effect of Z_{LC} on the series RLC bandpass response.*

EXAMPLE 12-13

(a) Show that the current transfer function $T(s) = I_2(s)/I_1(s)$ in Figure 12-35 has a bandpass gain response with a center frequency at $\omega_0 = 1/\sqrt{LC}$.

(a) Derive expression relating the descriptive parameters B, Q, ω_{C1}, and ω_{C2} to the circuit parameters R, L, and C.

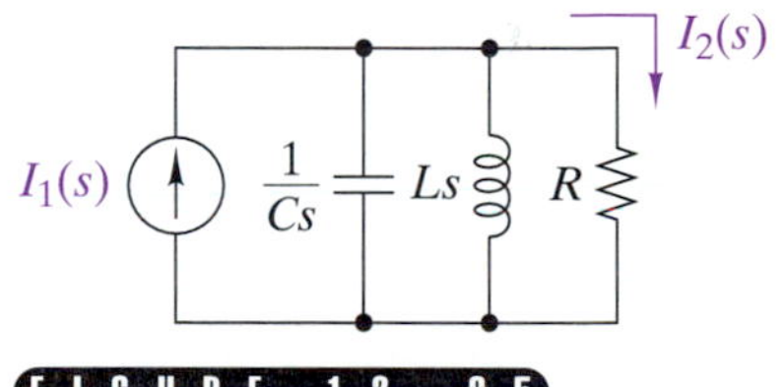

FIGURE 12-35
Parallel RLC bandpass circuit.

SOLUTION:

(a) The current transfer function is derived using current division as

$$T(s) = \frac{I_2(s)}{I_1(s)} = \frac{Y_R}{Y_L + Y_C + Y_R} = \frac{1/R}{1/Ls + Cs + 1/R}$$

$$= \frac{\dfrac{s}{RC}}{s^2 + \dfrac{s}{RC} + \dfrac{1}{LC}}$$

Comparing this transfer function to the standard bandpass form in Eq. (12-14), we see that this is a bandpass response with

$$K = \frac{1}{RC} \quad \omega_0 = \frac{1}{\sqrt{LC}} \quad 2\zeta\omega_0 = \frac{1}{RC}$$

(b) In general, the bandwidth of a second-order bandpass response is $B = 2\zeta\omega_0$. Hence for the parallel RLC circuit the bandwidth and Q are

$$B = \frac{1}{RC} \quad \text{and} \quad Q = \frac{\omega_0}{B} = \frac{R}{\sqrt{L/C}}$$

Inserting these results into the Eq. (12–24) leads to the following expressions:

$$\omega_{C1} = -\frac{1}{2RC} + \sqrt{\left(\frac{1}{2RC}\right)^2 + \frac{1}{LC}}$$

$$\omega_{C2} = +\frac{1}{2RC} + \sqrt{\left(\frac{1}{2RC}\right)^2 + \frac{1}{LC}}$$

■

Exercise 12–10

A series RLC circuit has cutoff frequencies of $\omega_{C1} = 100$ rad/s and $\omega_{C2} = 10$ krad/s. Find the values of B, ω_0, and Q. Does the circuit have a broadband or narrowband response?

Answers:
$B = 9.9$ krad/s, $\omega_0 = 1$ krad/s, $Q = 0.101$, broadband

Exercise 12–11

A parallel RLC bandpass circuit has a center frequency at $\omega_0 = 200$ krad/s, bandwidth of $B = 10$ krad/s, and a resistance of $R = 10$ kΩ. Find ω_0 and B when the resistance is increased to 40 kΩ.

Answers:
$\omega_0 = 200$ krad/s, $B = 2.5$ krad/s

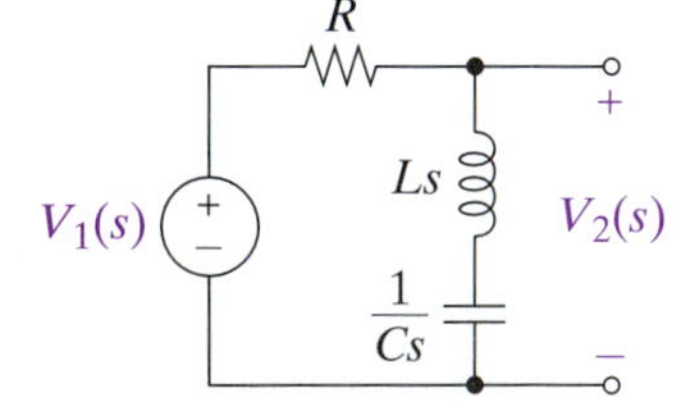

FIGURE 12–36
Series RLC bandstop circuit.

THE SERIES *RLC* BANDSTOP CIRCUIT

The transfer function of the series RLC circuit in Figure 12–36 can be derived by voltage division as

$$T(s) = \frac{Ls + 1/Cs}{Ls + 1/Cs + R} = \frac{s^2 + \dfrac{1}{LC}}{s^2 + \dfrac{R}{L}s + \dfrac{1}{LC}}$$

If we define $\omega_0 = 1/\sqrt{LC}$ then $|T(j\omega_0)| = 0$ because the transfer function has zeros on the j-axis at $s = \pm j\omega_0$. The dc gain is $|T(0)| = 1$ and the infinite frequency gain is $|T(\infty)| = 1$. Thus, this transfer function has finite gain at dc and infinite frequency, and zero gain at an intermediate frequency. These features are indicative of a bandstop response.

The bandstop circuit in Figure 12–36 and the bandpass circuit in Figure 12–32 are both series *RLC* circuits. The difference is that the bandstop circuit takes its output across the inductor and capacitor in series while the bandpass circuit defines its output across the resistor. In either case, the shape of the frequency response is controlled by the impedance $Z_{LC}(j\omega) = j\omega L + 1/j\omega C$.

Figure 12–37 shows how this impedance controls the shape of the bandstop response. At dc and infinite frequency Z_{LC} acts like an open circuit so the output voltage equals the input voltage and the passband gains are both one. At $\omega = \omega_0$ the Z_{LC} acts like a short circuit so the output voltage and the gain are both zero. At the cutoff frequencies $Z_{LC} = \pm jR$, so the passband gains are reduced to $1/\sqrt{2}$. In sum, the factors defining the shape of the bandstop response are the same as those defining the shape of the bandpass response.

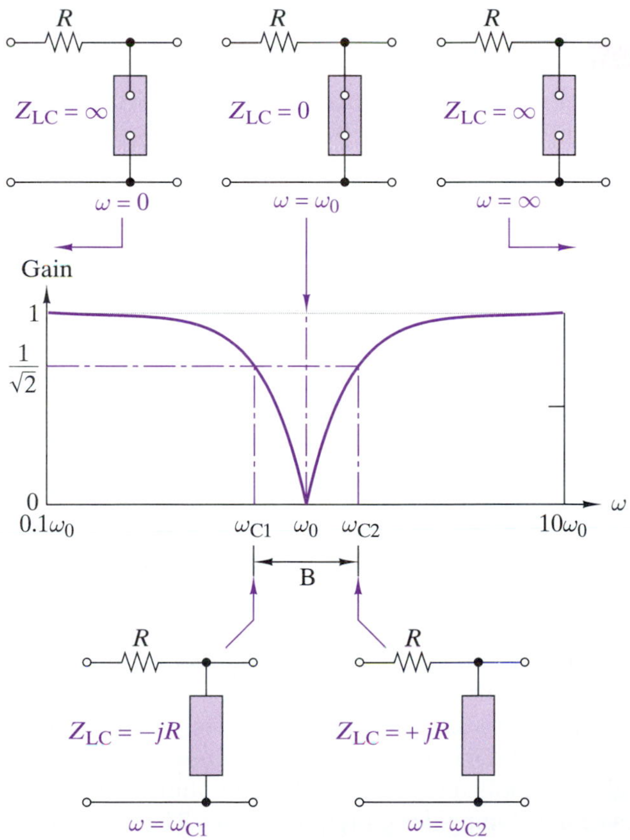

FIGURE 12–37 *Effect of Z_{LC} on the series RLC bandstop response.*

The net result is that the equations relating circuit parameters and the stopband descriptive parameters are the same as the equations for the bandpass case. That is, we can use Eqs. (12–39), (12–40), and (12–41) for both the bandpass and bandstop series *RLC* circuits. The difference is that B, ω_{C1}, and ω_{C2} describe the passband in the former and the stopband in the latter.

D DESIGN EXAMPLE 12–14

Series *RLC* Circuit Design

A series connection of an inductor and capacitor are to be connected across the output of a source whose Thévenin resistance is 50 Ω. The goal is to create a bandstop filter to eliminate a spurious (undesirable) source output at 25 krad/s. Select the values of L and C that eliminate the spurious response and produce a stopband bandwidth less than 1 krad/s.

SOLUTION:

Using Eq. (12–40), we have $B = R/L < 1000$. Since $R = 50\ \Omega$, this constraint requires $L > 50$ mH. Using Eq. (12–39), the bandstop notch must be located at $\omega_0 = 1/\sqrt{LC} = 25{,}000$. Selecting $L = 100$ mH to meet the bandwidth constraint means that $C = 1/\omega_0{}^2 L = 16$ nF. ■

Exercise 12–12

A series *RLC* circuit has a bandstop response with a B of 2 krad/s and a notch at $\omega_0 = 10$ krad/s. Find the circuit gain at $\omega = 9$ krad/s and $\omega = 11$ krad/s.

Answers: 0.726, 0.690

12–5 BODE DIAGRAMS

Bode diagrams are separate graphs of the gain $|T(j\omega)|_{\text{dB}}$ and phase $\theta(j\omega)$ versus log-frequency scales. The frequency-response performance of devices, circuits, and systems is often presented in this format. The poles and zeros of the transfer functions can be estimated from Bode plots of experimental frequency-response data. Thus, the Bode plot format is a very useful way to develop an understanding of frequency response of circuits and systems. Any of our computer-aided analysis tools can precisely calculate and plot Bode diagrams. However, often a simple hand-calculated approximation will tell us what we want to know about the frequency response of a circuit.

The purpose of this section is to present a method of quickly drawing straight-line approximations to Bode plot of transfer functions with real poles and zeros. In analysis situation the straight-line approximations tell us how the poles and zeros of $T(s)$ affect frequency response. In circuit design these straight-line plots serve as a shorthand notation for outlining design approaches or developing design requirements. The straight-line plots help us use computer-aided analysis effectively because they tell us what frequency ranges are important and what features of the response need to be investigated in greater detail.

The straight-line versions of Bode plots are particularly useful when the poles and zeros are located on the real axis in the s-plane. As a starting place, consider the transfer function

$$T(s) = \frac{Ks(s+\alpha_1)}{(s+\alpha_2)(s+\alpha_3)} \qquad (12\text{–}43)$$

where K, α_1, α_2, and α_3 are real. This function has zeros at $s = 0$ and $s = -\alpha_1$, and poles at $s = -\alpha_2$ and $s = -\alpha_3$. All of these critical frequencies lie on the real axis in the s plane. When making Bode plots we put $T(j\omega)$ in a standard format obtained by factoring out α_1, α_2, and α_3:

$$T(j\omega) = \left(\frac{K\alpha_1}{\alpha_2\alpha_3}\right)\frac{j\omega(1+j\omega/\alpha_1)}{(1+j\omega/\alpha_2)(1+j\omega/\alpha_3)} \qquad (12\text{–}44)$$

Using the following notation

$$\begin{aligned}\text{Magnitude} &= M = |1+j\omega/\alpha| = \sqrt{1+(\omega/\alpha)^2}\\ \text{Angle} &= \theta = \angle(1+j\omega/\alpha) = \tan^{-1}(\omega/\alpha) \qquad (12\text{–}45)\\ \text{Scale Factor} &= K_0 = \frac{K\alpha_1}{\alpha_2\alpha_3}\end{aligned}$$

we can write the transfer function in Eq. (12–44) in the form

$$T(j\omega) = K_0\frac{(\omega\, e^{j90^\circ})\,(M_1\, e^{j\theta_1})}{(M_2\, e^{j\theta_2})\,(M_3\, e^{j\theta_3})} = \frac{|K_0|\omega M_1}{M_2M_3}\, e^{j(\angle K_0 + 90^\circ + \theta_1 - \theta_2 - \theta_3)} \qquad (12\text{–}46)$$

The gain (in dB) and phase responses are

$$\begin{aligned}|T(j\omega)|_{\text{dB}} &= \underbrace{20\log_{10}|K_0|}_{\text{Scale Factor}} + \underbrace{20\log_{10}\omega}_{\text{Zero}} + \underbrace{20\log_{10}M_1}_{\text{Zero}} - \underbrace{20\log_{10}M_2}_{\text{Pole}} - \underbrace{20\log_{10}M_3}_{\text{Pole}}\\ \theta(\omega) &= \overbrace{\angle K_0} + \overbrace{90^\circ} + \overbrace{\theta_1} - \overbrace{\theta_2} - \overbrace{\theta_3}\end{aligned} \qquad (12\text{–}47)$$

The terms in Eq. (12–47) caused by zeros have positive signs and increase the gain and phase angle, while the pole terms have negative signs and decrease the gain and phase.

The summations in Eq. (12–47) illustrate a general principle. In a Bode plot, the gain and phase responses are determined by the following types of factors:

1. The scale factor K_0
2. A factor of the form $j\omega$ due to a zero or a pole at the origin
3. Factors of the form $(1 + j\omega/\alpha)$ caused by a zero or pole at $s = -\alpha$.

We can construct Bode plots by considering the contributions of these three factors.

The Scale Factor. The gain and phase contributions of the scale factor are constants that are independent of frequency. The gain contribution $20 \log_{10} |K_0|$ is positive when $|K_0| > 1$ and negative when $|K_0| < 1$. The phase contribution $\angle K_0$ is 0° when $K_0 > 0$ and ±180° when $K_0 < 0$.

The Factor jω. A simple zero or pole at the origin contributes $\pm 20 \log_{10}\omega$ to the gain and ±90° to the phase, where the plus sign applies to a zero and the minus to a pole. When T(s) has a factor s^n in the numerator (denominator), it has a zero (pole) of order n at the origin. Multiple zeros or poles at $s = 0$ contribute $\pm 20n \log_{10} \omega$ to the gain and $\pm n90°$ to the phase. Figure 12–38 shows that the gain factors contributed by zeros and poles at the origin are straight lines that pass through a gain of 1 (0 dB) at $\omega = 1$.[4]

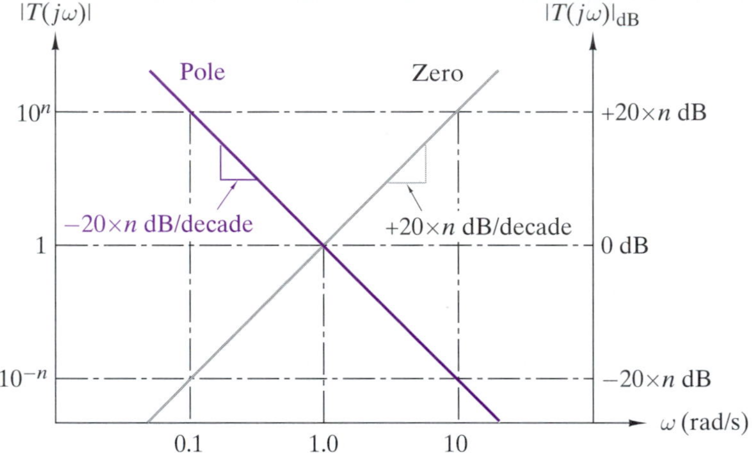

FIGURE 12–38 *Gain responses of poles and zeros at s = 0.*

The Factor $1 + j\omega/a$. The gain contributions of first-order zeros and poles are shown in Figure 12–39. Like the first-order transfer functions studied earlier in this chapter, these factors produce straight-line gain asymptotes at low and high frequency. In a Bode plot the low-frequency ($\omega << \alpha$) asymptotes are horizontal lines at with gain = 1 (0 dB). The high-frequency ($\omega >> \alpha$) asymptotes are straight lines of the form $\pm\omega/a$ ($\pm 20 \log(\omega/\alpha)$ dB), where the plus sign applies to a zero and the minus to a pole. The high-frequency gain asymptote is proportional to the frequency ω (slope = +1 or +20 dB/decade) for a zero and proportional to $1/\omega$ (slope = −1 or −20 dB/decade) for a pole. In either case, the low- and high-frequency asymptotes intersect at the corner frequency $\omega = \alpha$.

To construct straight-line (SL) gain approximations, we develop a piecewise linear function $|T(j\omega)|_{SL}$ defined by the asymptotes of each of the factor in $T(j\omega)$. The function $|T(j\omega)|_{SL}$ has a corner frequency at each of the critical frequencies of the transfer function. At frequencies below a corner ($\omega < \alpha$) a first-order factor is represented by a gain of 1. Above the corner frequency ($\omega > \alpha$) the factor is represented by its high-frequency asymptote ω/α. To generate $|T(j\omega)|_{SL}$ we start out below the lowest critical frequency with a low-frequency baseline that accounts for the scale factor K_0 and any poles or zeros at the origin. We increase frequency and change the form of $|T(j\omega)|_{SL}$ whenever we pass a corner frequency. We proceed up-

4 Strictly speaking, a circuit with a natural pole at the origin is unstable and does not have a sinusoidal steady-state response. Nevertheless, it is traditional to treat poles at the origin in Bode diagrams because there are practical applications in which such poles are important considerations.

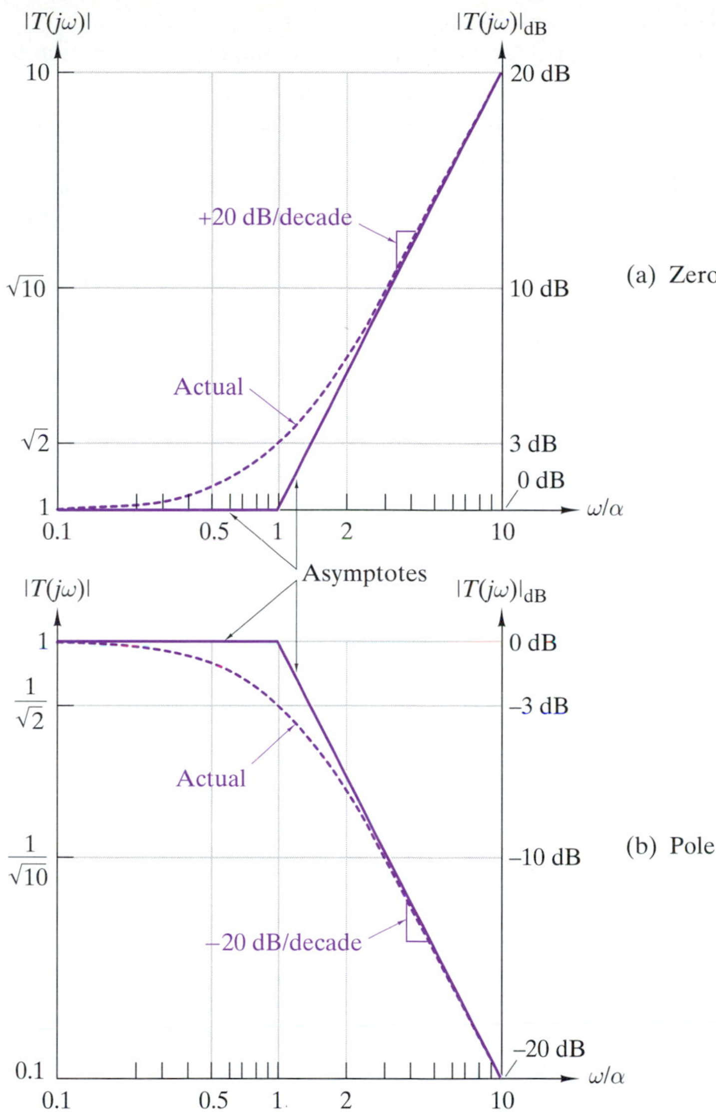

FIGURE 12–39 *Gain response of real poles and zeros.*

ward in frequency until we have gone beyond the highest critical frequency, at which point we have a complete expression for $|T(j\omega)|_{SL}$.

The following example illustrates the process.

EXAMPLE 12–15

(a) Construct the Bode plot of the straight-line approximation of the gain of the transfer function

$$T(s) = \frac{12{,}500\,(s + 10)}{(s + 50)\,(s + 500)}$$

(b) Find the point at which the high-frequency gain falls below the dc gain.

SOLUTION:

(a) Written in the standard form for a Bode plot, the transfer function is

$$T(j\omega) = \frac{5(1 + j\omega/10)}{(1 + j\omega/50)\,(1 + j\omega/500)}$$

The scale factor is $K_0 = 5$ and the corner frequencies are at $\omega_C = 10$ (zero), 50 (pole), and 500 (pole) rad/s. At low frequency ($\omega < 10$ rad/s) all of the first-order factors are represented by their low-frequency asymptotes. As a result $|T(j\omega)| \approx 5(1)/[(1)(1)] = 5$, so the low-frequency baseline is $|T(j\omega)|_{SL} = 5$ for $\omega \leq 10$. At $\omega = 10$ rad/s we encounter the first critical frequency. Beginning at this point the factor $(1 + j\omega/10)$ is represented by its high-frequency asymptote $\omega/10$ and the straight-line gain becomes $|T(j\omega)|_{SL} = 5(\omega/10) = \omega/2$. This expression applies until we pass the critical frequency at $\omega_C = 50$ due to the pole as $s = -50$. After this point the gain contribution due to the pole factor $1/(1 + j\omega/50)$ is represented by its high-frequency asymptote $\omega/50$ and $|T(j\omega)|_{SL} = 5(\omega/10)/(\omega/50) = 25$. This version applies until we pass the final critical frequency at $\omega_C = 500$ beyond which the gain contribution of last pole is approximated by $\omega/500$ and the high-frequency gain rolls off as $|T(j\omega)|_{SL} = 5(\omega/10)/[(\omega/50)(\omega/500)] = 12500/\omega$. In summary, the straight-line approximation to the gain is

$$|T(j\omega)|_{SL} = \begin{vmatrix} 5 & \text{if} & 0 < \omega \leq 10 \\ \omega/2 & \text{if} & 10 < \omega \leq 50 \\ 25 & \text{if} & 50 < \omega \leq 500 \\ 12{,}500/\omega & \text{if} & 500 < \omega \end{vmatrix}$$

Given this function, we can easily plot the straight-line gain response in Figure 12–40. At low frequency ($\omega < 10$) the gain is flat at value of 5 (14 dB). At $\omega = 10$ the zero causes the gain to increase as ω (slope = +1 or +20 dB/decade). This increasing gain continues until $\omega = 50$, where the first pole cancels the effect of the zero and the gain is flat at a value of 25 (28 dB). The gain remains flat until the final poles causes a corner at $\omega = 500$. Thereafter the gain falls off as $1/\omega$ (slope = –1 or –20 dB/decade).

(b) The dc gain is 5. A quick look at the sketch in Figure 12–40 shows that the high-frequency gain falls below the dc gain in the region above $\omega = 500$, where the straight-line gain is $12{,}500/\omega$. Hence we estimate the required frequency to be $\omega = 12{,}500/5 = 2500$ rad/s. ■

EXAMPLE 12–16

(a) Construct the Bode plot of the straight-line approximation of the gain of the transfer function:

$$T(s) = \frac{10s^2}{(s + 40)(s + 200)}$$

(b) Find the point at which the low-frequency gain falls –40 dB below the passband gain.

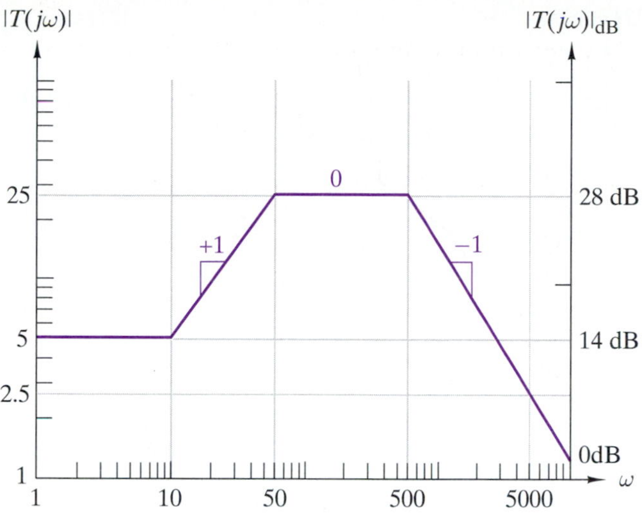

SOLUTION:

Writing $T(j\omega)$ in standard form produces

$$T(j\omega) = \frac{1}{800}\left[\frac{(j\omega)^2}{(1 + j\omega/40)(1 + j\omega/200)}\right]$$

In this form $T(j\omega)$ has a scale factor of $K_0 = 1/800$, a double zero ($n = 2$) at the origin, and finite critical frequencies at $\omega = 40$ and 200, both due to poles. At low frequency ($\omega < 40$) the two first-order factors are represented by their low-frequency asymptote. As a result, the low-frequency gain baseline is $|T(j\omega)|_{SL} = \omega^2/800$. This trend continues until we pass the critical frequency at $\omega = 40$. After this point the straight-line gain is

$$|T(j\omega)|_{SL} = (\omega^2/800)/(\omega/40) = \omega/20$$

The gain continues to increase at a reduced rate until we pass the final critical frequency at $\omega = 200$. Beyond this point the straight-line gain is constant at the high frequency of

$$|T(j\omega)|_{SL} = (\omega^2/800)/[(\omega/40)(\omega/200)] = 10$$

In summary, the straight-line approximation to the gain response is

$$|T(j\omega)|_{SL} = \begin{vmatrix} \omega^2/800 & \text{if} & 0 < \omega \leq 40 \\ \omega/20 & \text{if} & 40 < \omega \leq 200 \\ 10 & \text{if} & 200 < \omega \end{vmatrix}$$

We can easily plot the straight-line gain response shown in Figure 12–41. At low frequency ($\omega < 20$) the gain is increasing as ω^2 (slope = +2 or +40 dB/decade). This upward trend lasts until the critical frequency (a pole) at $\omega = 40$, at which point the gain is $(40)^2/800 = 2$. Thereafter the gain increases as ω (slope = +1 or +20 dB/decade) until the final critical frequency at $\omega = 200$ reduces the slope to zero at a flat gain of 10 (20 dB).

FIGURE 12–41

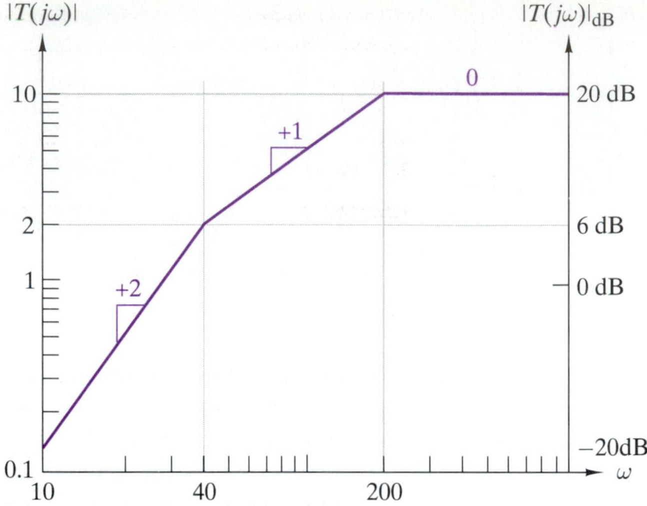

(b) A quick look at the plot in Figure 12–41 shows that the gain response has a high-pass characteristic with a passband above $\omega = 200$, where the passband gain is 20 dB. The low-frequency gain will be –40 dB below this level in the frequency range below $\omega = 40$, where the straight-line gain is $\omega^2/800$. The actual gain must be 20 dB – 40 dB = –20 dB or 0.1. This gain occurs when $\omega^2/800 = 0.1$ at $\omega = 8.9$ rad/s ■

Exercise 12–13

(a) Derive an expression for the straight-line approximation to the gain response of the following transfer function:

$$T(s) = \frac{500\,(s+50)}{(s+20)(s+500)}$$

(b) Find the straight-line gains at $\omega = 10$, 30, and 100 rad/s.
(c) Find the frequency at which the high-frequency gain asymptote falls below –20 dB.

Answers:

(a) $$|T(j\omega)|_{SL} = \begin{vmatrix} 2.5 & \text{if} & 0 < \omega \leqslant 2 \\ 50/\omega & \text{if} & 20 < \omega \leqslant 50 \\ 1 & \text{if} & 50 < \omega \leqslant 500 \\ 500/\omega & \text{if} & 500 < \omega \end{vmatrix}$$

(b) 8 dB, 4.4 dB, 0 dB
(c) 5 krad/s

Exercise 12–14

Given the following transfer function

$$T(s) = \frac{4000s}{(s+100)(s+2000)}$$

(a) Find the straight-line approximation to the gain at ω = 50, 100, 500, 2000, and 4000 rad/s.
(b) Estimate the actual gain at the frequencies in (a).

Answers:
(a) 0 dB, 6 dB, 6 dB, 6 dB, 0 dB
(b) –1 dB, 3 dB, 6 dB, 3 dB, –1 dB

In many situations the straight-line Bode plot tells us all we need to know. When greater accuracy is needed the straight-line gain plot can be refined by adding gain corrections in the neighborhood of the corner frequency. Figure 12–39 shows that the actual gains and the straight-line approximations differ by ±3 dB at the corner frequency. They differ by roughly ±1 dB an octave above or below the corner frequency. When these "corrections" are included, we can sketch the actual response and achieve somewhat greater accuracy. However, making the graphical gain corrections is usually not worth the trouble. First, the gain corrections overlap unless the corner frequencies are separated by more than two octaves. More important, the purpose of a straight-line gain analysis is to provide insight, not to generate accurate frequency-response data. The straight-line plots are useful in preliminary analysis and in the early stages of design. At some point accurate response data will be needed, in which case it is better to use computer-aided analysis rather than trying to "correct the errors" graphically in a straight-line plot.

EXAMPLE 12–17

Use computer-aided analysis to compare the actual and straight-line approximation to the gain of the transfer function in Example 12–15.

SOLUTION:

Figure 12–42 shows a Mathcad worksheet that calculates both the straight-line gain and the actual gain. In Mathcad we can write the transfer function $T(s)$ exactly as it is given in Example 12–15 and then have Mathcad calculate and plot the gain $|T(j\omega)|$. Similarly, we can use an extended conditional statement to write the straight-line gain $|T(j\omega)|_{SL}$ exactly as it appears in Example 12–15 and then have Mathcad calculate and plot this function as well. The frequency range of interest extends from one decade below the lowest critical frequency (ω = 10) to the first decade point above the highest critical frequency (ω = 500). The resulting graph shows that the straight-line gain (the solid line) is a reasonable approximation that captures the major features of the actual gain (the dashed curve). When numerical accuracy is important it is best to have a program like Mathcad calculate values of $|T(j\omega)|$ rather than try graphically to correct the plot of $|T(j\omega)|_{SL}$. ■

FIGURE 12–42

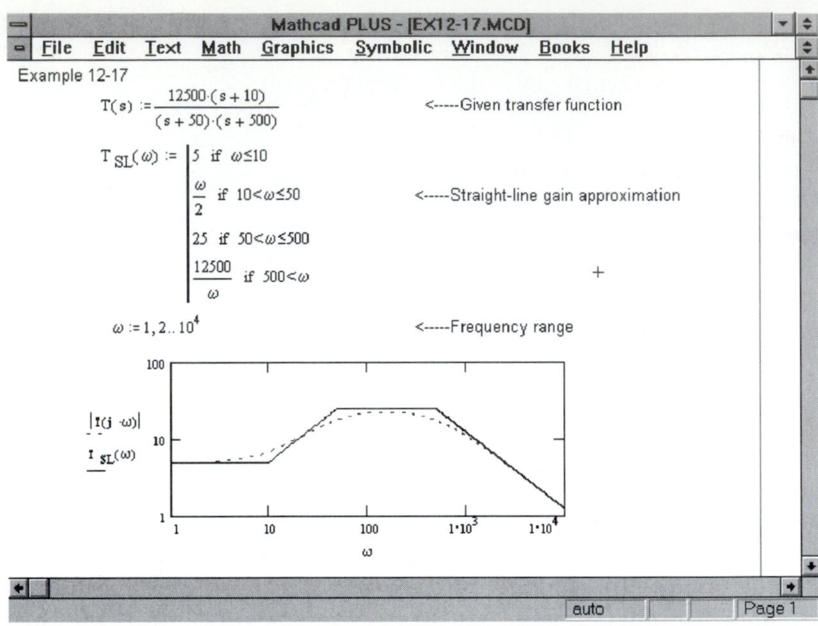

STRAIGHT-LINE PHASE ANGLE PLOTS

Figure 12–43 shows the phase contributions of first-order zeros and poles. The straight-line approximations are similar to the gain asymptotes except that there are two slope changes. The first occurs a decade below the gain corner frequency, and the second occurs a decade above. The total phase changes by 90° over this two-decade range, so the straight-line approximations have slopes of ±45° per decade, where the plus sign applies to a zero and the minus to a pole. Poles and zeros at the origin contribute a constant phase angle of $\pm n90°$, where n is the order of the critical frequency and the plus (minus) sign applies to zeros (poles).

To generate a straight-line phase plot, we begin with the low-frequency phase asymptote. This low-frequency baseline accounts for the effect of the scale factor K_0 and any poles or zeros at the origin. We account for the effect of other critical frequencies by introducing a slope change of ±45°/decade one decade below and one decade above each gain corner frequency. These slope changes generate a straight-line phase plot as we proceed from the low-frequency baseline to a high frequency that is at least a decade above the highest gain corner frequency.

It is important to remember that a decade above the highest corner frequency the phase asymptote is a constant value with zero slope. That is, at high frequency the straight-line phase plot is a horizontal line at $\theta(j\omega) = (m - n)90°$, where m is the number of finite zeros and n is the number of poles.

EXAMPLE 12–18

Find the straight-line approximation to the phase response of the transfer function in Example 12–15.

FIGURE 12-43 *Phase response of real poles and zeros.*

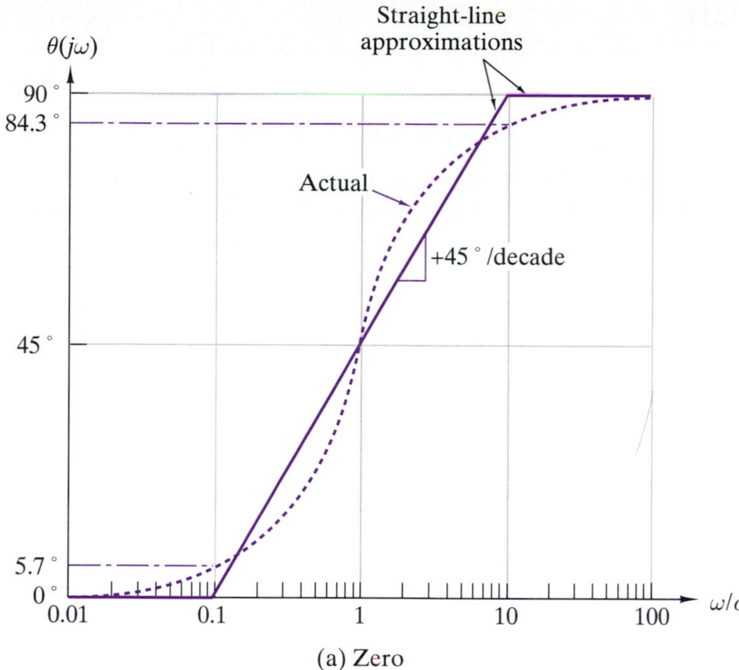

(a) Zero

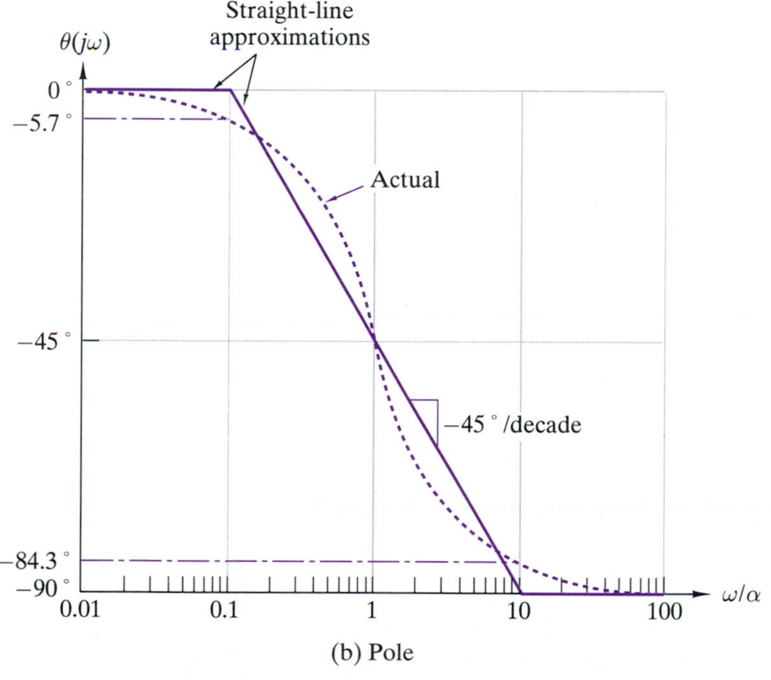

(b) Pole

SOLUTION:

In Example 12–15 the standard from of $T(j\omega)$ is shown to be

$$T(j\omega) = \frac{5(1 + j\omega/10)}{(1 + j\omega/50)(1 + j\omega/500)}$$

The scale factor is $K_0 = 5$ and the corner frequencies are $\omega_C = 10$ (zero), 50 (pole), and 500 (pole) rad/s. At low frequency $T(j\omega) \to K_0 = 5$, so the low-frequency phase asymptote is $\theta(\omega) \to \angle K_0 = 0°$. Proceeding from one decade below the lowest corner frequency (1 rad/s) to one decade above the highest corner frequency (5000 rad/s), we encounter the following slope changes:

FREQUENCY	CAUSED BY	SLOPE CHANGE	NET SLOPE
1	zero at $s = -10$	+45°/decade	+45°/decade
5	pole at $s = -50$	–45°/decade	0°/decade
50	pole at $s = -500$	–45°/decade	–45°/decade
100	zero at s = –10	–45°/decade	–90°/decade
500	pole at $s = -50$	+45°/decade	–45°/decade
5000	pole at $s = -500$	+45°/decade	0°/decade

Figure 12–44 shows the straight-line approximation and the actual phase response. ■

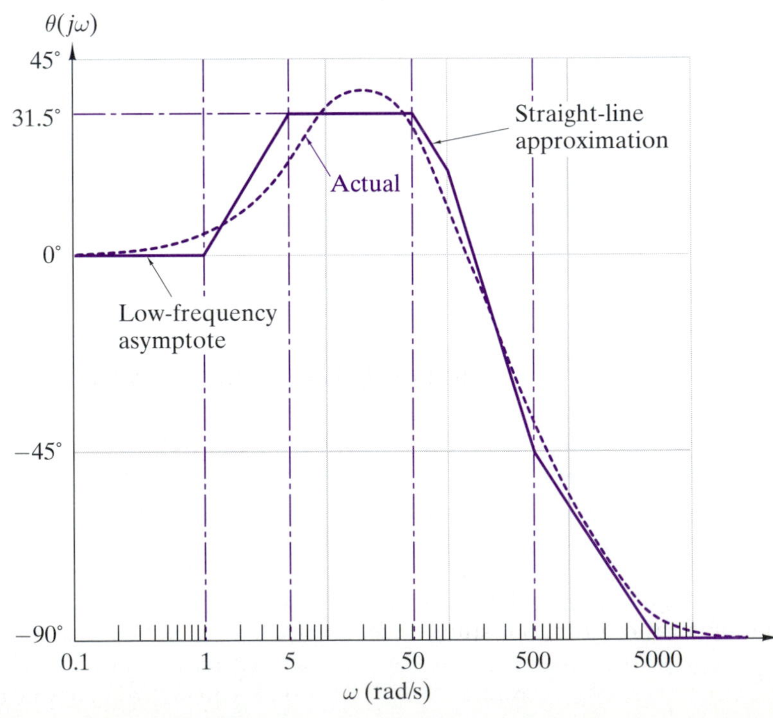

Exercise 12–15

Construct a Bode plot of the straight-line approximation to the phase response of the transfer function in Exercise 12–13. Use the plot to estimate the phase angles at $\omega = 1, 15, 300$, and 10^4 rad/s.

Answers: 0°, –18°, –45°, –90°

12–6 BODE DIAGRAMS WITH COMPLEX CRITICAL FREQUENCIES

The frequency response of transfer functions with complex poles and zeros can be analyzed using straight-line gain plots. However, complex critical frequencies may produce resonant peaks (or valleys) where the actual gain response departs significantly from the straight-line approximation. Straight-line plots can be used to define a starting place for describing the frequency response of these highly resonant circuits.

Complex poles and zeros occur in conjugate pairs that appear as quadratic factors of the form

$$s^2 + 2\zeta\omega_0 s + \omega_0^2 \tag{12–48}$$

where ζ and ω_0 are the damping ratio and undamped natural frequency. In a Bode diagram the appropriate standard form of the quadratic factor is obtained by factoring out ω_0^2 and replacing s by $j\omega$ to obtain

$$1 - (\omega/\omega_0)^2 + j2\zeta(\omega/\omega_0) \tag{12–49}$$

In a Bode diagram this quadratic factor introduces gain and phase terms of the following form:

$$|T(j\omega)|_{\text{dB}} = \pm\, 20\log_{10}\sqrt{[1-(\omega/\omega_0)^2]^2 + (2\zeta\omega/\omega_0)^2} \tag{12–50a}$$

$$\theta(\omega) = \pm\tan^{-1}\frac{2\zeta\omega/\omega_0}{1-(\omega/\omega_0)^2} \tag{12–50b}$$

where the plus sign applies to complex zeros of $T(s)$ and the minus sign to complex poles.

Figure 12–45 shows the gain contribution of complex poles and zeros for several values of the damping ratio ζ. The low-frequency ($\omega << \omega_0$) asymptotes for these plots is a gain of unity (0 dB). The high-frequency ($\omega >> \omega_0$) gain asymptotes are of the form $(\omega/\omega_0)^{\pm 2}$. Expressed in dB the high-frequency asymptote is $\pm 40\log_{10}(\omega/\omega_0)$, which in a Bode diagram is a straight line with a slope of ±2 or ±40 dB/decade, where again the plus sign applies to zeros and the minus to poles.

These asymptotes intersect at a corner frequency of $\omega_C = \omega_0$. The gains in the neighborhood of the corner frequency are strong functions of the damping ratio. From our study of second-order low pass transfer functions we can infer the following. For $\zeta > 1/\sqrt{2}$ the actual gain lies entirely above the asymptotes for complex zeros and entirely below for complex poles.

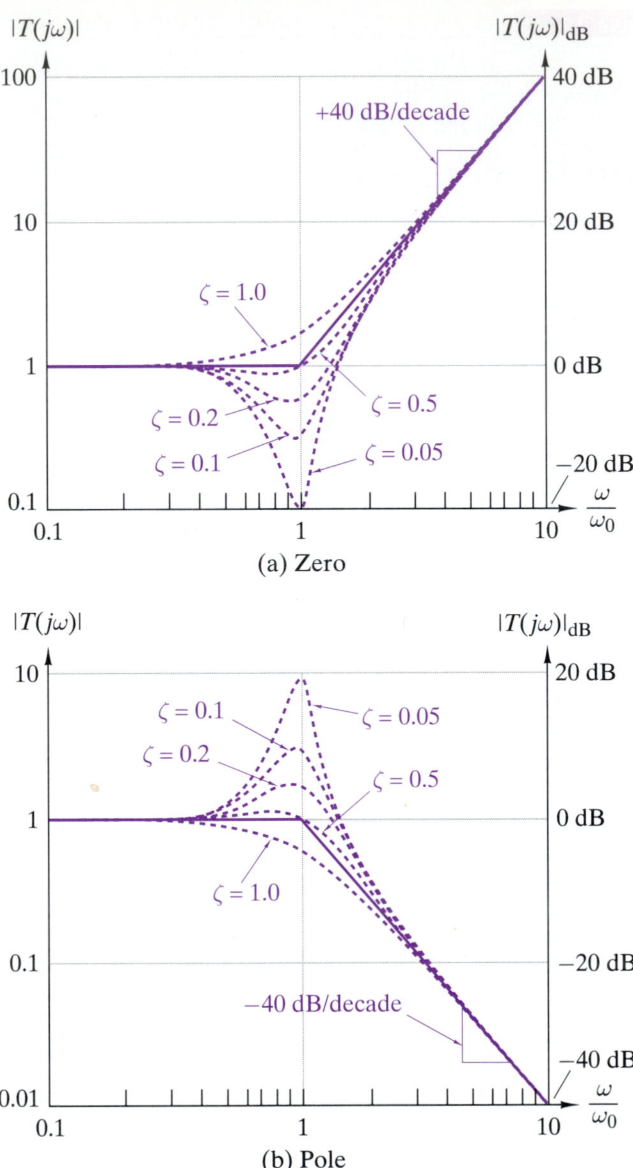

FIGURE 12–45 *Gain response of complex poles and zeros.*

For $\zeta < 1/\sqrt{2}$ the gain is a minimum at $\omega = \omega_0\sqrt{1 - 2\zeta^2}$ for complex zeros and a maximum for complex poles. These valleys (for zeros) and peaks (for poles) are not particularly conspicuous until $\zeta < 0.5$.

To develop a straight-line gain plot for complex critical frequencies we insert a corner frequency at $\omega = \omega_0$. Below this corner frequency we use the low-frequency asymptote to approximate the gain and above the corner we use the high-frequency asymptote. The actual gain around the corner frequency depends on ζ. But generally speaking, the straight-line gain is within ±3 dB of the actual gain for ζ in the range from about 0.3 to about 0.7. When ζ falls outside this range we can calculate the actual gain at the corner frequency and perhaps a few points on either side of the corner frequency. These gains may give us a better picture of the gain plot in the vicinity of the corner frequency.

However, we should keep in mind that the purpose of straight-line gain analysis is insight into the major features of a circuit's frequency response. If greater accuracy is required, then computer-aided analysis is the best approach. The straight-line gain gives useful results when the resonant peaks and valleys are not too abrupt. When a circuit has lightly damped critical frequencies, the straight-line approach may not be particularly helpful. The following examples illustrate both of these cases.

EXAMPLE 12–19

(a) Construct the straight-line gain plot for the transfer function

$$T(s) = \frac{5000(s + 100)}{s^2 + 400s + (500)^2}$$

(b) Use the straight-line plot to estimate the maximum gain and the frequency at which it occurs.

SOLUTION:

(a) The transfer function has a real zero at $s = -100$ rad/s and a pair of complex poles with $\zeta = 0.4$ and $\omega_0 = 500$ rad/s. This damping ratio falls in the range (0.3 to 0.7) in which the resonant peak due to the complex poles is not too pronounced. Hence we expect the straight-line gain to give a useful approximation. Written in standard form, $T(j\omega)$ is

$$T(j\omega) = 2\left(\frac{1 + j\omega/100}{1 - (\omega/500)^2 + j400\omega/500}\right)$$

The scale factor is $K_0 = 2$, and there are corner frequencies at $\omega =$ 100 rad/s due to the zero and $\omega = 500$ rad/s due to the pair of complex poles. At low frequency $T(j\omega) \to 2$, so the low-frequency ($\omega < 100$) baseline is $|T(j\omega)|_{SL} = 2$. This gain applies until we pass the first critical frequency at $\omega = 100$. Beginning at that point, the zero is represented by its high-frequency asymptote ($\omega/100$) and the straight-line gain becomes

$$|T(j\omega)|_{SL} = 2(\omega/100) = \omega/50$$

This linearly increasing gain applies until we pass the critical frequency at $\omega_0 = 500$. Thereafter the complex poles are represented by their high-frequency asymptote ($500^2/\omega^2$). After this point the gain rolls off as

$$|T(j\omega)|_{SL} = 2(\omega/100)(500^2/\omega^2) = 5000/\omega$$

In summary, the straight-line gain function is

$$|T(j\omega)|_{SL} = \begin{vmatrix} 2 & \text{if} & 0 < \omega \leq 100 \\ \omega/50 & \text{if} & 100 < \omega \leq 500 \\ 5000/\omega & \text{if} & 500 < \omega \end{vmatrix}$$

Figure 12–46 shows a plot of the straight-line gain. We expect to see a gain peak around $\omega = 500$ rad/s due to the complex poles. The plot in Figure 12–46 shows that the zero at $s = -100$ rad/s causes the gain to bend upward prior to the corner frequency at $\omega = 500$ rad/s. This upward bend enhances the height of the resonant peak caused by the complex poles.

FIGURE 12–46

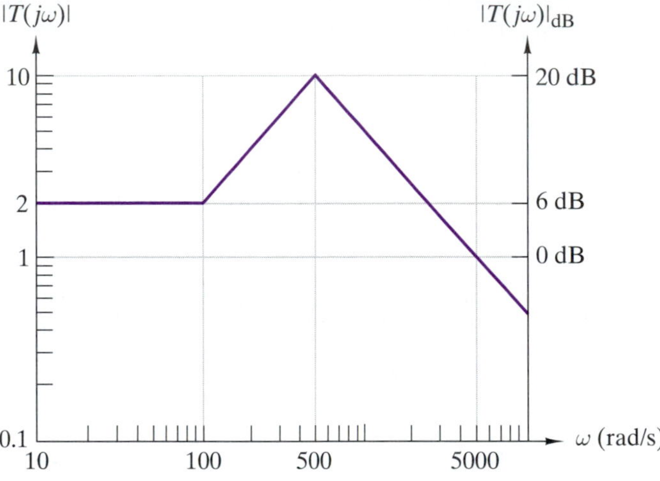

(b) The straight-line gain predicts a maximum gain of 10 (20 dB) at $\omega = 500$ rad/s. The actual gain at that point is

$$|T(j500)| = 2\left|\frac{1 + j5}{j0.8}\right| = 12.7 \text{ (22 dB)}$$

In this case the straight-line plot gives us a useful approximation of the gain in the vicinity of the resonant peak. ■

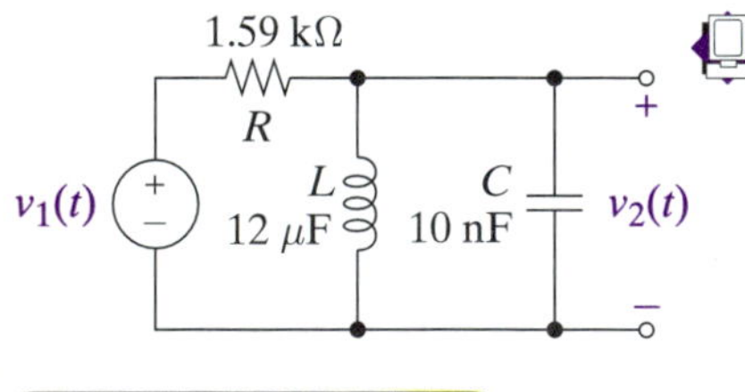

FIGURE 12–47

EXAMPLE 12–20

Calculate straight-line and the actual gain response of the *RLC* circuit shown in Figure 12–47.

SOLUTION:

The analysis of this circuit is in Example 12–9, where its transfer function is shown to be

$$T(s) = \frac{s/RC}{s^2 + s/RC + 1/LC}$$

This is a second-order bandpass transfer function with a center frequency at $\omega_0 = 1/\sqrt{LC}$. The appropriate standard form for straight-line gain analysis is

$$|T(j\omega)| = \left|\frac{j\omega L/R}{1 - LC\omega^2 + j\omega L/R}\right|$$

At low frequency ($\omega << \omega_0$) the gain asymptote is $\omega L/R$. At high frequency ($\omega >> \omega_0$) the gain asymptote is $1/\omega RC$. These asymptotes intersect when $\omega L/R = 1/\omega RC$, which occurs at $\omega^2 = 1/LC$; that is, at the center frequency $\omega_0 = 1/\sqrt{LC}$. The straight-line gain for this circuit is

$$|T(j\omega)|_{SL} = \begin{vmatrix} \omega L/R & \text{if} \quad 0 < \omega \leq \omega_0 \\ 1/\omega RC & \text{if} \quad \omega_0 < \omega \end{vmatrix}$$

Figure 12–48 shows a Mathcad worksheet that includes the circuit parameters, the circuit transfer function, the straight-line gain function, and a frequency range from a decade below to a decade above the center frequency. The Mathcad worksheet includes a plot of the actual gain (the dashed curve) and the straight-line gain (the solid lines). In this case the straight-line gain plot indicates a bandpass response but does not tell us the bandwidth.

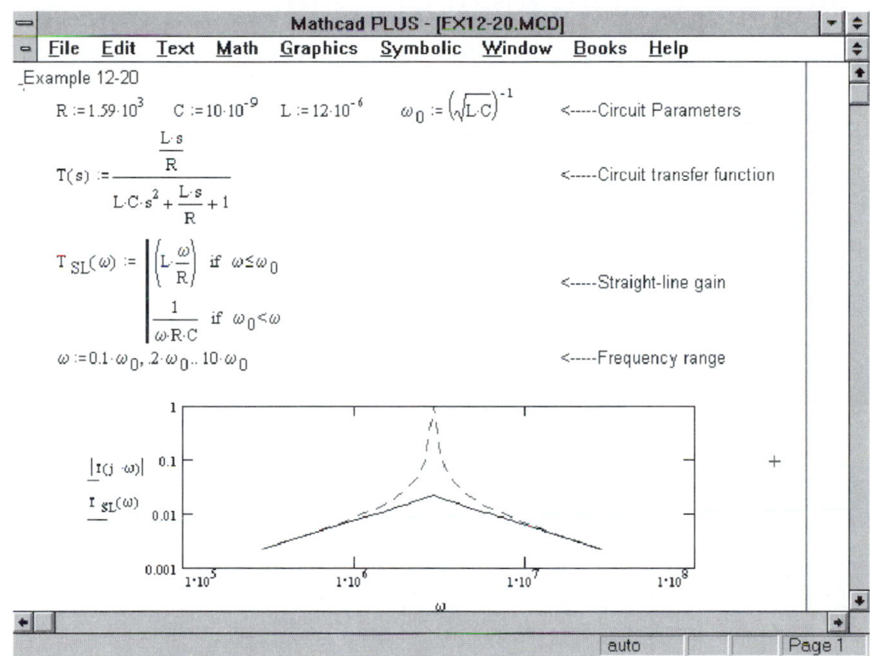

FIGURE 12–48

In Example 12–9 the circuit element values used are selected to produce a center frequency at 455 kHz and a bandwidth of 10 kHz. The damping ratio of this circuit is

$$\zeta = \frac{BW}{2\omega_0} = \frac{10 \times 10^3}{2 \times 455 \times 10^3} = 0.011$$

Since $\zeta << 0.5$, the circuit has a very narrow resonant peak at 455 kHz. For highly resonant circuits like this one the straight-line gain is not particularly helpful. ■

Exercise 12–16

(a) Construct the straight-line gain function for the transfer function

$$T(s) = \frac{10^5}{[s^2 + 100s + 10^4](s + 10)}$$

(b) Find the straight-line gain at ω = 1, 10, 100, 1000 rad/s.

Answers:

(a) $$|T(j\omega)|_{SL} = \begin{vmatrix} 1 & \text{if} & 0 < \omega < 10 \\ 10/\omega & \text{if} & 10 < \omega \leq 100 \\ 10^5/\omega^3 & \text{if} & 100 < \omega \end{vmatrix}$$

(b) 0 dB, 0 dB, –20 dB, –80 dB

PHASE PLOTS FOR COMPLEX CRITICAL FREQUENCIES

Figure 12–49 shows the phase contribution from complex poles or zeros for several values of ζ. The low-frequency phase asymptotes are 0° and the high-frequency limits are ±180°. The phase is always ±90° at $\omega = \omega_0$ regardless of the value of the damping ratio. The total phase change is ±180°, and most of this change occurs in a two-decade range from $\omega_0/10$ to $10\omega_0$. As a result, the straight lines in Figure 12–49 offer crude approximations to the phase shift. The shape of the phase curves change radically with the damping ratio, so these straight-line approximations are of little use except at ω_0 and around the end points.

The net result is that phase angle plots for complex critical frequencies are best generated by computer-aided analysis. In practical applications we can often derive useful information from the gain plot alone without generating phase response. However, the converse is not true. When we need phase response we usually need gain as well. The next example shows how to obtain both using a computer-aided analysis tool.

EXAMPLE 12–21

Plot the gain and phase response of the transfer function

$$T(s) = \frac{5000(s + 100)}{s^2 + 400s + (500)^2}$$

SOLUTION:

The straight-line gain plot for this transfer function is found in Example 12–19. The function has a zero at s = –100 rad/s and a pair of complex poles with ζ = 0.4 and ω_0 = 500 rad/s. Written in standard form, $T(j\omega)$ is

$$T(j\omega) = 2\left(\frac{1 + j\omega/100}{1 - (\omega/500)^2 + j0.8\omega/500}\right)$$

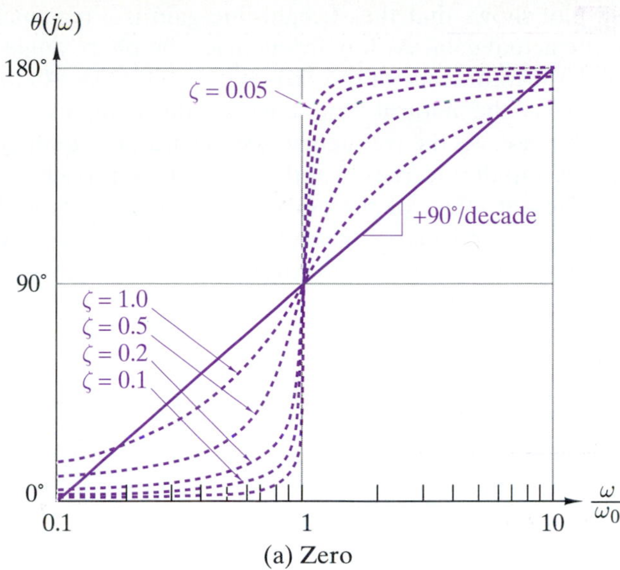

(a) Zero

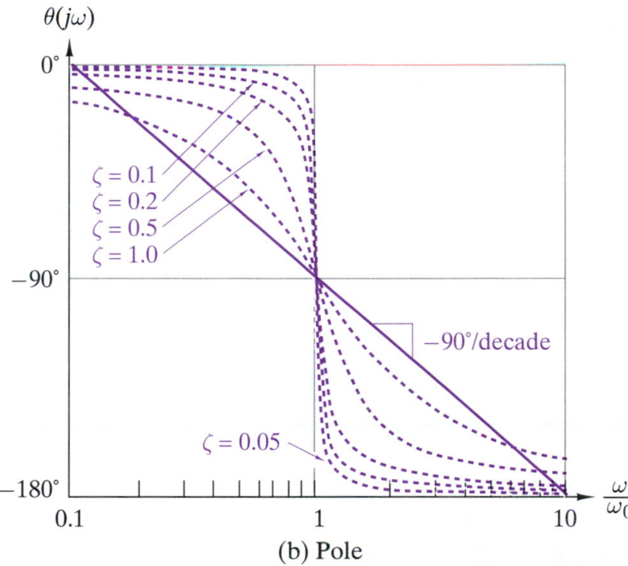

(b) Pole

FIGURE 12–49 *Phase response of complex poles and zeros.*

The analytical expressions for the gain and phase of $T(j\omega)$ are

$$|T(j\omega)| = 2\sqrt{\frac{1 + (\omega/100)^2}{\{1 - (\omega/500)^2\}^2 + (0.8\omega/500)^2}}$$

$$\theta(\omega) = +\tan^{-1}(\omega/100) - \tan^{-1}\left(\frac{0.8\omega/500}{1 - (\omega/500)^2}\right)$$

Figure 12–50 shows a Quattro Pro spreadsheet that uses these expressions to calculate and plot the gain and phase responses (the dashed curves) on a frequency range from 10 rad/s to 10 krad/s. For comparison the spreadsheet also calculates the straight-line gain (the solid line) found in Example

12–19. The gain plot shows that the straight-line gain is a reasonable approximation to the actual gain. At low frequencies the phase angle gradually increases under the influence of the zero at $s = -100$ rad/s. As the input frequency approaches the natural frequency of the complex poles the phase begins to decrease. As the frequency passes natural frequency at $\omega = 500$ rad/s the phase rapidly decreases and eventually approaches –90° at high frequency. The net effect of the zero and the two poles is that the phase initially increases and then decreases as the poles come into play. The result is that the phase has a maximum of about 42° at around 200 rad/s. ■

FIGURE 12–50

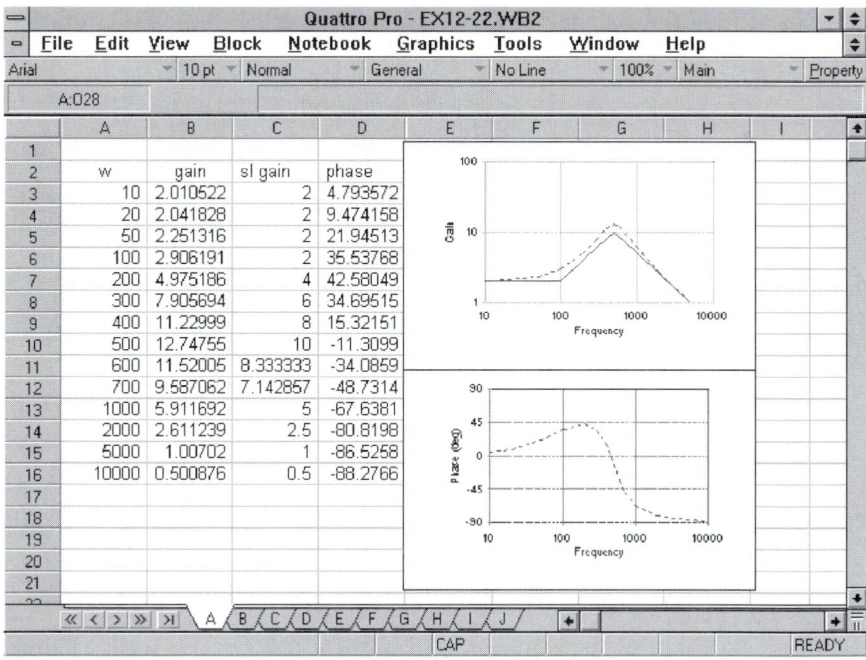

Quattro Pro - EX12-22.WB2

w	gain	sl gain	phase
10	2.010522	2	4.793572
20	2.041828	2	9.474158
50	2.251316	2	21.94513
100	2.906191	2	35.53768
200	4.975186	4	42.58049
300	7.905694	6	34.69515
400	11.22999	8	15.32151
500	12.74755	10	-11.3099
600	11.52005	8.333333	-34.0859
700	9.587062	7.142857	-48.7314
1000	5.911692	5	-67.6381
2000	2.611239	2.5	-80.8198
5000	1.00702	1	-86.5258
10000	0.500876	0.5	-88.2766

12–7 FREQUENCY RESPONSE AND STEP RESPONSE

Frequency response and time-domain step response are often used to describe the performance of devices, circuits, and systems. In Chapter 11 we found that a transfer function contains all of the data needed to construct the step response as $g(t) = \mathscr{L}^{-1}\{T(s)/s\}$. In this chapter we showed that a transfer function also gives us the frequency response in the form of gain $|T(j\omega)|$ and phase $\angle T(j\omega)$. This section explores the relationship between the step response of a circuit and its frequency response.

To begin we show that the end point of the step response and the end points of the gain response are related. Since $G(s) = T(s)/s$, applying the initial and final value properties from Chapter 9 reveals that

$$\text{Initial Value: } \lim_{t\to 0} g(t) = \lim_{s\to\infty} sG(s) = \lim_{s\to\infty} T(s)$$

$$\text{Final Value: } \lim_{t\to\infty} g(t) = \lim_{s\to 0} sG(s) = \lim_{s\to 0} T(s) \qquad (12\text{–}51)$$

or, more succinctly,

$$g(0) = T(\infty) \quad \text{and} \quad g(\infty) = T(0) \qquad (12\text{–}52)$$

But the quantities $T(0)$ and $T(\infty)$ are the dc gain and the infinite frequency gain, respectively. The dc gain gives us the final value of the step response, which is nothing more than the dc steady-state response. Regarding the initial value of $g(t)$, we need to remember that the step response is a zero-state response. Hence the initial value $g(0)$ is zero unless the application of a step input causes the output to have a jump discontinuity at $t = 0$. What Eq. (12–52) points out is that we can tell whether or not a jump will occur by looking at the infinite frequency gain of the circuit. In the laboratory we cannot actually measure infinite frequency gain, so we look at the high-frequency gain, where high frequency means values beyond the highest critical frequency in $T(s)$.

Using these observations, we can construct a table listing the step response end points for each of the prototype frequency responses:

Type of Response	Step Response at $t = \infty$	$t = 0$
Low Pass	Finite	0
High Pass	0	Finite
Bandpass	0	0
Bandstop	Finite	Finite

Since each prototype has a unique pattern, we can predict the type of frequency response by examining the end points of its step response. Conversely, given the type of frequency response, we can predict the end points of the step response.

The correlations between the end points of gain response and step response provide insight into the relationship between time and frequency responses. If we have the frequency response of a circuit and we want to learn about the late-time characteristics of its step response (including the final value), then we must examine the circuit's low-frequency characteristics. Conversely, if we want to learn about the early-time characteristics of the step response (including the initial value), then we must examine the high-frequency characteristics of the circuit. The reciprocal relationship between time- and frequency-domain characteristics is an important idea in developing an understanding of circuits and signals.

But the larger question is can we go beyond the end points and predict the entire waveform $g(t)$ from the gain response $|T(j\omega)|$, or vice versa. The answer is yes, provided we can determine the circuit transfer function from the given response. The transfer function serves as an intermediary that allows us to calculate the response due to any input, including the step response and gain response. It is important to be able to go from time-domain to frequency-domain characteristics since design requirements are sometimes specified in both domains.

The following examples illustrate the process of going between frequency response and step response.

EXAMPLE 12–22

Find the time at which the step response corresponding to the straight-line gain response in Figure 12–51 is within 10% of its final value.

FIGURE 12–51

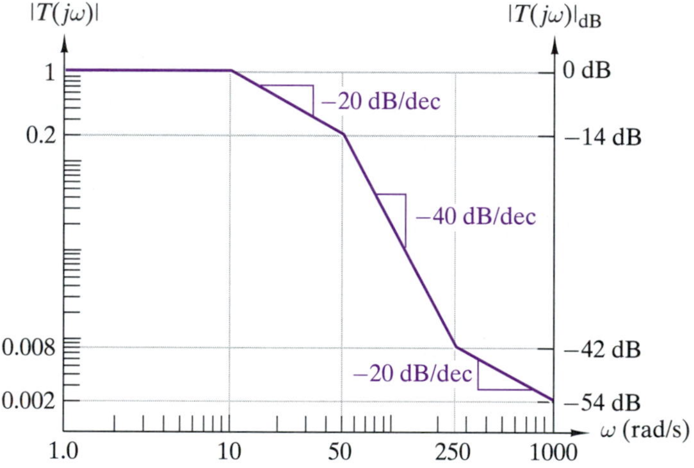

SOLUTION:

The gain plot shows corner frequencies at $\omega = 10$, 50, and 250 rad/s. The following observations determine whether the critical frequencies are poles or zeros:

- The gain slope between $\omega = 10$ and 50 is $m = (-14 - 0)/(\log 50 - \log 10) = -20$ dB/decade, so the critical frequency at $\omega = 10$ is a pole.
- The slope between $\omega = 50$ and 250 is $m = [-42 - (-14)]/(\log 250 - \log 50) = -40$ dB/dec, so the critical frequency at $\omega = 50$ is a pole.
- The gain slope between $\omega = 250$ and 1000 is $m = [-54 - (-42)]/(\log 1000 - \log 250) = -20$ dB/dec, so the critical frequency at $\omega = 250$ is a zero.

Combining these observations, the transfer function must have the form

$$T(s) = \frac{K(s + 250)}{(s + 10)(s + 50)}$$

The dc gain of this transfer function is $T(0) = K/2$. The dc gain in Figure 12–51 is 1, hence $K = 2$. Given $T(s)$, we write the transform of the step response as

$$G(s) = \frac{2(s+250)}{s(s+10)(s+50)}$$

Expanding $G(s)$ by partial fractions yields

$$G(s) = \frac{1}{s} - \frac{48/40}{s+10} + \frac{4/20}{s+50}$$

The inverse Laplace transformation produces the step response waveform as

$$g(t) = [1 - 1.2\,e^{-10t} + 0.2e^{-50t}]u(t)$$

The dc gain in Figure 12–51 is 1; hence the final value of the step response is 1. The exponential term $1.2e^{-10t}$ dominates the late-time step response since the term $0.2e^{-50t}$ is smaller in amplitude and decays five times as fast. Hence the step response will be within 10% of its final value when $1.2e^{-10t} = 0.1$ or $t = 248$ ms. ■

EXAMPLE 12–23

The step response of a circuit is

$$g(t) = 2[e^{-500t}\sin(2000t)]u(t)$$

Describe the frequency response of the circuit, including bandwidth, cutoff frequencies, and passband gain.

SOLUTION:

The circuit transfer function is

$$T(s) = sG(s) = s\mathscr{L}\{g(t)\} = \frac{4000s}{(s+500)^2 + 2000^2}$$

$$= \frac{4000s}{s^2 + 1000\,s + 4.25 \times 10^6}$$

This is a second-order bandpass response with $K = 4000$, $\omega_0 = 2.06$ krad/s, and $\zeta = 0.242$. The descriptive parameters of the gain response are obtained using Eqs. (12–19), (12–24), and (12–26).

$$|T(j\omega)|_{\mathrm{MAX}} = \frac{K}{2\zeta\omega_0} = 4$$

$$B = 2\zeta\omega_0 = 1000 \text{ rad/s}$$

$$\omega_{C1} = \omega_0(-\zeta + \sqrt{1+\zeta^2}) = 1.62 \text{ krad/s}$$

$$\omega_{C2} = \omega_0(+\zeta + \sqrt{1+\zeta^2}) = 2.62 \text{ krad/s}$$

■

SUMMARY

- The frequency response of a circuit is the variation of the gain $|T(j\omega)|$ and phase $\angle T(j\omega)$ with frequency. The gain function is usually expressed in dB in frequency-response plots. Logarithmic frequency scales are used on frequency-response plots of the gain and phase functions.
- A passband is a range of frequencies over which the steady-state output is essentially constant with very little attenuation. A stopband is a range of frequencies over which the steady-state output is significantly attenuated. The cutoff frequency is the boundary between a passband and the adjacent stopband.
- Circuit gain responses are classified as low pass, high pass, bandpass, and bandstop depending on the number and location of the stop and passbands. The performance of devices and circuits is often specified in terms of frequency-response descriptors such as bandwidth, passband gain, and cutoff frequency.
- The low- and high-frequency gain asymptotes of a first-order circuit intersect at a corner frequency determined by the location of its pole. The total phase change from low to high frequency is $\pm 90^\circ$. First-order circuits can be connected to produce bandpass and bandstop responses.
- The low- and high-frequency gain asymptotes of second-order circuits intersect at a corner frequency determined by the natural frequency of the poles. The total phase change from low to high frequency is 180°. Second-order circuits with complex critical frequencies may exhibit narrow resonant peaks and valleys.
- Series and parallel *RLC* circuits provide bandpass and bandstop gain characteristics that are easily related to the circuit parameters.
- Bode plots are graphs of the gain (in dB) and phase angle (in degrees) versus log-frequency scales. Straight-line approximations to the gain and phase can be constructed using the corner frequencies defined by the poles and zeros of $T(s)$. The purpose of the straight-line approximations is to develop a conceptual understanding of frequency response. The straight-line plots do not necessarily provide accurate data at all frequencies, especially for circuits with complex poles.
- Computer-aided circuit analysis programs can accurately generate and plot frequency-response data. The user must have a rough idea of the gain and frequency ranges of interest to use these tools intelligently.
- The equations $g(0) = T(\infty)$ and $g(\infty) = T(0)$ relate the end points of the step response and frequency response of a circuit.

EN ROUTE OBJECTIVES AND ASSOCIATED PROBLEMS

ERO 12–1 FIRST-ORDER CIRCUIT FREQUENCY RESPONSE (SECTS. 12–1, 12–2)

Given a first-order linear circuit or its transfer function,

(a) Determine frequency-response descriptors and classify the circuit response.
(b) Draw the straight-line approximations of the gain and phase responses.
(c) Use the straight-line approximations to calculate the steady-state output for a specified input.
(d) Select circuit parameters to produce specified descriptors.

12–1 **(a)** Find the transfer function $T_V(s) = V_2(s)/V_1(s)$ for the RL circuit in Figure P12–1.
(b) Determine the dc gain, infinite frequency gain, and the cutoff frequency ω_C. Is the gain response low pass, high pass, or bandpass?
(c) Draw the straight-line approximations of the gain and phase of $T_V(j\omega)$.
(d) Use the straight-line approximations to calculate the gain at $\omega = 0.5\omega_C$, ω_C, and $2\omega_C$. Compare these straight-line gains to the actual value of $|T_V(j\omega)|$ at the same frequencies.

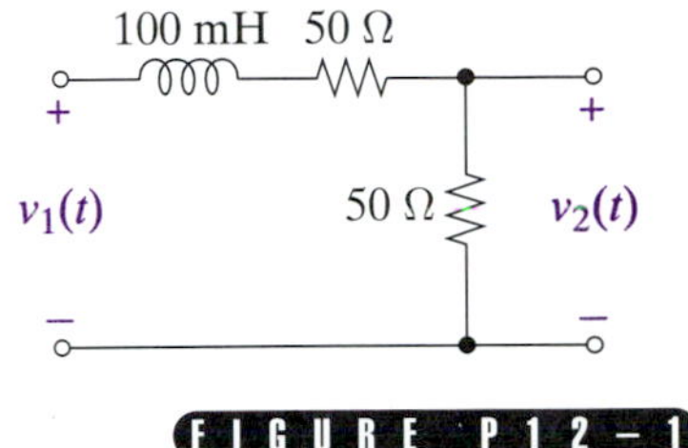

FIGURE P12–1

12–2 **(a)** Find the transfer function $T_V(s) = V_2(s)/V_1(s)$ for the RL circuit in Figure P12–2.
(b) Determine the dc gain, infinite frequency gain, and the cutoff frequency ω_C. Is the gain response low pass, high pass, or bandpass?
(c) Draw the straight-line approximations of the gain and phase of $T_V(j\omega)$.
(d) Use the straight-line approximations to calculate the gain at $\omega = 0.5\omega_C$, ω_C, and $2\omega_C$. Compare these straight-line gains to the actual value of $|T_V(j\omega)|$ at the same frequencies.

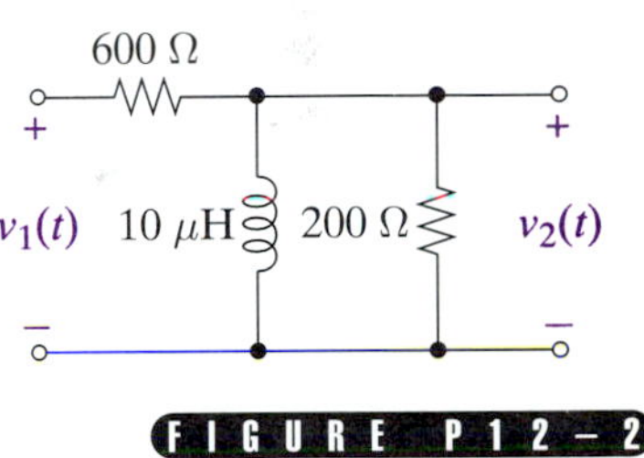

FIGURE P12–2

12–3 **(a)** Find the transfer function $T_V(s) = V_2(s)/V_1(s)$ for the RC OP AMP circuit in Figure P12–3.
(b) Determine the dc gain, infinite frequency gain, and the cutoff frequency ω_C. Is the gain response low pass, high pass, or bandpass?
(c) Draw the straight-line approximations of the gain and phase of $T_V(j\omega)$.
(d) Use the straight-line approximations to calculate the gain at $\omega = 0.5\omega_C$, ω_C, and $2\omega_C$. Compare these straight-line gains to the actual value of $|T_V(j\omega)|$ at the same frequencies.

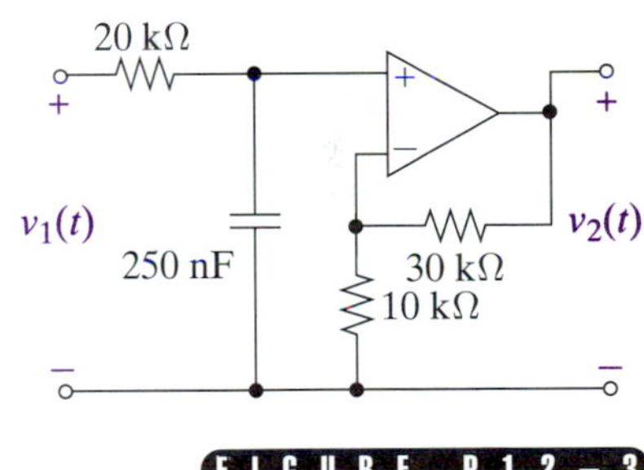

FIGURE P12–3

12–4 **(a)** Find the transfer function $T_V(s) = V_2(s)/V_1(s)$ for the RC OP AMP circuit in Figure P12–4.
(b) Determine the dc gain, infinite frequency gain, and the cutoff frequency ω_C. Is the gain response low pass, high pass, or bandpass?
(c) Draw the straight-line approximations of the gain and phase of $T_V(j\omega)$.
(d) Use the straight-line approximations to calculate the gain at $\omega = 0.5\omega_C$, ω_C, and $2\omega_C$. Compare these straight-line gains to the actual value of $|T_V(j\omega)|$ at the same frequencies.

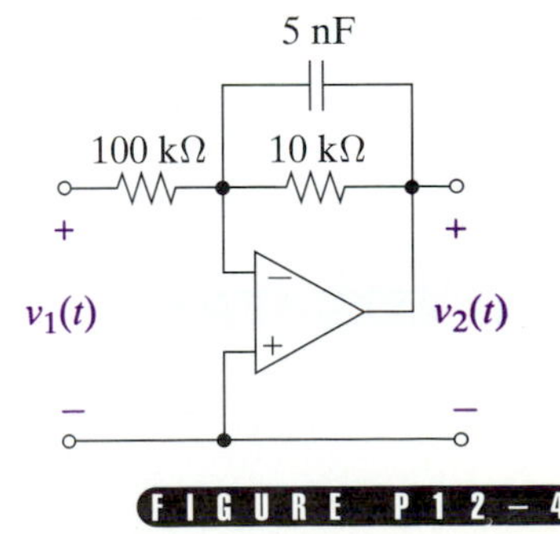

FIGURE P12–4

12–5 **(a)** Find the transfer function $T_V(s) = V_2(s)/V_1(s)$ for the *RC* OP AMP circuit in Figure P12–5.

FIGURE P12–5

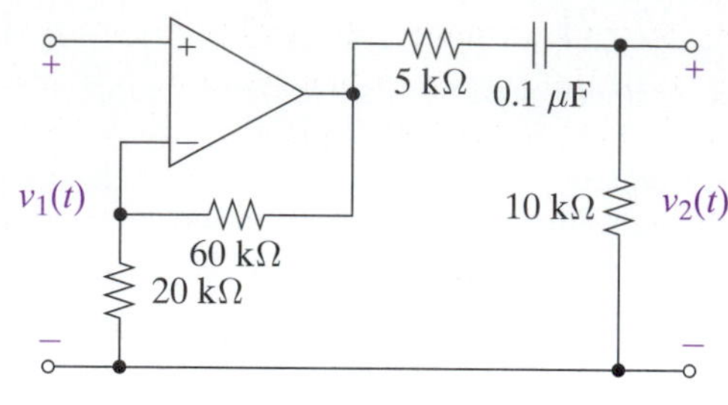

(b) Determine the dc gain, infinite frequency gain, and the cutoff frequency ω_C. Is the gain response low pass, high pass, or bandpass?

(c) Draw the straight-line approximations of the gain and phase of $T_V(j\omega)$.

(d) Use the straight-line approximations to calculate the gain at $\omega = 0.5\omega_C$, ω_C, and $2\omega_C$. Compare these straight-line gains to the actual value of $|T_V(j\omega)|$ at the same frequencies.

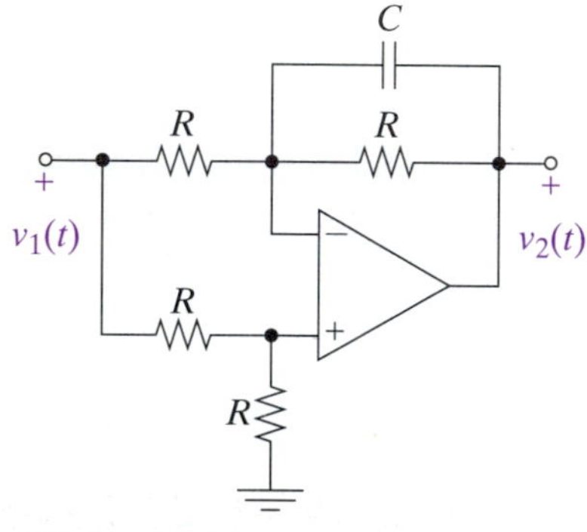

FIGURE P12–6

12–6 Determine the dc and infinite frequency gain of the circuit in Figure P12–6. Is this a low-pass, bandpass, or high-pass circuit? Derive expressions for the passband gain and the cutoff frequency in terms of *R* and *C*. Select values of *R* and *C* to produce a cutoff frequency of 20 rad/s.

12–7 The circuit in Figure P12–7 is a small-signal model of a transistor circuit. Determine the gain of $T_V(s) = V_2(s)/V_1(s)$ at $\omega = 0$ and $\omega = \infty$. Is this a low-pass, bandpass, or high-pass circuit? What are the passband gain and the cutoff frequency for $R_S = 1$ kΩ, $R_g = 500$ kΩ, $R_O = 10$ kΩ, $R_L = 5$ kΩ, $C_L = 5$ pF, and $\beta = 100$?

FIGURE P12–7

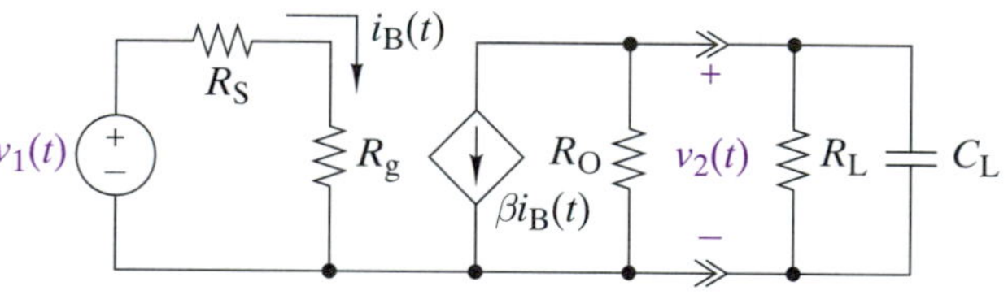

12–8 The circuit in Figure P12–8 is a small-signal model of a transistor circuit. Determine the gain of $T_V(s) = V_2(s)/V_1(s)$ at $\omega = 0$ and $\omega = \infty$. Is this a low-pass, bandpass, or high-pass circuit? What are the passband gain and the cutoff frequency for $R_S = 1$ kΩ, $R_g = 500$ kΩ, $R_D = 10$ kΩ, $R_L = 5$ kΩ, $C_C = 5$ μF, and $g = 0.01$ S.

FIGURE P12–8

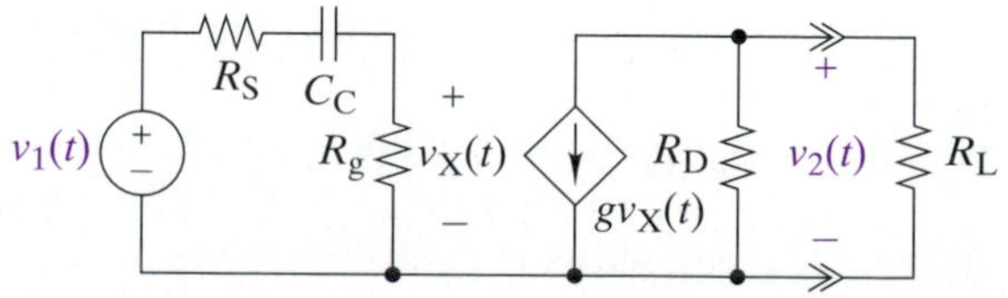

12–9 **D** The circuit in Figure P12–9 produces a bandpass response for a suitable choice of element values. Select element values so that passband gain is 10 and the cutoff frequencies are $\omega_{C1} = 100$ rad/s and $\omega_{C2} = 2500$ rad/s. The element values must be in the range $R > 10$ kΩ and $C < 1$ μF. Calculate gains in passband at $\omega = 200$, 500, and 1000 rad/s. Calculate gains in the stopbands at $\omega = 10$ rad/s and $\omega = 25$ krad/s.

FIGURE P12–9

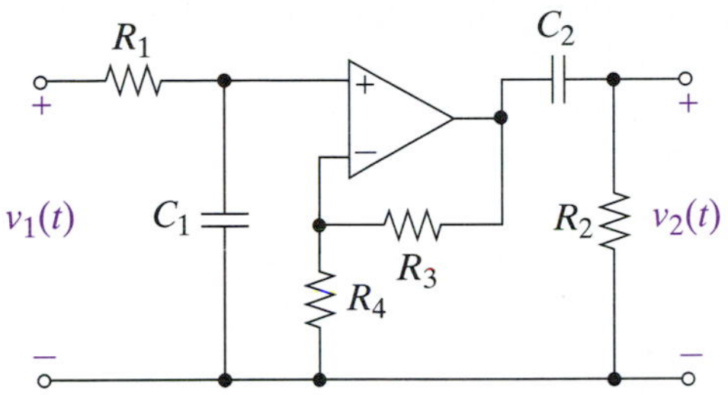

12–10 **D** The circuit in Figure P12–10 produces a bandstop response for a suitable choice of element values. Select element values so that the cutoff frequencies are $\omega_{C1} = 100$ rad/s and $\omega_{C2} = 2500$ rad/s. The element values must be in the range $L < 100$ mH and $C < 1$ μF. Calculate the gain in the stopband at $\omega = 200$, 500, and 1000 rad/s.

FIGURE P12–10

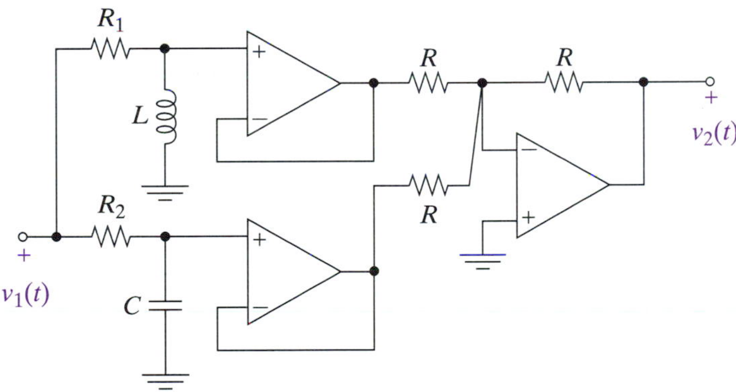

ERO 12–2 SECOND-ORDER CIRCUIT FREQUENCY RESPONSE (SECT. 12–3)

Given a second-order linear circuit or its transfer function,

(a) Determine frequency-response descriptors and classify the circuit response.
(b) Draw the straight-line approximations of the gain and phase responses.
(c) Use the straight-line approximations to calculate the steady-state output for a specified input.
(d) Select circuit parameters to produce specified descriptors.

12–11 **(a)** Find the transfer function $T_V(s) = V_2(s)/V_1(s)$ for the *RLC* circuit in Figure P12–11.

(b) Determine the dc gain, infinite frequency gain, damping ratio ζ, and undamped natural frequency ω_0. Is the gain response low-pass, high-pass, or bandpass?

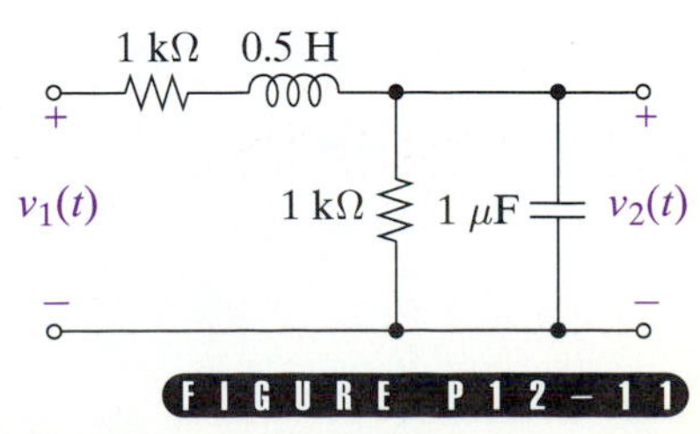

FIGURE P12–11

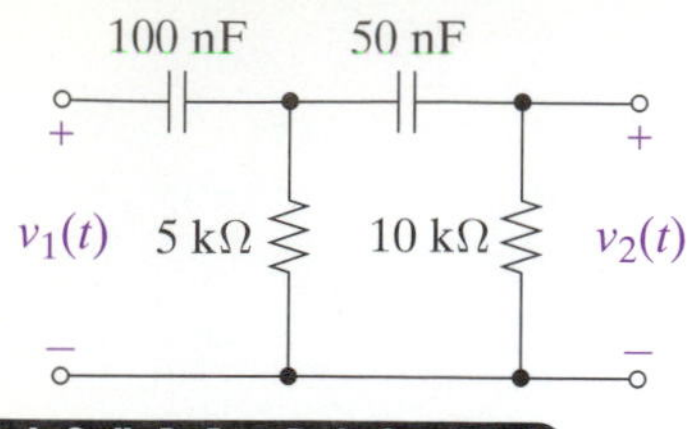

FIGURE P12–12

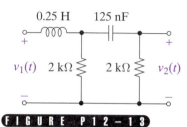

FIGURE P12–13

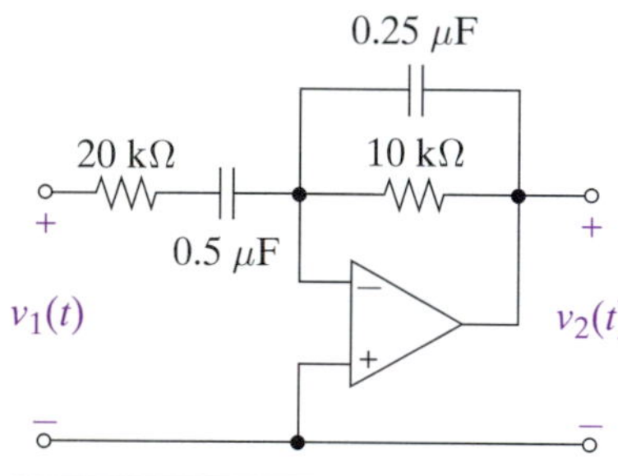

FIGURE P12–14

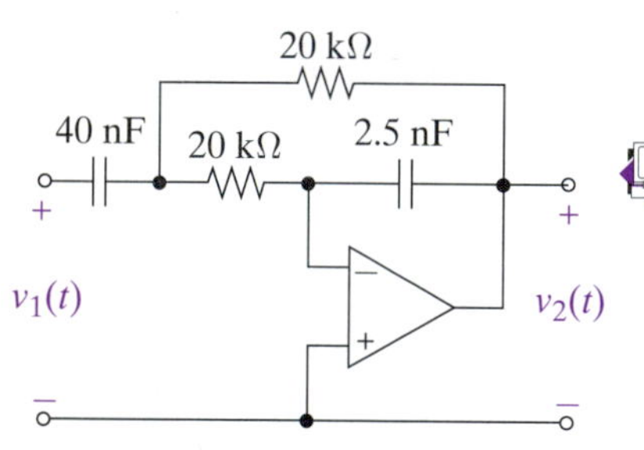

FIGURE P12–15

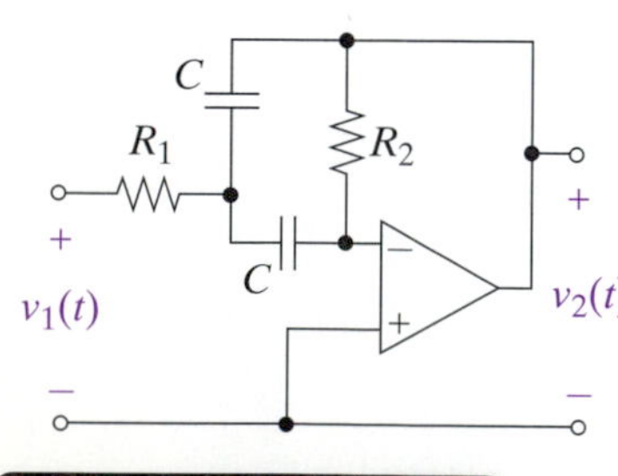

FIGURE P12–16

(c) Draw the straight-line approximation of the gain of $T_V(j\omega)$.

(d) Use the straight-line approximation to calculate the gain at $\omega = 0.5\omega_0$, ω_0, and $2\omega_0$. Compare these straight-line gains with the actual values of $|T_V(j\omega)|$ at the same frequencies.

12–12 **(a)** Find the transfer function $T_V(s) = V_2(s)/V_1(s)$ for the *RC* circuit in Figure P12–12.

(b) Determine the dc gain, infinite frequency gain, damping ratio ζ, and undamped natural frequency ω_0. Is the gain response low pass, high pass, or bandpass?

(c) Draw the straight-line approximation of the gain of $T_V(j\omega)$.

(d) Use the straight-line approximation to calculate the gain at $\omega = 0.5\omega_0$, ω_0, and $2\omega_0$. Compare these straight-line gains with the actual values of $|T_V(j\omega)|$ at the same frequencies.

12–13 **(a)** Find the transfer function $T_V(s) = V_2(s)/V_1(s)$ for the *RLC* circuit in Figure P12–13.

(b) Determine the dc gain, infinite frequency gain, damping ratio ζ, and undamped natural frequency ω_0. Is the gain response low pass, high pass, or bandpass?

(c) Draw the straight-line approximation of the gain of $T_V(j\omega)$.

(d) Use the straight-line approximation to calculate the gain at $\omega = 0.5\omega_0$, ω_0, and $2\omega_0$. Compare these straight-line gains with the actual values of $|T_V(j\omega)|$ at the same frequencies.

12–14 **(a)** Find the transfer function $T_V(s) = V_2(s)/V_1(s)$ for the OP AMP circuit in Figure P12–14.

(b) Determine the dc gain, infinite frequency gain, damping ratio ζ, and undamped natural frequency ω_0. Is the gain response low pass, high pass, or bandpass?

(c) Draw the straight-line approximation of the gain of $T_V(j\omega)$.

(d) Use the straight-line approximation to calculate the gain at $\omega = 0.5\omega_0$, ω_0, and $2\omega_0$. Compare these straight-line gains with the actual values of $|T_V(j\omega)|$ at the same frequencies.

12–15 **(a)** Find the transfer function $T_V(s) = V_2(s)/V_1(s)$ for the OP AMP circuit in Figure P12–15.

(b) Determine the dc gain, infinite frequency gain, damping ratio ζ, and undamped natural frequency ω_0. Is the gain response low pass, high pass, or bandpass?

(c) Draw the straight-line approximation of the gain of $T_V(j\omega)$.

(d) Use the straight-line approximation to calculate the gain at $\omega = 0.5\omega_0$, ω_0, and $2\omega_0$. Compare these straight-line gains with the actual values of $|T_V(j\omega)|$ at the same frequencies.

12–16 **D** Find the transfer function $T_V(s) = V_2(s)/V_1(s)$ for the OP AMP circuit in Figure P12–16. Is this a low-pass, high-pass, bandpass, or bandstop circuit? Derive expressions for the damping ratio ζ and the undamped natural frequency ω_0 in terms of circuit parameters. Select values of the circuit parameters so that $\zeta = 0.5$ and $\omega_0 = 2500$ rad/s. What is the passband gain for your choice?

12–17 **D** Find the transfer function $T_V(s) = V_2(s)/V_1(s)$ for the *RLC* circuit in Figure P12–17. Is this a low-pass, high-pass, bandpass, or bandstop circuit? Derive expressions for the damping ratio ζ and the undamped natural frequency ω_0 in terms of circuit parameters. Select values of the circuit parameters so that $\zeta = 2$ and $\omega_0 = 5$ krad/s. What is the passband gain for your choice?

12–18 **D** Find the transfer function $T_V(s) = V_2(s)/V_1(s)$ for the *RC* bridge circuit in Figure P12–18. Is this a low-pass, high-pass, bandpass, or bandstop circuit? Derive expressions for the damping ratio ζ and the undamped natural frequency ω_0 in terms of circuit parameters. Select values of the circuit parameters so that $\omega_0 = 2500$ rad/s. What are the passband gains for your choice? What is the gain at $\omega = \omega_0$?

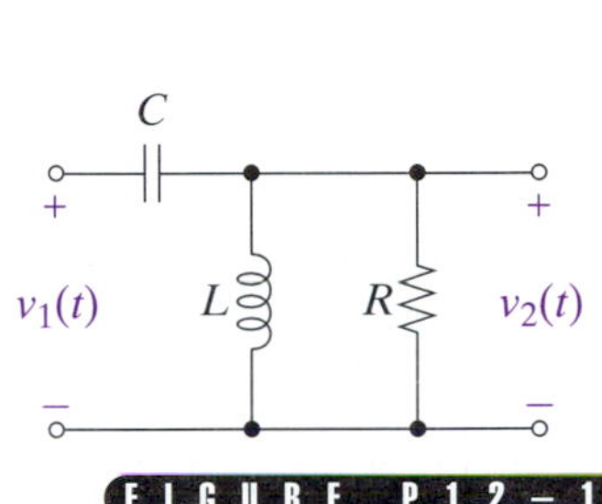

FIGURE P12–17

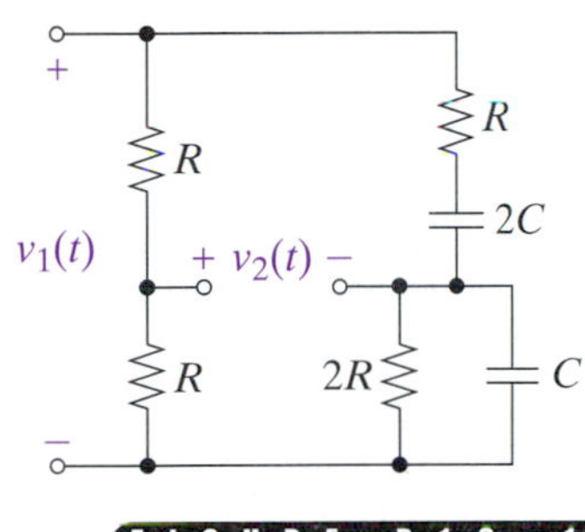

FIGURE P12–18

12–19 **D** Find the transfer function $T_V(s) = V_2(s)/V_1(s)$ for the OP AMP circuit in Figure P12–19. Is this a low-pass, high-pass, bandpass, or bandstop circuit? Derive expressions for the damping ratio ζ and the undamped natural frequency ω_0 in terms of circuit parameters. Select values of the circuit parameters so that $\zeta = 0.7$ and $\omega_0 = 500$ rad/s. What is the passband gain for your choice?

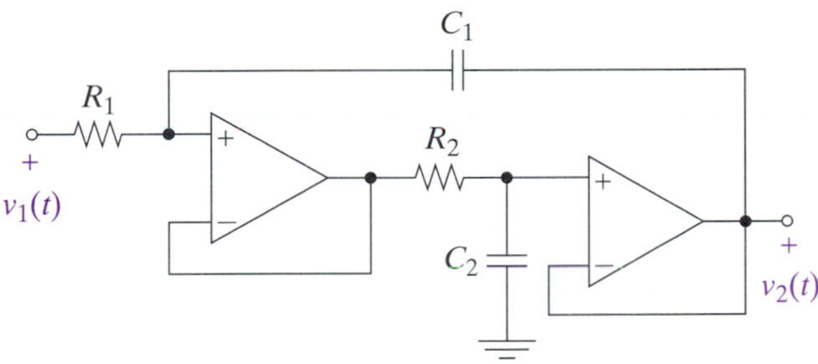

FIGURE P12–19

12–20 Given a second-order low pass transfer function of the form

$$T(s) = \frac{K}{s^2 + 2\zeta\omega_0 s + \omega_0^2}$$

Show that the maximum gain is

$$|T(j\omega_{MAX})| = \frac{|T(0)|}{2\zeta\sqrt{1 - \zeta^2}}$$

where $\omega_{MAX} = \omega_0\sqrt{1 - 2\,\zeta^2}$.

ERO 12–3 FREQUENCY RESPONSE OF *RLC* CIRCUITS (SECT. 12–4)

Given a series or parallel *RLC* circuit connected as a bandpass or bandstop filter,

(a) Find the circuit parameters or frequency-response descriptors.
(b) Select the circuit parameters to achieve specified filter characteristics.
(c) Derive expressions for the frequency-response descriptors.

12–21 A series *RLC* circuit is designed to have a bandwidth of 8 Mrad/s and an input impedance of 24 Ω at its resonant frequency of 50 Mrad/s. Determine the values *L*, *C*, *Q*, and the upper and lower cutoff frequencies.

12–22 A 20-mH inductor with an internal series resistance of 20 Ω is connected in series with a capacitor and a voltage source with a Thévenin resistance of 50 Ω.

(a) Determine the value of capacitance *C* required to produce resonance at 7 krad/s.

(b) Calculate the *Q* and bandwidth of the circuit.

12–23 A series *RLC* circuit with $R = 100\ \Omega$, $L = 25$ mH, and $C = 100$ nF is driven by a sinusoidal voltage source with a peak amplitude of 10 V.

(a) Calculate the circuit bandwidth and the upper and lower cutoff frequencies.

(b) Calculate the amplitude of the steady-state voltage across the capacitor and the inductor at the resonant frequency.

12–24 A series *RLC* circuit has a bandwidth of 5 krad/s and a driving-point impedance of 800 Ω at its resonant frequency of 100 krad/s. Determine the values *L*, *C*, *Q*, and the upper and lower cutoff frequencies.

12-25 A parallel *RLC* circuit with $R = 40$ kΩ is to have a resonant frequency of 100 MHz. Calculate the values of *L* and *C* required to produce a bandwidth of 100 kHz.

12-26 **D** A series *RLC* bandpass filter is required to have a resonance at $f_0 = 100$ kHz. The series connected *L* and *C* are to be driven by a sinusoidal source with a Thévenin resistance of 50 Ω. The following standard capacitors are available in the stock room: 1 μF, 680 nF, 470 nF, 330 nF, 220 nF, and 150 nF. The inductor will be custom designed to match the capacitor used. Select from the available capacitors the one that maximizes the circuit bandwidth.

12-27 **D** A series *RLC* circuit is to be used as a notch filter to eliminate a bothersome 60-Hz hum in an audio channel. The signal source has a Thévenin resistance of 600 Ω. Select values of *L* and *C* so the upper cutoff frequency is below 200 Hz.

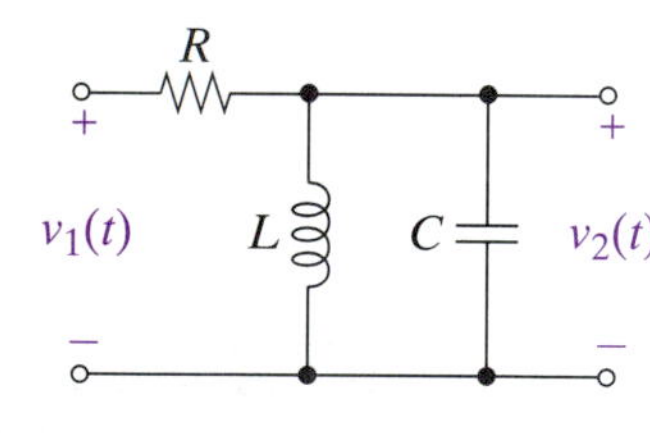

FIGURE P12–28

12–28 Show that the circuit in Figure P12–28 has a bandpass filter characteristic with a center frequency at $\omega_0 = 1/\sqrt{LC}$. Derive expressions relating the descriptive parameters *B*, *Q*, ω_{C1}, and ω_{C2} to the circuit parameters *R*, *L*, and *C*.

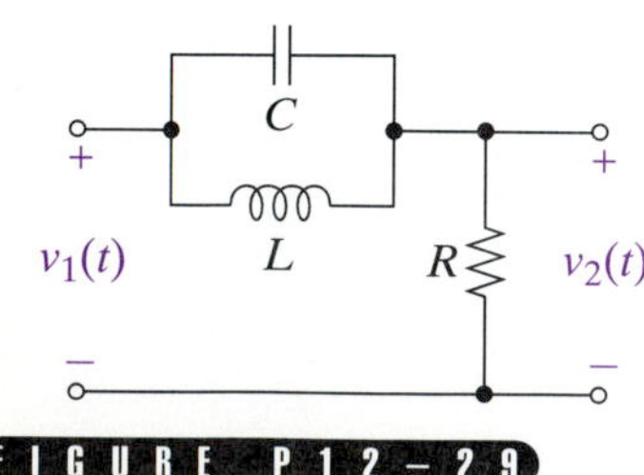

FIGURE P12–29

12–29 Show that the circuit in Figure P12–29 has a bandstop filter characteristic with a notch at $\omega_0 = 1/\sqrt{LC}$. Derive expressions relating the descriptive parameters *B*, *Q*, ω_{C1}, and ω_{C2} to the circuit parameters *R*, *L*, and *C*.

12–30 For the circuit in Figure P12–30, show that the transfer impedance $T_Z(s) = V_2(s)/I_1(s)$ has a bandpass characteristic with a resonant peak in the gain at $\omega_0 = 1/\sqrt{LC}$. Derive expressions relating the descriptive parameters B, Q, ω_{C1}, and ω_{C2} to the circuit parameters R, L, and C.

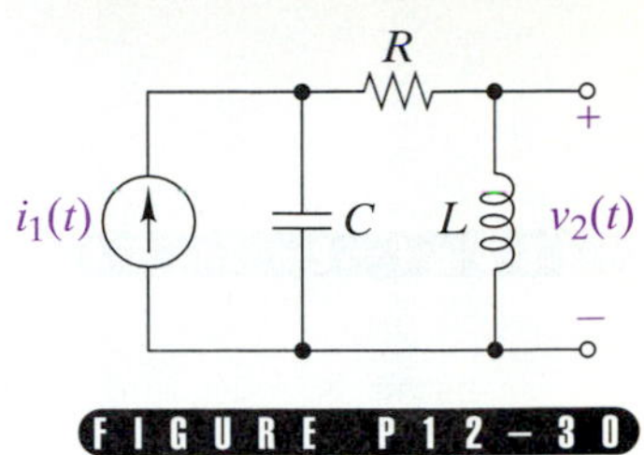

FIGURE P12–30

ERO 12–4 BODE PLOTS (SECTS. 12–5, 12–6)

(a) Construct Bode plots of the asymptotic gain and phase responses of a given circuit or transfer function. .

(b) Construct the transfer function corresponding to the Bode plots of a given asymptotic gain. (c) Use the asymptotic gain plots to estimate circuit parameters or frequency-response descriptors.

12–31 Construct a Bode plot of the straight-line approximation to gain responses of the circuit in Figure P12–31. Use the straight-line gain plot to calculate the amplitude of the steady-state output when the input is $v_1(t) = 10 \sin 30t$ V. Use the circuit transfer function to calculate the amplitude of the steady-state output for the same input and compare the two results.

12–32 Repeat Problem 12–31 using the circuit in Figure P12–32.

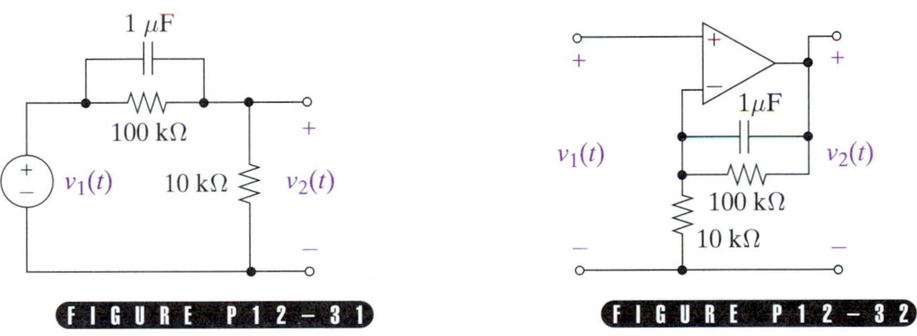

FIGURE P12–31

FIGURE P12–32

12–33 Construct the Bode plot of the straight-line approximation to the gain response of the circuit in Figure P12–33. Is this a low-pass, high-pass, bandpass, or bandstop response? Use the straight-line gain plot to estimate the cutoff frequency and passband gain.

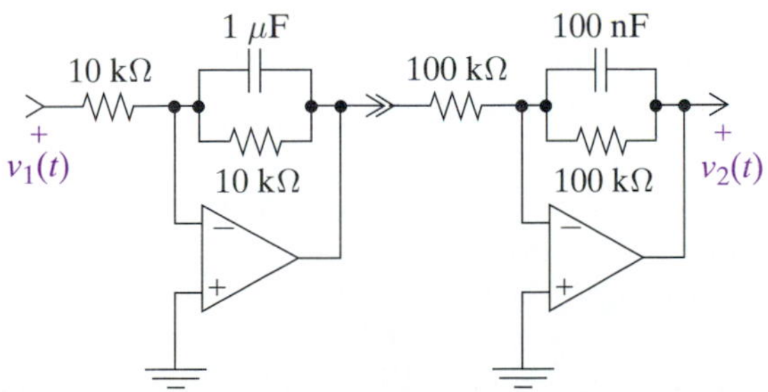

FIGURE P12–33

12–34 Construct the Bode plot of the straight-line approximation to the gain response of the circuit in Figure P12–34. Is this a low-pass, high-pass, bandpass, or bandstop response? Use the straight-line gain plot to estimate the cutoff frequency and passband gain.

FIGURE P12–34

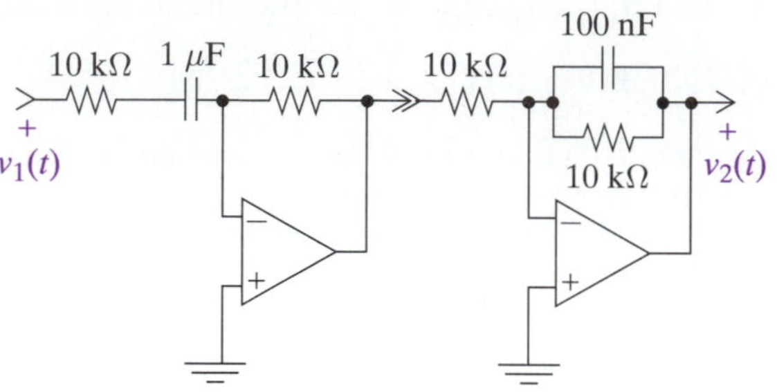

12–35 Construct Bode plots of the straight-line approximations to the gain and phase responses of the following transfer functions. Are these low-pass, high-pass, bandpass, or bandstop functions? Estimate the cutoff frequency and passband gain.

$$\text{(a) } T(s) = \frac{(0.02s + 1)}{(0.2s + 1)(2s + 1)}$$

$$\text{(b) } T(s) = \frac{(0.2s + 1)}{(0.02s + 1)(2s + 1)}$$

12–36 Construct Bode plots of the straight-line approximations to the gain and phase responses of the following transfer functions. Are these low-pass, high-pass, bandpass, or bandstop functions? Estimate the cutoff frequency and passband gain.

$$\text{(a) } T(s) = \frac{s(s + 25)}{(0.01s + 1)(0.4s + 1)}$$

$$\text{(b) } T(s) = \frac{s^2}{(0.01s + 1)(0.4s + 1)}$$

12–37 Construct Bode plots of the straight-line approximations to the gain response of the following transfer functions. Are these low-pass, high-pass, or bandpass functions? What is the passband gain and the maximum gain?

$$\text{(a) } T(s) = \frac{20}{(0.01s^2 + 0.05s + 1)}$$

$$\text{(b) } T(s) = \frac{40s^2}{(4s^2 + 0.2s + 1)}$$

12–38 Construct Bode plots of the straight-line approximations to the gain response of the following transfer functions. Are these low-pass, high-pass, or bandpass functions? What is the passband gain and the maximum gain?

$$\text{(a) } T(s) = \frac{5(0.5s + 1)}{(0.04s^2 + 0.04s + 1)}$$

$$\text{(b) } T(s) = \frac{5s}{(0.25s^2 + 0.5s + 1)}$$

12–39 Find the transfer function corresponding to the straight-line gain plot in Figure P12–39. Draw the straight-line approximation to the phase response of the transfer function.

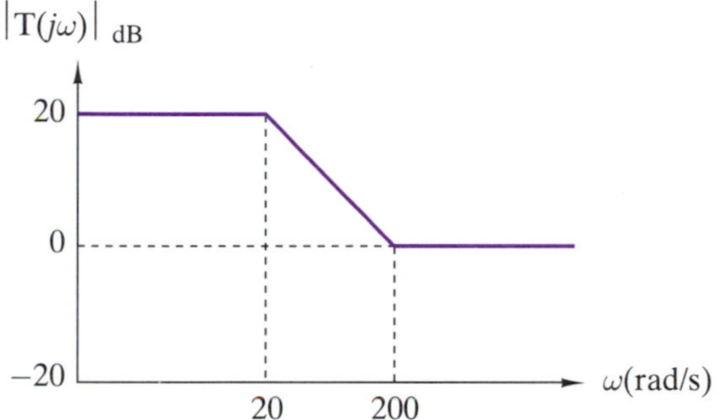

FIGURE P12–39

12–40 Find the transfer function corresponding to the straight-line gain plot in Figure P12–40. Draw the straight-line approximation to the phase response of the transfer function.

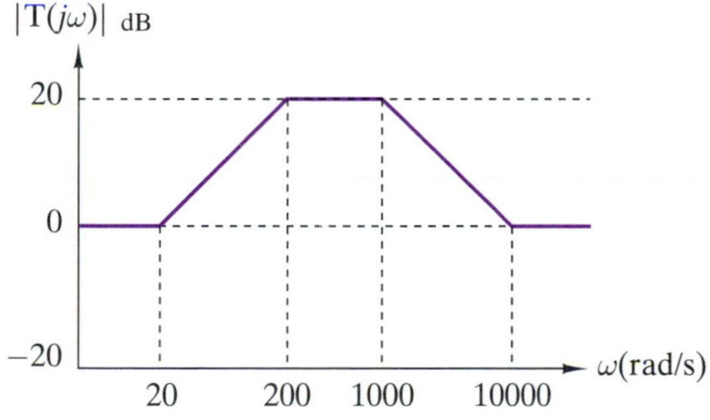

FIGURE P12–40

ERO 12–5 FREQUENCY RESPONSE AND STEP RESPONSE (SECT. 12–7)

(a) Given an asymptotic gain or phase response of a linear circuit, determine its step response.
(b) Given the step response of a linear circuit, construct the asymptotic gain and phase responses.
(c) Construct a transfer function that meets constraints on both the frequency and step responses.

12–41 Figure P12–41 shows the straight-line approximations to the gain response of a linear circuit. Find the time-domain step response $g(t)$.

FIGURE P12–41

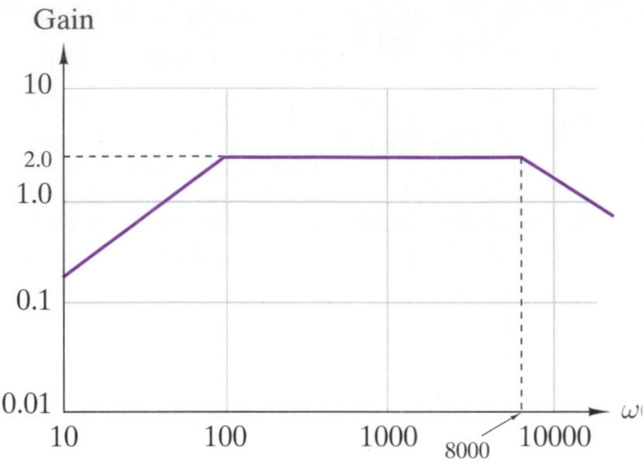

12–42 Repeat Problem 12–41 for the gain response in Figure P12–39.

12–43 Repeat Problem 12–41 for the gain response in Figure P12–40.

 **12–44** The step response of a linear circuit is

$$g(t) = 12 - 10e^{-10t} - 2e^{-100t} \qquad t > 0$$

Is the circuit a low-pass, high-pass, bandpass, or bandstop filter? Construct Bode plots of the straight-line approximations to the gain and phase responses of the circuit.

12–45 The step response of a linear circuit is

$$g(t) = 5 - 5e^{-100t} \sin 200\,t \qquad t > 0$$

Is the circuit a low-pass, high-pass, bandpass, or bandstop filter? Construct Bode plots of the straight-line approximations to the gain and phase responses of the circuit.

12–46 The step response of a linear circuit is

$$g(t) = 10e^{-100t} \cos 200\,t \qquad t > 0$$

Is the circuit a low-pass, high-pass, bandpass, or bandstop filter? Construct Bode plots of the straight-line approximations to the gain response of the circuit.

12–47 The step response of a linear circuit is

$$g(t) = e^{-100t} + 2e^{-2000t} \qquad t > 0$$

Is the circuit a low-pass, high-pass, bandpass, or bandstop filter? Construct Bode plots of the straight-line approximations to the gain and phase responses of the circuit.

12–48 **D** Construct a first-order low-pass transfer function with a dc gain of 10, a bandwidth less than 200 rad/s, and a step response that rises to 50% of its final value in less than 5 ms.

12–49 **D** Construct a first-order high-pass transfer function whose step response decays to 10% of its peak value in less than 10 μs and whose cutoff frequency is less than 100 kHz.

12–50 **D** Construct a second-order bandpass transfer function with a midband gain of 10, a center frequency of 100 kHz, a bandwidth less than 10 kHz, and a step response that decays to less that 10 % of its peak value in less than 5 μs.

CHAPTER-INTEGRATING PROBLEMS

12–51 A TRANSFORMER TRANSFER FUNCTION

Figure P12–51 shows a transformer modeled as two coupled coils.

(a) Use the s-domain i–v relationships for the coupled coils to find the transfer function $V_2(s)/V_1(s)$.

(b) Show that the transfer function has a second-order bandpass characteristic.

(c) Using $L_1 = 0.25$ H, $L_2 = 1$ H, $M = 0.499$ H, $R_1 = 50\ \Omega$, and $R_L = 200\ \Omega$ calculate the center frequency, upper and lower cutoff frequencies, and bandwidth.

(d) Does the transformer have a wideband or narrowband bandpass frequency response?

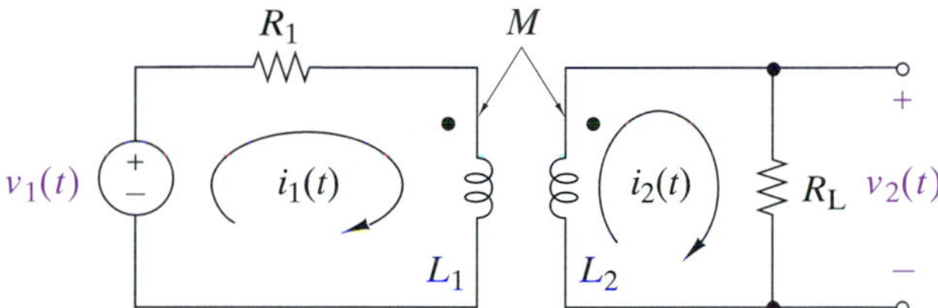

FIGURE P12–51

12–52 A BANDPASS TO BANDSTOP TRANSFORMATION

The circuit in Figure P12–52(a) is a second-order bandpass filter with a midband gain of unity. That is, the transfer function of the three-terminal circuit in Figure 12–52(a) is

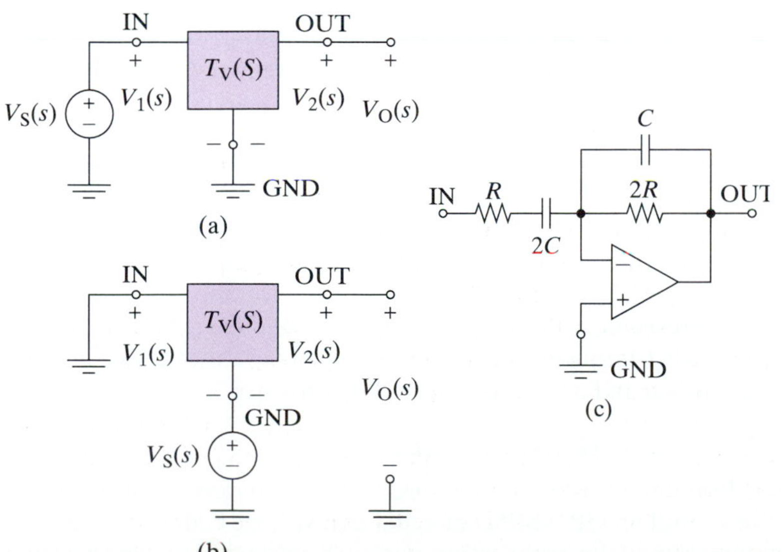

FIGURE P12–52

$$T_V(s) = \frac{V_2(s)}{V_1(s)} = \frac{2\zeta\omega_0 s}{s^2 + 2\zeta\omega_0 s + \omega_0^2}$$

The circuit in Figure P12–52(b) is formed by interchanging the input and ground connections in Figure P12–52(a). Show that the transfer function $V_O(s)/V_S(s)$ in Figure 12–52(b) is a second-order bandstop filter with unity gain in both passbands. That is, show that interchanging the input and ground changes a unity gain bandpass circuit into a unity gain bandstop circuit.

12–53 A D BLOCK DIAGRAM ANALYSIS AND DESIGN

Figure P12–53 shows an s-domain block diagram consisting of a summing point, an integrator, and a gain block.

(a) Show that the transfer function $V_2(s)/V_1(s)$ is a first-order low pass filter with unity passband gain and that the transfer function $V_3(s)/V_1(s)$ is a first-order high pass filter with unity passband gain.

(b) Design an OP AMP circuit that implements the block diagram using only resistors, capacitors, and no more than two OP AMPs.

FIGURE P12–53

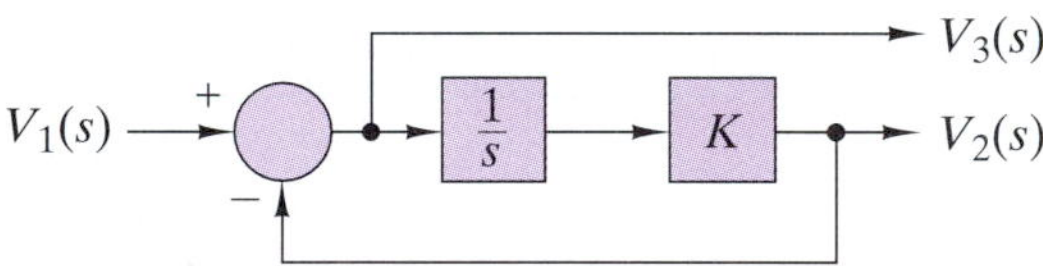

12–54 A HIGH-FREQUENCY MODEL OF A RESISTOR

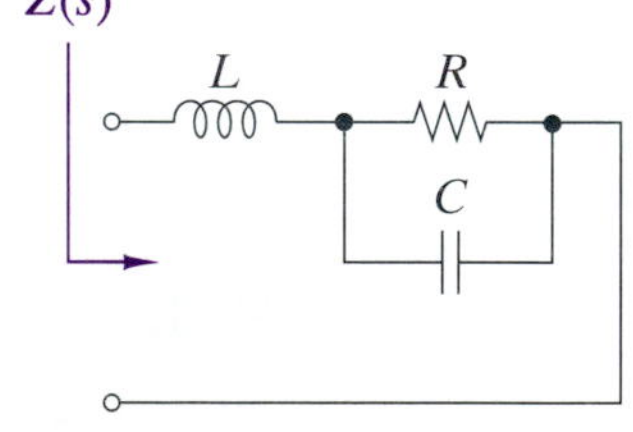

FIGURE P12–54

Figure P12–54 shows a circuit model of a resistor R that includes parasitic capacitance C and parasitic lead inductance L. The purpose of this problem is to investigate the effect of these parasitic elements on the high-frequency characteristics of the resistor device.

(a) Derive an expression for the impedance $Z(s)$ of the circuit model in Figure P12–54 in terms of the circuit parameters R, L, and C.

(b) For $R = 10\ \text{k}\Omega$, $L = 2\ \mu\text{H}$, and $C = 4$ pF find the poles and zeros of $Z(s)$. Construct a Bode plot of the straight-line asymptotes of $|Z(j\omega)|$. Do not express $|Z(j\omega)|$ in dB. Use a logarithmic scale with the impedance magnitude expressed in ohms. Identify the corner frequencies and slopes (in ohms/decade) in this plot.

(c) Use the straight-line Bode plot in (b) to identify the frequency range (in Hz) over which the resistor device appears to be: (1) a 10-kΩ resistance, (2) a 4-pF capacitance, and (3) a 2-μH inductor.

(d) Over what frequency range can you safely use this device in a circuit design and treat it as a pure 10-kΩ resistor?

12–55 A E PACKAGED CIRCUIT EVALUATION

The hybrid circuit package in Figure P12–55 contains a resistor R, capacitor C, and an OP AMP connected as a voltage follower. The sales literature claims that connecting two such packages as shown in the

FIGURE P12–55

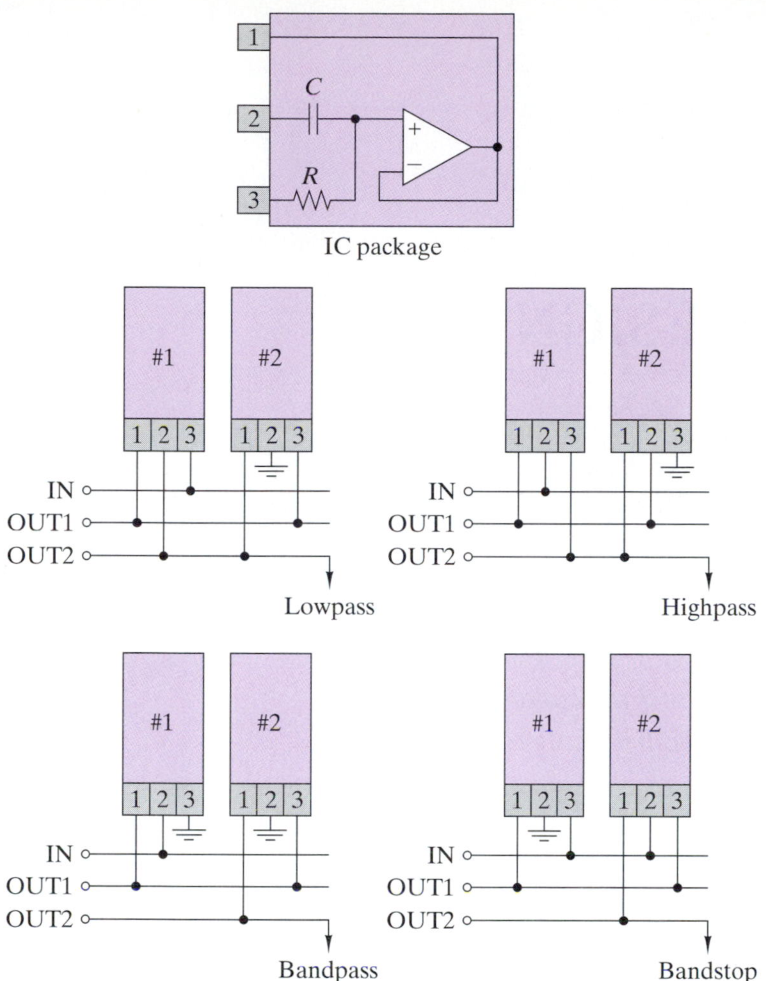

figure will produce second-order low-pass, high-pass, bandpass, and bandstop filters with $\omega_0 = 1/RC$ and $\zeta = 0.5$. Prove or disprove this claim.

CHAPTER 13

ANALOG FILTER DESIGN

In its usual form the electric wave-filter transmits currents of all frequencies lying within one or more specified ranges, and excludes currents of all other frequencies.

George A. Campbell, 1922,
American Engineer

The electric filter was independently invented during World War I by George Campbell in the United States and by K. W. Wagner in Germany. Electric filters and vacuum tube amplifiers were key technologies that triggered the growth of telephone and radio communication systems in the 1920s and 1930s. The emergence of semiconductor electronics in the 1960s, especially the integrated circuit OP AMP, allowed the functions of filtering and amplification to be combined into what are now called active filters.

This chapter treats an important type of electric wave filters made possible by operational amplifiers. These circuits are often called active filters, although the term *analog filter* is also common. Modern integrated circuit technology allows signal-processing systems to use both analog and digital filters, sometimes on the same chip. Although analog and digital filters have some common attributes, the subject of digital filtering is covered in courses in discrete-time signal processing.

Some signal-processing functions performed by analog filters are described in the first section of this chapter. The second section introduces filter design techniques using a cascade connection of first-order circuits. The third section treats the design of second-order low-pass, high-pass, and bandpass circuits. The fourth section develops cascade realizations of low-pass transfer functions using the first- and second-order building blocks. The fifth section shows how the low-pass filter serves as a prototype for designing high-pass filters. The final section illustrates that low-pass and high-pass filters are the building blocks for bandpass and bandstop filters.

13–1 FREQUENCY-DOMAIN SIGNAL PROCESSING

The spectrum of a signal is a description of the amplitude and phase angle of its sinusoidal components. When viewed as a spectrum, we can think of a signal as the sum of a large number of voltage sources, each producing a sinusoid with a specified frequency, amplitude, and phase angle. In frequency-domain signal processing the spectrum of the output signal is obtained by selectively altering the amplitudes and phase angles of the frequencies contained in the input signal. The idea that signals can be described and processed in terms of their frequency components is one of the fundamental concepts in electrical engineering.

For example, the touch-tone telephone shown in Figure 13–1 transmits two frequencies when the button for a digit is pressed. One frequency comes from the low group (697, 770, 852, and 941 Hz) and the other from the high group (1209, 1336, and 1477 Hz). When the no. 3 button is pressed the instrument transmits a sum of sinusoids at 697 Hz and 1477 Hz. When the no. 5 button is pressed the dial signal is a combination of 770 Hz and 1336 Hz. The details of the time-domain waveform produced are not important. The important point is that the touch-tone telephone produces signals whose frequency spectrum lies in the range from 697 Hz to 1477 Hz. The telephone-switching equipment decodes a dial signal by detecting the frequencies it contains.

A **filter** is a signal processor that transmits signals in some frequency bands and rejects or attenuates signals in other bands. Figure 13–2 shows how an input spectrum containing three frequencies is modified by the

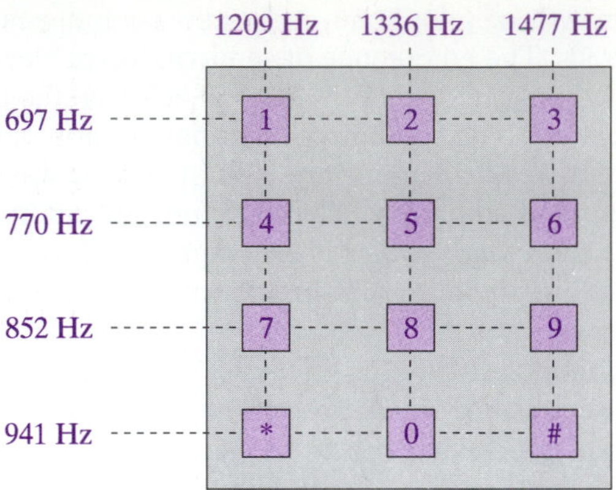

FIGURE 13–1 *Touch-tone dialing frequencies.*

four prototype filter responses described in Chapter 12. The low-pass filter passes frequencies below its cutoff frequency ω_C and attenuates the high-frequency components in the stopband above the cutoff frequency. The high-pass filter passes frequencies above its cutoff frequency and attenuates the low-frequency components below cutoff. The bandpass filter passes the intermediate frequency and attenuates the low- and high-frequency components on either side. Finally, the bandstop filter is the inverse of the bandpass case, attenuating the intermediate frequency and passing the low- and high-frequency components.

This chapter introduces methods of designing filter circuits with prescribed frequency-domain signal-processing characteristics. A filter design problem is defined by specifying a frequency-response gain function $|T(j\omega)|$. The objective is to design one or more circuits that produce the desired gain function. In general, a given gain response can be realized by many different circuits, including passive circuits containing only resistors, capacitors, and inductors. We limit our study to **active RC filter** realizations involving resistors, capacitors, and OP AMPs. These filters offer the following advantages:

1. They combine amplifier gain with the frequency-response characteristics of passive *RLC* filters.
2. The transfer function can be divided into stages that can be designed independently and then connected in cascade to realize the required gain function.
3. They are often smaller and less expensive than *RLC* filters because they do not require inductors, which can be quite large in low-frequency applications.

The design approaches described produce circuits that approximate the specified filter gain characteristics. The filter phase response is not directly controlled, since the design process concentrates on the gain response. Designing circuits with specified phase characteristics involves similar ideas but will not be treated in detail.

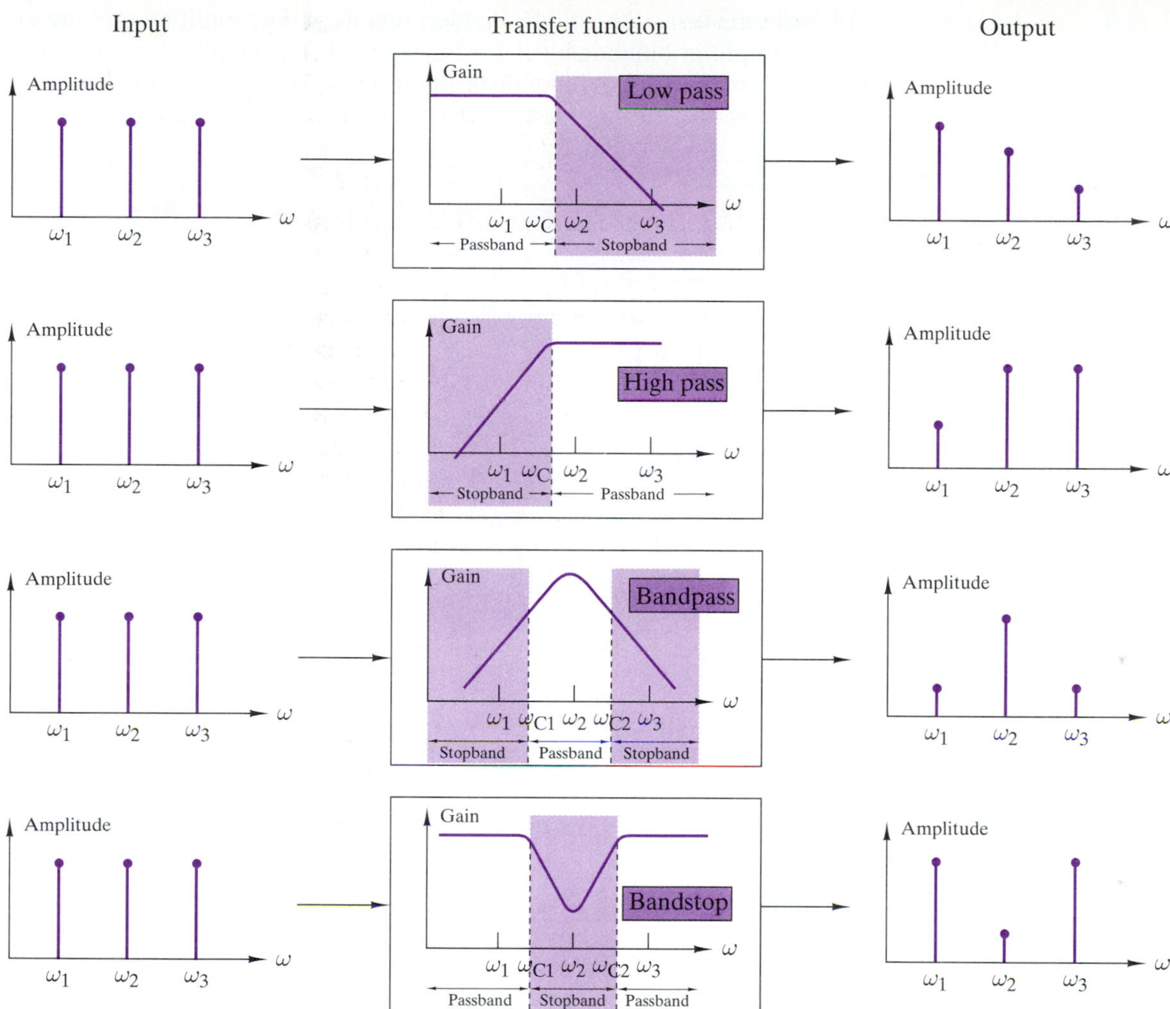

FIGURE 13–2 *Four prototype filter characteristics.*

13–2 DESIGN WITH FIRST-ORDER CIRCUITS

In this section we begin the study of filter design problems in which characteristics of the gain response $|T(j\omega)|$ are specified. Our objective is to obtain a circuit whose transfer function has the specified gain response and whose element values are in practical ranges. The design process begins by constructing a transfer function whose gain response meets the specification. Except in the case of simple first- and second-order filters, we partition the transfer function into a product of the form

$$T(s) = T_1(s) \times T_2(s) \times T_3(s) \times \dots T_n(s) \qquad (13-1)$$

where each $T_k(s)$ in this equation is a first-order transfer function with one pole and no more than one finite zero. We then design prototype first-order circuits using the voltage divider, noninverting amplifier, and the inverting amplifier building blocks in Figure 13–3. The circuit element values in the prototype may be unrealistically large or small, so we use a magnitude scale factor to bring the element values into practical ranges.

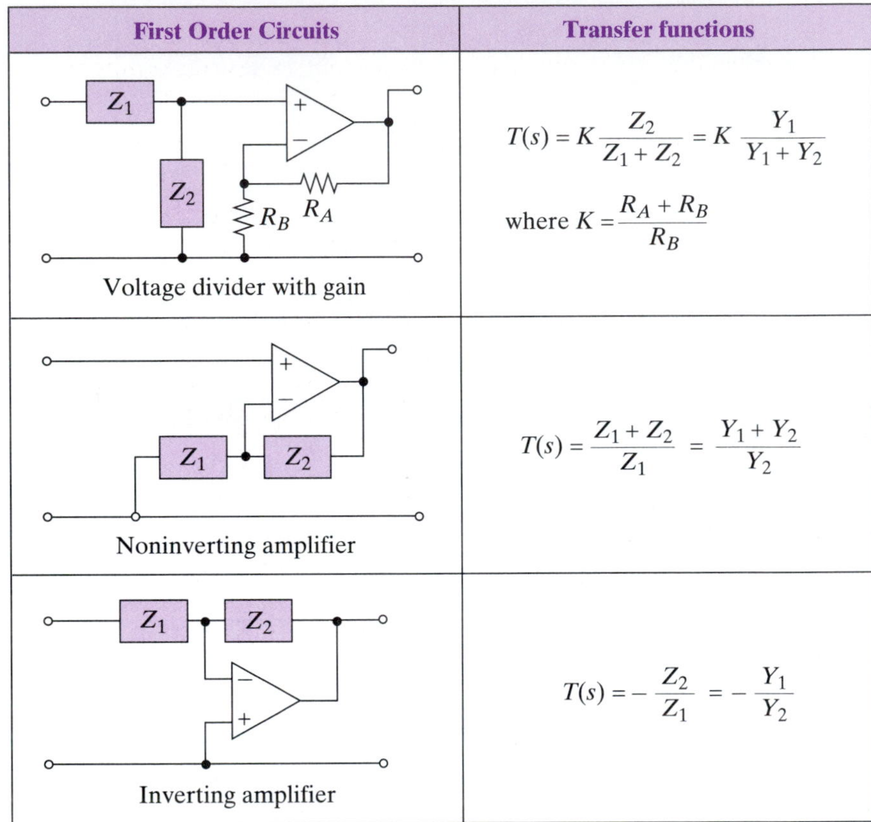

First Order Circuits
Transfer functions
Z_1
Z_2
R_B
R_A
Voltage divider with gain
$T(s) = K\dfrac{Z_2}{Z_1 + Z_2} = K\dfrac{Y_1}{Y_1 + Y_2}$
where $K = \dfrac{R_A + R_B}{R_B}$
Noninverting amplifier
$T(s) = \dfrac{Z_1 + Z_2}{Z_1} = \dfrac{Y_1 + Y_2}{Y_2}$
Inverting amplifier
$T(s) = -\dfrac{Z_2}{Z_1} = -\dfrac{Y_1}{Y_2}$

FIGURE 13–3 *First-order circuit building blocks.*

The required transfer function $T(s)$ is realized by connecting the scaled circuit for each stage in cascade, as shown in Figure 13–4. The cascade connection produces the required $T(s)$ because the building blocks in Figure 13–3 have OP AMP outputs. As a result, loading does not change the stage transfer functions and the chain rule in Eq. (13–1) applies. The noninverting and inverting amplifier circuits in Figure 13–3 inherently have low-impedance outputs. Adding a noninverting amplifier to the output of the basic voltage-divider circuit in Figure 13–3 produces a circuit that can be connected in cascade without changing the stage transfer function.

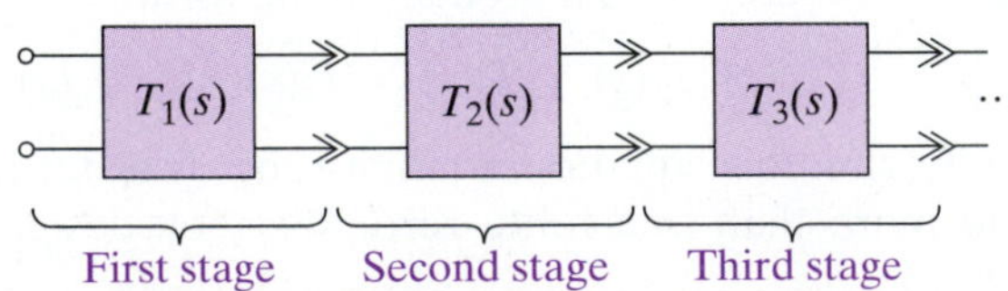

FIGURE 13–4 *A cascade connection.*

The end result is a cascade circuit whose gain response has the attributes required by the specification. The aforementioned procedure does not produce a unique solution for the following reasons:

1. Several transfer functions may exist that adequately approximate the required gain characteristics.
2. Partitioning the selected transfer function into a product of first-order transfer functions can be carried out in several different ways.
3. Any of the three building blocks in Figure 13–3 can be used to realize the first-order transfer functions in the selected partitioning.
4. There usually are several ways to assign numerical values to circuit elements in the selected building block for each stage.
5. Each stage normally requires a different magnitude scale factor to bring the assigned numerical values into practical ranges.

In summary, since there are many choices, there are no unique answers to the circuit design problem. The following examples illustrate the design of active *RC* circuits.

D DESIGN EXAMPLE 13–1

Active *RC* Low-Pass Filter Design

Design two active *RC* circuits that realize a first-order low-pass filter with a cutoff frequency of 2 krad/s and a passband gain of 5.

SOLUTION:

In Chapter 12 we found that a first-order low-pass transfer function has a pole at $s = -\alpha$, cutoff frequency of $\omega_C = \alpha$, and passband gain of $T(0)$. For design puposes it is convenient to write the first-order lowpass transfer function in the Bode plot standard format

$$T(s) = \frac{K}{s/\alpha + 1}$$

Written in this form, we see that the design specification requires that $\omega_C = \alpha = 2000$ and that passband gain $T(0) = K = 5$. Thus, the required transfer function is

$$T(s) = \frac{\pm 5}{s/2000 + 1}$$

where the ± sign indicates that the phase response is not specified.

First Design: Using the voltage divider circuit in Figure 13–3, we use the plus sign and partition $T(s)$ as

$$T(s) = [K]\left[\frac{Y_1}{Y_1 + Y_2}\right] = [+5]\left[\frac{1}{s/2000 + 1}\right]$$

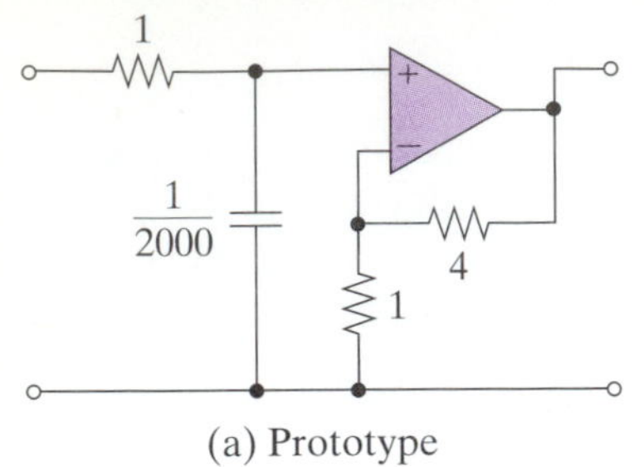

(a) Prototype

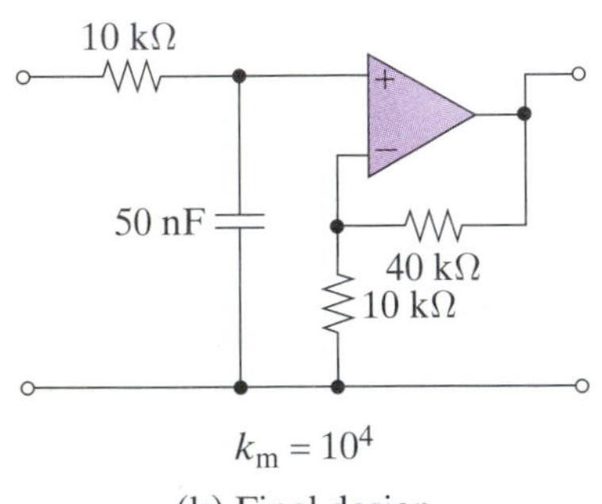

$k_m = 10^4$

(b) Final design

FIGURE 13–5

from which we identify $K = 5$, $R_A = (5-1)R_B$, $Y_1 = 1$, and $Y_2 = s/2000$. Selecting $R_B = 1\ \Omega$, we obtain $R_A = 4\ \Omega$. The admittance Y_1 can be realized by a resistor $R_1 = 1\ \Omega$, and admittance Y_2 by a capacitor $C_2 = 1/2000$ F. These results lead to the prototype design in Figure 13–5(a). To obtain practical element values, we apply a magnitude scale factor of $k_m = 10^4$ to produce the final design shown in Figure 13–5(b).

Second Design: Using the inverting amplifier circuit in Figure 13–3, we use the minus sign and write $T(s)$ as

$$T(s) = \left[-\frac{Y_1}{Y_2}\right] = \left[-\frac{5}{s/2000 + 1}\right]$$

from which we identify $Y_1 = 5$ and $Y_2 = s/2000 + 1$. The admittance Y_1 can be realized by a resistor $R_1 = 1/5\ \Omega$. The admittance Y_2 is of the form $C_2 s + G_2$ and hence can be realized by capacitor $C_2 = 1/2000$ F connected in parallel with a resistor $R_2 = 1\ \Omega$. These results lead to the prototype design in Figure 13–6(a). To obtain practical element values, we apply a magnitude scale factor of $k_m = 5 \times 10^4$ to produce the final design shown in Figure 13–6(b). ■

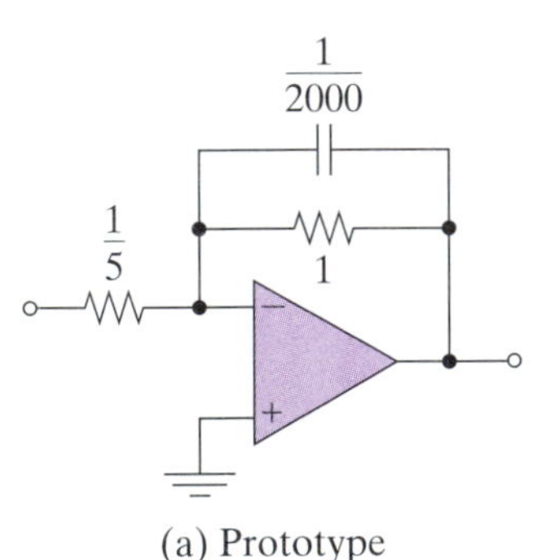

(a) Prototype

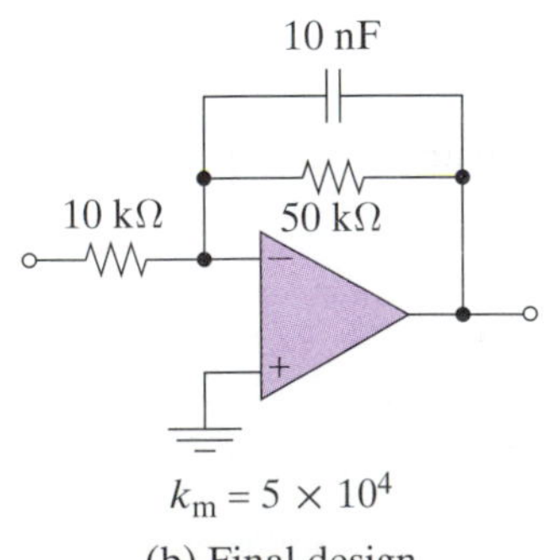

$k_m = 5 \times 10^4$

(b) Final design

FIGURE 13–6

DESIGN EXAMPLE 13–2

First-Order Active *RC* Cascade Design

(a) Construct a transfer function $T(s)$ with the straight-line gain response shown in Figure 13–7.
(b) Design an active *RC* circuit to realize the $T(s)$ found in (a).

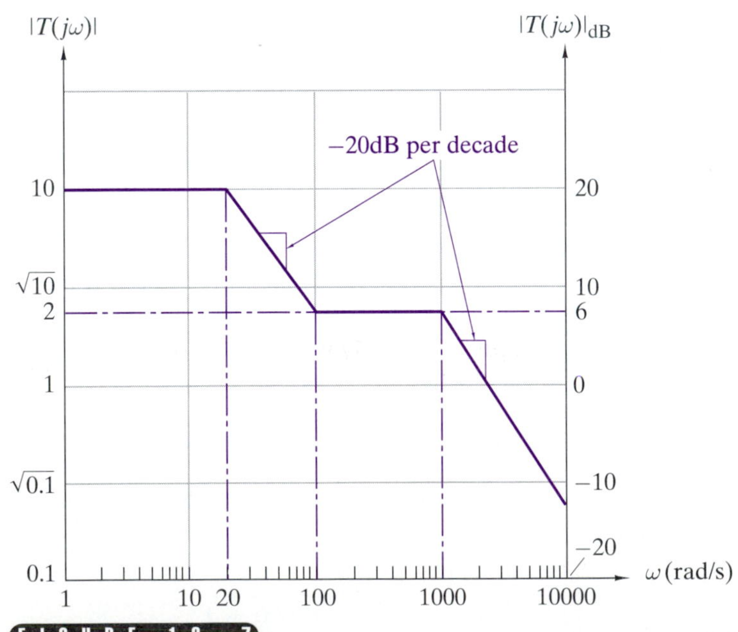

FIGURE 13–7

SOLUTION:

(a) The gain response shows slope changes at ω = 20 rad/s, 100 rad/s, and 1000 rad/s. Since the net slope changes at ω = 20 rad/s and 1000 rad/s are both –20 dB/decade, the denominator of $T(s)$ must have poles at

Item	First Stage	Second Stage
Transfer function	$T_1(s) = -\dfrac{(s/100)+1}{(s/20)+1}$	$T_2(s) = -\dfrac{10}{(s/1000)+1}$
Design constraints	Inverting Amplifier $\dfrac{Z_2}{Z_1} = \dfrac{(s/100)+1}{(s/20)+1}$	Inverting Amplifier $\dfrac{Z_2}{Z_1} = \dfrac{10}{(s/1000)+1}$
Z_1	$\dfrac{1}{(s/100)+1}$ 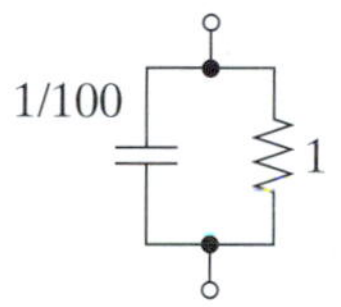 1/100 1	$\dfrac{1}{10}$ 1/10 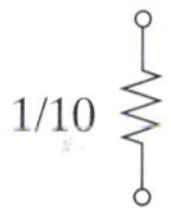
Z_2	$\dfrac{1}{(s/20)+1}$ 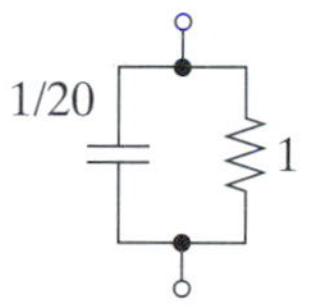 1/20 1	$\dfrac{1}{(s/1000)+1}$ 1/1000 1 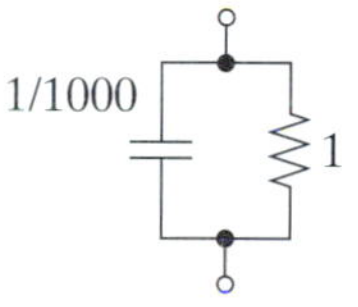
Prototype designs	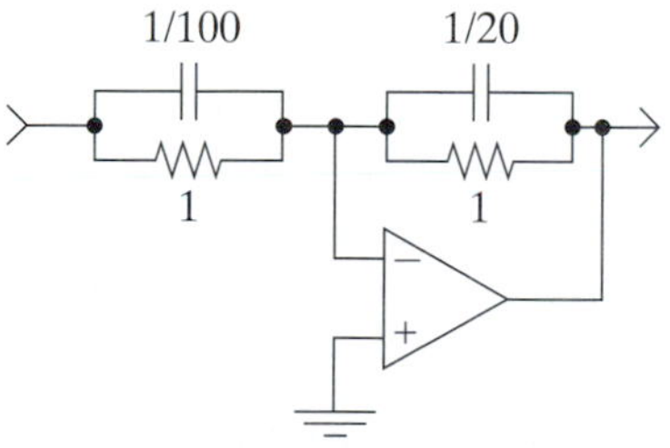 1/100 1/20 1 1	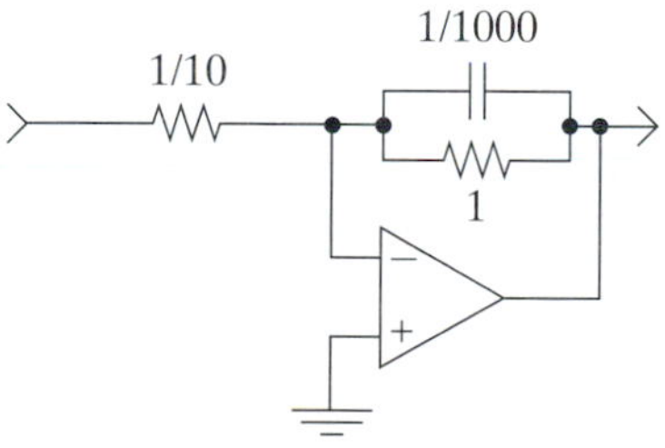 1/10 1/1000 1
Final designs	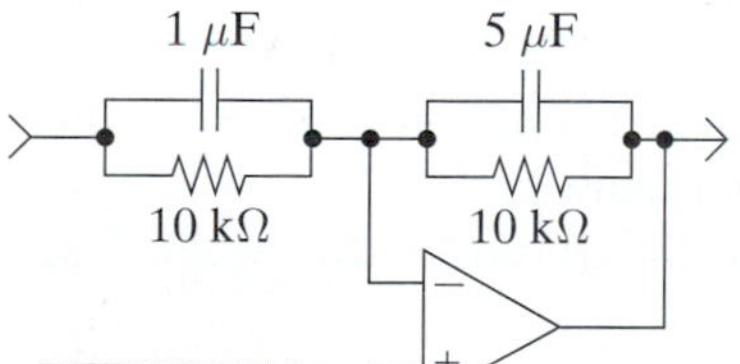 1 μF 5 μF 10 kΩ 10 kΩ $k_m = 10^4$	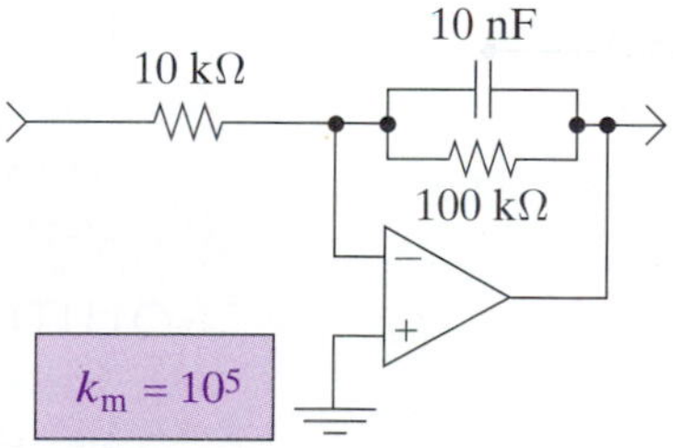 10 kΩ 10 nF 100 kΩ $k_m = 10^5$

FIGURE 13–8 *Design sequence for Example 13–2.*

$s = -20$ rad/s and $s = -1000$ rad/s. Since the net slope change at $\omega = 100$ rad/s is +20 dB/decade, the numerator of $T(s)$ must have a zero at $s = -100$ rad/s. These critical frequencies account for all of the slope changes, so the required transfer function has the form

$$T(s) = K\frac{s/100 + 1}{(s/20 + 1)(s/1000 + 1)}$$

where the gain K is yet to be determined. The dc gain of the proposed transfer function is $T(0) = K$ and the specified dc gain in Figure 13–7 is +20 dB; hence $K = 10$.

(b) To design first-order circuits, we partition $T(s)$ into a product of first-order transfer functions:

$$T(s) = T_1(s)T_2(s) = \left(\frac{s/100 + 1}{s/20 + 1}\right)\left(\frac{10}{s/1000 + 1}\right)$$

This partitioning is not unique because the overall gain $K = K_1 \times K_2 = 10$ can be distributed between the two functions in any number of ways (for example, $K_1 = 2$ and $K_2 = 5$). We could move the zero from the first function to the second or reverse the order in which the functions are assigned to stages in the cascade design. Selecting the inverting amplifier building block in Figure 13–3 for both stages leads to the design sequence shown in Figure 13–8.

The transfer function of the inverting amplifier is $-Z_2(s)/Z_1(s)$, so the selected building block places constraints on Z_1 and Z_2, as indicated in the second row in Figure 13–8. Equating $Z_1(s)$ to the reciprocal of the transfer function numerator and $Z_2(s)$ to the reciprocal of the denominator yields impedances of the form $1/(Cs + G)$. An impedance of this form is a resistor in parallel with a capacitor, as shown in the third and fourth rows in Figure 13–8. The element values of the prototype designs shown in the fifth row are not within practical ranges. To make all resistors 10 kΩ or greater, we use a magnitude scale factor of $k_m = 10^4$ in the first stage and $k_m = 10^5$ in the second stage. Applying these scale factors to the prototype designs produces the final designs shown in the last row of Figure 13–8. ■

D DESIGN EXAMPLE 13–3

First-Order Active *RC* Cascade Design

(a) Construct a transfer function $T(s)$ with the straight-line gain response shown in Figure 13–9.

(b) Design an active *RC* circuit to realize the $T(s)$ found in (a).

SOLUTION:

(a) The straight-line gain response shows slope changes at $\omega = 10$ rad/s, 100 rad/s, 500 rad/s, and 5000 rad/s. The net slope changes at $\omega = 10$ rad/s and 5000 rad/s are –20 dB/decade. The net slope changes at $\omega = 100$ rad/s and 500 rad/s are +20 dB/decade. Therefore, $T(s)$ must

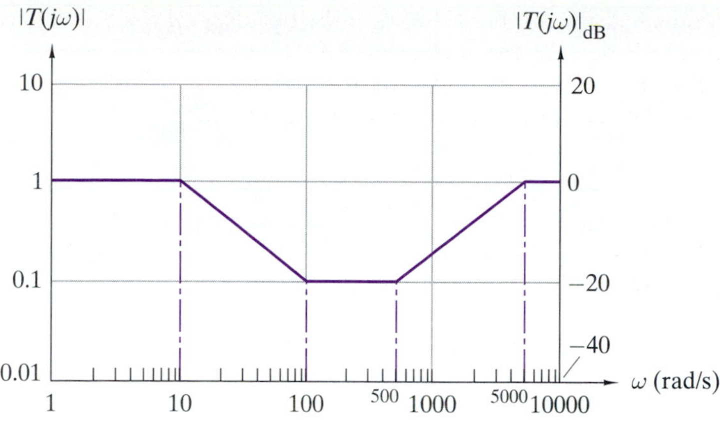

have poles at $s = -10$ rad/s and $s = -5000$ rad/s and zeros at $s = -100$ rad/s and $s = -500$ rad/s. The required transfer function has the form

$$T(s) = K\frac{(s/100 + 1)(s/500 + 1)}{(s/10 + 1)(s/5000 + 1)}$$

where the gain K is yet to be determined. The gain plot in Figure 13–9 indicates that the required dc gain is 0 dB. The dc gain of the proposed transfer function is $T(0) = K$, so we conclude that $K = 1$.

(b) To begin the circuit design, we partition $T(s)$ into the following product of first-order transfer functions:

$$T(s) = T_1(s)T_2(s) = \left(\frac{s/100 + 1}{s/10 + 1}\right)\left(\frac{s/500 + 1}{s/5000 + 1}\right)$$

This partitioning of $T(s)$ is not unique, since we could, for example, interchange the zeros or reverse the order in which the stages are listed. The design sequence shown in Figure 13–10 uses a voltage-divider circuit for the first stage and a noninverting amplifier for the second stage.

Factoring an s out of the numerator and denominator of the stage transfer functions produces the design constraints in the second row of Figure 13–10. Equating numerators and denominators of the design constraint equations leads to the RC circuits shown in the fourth and fifth rows of Figure 13–10. The gain of the voltage-divider stage is unity ($K = 1$) so the OP AMP in the first stage is a voltage follower, as indicated in the prototype design. However, the output of the first stage drives the noninverting input of the second-stage OP AMP. Since OP AMP inputs draw negligible current, no loading occurs when the voltage follower in the first stage is eliminated. The final design in the last row of Figure 13–10 eliminates the first-stage OP AMP and uses magnitude scale factors of $k_m = 10^6$ and $k_m = 5 \times 10^7$ to make all resistors greater than 10 kΩ. ■

Item	First Stage	Second Stage
Transfer function	$T_1(s) = \frac{(s/100) + 1}{(s/10) + 1}$	$T_2(s) = \frac{(s/500) + 1}{(s/5000) + 1}$
Design constraints	Voltage Divider $K\frac{Z_2}{Z_1 + Z_2} = \frac{1/100 + 1/s}{(1/10) + 1/s}$	Noninverting Amplifier $\frac{Z_1 + Z_2}{Z_1} = \frac{1/500 + 1/s}{(1/5000) + 1/s}$
K	1	Not Applicable
Z_1	$\frac{9}{100}$ 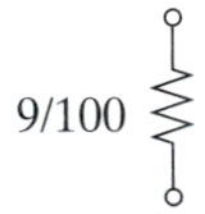 9/100	$\frac{1}{s} + \frac{1}{5000}$ 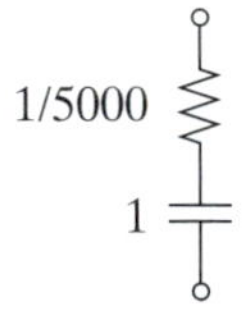 1/5000 1
Z_2	$\frac{1}{s} + \frac{1}{1000}$ 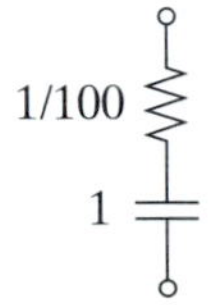 1/100 1	$\frac{9}{5000}$ 9/5000 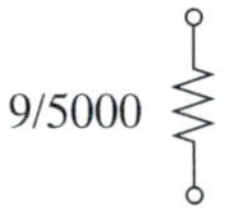
Prototype designs	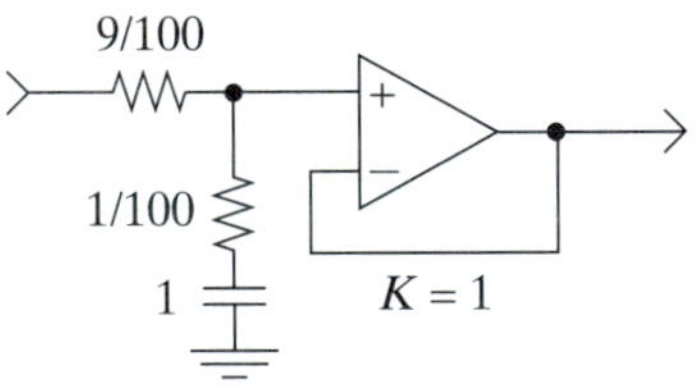 9/100 + − 1/100 1 $K = 1$	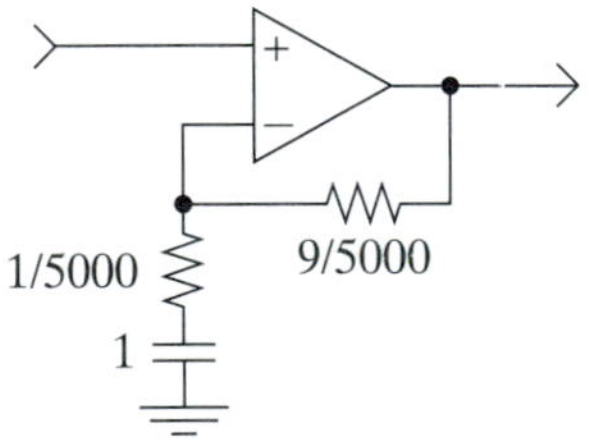 + − 1/5000 9/5000 1
Final designs	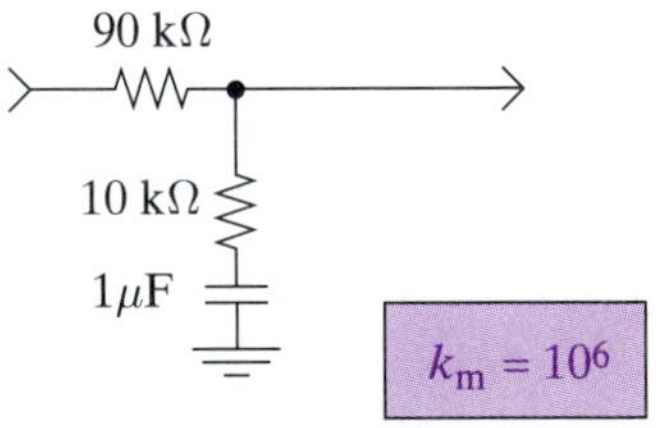 90 kΩ 10 kΩ 1μF $k_m = 10^6$	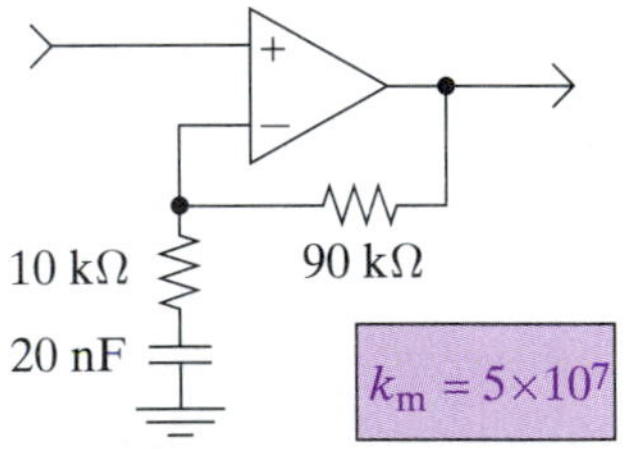 + − 10 kΩ 90 kΩ 20 nF $k_m = 5\times10^7$

FIGURE 13–10 *Design sequence for Example 13–3.*

D DESIGN EXERCISE: 13–1

Design an active RC circuit that realizes a first-order high-pass filter with a cutoff frequency of 500 rad/s and a passband gain of 10.

Answers:

There are no unique answers. Two possible unscaled prototypes are shown in Figure 13–11.

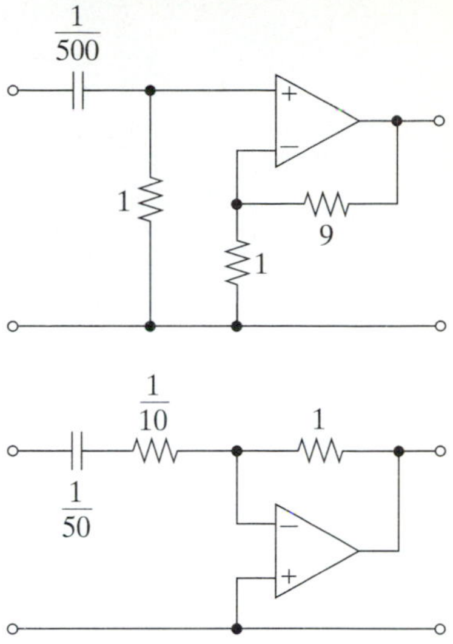

FIGURE 13–11

D DESIGN EXERCISE: 13–2

(a) Construct a transfer function $T(s)$ with the asymptotic gain response shown in Figure 13–12.

(b) Design an active RC circuit to realize the $T(s)$ found in (a).

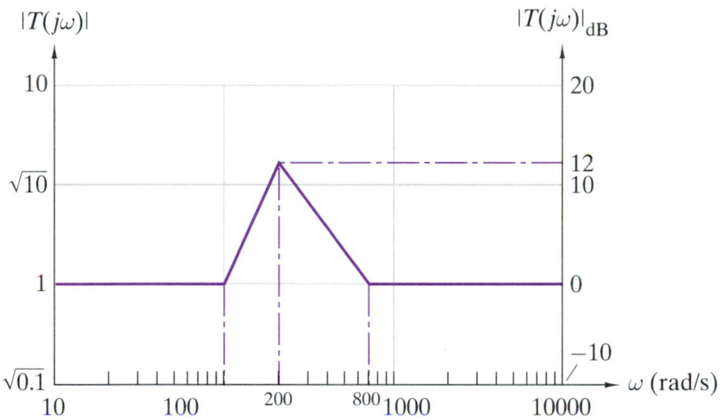

FIGURE 13–12

Answers:

(a) $T(s) = \dfrac{(s/100 + 1)^2\,(s/800 + 1)}{(s/200 + 1)^3}$

(b) There is no unique answer. One possible unscaled prototype design is shown in Figure 13–13.

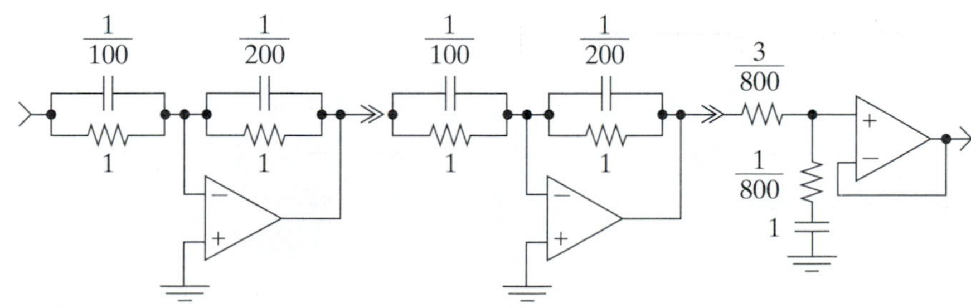

FIGURE 13–13

13–3 DESIGN WITH SECOND-ORDER CIRCUITS

Cascade connections of first-order circuit can only produce transfer functions with poles on the negative real axis in the s plane. The complex poles available in second-order circuits produce highly selective filter characteristics that cannot be realized using only real poles. While passive RLC circuits can produce complex poles, our interest centers on active RC circuits. In this regard we need second-order building block circuits analogous to the first-order circuits in Figure 13–3.

SECOND-ORDER LOW-PASS CIRCUITS

The active RC circuit in Figure 13–14(a) is analyzed in Chapter 11 (Example 11–6), where its voltage transfer function is shown to be

$$T(s) = \frac{V_2(s)}{V_1(s)} = \frac{\mu}{R_1R_2C_1C_2s^2 + (R_1C_1 + R_2C_2 + R_1C_2 - \mu R_1C_1)s + 1} \qquad (13\text{–}2)$$

In circuit applications the dependent source in Figure 13–14(a) is replaced by the noninverting OP AMP circuit in Figure 13–14(b). The OP AMP circuit simulates the dependent source because it draws negligible input current and has very low output resistance. To serve as a replacement for the dependent source, the gain of the noninverting OP AMP circuit must be

FIGURE 13–14 *A second-order low-pass circuit.*

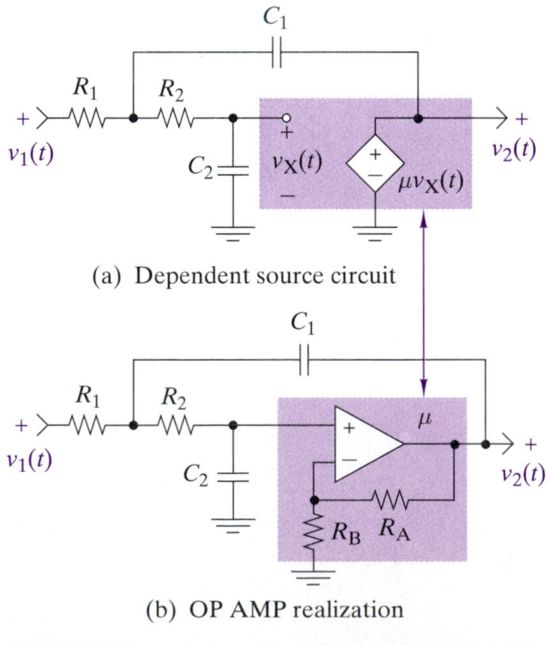

$$\frac{R_A + R_B}{R_B} = \mu \quad (13\text{–}3)$$

where μ is the gain of the dependent source in Figure 13–14(a).

In second-order circuit design we select element values to produce specified values of the natural frequency ω_0 and damping ratio ζ. Comparing the denominator of Eq. (13–2) with the standard form $(s/\omega_0)^2 + 2\zeta(s/\omega_0) + 1$ gives

$$\omega_0 = \frac{1}{\sqrt{R_1R_2C_1C_2}} \text{ and } 2\zeta = \sqrt{\frac{R_2C_2}{R_1C_1}} + \sqrt{\frac{R_1C_2}{R_2C_1}} + (1-\mu)\sqrt{\frac{R_1C_1}{R_2C_2}} \quad (13\text{–}4)$$

Since this yields two design constraints and five unknown element values, the designer has more options than are actually needed. Two common methods of selecting element values are discussed next.

The equal R and equal C method requires that $R_1 = R_2 = R$ and $C_1 = C_2 = C$. Using the equal element constraints together with Eqs. (13–3) and (13–4) yields the conditions

$$RC = \frac{1}{\omega_0} \text{ and } \frac{R_A}{R_B} = 2(1-\zeta) \quad (13\text{–}5)$$

The unity gain method requires that $R_1 = R_2 = R$ and $\mu = 1$. Using these constraints together with Eqs. (13–3) and (13–4) yields the conditions

$$R_A = 0,\ R\sqrt{C_1C_2} = \frac{1}{\omega_0},\ \text{and } \frac{C_2}{C_1} = \zeta^2 \quad (13\text{–}6)$$

Since $R_A = 0$, the noninverting OP AMP circuit in Figure 13–14(b) can be a voltage follower, so neither feedback resistor in the OP AMP circuit is needed.

Finally, combining Eqs. (13–2) and (13–3), we find that the dc gain is $T(0) = (R_A + R_B)/R_B$. That is, the dc gain of the transfer function equals the gain of the OP AMP circuit.

Note: Under the equal element or unity gain approaches, the designer does not control the dc gain since the OP AMP circuit gain is determined by the damping ratio or is set to unity. In some cases the design conditions may not specify the dc gain because what really matters in a filter is the relative gains in passband and stopband. An additional gain stage can be added if the dc gain is specified.

D DESIGN EXAMPLE 13–4

Second Order Low-Pass Active *RC* Design

(a) Construct a second-order low-pass transfer function with a natural frequency of $\omega_0 = 1000$ rad/s and with $|T(0)| = |T(j\omega_0)|$.

(b) Design second-order circuits that realize the transfer function found in (a).

SOLUTION:

(a) The transfer function has the form

$$T(s) = \frac{K}{(s/1000)^2 + 2\zeta(s/1000) + 1}$$

where K and ζ are to be determined. The dc gain of this function is $|T(0)| = |K|$. The gain at the natural frequency is $|T(j1000)| = |K|/2\zeta$. The condition $|T(0)| = |T(j\omega_0)|$ requires $\zeta = 0.5$. Hence a transfer function meeting the design statement is

$$T(s) = \frac{K}{(s/1000)^2 + (s/1000) + 1}$$

Note that the design conditions do not specify a value for the dc gain $|T(0)| = K$.

(b) We use both methods of assigning component values to obtain alternative designs.

Equal R and Equal C Design: Inserting the design constraints $\omega_0 = 1000$ rad/s and $\zeta = 0.5$ into Eq. (13–5) yields $RC = 10^{-3}$ s and $R_A = R_B$. Selecting $R = R_A = 10\ \text{k}\Omega$ requires $C = 100$ nF and $R_B = 10\ \text{k}\Omega$ and produces the circuit in Figure 13–15(a). The transfer function realized by the equal element value design has a dc gain of $K = (R_A + R_B)/R_B = 2$.

FIGURE 13–15

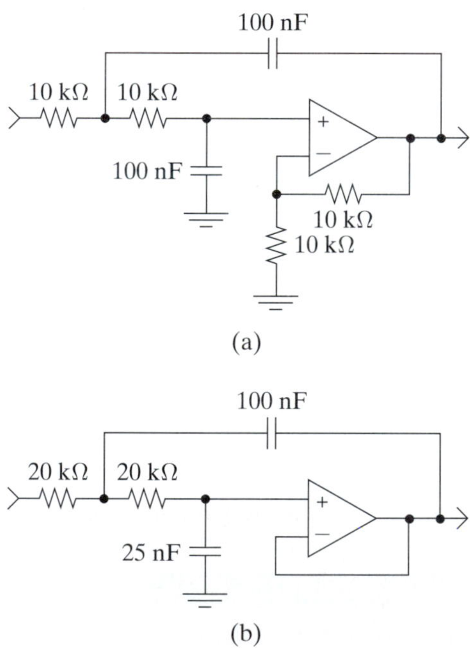

Unity Gain Design: Inserting the design constraints $\omega_0 = 1000$ rad/s and $\zeta = 0.5$ into Eq. (13–6) yields $R\sqrt{C_1C_2} = 10^{-3}$ rad/s and $C_2 = 0.25C_1$. Selecting $C_1 = 100$ nF dictates that $C_2 = 25$ nF and $R = 20\ \text{k}\Omega$ and yields the circuit in Figure 13–15(b). The unity gain design uses two fewer resistors since the

OP AMP is connected as a voltage follower. The transfer function realized by the method has a dc gain $K = 1$, which is less than our equal R and equal C design. ■

SECOND-ORDER HIGH-PASS CIRCUITS

The active *RC* circuit in Figure 13–16(a) has a second-order high-pass voltage transfer function of the form

$$T(s) = \frac{V_2(s)}{V_1(s)} = \frac{\mu R_1 R_2 C_1 C_2 s^2}{R_1 R_2 C_1 C_2 s^2 + (R_2 C_2 + R_1 C_1 + R_1 C_2 - \mu R_2 C_2)s + 1} \tag{13-7}$$

This high-pass circuit is obtained from the low-pass circuit in Figure 13–14(a) by interchanging the locations of the resistors and capacitors.[1] Derivation of the transfer function in Eq. (13–7) is left as an exercise (see Problem 13–26).

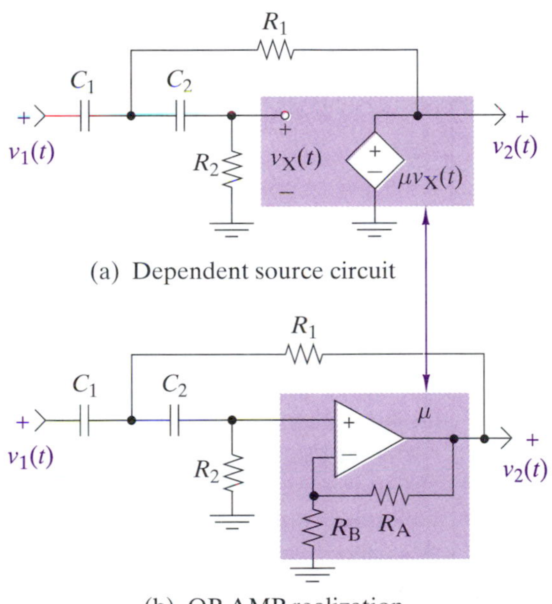

FIGURE 13–16 *A second-order high-pass circuit.*

In design applications the dependent source in Figure 13–16(a) is replaced by the noninverting OP AMP circuit in Figure 13–16(b). To serve as a replacement for the dependent source, the gain of the noninverting OP AMP circuit must be

1 Both circuits belong to a family of circuits originally proposed by R. P. Sallen and E. L. Key in "A Practical Method of Designing RC Active Filters," *IRE Transactions on Circuit Theory*, Vol. CT-2, pp. 74–85, 1955. In 1955 the controlled source was derived using vacuum tubes.

$$\frac{R_A + R_B}{R_B} = \mu \qquad (13\text{–}8)$$

where μ is the gain of the dependent source in Figure 13–16(a). Comparing the denominator of Eq. (13–7) with the standard form $(s/\omega_0)^2 + 2\zeta\,(s/\omega_0) + 1$ yields the following results:

$$\omega_0 = \frac{1}{\sqrt{R_1R_2C_1C_2}} \text{ and } 2\zeta = \sqrt{\frac{R_1C_1}{R_2C_2}} + \sqrt{\frac{R_1C_2}{R_2C_1}} + (1-\mu)\sqrt{\frac{R_2C_2}{R_1C_1}} \qquad (13\text{–}9)$$

As is the case with the low-pass circuit, we have two design constraints and five unknown element values. Two often used methods of defining element values are discussed next.

The equal R and equal C method requires that $R_1 = R_2 = R$ and $C_1 = C_2 = C$. Inserting these constraints into Eqs. (13–8) and (13–9) yields the conditions

$$RC = \frac{1}{\omega_0} \text{ and } \frac{R_A}{R_B} = 2(1-\zeta) \qquad (13\text{–}10)$$

which is the same as the result in Eq. (13–5) for the low-pass circuit. The unity gain method requires that $C_1 = C_2 = C$ and $\mu = 1$. Inserting these constraints into Eqs. (13–8) and (13–9) yields the conditions

$$R_A = 0,\ C\sqrt{R_1R_2} = \frac{1}{\omega_0},\ \text{and } \frac{R_1}{R_2} = \zeta^2 \qquad (13\text{–}11)$$

Since $R_A = 0$, the noninverting OP AMP circuit in Figure 13–16(b) can be a voltage follower, so neither feedback resistor is needed.

Combining Eqs. (13–7) and (13–8) shows that the passband gain of the high-pass transfer function is $|T(\infty)| = (R_A + R_B)/R_B$. As is the case for the low-pass circuit, the passband gain equals the gain of the OP AMP circuit.

Note: Under the equal element or unity gain approaches, the designer does not control the passband gain since the OP AMP circuit gain is determined by the damping ratio or is set to unity. An additional gain stage can be added if a different value of gain is specified.

The next example illustrates the problem of achieving both a specified damping ratio and a passband gain.

D DESIGN EXAMPLE 13–5

Second-Order High-Pass Active *RC* Design

(a) Design a second-order high-pass transfer function with a passband gain of 0 dB and a cutoff frequency of $\omega_C = \omega_0 = 20$ krad/s.
(b) Design active *RC* circuits that realize the transfer function.

SOLUTION:

(a) A high-pass transfer function with a natural frequency of $\omega_0 = 20$ krad/s has the form

$$T(s) = \frac{K(s/20{,}000)^2}{(s/20{,}000)^2 + 2\zeta(s/20{,}000) + 1}$$

where K and ζ are to be determined. The passband gain of this transfer function is $|T(\infty)| = |K|$. The specification calls for a passband gain of 0 dB so $|K| = 1$. For the natural frequency also to be the cutoff frequency requires that $|T(j\omega_0)| = |K|/\sqrt{2}$. This, in turn, means that $|T(j20{,}000)| = |K|\sqrt{2}\zeta = |K|\sqrt{2}$, or $2\zeta = \sqrt{2}$. A transfer function that meets the specification is

$$T(s) = \frac{(s/20{,}000)^2}{(s/20{,}000)^2 + \sqrt{2}(s/20{,}000) + 1}$$

(b) We use both methods of assigning component values to obtain alternative designs.

Equal R and Equal C Design: Substituting the conditions $\omega_0 = 20$ krad/s and $\zeta = 1/\sqrt{2}$ into Eq. (13–10) yields $RC = 5 \times 10^{-5}$ s and $R_A = (2 - \sqrt{2})R_B = 0.586R_B$. Selecting $C = 5$ nF and $R_B = 50$ kΩ requires $R = 10$ kΩ and $R_A = 29.3$ kΩ. The passband gain of the resulting second-order circuit is $|T(\infty)| = K = (R_A + R_B)/R_B = 1.586$ and not unity (0 dB), as given in the specification. To overcome this problem we partition the transfer function as

$$T(s) = \underbrace{\left(\frac{1}{1.586}\right)}_{\text{First Stage}}\underbrace{\left(\frac{1.586(s/20{,}000)^2}{(s/20{,}000)^2 + \sqrt{2}(s/20{,}000) + 1}\right)}_{\text{Second Stage}}$$

The second stage has a passband gain of $K = 1.586$ and can be realized using the second-order high-pass circuit designed previously. The first stage is a voltage divider providing an attenuation of 1/1.586 to bring the

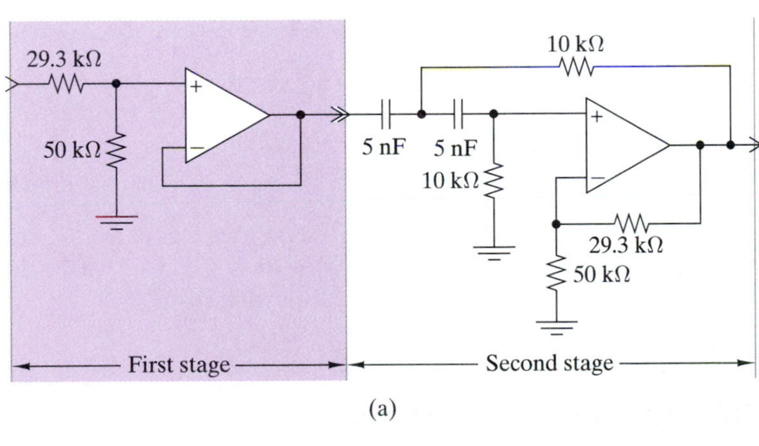

(a)

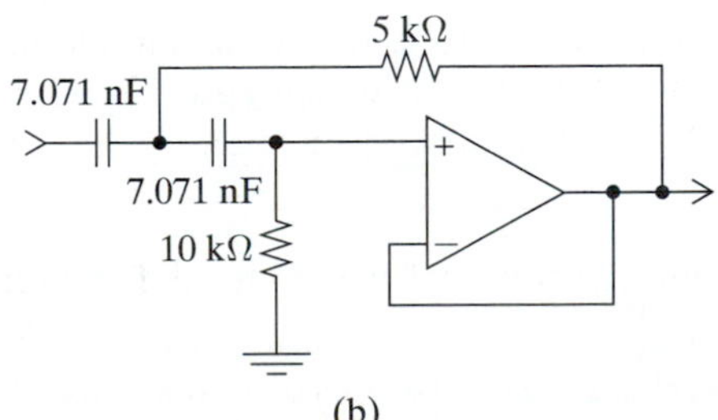

(b)

FIGURE 13–17

overall passband gain down to the 0 dB level specified. Figure 13–17(a) shows the resulting two-stage cascade design.

Unity Gain Design: Substituting the conditions $\omega_0 = 20$ krad/s and $\zeta = 1/\sqrt{2}$ into Eq. (13–11) yields $R_A = 0$, $C\sqrt{R_1R_2} = 5 \times 10^{-5}$ rad/s, and $R_1 = 0.5R_2$. Selecting $R_2 = 10$ kΩ dictates that $R_1 = 5$ kΩ and $C = 7.071$ nF. The transfer function realized by the method has a passband gain $|T(\infty)| = (R_A + R_B)/R_B = 1$, which matches the 0 dB condition in the specification. Since no gain correction is needed, the single stage design in Figure 13–17(b) suffices. ■

SECOND-ORDER BANDPASS CIRCUITS

The active *RC* circuit in Figure 13–18 has a second-order bandpass transfer function of the form

$$T(s) = \frac{V_2(s)}{V_1(s)} = \frac{-R_2C_2s}{R_1R_2C_1C_2s^2 + (R_1C_1 + R_1C_2)s + 1} \tag{13-12}$$

Derivation of the transfer function in Eq. (13–12) is left as an exercise (see Problem 13–27). This bandpass circuit has two negative feedback paths, one provided by the resistor R_2 and the other by the capacitor C_2. This arrangement identifies this circuit as a member of a class of active *RC* circuits called multiple feedback circuits.[2]

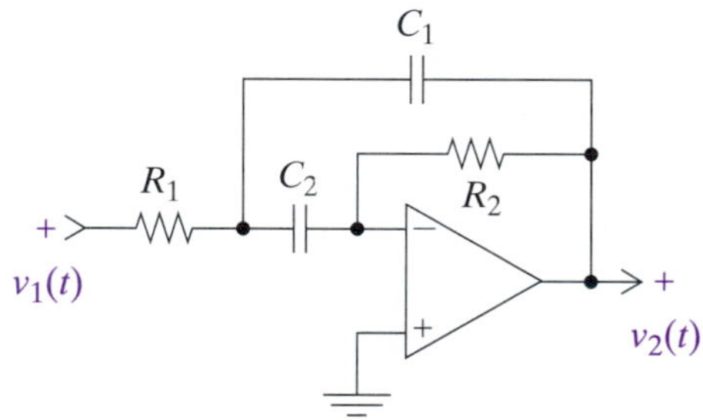

FIGURE 13–18 *A second-order bandpass circuit.*

The key descriptors of a bandpass filter are its center frequency ω_0 and its bandwidth $2\zeta\omega_0$. Comparing the denominator of Eq. (13–12) with the standard form $(s/\omega_0)^2 + 2\zeta\,(s/\omega_0) + 1$ yields the following results:

$$\omega_0 = \frac{1}{\sqrt{R_1R_2C_1C_2}} \quad \text{and} \quad 2\zeta = \sqrt{\frac{R_1C_1}{R_2C_2}} + \sqrt{\frac{R_1C_2}{R_2C_1}} \tag{13-13}$$

In the multiple feedback bandpass case we have two design constraints and four unknown element values. One way to assign element values is to use equal capacitors ($C_1 = C_2 = C$), in which case Eq. (13–13) yields the conditions

2 For an extensive discussion of this family of circuits, see Wai-Kai Chen, Ed., *The Circuits and Filters Handbook*, Boca Raton, Fla., CRC Press, 1995, Chapter 76, p. 2372ff. The bandpass circuit in Figure 13–18 is sometimes called the Delyannis-Friend circuit. See M. E. Van Valkenburg, *Analog Filter Design*, New York, Holt, Rinehart and Winston, 1982, p. 203.

$$C\sqrt{R_1R_2} = \frac{1}{\omega_0} \quad \text{and} \quad \frac{R_1}{R_2} = \zeta^2 \qquad (13-14)$$

For this choice of element values the gain at the center frequency is $|T(j\omega_0)| = R_2/2R_1 = 1/2\zeta$. As is the case for the low-pass and high-pass circuits, we cannot independently choose the damping ratio and the passband gain.

Bandpass filters are traditionally described in terms of center frequency ω_0 and a quality factor $Q = 1/2\zeta$. For second-order functions the filter bandwidth is

$$B = 2\zeta\omega_0 = \omega_0/Q$$

When $Q > 1$ ($\zeta < 0.5$) the filter is said to be narrowband because the bandwidth is less than the center frequency. Conversely, $Q < 1$ ($\zeta > 0.5$) describes a broadband filter. The active *RC* circuit shown in Figure 13–18 is best suited to narrowband applications. The design of broadband filters is discussed in Sect. 13–6.

D DESIGN EXAMPLE 13–6

Second-Order Band-Pass Active *RC* Design

Design an active *RC* bandpass circuit that has a center frequency of 10 kHz and a bandwidth of 2 kHz.

SOLUTION:

From the definitions of center frequency and bandwidth we have

$$\omega_0 = 2\pi \times 10^4 = 6.283 \times 10^4 \text{ rad/s} \quad \text{and} \quad Q = \frac{\omega_0}{B} = 5$$

Selecting $R_2 = 100$ kΩ and using $\zeta = 1/2Q = 0.1$ in Eq. (13–14) yields $R_1 =$ 1 kΩ and $C_1 = C_2 = 1.592$ nF. The passband gain produced by this design is $|T(j\omega_0)| = 1/2\,\zeta = 5$.

D DESIGN EXERCISE: 13–3

Design an active *RC* circuit that has the same transfer function $T(s) = V_2(s)/V_1(s)$ as the *RLC* circuit in Figure 13–19.

Answer: One possible solution is shown in Figure 13–20.

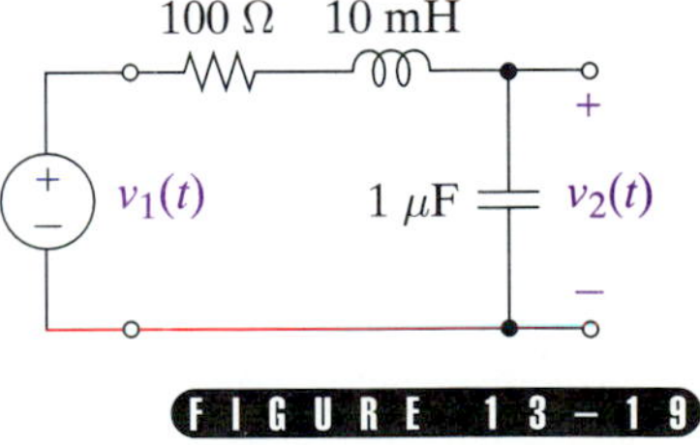

FIGURE 13–19

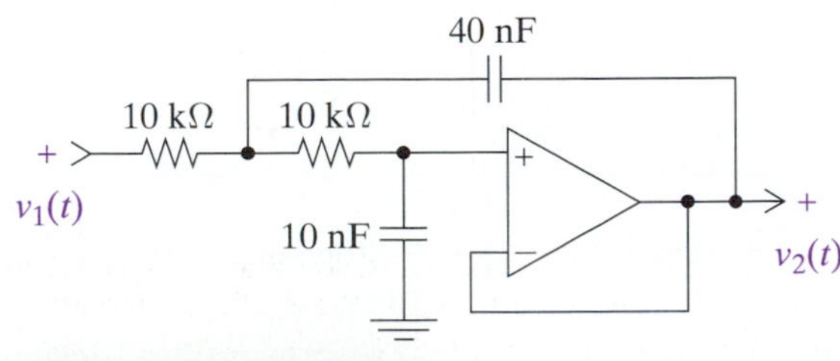

FIGURE 13–20

DISCUSSION: *At first glance the* RLC *filter in Figure 13–19 seems simpler than the active* RC *circuit in Figure 13–20. However, active* RC *filters offer the advantages discussed in the first section of this chapter. Briefly, the advantages are that they produce both gain and frequency selectivity, they can be connected in cascade to produce high-order filters, and they are often smaller and less expensive in low-frequency applications.*

D DESIGN EXERCISE: 13–4

Design a second-order active RC high-pass circuit with $\omega_0 = 500$ rad/s and Q = 0.5 using only 10-kΩ resistors.

Answers: Two possible solutions are shown in Figure 13–21.

FIGURE 13–21

13–4 LOW-PASS FILTER DESIGN

The gain of the ideal low-pass filter response in Figure 13–22 is unity (0 dB) in the passband and zero (–∞ dB) in the stopband. The transfer functions of physically realizable (real) low-pass filters are rational functions that can only approximate the ideal response. These rational functions have asymptotic high-frequency responses that roll off as ω^{-n} ($-20n$ dB/decade), where n is the number of poles in $T(s)$. Increasing the number of poles improves the approximation, as indicated in Figure 13–22. On the other hand, increasing the number of poles makes the circuit realizing $T(s)$ more complicated. Since cost and circuit complexity are usually related, there is an important trade-off between circuit complexity and how closely different filters approximate the ideal response.

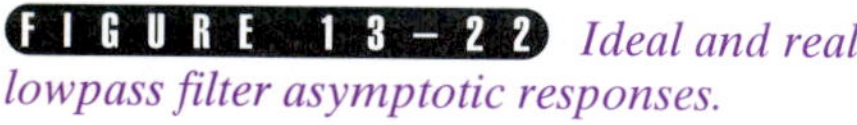

FIGURE 13–22 *Ideal and real lowpass filter asymptotic responses.*

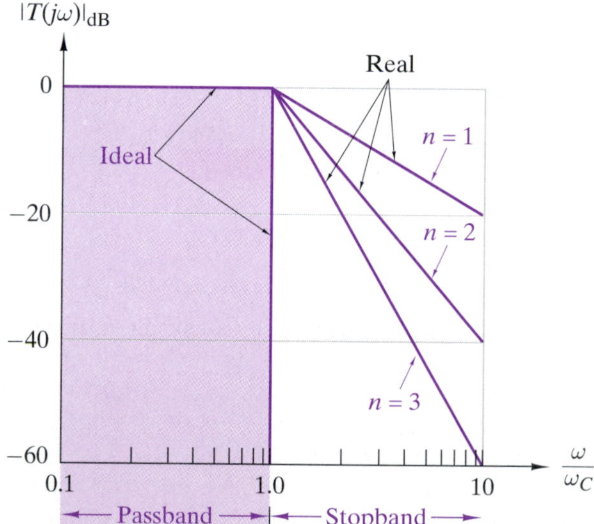

Since we can only approximate the ideal response filter, design requirements specify how closely we must approach the ideal. A commonly used way to specify this is to require that the gain response fall within the unshaded region in Figure 13–23. Many different transfer functions can meet this restriction, as illustrated by two responses shown in the figure. The allowable region in Figure 13–23 is defined by four parameters. The parameter T_{MAX} is the maximum gain in the passband, called simply the **passband gain**. Within the passband the gain $|T(j\omega)|$ must remain in the range

$$\frac{T_{MAX}}{\sqrt{2}} \leq |T(j\omega)| \leq T_{MAX}$$

and must equal $T_{MAX}/\sqrt{2}$ at the **cutoff frequency** ω_C. In the stopband the gain must decrease to and remain below T_{MIN} for all $\omega \geq \omega_{MIN}$. In sum, the parameters T_{MAX} and ω_C specify the passband response and the parameters T_{MIN} and ω_{MIN} specify how rapidly the stopband response must decrease.

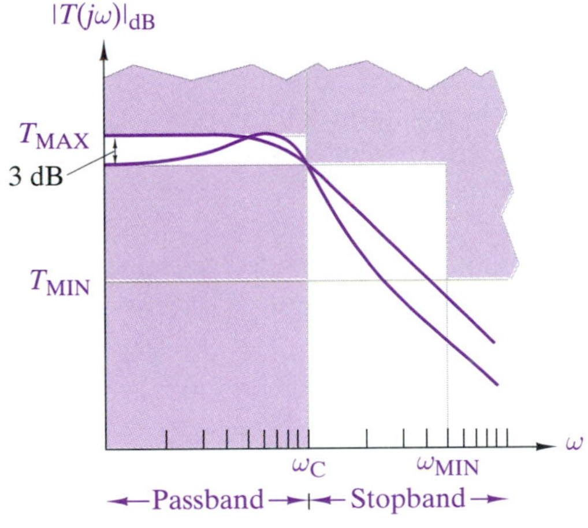

FIGURE 13–23 *Gain responses meeting a low-pass filter specification.*

To design a low-pass filter we must construct a transfer function whose gain $|T(j\omega)|$ approximates the ideal filter response within the tolerances allowed by the four parameters T_{MAX}, T_{MIN}, ω_C, and ω_{MIN}. Such a low-pass transfer function has the form

$$T_n(s) = \frac{K}{q_n(s)}$$

where $q_n(s)$ is an nth-order polynomial defining the poles. Thus, filter design involves two major tasks: (1) Construct a transfer function $T_n(s)$ whose gain response meets the filter performance specification and (2) devise one or more circuits that produce the transfer function $T_n(s)$.

We will consider three approaches to the first task: first-order cascade responses, Butterworth responses, and Chebychev responses. For the second task we partition the transfer function into a product of first- and second-order functions each of which can be realized using the building block circuits described in the preceding sections. A circuit realizing the transfer function is obtained by a cascade connection of these first- and second-order stages.

FIRST-ORDER CASCADE RESPONSES

A simple way to produce an n-th order low-pass filter is to connect n identical first-order low-pass filters in cascade. When we connect n identical filters in cascade the overall transfer function is

$$T_n(s) = \underbrace{\left[\frac{K}{s/\alpha + 1}\right] \times \left[\frac{K}{s/\alpha + 1}\right] \times \ldots \left[\frac{K}{s/\alpha + 1}\right]}_{n \text{ Stages}} = \frac{K^n}{(s/\alpha + 1)^n} \qquad (13-15)$$

In a design problem we must select K, α, and n such that the gain response of this transfer function meets the performance requirements defined by T_{MAX}, T_{MIN}, ω_C, and ω_{MIN}.

The transfer function in Eq. (13–15) produces a gain response of

$$|T_n(j\omega)| = \frac{|K|^n}{\left[\sqrt{1 + (\omega/\alpha)^2}\right]^n} \qquad (13-16)$$

Note that the low-frequency gain asymptote is $|K|^n$ and the high-frequency asymptote is $(|K|\alpha/\omega)^n$. These asymptotes intersect (i.e., are equal) at a corner frequency located at $\omega = \alpha$. However, when $n > 1$ this corner frequency is *not* the filter cutoff frequency.

The maximum gain in Eq. (13–16) occurs at $\omega = 0$, where gain is $|T(0)| = |K|^n$. To meet the passband gain requirement, we select $|K|^n = T_{MAX}$. The passband specification also requires the gain at the cutoff frequency to be

$$|T_n(j\omega_C)| = \frac{|K|^n}{\left[\sqrt{1 + (\omega_C/\alpha)^2}\right]^n} = \frac{T_{MAX}}{\sqrt{2}}$$

With $|K|^n = T_{MAX}$ we can equate the denominators on the right side of this expression and solve for α as

$$\alpha = \frac{\omega_C}{\sqrt{2^{1/n} - 1}} \qquad (13-17)$$

Each first-order function in the cascade has a corner frequency at $\omega = \alpha$ whose value depends on ω_C and the number of poles n. Since $2^{1/n} - 1 \leq 1$ it follows that $\alpha \geq \omega_C$; that is, the corner frequency is higher than the cutoff frequency for all $n > 1$. Said another way, increasing the order of a cascade filter requires that we increase the corner frequency to maintain the same bandwidth.

Figure 13–24 shows normalized gain responses of first-order low-pass cascades for $n = 1$ to $n = 8$. All of these responses meet the passband requirements. As expected, the stopband attenuation increases as the number of poles n increases since the high-frequency asymptote is proportional to $(\alpha/\omega)^n$. We can estimate the number of poles needed to meet the stopband requirements from the graphs in Figure 13–24. For example, suppose the stopband requirement is $T_{MIN}/T_{MAX} = 0.01$ (–40 dB) at $\omega_{MIN} = 10\omega_C$. In Figure 13–24 we see that at $\omega/\omega_C = 10$ the normalized gain $|T(j\omega)|/T_{MAX}$ is –32 dB for $n = 2$ and –42 db for $n = 3$. Hence $n = 3$ is the smallest number of poles in a first-order cascade response that meets these requirements.

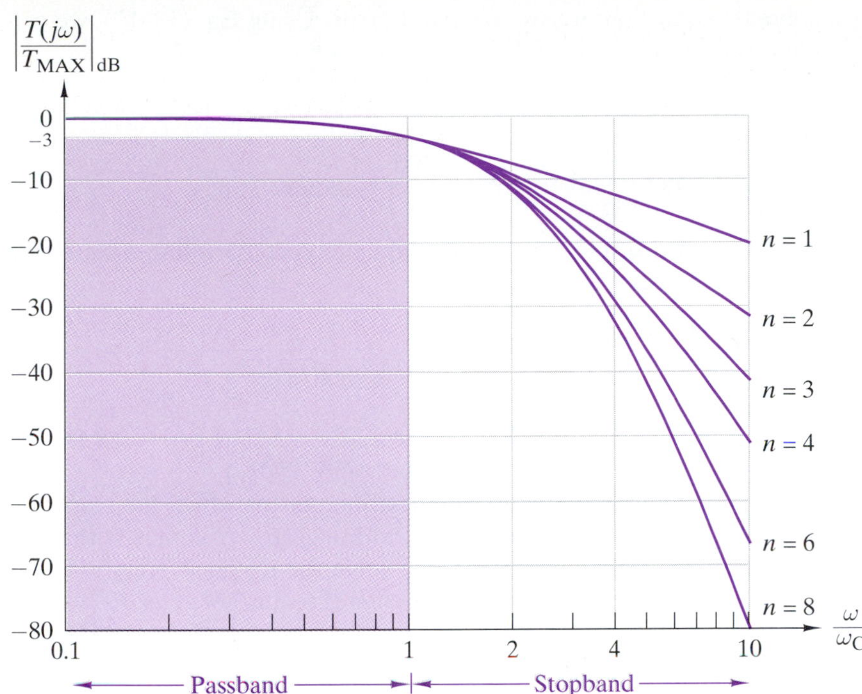

FIGURE 13–24
First-order low-pass cascade filter responses.

In summary, to construct a first-order cascade transfer function, we proceed as follows. Given values of T_{MAX}, T_{MIN}, ω_C, and ω_{MIN}, we set $|K|^n = T_{MAX}$ and use Figure 13–24 (or trial and error) to find the smallest integer n that meets the stopband requirements. Given n and ω_C, we calculate α using Eq. (13–17) and obtain the required transfer function $T_n(s)$ from Eq. (13–15). The transfer function is partitioned into a product of identical first-order functions, each of which can be obtained using a first-order circuit. The design process is relatively simple and yields identical stages, which may reduce manufacturing and logistical support costs. The next example illustrates these features.

D DESIGN EXAMPLE 13–7

Low-Pass Design with First-Order Poles

(a) Construct a first-order cascade transfer function that meets the following requirements: $T_{MAX} = 10$ dB, $\omega_C = 200$ rad/s, $T_{MIN} = -20$ dB, and $\omega_{MIN} = 800$ rad/s.
(b) Design a cascade of active *RC* circuits that realizes the transfer function developed in (a).

SOLUTION:

(a) The stopband requirement is that the normalized gain be less than −30 dB at $\omega/\omega_C = 800/200 = 4$. Figure 13–24 suggests that $n = 7$ might work, but we cannot be sure since the curve for $n = 7$ is not shown. To resolve this question, we use trial and error. Using Eq. (13–17), we calculate corner frequencies for $n = 7$ and $n = 8$.

$$\text{For } n = 7, \quad \alpha = \frac{200}{\sqrt{2^{1/7} - 1}} = 620 \quad \text{rad/s}$$

$$\text{For } n = 8, \quad \alpha = \frac{200}{\sqrt{2^{1/8} - 1}} = 665 \quad \text{rad/s}$$

Next we use Eq. (13–16) to calculate the corresponding normalized stopband gains:

$$\text{For } n = 7, \left|\frac{T_7(j\omega_{\text{MIN}})}{T_{\text{MAX}}}\right| = 20\log\left(\frac{1}{\left[\sqrt{1 + (800/620)^2}\,\right]^7}\right) = -29.8 \text{ dB}$$

$$\text{For } n = 8, \left|\frac{T_8(j\omega_{\text{MIN}})}{T_{\text{MAX}}}\right| = 20\log\left(\frac{1}{\left[\sqrt{1 + (800/665)^2}\,\right]^8}\right) = -31.1 \text{ dB}$$

Strictly speaking, $n = 8$ is the smallest integer for which the stopband gain meets the design requirement, although $n = 7$ comes within 0.2 dB (roughly 2.3%). Using $n = 8$, we solve for K. Since $T_{\text{MAX}} = 10$ dB (factor of $10^{1/2}$), we can write the passband requirement as $|K|^8 = 10^{1/2}$; hence $K = 1.155$. So, finally, the required first-order cascade transfer function is

$$T_8(s) = \left(\frac{1.155}{s/665 + 1}\right)^8$$

Note that the corner frequency is 665 rad/s while the cutoff frequency is 200 rad/s.

(b) The transfer function developed in (a) can be partitioned into a product of eight identical first-order functions of the form $1.155/(s/665 + 1)$. Using the voltage-divider building block in Figure 13–3 produces the following design constraints:

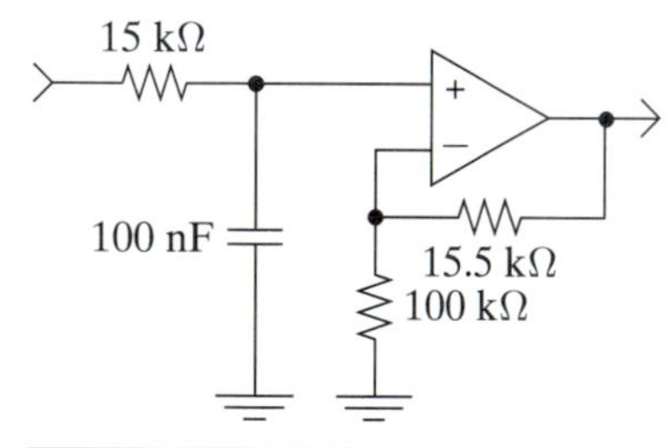

FIGURE 13–25

$$K\frac{Z_2}{Z_1 + Z_2} = 1.155 \times \frac{1/s}{1/665 + 1/s}$$

These conditions yield $K = (R_A + R_B)/R_B = 1.155$, $Z_2(s) = 1/s$, and $Z_1(s) = 1/665$. Selecting $R_B = 100$ kΩ leads to $R_A = 15.5$ kΩ. Using the magnitude scale factor of $k_m = 10^7$ on the RC voltage divider circuit produces the first-order low-pass circuit in Figure 13–25. A cascade connection of eight such circuits produces a low-pass filter that meets the design requirements. ■

BUTTERWORTH LOW-PASS RESPONSES

All Butterworth low-pass filters produce a gain response of the form

$$|T_n(j\omega)| = \frac{|K|}{\sqrt{1 + (\omega/\omega_C)^{2n}}} \qquad (13\text{–}18)$$

where ω_C is the cutoff frequency and n is the number of poles in $T_n(s)$. By inspection, the maximum passband gain occurs at $\omega = 0$, where the gain is

$|T(0)| = |K| = T_{MAX}$. At the cutoff frequency the gain is $|T_n(j\omega_C)| = |K|/\sqrt{2}$ for all n. Thus, selecting $|K| = T_{MAX}$ ensures that the Butterworth gain response in Eq. (13–18) satisfies the passband requirements for all values of n.

The low-frequency gain asymptote in Eq. (13–18) is $|K|$, while the high-frequency asymptote is $|K|\,(\omega_C/\omega)^n$. These two asymptotes intersect at a corner frequency of $\omega = \omega_C$. In a Butterworth response the corner frequency is always equal to the cutoff frequency, which means that it is independent of the order of the filter. This feature is different from the first-order cascade response, where the corner frequency increases with filter order.

Figure 13–26 compares normalized first-order cascade and Butterworth gain responses for $n = 4$. Both responses meet the passband requirements, and both have high-frequency asymptotic slopes of $-20n = -80$ dB/decade. However, the Butterworth response provides greater attenuation in the stopband because its corner frequency is lower and hence it approaches its high-frequency asymptote at lower frequencies than does the first-order cascade response.

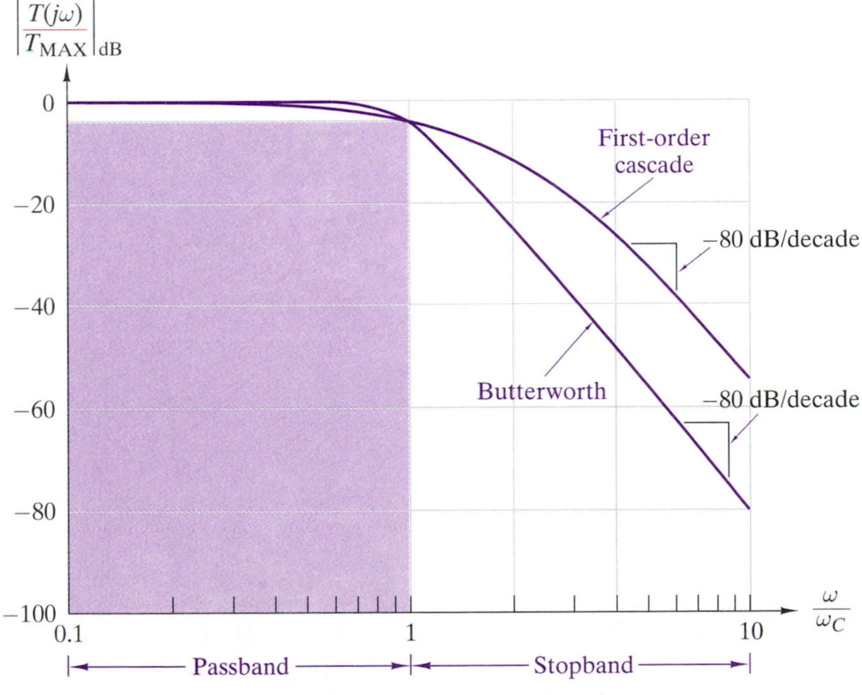

FIGURE 13–26 *First-order cascade and Butterworth low-pass filter responses for* n = 4.

With the Butterworth response we can analytically solve for the required number of poles. Since $|K| = T_{MAX}$, we insert the stopband requirements in Eq. (13–18) to obtain

$$|T(j\omega_{MIN})| = \frac{T_{MAX}}{\sqrt{1 + (\omega_{MIN}/\omega_C)^{2n}}} \leq T_{MIN} \qquad (13\text{–}19)$$

Solving this equation for n yields the constraint

$$n \geqslant \frac{1}{2}\frac{\ln[(T_{MAX}/T_{MIN})^2 - 1]}{\ln[\omega_{MIN}/\omega_C]} \tag{13-20}$$

For example, the stopband requirement of $T_{MAX}/T_{MIN} = 10^{3/2}$ (30 dB) at $\omega_{MIN} = 4\omega_C$ yields

$$n \geqslant \frac{1}{2}\frac{\ln[(10^{3/2})^2 - 1]}{\ln[4]} = 2.49$$

The smallest integer meeting this constraint is $n = 3$.

Figure 13–27 shows normalized plots of the Butterworth gain response in Eq. (13–18) for $n = 1$ to $n = 6$. These graphs can be used to estimate the number of poles required to meet the stopband requirements. For example, consider the requirements used previously, namely, $|T_{MIN}/T_{MAX}|_{dB} =$ –30 dB at $\omega_{MIN} = 4\omega_C$. In Figure 13–27 we see that a $\omega/\omega_C = 4$, $|T(j\omega)/T_{MAX}|_{dB}$ is –24 dB for $n = 2$, and is –36 dB for $n = 3$. Hence $n = 3$ is the smallest number of poles in a Butterworth response that meets these stopband requirements. Thus, either Eq. (13–20) or Figure 13–27 can be used to determine n.

FIGURE 13–27 *Butterworth low-pass filter responses.*

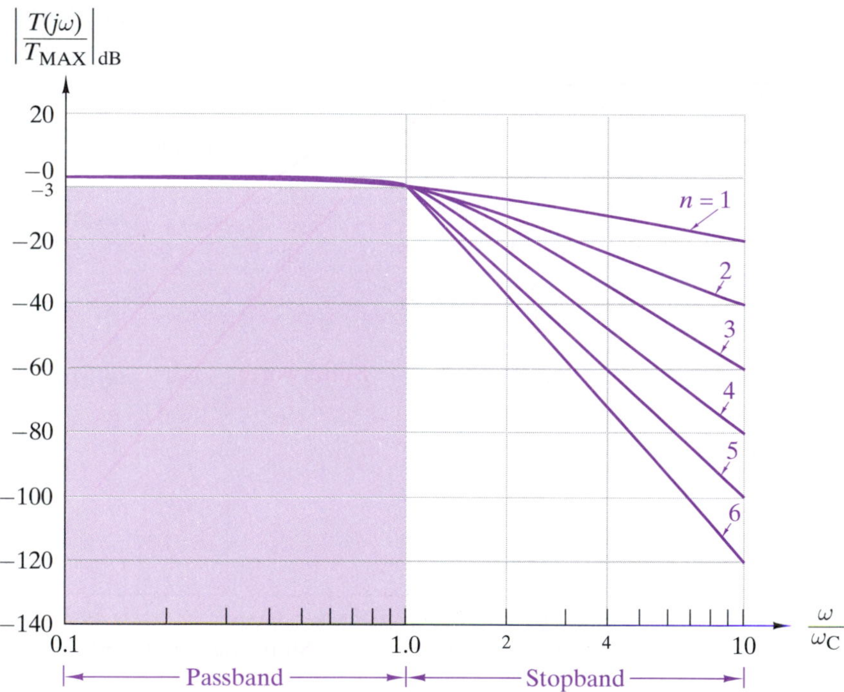

To design low-pass filters we need polynomials $q_n(s)$ such that the transfer function

$$T_n(s) = \frac{K}{q_n(s)}$$

produces the Butterworth gain response in Eq. (13–18). We begin with a first-order polynomial of the form $q_1(s) = s/\omega_C + 1$, which produces the gain response

$$|T_1(j\omega)| = \frac{|K|}{\sqrt{1 + (\omega/\omega_C)^2}} \tag{13–21}$$

This response has the Butterworth form for $n = 1$. Next consider a second-order polynomial of the form $q_2(s) = (s/\omega_C)^2 + 2\zeta(s/\omega_C) + 1$, which produces the gain response

$$\begin{aligned} |T_2(j\omega)| &= \frac{|K|}{\sqrt{[1 - (\omega/\omega_C)^2]^2 + (2\zeta\omega/\omega_C)^2}} \\ &= \frac{|K|}{\sqrt{1 + (4\zeta^2 - 2)(\omega/\omega_C)^2 + (\omega/\omega_C)^4}} \end{aligned} \tag{13–22}$$

When $4\zeta^2 = 2$ this response has the Butterworth form for $n = 2$. As a final example, consider a third-order polynomial of the form $q_3(s) = (s/\omega_C + 1)[(s/\omega_C)^2 + 2\zeta(s/\omega_C) + 1]$, which produces a gain response

$$\begin{aligned} |T_3(j\omega)| &= \frac{|K|}{\sqrt{1 + (\omega/\omega_C)^2}\sqrt{[1 - (\omega/\omega_C)^2]^2 + 2\zeta(\omega/\omega_C)^2}} \\ &= \frac{|K|}{\sqrt{1 + (4\zeta^2 - 1)(\omega/\omega_C)^2 + (4\zeta^2 - 1)(\omega/\omega_C)^4 + (\omega/\omega_C)^6}} \end{aligned} \tag{13–23}$$

When $4\zeta^2 = 1$ this response has the Butterworth form of Eq. (13–18) for $n = 3$.

The preceding analysis shows that the polynomials

$$\begin{aligned} q_1(s) &= s/\omega_C + 1 \\ q_2(s) &= (s/\omega_C)^2 + \sqrt{2}(s/\omega_C) + 1 \\ q_3(s) &= (s/\omega_C + 1)[(s/\omega_C)^2 + (s/\omega_C) + 1] \end{aligned}$$

produce the Butterworth gain response in Eq. (13–18) for $n = 1$, 2, and 3. Proceeding in this fashion, we can generate the normalized ($\omega_C = 1$) polynomials in Table 13–1 for values of n up to 6.

TABLE 13–1 NORMALIZED POLYNOMIALS THAT PRODUCE BUTTERWORTH RESPONSES

ORDER	NORMALIZED DENOMINATOR POLYNOMIALS
1	$(s + 1)$
2	$(s^2 + 1.414s + 1)$
3	$(s + 1)(s^2 + s + 1)$
4	$(s^2 + 0.7654s + 1)(s^2 + 1.848s + 1)$
5	$(s + 1)(s^2 + 0.6180s + 1)(s^2 + 1.618s + 1)$
6	$(s^2 + 0.5176s + 1)(s^2 + 1.414s + 1)(s^2 + 1.932s + 1)$

A general Butterworth low-pass transfer function with a cutoff frequency of ω_C is

$$T_n(s) = \frac{K}{q_n(s/\omega_C)} \tag{13–24}$$

where $q_n(s)$ is the nth-order normalized polynomial in Table 13–1. With $|K| = T_{MAX}$ this transfer function meets the passband conditions because the normalized polynomials produce Butterworth gain responses. The order of the polynomial, and hence the number of poles, is determined from the stopband requirement using Figure 13–27 or Eq. (13–20).

Once we have constructed the required $T_n(s)$, we partition it into a product of first- and second-order functions and realize each function using the building blocks developed in the previous sections. The next example illustrates the design procedure for a Butterworth low-pass filter.

DESIGN EXAMPLE 13–8

Low-Pass Design with Butterworth Poles

(a) Construct a Butterworth low-pass transfer function such that T_{MAX} = 20 dB, ω_C = 1000 rad/s, and T_{MIN} = −20 dB at ω_{MIN} = 4000 rad/s.

(b) Design a cascade of active *RC* circuits that realizes the transfer function found in part (a).

SOLUTION:

(a) The passband gain condition requires that $K = 10$ in Eq. (13–24). The stopband requirement specifies that the gain at $\omega_{MIN}/\omega_C = 4$ must be 40 dB (factor of 100) less than the passband gain. Using Eq. (13–20) yields

$$n \geqslant \frac{1}{2}\frac{\ln[(100)^2 - 1]}{\ln[4]} = 3.32$$

from which we see that $n = 4$ is the lowest-order polynomial that meets the stopband requirements. Using the fourth-order polynomial from Table 13–1, the required Butterworth low-pass transfer function is

$$T(s) = \frac{K}{q_4(s/\omega_C)}$$

$$= \frac{10}{\left[\left(\frac{s}{1000}\right)^2 + 0.7654\left(\frac{s}{1000}\right) + 1\right]\left[\left(\frac{s}{1000}\right)^2 + 1.848\left(\frac{s}{1000}\right) + 1\right]}$$

(b) The transfer function developed in (a) can be partitioned as follows:

$$\frac{T(s)}{10} = \left[\frac{1}{\left(\frac{s}{1000}\right)^2 + 0.7654\left(\frac{s}{1000}\right) + 1}\right]\left[\frac{1}{\left(\frac{s}{1000}\right)^2 + 1.848\left(\frac{s}{1000}\right) + 1}\right]$$

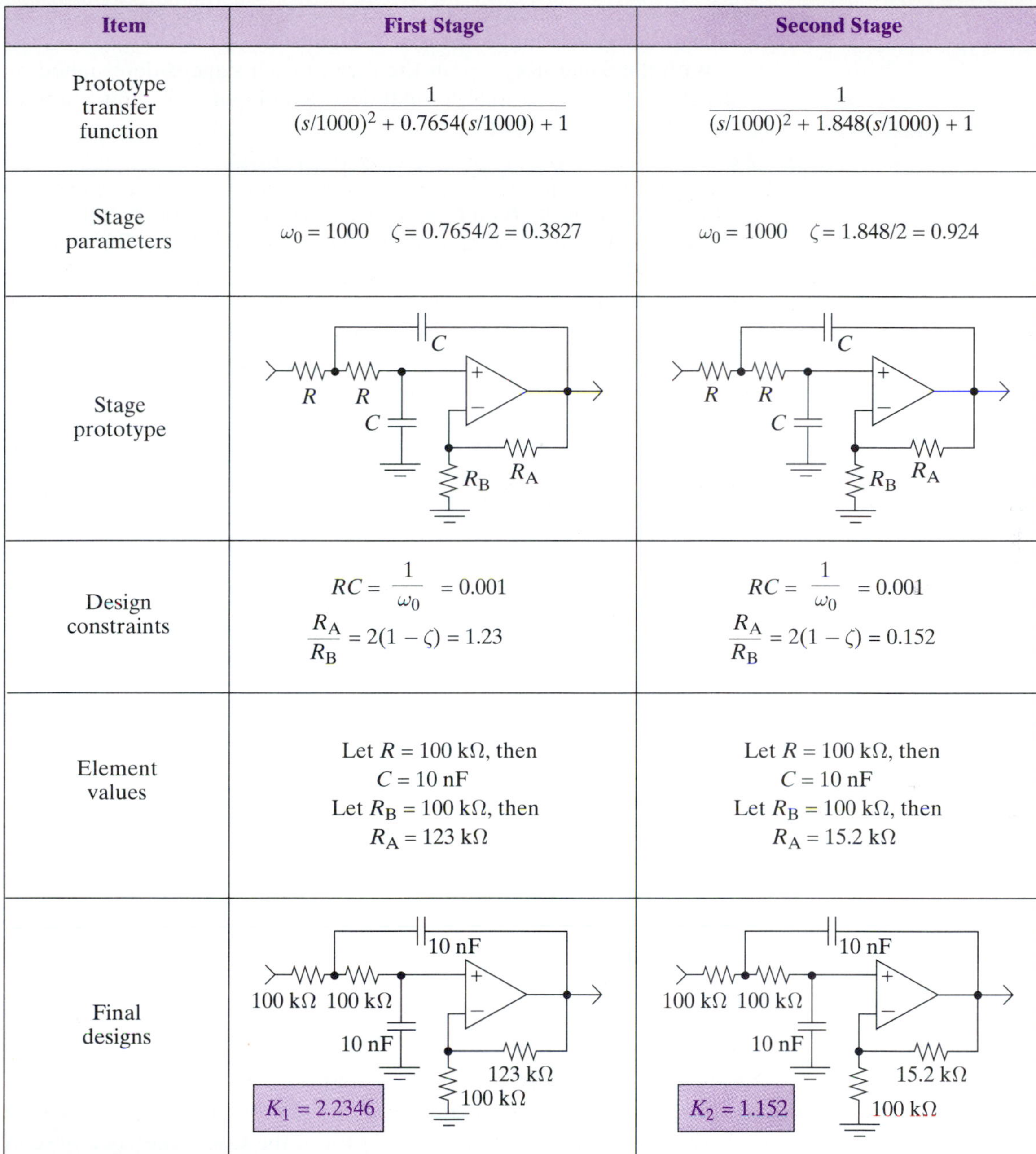

Item	First Stage	Second Stage
Prototype transfer function	$\dfrac{1}{(s/1000)^2 + 0.7654(s/1000) + 1}$	$\dfrac{1}{(s/1000)^2 + 1.848(s/1000) + 1}$
Stage parameters	$\omega_0 = 1000 \quad \zeta = 0.7654/2 = 0.3827$	$\omega_0 = 1000 \quad \zeta = 1.848/2 = 0.924$
Stage prototype	C, R, R, C, R_B, R_A	C, R, R, C, R_B, R_A
Design constraints	$RC = \dfrac{1}{\omega_0} = 0.001$ $\dfrac{R_A}{R_B} = 2(1 - \zeta) = 1.23$	$RC = \dfrac{1}{\omega_0} = 0.001$ $\dfrac{R_A}{R_B} = 2(1 - \zeta) = 0.152$
Element values	Let $R = 100$ kΩ, then $C = 10$ nF Let $R_B = 100$ kΩ, then $R_A = 123$ kΩ	Let $R = 100$ kΩ, then $C = 10$ nF Let $R_B = 100$ kΩ, then $R_A = 15.2$ kΩ
Final designs	10 nF, 100 kΩ, 100 kΩ, 10 nF, 123 kΩ, 100 kΩ $K_1 = 2.2346$	10 nF, 100 kΩ, 100 kΩ, 10 nF, 15.2 kΩ, 100 kΩ $K_2 = 1.152$

FIGURE 13–28 *Design sequence for Example 13–8.*

Figure 13–28 shows a design sequence for these second-order transfer functions using the Sallen-Key low-pass circuit shown in Figure 13–14. The first and second rows in the figure give the transfer functions for each stage and the stage parameters. Using the equal R and equal C design method [see Eq. (13–5)] leads to the design constraints in the fourth row. The element values selected in the fifth row produce the final design shown in the last row of Figure 13–28.

With the Sallen-Key circuit the gain of each stage is determined by the stage damping ratio. The final designs in Figure 13–28 produce an overall passband gain of

$$K = K_1K_2 = 2.23 \times 1.152 = 2.57$$

which is less that the requirement of $K = 10$. To meet the gain requirement, we add a third stage with a gain of $K_3 = 10/2.57 = 3.89$. Figure 13–29 shows a final three-stage cascade design that meets all of the design requirements. ■

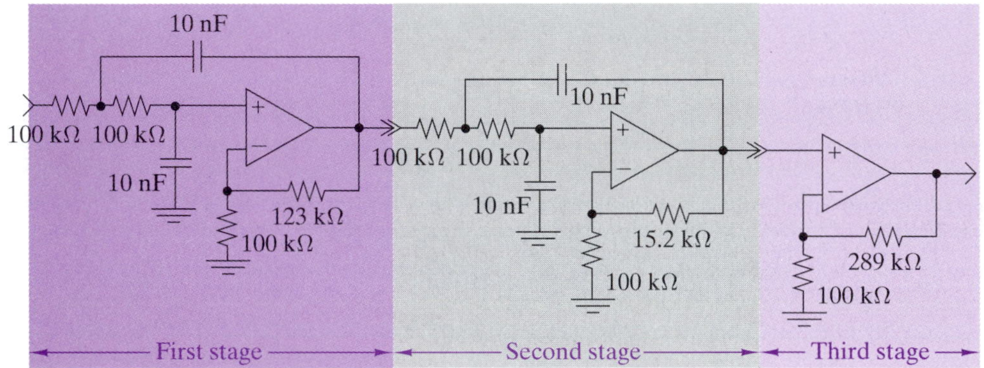

FIGURE 13–29

CHEBYCHEV LOW-PASS RESPONSES

All Chebychev low-pass filters produce a gain response of the form

$$|T_n(j\omega)| = \frac{|K|}{\sqrt{1 + C_n^2(\omega/\omega_C)}} \quad (13\text{–}25)$$

where $C_n(x)$ is an nth-order Chebychev polynomial defined by

$$C_n(x) = \cos[n \times \cos^{-1}(x)] \quad \text{for} \quad x \leq 1 \quad (13\text{–}26\text{a})$$

and

$$C_n(x) = \cosh[n \times \cosh^{-1}(x)] \quad \text{for} \quad x > 1 \quad (13\text{–}26\text{b})$$

In the passband ($x = \omega/\omega_C \leq 1$) the function $C_n(x)$ in Eq. (13–26a) is a cosine function that varies between –1 and +1. Hence $C_n^2(x)$ varies between 0 and 1 with the result that the passband gain of the Chebychev response in Eq. (13–25) varies over the range

$$\frac{|K|}{\sqrt{2}} \leq |T_n(j\omega)| \leq |K| \quad \text{for} \quad \omega \leq \omega_C$$

and, in particular at $\omega = \omega_C$,

$$|T_n(j\omega_C)| = \frac{|K|}{\sqrt{1 + C_n^2(1)}} = \frac{|K|}{\sqrt{2}}$$

for all values of n. By selecting $|K| = T_{MAX}$ we ensure that the Chebychev response in Eq. (13–25) meets the passband gain requirements for all n.

Like Butterworth responses, the Chebychev order is determined by the stopband requirements. Inserting these requirements into Eq. (13–25) produces

$$|T_n(j\omega_{MIN})| = \frac{|T_{MAX}|}{\sqrt{1 + C_n^2(\omega_{MIN}/\omega_C)}} \leq T_{MIN} \qquad (13\text{–}27)$$

Solving this constraint for $C_n(\omega_{MIN}/\omega_C)$ yields

$$C_n(\omega_{MIN}/\omega_C) \geq \sqrt{\left(\frac{T_{MAX}}{T_{MIN}}\right)^2 - 1}$$

In the stopband ($x = \omega/\omega_C \geq 1$) the function $C_n(x)$ is defined by the hyperbolic cosine function in Eq. (13–26b). Inserting this definition into the preceding constraint and then solving for n yields

$$n \geq \frac{\cosh^{-1}\left(\sqrt{(T_{MAX}/T_{MIN})^2 - 1}\right)}{\cosh^{-1}(\omega_{MIN}/\omega_C)} \qquad (13\text{–}28)$$

In Example 13–8 the Butterworth response requires $n = 4$ to meet the stopband conditions $T_{MAX}/T_{MIN} = 100$ (40 dB) at $\omega_{MIN} = 4\omega_C$. Inserting these conditions into Eq. (13–28) yields

$$n \geq \frac{\cosh^{-1}\left(\sqrt{(100)^2 - 1}\right)}{\cosh^{-1}(4)} = 2.57$$

The Chebychev response can meet the same stopband conditions using $n = 3$.

Figure 13–30 compares the Butterworth and Chebychev gain responses for $n = 4$. Both responses have stopband asymptotic slopes of –80 dB/decade. The Butterworth response is relatively flat in the passband and has a smooth transition to its high-frequency asymptote. In contrast, the Chebychev passband gain displays a succession of resonant peaks and valleys with a more abrupt transition to the stopband asymptote. Because $C_n(\omega)$ varies as cosine function in the passband, the resonant peaks in the Chebychev gain characteristic are all equal to T_{MAX} and the valleys all equal to $T_{MAX}/\sqrt{2}$. For this reason the Chebychev gain response in Eq. (13–25) is called the **equal-ripple response**. The net result of these resonances is that the Chebychev response transitions to its high-frequency asymptote rather abruptly.

To design a low-pass filter we need polynomials $q_n(s)$ such that the transfer function

$$T_n(s) = \frac{K}{q_n(s)}$$

produces a Chebychev gain response. Derivation of these polynomials involves complex variable theory beyond the scope of our study.[3] The analy-

3 For example, see M. E. Van Valkenburg, *Analog Filter Design*, Chicago: Holt, Rinehart, and Winston, 1982, pp. 233–241.

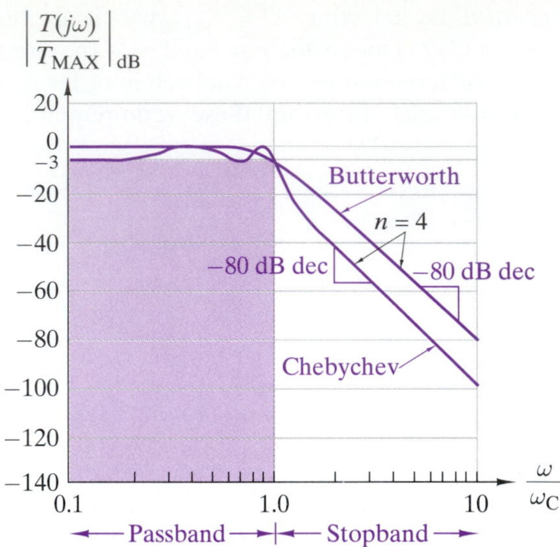

FIGURE 13–30 *Butterworth and Chebychev low-pass filter responses for* n = 4.

sis carried out in the reference allows us to write the normalized ($\omega_C = 1$) polynomials in Table 13–2. The transfer function of an nth-order Chebychev low-pass filter with a cutoff frequency of ω_C is then written as follows

$$T_n(s) = \frac{K}{q_n(s/\omega_C)} \qquad n \text{ odd} \tag{13–29a}$$

or

$$T_n(s) = \frac{K/\sqrt{2}}{q_n(s/\omega_C)} \qquad n \text{ even} \tag{13–29b}$$

where $q_n(s)$ is the nth-order normalized polynomial in Table 13–2. When we select $|K| = T_{MAX}$ the scale factor adjustment of $1/\sqrt{2}$ in Eq. (13–29b) is needed to ensure that $|T_n(j\omega)|$ meets the passband requirements when n is even. As with the Butterworth response, the order of the denominator polynomial can be found analytically from Eq. (13–28) or graphically using the normalized gain plots in Figure 13–31.

TABLE 13–2 NORMALIZED POLYNOMIALS THAT PRODUCE CHEBYCHEV RESPONSES

ORDER	NORMALIZED DENOMINATOR POLYNOMIALS
1	$(s + 1)$
2	$[(s/0.8409)^2 + 0.7654(s/0.8409) + 1]$
3	$[(s/0.2980) + 1][(s/0.9159)^2 + 0.3254(s/0.9159) + 1]$
4	$[(s/0.9502)^2 + 0.1789(s/0.9502) + 1)][(s/0.4425)^2 + 0.9276(s/0.4425) + 1]$
5	$[(s/0.1772) + 1][(s/0.9674)^2 + 0.1132(s/0.9674) + 1][(s/0.6139)^2 + 0.4670(s/0.6139) + 1]$
6	$[(s/0.9771)^2 + 0.0781(s/0.9771) + 1][(s/0.7223)^2 + 0.2886(s/0.7223) + 1][(s/0.2978)^2 + 0.9562(s/0.2978) + 1]$

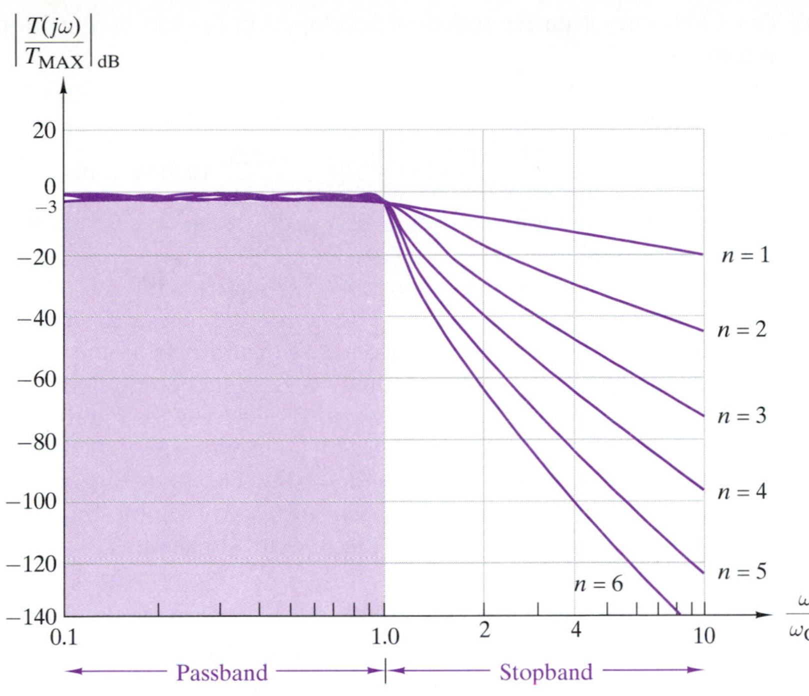

FIGURE 13–31 *Chebychev low-pass filter responses.*

D DESIGN EXAMPLE 13–9

Low-Pass Design with Chebychev Poles

(a) Construct a Chebychev low-pass transfer function that meets a passband requirement of T_{MAX} = 20 dB and ω_C = 10 rad/s, and a stopband requirement of T_{MIN} = –30 dB at ω_{MIN} = 50 rad/s.
(b) Design a cascade of active *RC* circuits that produces the transfer function found in part (a).

SOLUTION:

(a) The passband gain condition requires K = 10. The stopband requirement specifies that the stopband gain at $\omega_{MIN}/\omega_C = 5$ must be 50 dB (factor of $10^{5/2}$) less than the passband gain. Using Eq. (13–28) yields

$$n \geqslant \frac{\cosh^{-1}(\sqrt{(10^{2.5})^2 - 1})}{\cosh^{-1}(5)} = 2.81$$

Hence $n = 3$ is the smallest integer meeting the stopband requirement. Using the third-order polynomial from Table 13–2, we construct the required Chebychev low-pass transfer function:

$$T(s) = \frac{K}{q_3(s/\omega_C)}$$

$$= \frac{10}{\left[\left(\frac{s}{0.298 \times 10}\right) + 1\right]\left[\left(\frac{s}{0.9159 \times 10}\right)^2 + 0.3254\left(\frac{s}{0.9159 \times 10}\right) + 1\right]}$$

(b) The Chebychev transfer function developed in (a) can be partitioned as follows:

$$\frac{T(s)}{10} = \left[\frac{1}{\left(\frac{s}{0.298 \times 10}\right) + 1}\right]\left[\frac{1}{\left(\frac{s}{0.9159 \times 10}\right)^2 + 0.3254\left(\frac{s}{0.9159 \times 10}\right) + 1}\right]$$

Realizing this partition requires a first-order stage in cascade with a second-order stage.

The design sequence in Figure 13–32 begins with the required transfer functions in the first row. The next three rows show the stage parameters, stage prototype, and design constraints for the selected prototypes. The constraints are then used to select element values that produce the final designs shown in the last row of Figure 13–32. The second stage is a Sallen-Key circuit, so its gain ($K_2 = 2.675$) is determined by the second-stage damping ratio. The first stage is a voltage divider circuit whose gain can be adjusted without changing its pole location. Thus, we can adjust the first-stage gain at $K_1 = 10/K_2$ so that the overall passband gain is $K_1 \times K_2 = K = 10$. A cascade connection of the final designs in the last two of Figure 13–32 meets all design requirements without introducing an additional gain stage. ■

Exercise 13–5

What is the minimum order of the first-order cascade, Butterworth, and Chebychev transfer functions that meet the following stopband conditions?

(a) $T_{MIN}/T_{MAX} = -20$ dB at $4\omega_C$
(b) $T_{MIN}/T_{MAX} = -30$ dB at $5\omega_C$
(c) $T_{MIN}/T_{MAX} = -40$ dB at $6\omega_C$
(d) $T_{MIN}/T_{MAX} = -60$ dB at $8\omega_C$

Answers:

	First Order	Butterworth	Chebychev
(a)	$n = 3$	$n = 2$	$n = 2$
(b)	$n = 4$	$n = 3$	$n = 2$
(c)	$n = 5$	$n = 3$	$n = 3$
(d)	$n = 7$	$n = 4$	$n = 3$

COMPARISON OF LOW-PASS FILTER RESPONSES

We have described low-pass filter design methods for three responses, the first-order cascade, the Butterworth, and the Chebychev. At this point we want to compare the methods and discuss how we might choose between them. In filter applications the gain response is obviously important. Figure 13–33 shows the three straight-line asymptotes (solid lines) and the actual gain responses (dashed curves) for $n = 4$. All three responses meet the same passband requirements, have the same cutoff frequency, and have high-frequency asymptotes with slopes of $-20n = -80$ dB/decade. However, the three responses have different corner frequencies. At one extreme the corner frequency of the first-order cascade response is above the cutoff

Item	First Stage	Second Stage
Prototype transfer function	$\dfrac{1}{(s/2.98)+1}$	$\dfrac{1}{(s/9.159)^2+0.3254(s/9.159)+1}$
Stage parameters	$\omega_0 = 2.980$	$\omega_0 = 9.159 \quad \zeta = 0.3254/2 = 0.1627$
Stage prototype	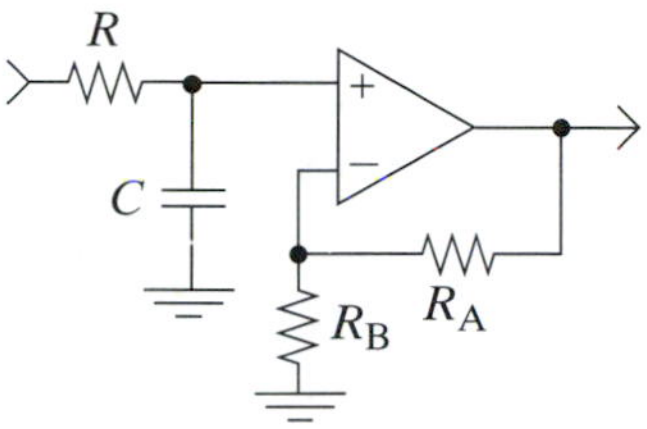 R, C, R_B, R_A, +, −	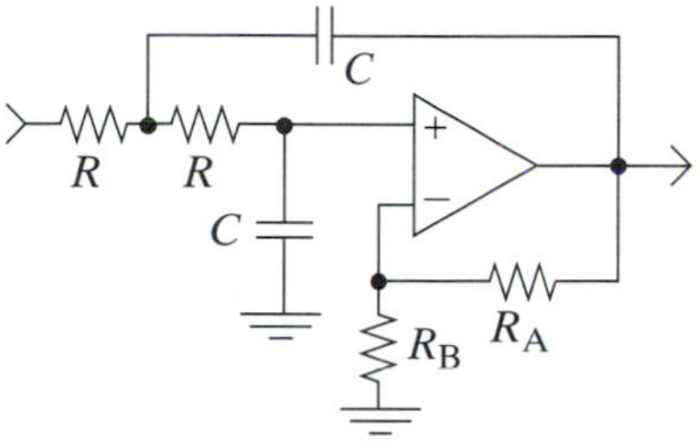 C, R, R, C, R_B, R_A, +, −
Design constraints	$RC = \dfrac{1}{\omega_0} = 0.3357$ $\dfrac{R_A}{R_B} = K_1 - 1 = 2.74$	$RC = \dfrac{1}{\omega_0} = 0.1092$ $\dfrac{R_A}{R_B} = 2(1-\zeta) = 1.67$
Element values	Let $R = 100$ kΩ, then $C = 3.36\ \mu$F Let $R_B = 100$ kΩ, then $R_A = 274$ kΩ	Let $R = 100$ kΩ, then $C = 1.092\ \mu$F Let $R_B = 100$ kΩ, then $R_A = 167$ kΩ
Final designs	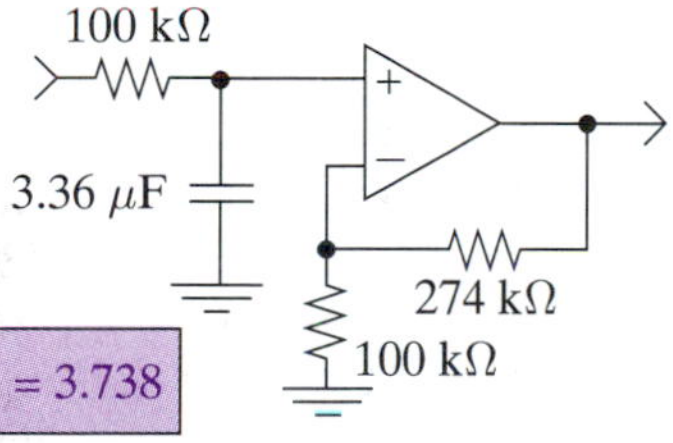 100 kΩ, 3.36 μF, 274 kΩ, 100 kΩ, +, − $K_1 = 3.738$	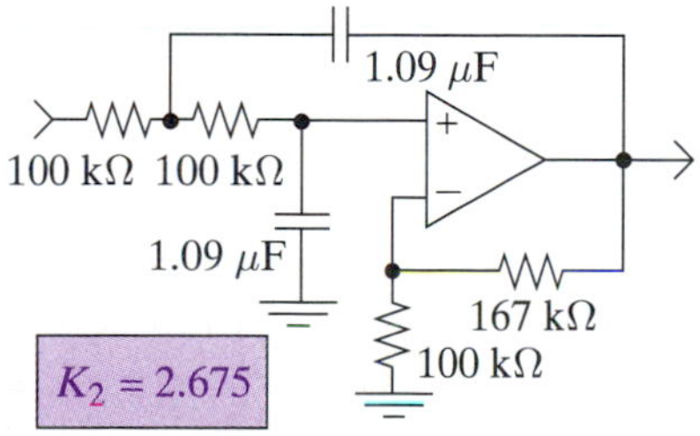 1.09 μF, 100 kΩ, 100 kΩ, 1.09 μF, 167 kΩ, 100 kΩ, +, − $K_2 = 2.675$

FIGURE 13–32 *Design sequence for Example 13–9.*

frequency, so its actual gain response approaches its asymptote very gradually. At the other extreme the Chebychev corner frequency lies below the cutoff frequency and the actual response has a resonant peak that fills the gap between the corner frequency and the cutoff frequency. This resonance causes the Chebychev response to decrease rapidly in the neighborhood of the cutoff frequency. The Butterworth response has its corner frequency at the cutoff frequency, so its gain response falls between these two extremes.

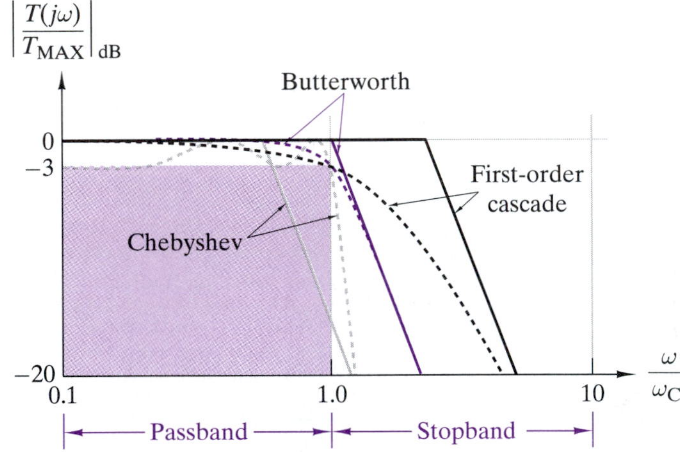

FIGURE 13–33 *First-order cascade, Butterworth, and Chebychev low-pass responses for* n = 4.

The differences in gain response can be understood by examining the pole-zero diagram in Figure 13–34. The Butterworth poles are evenly distributed on a circle of radius ω_C. The Chebychev poles lie on an ellipse whose minor axis is much smaller than ω_C. As a result, the Chebychev poles are closer to the *j*-axis, have lower damping ratios, and produce a gain response with pronounced resonant peaks. These resonant peaks lead to the equal-ripple response in the passband and the steep gain slope in the neighborhood of the cutoff frequency. At the other extreme the first-order cascade response has a fourth-order pole (quadruple pole) located on the

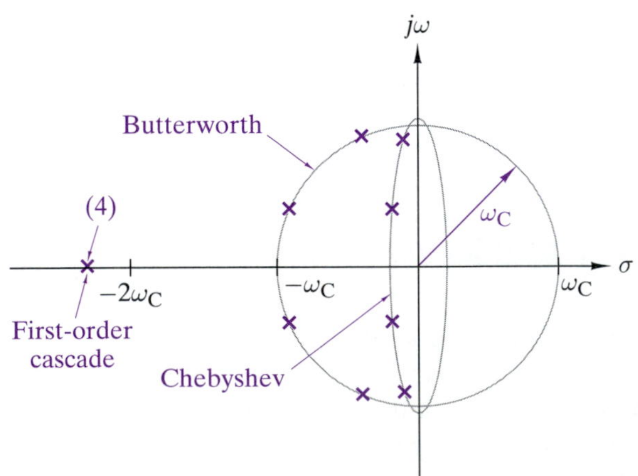

FIGURE 13–34 *First-order cascade, Butterworth, and Chebychev pole locations for* n = 4.

negative real axis. The distance from the j-axis to the first-order cascade poles is much larger than ω_C, which explains the rather leisurely way its gain response transitions from the passband to stopband asymptote. As might be expected, the Butterworth poles fall between these two extremes.

This discussion illustrates the following principle. For any given value of n, the Chebychev response produces more stopband attenuation than the Butterworth response, which, in turn, produces more than the first-order cascade response. If stopband performance is the only consideration, then we should choose the Chebychev response. However, the Chebychev response comes at a price.

Figure 13–35 shows the step response of these three low-pass filters for $n = 4$. The step response of the Chebychev filter has lightly damped oscillations that produce a large overshoot and a long settling time. These undesirable features of the Chebychev step response are a direct result of the low-damping-ratio complex poles that produce the desirable features of its gain response. At the other extreme the step response of the first-order cascade filter rises rapidly to its final value without overshooting. This result should not be surprising since the remote poles of the first-order cascade produce exponential waveforms that have relatively short durations. In other words, the desirable features of the first-order cascade step response are a direct result of the remote real poles that produce the undesirable features of its gain response. Not surprisingly, the step response of the Butterworth filter lies between these two extremes.

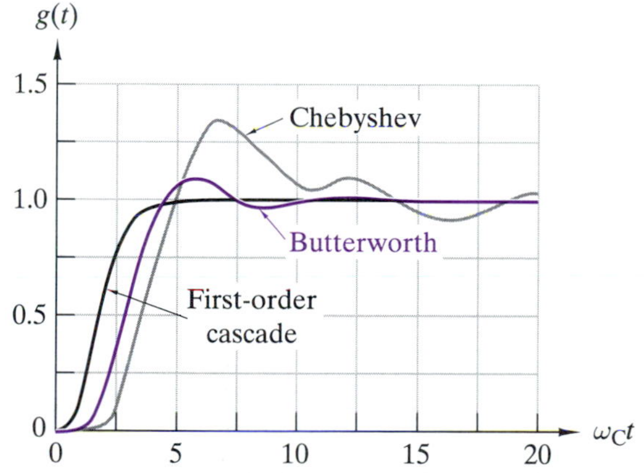

FIGURE 13–35 *First-order cascade, Butterworth, and Chebychev step responses for* n = 4.

Finally, consider the element values in the circuit realizations of these filters. Examination of Table 13–2 reveals that each pair of complex poles in a Chebychev filter has a different ω_0 and a different ς. These parameters define the constraints on the element values for each stage in the filter. As a result, each stage in a cascade realization of a Chebychev filter has a different set of element values. In contrast, the stages in a first-order cascade filter can be exactly the same. From a manufacturing point of view, it may be better to produce and stock identical circuits rather than uniquely different circuits.

The essential point is that stopband attenuation is important, but it does not tell the whole story. Filter design, and indeed all design, involves tradeoffs between conflicting requirements. The choice of a design approach is driven by the weight assigned to conflicting requirements.

13–5 HIGH-PASS FILTER DESIGN

High-pass transfer functions can be derived from low-pass prototypes using a transformation of the complex frequency variable s. If a low-pass transfer function $T_{LP}(s)$ has a passband gain of T_{MAX} and cutoff frequency of ω_C, then the transfer function $T_{HP}(s)$ defined as

$$T_{HP}(s) = T_{LP}(\omega_C^2/s) \qquad (13-30)$$

has high-pass characteristics with the same cutoff frequency and passband gain. On a logarithmic frequency scale this transformation amounts to a horizontal reflection of the gain response about ω_C. In other words, replacing s by $\omega_C{}^2/s$ changes a low-pass transfer function into a high-pass function without changing the parameters defining passband and stopband performances.

The first-order low-pass transfer function provides a simple example of the low-pass to high-pass transformation. Given a first-order low-pass

$$T_{LP}(s) = \frac{T_{MAX}}{\dfrac{s}{\omega_C} + 1}$$

replacing s by ω_C^2/s yields a first-order high-pass transfer function

$$T_{HP}(s) = \frac{T_{MAX}}{\dfrac{\omega_C^2/s}{\omega_C} + 1} = \frac{T_{MAX}s}{s + \omega_C}$$

Note that the cutoff frequency and passband gain of the high-pass function are the same as those of the low-pass function from which it was derived.

Figure 13–36 shows the high-pass responses derived from the fourth-order Butterworth and Chebychev low-pass responses in Figure 13–30. From these plots we see that the transformation interchanges the pass and stopbands. The cutoff frequency is unchanged because it lies at the boundary between the two bands. Moreover, the same maximally flat or equal-ripple features appear in the passband of the high-pass response. Finally, the high-pass stopband gain is a mirror image about $\omega/\omega_C = 1$ of the low-pass stopband response. For example, if a low-pass function has –40 dB gain one octave above cutoff, then the corresponding high-pass function will have –40 dB gain one octave below cutoff.

A high-pass filter design problem is defined by specifying four parameters: T_{MAX}, ω_C, T_{MIN}, and ω_{MIN}. To obtain a high-pass transfer function that meets these requirements, we first construct a low-pass prototype $T_{LP}(s)$. The passband parameters for the low-pass prototype are the same as T_{MAX} and ω_C for the high pass. The stopband requirement for the low-pass prototype is T_{MIN} at $\omega_C^2/s\omega_{MIN}$. Given these design requirements, we construct

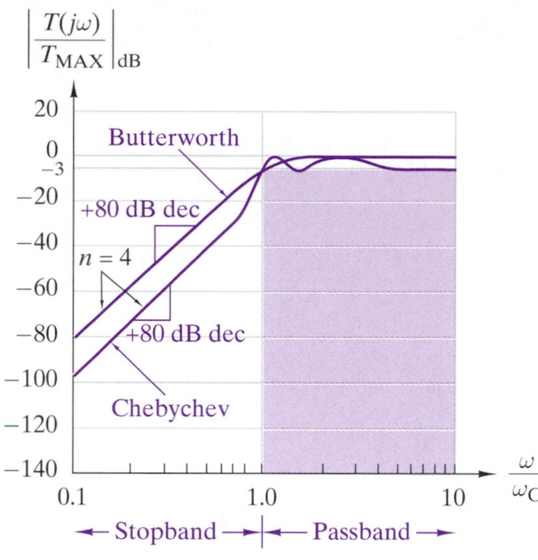

FIGURE 13–36 *Butterworth and Chebychev high-pass filter responses for* n = 4.

a low-pass prototype $T_{LP}(s)$ using the methods described in Sect. 13–4. Replacing s by ω_C^2/s transforms the low-pass prototype into a high-pass transfer function $T_{HP}(s)$. The high-pass function is then partitioned into first- and second-order factors and realized using high-pass building blocks discussed in previous sections.

The next examples illustrate the method of designing high-pass filters using a low-pass prototype.

D DESIGN EXAMPLE 13–10

High-Pass Design with Butterworth Poles

(a) Construct a Butterworth high-pass transfer function with T_{MAX} = 20 dB, ω_C = 10 rad/s, and a stopband requirement of T_{MIN} = −10 dB at ω_{MIN} = 3 rad/s.

(b) Design a cascade of active *RC* circuits that realizes the transfer function found in part (a).

SOLUTION:

(a) The passband requirements for the low-pass prototype are $K = 10$ and ω_C = 10 rad/s. The stopband requirement for the low-pass prototype is T_{MIN} = −10 dB at $\omega_{MIN} = \omega_C^2/3 = 33.3$. The total range from T_{MIN} to T_{MAX} is 30 dB; hence $T_{MAX}/T_{MIN} = 10^{3/2}$. Using Eq. (13–20) yields

$$n \geqslant \frac{1}{2}\,\frac{\ln[(10^{3/2})^2 - 1]}{\ln(33.3/10)} = 2.87$$

We find that $n = 3$ is the lowest-order Butterworth response that meets the low-pass design requirements. Using the third-order polynomial from Table 13–1, the low-pass prototype is

$$T_{LP}(s) = \frac{K}{q_3(s/10)} = \frac{10}{\left[\left(\frac{s}{10}\right)^2 + \left(\frac{s}{10}\right) + 1\right]\left[\left(\frac{s}{10}\right) + 1\right]}$$

The high-pass transfer function is obtained by replacing s with ω_C^2/s = $100/s$:

$$T_{HP}(s) = \frac{10}{\left[\left(\frac{100/s}{10}\right)^2 + \left(\frac{100/s}{10}\right) + 1\right]\left[\left(\frac{100/s}{10}\right) + 1\right]}$$

$$= \left[\frac{(s/10)^2}{(s/10)^2 + (s/10) + 1}\right]\left[\frac{10(s/10)}{(s/10) + 1}\right]$$

The function $T_{HP}(s)$ is a high-pass transfer function that meets the filter design requirements.

(b) Figure 13–37 shows a design sequence for realizing $T_{HP}(s)$ using the first- and second-order high-pass active *RC* building blocks. The stage transfer functions given in the first row yield the stage parameters in the second row. The stage prototypes are a second-order high-pass section with unity gain and a first-order high-pass section with an adjustable gain. The stage prototypes together with the stage parameters yield the design constraints in the fourth row. Selecting element values within these constraints produces the final stage designs shown in the last row of Figure 13–37. The required passband gain is included in the first-order circuit, so no gain correction stage is required in this example. In other words, connecting the two stages in Figure 13–37 in cascade meets all design requirements, including the passband gain of 20 dB. ■

EXAMPLE 13–11

Use Microsim Design Center to verify the high-pass design developed in Example 13–10.

SOLUTION:

One of the most important uses of computer-aided analysis is to simulate a proposed circuit design and confirm that it meets the performance requirements. Figure 13–38 shows the two-stage design in the last row of Figure 13–37 as constructed using Microsim Schematics. The input source V1 is set to produce a 1-V ac input. As a result, the ac voltage at the output bubble is the overall filter circuit gain function. Using the **Analysis\Setup\AC Sweep** command, we set the frequency of the source V1 to sweep across range from 0.1 Hz to 100 Hz. The **Analysis\Simulate** command causes Microsim PSpice to execute a sequence of ac analysis runs that lead to the gain plot shown in Figure 13–38. Microsim Probe constructs plots of vdb(out) versus frequency. The suffix “db” means that the vertical axis is the gain in dB. Although Microsim Probe labels the horizontal axis in Hz, the units are actually $2\pi f = \omega$ in rad/s. The plot confirms that the circuit has

Item	First Stage	Second Stage
Prototype transfer function	$\dfrac{(s/10)^2}{(s/10)^2 + (s/10) + 1}$	$\dfrac{10\,(s/10)}{(s/10) + 1}$
Stage parameters	$\omega_0 = 10 \quad \zeta = 0.5 \quad K_1 = 1$	$\omega_0 = 10 \quad K_2 = 10$
Stage prototype	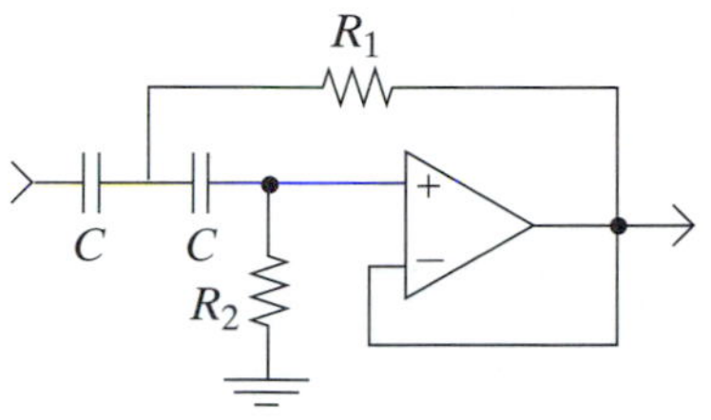	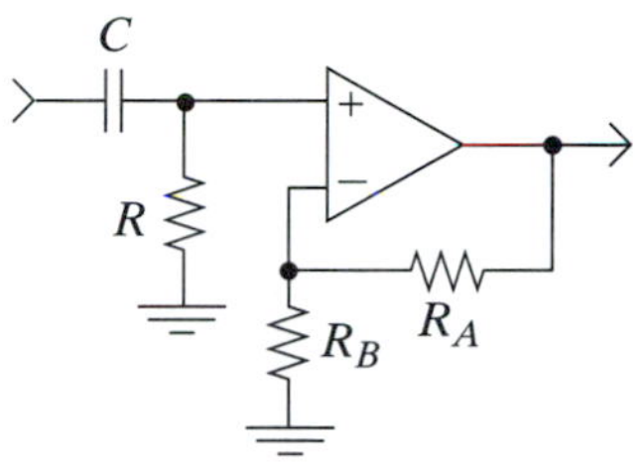
Design constraints	$\sqrt{R_1R_2}C = 1/\omega_0 = 0.1$ $R_1/R_2 = \zeta^2 = 0.25$	$RC = 1/\omega_0 = 0.1$ $R_A/R_B = K_2 - 1 = 9$
Element values	Let $R_2 = 100$ kΩ, then $R_1 = 25$ kΩ and $C = 2\ \mu$F	Let $R = 50$ kΩ, then $C = 2\ \mu$F Let $R_B = 10$ kΩ, then $R_A = 90$ kΩ
Final designs	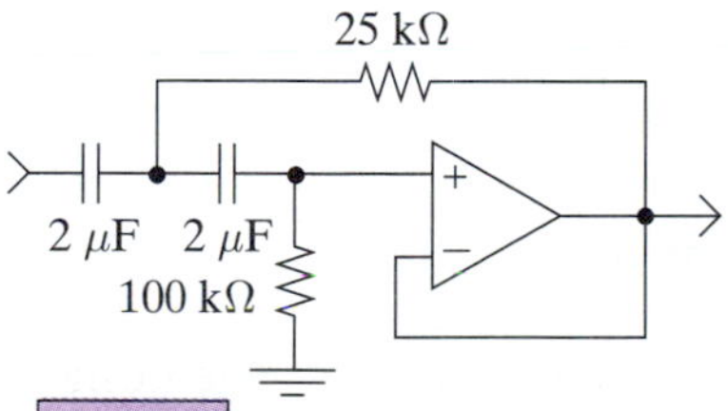	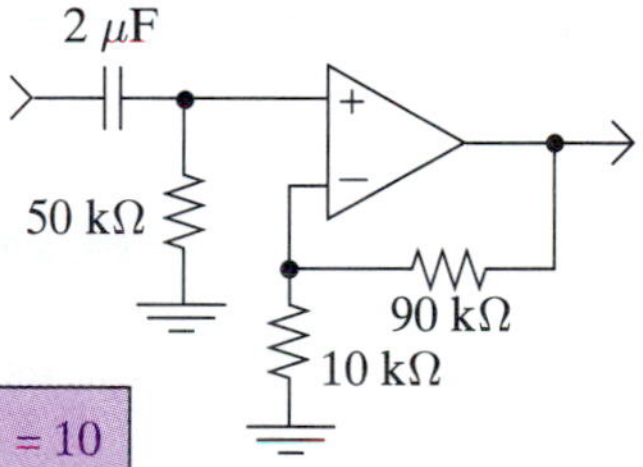

FIGURE 13–37 *Design sequence for Example 13–10.*

a high-pass characteristic with a passband above $\omega = 10$ rad/s, a passband gain of 20 dB, and stopband gain that falls below –10 dB at $\omega = 3$ rad/s. ■

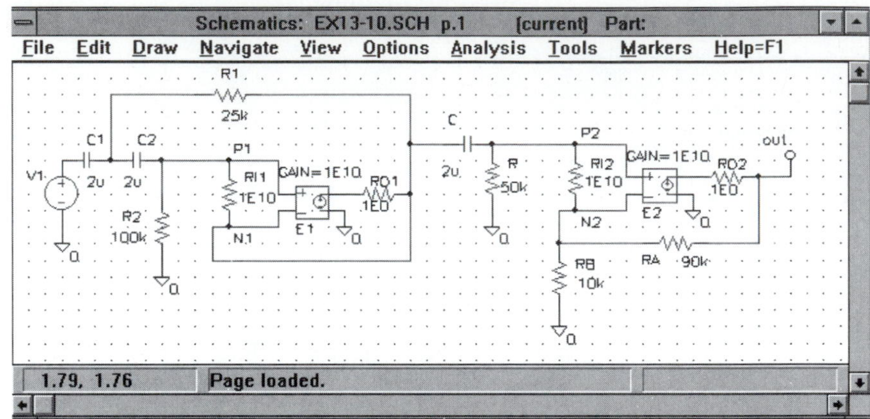

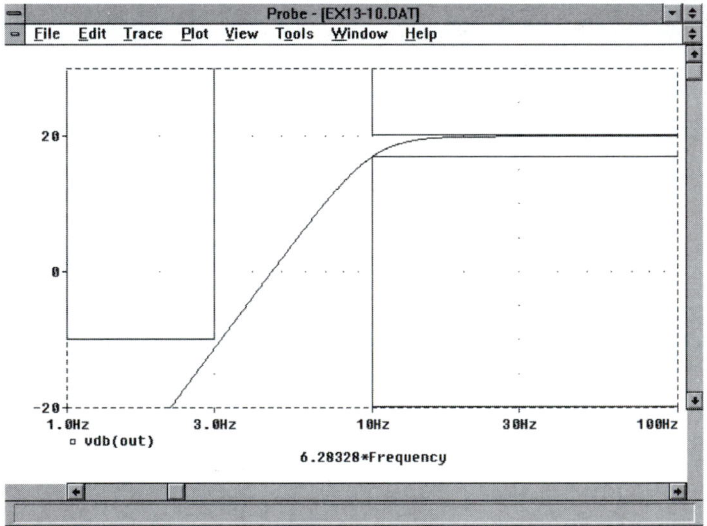

FIGURE 13–38

Exercise 13–6

Construct first-order cascade and Butterworth high-pass transfer functions that have passband gains of 0 dB, cutoff frequencies of 50 rad/s, and $T_{MIN} = -40$ dB at $\omega_{MIN} = 10$ rad/s.

Answers:

$$T_{FO}(s) = \frac{s^8}{(s+15)^8},\quad T_{BU}(s) = \frac{s^3}{(s+50)(s^2+50s+2500)}$$

13–6 BANDPASS AND BANDSTOP FILTER DESIGN

In Chapter 12 we found that the cascade connection in Figure 13–39 can produce a bandpass filter. When the cutoff frequency of the low-pass filter (ω_{CLP}) is higher than the cutoff frequency of the high-pass filter (ω_{CHP}), the interval between the two frequencies is a passband separating two stopbands. The low-pass filter provides the high-frequency stopband and the high-pass filter the low-frequency stopband. Frequencies between the two cutoffs fall in the passband of both filters and are transmitted through the cascade connection, producing the passband of the resulting bandpass filter.

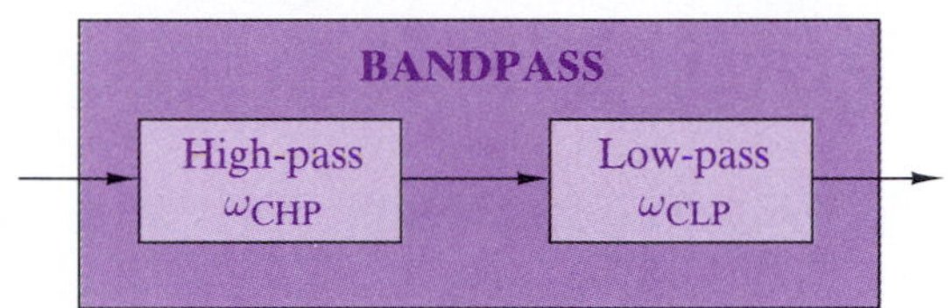

FIGURE 13–39 *Cascade connection of high-pass and low-pass filters.*

When $\omega_{CLP} >> \omega_{CHP}$, two bandpass cutoff frequencies are approximately $\omega_{C1} \approx \omega_{CHP}$ and $\omega_{C2} \approx \omega_{CLP}$. Under these conditions the center frequency and bandwidth of the bandpass filter are

$$\omega_0 = \sqrt{\omega_{CHP}\omega_{CLP}} \text{ and } B = \omega_{CLP} - \omega_{CHP}$$

When $\omega_{CLP} >> \omega_{CHP}$, the ratio of the center frequency over the bandwidth is approximately

$$\frac{\omega_0}{B} = Q \approx \sqrt{\frac{\omega_{CHP}}{\omega_{CLP}}} << 1$$

Since the quality factor is less than 1, this method of bandpass filter design produces a broadband filter, as contrasted with the narrowband response ($Q > 1$) produced by the active RC bandpass circuit studied earlier in Sect. 13–3.

D DESIGN EXAMPLE 13–12

Bandpass Design with Butterworth Poles

Construct a Butterworth bandpass filter with a passband gain of 0 dB and cutoff frequencies at $\omega_{C1} = 10$ rad/s and $\omega_{C2} = 50$ rad/s. The stopband gains must be less than –20 db at 2 rad/s and 250 rad/s.

SOLUTION:

In the upper stopband the –20-dB gain is specified at 250 rad/s = $5\omega_{C2}$. Using either Eq. (13–20) or Figure 13–27 shows that this requirement can be met by a second-order Butterworth polynomial. Hence the required low-pass function is

$$T_{LP}(s) = \frac{1}{(s/50)^2 + \sqrt{2}(s/50) + 1}$$

In the lower stopband the –20-dB gain is specified at 2 rad/s = $\omega_{C1}/5$. Hence a second-order Butterworth polynomial will meet this requirement as well and the required high-pass function is

$$T_{HP}(s) = \frac{(s/10)^2}{(s/10)^2 + \sqrt{2}(s/10) + 1}$$

When circuits realizing these two functions are connected in cascade, the overall transfer function is $T_{HP}(s) \times T_{LP}(s)$. Figure 13–40 is a Mathcad worksheet showing that the product of these two functions produces the specified bandpass response. Note that the center frequency of the response is $\omega_0 = \sqrt{10 \times 50} = 22.4$ rad/s and the bandwidth is $B = 50 - 10 = 40$ rad/s; hence the filter quality factor is $Q = \omega_0/B = 0.56 < 1$, indicating a broadband response. ■

FIGURE 13–40

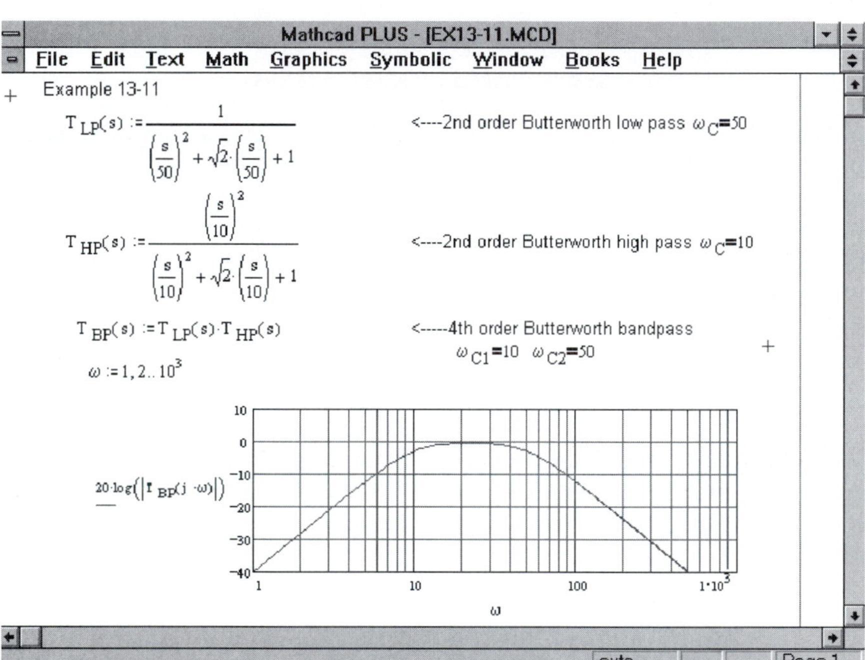

Figure 13–41 shows the dual situation in which a high-pass and a low-pass filter are connected in parallel to produce a bandstop filter. When $\omega_{CLP} << \omega_{CHP}$, the region between the two cutoff frequencies is a stopband separating two passbands. The low-pass filter provides the low-frequency passband via the lower path and the high-pass filter the high-frequency passband via the upper path. Frequencies between the two cutoffs fall in the stopband of both filters and are not transmitted through either path in the parallel connection. As a result, the two filters produce the stopband of the resulting bandstop filter. When $\omega_{CHP} >> \omega_{CLP}$, two cutoff frequencies are approximately $\omega_{C1} \approx \omega_{CLP}$ and $\omega_{C2} \approx \omega_{CHP}$.

In Example 13–11 we produced a fourth-order Butterworth bandpass function using the product of second-order high-pass and low-pass func-

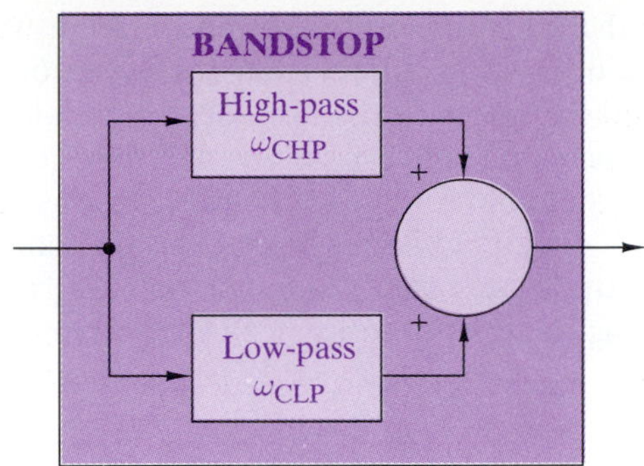

FIGURE 13–41 *Parallel connection of high-pass and low-pass filters.*

tions. If we interchange the cutoff frequencies of these functions, we produce the functions

$$T_{LP}(s) = \frac{1}{(s/10)^2 + \sqrt{2}(s/10) + 1}$$

$$T_{HP}(s) = \frac{(s/50)^2}{(s/50)^2 + \sqrt{2}(s/50) + 1}$$

where $\omega_{CLP} = 10 << \omega_{CHP} = 50$. When circuits realizing these two functions are connected in parallel, the overall transfer function is $T_{HP}(s) + T_{LP}(s)$. Figure 13–42 is a Mathcad worksheet showing that the sum of these two functions produces a bandstop response. Note that the center of the stopband is at $\omega_0 = \sqrt{10 \times 50} = 22.4$ rad/s, which is the center frequency of the bandpass response used to derive this bandstop response.

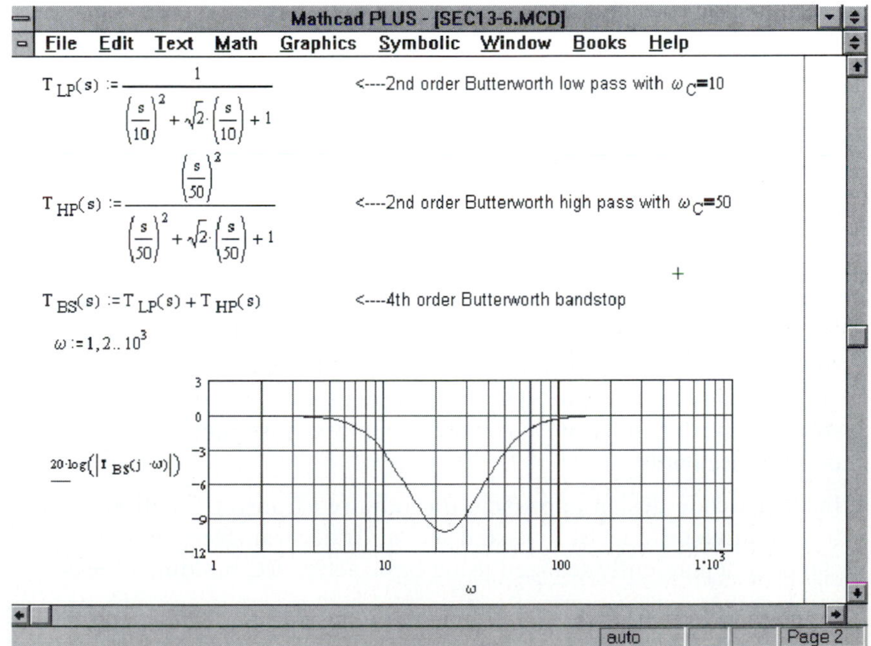

FIGURE 13–42

When the two cutoff frequencies are widely separated, we can realize broadband bandpass and bandstop filters using a cascade or parallel connection of low-pass and high-pass filters. The design problem reduces to designing separate low-pass and high-pass filters and then connecting them in cascade or parallel to obtain the required overall response. In the bandpass case the active *RC* circuits building blocks can be connected in cascade without violating the chain rule. The bandstop case requires a summation, which can be implemented using an OP AMP summer.

Exercise 13–7

Construct Butterworth low-pass and high-pass transfer functions whose cascade connection produces a bandpass function with cutoff frequencies at 20 rad/s and 500 rad/s, a passband gain of 0 dB, and a stopband gain less than –20 dB at 5 rad/s and 2000 rad/s.

Answer:

$$T(s) = \left[\frac{500^2}{s^2 + 707s + 500^2}\right]\left[\frac{s^2}{s^2 + 28.3s + 400}\right]$$

Exercise 13–8

Develop Butterworth low-pass and high-pass transfer functions whose parallel connection produces a bandstop filter with cutoff frequencies at 2 rad/s and 800 rad/s, passband gains of 20 dB, and stopband gains less than –30 dB at 20 rad/s and 80 rad/s.

SOLUTION:

$$T_{\mathrm{LP}}(s) = \frac{80}{(s^2 + 2s + 4)(s + 2)}$$

$$T_{\mathrm{HP}}(s) = \frac{10s^3}{(s^2 + 800s + 800^2)(s + 800)}$$

SUMMARY

- A filter design problem is defined by specifying attributes of the gain response such as a straight-line gain plot, cutoff frequency, passband gain, and stopband attenuation. The first step in the design process is to construct a transfer function $T(s)$ whose gain response meets the specification requirements.
- In the cascade design approach, the required transfer function is partitioned into a product of first- and second-order transfer functions, which can be independently realized using basic active *RC* building blocks.
- Transfer functions with real poles and zeros can be realized using the voltage divider, noninverting amplifier, or inverting amplifier building

blocks. Transfer functions with complex poles can be realized using second-order active *RC* circuits.

- Transfer functions meeting low-pass filter specifications can be constructed using first-order cascade, Butterworth, or Chebychev poles. First-order cascade filters are easy to design but have poor stopband performance. Butterworth responses produce maximally flat passband responses and more stopband attenuation than a first-order cascade with the same number of poles. The Chebychev responses produce equal-ripple passband responses and more stopband attenuation than the Butterworth response with the same number of poles.
- A high-pass transfer function can be constructed from a low-pass prototype by replacing s with ω_C^2/s. Bandpass (bandstop) filters can be constructed using a cascade (parallel) connection of a low-pass and a high-pass filter.

EN ROUTE OBJECTIVES AND RELATED PROBLEMS

ERO 13–1 DESIGN WITH FIRST-ORDER CIRCUITS (SECT. 13–2)

Given a filter specification or a Bode plot of a straight-line gain,

(a) Construct a transfer function $T(s)$ that has the specified characteristics.
(b) Design a cascade of first-order circuits that realizes $T(s)$.

13–1 **D** Design a first-order low-pass filter with a cutoff frequency of 500 Hz and a passband gain of 14 dB. Scale the circuit so the element values are in practical ranges.

13–2 **D** Design a first-order high-pass filter with a passband gain of 12 dB, a gain of at least 9 dB at 2.5 kHz, and a gain of less than –5 dB at 250 Hz. Scale the circuit so the element values are in practical ranges.

13–3 **D** Use a cascade connection of a first-order low-pass and high-pass circuits to design a bandpass filter with cutoff frequencies at 200 rad/s and 3000 rad/s. The passband gain of the bandpass circuit must be at least 30 dB. Scale the circuit so the element values are in practical ranges.

13–4 **D** The open-circuit voltage of the source in Figure P13–4 is

$$v_S(t) = 5 + 0.02\sin(2000\pi t) \quad \text{V}$$

The purpose of the bypass capacitor is to reduce the ac voltage delivered to the 20-Ω load below 10-mV peak. Select a value of C.

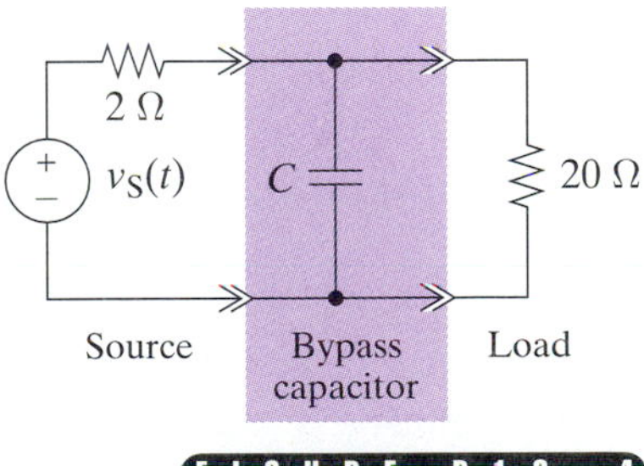

FIGURE P13–4

13–5 **D** The open-circuit voltage of the signal source in Figure P13–5 is

$$v_S(t) = 5 + 0.02\sin(50000\pi t) \quad \text{V}$$

Design an interface circuit so that no dc voltage appears across the 50-Ω load and the ac voltage to the load has a peak amplitude of at least 2 V.

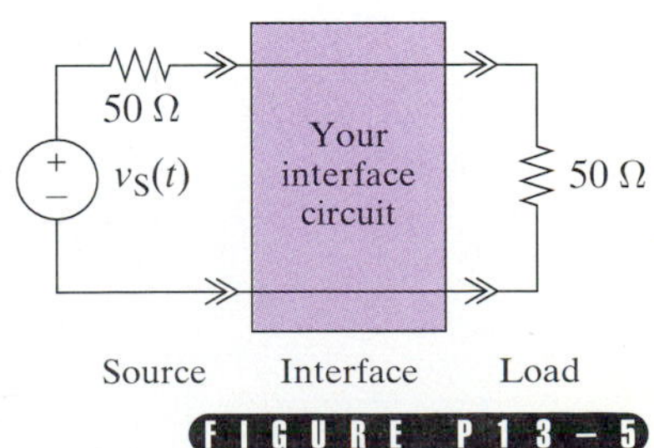

FIGURE P13–5

13–6 **D** The open-circuit voltage of the signal generator in Figure P13–5 is a 5-kHz sinusoid with a 1-V peak amplitude plus a spurious (undesirable) sinusoid at 100 kHz with a 0.5-V peak amplitude. Design an interface circuit filter so that the voltage delivered to the 50-Ω load is a 5-kHz sinusoid with a peak amplitude of at least 4 V and a 100-kHz sinusoid with a peak amplitude of less than 200 mV.

13–7 **D** The straight-line gain plot in Figure P13–7 emphasizes the frequencies below 50 rad/s and deemphasizes the frequencies above 250 rad/s.

(a) Construct a transfer function that has this gain response using only real poles and zeros.

(b) Design a cascade of first-order active *RC* circuits to realize the $T(s)$ found in (a). Scale the circuits so the element values are in practical ranges.

FIGURE P13–7

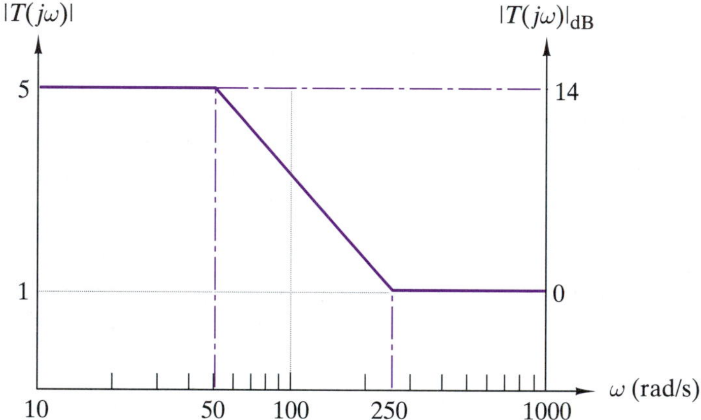

13–8 **D** The straight-line plot in Figure P13–8 has a low-pass characteristic with a two-pole stopband roll-off.

(a) Construct a transfer function $T(s)$ that has this gain response using only real poles and zeros.

(b) Design a cascade of first-order active *RC* circuits to realize the transfer function found in (a). Scale the circuits so the element values are in practical ranges.

FIGURE P13–8

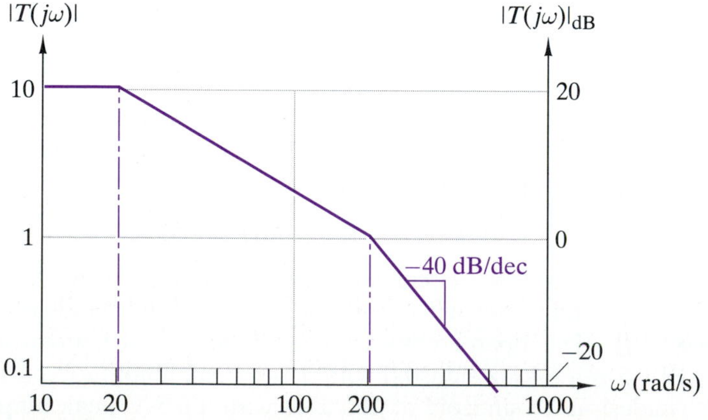

13–9 **D** The straight-line gain response in Figure P13–9 emphasizes the frequencies between 100 rad/s and 2000 rad/s and deemphasizes the frequencies below 10 rad/s and above 20 krad/s.

(a) Construct a transfer function $T(s)$ that has this gain response using only real poles and zeros.

(b) Design a cascade of first-order active RC circuits to realize the $T(s)$ found in (a). Scale the circuits so the element values are in practical ranges.

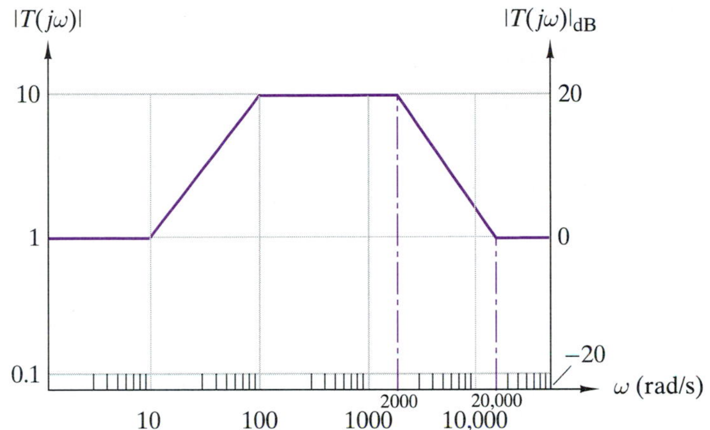

FIGURE P13–9

13–10 **D** The gain response in Figure P13–10 has a passband between 40 Hz and 2 kHz.

(a) Construct a transfer function $T(s)$ that has this gain response using only real poles and zeros.

(b) Design a cascade of first-order active RC circuits to realize the transfer function found in (a). Scale the circuits so the element values are in practical ranges.

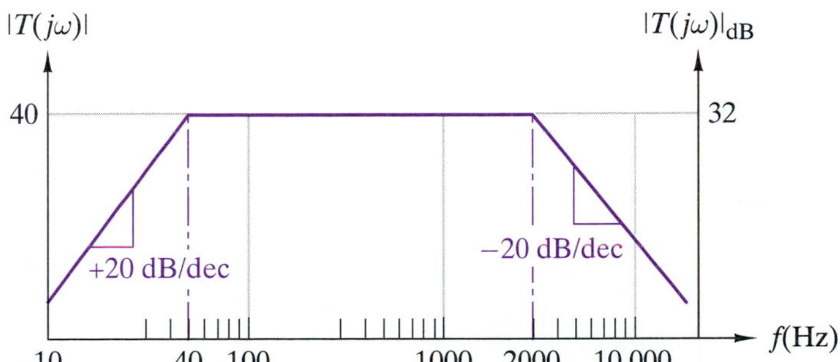

FIGURE P13–10

13–11 **D** The high-pass straight-line gain response in Figure P13–11 provides a two-pole stopband roll-off at low frequencies.

(a) Construct a transfer function $T(s)$ that has this gain response using only real poles and zeros.

(b) Design an active *RC* circuit to realize the $T(s)$ found in (a) using only one OP AMP. Scale the circuit so the element values are in practical ranges.

FIGURE P13–11

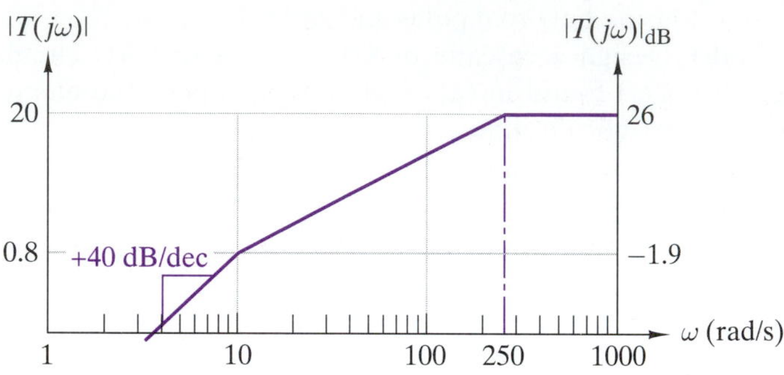

13–12 D The straight-line gain response in Figure P13–12 is the design specification for an audio preamplifier. Note that frequencies are specified in Hz.

(a) Construct a transfer function $T(s)$ that has this gain response using only real poles and zeros.

(b) Design an active *RC* circuit to realize the $T(s)$ found in (a) using only one OP AMP. Scale the circuit so the element values are in practical ranges.

FIGURE P13–12

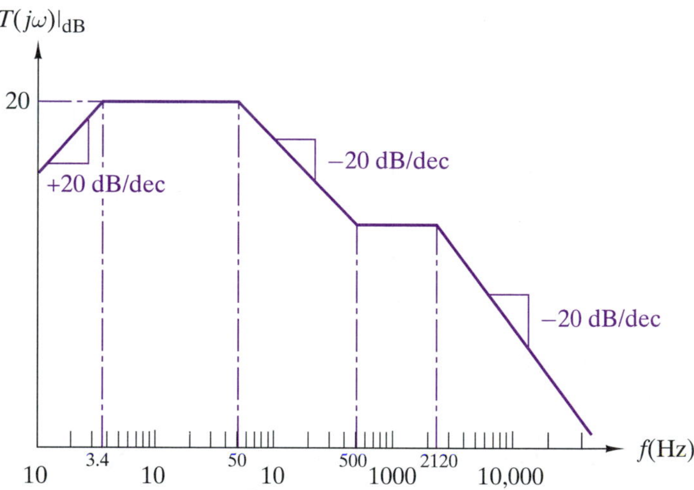

13–13 D A first-order low-pass power amplifier has a dc gain of 7 dB and a cutoff frequency of 2 kHz. Design an active *RC* preamp to connect in cascade with the power amplifier so that the overall circuit has a first-order low-pass response with a dc gain of 20 dB and a cutoff frequency of 5 kHz. Scale the circuit so the element values are in practical ranges.

13–14 **D** A first-order low-pass amplifier has a dc gain of 10 dB and a cutoff frequency of 10 kHz. Design an active *RC* preamp circuit to connect in cascade with the amplifier so that the resulting combination has a bandpass characteristic with cutoff frequencies at 10 Hz and 10 kHz and a passband gain of 20 dB. Scale the circuit so the element values are in practical ranges

13–15 **D** Your boss asks you to design a cost-effective *RC* circuit that realizes the following transfer function. You are cautioned that *cost effective* means using as few devices as possible and using standard values wherever possible. In addition, your boss would like you to use some of those 10-nF capacitors left over from the research project that he canceled.

$$T(s) = \pm\frac{Ks}{(s+10^3)(s+10^5)}$$

ERO 13–2 DESIGN WITH SECOND-ORDER CIRCUITS (SECT. 13–3)

A Given a circuit that realizes a second-order transfer function, develop a method of selecting circuit parameters to achieve specified filter characteristics.

D Given a filter specification, develop a second-order transfer function that has the required characteristics and design an active *RC* circuit that realizes the transfer function.

Design second-order active RC circuits to meet the following requirements:

Problem	Type	ω_0(rad/s)	ζ	Constraints
13–16 D	Low pass	2000	0.5	Use 20-nF capacitors.
13–17 D	Low pass	1000	0.2	Gain of 10 dB at dc
13–18 D	Low pass	500	?	Cutoff frequency at 500 rad/s
13–19 D	High pass	1000	?	20-dB gain at corner frequency
13–20 D	High pass	20	0.75	Use 20-kΩ resistors.
13–21 D	High pass	500	0.5	High-frequency gain of 40 dB
13–22 D	Bandpass	5000	?	$Q = 2$
13–23 D	Bandpass	1000	?	Bandwidth of 300 rad/s

13–24 **D** A second-order bandpass filter is required with cutoff frequencies at 97 kHz and 103 kHz. What are the values of ω_0, Q, and ζ? Design an active *RC* circuit that meets the design requirements.

13–25 **D** A digital data system requires a bandwidth of 2 kHz and a center frequency of 10 kHz. Design an active *RC* bandpass filter to meet these requirements. The system transmits two sinusoidal tones, one at 9 kHz and the other at 11 kHz. For your design, what is the maximum allowable amplitude of these tones when $V_{CC} = 15$ V?

13–26 Show that the Sallen-Key high-pass circuit in Figure 13–16 has the transfer function given in Eq. (13–7).

13–27 Show that the active *RC* bandpass circuit in Figure 13–18 has the transfer function given in Eq. (13–12).

13–28 The Sallen-Key low-pass circuit in Figure 13–14 can be designed using the conditions $R_A = R_B = R_1 = R_2 = R$. Develop a method of selecting R, C_1, and C_2 to achieve specified values of ω_0 and ζ.

13–29 Figure P13–29 shows the Sallen-Key bandpass circuit with equal resistors and capacitors. Show that the circuit has a transfer function

$$T(s) = \frac{V_2(s)}{V_1(s)} = \frac{\mu RC\,s}{(RCs)^2 + (4-\mu)(RCs) + 2}$$

Develop a method of selecting R, C, and μ to achieve specified values of ω_0 and ζ.

FIGURE P13–29

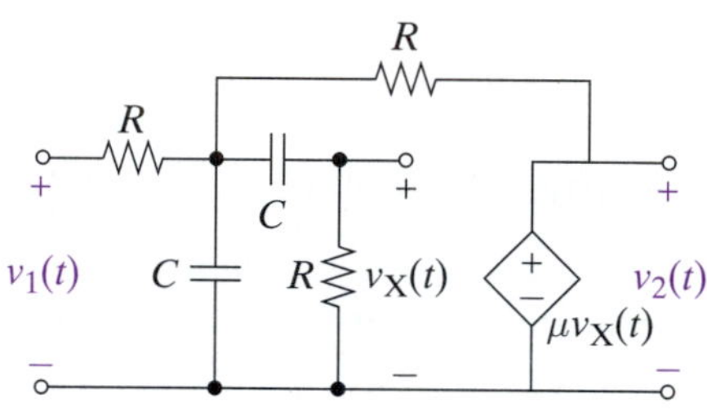

13–30 Show that the active RC circuit in Figure P13–30 has a bandpass transfer function of the form

$$T(s) = \frac{V_2(s)}{V_1(s)} = \frac{-\dfrac{s}{R_1C_2}}{s^2 + \dfrac{1}{R_3}\times\left(\dfrac{1}{C_1}+\dfrac{1}{C_2}\right)s + \dfrac{1}{R_3C_1C_2}\times\left(\dfrac{1}{R_1}+\dfrac{1}{R_2}\right)}$$

For the condition $R_1 = R_2 = R$ and $C_1 = C_2 = C$, develop a method of selecting R, C, and R_3 to achieve specified values of ω_0 and ζ.

FIGURE P13–30

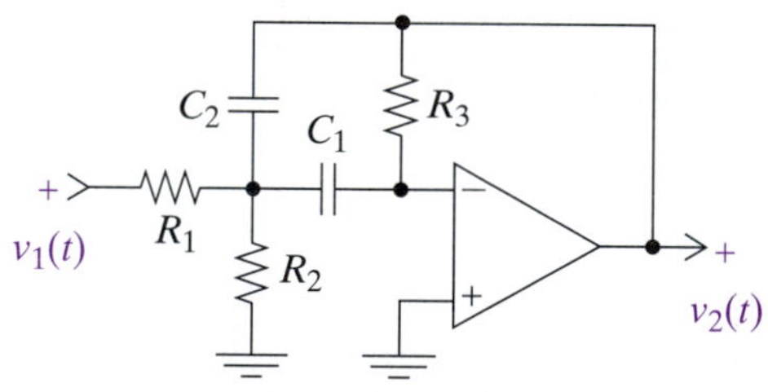

ERO 13–3 LOW-PASS FILTER DESIGN (SECT. 13–4)

Given a low-pass filter specification,

(a) Construct a transfer function $T(s)$ that meets the specification using first-order cascade, Butterworth, or Chebychev poles.
(b) Design a cascade of first- and second-order circuits that realizes $T(s)$.

13–31 Construct a transfer function with a first-order cascade low-pass gain response for $n = 5$, $\omega_C = 400$ rad/s, and a gain of 7 dB at its cutoff frequency. Find the gain (in dB) at $2\omega_C$, $5\omega_C$, and $10\omega_C$. Plot the straight-line gain response on the range $0.1\omega_C \le \omega \le 10\omega_C$ and sketch the actual response.

13–32 Construct a transfer function with a third-order Butterworth low-pass response with $\omega_C = 2500$ rad/s and a passband gain of 10 dB. Find the gain (in dB) at $2\omega_C$, $5\omega_C$, and $10\omega_C$. Plot the straight-line gain response on the range $0.1\omega_C \le \omega \le 10\omega_C$ and sketch the actual response.

13–33 Construct a transfer function with a fourth-order Chebychev low-pass response with $\omega_C = 500$ rad/s and a passband gain of 0 dB. Find the gain (in dB) at $2\omega_C$, $5\omega_C$, and $10\omega_C$. Plot the straight-line gain response on the range $0.1\omega_C \le \omega \le 10\omega_C$ and sketch the actual response.

13–34 **D** A low-pass filter specification requires $\omega_C = 2$ krad/s, a passband gain of 0 dB, and a stopband gain less than –30 dB at 10 krad/s.

(a) Find the lowest order (n) of a first-order cascade response that meets these requirements.

(b) Repeat (a) using a Butterworth response and a Chebychev response.

(c) Calculate the actual stopband gain at $\omega = 10$ krad/s for the responses found in (a) and (b).

(d) Which of these responses would you use to minimize the number of stages in a cascade design?

13–35 **D** A low-pass filter specification requires $\omega_C = 500$ rad/s, a passband gain of 0 dB, and a stopband gain less than –30 dB at 4 krad/s.

(a) Find the lowest order (n) of a first-order cascade response that meets these requirements.

(b) Repeat (a) using a Butterworth response and a Chebychev response.

(c) Calculate the actual stopband gain at $\omega = 4$ krad/s for the responses found in (a) and (b).

(d) Which of these responses would you use to minimize settling time of the step response?

13–36 **D** A low-pass filter specification requires $\omega_C = 300$ rad/s, a passband gain of 10 dB, and a stopband gain less than –30 dB at 2.4 krad/s.

(a) Find the lowest order (n) of a Butterworth response that meets these requirements.

(b) Repeat (a) using a Chebychev response.

(c) Calculate the actual stopband gain at $\omega = 2.4$ krad/s for the responses found in (a) and (b).

(d) Which or these responses would you use to obtain the most attenuation at $\omega = 2.4$ krad/s?

13–37 **D** A low-pass filter specification requires $\omega_C = 5$ krad/s, a passband gain of 9 dB, and a stopband gain less than –10 dB at 40 krad/s.

(a) Construct a transfer function $T(s)$ that meets the specification using first-order cascade poles.

(b) Design an active RC circuit that realizes the transfer function in (a) using only 100-kΩ resistors.

13–38 **D** A low-pass filter specification requires $\omega_C = 200$ rad/s, a passband gain of 20 dB, and a stopband gain less than –15 dB at 1 krad/s.

(a) Construct a transfer function $T(s)$ that meets the specification using Butterworth poles.

(b) Design an active *RC* circuit that realizes the transfer function in (a) using only 100-nF capacitors.

13–39 **D** Design a low-pass filter with 0-dB passband gain, a cutoff frequency of 3.2 kHz, and stopband gains less than –20 dB at 6.4 kHz and –40 dB at 16 kHz. Calculate the gains realized by your design at 3.2 kHz, 6.4 kHz, and 16 kHz.

13–40 **D** A pesky signal at 200 kHz is interfering with a desired signal at 50 kHz. Careful analysis suggests that reducing the interfering signal by 40 dB will eliminate the problem, provided that the desired signal is not reduced by more than 3 dB. Design an active *RC* filter that meets these requirements.

ERO 13–4 HIGH-PASS, BANDPASS, AND BANDSTOP FILTER DESIGN (SECTS. 13–5, 13–6)

Given a high-pass, broadband bandpass, or bandstop filter specification,

(a) Construct a transfer function $T(s)$ that meets the specification using first-order cascade, Butterworth, or Chebychev poles.

(b) Design a cascade or parallel connection of first- and second-order circuits that realizes $T(s)$.

13–41 **D** A high-pass filter specification requires $\omega_C = 20$ krad/s, a passband gain of 20 dB, and a stopband gain less than –20 dB at 5 krad/s.

(a) Construct a high-pass transfer function $T(s)$ that meets the specification using first-order cascade poles.

(b) Repeat (a) using Butterworth poles.

(c) Which of these responses would you use and why?

13–42 **D** A high-pass filter specification requires $\omega_C = 25$ krad/s, a passband gain of 0 dB, a stopband gain less than –20 dB at 10 krad/s, and a stopband gain less than –50 dB at 5 krad/s.

(a) Construct a high-pass transfer function $T(s)$ that meets the specification using Chebychev poles.

(b) Calculate the actual stopband gain of $T(s)$ at $\omega = 5$ krad/s and 10 krad/s. Which stopband requirement determines the number of poles in $T(s)$?

13–43 **D** A high-pass filter specification requires $\omega_C = 8$ krad/s, a passband gain of 10 dB, and a stopband gain less than –10 dB at 1 krad/s.

(a) Construct a transfer function $T(s)$ that meets the specification using first-order cascade poles.

(b) Design an active *RC* circuit that realizes the transfer function in (a) using only 100-kΩ resistors.

13–44 **D** A high-pass filter specification requires $\omega_C = 200$ rad/s, a passband gain of 5 dB, and a stopband gain less than –25 dB at 40 rad/s. Design an active *RC* circuit that meets these requirements using only 100-nF capacitors.

13–45 **D** A filter is required to attenuate 60 Hz noise by at least 30 dB and to pass a 500-Hz tone with no more than 3 dB attenuation. Design an active *RC* filter to meet the requirement.

13–46 **D** A bandpass filter specification requires cutoff frequencies at 100 rad/s and 1000 rad/s, a passband gain of 0 dB, and stopband gains less than –20 dB at 25 rad/s and 4 krad/s.

(a) Construct a bandpass transfer function $T(s)$ that meets the specification using Butterworth poles.

(b) Repeat (a) using Chebychev poles.

(c) Calculate the stopband gain at 25 rad/s and 4 krad/s for the transfer functions found in (a).

(d) Which one of these responses would you choose and why?

13–47 **D** A bandpass filter specification requires cutoff frequencies at 2 krad/s and 30 krad/s, a passband gain of 0 dB, a stopband gain less than –20 dB at 500 rad/s, and a stopband gain less than –30 dB at 200 krad/s.

(a) Construct a transfer function $T(s)$ that meets the specification.

(b) Calculate the actual stopband gain of $T(s)$ at ω = 500 rad/s and 200 krad/s.

13–48 **D** A bandstop filter specification requires cutoff frequencies at 100 rad/s and 3 krad/s, passband gains of 0 dB, and stopband gain less than –30 dB at 500 rad/s and at 600 rad/s.

(a) Construct a transfer function $T(s)$ that meets the specification.

(b) Calculate the actual stopband gain of $T(s)$ at ω = 500 rad/s and 600 rad/s.

13–49 **D** Design a Butterworth bandpass filter that passes sinusoidal tones at 1175 Hz and 2275 Hz with a gain of at least –3 dB and has gains no greater than –40 dB for sinusoidal tones at 60 Hz and 25 kHz.

13–50 **D** Design a bandstop filter that has passbands below 100 rad/s and above 2000 rad/s and has a stopband gain at least 20 dB below the passband gains at 500 rad/s.

CHAPTER-INTEGRATING PROBLEMS

13–51 **E** UNIVERSAL FILTER CIRCUIT

The circuit in Figure P13–51 consists of two OP AMP integrators and an inverting summer. In this circuit the capacitors have the same value *C* and all of the resistors have the same value *R*, except the resistor labelled R_X. It is claimed that this circuit produces second-order low-pass, high-pass, and bandpass responses. Specifically it is claimed that the transfer functions $T_1(s) = V_1(s)/V_S(s)$ is high pass, $T_2(s) = V_2(s)/V_S(s)$ is bandpass, and $T_3(s) = V_3(s)/V_S(s)$ is low pass.

(a) Prove or disprove this claim.

(b) If the claim is true develop a method of selecting *R*, *C*, and R_X to achieve specified values of ω_0 and ζ.

(c) If the claim is false suggest a simple modification that would make it true.

FIGURE P13–51

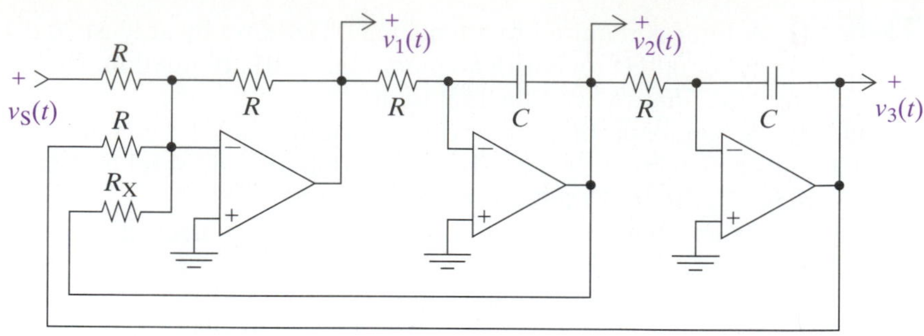

13–52 D MODIFYING AN EXISTING DESIGN

An existing digital data channel uses a second-order Butterworth low-pass filter with a cutoff frequency of 10 kHz. Field experience reveals that noise is causing the equipment performance to fall below advertised levels. Analysis by the engineering department suggests that decreasing the filter gain by 20 dB at 40 kHz will solve the problem, provided that the cutoff frequency does not change. The manufacturing department reports that adding anything more than one second-order stage will cause a major redesign and an unacceptable slip in scheduled deliveries. Design a second-order low-pass filter to connect in cascade with the existing second-order Butterworth filter. The frequency response of the circuit consisting of your second-order circuit in cascade with the original second-order Butterworth circuit must have a cutoff frequency of 10 kHz and reduce the gain at 40 kHz by at least 20 dB.

13–53 A BUTTERWORTH POLES

The poles of nth-order Butterworth low-pass responses are located at

$$s_k = \omega_C\left\{-\sin\left[\frac{(1+2k)\pi}{2n}\right] + j\cos\left[\frac{(1+2k)\pi}{2n}\right]\right\}$$

where $k = 0, 1, 2, \ldots (n-1)$ and ω_C is the cutoff frequency.

(a) Use this expression to verify the entries in Table 13–1 for $n = 3$ and $n = 4$.

(b) Show that the poles lie on a circle of radius ω_C.

(c) Calculate the damping ratios of the complex poles for $n = 3, 4, 5$, and 6.

(d) Your company's filter design guidelines require that the damping ratio of all complex poles must be greater than 0.2. What is the largest value of n that meets this guideline?

13–54 A E SECOND-ORDER CASCADE RESPONSE

The transfer function of a second-order Butterworth low-pass filter is

$$T_2(s) = \frac{K}{\left(\dfrac{s}{\omega_0}\right)^2 + \sqrt{2}\left(\dfrac{s}{\omega_0}\right) + 1}$$

where ω_0 is the cutoff frequency of the second-order response. A second-order cascade response is obtained by a cascade connection of n stages each of which has a transfer function $T_2(s)$.

(a) Derive an expression relating the cutoff frequency (ω_C) of an n-stage second-order cascade to the cutoff frequency (ω_0) of the individual stages. *Hint:* Review the derivation of the first-order cascade response.

(b) Derive an expression relating the corner frequency (ω_{CORNER}) to the cutoff frequency (ω_C) of an n-stage second-order cascade.

(c) Plot the normalized gain response of a two-stage second-order cascade response on the range $0.1\omega_C \le \omega \le 10\omega_C$. Plot the normalized gain response of a first-order cascade response with the same number of poles. Which response produces the most stopband attenuation and why?

(d) Discuss the advantages the second-order cascade has over other low-pass responses.

13–55 A ASYMPTOTIC CHEBYCHEV GAIN RESPONSE

For $\omega >> \omega_C$ a Chebychev polynomial is approximately

$$C_n(\omega/\omega_C) = 2^{n-1}\left(\frac{\omega}{\omega_C}\right)^n$$

(a) Derive an expression relating the corner frequency (ω_{CORNER}) to the cutoff frequency (ω_C) of an nth-order Chebychev response.

(b) Show that for $\omega > \omega_C$ the straight-line gain of an nth-order Chebychev filter is $6(n - 1)$ dB less than the straight-line gain of an nth-order Butterworth filter.

CHAPTER 14

POWER IN THE SINUSOIDAL STEADY STATE

George Westinghouse was, in my opinion, the only man on the globe who could take my alternating current (power) system under the circumstances then existing and win the battle against prejudice and money power.

Nikola Tesla, 1932,
American Engineer

In the last decade of the nineteenth century there were two competing electrical power systems in this country. The direct current approach was developed by Thomas Edison, who installed the first of his dc power systems at the famous Pearl Street Station in New York City in 1882. By 1884 there were more than 20 such power stations operating in the United States. The competing alternating current technology was hampered by the lack of practical motors for the single-phase systems initially produced. The three-phase ac induction motor that met this need was the product of the mind of the brilliant Serbian immigrant Nikola Tesla (1856–1943). Tesla was educated in Europe and in 1884 emigrated to the United States, where he initially worked for Edison. In 1887 Tesla founded his own company to develop his inventions, eventually producing some 40 patents on three-phase equipment and controls. The importance of Tesla's work was recognized by George Westinghouse, a hard-driving electrical pioneer who purchased the rights to Tesla's patents. In the early 1890s the competition between the older dc system championed by Edison and the newer ac technology sponsored by Westinghouse developed into a heated controversy called the "war of the currents." The showdown came over the equipment to be installed in a large electric power station at Niagara Falls, New York. The choice of an ac system for Niagara Falls established a trend that led to large interconnected ac systems that form the backbone of modern industry today.

In this chapter we study the flow of electrical power in the sinusoidal steady state. The first section shows that the instantaneous power at an interface can be divided into two components called real and reactive power. The unidirectional real component produces a net transfer of energy from the source to the load. The oscillatory reactive power represents an interchange between the source and load with no net transfer of energy. The concept of complex power developed in the second section combines these two components into a single complex entity relating power flow to the interface voltage and current phasors. The third and fourth sections develop the basic tools for using complex power to analyze power flow in ac circuits. The final three sections discuss the three-phase circuits and systems that deal with the large blocks of electrical power required in a modern industrial society.

14–1 AVERAGE AND REACTIVE POWER

We begin our study of electric power circuits with the two-terminal interface in Figure 14–1. In power applications we normally think of one circuit as the source and the other as the load. Our objective is to describe the flow of power across the interface when the circuit is operating in the sinusoidal steady state. To this end, we write the interface voltage and current in the time domain as sinusoids of the form

$$v(t) = V_A \cos(\omega t + \theta)$$
$$i(t) = I_A \cos \omega t \qquad (14\text{–}1)$$

In Eq. (14–1) V_A and I_A are real, positive numbers representing the peak amplitudes of the voltage and current, respectively.

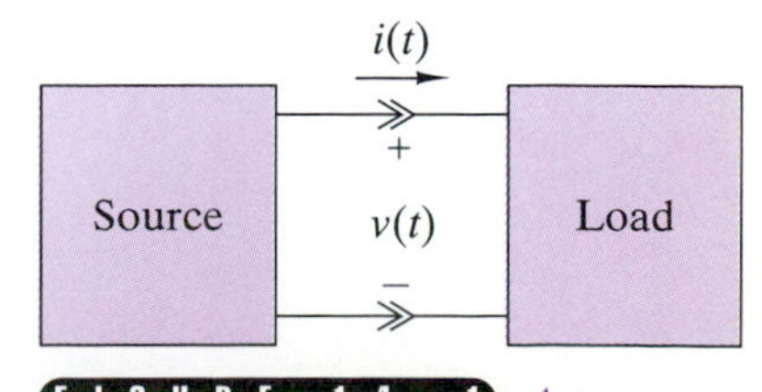

FIGURE 14–1 *A two-terminal interface.*

In Eq. (14–1) we have selected the $t = 0$ reference at the positive maximum of the current $i(t)$ and assigned a phase angle to $v(t)$ to account for the fact that the voltage maximum may not occur at the same time. In the phasor domain the angle $\theta = \phi_V - \phi_I$ is the angle between the phasors $\mathbf{V} = V_A\angle\phi_V$ and $\mathbf{I} = I_A\angle\phi_I$. In effect, choosing $t = 0$ at the current maximum shifts the phase reference by an amount $-\phi_I$ so that the voltage and current phasors become $\mathbf{V} = V_A\angle\,\theta$ and $\mathbf{I} = I_A\angle 0$.

A method of relating power to phasor voltage and current will be presented in the next section, but at the moment we write the instantaneous power in the time domain.

$$\begin{aligned} p(t) &= v(t) \times i(t) \\ &= V_A I_A \cos(\omega t + \theta)\cos \omega t \end{aligned} \qquad (14-2)$$

This expression for instantaneous power contains dc and ac components. To separate the components, we first use the identity $\cos(x + y) = \cos x \cos y - \sin x \sin y$ to write $p(t)$ in the form

$$\begin{aligned} p(t) &= V_A I_A[\cos \omega t \cos \theta - \sin \omega t \sin \theta] \cos \omega t \\ &= [V_A I_A \cos \theta]\cos^2 \omega t - [V_A I_A \sin \theta]\cos \omega t \sin \omega t \end{aligned} \qquad (14-3)$$

Using the identities $\cos^2 x = ½(1 + \cos 2x)$ and $\cos x \sin x = ½ \sin 2x$, we write $p(t)$ in the form

$$p(t) = \underbrace{\left[\frac{V_A I_A}{2}\cos\theta\right]}_{\text{dc Component}} + \underbrace{\left[\frac{V_A I_A}{2}\cos\theta\right]\cos 2\omega t - \left[\frac{V_A I_A}{2}\sin\theta\right]\sin 2\omega t}_{\text{ac Component}} \qquad (14-4)$$

Written this way, we see that the instantaneous power is the sum of a dc component and a double-frequency ac component. That is, the instantaneous power is the sum of a constant plus a sinusoid whose frequency is 2ω, which is twice the angular frequency of the voltage and current in Eq. (14–1).

Note that instantaneous power in Eq. (14–4) is periodic. In Chapter 6 we defined the average value of a periodic waveform as

$$P = \frac{1}{T}\int_0^T p(t)dt$$

where $T = 2\pi/2\omega$ is the period of $p(t)$. In Chapter 6 we also showed that the average value of a sinusoid is zero, since the area under the waveform during a positive half cycle is canceled by the area under a subsequent negative half cycle. Therefore, the **average value** of $p(t)$, denoted as P, is equal to the constant or dc term in Eq. (14–4):

$$P = \frac{V_A I_A}{2}\cos\theta \qquad (14-5)$$

The amplitude of the sin $2\omega t$ term in Eq. (14–4) has a form much like the average power in Eq. (14–5), except it involves $\sin\theta$ rather than $\cos\theta$.

This amplitude factor is called the **reactive power** of $p(t)$, where reactive power Q is defined as

$$Q = \frac{V_A I_A}{2} \sin \theta \qquad (14\text{–}6)$$

Substituting Eqs. (14–5) and (14–6) into Eq. (14–4) yields the instantaneous power in terms of the average power and reactive power:

$$p(t) = \underbrace{P(1 + \cos 2\omega t)}_{\text{Unipolar}} - \underbrace{Q \sin 2\omega t}_{\text{Bipolar}} \qquad (14\text{–}7)$$

The first term in Eq. (14–7) is said to be unipolar because the factor $1 + \cos 2\omega t$ never changes sign. As a result, the first term is either always positive or always negative depending on the sign of P. The second term is said to be bipolar because the factor $\sin 2\omega t$ alternates signs every half cycle.

The energy transferred across the interface during one cycle $T = 2\pi/2\omega$ of $p(t)$ is

$$\begin{aligned} W &= \int_0^T p(t)dt \\ &= P\underbrace{\int_0^T (1 + \cos 2\omega t)dt}_{\text{Net Energy}} - Q\underbrace{\int_0^T \sin 2\omega t\, dt}_{\text{No Net Energy}} \qquad (14\text{–}8) \\ &= \qquad P \times T \qquad - \qquad 0 \end{aligned}$$

Only the unipolar term in Eq. (14–7) provides any net energy transfer, and that energy is proportional to the average power P. With the passive sign convention the energy flows from source to load when $W > 0$. Equation (14–8) shows that the net energy will be positive if the average power $P > 0$. Equation (14–5) points out that the average power P is positive when $\cos \theta > 0$, which in turn means $|\theta| < 90°$. We conclude that

The net energy flow in Figure 14–1 is from source to load when the angle between the interface voltage and current is bounded by $-90° < \theta < 90°$; otherwise the net energy flow is from load to source.

The bipolar term in Eq. (14–7) is a power oscillation that transfers no net energy across the interface. In the sinusoidal steady state the load in Figure 14–1 borrows energy from the source circuit during part of a cycle and temporarily stores it in the load inductance or capacitance. In another part of the cycle the borrowed energy is returned to the source unscathed. The amplitude of the power oscillation is called reactive power because it involves periodic energy storage and retrieval from the reactive elements of the load. The reactive power can be either positive or negative depending on the sign of $\sin \theta$. However, the sign of Q tells us nothing about the net energy transfer, which is controlled by the sign of P.

We are obviously interested in average power, since this component carries net energy from source to load. For most power system customers the basic cost of electrical service is proportional to the net energy delivered to the load. Large industrial users may also pay a service charge for their reactive power. This may seem unfair, since reactive power transfers no net energy. However, the electric energy borrowed and returned by the load is generated within a power system that has losses. From a power company's viewpoint, the reactive power is not free because there are losses in the system connecting the generators in the power plant to source/load interface at which the lossless interchange of energy occurs.

In ac power circuit analysis, it is necessary to keep track of both the average power and reactive power. These two components of power have the same dimensions, but because they represent quite different effects they traditionally are given different units. The average power is expressed in watts (W) while reactive power is expressed in VARs, which is an acronym for "volt-amperes reactive."

Exercise 14–1

Using the reference marks in Figure 14–1, calculate the average and reactive power for the following voltages and currents. State whether the load is absorbing or delivering net energy.

(a) $v(\text{t}) = 168 \cos(377t + 45°)$ V, $i(t) = 0.88 \cos 377t$ A
(b) $v(t) = 285 \cos(2500t - 68°)$ V, $i(t) = 0.66 \cos 2500t$ A
(c) $v(t) = 168 \cos(377t + 45°)$ V, $i(t) = 0.88 \cos(377t - 60°)$ A
(d) $v(t) = 285 \cos(2500t - 68°)$ V, $i(t) = 0.66 \sin 2500t$ A

Answers:
(a) $P = +52.3$ W, $Q = +52.3$ VAR, absorbing
(b) $P = +35.2$ W, $Q = -87.2$ VAR, absorbing
(c) $P = -19.1$ W, $Q = +71.4$ VAR, delivering
(d) $P = +87.2$ W, $Q = +35.2$ VAR, absorbing

14–2 COMPLEX POWER

It is important to relate average and reactive power to phasor quantities because ac circuit analysis is conveniently carried out using phasors. In our previous work the magnitude of a phasor represented the peak amplitude of a sinusoid. However, in power circuit analysis it is convenient to express phasor magnitudes in rms (root mean square) values. In this chapter phasor voltages and currents are expressed as

$$\mathbf{V} = V_{\text{rms}} e^{j\phi_{\text{V}}} \quad \text{and} \quad \mathbf{I} = I_{\text{rms}} e^{j\phi_{\text{I}}} \qquad (14\text{–}9)$$

In this chapter phasor magnitudes are the rms amplitude of the corresponding sinusoid.

Equations (14–5) and (14–6) express average and reactive power in terms of peak amplitudes V_{A} and I_{A}. In Chapter 6 we showed that the peak and rms values of a sinusoid are related by $V_{\text{rms}} = V_{\text{A}}/\sqrt{2}$. The expression for average power easily can be converted to rms amplitudes since we can write Eq. (14–5) as

$$P = \frac{V_A I_A}{2}\cos\theta = \frac{V_A}{\sqrt{2}}\frac{I_A}{\sqrt{2}}\cos\theta$$
$$= V_{rms} I_{rms} \cos\theta \qquad (14\text{–}10)$$

where $\theta = \phi_V - \phi_I$ is the angle between the voltage and current phasors. By similar reasoning, Eq. (14–6) becomes

$$Q = V_{rms} I_{rms} \sin\theta \qquad (14\text{–}11)$$

Using rms phasors the **complex power** *(S)* at a two-terminal interface is defined as follows:

$$S = \mathbf{VI}^* \qquad (14\text{–}12)$$

That is, the complex power at an interface is the product of the voltage phasor times the conjugate of the current phasor. Substituting Eq. (14–9) into this definition yields

$$S = \mathbf{VI}^* = V_{rms}e^{j\phi_V} I_{rms}e^{-j\phi_I}$$
$$= [V_{rms} I_{rms}]e^{j(\phi_V - \phi_I)} \qquad (14\text{–}13)$$

Using Euler's relationship and the fact that the angle is $\theta = \phi_V - \phi_I$, we can write complex power as

$$S = [V_{rms} I_{rms}]e^{j\theta}$$
$$= [V_{rms} I_{rms}]\cos\theta + j[V_{rms} I_{rms}]\sin\theta \qquad (14\text{–}14)$$
$$= P + jQ$$

The real part of the complex power S is the average power, and the imaginary part is the reactive power. Although S is a complex number, it is not a phasor. However, it is a convenient variable for keeping track of the two components of power when the voltage and currents are expressed as phasors.

The power triangles in Figure 14–2 provide a convenient way to remember complex power relationships and terminology. We confine our study to cases in which net energy is transferred from source to load. In such cases $P > 0$ and the power triangles fall in the first or fourth quadrant, as indicated in Figure 14–2.

The magnitude $|S| = V_{rms}I_{rms}$ is called **apparent power** and is expressed using the unit volt-ampere (VA). The ratio of the average power to the apparent power is called the **power factor** (pf). Using Eq. (14–10), we see that the power factor is

$$\text{pf} = \frac{P}{|S|} = \frac{V_{rms}I_{rms}\cos\theta}{V_{rms}I_{rms}} = \cos\theta \qquad (14\text{–}15)$$

Since $\text{pf} = \cos\theta$, the angle θ is called the **power factor angle**.

When the power factor is unity the phasors **V** and **I** are in phase ($\theta = 0°$) and the reactive power is zero since $\sin\theta = 0$. When the power factor is less than unity, the reactive power is not zero and its sign is indicated by the modifiers lagging or leading. The term *lagging power factor* means the cur-

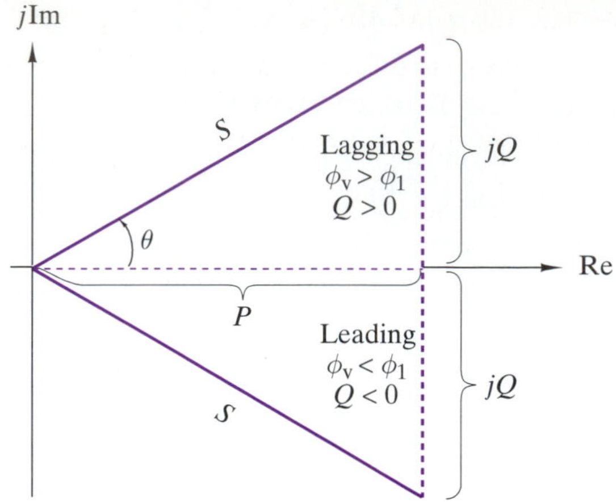

FIGURE 14–2 *Power triangles.*

rent phasor lags the voltage phasor so that $\theta = \phi_V - \phi_I > 0$. For a lagging power factor S falls in the first quadrant in Figure 14–2 and the reactive power is positive since $\sin \theta > 0$. The term *leading power factor* means the current phasor leads the voltage phasor so that $\theta = \phi_V - \phi_I < 0$. In this case S falls in the fourth quadrant in Figure 14–2 and the reactive power is negative since $\sin \theta < 0$. Most industrial and residential loads have lagging power factors.

The apparent power rating of electrical power equipment is an important design consideration. The ratings of generators, transfomers, and transmission line are normally stated in kVA. The ratings of most loads are stated in kW and power factor. The wiring must be large enough to carry the required current and insulated well enough to withstand the rated voltage. However, only the average power is potentially available as useful output, since the reactive power represents a lossless interchange between the source and device. Because reactive power increases the apparent power rating without increasing the net energy output, it is desirable for electrical devices to operate with zero reative power or, equivalently, at unity power factor.

Exercise 14–2

Determine the average power, reactive power, and apparent power for the following voltage and current phasors. State whether the power factor is lagging or leading.

(a) $\mathbf{V} = 208\angle{-90°}$ V (rms), $\mathbf{I} = 1.75\angle{-75°}$ A (rms)
(b) $\mathbf{V} = 277\angle{+90°}$ V (rms), $\mathbf{I} = 11.3\angle{0°}$ A (rms)
(c) $\mathbf{V} = 120\angle{-30°}$ V (rms), $\mathbf{I} = 0.30\angle{-90°}$ A (rms)
(d) $\mathbf{V} = 480\angle{+75°}$ V (rms), $\mathbf{I} = 8.75\angle{+105°}$ A (rms)

Answers:

(a) $P = 352$ W, $Q = -94.2$ VAR, $|S| = 364$ VA, leading
(b) $P = 0$ W, $Q = +3.13$ kVAR, $|S| = 3.13$ kVA, lagging
(c) $P = 18$ W, $Q = +31.2$ VAR, $|S| = 36$ VA, lagging
(d) $P = 3.64$ kW, $Q = -2.1$ kVAR, $|S| = 4.20$ kVA, leading

COMPLEX POWER AND LOAD IMPEDANCE

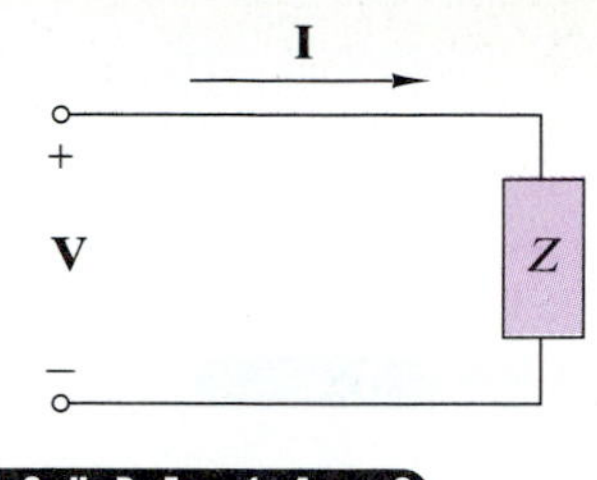

FIGURE 14–3
Two-terminal impedance.

In many cases power circuit loads are described in terms of their power ratings at a specified voltage or current level. To find voltages and current elsewhere in the circuit, it is necessary to know the load impedance. For this reason we need to relate complex power and load impedance.

Figure 14–3 shows the general case for a two-terminal load. For the assigned reference directions the load produces the element constraint $\mathbf{V} = Z\mathbf{I}$. Using this constraint in Eq. (14–12), we write the complex power of the load as

$$\begin{aligned} S &= \mathbf{V} \times \mathbf{I}^* = Z\mathbf{I} \times \mathbf{I}^* = Z|\mathbf{I}|^2 \\ &= (R + jX)\, I_{\text{rms}}^2 \end{aligned}$$

where R and X are the resistance and reactance of the load, respectively. Since $S = P + jQ$, we conclude that

$$R = \frac{P}{I_{\text{rms}}^2} \quad \text{and} \quad X = \frac{Q}{I_{\text{rms}}^2} \tag{14–16}$$

The load resistance and reactance are proportional to the average and reactive power of the load, respectively.

The first condition in Eq. (14–16) demonstrates that resistance cannot be negative, since P cannot be negative for a passive circuit. That is, a passive circuit cannot produce average power in the sinusoidal steady state; otherwise, perpetual motion would be possible and the energy crisis would be a small footnote in the great sweep of human history. The second condition in Eq. (14–16) points out that when the reactive power is positive the load is inductive, since $X_L = \omega L$ is positive. Conversely, when the reactive power is negative the load is capacitive, since $X_C = -1/\omega C$ is negative. The terms *inductive load, lagging power factor,* and *positive reactive power* are synonymous, as are the terms *capacitive load, leading power factor,* and *negative reactive power.*

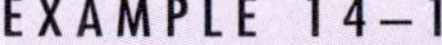

EXAMPLE 14–1

At 440 V (rms) a two-terminal load draws 3 kVA of apparent power at a lagging power factor of 0.9. Find

(a) I_{rms}
(b) P
(c) Q
(d) the load impedance.

Draw the power triangle for the load.

SOLUTION:

(a) $I_{\text{rms}} = |S|/V_{\text{rms}} = 3000/440 = 6.82$ A (rms)
(b) $P = V_{\text{rms}} I_{\text{rms}} \cos\theta = 3000 \times 0.9 = 2.7$ kW

(c) For $\cos\theta = 0.9$ lagging, $\sin\theta = 0.436$ and $Q = V_{rms}I_{rms}\sin\theta = 1.31$ kVAR
(d) $Z = (P + jQ)/(I_{rms})^2 = (2700 + j1310)/46.5 = 58.0 + j28.2\ \Omega$.

Figure 14–4 shows the power triangle for this load. ■

FIGURE 14–4

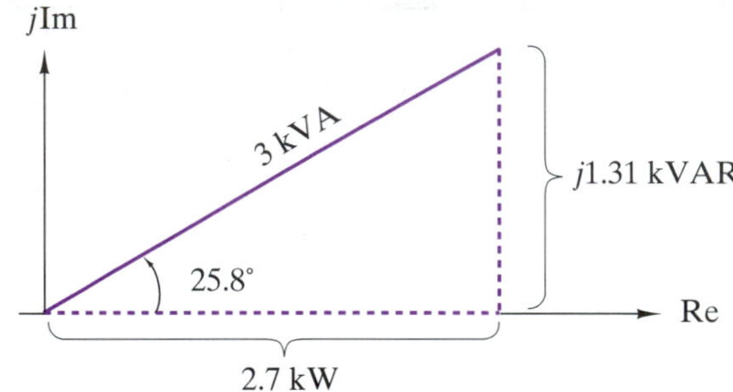

Exercise 14–3

Find the impedance of a two-terminal load under the following conditions.
(a) $\mathbf{V} = 120\angle 30°$ V (rms) and $\mathbf{I} = 20\angle 75°$ A (rms)
(b) $|S| = 3.3$ kVA, $Q = -1.8$ kVAR, and $I_{rms} = 7.5$ A
(c) $P = 3$ kW, $Q = 4$ kVAR, and $V_{rms} = 880$ V
(d) $V_{rms} = 208$ V, $I_{rms} = 17.8$ A, and $P = 3$ kW

Answers:
(a) $Z = 4.24 - j4.24\ \Omega$
(b) $Z = 49.2 - j32\ \Omega$
(c) $Z = 92.9 + j124\ \Omega$
(d) $Z = 9.47 \pm j6.85\ \Omega$

14–3 AC POWER ANALYSIS

The nature of ac power analysis can be modeled in terms of the phasor voltage, phasor current, and complex power at the source/load interface in Figure 14–1. Two different types of problems are treated using this model. In the **direct analysis** problem the source and load circuit are given and we are required to find the steady-state responses at one or more interfaces. This type of problem is essentially the same as the phasor circuit analysis problems in Chapter 8, except that we calculate complex powers as well as phasor responses. In the **load-flow** problem we are required to adjust the source so that a prescribed complex power is delivered to the load at a specified interface voltage magnitude. This type of problem arises in electrical power systems where the objective is to supply changing energy demands at a fixed voltage level.

The following examples are direct analysis problems that illustrate the computational tools needed to deal with the load-flow problems discussed in the next section. One of the useful tools is the principle of the **conservation of complex power**, which can be stated as follows:

In a linear circuit operating in the sinusoidal steady state, the sum of the complex powers produced by each independent source is equal to the sum of the complex power absorbed by all other two-terminal elements in the circuit.

To apply this principle, it is important to distinguish between the complex power "produced by" and "absorbed by" a two-terminal element. To do so, we modify our practice of using the passive sign convention. We continue to use the passive convention (current reference directed in at the + voltage mark) for loads, but use the active convention (current reference directed out at the + voltage mark) for sources. In either case, the complex power is always calculated as $S = \mathbf{VI}^* = P + jQ$. The net result is that the average power produced by a source is positive and the average power absorbed by a load is positive.

EXAMPLE 14–2

(a) Calculate the complex power absorbed by each parallel branch in Figure 14–5.

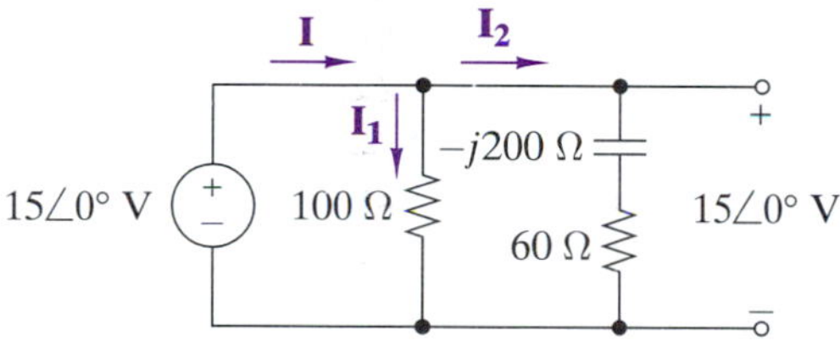

FIGURE 14–5

(b) Calculate the complex power produced by the source and the power factor of the load seen by the source.

SOLUTION:

(a) The voltage across each branch is $15\angle 0°$ V and the branch impedances are $Z_1 = 100$ and $Z_2 = 60 - j200$. Therefore, the branch currents are

$$\mathbf{I}_1 = \frac{15\angle 0°}{100} = 0.15\angle 0° \text{ A}$$

$$\mathbf{I}_2 = \frac{15\angle 0°}{60 - j200} = 0.0718\angle 73.3° \text{ A}$$

The reference marks for the voltage across and currents through these loads follow the passive sign convention. Hence the complex powers absorbed by the loads are

$$S_1 = (15\angle 0°)\mathbf{I}_1^* = (15\angle 0°)(0.15\angle -0°) = 2.25\angle 0° \text{ VA}$$

$$S_2 = (15\angle 0°)\mathbf{I}_2^* = (15\angle 0°)(0.0718\angle -73.3°) = 1.08\angle -73.3° \text{ VA}$$

(b) Using KCL, the source current **I** is

$$\mathbf{I} = (\mathbf{I}_1 + \mathbf{I}_2) = (0.15\angle 0^\circ + 0.0718\angle 73.3^\circ)$$
$$= 0.171 + j0.0688 = 0.184\angle 21.9^\circ \text{ A}$$

The reference marks for the source current **I** and source voltage $15\angle 0^\circ$ conform to the active sign convention, and the complex power produced by the source is

$$S = (15\angle 0^\circ)\mathbf{I}^* = (15\angle 0^\circ)(0.184\angle -21.9^\circ)$$
$$= 2.76\angle -21.9^\circ \text{ VA}$$

The power factor is cos(–21.9°) = 0.928 leading. Alternatively, we can use the conservation of complex power to obtain the complex power produced by the source as the sum of the complex powers delivered to the passive elements:

$$S_1 + S_2 = 2.25\angle 0^\circ + 1.08\angle -73.3^\circ$$
$$= 2.25 + j0 + 0.310 - j1.03$$
$$= 2.56 - j1.03 = 2.76\angle -21.9^\circ \text{ VA}$$

This result is the same as the answer obtained previously. ■

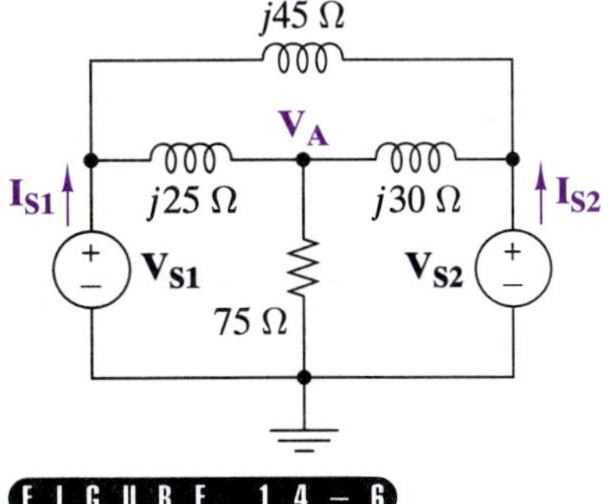

FIGURE 14–6

EXAMPLE 14–3

Find the complex power produced by each source in Figure 14–6 when $\mathbf{V}_{S1} = 440\angle 0^\circ$ V (rms) and $\mathbf{V}_{S2} = 500\angle 0^\circ$ V (rms).

SOLUTION:

Since both the voltage sources are connected to ground, the voltage at node A is the only unknown node voltage in the circuit. By inspection, the node equation at node A is

$$\left[\frac{1}{75} + \frac{1}{j25} + \frac{1}{j30}\right]\mathbf{V}_A = \frac{\mathbf{V}_{S1}}{j25} + \frac{\mathbf{V}_{S2}}{j30} = -j34.27$$

which yields $\mathbf{V}_A = 452 - j82.2$ V. The current supplied by source no. 1 is

$$\mathbf{I}_{S1} = \frac{\mathbf{V}_{S1} - \mathbf{V}_A}{j25} + \frac{\mathbf{V}_{S1} - \mathbf{V}_{S2}}{j45} = 3.29 + j1.81 \text{ A (rms)}$$

The complex power supplied by source no. 1 is

$$S_{S1} = \mathbf{V}_{S1}\mathbf{I}_{S1}^* = 440 \times (3.29 - j1.83)$$
$$= 1450 - j796 \quad \text{VA}$$

The current supplied by source no. 2 is

$$\mathbf{I}_{S2} = \frac{\mathbf{V}_{S2} - \mathbf{V}_A}{j30} + \frac{\mathbf{V}_{S2} - \mathbf{V}_{S1}}{j45} = 2.74 - j2.93 \quad \text{A (rms)}$$

and the complex power supplied by source no. 2 is

$$S_{S2} = \mathbf{V}_{S2}\mathbf{I}^*_{S2} = 500 \times (2.74 + j2.93)$$
$$= 1370 + j1460 \quad \text{VA}$$

EXAMPLE 14–4

Given the transformer circuit in Figure 14–7, find the complex power produced by the input voltage source and the power absorbed by the 100-Ω load resistor.

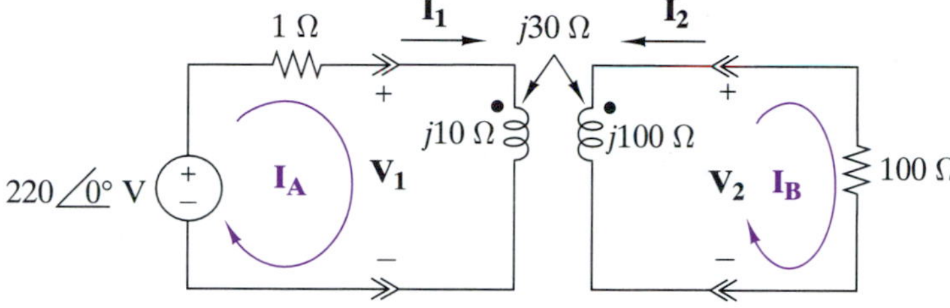

FIGURE 14–7

SOLUTION:

Using the coil voltages and mesh currents in Figure 14–7, the KVL equations around the primary and secondary circuits are

$$1 \times \mathbf{I}_A + \mathbf{V}_1 = 220\angle 0°$$
$$100\,\mathbf{I}_B - \mathbf{V}_2 = 0$$

The coil currents are related to the mesh currents as $\mathbf{I}_1 = \mathbf{I}_A$ and $\mathbf{I}_2 = -\mathbf{I}_B$. Both coil currents are directed inward at the coil dots, so the mutual inductive coupling is additive and the *i–v* characteristics of the coupled coils in terms of the mesh currents are

$$\mathbf{V}_1 = j10\mathbf{I}_A + j30(-\mathbf{I}_B)$$
$$\mathbf{V}_2 = j30\mathbf{I}_A + j100(-\mathbf{I}_B)$$

Substituting the coil *i–v* characteristics into the KVL equation produces the two mesh current equations for the transformer:

$$(1 + j10)\mathbf{I}_A - j30\mathbf{I}_B = 220$$
$$-j30\mathbf{I}_A + (100 + j100)\mathbf{I}_B = 0$$

Solving for the two mesh current produces

$$\mathbf{I}_A = 20 - j20 \text{ A (rms)}$$
$$\mathbf{I}_B = 6 + j0 \text{ A (rms)}$$

Using mesh current $\mathbf{I}_A$, the complex power produced by the source is

$$S_{IN} = (220\angle 0°)\mathbf{I}^*_A = 4400 + j4400 \quad \text{VA}$$

and the power absorbed by the 100-Ω output resistor is

$$S_{OUT} = (100\mathbf{I}_B)\mathbf{I}_B^* = 3600 + j0 \text{ VA}$$ ■

Exercise 14–4

Calculate the complex power delivered by each source in Figure 14–8.

FIGURE 14–8

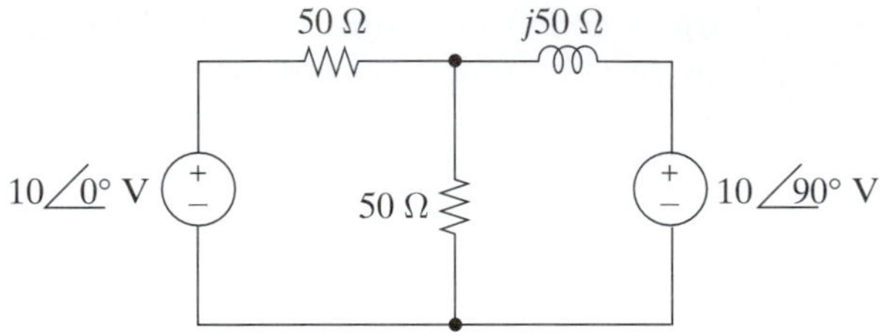

Answers: $S_1 = 0.4 + j0.8$ VA, $S_2 = 1.6 + j1.2$ VA

14–4 LOAD-FLOW ANALYSIS

The analysis of ac electrical power systems is one of the major applications of phasor circuit analysis. Although the loads on power systems change during the day, these variations are extremely slow compared with the period of the 50/60-Hz sinusoid involved.[1] Consequently, electrical power system analysis can be carried out using steady-state concepts and phasors. In fact, it was the study of the steady-state performance of ac power equipment that led Charles Steinmetz to advocate phasors in the first place.

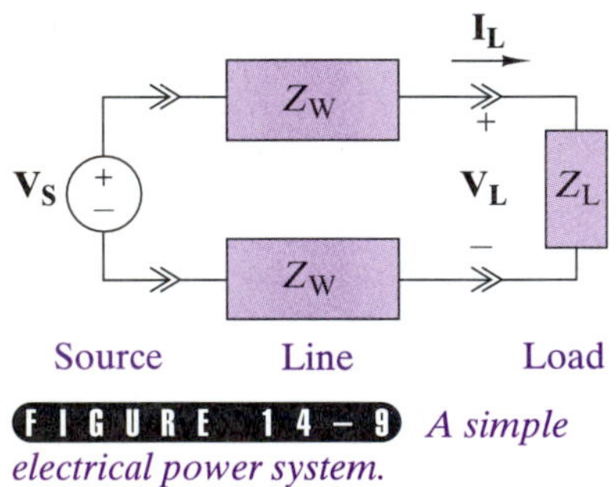

FIGURE 14–9 *A simple electrical power system.*

In this section we treat ac power analysis using the simple model of an electrical power system in Figure 14–9. This model is a series circuit with an ac source connected to a load via power lines whose wire impedances are Z_W. In a **load-flow problem** the complex power delivered to the load is specified and we are asked to find either the source voltage for a given load voltage or the load voltage for a given source voltage. The analysis approach is similar to the unit output method. That is, we begin with conditions at the load and work backward through the circuit to establish the required source voltage. The load-flow problem is different from the maximum power transfer problem studied in Chapter 8. In a maximum power transfer problem the source is fixed and the load is adjusted to achieve a conjugate match. Conjugate matching does not apply to electrical power systems because the load power is fixed and the source is adjusted to meet customer demands.

Large industrial customers are charged for their reactive power, so in some cases it is desirable to reduce the load reactance. Since power system

1 In the United States commercial ac power systems operate at 60 Hz. In most of the rest of the world the standard operating frequency is 50 Hz.

loads are normally inductive, the net reactive power of the load can be reduced by adding a capacitor in parallel with the load. The amount of the negative reactive power taken by the capacitor is selected to cancel some or all of the positive reactance power drawn by the inductive load. Physically, this means that the oscillatory interchange of energy represented by reactive power takes place between the capacitor and inductance in the load, rather than between the load inductance and the lossy power system.

Adding parallel capacitance is called **power factor correction**, since the net power factor of the composite load is increased. If the power factor is increased to unity, then the net reactance is zero and the load is in resonance. Power factor correction reduces the reactive power drain on the power system but does not change the average power delivered to the load.

The following examples illustrate ac power analysis problems, including load flow and power factor correction.

EXAMPLE 14–5

In this problem the two parallel connected impedances in Figure 14–10 are the load in the power system model in Figure 14–9. With $V_L = 480$ V (rms), load Z_1 draws an average power of 10 kW at a lagging power factor of 0.8 and load Z_2 draws 12 kW at a lagging power factor of 0.75. The line impedances shown in Figure 14–9 are $Z_W = 0.35 + j1.5\ \Omega$.

(a) Find the total complex power delivered to the composite load.
(b) Find the apparent power delivered by the source and the source voltage phasor $\mathbf{V}_S$.
(c) Calculate the transmission efficiency of the system.

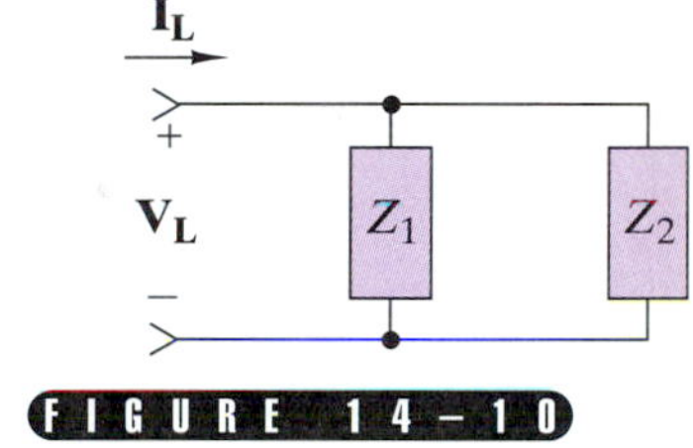

FIGURE 14–10

SOLUTION:

(a) The complex powers delivered to each load are

$$S_{L1} = 10 + j10\tan(\cos^{-1} 0.8) = 10 + j7.5 \text{ kVA}$$

$$S_{L2} = 12 + j12\tan(\cos^{-1} 0.75) = 12 + j10.6 \text{ kVA}$$

The total complex power delivered to the composite load is

$$S_L = S_{L1} + S_{L2} = 22 + j18.1 = 28.5\angle 39.4^\circ \text{ k}VA$$

(b) Using the load voltage as the phase reference, we find the load current to be

$$\mathbf{I}_L^* = \frac{S_L}{\mathbf{V}_L} = \frac{28500\angle 39.4^\circ}{480\angle 0^\circ} = 59.4\angle 39.4^\circ \quad \text{A (rms)}$$

or $\mathbf{I}_L = 59.4\angle{-39.4^\circ}$ A (rms). To find the source power, we need to find the complex power lost in the transmission to the line:

$$\begin{aligned} S_W &= 2|\mathbf{I}_L|^2(R_W + jX_W) = 2 \times (59.4)^2\,(0.35 + j1.5) \\ &= 2.47 + j10.6 \text{ kVA} \end{aligned}$$

Using the conservation of complex power, we find that the source must produce

$$S_S = S_L + S_W = 24.5 + j28.7 = 37.7\angle 49.5° \quad \text{kVA}$$

For the series model in Figure 14–9 the source and load currents are equal so the source power is $S_S = \mathbf{V}_S(\mathbf{I}_L)^*$. Given the source power and load current, we find that the required source voltage is

$$\mathbf{V}_S = \frac{S_S}{\mathbf{I}^*_L} = \frac{37700\angle 49.5°}{59.4\angle 39.4°} = 635\angle 10.1° \quad \text{V (rms)}$$

(b) The transmission efficiency is defined in terms of source and load average power as

$$\eta = \frac{P_L}{P_S} \times 100\% = \frac{22}{24.5} \times 100 = 89.8\%$$

EXAMPLE 14–6

A power system modeled by the circuit in Figure 14–9 delivers a load power of $S_L = 25 + j10$ kVA when the source voltage is $\mathbf{V}_S = 600\angle 0°$. The line impedances are $Z_W = 0.35 + j1.5\ \Omega$.

(a) Find the load voltage and current.
(b) Calculate the efficiency of the system.

SOLUTION:

(a) In the preceding example specified quantities are the load power and load voltage. In this example the load power and the source voltage are specified. As a result, both the load current and the load voltage are unknowns. We can write two constraints on these unknowns. First, the specified complex power delivered to the load requires that

$$S_L = 25{,}000 + j10{,}000 = \mathbf{V}_L\mathbf{I}^*_L$$

Next, writing a KVL equation around the loop in Figure 14–9 yields $\mathbf{V}_S - \mathbf{V}_L - 2Z_W\mathbf{I}_L = 0$. Inserting the known quantities into this constraint produces

$$600 + j0 - \mathbf{V}_L - (0.7 + j3)\mathbf{I}_L = 0$$

We have two equations in the two unknowns. Deriving a closed-form solution is not an easy matter since both equations involve complex quantities and the load power constraint is a nonlinear equation.

Figure 14–11 shows a Mathcad worksheet that numerically solves these equations. The first two lines define the specified quantities in the problem. The third line contains initial guesses for $\mathbf{V}_L$ and $\mathbf{I}_L$. The initial guess of $\mathbf{V}_L = 400 - j100$ recognizes that the load voltage will lag the source voltage and be somewhat smaller in magnitude because of the voltage drop in the line. The load-power constraint is then used to calculate an initial guess for the load current.

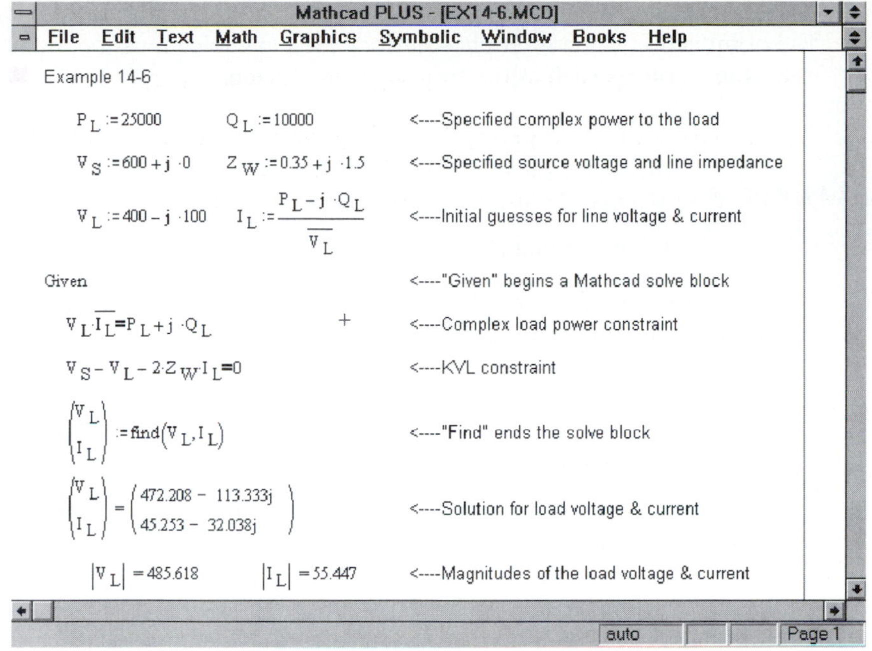

FIGURE 14–11

The reserve word "given" marks the beginning of a Mathcad solve block that includes the load-power constraint and the KVL constraint. Mathcad solves these constraints iteratively starting with the initial estimates of the load voltage and current. If the initial estimates are too far off, the iterative process does not converge. As always, intelligent use of computer-aided circuit analysis requires that the user have at least a rough idea of the expected answer. The reserve word "find" ends the solve block and yields a solution for the unknown load voltage and current.

(b) The apparent power delivered by the source is

$$S_S = \mathbf{V}_S\mathbf{I}_L^* = (600 + j0)(45.3 + j32.0)$$
$$= 27.2 + j19.2 \quad \text{kVA}$$

Hence the transmission efficiency is

$$\eta = \frac{P_L}{P_S} \times 100\% = \frac{25}{27.2} \times 100 = 91.9\%$$

Several comments are in order. First, with this type of load-flow problem it is possible to define conditions that do not have any solutions. For instance, if in the present case we say that the source voltage is only 1 V, then the system cannot possibly deliver $P = 25$ kW via the given transmission line to any load. Second, with this type of load-flow problem there may be many solutions. In the present case there is another solution that yields $|\mathbf{V}_L| = 170.8$ V and $|\mathbf{I}_L| = 157.6$ A. This alternative solution involves a larger line current so the power losses in the transmission line are much larger. Thus, on the basis of transmission efficiency we are inclined to choose the solution given in Figure 14–11. The point is that when multiple solutions exist, a choice must be made using some criteria such as the transmission efficiency. ■

EXAMPLE 14–7

Using the loads and line impedances defined in Example 14–5,

(a) Find the parallel capacitance needed so that the load power factor is at least 0.95. The power system frequency is 60 Hz.
(b) Find the transmission efficiency with the capacitor connected.

SOLUTION:

(a) To determine the capacitance, it is necessary to relate the reactive power of a capacitor to the load voltage. Since the capacitor is in parallel with the load, the current through it is $\mathbf{I}_C = j\omega C\mathbf{V}_L$. Therefore, the reactive power of the capacitor can be written as

$$\begin{aligned} Q_C &= |\mathbf{I}_C|^2 X_C = |j\omega C\mathbf{V}_L|^2\left(\frac{-1}{\omega C}\right) \\ &= |\mathbf{V}_L|^2(-\omega C) \end{aligned}$$

Note that Q_C is negative. In Example 14–5 the complex power of the two parallel loads is found to be

$$S_L = P_L + jQ_L = 22 + j18.1 \quad \text{kVA}$$

When the capacitor is connected the complex power delivered to the composite load becomes

$$S_L = P_L + j(Q_L + Q_C)$$

Since the capacitor is a reactive element, it only changes the reactive power and not the average power. To correct the power factor to at least 0.95 requires that

$$\cos\theta = \frac{P_L}{\sqrt{P_L^2 + (Q_L + Q_C)^2}} \geqslant 0.95$$

Solving for $-Q_C$ yields

$$-Q_C \geqslant Q_L - P_L\sqrt{1/(0.95)^2 - 1} = 10.9 \quad \text{kVAR}$$

which means that a lower bound on the capacitance is

$$C = \frac{-Q_C}{V_L^2\omega} \geqslant \frac{10{,}900}{(480)^2(2\pi 60)} = 125\ \mu\text{F}$$

This yields a lower bound on the required capacitance. An upper bound is found by increasing the load-power factor to unity ($\cos\theta = 1$). The required capacitive reactance is

$$-Q_C = Q_L = 18.1 \quad \text{kVAR}$$

which yields an upper bound on the capacitance of

$$C = \frac{-Q_C}{V_L^2 \omega} \leq \frac{18{,}100}{(480)^2(2\pi 60)} = 208\ \mu\text{F}$$

Thus, the design requirement can be met by any capacitance in the range from 125 μF to 208 μF.

(b) With the minimum capacitance of $C = 125$ μF connected in parallel with the load, the apparent power delivered to the composite load is $S_L = 22 + j7.2$ kVA. Using the load voltage for the phase reference, we find that the load current is

$$\mathbf{I}_L^* = \frac{S_L}{\mathbf{V}_L} = \frac{22{,}000 + j7200}{480\angle 0^\circ}$$
$$= 48.2\angle 18.1^\circ \quad \text{A (rms)}$$

The apparent power lost in the line is

$$S_W = |\mathbf{I}_L|^2\, 2(R_W + jX_W) = 1.62 + j6.97 \quad \text{kVA}$$

Hence with power factor correction the source produces

$$S_S = S_L + S_W = 23.6 + j14.2 \quad \text{kVA}$$

and the transmission efficiency is

$$\eta = \frac{P_L}{P_S} \times 100\% = \frac{22}{23.6} \times 100 = 93.2\%$$

In Example 14–5 we found the transmission efficiency without power factor correction to be 89.8%. With power factor correction the source delivers the same average power to the load with an increase in efficiency. Reactive power is a burden to a power system even though it represents a lossless interchange of energy at the terminals of the load. ■

Exercise 14–5

Find the source voltage and apparent power required to deliver 2400 V (rms) to a load that draws 25 kVA at a 0.85 lagging power factor from a line with a total line impedance of $2Z_W = 4 + j20\ \Omega$.

Answers: 2.55 kV (rms) and 26.6 kVA at a lagging power factor of 0.82

APPLICATION NOTE: EXAMPLE 14–8

The electrical power for most residential customers in the United States is supplied by the 60-Hz, 110/220-V (rms) single-phase, three-wire system modeled in Figure 14–12. The term *single phase* means that the phasors representing the two source voltages are in phase. The three lines connecting the sources and loads are labeled A, B, and N (for neutral). The impedances Z_W and Z_N are small compared with the load impedances, so the load voltages differ from the source voltages by only a few percent. The impedances Z_1 and Z_2 connected from Lines A or B to neutral represent small appliance and lighting loads which require 110 V(rms) service. The impedances Z_3 connected between lines A and B are heavier loads that require 220 V (rms) service, such as water heaters or clothes dryers.

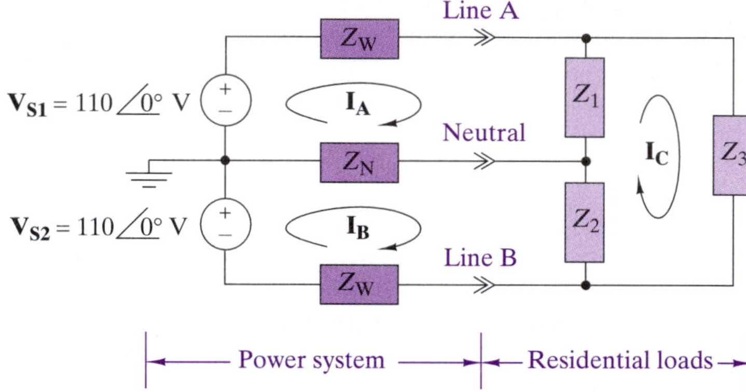

FIGURE 14–12 *Residential power distribution circuit.*

When the two source voltages are exactly equal and $Z_1 = Z_2$ the system is said to be balanced. Under balanced conditions the current in the neutral wire is zero. To show why the neutral current is zero, we write two mesh-current equations:

$$\text{Mesh A: } (Z_W + Z_1 + Z_N)\mathbf{I}_A - Z_N\mathbf{I}_B - Z_1\mathbf{I}_C = \mathbf{V}_{S1}$$

$$\text{Mesh B: } -Z_N\mathbf{I}_A + (Z_W + Z_2 + Z_N)\mathbf{I}_B - Z_2\mathbf{I}_C = \mathbf{V}_{S2}$$

For balanced conditions $\mathbf{V}_{S1} = \mathbf{V}_{S2}$ and $Z_1 = Z_2 = Z_L$. Subtracting the mesh B equation from the mesh A equation yields the condition

$$(Z_W + Z_L + 2Z_N)(\mathbf{I}_A - \mathbf{I}_B) = 0$$

This condition requires $\mathbf{I}_A - \mathbf{I}_B = 0$, since the impedance sum cannot be zero for all loads. Therefore, the net current in the neutral line is zero and theoretically the neutral wire can be disconnected. In practice, the balance is never perfect and the neutral line is included for safety reasons. But even so, the current in the neutral is usually less than the line currents, so losses in the feeder lines are reduced.

14–5 THREE-PHASE CIRCUITS

The three-phase system shown in Figure 14–13 is the predominant method of generating and distributing ac electrical power. The system uses four lines (A, B, C, N) to transmit power from the source to the loads. The symbols stand for the three phases A, B, and C, and a neutral line labeled N. The three-phase generator in Figure 14–13 is modeled as three independent sources, although the physical hardware is a single unit with three separate windings. Similarly, the loads are modeled as three separate impedances, although the actual equipment may be housed within a single container.

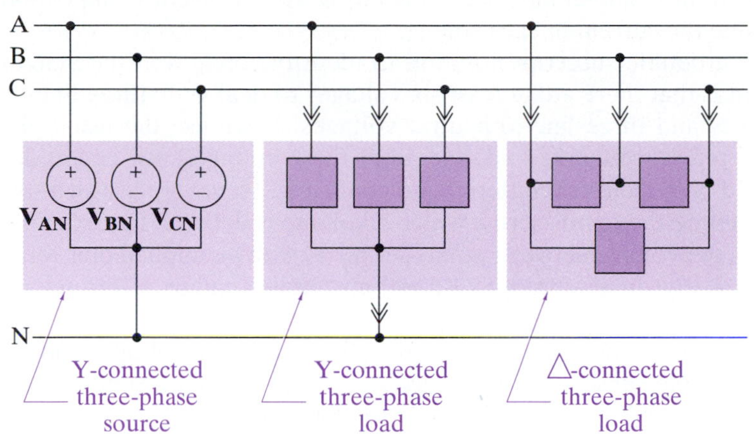

FIGURE 14–13 *A three-phase ac electrical power system.*

A three-phase system involves three voltages and three currents. In a balanced three-phase system the generator produces phasor voltages that are equal in magnitude and symmetically displaced in phase at 120° intervals. When the three-phase load is balance (equal impedances), the resulting phasor currents have equal magnitude and are symmetically displaced in phase at 120° intervals. Thus, a **balanced three-phase** system is one in which the phasor currents and voltages have equal magnitudes and phase differences of 120°.

The terminology Y-connected and Δ-connected refers to the two ways the source and loads can be electrically connected. Figure 14–14 shows the same electrical arrangement as Figure 14–13 with the elements rearranged to show the Y and Δ nature of the connections (the Δ is upside down in the figure). The circuit diagrams in the two figures are electrically equivalent, but we will use the form in Figure 14–13 because it highlights the purpose of the system. You need only remember that in a Y-connection the three elements are connected from line to neutral, while in the Δ-connection they are connected from line to line. In most systems the source is Y-connected while the loads can be either Y or Δ, although the latter is more common.

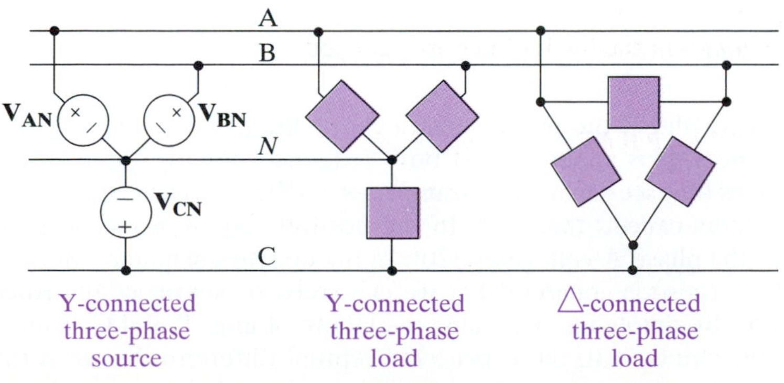

FIGURE 14–14 *A three-phase power system with the loads rearranged.*

Three-phase sources usually are Y-connected because the Δ-connection involves a loop of voltage sources. Large currents may circulate in this loop if the three voltages do not exactly sum to zero. In analysis situations, a Δ-connection of ideal voltage sources is awkward because it is impossible to determine the current in each source.

We use a double subscript notation to identify voltages in the system. The reason is that there are at least six voltages to deal with: three line-to-line voltages and three line-to-neutral voltages. If we use the usual plus and minus reference marks to define all of these voltages, our circuit diagram would be hopelessly cluttered and confusing. Hence we use two subscripts to define the points across which a voltage is defined. For example, $\mathbf{V}_{XY}$ means the voltage between points X and Y, with an implied plus reference mark at the first subscript (X) and an implied minus at the second subscript (Y).

The three line-to-neutral voltages are called the **phase voltages** and are written in double subscript notation as $\mathbf{V}_{AN}$, $\mathbf{V}_{BN}$, and $\mathbf{V}_{CN}$. Similarly, the three line-to-line voltages, called simply the **line voltages**, are identified as $\mathbf{V}_{AB}$, $\mathbf{V}_{BC}$, and $\mathbf{V}_{CA}$. From the definition of the double subscript notation it follows that $\mathbf{V}_{XY} = -\mathbf{V}_{YX}$. Using this result and KVL, we derive the relationships between the line voltages and phase voltages:

$$\begin{aligned} \mathbf{V}_{AB} &= \mathbf{V}_{AN} + \mathbf{V}_{NB} = \mathbf{V}_{AN} - \mathbf{V}_{BN} \\ \mathbf{V}_{BC} &= \mathbf{V}_{BN} + \mathbf{V}_{NC} = \mathbf{V}_{BN} - \mathbf{V}_{CN} \\ \mathbf{V}_{CA} &= \mathbf{V}_{CN} + \mathbf{V}_{NA} = \mathbf{V}_{CN} - \mathbf{V}_{AN} \end{aligned} \tag{14-17}$$

A balanced three-phase source produces phase voltages that obey the following two constraints:

$$\begin{aligned} |\mathbf{V}_{AN}| = |\mathbf{V}_{BN}| &= |\mathbf{V}_{CN}| = V_P \\ \mathbf{V}_{AN} + \mathbf{V}_{BN} + \mathbf{V}_{CN} &= 0 + j0 \end{aligned}$$

That is, the phase voltages have equal amplitudes (V_P) and sum to zero. There are two ways to satisfy these constraints:

Positive Phase Sequence	Negative Phase Sequence	
$\mathbf{V}_{AN} = V_P\angle 0°$	$\mathbf{V}_{AN} = V_P\angle 0°$	
$\mathbf{V}_{BN} = V_P\angle -120°$	$\mathbf{V}_{BN} = V_P\angle -240°$	(14–18)
$\mathbf{V}_{CN} = V_P\angle -240°$	$\mathbf{V}_{CN} = V_P\angle -120°$	

Figure 14–15 shows the phasor diagrams for the positive and negative phase sequences. It is apparent that both sequences involve three equal-length phasors that are separated by angles of 120°. As a result, the sum of any two phasors cancels the third. In the positive sequence the phase B voltage lags the phase A voltage by 120°. In the negative sequence phase B lags by 240°. It also is apparent that we can convert one phase sequence into the other by simply interchanging the labels on lines B and C. From a circuit analysis viewpoint, there is no conceptual difference between the

two sequences. Consequently, in analysis problems we will use the positive phase sequence unless otherwise stated.

However, the phrase *no conceptual difference* does not mean that phase sequence is unimportant. It turns out that three-phase motors run in one direction when the positive sequence is applied, and in the opposite direction for the negative sequence. This could be a matter of some importance if the motor is driving a conveyor belt at a sewage treatment facility. In practice, it is essential that there be no confusion about which is line A, B, and C and whether the source phase sequence is positive or negative.

A simple relationship between the line and phase voltages is obtained by substituting the positive phase sequence voltages from Eq. (14–18) into the phasor sums in Eq. (14–17). For the first sum

$$\begin{aligned}\mathbf{V}_{AB} &= \mathbf{V}_{AN} - \mathbf{V}_{BN}\\ &= V_P\angle 0° - V_P\angle -120°\\ &= V_P(1 + j0) - V_P(-1/2 - j\sqrt{3}/2)\\ &= V_P(3/2 + j\sqrt{3}/2)\\ &= \sqrt{3}V_P\angle 30°\end{aligned} \quad (14\text{–}19)$$

Using the other sums, we find the other two positive sequence line voltages as

$$\begin{aligned}\mathbf{V}_{BC} &= \sqrt{3}V_P\angle -90°\\ \mathbf{V}_{CA} &= \sqrt{3}V_P\angle -210°\end{aligned} \quad (14\text{–}20)$$

Figure 14–16 shows the phasor diagram of these results. The line voltage phasors have the same amplitude and are displaced from each other by 120°. Hence they obey equal-amplitude and zero-sum constraints like the phase voltages.

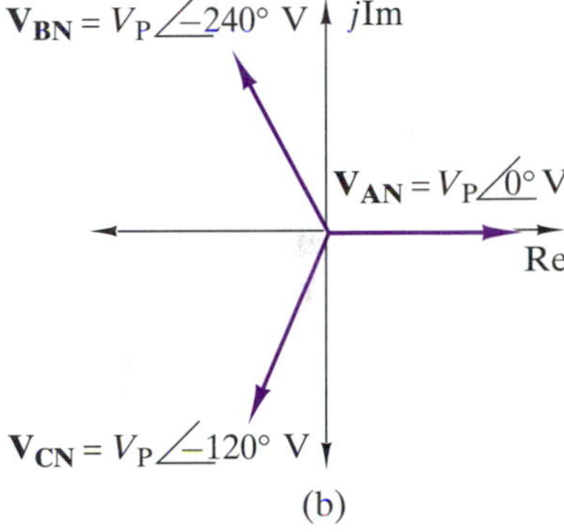

FIGURE 14–15 *Two possible phase sequences: (a) Positive. (b) Negative.*

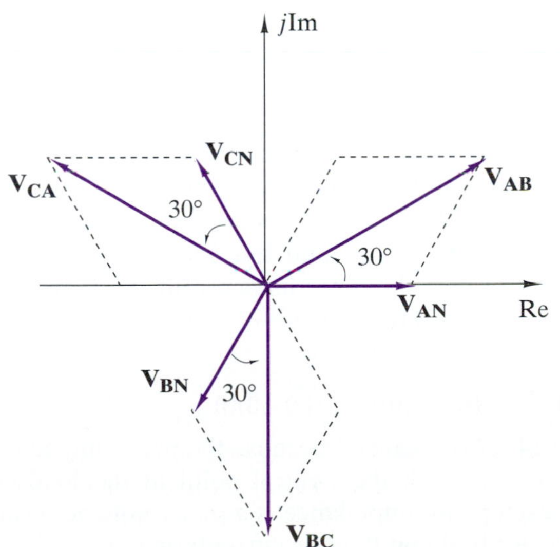

FIGURE 14–16 *Phasor diagram showing phase and line voltages for the positive phase sequence.*

If we denote the amplitude of the line voltages as V_L, then

$$V_L = \sqrt{3}V_P \tag{14-21}$$

In a balanced three-phase system the line voltage amplitude is $\sqrt{3}$ times the phase voltage amplitude. This ratio appears in equipment descriptions such as 277/480 V three phase, where 277 is the phase voltage and 480 the line voltage.

It is necessary to choose one of the phasors as the zero-phase reference when defining three-phase voltages and currents. Usually the reference is the line A phase voltage (i.e., $\mathbf{V}_{AN} = V_P\angle 0°$), as illustrated in Figures 14–15 and 14–16. Unless otherwise stated, $\mathbf{V}_{AN}$ will be used as the phase reference in this chapter.

Exercise 14–6

A balanced Y-connected three-phase source produces positive sequence phase voltages with 2400-V (rms) amplitudes. Write expressions for the phase and line voltage phasors.

Answers:

$\mathbf{V}_{AN} = 2400\angle 0°$ $\quad\mathbf{V}_{BN} = 2400\angle -120°$ $\quad\mathbf{V}_{CN} = 2400\angle -240°$
$\mathbf{V}_{AB} = 4160\angle +30°$ $\quad\mathbf{V}_{BC} = 4160\angle -90°$ $\quad\mathbf{V}_{CA} = 4160\angle -210°$

Exercise 14–7

Given that $\mathbf{V}_{BC} = 480\angle +135°$ in a balanced, positive sequence, three-phase system, write expressions for the three phase-voltage phasors.

Answer:

$\mathbf{V}_{AN} = 277\angle -135°$ $\quad\mathbf{V}_{BN} = 277\angle +105°$ $\quad\mathbf{V}_{CN} = 277\angle -15°$

14–6 THREE-PHASE AC POWER ANALYSIS

This section treats the analysis of balanced three-phase circuits. We first treat the direct analysis problem beginning with the Y-connected source and load shown in Figure 14–17. In a direct analysis problem we are given the source phase voltages $\mathbf{V}_{AN}$, $\mathbf{V}_{BN}$, and $\mathbf{V}_{CN}$ and the load impedances Z. Our objective is to determine the three line currents $\mathbf{I}_A$, $\mathbf{I}_B$, and $\mathbf{I}_C$ and the total complex power delivered to the load.

Y-CONNECTED SOURCE AND Y-CONNECTED LOAD

The load in Figure 14–17 is balanced because the phase impedances in the legs of the Y are equal. With the neutral point at the load connected, the voltage across each phase impedance is a phase voltage. Using $\mathbf{V}_{AN}$ as the phase reference, we find that the line currents are

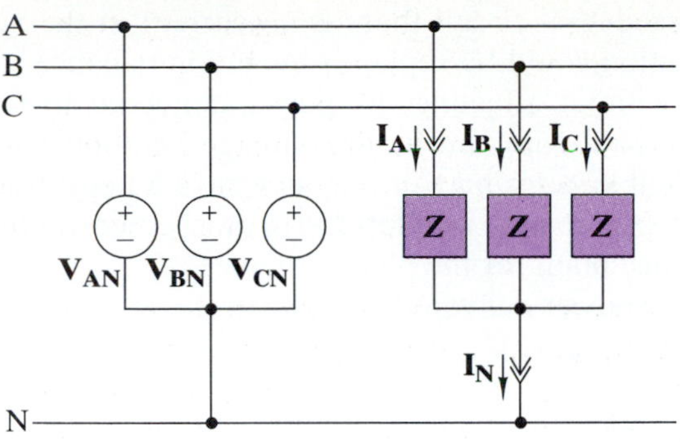

FIGURE 14–17 A balanced three-phase system with a Y-connected source and load.

$$\begin{aligned}
\mathbf{I}_A &= \frac{\mathbf{V}_{AN}}{Z} = \frac{V_P\angle 0^\circ}{|Z|\angle\theta} = \frac{V_P}{|Z|}\angle -\theta \\
\mathbf{I}_B &= \frac{\mathbf{V}_{BN}}{Z} = \frac{V_P\angle -120^\circ}{|Z|\angle\theta} = \frac{V_P}{|Z|}\angle -120^\circ - \theta \\
\mathbf{I}_C &= \frac{\mathbf{V}_{CN}}{Z} = \frac{V_P\angle -240^\circ}{|Z|\angle\theta} = \frac{V_P}{|Z|}\angle -240^\circ - \theta
\end{aligned} \tag{14–22}$$

Figure 14–18 shows the phasor diagram of the line currents and phase voltages.

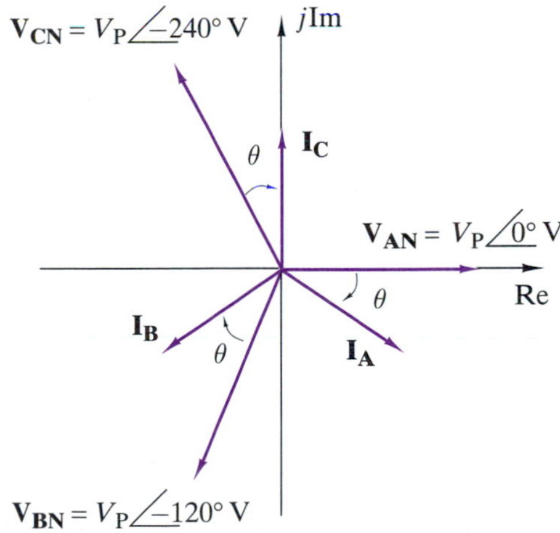

FIGURE 14–18 Line currents and phase voltages in a balanced three-phase system.

The line current phasors in Eq. (14–22) and Figure 14–18 have the same amplitude I_L, where

$$I_L = \frac{V_P}{|Z|} \text{ (Y-connected Load)} \tag{14–23}$$

The line currents have equal amplitudes and are symmetrically disposed at 120° intervals, so they obey the zero-sum condition $\mathbf{I}_A + \mathbf{I}_B + \mathbf{I}_C = 0$. Applying KCL at the neutral point of the load in Figure 14–17, we find that $\mathbf{I}_N = \mathbf{I}_A + \mathbf{I}_B + \mathbf{I}_C = 0$.

Thus, in a balanced Y-Y circuit there is no current in the neutral line. The neutral connection could be replaced by any impedance whatsoever, including infinity, without affecting the power delivered to the load. In other words, the neutral wire can be disconnected without changing the circuit response. Real systems may or may not have a neutral wire, but in solving three-phase problems it is helpful to draw the neutral line because it serves as a reference point for the phase voltages.

The total complex power delivered to the load is

$$\begin{aligned} S_L &= \mathbf{V}_{AN}\mathbf{I}_A^* + \mathbf{V}_{BN}\mathbf{I}_B^* + \mathbf{V}_{CN}\mathbf{I}_C^* \\ &= (V_P\angle 0)(I_L\angle\theta) + (V_P\angle -120°)(I_L\angle 120°+\theta) + \\ &\quad (V_P\angle -240°)(I_L\angle 240°+\theta) \\ &= 3V_P I_L\angle\theta \end{aligned} \tag{14-24}$$

Since $V_P = V_L/\sqrt{3}$, the expression for complex power can also be written using the line voltage:

$$S_L = \sqrt{3}V_L I_L\angle\theta \tag{14-25}$$

In either Eq. (14–24) or (14–25) the power factor angle θ is the angle of the per-phase impedance of the Y-connected load.

EXAMPLE 14–9

When the line voltage is 480 V (rms), a balanced Y-connected load draws an apparent power of 40 kVA at a lagging power factor of 0.9.

(a) Find the per-phase impedance of the load.
(b) Find the three line current phasors using $\mathbf{V}_{AN}$ as the phase reference.

SOLUTION:

(a) For the given conditions the phase voltage, line current, and power factor angle are

$$V_P = \frac{V_L}{\sqrt{3}} = \frac{480}{\sqrt{3}} = 277 \quad \text{V (rms)}$$

$$I_L = \frac{|S_L|}{\sqrt{3}V_L} = \frac{4\times 10^4}{\sqrt{3}\times 480} = 48.1 \text{ A (rms)}$$

$$\theta = \cos^{-1}(0.9) = 25.8°$$

and the per-phase impedance of the Y-connected load is

$$\begin{aligned} Z_L &= \frac{V_P}{I_L}\angle\theta = \frac{277}{48.1}\angle 25.8° \\ &= 5.18 + j2.51 \quad \Omega \end{aligned}$$

(b) With $\mathbf{V}_{AN} = 277\angle 0°$ as the phase reference, we calculate the line current $\mathbf{I}_A$ as

$$\mathbf{I}_A = \frac{\mathbf{V}_{AN}}{Z_L} = I_L\angle -\theta = 48.1\angle -25.8° \text{ A (rms)}$$

Hence for a balanced load the other two line current phasors are

$$\mathbf{I}_B = I_L\angle -120° - \theta = 48.1\angle -145.8° \quad \text{A (rms)}$$
$$\mathbf{I}_C = I_L\angle -240° - \theta = 48.1\angle -265.8° \quad \text{A (rms)}$$

Exercise 14–8

A Y-connected load with $Z = 10 + j4\ \Omega$/phase is driven by a balanced, positive sequence three-phase generator with $V_L = 4.16$ kV (rms). Using $\mathbf{V}_{AN}$ as the phase reference,

(a) Find the line currents.
(b) Find the average and reactive power delivered to the load.

Answers:
(a) $\mathbf{I}_A = 223\angle{-21.8°}$ A $\quad \mathbf{I}_B = 223\angle{-141.8°}$ A $\quad \mathbf{I}_C = 223\angle{-261.8°}$ A
(b) $P_L = 1.49$ MW $\quad Q_L = 0.597$ MVAR

Y-CONNECTED SOURCE AND Δ-CONNECTED LOAD

We now turn to the balanced Δ-connected load shown in Figure 14–19. When the objective is to determine the line currents and total complex power, we can convert the load into an equivalent Y using a Δ-to-Y transformation. As discussed in Sect. 8-3, the balanced Δ-connected load in Figure 14–19 can be replaced by an the equivalent Y-connected load with leg impedances

$$Z_Y = \frac{Z}{3} \tag{14-26}$$

Using the Δ-to-Y transformation, we reduce the problem to a circuit in which the source and load are Y-connected. The resulting Y-Y configuration can then be analyzed to determine line currents and total power, as discussed previously.

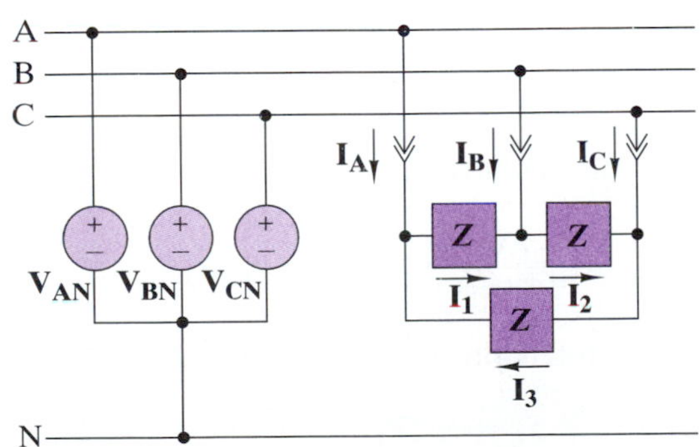

FIGURE 14–19 *A balanced three-phase system with a Y-connected source and a Δ-connected load.*

However, when we need to know the current or power delivered to each leg of the delta load, we must determine the phase currents $\mathbf{I}_1$, $\mathbf{I}_2$, and $\mathbf{I}_3$ shown in Figure 14–19. The phase currents can be expressed in terms of the phase impedances and the line voltage. Assuming the positive phase sequence and using $\mathbf{V}_{AN}$ as the phase reference, these expressions are

$$\mathbf{I}_1 = \frac{\mathbf{V}_{AB}}{Z} = \frac{V_L\angle 30^\circ}{|Z|\angle\theta} = \frac{V_L}{|Z|}\angle 30^\circ-\theta$$

$$\mathbf{I}_2 = \frac{\mathbf{V}_{BC}}{Z} = \frac{V_L\angle -90^\circ}{|Z|\angle\theta} = \frac{V_L}{|Z|}\angle -90^\circ-\theta \qquad (14\text{–}27)$$

$$\mathbf{I}_3 = \frac{\mathbf{V}_{CA}}{Z} = \frac{V_L\angle -210^\circ}{|Z|\angle\theta} = \frac{V_L}{|Z|}\angle -210^\circ-\theta$$

The phase currents have the same amplitude I_P defined as

$$I_P = \frac{V_L}{|Z|} \text{ (}\Delta\text{-connected Load)} \qquad (14\text{–}28)$$

Although of no immediate physical importance, note that the phase currents sum to zero because they have equal amplitudes and are symmetrically disposed at 120° intervals.

Using the results in Eq. (14–27), the complex power delivered to each leg of the delta load is

$$S_1 = \mathbf{V}_{AB} \times \mathbf{I}_1^* = (V_L\angle 30^\circ)\,(I_P\angle\theta-30^\circ) = V_L I_P\angle\theta$$

$$S_2 = \mathbf{V}_{BC} \times \mathbf{I}_2^* = (V_L\angle -90^\circ)\,(I_P\angle\theta+90^\circ) = V_L I_P\angle\theta \qquad (14\text{–}29)$$

$$S_3 = \mathbf{V}_{CA} \times \mathbf{I}_3^* = (V_L\angle -210^\circ)\,(I_P\angle\theta+210^\circ) = V_L I_P\angle\theta$$

The total complex power delivered to the Δ-connected load is

$$S_L = S_1 + S_2 + S_3 = 3V_L I_P\angle\theta \qquad (14\text{–}30)$$

where the power factor angle θ is the angle of the per-phase impedance of the Δ-connected load.

The result in Eq. (14–30) can be put in the same form as Eq. (14–25) by replacing the phase current I_P by the line current I_L. As noted previously, the line currents for a balanced Δ-connected load can be calculated using a Δ-to-Y transformation. In the transformed circuit the line current amplitude is $I_L = V_P/|Z_Y|$, where Z_Y is the impedance in each leg of the equivalent Y-connected load. But in a balanced system $V_P = V_L/\sqrt{3}$, and according to Eq. (14–26) $Z_Y = Z/3$. Therefore, the amplitudes of the line and phase currents in a Δ-connected load are related as follows:

$$I_L = \frac{V_L/\sqrt{3}}{|Z/3|} = \sqrt{3}\frac{V_L}{|Z|} = \sqrt{3}I_P \qquad (14\text{–}31)$$

When $I_P = I_L/\sqrt{3}$ is substituted into Eq. (14–30), we obtain

$$S_L = \sqrt{3}V_L I_L\angle\theta \qquad (14\text{–}32)$$

Equations (14–25) and (14–32) are identical, which means that the relationship applies to balanced three-phase loads whether Y- or Δ-connected. In either case the power factor angle θ is the angle of the per-phase impedance of the load because the transformation $Z_Y = Z/3$ does not alter the phase angle of the phase impedance.

EXAMPLE 14–10

A Δ-connected load with $Z = 40 + j30\ \Omega$/phase is driven by a balanced, positive sequence three-phase generator with $V_L = 2400$ V (rms). Using $\mathbf{V}_{AN}$ as the phase reference,

(a) Find the phase currents.
(b) Find the line currents.
(c) Find the average and reactive power delivered to the load.

SOLUTION:

(a) The first phase current is

$$\mathbf{I}_1 = \frac{\mathbf{V}_{AB}}{Z} = \frac{2400\angle 30^\circ}{40 + j30} = 48.0\angle -6.87^\circ \text{ A (rms)}$$

Since the circuit is balanced, the other phase currents all have amplitudes of $I_P = 48.0$ A and are displaced at 120° intervals.

$$\mathbf{I}_2 = 48.0\angle -126.87^\circ \text{ A (rms)}$$

$$\mathbf{I}_3 = 48.0\angle -246.87^\circ \text{ A (rms)}$$

(b) Using $V_P = 2400/\sqrt{3}$ and Δ-Y transformation with $Z_Y = (40 + j30)/3$, we find that the phase A line current is

$$\mathbf{I}_A = \frac{\mathbf{V}_{AN}}{Z_Y} = \frac{2400/\sqrt{3}}{(40 + j30)/3} = 83.1\angle -36.9^\circ \text{ A (rms)}$$

Since the circuit is balanced, the other line currents have amplitudes of $I_L = 83.1$ A and are displaced at 120° intervals.

$$\mathbf{I}_B = 83.1\angle -156.9^\circ \text{ A (rms)}$$

$$\mathbf{I}_C = 83.1\angle -276.9^\circ \text{ A (rms)}$$

(c) The complex power delivered to the load is

$$S_L = \sqrt{3}V_L I_L \angle\theta = \sqrt{3} \times 2400 \times 83.1\angle 36.9^\circ$$
$$= 345\angle 36.9^\circ \text{ kVA}$$

Therefore, $P_L = 276$ kW and $Q_L = 207$ kVAR. ■

Exercise 14–9

Exercise 14–8 involved a balanced Y-connected load with $Z = 10 + j4\ \Omega$/phase and a line voltage of $V_L = 4.16$ kV (rms). In this exercise these same parameters apply to a Δ-connected load. Using $\mathbf{V}_{AN}$ as the phase reference,

(a) Find phase currents.
(b) Find the line currents.
(c) Find the average and reactive power delivered to the load.

Answers:

(a) $\mathbf{I}_1 = 386\angle{+8.20^\circ}$ A, $\mathbf{I}_2 = 386\angle{-111.8^\circ}$ A, $\mathbf{I}_3 = 386\angle{-231.8^\circ}$ A
(b) $\mathbf{I}_A = 669\angle{-21.8^\circ}$ A, $\mathbf{I}_B = 669\angle{-141.8^\circ}$ A, $\mathbf{I}_C = 669\angle{-261.8^\circ}$ A
(c) $P_L = 4.47$ MW, $Q_L = 1.79$ MVAR

THREE-PHASE LOAD-FLOW ANALYSIS

The analysis and examples given thus far treat direct analysis problems in which the source parameters are given and the power flow is unknown. In a load-flow problem we are required to find the source or load voltages when the power flow is given.

A simple model of the three-phase circuit for the load-flow problem is shown in Figure 14–20. The impedance Z_W represents the wire impedances of the power lines connecting the source and load. It is clear even in this very simple case that including all three phases in a circuit diagram is unwieldy. In more complicated situations, including all three phases in circuit diagrams tends to obscure the working of the system. In a balanced three-phase system we have seen that once we find one of the line currents or voltages, the others are easily derived by shifting the known response at 120° intervals. Thus, in effect, we really do not need all three phases in the circuit diagram to analyze balanced three-phase systems.

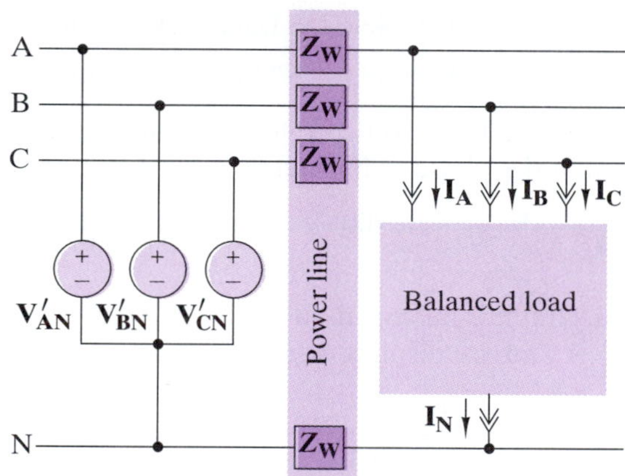

FIGURE 14–20 *A balanced three-phase system with line impedances.*

A simpler representation of a balanced three-phase system is obtained by omitting the neutral and using one line to represent all three phases. Figure 14–21 is a single-line representation of the circuit in Figure 14–20. In power system terminology a **bus** is a group of conductors that serve as a common connection for two or more circuits. In the single-line diagram in Figure 14–20 the buses are represented by short horizontal lines. Bus no. 1 is a generator bus connecting a three-phase source represented by the circle and a transmission line represented by Z_W. Bus no. 2 is a load bus connecting the transmission line to a balanced three-phase load represented by an arrow indicating the delivery of complex power. The line voltages and complex power flow are written beside the buses using a subscript that identifies the bus.

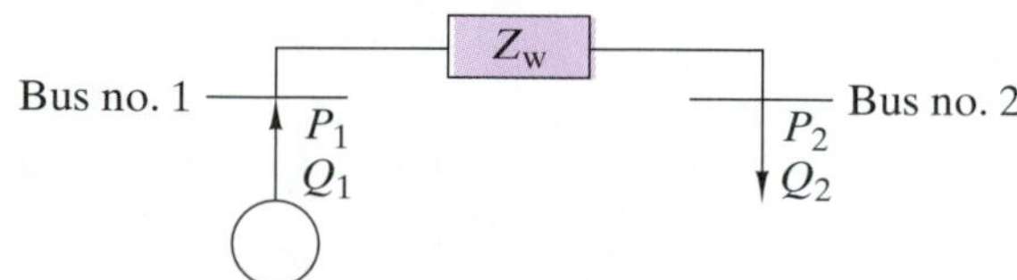

FIGURE 14–21 *Single-line representation of a three-phase system.*

Using single-line diagrams makes three-phase load-flow analysis similar to the single-phase two-wire load-flow problems in Sect. 14–5. The only complication here is that we must account for the power in all three phases and we must distinguish between the line and phase voltages. In a three-phase load-flow problem the bus voltages and line currents are represented by their phasor magnitudes without reference to their phase angles. A load-flow problem does not require that we find these phase angles since the required phase information is carried by the specified complex power.

EXAMPLE 14–11

The single-line diagram in Figure 14–22 shows a power system with a generator bus connected to a load bus via power lines with $Z_W = 4 + j16\ \Omega$. The line voltage at the load bus is $V_{L2} = 4800$ V (rms) and the load draws $P_2 = 100$ kW at 0.8 lagging power factor. Find the complex power produced by the source, the line voltage at the source bus, and the transmission efficiency.

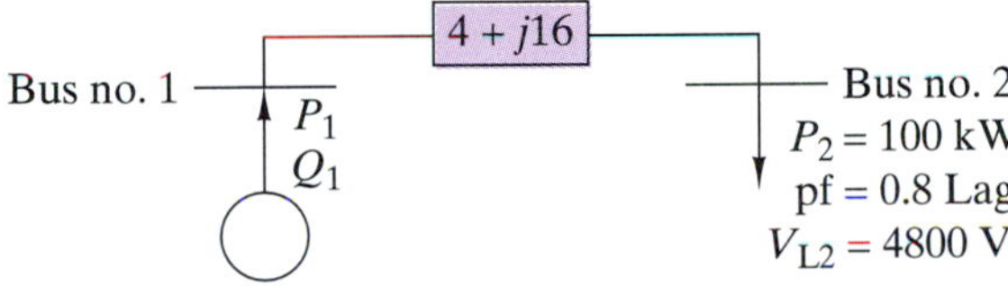

FIGURE 14–22

SOLUTION:

The total complex power delivered to the three-phase load connected to bus no. 2 is

$$S_2 = 100 + j100\tan(\cos^{-1} 0.8) = 100 + j75$$
$$= 125\angle 36.9^\circ \text{ kVA}$$

Using Eq. (14–32) to calculate the line current at the load bus yields

$$I_L = \frac{|S_2|}{\sqrt{3}\, V_{L2}} = \frac{125000}{\sqrt{3} \times 4800} = 15.04 \text{ A (rms)}$$

The total complex power absorbed by the power line is

$$S_W = 3I_L^2(R_W + jX_W) = 3(15.04)^2(4 + j16)$$
$$= 2.71 + j10.8 \text{ kVA}$$

The preceding computation includes the three lines for phases A, B, and C but does not include the neutral wire since the circuit is balanced and there is no current in the neutral line. Using the conservation of complex power yields the source power as

$$S_1 = S_2 + S_W = 102.7 + j85.8$$
$$= 133.8\angle 39.9^\circ \text{ kVA}$$

We now use Eq. (14–32) again to find the line voltage at the source bus as

$$V_{L1} = \frac{|S_1|}{\sqrt{3}I_L} = \frac{133800}{\sqrt{3} \times 15.04}$$
$$= 5.14 \text{ kV (rms)}$$

The transmission efficiency is

$$\eta = \frac{P_2}{P_1} \times 100\% = \frac{100}{102.7} \times 100 = 97.4\%$$

EXAMPLE 14–12

The transmission line in Figure 14–23 has a maximum rated capacity of 250 kVA at line voltage of 4160 V (rms). When operating at rated capacity, the resistive and reactive voltage drops in the line are 2.5% and 6% of the rated voltage, respectively.

FIGURE 14–23

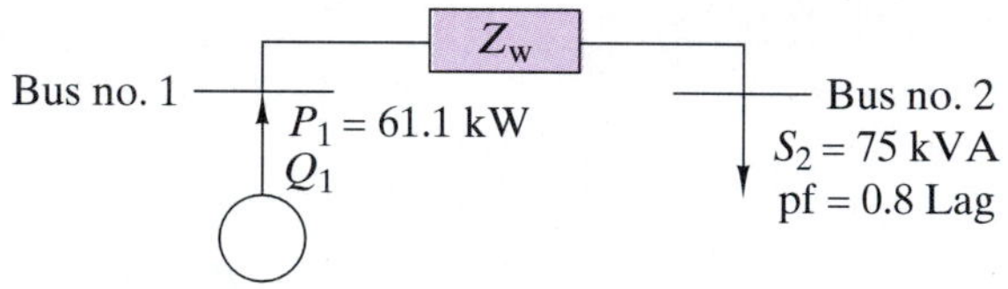

(a) Find the wire impedance Z_W.
(b) The system is operating with $P_1 = 61.1$ kW and $S_2 = 75$ kVA at pf = 0.8 lagging. Find the line voltage at the load bus.

SOLUTION:

(a) When the power line is operating at maximum rated capacity, the line current is

$$I_L = \frac{|S_L|}{\sqrt{3}\,V_L} = \frac{250{,}000}{\sqrt{3} \times 4160} = 34.7 \text{ A (rms)}$$

The magnitudes of the voltage across line resistance and reactance are

$$I_L R_W = 4160 \times 0.025 = 104 \text{ V}$$
$$I_L X_W = 4160 \times 0.060 = 250 \text{ V}$$

Hence the wire impedance of the line is

$$Z_W = \frac{104 + j250}{I_L} = 3 + j7.2\ \Omega$$

(b) When the system operates with $P_1 = 61.1$ kW and $S_2 = 75$ kVA at pf = 0.8 lagging, the average power lost in the line is $P_W = P_1 - S_2 \times 0.8 = 1.1$ kW. The line current is

$$I_L = \sqrt{\frac{P_W}{3\,R_W}} = \sqrt{\frac{1100}{3 \times 3}} = 11.06 \text{ A (rms)}$$

and the line voltage at load bus is

$$V_{L2} = \frac{|S_2|}{\sqrt{3}I_L} = 3.92 \text{ kV (rms)}$$

■

Exercise 14–10

A balanced three-phase load draws 8 kVA at lagging power factor of 0.9 when the phase voltage is 277 V (rms). The load is fed by a balanced three-phase source via lines with $Z_W = 0.3 + j5\ \Omega$.

(a) Find the line current.
(b) Find the line voltage at the source.

Answers:
(a) 9.63 A
(b) 526 V

APPLICATION NOTE: EXAMPLE 14–13

Electrical power is generated and transmitted in three-phase form even though most residential and small commercial customers are single-phase loads. The primary reason is that three-phase devices and transmission lines (see Problem 14–54) are smaller and more efficient than the corresponding single-phase equipment handling the same power. Part of the advantage enjoyed by three phase is that the instantaneous power in a balanced three-phase circuit or device is constant.

To show that $p_T(t)$ is constant, we write the instantaneous power in each phase of the balanced three-phase circuit:

$$p_A(t) = v_{AN}(t) \times i_A(t) = [\sqrt{2}V_P \cos(\omega t)] \times [\sqrt{2}I_L \cos(\omega t - \theta)]$$

$$p_B(t) = v_{BN}(t) \times i_B(t) = \sqrt{2}V_P \cos(\omega t - 120°)] \times [\sqrt{2}I_L \cos(\omega t - 120° - \theta)]$$

$$p_C(t) = v_{CN}(t) \times i_C(t) = [\sqrt{2}V_P \cos(\omega t - 240°)] \times [\sqrt{2}I_L \cos(\omega t - 240° - \theta)]$$

where $\sqrt{2}V_P$ is the peak amplitude of each line-to-neutral voltage and $\sqrt{2}I_L$ is the peak amplitude of each line current. Using the trigonometric identity

$$[\cos x] \times [\cos y] = \frac{1}{2}\cos(x - y) + \frac{1}{2}\cos(x + y)$$

the phase powers can be put into the form

$$p_A(t) = V_P I_L \cos\theta + V_P I_L \cos(2\omega t - \theta)$$

$$p_B(t) = V_P I_L \cos\theta + V_P I_L \cos(2\omega t - 240° - \theta)$$

$$p_C(t) = V_P I_L \cos\theta + V_P I_L \cos(2\omega t - 480° - \theta)$$

Each phase power is a constant or dc term $V_P I_L \cos\theta$ plus a double-frequency ac term. The double-frequency terms all have the same amplitude $V_P I_L$ and are symmetrically disposed at 120° intervals because –480° is the same as –120°. Therefore, the double-frequency sinusoidal terms sum to zero and the total instantaneous power is

$$p_T(t) = p_A(t) + p_B(t) + p_C(t) = 3V_P I_L \cos\theta$$

The fact that the total instantaneous power is constant means that operating three-phase generators and motors involves constant mechanical torque. As a result, there is smoother operation with less vibration at the electromechanical interfaces of the system.

14–7 THREE-PHASE POWER MEASUREMENT

A **wattmeter** is an instrument that measures average power in the sinusoidal steady state. Figure 14–24 shows a typical connection of a wattmeter at a two-terminal interface. The device contains a movable high-resistance **potential** (voltage) **coil** (PC) that is connected across the load and a fixed low-resistance **current coil** (CC) connected in series with the load. The current coil responds to the interface current and the potential coil to the interface voltage. The two coils interact in such a way that the deflection of the meter indicates the average power flow.

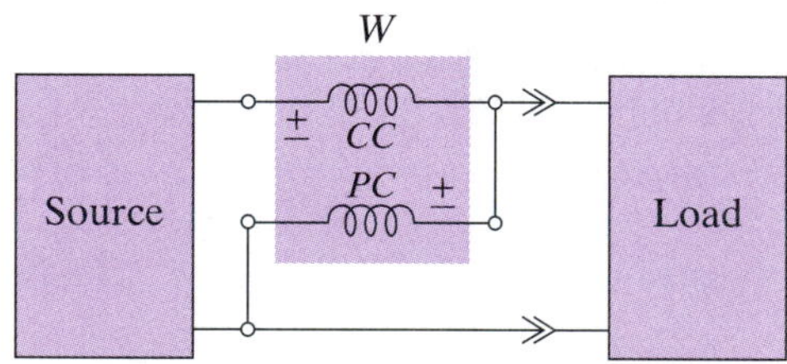

FIGURE 14–24 *Wattmeter connection to measure single-phase power.*

Both coils have a reference mark, usually a ± symbol, but sometimes other symbols are used. In Figure 14–24 the current coil terminal with the reference mark is connected to the source and the potential coil terminal with the reference mark is connected to the line in which the current coil is inserted. When the average power flows from source to load, this connection causes the meter to deflect upscale by an amount proportional to the average power delivered to the load. If the power flow is actually from load to source, the meter deflects downscale. Most meters do not read in both directions, so it is necessary to reverse the connection to one (but not both) of the coils to obtain a positive deflection. But having reversed the connections on one coil, we must remember that the resulting positive deflection measures the average power flow from load to source. In other words, with appropriate connections a wattmeter can measure average power flow from source to load or load to source, but it is up to the user to figure out what connections to make.

Three-phase power can be measured using three wattmeters with their current coils inserted in the lines and the potential coils connected from line to neutral. If the circuit is balanced, we could measure the power in one phase and then multiply by 3. However, a neutral point does not exist in a Δ-connected circuit and may not be accessible in a Y-connected device. What is needed is a method of measuring three-phase power that only uses the three accessible lines. The two-wattmeter connection in Figure 14–25 accomplishes this objective. Our first task is to show that the sum of the two wattmeter readings is the total average power delivered to the three-phase load.

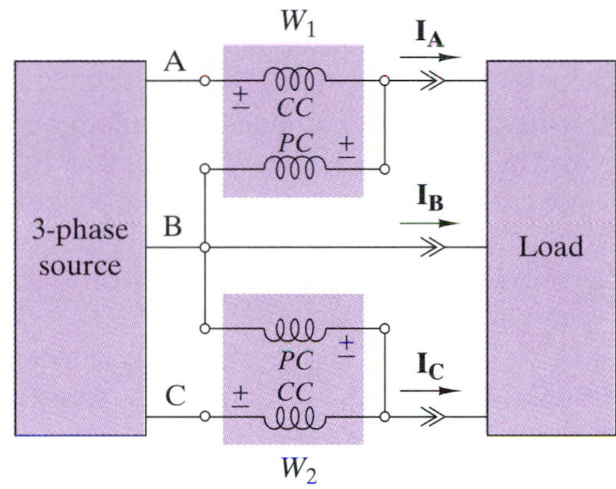

FIGURE 14–25 *Two-wattmeter connection to measure three-phase power.*

Written in terms of line voltage and line current phasors, the two wattmeter readings are

$$W_1 = \text{Re}\{\mathbf{V}_{AB}\mathbf{I}_A^*\}$$
$$W_2 = \text{Re}[\mathbf{V}_{CB}\mathbf{I}_C^*\} \qquad (14\text{–}33)$$

If $\mathbf{V}_{AN}$ is the phase reference, then according to Eqs. (14–19) and (14–20) the line voltages can be written as $\mathbf{V}_{AB} = V_L\angle 30°$ and $\mathbf{V}_{CB} = -\mathbf{V}_{BC} = V_L\angle 90°$. Similarly, according to Eqs. (14–22) and (14–23) the line currents are $\mathbf{I}_A = I_L\angle{-\theta}$ and $\mathbf{I}_C = I_L\angle{-\theta} -240°$, where $\cos\theta$ is the load power factor. Inserting these expression into Eq. (14–33) yields

$$W_1 = \text{Re}\{V_L\angle 30° I_L\angle\theta\} = V_L I_L \cos(\theta + 30°)$$
$$W_2 = \text{Re}\{V_L\angle 90° I_L\angle\theta + 240°\} = V_L I_L \cos(\theta - 30°) \qquad (14\text{–}34)$$

The sum of the two wattmeter readings is

$$\begin{aligned} W_1 + W_2 &= V_L I_L[\cos(\theta + 30°) + \cos(\theta - 30°)] \\ &= 2V_L I_L \cos\theta \cos 30° \qquad (14\text{–}35) \\ &= \sqrt{3} V_L I_L \cos\theta \end{aligned}$$

The last line in this equation has the same form as the real part of total three-phase power in Eq. (14–32), which shows that the two wattmeter readings sum to the total average power delivered to the load.

Several comments are worth making regarding the two-wattmeter method. It is a simple matter to show that the reactive power is proportional to $W_2 - W_1$ (see Problem 14–55). The foregoing derivation assumes that the three-phase circuit is balanced, but it turns out that the final conclusion in Eq. (14–35) applies whether or not the circuit is balanced. Examination of Eq. (14–34) shows that both wattmeter readings are positive when the load power factor is greater than 0.5 ($-60^0 < \theta < 60°$). When the power factor is less than 0.5 ($-90^0 < \theta < -60°$ or $60^0 < \theta < 90°$), one of the readings is negative. In such an event, we find the total power by reversing a connection on the meter reading downscale and subtracting the resulting upscale reading from other meter reading.

In a three-wire, three-phase circuit, KVL requires that $\mathbf{V}_{AB} + \mathbf{V}_{BC} + \mathbf{V}_{CA} = 0$, which means that only two of the three line voltages can be independent variables. Similarly, KCL requires that $\mathbf{I}_A + \mathbf{I}_B + \mathbf{I}_C = 0$, which means that only two of the three line currents can be independent variables. As a result, wattmeters measuring the interaction between a total of only two line voltages and two line currents can determine the total power flow. The generalization is obvious. The power flow in a circuit with n wires can be measured using $n - 1$ wattmeters. If a neutral wire is included in a three-phase circuit, then in general a third wattmeter must be added to measure the total power flow. However, if the circuit is balanced the neutral wire carries no current, so two wattmeters are enough to measure the total three-phase power.

EXAMPLE 14–14

The balanced three-phase load in Figure 14–25 draws an apparent power of 4 kVA at a lagging power factor of 0.75 when the line voltage is 230 V (rms). Find the readings of the two wattmeters shown in the figure.

SOLUTION:

With $\mathbf{V}_{AN}$ as the phase reference and $V_L = 230$ V the line currents and power factor angle are

$$\theta = \cos^{-1} 0.75 = 41.41° \quad \text{and} \quad I_L = \frac{|S|}{\sqrt{3}V_L} = 10.04 \text{ A (rms)}$$

Using Eq. (14–34), we calculate

$$W_1 = V_L I_L \cos(\theta + 30°) = 736 \text{ W}$$

$$W_2 = V_L I_L \cos(\theta - 30°) = 2264 \text{ W}$$

Note that $W_1 + W_2 = 3000$ W, which is the same as $S \times \text{pf} = 4000 \times 0.75 = 3000$ W. ■

SUMMARY

- In the sinusoidal steady state the instantaneous power at a two-terminal interface contains average and reactive power components. The average power represents a unidirectional transfer of energy from source to load.

The reactive power represents a lossless interchange of energy between the source and load.

- In ac power analysis problems amplitudes of voltage and current phasors are expressed in rms values. Complex power is defined as the product of the voltage phasor and the conjugate of the current phasor. The real part of the complex power is the average power in watts (W), the imaginary part is the reactive power in volt-amperes reactive (VAR), and the magnitude is the apparent power in volt-amperes (VA).
- In a direct analysis problem the load impedance, line impedances, and source voltage are given, and the load voltage, current, and power are the unknowns. In a load-flow problem the source and load powers are given, and the unknowns are line voltages and currents at different points.
- Three-phase systems transmit power from source to load on four lines labeled A, B, C, and N. The three line-to-neutral voltages $\mathbf{V}_{AN}$, $\mathbf{V}_{BN}$, and $\mathbf{V}_{CN}$ are called the phase voltages. The three line-to-line voltages $\mathbf{V}_{AB}$, $\mathbf{V}_{BC}$, and $\mathbf{V}_{CA}$ are called line voltages.
- In a balanced three-phase system, (1) the neutral wire carries no current, (2) the line-voltage amplitude V_L is related to the phase voltage amplitude V_P by $V_L = \sqrt{3}\,V_P$, (3) the three line currents $\mathbf{I}_A$, $\mathbf{I}_B$ and $\mathbf{I}_C$ have the same amplitude I_L, and (4) the total complex power delivered to a Y- or a Δ-connected load is $\sqrt{3}V_L I_L \angle\theta$, where θ is the angle of the phase impedance.
- A wattmeter has a low-resistance current coil and a high-resistance potential (voltage) coil that interact to indicate the average power flow in the sinusoidal steady state. The average power flow in a three-wire three-phase circuit can be measured by the two-wattmeter method.

EN ROUTE OBJECTIVES AND ASSOCIATED PROBLEMS

ERO 14–1 COMPLEX POWER (SECTS. 14–1, 14–2)

Given a linear circuit operating in the sinusoidal steady state,

(a) Find the complex power delivered at a specified interface.
(b) Find the phasor voltages or currents required to deliver a specified complex power at an interface.
(c) Find the load impedance required to draw a specified complex power at a given voltage level.

14–1 Calculate average power, reactive power, and power factor for the circuit in Figure P14–1 using the following voltages and currents. State whether the circuit is absorbing or delivering net energy.

(a) $v(t) = 170\cos(\omega t - 45°)$ V, $i(t) = 12\cos(\omega t - 30°)$ A

(b) $v(t) = 280\cos(\omega t + 90°)$ V, $i(t) = 1.5\cos(\omega t - 30°)$ A

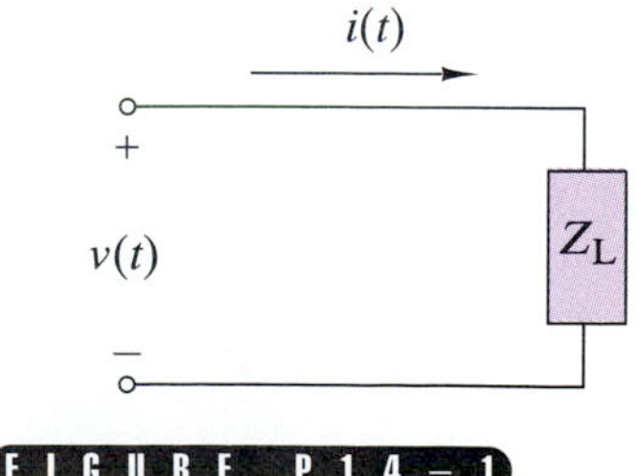

FIGURE P14–1

14–2 Calculate average power, reactive power, and power factor for the circuit in Figure P14–1 using the following voltages and currents. State whether the circuit is absorbing or delivering net energy.

(a) $v(t) = 135\cos(\omega t)$ V, $i(t) = 1.5\cos(\omega t + 30°)$ A

(b) $v(t) = 370\sin(\omega t)$ V, $i(t) = 11.5\cos(\omega t + 130°)$ A

14–3 Calculate average power, reactive power, and power factor for the circuit in Figure P14–1 using the following conditions:

(a) $V = 22.5\angle 0°$ V (rms), $I = 250\angle{-105°}$ mA (rms)

(b) $V = 120\angle 35°$ V (rms), $I = 12.5\angle 115°$ A (rms)

14–4 Calculate average power, reactive power, and power factor for the circuit in Figure P14–1 using the following conditions:

(a) $V = 2.4\angle 0°$ kV (rms), $Z_L = 250\angle{-10.5°}\ \Omega$

(b) $Z_L = 300 - j400\Omega$, $I = 120\angle 125°$ mA (rms)

14–5 Find the power factor of the circuit in Figure P14–1 under the following conditions. State whether the power factor is lagging or leading.

(a) $S = 1000 + j250$ kVA

(b) $|S| = 12$ kVA, $Q = -9$ kVA, $\cos\theta > 0$

14–6 The instantaneous power absorbed by the load in Figure P14–1 is $p(t) = 2400 + 2400 \cos 2\omega t + 1800 \sin 2\omega t$ VA.

(a) Find P, Q, and the power factor.

(b) Find the load impedance when the voltage level is 440 V (peak).

14–7 At 2400 V (rms) the load in Figure P14–1 absorbs an apparent power of 20 kVA at a power factor of 0.75 lagging.

(a) Find the average power, reactive power, and the rms current delivered to the load.

(b) Find the load impedance.

14–8 The load in Figure P14–1 draws an average power of 25 kW of average power and 12.1 A (rms) from a 2400-V (rms) line.

(a) Find the apparent power delivered to the load and the power factor.

(b) Find the load impedance.

14–9 The load in Figure P14–1 draws 12 A (rms) and 4.8 kVARS from a 440 V (rms) 60-Hz source. Find the load power factor and impedance.

14–10 An electrical load is rated at 220 V (rms) and 20 A (rms). Find the load impedance when it operates at its rating with a power factor of 0.8 lagging.

ERO 14–2 AC POWER ANALYSIS (SECT. 14–3)

Given a linear circuit operating in the sinusoidal steady state,

(a) Find the complex power associated with any element.
(b) Find the load impedance required to draw a given complex from a source.

14–11 A load consisting of a 100-Ω resistor in series with a 150-mH inductor is connected across a 60-Hz voltage source that delivers 240 V (rms). Find the complex power delivered to the load.

14–12 A load consisting of a 50-Ω resistor in parallel with a 10-μF capacitor is connected across a 400-Hz voltage source that delivers 110 V (rms). Find the complex power delivered to the load.

14–13 A load consisting of a resistor and capacitor connected in parallel absorbs a complex power $S = 10 - j126$ VA when connected to a 440-V (rms) 60-Hz line. Find the values of R and C.

14–14 The load in Figure P14–14 consists of a 400-Ω resistor in parallel with an inductor whose reactance is 600 Ω. The voltage source produces 440 V (rms) at 60 Hz, and the wire impedance of the line is $Z_W = 1 + j10\ \Omega$.

(a) Find the rms current in the line.

(b) Find the complex power absorbed by the load and line.

(c) Calculate the transmission efficiency (η).

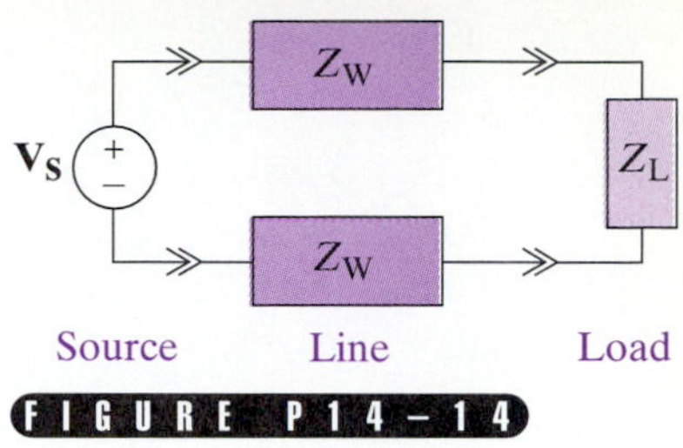

FIGURE P14–14

14–15 The load in Figure P14–14 consists of a 60-Ω resistor in series with an inductor whose reactance is 40 Ω. The voltage source produces 220 V (rms) at 60 Hz, and the wire impedance of the line is $Z_W = 2 + j5\ \Omega$.

(a) Find the rms current in the line.

(b) Find the complex power absorbed by the load and line.

(c) Calculate the transmission efficiency (η).

14–16 The transmission line in Figure P14–14 has a maximum rated capacity of 25 kVA at 2400-V (rms). When operated at rated capacity, the resistive voltage drop in the line is 5% and the reactive drop is 8% of the rated voltage. Find the line impedance. Find the transmission efficiency when the load is a 500-Ω resistor and the source voltage is 2400 V (rms).

14–17 The power line in Figure 14–14 has a transmission efficiency of η = 90% when it delivers 25 kW to the load. To improve efficiency, a second identical transmission line is added in parallel with this line. Find the transmission efficiency when the two lines in parallel deliver 25 kW to the load.

14–18 The three load impedances in Figure P14–18 are $Z_1 = 25 + j6\ \Omega$, $Z_2 = 16 + j4\ \Omega$, and $Z_3 = 10 + j0\ \Omega$.

(a) Find the current in lines A, B, and N.

(b) Find the complex power produced by each source.

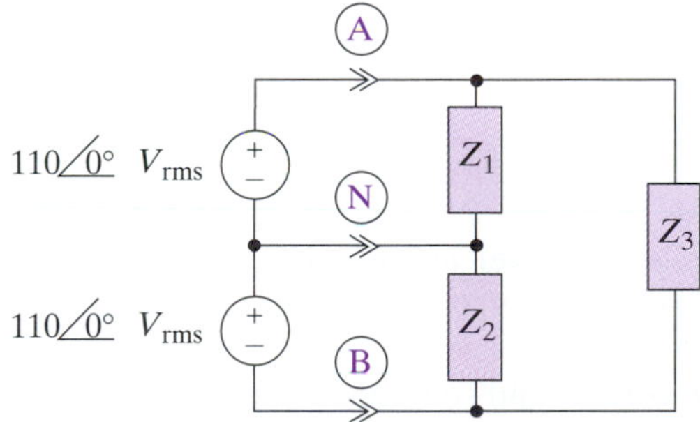

FIGURE P14–18

14–19 The three loads in Figure P14–18 are absorbing the following complex powers:

$$S_1 = 1250 + j250\ \text{VA},\ S_2 = 800 + j400\ \text{VA},\ S_3 = 2000 + j0\ \text{VA}.$$

(a) Find the current in lines A, B and N.

(b) Find the complex power produced by each source.

14–20 A load is rated at 10 kW at 0.75 lagging power factor when the voltage across the load is 440 V(rms). The load is supplied by 440-V source via a two-wire line with wire impedances of $0.3 + j2\ \Omega$. Find the voltage and apparent power delivered to the load.

ERO 14–4 LOAD-FLOW ANALYSIS (SECT. 14–4)

Given a specified power flow in linear circuit, find the unknown voltages and power levels.

14–21 The load in Figure P14–14 draws 30 kW at 2400 V (rms) with a power factor of 0.75 lagging. The wire impedance is 2.3 + $j8$ Ω. Find the complex power produced by the source and the transmission efficiency (η).

14–22 The apparent power delivered to the load in Figure P14–14 is 20 kVA at a power factor of 0.8 lagging when the source voltage is 2400 V (rms). The wire impedance is 3 + $j10$ Ω. Find the voltage across and current through the load.

14–23 The source in Figure P14–14 delivers 37 kW when the apparent power delivered to the load is 35 + $j20$ kVA. The wire impedance is 2.1 + $j12$ Ω. Find the load and source voltages.

14–24 The two loads in Figure P14–24 absorb complex powers of $S_1 = 12 + j6$ kVA and $|S_2| = 25$ kVA at 0.9 lagging power factor. The load voltage is $|\mathbf{V}_L| = 2400$ V (rms) and the line impedances are $Z_W = 0.5 + j2\ \Omega$.

(a) Find the line current and source voltage.

(b) Find the complex power produced by the source.

(c) Calculate the transmission efficiency (η).

FIGURE P14–24

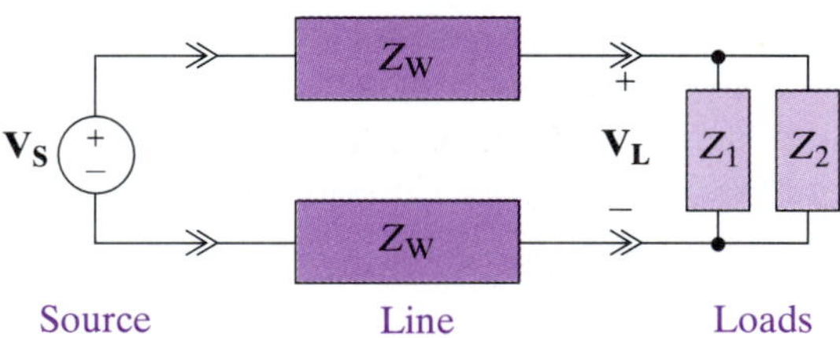

14–25 The two loads in Figure P14–24 absorb complex powers of $|S_1| = 16$ kVA at 0.75 lagging power factor and $|S_2| = 25$ kVA at unity power factor. The load voltage is $|\mathbf{V}_L| = 277$ V (rms) and the line impedances are $Z_W = 0.1 + j0.5\ \Omega$.

(a) Find the line current and source voltage.

(b) Find the complex power absorbed by the line and the source power factor.

14–26 A 440-V source delivers 5 kW at 0.75 lagging power factor to a load via a two-wire line with wire impedances of 0.5 + $j4$ Ω. Find the load voltage and the apparent power produced by the source.

14–27 The load in Figure P14–27 operates at 440 V (rms), 60 Hz, and draws 33 kVA at 0.7 power factor lagging.

(a) Calculate the value of C required to produce an overall power factor of at least 0.90.

(b) Calculate the transmission efficiency with and without the capacitor found in (a).

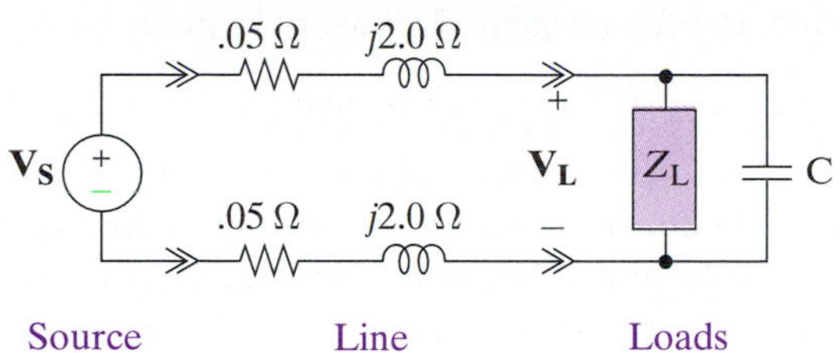

FIGURE P14–27

14–28 A load draws an average power of 25 kW at a lagging power factor 0.7 from a 60-Hz voltage source whose output is 208 V (rms). Find the capacitance to be connected in parallel with the load so that the combined load has a power factor of unity.

14–29 The load in Figure P14–29 operates at 60 Hz. With $\mathbf{V}_L = 12\angle 0°$ kV (rms) the load draws 1.2 MVA at 0.9 power factor lagging. The first source voltage is $\mathbf{V}_{S1} = 12.6 + j1.2$ kV (rms). Find the complex power supplied by each of the sources.

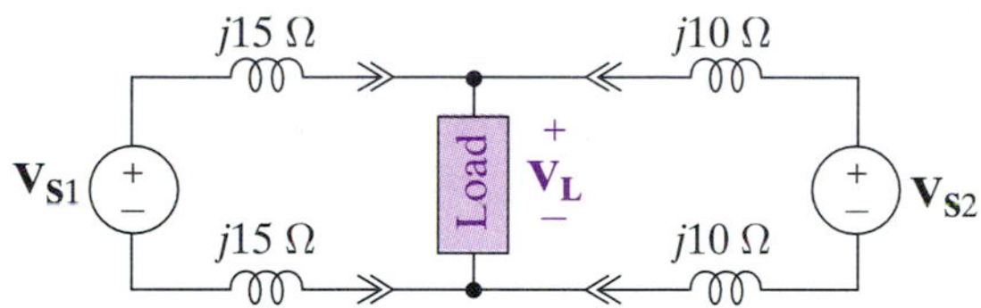

FIGURE P14–29

14–30 A two-wire power line has wire impedances of $Z_W = 2 + j4$ Ω. The voltage between wires at bus A is 200 + *j*0 V (rms) and at bus B is 200 – *j*100 V (rms). What is the direction of power flow in the line?

ERO 14–5 THREE-PHASE POWER (SECTS. 14–5, 14–6, 14–7)

Given a balanced three-phase circuit operating in the sinusoidal steady state,

(a) Find the line (phase) voltages or currents when given the phase sequence and the phase (line) voltages or currents.
(b) Find the line current and total complex power (load impedance) when given the line or phase voltage and the load impedance (total complex power).
(c) Find unknown voltages required to produce a specified power flow.
(d) Find the readings of two wattmeters in a three-phase circuit.

14–31 In a balanced Y-connected three-phase circuit the magnitude of the line voltage is 208 V (rms) and the phase sequence is positive.

(a) Write the line and phase-voltage phasors in polar form using $\mathbf{V}_{AN}$ as the reference phasor.

(b) Draw a phasor diagram of the line and phase voltages.

14–32 In a balanced Y-connected three-phase circuit the magnitude of the phase voltage is 2400 V (rms) and the phase sequence is positive.

(a) Write the line and phase voltage phasors in polar form using $\mathbf{V}_{AB}$ as the reference phasor.

(b) Draw a phasor diagram of the line and phase voltages.

14–33 In a balanced Δ-connected three-phase circuit the magnitude of the phase current is $I_P = 23.1$ A (rms) and the phase sequence is negative.

(a) Write the line and phase current phasors in polar form using $\mathbf{I}_A$ as the reference phasor.

(b) Draw a phasor diagram of the line and phase currents.

14–34 A balanced Y-connected three-phase load with a per-phase impedance of $10 + j5\ \Omega$ operates with a line voltage magnitude of 208 V (rms) using a positive phase sequence. Using $\mathbf{V}_{AN}$ as the reference phasor,

(a) Find the line current phasors in rectangular form.

(b) Calculate the total complex power delivered to the load.

(c) Draw a phasor diagram showing the line currents and phase voltages.

14–35 A balanced Y-connected three-phase load with a per-phase impedance of $5 - j2\ \Omega$ operates with a line voltage magnitude of 480 V (rms) using a negative phase sequence. Using $\mathbf{V}_{AN}$ as the reference,

(a) Find the line current phasors in rectangular form.

(b) Calculate the total complex power delivered to the load.

(c) Draw a phasor diagram showing the line currents and phase voltages.

14–36 A balanced Δ-connected three-phase load with a per-phase impedance of $50\angle 20°\ \Omega$ operates with a line voltage magnitude of 2400 V (rms) using a positive phase sequence. Using $\mathbf{I}_A$ as the reference,

(a) Find the line current phasors in rectangular form.

(b) Calculate the total complex power delivered to the load.

14–37 A balanced Δ-connected three-phase load with a per-phase impedance of $6 - j8\ \Omega$ is connected in parallel with a balanced Y-connected three-phase load with a per-phase impedance of $12\angle 30°\ \Omega$. The line voltage magnitude is 480 V (rms). Find the magnitude of the line current and the power factor of the combined loads.

14–38 In a balanced Δ-connected three-phase load the phase A line current is $\mathbf{I}_A = 100\angle -30°$ A (rms) with a line voltage of $\mathbf{V}_{AB} = 480\angle 30°$ V (rms). Find the phase impedance of the load, assuming a positive phase sequence.

14–39 A balanced Y-connected three-phase load absorbs 30 kVA at a power factor of 0.75 lagging when the line voltage magnitude is 480 V (rms).

(a) Find the magnitude of the line current.

(b) Calculate the resistance and reactance of the per-phase impedance.

14–40 A balanced Y-connected three-phase load absorbs 20 kW when the line current magnitude is 83 A (rms) and the line voltage magnitude is 480 V (rms). Find the resistance and reactance of the per-phase impedance assuming a lagging power factor.

14–41 A balanced Δ-connected three-phase load absorbs 30 kVA at a power factor of 0.9 lagging when the line voltage magnitude is 2400 V (rms).

(a) Find the magnitude of the line current.

(b) Calculate the resistance and reactance of the per-phase impedance.

14–42 Two three-phase loads are connected in parallel. The first is a balanced Y-connected circuit absorbing 30 kVA at a power factor of 0.85 lagging. The second is a balanced Δ-connected load with a per-phase impedance of $20 + j15\ \Omega$. The magnitude of the line voltage at the loads is 480 V (rms). Find the magnitude of the total line current and the total complex power delivered to the loads.

14–43 The wire impedances in the single-line diagram of Figure P14–43 are $Z_W = 0.6 + j4\ \Omega$ per phase. The balanced load connected to bus no. 2 is rated at $S_2 = 16 + j12$ kVA when the line voltage is 440 V(rms). The generator connected to bus no. 1 produces a line voltage is 420 V (rms). Find the line voltage at bus no. 2 and the complex power produced by the source.

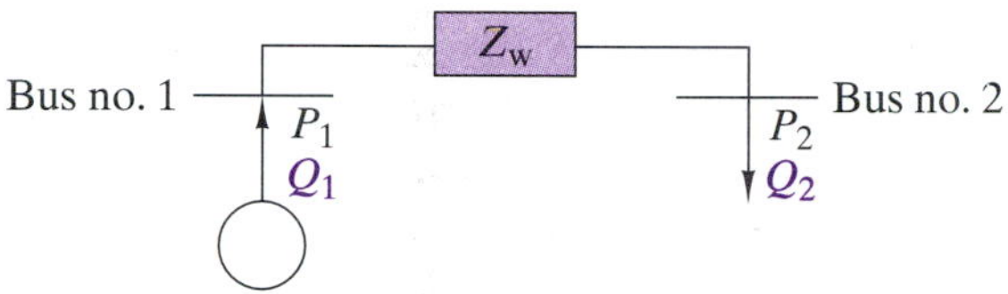

FIGURE P14–43

14–44 The source at bus no. 1 in Figure P14–43 is a Y-connected generator with an internal impedance of $j2\ \Omega$/phase and a Thévenin voltage of 2400 V/phase. The load connected to bus no. 2 is a Y-connected three-phase load with a phase impedance of $80 + j60\ \Omega$/phase. The power lines connecting the two buses have wire impedances of $1 + j5\ \Omega$/phase.

(a) Find the line current.

(b) Find the complex power delivered to the load and phase voltage at bus no. 2.

(c) Find the total complex power produced by the source.

(d) Find the transmission efficiency (η).

14–45 The three-phase line in Figure P14–43 has wire impedances of $Z_W = 0 + j8\ \Omega$ per phase. The line voltage at bus no. 2 is 3800 V (rms), and the load absorbs 800 kVA at 0.8 power factor lagging. Find the line current, the line voltage at bus no. 1, and the complex power produced by the source.

14–46 The three-phase line in Figure P14–43 has wire impedances of $Z_W = 3 + j6\ \Omega$ per phase. The line voltage at bus no. 1 is 10 kV (rms), and the load at bus no. 2 absorbs 600 kW at 0.8 power factor lagging. Find the line current and the line voltage at bus no. 2.

14–47 The three-phase line in Figure P14–43 has wire impedances of $Z_W = 2.5 + j8\ \Omega$ per phase. The generator at bus no. 1 produces an average power of $P_1 = 500$ kW. The load at bus no. 2 absorbs an average power of $P_2 = 494$ kW at 0.9 power factor lagging. Find the line current and the line voltages at bus no. 1 and bus no. 2.

14–48 The three-phase load connected to bus no. 2 in Figure P14–48 draws an average power of $P_2 = 100$ MW at a power factor of 0.8 lagging. At bus no. 2 the phase A voltage phasor is $90\angle 0°$ kV (rms). At the bus no. 3 the phase A voltage phasor is 99.9∠10° kV (rms). Find the complex power produced by each source.

FIGURE P14–48

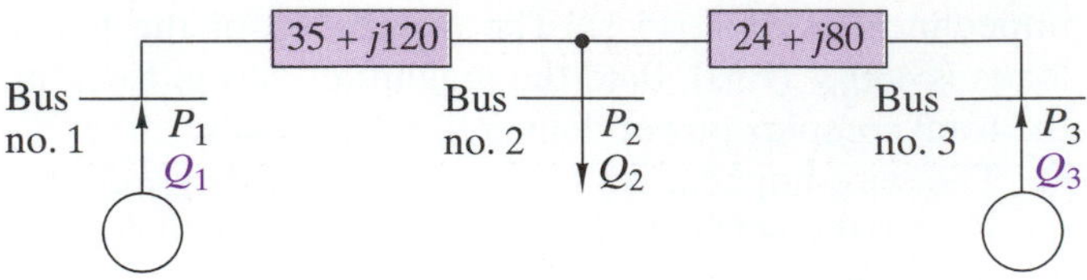

14–49 The balanced three-phase load in Figure P14–49 draws 60 kW at a lagging power factor of 0.8. The line voltage is 2400 V (rms). Find the reading of each wattmeter.

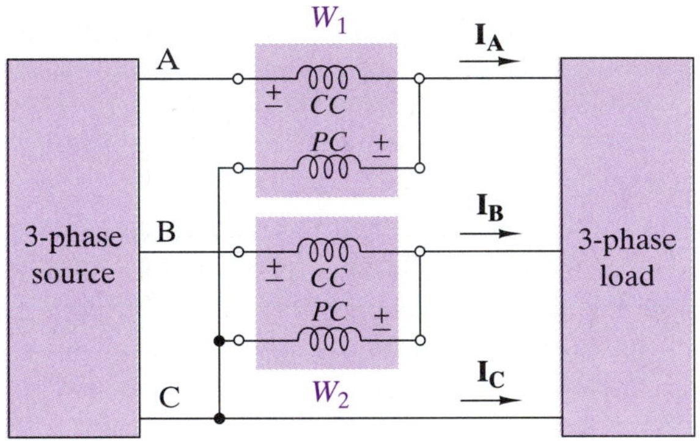

14–50 The three-phase load in Figure P14–49 is a balance Δ-connection with phase impedances of 60 + j30 Ω. The line voltage is 208 V (rms). Find the reading of each wattmeter.

CHAPTER-INTEGRATING PROBLEMS

14–51 A UNBALANCED THREE-PHASE LOAD

The three-phase source in Figure P14–51 is balanced with $V_P = 120$ V (rms). The Y-connected three-phase load has phase impedances $Z_A = 100\ \Omega$, $Z_B = 100\ \Omega$, and $Z_C = j100\ \Omega$.

(a) Calculate the line currents, line voltages, and total complex power delivered to the load.

(b) Find the reading of the two wattmeters. Does the sum of the two readings equal the average power found in part (a)?

(c) Repeat parts (a) and (b) when a zero-impedance neutral wire is connected between points N and N′ in Figure P14–51.

14–52 A E THREE-PHASE POWER FACTOR CORRECTIONS

The line voltage in Figure P14–52 is 480 V (rms). The balanced three-phase load operates 8 hours/day and draws 75 kVA at a lagging power

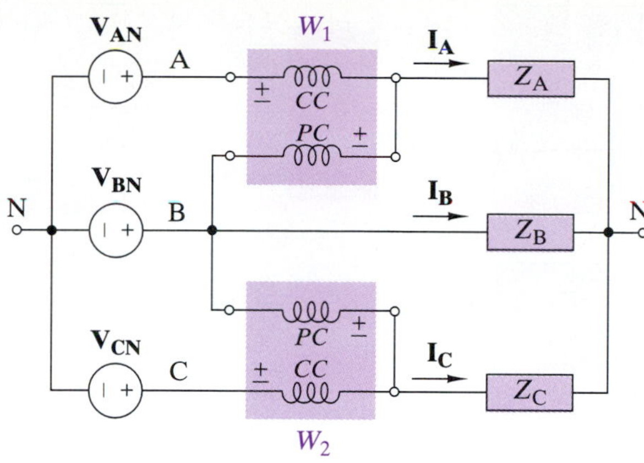

FIGURE P14–51

factor of 0.75. The electric power supplier charges 6¢/kW-hr when the load power factor is greater than 0.95 and 8¢/kW-hr when the power factor is less than 0.95. The following three-phase capacitor banks are commercially available:

480-V THREE-PHASE CAPACITOR EQUIPMENT					
KVAR	PART NUMBER	UNIT PRICE	KVAR	PART NUMBER	UNIT PRICE
10	1N0240A05	$500	40	1N0240A17	$900
20	1N0240A09	$600	50	1N0240A19	$1100
30	1N0240A11	$700	60	1N0240A23	$1500

If one or more capacitor banks are purchased to increase the power factor above 0.95, about how long will it take for the accumulated savings in operating costs to equal the equipment capital investment?

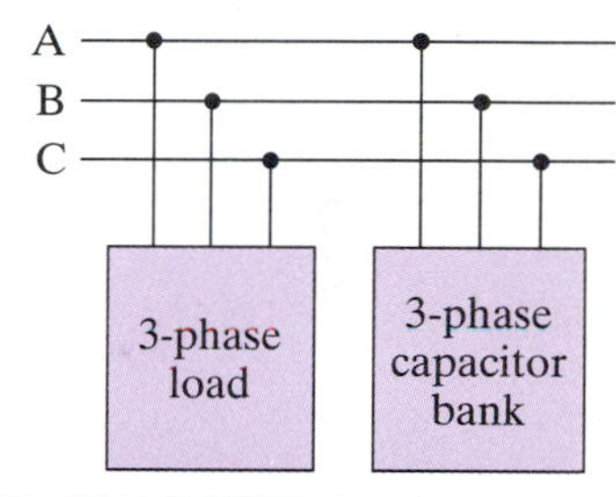

FIGURE P14–52

14–53 A THREE-PHASE TRANSFORMER BANK

Figure P14–53 shows a three-phase transformer bank modeled as three identical ideal transformers. The primary windings are Δ-connected and the secondary windings are Y-connected. The line current and line voltage phasors on the primary side are denoted as $\mathbf{V}_L$ and $\mathbf{I}_L$, respectively. Derive an expression relating the line voltage and line current phasors on the secondary side of the transformers to $\mathbf{V}_L$ and $\mathbf{I}_L$.

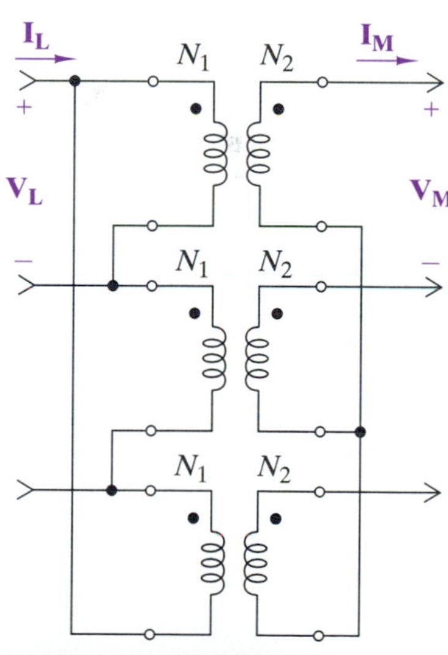

FIGURE P14–53

14–54 E COMPARISON OF THREE-PHASE AND SINGLE-PHASE SYSTEMS

The three-phase and single-phase power systems in Figure P14–54 operate under the following conditions:

(a) The two systems deliver the same total complex power to the load.

FIGURE P14–54

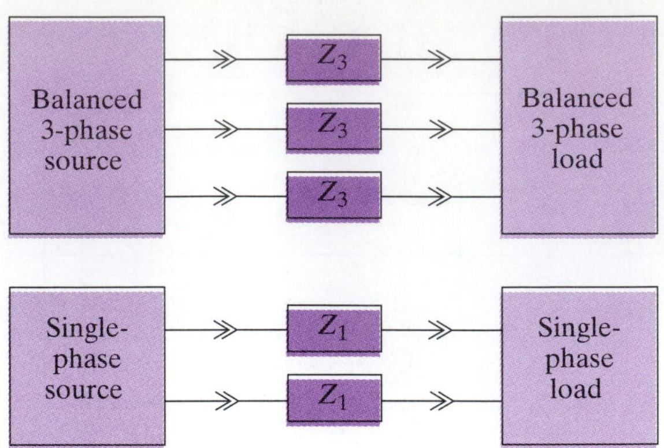

(b) The two systems have the same line-to-line voltage.
(c) The two systems have the same transmission efficiency.
(d) The distance from source to load is the same.
(e) The resistance of a line is proportional to its length divided by the cross-sectional area of the wire.

Show that the transmission line in three-phase system requires 25% less copper than the single-phase system.

14–55 A THREE-PHASE REACTIVE POWER MEASUREMENT

Starting with Eq. (14–34), show that the reactive power flowing in Figure 14–25 is $\sqrt{3}(W_2 - W_1)$, where W_1 and W_2 are the readings of the two wattmeters.

CHAPTER 15

FOURIER SERIES

The series formed of sines or cosines of multiple arcs are therefore adapted to represent between definite limits all possible functions, and the ordinates of lines or surfaces whose form is discontinuous.

Jean Baptiste Joseph Fourier, 1822,
French Physicist

The analysis techniques in this chapter have their roots in the works of the French physicist J. J. B. Fourier (1768–1830). While studying heat transfer, Fourier found that he could represent discontinuous functions by an infinite series of harmonic sinusoids, or sines of multiple arcs as he called them. Fourier was guided by his physical intuition and presented experimental evidence to support his claim, but he left the question of series convergence unanswered. As a result, his theory was incomplete and his 1807 treatise was initially rejected by the scientific community of his day. Some years later an acceptable proof of the "Fourier theorem" was supplied by the German mathematician P. G. L. Dirichlet (1805–1859). The basic ideas behind Fourier analysis were eventually accepted during his lifetime and are now firmly entrenched in all branches of science and engineering.

Originally, Fourier's motivation was to represent a single-valued function on a finite interval. Since his series consists of harmonic sinusiods, it has values outside of the interval, and in fact represents the function not only on the given finite interval but on periodic extensions of that interval as well. In other words, the given finite interval is but one cycle of a periodic function that extends indefinitely in both directions.

Applying the Fourier techniques in circuit analysis involves two basic steps: (1) finding the Fourier series for periodic waveforms that drive the circuit and (2) solving for the steady-state response of a circuit driven by a periodic input. The first three sections of this chapter treat the first step by deriving and exploring the properties of the Fourier series of common period waveforms. The fourth and fifth sections then use these results to solve for circuit responses, including average power. The chapter closes with a development of the exponential form of the Fourier series that serves as a stepping stone to the Fourier transformation treated in Chapter 16.

15–1 OVERVIEW OF FOURIER ANALYSIS

In this chapter we develop a method of finding the steady-state response of circuits to periodic inputs such as the waveforms in Figure 15–1. These periodic waveforms can be written as a Fourier series consisting of an infinite sum of harmonically related sinusoids. More specifically, if $f(t)$ is periodic with period T_0 and is reasonably well behaved, then $f(t)$ can be expressed as a **Fourier series** of the form

$$\begin{aligned} f(t) &= a_0 + a_1\cos(2\pi f_0 t) + a_2\cos(2\pi 2 f_0 t) + \ldots + a_n\cos(2\pi n f_0 t) + \ldots \\ &\quad + b_1\sin(2\pi f_0 t) + b_2\sin(2\pi 2 f_0 t) + \ldots + b_n\sin(2\pi n f_0 t) + \ldots \end{aligned} \tag{15-1}$$

or, more compactly,

$$f(t) = \underbrace{a_0}_{\text{dc}} + \underbrace{\sum_{n=1}^{\infty}[a_n\cos(2\pi n f_0 t) + b_n\sin(2\pi n f_0 t)]}_{\text{ac}} \tag{15-2}$$

The coefficient a_0 is the dc component or average value of $f(t)$. The constants a_n and b_n ($n = 1, 2, 3, \ldots$) are the **Fourier coefficients** of the sinusoids

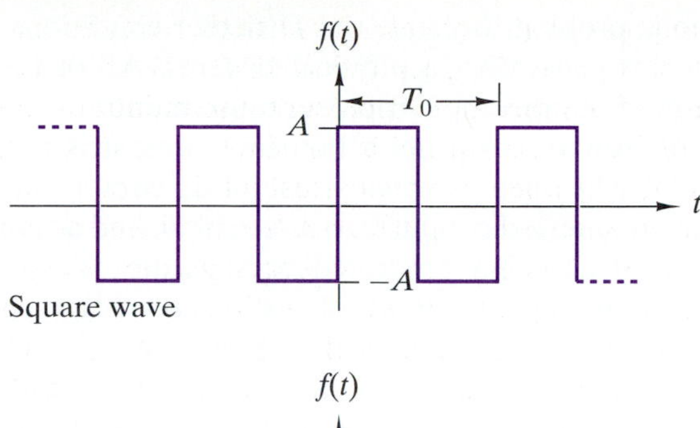

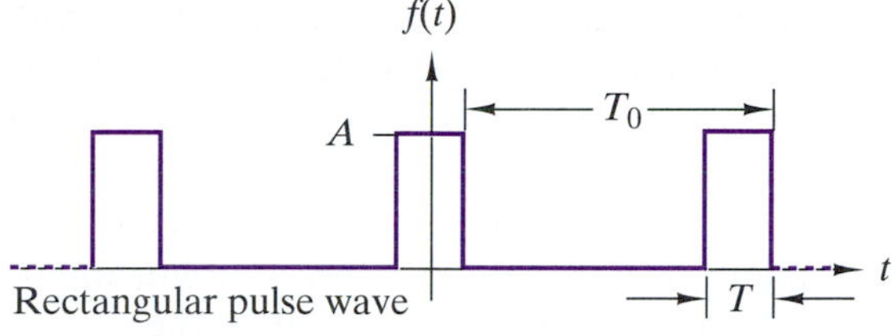

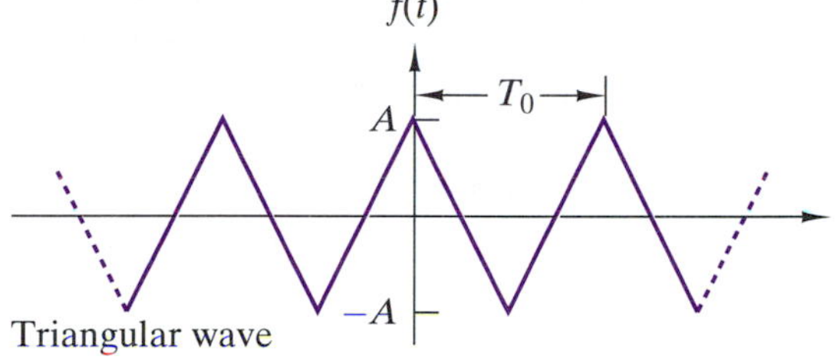

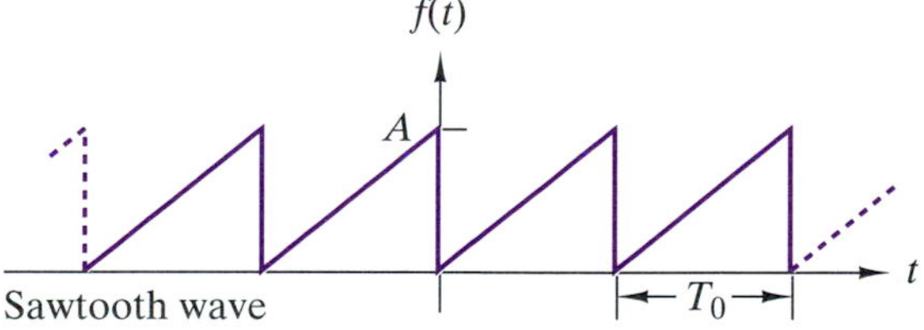

FIGURE 15–1 *Some examples of periodic waveforms.*

in the ac component. The lowest frequency in the ac component occurs for $n = 1$ and is called the **fundamental frequency** defined as $f_0 = 1/T_0$. The other frequencies are integer multiples of the fundamental called the second harmonic ($2f_0$), third harmonic ($3f_0$) and, in general, the nth harmonic (nf_0).

Since Eq. (15–2) is an infinite series, there is always a question of convergence. We have said that the series converges as long as $f(t)$ is reasonably well behaved. Basically, this means that $f(t)$ is single valued, the integral of $|f(t)|$ over a period is finite, and $f(t)$ has a finite number of discontinuities in any one period. These requirements, called the **Dirichlet conditions**, are sufficient to assure convergence. Every periodic waveform that meets the Dirichlet conditions has a convergent Fourier series. However, there are waveforms that do not meet the Dirichlet conditions that also have convergent Fourier series. That is, while the Dirichlet conditions are sufficient, they are not necessary and sufficient. This limitation does not present a serious problem because the Dirichlet conditions are satisfied by the waveforms generated in physical systems. All of the periodic waveforms in Figure 15–1 meet the Dirichlet requirements.

Before discussing how to construct a Fourier series, it is important to have an overview of why such a series is useful in circuit analysis. The Fourier series resolves a periodic input into a sum of dc and ac components that can be thought of as being generated by separate dc and ac signal sources. For linear circuits we can think of the steady-state response to a periodic input as the sum of the steady-state responses to each of these sources acting alone. Since we know how to find the steady-state response to dc inputs (Chapters 2, 3, and 4) and sinusoidal (ac) inputs (Chapters 8, 11, and 12), we can calculate the steady-state response to a periodic input using superposition. The net result is that both the input and the steady-state output are expressed as Fourier series.

At first glance it may seem awkward to express circuit inputs and outputs as infinite series. However, it turns out that the Fourier series tells us a great deal about signals and circuits. With experience you will see that Fourier analysis is not simply another circuit analysis technique, but a point of view that pervades analog signal progressing. We think of periodic signals as having a spectrum containing components at the discrete frequencies nf_0 ($n = 0, 1, 2, 3, \ldots$). The manner in which the circuit alters the spectral components tells us much that is useful in analog circuit analysis and design.

15–2 FOURIER COEFFICIENTS

The Fourier coefficients for any periodic waveform $f(t)$ satisfying the Dirichlet conditions can be obtained from the equations

$$
\begin{aligned}
a_0 &= \frac{1}{T_0}\int_{-T_0/2}^{+T_0/2} f(t)dt \\
a_n &= \frac{2}{T_0}\int_{-T_0/2}^{+T_0/2} f(t)\cos(2\pi nt/T_0)dt \\
b_n &= \frac{2}{T_0}\int_{-T_0/2}^{+T_0/2} f(t)\sin(2\pi nt/T_0)dt
\end{aligned}
\tag{15–3}
$$

The integration limits in these equations extend from $-T_0/2$ to $+T_0/2$. However, the limits can span any convenient interval as long as it is exactly one period. For example, the limits could be from 0 to T_0 or $-T_0/4$ to $3T_0/4$. We will show where Eq. (15–3) comes from in a moment, but first we use these equations to obtain the Fourier coefficients of the sawtooth wave.

EXAMPLE 15–1

Find the Fourier coefficients for the sawtooth wave in Figure 15–1.

SOLUTION:

An expression for a sawtooth wave on the interval $0 \le t \le T_0$ is

$$f(t) = \frac{At}{T_0} \qquad 0 \le t < T_0$$

For this definition of $f(t)$ we use 0 and T_0 as the limits in Eq. (15–3). The first expression in Eq. (15–3) yields a_0 as

$$a_0 = \frac{1}{T_0}\int_0^{T_0} \frac{At}{T_0} dt = \frac{A}{T_0^2}\frac{t^2}{2}\bigg|_0^{T_0} = \frac{A}{2}$$

This result states that the average or dc value is $A/2$, which is easy to see because the area under one cycle of the sawtooth wave is $AT_0/2$. The second expression in Eq. (15–3) yields a_n as

$$a_n = \frac{2}{T_0}\int_0^{T_0} \frac{At}{T_0}\cos(2\pi nt/T_0)dt$$

$$= \frac{2A}{T_0^2}\left[\frac{\cos(2\pi nt/T_0)}{(2\pi n/T_0)^2} + \frac{t \times \sin(2\pi nt/T_0)}{(2\pi n/T_0)}\right]_0^{T_0}$$

$$= \frac{2A}{T_0^2}\left[\frac{\cos(2\pi n) - \cos(0)}{(2\pi n/T_0)^2}\right] = 0 \qquad \text{for all } n$$

Since $a_n = 0$ for all n, there are no cosine terms in the series. The b_n coefficients are found using the third expression in Eq. (15–3):

$$b_n = \frac{2}{T_0}\int_0^{T_0} \frac{At}{T_0}\sin(2\pi nt/T_0)dt$$

$$= \frac{2A}{T_0^2}\left[\frac{\sin(2\pi nt/T_0)}{(2\pi n/T_0)^2} - \frac{t \times \cos(2\pi nt/T_0)}{(2\pi n/T_0)}\right]_0^{T_0}$$

$$= \frac{2A}{T_0^2}\left[\frac{T_0 cos(2\pi n)}{(2\pi n/T_0)}\right] = -\frac{A}{n\pi} \qquad \text{for all } n$$

Given the coefficients a_n and b_n found above, the Fourier series for the sawtooth wave is

$$f(t) = \frac{A}{2} + \sum_{n=1}^{\infty}\left[-\frac{A}{n\pi}\right]\sin(2\pi n f_0 t)$$

■

EXAMPLE 15–2

In this example we use a computer tool to show that a truncated Fourier series approximates a periodic waveform. The waveform is a sawtooth with $A = 10$ and $T_0 = 2$ ms. Calculate the Fourier coefficients of the first 20 harmonics and plot the truncated series representation of the waveform using the first 5 harmonics and the first 10 harmonics.

SOLUTION:

From Example 15–1 the Fourier coefficients for the sawtooth wave are

$$a_0 = A/2 \quad a_n = 0 \quad \text{and} \quad b_n = -\frac{A}{n\pi} \quad \text{for all } n$$

Figure 15–2 shows a Mathcad worksheet that generates truncated Fourier series. The first line defines the waveform amplitude and period. The Fourier coefficients of the first 20 harmonics are calculated in the second line using the index variable $n = 1,2, \ldots 20$. In Mathcad syntax $n = I, J, \ldots K$ means FOR $n = I$ TO K STEP $J - I$ DO. The next line defines a truncated Fourier series $f(k,t)$ consisting of the dc component a_0 plus the sum of the first k harmonics. Specifically, the function $f(5, t)$ is the sum of the dc component plus the first 5 harmonics and $f(10, t)$ is the sum of the dc component plus the first 10 harmonics. The plots of these two functions at the bottom of the worksheet show how function $f(k, t)$ approaches the sawtooth wave as more harmonics are added. Infinitely many harmonics are needed to represent a sawtooth wave exactly. However, the plots suggest that a relatively small number, say 5 or 10, provides a reasonable approximation of the major features of the sawtooth wave.

FIGURE 15–2

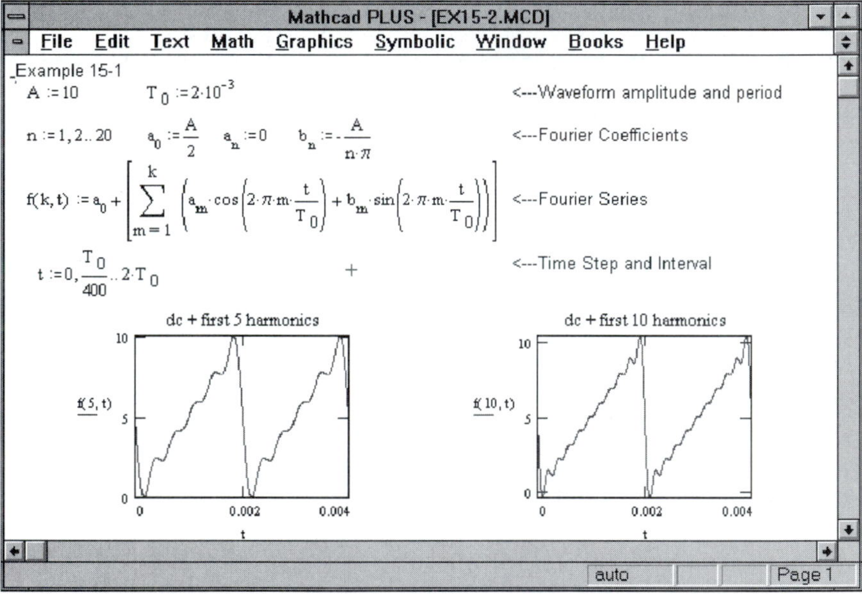

The Mathcad worksheet in Figure 15–2 is a template for generating truncated Fourier series. Changing the amplitude and period in the first line and the Fourier coefficients in the second line generates plots of the truncated Fourier series for other periodic waveforms. The index for n in the second line may need to be changed as well. For example, if only odd harmonics are present in the series, then the index should be $n = 1,3, \ldots 21$. ■

DERIVING EQUATIONS FOR a_n AND b_n

The sawtooth wave example shows how to calculate the Fourier coefficients using Eq. (15–3). We now turn to the derivation of these equations. An equation for a Fourier coefficient is derived by multiplying both sides of Eq. (15–2) by the sinusoid associated with the coefficient and then integrating the result over one period. This multiply and integrate process isolates one coefficient because it turns out that all of the integrations produce zero except one.

The following derivation makes use of the fact that the area under a sine or cosine wave over an integer number of cycles is zero. That is,

$$\begin{aligned} &\int_{-T_0/2}^{+T_0/2} \sin(2\pi k f_0 t)dt = 0 && \text{for all } k \\ &\int_{-T_0/2}^{+T_0/2} \cos(2\pi k f_0 t)dt = 0 && \text{for } k \neq 0 \\ &\qquad\qquad = T_0 && \text{for } k = 0 \end{aligned} \tag{15-4}$$

where k is an integer. These equations state that integrating a sinusoid over $k \neq 0$ cycles produces zero, since the areas under successive half cycles cancel. The single exception occurs when $k = 0$, in which case the cosine function reduces to one and the net area for one period is T_0.

We derive the equation for the amplitude of the dc component a_0 by integrating both sides of Eq. (15–2):

$$\begin{aligned} &\int_{-T_0/2}^{+T_0/2} f(t)dt = \\ &a_0 \int_{-T_0/2}^{+T_0/2} dt + \sum_{n=1}^{\infty} \left[a_n \int_{-T_0/2}^{+T_0/2} \cos(2\pi n f_0 t)dt + b_n \int_{-T_0/2}^{+T_0/2} \sin(2\pi n f_0 t)dt \right] \\ &= a_0 T_0 + \qquad 0 + \qquad 0 \end{aligned} \tag{15-5}$$

The integrals of the ac components vanish because of the properties in Eq. (15–4), and the right side of this expression reduces to a_0T_0. Solving for a_0 yields the first expression in Eq. (15–3).

To derive the expression for a_n we multiply Eq. (15–2) by $\cos(2\pi m f_0 t)$ and integrate over the interval from $-T_0/2$ to $+T_0/2$:

$$\begin{aligned} \int_{-T_0/2}^{+T_0/2} f(t) \cos(2\pi m f_0 t)dt &= a_0 \int_{-T_0/2}^{+T_0/2} \cos(2\pi m f_0 t)dt \\ &+ \sum_{n=1}^{\infty} \left[a_n \int_{-T_0/2}^{+T_0/2} \cos(2\pi m f_0 t) \cos(2\pi n f_0 t)dt + \right. \\ &\left. b_n \int_{-T_0/2}^{+T_0/2} \cos(2\pi m f_0 t) \sin(2\pi n f_0 t)dt \right] \end{aligned} \tag{15-6}$$

All of the integrals on the right side of this equation are zero except one. To show this we use identities

$$\cos(x)\cos(y) = \frac{1}{2}\cos(x - y) + \frac{1}{2}\cos(x + y)$$

$$\cos(x)\sin(y) = \frac{1}{2}\sin(x - y) + \frac{1}{2}\sin(x + y)$$

to change Eq. (15–6) into the following form:

$$\int_{-T_0/2}^{+T_0/2} f(t)\cos(2\pi m f_0 t)dt = a_0\int_{-T_0/2}^{+T_0/2}\cos(2\pi m f_0 t)dt$$

$$+\sum_{n=1}^{\infty}\left\{\frac{a_n}{2}\left[\int_{-T_0/2}^{+T_0/2}\cos[2\pi(m-n)f_0 t]dt + \int_{-T_0/2}^{+T_0/2}\cos[2\pi(m+n)f_0 t]dt\right]\right\} \tag{15-7}$$

$$+\sum_{n=1}^{\infty}\left\{\frac{b_n}{2}\left[\int_{-T_0/2}^{+T_0/2}\sin[2\pi(m-n)f_0 t]dt + \int_{-T_0/2}^{+T_0/2}\sin[2\pi(m+n)f_0 t]dt\right]\right\}$$

All of the integrals are now in the form of expressions in Eq. (15–4). Consequently, we see all of the integrals on the right side of Eq. (15–7) vanish, except for one cosine integral when $m = n$. This one survivor corresponds to the $k = 0$ case in Eq. (15–4), and the right side of Eq. (15–7) reduces to

$$\int_{-T_0/2}^{T_0/2} f(t)\cos(2\pi n f_0 t)dt = \frac{a_n}{2}\int_{-T_0/2}^{T_0/2}\cos[2\pi(n-n)f_0 t]dt$$

$$= \frac{a_n}{2}T_0$$

Solving Eq. (15–7) for a_n yields the second expression in Eq. (15–3).

To obtain the expression for b_n we multiply Eq. (15–2) by $\sin(2\pi m f_0 t)$ and integrate over the interval $t = -T_0/2$ to $+T_0/2$. The derivation steps then parallel the approach used to find a_n. The end result is that the dc component integral vanishes and the ac component integrals reduce to $b_n T_0/2$, which yields the expression for b_n in Eq. (15–3). The details of the development for b_n are left as a problem (see Problem 15–14).

The derivation of Eq. (15–3) focuses on the problem of finding the Fourier coefficients of a given periodic waveform. Some experience and practice are necessary to understand the implications of this procedure. On the other hand, it is not necessary to go through these mechanics for every newly encountered periodic waveform because tables of Fourier series expansions are available. For our purposes the listing in Figure 15–3 will suffice. For each waveform defined graphically, the figure lists the expressions for a_0, a_n, and b_n as well as restrictions on the integer n.

EXAMPLE 15–3

Verify the Fourier coefficients given for the square wave in Figure 15–3 and write the first three nonzero terms in its Fourier series.

Waveform	Fourier Coefficients	Waveform	Fourier Coefficients
Constant (dc) 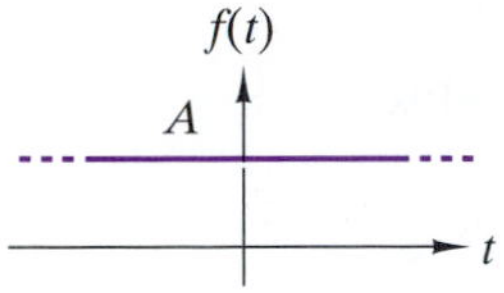	$a_0 = A$ $a_n = 0$ all n $b_n = 0$ all n	Sawtooth wave 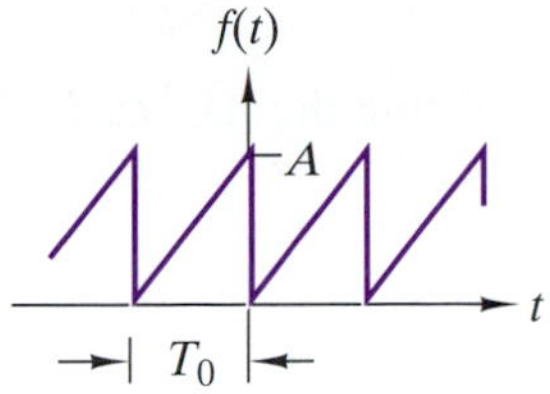	$a_0 = \frac{A}{2}$ $a_n = 0$ all n $b_n = -\frac{A}{n\pi}$ all n
Cosine wave 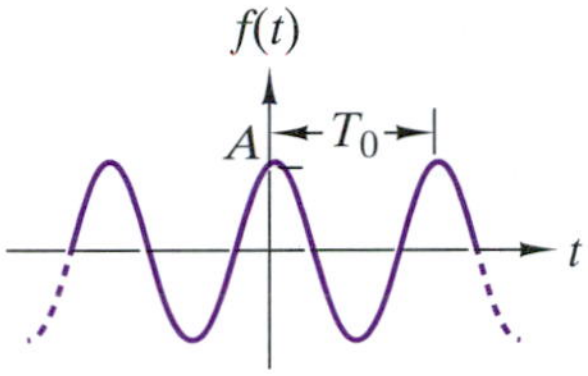	$a_0 = 0$ $a_1 = A$ $a_n = 0$ $n \neq 1$ $b_n = 0$ all n	Triangular wave 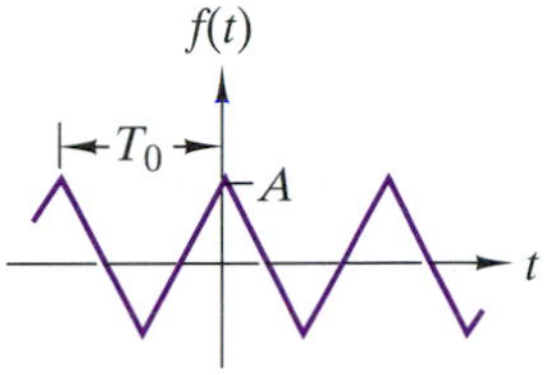	$a_0 = 0$ $a_n = \frac{8A}{(n\pi)^2}$ n odd $a_n = 0$ n even $b_n = 0$ all n
Sine wave 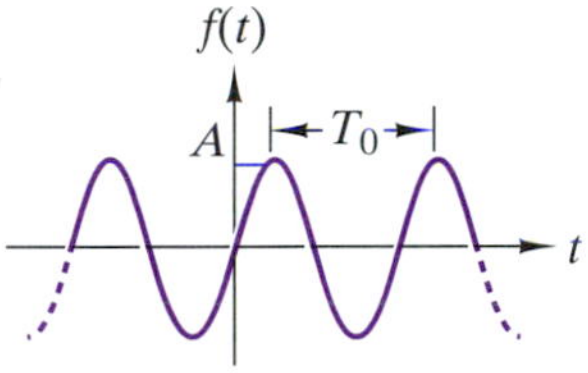	$a_0 = 0$ $a_n = 0$ all n $b_1 = A$ $b_n = 0$ $n \neq 1$	Half-wave rectified sine wave 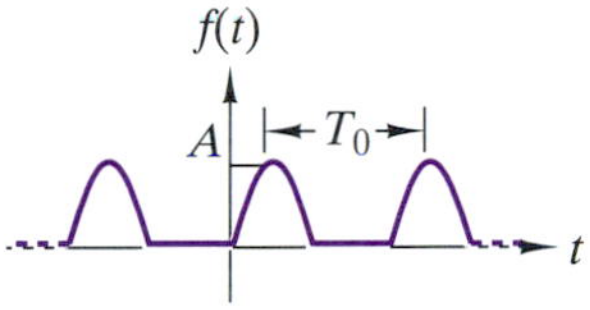	$a_0 = \frac{A}{\pi}$ $a_n = \frac{2A/\pi}{1-n^2}$ n even $a_n = 0$ n odd $b_1 = \frac{A}{2}$ $n = 1$ $b_n = 0$ $n \neq 1$
Square wave 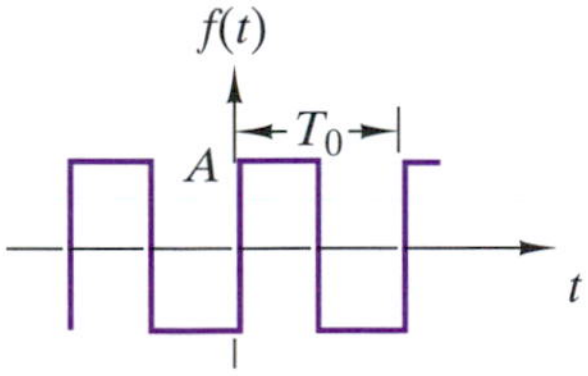	$a_0 = 0$ $a_n = 0$ all n $b_n = \frac{4A}{n\pi}$ n odd $b_n = 0$ n even	Full-wave rectified sine wave 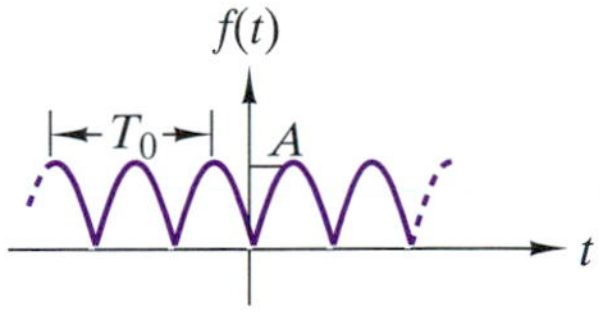	$a_0 = 2A/\pi$ $a_n = \frac{4A/\pi}{1-n^2}$ n even $a_n = 0$ n odd $b_n = 0$ all n
Rectangular pulse 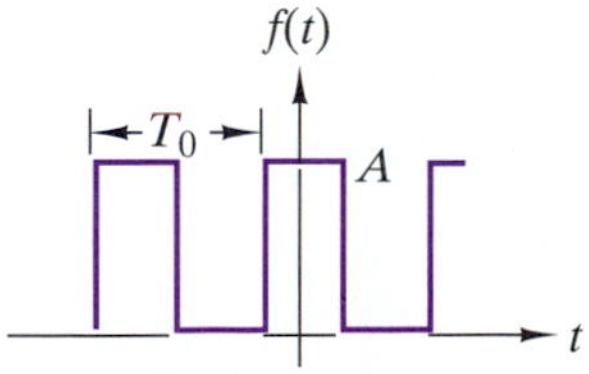	$a_0 = \frac{AT}{T_0}$ $a_n = \frac{2A}{n\pi}\sin\left(\frac{n\pi T}{T_0}\right)$ $b_n = 0$ all n	Parabolic wave 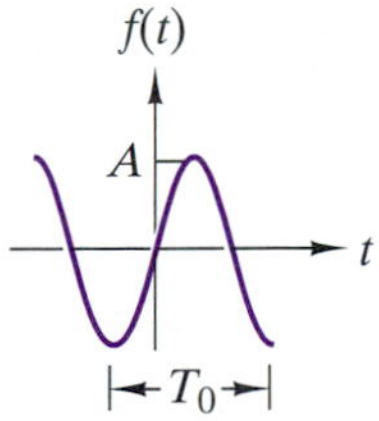	$a_0 = 0$ $a_n = 0$ all n $b_n = \frac{32A}{(n\pi)^3}$ n odd $b_n = 0$ n even

FIGURE 15-3 *Fourier coefficients for some periodic waveforms.*

SOLUTION:

An expression for a square wave on the interval $0 < t <$ to T_0 is

$$f(t) = \begin{cases} A & 0 < t < T_0/2 \\ -A & T_0/2 < t < T_0 \end{cases}$$

Using the first expression in Eq. (15–3) to find a_0 yields

$$\begin{aligned} a_0 &= \frac{1}{T_0}\int_0^{T_0/2} A\,dt + \frac{1}{T_0}\int_{T_0/2}^{T_0} (-A)dt \\ &= \frac{A}{T_0}\left[\frac{T_0}{2} - 0 - T_0 + \frac{T_0}{2}\right] = 0 \end{aligned}$$

The result $a_0 = 0$ means that the dc value of the square wave is zero, which is easy to see because the area under a positive half cycle cancels the area under a negative half cycle. Using the second expression in Eq. (15–3) to find a_n produces

$$\begin{aligned} a_n &= \frac{2}{T_0}\int_0^{T_0/2} A\cos(2\pi nt/T_0)dt + \frac{2}{T_0}\int_{T_0/2}^{T_0} (-A)\cos(2\pi nt/T_0)dt \\ &= \frac{2A}{T_0}\left[\frac{\sin(2\pi nt/T_0)}{2\pi n/T_0}\right]_0^{T_0/2} - \frac{2A}{T_0}\left[\frac{\sin(2\pi nt/T_0)}{2\pi n/T_0}\right]_{T_0/2}^{T_0} \\ &= \frac{A}{n\pi}[\sin(n\pi) - \sin(0) - \sin(2n\pi) + \sin(n\pi)] = 0 \end{aligned}$$

Since $a_n = 0$ for all n there are no cosine terms in the series. This makes some intuitive sense because a sinewave with the same fundamental frequency as the square wave fits nicely inside the square wave with zeros crossing at the same points, whereas a cosine with the same frequency does not fit at all. The b_n coefficients for the sine terms are found using the third expression in Eq. (15–3):

$$\begin{aligned} b_n &= \frac{2}{T_0}\int_0^{T_0/2} A\sin(2\pi nt/T_0)dt + \frac{2}{T_0}\int_{T_0/2}^{T_0} (-A)\sin(2\pi nt/T_0)dt \\ &= \frac{2A}{T_0}\left[-\frac{\cos(2\pi nt/T_0)}{2\pi n/T_0}\right]_0^{T_0/2} - \frac{2A}{T_0}\left[-\frac{\cos(2\pi nt/T_0)}{2\pi n/T_0}\right]_{T_0/2}^{T_0} \\ &= \frac{A}{n\pi}[-\cos(n\pi) + \cos(0) + \cos(2n\pi) - \cos(n\pi)] \\ &= \frac{2A}{n\pi}[1 - \cos(n\pi)] \end{aligned}$$

The term $[1 - \cos(n\pi)] = 2$ if n is odd and zero if n is even. Hence b_n can be written as

$$b_n = \begin{cases} \dfrac{4A}{n\pi} & n \text{ odd} \\ 0 & n \text{ even} \end{cases}$$

The first three nonzero terms in the Fourier series of the square wave are

$$f(t) = \frac{4A}{\pi}\left[\sin 2\pi f_0 t + \frac{1}{3}\sin 2\pi 3 f_0 t + \frac{1}{5}\sin 2\pi 5 f_0 t + \ldots\right]$$

Note that this series contains only odd harmonic terms. ■

Exercise 15–1

The triangular wave in Figure 15–3 has a peak amplitude of $A = 10$ and $T_0 = 2$ ms. Calculate the Fourier coefficients of the first nine harmonics.

Answers:
$a_1 = 8.11$, $a_2 = 0$, $a_3 = 0.901$, $a_4 = 0$, $a_5 = 0.324$, $a_6 = 0$, $a_7 = 0.165$, $a_8 = 0$, $a_9 = 0.100$, $b_n = 0$ for all n

ALTERNATIVE FORM OF THE FOURIER SERIES

The series in Eq. (15–1) can be written in several alternative yet equivalent forms. From our study of sinusoids in Chapter 5, we recall that the Fourier coefficients determine the amplitude and phase angle of the general sinusoid. Thus, we can write a general Fourier series in the form

$$f(t) = A_0 + A_1\cos(2\pi f_0 t + \phi_1) + A_2\cos(2\pi 2 f_0 t + \phi_2) + \ldots + A_n\cos(2\pi n f_0 t + \phi_n) + \ldots \qquad (15\text{–}8)$$

where

$$A_n = \sqrt{a_n^2 + b_n^2} \quad \text{and} \quad \phi_n = \tan^{-1}\frac{-b_n}{a_n} \qquad (15\text{–}9)$$

The coefficient A_n is the amplitude of the nth harmonic and ϕ_n is its phase angle.[1]

Note that the amplitude A_n and phase angle ϕ_n contain all of the information needed to construct the Fourier series in the form of Eq. (15–8). Figure 15–4 shows how plots of this information are used to display the spectral content of a periodic waveform $f(t)$. The plot of A_n versus nf_0 (or $n\omega_0$) is called the **amplitude spectrum**, while the plot of ϕ_n versus nf_0 (or $n\omega_0$) is called the **phase spectrum**. Both plots are **line spectra** because spectral content can be represented as a line at discrete frequencies. In the next chapter we use Fourier transforms to obtain continuous spectra for aperiodic waveforms. In this chapter we concentrate on the line spectrum of the Fourier series as a means of describing periodic signals and solving circuit analysis problems.

1 There is a 180° ambiguity in the value returned by the inverse tangent function in most computational tools. The ambiguity is resolved by the following rule: $b_n < 0$ implies that the angle is in the range 0 to –180°, while $b_n > 0$ implies the 0 to +180° range.

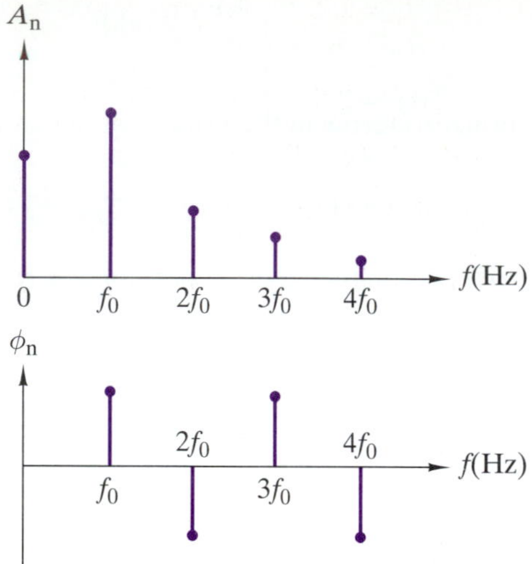

FIGURE 15–4 *Amplitude and phase spectra.*

In theory, a Fourier series includes infinitely many harmonics, although the harmonics tend to decrease in amplitude at high frequency. For example, the summary in Figure 15–3 shows that the amplitudes of the square wave decrease as $1/n$, the triangular wave as $1/n^2$, and the parabolic wave as $1/n^3$. The $1/n^3$ dependence means that the amplitude of the fifth harmonic in a parabolic wave is less than 1% of the amplitude of the fundamental (actually 1/125th of the fundamental). In practical signals the harmonic amplitudes decrease at high frequency so that at some point the higher-order components become negligibly small. This means that we can truncate the series at some point and still retain the important features of the signal.

EXAMPLE 15–4

Derive expressions for the amplitude A_n and phase angle ϕ_n of the Fourier series of the sawtooth wave in Figure 15–3. Sketch the amplitude and phase spectra of a sawtooth wave with $A = 5$ and $T_0 = 4$ ms.

SOLUTION:

Figure 15–3 gives the Fourier coefficients of the sawtooth wave as

$$a_0 = \frac{A}{2} \qquad a_n = 0 \qquad b_n = -\frac{A}{n\pi} \qquad \text{for all } n$$

Using Eq. (15–9) yields

$$A_n = \sqrt{a_n^2 + b_n^2} = \begin{cases} \dfrac{A}{2} & n = 0 \\ \dfrac{A}{n\pi} & n > 0 \end{cases}$$

and

$$\phi_n = \tan^{-1}\frac{-b_n}{a_n} = \begin{cases} \text{undefined} & n = 0 \\ 90^\circ & n > 0 \end{cases}$$

For $A = 5$ and $f_0 = 1/T_0 = 250$ Hz the first four nonzero terms in the series are

$$f(t) = 2.5 + 1.59\cos(2\pi 250t + 90°)$$
$$+ 0.796\cos(2\pi 500t + 90°) + 0.531\cos(2\pi 750t + 90°) + \ldots$$

Figure 15–5 shows the amplitude and phase spectra for this signal. ■

FIGURE 15–5

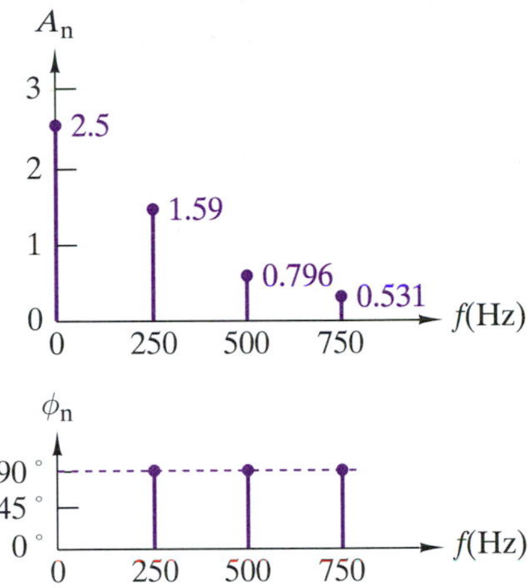

Exercise 15–2

Derive expressions for the amplitude A_n and phase angle ϕ_n for the triangular wave in Figure 15–3 and write an expression for the first three nonzero terms in the Fourier series with $A = \pi^2/8$ and $T_0 = 2\pi/5000$ s.

Answers:

$$A_n = \frac{8A}{(n\pi)^2} \quad \phi_n = 0° \qquad n \text{ odd}$$

$$A_n = 0 \quad \phi_n \text{ undefined} \qquad n \text{ even}$$

$$f(t) = \cos(5000t) + \frac{1}{9}\cos(15{,}000t) + \frac{1}{25}\cos(25{,}000t) + \ldots$$

15–3 WAVEFORM SYMMETRIES

Many of the Fourier coefficients are zero when a periodic waveform has certain types of symmetries. It is helpful to recognize these symmetries, since they may simplify the calculation of the Fourier coefficients.

The first expression in Eq. (15–3) shows that the amplitude of the dc component a_0 is the average value of the periodic waveform $f(t)$. If the waveform has equal area above and below the time axis, then the integral over one cycle vanishes, the average value is zero, and $a_0 = 0$. The square wave, triangular wave, and parabolic wave in Figure 15–3 are examples of periodic waveforms with zero average value.

A waveform is said to have **even symmetry** if $f(-t) = f(t)$. The cosine wave, rectangular pulse, and triangular wave in Figure 15–3 are examples of waveforms with even symmetry. The Fourier series of an even waveform is made up entirely of cosine terms: that is, all of the b_n coefficients are zero. To show this we write the Fourier series for $f(t)$ in the form

$$f(t) = a_0 + \sum_{n=1}^{\infty}[a_n \cos(2\pi n f_0 t) + b_n \sin(2\pi n f_0 t)] \tag{15-10}$$

Given the Fourier series for $f(t)$, we use the identities $\cos(-x) = \cos(x)$ and $\sin(-x) = -\sin(x)$ to write the Fourier series for $f(-t)$ as follows:

$$f(-t) = a_0 + \sum_{n=1}^{\infty}[a_n \cos(2\pi n f_0 t) - b_n \sin(2\pi n f_0 t)] \tag{15-11}$$

For even symmetry $f(t) = f(-t)$ and the right sides of Eqs. (15–10) and (15–11) must be equal. Comparing the Fourier coefficients term by term, we find that $f(t) = f(-t)$ requires $b_n = -b_n$. The only way this can happen is for $b_n = 0$ for all n.

A waveform is said to have **odd symmetry** if $-f(-t) = f(t)$. The sine wave, square wave, and parabolic wave in Figure 15–3 are examples of waveforms with this type symmetry. The Fourier series of odd waveforms are made up entirely of sine terms: that is, all of the a_n coefficients are zero. Given the Fourier series for $f(t)$ in Eq. (15–10), we use the identities $\cos(-x) = \cos(x)$ and $\sin(-x) = -\sin(x)$ to write the Fourier series for $-f(-t)$ in the form

$$-f(-t) = -a_0 + \sum_{n=1}^{\infty}[-a_n \cos(2\pi n f_0 t) + b_n \sin(2\pi n f_0 t)] \tag{15-12}$$

With odd symmetry $f(t) = -f(-t)$ and the right sides of Eq. (15–10) and (15–12) must be equal. Comparing the Fourier coefficients term by term, we find that odd symmetry requires $a_0 = -a_0$ and $a_n = -a_n$. The only way this can happen is for $a_n = 0$ for all n, including $n = 0$.

A waveform is said to have **half-wave symmetry** if $-f(t - T_0/2) = f(t)$. This requirement states that inverting the waveform $[-f(t)]$ and then time shifting by half a cycle ($T_0/2$) must produce the same waveform. Basically, this means that successive half cycles have the same waveshape but opposite polarities. In Figure 15–3 the sine wave, cosine wave, square wave, triangular wave, and parabolic wave have half-wave symmetry. The sawtooth wave, half-wave sine, rectangular pulse train, and full-wave sine do not have this symmetry.

With half-wave symmetry the amplitudes of all even harmonics are zero. To show this we use the identities $\cos(x - n\pi) = (-1)^n \cos(x)$ and $\sin(x - n\pi) = (-1)^n \sin(x)$ to write the Fourier series of $-f(t - T_0/2)$ in the form

$$-f(t - T_0/2) = -a_0 + \sum_{n=1}^{\infty}[-(-1)_n a_n \cos(2\pi n f_0 t) - (-1)^n b_n \sin(2\pi n f_0 t)] \tag{15-13}$$

For half-wave symmetry the right sides of Eqs. (15–10) and (15–13) must be equal. Comparing the coefficients term by term, we find that equality requires $a_0 = -a_0$, $a_n = -(-1)^n a_n$, and $b_n = -(-1)^n b_n$. The only way this can happen is for $a_0 = 0$ and for $a_n = b_n = 0$ when n is even. In other words, the only nonzero Fourier coefficients occur when n is odd.

A waveform may have more than one symmetry. For example, the triangular wave in Figure 15–3 has even symmetry and half-wave symmetry, while the square wave has both odd and half-wave symmetries. The sawtooth wave in Figure 15–3 is an example where an underlying odd symmetry is masked by a dc component. A symmetry that is not apparent until the dc component is removed is sometimes called a **hidden symmetry**.

Finally, whether a waveform has even or odd symmetry (or neither) depends on where we choose to define $t = 0$. For example, the triangular wave in Figure 15–3 has even symmetry because the $t = 0$ vertical axis is located at a local maximum. If the axis is shifted to a zero crossing, the waveform has odd symmetry and the cosine terms in the series are replaced by sine terms. If the vertical axis is shifted to a point between a zero cross and a maximum, then the resulting waveform is neither even nor odd and its Fourier series contains both sine and cosine terms.

EXAMPLE 15–5

Given that $f(t)$ is a square wave of amplitude A and period T_0, use the Fourier coefficients in Figure 15–3 to find the Fourier coefficients of $g(t) = f(t + T_0/4)$.

SOLUTION:

Figure 15–6 compares the square waves $f(t)$ and $g(t) = f(t + T_0/4)$. The square wave $f(t)$ has odd symmetry (sine terms only) and half-wave symmetry (odd harmonics only). Using the coefficients in Figure 15–3, the Fourier series for $f(t)$ is

$$f(t) = \sum \frac{4A}{n\pi} \sin(2\pi nt/T_0) \quad n \text{ odd}$$

The Fourier series for $g(t) = f(t + T_0/4)$ can be written in the form

$$\begin{aligned} g(t) = f(t + T_0/4) &= \sum \frac{4A}{n\pi} \sin[2\pi n(t + T_0/4)/T_0] \quad n \text{ odd} \\ &= \sum \frac{4A}{n\pi} \sin(2\pi nt/T_0 + n\pi/2) \\ &= \sum \frac{4A}{n\pi} \cos(2\pi nt/T_0)\sin(n\pi/2) \\ &= \sum \frac{4A}{n\pi} \cos(2\pi nt/T_0)(-1)^{\frac{n-1}{2}} \quad n \text{ odd} \end{aligned}$$

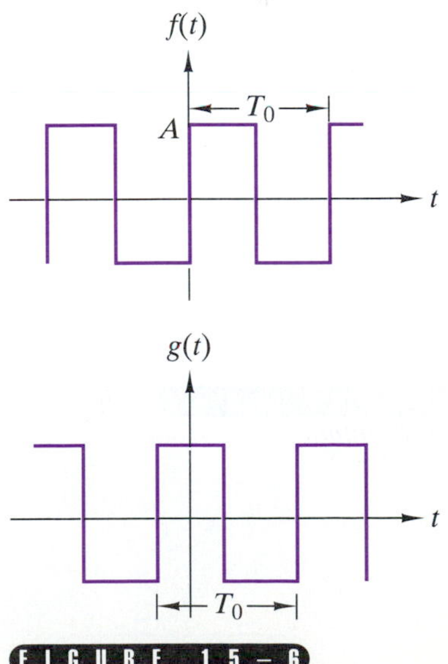

FIGURE 15–6

Figure 15–6 shows that $g(t)$ has even and half-wave symmetry so its Fourier series has only cosine terms and odd harmonics. The Fourier coefficients for $g(t)$ are

$$a_0 = 0 \quad a_n = \begin{cases} 0 & n \text{ even} \\ \left[\dfrac{4A}{n\pi}\right](-1)^{\frac{2n-1}{2}} & n \text{ odd} \end{cases}$$
$$b_n = 0 \quad \text{all } n$$

Shifting the time origin alters the even or odd symmetry properties of a periodic waveform because these symmetries depend on values of $f(t)$ on opposite sides of the vertical axis at $t = 0$. The half-wave symmetry of a waveform is not changed by time shifting because this symmetry only requires successive half cycles to have the same form but opposite polarities. ■

Exercise 15–3

(a) Identify the symmetries in the waveform $f(t)$ whose Fourier series is

$$f(t) = \frac{2\sqrt{3}A}{\pi}\left[\cos(\omega_0 t) - \frac{1}{5}\cos(5\,\omega_0 t) + \frac{1}{7}\cos(7\,\omega_0 t) - \frac{1}{11}\cos(11\,\omega_0 t) + \frac{1}{13}\cos(13\,\omega_0 t) + \ldots\right]$$

(b) Write the corresponding terms of the function $g(t) = f(t - T_0/4)$.

Answers:

(a) Even symmetry, half-wave symmetry, zero average value.

(b) $$g(t) = \frac{2\sqrt{3}A}{\pi}\left[\sin(\omega_0 t) - \frac{1}{5}\sin(5\,\omega_0 t) - \frac{1}{7}\sin(7\,\omega_0 t) + \frac{1}{11}\sin(11\,\omega_0 t) + \frac{1}{13}\sin(13\,\omega_0 t) + \ldots\right]$$

15–4 CIRCUIT ANALYSIS USING FOURIER SERIES

Up to this point we have concentrated on finding the Fourier series description of periodic waveforms. We are now in a position to address circuit analysis problems of the type illustrated in Figure 15–7. This first-order RL circuit is driven by a periodic sawtooth voltage, and the objective is to find the steady-state current $i(t)$.

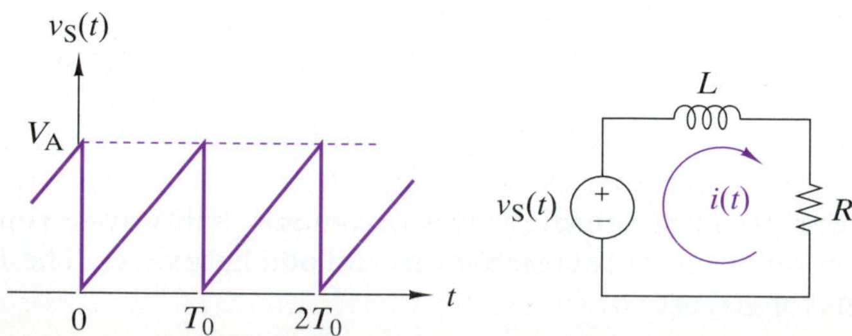

FIGURE 15–7 *Linear circuit with a periodic input.*

We begin by using the results in Example 15–4 to express the input voltage as a Fourier series in the form

$$v_S(t) = \underbrace{\frac{V_A}{2}}_{\text{dc}} + \underbrace{\sum_{n=1}^{\infty} \frac{V_A}{n\pi}\cos(n\omega_0 t + 90°)}_{\text{ac}} \quad (15\text{–}14)$$

This result expresses the input driving force as the sum of a dc component plus ac components at harmonic frequencies $n\omega_0 = 2\pi n f_0$, $n = 1, 2, 3, \ldots$. Since the circuit is linear, we find the steady-state response caused by each component acting alone and then obtain the total response by superposition.

In the dc steady state the inductor acts like a short circuit, so the steady-state current due to the dc input $V_A/2$ is simply $i_0(t) = V_A/(2R)$. The nth ac component in Eq. 15–14 can be written in phasor form as

$$\mathbf{V}_n = \frac{V_A}{n\pi}\angle 90°$$

The impedance of the series connection at the nth harmonic frequency is

$$Z_n = R + jn\omega_0 L = R\sqrt{1 + (n\omega_0 L/R)^2}\angle\theta_n$$

where $\theta_n = \tan^{-1}(n\omega_0 L/R)$. Hence the phasor representation of the steady-state current due to the nth harmonic of the input is

$$\mathbf{I}_n = \frac{\mathbf{V}_n}{Z_n} = \frac{V_A}{n\pi R}\frac{1}{\sqrt{1 + (n\omega_0 L/R)^2}}\angle(90° - \theta_n)$$

The sinusoidal waveform corresponding to this phasor is

$$i_n(t) = \frac{V_A}{n\pi R}\frac{1}{\sqrt{1 + (n\omega_0 L/R)^2}}\cos(n\omega_0 t + 90° - \theta_n)$$

We have now found the steady-state response of the circuit due to the dc component acting alone and the nth harmonic ac component acting alone. Since the circuit is linear, superposition applies and we find the steady-state response caused the sawtooth input triangular summing the contributions of each of these sources:

$$\begin{aligned} i(t) &= i_0(t) + \sum_{n=1}^{\infty} i_n(t) \\ &= \frac{V_A}{2R} + \frac{V_A}{R}\sum_{n=1}^{\infty}\frac{1}{n\pi\sqrt{1 + (n\omega_0 L/R)^2}}\cos(n\omega_0 t + 90° - \theta_n) \end{aligned} \quad (15\text{–}15)$$

The Fourier series in Eq. (15–15) represents the steady-state current due to a sawtooth driving force whose Fourier series is in Eq. (15–14).

Given the Fourier series of a periodic input, it is a straightforward procedure to obtain the Fourier series of the steady-state response. But interpreting the analysis result requires some thought since the response is presented as an infinite series. In practice the series converges rather rapidly, so we can calculate specific values or generate plots using computer tools to sum a truncated version of the infinite series. Before doing so let us look closely at Eq. (5-15) to see what we can infer about the response.

First note that if $L = 0$ Eq. (15–15) reduces to

$$i(t) = \frac{V_A/R}{2} + \sum_{n=1}^{\infty} \frac{V_A/R}{n\pi}\cos(n\omega_0 t + 90°)$$

which is the Fourier series of sawtooth wave of amplitude V_A/R. This makes sense because without the inductor the circuit in Figure 15–7 is a simple resistive circuit in which $i(t) = v_S(t)/R$, so the input and response must have the same waveform.

When $L \neq 0$ the response is not a sawtooth, but we can infer some features of its waveform if we examine the amplitude spectrum. At high frequency $[(n\omega_0 L/R) >> 1]$ Eq. (15–15) points out that the amplitudes of the ac components are approximately

$$I_n \approx \frac{V_A}{R}\frac{1}{n^2\pi\omega_0 L/R}$$

In the steady-state response the amplitudes of the high-frequency ac components decrease as $1/n^2$, whereas the ac components in the input sawtooth decrease as $1/n$. In other words, the relative amplitudes of the high-frequency components are much smaller in the response than in the input. This makes sense because the inductor's impedance increases with frequency and thereby reduces the amplitudes of the high-frequency ac currents. We would expect the circuit to filter out the high-frequency components in the input and produce a response without the sharp corners and discontinuities in the input sawtooth.

The next example examines this thought for a specific set of parameters.

EXAMPLE 15–6

The parameters of the steady-state waveform in Eq. (15–15) are V_A = 25 V, $T_0 = 5$ μs, $L = 40$ μH, and $R = 50$ Ω. Calculate and plot a truncated Fourier series representation of the steady-state current using the first 5 harmonics and the first 10 harmonics.

SOLUTION:

Figure 15–8 shows a Mathcad worksheet that calculates truncated Fourier series of the steady-state current in Eq. (15–15). The first two lines define the waveform and circuit parameters. The Fourier parameters for the first 20 harmonics are calculated in the third line using the index variable n = 1,2, . . . 20. The next line defines a truncated Fourier series $i(k, t)$ consisting of the dc component I_0 plus the sum of the first k harmonics. The responses $I(5, t)$ and $I(10, t)$ are plotted at the bottom of the worksheet. There is not much change between the two plots, suggesting that a truncated series converges rather rapidly and gives a reasonable approximation to the steady-state current.

The plots in Figure 15–8 show that the steady-state current is indeed smoother than the input driving force. The reason is that the inductor suppresses the high-frequency components that are important contributors to the discontinuities in the sawtooth waveform. As a result, the response

FIGURE 15-8

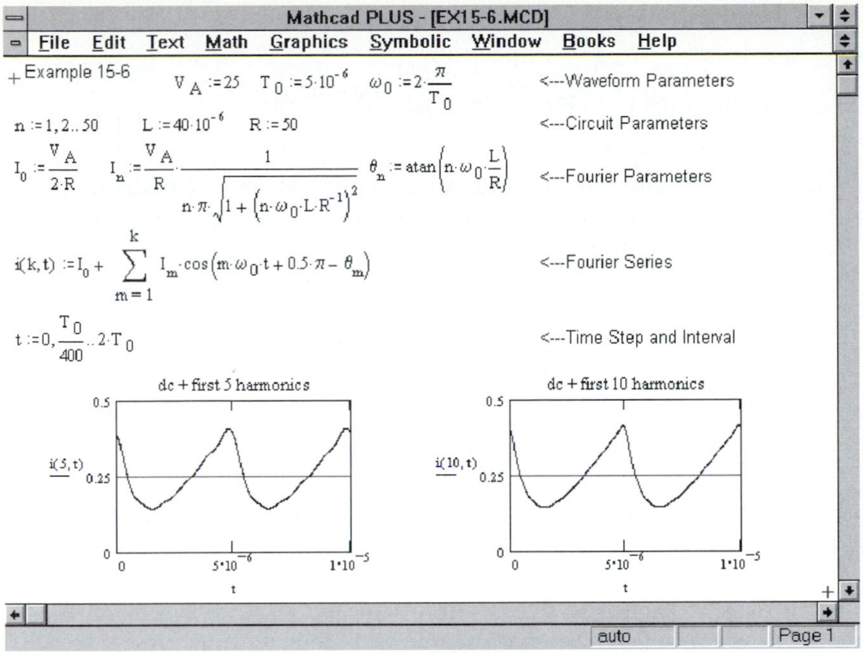

Mathcad PLUS - [EX15-6.MCD]

File Edit Text Math Graphics Symbolic Window Books Help

Example 15-6

$V_A := 25 \quad T_0 := 5\cdot 10^{-6} \quad \omega_0 := 2\cdot\frac{\pi}{T_0}$ <---Waveform Parameters

$n := 1, 2 .. 50 \quad L := 40\cdot 10^{-6} \quad R := 50$ <---Circuit Parameters

$I_0 := \frac{V_A}{2\cdot R} \quad I_n := \frac{V_A}{R}\cdot\frac{1}{n\cdot\pi\cdot\sqrt{1+\left(n\cdot\omega_0\cdot L\cdot R^{-1}\right)^2}} \quad \theta_n := \text{atan}\left(n\cdot\omega_0\cdot\frac{L}{R}\right)$ <---Fourier Parameters

$i(k,t) := I_0 + \sum_{m=1}^{k} I_m\cdot\cos\left(m\cdot\omega_0\cdot t + 0.5\cdot\pi - \theta_m\right)$ <---Fourier Series

$t := 0, \frac{T_0}{400} .. 2\cdot T_0$ <---Time Step and Interval

dc + first 5 harmonics — $i(5,t)$ vs. t (0 to $1\cdot 10^{-5}$)

dc + first 10 harmonics — $i(10,t)$ vs. t (0 to $1\cdot 10^{-5}$)

auto Page 1

does not have the abrupt changes and sharp corners present in the sawtooth input.

Exercise 15–4

Derive an expression for the steady-state current of the *RL* circuit in Figure 15–7 when the input voltage is a triangular wave with amplitude V_A and frequency ω_0.

Answer:

$$i(t) = \sum_{n=1}^{\infty} \frac{8V_A/R}{(n\pi)^2\sqrt{1 + (n\omega_0 L/R)^2}} \cos(n\omega_0 t - \theta_n) \qquad n \text{ odd}$$

where

$$\theta_n = \tan^{-1}(n\omega_0 L/R)$$

The transfer function offers another approach to circuit analysis with Fourier series. In Chapter 12 we found that in the sinusoidal steady state the relationship between the input and output sinusoids can be summarized in the following statements:

(Output Amplitude) = (Input Amplitude) × (Magnitude of $T(j\omega)$)
(Output Phase) = (Input Phase) + (Angle of $T(j\omega)$)

When the driving force is periodic, the input and output signals are represented by their amplitude and phase spectra. When the circuit is linear, the generalization of the preceding result for periodic driving forces is

$$\begin{pmatrix}\text{Output Amplitude}\\ \text{Spectrum}\end{pmatrix} = \begin{pmatrix}\text{Input Amplitude}\\ \text{Spectrum}\end{pmatrix} \times \begin{pmatrix}\text{Magnitude of}\\ T(jn\omega_0)\end{pmatrix}$$

$$\begin{pmatrix}\text{Output Phase}\\ \text{Spectrum}\end{pmatrix} = \begin{pmatrix}\text{Input Phase}\\ \text{Spectrum}\end{pmatrix} + \begin{pmatrix}\text{Angle of}\\ T(jn\omega_0)\end{pmatrix} \quad (15\text{–}16)$$

where the spectrum product and sum operations are carried out at dc ($n = 0$) and each of the harmonic ac frequencies ($n = 1, 2, 3, \ldots$). In some cases the output amplitude spectrum suffices as the solution for a problem.

EXAMPLE 15–7

Figure 15–9 shows a block diagram of a dc power supply. The ac input is a sinusoid that is converted to a full-wave sine by the rectifier. The filter passes the dc component in the rectified sine and suppresses the ac components. The result is an output consisting of a small residual ac ripple riding on top of a much larger dc signal.

FIGURE 15–9

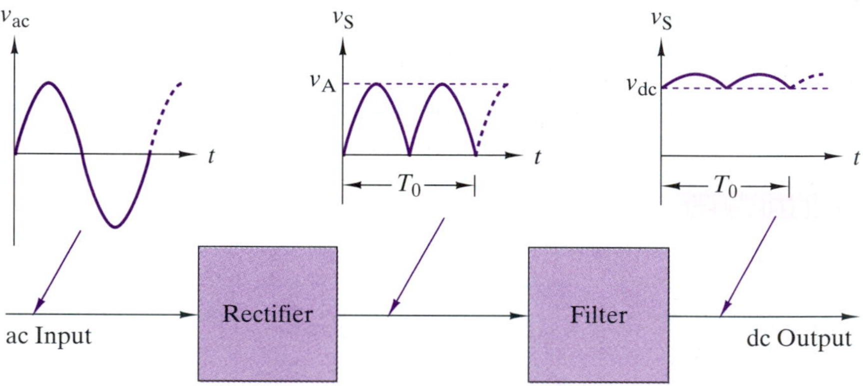

Calculate and plot the first 10 harmonics in amplitude spectra of the filter input and output for $V_A = 23.6$ V, $T_0 = 1/60$ s, and a lowpass filter transfer function of

$$T(s) = \frac{(200)^2}{s^2 + 280s + (200)^2}$$

SOLUTION:

The amplitude spectrum of the filter input is obtained using the Fourier coefficients for the full-wave rectified sine in Figure 15–3:

$$V_0 = 2V_A/\pi = 15.02\ V$$

$$V_n = \begin{cases} 0 & n \text{ odd} \\ \left|\dfrac{4V_A/\pi}{1-n^2}\right| = \dfrac{30.04}{n^2-1} & n \text{ even} \end{cases} \quad (15\text{–}17)$$

The magnitude of the transfer function at each of these discrete frequencies is

$$|T(jn\omega_0)| = \frac{(200)^2}{\sqrt{[(200)^2 - (n\omega_0)^2]^2 + (280\, n\omega_0)^2}} \tag{15–18}$$

To obtain the specified output spectrum, we must generate the product of the input amplitude times the transfer function magnitude for $n = 0, 1, 2, 3, \ldots 10$.

Spreadsheets are ideally suited to making repetitive calculations of this type. Figure 15–10 shows a Quattro Pro spreadsheet that implements the required calculations. Column A gives the index n and column B gives the corresponding frequencies in Hz. The input amplitudes in column C are calculated using Eq. (15–17), while the entries in column D are based on Eq. (15–18). Finally, the entries in column E are the product of those in columns C and D. Since the lowpass filter has unity gain at zero frequency, the dc components in the input and output are equal. The first nonzero ac component is the second harmonic, which has an amplitude of 10 V in the input but less than 1 V in the output. By the time we get to the next nonzero harmonic at 240 Hz, the ac amplitudes in the output are entirely negligible. ■

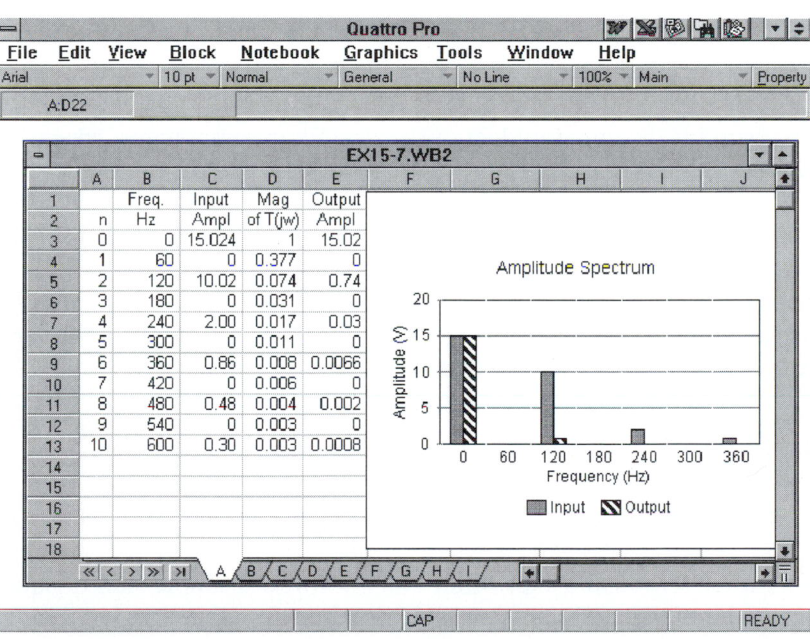

n	Freq. Hz	Input Ampl	Mag of T(jw)	Output Ampl
0	0	15.024	1	15.02
1	60	0	0.377	0
2	120	10.02	0.074	0.74
3	180	0	0.031	0
4	240	2.00	0.017	0.03
5	300	0	0.011	0
6	360	0.86	0.008	0.0066
7	420	0	0.006	0
8	480	0.48	0.004	0.002
9	540	0	0.003	0
10	600	0.30	0.003	0.0008

FIGURE 15–10

Exercise 15–5

Derive an expression for the first three nonzero terms in the Fourier series of the steady-state output voltage in Example 15–7.

Answer:

$v_O(t) = 15.02 + 0.736\cos(2\pi\, 120t + 21.5°) + 0.0349\cos(2\pi\, 240t + 10.6°)$ V

15–5 RMS VALUE AND AVERAGE POWER

In Chapter 5 we introduced the rms value of a periodic waveform as a descriptor of the average power carried by a signal. In this section we relate the rms value of the waveform to the amplitudes of the dc and ac components in its Fourier series. The rms value of a periodic waveform is defined as

$$F_{\text{rms}} = \sqrt{\frac{1}{T_0}\int_0^{T_0}[f(t)]^2\,dt} \qquad (15\text{–}19)$$

The waveform $f(t)$ can be expressed as a Fourier series of the form

$$f(t) = A_0 + \sum_{n=1}^{\infty} A_n \cos(n\omega_0 t + \phi_n)$$

Substituting this expression into Eq. (15–19), we can write F^2rms as

$$F^2_{\text{rms}} = \frac{1}{T_0}\int_0^{T_0}\left[A_0 + \sum_{n=1}^{\infty} A_n \cos(n\omega_0 t + \phi_n)\right]^2 dt \qquad (15\text{–}20)$$

Squaring and expanding the integrand on the right side of this equation produces three types of terms. The first is the square of the dc component:

$$\frac{1}{T_0}\int_0^{T_0}[A_0]^2\,dt = A_0^2 \qquad (15\text{–}21)$$

The second is the cross product of the dc and ac components, which takes the form

$$\frac{1}{T_0}\sum_{n=1}^{\infty} 2A_0\int_0^{T_0} A_n \cos(n\omega_0 t + \phi_n)dt = 0 \qquad (15\text{–}22)$$

These terms all vanish because they involve integrals of sinusoids over an integer number of cycles. The third and final type of term is the square of the ac components, which can be written as

$$\frac{1}{T_0}\sum_{n=1}^{\infty}\sum_{m=1}^{\infty}\int_0^{T_0} A_n \cos(n\omega_0 t + \phi_n)A_m \cos(m\omega_0 t + \phi_m)dt = \frac{1}{2}\sum_{n=1}^{\infty} A_n^2 \qquad (15\text{–}23)$$

This rather formidable expression boils down to a simple sum of squares because all of the integrals vanish except when $m = n$.

Combining Eqs. (15–19) through (15–23), we obtain the rms value as

$$F_{\text{rms}} = \sqrt{A_0^2 + \sum_{n=1}^{\infty}\frac{A_n^2}{2}}$$

$$= \sqrt{A_0^2 + \sum_{n=1}^{\infty}\left(\frac{A_n}{\sqrt{2}}\right)^2} \qquad (15\text{–}24)$$

Since the rms value of a sinusoid of amplitude A is $A/\sqrt{2}$, we conclude that

The rms value of a periodic waveform is equal to the square root of the sum of the square of the dc value and the square of the rms value of each of the ac components.

In Chapter 5 we found that the average power delivered to a resistor is related to its rms voltage or current as

$$P = \frac{V_{\text{rms}}^2}{R} = I_{\text{rms}}^2 R$$

Combining these expressions with the result in Eq. (15–24), we can write the average power delivered by a periodic waveform to the average power delivered by each of its Fourier components:

$$P = \frac{V_0^2}{R} + \sum_{n=1}^{\infty} \frac{V_n^2}{2R} = I_0^2 R + \sum_{n=1}^{\infty} \frac{I_n^2}{2} R$$

$$= P_0 + \sum_{n=1}^{\infty} P_n \qquad (15\text{–}25)$$

where P_0 is the average power delivered by the dc component and P_n is the average power delivered by the nth ac component. This additive feature is important because it means we can find the total average power by adding the average power carried by the dc plus that carried by each of the ac component.

Caution: In general, we cannot find the total power by adding the power delivered by each component acting alone because the superposition principle does not apply to power. However, the average power carried by harmonic sinusoids is additive because they belong to a special class call orthogonal signals.

EXAMPLE 15–8

Derive an expression for the average power delivered to a resistor by a sawtooth voltage of amplitude V_A and period T_0. Then calculate the fraction of the average power carried by the dc component plus the first three ac components.

SOLUTION:

An equation for the sawtooth voltage is $v(t) = V_A t/T_0$ for the range $0 < t < T_0$. The square of the rms value of a sawtooth is

$$V_{\text{rms}}^2 = \frac{1}{T_0}\int_0^{T_0}\left(\frac{V_A t}{T_0}\right)^2 dt = V_A^2\left[\frac{t^3}{3T_0^3}\right]_0^{T_0} = \frac{V_A^2}{3}$$

The average power delivered to a resistor is

$$P = \frac{V_{\text{rms}}^2}{R} = \frac{V_A^2}{3R} = 0.333\,\frac{V_A^2}{R}$$

This result is obtained directly from the sawtooth waveform without having to sum an infinite series. The same answer could be obtained by summing an infinite series. The question this example asks is, How much of the average power is carried by the first four components in the Fourier series of the sawtooth wave? The amplitude spectrum of the sawtooth wave (see Example 15–4) is

$$V_n = \begin{cases} \dfrac{V_A}{2} & n = 0 \\ \dfrac{V_A}{n\pi} & n > 0 \end{cases}$$

From Eq. (15–25) the average power in terms of amplitude spectrum is

$$P = \frac{(V_A/2)^2}{R} + \sum_{n=1}^{\infty} \frac{(V_A/n\pi)^2}{2R}$$

which can be arranged in the form

$$P = \frac{V_A^2}{R}\left\{\underbrace{\underbrace{\frac{1}{(2)^2} + \frac{1}{2(\pi)^2} + \frac{1}{2(2\pi)^2} + \frac{1}{2(3\pi)^2}}_{0.319(96\%)} + \frac{1}{2(4\pi)^2} + \dots}_{0.333}\right\}$$

The infinite series within the braces must sum to 0.333 to match the average power we calculated directly from the waveform itself. The dc component plus the first three ac terms contribute 0.319 to the infinite sum. In other words, these four components alone deliver 96% of the average power carried by the sawtooth wave. ■

EXAMPLE 15–9

Calculate the average power delivered to the 50-Ω resistor in Example 15–6.

SOLUTION:

In Example 15–6 we calculated the Fourier series of the current in a series *RL* circuit that was driven by a sawtooth voltage. We cannot directly calculate the average power carried by the current because we do not have a closed-form expression for the current. In this case we must use a truncated series to estimate the average power. The Mathcad worksheet in Figure 15–11 is a modified version of the worksheet used in Example 15–6. The first two lines define the input waveform and the circuit parameters while the third line gives the amplitude spectrum of the current as found in Example 15–6. The fourth line of Figure 15–11 defines a summation for a truncated average power $P(k)$ that includes the average power carried by the dc component plus the contributions of the first k ac components. The question is, How many harmonics must we include to obtain a reasonable approximation? The fifth line defines a function $\Delta(k)$ that calculates the percentage change in average power $P(k)$ resulting from adding the contribution of the kth harmonic. The result $\Delta(2) = 0.913$ means that adding the second harmonic changes the truncated average power by less than 1%. Likewise, $\Delta(5) = 0.028$ means that adding the fifth harmonic changes the truncated average power by less than 0.03%. Clearly, $P(5) = 3.48$ W is a reasonable approximation. ■

Mathcad PLUS - [EX15-9.MCD]

File Edit Text Math Graphics Symbolic Window Books Help

Example 15-9 $V_A := 25 \quad T_0 := 5 \cdot 10^{-6} \quad \omega_0 := 2 \cdot \frac{\pi}{T_0}$ <---Waveform Parameters

$n := 1, 2 .. 20 \quad L := 40 \cdot 10^{-6} \quad R := 50$ <---Circuit Parameters

$I_0 := \frac{V_A}{2 \cdot R} \quad I_n := \frac{V_A}{R} \cdot \frac{1}{n \cdot \pi \cdot \sqrt{1 + \left(n \cdot \omega_0 \cdot L \cdot R^{-1}\right)^2}}$ <---Amplitude Spectrum

$P(k) := \left(I_0\right)^2 \cdot R + \sum_{m=1}^{k} \frac{\left(I_m\right)^2}{2} \cdot R$ <---Truncated Average Power

$\Delta(k) := \frac{P(k) - P(k-1)}{P(k-1)} \cdot 100 \quad \Delta(2) = 0.913 \quad \Delta(5) = 0.028$ <---Percent Change

$P(5) = 3.48$ <----Estimated Average Power

auto Page 1

FIGURE 15–11

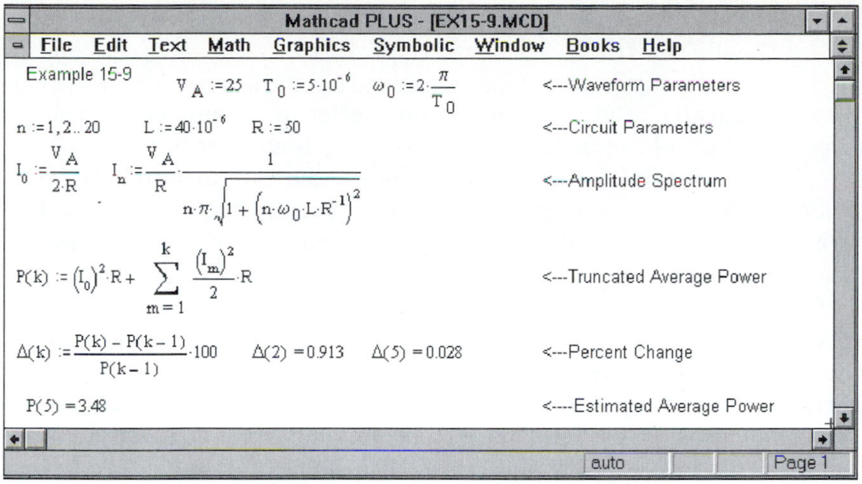

APPLICATION NOTE: EXAMPLE 15–10

When a pure sinewave is applied at the input of a linear circuit, the steady-state output will be a sinusoid of the same frequency as the input. When the circuit is nonlinear the output can be a distorted version of the input sinusoid. For typical nonlinearities, the output will still be a periodic waveform at the same fundamental frequency as the input. If the input is the sinusoid

$$x(t) = X_A \cos \omega_0 t$$

then the steady-state output can be represented by a Fourier series of the form

$$y(t) = Y_0 + Y_1 \cos(\omega_0 t + \phi_1) + Y_2 \cos(2\omega_0 t + \phi_2) + \ldots + Y_n \cos(n\omega_0 t + \phi_n) + \ldots$$

Note that the input contains a single frequency, whereas the output contains a multiplicity of frequencies.

Under sinusoidal excitation the output of a nonlinear circuit will contain harmonic frequencies that are not present in the input. Active devices like transistors and OP AMPs are slightly nonlinear even in their "linear" operating modes. Hence different harmonics can appear in the output of an active circuit that is nominally linear. These harmonics represent distortion of the desired output signal. The quality of a quasi-linear amplifier is indicated by the amount of harmonic distortion present when a pure sinusoid is applied at its input. The **total harmonic distortion (THD)** is defined to be the ratio of the rms value of the harmonic components to the amplitude of the fundamental component.

$$\text{THD} = \frac{\sqrt{Y_2^2 + Y_3^2 + \ldots + Y_n^2 + \ldots}}{|Y_1|}$$

For nonlinearities of interest, the infinite series in the numerator converges rapidly and can be truncated after a small number of terms. For any given device the harmonic distortion in the output normally increases as the output power increases. Consequently, the output power capabilities are specified in terms of the available power at a given harmonic distortion.

Total harmonic distortion is measured in the laboratory using a spectrum analyzer to detect the harmonics in the output. This type of testing requires a very pure sinusoidal source to avoid introducing harmonics at the input to the amplifier under test. Circuit simulation programs such as MicroSim PSpice can perform Fourier analysis to calculate the harmonics in the nonsinusoidal output of the simulated nonlinear circuit. This type of analysis may require long simulation times since a transient analysis run must be long enough for the circuit to reach a periodic steady-state condition. ■

Exercise 15–6

The full-wave rectified sine in Figure 15–3 has an rms value of $A/\sqrt{2}$. What fraction of the average power that the waveform delivers to a resistor is carried by the first two nonzero terms in its Fourier series?

Answer: $88/9\pi^2 = 99.07\%$

15–6 THE EXPONENTIAL FOURIER SERIES

The trigonometric form of the Fourier series of $f(t)$ is written in the form

$$f(t) = a_0 + \sum_{n=1}^{\infty} a_n \cos n\omega_0 t + b_n \sin n\omega_0 t \tag{15–26}$$

An equivalent way to write the series is the exponential form

$$f(t) = \sum_{n=-\infty}^{\infty} c_n e^{jn\omega_0 t} \tag{15–27}$$

In this form the summation extends over both positive ($n > 0$) and negative ($n < 0$) frequencies $n\omega_0$. The exponential form compactly describes the Fourier series in terms of a single complex parameter c_n defined as

$$c_n = \frac{a_n - jb_n}{2} \tag{15–28}$$

Our first task is to show that Eqs. (15–26) and (15–27) are equivalent. We begin with the exponential representation of the cosine and sine functions:

$$\cos n\omega_0 t = \frac{e^{jn\omega_0 t} + e^{-jn\omega_0 t}}{2}$$

$$\sin n\omega_0 t = \frac{e^{jn\omega_0 t} - e^{-jn\omega_0 t}}{j2} \qquad (15\text{–}29)$$

Substituting these expressions into Eq. (15–3) and using the definition in Eq. (15–28), we can relate c_n to $f(t)$ as

$$\begin{aligned} c_n &= \frac{1}{2}\left[\frac{2}{T_0}\int_{-T_0/2}^{T_0/2} f(t)\frac{e^{jn\omega_0 t} + e^{-jn\omega_0 t}}{2}dt - j\frac{2}{T_0}\int_{-T_0/2}^{T_0/2} f(t)\frac{e^{jn\omega_0 t} - e^{-jn\omega_0 t}}{j2}dt\right] \\ &= \frac{1}{2T_0}\left[\int_{-T_0/2}^{T_0/2} (f(t)e^{jn\omega_0 t} + f(t)e^{-jn\omega_0 t} - f(t)e^{jn\omega_0 t} + f(t)e^{-jn\omega_0 t})dt\right] \\ &= \frac{1}{T_0}\int_{-T_0/2}^{T_0/2} f(t)e^{-jn\omega_0 t}\,dt \qquad (15\text{–}30) \end{aligned}$$

Substituting Eq (15–29) into Eq. (15–26) and grouping the factors involving like exponential terms produces

$$\begin{aligned} f(t) &= a_0 + \sum_{n=1}^{\infty}\left(\frac{a_n - jb_n}{2}\right)e^{jn\omega_0 t} + \sum_{n=1}^{\infty}\left(\frac{a_n + jb_n}{2}\right)e^{-jn\omega_0 t} \\ &= a_0 + \sum_{n=1}^{\infty} c_n e^{jn\omega_0 t} + \sum_{n=1}^{\infty} c_n^* e^{-jn\omega_0 t} \qquad (15\text{–}31) \end{aligned}$$

The last line in Eq. (15–30) points out that $a_0 = c_0$ and that $c_n^* = c_{-n}$ (c_n with n replaced by $-n$). Hence the second line in Eq. (15–31) can be written as

$$f(t) = \sum_{n=0}^{\infty} c_n e^{jn\omega_0 t} + \sum_{n=1}^{\infty} c_{-n} e^{-jn\omega_0 t}$$

The second summation in this result, which runs from $n = 1$ to ∞, is unchanged when c_{-n} is replaced by c_n and the summation runs from $n = -\infty$ to $n = -1$, in which case the expression for $f(t)$ takes the form

$$\begin{aligned} f(t) &= \sum_{n=0}^{\infty} c_n e^{jn\omega_0 t} + \sum_{n=-\infty}^{-1} c_n e^{jn\omega_0 t} \\ &= \sum_{n=-\infty}^{\infty} c_n e^{jn\omega_0 t} \end{aligned}$$

which is the result given in Eq. (15–27).

This completes the development of the exponential Fourier series. Summarizing the main results, the exponential form of the Fourier series is

$$f(t) = \sum_{n=-\infty}^{\infty} c_n e^{jn\omega_0 t} \qquad (15\text{–}32)$$

where the complex coefficients c_n are obtained from the periodic waveform $f(t)$ by the equation

$$c_n = \frac{1}{T_0}\int_{-T_0/2}^{T_0/2} f(t)e^{-jn\omega_0 t}\,dt \qquad (15\text{–}33)$$

Written in this way the exponential form highlights the basic elements of the Fourier series as a waveform transformation. We think of Eq. (15–33) as the direct transformation that converts a periodic waveform $f(t)$ into a complex spectrum c_n. Conversely, we think of Eq. (15–32) as the inverse transformation that converts the spectrum c_n into the periodic waveform $f(t)$.

The exponential form yields a discrete spectrum since it contains components only at the discrete harmonics $n\omega_0$. We call it a two-sided spectrum because both positive and negative frequencies are included; that is, $n = 0, \pm 1, \pm 2, \pm 3, \ldots$. The magnitude and angle of c_n are related to the Fourier coefficients by

$$|c_n| = \frac{A_n}{2} = \frac{\sqrt{a_n^2 + b_n^2}}{2} \quad \text{and} \quad \angle c_n = \phi_n = \tan^{-1}(-b_n/a_n) \qquad (15\text{–}34)$$

Thus, $|c_n|$ is the two-sided amplitude spectrum and $\angle c_n$ is the two-sided phase spectrum of the periodic waveform $f(t)$.

When given the Fourier coefficients a_n and b_n of a waveform, we use the definition in Eq. (15–28) to determine c_n. Given a periodic waveform $f(t)$, we use Eq. (15–33). Both methods are illustrated in the following example.

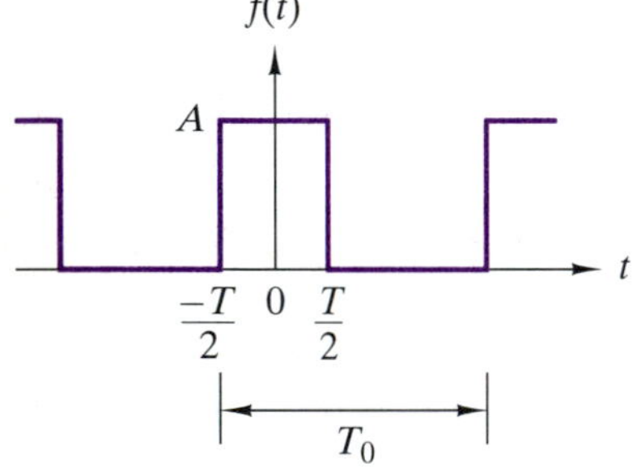

FIGURE 15–12

EXAMPLE 15–11

Given the periodic pulse train in Figure 15–12,

(a) Find the coefficient c_n using Eq. (15–33).
(b) Find the coefficient c_n using the definition in Eq. (15–28) and the expressions for a_n and b_n from Figure 15–3.
(c) Sketch the two-sided amplitude spectrum $|c_n|$ of the signal.

SOLUTION:

(a) In Figure 15–12 the cycle centered at the origin ($t = 0$) has zero amplitude except on the range $-T/2 \le t \le +T/2$. The integration in Eq. (15–33) takes the form

$$c_n = \frac{1}{T_0}\int_{-T/2}^{T/2} Ae^{-jn\omega_0 t}\,dt = \left[\frac{A}{T_0}\right]\frac{e^{-jn\omega_0 t}}{-jn\omega_0}\Bigg|_{-T/2}^{T/2}$$
$$= \frac{2A}{n\omega_0 T_0}\left[\frac{e^{jn\omega_0 T/2} - e^{-jn\omega_0 T/2}}{j2}\right]$$
$$= \frac{2A}{T_0}\,\frac{\sin(n\omega_0 T/2)}{n\omega_0}$$

For this waveform the imaginary part of $c_n = (a_n - jb_n)/2$ is zero, since the pulse train in Figure 15–12 has even symmetry.

It is convenient to write c_n in the form of the function $(\sin x)/x$. Multiplying and dividing the right side of the expression for c_n by T and rearranging terms yields

$$c_n = \frac{AT}{T_0}\left[\frac{\sin(n\omega_0 T/2)}{(n\omega_0 T/2)}\right]$$

(b) Figure 15–3 gives the Fourier coefficients a_n and b_n of the pulse train as

$$a_n = \frac{2A}{n\pi}\sin(n\pi T/T_0) \text{ and } b_n = 0$$

Since $b_n = 0$ the definition of c_n in Eq. (15–28) yields

$$c_n = \frac{A}{n\pi}\sin(n\pi T/T_0)$$

This expression can be put in the form (sin x)/x by rearranging terms as

$$n\pi T/T_0 = n\frac{2\pi}{T_0}T/2 = n\omega_0 T/2$$

and

$$\frac{A}{n\pi}\frac{T/T_0}{T/T_0} = \frac{AT}{T_0}\frac{1}{n\dfrac{2\pi}{T_0}T/2} = \frac{AT}{T_0}\frac{1}{n\omega_0 T/2}$$

producing

$$c_n = \frac{AT}{T_0}\left[\frac{\sin(n\omega_0 T/2)}{(n\omega_0 T/2)}\right]$$

which is the same result found in (a).

(c) Figure 15–13 shows a plot of $|c_n|$ versus angular frequency ω for $T = T_0/4$. The spacing between lines in the spectrum is the fundamental frequency ω_0. The envelope of the amplitude spectrum is defined by a function of the form $K|(\sin x)/x|$, where $x = \omega T/2$. Evaluating (sin x)/x at $x = 0$ yields the indeterminant form 0/0. Applying l'Hôpital's rule shows that (sin x)/x = 1 at x = 0. The maximum value of the spectral

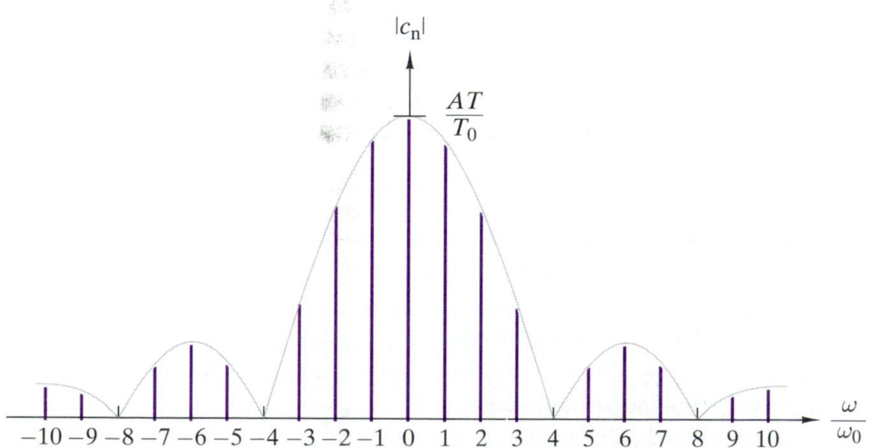

FIGURE 15–13

envelope occurs at $\omega = 0$ and is $K = AT/T_0$. The null values in the envelope of $|c_n|$ occur when $\sin x = 0$. These nulls occur when $x = m\pi$ ($m = \pm 1, \pm 2, \ldots$) or at frequencies $\omega = \pm 2\pi m/T$. ■

Exercise 15–7

Find c_n for the square wave in Figure 15–3.

Answer: $c_n = -jA(1 - \cos n\pi)/(n\pi)$

SUMMARY

- The Fourier series resolves a periodic waveform into a dc component plus an ac component containing an infinite sum of harmonic sinusoids. The dc component is equal to the average value of the waveform. The amplitudes of the sine and cosine terms in the ac component are called Fourier coefficients.
- The fundamental frequency of the ac component is determined by the period T_0 of the waveform ($f_0 = 1/T_0$). The harmonic frequencies in the ac component are integer multiples of the fundamental frequency.
- Waveform symmetries cause the amplitudes of some terms in a Fourier series to be zero. Even symmetry causes all of the sine terms in the ac component to be zero. Odd symmetry causes all of the cosine terms to be zero. Half-wave symmetry causes all of the even harmonics to be zero.
- An alternative form of the Fourier series represents each harmonic in the ac component by its amplitude and phase angle. A plot of amplitudes versus frequency is called the amplitude spectrum. A plot of phase angles versus frequency is called the phase spectrum. A periodic waveform has spectral components at the discrete frequencies present in its Fourier series.
- The steady-state response of a linear circuit for a periodic driving force can be found by first finding the steady-state response due each term in the Fourier series of the input. The Fourier series of the steady-state response is then found by adding (superposing) responses due to each term acting alone. The individual responses can be found using either phasor or s-domain analysis.
- The rms value of a periodic waveform is equal to the square root of the sum of the square of the dc value and the square of the rms value of each of the ac components. The average power delivered by a periodic waveform is equal to the average power delivered by the dc component plus the sum of average powers delivered by each of the ac components.
- The exponential Fourier series is an alternate form that expresses a periodic waveform as an infinite sum of complex exponentials at positive and negative harmonic frequencies. The exponential form leads to two-sided amplitude and phase spectra.

EN ROUTE OBJECTIVES AND ASSOCIATED PROBLEMS

ERO 15–1 THE FOURIER SERIES (SECTS. 15–1, 15–2, 15–3)

(a) Given an equation or graph of a periodic waveform, find its Fourier coefficients.
(b) Construct a periodic waveform whose Fourier coefficients have prescribed characteristics.
(c) Derive properties of the Fourier series.

15–1 Verify the expressions in Figure 15–3 for the Fourier coefficients of the rectangular pulse train.

15–2 Verify the expressions in Figure 15–3 for the Fourier coefficients of the triangular wave.

15–3 Verify the expressions in Figure 15–3 for the Fourier coefficients of the full-wave rectified sine wave.

15–4 The full-wave rectified sine wave in Figure 15–3 has an amplitude of 250 V and a fundamental frequency of 60 Hz. Write an expression for the first four nonzero terms in the Fourier series and plot the amplitude spectrum of the signal.

15–5 A composite waveform is formed by summing 5-V dc and a 1-kHz square wave with a peak-to-peak amplitude of 5 V. Write an expression for the first four nonzero terms in the Fourier series and plot the amplitude spectrum of the signal.

15–6 The parabolic wave in Figure 15–3 has a peak-to-peak amplitude of 30 V and a fundamental frequency of 500 Hz. Write an expression for the first four nonzero terms in the Fourier series and plot the amplitude spectrum of the signal.

15–7 The equation for the first cycle ($0 \le t \le T_0$) of a periodic waveform is $v(t) = V_A(t/T_0 - 1)$.

(a) Sketch the first two cycles of the waveform.
(b) Derive expressions for the Fourier coefficients for a_n and b_n.

15–8 The equation for the first cycle ($0 \le t \le T_0$) of a periodic pulse train is

$$v(t) = V_A[u(4t - T_0) - u(4t - 3T_0)]$$

(a) Sketch the first two cycles of the waveform.
(b) Derive expressions for the Fourier coefficients for a_n and b_n.

15–9 Find the Fourier coefficients for the periodic waveform in Figure P15–9.

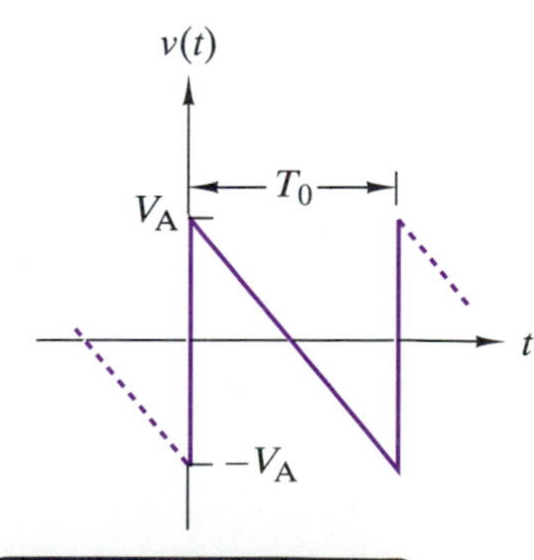

FIGURE P15–9

15–10 Given the Fourier coefficients of the rectangular pulse train $f(t)$ in Figure 15–3, find the Fourier coefficients when the waveform is shifted by a quarter of a cycle. That is, find the Fourier coefficients of the periodic waveform $g(t) = f(t - T_0/4)$.

15–11 Given the Fourier coefficients of the triangular wave $f(t)$ in Figure 15–3, find the Fourier coefficients when the waveform is shifted by a quarter of a cycle. That is, find the Fourier coefficients of the periodic waveform $g(t) = f(t - T_0/4)$.

15–12 The four terms in the Fourier series of a periodic signal are

$$v(t) = 25\left[\sin(200t) - \frac{1}{9}\sin(600t) + \frac{1}{25}\sin(1000t) - \frac{1}{49}\sin(1400t) + \ldots\right]$$

(a) Find the fundamental frequency in rad/s and Hz. Find the period.
(b) Does the waveform have even or odd symmetry?
(c) Plot the waveform using the foregoing truncated series to confirm your answer in (b). Can you identify the waveform from this plot?

15–13 The four terms in the Fourier series of a periodic signal are

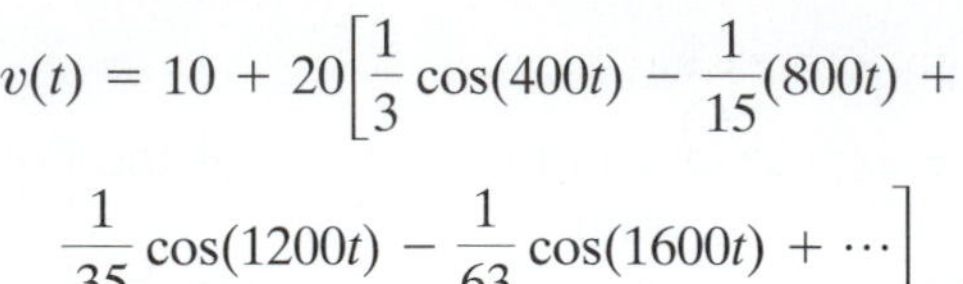

$$v(t) = 10 + 20\left[\frac{1}{3}\cos(400t) - \frac{1}{15}(800t) + \frac{1}{35}\cos(1200t) - \frac{1}{63}\cos(1600t) + \cdots\right]$$

(a) Find the fundamental frequency in rad/s and Hz. Find the period.
(b) Does the waveform have even or odd symmetry?
(c) Plot the waveform using the foregoing truncated series to confirm your answer in (b). Can you identify the waveform from this plot?

15–14 Derive the expression for b_n in Eq. (15–3). *Suggestion:* The text gives the derivation of the expression for a_n. Review this derivation and follow the hint given at the end of the derivation.

15–15 The periodic waveform $f(t)$ has Fourier coefficients a_n and b_n. Derive expressions relating the Fourier coefficients of the periodic waveform $f(-t)$ to a_n and b_n. *Hint:* Write down all of the expressions in Eq. (15–3) and replace $f(t)$ by $f(-t)$.

ERO 15–2 FOURIER SERIES AND CIRCUIT ANALYSIS (SECT. 15–4)

Given a linear circuit with a periodic input waveform, find the Fourier series representation of the steady-state response.

15–16 The periodic pulse train in Figure P15–16 is applied to the *RL* circuit shown in the figure.
(a) Derive an expression for the Fourier series of the steady-state output voltage $v_O(t)$.
(b) Write the first four nonzero terms in the Fourier series for $v_O(t)$ when $V_A = 125$ V, $T_0 = \pi/2$ ms, $T = T_0/2$, $R = 200\ \Omega$, and $L = 100$ mH.

FIGURE P15–16

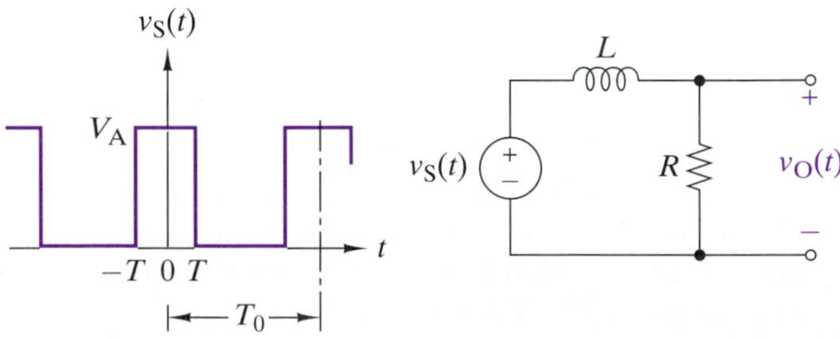

15–17 The periodic triangular wave in Figure P15–17 is applied to the *RC* circuit shown in the figure. The Fourier coefficients of the input are

$$a_0 = a_n = 0 \quad \text{all } n$$

$$b_n = 0 \quad n \text{ even}$$

$$b_n = \frac{8V_A}{(n\pi)^2} \sin\left(n\frac{\pi}{2}\right) \quad n \text{ odd}$$

(a) Derive an expression for the Fourier series of the steady-state output voltage $v_O(t)$.

(b) Write the first four nonzero terms in the Fourier series for $v_O(t)$ when $V_A = 15$ V, $T_0 = 20\pi$ μs, $R = 10$ kΩ, and $C = 500$ pF.

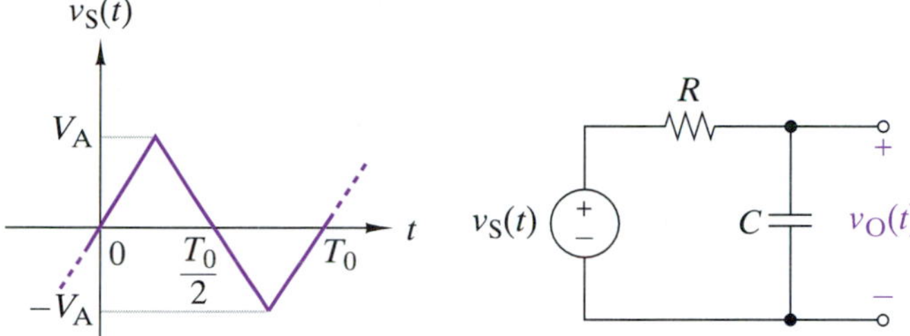

FIGURE P15–17

15–18 The periodic sawtooth wave in Figure P15–18 drives the OP AMP circuit shown in the figure.

(a) Derive an expression for the Fourier series of the steady-state output voltage $v_O(t)$.

(b) Write the first four nonzero terms in the Fourier series for $v_O(t)$ when $V_A = 5$ V, $T_0 = 400\pi$ μs, $R_1 = 10$ kΩ, $R_2 = 50$ kΩ, and $C = 200$ nF.

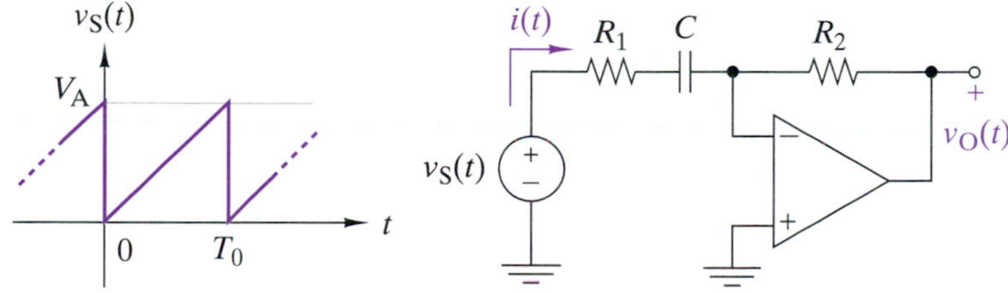

FIGURE P15–18

15–19 The periodic sawtooth wave in Figure P15–18 drives the OP AMP circuit shown in the figure.

(a) Derive an expression for the Fourier series of the steady-state input current $i(t)$.

(b) Write the first four nonzero terms in the Fourier series for $i(t)$ when $V_A = 4$ V, $T_0 = 800\pi$ μs, $R_1 = 10$ kΩ, $R_2 = 50$ kΩ, and $C = 400$ nF.

15–20 The periodic triangular wave in Figure P15–20 is applied to the *RLC* circuit shown in the figure. The Fourier coefficients of the input are

$$a_0 = a_n = 0 \qquad \text{all } n$$

$$b_n = 0 \qquad n \text{ even}$$

$$b_n = \frac{8V_A}{(n\pi)^2}\sin\left(n\frac{\pi}{2}\right) \qquad n \text{ odd}$$

(a) Derive an expression for the Fourier series of the steady-state current $i(t)$.

(b) Write the first four nonzero terms in the Fourier series for $v_O(t)$ when $V_A = 1\text{V}$, $T_0 = 10\pi$ μs, $R = 10\ \Omega$, $L = 2$ mH, and $C = 800$ nF.

(c) What term in the Fourier series tends to dominate the response? Explain.

FIGURE P15–20

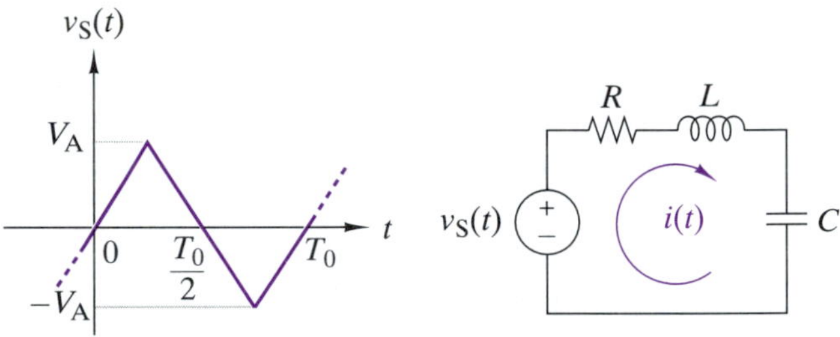

15–21 The parabolic wave in Figure 15–3 with $V_A = 10$ V and $T_0 = 20\pi$ ms drives a circuit with a transfer function $T(s) = 200/(s + 200)$. Find the amplitude of the first four nonzero terms in the Fourier series of the steady-state output. What term in the Fourier series tends to dominate the response? Explain.

15–22 The sawtooth wave in Figure 15–3 with $V_A = 12$ V and $T_0 = 10\pi$ ms drives a circuit with a transfer function $T(s) = s/(s + 10)$. Find the first four nonzero terms in the Fourier series of the input and steady-state output. Sketch the output waveform.

15–23 The half-wave rectified sine in Figure 15–3 with $V_A = 8$ V and $T_0 = 2\pi$ ms drives a circuit with a transfer function $T(s) = 10s/(s^2 + 10s + 10^6)$. Find the first four nonzero terms in the Fourier series of the input and steady-state output. Sketch the output waveform.

15–24 A square wave with $V_A = 5\pi$ V and $T_0 = 20\pi$ ms drives a first-order filter with unity passband gain. The amplitudes of the first four ac components in the steady-state output voltage are observed to be 19.4 V at ω_0, 5.33 V at $3\omega_0$, 2.5 V at $5\omega_0$, and 1.42 V at $7\omega_0$. Is the filter high pass or low pass? Estimate the cutoff frequency of the filter.

15–25 A square wave with $V_A = 5\pi$ V and $T_0 = 20\pi$ ms drives a first-order filter with unity passband gain. The amplitudes of the first four ac components in the steady-state output voltage are observed to be 5.49 V at ω_0, 4.34 V at $3\omega_0$, 3.28 V at $5\omega_0$, and 2.56 V at $7\omega_0$. Is the filter high pass or low pass? Estimate the cutoff frequency of the filter.

ERO 15–3 RMS VALUE AND AVERAGE POWER (SECT. 15–5)

Given a periodic input waveform, find the fraction of the average power carried by specified components and average power delivered to a specified load in a linear circuit.

15–26 Find the rms value of the square wave in Figure 15–3 and write an expression for the total average power the square wave delivers to a resistor R. What fraction of the total average power is carried by the first three nonzero harmonics in the square wave?

15–27 Find the rms value of the triangular wave in Figure 15–3 and write an expression for the total average power the square wave delivers to a resistor R. What fraction of the total average power is carried by the first three nonzero harmonics in the square wave?

15–28 Find the rms value of the full-wave rectified sine in Figure 15–3 and write an expression for the total average power the square wave delivers to a resistor R. What fraction of the total average power is carried by the first three nonzero harmonics in the square wave?

15–29 Find the rms value of the periodic waveform in Figure P15–29 and write an expression for the total average power the waveform delivers to a resistor R. Find the Fourier coefficients of the waveform. What fraction of the total average power is carried by dc component plus the first three nonzero ac components in the Fourier series of the waveform?

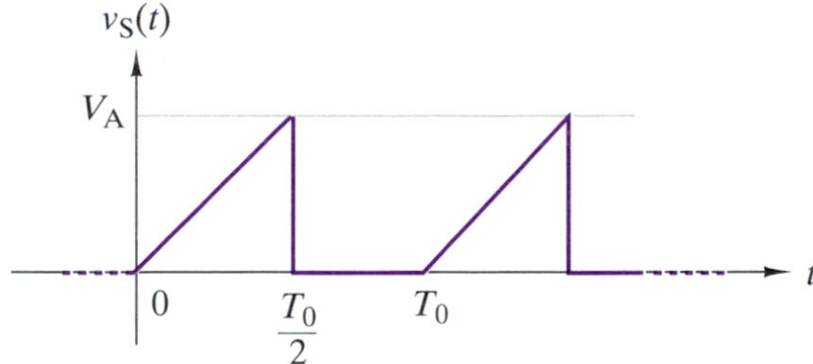

FIGURE P15–29

15–30 Find the rms value of the periodic waveform in Figure P15–30 and write an expression for the total average power the waveform delivers to a resistor R. Find the Fourier coefficients of the waveform. What fraction of the total average power is carried by dc component plus the first three nonzero ac components in the Fourier series of the waveform?

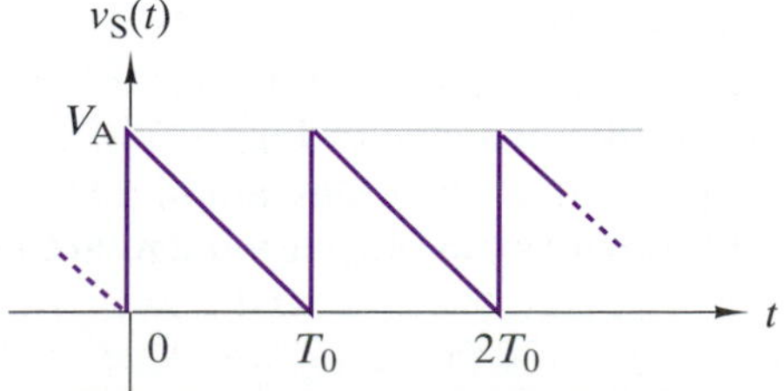

FIGURE P15–30

15–31 A low-pass filter has a cutoff frequency of 100 rad/s and a pass-band gain of 6 dB. The input to the filter is $v_1(t) = 30 \sin 200t + 10 \cos 600t$ V. Find the rms value of the steady-state output.

15–32 The Fourier series of a certain periodic function is

$$f(t) = V_A\left[\ln 2 + \sum_{n=1}^{\infty} \frac{1}{n} \cos n\omega_0 t\right]$$

Estimate the fraction of the total average power carried by the fundamental component. Repeat for the third harmonic.

15–33 The Fourier series of a certain periodic function is

$$f(t) = V_A\left[\frac{\pi^2}{12} - \cos \omega_0 t + \frac{1}{4}\cos 2\omega_0 t - \frac{1}{9}\cos 3\omega_0 t + \ldots\right]$$

Estimate the fraction of the average power carried by the dc component plus the fundamental component.

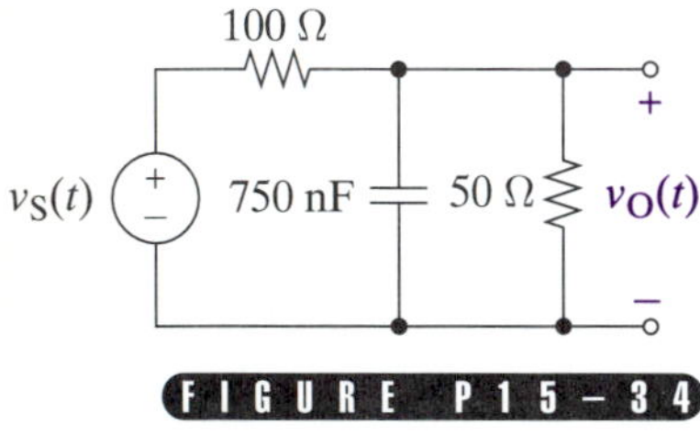

FIGURE P15–34

15–34 A square wave voltage with $V_A = 5$ V and $T_0 = 50\pi$ μs is applied at the input to the circuit in Figure P15–34. Calculate the average power delivered to the 50-Ω resistor.

15–35 A sawtooth voltage with $V_A = 4$ V and $T_0 = 50\pi$ μs is applied at the input to the circuit in Figure P15–34. Calculate the average power delivered to the 50-Ω resistor.

ERO 15–4 THE EXPONENTIAL FOURIER SERIES (SECT. 15–6)

Given an equation or graph or the Fourier coefficients of a periodic waveform, derive expressions for the coefficients of the exponential Fourier series and plot two-sided spectra.

15–36 Find the coefficients c_n of the exponential Fourier series for the following periodic waveforms:

(a) $f_1(t) = 12 + 8 \cos \omega_0 t + 6 \sin \omega_0 t + 2 \cos 2\omega_0 t + 5 \sin 4\omega_0 t$

(b) $f_2(t) = -5 \cos \omega_0 t + 6 \sin 3\omega_0 t - 8 \cos 3\omega_0 t + 2 \sin 5\omega_0 t$

15–37 Write the trigonometric Fourier series corresponding to the following exponential series:

$$f(t) = \sum_{n=-3}^{3} [(0.5)^{|n|}] \times [e^{jn\omega_0 t}]$$

15–38 Derive an expression for c_n of the exponential Fourier series representing the periodic waveform in Figure P15–29. Plot the two-sided amplitude and phase spectra of the signal.

15–39 Derive an expression for c_n of the exponential Fourier series representing the periodic waveform in Figure P15–30. Plot the two-sided amplitude and phase spectra of the signal.

15–40 Derive an expression for c_n of the exponential Fourier series representing the full-wave rectified sine in Figure 15–3. Sketch the two-sided amplitude and phase spectra of the signal.

15–41 The exponential Fourier series of a periodic waveform is

$$f(t) = \frac{-j2}{3}e^{-j45t} - je^{-j30t} - j2\,e^{-j15t} + 3 + j2e^{j15t} + je^{j30t} + \frac{j2}{3}e^{j45t}$$

(a) What is the period of the waveform?
(b) What is the rms value of the waveform?
(c) Does the waveform have even or odd symmetry?

15–42 The coefficients of a trigonometric Fourier series are

$$a_0 = 0 \quad a_n = 0 \quad b_n = \frac{8A}{(n\pi)^2}\sin\left(\frac{n\pi}{2}\right) \quad n = 1, 2, 3, \ldots$$

Derive an expression for the coefficients of the exponential Fourier series and sketch the two-sided amplitude and phase spectra.

15–43 The coefficients of a trigonometric Fourier series are

$$a_0 = 0 \quad a_n = \frac{4A}{(n\pi)^2}\sin\left(\frac{n\pi}{2}\right) \quad b_n = -\frac{2A}{\pi n}\sin\left(\frac{n\pi}{2}\right) \quad n = 1, 2, 3, \ldots$$

Derive an expression for the coefficients of the exponential Fourier series and sketch the amplitude and phase spectra.

15–44 The signal $f(t)$ has a periodic waveform with a fundamental frequency ω_0 and exponential Fourier series coefficients c_n, $n = 0, \pm1, \pm2, \ldots$ Derive an expression for the Fourier coefficients of the signal $g(t)$ in terms of c_n when
(a) $g(t) = f(t - T)$, where T is a real positive constant
(b) $g(t) = f(-t)$.

15–45 The signal $f(t)$ has a periodic waveform with a fundamental frequency ω_0 and exponential Fourier series coefficients c_n, $n = 0, \pm1, \pm2, \ldots$ Derive an expression for rms value of $f(t)$ in terms of c_n.

CHAPTER-INTEGRATING PROBLEMS

15–46 A FOURIER SERIES FROM A BODE PLOT

Figure P15–46 shows the straight-line Bode plots of the magnitude and phase angle of a transfer function. The circuit is driven by a sawtooth wave with $V_A = 10$ V and $T_0 = 20\pi$ ms.
(a) Write the first five terms in the Fourier series of the input.
(b) Use the straight-line Bode plot and the input Fourier series in (a) to obtain an approximation to the first five terms in the Fourier series of the steady-state output.
(c) Find the function $T(s)$ that matches the Bode plots shown in the figure. Use $T(j\omega)$ and the Fourier series of the input found in (a) to calculate the exact values of the first five terms of the Fourier series of the steady-state output.
(d) Compare your results in (b) and (c) and discuss the differences.

FIGURE P15–46

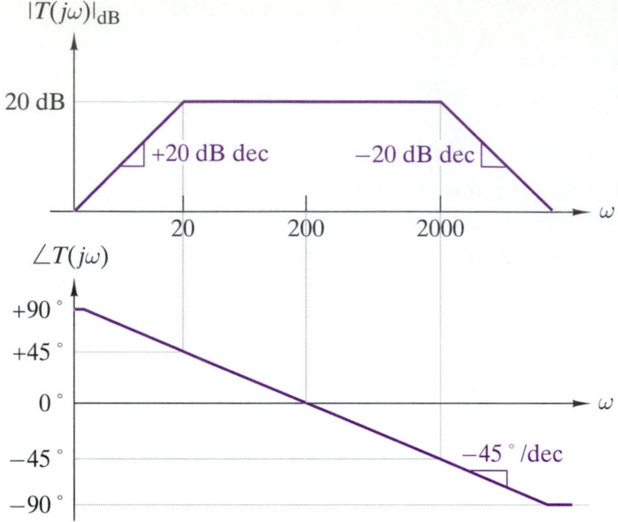

15–47 A STEADY-STATE RESPONSE FOR A PERIODIC IMPULSE TRAIN

A periodic impulse train can approximate a pulse train when the individual pulse durations are very short compared with the circuit response time. This example explores the response of a first-order circuit to a periodic impulse train. A linear circuit whose impulse response is

$$h(t) = \frac{1}{T_0} e^{-t/T_0} u(t)$$

is driven by a periodic impulse train

$$x(t) = T_0 \sum_{n=-\infty}^{\infty} \delta(t - nT_0)$$

(a) Use Eq. (15–3) to find the Fourier coefficients of $x(t)$. Write a general expression for the Fourier series of the input $x(t)$.

(b) Drive expressions for the Fourier coefficients of the steady-state output $y(t)$ when the input is the periodic impulse train $x(t)$.

(c) Write a general expression for the Fourier series of the steady-state output $y(t)$.

(d) Use a computer tool to generate a plot of a truncated Fourier series that gives a reasonable approximation of the steady-state response found in (c).

15–48 A ORTHOGONAL FUNCTIONS AND FOURIER COEFFICIENTS

Deriving closed form expressions for Fourier coefficients is greatly simplified by the orthogonality of the functions used in the Fourier series. The purpose of this problem is to use orthogonality to derive Eq. (15–33). The complex exponential $f_n(t) = \exp(j2n\pi t/T_0)$ is said to be orthogonal on the interval $-T_0/2 \leq t \leq - T_0/2$ if

$$\int_{-T_0/2}^{+T_0/2} f_n(t) f_m^*(t) dt = \begin{cases} = 0 \text{ for } n \neq m \\ = T_0 \text{ for } n = m \end{cases}$$

where $f_m^*(t) = \exp(-j2m\pi t/T_0)$ is the conjugate of

$$f_m(t) = \exp(j2m\pi t/T_0)$$

(a) Verify that the complex exponential is orthogonal on the stated interval.

(b) Multiply the exponential Fourier series

$$f(t) = \sum_{n=-\infty}^{\infty} c_n e^{j2n\pi/T_0}$$

by $e^{-j2m\pi t/T_0}$. Then integrate both sides over the interval $-T_0/2 \leq t \leq -T_0/2$ and use orthogonality to derive an equation for c_n.

(c) Compare your equation with Eq. (15–33). They should be the same.

15–49 A SLEW RATE DISTORTION

The rate of change of the output voltage of an OP AMP cannot exceed a maximum value called the **slew rate**. When an OP AMP is driven to its slew rate limit, the output becomes a ramp whose slope equals the slew rate limit. When a sinusoid drives an OP AMP to its slew rate limit, the output voltage becomes a periodic triangular wave whose fundamental frequency equals the frequency of the input. This nonlinear response causes harmonic distortion since the output contains harmonic frequencies that are not present in the input. When the input to an amplifier is a sinusoid, the total harmonic distortion (THD) in the output is defined as

$$\text{THD} = \frac{\sqrt{V_2^2 + V_3^2 + \ldots + V_n^2 + \ldots}}{V_1}$$

where V_1 is the amplitude of the fundamental frequency and $V_n (n = 2, 3, \ldots)$ is the amplitude of the nth harmonic in the output. Calculate the total harmonic distortion for slew rate limiting.

15–50 A ESTIMATING PERIODIC SIGNAL BANDWIDTHS

One way to define periodic signal bandwidth is to require the harmonics within the bandwidth to carry a specified fraction of the average power carried by the waveform. For a square wave, calculate the bandwidth required for the harmonics to carry 90%, 95%, and 98% of the average power carried by the waveform.

CHAPTER 16

FOURIER TRANSFORMS

I had become filled with the utmost admiration for the splendor and poetry of Fourier.

William Thomson, Lord Kelvin,
British Physicist

Fourier's claim that any periodic function could be represented by an infinite sum of harmonic sinusoids was a startling idea in the early nineteenth century. His notion that an aperiodic function could be described by an integral of sinusoids was even more surprising. Much of the credit for demonstrating the applications of these powerful tools belongs to Sir William Thomson (1824–1907). Like most natural philosophers of that era, Thomson had wide-ranging interests, and he published more than 600 papers in scientific journals. Those interests included the application of Fourier analysis to the problem of transmitting telegraph signals in transatlantic underseas cables. His research afforded him a clear understanding of the problem that allowed him to recommend cable characteristics and predict the signaling rate. He also invented a sensitive detector. While his efforts contributed greatly to one of the major technological advances of the nineteenth century, his enduring legacy is the wide range of application of Fourier methods in today's technology.

Why introduce another transform method when we already have Laplace transforms? There are several reasons. The analysis and design of many signal-processing functions involve signal and circuit models for which Fourier transforms exist and Laplace transforms do not. Fourier transforms lend themselves to computer software implementation far better than do Laplace transforms. As a result, digital signal processing is invariably based on Fourier transforms rather than Laplace transforms. Introducing Fourier transforms at this point serves as a bridge between the Laplace transform–based circuit analysis and design in earlier chapters and the Fourier transform–based signal-processing topics in subsequent courses.

The chapter is divided into three main topics. The first two sections define Fourier transforms and show their relationship to Laplace transforms. The next two sections derive basic transform pairs and the key mathematical properties of the Fourier transformation. The final three sections present applications of Fourier transforms in circuit and system analysis.

16–1 DEFINITION OF FOURIER TRANSFORMS

For periodic waveforms the Fourier series provides a frequency-domain description in terms of spectral lines at discrete harmonic frequencies. Aperiodic waveforms like the exponential or step function cannot be represented by a Fourier series. In some cases we can think of an aperiodic waveform as a limiting case of a periodic signal as the period becomes infinite. For instance, in Example 15–11 we found the line spectrum of a periodic pulse train to be

$$c_n = \frac{AT}{T_0}\left[\frac{\sin(n\omega_0 T/2)}{n\omega_0 T/2}\right]$$

Figure 16–1 shows how the amplitude spectrum $|c_n|$ changes with different values of the period T_0. As T_0 increases the envelope of the spectrum retains its $K|(\sin x)/x|$ form, but the height of the envelope ($K = AT/T_0$) decreases. Similarly, the spacing between spectral lines ($\omega_0 = 2\pi/T_0$) decreases. Ultimately, if we let T_0 approach infinity, we get a single aperiodic pulse whose spectral lines are so densely packed as to be indistinguishable.

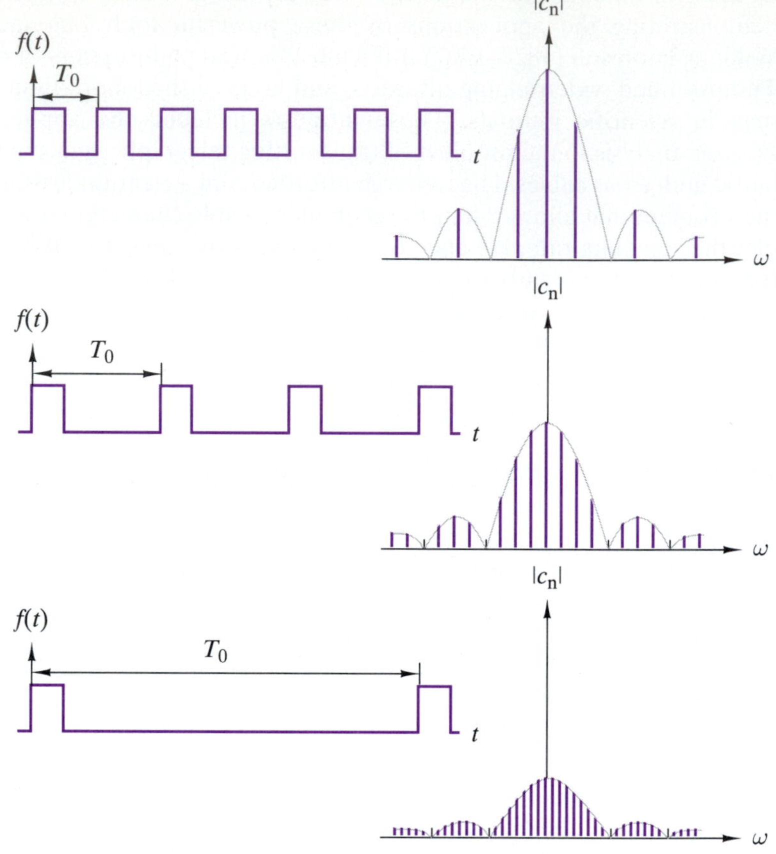

FIGURE 16–1 *Rectangular pulse train waveform and amplitude spectrum as the period increases.*

The Fourier transformation can be thought of as the result of applying the limiting condition $T_0 \to \infty$ to the exponential Fourier series. In Chapter 15 the defining equations for the exponential series were shown to be

$$f(t) = \sum_{n=-\infty}^{\infty} c_n e^{jn\omega_0 t} \tag{16–1a}$$

$$c_n = \frac{1}{T_0}\int_{-T_0/2}^{T_0/2} f(t)e^{-jn\omega_0 t}\,dt \tag{16–1b}$$

The periodic waveform $f(t)$ in Eq. (16–1a) is expressed as a sum of complex exponentials each weighted by a Fourier coefficient c_n. The Fourier coefficients describe the amplitude and phase spectra of the signal and are derived from $f(t)$ using Eq. (16–1b).

Inserting Eq. (16–1b) into (16–1a) expresses $f(t)$ in the form

$$\begin{aligned} f(t) &= \sum_{n=-\infty}^{\infty}\left[\frac{1}{T_0}\int_{-\infty}^{\infty} f(t)e^{-jn\omega_0 t}\,dt\right]e^{jn\omega_0 t} \\ &= \frac{1}{2\pi}\sum_{n=-\infty}^{\infty}\left[\int_{-\infty}^{\infty} f(t)e^{-jn\omega_0 t}\,dt\right]\omega_0 e^{jn\omega_0 t} \end{aligned} \tag{16–2}$$

where the $1/T_0$ in the expression for c_n has been written as $\omega_0/(2\pi)$. As $T_0 \rightarrow \infty$ the separation between successive harmonics becomes vanishingly small so that the nth harmonic $n\omega_0$ becomes indistinguishable from the adjacent harmonics. In other words, $n\omega_0$ merges into a continuous variable $n\omega_0 \rightarrow \omega$ and the distance between harmonics ω_0 becomes a differential $d\omega$. Finally, as T_0 goes to infinity the summation in Eq. (16–2) can be replaced by a continuous integration because the sum consists of spectral components that are indistinguishably close together.

When these limiting conditions are applied in Eq. (16–2) the result is

$$f(t) = \frac{1}{2\pi}\int_{-\infty}^{\infty}\left[\int_{-\infty}^{\infty} f(t)e^{-j\omega t}\,dt\right]e^{+j\omega t}\,d\omega \qquad (16-3)$$

The integral inside the brackets in Eq. (16–3) is a function of a continuous variable ω, since time is the integration variable. This integral is called the Fourier transform of $f(t)$ and is denoted by $F(\omega)$.

In other words, the **direct Fourier transformation** is defined to be

$$F(\omega) = \int_{-\infty}^{\infty} f(t)e^{-j\omega t}\,dt \qquad (16-4)$$

In general, $F(\omega)$ is a complex function of the real variable ω. The magnitude $|F(\omega)|$ is called the **amplitude spectrum** and the angle $\angle F(\omega)$ the **phase spectrum.** Given the definition of $F(\omega)$ in Eq. (16–4), we see that Eq. (16–3) also indicates that the **inverse Fourier transformation** is

$$f(t) = \frac{1}{2\pi}\int_{-\infty}^{\infty} F(\omega)e^{j\omega t}\,d\omega \qquad (16-5)$$

The integration in the inverse operation extends from $\omega = -\infty$ to $\omega = \infty$, which shows that the Fourier transformation yields a two-sided spectrum that spans both positive and negative frequencies. The waveform $f(t)$ and transform $F(\omega)$ comprise a **Fourier transform pair**. We say that $F(\omega)$ is the Fourier transform of $f(t)$ and, conversely, $f(t)$ is the inverse transform of $F(\omega)$. The shorthand notation $F(\omega) = \mathcal{F}\{f(t)\}$ and $f(t) = \mathcal{F}^{-1}\{F(\omega)\}$ is used to denote these operations.

The integral definition in Eq. (16–4) shows that transforming a voltage $v(t)$ (in V) yields a transform $V(\omega)$ with units of volt-seconds (V-s). Similarly, transforming a current waveform $i(t)$ (in A) produces $I(\omega)$ with units of ampere-seconds (A-s). Thus, waveforms and Fourier transforms do not have the same units, as is the case for waveforms and Laplace transforms. Even though they do not have the same units, we usually refer to both $V(\omega)$ and $v(t)$ as voltages and both $I(\omega)$ and $i(t)$ as currents.

The fact that the integral in Eq. (16–4) has infinite limits should alert you to the question of convergence and existence of $F(\omega)$. One set of sufficient conditions, called the **Dirichlet conditions**, requires that the waveform $f(t)$ meet the following conditions:

1. Have a finite number of discontinuities
2. Have a finite number of maxima and minima in any finite interval

3. Be absolutely integrable. That is,

$$\int_{-\infty}^{\infty} |f(t)|dt < \infty$$

A number of useful waveforms meet the Dirichlet conditions—for example, the rectangular pulse $[u(t) - u(t - T)]$ $(|T| < \infty)$] and the causal exponential $u(t)e^{-\alpha t}$ $(\alpha > 0)$. However, signals such as the step function $u(t)$ and the eternal sinewave $\cos \beta t$ do not. Since step functions and sinusoids are important in circuit analysis, we cannot limit ourselves to the Dirichlet conditions. Bear in mind that the Dirichlet conditions are sufficient to establish the existence of $F(\omega)$. They are not necessary and sufficient. Happily, there are ways of extending the Fourier transformation to signals that do not meet the Dirichlet conditions.

Finally, whenever $F(\omega)$ exists there is a unique, one-to-one correspondence between a waveform $f(t)$ and its Fourier transform $F(\omega)$. Uniqueness means that a transform pair can be used to go from waveform to transform or transform to waveform. Once we have developed a basic set of pairs, we will summarize our results in a table of Fourier transform pairs similar to the table of Laplace transform pairs in Chapter 9.

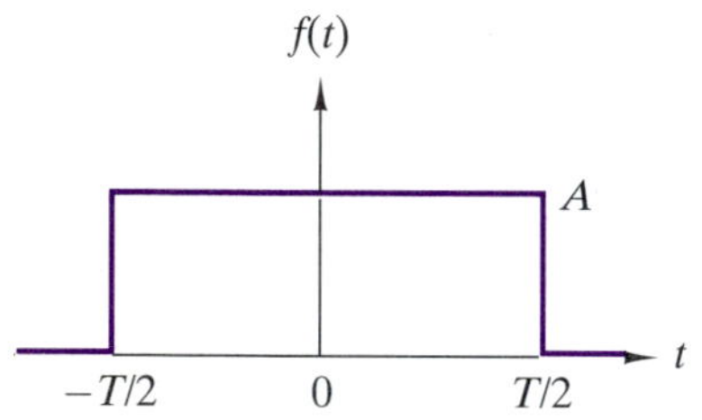

FIGURE 16–2

EXAMPLE 16–1

Find the Fourier transform of the rectangular pulse in Figure 16–2 and plot its amplitude spectrum.

SOLUTION:

The waveform in Figure 16–2 meets the Dirichlet conditions since it only has two isolated discontinuities and is zero everywhere except in the range from $t = -T/2$ to $t = +T/2$, where it is finite. For this waveform the integration in Eq. (16–4) can be written in the form

$$F(\omega) = \int_{-T/2}^{T/2} Ae^{-j\omega t}\, dt = -\frac{A}{j\omega}e^{-j\omega t}\Big|_{-T/2}^{T/2}$$

$$= \frac{A}{\omega/2}\left[\frac{e^{j\omega T/2} - e^{-j\omega T/2}}{j2}\right]$$

$$= AT\frac{\sin(\omega T/2)}{\omega T/2}$$

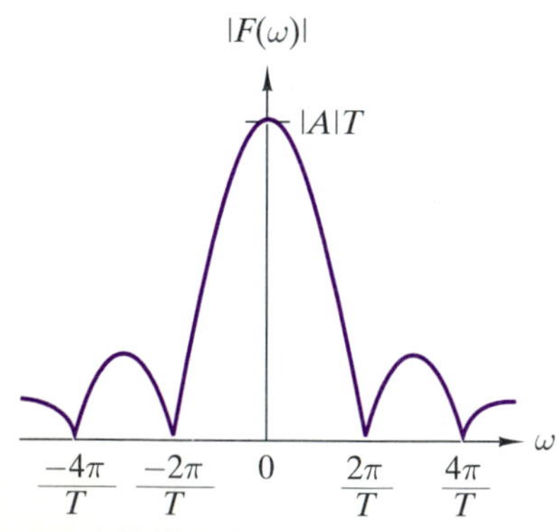

FIGURE 16–3

The final result has been put in the form $(\sin x)/x$ because this function plays a key role in Fourier analysis. Figure 16–3 shows a plot of the amplitude spectrum $|F(\omega)|$ versus ω. Note that $|F(\omega)|$ is a two-sided spectrum containing both positive and negative frequencies. The zeros in the spectral plot occur when $\sin(\omega T/2) = 0$ at the frequencies $\omega = 2k\pi/T$ $(k = \pm 1, \pm 2, \ldots)$. The maximum value of $|F(\omega)|$ occurs at $\omega = 0$. At $x = 0$ the value of $\sin(x)/x = 1$ and so the maximum value of $|F(\omega)|$ is $|A|T$. ■

EXAMPLE 16–2

Find the Fourier transform of the exponential $f(t) = \{Ae^{-\alpha t}\}u(t)$ and plot its amplitude and phase spectra. Assume $\alpha > 0$.

SOLUTION:

This waveform also meets the Dirichlet conditions since it has only one isolated discontinuity and is absolutely integrable in the sense of Eq. (16–6). The waveform is causal, so the integration in Eq. (16–4) extends from $t = 0$ to $t = +\infty$.

$$F(\omega) = \int_0^\infty Ae^{-\alpha t}e^{-j\omega t}\,dt = A\int_0^\infty e^{-(\alpha+j\omega)t}\,dt$$

$$= -A\left.\frac{e^{-(\alpha+j\omega)t}}{\alpha + j\omega}\right|_0^\infty$$

For $\alpha > 0$ the integral vanishes at the upper limit and $F(\omega)$ becomes

$$F(\omega) = \frac{A}{\alpha + j\omega} \quad (\alpha > 0)$$

The amplitude and phase spectra of $F(\omega)$ are

$$|F(\omega)| = \frac{|A|}{\sqrt{\alpha^2 + \omega^2}} \quad \text{(Amplitude)}$$

and

$$\phi(\omega) = \angle F(\omega) = -\tan^{-1}(\omega/\alpha) \quad \text{(Phase)}$$

The plots in Figure 16–4 show the two-sided amplitude and phase spectra. The Fourier transform does not exist for $\alpha < 0$ because the exponential waveform becomes unbounded and the integral in Eq. (16–4) does not converge. ■

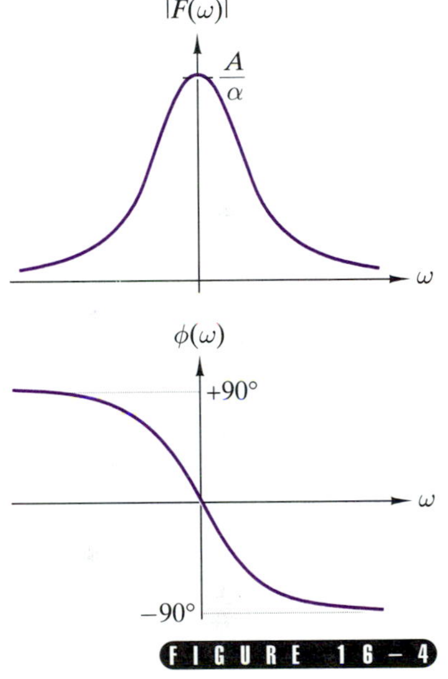

FIGURE 16–4

Exercise 16–1

Find the Fourier transform of the waveform in Figure 16–5.

Answer:

$$F(\omega) = -jAT\frac{1 - \cos(\omega T/2)}{\omega T/2}$$

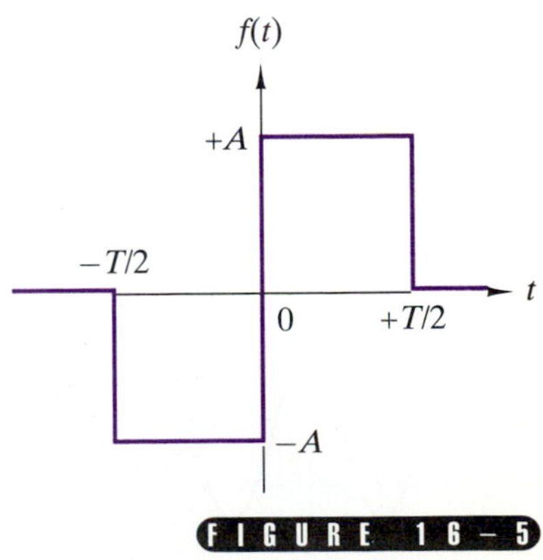

FIGURE 16–5

INVERSE FOURIER TRANSFORMS

The formal inversion integral for Laplace transforms given in Chapter 9 is rarely used because most applications are easily handled by partial fraction expansion. In contrast, the inverse Fourier transformation integral in Eq.

(16–5) is relatively easy to apply and often quite useful. As an example, consider the transform

$$F(\omega) = 2\pi\delta(\omega - \beta) \tag{16–7}$$

The transform is a frequency-domain impulse located at $\omega = \beta$ with an area of 2π. The time-domain waveform $f(t)$ corresponding to this transform is found by applying the inversion integral in Eq. (16–5). Because $F(\omega)$ is zero except at $\omega = \beta$, the integration limits need only span the range from $\omega = \beta-$ to $\omega = \beta+$, just slightly above and below the frequency $\omega = \beta$.

$$\begin{aligned} f(t) &= \frac{1}{2\pi}\int_{\beta-}^{\beta+} 2\pi\delta(\omega - \beta)e^{j\omega t}\,d\omega \\ &= e^{j\beta t}\int_{\beta-}^{\beta+} \delta(\omega - \beta)d\omega = e^{j\beta t} \end{aligned} \tag{16–8}$$

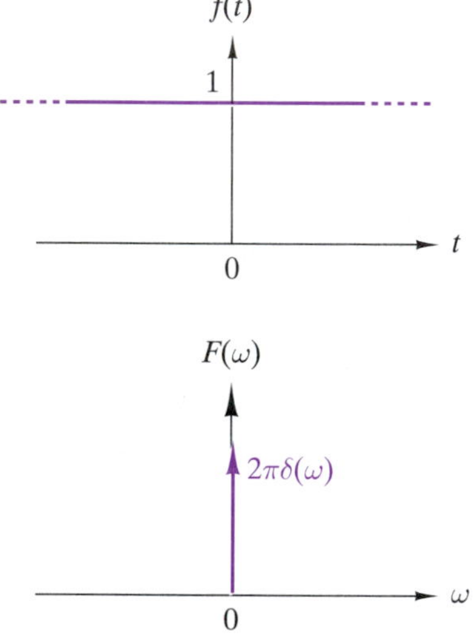

FIGURE 16–6

By direct application of the inversion integral, we find that the inverse transform of $2\pi\delta(\omega - \beta)$ is the complex exponential $e^{j\beta t}$. Because the Fourier transform is unique, we also have that $\mathcal{F}\{e^{j\beta t}\} = 2\pi\delta(\omega - \beta)$.

In particular, if $\beta = 0$, then $f(t) = e^{j0} = 1$ for all time t and $F(\omega) = 2\pi\delta(\omega)$. In other words, the Fourier transform of a dc waveform with amplitude $A = 1$ is an impulse of area 2π at $\omega = 0$. Figure 16–6 shows the waveform and Fourier transform of the unity amplitude dc signal. The dc waveform is noncausal, so it cannot be represented by a Laplace transform pair. Likewise, the dc waveform does not meet the Dirichlet conditions because it is not absolutely integrable as defined in Eq. (16–6). Nonetheless, its Fourier transform exists as an impulse at $\omega = 0$.

EXAMPLE 16–3

Use the inversion integral to find the waveform corresponding to the rectangular transform

$$F(\omega) = \frac{\pi A}{\beta}[u(\omega + \beta) - u(\omega - \beta)]$$

SOLUTION:

Since $F(\omega)$ is zero everywhere except in the range from $\omega = -\beta$ to $\omega = +\beta$, the inversion integral in Eq. (16–5) takes the form

$$\begin{aligned} f(t) &= \frac{1}{2\pi}\int_{-\beta}^{\beta} \pi\frac{A}{\beta}e^{j\omega t}\,d\omega = \frac{A}{2\beta}\frac{e^{j\omega t}}{jt}\bigg|_{-\beta}^{\beta} \\ &= \frac{A}{\beta t}\frac{e^{j\beta t} - e^{-j\beta t}}{j2} = A\frac{\sin(\beta t)}{\beta t} \end{aligned}$$

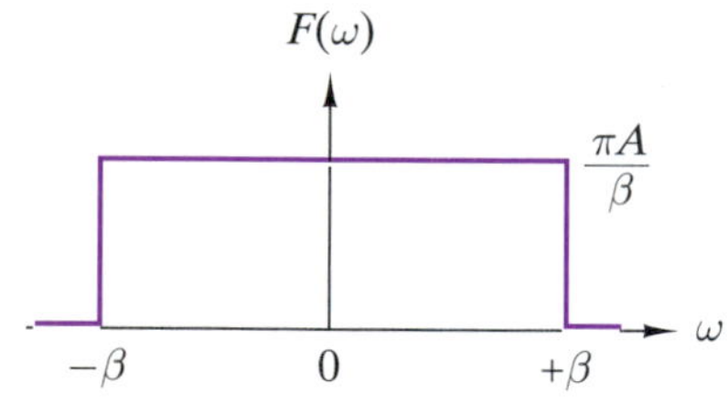

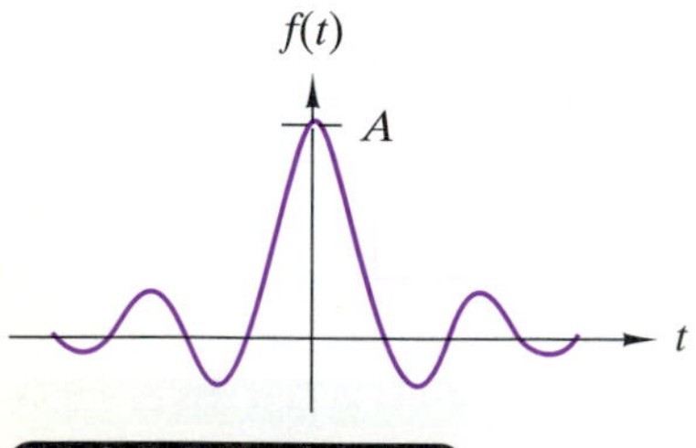

FIGURE 16–7

Figure 16–7 shows the given amplitude spectrum $|F(\omega)|$ and the resulting waveform $f(t)$ derived from the inverse transform. The Fourier transform pair $f(t) = A\sin(\beta t)/(\beta t)$ and $F(\omega) = (A\pi/\beta)[u(\omega + \beta) - u(\omega - \beta)]$ is yet another example of a noncausal signal for which there is no corresponding Laplace transform pair. ■

Exercise 16–2

Use the inversion integral to find the waveform corresponding to the transform $F(\omega) = \pi\alpha A e^{-\alpha|\omega|}$. Assume that $\alpha > 0$.

Answer:

$$f(t) = \frac{A}{1 + (t/\alpha)^2}$$

16–2 LAPLACE TRANSFORMS AND FOURIER TRANSFORMS

For many useful signals there is a simple relationship between the Laplace and Fourier transforms. In Chapter 9 the integral definition of the direct Laplace transformation is given as

$$\mathscr{L}\{f(t)\} = \int_0^\infty f(t)e^{-st}\,dt = F(s) \qquad (16\text{–}9)$$

where $s = \sigma + j\omega$ is the complex frequency variable. The lower limit of this integration reminds us that $f(t)$ must be causal for a unique transform pair to exist. If $f(t)$ is absolutely integrable in the sense defined in Eq. (16–6), then the integration in Eq. (16–9) converges when $\sigma = 0$, in which case Eq. (16–9) becomes

$$\mathscr{L}\{f(t)\} = \int_0^\infty f(t)e^{-j\omega t}\,dt = F(s)\Big|_{\sigma=0} \qquad (16\text{–}10)$$

On the other hand, when $f(t)$ is causal and absolutely integrable its Fourier transform exists and is found from Eq. (16–4) to be

$$\mathscr{F}\{f(t)\} = \int_0^\infty f(t)e^{-j\omega t}\,dt = F(\omega) \qquad (16\text{–}11)$$

Comparing Eqs. (16–10) and (16–11), we conclude that

$$F(\omega) = F(s)\Big|_{\sigma=0} \qquad (16\text{–}12)$$

provided that $f(t)$ is causal and absolutely integrable.

For $f(t)$ to be absolutely integrable, it must have finite duration or decay to zero rapidly enough so that the integral of $|f(t)|$ from $t = 0$ to $t = \infty$ converges. A sufficient condition for $f(t)$ to decay to zero is that all of the poles of $F(s)$ lie in the left half plane. For example, the Laplace transform of the causal exponential $Ae^{-\alpha t}u(t)$ is $A/(s + \alpha)$. The transform has a pole at $s = -\alpha$, which lies in the left half of the s-plane for $\alpha > 0$. When $\alpha > 0$ the Fourier transform of the causal exponential is found from its Laplace transform to be

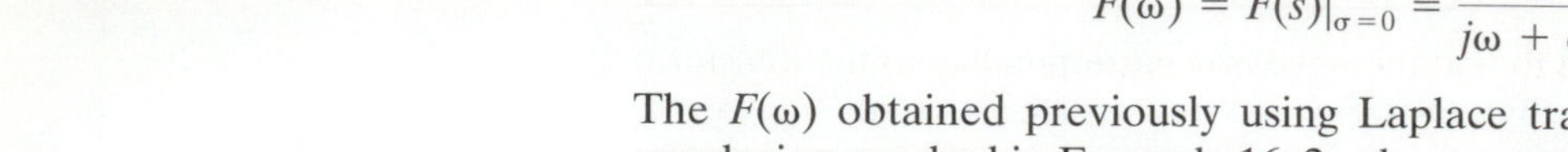

$$F(\omega) = F(s)\big|_{\sigma=0} = \frac{A}{j\omega + \alpha}$$

The $F(\omega)$ obtained previously using Laplace transforms agrees with the conclusion reached in Example 16–2, where we used the integral definition of the Fourier transformation.

We can use the conditions in Eq. (16–12) to find $F(\omega)$ from $F(s)$ provided that all poles of $F(s)$ lie in the left half of the s-plane. The poles cannot lie in the right half plane or on the j-axis boundary. For example, the Laplace transform method cannot be used to find the Fourier transform of a step function because $F(s) = 1/s$ has a pole on the j-axis at $s = 0$. Likewise, the Laplace transform method will not work for the causal sine wave $f(t) = u(t)[\sin \beta t]$ since $F(s) = 1/(s^2 + \beta^2)$ has poles on the j-axis at $s = \pm j\beta$.

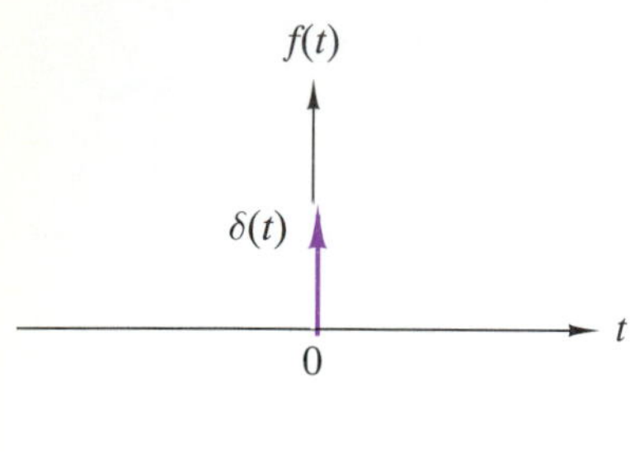

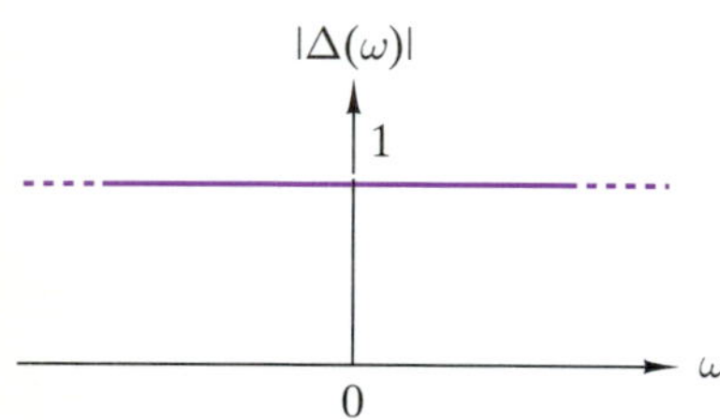

FIGURE 16–8 *Waveform and Fourier transform of the unit impulse signal.*

The Laplace transform method can be used to find the Fourier transform of the unit impulse because $\delta(t)$ is causal and absolutely integrable. Applying Eq. (16–12), we obtain

$$\mathscr{F}[\delta(t)] = \mathscr{L}[\delta(t)]\big|_{\sigma=0} = 1 \qquad (16\text{–}13)$$

Figure 16–8 shows impulse waveform $\delta(t)$ and its constant amplitude spectrum $|\Delta(\omega)|$. Note the symmetry between plots in Figure 16–8 and those in Figure 16–6. A constant time-domain waveform leads to the impulsive frequency spectrum in Figure 16–6. Conversely, an impulsive time-domain waveform leads to the constant frequency-domain spectrum in Figure 16–8.

Laplace transform concepts can be used to find inverse Fourier transforms as well. Given a Fourier transform $F(\omega)$, we form the Laplace transform $F(s)$ by replacing $j\omega$ by s or, equivalently, replacing ω by $-js$. If the poles of $F(s)$ all lie in the left half of the s-plane, then by the uniqueness property of Fourier and Laplace transforms we have

$$f(t) = \mathscr{F}^{-1}\{F(\omega)\} = \mathscr{L}^{-1}\{F(s)\} \quad (t > 0) \qquad (16\text{–}14)$$

The inverse transform of $F(s)$ in this equation can be obtained using partial-fraction expansion if need be. However, keep in mind that the Laplace transform method requires either (1) $f(t)$ to be causal and absolutely integrable, or (2) all of the poles of $F(s)$ to be in the left half of the s-plane.

Exercise 16–3

Use Laplace transforms to find the Fourier transforms of the following causal waveforms. Assume that $\alpha > 0$.

(a) $f(t) = A[e^{-\alpha t} \sin \beta t]u(t)$
(b) $f(t) = A[\alpha t e^{-\alpha t}]u(t)$

Answers:

(a) $F(\omega) = \dfrac{A\beta}{\beta^2 + \alpha^2 - \omega^2 + j2\alpha\omega}$

(b) $F(\omega) = \dfrac{A\alpha}{\alpha^2 - \omega^2 + j2\alpha\omega}$

EXAMPLE 16–4

Use Laplace transforms to find the inverse Fourier transform of

$$F(\omega) = \frac{10}{(j\omega + 2)(j\omega + 4)}$$

SOLUTION:

Replacing $j\omega$ by s yields $F(s)$ yields

$$F(s) = \frac{10}{(s + 2)(s + 4)}$$

$F(s)$ is a rational function of s with poles at $s = -2$ and $s = -4$. Both poles are in the left half plane, so the inverse transform of $F(s)$ is the inverse transform of $F(\omega)$. Expanding $F(s)$ by partial fractions yields

$$F(s) = \frac{k_1}{s + 2} + \frac{k_2}{s + 4}$$

The poles are simple, so the residues k_1 and k_2 are

$$k_1 = (s + 2)F(s)|_{s=-2} = 5$$
$$k_2 = (s + 4)F(s)|_{s=-4} = -5$$

and the inverse transform of $F(\omega)$ is

$$f(t) = \mathcal{L}^{-1}\{F(s)\} = \mathcal{L}^{-1}\left\{\frac{5}{s + 2}\right\} + \mathcal{L}^{-1}\left\{\frac{-5}{s + 4}\right\}$$
$$= [5e^{-2t} - 5e^{-4t}]u(t)$$

Exercise 16–4

Use the Laplace transform method to find the causal waveform corresponding to the following Fourier transform:

$$F(\omega) = \frac{5(j\omega - 3)}{(j\omega + 1)(j\omega + 5)}$$

Answer:

$$f(t) = [-5e^{-t} + 10e^{-5t}]\,\mu(t)$$

Exercise 16–5

Explain why Laplace transforms cannot be used to find the Fourier transforms of the following waveforms. Assume that $\alpha > 0$.

(a) $f(t) = A\alpha t u(t)$
(b) $f(t) = Ae^{-\alpha|t|}$
(c) $f(t) = A \sin \alpha t$

Answers:

(a) $F(s)$ has a double pole at $s = 0$.
(b) $f(t)$ is not causal.
(c) $f(t)$ is not absolutely integrable.

Exercise 16–6

Explain why Laplace transforms cannot be used to find the waveforms corresponding to the following Fourier transforms. Assume that $\alpha > 0$.

(a) $F(\omega) = \dfrac{2\alpha}{\alpha^2 + \omega^2}$
(b) $F(\omega) = u(\omega + \alpha) - u(\omega - \alpha)$

Answers:

(a) $F(s)$ has a pole at $s = +\alpha$.
(b) $F(s)$ is not a rational function.

16–3 BASIC FOURIER TRANSFORM PROPERTIES AND PAIRS

This section introduces the important basic mathematical properties of the Fourier transformation. The basic properties are then applied to derive additional Fourier transform pairs.

LINEARITY

Like Laplace transforms, the foremost property of Fourier transforms is **linearity**. Stated formally,

$$\mathscr{F}\{Af_1(t) + Bf_2(t)\} = AF_1(\omega) + BF_2(\omega) \qquad (16\text{–}15)$$

where A and B are constants. Proof of this property follows directly from the integral definition of the direct Fourier transformation in Eq. (16–4) using the same logic applied in Sect. 9–2 to derive the linearity property of the Laplace transforms. The following example illustrates an application of linearity.

EXAMPLE 16–5

Find the Fourier transforms of $\cos \beta t$ and $\sin \beta t$.

SOLUTION:

We cannot use the Laplace transform method because these waveforms are noncausal, eternal sinusoids. In Sect. 16–1 we found that

$$\mathscr{F}\{e^{j\beta t}\} = 2\pi\delta(\omega - \beta)$$

Using Euler's relationship for $\cos \beta t$ and the linearity property of the Fourier transform, we can write

$$\mathscr{F}\{\cos \beta t\} = \mathscr{F}\left\{\frac{e^{j\beta t} + e^{-j\beta t}}{2}\right\} = \frac{1}{2}\mathscr{F}\{e^{j\beta t}\} + \frac{1}{2}\mathscr{F}\{e^{-j\beta t}\}$$
$$= \pi[\delta(\omega - \beta) + \delta(\omega + \beta)]$$

Similarly, for sin βt we obtain

$$\mathscr{F}[\sin \beta t\} = \mathscr{F}\left\{\frac{e^{j\beta t} - e^{-j\beta t}}{j2}\right\} = \frac{1}{j2}\mathscr{F}\{e^{j\beta t}\} - \frac{1}{j2}\mathscr{F}\{e^{-j\beta t}\}$$
$$= -j\pi[\delta(\omega - \beta) - \delta(\omega + \beta)]$$

We previously found that the Fourier transform of a dc waveform is an impulse at zero frequency ($\omega = 0$). Here we see that the transforms of ac waveforms have impulses located at $\omega = \pm\beta$, where β is the radian frequency of the sinusoids. ■

TIME DIFFERENTIATION AND INTEGRATION

The **time differentiation** property of Fourier transforms states that

$$\mathscr{F}\left\{\frac{df(t)}{dt}\right\} = j\omega F(\omega) \tag{16-16}$$

Derivation of this property of Fourier transforms begins with the inverse transformation integral:

$$f(t) = \frac{1}{2\pi}\int_{-\infty}^{\infty} F(\omega)e^{j\omega t}\, d\omega \tag{16-17}$$

We first differentiate both sides of this equation with respect to time:

$$\frac{df(t)}{dt} = g(t) = \frac{d}{dt}\left[\frac{1}{2\pi}\int_{-\infty}^{\infty} F(\omega)e^{j\omega t}\, d\omega\right]$$

Assuming that the order of integration and differentiation on the right side of this equation can be interchanged, we obtain

$$\frac{df(t)}{dt} = g(t) = \frac{1}{2\pi}\int_{-\infty}^{\infty}\left[\frac{d}{dt}F(\omega)e^{j\omega t}\right] d\omega$$
$$= \frac{1}{2\pi}\int_{-\infty}^{\infty} j\omega F(\omega)e^{j\omega t}\, d\omega$$

The right side of the last line in this equation implies $\mathscr{F}[g(t)] = j\omega F(\omega)$. Since $g(t) = df/dt$, we conclude that

$$\mathscr{F}\left[\frac{df(t)}{dt}\right] = j\omega F(\omega) \tag{16-18}$$

Differentiating $f(t)$ in the time domain corresponds to multiplying $F(\omega)$ by $j\omega$ in the frequency domain.

Given the differentiation property, it is reasonable to expect that integrating $f(t)$ in the time domain corresponds to dividing $F(\omega)$ by $j\omega$ in the frequency domain. This expectation is correct, except that integrating a waveform may produce a constant offset or dc component. As we have seen, the Fourier transform of a dc component is an impulse at $\omega = 0$ in the frequency domain. As a result, the statement of the **integration property** is

$$\mathscr{F}\left[\int_{-\infty}^{t} f(x)dx\right] = \frac{F(\omega)}{j\omega} + \pi F(0)\delta(\omega) \qquad (16\text{–}19)$$

Integrating $f(t)$ in the time domain leads to division of $F(\omega)$ by $j\omega$ plus an additive term $\pi F(0)\delta(\omega)$ to account for the possibility of a dc component in the integral of $f(t)$. The factor $F(0)$ is related to $f(t)$ via the integral defining the direct Fourier transformation. Replacing ω by 0 reduces Eq. (16–4) to

$$F(0) = \int_{-\infty}^{\infty} f(t)dt \qquad (16\text{–}20)$$

The zero frequency or dc component $F(0)$ is zero when the integral of $f(t)$ over all time is zero. In such a case, the second term on the right-hand side in Eq. (16–19) vanishes, and time integration corresponds to division by $j\omega$ in the frequency domain.

EXAMPLE 16–6

Use the integration property to find the Fourier transform of the step function $u(t)$.

SOLUTION:

We cannot use the Laplace transform method here because the step function is not absolutely integrable. The Fourier transform of a time-domain impulse was previously found to be $\mathscr{F}[\delta(t)] = 1$. Since the step function is the integral of an impulse, the integration property yields the Fourier transform of the unit step function.

$$\mathscr{F}\{u(t)\} = \mathscr{F}\left\{\int_{-\infty}^{t} \delta(x)dx\right\} = \frac{1}{j\omega} + \pi\delta(\omega)$$

The Fourier and Laplace transforms of the step function have the same form when s is replaced by $j\omega$, except for the frequency-domain impulse $\pi\delta(\omega)$, which is required to account for the dc component in $u(t)$. ■

REVERSAL

A waveform $f(t)$ is said to be reversed when t is replaced by $-t$. The waveform $f(-t)$ is reversed because everything happens in reverse order, with events that previously happened for $t > 0$ now occurring for $t < 0$, and vice versa. If the Fourier transform of $f(t)$ is $F(\omega)$, what can be said about the transform of $f(-t)$? The **reversal** property of the Fourier transformation is formally stated as follows:

$$\text{If } \mathscr{F}[f(t)] = F(\omega) \text{ then } \mathscr{F}[f(-t)] = F(-\omega) \qquad (16\text{–}21)$$

Simply stated, reversing $f(t)$ reverses $F(\omega)$.

Deriving this property begins by noting that by definition the Fourier transform of $f(t)$ is

$$F(\omega) = \int_{-\infty}^{\infty} f(t)e^{-j\omega t}\,dt \qquad (16\text{–}22)$$

and the Fourier transform of the reversed waveform is

$$G(\omega) = \int_{-\infty}^{\infty} f(-t)e^{-j\omega t}\,dt \qquad (16\text{–}23)$$

Changing the dummy variable of integration in Eq. (16–23) to $\tau = -t$ produces

$$\begin{aligned} G(\omega) &= -\int_{\infty}^{-\infty} f(\tau)e^{j\omega\tau}\,d\tau \\ &= \int_{-\infty}^{\infty} f(\tau)e^{-j(-\omega)\tau}\,d\tau \end{aligned} \qquad (16\text{–}24)$$

Comparing the last line in Eq. (16–24) with the definition in Eq. (16–22), we conclude that $\mathscr{F}\{f(-t)\} = G(\omega) = F(-\omega)$.

The reversal property is used to derive the Fourier transforms of waveforms of the type shown in Figure 16–9. The mathematical expressions for these two waveforms are

$$\begin{aligned} \text{sgn}(t) &= u(t) - u(-t) \\ e^{-\alpha|t|} &= u(t)e^{-\alpha t} + u(-t)e^{-\alpha(-t)} \end{aligned} \qquad (16\text{–}25)$$

The first waveform is called the **signum function**. By definition, sgn(t) is +1 for $t > 0$, –1 for $t < 0$, and zero for $t = 0$. As indicated in Eq. (16–25), sgn(t) can be constructed by adding a step $u(t)$ to a reversed step $-u(-t)$.

The second waveform in Figure 16–9 is called a **double-sided** exponential. This waveform is unity at $t = 0$ and exponentially decays (for $\alpha > 0$) to zero in both directions along the time axis. As shown in Eq. (16–25), the double-sided exponential is the sum of a causal exponential and a reversed causal exponential.

The signum and double-sided exponential are examples of noncausal waveforms that can be written as $f(t) = g(t) \pm h(-t)$, where $g(t)$ and $h(t)$ are causal. If the Fourier transforms of $g(t)$ and $h(t)$ are known, then using the reversal and linearity properties shows that $F(\omega) = G(\omega) \pm H(-\omega)$. When $g(t)$ and $h(t)$ are also absolutely integrable, we can use Laplace transforms to find $G(\omega)$ and $H(\omega)$.

The next example illustrates the possibilities.

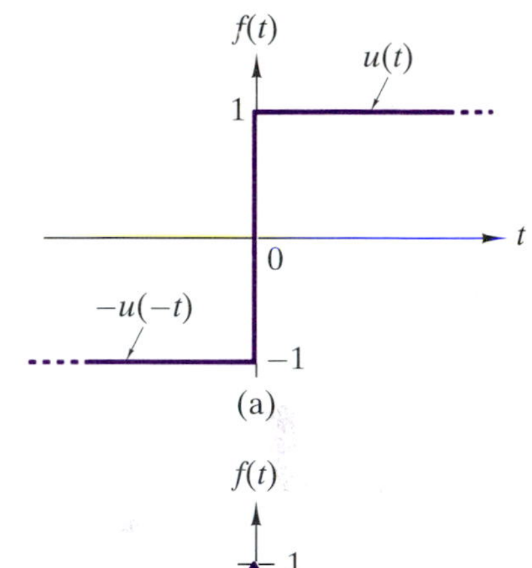

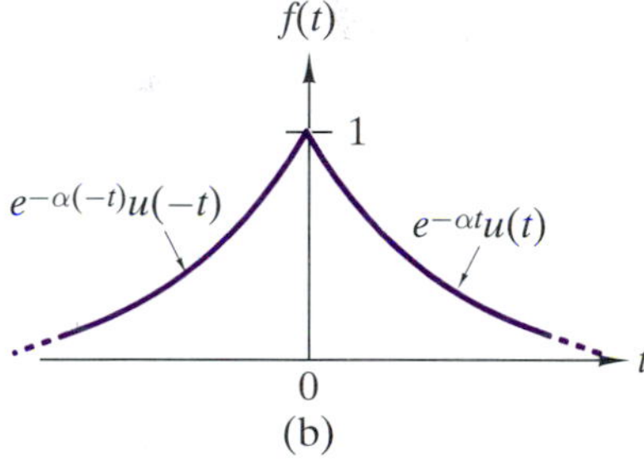

FIGURE 16–9 *Waveforms of the signum and double-sided exponential signals.*

EXAMPLE 16–7

Use the linearity and reversal properties to find the Fourier transform of

(a) sgn(t)
(b) $e^{-\alpha|t|}$

SOLUTION:

(a) The signum function is of the form $f(t) = g(t) - g(-t)$, where $g(t) = u(t)$. In Example 16–6 the transform of a unit step function is shown to be $\mathcal{F}\{u(t)\} = 1/j\omega + \pi\delta(\omega)$. Using the linearity and reversal properties yields the Fourier transform of sgn(t).

$$\begin{aligned}\mathcal{F}\{\text{sgn}(t)\} &= G(\omega) - G(-\omega)\\ &= \left[\frac{1}{j\omega} + \pi\delta(\omega)\right] - \left[\frac{1}{j(-\omega)} + \pi\delta(-\omega)\right]\\ &= \frac{2}{j\omega}\end{aligned}$$

In the last line of this equation we have used the fact that $\pi\delta(\omega) - \pi\delta(-\omega) = 0$ since both $\delta(\omega)$ and $\delta(-\omega)$ are impulses at $\omega = 0$.

(b) For the double-sided exponential, $f(t) = g(t) + g(-t)$, where $g(t) = [e^{-\alpha t}]u(t)$. The Fourier transform of $g(t)$ is $G(\omega) = 1/(\alpha + j\omega)$. Using the linearity and reversal properties yields the Fourier transform of the double-sided exponential.

$$\begin{aligned}\mathcal{F}\{e^{-\alpha|t|}\} &= G(\omega) + G(-\omega)\\ &= \left[\frac{1}{\alpha + j\omega}\right] + \left[\frac{1}{\alpha + j(-\omega)}\right]\\ &= \frac{2\alpha}{\alpha^2 + \omega^2}\end{aligned}$$

■

Exercise 16–7

Use linearity and reversal properties to find the Fourier transform of

$$f(t) = [e^{-\alpha t}]u(t) + u(-t)$$

Assume that $\alpha > 0$.

Answer:

$$F(\omega) = \pi\delta(\omega) - \frac{\alpha}{j\omega(j\omega + \alpha)}$$

16–4 MORE FOURIER TRANSFORM PROPERTIES

Uniqueness, linearity, time differentiation, time integration, and reversal are basic properties of the Fourier transforms commonly used in circuit analysis. This section discusses some additional properties that provide insight into the nature of Fourier transforms and the relationships between the time and frequency domains.

EVEN AND ODD PARTS OF $F(\omega)$

In general, a Fourier transform $F(\omega)$ is a complex function that can be written in rectangular and polar form.

$$F(\omega) = A(\omega) + jB(\omega) = |F(\omega)|e^{j\theta(\omega)}$$

The functions $A(\omega)$ and $B(\omega)$ are the real and imaginary parts of $F(\omega)$, while $|F(\omega)|$ and $\theta(\omega)$ are the magnitude and angle of $F(\omega)$. The next example shows how to calculate these functions for a given transform.

EXAMPLE 16–8

Find the real part, imaginary parts, magnitude, and angle of the Fourier transform of the causal exponential $f(t) = [e^{-\alpha t}]u(t)$.

SOLUTION:

Example 16–2 shows that $F(\omega) = 1/(\alpha + j\omega)$. Multiplying the numerator and denominator of $F(\omega)$ by the conjugate of the denominator yields

$$F(\omega) = \frac{1}{\alpha + j\omega}\frac{\alpha - j\omega}{\alpha - j\omega} = \frac{\alpha - j\omega}{\alpha^2 + \omega^2}$$

$$= \frac{\alpha}{\alpha^2 + \omega^2} + \frac{-j\omega}{\alpha^2 + \omega^2}$$

The real and imaginary parts are

$$A(\omega) = \frac{\alpha}{\alpha^2 + \omega^2} \quad \text{and} \quad B(\omega) = \frac{-\omega}{\alpha^2 + \omega^2}$$

The magnitude and angle of $F(\omega)$ are

$$|F(\omega)| = \frac{1}{\sqrt{\alpha^2 + \omega^2}} \quad \text{and} \quad \theta(\omega) = \tan^{-1}(-\omega/\alpha)$$

Note that the real part and magnitude are even functions of ω, while the imaginary part and angle are odd functions. ■

The conclusion reached in the preceding example regarding the even and odd parts of $F(\omega)$ can be generalized as follows. Using Euler's equation $e^{-j\omega t} = \cos \omega t - j \sin \omega t$ in the integral defining the Fourier transformation yields

$$F(\omega) = \int_{-\infty}^{\infty} f(t)\cos \omega t \, dt - j\int_{-\infty}^{\infty} f(t) \sin \omega t \, dt$$

from which we conclude that

$$A(\omega) = \int_{-\infty}^{\infty} f(t)\cos \omega t \, dt \qquad (16\text{–}26)$$

$$B(\omega) = -\int_{-\infty}^{\infty} f(t)\sin \omega t \, dt \qquad (16\text{–}27)$$

and

$$|F(\omega)| = \sqrt{A^2(\omega) + B^2(\omega)} \tag{16–28}$$

$$\theta(\omega) = \tan^{-1}\left(\frac{B(\omega)}{A(\omega)}\right) \tag{16–29}$$

When $f(t)$ is a real-valued function, we can make the following observations:

1. The real part of $F(\omega)$ is an even function since replacing ω by $-\omega$ in Eq. (16–26) shows that $A(-\omega) = A(\omega)$.
2. The imaginary part of $F(\omega)$ is an odd function since replacing ω by $-\omega$ in Eq. (16–27) shows that $B(-\omega) = -B(\omega)$.
3. The magnitude of $F(\omega)$ is an even function since replacing ω by $-\omega$ in Eq. (16–28) shows that $|F(-\omega)| = |F(\omega)|$ because $A^2(\omega)$ and $B^2(\omega)$ are even functions.
4. The angle of $F(\omega)$ is an odd function since replacing ω by $-\omega$ in Eq. (16–29) shows that $\theta(-\omega) = -\theta(\omega)$ because $B(\omega)$ is an odd function and $A(\omega)$ is an even function.
5. As a result of observations 1 and 2, we have $F(-\omega) = A(\omega) - jB(\omega) = F^*(\omega)$, which means that the reversal of $F(\omega)$ is its complex conjugate.
6. As a result of observation 5, the product of $F(\omega)$ and its reversal is its squared magnitude since $F(\omega)F(-\omega) = A^2(\omega) + B^2(\omega) = |F(\omega)|^2$.
7. When $f(t)$ is an even function, $B(\omega) = 0$ since the integrand $f(t)\sin \omega t$ in Eq. (16–27) is odd. That is, when $f(t)$ is even $F(\omega)$ is real.
8. When $f(t)$ is an odd function, $A(\omega) = 0$ since the integrand $f(t)\cos \omega t$ in Eq. (16–26) is odd. That is, when $f(t)$ is odd $F(\omega)$ is imaginary. For example, the double-sided exponential waveform in Figure 16–9 is even and its Fourier transform $F(\omega) = 2\alpha/(\alpha^2 + \omega^2)$ is real. Conversely, the signum waveform in Figure 16–9 is odd and its transform $F(\omega) = 2/j\omega$ is imaginary.

Exercise 16–8

(a) Find the real part, imaginary part, magnitude, and angle of the Fourier transform in Exercise 16–1.

(b) Repeat for Exercise 16–2. Indicate whether the waveform is even, odd, or neither.

Answers:

(a) $A(\omega) = 0$, $B(\omega) = -2A[1 - \cos(\omega T/2)]/\omega$
$|F(\omega)| = |B(\omega)|$, $\theta(\omega) = -90°$, $f(t)$ is odd

(b) $A(\omega) = \pi\alpha A e^{-\alpha|\omega|}$, $B(\omega) = 0$
$|F(\omega)| = |A(\omega)|$, $\theta(\omega) = 0°$, $f(t)$ is even

SYMMETRY

The general statement of the **symmetry property** is

$$\text{If } \mathcal{F}\{f(t)\} = F(\omega) \text{ then } \mathcal{F}\{F(t)\} = 2\pi f(-\omega) \qquad (16\text{–}30)$$

When $\mathcal{F}\{f(t)\} = F(\omega)$, the inverse Fourier transform can be written in the form

$$2\pi f(t) = \int_{-\infty}^{\infty} F(\omega)e^{j\omega t}\, d\omega$$

Replacing t by $-t$ yields

$$2\pi f(-t) = \int_{-\infty}^{\infty} F(\omega)e^{-j\omega t}\, d\omega$$

Now interchanging t and ω produces

$$2\pi f(-\omega) = \int_{-\infty}^{\infty} F(t)e^{-j\omega t}\, dt$$

This equation is the conclusion part of the statement in Eq. (16–30).

The symmetry property states that waveforms and Fourier transforms can be interchanged within a factor of 2π. The origin of this symmetry traces back to the similarity of the direct transformation in Eq. (16–4) and the inverse transformation in Eq. (16–5). Except for the factor of 2π, these two equations are similar in form.

Figure 16–10 illustrates the waveforms/transforms duality implied by the symmetry property. The upper pair comes from Example 16–1, where we found that a rectangular pulse waveform has an oscillatory Fourier transform of the form $K \sin(x)/x$. The lower pair comes from Example 16–3, where we found that a rectangular Fourier transform has an oscillatory waveform of the form $K \sin(x)/x$.

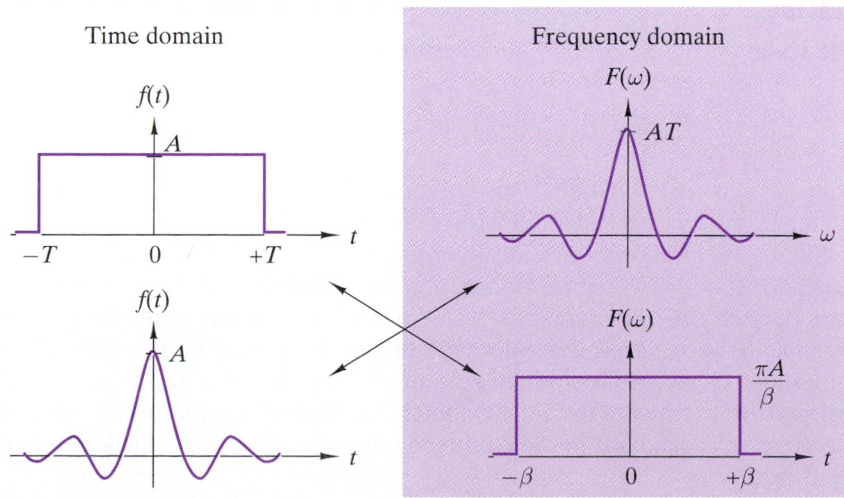

FIGURE 16–10 *Example of the symmetry property of Fourier transforms.*

Exercise 16–9

Given that $\mathscr{F}\{e^{-\alpha|t|}\} = 2\alpha/(\alpha^2 + \omega^2)$, use the symmetry and linearity properties to find the Fourier transform of $f(t) = 1/[1 + (t/\alpha)^2]$.

Answer:
$F(\omega) = \pi\alpha e^{-\alpha|\omega|}$

TIME AND FREQUENCY SHIFTING

Two important Fourier transform properties that are easily derived from the defining integrals are

$$\text{If } \mathscr{F}\{f(t)\} = F(\omega) \text{ then } \mathscr{F}\{f(t - T)\} = e^{-j\omega T}F(\omega)$$
$$\text{If } \mathscr{F}^{-1}\{F(\omega)\} = f(t) \text{ then } \mathscr{F}^{-1}\{F(\omega - \beta)\} = e^{j\beta t}f(t) \qquad (16\text{–}31)$$

The first statement indicates that shifting the time-domain origin by an amount T is equivalent to multiplying the transform by $e^{-j\omega T}$. The time-domain shifting property means that delaying a waveform ($T > 0$) does not change the amplitude spectrum since

$$|F(\omega)e^{-j\omega T}| = |F(\omega)|\,|e^{-j\omega T}| = |F(\omega)|$$

but does change the phase spectrum since

$$\angle[F(\omega)e^{-j\omega T}] = \angle[F(\omega)]\angle[e^{-j\omega T}] = \angle F(\omega) - \omega T$$

The second statement in Eq. (16–31) says that multiplying a waveform by $e^{j\beta t}$ shifts its spectrum by an amount β. The frequency-domain shifting property is the basis for a signal-processing operation called modulation, in which the spectral content of a signal is shifted from one frequency range to another.

SCALING

The **scaling** property of the Fourier transformation is

$$\text{If } \mathscr{F}[f(t)] = F(\omega) \text{ then } \mathscr{F}[f(at)] = \frac{1}{|a|}F(\omega/a) \qquad (16\text{–}32)$$

where a is a real constant. This statement is essentially the same as the scaling property of Laplace transforms in Sect. 9–7.

Figure 16–11 shows the transform pairs for a rectangular pulse for two pulse durations. The figure points out that compressing the pulse in the time domain ($a < 1$) causes the transform to spread out in the frequency domain, or vice versa. For this reason the statement in Eq. (16–32) is sometimes called the reciprocal spreading property. An important implication is that reducing the time-domain duration of a waveform causes its spectrum to spread out in the frequency domain, dictating a larger system bandwidth.

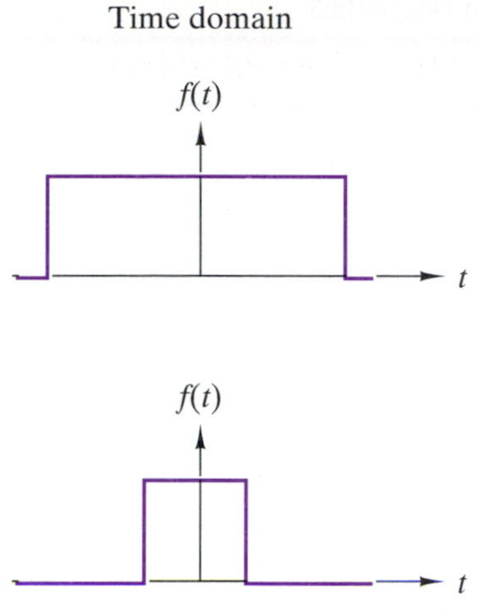

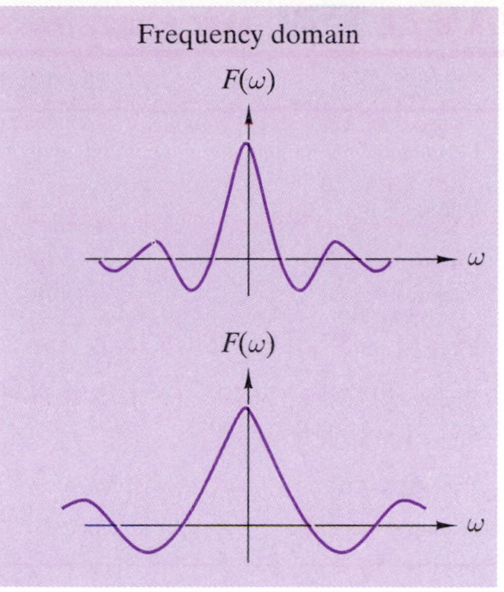

FIGURE 16–11 *Example of the scaling property of Fourier transforms.*

SUMMARY TABLES

Table 16–1 lists a basic set of Fourier transform pairs. Additional pairs are easy to derive using Laplace transform methods or the transform properties summarized in Table 16–2.

TABLE 16–1 BASIC FOURIER TRANSFORM PAIRS

SIGNAL	WAVEFORM F(t)	TRANSFORM F(ω)
Impulse	$\delta(t)$	1
Constant (dc)	1	$2\pi\delta(\omega)$
Step function	$u(t)$	$\frac{1}{j\omega} + \pi\delta(\omega)$
Signum	$\text{sgn}(t)$	$\frac{2}{j\omega}$
Causal exponential	$[e^{-\alpha t}]u(t)$	$\frac{1}{\alpha + j\omega}$
Two-sided exponential	$e^{-\alpha\|t\|}$	$\frac{2\alpha}{\alpha^2 + \omega^2}$
Complex exponential	$e^{j\beta t}$	$2\pi\delta(\omega - \beta)$
Cosine (ac)	$\cos \beta t$	$\pi[\delta(\omega - \beta) + \delta(\omega + \beta)]$
Sine (ac)	$\sin \beta t$	$-j\pi[\delta(\omega - \beta) - \delta(\omega + \beta)]$
Sinc	$\frac{\sin \beta t}{\pi t}$	$u(\omega - \beta) - u(\omega + \beta)$

TABLE 16–1 BASIC FOURIER TRANSFORM PROPERTIES

PROPERTY	TIME DOMAIN	FREQUENCY DOMAIN
Linearity	$Af_1(t) + Bf_2(t)$	$AF_1(\omega) + BF_2(\omega)$
Differentiation	$\dfrac{df(t)}{dt}$	$j\omega F(\omega)$
Integration	$\int_{-\infty}^{t} f(x)dx$	$\dfrac{F(\omega)}{j\omega} + \pi F(0)\delta(\omega)$
Reversal	$f(-t)$	$F(-\omega)$
Symmetry	$F(t)$	$2\pi f(-\omega)$
Time shift	$f(t - T)$	$e^{-j\omega T}F(\omega)$
Frequency shift	$e^{j\beta t}f(t)$	$F(\omega - \beta)$
Scaling	$\lvert a \rvert f(at)$	$F(\omega/a)$

16–5 CIRCUIT ANALYSIS USING FOURIER TRANSFORMS

Previous chapters showed that Laplace transforming a circuit into the s-domain can greatly simplify circuit analysis. It should come as no surprise that we can transform circuits using the Fourier transformation. To see how the Fourier transformation applies to circuit analysis, we must examine how the transformation affects the connection and device constraints. Because of the linearity property, the Fourier transform of a typical KVL constraint such as

$$v_1(t) + v_2(t) - v_3(t) = 0$$

takes the form

$$V_1(\omega) + V_2(\omega) - V_3(\omega) = 0$$

This example obviously generalizes to any KVL or KCL constraint. The Fourier transformation changes the waveforms into transforms but leaves the form of the connection constraints unchanged.

The frequency-domain element constraints are found by transforming the i–v characteristics of the passive elements. Using the differentiation property of the Fourier transforms, we write the time-domain and frequency-domain element constraints as follows:

	TIME DOMAIN	FREQUENCY DOMAIN
Resistor:	$v(t) = Ri(t)$	$V(\omega) = RI(\omega)$
Inductor:	$v(t) = L\dfrac{di}{dt}$	$V(\omega) = j\omega LI(\omega)$
Capacitor:	$i(t) = C\dfrac{dv}{dt}$	$I(\omega) = j\omega CV(\omega)$

As might be expected, in the frequency domain the element constraints are algebraic equations similar in form to Ohm's law. The proportionality factors relating the voltage and current transforms are the ac impedance of the passive elements:

$$Z_R = R \quad Z_L = j\omega L \quad Z_C = \frac{1}{j\omega C} \tag{16-33}$$

The form of the frequency-domain connection and element constraints have a familiar ring because we have seen similar results before in Chapter 10. In the present context the central points are that (1) the Fourier transformation does not change the form of the connection constraints, and (2) the transformed element constraints are similar to Ohm's law. From our previous experience, we know that our vast repertoire of algebraic circuit analysis techniques can be applied to the transformed circuit.

To transform a circuit, we change waveforms into Fourier transforms and replace passive elements by what amounts to their ac impedance. We then use algebraic techniques such as voltage division, equivalence, node analysis, or mesh analysis to solve for the unknown current or voltage transforms. The inverse Fourier transform is then used to obtain the response waveform in the time domain.

The preceding discussion closely parallels the development in Chapter 10, except for one thing—there is no mention of initial conditions. The reason for this omission is that there is a lower limit of $t = -\infty$ on the integral in Eq. (16–4). In other words, the Fourier transformation takes into account the entire history of a circuit beginning at $t = -\infty$ and ending at $t = +\infty$. For the Laplace transformation the lower limit on the defining integral [see Eq. (9-2)] is $t = 0$, and the effect of inputs prior to $t = 0$ are represented by the initial conditions.

In summary, the Fourier circuit analysis method inherently takes into account all inputs, including those that happened for $t < 0$. The Fourier transforms exist for noncausal waveforms such as $\text{sgn}(t)$, and so Fourier methods yield response waveforms that are valid from $t = -\infty$ to $t = \infty$. As a result, Fourier analysis cannot handle initial value circuit analysis problems in which the effects of inputs prior to $t = 0$ are represented as initial conditions.

EXAMPLE 16–9

Use Fourier transforms to find $v_2(t)$ in the circuit in Figure 16–12 for a unit step function input $v_1(t) = u(t)$.

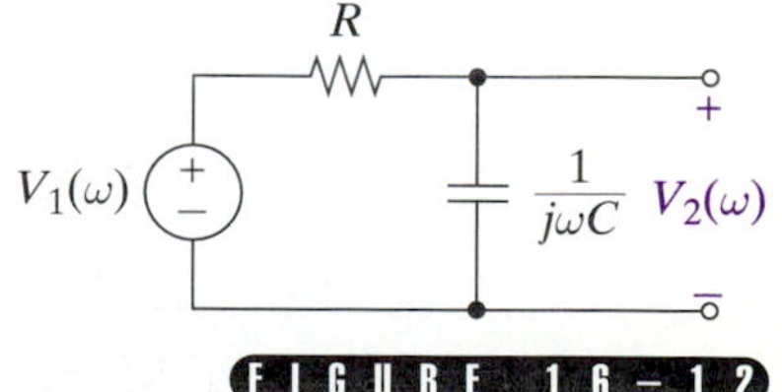

FIGURE 16–12

SOLUTION:

We first encountered the step response of a first-order *RC* circuit in Chapter 7 and revisited it again in Chapters 9, 10, and 11. From this previous experience we know that the zero-state step response is $v_2(t) = [1 - e^{-t/RC}]u(t)$. The purpose of analyzing this circuit yet again is simply to show that the Fourier transform method produces the same result.

The circuit in Figure 16–12 has been transformed into the frequency domain, so we proceed directly to the analysis process. We find the output transform using voltage division:

$$V_2(\omega) = \left[\frac{\dfrac{1}{j\omega C}}{R + \dfrac{1}{j\omega C}}\right] V_1(\omega) = \left[\frac{1/RC}{j\omega + 1/RC}\right] V_1(\omega)$$

For a unit step function input $V_1(\omega) = 1/j\omega + \pi\delta(\omega)$, and so the response transform is

$$V_2(\omega) = \frac{1/RC}{j\omega(j\omega + 1/RC)} + \frac{\pi\delta(\omega)/RC}{j\omega + 1/RC}$$

The first term on the right-hand side can be expanded by partial fractions. The second term on the right reduces to $\pi\delta(\omega)$ because, in general, a function $F(\omega)\delta(\omega) = F(0)\delta(\omega)$ since the impulse is zero everywhere except at $\omega = 0$. The partial-fraction expansion of the response yields three terms:

$$V_2(\omega) = \frac{1}{j\omega} - \frac{1}{j\omega + 1/RC} + \pi\delta(\omega)$$

which can be rearranged as

$$V_2(\omega) = \underbrace{\frac{1}{j\omega} + \pi\delta(\omega)}_{\substack{\text{Step}\\ \text{Function}}} - \underbrace{\frac{1}{j\omega + 1/RC}}_{\substack{\text{Causal}\\ \text{Exponential}}}$$

Each term in this expansion is the transform of a basic signal listed in Table 16–1. As expected, the step response waveform is

$$v_2(t) = [1 - e^{-t/RC}]u(t)$$

■

EXAMPLE 16–10

Find the output waveform of the *RC* circuit in Figure 16–12 for an input $v_1(t) = \text{sgn}(t)$.

SOLUTION:

This example uses the circuit in Example 16–9 with a signum input. From Table 16–1 the input transform is $V_1(\omega) = 2/j\omega$. Using the voltage division result from Example 16–9, we write the output transform in the form

$$V_2(\omega) = \left[\frac{1/RC}{j\omega + 1/RC}\right]\frac{2}{j\omega}$$

The output $V_2(\omega)$ can be expanded by partial fractions:

$$V_2(\omega) = \frac{2/RC}{j\omega(j\omega + 1/RC)} = \underbrace{\frac{2}{j\omega}}_{\text{Signum}} - \underbrace{\frac{2}{j\omega + 1/RC}}_{\text{Exponential}}$$

Each term in this expansion is listed in Table 16–1. Performing the inverse transformation produces the response waveform.

$$v_2(t) = \text{sgn}(t) - 2[e^{-t/RC}]u(t)$$

Figure 16–13 shows how the noncausal sgn(t) and the causal exponential combine to produce the response $v_2(t)$. A physical interpretation of this response is that signum waveform applies an input of –1 V at $t = -\infty$ (a long time ago). After about five time constants ($t = -\infty + 5RC$, still a long time ago) the circuit output reaches a steady-state condition of $v_2(t) = -1$ V. Thus, for all practical purposes $v_2(t) = -1$ V for all $t < 0$. At $t = 0$ the input jumps to +1 V, driving the output response from –1 V at $t = 0$ to a final steady-state condition of 1 V as $t \to \infty$. Both causal and noncausal waveforms are required to show how a circuit responds to the noncausal signum input. ■

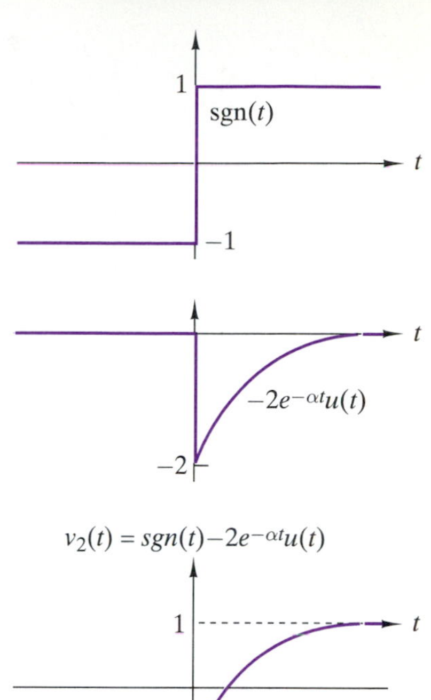

FIGURE 16–13

Exercise 16–10

Find the output waveform of the RC circuit in Figure 16–12 when the input is $v_1(t) = \text{sgn}(t) - 1$.

Answer:
$v_2(t) = -2u(-t) + 2[e^{-t/RC}]u(t)$

16–6 IMPULSE RESPONSE AND CONVOLUTION

The examples in the previous section show that Fourier transform methods can solve for the time-domain response of linear circuits. Once we become accustomed to the idea of noncausal waveforms, the process is quite similar to Laplace transform methods. However, Fourier transforms offer much more than just another way to find zero-state responses.

Fourier transforms are interesting because they can represent idealized models of signals and signal processors. These ideal signal processors usually involve noncausal responses so they cannot be represented by Laplace transforms. Of course, real physical systems must have causal responses so these models cannot actually be realized as engineering hardware. Nevertheless, ideal models are very useful in feasibility design and as benchmark standards for evaluating the performance of hardware that approximates ideal processors.

These ideal processors are normally described in the frequency domain by the Fourier transform equivalent of the s-domain transfer function. To develop the Fourier equivalent, we begin with the convolution integral from Chapter 11:

$$y(t) = \int_0^t x(\tau)h(t - \tau)d\tau$$

In this expression $h(t)$ is the system impulse response and $y(t)$ is the output caused by the input $x(t)$. The limits of integration are $\tau = 0$ to $\tau = t$ because Chapter 11 assumes that $h(t)$ and $x(t)$ are causal waveforms. To overcome this limitation the integration limits are extended backward to $t = -\infty$ to accommodate a noncausal input $x(\tau)$ and forward to $t = \infty$ to accommodate a noncausal $h(t - \tau)$. The result is

$$y(t) = \int_{-\infty}^{\infty} x(\tau)h(t-\tau)d\tau \qquad (16\text{–}34)$$

Equation (16–34) is the general form of the convolution integral, a form that applies to causal and noncausal waveforms.

We now take the Fourier transformation on both sides of Eq. (16–34):

$$\mathcal{F}\{y(t)\} = Y(\omega) = \mathcal{F}\left\{\int_{\tau=-\infty}^{\infty} x(\tau)h(t-\tau)d\tau\right\}$$

$$= \int_{t=-\infty}^{\infty}\left[\int_{\tau=-\infty}^{\infty} x(\tau)h(t-\tau)d\tau\right]e^{-j\omega t}\,dt \qquad (16\text{–}35)$$

Next we interchange the order of integration and factor out $x(\tau)$, since it does not depend on t:

$$Y(\omega) = \int_{\tau=-\infty}^{\infty} x(\tau)\left[\int_{t=-\infty}^{\infty} h(t-\tau)e^{-j\omega t}\,dt\right]d\tau \qquad (16\text{–}36)$$

According to the time-shift property in Eq. (16–31), the quantity within the brackets is $H(\omega)e^{-j\omega\tau}$. Substituting this into Eq. (16–36) produces

$$Y(\omega) = \int_{\tau=-\infty}^{\infty} x(\tau)H(\omega)e^{-j\omega\tau}\,d\tau$$

$$= H(\omega)\int_{\tau=-\infty}^{\infty} x(\tau)e^{-j\omega\tau}\,d\tau \qquad (16\text{–}37)$$

The remaining integral in the last line of Eq. (16–37) is $\mathcal{F}\{x(t)\}$. We conclude that

$$Y(\omega) = H(\omega)X(\omega) \qquad (16\text{–}38)$$

Thus, the Fourier transform of the output equals the Fourier transform of the system impulse response times the Fourier transform of the input.

Equation (16–38) looks suspiciously like the s-domain relationship $Y(s) = T(s)X(s)$, where $T(s)$ is the s-domain transfer function. Since the two input-output relationships have the same form, we call $H(\omega)$ the **Fourier-domain transfer function**. The differences between T(s) and $H(\omega)$ are that (1) $H(\omega)$ exists for noncausal impulse response waveforms for which $T(s)$ does not exist; and (2) $T(s)$ exists for unstable or unbounded impulse response waveforms for which $H(\omega)$ does not exist. Except for these differences, we can say that for a stable causal system $H(\omega) = T(s)\rceil_{\sigma=0}$.

In other words, the transfer function $H(\omega)$ represents the frequency response of a system, including noncausal systems that cannot be treated using Laplace transforms. For example, consider the $H(\omega)$ shown in Figure 16–14. In the filter terminology the gain $|H(\omega)|$ is an **ideal low-pass filter** with a passband gain of unity, a stopband gain of zero, and a bandwidth of β. In Example 16–5 we found that the waveform corresponding to a rectangular transform is the noncausal $h(t)$ shown in Figure 16–14. The noncausal form of $h(t)$ means that an ideal low-pass filter responds before the impulse is applied at $t = 0$. Such anticipatory behavior is physically impossible, so actually building an ideal filter using physical hardware is an impossibility. Nevertheless, the ideal low-pass filter model is used in conceptual design work because it is easily understood and can be implemented in the software simulating a proposed design. Moreover, the ideal filter provides a standard for specifying and evaluating the performance of the real filters that only approximate the ideal response.

Fourier transforms highlight the relationship between impulse response and frequency response. A modern approach to signal-processing design involves defining an impulse response $h(t)$ whose Fourier transform $H(\omega)$ has specified frequency-response characteristics. The signal-processing action is actually carried out using software to convolve $h(t)$ and an input $x(t)$ in the time domain. The fast algorithms for performing time-domain convolution are readily available in commercial software. Thus, one of the reasons that Fourier transforms play a key role in the analysis and design of signal processing is that they offer a computationally efficient way to relate the time and frequency domains.

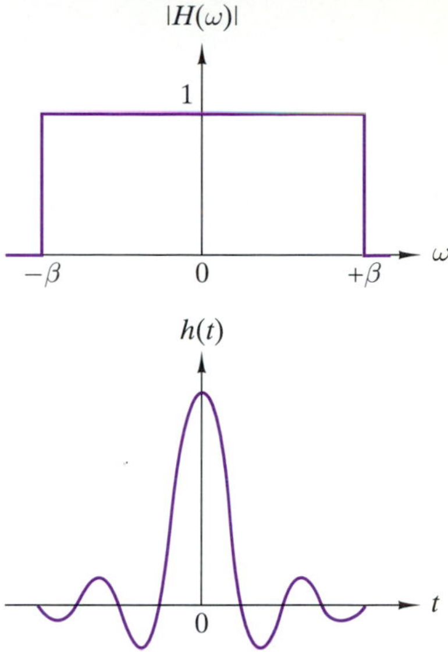

FIGURE 16–14 *Impulse response of an ideal low-pass filter.*

EXAMPLE 16–11

Characterize the frequency response of a system whose impulse response of a system is

$$h(t) = \frac{\alpha}{2}e^{-\alpha|t|}$$

SOLUTION:

The given $h(t)$ is a two-sided exponential whose transform is listed in Table 16–1, so the system transfer function is

$$H(\omega) = \frac{\alpha}{2}\mathscr{F}\{e^{-\alpha|t|}\} = \frac{\alpha^2}{\alpha^2 + \omega^2}$$

The system acts like a low-pass filter since the maximum gain occurs at dc where $H(0) = 1$ and the high-frequency gain monotonically approaches zero. The high-frequency gain rolls off as $1/\omega^2$, or −40 dB/decade. The 3-dB cutoff frequency occurs when $|H(\omega_C)| = H(0)/\sqrt{2}$. Cutoff occurs at

$$\omega_C = \alpha\sqrt{\sqrt{2} - 1} = 0.644\alpha$$

Figure 16–15 shows a plot of the two-sided magnitude of the transfer function. ■

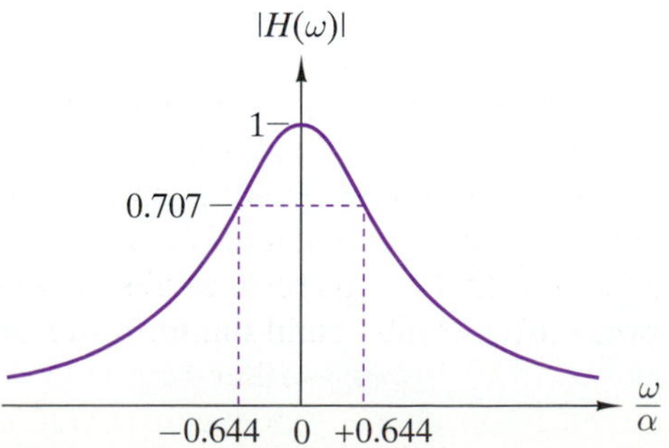

FIGURE 16–15

Exercise 16–11

Characterize the frequency response of a system whose impulse response is $h(t) = \delta(t) - \alpha e^{-\alpha|t|}$.

Answer:
Bandstop filter with $|H(0)| = |H(\infty)| = 1$, $|H(\alpha)| = 0$, and cutoff frequencies at $\pm(\sqrt{2} - 1)\alpha$ and $\pm(\sqrt{2} + 1)\alpha$

As a final signal-processing example, consider an **ideal differentiator** whose output is the time derivative of the input.

$$y(t) = \frac{dx(t)}{dt}$$

According to the derivative property, the Fourier transform of this relationship is

$$Y(\omega) = j\omega X(\omega)$$

from which we conclude that $H(\omega) = j\omega$. The gain of this transfer function increases linearly with frequency, so it tends to accentuate high-frequency noise. To avoid this problem we define a band-limited differentiator as a processor with the following transfer function:

$$H(\omega) = j\omega[u(\omega + \beta) - u(\omega - \beta)] \qquad (16\text{–}39)$$

Figure 16–16 shows the frequency response of the band-limited and the ideal differentiator. In the frequency band from $-\beta$ to $+\beta$ the band-limited processor acts like a differentiator with a gain proportional to frequency. Signals whose amplitude spectrum falls within this band will be differentiated. Signals whose amplitude spectrum lie outside this band (high-frequency noise, for instance) are eliminated. To implement band-limited differentiation via a time-domain convolution, we need to know its impulse response $h(t)$.

FIGURE 16–16

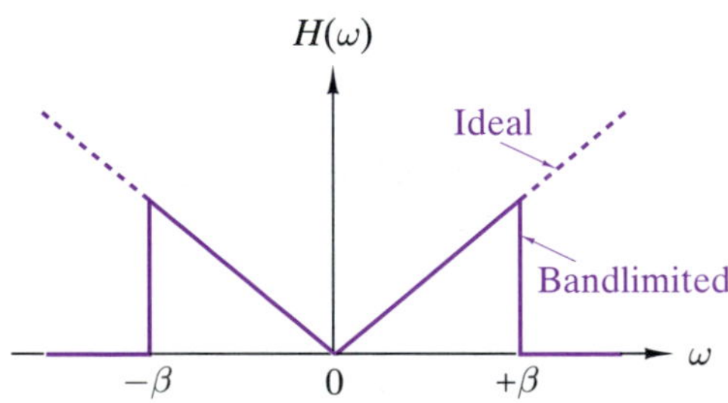

EXAMPLE 16–12

Find the impulse response $h(t)$ of the band-limited differentiator defined in Eq. (16–39).

SOLUTION:

Equation (16–39) gives the impulse response transform. Using the inverse Fourier transformation in Eq. (16–5), we calculate $h(t)$ as

$$h(t) = \frac{1}{2\pi}\int_{-\infty}^{+\infty} H(\omega)e^{j\omega t}\, d\omega$$

$$= \frac{1}{2\pi}\int_{-\beta}^{+\beta} j\omega e^{j\omega t}\, d\omega = \frac{j}{2\pi}\left[\frac{e^{j\omega t}(-j\omega t + 1)}{t^2}\right]_{-\beta}^{\beta}$$

$$= \frac{j}{2\pi t^2}\left[e^{j\beta t}(-j\beta t + 1) - e^{-j\beta t}(j\beta t + 1)\right]$$

$$= \frac{1}{\pi}\left[\frac{\beta t\cos\beta t - \sin\beta t}{t^2}\right]$$

Figure 16–17 shows a plot of this noncausal impulse response. ■

FIGURE 16–17

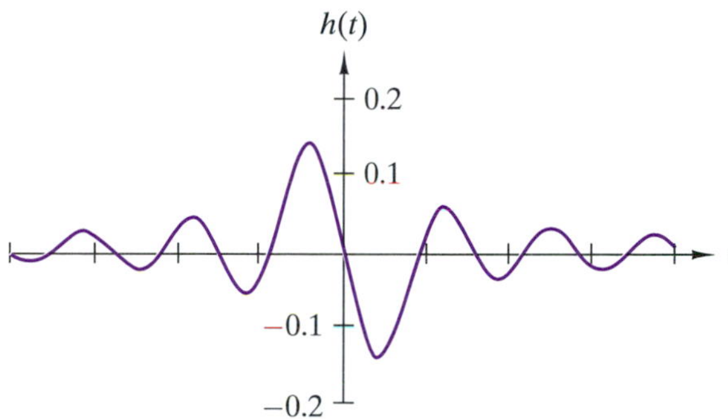

16–7 PARSEVAL'S THEOREM

Parseval's theorem relates the energy carried by a waveform to the amplitude spectrum of its Fourier transform. The total energy carried by any waveform is defined to be

$$W_T = \int_{-\infty}^{+\infty} p(t)dt$$

where $p(t)$ is the power the waveform delivers to a specified load. For a resistive load $p(t) = v^2(t)/R = i^2(t)R$, so the energy delivered to a 1-Ω resistive load can be written in the form

$$W_{1\Omega} = \int_{-\infty}^{+\infty} f^2(t)dt \qquad (16\text{–}40)$$

where $f(t)$ can be either a voltage or a current waveform. Equation (16–40) is often used as the definition of the energy carried by a waveform, although an implied 1-Ω resistance is required for the result to have the dimensions of energy.

Parseval's theorem states that the total energy carried by a waveform can be calculated in either the time domain or the frequency domain.

$$W_{1\Omega} = \int_{-\infty}^{+\infty} f^2(t)dt = \frac{1}{2\pi}\int_{-\infty}^{+\infty} |F(\omega)|^2\, d\omega \qquad (16-41)$$

That is, the total 1-Ω energy can be found from either the waveform $f(t)$ or its transform $F(\omega)$. In the time domain the total energy is the integral over all time of the square of the waveform. In the frequency domain total energy equals $1/2\pi$ times the integral over all frequencies of the square of the amplitude spectrum. Because the squared magnitude $|F(\omega)|^2$ is an even function of ω, the integral over all frequencies is twice the integral over the positive frequencies. Thus, the energy also can be calculated in the frequency domain by

$$W_{1\Omega} = \frac{1}{\pi}\int_{0}^{+\infty} |F(\omega)|^2\, d\omega \qquad (16-42)$$

Parseval's theorem assumes that the integrals in Eqs. (16–41) and (16–42) converge to finite values. Signals for which $W_{1\Omega}$ is finite are called **energy signals**. Examples of energy signals are the causal exponential, the two-sided exponential, the rectangular pulse, and the damped sine. Finite energy is a stronger requirement than the absolutely integrable requirement in Dirichlet conditions. As a result, not all signals that have Fourier transforms are energy signals. The impulse, step, sgn(t), and eternal sinusoid are examples of signals that have Fourier transforms but do not have finite energy.

The derivation of Parseval's theorem begins with energy in the time domain. Assuming the Fourier transform of $f(t)$ exists, this energy can be written in the form

$$W_{1\Omega} = \int_{-\infty}^{+\infty} [f(t)][f(t)]dt = \int_{-\infty}^{+\infty} [f(t)]\left[\frac{1}{2\pi}\int_{-\infty}^{+\infty} F(\omega)e^{j\omega t}\, d\omega\right]dt$$

The integration within the bracket does not involve time, so $f(t)$ can be moved inside the second integral and the $1/2\pi$ moved outside the first integral to produce

$$W_{1\Omega} = \int_{-\infty}^{+\infty} [f(t)][f(t)]dt = \frac{1}{2\pi}\int_{-\infty}^{+\infty}\int_{-\infty}^{+\infty} f(t)F(\omega)e^{j\omega t}\, d\omega\, dt$$

We now reverse the order of integration and factor out $F(\omega)$ to obtain

$$W_{1\Omega} = \int_{-\infty}^{+\infty} [f(t)][f(t)]dt = \frac{1}{2\pi}\int_{-\infty}^{+\infty} F(\omega)\underbrace{\left[\int_{-\infty}^{+\infty} f(t)e^{-j(-\omega)t}\, dt\right]}_{F(-\omega)}d\omega$$

The function inside the brackets is $F(-\omega)$. In Sect. 16–5 we found that $F(\omega)F(-\omega) = |F(\omega)|^2$. As a result, the right side of Eq. (16–43) reduces to the right side of the statement of Parseval's theorem in Eq. (16–41).

EXAMPLE 16–13

(a) Find the 1-Ω energy carried by causal exponential $v(t) = V_A[e^{-\alpha t}]u(t)$ in the time domain.
(b) Repeat (a) in the frequency domain.

SOLUTION:

(a) The given waveform is causal, so the time integration in Eq. (16–40) extends from $t = 0$ to $t = +\infty$.

$$W_{1\Omega} = \int_{0}^{+\infty} (V_A e^{-\alpha t})^2\, dt = \frac{V_A^2}{-2\alpha} e^{-2\alpha t}\bigg|_{0}^{+\infty} = \frac{V_A^2}{2\alpha}$$

This result applies provided that $\alpha > 0$. If $\alpha < 0$ the waveform is unbounded and is not an energy signal.

(b) The Fourier transform of the signal is $V(\omega) = V_A/(j\omega + \alpha)$ provided that $\alpha > 0$. In the frequency domain the 1-Ω energy is found to be

$$W_{1\Omega} = \frac{1}{2\pi}\int_{-\infty}^{+\infty} \frac{V_A^2}{\alpha^2 + \omega^2}\, d\omega = \frac{V_A^2}{2\pi\alpha} \tan^{-1}\frac{\omega}{\alpha}\bigg|_{-\infty}^{+\infty}$$

$$= \frac{V_A^2}{2\pi\alpha}\left[\frac{\pi}{2} - \left(-\frac{\pi}{2}\right)\right] = \frac{V_A^2}{2\alpha}$$

which is the same as the result in (a). This result applies only for $\alpha > 0$ because $F(\omega)$ does not exist for $\alpha < 0$. ■

APPLICATIONS OF PARSEVAL'S THEOREM

The function $|F(\omega)|^2$ is called the **energy spectral density** because it describes how the total energy carried by $f(t)$ is distributed among the frequencies in its spectrum. In this sense we think of the integral

$$W_{12} = \frac{1}{\pi}\int_{\omega_1}^{\omega_2} |F(\omega)|^2\, d\omega$$

as the amount of energy carried by frequencies in the range from ω_1 to ω_2. The energy viewpoint offers a way to quantify the performance of frequency selective filters. Since the output of a filter is $Y(\omega) = H(\omega)X(\omega)$, the energy spectral density of the output signal is

$$|Y(\omega)|^2 = |H(\omega)|^2 |X(\omega)|^2 \qquad (16\text{–}44)$$

The squared magnitude of the filter transfer function $|H(\omega)|^2$ multiplies the input spectral density $|X(\omega)|^2$ to produce the output spectral density $|Y(\omega)|^2$. We can calculate the total amount of energy in the output signal by combining Eqs. (16–42) and (16–44) to obtain

$$W_{1\Omega} = \frac{1}{\pi}\int_{0}^{+\infty} |H(\omega)|^2 |X(\omega)|^2\, d\omega \qquad (16\text{–}45)$$

We can view frequency selective filtering as a process that rejects the input energy carried by frequencies in the stopband and transfers energy carried by frequencies in the passband. Note that we can calculate these energies directly using Fourier transforms without finding signal waveforms.

EXAMPLE 16–14

(a) Find the percentage of the total 1-Ω energy in the causal exponential that is carried by frequencies between $\omega = -\alpha$ and $\omega = \alpha$.
(b) Find the bandwidth required to pass 90% of the total 1-Ω energy in the causal exponential.

SOLUTION:

(a) In Example 16–13 the total 1-Ω energy of this signal was found to be $V_A^2/(2\alpha)$. Using Eq. (16–42), the amount of energy carried by frequencies between $-\alpha$ and α is

$$W_\alpha = \frac{1}{\pi}\int_0^\alpha \frac{V_A^2}{\alpha^2+\omega^2}\,d\omega = \frac{V_A^2}{\pi\alpha}\tan^{-1}\frac{\omega}{\alpha}\bigg|_0^\alpha$$
$$= \frac{V_A^2}{4\alpha}$$

The ratio of the energy in this band to the total energy is

$$\frac{W_\alpha}{W_{1\Omega}} = \frac{V_A^2/4\alpha}{V_A^2/2\alpha} = \frac{1}{2}$$

That is, 50% of the total energy of the causal exponential is carried by the frequencies between $\omega = -\alpha$ and $\omega = \alpha$.

(b) Let $\omega = \beta$ be the bandwidth required to pass 90% of the total energy. The total energy in this band is

$$W_\beta = \frac{1}{\pi}\int_0^\beta \frac{V_A^2}{\alpha^2+\omega^2}\,d\omega = \frac{V_A^2}{\pi\alpha}\tan^{-1}\frac{\omega}{\alpha}\bigg|_0^\beta$$
$$= \frac{V_A^2}{\pi\alpha}\tan^{-1}(\beta/\alpha) = 0.9\frac{V_A^2}{2\alpha}$$

The equality sign in the last line of this equation requires

$$\tan^{-1}(\beta/\alpha) = 0.9\frac{\pi}{2} \quad \text{or} \quad \beta = \alpha\tan(9\pi/20) = 6.31\alpha$$ ■

EXAMPLE 16–15

The input to an ideal, unity-gain low-pass filter is $x(t) = 10[e^{-20t}]u(t)$. Find the percentage of the input 1-Ω energy contained in the output signal when the filter cutoff frequency is $\omega_C = 100$ rad/s.

SOLUTION:

The 1-Ω energy in the input signal is

$$W_{1\Omega,\,IN} = \int_0^{+\infty} 100e^{-40t}\,dt = -\frac{100e^{-40t}}{40}\bigg|_0^\infty = 2.5\text{ J}$$

The Fourier transform of the input signal is $10/(20 + j\omega)$. The frequency response of the ideal low-pass filter is $|H(\omega)| = 1$ for $-100 < \omega < 100$ and

$|H(\omega)| = 0$ elsewhere. Using Eq. (16–45), we obtain the 1-Ω energy in the output signal.

$$W_{1\Omega,\,\mathrm{OUT}} = \frac{1}{\pi}\int_0^{100} \frac{100}{400 + \omega^2}d\omega = \frac{100}{20\pi}\tan^{-1}\frac{\omega}{20}\bigg|_0^{100}$$

$$= \frac{100}{20\pi}\tan^{-1} 5 = 2.19 \text{ J}$$

The fraction of the input energy in the output signal is 2.19/2.5, or about 87.6%. ■

EXAMPLE 16–16

The transfer function of a first-order low-pass filter is $H(\omega) = 100/(100 + j\omega)$. The input to the filter is $x(t) = 10[e^{-20t}]u(t)$.

(a) Find the percentage of the input energy in the output signal.
(b) Find the percentage of the output energy that lies within the filter passband.

SOLUTION:

(a) The input signal is the same as in Example 16–15, where we found $W_{1\Omega,\mathrm{IN}} = 2.5$ J. Using Eq. (16–45), the energy in the output signal is

$$W_{1\Omega,\mathrm{OUT}} = \frac{1}{\pi}\int_0^{\infty} |H(\omega)|^2\,|X(\omega)|^2\,d\omega = \frac{1}{\pi}\int_0^{\infty}\left(\frac{100^2}{100^2 + \omega^2}\right)\left(\frac{10^2}{20^2 + \omega^2}\right)d\omega$$

The integrand in this expression can be expanded by partial fractions as

$$\frac{10^6}{(100^2 + \omega^2)(20^2 + \omega^2)} = \frac{k_1}{100^2 + \omega^2} + \frac{k_2}{20^2 + \omega^2}$$

The constants in this expansion are

$$k_1 = \frac{10^6}{20^2 + \omega^2}\bigg|_{\omega^2 = -10^4} = -\frac{10^6}{9600}$$

$$k_2 = \frac{10^6}{10^4 + \omega^2}\bigg|_{\omega^2 = -20^2} = -k_1$$

The output energy is

$$W_{1\Omega,\,\mathrm{OUT}} = \frac{10^6}{9600\,\pi}\left[\int_0^{\infty} -\frac{d\omega}{100^2 + \omega^2} + \int_0^{\infty}\frac{d\omega}{20^2 + \omega^2}\right] =$$

$$\frac{10^6}{9600\,\pi}\left[\frac{\pi}{40} - \frac{\pi}{200}\right] = 2.08 \text{ J}$$

The fraction of the input energy in the output signal is 2.08/2.5, or about 83.2%.

(b) The cutoff frequency of the lowpass filter is 100 rad/s. The output energy in the passband is

$$W_{1\Omega,\,\text{OUT}} = \frac{10^6}{9600\,\pi}\left[-\int_0^{100}\frac{d\omega}{100^2+\omega^2}+\int_0^{100}\frac{d\omega}{20^2+\omega^2}\right]$$

$$= \frac{10^6}{9600\,\pi}\left[-\frac{\tan^{-1}100/100}{100}+\frac{\tan^{-1}100/20}{20}\right] = 2.02\text{ J}$$

The fraction of the output energy in the filter passband is 2.02/2.08, or about 97.1%. ■

Exercise 16–12

(a) Find the total 1-Ω energy carried by $v(t) = V_A e^{-\alpha|t|}$.

(b) Find the fraction of the energy found in (a) that is carried by frequencies in the range from $\omega = -\alpha$ to $\omega = \alpha$.

Answers:

(a) $V_A^{\,2}/\alpha$

(b) $0.5 + 1/\pi$

Exercise 16–13

Repeat Exercise 16–12 for $v(t) = V_A \alpha t e^{-\alpha t} u(t)$.

Answers:

(a) $V_A^{\,2}/4\alpha$

(b) $0.5 + 1/\pi$

Exercise 16–14

The current in a 5-kΩ resistor is $i(t) = 12\,[e^{-200t}]u(t)$ mA. Find the total energy delivered to the resistor.

Answer: 1.8 mJ

Exercise 16–15

The input $x(t) = 5[e^{-10t}]u(t)$ drives an ideal unity-gain highpass filter with ω_C = 1 krad/s. Find the percentage of the input energy that appears in the filter passband.

Answer: 0.636%

SUMMARY

- The Fourier transformation applies to causal and noncausal waveforms. The inverse transformation is often used to convert transforms into waveforms. When it exists, a Fourier transform pair is unique.

- Sufficient conditions for the existence of $F(\omega)$ are that $f(t)$ be absolutely integrable and have a finite number of discontinuities in any finite interval. Signals not meeting these conditions may still have a Fourier transform.
- If $f(t)$ is causal and absolutely integrable, then its Fourier transform can be obtained from its Laplace transform $F(s)$ by replacing s by $j\omega$. A causal waveform $f(t)$ is absolutely integrable if all of the poles of $F(s)$ lie in the left half of the s-plane.
- The basic Fourier transform properties are uniqueness, linearity, integration, differentiation, and reversal. Other useful properties are symmetry, scaling, time shifting, and frequency shifting.
- Finding circuit responses using Fourier transforms involves transforming the circuit into the frequency domain, solving for the unknown response transforms, and performing the inverse transform to obtain the response waveform.
- Fourier transforms exist for signal and system models that do not have Laplace transforms and are not physically realizable. These ideal models are often used in conceptual system design and as standards for specifying the performance of real systems.
- Parseval's theorem relates the energy carried by a waveform $f(t)$ to the squared magnitude of its Fourier transform. The function $|F(\omega)|^2$ is called the energy spectral density of the signal.

EN ROUTE OBJECTIVES AND ASSOCIATED PROBLEMS

ERO 16–1 FOURIER TRANSFORMS (SECTS. 16–1, 16–2, 16–3, 16–4)

Given a signal waveform (transform), find its transform (waveform) using the integral definitions of the Fourier transformation or basic properties and pairs.

16–1 Use the integral definition in Eq. (16–4) to find the Fourier transform of the sawtooth pulse defined by

$$f(t) = \frac{At}{T}[u(t) - u(t - T)]$$

16–2 Use the integral definition in Eq. (16–4) to find the Fourier transform of the cosine pulse defined by

$$f(t) = A\cos(2\pi t/T)\,[u(t + T/4) - u(t - T/4)]$$

16–3 Use the integral definition in Eq. (16–4) to find the Fourier transform of the sine pulse defined by

$$f(t) = A[\sin(2\pi t/T)]\,[u(t) - u(t - T/2)]$$

16–4 Use the integral definition in Eq. (16–4) to find the Fourier transform of the triangular pulse defined by

$$f(t) = A[1 - |t|/T]\,[u(t + T) - u(t - T)]$$

16–5 Use the integral definition in Eq. (16–5) to find the inverse Fourier transform of

$$F(\omega) = \frac{\pi}{\alpha} e^{-\alpha|\omega|}$$

where α is real and positive.

16–6 Use the integral definition in Eq. (16–5) to find the inverse Fourier transform of

$$F(\omega) = \frac{\pi A}{\beta}[u(\omega + \beta) - u(\omega - \beta)]$$

where A and β are real and positive.

16–7 Use partial-fraction expansion and the basic transform pairs in Table 16–1 to find the inverse transforms of the following functions:

(a) $F_1(\omega) = \dfrac{400}{(j\omega + 20)(j\omega + 40)}$ (b) $F_2(\omega) = \dfrac{j\omega}{(j\omega + 20)(j\omega + 40)}$

(c) $F_3(\omega) = \dfrac{400}{j\omega\,(j\omega + 20)(j\omega + 40)}$ (d) $F_4(\omega) = \dfrac{-\omega^2}{(j\omega + 20)(j\omega + 40)}$

16–8 Use partial-fraction expansion and the basic transform pairs in Table 16–1 to find the inverse transforms of the following functions:

(a) $F_1(\omega) = \dfrac{5000}{-\omega^2 + j200\,\omega + 3600}$ (b) $F_2(\omega) = \dfrac{5000}{j\omega(-j\omega + 50)(j\omega + 50)}$

(c) $F_3(\omega) = \dfrac{5j\omega}{(j\omega + 50)(j\omega + 50)}$ (d) $F_4(\omega) = \dfrac{500j\omega}{(-j\omega + 50)(j\omega + 50)}$

16–9 Use the transform pairs in Table 16–1 and the transform properties in Table 16–2 to find the Fourier transforms of the following waveforms:

(a) $f_1(t) = 2 - 2u(t)$
(b) $f_2(t) = 2\,\text{sgn}(t) - 6u(t)$
(c) $f_3(t) = [2e^{-2t}u(t) + 2\,\text{sgn}(t)]\delta(t + 2)$
(d) $f_4(t) = 2e^{-2(t-2)}u(t-2) + 2e^{-2(t+2)}u(t+2)$

16–10 Use the transform pairs in Table 16–1 and the transform properties in Table 16–2 to find the waveforms corresponding to the following Fourier transforms:

(a) $F_1(\omega) = 4\pi\delta(\omega) + 4(j\omega + 1)/[j\omega(2 + j\omega)]$
(b) $F_2(\omega) = 4\pi\delta(\omega - 4)e^{-j2\omega}/j\omega$
(c) $F_3(\omega) = 4\pi\delta(\omega) + 4\pi\delta(\omega - 2) + 4\pi\delta(\omega + 2)$
(d) $F_4(\omega) = 4\pi\delta(\omega) + e^{-j2\omega}$

ERO 16–2 FOURIER TRANSFORM PROPERTIES (SECTS. 16–3, 16–4)

Use specified Fourier transform properties and pairs to derive other properties and pairs.

Fourier transform pairs can be derived from a wide range of starting places. The following series of problems gives you a transform pair and one or more properties, and then asks you to derive another transform pair using only the given information.

16–11 Given that $\mathcal{F}\{\delta(t)\} = 1$, use the reversal and time derivative properties of Fourier transforms to show that $\mathcal{F}\{\text{sgn}(t)\} = 2/j\omega$.

16–12 Given that $\mathcal{F}\{\cos(\beta t)\} = \pi[\delta(\omega - \beta) + \delta(\omega + \beta)]$, use the time derivative property of Fourier transforms to show that $\mathcal{F}\{\sin(\beta t)\} = -j\pi[\delta(\omega - \beta) - \delta(\omega + \beta)]$.

16–13 Given that $\mathcal{F}\{Au(t)e^{-\alpha t}\} = A/(\alpha + j\omega)$, use the time integration property to find $\mathcal{F}\{(1 - e^{-\alpha t})u(t)\}$.

16–14 Given that $\mathcal{F}\{Au(t)e^{-\alpha t}\} = A/(\alpha + j\omega)$, use the linearity and reversal properties to find $\mathcal{F}\{A\ \text{sgn}(t)e^{-\alpha|t|}\}$. Then let $\alpha \to 0$ to verify that your answer reduces to $\mathcal{F}\{A\ \text{sgn}(t)\} = 2A/j\omega$.

16–15 Given $\mathcal{L}\{e^{-\alpha t}\sin(\beta t)u(t)\} = \beta/[(s + \alpha)^2 + \beta^2]$, use the reversal property of Fourier transforms to find $\mathcal{F}\{e^{-\alpha|t|}\sin \beta t\}$.

16–16 Given the function $f(t) = \delta(t) - \delta(t - T)$, use the time-shifting property of Fourier transforms to show that $|F(\omega)| = 0$ at $\omega = \pm 2n\pi/T$, $n = 1, 2, 3, \ldots$.

16–17 Given the function $F(\omega) = 2\pi\delta(\omega) - \pi[\delta(\omega + \beta) + \delta(\omega - \beta)]$, use the frequency-shifting property of Fourier transforms to show that $f(t) = 0$ at $t = \pm 2n\pi/\beta$, $n = 1, 2, 3, \ldots$.

16–18 Given that $\mathcal{F}\{u(t)\} = 1/j\omega + \pi\delta(\omega)$,

(a) Use the frequency-shifting property to show that

$$\mathcal{F}\{e^{j\beta t}u(t)\} = \frac{1}{j(\omega - \beta)} + \pi\delta(\omega - \beta)$$

(b) Use the result in part (a) and linearity to show that

$$\mathcal{F}\{[\cos \beta t]u(t)\} = \frac{j\omega}{\beta^2 - \omega^2} + \frac{\pi}{2}[\delta(\omega - \beta) + \delta(\omega + \beta)]$$

(c) Since $\mathcal{L}\{\cos \beta t\ u(t)\} = s/(s^2 + \beta^2)$, explain why replacing s by $j\omega$ in the Laplace transform does not yield the result in (b).

16–19 Use the integral definition in Eq. (16–4) to derive the time-shifting property

$$\text{If } \mathcal{F}\{f(t)\} = F(\omega) \text{ then } \mathcal{F}\{f(t - T)\} = e^{-j\omega T}F(\omega)$$

16–20 Use the integral definition in Eq. (16–4) to derive the time-domain sampling property of the impulse function.

$$\text{If } \mathcal{F}\{f(t)\} = F(\omega) \text{ then } \mathcal{F}\{f(t)\delta(t - T)\} = f(T)e^{-j\omega T}$$

ERO 16–3 CIRCUIT ANALYSIS USING FOURIER TRANSFORMS (SECT. 16–7)

Given a linear circuit and a Fourier transformable input waveform,

(a) Use the transformed circuit to solve for transfer functions and output transforms.

(b) Use inverse Fourier transforms to find output waveforms.

The following series of problems use different versions of the general circuit in Figure P16–21. In each problem the switch has been in position A since $t = -\infty$ and is moved to position B at $t = 0$, where it remains until $t = \infty$.

FIGURE P16–21

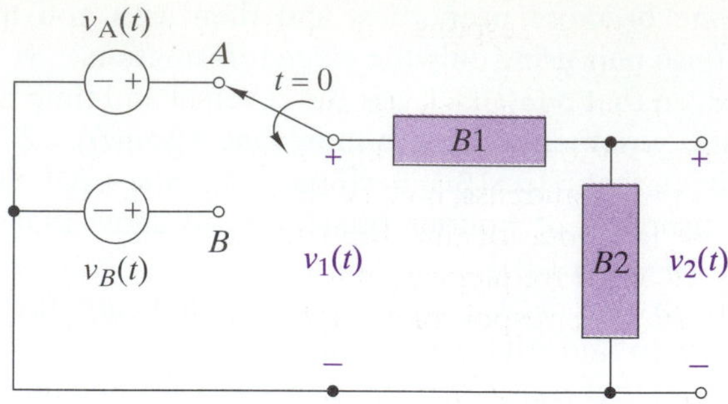

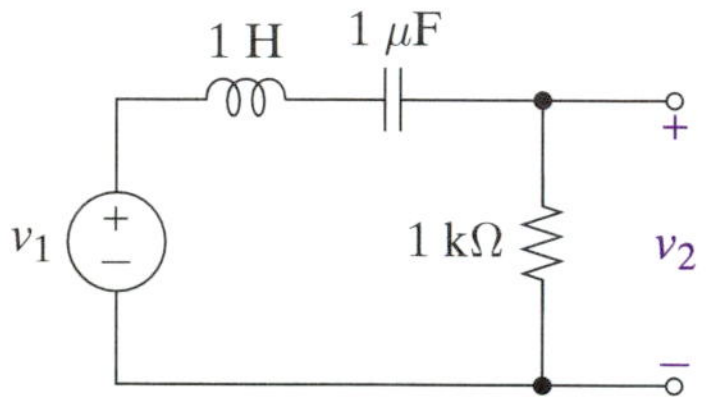

FIGURE P16–26

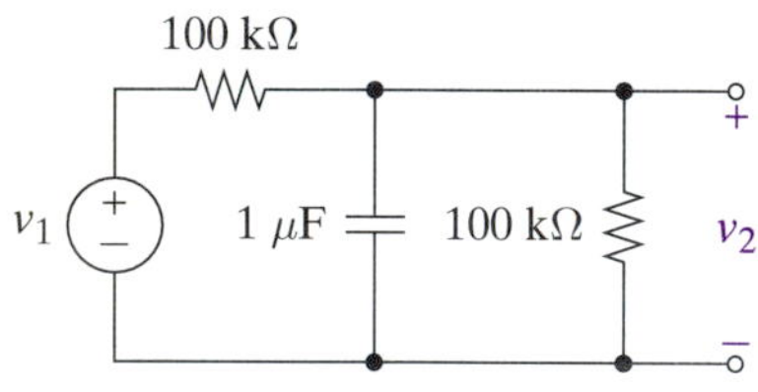

FIGURE P16–27

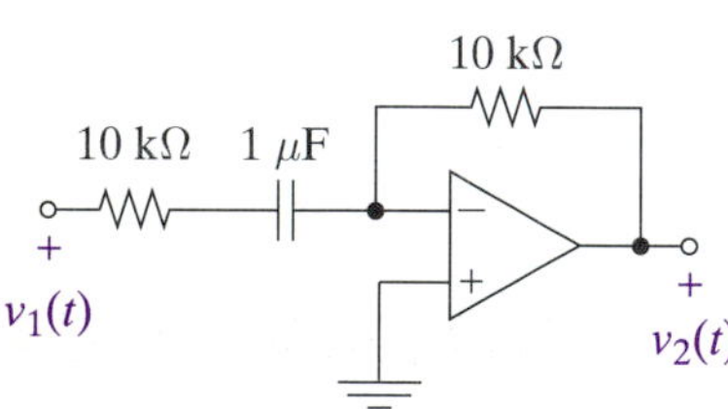

FIGURE P16–29

For each problem
(a) Write an expression for $v_1(t)$ and find its transform $V_1(\omega)$.
(b) Fourier transform the circuit and solve for $V_2(\omega)$.
(c) Use the inverse transform to solve for $v_2(t)$.

Problem	$v_A(t)$ is	$v_B(t)$ is	Branch B1 is	Branch B2 is
16–21	10 V	–10 V	10-kΩ resistor	1-μF capacitor
16–22	$10e^{100t}$ V	$10e^{-100t}$ V	1-H inductor	500-Ω resistor
16–23	10 V	$10e^{-100t}$ V	1-H inductor	100-Ω resistor
16–24	$10e^{100t}$ V	$-10e^{-100t}$ V	500-Ω resistor	1-H inductor
16–25	–10 V	+15 V	1-μF capacitor	20-kΩ resistor

16–26 The circuit in Figure P16–26 is driven by $v_1(t) = 10\ \text{sgn}(t)$ V. Use Fourier transforms to find $v_2(t)$.

16–27 The circuit in Figure P16–27 is driven by $v_1(t) = 20e^{-5t}u(t)$ V. Use Fourier transforms to find $v_2(t)$.

16–28 The input to the circuit in Figure P16–27 is $v_1(t) = 20\ \text{sgn}(t)$ V. Use Fourier transforms to find $v_2(t)$.

16–29 The input to the OP AMP circuit in Figure P16–29 is $v_1(t) = 20e^{-5t}u(t)$ V. Use Fourier transforms to find $v_2(t)$.

16–30 The input to the OP AMP circuit in Figure P16–29 is $v_1(t) = 5\ \text{sgn}(t)$ V. Use Fourier transforms to find $v_2(t)$.

ERO 16–4 IMPULSE RESPONSE AND CONVOLUTION (SECT. 16–6)

(a) Given the impulse response of a signal processor, find its transfer function and characterize the processor's frequency response.
(b) Given the frequency response of a signal processor, find its impulse response.
(c) Given the impulse or frequency response of a linear processor, find the response for a specified input.

16–31 The impulse response of a linear signal processor is $h(t) = Ae^{-\alpha|t|}$ with $\alpha > 0$.
(a) Find $H(\omega)$ and sketch $|H(\omega)|$.
(b) Identify the passbands and stopbands. Classify the processor as low pass, bandpass, high pass, or bandstop.
(c) Find the slope of the stopband asymptote in dB/decade and the 3-dB cutoff frequencies in terms of α.

16–32 The impulse response of a linear circuit is $h(t) = A[\delta(t) - 2\alpha u(t)e^{-\alpha t}]$ with $\alpha > 0$.

(a) Find $H(\omega)$ and sketch $|H(\omega)|$.

(b) Identify the passbands and stopbands. Classify the processor as low pass, bandpass, high pass, or bandstop.

(c) Find the slope of the stopband asymptote in dB/decade and the 3-dB cutoff frequencies in terms of α.

16–33 The impulse response of a linear circuit is $h(t) = A[\delta(t)/\alpha - u(t)e^{-\alpha t}]$ with $\alpha > 0$.

(a) Find $H(\omega)$ and sketch $|H(\omega)|$.

(b) Identify the passbands and stopbands. Classify the processor as low pass, bandpass, high pass, or bandstop.

(c) Find the slope of the stopband asymptote in dB/decade and the 3-dB cutoff frequencies in terms of α.

16–34 The transfer function of an ideal low-pass filter is

$$H(\omega) = [u(\omega + \beta) - u(\omega - \beta)]e^{-j\omega T}$$

Use the inverse transform integral in Eq. (16–5) to find the filter impulse response $h(t)$.

16–35 The gain of an ideal low-pass filter is $|H(\omega)| = u(\omega + \beta) - u(\omega - \beta)$. The phase shift of the filter is

$$\angle H(\omega) = \begin{cases} \pi/2 \text{ for } \omega > 0 \\ -\pi/2 \text{ for } \omega < 0 \end{cases}$$

Use the inverse transform integral in Eq. (16–5) to find the filter impulse response $h(t)$.

16–36 The transfer function of an ideal high-pass filter is

$$H(\omega) = u(-\omega - \beta) + u(\omega - \beta)$$

Use the inverse transform integral in Eq. (16–5) to find the filter impulse response $h(t)$.

16–37 The frequency response of a linear signal processor is shown in Figure P16–37. Find the impulse response $h(t)$ of the processor.

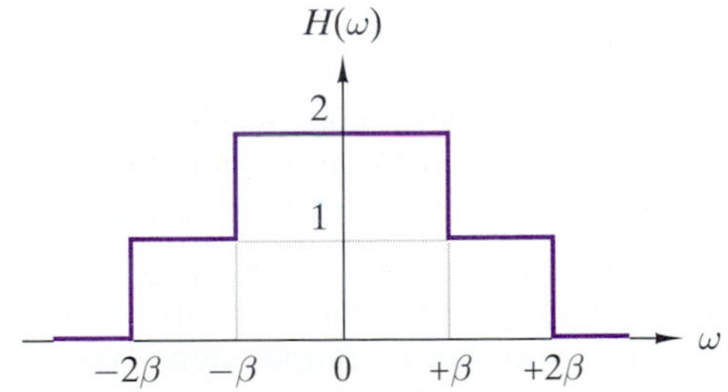

FIGURE P16–37

16–38 The frequency response of a linear signal processor is shown in Figure P16–38. Find the impulse response $h(t)$ of the processor.

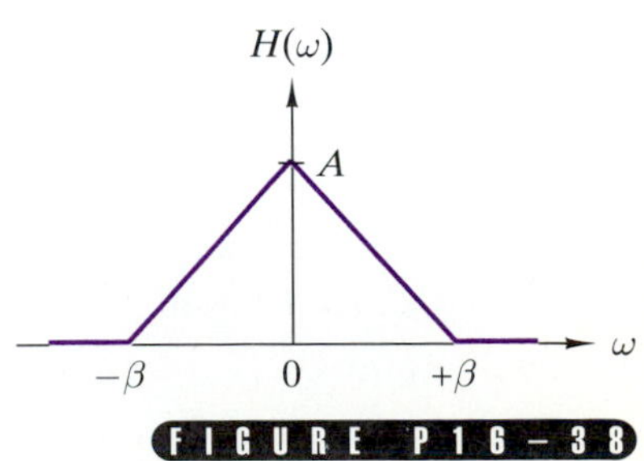

FIGURE P16–38

16–39 The impulse response of a linear signal processor is

$$h(t) = -Au(t)e^{-\alpha t} + Au(-t)e^{-\alpha(-t)}$$

Assume that $\alpha > 0$. Show that the input $x(t) = 2\,u(t)$ and $x(t) = \text{sgn}(t)$ produce the same output $y(t)$.

16–40 The impulse response of a certain linear signal processor is

$$h(t) = 2\frac{\sin 2\beta t}{\pi t}$$

Find the output $y(t)$ when the input is $x(t) = A\sin(\beta t)/(\beta t)$.

ERO 16–5 PARSEVAL'S THEOREM (SECT. 16–7)

Given a signal waveform or transform, find the total 1-Ω energy carried by the signal and the percentage of the total energy in specified frequency bands.

16–41 Find the total 1-Ω energy carried by the waveform $v(t) = V_A \alpha t e^{-\alpha t}u(t)$. Then find the percentage of the 1-Ω energy carried by frequencies in the range $-\alpha \leq \omega \leq \alpha$.

16–42 Find the total 1-Ω energy carried by the waveform $v(t) = V_A(1 - \alpha t)e^{-\alpha t}u(t)$. Then find the percentage of the 1-Ω energy carried by frequencies in the range $-\alpha \leq \omega \leq \alpha$.

16–43 Find the total 1-Ω energy carried by the following signal transform. Then find the percentage of the 1-Ω energy carried by frequencies in the range $-\alpha \leq \omega \leq \alpha$.

$$V(\omega) = \frac{2\alpha V_A}{\omega^2 + \alpha^2}$$

16–44 Find the total 1-Ω energy carried by the following signal transform. Then find the percentage of the 1-Ω energy carried by frequencies in the range $-\alpha \leq \omega \leq \alpha$.

$$V(\omega) = \frac{j\omega V_A}{\omega^2 + \alpha^2}$$

16–45 The transfer function of an ideal high-pass filter is $H(\omega) = [u(-\omega - \beta) + u(\omega - \beta)]$, where $\beta = 2$ krad/s. Find the percentage of the input signal's 1-Ω energy that lies in the filter passband when the input signal is $x(t) = 10e^{-2000|t|}$.

16–46 The transfer function of an ideal low-pass filter is $H(\omega) = [u(-\omega + \beta) - u(\omega - \beta)]$, where $\beta = 2$ krad/s. Find the percentage of the input signal's 1-Ω energy that lies in the filter passband when the input signal is $x(t) = 10\,\text{sgn}(t)e^{-2000|t|}$.

16–47 An ideal unity-gain bandpass filter has cutoff frequencies at $\omega_{C1} = \pm 1$ krad/s and $\omega_{C2} = \pm 1.1$ krad/s and an input signal $x(t) = 10e^{-5000t}u(t)$.

(a) Sketch the squared magnitude of the filter frequency response and the input signal energy spectral density on the same frequency scale.

(b) Estimate the 1-Ω energy that lies in the filter passband without formally integrating the output energy spectral density.

16–48 This problem deals with estimating the amount of energy in the output of a filter for two inputs $v_{S1}(t) = 40e^{-20t}u(t)$ and $v_{S2}(t) = 5e^{-20|t|}$.

(a) Sketch the energy spectral density functions $|V_{S1}(\omega)|^2$ and $|V_{S2}(\omega)|^2$.

(b) Sketch the squared magnitude of the filter frequency response for $H(\omega) = 10/(j\omega + 10)$.

(c) Without formally integrating the energy density, determine which input produces the most 1-Ω energy in the output.

16–49 The input to the RC filter circuit in Figure P16–27 is $v_1(t) = 20e^{-5t}u(t)$ V. Determine the total 1-Ω energy in the filter output.

16–50 Repeat Problem 16–49 using the OP AMP circuit in Figure P16–29.

CHAPTER-INTEGRATING PROBLEMS

16–51 A AC CIRCUIT ANALYSIS USING FOURIER TRANSFORMS

The sinusoidal steady-state response can be found as the forced response of the circuit differential equation (Chapter 7), using phasor circuit analysis (Chapter 8), using Laplace transforms (Chapter 9), or from the circuit transfer function $T(s)$ (Chapter 11). The purpose of this problem is to show that the ac response can also be found using Fourier methods.

The RC circuit in Figure P16–51 is driven by an input $v_1(t) = V_A \cos \beta t$. Fourier transform the circuit and solve for $V_2(\omega)$. Use inverse Fourier transforms to find $v_2(t)$. You will find the following relationship to be quite useful: $H(\omega)\delta(\omega - \beta) = H(\beta)\delta(\omega - \beta)$. Explain why this relationship holds. Check your answer for $v_2(t)$ using phasor circuit analysis.

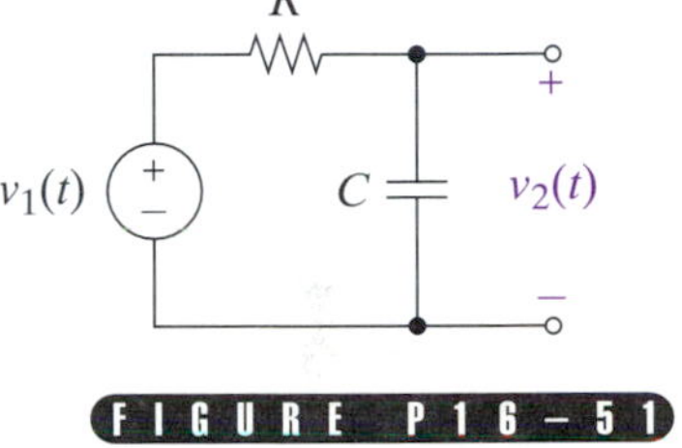

FIGURE P16–51

16–52 A BODE PLOTS AND PARSEVAL'S THEOREM

The purpose of this problem is to explore using the straight-line approximations of the Bode gain diagram to estimate the area under the energy density function of a causal waveform. Consider the waveform $v(t) = V_A e^{-\alpha t}u(t)$ V.

(a) Find the low- and high-frequency asymptotes of the energy density function $|V(\omega)|^2$. Show that these intercepts intersect at $|\omega| = \alpha$. Sketch the asymptotic approximation of $|V(\omega)|^2$.

(b) Use Parseval's theorem and the asymptotic approximation in part (a) to estimate the 1-Ω energy carried by the signal.

(c) Show that the estimate found in (b) overstates the true value of the 1-Ω energy by a multiplicative factor of $4/\pi$.

16–53 A IMPULSE EQUIVALENT BANDWIDTH

Bandwidth is an important concept in circuit and system analysis. Generally in this book we have used the half-power or 3-dB concept to define bandwidth. There are many other ways to define bandwidth. This problem explores one of them.

The impulse equivalent bandwidth of a low-pass filter is defined to be the bandwidth of an ideal low-pass filter with the same dc gain and whose impulse response has the same peak amplitude. That is, let $T(\omega)$ be the transfer function of a low-pass filter. Let $H(\omega)$ be an ideal low-pass filter defined as $H(\omega) = K[u(-\omega + \beta) - u(\omega - \beta)]$. When the parameters K and β are selected such that

$$H(0) = T(0) \quad \text{and} \quad |\mathcal{F}^{-1}\{H(\omega)\}|_{\max} = |\mathcal{F}^{-1}\{T(\omega)\}|_{\max}$$

then β is the impulse equivalent bandwidth of the low-pass filter $T(\omega)$. Find the impulse equivalent bandwidth of a second-order Butterworth low-pass filter defined as

$$T(\omega) = \frac{1}{\left(\dfrac{j\omega}{\omega_C}\right)^2 + \sqrt{2}\left(\dfrac{j\omega}{\omega_C}\right) + 1}$$

Note that ω_C is the 3-dB bandwidth of the filter.

16–54 A IMPULSE GENERATOR

The theoretical impulse has an amplitude spectrum that is constant at all frequencies. In practice, a constant spectrum cannot be achieved, nor is it really necessary. What is required is an amplitude spectrum that is relatively constant over the frequency range of interest. Under this concept an impulse generator is a signal source that produces a pulse waveform whose amplitude spectrum does not vary more than a prescribed amount over a specified frequency range.

Given a rectangular pulse

$$f(t) = A[u(t + T/2) - u(t - T/2)]$$

(a) Find $F(\omega)$ and sketch its amplitude spectrum $|F(\omega)|$.

(b) Show that the maximum value of the amplitude spectrum occurs at $\omega = 0$ and is equal to the area of under $f(t)$.

(c) Select the pulse duration T such that the amplitude spectrum does not change by more than 10% over a frequency range from 1 MHz to 10 MHz.

16–55 A PHASE DISTORTION

The output of an ideal delay is an exact replica of the input except that it is shifted in time. An ideal time delay of T seconds has a Fourier domain transfer function $H(\omega) = e^{-j\omega T}$. The gain and phase of this response are $|H(\omega)| = 1$ and $\angle H(\omega) = -\omega T$. That is, the ideal delay has a gain of 1 and a phase shift that varies linearly with frequency.

Now consider the transfer function

$$H(\omega) = \frac{j\omega - \alpha}{j\omega + \alpha}$$

(a) Show that the gain of this transfer function is unity at all frequencies.

(b) Find the output when the input is $x(t) = e^{-\beta t}u(t)$ when $\alpha \neq \beta$. Is the output a replica of the input? If not, what is the source of the distortion?

PART 3

APPLICATIONS

COURSE-INTEGRATING PROBLEMS
COURSE OBJECTIVES

A Analysis Given a dynamic circuit with sinusoidal input signals, select an analysis technique and find the circuit's response in terms of complex power flow, frequency response, harmonic spectrum response, or continuous spectrum response.

D Design Given a specified ac signal- or power-processing function, design one or more circuits that implement the stated function within given constraints.

E Evaluation Given several dynamic circuits that reportedly perform the same ac signal- or power-processing function, verify the claim and rank order the circuits using stated evaluation criteria.

I–21 A DC, AC, AND IMPULSE RESPONSES

A linear circuit is driven by an input $v_1(t) = 4\cos(1000t)$. The zero-state response for this input is observed to be $v_2(t) = 4\sin(1000t) + 8\cos(1000t) - e^{-1000t}[6\sin(2000t) + 8\cos(2000t)]$.

(a) Find the phasor representation of the steady-state output when the input is

$$v_1(t) = 4\cos(2000t)$$

(b) Find the steady-state output when the input is 5 V dc.

(c) Construct the Bode plot of the circuit gain as a function of frequency.

(d) Determine the circuit impulse response.

I–22 A BANDPASS FILTER STEP RESPONSES

The step responses of the two second-order bandpass filters are

$$g_1(t) = 0.2e^{-20t}\sin(2000t)u(t)$$

$$g_2(t) = (e^{-10t} - e^{-4000t})u(t)$$

(a) Find the center frequency and bandwidth of each filter.

(b) Which filter has a gain less than –20 dB two octaves above and below the center frequency?

(c) Which filter has a gain greater than –3 dB one decade above and below the center frequency?

(d) Which filter has phase shift within ±15° over the frequency range from one octave above to one octave below the center frequency?

I–23 E NEW PRODUCT EVALUATION

The RonAl Corporation has issued Application Note No. 2 on the USPTS integrated circuit described in Problem I–16 of Chapter 11. The note claims that interconnecting three USPTS circuits as indicated in Figure PI–23 produces a third-order Butterworth low-pass filter with $\omega_C = 1/RC$. Verify this claim.

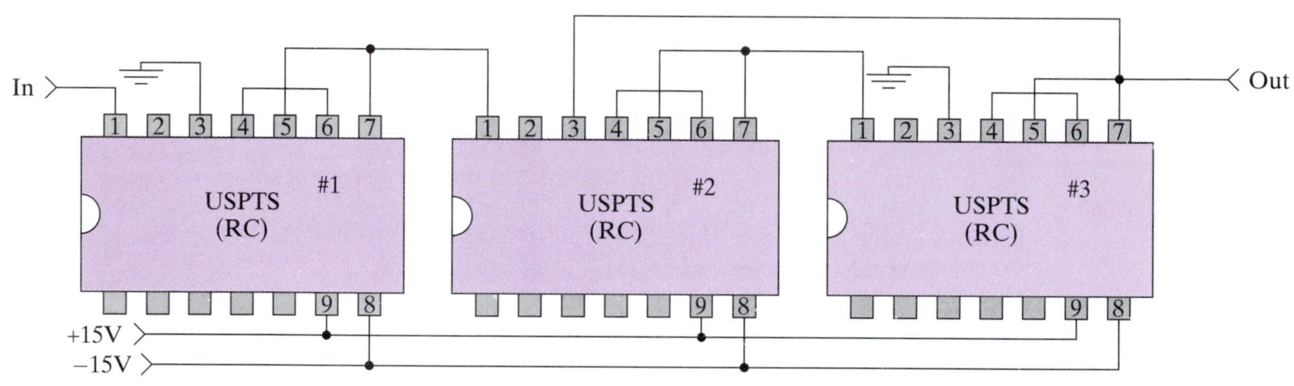

FIGURE PI–23

I–24 A FILTER INSERTION LOSS

Filter characteristics are sometimes specified in terms of insertion loss, defined as the ratio of average power delivered to a load when the filter is not present over the average power with the filter present.

(a) Circuit C1 in Figure PI–24 shows a sinusoidal source connected directly to a resistive load. Use phasor circuit analysis to derive an expression for the average power delivered to the load in the sinusoidal steady state in terms of V_A, R_0.

(b) Circuit C2 shows the same source and load with an inductor inserted between them. With the inductor inserted, use phasor circuit analysis to derive an expression for the average power delivered to the load in the sinusoidal steady state.

(c) Insertion loss is the ratio of power found in (a) and the power found in (b). Derive an expression for the insertion loss of the inductor in terms of R_0, L, and ω.

(d) Show that the insertion loss is unity at zero frequency and explain this result in terms of the inductor impedance. Show that the insertion loss is infinite at infinite frequency and explain this result physically. Find the frequency at which the insertion loss is +3 dB.

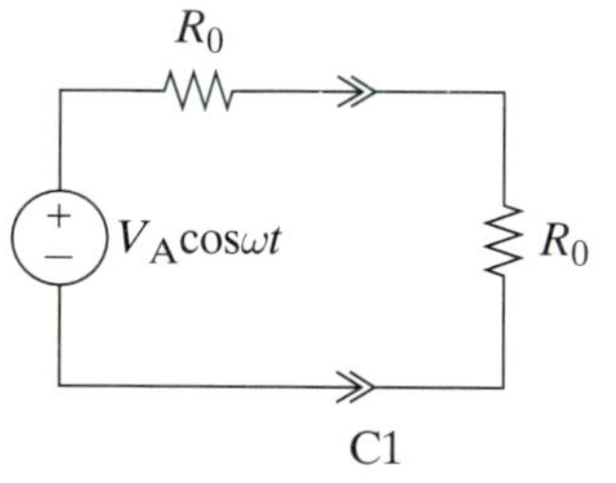

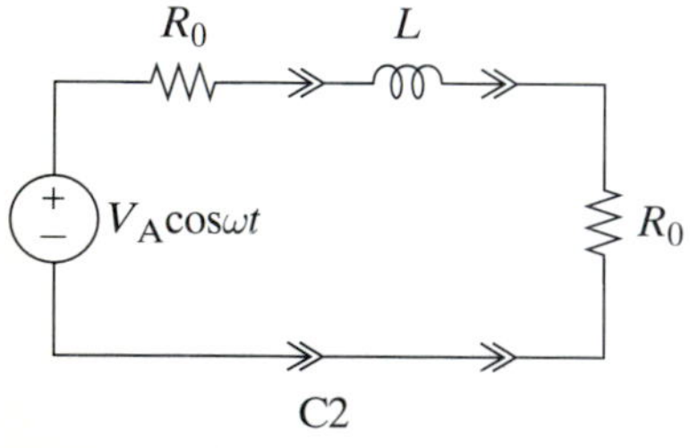

FIGURE PI–24

I–25 D FILTER DESIGN WITH INPUT IMPEDANCE SPECIFIED

Design a circuit whose gain responses lie entirely within the unshaded region in Figure PI–25 and whose input impedance is around 50-Ω for most of the frequencies in the passband.

FIGURE PI–25

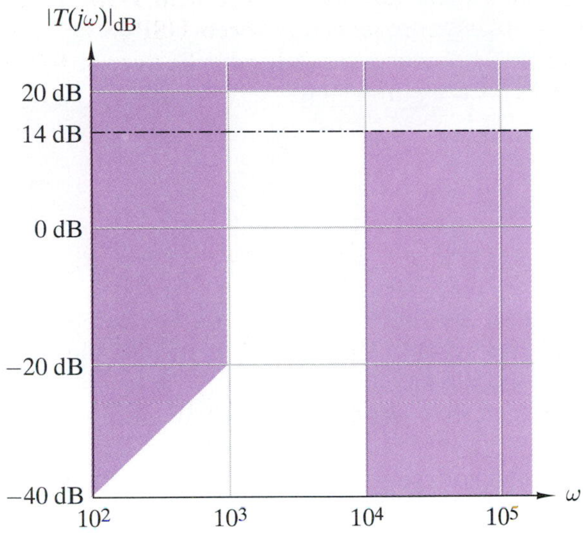

I–26 A D E INVERSE SYSTEM

During a missile flight test a telemetry system monitors a quantity $x(t)$ and records an output signal $y(t)$. The transfer function relating $x(t)$ and $y(t)$ has been calibrated and shown to have a bandpass characteristic of the form

$$\frac{Y(s)}{X(s)} = \frac{Ks}{s^2 + 2\zeta\omega_0 s + \omega_0^2}$$

where K, ζ, and ω_0 are known parameters. During post-test analysis it is necessary to estimate the quantity $x(t)$ from the recorded output $y(t)$.

(a) A For the given transfer function show that $x(t)$ can be recovered from $y(t)$ as follows:

$$x(t) = \frac{1}{K}\frac{dy(t)}{dt} + \frac{2\zeta\omega_0}{K}y(t) + \frac{\omega_0^2}{K}\int_0^t y(x)dx$$

(b) D Design an RC OP AMP circuit that implements this relationship.

(c) E Suppose that small imperfections cause the signal recorded by the telemetry system to be the desired signal plus a small dc offset. That is, the recorded signal is $y(t) + V_{dc}$, where V_{dc} is a small (but unknown and unpredictable) dc value. Describe the way this small offset will affect the output signal produced by the circuit you designed in (b).

I–27 A POWER TRANSFORMER LOAD FLOW

Figure PI–27 shows a model of a power transformer consisting of an ideal transformer with $n = 5$, a resistance $R_{EQ} = 0.02\ \Omega$, and a reactance $X_{EQ} = 0.12\ \Omega$. The transformer's rated output is 50 kVA at a power factor of 0.8 lagging.

FIGURE PI–27

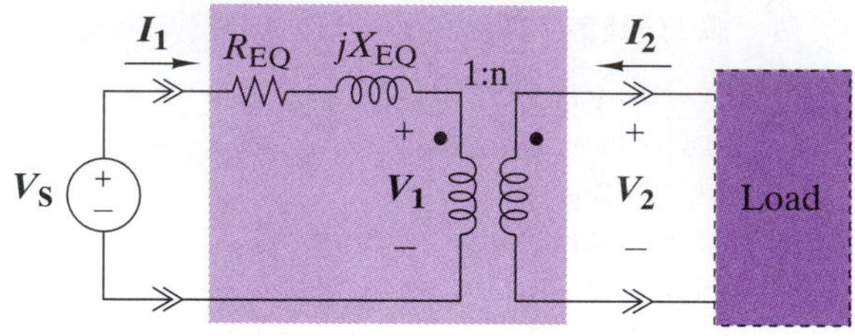

(a) Find the source voltage $\mathbf{V}_S$ required to deliver the rated output with $|\mathbf{V}_2| = 2400$ V (rms).

(b) Find the transformer efficiency under the full-load conditions found in (a).

(c) The percentage voltage regulation (PVR) of a transformer is defined as

$$\text{PVR} = \frac{|\mathbf{V}_2|(\text{at no load}) - |\mathbf{V}_2|(\text{at rated load})}{|\mathbf{V}_2|(\text{at rated load})} \times 100\%$$

Calculate the PVR of this transformer.

I–28 A D E COMPENSATOR DESIGN

A modification is required to improve the performance of an existing output transducer. The compensator/transducer combination must meet the following performance specification:

dc gain 0 dB, gain = 0 ±5 dB for ω between 20 rad/s and 200 rad/s, gain slope of –40 dB/decade for ω > 1000 rad/s. The two designs in Figure PI–28 have been proposed.

FIGURE PI–28

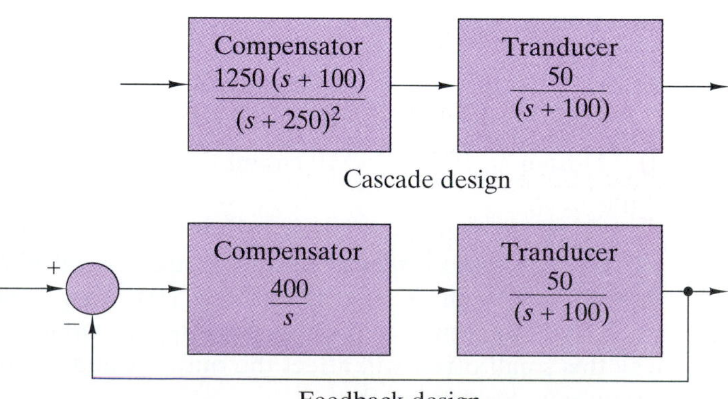

(a) **A** Verify that both designs meet the performance specification.

(b) **E** The compensator is to be built using an RC OP AMP circuit with no more than one OP AMP. Which of the two designs would you recommend and why?

(c) **D** Design an OP AMP circuit to implement your recommendation in (b).

I–29 A D E THIRD-ORDER BUTTERWORTH CIRCUIT

(a) **A** Show that the circuit in Figure PI–29 produces a third-order Butterworth low-pass filter with a cutoff frequency of $\omega_C = 1/RC$ and a passband gain of $K = 4$.

(b) **D** Use the cascade design method in Sect. 13–4 to produce a two-stage circuit that produces the same low-pass filter response.

(c) **E** Rank order the two circuits using each of the following criteria: (1) smallest number of components required, (2) smallest OP AMP gain bandwidth required, (3) smallest number of different component values required, and (4) ease of fine-tuning the cutoff frequency in production.

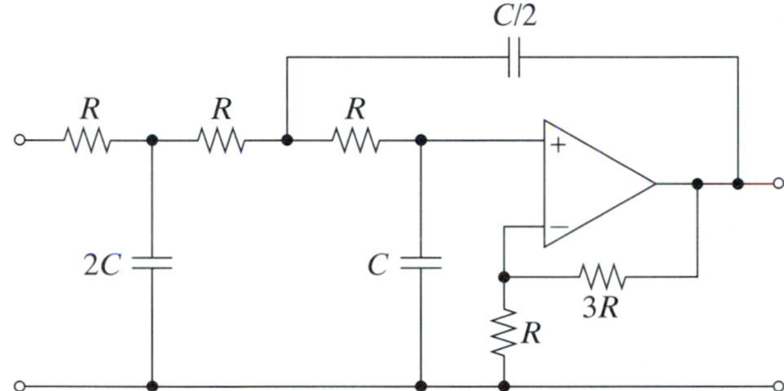

FIGURE PI–29

I–30 A FORCED RESPONSE FOR A PERIODIC INPUT

In Chapter 7 we found that a first-order *RC* circuit is governed by the differential equation

$$R_T C\frac{dv(t)}{dt} + v(t) = v_T(t)$$

In Chapter 15 we found that a periodic waveform can be represented by an exponential Fourier series. Suppose that $v_T(t)$ is a periodic waveform with a convergent Fourier series of the form

$$v_T(t) = \sum_{n=-\infty}^{+\infty} c_n e^{jn\omega_0 t}$$

The forced response for this input is also periodic. Let

$$v_F(t) = \sum_{n=-\infty}^{+\infty} d_n e^{jn\omega_0 t}$$

represent the exponential Fourier series of the forced response $v_F(t)$. Derive an expression relating the Fourier coefficients of the forced response to the Fourier coefficients of the periodic input.

APPENDIX A

COMPONENTS

This appendix describes some of the physical characteristics and limitations of resistors, OP AMPs, capacitors, and inductors. Circuit analysis generally involves ideal models of these devices. Some knowledge of the limitations of ideal models is necessary to appreciate the restrictions of circuit analysis. Circuit design involves choosing circuit component types and values. Some knowledge of the physical characteristics influencing these choices is necessary to appreciate the scope of the circuit design problem.

This appendix provides some background for designing practical electronic circuits. It discusses only a few key features of electronic devices and is not intended to be a comprehensive treatment of device characteristics or circuit design considerations.[1]

RESISTORS

The prototype physical model for a resistor is a homogeneous conductor with a constant cross section. The **resistance** of a uniform bar of length ℓ (m) and cross-sectional area A (m^2) is

$$R = \frac{\rho\ell}{A}\,\Omega$$

where ρ is the **resistivity** of the conducting material in Ω-m. Manufacturing processes achieve specific values of resistance by adjusting device geometry (ℓ and A) or material properties (ρ) or both.

1 For a more detailed discussion see C. A. Harper, editor-in-chief, *Handbook of Components for Electronics*, New York, McGraw-Hill, 1977.

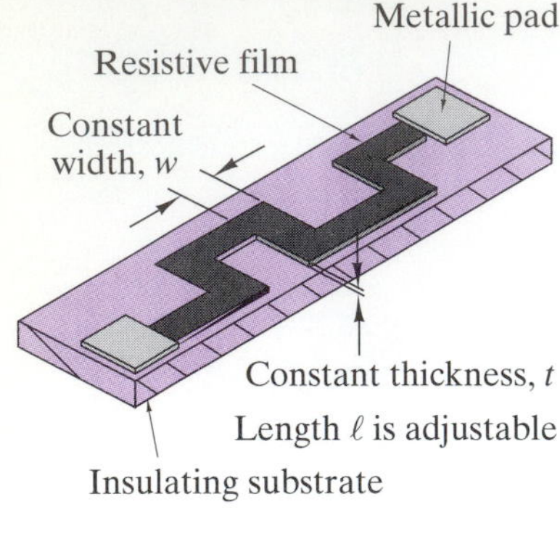

(a)

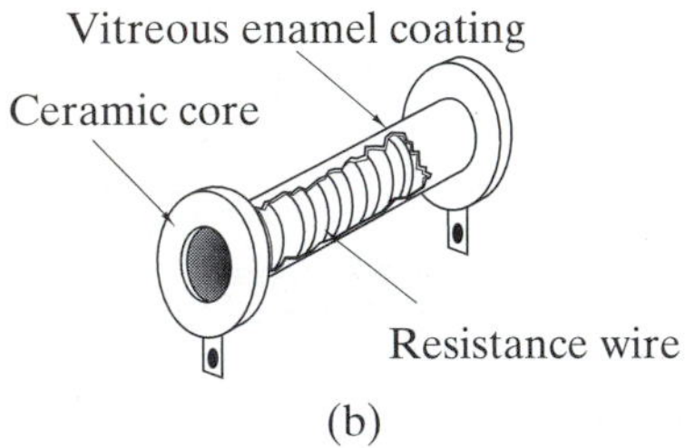

(b)

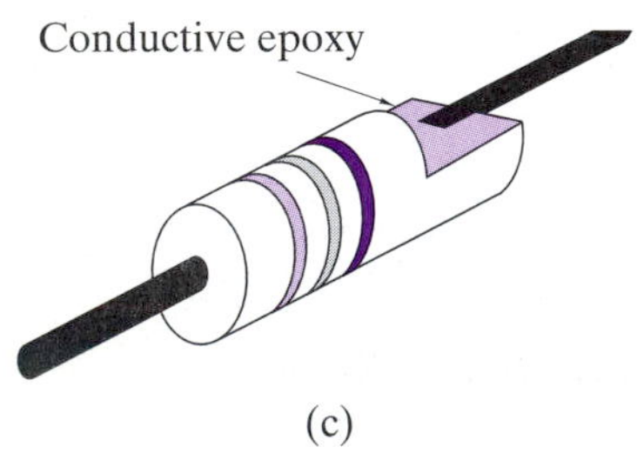

(c)

FIGURE A–1 *Resistor types: (a) Thin or thick film. (b) Wirewound. (c) Composition.*

Figure A–1 shows three basic resistor types. A wirewound resistor consists of a length of wire wrapped around an insulating cylinder. The length of the wire and its resistance per unit length are varied to control the amount of resistance. Composition resistors are made from epoxy material molded into a cylindrical shape. Impregnating the epoxy with a known amount of highly conductive material (usually graphite) changes its resistivity and controls the amount of resistance. Film resistors are made by vacuum depositing a thin layer of metal, or silk screening a thicker layer of conductive paste onto an insulating substrate. The resistivity of the conductive layer is held constant while its thickness, width, or length is varied to control the resistance. These thin- and thick-film techniques can be combined with integrated circuits to produce hybrid circuits.

Resistors in integrated circuits are made by a photolithographic process similar to the thin-film process described previously. The photographic part of the process controls the geometry of the resistors. The resistivity properties are controlled by a diffusion process in which certain pure elements (e.g., B, As, P, or Ga) are introduced into the very pure silicon substrate. The resistors thus fabricated are interconnected with other integrated circuit devices, such as transistors, diodes, and capacitors, directly on the silicon substrate.

To reduce inventory costs the electrical industry has agreed on standard values and tolerances for commonly used discrete components such as resistors, capacitors, and zener diodes. The standard values for resistors and capacitors with 5%, 10%, and 20% tolerances are shown in Table A–1. Standard resistances are obtained by multiplying the values in the table by different powers of 10. For example, multiplying the values for ±20% tolerance by 10^4 yields a decade range of standard resistances of 100 kΩ, 150 kΩ, 220 kΩ, 330 kΩ, 470 kΩ, and 680 kΩ. Standard values for tolerances down to ±0.1% are defined, although the resulting proliferation of values tends to defeat the purpose of standardization.

Table A–2 lists resistor types with their range, typical tolerances, power ratings, and relative cost. Not all types are available in all possible combinations of resistance, tolerance, and power ratings. A lower tolerance or

TABLE A–1 STANDARD VALUES FOR RESISTORS AND CAPACITORS

Value	Tolerances	Value	Tolerances	Value	Tolerances
10	±5%, ±10%, ±20%	22	±5%, ±10%, ±20%	47	±5%, ±10%, ±20%
11	±5%	24	±5%	51	±5%
12	±5%, ±10%	27	±5%, ±10%	56	±5%, ±10%
13	±5%	30	±5%	62	±5%
15	±5%, ±10%, ±20%	33	±5%, ±10%, ±20%	68	±5%, ±10%, ±20%
16	±5%	36	±5%	75	±5%
18	±5%, ±10%	39	±5%, ±10%	82	±5%, ±10%
20	±5%	43	±5%	91	±5%

higher power rating usually means higher initial component costs. The relative costs in the table are only rough guidelines. The total cost of including a resistor in a system depends on many other factors, such as quality control testing, engineering design costs, circuit manufacturing methods, and spare part requirements. These value-added costs usually greatly exceed the catalog price of the resistor.

TABLE A–2 TYPICAL CHARACTERISTICS OF RESISTORS

Type and Range	Tolerances (±%)	Power Ratings(W)	Relative Cost
Composition 1 Ω–20 MΩ	5, 10, 20	⅛, ¼, ½, 1, 2	Low
Carbon film 1 Ω–20 MΩ	1, 2, 5	½–2	Medium
Metal film 10 Ω–10 MΩ	0.01–1	1/20–¼	Medium
Wirewound 0.1 Ω–200 kΩ	0.1–2	1, 2, 5, 10, 25	High
Diffused on IC 20 Ω–50 kΩ	20	—	Very low as part of IC

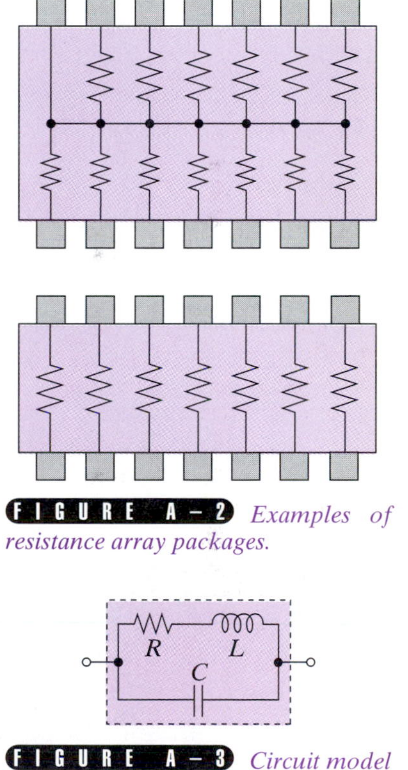

FIGURE A–2 *Examples of resistance array packages.*

FIGURE A–3 *Circuit model for a resistor.*

The advent of integrated circuits has given rise to packaged resistance arrays. Figure A–2 shows some examples of arrays available in 14-pin dual-in-line packages (DIP). Resistance arrays can be fabricated using either thick- or thin-film technology. They generally offer tighter tolerances and closer tracking than discrete resistors of comparable price. These packages also are better suited to automated manufacturing and can be less costly than discrete resistors in large production runs.

Resistors follow the Ohm's law model reasonably well as long as the device is operated within nominal ratings, especially the power rating. The equivalent circuit in Figure A–3 may be needed to model a resistor adequately in high-frequency applications. The inductance L and capacitance C are parasitic elements that unavoidably accompany the desired resistance R. These parasitic elements cause high-frequency effects that limit the frequency range over which Ohm's law adequately describes the device. These high-frequency effects may cause puzzling malfunctions that are difficult to diagnose by studying the nominal circuit schematic. Except for low values of resistance and wirewound resistors, the effect of the series inductance is generally negligible compared with the parallel capacitance.

VARIABLE RESISTORS

A variable resistor, or potentiometer, is a three-terminal device with two terminals connected to the ends of a resistive element, and a third terminal making movable contact with the resistive element at an intermediate point. By connecting the two fixed ends of the potentiometer to a voltage source, an adjustable fraction of the source voltage is available at the movable terminal. Basically, a variable resistor functions as an adjustable voltage divider.

Figure A–4 shows two common types of potentiometers. The rotary devices are used in applications requiring frequent adjustments and the linear devices (trim "pots" being the most common) for infrequent adjustments. Both kinds can be fabricated using composition, film, or wirewound techniques. Some typical potentiometer characteristics are given in Table A–3.

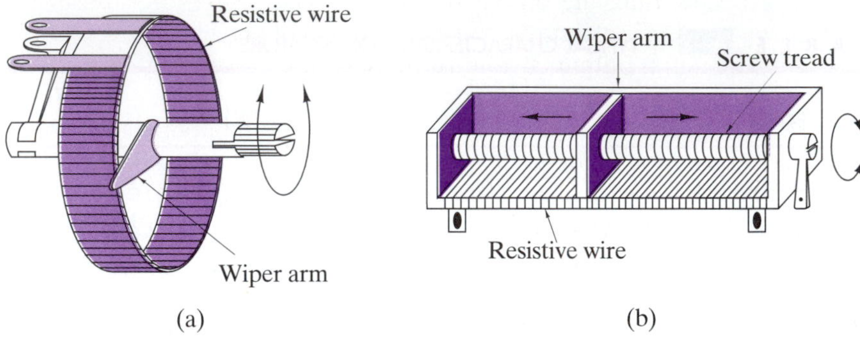

FIGURE A–4 *Variable resistors: (a) Rotary. (b) Linear.*

TABLE A–3 CHARACTERISTICS OF POTENTIOMETERS

Type and Range	Tolerances (±%)	Power Ratings(W)	Relative Cost
Composition 50 Ω–5 MΩ	10	2	Low
Metal film 50 Ω–10 kΩ	2.5	½–1	Medium
Wirewound 10 Ω–100 kΩ	2.5	1–1000	High

Operational Amplifiers

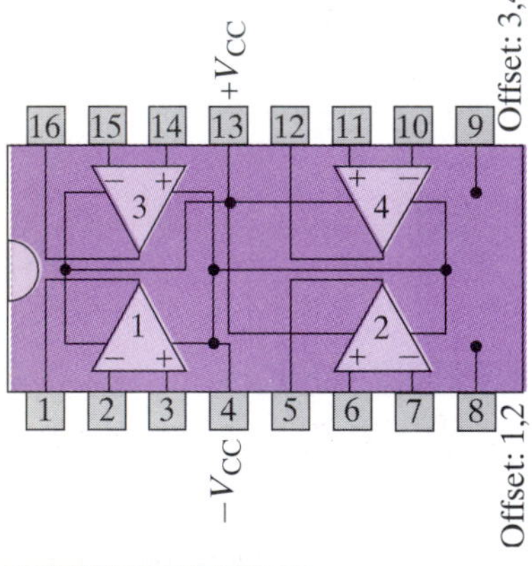

FIGURE A–5 *Quad OP AMP integrated circuit package.*

A typical integrated circuit (IC) operational amplifier (OP AMP) consists of a dozen or so transistors, roughly the same number of resistors, and perhaps one or two capacitors. All of these components are fabricated and interconnected on a tiny piece of silicon, and then packaged as a complete amplifier with only a few key terminals brought out to the external world. The finished package may contain more than one amplifier, as illustrated by the 16-pin quad OP AMP package shown in Figure A–5.

Important OP AMP parameters are input offset, voltage gain, unity gain bandwidth, slew rate, and maximum output current. Offset refers to the fact that the amplifier output may not be zero when the external input is zero. Offset is specified in terms of the input voltage (usually in mV) required to reduce the output voltage to zero. The input offset current (usually in pA) is the input current that exists when the output offset voltage has been reduced to zero. Offset is important in low-level applications where the signal output may be small compared with the no-signal output (i.e., the offset). Offset can be adjusted to zero by applying dc signals to the offset control pins. However, offset varies with temperature and from unit to unit.

The amplifier voltage gain is usually specified in volts per millivolt. For example, a gain of 50 V/mV is the same as a gain of 50,000. The frequency range over which an OP AMP voltage follower has a gain of unity is called the unity gain bandwidth (usually in MHz), or sometimes the gain-bandwidth product. Slew rate refers to the maximum allowable rate of change of the output voltage (usually in V/μs). If the output rate of change exceeds the slew rate, the output becomes a ramp waveform. Slew rate limiting is a nonlinear effect that must be avoided in linear applications. Finally, the maximum output current (usually in mA) is defined for a specified load.

Table A–4 lists some representative values of these parameters for different amplifier types. The table is not definitive, but only shows typical characteristics of several classes of OP AMPs. Some of the OP AMP parameters in the table can be optimized for specific applications, but generally only at the expense of one or more of the other characteristics. For example, a high-power OP AMP can deliver a large output current but has relatively large offset parameters. Conversely, a precision input amplifier has low offset and high gain, but at the price of bandwidth, slew rate, and output current. As the name suggests, the general-purpose amplifier strikes a balance between these extremes.

TABLE A–4 SOME TYPICAL OP AMP CHARACTERISTICS

Type	Input Offset Voltage (mV)	Input Offset Current (pA)	Voltage Gain (V/mV)	Gain Bandwidth (MHz)	Slew Rate (V/μs)	Maximum Output Current (mA)
High power	5	200	75	1	3	500
Wideband	3	200	15	30	30	50
High slew rate	5	100	4	50	400	50
Precision input	0.05	2	500	0.4	0.06	1
General purpose	2	50	100	1	3	10

CAPACITORS

The prototype physical model for a capacitor is two parallel conducting plates separated by an insulating dielectric material. The capacitance of two parallel plates of area A separated a distance d is

$$C = \frac{\varepsilon A}{d}\ \text{F}$$

where ε is the permittivity of the dielectric material between the plates. Although capacitors are realized by several methods, all approaches adjust device geometry (A and d) or material properties (ε) or both to obtain a given value of capacitance.

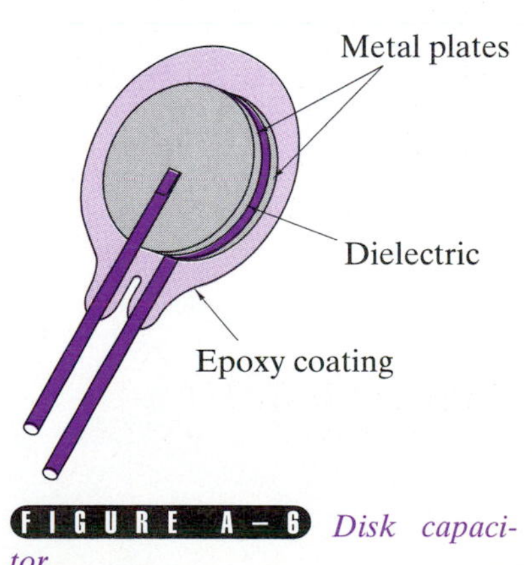

FIGURE A–6 *Disk capacitor.*

The disk capacitor in Figure A–6 consists of two disk-shaped metal plates separated by a dielectric insulator. This geometry closely resembles the parallel plate model. In the final package the disk structure is epoxy coated for mechanical strength and electrical isolation. Disk capacitors are suitable for small values of capacitance, usually in the picofarad range.

The tubular capacitor in Figure A–7 produces capacitances from a few hundred picofarads to a microfarad or so. The device is constructed by rolling up two strips of metal foil that are separated by a dielectric strip such as mylar. The two external leads of the capacitor are connected to the foil strips and the completed roll packaged in a cylindrical tube (hence the name) to provide mechanical strength and electrical isolation.

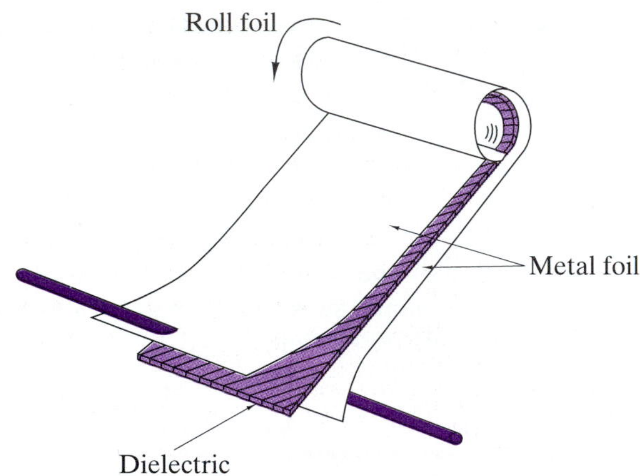

FIGURE A–7 *Tubular capacitor.*

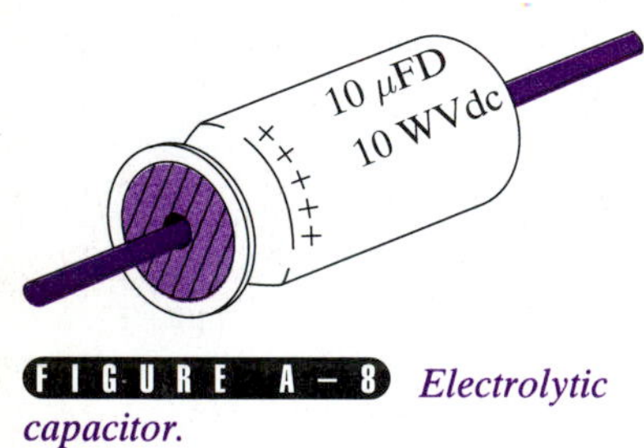

FIGURE A–8 *Electrolytic capacitor.*

Larger capacitances (up to several thousand μF) are made by forming an oxide coating electrochemically on the surface of a metal plate (usually aluminum). These electrolytic devices achieve larger capacitance because the very thin oxide coating serves as the dielectric separating the capacitor plates. The oxide layer is polarized, and voltages applied to these devices must agree with reference polarity marks. An example device with polarity marks is shown in Figure A–8.

Breakdown voltage is a basic limitation of all capacitors. Above the breakdown level, the dielectric becomes conductive and supports an arc that disrupts the capacitive function of the device. For this reason capacitor markings indicate their capacitance and their breakdown voltage, where the latter is usually expressed in dc working volts. Electrolytic capacitors also have polarity marks that must be complied with to avoid improper operation or even damage to the device.

Table A–5 lists the range of capacitances, tolerances, and breakdown voltages for capacitors using different types of dielectric materials. The values in the table give typical ranges for general-purpose capacitors. Capacitors come in standard values that are negative powers of 10 times the preferred values listed in Table A–1. For example, using a multiplicative factor 10^{-7} on the standard values for ±20% tolerance in Table A–1 yields standard capacitances of 1.0 μF, 1.5 μF. 2.2 μF, 3.3 μF, 4.7 μF, and 6.8 μF. Not all capacitor types are available in every possible combination of capacitance, tolerance, and breakdown voltage.

TABLE A–5 CHARACTERISTICS OF CAPACITORS

DIELECTRIC	RANGE	TOLERANCES (±%)	RATED VOLTAGE (DWV)
Glass	1–10^4 pF	5	100–1250
Mica	1–10^5 pF	1, 2, 5	50–500
Paper	10 pF–10 μF	10	50–400
Plastic	1 pF–1 μF	2, 5, 10	50–600
Ceramic	10–10^6 pF	5, 10, 20	50–1600
Electrolytic			
Aluminum oxide	1μ F–2 mF	−10, +5, +30, +50	5–450
Solid tantalum	2 pF–300 μF	5, 10, 20	6–100

Capacitors follow the theoretical model rather closely as long as they are operated within their voltage rating. The equivalent circuit in Figure A–9 may be needed to model a capacitive device adequately. The values of R_P, R_S, and L vary widely between capacitor types. For example, the parallel resistance R_P ranges from as low as 10^7 Ω for some electrolytic capacitors to as high as 10^{12} Ω for high-quality disk capacitors. The parallel resistance models the insulation resistance of the device. The series resistance and inductance limit the frequency range over which the ideal element model adequately describes the device.

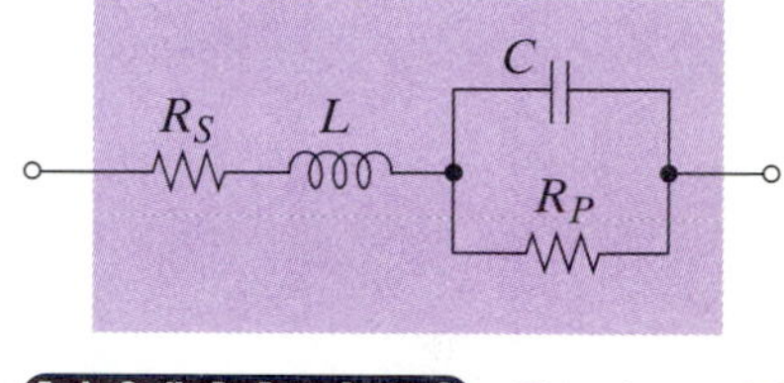

FIGURE A–9 *Circuit model for a capacitor.*

The electronic tuning in modern electronic equipment such as car radios employs a special type of voltage-dependent capacitor called a varactor. These semiconductor devices capitalize on variable space-charge layers that can be analyzed in a manner quite similar to a classical parallel plate capacitor. Applying a control voltage effectively changes the spacing between the space-charge layers or "plates," thereby changing the capacitance of the device.

INDUCTORS

The physical prototype for an inductor is a coil of wire wrapped around a central core. A long helical coil with N turns around a concentric core of cross section A and length ℓ has an inductance of

$$L = \mu \frac{N^2 A}{\ell} \text{ H}$$

where μ is the magnetic permeability of the core material. The value of inductance, like resistance and capacitance, depends on the device geometry and material properties.

Inductors have a wide range of applications that generate a vast assortment of specialized types. For example, there are more than 1500 types and sizes of radio frequency coils alone. Although inductors have many applications, the total demand does not even remotely approach the consumption of resistors and capacitors. Thus, inductors do not lend themselves to industrywide standardization to the same degree as the more

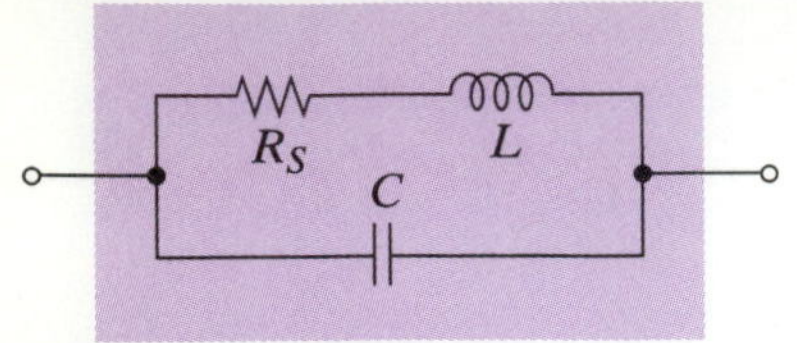

FIGURE A–10 *Circuit model for an inductor.*

frequently used devices. Inductors are not amenable to fabrication by integrated circuit technology except in very special and limited applications. Unlike resistors and capacitors, inductors are often custom designed for an application. Inductors tend to be relatively bulky and expensive, especially in low-frequency applications.

Inductors depart from the ideal element model to a greater degree than resistors or capacitors. The circuit model in Figure A–10 is often needed to represent an inductor adequately across all frequencies. The series resistance represents an inherent feature of a coil of wire. The parallel capacitance is a lumped representation of the distributed capacitance between individual coil turns. At low frequencies the series resistance is the dominant element in the model, while at high frequencies the capacitance dominates. At best there is an intermediate frequency range in which inductance is the primary feature of an inductor.

APPENDIX B

SOLUTION OF LINEAR EQUATIONS

The purpose of this appendix is to review the methods of solving systems of linear algebraic equations. Circuit analysis often requires solving linear algebraic equations of the type

$$\begin{aligned} 5x_1 - 2x_2 - 3x_3 &= 4 \\ -5x_1 + 7x_2 - 2x_3 &= -10 \\ -3x_1 - 3x_2 + 8x_3 &= 6 \end{aligned} \tag{B-1}$$

where x_1, x_2, and x_3 are unknown voltages or currents. Often some of the unknowns may be missing from one or more of the equation. For example, the equations

$$\begin{aligned} 5x_1 - 2x_2 &= 5 \\ -4x_1 + 7x_2 &= 0 \\ -3x_2 + 8x_3 &= 0 \end{aligned}$$

involve three unknowns with one variable missing in each equation. Such equations can always be put in the standard square form by inserting the missing unknowns with a coefficient of zero.

$$\begin{aligned} 5x_1 - 2x_2 - 0x_3 &= 5 \\ -4x_1 + 7x_2 - 0x_3 &= 0 \\ 0x_1 - 3x_2 + 8x_3 &= 0 \end{aligned} \tag{B-2}$$

Equations (B–1) and (B–2) will be used to illustrate the different methods of solving linear equations.

CRAMER'S RULE

Cramer's rule states that the solution of a system of linear equations for any unknown x_k is found as the ratio of two determinants

$$x_k = \frac{\Delta_k}{\Delta} \tag{B-3}$$

where Δ and Δ_k are determinants derived from the given set of equations. A **determinant** is a square array of numbers or symbols called **elements**. The elements are arranged in horizontal rows and vertical columns and are bordered by two vertical straight lines. In general, a determinant contains n^2 elements arranged in n rows and n columns. The value of the determinant is a function of the value and position of its n^2 elements.

The **system determinant** Δ in Eq. (B–3) is made up of the coefficients of the unknowns in the given system of equations. For example, the system determinant for Eq. (B–1) is

$$\Delta = \begin{vmatrix} 5 & -2 & -3 \\ -5 & 7 & -2 \\ -3 & -3 & 8 \end{vmatrix}$$

and for Eq. (B–2) is

$$\Delta = \begin{vmatrix} 5 & -2 & 0 \\ -4 & 7 & 0 \\ 0 & -3 & 8 \end{vmatrix}$$

These two equations are examples of the general 3×3 determinant

$$\Delta = \begin{vmatrix} a_{11} & a_{12} & a_{13} \\ a_{21} & a_{22} & a_{23} \\ a_{31} & a_{32} & a_{33} \end{vmatrix} \tag{B-4}$$

where a_{ij} is the element in the ith row and jth column.

The determinant Δ_k in Eq. (B–3) is derived from the system determinant by replacing the kth column by the numbers on the right side of the system of equations. For example, Δ_1 for Eq. (B–1) is

$$\Delta_1 = \begin{vmatrix} 4 & -2 & -3 \\ -10 & 7 & -2 \\ 6 & -3 & 8 \end{vmatrix}$$

and Δ_3 for Eq. (B–2) is

$$\Delta_3 = \begin{vmatrix} 5 & -2 & 5 \\ -4 & 7 & 0 \\ 0 & -3 & 0 \end{vmatrix}$$

These examples are 3×3 determinants because the system determinants from which they are derived are 3×3.

In summary, using Cramer's rule to solve linear equations boils down to evaluating the determinants formed using the coefficients of the unknowns and the right side of the system of equations.

EVALUATING DETERMINANTS

The **diagonal rule** gives the value of a 2×2 determinant as the difference in the product of the elements on the main diagonal ($a_{11}a_{22}$) and the product of the elements on the off diagonal ($a_{21}a_{12}$). That is, for a 2×2 determinant

$$\Delta = \begin{vmatrix} a_{11} & a_{12} \\ a_{21} & a_{22} \end{vmatrix} = a_{11}a_{22} - a_{21}a_{12} \qquad \text{(B-5)}$$

The value of 3×3 and higher-order determinants can be found using the method of minors. Every element a_{ij} has a **minor** M_{ij}, which is formed by deleting the row and column containing a_{ij}. For example, the minor M_{21} of the general 3×3 determinant in Eq. (B–4) is

$$M_{21} = \begin{vmatrix} a_{12} & a_{13} \\ a_{32} & a_{33} \end{vmatrix} = a_{12}a_{33} - a_{32}a_{13}$$

The **cofactor** C_{ij} of the element a_{ij} is its minor M_{ij} multiplied by $(-1)^{i+j}$.

$$C_{ij} = (-1)^{i+j}M_{ij}$$

The signs of the cofactors alternate along any row or column. The appropriate sign for cofactor C_{ij} is found by starting in position a_{11} and counting plus, minus, plus, minus . . . along any combination of rows or columns leading to the position a_{ij}.

To use the **method of minors** we select one (and only one) row or column. The determinant is the sum of the products of the elements in the selected row or column and their cofactors. For example, selecting the first column in Eq. (B–4), we obtain Δ as follows:

$$\begin{aligned} \Delta &= a_{11}C_{11} + a_{21}C_{21} + a_{31}C_{31} \\ &= a_{11}(-1)^2\begin{vmatrix} a_{22} & a_{23} \\ a_{32} & a_{33} \end{vmatrix} + a_{21}(-1)^3\begin{vmatrix} a_{12} & a_{13} \\ a_{32} & a_{33} \end{vmatrix} + a_{31}(-1)^4\begin{vmatrix} a_{12} & a_{13} \\ a_{22} & a_{23} \end{vmatrix} \\ &= a_{11}(a_{22}a_{33} - a_{32}a_{23}) - a_{21}(a_{12}a_{33} - a_{32}a_{13}) + a_{31}(a_{12}a_{23} - a_{22}a_{13}) \end{aligned}$$

An identical expression for Δ is obtained using any other row or column. For determinants greater than 3×3 the minors themselves can be evaluated using this approach. However, a system of equations leading to determinants larger than 3×3 is probably better handled using computer tools.

EXAMPLE B–1

Solve for the three unknowns in Eq. (B–1) using Cramer's rule.

SOLUTION:

Expanding the system determinant about the first column yields

$$\Delta = \begin{vmatrix} 5 & -2 & -3 \\ -5 & 7 & -2 \\ -3 & -3 & 8 \end{vmatrix} = 5\begin{vmatrix} 7 & -2 \\ -3 & 8 \end{vmatrix} - (-5)\begin{vmatrix} -2 & -3 \\ -3 & 8 \end{vmatrix} + (-3)\begin{vmatrix} -2 & -3 \\ 7 & -2 \end{vmatrix}$$

$$= 5[7 \times 8 - (-2)(-3)] - (-5)[(-2) \times 8 - (-3)(-3)] + (-3)[(-2)(-2) - (7)(-3)]$$

$$= 250 - 125 - 75 = 50$$

Expanding Δ_1 about the first column yields

$$\Delta_1 = \begin{vmatrix} 4 & -2 & -3 \\ -10 & 7 & -2 \\ 6 & -3 & 8 \end{vmatrix} = 4\begin{vmatrix} 7 & -2 \\ -3 & 8 \end{vmatrix} - (-10)\begin{vmatrix} -2 & -3 \\ -3 & 8 \end{vmatrix} + (6)\begin{vmatrix} -2 & -3 \\ 7 & -2 \end{vmatrix}$$

$$= 200 - 250 + 150 = 100$$

Expanding Δ_2 about the first column yields

$$\Delta_2 = \begin{vmatrix} 5 & 4 & -3 \\ -5 & -10 & -2 \\ -3 & 6 & 8 \end{vmatrix} = 5\begin{vmatrix} -10 & -2 \\ 6 & 8 \end{vmatrix} - (-5)\begin{vmatrix} 4 & -3 \\ 6 & 8 \end{vmatrix} + (-3)\begin{vmatrix} 4 & -3 \\ -10 & -2 \end{vmatrix}$$

$$= -340 + 250 + 114 = 24$$

Expanding Δ_3 about the first column yields

$$\Delta_3 = \begin{vmatrix} 5 & -2 & 4 \\ -5 & 7 & -10 \\ -3 & -3 & 6 \end{vmatrix} = 5\begin{vmatrix} 7 & -10 \\ -3 & 6 \end{vmatrix} - (-5)\begin{vmatrix} -2 & 4 \\ -3 & 6 \end{vmatrix} + (-3)\begin{vmatrix} -2 & 4 \\ 7 & -10 \end{vmatrix}$$

$$= 60 - 0 + 24 = 84$$

Now, applying Cramer's rule, we solve for the three unknowns.

$$x_1 = \frac{\Delta_1}{\Delta} = \frac{100}{50} = 2$$

$$x_2 = \frac{\Delta_2}{\Delta} = \frac{24}{50} = 0.48$$

$$x_3 = \frac{\Delta_3}{\Delta} = \frac{84}{50} = 1.68$$

■

Exercise B–1

Evaluate Δ, Δ_1, Δ_2, and Δ_3 for Eq. (B–2).

Answer: 216, 280, 160, and 60

GAUSSIAN ELIMINATION

Gaussian elimination is the basis for most computer programs for solving linear equations. Basically, this method reduces the system of equations to a triangular form by systematically eliminating one variable at a time. Given three equations in three unknowns

$$a_{11}x_1 + a_{12}x_2 + a_{13}x_3 = b_1$$
$$a_{21}x_1 + a_{22}x_2 + a_{23}x_3 = b_2$$
$$a_{31}x_1 + a_{32}x_2 + a_{33}x_3 = b_3$$

we multiply or divide these equations by constants and add or subtract equations to reduce the equations to an equivalent form:

$$x + c_{12}x_2 + c_{13}x_3 = d_1$$
$$x_2 + c_{23}x_3 = d_2$$
$$x_3 = d_3$$

When reduced to this format, these equations immediately yield the solution for x_3. The value of x_3 is then back substituted into the second equation to solve for x_2. Finally, the values of x_2 and x_3 are back substituted into the first equation to find x_1.

Gaussian elimination produces the solution of the original equations because multiplying equations by nonzero constants or adding equations yields an equivalent set of equations that has the same solution.

EXAMPLE B–2

Solve for the three unknowns in Eq. (B–1) using Gaussian elimination.

SOLUTION:

The given equations are

$$5x_1 - 2x_2 - 3x_3 = 4$$
$$-5x_1 + 7x_2 - 2x_3 = -10$$
$$-3x_1 - 3x_2 + 8x_3 = 6$$

Dividing the first equation by 5, the second by –5, and the third by –3 yields

$$x_1 - \frac{2}{5}x_2 - \frac{3}{5}x_3 = \frac{4}{5}$$

$$x_1 - \frac{7}{5}x_2 + \frac{2}{5}x_3 = 2$$

$$x_1 + x_2 - \frac{8}{3}x_3 = -2$$

Subtracting the first equation from the second and third equations eliminates x_1 from these equations:

$$x_1 - \frac{2}{5}x_2 - \frac{3}{5}x_3 = \frac{4}{5}$$
$$-x_2 + x_3 = \frac{6}{5}$$
$$\frac{7}{5}x_2 - \frac{31}{15}x_3 = -\frac{14}{5}$$

Dividing the second equation by –1 and the third equation by 5/7 yields

$$x_1 - \frac{2}{5}x_2 - \frac{3}{5}x_3 = \frac{4}{5}$$
$$x_2 - x_3 = -\frac{6}{5}$$
$$x_2 - \frac{31}{21}x_3 = -2$$

Subtracting the second equation from the third eliminates x_2 from the last equation:

$$x_1 - \frac{2}{5}x_2 - \frac{3}{5}x_3 = \frac{4}{5}$$
$$x_2 - x_3 = -\frac{6}{5}$$
$$-\frac{10}{21}x_3 = -\frac{4}{5}$$

The third equation yields $x_3 = 84/50$. Substituting x_3 back into the second equation gives

$$x_2 - \frac{84}{50} = -\frac{6}{5}$$

which yields $x_2 = 24/50$. Substituting x_2 and x_3 into the first equation gives

$$x_1 - \frac{2}{5}\left(\frac{24}{50}\right) - \frac{3}{5}\left(\frac{84}{50}\right) = \frac{4}{5}$$

which yields $x_1 = 2$. These are the same answers found in Example B–1 using Cramer's rule. ■

Exercise B–2

Use Gaussian elimination to solve the following linear equations:

$$2x_1 - x_2 - x_3 = 6$$
$$-x_1 + 3x_2 = 3$$
$$-x_1 + 6x_3 = 0$$

Answers: $x_1 = 4.667, x_2 = 2.556, x_3 = 0.7778$

MATRICES AND LINEAR EQUATIONS

Circuit equations can be formulated and solved in matrix format. By definition, a **matrix** is a rectangular array written as

$$\mathbf{A} = \begin{bmatrix} a_{11} & a_{12} & a_{13} & \dots & a_{1n} \\ a_{21} & a_{22} & a_{23} & \dots & a_{2n} \\ \dots & \dots & \dots & \dots & \dots \\ a_{m1} & a_{m2} & a_{m3} & \dots & a_{mn} \end{bmatrix} \quad \text{(B-6)}$$

The matrix **A** in Eq. (B–6) contains *m* rows and *n* columns and is said to be of order *m by n* (or $m \times n$). The matrix motation in Eq. (B–6) can be abbreviated as follows:

$$\mathbf{A} = [a_{ij}]_{mn} \quad \text{(B-7)}$$

where a_{ij} is the element in the *i*th row and *j*th column.

SOME DEFINITIONS

Different types of matrices have special names. A **row matrix** has only one row ($m = 1$) and any number of columns. A **column matrix** has only one column ($n = 1$) and any number of rows. A **square matrix** has the same number of rows as columns ($m = n$). A **diagonal matrix** is a square matrix in which all elements not on the main diagonal are zero ($a_{ij} = 0$ for $i \neq j$). An **identity matrix** is a diagonal matrix for which the main diagonal elements are all unity ($a_{ii} = 1$).

For example, given

$$\mathbf{A} = [1 \quad -2 \quad 0 \quad 4] \quad \mathbf{B} = \begin{bmatrix} 3 \\ -2 \\ 6 \\ 0 \end{bmatrix} \quad \mathbf{C} = \begin{bmatrix} 1 & 0 & -7 \\ -3 & 12 & 0 \\ 0 & 0 & -4 \end{bmatrix} \quad \mathbf{U} = \begin{bmatrix} 1 & 0 & 0 & 0 \\ 0 & 1 & 0 & 0 \\ 0 & 0 & 1 & 0 \\ 0 & 0 & 0 & 1 \end{bmatrix}$$

we say that **A** is a 1×4 row matrix, **B** is a 4×1 column matrix, **C** is a 3×3 square matrix, and **U** is a 4×4 identity matrix.

The **determinant** of a square matrix **A** (denoted det **A**) has the same elements as the matrix itself. For example, given

$$\mathbf{A} = \begin{bmatrix} 4 & -6 \\ 1 & -2 \end{bmatrix} \text{ then } \det \mathbf{A} = \begin{vmatrix} 4 & -6 \\ 1 & -2 \end{vmatrix} = -8 + 6 = -2$$

The **transpose** of a matrix **A** (denoted $\mathbf{A}^T$) is formed by interchanging the rows and columns. For example, given

$$\mathbf{A} = \begin{bmatrix} 1 & 2 & 0 & 8 \\ 4 & 7 & -1 & -3 \end{bmatrix} \text{ then } \mathbf{A}^T = \begin{bmatrix} 1 & 4 \\ 2 & 7 \\ 0 & -1 \\ 8 & -3 \end{bmatrix}$$

The **adjoint** of a square matrix **A** (denoted adj **A**) is formed by replacing each element a_{ij} by its cofactor C_{ij} and then transposing.

$$\text{adj } \mathbf{A} = [C_{ij}]^T \quad \text{(B-8)}$$

For example, if

$$\mathbf{A} = \begin{bmatrix} -3 & 2 \\ 0 & 5 \end{bmatrix} \text{ then } C_{11} = 5 \quad C_{12} = 0 \quad C_{21} = -2 \quad C_{22} = -3$$

and therefore

$$\text{adj } \mathbf{A} = \begin{bmatrix} 5 & 0 \\ -2 & -3 \end{bmatrix}^T = \begin{bmatrix} 5 & -2 \\ 0 & -3 \end{bmatrix}$$

MATRIX ALGEBRA

The matrices **A** and **B** are equal if and only if they have the same number of rows and columns, and $a_{ij} = b_{ij}$ for all i and j. Matrix addition is only possible when two matrices have the same number of rows and columns. When two matrices are of the same order, their sum is obtained by adding the corresponding elements: that is,

$$\text{If } \mathbf{C} = \mathbf{A} + \mathbf{B} \text{ then } c_{ij} = a_{ij} + b_{ij} \quad \text{(B-9)}$$

For example, given

$$\mathbf{A} = \begin{bmatrix} -1 & 4 \\ -3 & -2 \end{bmatrix} \text{ and } \mathbf{B} = \begin{bmatrix} 3 & 0 \\ 2 & -4 \end{bmatrix} \text{ then } \mathbf{C} = \mathbf{A} + \mathbf{B} = \begin{bmatrix} 2 & 4 \\ -1 & -6 \end{bmatrix}$$

Multiplying a matrix **A** by a scalar constant k is accomplished by multiplying every element by k; that is, $k\mathbf{A} = [ka_{ij}]$. In particular, if $k = -1$ then $-\mathbf{B} = [-b_{ij}]$, and applying the matrix addition rule yields matrix **subtraction**.

$$\text{If } \mathbf{C} = \mathbf{A} - \mathbf{B} \text{ then } c_{ij} = a_{ij} - b_{ij} \quad \text{(B-10)}$$

Multiplication of two matrices **AB** is defined only if the number of columns in **A** equals the number of rows in **B**. In general, if **A** is of order $m \times n$ and **B** is of order $n \times r$, then the product $\mathbf{C} = \mathbf{AB}$ is a matrix of order $m \times r$. The element c_{ij} is found by summing the products of the elements in the ith row of **A** and the jth column of **B**.

$$c_{ij} = [a_{i1}\ a_{i2}\ \dots\ a_{in}] \begin{bmatrix} b_{1j} \\ b_{2j} \\ \cdot\cdot \\ \cdot\cdot \\ \cdot\cdot \\ b_{nj} \end{bmatrix} = a_{i1}b_{1j} + a_{i2}b_{2j} + \cdots a_{in}b_{nj}$$

$$= \sum_{k=1}^{n} a_{ik}b_{kj} \quad \text{(B-11)}$$

In other words, matrix multiplication is a row by column operation.

Matrix multiplication is not commutative so usually $\mathbf{AB} \neq \mathbf{BA}$. Two important exceptions are (1) the product of a square matrix **A** and an identity matrix **U** for which $\mathbf{UA} = \mathbf{AU} = \mathbf{A}$, and (2) the product of a square matrix **A** and its **inverse** (denoted $\mathbf{A}^{-1}$) for which $\mathbf{A}^{-1}\mathbf{A} = \mathbf{AA}^{-1} = \mathbf{U}$. A closed-form formula for the inverse of a square matrix is

$$\mathbf{A}^{-1} = \frac{\text{adj}\,\mathbf{A}}{\det \mathbf{A}} \tag{B-12}$$

That is, the inverse can be found by multiplying the adjoint matrix of **A** by the scalar 1/det **A**. If det **A** = 0 then **A** is said to be **singular** and $\mathbf{A}^{-1}$ does not exist. Equation (B–12) is useful for deriving properties of the inverse of a matrix. It is not, however, a very efficient way to calculate the inverse of a matrix of order greater than 3×3.

Exercise B–3

Given:

$$\mathbf{A} = \begin{bmatrix} -5 & 7 \\ 7 & 11 \end{bmatrix} \text{ and } \mathbf{B} = \begin{bmatrix} 3 & -1 \\ 6 & -2 \end{bmatrix}$$

Calculate AB, BA, A^{-1}, and B^{-1}.

Answers:

$$\mathbf{AB} = \begin{bmatrix} 27 & -9 \\ 87 & -29 \end{bmatrix} \quad \mathbf{BA} = \begin{bmatrix} -22 & 10 \\ -44 & 20 \end{bmatrix}$$

$$\mathbf{A}^{-1} = \frac{1}{104}\begin{bmatrix} -11 & 7 \\ 7 & 5 \end{bmatrix} \quad \mathbf{B}^{-1} \text{ does not exist}$$

MATRIX SOLUTION OF LINEAR EQUATIONS

The three linear equations in Eq. (B–1) are

$$\begin{aligned} 5x_1 - 2x_2 - 3x_3 &= 4 \\ -5x_1 + 7x_2 - 2x_3 &= -10 \\ -3x_1 - 3x_2 + 8x_3 &= 6 \end{aligned}$$

These equations are expressed in matrix form as follows:

$$\begin{bmatrix} 5 & -2 & -3 \\ -5 & 7 & -2 \\ -3 & -3 & 8 \end{bmatrix} \begin{bmatrix} x_1 \\ x_2 \\ x_3 \end{bmatrix} = \begin{bmatrix} 4 \\ -10 \\ 6 \end{bmatrix} \tag{B-13}$$

The left side of Eq. (B–13) is the product of a 3×3 square matrix and a 3×1 column matrix of unknowns. The elements in the square matrix are the coefficients of the unknown in the given equations. The matrix product on the left side in Eq. (B–13) produces a 3×1 matrix, which equals the

3×1 column matrix on the right side. The elements of the 3×1 on the right side are the constants on the right sides of the given equations.

In symbolic form we write the matrix equation in Eq. (B–13) as

$$\mathbf{AX} = \mathbf{B} \tag{B-14}$$

where

$$\mathbf{A} = \begin{bmatrix} 5 & -2 & -3 \\ -5 & 7 & -2 \\ -3 & -3 & 8 \end{bmatrix}, \quad \mathbf{X} = \begin{bmatrix} x_1 \\ x_2 \\ x_3 \end{bmatrix} \text{ and } \mathbf{B} = \begin{bmatrix} 4 \\ -10 \\ 6 \end{bmatrix}$$

Left multiplying Eq. (B–14) by $\mathbf{A}^{-1}$ yields

$$\mathbf{A}^{-1}\mathbf{AX} = \mathbf{A}^{-1}\mathbf{B}$$

But by definition $\mathbf{A}^{-1}\mathbf{A} = \mathbf{U}$ and $\mathbf{UX} = \mathbf{X}$; therefore

$$\mathbf{X} = \mathbf{A}^{-1}\mathbf{B} \tag{B-15}$$

To solve linear equations by matrix methods we calculate the product $\mathbf{A}^{-1}\mathbf{B}$.

To implement the matrix approach we must first find $\mathbf{A}^{-1}$ using Eq. (B–12). The determinant of the coefficient matrix is

$$\det \mathbf{A} = \begin{vmatrix} 5 & -2 & -3 \\ -5 & 7 & -2 \\ -3 & -3 & 8 \end{vmatrix} = 50$$

The cofactors of the first row of the coefficient matrix are

$$C_{11} = -\begin{vmatrix} +7 & -2 \\ -3 & 8 \end{vmatrix} = 50 \quad C_{12} = \begin{vmatrix} -5 & -2 \\ -3 & 8 \end{vmatrix} = 46$$

$$C_{13} = -\begin{vmatrix} -5 & +7 \\ -3 & -3 \end{vmatrix} = 36$$

The cofactors for the second and third rows are

$$C_{21} = 25 \quad C_{22} = 31 \quad C_{23} = 21$$

$$C_{31} = 25 \quad C_{32} = 25 \quad C_{33} = 25$$

Now, using Eq. (B–12), we obtain $\mathbf{A}^{-1}$ as

$$\mathbf{A}^{-1} = \frac{\text{adj } \mathbf{A}}{\det \mathbf{A}} = \frac{1}{50}\begin{bmatrix} 50 & 46 & 36 \\ 25 & 31 & 21 \\ 25 & 25 & 25 \end{bmatrix}^T = \frac{1}{50}\begin{bmatrix} 50 & 25 & 25 \\ 46 & 31 & 25 \\ 36 & 21 & 25 \end{bmatrix}$$

Using Eq. (B–15), we solve for the column matrix of unknowns as

$$\begin{bmatrix} x_1 \\ x_2 \\ x_3 \end{bmatrix} = \mathbf{X} = \mathbf{A}^{-1}\mathbf{B} = \frac{1}{50}\begin{bmatrix} 50 & 25 & 25 \\ 46 & 31 & 25 \\ 36 & 21 & 25 \end{bmatrix}\begin{bmatrix} 4 \\ -10 \\ 6 \end{bmatrix} = \frac{1}{50}\begin{bmatrix} 100 \\ 24 \\ 84 \end{bmatrix}$$

which yields $x_1 = 2$, $x_2 = 24/50$, and $x_3 = 84/50$. These are, of course, the same results previously obtained using Cramer's rule and Gaussian elimination.

Exercise B–4

Find the inverse of the coefficient matrix for Eq. (B–2).

Answer:

$$\mathbf{A}^{-1} = \frac{1}{216}\begin{bmatrix} 56 & 16 & 0 \\ 32 & 40 & 0 \\ 12 & 15 & 27 \end{bmatrix}$$

USING COMPUTER TOOLS

Computer tools for solving linear equations range from inexpensive hand-held calculators to mainframe packages capable of solving hundreds of such equations. At the personal computer level there are math analysis software packages such as Mathcad. Spreadsheets such as Quattro Pro can perform the basic operations of linear algebra and offer yet another set of computer tools for solving linear equations. Under what circumstances should you consider using these tools in linear circuit analysis?

There are no hard and fast rules here. Somewhere around four or five equations, the burden of hand calculations becomes mildly excruciating. Sets of equations with N up to 20 or 30 are routinely solved using computer tools, except when the equations are ill conditioned (several equations are almost linearly dependent). Well-conditioned systems of equations with $N = 50$ or more can be solved using sophisticated numerical methods. On the other hand, these sophisticated computer tools probably do not buy you very much in linear circuit design applications. They only allow you to tackle problems that you probably should not tackle directly anyway. If you encounter a circuit design problem that requires solving, say, 20 or more linear equations, you should probably partition the problem into smaller pieces because it is difficult to formulate the equations and interpret results correctly.

Mathcad and Quattro Pro are specific examples of computer tools available. Figure B–1 shows a Mathcad worksheet that solves the matrix equation in Eq. (B–13). The format and appearance of the mathematical operations in the worksheet are virtually self-defining. Perhaps the only surprise is the last step, where the matrix product **AX** is formed to see if it equals the matrix **B** given in the first line. This checking step is always advisable, particularly when the problem involves several equations with irrational coefficients.

Many spreadsheet programs can perform the matrix operations needed to solve linear equations. Figure B–2 shows the same system of equations as solved by Quattro Pro. The **A** matrix is entered in the first three rows. Selecting **Tools/Numeric Tools/Invert** from the menu bar then produces

FIGURE B–1

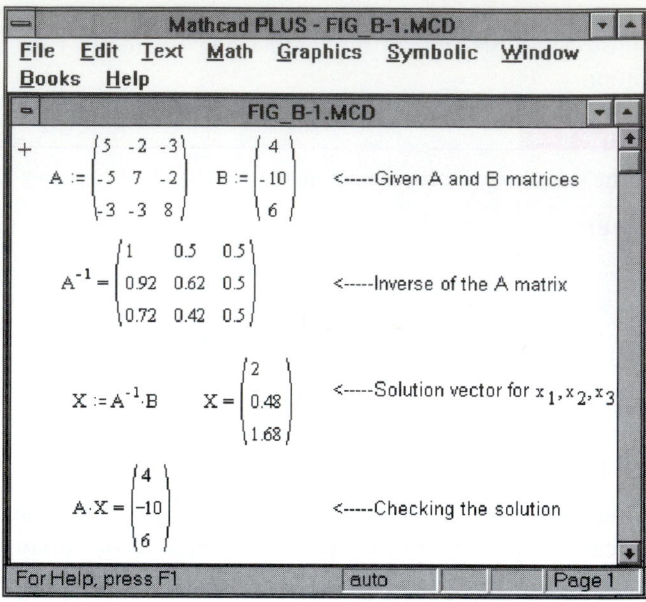

$\mathbf{A}^{-1}$ in the fifth, sixth, and seventh rows. The **B** column matrix is entered in the next three rows. Finally, selecting **Tools/Numeric Tools/Multiply** from the menu bar produces the product $\mathbf{A}^{-1}\mathbf{B}$ in the last three rows.

FIGURE B–2

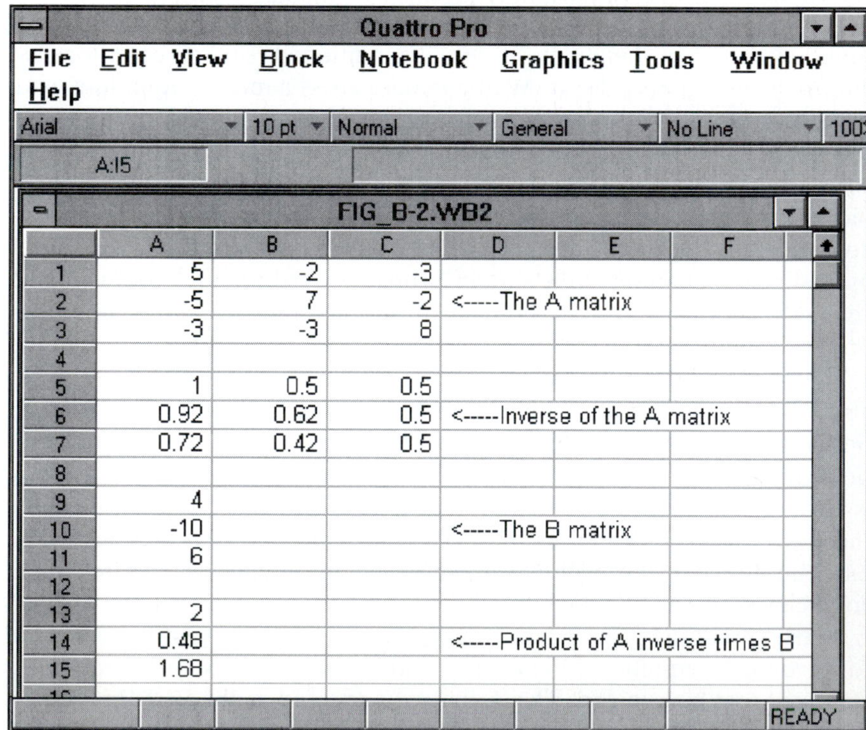

	A	B	C	D	E	F
1	5	-2	-3			
2	-5	7	-2	<-----The A matrix		
3	-3	-3	8			
4						
5	1	0.5	0.5			
6	0.92	0.62	0.5	<-----Inverse of the A matrix		
7	0.72	0.42	0.5			
8						
9	4					
10	-10			<-----The B matrix		
11	6					
12						
13	2					
14	0.48			<-----Product of A inverse times B		
15	1.68					

APPENDIX C

COMPLEX NUMBERS

Using complex numbers to represent signals and circuits is a fundamental tool in electrical engineering. This appendix reviews complex-number representations and arithmetic operations. These procedures, though rudimentary, must be second nature to all who aspire to be electrical engineers. Exercises are provided to confirm your mastery of these basic skills.

COMPLEX-NUMBER REPRESENTATIONS

A complex number z can be written in rectangular form as

$$z = x + jy \tag{C-1}$$

where j represents $\sqrt{-1}$. Mathematicians customarily use i to represent $\sqrt{-1}$, but i represents current in electrical engineering so we use the symbol j instead.

The quantity z is a two-dimensional number represented as a point in the complex plane, as shown in Figure C–1. The x component is called the **real part** and y (not jy) the **imaginary part** of z. A special notation is sometimes used to indicate these two components:

$$x = \text{Re}\{z\} \quad \text{and} \quad y = \text{Im}\{z\} \tag{C-2}$$

where Re$\{z\}$ means the real part and Im$\{z\}$ the imaginary part of z.

Figure C–1 also shows the polar representation of the complex number z. In polar form a complex number is written

$$z = M\angle\theta \tag{C-3}$$

where M is called the **magnitude** and θ the **angle** of z. A special notation is also used to indicate these two components.

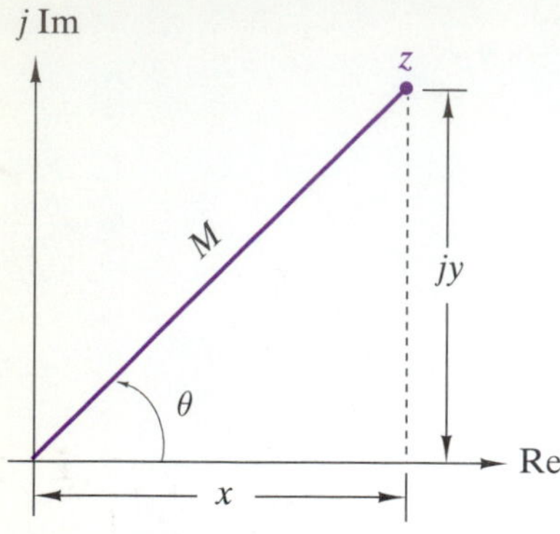

FIGURE C–1 *Graphical representation of complex numbers.*

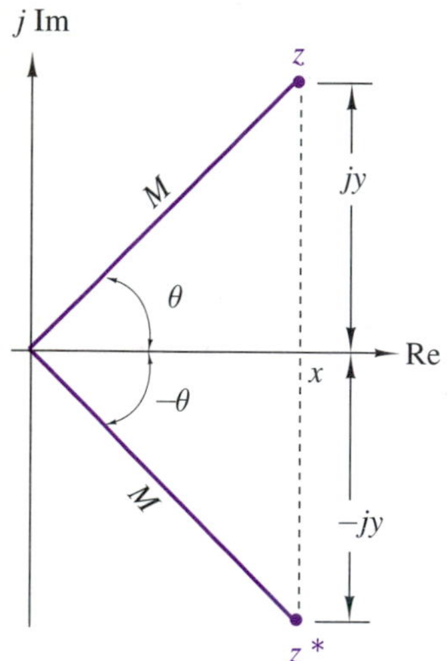

FIGURE C–2 *Graphical representation of conjugate complex numbers.*

$$|z| = M \quad \text{and} \quad \angle z = \theta \tag{C–4}$$

where $|z|$ means the magnitude and $\angle z$ the angle of z.

The real and imaginary parts and magnitude and angle of z are all shown geometrically in Figure C–1. The relationships between the rectangular and polar forms are easily derived from the geometry in Figure C–1:

$$\text{Rectangular to Polar} \quad M = \sqrt{x^2 + y^2} \quad \theta = \tan^{-1}\frac{y}{x}$$

$$\text{Polar to Rectangular} \quad x = M\cos\theta \quad y = M\sin\theta \tag{C–5}$$

The inverse tangent relation for θ involves an ambiguity that can be resolved by identifying the correct quadrant in the z-plane using the signs of the two rectangular components. [See Exercise C–1(b) and (c).]

Another version of the polar form is obtained using Euler's relationship:

$$e^{j\theta} = \cos\theta + j\sin\theta \tag{C–6}$$

We can write the polar form as

$$z = Me^{j\theta} = M\cos\theta + jM\sin\theta \tag{C–7}$$

This polar form is equivalent to Eq. (C–3), since the right side yields the same polar-to-rectangular relationships as Eq. (C–5). Thus, a complex number can be represented in three ways:

$$z = x + jy \quad z = M\angle\theta \quad z = Me^{j\theta} \tag{C–8}$$

The relationships between these forms are given in Eq. (C–5).

The quantity z^* is called the conjugate of the complex number z. The asterisk indicates the **conjugate** of a complex number formed by reversing the sign of the imaginary component. In rectangular form the conjugate of $z = x + jy$ is written as $z^* = x - jy$. In polar form the conjugate is obtained by reversing the sign of the angle of z, $z^* = Me^{-j\theta}$. The geometric interpretation in Figure C–2 shows that conjugation simply reflects a complex number across the real axis in the complex plane.

Exercise C–1

Convert the following complex numbers to polar form.
(a) $1 + j\sqrt{3}$ (b) $-10 + j20$ (c) $-2000 - j8000$ (d) $60 - j80$

Answers: (a) $2e^{j60°}$ (b) $22.4e^{j117°}$ (c) $8246e^{j256°}$ (d) $100e^{j307°}$

Exercise C–2

Convert the following complex numbers to rectangular form.
(a) $12e^{j90°}$ (b) $3e^{j45°}$ (c) $400\angle\pi$ (d) $8e^{-j60°}$ (e) $15e^{j\pi/6}$

Answers: (a) $0 + j12$ (b) $2.12 + j2.12$ (c) $-400 + j0$ (d) $4 - j6.93$ (e) $13 + j7.5$

Exercise C–3

Evaluate the following expressions.

(a) $\text{Re}(12e^{j\pi})$ (b) $\text{Im}(100\angle 60°)$ (c) $\angle(-2 + j6)$ (d) $\text{Im}[(4e^{j\frac{\pi}{4}})^*]$

Answers:

(a) −12 (b) 86.6 (c) 108.4° (d) −2.83

ARITHMETIC OPERATIONS: ADDITION AND SUBTRACTION

Addition and subtraction are defined in terms of complex numbers in rectangular form. Two complex numbers

$$z_1 = x_1 + jy_1 \quad \text{and} \quad z_2 = x_2 + jy_2 \qquad \text{(C–9)}$$

are added by separately adding the real parts and imaginary parts. The sum $z_1 + z_2$ is defined as

$$z_1 + z_2 = (x_1 + x_2) + j(y_1 + y_2) \qquad \text{(C–10)}$$

Subtraction follows the same pattern except that the components are subtracted:

$$z_1 - z_2 = (x_1 - x_2) + j(y_1 - y_2) \qquad \text{(C–11)}$$

Figure C–3 shows a geometric interpretation of addition and subtraction. In particular, note that $z + z^* = 2x$ and $z - z^* = j2y$.

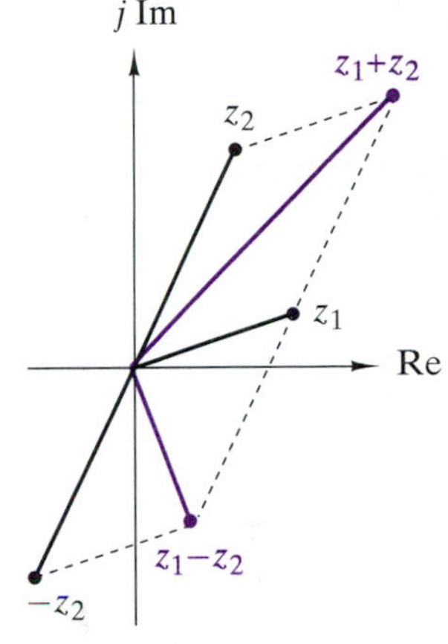

FIGURE C–3 *Graphical representation of addition and subtraction of complex numbers.*

MULTIPLICATION AND DIVISION

Multiplication and division of complex numbers can be accomplished with the numbers in either rectangular or polar form. For complex numbers in rectangular form the multiplication operation yields

$$\begin{aligned} z_1 z_2 &= (x_1 + jy_1)(x_2 + jy_2) \\ &= (x_1x_2 + j^2y_1y_2) + j(x_1y_2 + x_2y_1) \\ &= (x_1x_2 - y_1y_2) + j(x_1y_2 + x_2y_1) \end{aligned} \qquad \text{(C–12)}$$

For numbers in polar form the product is

$$\begin{aligned} z_1 z_2 &= (M_1 e^{j\theta_1})(M_2 e^{j\theta_2}) \\ &= (M_1 M_2) e^{j(\theta_1 + \theta_2)} \end{aligned} \qquad \text{(C–13)}$$

Multiplication is somewhat easier to carry out with the numbers in polar form, although both methods should be understood. In particular, the product of a complex number z and it conjugate z^* is the square of its magnitude, which is always positive.

$$zz^* = (Me^{j\theta})(Me^{-j\theta}) = M^2 \qquad \text{(C–14)}$$

For complex numbers in polar form the division operation yields

$$\frac{z_1}{z_2} = \frac{Me^{j\theta_1}}{M_2e^{j\theta_2}}$$

$$= \left(\frac{M_1}{M_2}\right)e^{j(\theta_1 - \theta_2)} \qquad \text{(C–15)}$$

When the numbers are in rectangular form the numerator and denominator of the quotient are multiplied by the conjugate of the denominator.

$$\frac{z_1}{z_2}\frac{z_2^*}{z_2^*} = \frac{(x_1 + jy_1)(x_2 - jy_2)}{(x_2 + jy_2)(x_2 - jy_2)}$$

Applying the multiplication rule from Eq. (C–12) to the numerator and denominator yields

$$\frac{z_1}{z_2} = \frac{(x_1x_2 + y_1y_2) + j(x_2y_1 - x_1y_2)}{x_2^2 + y_2^2} \qquad \text{(C–16)}$$

Complex division is easier to carry out with the numbers in polar form, although both methods should be understood.

Exercise C–4

Evaluate the following expressions using $z_1 = 3 + j4$, $z_2 = 5 - j7$, $z_3 = -2 + j3$, and $z_4 = 5\angle{-30°}$:

(a) z_1z_2 (b) $z_3 + z_4$ (c) z_2z_3/z_4 (d) $z_1{}^* + z_3z_1$ (e) $z_2 + (z_1z_4)^*$

Answers:
(a) $43 - j$ (b) $2.33 + j0.5$ (c) $-0.995 + j6.12$ (d) $-15 - j3$ (e) $28 - j16.8$

Exercise C–5

Given $z = x + jy = Me^{j\theta}$, evaluate the following statements:

(a) $z + z^*$ (b) $z - z^*$ (c) z/z^* (d) z^2 (e) $(z^*)^2$ (f) zz^*

Answers:
(a) $2x$ (b) $j2y$ (c) $e^{j2\theta}$ (d) $x^2 - y^2 + j2xy$ (e) $x^2 - y^2 - j2xy$ (f) $x^2 + y^2$

Exercise C–6

Given $z_1 = 1$, $z_2 = -1$, $z_3 = j$, and $z_4 = -j$, evaluate (a) z_1/z_3 (b) z_1/z_4 (c) z_3z_4 (d) z_3z_3 (e) z_4z_4 (f) $z_2z_3^*$.

Answers:
(a) $-j$ (b) $+j$ (c) 1 (d) -1 (e) -1 (f) j

Exercise C–7

Evaluate the expression $T(\omega) = j\omega/(j\omega + 10)$ at $\omega = 5, 10, 20, 50, 100$.

Answers: $0.447\angle 63.4°$, $0.707\angle 45°$, $0.894\angle 26.6°$, $0.981\angle 11.3°$, $0.995\angle 5.71°$

APPENDIX D

TWO-PORT CIRCUITS

The purpose of this appendix is to define and illustrate the network functions used to characterize linear two-port circuits. The circuit in Figure D–1 is in the zero state and contains only linear resistors, capacitors, inductors, mutual inductance, and dependent sources. The two pairs of external terminals are called ports, with port 1 referred to as the input and port 2 as the output. The variables $V_1(s)$ and $I_1(s)$ are associated with the input port and the variables $V_2(s)$ and $I_2(s)$ with the output port. Note that the reference marks for the port variables comply with the passive sign convention.

Two-port parameters are the network functions that relate the port variables. A specific set of two-port parameters is obtained by selecting two of the four port variables as independent variables and using the other two as dependent variables. The *i–v* characteristics relating dependent and independent variables involve network functions of four types: (1) driving-point functions at the input port, (2) driving-point functions at the output port, (3) forward transfer functions from the input port to the output port, and (4) reverse transfer functions from the output port to the input port. Although there are six possible sets of two-port parameters, we discuss only the impedance, admittance, hybrid, and transmission parameters.

IMPEDANCE PARAMETERS

The impedance parameters are defined by selecting $I_1(s)$ and $I_2(s)$ as the independent variables and $V_1(s)$ and $V_2(s)$ as the dependent variables. Because the circuit in Figure D–1 is linear, the *i–v* relationships of the two-port can be written in the form

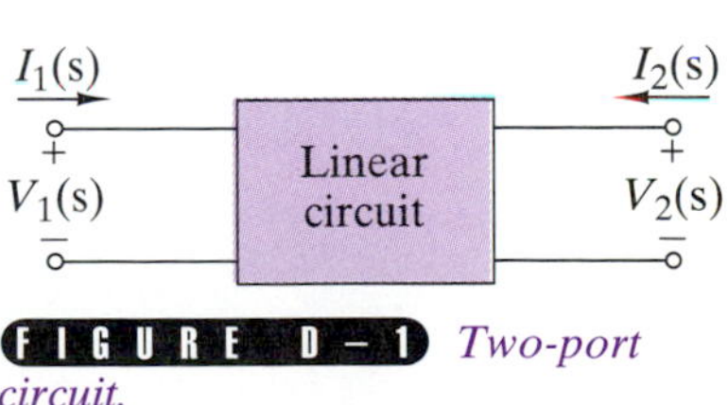

FIGURE D–1 *Two-port circuit.*

$$V_1(s) = z_{11}I_1(s) + z_{12}I_2(s)$$
$$V_2(s) = z_{21}I_1(s) + z_{22}I_2(s) \quad \text{(D-1)}$$

The network functions in these relationships are defined as follows:

$$z_{11} = \left.\frac{V_1}{I_1}\right|_{I_2=0} \quad \text{input driving-point impedance with port 2 open}$$

$$z_{12} = \left.\frac{V_1}{I_2}\right|_{I_1=0} \quad \text{reverse transfer impedance with port 1 open}$$

$$z_{21} = \left.\frac{V_2}{I_1}\right|_{I_2=0} \quad \text{forward transfer impedance with port 2 open}$$

$$z_{22} = \left.\frac{V_2}{I_2}\right|_{I_1=0} \quad \text{output driving-point impedance with port 1 open}$$

Collectively these network functions are called the impedance parameters because they all have dimensions of ohms. The impedance parameters are found by first measuring or calculating the input driving-point impedance and the forward transfer impedance with the output port open [$I_2(s) = 0$], and then measuring or calculating the output driving-point impedance and reverse transfer impedance with the input port open [$I_1(s) = 0$].

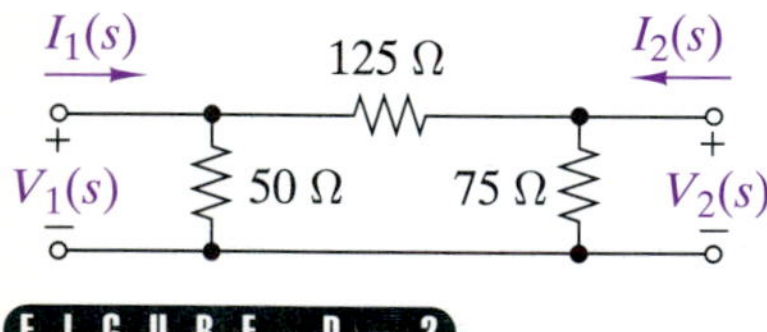

FIGURE D–2

EXAMPLE D–1

Find the impedance parameters of the circuit in Figure D–2.

SOLUTION:

The equivalent resistance looking in at port 1 with port 2 open is

$$z_{11} = 50\|(125 + 75) = 40\ \Omega$$

The current through the 75-Ω resistor with port 2 open is found using current division.

$$I_{75} = \frac{50}{50 + 125 + 75}I_1 = 0.2I_1$$

By Ohm's law the output voltage is $V_2 = I_{75} \times 75$. Therefore, the forward transfer impedance is

$$z_{21} = \left.\frac{V_2}{I_1}\right|_{I_2=0} = \frac{(0.2I_1) \times 75}{I_1} = 15\ \Omega$$

The current through the 50-Ω resistor with port 1 open is found using current division.

$$I_{50} = \frac{75}{50 + 125 + 75}I_2 = 0.3I_2$$

By Ohm's law the input voltage is $V_1 = I_{50} \times 50$. Therefore, the reverse transfer impedance is

$$z_{12} = \left.\frac{V_1}{I_2}\right|_{I_1=0} = \frac{(0.3I_2) \times 50}{I_2} = 15\ \Omega$$

The equivalent resistance looking in at port 2 with port 1 open is

$$z_{22} = 75\|(125 + 50) = 52.5\ \Omega$$

Using the impedance parameters, the *i–v* relationships of the two port in Figure D–2 are

$$V_1 = 40I_1 + 15I_2$$
$$V_2 = 15I_1 + 52.5I_2$$

■

ADMITTANCE PARAMETERS

The admittance parameters are defined by selecting $V_1(s)$ and $V_2(s)$ as the independent variables and $I_1(s)$ and $I_2(s)$ as the dependent variables. Because the circuit in Figure D–1 is linear the *i–v* relationships of the two port can be written in the form

$$I_1(s) = y_{11}V_1(s) + y_{12}V_2(s)$$
$$I_2(s) = y_{21}V_1(s) + y_{22}V_2(s) \qquad \text{(D – 3)}$$

The network functions in these relationships are defined as follows:

$$y_{11} = \left.\frac{I_1}{V_1}\right|_{V_2=0}$$ input driving−point admittance with port 2 shorted

$$y_{12} = \left.\frac{I_1}{V_2}\right|_{V_1=0}$$ reverse transfer admittance with port 1 shorted

$$y_{21} = \left.\frac{I_2}{V_1}\right|_{V_2=0}$$ forward transfer admittance with port 2 shorted

$$y_{22} = \left.\frac{I_2}{V_2}\right|_{V_1=0}$$ output driving−point admittance with port 1 shorted

Collectively these network functions are called the admittance parameters because they all have dimensions of siemens. The admittance parameters are found by first measuring or calculating the input driving-point admittance and the forward transfer admittance with the output port shorted $[V_2(s) = 0]$, and then measuring or calculating the output driving-point admittance and reverse transfer admittance with the input port shorted $[V_1(s) = 0]$.

EXAMPLE D–2

Find the admittance parameters of the circuit in Figure D–2.

SOLUTION:

The equivalent conductance looking in at port 1 with port 2 shorted is

$$y_{11} = \frac{1}{50} + \frac{1}{125} = 0.028 \text{ S}$$

The output current with port 2 shorted is $I_2 = -V_1/125$. Therefore, the forward transfer admittance is

$$y_{21} = \left.\frac{I_2}{V_1}\right|_{V_2=0} = -\frac{1}{125} = -0.008 \text{ S}$$

The input current with port 1 shorted is $I_1 = -V_2/125$. Therefore, the reverse transfer admittance is

$$y_{12} = \left.\frac{I_1}{V_2}\right|_{V_1=0} = -\frac{1}{125} = -0.008 \text{ S}$$

The equivalent conductance looking in at port 2 with port 1 shorted is

$$y_{22} = \frac{1}{75} + \frac{1}{125} = 0.0213 \text{ S}$$

Using admittance parameters, the *i–v* relationships of the two-port in Figure D–2 are

$$I_1 = 0.028V_1 - 0.008V_2$$
$$I_2 = -0.008V_1 + 0.0213V_2$$

■

HYBRID PARAMETERS

The hybrid parameters are defined by selecting $I_1(s)$ and $V_2(s)$ as the independent variables and $V_1(s)$ and $I_2(s)$ as the dependent variables. Because the circuit is linear the *i–v* relationships of the two-port can be written in the form

$$V_1(s) = h_{11}I_1(s) + h_{12}V_2(s)$$
$$I_2(s) = h_{21}I_1(s) + h_{22}V_2(s) \qquad \text{(D–5)}$$

The network functions in these relationships are defined as follows:

$$h_{11} = \left.\frac{V_1}{I_1}\right|_{V_2=0}$$ input driving–point impedance with port 2 shorted

$$h_{12} = \left.\frac{V_1}{V_2}\right|_{I_1=0}$$ reverse voltage transfer function with port 1 open

$$h_{21} = \left.\frac{I_2}{I_1}\right|_{V_2=0} \quad \text{forward current transfer function with port 2 shorted}$$

$$h_{22} = \left.\frac{I_2}{V_2}\right|_{I_1=0} \quad \text{output driving}-\text{point admittance with port 1 open}$$

Collectively these network functions are called the hybrid parameters because they involve a mixture of dimensionless and dimensioned parameters. The hybrid parameters are found by first measuring or calculating the input driving-point impedance and forward current gain with the output port shorted [$V_2(s) = 0$], and then measuring or calculating the output driving-point admittance and reverse voltage gain with the input port open [$I_1(s) = 0$].

EXAMPLE D–3

Figure D–3 shows a low-frequency small-signal transistor model. Find the hybrid parameters of this circuit when $r_{bc} >> r_{be}$.

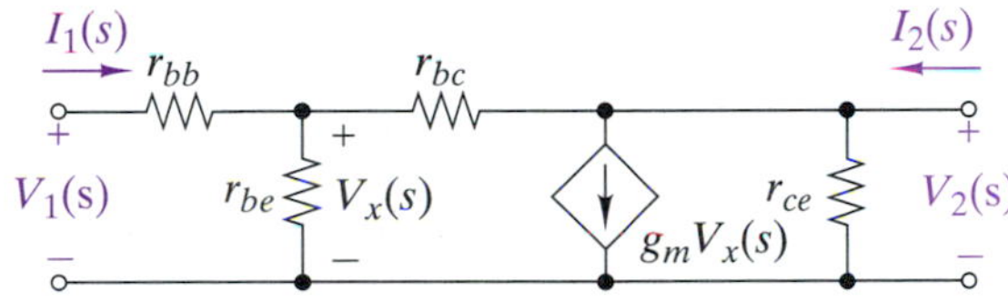

FIGURE D–3

SOLUTION:

The equivalent resistance looking in at port 1 with port 2 shorted is

$$h_{11} = r_{bb} + r_{be} \| r_{bc} \approx r_{bb} + r_{be}$$

where the approximation applies because $r_{bc} >> r_{be}$. The output current with port 2 shorted is $I_2 = g_m V_x$. The input current I_1 divides between r_{be} and r_{bc}. But since $r_{bc} >> r_{be}$, almost all of I_1 enters r_{be}. Using Ohm's law, $V_x \approx I_1 r_{be}$ and the forward current gain is

$$h_{21} = \left.\frac{I_2}{I_1}\right|_{V_2=0} \approx \frac{g_m(I_1 r_{be})}{I_1} = g_m r_{be}$$

Using voltage division with port 1 open produces

$$V_1 = V_x = \frac{r_{be}}{r_{be} + r_{bc}} V_2$$

The reverse voltage gain is

$$h_{12} = \left.\frac{V_1}{V_2}\right|_{I_1=0} = \frac{r_{be}}{r_{be} + r_{bc}} \approx \frac{r_{be}}{r_{bc}}$$

where the approximation applies because $r_{bc} >> r_{be}$. Writing a node equation at the output port with the input port open produces

$$I_2 = \frac{V_2}{r_{ce}} + g_m V_x + \frac{V_2}{r_{bc} + r_{be}}$$

Since $V_x = h_{12}V_2$ the output conductance with the input port open can be written as

$$h_{22} = \left.\frac{I_2}{V_2}\right|_{I_1=0} = \frac{1}{r_{ce}} + g_m h_{12} + \frac{1}{r_{be} + r_{bc}}$$

$$\approx \frac{1}{r_{ce}} + \frac{g_m r_{be} + 1}{r_{bc}}$$

■

TRANSMISSION PARAMETERS

The transmission parameters are obtained by selecting $V_2(s)$ and $I_2(s)$ as the independent variables and $V_1(s)$ and $I_1(s)$ as the dependent variables. Because the circuit is linear the *i–v* relationships of the two port can be written in the form

$$V_1(s) = AV_2(s) + BI_2(s)$$
$$I_1(s) = CV_2(s) + DI_2(s) \qquad \text{(D-7)}$$

The network functions in these relationships are defined as follows:

$A = \left.\frac{V_1}{V_2}\right|_{I_2=0}$ reciprocal of the forward voltage gain with port 2 open

$B = \left.\frac{V_1}{I_2}\right|_{V_2=0}$ reciprocal of the forward transfer admittance with port 2 shorted

$C = \left.\frac{I_1}{V_2}\right|_{I_2=0}$ reciprocal of the forward transfer impedance with port 2 open

$D = \left.\frac{I_1}{I_2}\right|_{V_2=0}$ reciprocal of the forward current gain with port 2 shorted

Collectively these network functions are called the transmission parameters because all four are reciprocals of forward transfer functions. The transmission parameters are found by first measuring or calculating the forward voltage gain and transfer impedance with the output port open [$I_2(s) = 0$], and then measuring or calculating the forward current gain and transfer admittance with the output port shorted [$V_2(s) = 0$].

EXAMPLE D–4

Figure D–4 shows an s-domain model of a transformer in the zero state. Find the impedance parameters and transmission parameters of this circuit.

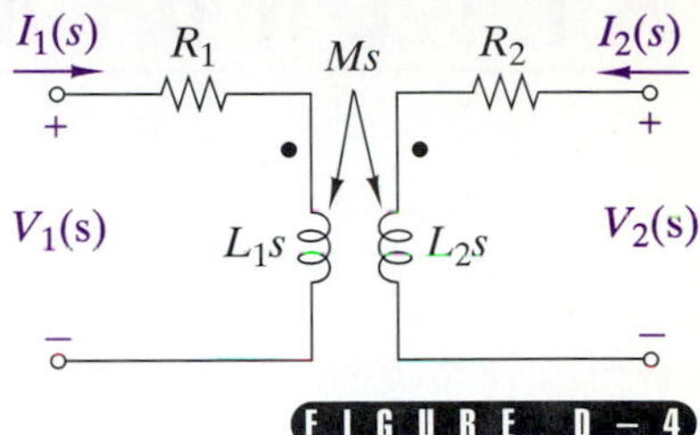

FIGURE D–4

SOLUTION:

The coupling in Figure D–4 is additive, so the *i–v* relationships of the transformer are

$$V_1 = (L_1s + R_1)I_1 + MsI_2$$

$$V_2 = MsI_1 + (L_2s + R_2)I_2$$

By inspection, the impedance parameters are

$$z_{11} = L_1s + R_1$$

$$z_{12} = z_{21} = Ms$$

$$z_{22} = L_2s + R_2$$

With the output port open $I_2 = 0$ and the transformer *i–v* relationships yield

$$A = \left.\frac{V_1}{V_2}\right|_{I_2=0} = \frac{(L_1s + R_1)I_1}{MsI_1} = \frac{L_1s + R_1}{Ms}$$

$$C = \left.\frac{V_2}{I_1}\right|_{I_2=0} = Ms$$

With the output port shorted $V_2 = 0$ and the second *i–v* relationship yields

$$I_1 = -\frac{L_2s + R_2}{Ms}I_2$$

Substituting this value of I_1 into the first *i–v* relationship produces

$$V_1 = \left[(L_1s + R_1)\left(-\frac{L_2s + R_2}{Ms}\right) + Ms\right]I_2$$

The remaining transmission parameters are

$$B = \left.\frac{V_1}{I_2}\right|_{V_2=0} = \frac{[-(L_1s + R_1)(L_2s + R_2)/Ms + Ms]I_2}{I_2}$$

$$= \frac{M^2s^2 - (L_1s + R_1)(L_2s + R_2)}{M^2s^2}$$

and

$$D = \left.\frac{I_1}{I_2}\right|_{V_2=0} = -\frac{L_2s + R_2}{Ms}$$

■

APPENDIX E

REFERENCES

CONTEMPORARY BOOKS ON CIRCUIT ANALYSIS

Balabanian, N., *Electric Circuits.* New York: McGraw-Hill, 1994.

Dorf, R. C., *Introduction to Electric Circuits*, 2nd ed. New York: John Wiley & Sons, 1993.

Hayt, W. H., Jr., and J. E. Kemmerly, *Engineering Circuit Analysis*, 5th ed. New York: McGraw-Hill, 1993.

Huelsman, L. P., *Basic Circuit Theory*, 3rd ed. Englewood Cliffs, N.J.: Prentice Hall, 1991.

Irwin, J. D., *Basic Engineering Circuit Analysis*, 5th ed. Englewood Cliffs, N.J.: Prentice Hall, 1996.

Johnson, D. E., J. R. Johnson, J. L. Hilburn, and P. D. Scott, *Electric Circuit Analysis*, 3rd ed. Englewood Cliffs, N.J.: Prentice Hall, 1997.

Nilsson, J. W., and S. A. Riedel, *Electric Circuits*, 5th ed. Reading, Mass.: Addison-Wesley, 1995.

CLASSICAL BOOKS ON CIRCUIT ANALYSIS

Bode, H. W., *Network Analysis and Feedback Amplifier Design.* Princeton, N.J.: D. Van Nostrand, 1945.

Gardner, M. F., and J. L. Barnes, *Transients in Linear Systems.* New York: John Wiley & Sons, 1942.

Guillemin, E. A., *Introductory Circuit Theory.* New York: John Wiley & Sons, 1953.

Skilling, H. H., *Transient Electric Currents.* New York: McGraw-Hill, 1937.

Van Valkenburg, M. E., *Network Analysis.* Englewood Cliffs, N.J.: Prentice Hall, 1st ed., 1955, 2nd ed., 1964, 3rd ed., 1974.

CIRCUIT DESIGN

Franca, J. E., and Y. Tsividis, editors, *Design of Analog-Digital VLSI Circuits for Telecommunications and Signal Processing*, 2nd ed. Englewood Cliffs, N.J.: Prentice Hall, 1994.

Huelsman, L. P., *Active and Passive Analog Filter Design.* New York: McGraw-Hill, 1993.

McConnell, R. L., W. L. Cooley, and N. T. Middleton, *Electrical Engineering Design Compendium.* Reading, Mass.: Addison-Wesley, 1993.

Meiksin, Z. H., and P. C. Thackray, *Electronic Design with Off-the-Shelf Integrated Circuits*, 2nd ed. Englewood Cliffs, N.J.: Prentice Hall, 1984.

Van Valkenburg, M. E., *Analog Filter Design.* Chicago: Holt, Rinehart & Winston, 1982.

Williams, J., *Analog Circuit Design.* Boston: Butterworth-Heinemann, 1991.

CIRCUIT ANALYSIS AND ELECTRONICS

Horenstein, M. N., *Microelectronic Circuits and Devices*, 2nd ed. Englewood Cliffs, N.J.: Prentice Hall, 1996.

Savant, C. J., Jr., M. S. Roden, and G. L. Carpenter, *Electronic Design: Circuits and Systems,* 2nd ed. Redwood City, Calif.: Bengamin Cummings, 1991.

Senturia, S. D., and B. D. Wedlock, *Electronic Circuits and Applications.* New York: Kreiger, 1993.

Wait, J. V., L. P. Huelsman, and G. A. Korn, *Introduction to Operational Amplifier Theory and Applications*, 2nd ed. New York: McGraw-Hill, 1993.

CIRCUIT ANALYSIS AND ELECTRIC POWER SYSTEMS

del Toro, V., *Electric Power Systems.* Englewood Cliffs, N.J.: Prentice Hall, 1992.

Elgerd, O. I., *Electrical Energy Systems Theory: An Introduction.* New York: McGraw-Hill, 1982.

El-Hawary, M. E., *Electrical Power Systems.* Piscataway, N.J.: IEEE Press, 1995.

SIGNAL AND SYSTEM ANALYSIS

Cooper, G. R., and C. D. MacGillem, *Continuous and Discrete Signals and Systems Analysis*, 3rd ed. Philadelphia: Saunders, 1991.

Dorf, R. C., *Modern Control Systems*, 6th ed. Reading, Mass.: Addison-Wesley, 1992.

Kuo, B. C., *Automatic Control Systems*, 6th ed. Englewood Cliffs, N.J.: Prentice Hall, 1991.

Oppenheim, A. V., A. S. Willsky, and I. T. Young, *Signals and Systems*, 2nd ed. Englewood Cliffs, N.J.: Prentice Hall, 1991.

COMPUTER-AIDED CIRCUIT ANALYSIS

Goody, R. W., *PSpice for Windows—A Circuit Simulation Primer.* Englewood Cliffs, N.J.: Prentice Hall, 1995.

Herniter, M. E., *Schematic Capture with PSpice.* New York: Merrill/Macmillan, 1994.

Rashid, M. H., *SPICE for Circuits and Electronics Using PSpice.* Englewood Cliffs, N.J.: Prentice Hall, 1990.

Roden, M. S., *The Student Edition of MICRO-CAP IV*. Redwood City, Calif.: Benjamin Cummings, 1993.

Tuinenga P., *SPICE: A Guide to Circuit Simulation & Analysis Using PSpice,* 2nd ed. Englewood Cliffs, N.J.: Prentice Hall, 1992.

MicroSim™ PSpice® Circuit Analysis User's Guide with Schematics, Version 6.2. Irvine, Calif.: MicroSim Corp., April 1995.

Matchcad User's Guide, Version 6.0. Cambridge, Mass.: MathSoft Inc., 1995.

Quattro Pro User's Guide, Version 6.0. Orem, Utah: Novell, Inc., 1994.

HANDBOOKS

Chen, Wai-Kai, editor-in-chief, *The Circuits and Filter Handbook.* Boca Raton, Fla.: CRC Press, 1995.

Dorf, R. C., editor-in-chief, *The Electrical Engineering Handbook.* Boca Raton, Fla.: CRC Press, 1993.

Harper, C. A., editor-in-chief, *Handbook of Components for Electronics.* New York: McGraw-Hill, 1977.

ANSWERS TO SELECTED PROBLEMS

CHAPTER ONE

1–3 (a) 2.2 MW; (b) 2.3 μF; (c) 6.2 kΩ; (d) 0.752 MJ; (e) 0.235 mH;

1–5 (a) 10^6; (b) 10^{-3}; (c) 10^3; (d) 10^{-6}

1–7 (a) 1.08×10^7 C; (b) 250 A

1–9 $i(0) = 0$ A; $i(1) = 6$ A; $i(3) = 18$ A

1–10 $q(0) = 0$; $q(5) = 0.625$ C

1–13 (a) 4.167 A; (b) 48 hrs

1–15 2.16 MJ

1–19 33.3 mA

1–20 10 mW

1–26 49.05 dB

1–27 0.184 mW/°C

CHAPTER TWO

2–1 (a) $i = 1.2$ mA; $p = 14.4$ mW;
(b) $v = -2$ V;
(c) $p = -120$ mW;
(d) $v = 0$; $p = 0$

2–3 (a) $i = 2$ mA; $v = 2$ V; $p = 4$ mW;
(b) $i = 5$ A; $v = 0$; $p = 0$;
(c) $i = 5$ A; $v = -1$ kV; $p = -5$ kW

2–5 Red devices are 1.5-V batteries; black devices are 4-kΩ resistors

2–11 (a) Nodes A, B, C; Loops 1,2; 2,3,4; 1,3,4
(b) Series, 3 & 4; Parallel, 1 & 2
(c) KCL: $i_1 + i_2 + i_3 = 0$;
$-i_3 + i_4 = 0$;
$-i_1 - i_2 - i_4 = 0$
KVL: $-v_1 + v_2 = 0$;
$-v_2 + v_3 + v_4 = 0$;
$-v_1 + v_3 + v_4 = 0$
(d) $i_3 = i_4 = -2$ mA

2–13 (a) Nodes A, B, C, D; Loops 1,3,2; 2,4,5; 3,6,4; 1,5,6; 2,3,5,6
(b) Series, none; Parallel, none
(c) KCL: $i_2 + i_3 + i_4 = 0$;
$i_1 - i_3 + i_6 = 0$;
$-i_1 - i_2 - i_5 = 0$;
$-i_4 + i_5 - i_6 = 0$
KVL: $-v_1 + v_2 - v_3 = 0$;
$-v_2 + v_4 + v_5 = 0$;
$v_3 + v_6 - v_4 = 0$
(d) $v_2 = 1$ V; $v_1 = 9$ V; $v_6 = 0$ V

2–15 (a) Nodes A, B, C, D; Loops 1,3,2; 2,4,5; 3,6,4; 1,5,6
(b) KCL: $i_2 + i_3 + i_4 = 0$;
$i_1 - i_3 + i_6 = 0$;
$-i_1 - i_2 - i_5 = 0$;
$-i_4 + i_5 - i_6 = 0$
(c) $i_2 = -3$ mA; $i_1 = -2$mA; $i_6 = 17$ mA

2–20 C1: $i_x = -1$ A; $v_x = 5$ V; C2: $i_x = 0.4$ A; $v_x = 12$ V

2–21 C3: $i_x = 1.41$ mA; $v_x = 7.89$ V; C4: $i_x = -2.05$ mA; $v_x = -18.7$ V

2–22 $v_4 = -5$ V; $v_5 = 5$ V; $v_6 = 0$ V;
$i_1 = -50$ mA; $i_2 = 100$ mA;
$i_3 = -50$ mA; $i_4 = -50$ mA;
$i_5 = 50$ mA; $i_6 = 0$

2–24 (a) $i_x = -1$ mA; $v_x = -10$ V;
(b) $-i_1 + 0.01 - 0.005 + i_x = 0$

2–30 $R_{AB} = 60\ \Omega$; $R_{BC} = 0\ \Omega$; $R_{AC} = 60\ \Omega$; $R_{CD} = 50\ \Omega$; $R_{BD} = 50\ \Omega$; $R_{AD} = 110\ \Omega$

2–31 $R_{AB} = 90\ \Omega$; $R_{AC} = 60\ \Omega$; $R_{AD} = 40\ \Omega$; $R_{BC} = 130\ \Omega$; $R_{BD} = 110\ \Omega$; $R_{CD} = 40\ \Omega$

2–32 C1: $R_{AB} = 20\ \Omega$; C2: $R_{AB} = 20\ \Omega$; C3: $R_{AB} = 30\ \Omega$; C4: $R_{AB} = 40\ \Omega$; C5: $R_{AB} = 232.8\ \Omega$

2–33 (a) $v_S = 8$ V; $R = 40\ \Omega$;
(b) $i_S = 150.4$ mA; $R = 133\ \Omega$;
(c) $i_S = 350.3$ mA; $R = 30.75\ \Omega$

2–40 $R = 81\ \Omega$

2–42 C1: $v_x = 0.1v_S$; C2: $v_x = 1.898$ V

2–43 C1: $i_x = 2.5$ A; C2: $v_x = 0.666$ V

2–44 C3: $i_x = 1.67$ A; $v_x = 2.5$ V; C4: $i_x = 0.6$ A; $v_x = 12$ V

2–50 $x = 61.8$ %

2–51 $i_x = -1.25$ A; $v_x = -12.5$ V

2–52 $i_x = 62.5$ mA

2–53 $i_x = 0.833$ A; $v_x = 1.67$ V

2–54 $i_x = -0.1$ A; $v_x = -0.75$ V

Chapter Three

3–5 (b) $i_x = -0.5$ m A; $v_x = 0$

3–6 (b) $i_x = -5.36$ A; $v_x = 10.7$ V

3–7 (b) $i_x = 73.7$ mA; $v_x = 21.05$ V;
(c) $p_{total} = -7.37$ W

3–8 (b) $i_x = 0.420$ mA; $v_x = 104$ mV;
(b) $p_{R2} = 0.411$ mW

3–9 (b) $i_x = -0.50$ mA; $v_x = 10$ V;
(c) $p_{R1} = 2.50$ mW

3–11 (b) $i_x = -167$ mA; $v_x = 0$;
(c) $p_{vs} = -10$ W

3–13 (b) $i_x = 3.35$ mA; $v_x = -3$ V;
(c) $p_{S1} = -40.2$ mW

3–21 $K = \dfrac{R_1R_3}{R_1 + R_2 + R_3}$

3–23 $K = \dfrac{R_2R_3 - R_1R_4}{R_1 + R_2 + R_3 + R_4}$

3–25 $i_O = 63.5$ mA

3–29 $i_O = 0.923$ mA

3–31 $v_O = R(0.333i_1 - i_2)$

3–34 $k_1 = 0.8333$; $k_2 = 0.08333$; $k_3 = 0.05556$

3–36 (a) $v_T = R_1 i_S$; $i_N = R_1 i_S/(R_1 + R_2)$; $R_T = R_1 + R_2$;
(b) and (c) $i_L = R_1 i_S/(R_1 + R_2 + R_L)$

3–38 (a) $v_T = 40$ V; $R_T = 30$ kΩ;
(b) If $R_L = 10$ kΩ; $p_L = 10$ mW;
(c) If $R_L = 20$ kΩ; $p_L = 12.8$ mW; If $R_L = 40$ kΩ; $p_L = 13.1$ mW;
If $R_L = 80$ kΩ; $p_L = 10.6$ mW

3–40 (a) $v_T = 21$ V; $R_T = 18\ \Omega$; $i_N = 1.167$ A;
(b) $p_L = 5.63$ W;
(c) $p_L = 4.44$ W

3–42 (a) $v_T = 8$ V; $R_T = 1\ \text{k}\Omega$;
(b) If $R_L = 500\ \Omega$; $p_L = 14.2$ mW; If $R_L = 1\ \text{k}\Omega$; $p_L = 16$ mW; If $R_L = 2\ \text{k}\Omega$; $p_L = 14.2$ mW

3–44 (b) $v_T = 15$ V; $R_T = 5\ \text{k}\Omega$

3–51 (a) $R_L = 13.3\ \Omega$; $p_{max} = 33.3$ mW;
(b) $R_L = \infty$; $v_{max} = 1.33$ V;
(c) $R_L = 0$; $i_{max} = 100$ mA

3–52 (a) $R_L = 600\ \Omega$; $p_{max} = 38.4$ mW;
(b) $R_L = \infty$; $v_{max} = 9.6$ V;
(c) $R_L = 0$; $i_{max} = 16$ mA

3–53 (a) $R_L = 21.7\ \Omega$; $p_{max} = 801$ mW;
(b) $R_L = \infty$; $v_{max} = 8.33$ V;
(c) $R_L = 0$; $i_{max} = 385$ mA

3–54 $v_L = 20$ V; $p_L = 100$ mW; $R = 12\ \text{k}\Omega$

3–61 For a series resistor $R = 25\ \Omega$; many other designs are possible

3–62 For a series resistor $R = 6230\ \Omega$; many other designs are possible

3–63 For a series resistor $R = 400\ \Omega$ (nominal);
R = 100 + 470 || 680 = 378 ±5% Ω

Chapter Four

4–2 (a) –200/3; (b) –5/3;
(c) $p_{IN} = 0.2$ mW; $p_{OUT} = 22.2$ mW

4–3 $v_3 = 2.27$ V; $K_I = 3.33 \times 10^5$

4–4 (a) $v_2 = -0.398$ V; $K_I = -49.8$;
(b) $R_{IN} = 249\ \Omega$

4–5 (a) $i_2 = -0.461$ mA; $K_V = 3.98$;
(b) $R_{IN} = 62.8\ \text{k}\Omega$

4–10 10.58 kΩ

4–14 (a) $0.6 < v_S < 8.6$ V;
(b) $0.6 < v_S < 4.6$ V

4–15 (a) $0.7 < v_S < 6.02$ V;
(b) $0.7 < v_S < 3.89$ V

4–16 (a) $R_B = 113\ \text{k}\Omega$;
(b) $R_B = 226\ \text{k}\Omega$

4–23 (a) $v_O = 2v_S$;
(b) $p_S = 0$; $p_O = 1.8$ mW

4–24 (a) $v_O = -2v_{S1} + 0.6v_{S2}$;
(c) $8.33 < v_{S2} < 58.3$ V
(d) $v_{S2} = 16.667$ V

4–25 (a) $R_1 = 54$ kΩ; $R_2 = 18$ kΩ; $R_3 = 9$ kΩ;
(b) $-10.5 < v_1 < 19.5$ V

4–26 $v_O = K(v_S - V_{BB})$; $K = (R_1 + R_2)/R_1$

4–27 (a) $v_{max} = 5$ V; $i_{max} = 0.417$ mA; $p_{max} = 0.521$ mW;
(b) $v_O = -8.70$ V; $i_O = -1.74$ mA; $p_O = 15.2$ mW;

4–46 (a) $V_{OH} = 15$ V; $V_{OL} = 0$ V;
(b) $v_O = V_{OH}$ if $v_S > 7.5$ V;
$v_O = V_{OL}$ if $v_S < 7.5$ V

4–47 (a) $V_{OH} = 15$ V; $V_{OL} = 0$ V;
(b) $v_O = V_{OH}$ if $v_S > -2$ V;
$v_O = V_{OL}$ if $v_S < -2$ V

4–52 (a) Circuit is a ladder. Use circuit reduction.
(b) Select node D as reference and write node equations at B and C.
(c) Modify node equations in (b).

4–53 (a) Use series equivalence.
(b) Use superposition.
(c) Use KVL and Ohm's Law.

4–56 (a) Use superposition and voltage division.
(b) Use superposition and the lookback resistance.
(c) Use Ohm's law and the lookback resistance.

4–63 (a) $K = (R_F/R)(2 + R/R_F)^{-1}$;
(b) $V_{REF} = 15$ V; $R_F = 100.05$ kΩ

Chapter Five

5–4 $5 \times [u(0.003 - t) + u(t - 0.005)]$

5–6 (a) $V_A = 10$ V; $T_C = 0.5$ s;
(b) $V_A = 10$ V; $T_C = 2$ s;
(c) $V_A = -10$ V; $T_C = 50$ ms;
(d) $V_A = -10$ V; $T_C = 20$ s

5–8 $V_A = 13.9$ V; $T_C = 3.92$ ms

5–12 $T_0 = 1$ ms; $\phi = 2.68$ rad; $T_S = -0.426$ ms; $V_A = 22.36$ V

5–14 $a = 10$ V; $b = 10$ V;
$\phi = -0.785 \text{ rad} = -45^\circ$

5–19 (a) $u(t) - u(t-2)$;
(b) $u(t) - 2u(t-1) + u(t-2)$

5–20 $V_A = 10$ V; $V_B = 5$ V; $\alpha = 1.386 \times 10^5$ rad/s

5–21 $V_A = 9.951$ V; $\alpha = 994.7$ rad/s; $\beta = 1257$ rad/s

5–24 $V_A = 10$ V; $V_B = 12$ V; $\beta = 2.513 \times 10^5$ rad/s

5–29 $V_A = 24.5$ V; $\alpha = 235$ rad/s; $\beta = 1257$ rad/s

5–34 $V_p = 3$ V; $V_{pp} = 3$ V; $V_{avg} = 1.5$ V; $V_{rms} = 1.87$ V

5–35 $V_p = 2$ V; $V_{pp} = 3$ V; $V_{avg} = 0.25$ V; $V_{rms} = 1.12$ V

5–36 $V_A = 5$ V; $V_B = 10$ V

5–43 $B = 500$ Hz

5–44 $B = 50$ kHz

5–45 $B = 20$ kHz

5–50 Triangular wave

Chapter Six

6–2 $\beta = 5$ krad/s; $i_C(t) = -15 \sin(\beta t)$ mA; $p_C(t) = -0.225 \sin(2\beta t)$ W; $w_C(t) = 22.5\,[1 + \cos(2\beta t)]$ μJ; both

6–3 $\alpha = 5$ krad/s; $v_C(t) = 80\,[1 - \exp(-\alpha t)]$ V; $p_C(t) = 4[\exp(-\alpha t) - \exp(-2\alpha t)]$ W; $w_C(t) = 400[1 - \exp(-\alpha t)]^2$ μJ; absorbing

6–7 50 V; 100 V; 100 V

6–8 $\alpha = 1$ krad/s; $v_L(t) = 2 \exp(-\alpha t)$ V; $p_L(t) = 2[\exp(-\alpha t) - \exp(-2\alpha t)]$ W; $w_L(t) = [1 - \exp(-\alpha t)]^2$ mJ; absorbing

6–11 $\alpha = 1$ krad/s; $i_L(t) = 20[1 - \exp(-\alpha t)]$ mA; $p_L(t) = 20[\exp(-\alpha t) - \exp(-2\alpha t)]$ mW; $w_L(t) = 10[1 - \exp(-\alpha t)]^2$ μJ; absorbing

6–13 0.125 A; 0.5 A; 1.5 A; absorbing

6–14 $\alpha = 5$ krad/s; $i_C(t) = -1.25\exp(-\alpha t)$ A; $p_C(t) = -31.25 \exp(-2\alpha t)$ W; delivering

6–20 $C = 1$ μF

6–24 $v_O(t) = 10 - 2500t$ V; $t = 10$ ms

6–25 No

6–26 $v_O(t) = 0.25 \times V_A \sin(2000t)$ V; $V_A < 60$ V

6–28 $v_O(t) = -50 \times R \cos(10^6 t)$ μV; $R < 300$ kΩ

6–36 C1: $C_{EQ} = 3.5$ μF; C2: $L_{EQ} = 1.065$ mH

6–39 $C_{EQ} = 5.339$ μF

6–40 $C_{AB} = 4.128$ μF

6–42 Four strings in parallel each consisting of four 20 μF in series

6–46 (b) $v_2(t) = 7 \sin(2000t)$ V

6–47 (b) $i_1(t) = -125 \cos(1000t)$ A; $i_2(t) = 175 \cos(1000t)$ A

6–49 (b) $v_1(t) = 1.5 \cos(1000t)$ V; $v_2(t) = -\cos(1000t)$ V

6–54 (a) $n = 1/5$;
(b) $v_1(t) = 120 \cos(120\pi t)$ V; $i_1(t) = 0.6 \cos(120\pi t)$ A

6–55 $i_1(t) = -36 \sin(377t)$ A

6–59 $n = 2.29$

6–61 (a) 1.03 mF;
(b) 11.9 kJ;
(c) 11.5 MW;
(d) 11.9 kW

Chapter Seven

7–1 (a) $v(t) = -15e^{-1500t}$ V;
(b) $i(t) = 10 - 30\, e^{-1000t}$ mA

7–3 C1: 0.367 ms;
C2: 0.4 ms

7–4 C1: 0.831 ms;
C2: 99.9 ms

7–7 (c) C1: $v_C(t) = V_A\left[-1 + 2\exp\left(-\dfrac{t}{RC}\right)\right]$;

C2: $i_L(t) = \dfrac{V_A}{R}\left[-1 + 2\exp\left(-\dfrac{Rt}{L}\right)\right]$

7–11 $v_C(t) = 4 - e^{-150t}$ V

7–13 $v_C(t) = 11.5(1 - e^{-10400t})$ V

7–21 (a) $s + 1000 = 0$; $T_C = 1$ ms; $v_C(0) = -5$ V;
(b) $v_T(t) = 5$ V for $t > 0$

7–23 (a) $s + 1000 = 0$; $T_C = 1$ ms; $v_C(0) = 5$ V;
(b) $v_T(t) = 20 \cos(1000t)$ V for $t > 0$

7–25 (a) $s + 1000 = 0$; $T_C = 1$ ms;
(b) $R = 600\ \Omega$; $C = 1.67\ \mu$F

7–32 $v(t) = 2 + e^{-5t}[3 \cos(10t) + 4 \sin(10t)]$ for $t > 0$

7–33 C1: $\omega_0 = 50$ krad/s; $\zeta = 0.005$; underdamped; C2: $\omega_0 = 31.62$ Mrad/s; $\zeta = 0.158$; underdamped

7–34 (c) $v_C(t) = 13.3\, e^{-10000t} - 3.33\, e^{-40000t}$ V;
$i_L(t) = -3.33\, e^{-10000t} + 3.33\, e^{-40000t}$ mA

7–36 (c) $v_C(t) = 12.5\, e^{-4000t} - 2.5\, e^{-20000t}$ V;
$i_L(t) = -1.25\, e^{-4000t} + 1.25\, e^{-20000t}$ mA

7–38 (c) $v_C(t) = -1.69\, e^{-1667t} \sin(9860t)$ V; $i_L(t) = 1.67\ e^{-1667t}\,[\cos(9860t) + 0.169 \sin(9860t)]$ mA

7–46 $v_O(t) = -7.73\, e^{-5359t} + 107.73\, e^{-74640t}$ V

7–51 (a) $\omega_0 = 4.243$ krad/s; $\zeta = 1.061$;
(b) $v_C(0) = 0$; $v_C(\infty) = 10$ V; $i_L(0) = 6$ mA; $i_L(\infty) = 0$; $v_T = 10$ V; (c) $C = 133$ nF

7–52 (a) $\omega_0 = 141.4$ rad/s; $\zeta = 0.707$;
(b) $v_C(0) = 10$ V; $v_C(\infty) = 10$ V; $i_L(0) = -0.5$ mA; $i_L(\infty) = 0$; $v_T = 10$ V; (c) $C = 1\ \mu$F

7–56 $v_T(t) = 4.375\ e^{-500t}$ V

7–63 (a) $\alpha = 190$ krad/s; $\beta = 866$ krad/s;
(b) $s^2 + 3.8 \times 10^5 s + 7.872\text{x}10^{11} = 0$;
(c) $L = 5.79$ mH; $C = 219$ pF

Chapter Eight

8–1 $\mathbf{V}_1 = 70.7 + j70.7$ V; $\mathbf{V}_2 = 150 + j200$ V; $v_1(t) + v_2(t) = 349\cos(\omega t + 50.8^\circ)$ V

8–3 (a) $v_1(t) = 10\cos(10^4 t - 30^\circ)$ V;
(b) $v_2(t) = 60\cos(10^4 t - 220^\circ)$ V;
(c) $i_1(t) = 5\cos(10^4 t + 90^\circ)$ A;
(d) $i_2(t) = 2\cos(10^4 t + 270^\circ)$ A

8–8 $v_3(t) = 69.95\cos(\omega t + 120.4^\circ)$ V

8–10 $v_2(t) = 10\cos(\omega t - 143.1^\circ)$ V

8–11 (a) $Z_{EQ} = 50 + j40\ \Omega$;
(b) $Z_{EQ} = 10 - j20\ \Omega$;
(c) $Z_{EQ} = 16.5 - j15.5\ \Omega$;
(d) $Z_{EQ} = 4.5 - j12.5\ \Omega$

8–12 $Z_{EQ} = 57.99 + j74.68 = 94.55\angle 52.2^\circ\ \Omega$

8–14 $Z_{EQ} = 0.333 + j124.5 = 124.5\angle 89.8^\circ\ \Omega$

8–19 $L = 0.181$ mH; $C = 6.03$ nF

8–21 $i(t) = 70.7\cos(2500t - 45^\circ)$ mA

8–23 $i_R(t) = 141\cos(377t - 62.05^\circ)$ mA; $i_C(t) = 265\cos(377t + 27.95^\circ)$ mA

8–25 $i_R(t) = 10\cos(1000t + 45^\circ)$ mA; $i_C(t) = 10\cos(1000t + 135^\circ)$ mA

8–27 $Z = 162.2 - j27.03\ \Omega$; $v_X(t) = 116\cos(1000t + 35.5^\circ)$ V

8–29 $\mathbf{I}_X = 0.125 - j1.13 = 1.14\angle -83.7^\circ$ A

8–33 $\mathbf{V}_X = 21.16 - j31.03 = 37.56\angle -55.71^\circ$ V

8–36 $Z_T = 30 + j40$ kΩ; $\mathbf{V}_T = 300 + j0$ V

8–41 $v_X(t) = 121.1\cos(4000t - 84.09^\circ)$ V

8–43 $K = j1.031$; $Z_{IN} = 9897 + j101\ \Omega$

8–45 $\mathbf{I}_X = -2.37 + j0.237$ mA; $\mathbf{V}_Y = 1.83 + j12.62$ V

8–47 $K = 0.847 - j0.028$; $Z_{IN} = 21.32 - j9.71$ kΩ

8–51 $Z_{IN} = 64.37 + j54.25\ \Omega$; $v_2(t) = 11.03\cos(2000t + 28.07^\circ)$ V

8–53 $i(t) = 20.1\cos(20000t - 161.2^\circ)$ mA

8–56 $Z_{IN} = 2.5 + j1.5$ kΩ; $i(t) = 3.43\cos(4000t - 121^\circ)$ mA

8–58 Two solutions possible: $\omega = 7.27, 7.94$ krad/s

8–61 $\mathbf{V}_L = 35 + j0$ V; $\mathbf{I}_L = 0.7 - j0.7$ A; $P = 12.25$ W

8–63 $R = 1280\ \Omega$; $C = 1.06\ \mu$F

8–65 (a) $P_L = 144$ mW;
(b) $P_{MAX} = 450$ mW;
(c) $Z_L = 1 - j2$ kΩ

8–71 (a) $R = 125\ \Omega$; $L = 60.47$ mH;
(b) $\mathbf{V}_1 = 2.6 - j3.04$ V; $\mathbf{V}_2 = 7.4 + j3.04$ V

Chapter Nine

9–1 (a) $F(s) = \dfrac{A(s - \alpha)}{s(s + \alpha)}$

(b) $F(s) = \dfrac{A(s^2 + \alpha^2)}{s(s + \alpha)^2}$

9–3 $F(s) = \dfrac{A(\beta - s)^2}{s(s^2 + \beta^2)}$

9–5 $F(s) = \dfrac{A(s + \alpha)^2}{(s + \alpha)^2 + \beta^2}$

9–7 (a) $F(s) = \dfrac{-5s}{(s + 10)(s + 20)}$

(b) $F(s) = \dfrac{450000\, s}{(s^2 + 100^2)(s^2 + 200^2)}$

9–9 $F(s) = \dfrac{(s + 36.5)(s + 68.5)}{(s + 50)^2}$

9–21 (a) $f_1(t) = 36(e^{-20t} - e^{-45t})u(t)$
(b) $f_2(t) = 900te^{-30t}\ u(t)$
(c) $f_3(t) = 37.5e^{-18t}\sin(24t)u(t)$

9–23 (a) $f_1(t) = \{2.67 - 1.5e^{-2t} - 0.167e^{-6t}\}u(t)$
(b) $f_2(t) = \{0.333 + 0.238\cos(3\sqrt{5}t) + 0.429\cos(4\sqrt{5}t)\}u(t)$

9–25 (a) $f(t) = \{t + 0.25 + 0.289e^{-3t}\cos(3\sqrt{3}t + 150^\circ)\}u(t)$
(b) $f(t) = \{23.4 - 13.4e^{-10t} - 24te^{-10t}\}u(t)$

9–27 (a) $\gamma = 20$; $K = 2/3$;
(b) $\gamma = 30$; $K = 1$;
(c) $\gamma = 40$; $K = 4/3$

9–31 (a) $y(t) = 5e^{-10t}u(t)$
(b) $y(t) = \{10 - 20e^{-10000t}\}u(t)$

9–32 $y(t) = \{-4.95e^{-100t} + 4.95\cos(10\text{t}) + 0.495\sin(10t)\}u(t)$

9–38 $y(t) = \{10 - 11.1e^{-t} + 1.11e^{-10t}\}u(t)$

9–39 (b) $i_L(t) = \{e^{-1000t}[5\cos(3000t) + 1.67\sin(3000t)]\}u(t)$ mA

9–41 (a) $f(t) = \frac{A}{T}tu(t) - \frac{A}{T}(t - T)u(t - T) - Au(t - T)$

(b) $F(s) = \frac{A[1 - (1 + Ts)e^{-Ts}]}{Ts^2}$

9–46 (a) Initial value does not apply; FV = 0;
(b) IV = 1/3; Final value does not apply

9–48 (a) IV = 0; Final value does not apply;
(b) IV = 10; FV = 2

Chapter Ten

10–1 $Z(s) = \frac{R(RCs + 1)}{2RCs + 1}$

$R = 10$ kΩ; $C = 50$ nF

10–3 $Z(s) = \frac{(s + j4472)(s - j4472)}{(s + 2764)(s + 7236)}$

10–5 $Z(s) = \frac{1000\,[(s + 2000)^2 + 2000^2)}{s(s + 2000)}$

10–7 $Z(s) = \frac{(RCs + 0.382)(RCs + 2.618)}{Cs(RCs + 2)}$

10–13 $V_C(s) = \frac{V_A(RCs - 1)}{s(RCs + 1)}$

10–15 $I_L(s) = 2.5 \times 10^{-3}\frac{(s + 160000)}{s(s + 100000)}$

10–17 $I_L(s) = \frac{-30}{s^2 + 1000s + 2000000}$

10–19 (a) $I_L(s) = \frac{(V_A - V_B)C}{LCs^2 + R_2Cs + 1}$;

$V_C(s) = \frac{V_A}{s} - \frac{(V_A - V_B)}{s(LCs^2 + R_2Cs + 1)}$

(b) $i_L(t) = 5te^{-1000t}u(t)$ A;

$v_C(t) = \{5 + 5(1 + 1000\,t)e^{-1000t}\}\,u(t)$ V

10–21 (a) $V_C(s) = \left(\frac{Ls}{RLCs^2 + Ls + R}\right)V_S(s)$

10–27 $C = 50$ pF

10–31 (b) $I_2(s) = \frac{R_1CsV_1(s)}{(R_1 + R_2)LCs^2 + (L + R_1R_2C)s + R_1}$

(c) $i_2(t) = 8.03e^{-10040t}\sin(10200\,t)u(t)$ mA

10–33 (b) $V_2(s) = \dfrac{R_1R_2C_1C_2s^2V_1(s)}{R_1R_2C_1C_2s^2 + (R_1C_1 + R_2C_2 + R_1C_2)s + 1}$

(c) $v_2(t) = [-2.493\,e^{-50.21t} + 12.49e^{-251.6t}]u(t)$ V

10–39 (a) $\Delta(s) = [(RCs)^2 + (3 - \mu)RCs + 1]/R^2$;
(b) $\mu = 3$; $RC = 1/5000$

10–41 (b) $v_2(t) = [-0.826e^{-90.9t}]u(t)$ V

10–45 $V_O(s) = \dfrac{4000}{s^2 + 3000s + 800000}$

10–50 $R_1C_1 = 1/100$; $R_2C_2 = 1/500$

10–52 $i(t) = \{0.1 - 200te^{-1000t}\}u(t)$ A

Chapter Eleven

11–1 (a) $Z(s) = \dfrac{(Ls + R_2)(R_1Cs + 1)}{LCs^2 + (R_1 + R_2)Cs + 1}$;

$T_V(s) = \dfrac{R_2}{Ls + R_2}$

(b) $Z(s) = 2000\,\dfrac{(s + 20000)(s + 2000)}{(s + 1026)(s + 38970)}$;

$T_V(s) = \dfrac{20000}{s + 20000}$

11–3 (a) $Z(s) = \dfrac{(R_1 + R_2)L_1s + R_1R_2}{L_1s + R_2}$

$T_Y(s) = \dfrac{L_1s}{(R_1 + R_2)L_1s + R_1R_2}$

(b) $Z(s) = 150\left(\dfrac{s + 66.7}{s + 100}\right)$;

$T_Y(s) = \dfrac{1}{150}\left(\dfrac{s}{s + 66.7}\right)$

11–5 $T_V(s) = \dfrac{(s + 2500)^2}{(s + 955)(s + 6545)}$

11–7 $T_V(s) = -\dfrac{2000}{s + 20000}$

11–11 $h(t) = 2000e^{-20000t}u(t)$

11–13 $h(t) = 5000e^{-5000t}\sin(5000\,t)u(t)$

11–15 $h(t) = \delta(t) - \{2309\,e^{-1000t}\cos(1732\,t - 60°)\}u(t)$

11–19 $i(t) = \delta(t) - \{0.99\,e^{-101t} + 1.01\,e^{-201t}\}u(t)$

11–21 $g(t) = 0.1\{1 - e^{-20000t}\}u(t)$

11–23 $g(t) = \{0.5 + 0.707\, e^{-5000t}\cos(5000\,t + 270°)\}u(t)$

11–25 $g(t) = \{1.155\, e^{-1000t}\cos(1732\,t + 30°)\}u(t)$

11–27 (a) $T(s) = \dfrac{-s}{s + 2000}$;

$h(t) = -\delta(t) + 2000\, e^{-2000t}u(t)$

(b) $T(s) = \dfrac{2000}{s + 2000}$;

$h(t) = 2000\, e^{-2000t}u(t)$

11–31 $v_{2SS}(t) = 0.098 \cos(10^5 t + 101.3°)$ V
$v_{2SS}(t) = 0.999 \sin(10^3 t + 177.1°)$ V

11–33 $v_{2SS}(t) = 0.447 \cos(10^4 t - 26.56°)$ V;
$v_{2SS}(t) = 0.999 \sin(10^3 t - 2.86°)$ V

11–35 $v_{2SS}(t) = 4.47 \cos(5000\,t - 63.4°)$ V;
$v_{2SS}(t) = 2.49 \cos(2000\,t - 23.56°)$ V

11–37 $y_{SS}(t) = 2.24 \cos(1000\,t + 63.4°)$ V

11–41 $y(t) = 0.25 \times 10^{-4}\{-1 + 20000\,t + e^{-20000t}\}u(t)$

11–43 $y(t) = 10t^2$ for $0 < t < 5$; $y(t) = 100t - 250$ for $5 < t$

11–45 $y(t) = 0.5t^2$ for $0 < t < 10$; $y(t) = 10t - 50$ for $10 < t$

11–47 $y(t) = 10(1 - e^{-200t})$ for $0 < t < 0.1$; $y(t) = 10(e^{-200(t-0.1)} - e^{-200t})$ for $0.1 < t$

11–62 (a) $\alpha = 4.77 \times 10^5$ rad/s; $\beta = 2.24 \times 10^6$ rad/s; $K = 3.16 \times 10^{13}$

Chapter Twelve

12–1 (a) $T_V(s) = \dfrac{500}{s + 1000}$;

(b) $|T_V(0)| = 0.5$; $|T_V(j\infty)| = 0$; $\omega_C = 1$ krad/s; low pass

12–3 (a) $T_V(s) = \dfrac{800}{s + 200}$;

(b) $|T_V(0)| = 4$; $|T_V(j\infty)| = 0$; $\omega_C = 200$ rad/s; low pass

12–5 (a) $T_V(s) = \dfrac{8s}{3s + 2000}$;

(b) $|T_V(0)| = 0$; $|T_V(j\infty)| = 2.67$; $\omega_C = 667$ rad/s; high pass

12–7 low pass; $K = 0.665$; $\omega_C = 60$ Mrad/s

12–11 (a) $T_V(s) = \dfrac{2000000}{s^2 + 3000\,s + 4 \times 10^6}$

(b) $\omega_0 = 2000$ rad/s; $\zeta = 0.75$; low pass

12–13 (a) $T_V(s) = \dfrac{4000\,s}{s^2 + 6000\,s + 16 \times 10^6}$;

(b) $\omega_0 = 4000$ rad/s; $\zeta = 0.75$; bandpass

12–15 (a) $T_V(s) = \dfrac{-RC_1 s}{R^2 C_1 C_2 s^2 + 2RC_2 s + 1}$

(b) $\omega_0 = 5000$ rad/s; $\zeta = 0.25$; bandpass

12–17 (a) $T_V(s) = \dfrac{RLCs^2}{RLC\,s^2 + Ls + R}$;

(b) $\omega_0 = 5000$ rad/s; $\zeta = 2$; high pass

12–21 $L = 3\ \mu$H; $C = 133$ pF; $Q = 6.25$; $\omega_{C2} = 54.2$ Mrad/s; $\omega_{C1} = 46.2$ Mrad/s

12–23 (a) $B = 4$ krad/s; $\omega_{C1} = 18.1$ krad/s; $\omega_{C2} = 22.1$ krad/s;

(b) $\mathbf{V}_L = j50$ V; $\mathbf{V}_C = -j50$ V

12–25 $L = 63.7$ nH; $C = 39.8$ pF

12–27 $L = 555$ mH; $C = 12.7\ \mu$F; other solutions are possible.

12–31 $$|T(j\omega)|_{SL} = \begin{vmatrix} 1/11 & \text{if } 0 < \omega \leq 10; \\ \omega/110 & \text{if } 10 < \omega \leq 110; \\ 1 & \text{if } 110 < \omega \end{vmatrix}$$

12–33 $$|T(j\omega)|_{SL} = \begin{vmatrix} 1 & \text{if } 0 < \omega \leq 100; \\ 100^2/\omega^2 & \text{if } 100 < \omega \end{vmatrix}$$

12–35 (a) $$|T(j\omega)|_{SL} = \begin{vmatrix} 1 & \text{if } 0 < \omega \leq 0.5; \\ 0.5/\omega & \text{if } 0.5 < \omega \leq 5; \\ 2.5/\omega^2 & \text{if } 5 < \omega \leq 50; \\ 0.05/\omega & \text{if } 50 < \omega \end{vmatrix}$$

(b) $$|T(j\omega)|_{SL} = \begin{vmatrix} 1 & \text{if } 0 < \omega \leq 0.5; \\ 0.5/\omega & \text{if } 0.5 < \omega \leq 5; \\ 0.1 & \text{if } 5 < \omega \leq 50; \\ 5/\omega & \text{if } 50 < \omega \end{vmatrix}$$

12–37 (a) $$|T(j\omega)|_{SL} = \begin{vmatrix} 1 & \text{if } 0 < \omega \leq 100; \\ 100/\omega^2 & \text{if } 10 < \omega \end{vmatrix}$$

(b) $$|T(j\omega)|_{SL} = \begin{vmatrix} 40\omega^2 & \text{if } 0 < \omega \leq 0.5; \\ 10 & \text{if } 0.5 < \omega \end{vmatrix}$$

12–41 $g(t) = \{2.025\,(e^{-100t} - e^{-8000t})\}u(t)$

12–43 $g(t) = \{1 + 11.03\,(e^{-200t} - e^{-1000t})\}u(t)$

12–45 $T(s) = \dfrac{5\,(s^2 + 50000)}{s^2 + 200s + 50000}$; bandstop

Chapter Thirteen

13–1 $T(s) = \dfrac{5.012}{s/3142 + 1}$

13–3 $T(s) = \left(\dfrac{s}{s + 200}\right)(31.6)\left(\dfrac{1}{s/3000 + 1}\right)$

13–5 $T(s) = \dfrac{150\,s}{s + 40000}$; many other answers are possible

13–7 $T(s) = \dfrac{s + 250}{s + 50}$

13–24 $\omega_0 = 628$ krad/s; $Q = 16.66$; $\zeta = 0.0300$

13–31 $T(s) = \dfrac{\sqrt{10}}{(s/1037 + 1)^5}$

13–32 $T(s) = \dfrac{\sqrt{10}}{(s/2500 + 1)[(s/2500)^2 + (s/2500) + 1]}$

13–33 $T(s) = \dfrac{0.707}{[q_1(s)][q_2(s)]}$

$q_1(s) = (s/475)^2 + 0.1789(s/475) + 1$

$q_2(s) = (s/221)^2 + 0.9276(s/221) + 1$

13–34 (a) First order cascade $n = 4$;
(b) Butterworth $n = 3$; Chebychev $n = 2$

13–41 (a) First order cascade $n = 24$;
(b) Butterworth $n = 4$; Chebychev $n = 3$

13–43 (a) $T(s) = \left(\dfrac{1.778\,s}{s + 5149}\right)^2$

Chapter Fourteen

14–1 (a) $P = 985$ W; $Q = -264$ VAR; pf = 0.966; absorbing;
(b) $P = -105$ W; $Q = 182$ VAR; pf = –0.5; delivering

14–3 (a) $P = -1.46$ W; $Q = 5.43$ VAR; pf = –0.259; delivering;
(b) $P = 260$ W; $Q = -1477$ VAR; pf = 0.174; absorbing

14–5 (a) pf = 0.97; lagging; (b) pf = 0.661; leading

14–7 (a) $P = 15$ kW; $Q = 13.2$ kVAR; $|\mathbf{I}| = 8.33$ A
(b) $Z_L = 216 + j190\ \Omega$

14–11 $S = 436 + j247$ VA

14–13 $R = 19.4$ kΩ; $C = 1.73$ μF

14–15 (a) $|\mathbf{I}| = 2.71$ A;
(b) $S_L = 440 + j294$ VA; $S_W = 29.4 + j73.4$ VA; $\eta = 93.8$ %

14–17 $\eta = 94.7$ %

14–21 $S_S = 31.3 + j30.9$ kVA; $\eta = 95.9$ %

14–23 $\mathbf{V}_L = 1847$ V; $\mathbf{V}_S = 2190 + j409$ V

14–25 (a) $\mathbf{I}_L = 134 - j38.2$ A; $\mathbf{V}_S = 342 + j126$ V;
(b) $S_W = 3.86 + j19.3$ kVA; pf = 0.807

14–31 (a) $\mathbf{V}_{AN} = 120\angle 0^\circ$ V; $\mathbf{V}_{BN} = 120\angle -120^\circ$ V; $\mathbf{V}_{CN} = 120\angle 120^\circ$ V;
$\mathbf{V}_{AB} = 208\angle 30^\circ$ V; $\mathbf{V}_{BC} = 208\angle -90^\circ$ V; $\mathbf{V}_{CA} = 208\angle 150^\circ$ V

14–33 (a) $\mathbf{I}_A = 40\angle 0^\circ$ A; $\mathbf{I}_B = 40\angle 120^\circ$ A; $\mathbf{I}_C = 40\angle -120^\circ$ A;
$\mathbf{I}_1 = 23.1\angle -30^\circ$ A; $\mathbf{I}_2 = 23.1\angle 90^\circ$ A; $\mathbf{I}_3 = 23.1\angle -150^\circ$ A

14–37 $|\mathbf{I}_L| = 88.9$ A; pf = 0.786

14–39 (a) $|\mathbf{I}_L| = 36.1$ A; (b) $Z = 5.76 - j5.08\ \Omega$

14–43 $|\mathbf{V}_{L2}| = 315.7$ V; $S_1 = 8.88 + j10.4$ kVA

14–49 $W_1 = 43$ kW; $W_2 = 17$ kW

Chapter Fifteen

15–5 $f(t) = 5 + 3.18\sin(2000\pi t) + 1.06\sin(6000\pi t) + 0.637\sin(10000\pi t)$

15–7 $a_0 = -V_A/2$; $a_n = 0$; $b_n = -V_A/n\pi$

15–9 $a_0 = 0$; $a_n = 0$; $b_n = 2V_A/n\pi$

15–11 $a_0 = 0$; $a_n = 0$; $b_n = 8A/(n\pi)^2$ for n odd; $b_n = 0$ for n even

15–16 (b) $v_O(t) = 62.55 + 35.6\cos(4000t - 63.4^\circ) - 4.36\cos(12000t - 80.5^\circ) + 1.58\cos(20000t - 84.3^\circ)$ V

15–17 (b) $v_O(t) = 10.87\sin(10^5 t - 26.6^\circ) - 0.749\sin(3\times 10^5 t - 56.3^\circ) + 0.181\sin(5\times 10^5 t - 68.2^\circ) - 0.068\sin(7\times 10^5 t - 74.1^\circ)$ V

15–19 (b) $i(t) = -127\sin(2500t - 5.71^\circ) - 63.6\sin(5000t - 2.86^\circ) - 42.4\sin(7500t - 1.91^\circ) - 31.8\sin(10000t - 1.43^\circ)$ μA

15–25 Highpass with $\omega_C = 350$ rad/s

15–27 $V_{rms} = \dfrac{V_A}{\sqrt{3}}$; 99.9%

15–29 $V_{rms} = \dfrac{V_A}{\sqrt{6}}$; 87.8%

15–31 19.1 V

15–33 78.4%

15–37 $f(t) = 2 + \cos(\omega_0 t) + 0.5\cos(2\omega_0 t) + 0.25\cos(3\omega_0 t) + \ldots$

15–39 $c_n = -jV_A/2n\pi$ for $n \neq 0$; $c_0 = V_A/2$

15–41 (a) 0.419; (b) 4.46; (c) odd symmetry

15–45 $F_{rms} = \sqrt{c_0^2 + 2\sum_{n=1}^{\infty} |c_n|^2}$

15–49 about 12%

CHAPTER SIXTEEN

16–1 $F(\omega) = \frac{A}{T}\left[\frac{(j\omega T + 1)e^{-j\omega T} - 1}{\omega^2}\right]$

16–5 $f(t) = \frac{1}{\alpha^2 + t^2}$

16–7 (a) $f_1(t) = 20(e^{-20t} - e^{-40t})u(t)$;
(b) $f_2(t) = (-e^{-20t} + 2e^{-40t})u(t)$;
(c) $f_3(t) = 0.25 \operatorname{sgn}(t) + (-e^{-20t} + 0.5e^{-40t})u(t)$;
(d) $f_4(t) = \delta(t) + (20e^{-20t} - 80e^{-40t})u(t)$

16–9 (a) $F_1(\omega) = -\frac{2}{j\omega} + 2\pi\delta(\omega)$;
(b) $F_2(\omega) = -\frac{2}{j\omega} - 6\pi\delta(\omega)$;
(c) $F_3(\omega) = -4\pi\delta(\omega)$;
(d) $F_4(\omega) = \frac{4\cos(2\omega)}{2 + j\omega}$

16–21 (c) $v_2(t) = 20e^{-100t}u(t) - 10 \operatorname{sgn}(t)$ V;

16–23 (c) $v_2(t) = (10 + 1000\, t)e^{-100t}u(t) + 10\, u(-t)$ V;

16–25 (c) $v_2(t) = 25\, e^{-50t}u(t)$ V;

16–27 (c) $v_2(t) = 13.3\,(e^{-5t} - e^{-20t})u(t)$ V

16–31 (a) $H(\omega) = 2A\alpha/((\omega)^2 + \alpha^2)$;
(b) low pass;
(c) $\omega_C = 0.6436\alpha$; –40 dB/decade

16–33 (a) $H(\omega) = j\omega A/[\alpha(j\omega + \alpha)]$;
(b) high pass;
(c) $\omega_C = \alpha$; +20 dB/decade

16–35 $h(t) = [\cos(\beta t) - 1]/(\pi t)$

16–41 $W_{1\Omega} = V_A^{\,2}/(4\alpha)$; 81.8%

16–43 $W_{1\Omega} = V_A^{\,2}/\alpha$; 81.8%

16–46 $W_{1\Omega} = 1/20$ J; 18.2%

16–49 $W_{1\Omega} = 8$ J

INDEX